Stephen Birnbaum Travel Guides

Canada
Caribbean, Bermuda, and the Bahamas
Disneyland
Europe
Europe for Business Travelers
Florida for Free
France
Great Britain and Ireland
Hawaii
Italy
Mexico
South America
United States
USA for Business Travelers
Walt Disney World

ADVISORY EDITORS David Walker
Claire Hardiman

CONTRIBUTING EDITORS

Ann Arrarte
Agostino Bono
John Branche
Peter Breslow
Tom Bridges
Renee Buencristiano
Rich Campagna
Mike Celizic
Fred Clayton
Ana Ezcurra
Ernesto Fahrenkrog
Richard Falsone
Kathleen Fliegel
Alice Garrard
Keith Grant

Arnold Greenberg
Harriet Greenberg
Donald Griffis
Earl Hanks
Elizabeth Herrington
Ellen Hoffman
John Howard
Laurie Kassman
Patrick Knight
Norman Langer
Gloria Matute
Alexandra Mayes
Anne Millman
Tom Murphy
Laurie Nadel

Helen O'Brien
Broewell Peregine
Dennis Puleston
Monica Ribero
Kathy Rich
Allan Rokach
Tim Ross
Nina Serafino
John Treacy
Hortensia de Valloton
Bill Verigan
Mary Vogt
Helen Wagg
Laurel Wentz

COVER Robert Anthony

SYMBOLS Gloria McKeown

A Stephen Birnbaum Travel Guide

Birnbaum's
SOUTH
AMERICA
1988

Stephen Birnbaum
EDITOR

Carla Hunt
AREA EDITOR

Brenda Goldberg
EXECUTIVE EDITOR

Kristin Moehlmann
Barbara Benton
Associate Editors

Kathleen McHugh
Eleanor O'Neill
Assistant Editors

Stephen Coleman
Editorial Assistant

HOUGHTON MIFFLIN COMPANY BOSTON   1987

For Alex, who merely makes this all possible

This book is published by special arrangement
with Eric Lasher and Maureen Lasher.

ISBN: 0–395–44538–8 (pbk.)
ISSN: 0749–2561 (Stephen Birnbaum Travel Guides)
ISSN: 0883–2463 (South America)

Printed in the United States of America

Q 10 9 8 7 6 5 4 3 2 1

Contents

GETTING READY TO GO

All the practical travel data you need to plan your vacation down to the final detail.

When and How to Go

Preparing

On the Road

FACTS IN BRIEF

A compilation of pertinent tourist information such as entry requirements and customs, sports, language, currency, clothing requirements, and more for all of the South American countries.

PERSPECTIVES

A cultural and historical survey of South America's past and present, its people, politics, and heritage.

THE CITIES

Thorough, qualitative guides to each of the 13 cities most visited by vacationers and businesspeople. Each section offers a comprehensive report of the city's most compelling attractions and amenities designed to be used on the spot. Directions and recommendations are immediately accessible because each guide is presented in consistent form.

DIVERSIONS

A selective guide to 17 active and cerebral vacations, including the places to pursue them where the quality of experience is likely to be highest.

DIRECTIONS

South America's most spectacular routes and roads, most arresting natural wonders, most magnificent archaeological ruins, all organized into 62 specific driving tours.

A Word from the Editor

Despite an early colonial history that closely parallels that of North America, the South American continent has lagged well behind its northern neighbor in recent times and, in terms of sophisticated political and economic progress, is still more notable for its potential than its tangible achievements. What's more, South America remains far less familiar to today's North American travelers than points on the globe that are more distant and less similar. So although both continents occupy the same hemisphere, their patterns of development over the past several centuries have been markedly different, and modern visitors to South America find a far greater frontier atmosphere than anything that exists in the northern half of the hemisphere.

Though the greedy European "colonists" were no less rapacious south of the equator than north — Pizarro's plundering of the Incas was just about as complete as Cortés's looting of the Aztecs — the ensuing years were very different. Whereas industrialization and ever more sophisticated technology came relatively quickly to most areas of North America, they are just now becoming pervasive in South America. And even as this industrial revolution is taking place, a revolution in tourism is also occurring. Indeed, never before have South America's abundant attractions seemed to tempt so many of the Northern Hemisphere's travelers as at this moment.

It's ironic that many of the same elements that hampered the economic development of South America are the very things that seem to appeal most to current visitors. Extraordinary stretches of deep, untrammeled jungle and vast, lonely *llanos* (prairies) still survive in many areas of the South American continent, as do the extraordinary, nearly hidden ruins of cultures that may go back to the time of the Egyptians. As recently as 1984, evidence of an entirely new ancient civilization was revealed at the Andean site of Gran Pajaten in Perú, and further such discoveries seem imminent. So it's no surprise that devotees of the ancients, who regularly make pilgrimages to the remaining altars of Greek and Roman civilizations, have come to recognize that similar stunning reminders of times past exist in abundance all over South America.

It would be easy to try to treat South America as a single entity with a common continental culture, but that would be very misleading. For within this single continent exists an enormous variety of experiences, ranging from the modern high-rise towers of Caracas and Rio de Janeiro to the Stone Age jungle civilizations of the Mato Grosso. And South America is much more than just North America turned upside down, though at least part of South America's allure to tourists from the Northern Hemisphere is the opportunity to ski on fresh powder at a time when northern temperatures are inspiring cases of heat prostration and, alternately, to sunbathe on one of a bounty of South American beaches while the snow blows above the equator and the wind chill factor falls out of sight.

And there's also much more to visiting South America than just enjoying a happily hedonistic holiday. There are extraordinarily diverse peoples to meet and very complex social and governmental structures to try to comprehend. As with any similarly large landmass, South America has its fair share of genuine heroes and its quota of petty tyrants, with a vast panoply of noteworthy (and notorious) characters in between. To the traveler, this complex human mosaic represents the sort of challenge that enlivens any trip, as the visitor tries to obtain a firsthand grasp of locations and lifestyles that were previously totally unfamiliar.

In creating and revising this book, I've renewed lots of old acquaintances with South America, and all the new images and impressions have been especially surprising. When I was a boy during the early 1950s, I spent a significant amount of time visiting and living in South America, and reacquainting myself with once familiar cities (and others not so well known) is an odd and often disorienting enterprise. In all candor, my boyhood memories are of a time when the purposeful exploitation of South America's resources by foreigners was at its height and when relations between outsiders and the native populations were at their nadir. Perhaps a measure of the extent of this insularity is indicated by the fact that the neighborhood in which we lived in Caracas had not a single Venezuelan family within many blocks.

The research for this book and its revisions has dramatically driven home the point that times have indeed changed. The level of nationalistic spirit and pride has never been higher, and a by-product of this strong sense of national identity is a burst of development almost everywhere on the South American continent. Unfortunately, local politics often serve to keep the benefits of this development from the mass of citizens, but it appears that the more repressive regimes are at least beginning to deteriorate.

Despite some less than enlightened politics, the travel opportunities to South America are almost always extraordinary. Whether lying on the beaches of Bahía, climbing the Andes to ski in Portillo, or exploring Inca ruins near Cuzco, visitors find the experience unforgettable, and there's perhaps more of an opportunity for genuine discovery in South America than anywhere else on this planet. It is the basic focus and intent of this guide to make a South American travel experience more accessible to visitors who want to immerse themselves in this unusually rewarding adventure.

At the same time, the increasing and broadening sophistication of our readers — no matter where they are headed — has made it essential that any contemporary South American guidebook reflect and keep pace with the real needs of today's travelers. That's why we've tried to create a guide that's specifically organized, written, and edited for this newly knowledgeable traveler, for whom qualitative information is infinitely more desirable than mere quantities of unappraised data. We think that this book, as well as the other guides in our series, represents a new generation of travel guides, ones that are especially responsive to modern needs and interests.

For years, dating back as far as Herr Baedeker, travel guides have tended to be encyclopedic, seemingly much more concerned with demonstrating expertise in geography and history than in any analysis of the sorts of things that genuinely concern a typical tourist. But today, when it is hardly necessary to tell a traveler where Buenos Aires is located, it is hard to justify devoting a ream of pages to historical perspective. It becomes, therefore, the responsibility of the guidebook editor to provide new insights and perceptions, and to suggest new directions to make his guide genuinely valuable.

That's exactly what we've tried to do in our series. I think you'll notice a different, more contemporary tone to the text, as well as an organization and focus that are distinctive and different. And even a random examination of what follows will demonstrate a substantial departure from previous guidebook orientation, for we've not only attempted to provide information of a different sort, but we've also tried to present it in an environment that makes it particularly accessible.

Needless to say, it's difficult to decide just what to include in a guidebook of this size — and what to omit. Early on, we realized that giving up the encyclopedic approach precluded the inclusion of every single route and restaurant, which helped define our overall editorial focus. Similarly, when we discussed the possibility of presenting certain information in other than strict geographical order, we found that the new format enabled us to arrange data in a way that we feel best answers the questions travelers typically ask.

Large numbers of specific questions have provided the real editorial skeleton for this book. The volume of mail I regularly receive seems to emphasize that modern travelers want very precise information, so we've tried to address these needs and have organized our material in the most responsive way possible. Readers who want to know the best restaurant in Lima or the best beach in Cartagena will have no trouble extracting that data.

Travel guides are, above all, reflections of personal taste, and putting one's name on a title page obviously puts one's preferences on the line. But I think I ought to amplify just what "personal" means. I do not believe in the sort of personal guidebook that's a palpable misrepresentation on its face. It is, for example, hardly possible for any single travel writer to visit thousands of restaurants (and nearly as many hotels) in any given year and provide accurate appraisals of each. And even if it were possible for one human being to do so, it would of necessity have to be done at a dead sprint, and the perceptions derived therefrom would probably be less valid than those of any other individual visiting these same establishments. It is, therefore, impossible (especially in an annually revised and updated guidebook *series* such as we offer) to have only one person provide all the data on the entire world.

I also happen to think that such individual orientation is of substantially less value to readers. Visiting a single hotel for just one night or eating one hasty meal in a given restaurant hardly equips anyone to provide appraisals of more than passing interest. No amount of doggedly alliterative or oppressively onomatopoeic text can camouflage a technique that is specious on its face. We have, therefore, chosen what I like to describe as the "thee and me" approach to restaurant and hotel appraisal and, to a somewhat more limited degree, to the sites and sights we have included in the other sections of our text. What this really reflects is personal sampling tempered by intelligent counsel from informed local sources, and these additional friends-of-the-editor are almost always residents of the city and/or area about which they are consulted.

Despite the presence of several editors, a considerable number of writers and researchers, and numerous insightful local correspondents, very precise editing and tailoring keep our text fiercely subjective. So what follows is purposely designed to be the gospel according to Birnbaum, and it represents as much of my own taste and insight as is humanly possible. It is probable, therefore, that if you like your cities distinctive and your beaches uncrowded, prefer hotels with personality to high-rise anonymities, and can't tolerate good meat or fresh fish that's been relentlessly overcooked, we're likely to have a long and meaningful relationship. Readers with dissimilar tastes may be less enraptured.

I also should point out something about the person to whom this guidebook is directed. Above all, he or she is a "visitor." This means that such elements as restaurants have been specifically picked to provide a representative, enlightening, stimulating, and, above all, pleasant experience. Since so many extraneous considerations can affect the reception and service accorded a regular restaurant patron, our choices can in no way be construed as a definitive guide to resident dining. We think we've listed all the best places, in various price ranges, but they were chosen with a visitor's viewpoint in mind.

Other evidence of how we've tried to tailor our text to reflect changing travel habits is most apparent in the section we call DIVERSIONS. Where once it was common for travelers to spend a South American visit nailed to a single spot, the emphasis today is far more likely to be directed toward pursuing some active enterprise or interest while seeing the surrounding countryside. Such is the amount of perspiration regularly stimulated by today's "leisurely" vacationer that a common by-product of a typical modern holiday is often the need to take another vacation to recover from the first. So we've selected every activity we could reasonably evaluate and organized the material in a way that is especially accessible to activists — of either athletic or cerebral bent. It is no longer necessary, therefore, to wade through a pound or two of extraneous prose just to find the best golf course or climbable peak within a reasonable radius of a given South American destination.

If there is a single thing that best characterizes the revolution in and evolution of current holiday habits, it is that Americans now consider travel a right rather than a privilege. No longer is a trip to the far corners of the world necessarily a once-in-a-lifetime thing, nor is the idea of visiting exotic, faraway places in the least worrisome. Travel today translates as the enthusiastic desire to sample all of the world's opportunities, to find that elusive quality of experience that is not only enriching but comfortable. For that reason, we've tried to make what follows not only helpful and enlightening, but the sort of welcome companion of which every traveler dreams.

Finally, I should point out that every good travel guide is a living enterprise; that is, no part of this text is cast in bronze. In our annual revisions, we refine, expand, and further hone all our material to serve your travel needs even better. To this end, no contribution is of greater value to us than your personal reaction to what we have written, as well as information reflecting your own experiences while using this book. We earnestly and enthusiastically solicit your comments on this book *and* your opinions and perceptions about places you have recently visited. In this way, we will be able to provide the most current information — including the actual experiences of the traveling public — and to make those experiences more readily available to others. So please write to me at 60 E 42nd St., New York, NY 10165.

We sincerely hope to hear from you.

STEPHEN BIRNBAUM

How to Use This Guide

? A great deal of care has gone into the organization of this guidebook, and we believe it represents a real breakthrough in the presentation of travel material. Our aim is to create a new generation of travel books, to make this guide the most useful and practical travel tool available today.

Our text is divided into six basic sections in order to present information on every possible aspect of a South American vacation in the best way. This organization itself should alert you to the vast and varied opportunities available on this continent — as well as indicating all the specific, detailed data necessary to plan a trip in South America. You won't find much of the conventional "blue skies and beautiful scenery" text in this guide; we've chosen instead to use the available space for more useful and purposeful information. Prospective South American itineraries speak for themselves, and with so many diverse travel opportunities, our main job is to explain them and to provide the basic information — how, when, where, how much, and what's best — to allow you to make the most intelligent choices possible.

What follows is a brief summary of the six basic sections of this book and what you can expect to find in each. We believe that you will find both your travel planning and en route enjoyment enhanced by using this book.

GETTING READY TO GO

This compendium of practical travel facts is a sort of know-it-all companion that can provide all the precise information you need to put together a trip through South America. There are entries on more than two dozen separate topics, including how to travel, what preparations to make before you leave, what to expect in the different regions of South America, what your trip is likely to cost, and how to avoid prospective problems. The individual entries are specific, realistic, and cost-oriented.

We expect that you will use this section most before your trip, for its ideas and suggestions are intended to facilitate the often confusing planning period. Entries are intentionally concise in an effort to get at the meat of the matter with the least possible extraneous prose. This information is augmented further by extensive lists of specific sources from which to obtain even more specialized information and some suggestions for obtaining travel information on your own.

FACTS IN BRIEF

Here is a compilation of pertinent tourist information such as entry requirements and customs, sports, languages, currency, clothing and climate, and so on, for all of the South American countries. When planning your trip, turn to this section for easy and immediate access to crucial yet sometimes hard-to-find details.

PERSPECTIVES

This cultural and historical survey looks at South America's past and present, its people, politics, religions, literature, music and dance, and crafts, providing a glimpse of the diversity found on the South American continent.

THE CITIES

Individual reports are presented on the 13 South American cities most visited by tourists and businesspeople, researched and written by professional journalists on their own turf. Useful at the planning stage, THE CITIES is really designed to be taken with you and used on the spot. Each report offers a short-stay guide to its city within a consistent format: an essay, introducing the city as a contemporary place to live; *At-a-Glance,* a site-by-site survey of the most important (and sometimes most eclectic) sights to see and things to do; *Sources and Resources,* a concise listing of pertinent tourist information, meant to answer a myriad of potentially pressing questions as they arise — from something simple like the address of the tourist office to something more difficult like where to find the best night spot, to see a show, to play tennis, or to get a taxi; and *Best in Town,* our cost-and-quality choices of the best places to eat and sleep on a variety of budgets.

DIVERSIONS

This very selective guide is designed to help travelers find the very best places in which to pursue a wide range of physical and cerebral activities without having to wade through endless pages of unrelated text. With a list of 17 theme vacations — for the body, the mind, and the experience — DIVERSIONS provides a guide to the special places in South America where the quality of experience is highest. Whether you seek golf or tennis, fishing or skiing, the continent's uncharted wilderness or simply its best beach, each entry is the equivalent of a comprehensive checklist of the absolute best in South America.

DIRECTIONS

Here are 61 South American itineraries, from the Panamá Canal to Tierra del Fuego and from Easter Island to the Brazilian jungle. These itineraries take you to South America's most magnificent ruins and through its most spectacular natural wonders. You can travel by car along the Pan-American Highway or use South America's public transportation system: buses, *colectivos* (taxi shared by several people), and trains. DIRECTIONS is the only section of the book organized geographically, and its itineraries cover the touring highlights of the entire continent in short, independent segments that describe journeys of one to three days' duration. Itineraries can be "connected" for longer trips or used individually for short explorations.

Each entry includes a guide to sightseeing highlights; a cost-and-quality guide to accommodations and food along the road (small hostels, country hotels, campgrounds, and off-the-main-road discoveries); and suggestions for activities.

Although each of the sections has a distinct format and a unique function, they have all been designed to be used together to provide a complete package of travel information. To use this book to full advantage, take a few minutes to read the table of contents and random entries in each section. This will give you an idea of how it all fits together.

Pick and choose information that you need from different sections. For example, assume that you have always been interested in exploring and camping out in South America's pre-Columbian archaeological sites but never knew exactly how to organize the trip or where to go. You might begin by reading the short informative section on camping and hiking in GETTING READY TO GO. This would provide you with plenty of ideas on how to organize the trip, where to go for more information, and what to take along. But where to go? Turn to *Lost Worlds: The Archaeological Heritage of South America,* DIVERSIONS, for a list and description of the most fascinating ruins in South America. A look through *History,* PERSPECTIVES, will give you some historical background about the civilizations of the cities you will see. Perhaps you choose as one of your destinations Machu Picchu, the dramatic mountain outpost of the Inca Empire and Perú's most famous archaeological zone. Turn next to DIRECTIONS for suggestions on what else to do while in Perú; for example, a flight over the Nazca Desert line drawings or a cruise down the Amazon in a riverboat. You may even decide to take a break from camping in the wilds and visit Perú's capital, Lima, which is fully covered in THE CITIES.

In other words, the sections of this book are building blocks to help you put together the best possible trip. Use them selectively as a tool, a source of ideas, a reference work for accurate facts, and a guide to the best buys, the most exciting sights, the most pleasant accommodations and delicious food, *the best travel experiences* that you can have.

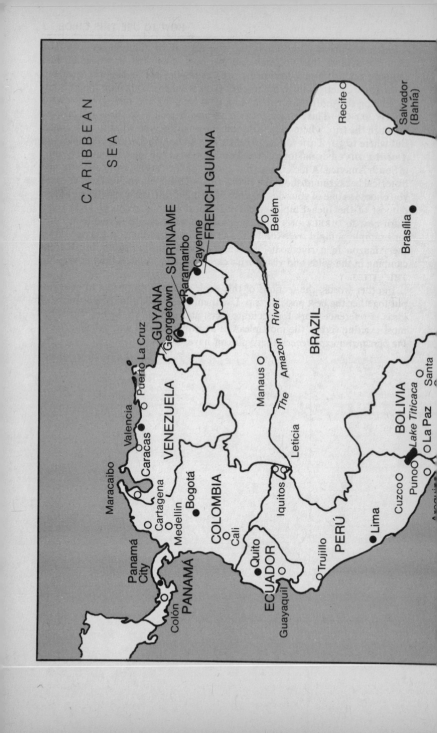

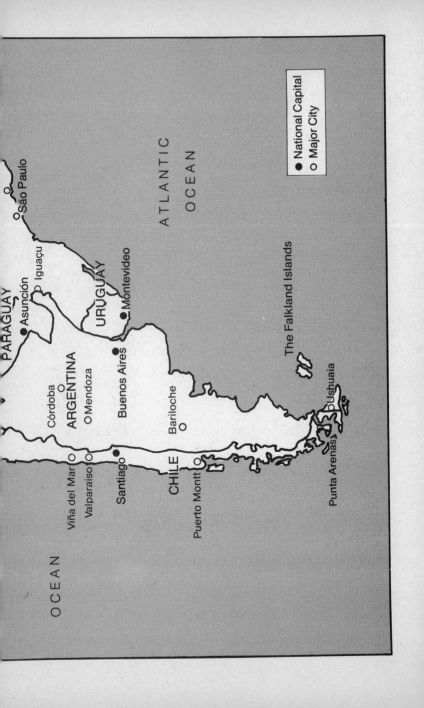

GETTING READY TO GO

When and How to Go

What's Where

The South American continent consists of 13 countries. Counterclockwise, they are Colombia, Ecuador, Perú, Bolivia, Chile, Argentina, Uruguay, Paraguay, Brazil, French Guiana, Suriname, Guyana, and Venezuela. Panamá links the South American landmass to Central America, with the Panamá Canal joining the Atlantic and Pacific oceans. The main body of the continent roughly resembles a lopsided, upside-down pear with a long, tapering end. South America covers approximately 6,464,037 square miles. Brazil, the largest country on the continent, covers approximately 3,268,473 square miles.

CLIMATE: With its great diversity of latitudes and three major temperature zones created by the western coastal desert, tropics, and mountains, South American climate fits few generalizations. In countries near the equator, such as Suriname, French Guiana, Guyana, Panamá, and a great part of Brazil, the weather is generally warm all year; the seasons are marked by the amount of rainfall rather than by temperature variation. On the other hand, the climate of other countries on or near the equator, such as Ecuador, Venezuela, and Colombia, which have vast mountain ranges, are affected by altitude as much as latitude.

Well south of the equator, seasonal changes in South America tend to run the reverse of those in North America. When it is summer in the US it is generally winter in those countries south of Perú. Spring arrives in the southern hemisphere in mid-September and lasts until December, when summer officially begins. Spring temperatures are in the 70s F during the day and cooler at night; in summer, they are in the 80s and 90s. In tropical regions, temperatures may climb as high as the 100s in summer. Autumn arrives around March, bringing cooler temperatures in the temperate southern zones and frequently damp fog. In Argentina and Chile, temperatures drop to the 50s and 40s in autumn, which falls between March and May. This is the prettiest season in the Andes, as the heavy summer rains abate and the mountain slopes turn green. During the height of summer along the coast, the mountains and the jungle have their rainy season. Roads are flooded, more often than not, and flying in and out of isolated regions is a difficult, if not totally impossible, proposition. Even after the rainy season, it can rain every afternoon for a few hours in the jungle — and often in the mountains as well. Winter is the dry season, but the temperature can drop into the 30s and occasionally even into the 20s in the Andes, southern Chile, Bolivia, and Argentina. The ribbon-like strip of mountainous, coastal desert running south from the Perú-Ecuador border to about 200 miles north of Santiago, Chile, is hot and dry all year except for a strip of land around Lima, Perú, which is foggy and humid much of the year.

TERRAIN: According to the US Department of State geographers, the South American continent's coastline runs approximately 13,415 miles, excluding Panamá. The Caribbean Sea, the Atlantic Ocean, and Panamá border the continent on the north. The Pacific Ocean forms the western border; the Drake Strait, the southern border; and the Atlantic Ocean, the eastern.

An aerial survey of the terrain reveals a narrow desert band along the Pacific coast from Colombia almost to Tierra del Fuego, bordered on the east by the Andes Mountains, a 4,500-mile ridge of giant peaks, the backbone of South America. The eastern slopes of the Andes are *montaña* — gently rolling mountain jungle that levels into *plano,* or flat jungle (*selva*), for nearly 2,700 miles to Brazil's northeastern coast. The Amazon basin takes up more than one-third of Brazil. In the south, the jungle rises to the highlands of the Mato Grosso. The pampas cover nearly 4,000 square miles of Argentina and Uruguay. South of the Río Colorado, in Argentina and Chile, the Patagonian plateau extends to the continent's base, meeting the apex of the triangular tip of the continent at the end of the 1,100-mile-long Tierra del Fuego archipelago. Stretching east-southeast from the isthmus of Panamá, the Caribbean and Atlantic coasts are tropical as far south as Patagonia. South America's four great rivers and their plains are: the Orinoco and its *llanos* in Venezuela; the Amazon and its *selva* in Perú, Colombia, Ecuador, and Brazil; the Paraguay and its Chaco in Paraguay; and the Paraná and its pampas in Argentina and Paraguay.

These are the major topographical and geographical features of the continent:

Isthmus of Panamá – A narrow neck of land connecting Central America with South America. The isthmus's terrain is mountainous, with agricultural valleys, forests, and thick jungle. The jungle swamps of the Darién region form the main impediment to the successful completion of the Pan-American Highway. International shipping traffic passes through the Panamá Canal between the Atlantic and Pacific oceans. Chiriqui Province is the biggest agricultural area. The San Blas Islands archipelago extends offshore along the Atlantic coast to Colombia.

Caribbean Coast – Extends for 1,978 nautical miles along the tropical shoreline of Colombia, Venezuela, French Guiana, Guyana, and Suriname. Barranquilla, Colombia; Caracas, Venezuela; and Georgetown, Guyana, are the major Caribbean ports. Lake Maracaibo, Venezuela, produces nearly three-quarters of that country's oil. Maracaibo is also a maritime export center for coffee, from Colombia and the Venezuelan interior, and shrimp.

Atlantic Coast – Stretching 6,117 nautical miles from Brazil, along Uruguay and Argentina, with tropical to sub-Arctic climates. The major Atlantic seaports are: Recife, Rio de Janeiro, and Santos, Brazil; Montevideo, Uruguay; and Buenos Aires, Argentina. The Atlantic Ocean beach resorts are considered the best in the Southern Hemisphere and among the finest in the world. The Falkland Islands, off the southern Argentine coast, belong to Great Britain under a contested treaty.

Pacific Coast – Extends from Panamá down to Colombia, Ecuador, Perú, and Chile for a total of 5,520 miles. The Colombian and Ecuadorian sections of the coast are tropical. Some areas are hilly. From Perú south to about 200 miles north of Santiago, the Chilean capital, the coast is a strip of mountainous, arid desert. In southern Perú, the flat Nazca plain has been marked with curious and gigantic drawings, believed by some people to have been carved into the sands to demarcate landing areas for extraterrestrial beings. In northern Chile, the Atacama Desert extends from the coast inland about 50 miles. This is copper mining country. Salt, nitrate, and iodine are mined here, too. The dry, reddish gold coastal sands give way to softer, gray beaches lined with scrub pines about 200 miles north of Santiago. From here to Puerto Montt, the Pacific coast is greener, although rocky cliffs break the shore in places. At Puerto Montt, the land breaks up into fjords, mountains, and glaciers for about 1,100 miles to the tip of Tierra del Fuego.

The Andes – Running the length of the continental mainland, some 4,500 miles from the Venezuelan highlands to Tierra del Fuego, the Andes form a spiny, north-south ridge of snow-covered mountains and volcanoes. The tallest, Mt. Aconcagua, towers 22,834 feet near the Chile-Argentina border at Mendoza, Argentina. In Ecuador, 50 volcanoes form the Avenue of the Volcanoes, of which the most famous is Mt. Chimborazo. At 19,347 feet, Mt. Cotopaxi is the tallest active volcano in the world. The Andes are separated into two mountain chains by the 600-mile-long altiplano, a grassy plain at an elevation of between 11,500 and 15,000 feet between Cuzco, Perú, and the Bolivian border at Lake Titicaca. At 12,500 feet, Lake Titicaca is the world's highest navigable lake. The altiplano is home to Indian potato farmers, llamas, and rare species of flamingo. At 15,000 feet and higher the *puna,* or high Andes, is even more sparsely settled. There are several ranches where cattle and other livestock are raised. La Paz, Bolivia, at 12,000 feet, one of the world's highest cities, is built in a valley cut into sediments of the altiplano. Around San Carlos de Bariloche in Argentina, the Andes Lake District resorts offer skiing, mountain climbing, and fishing. The eastern slopes of the Andes form the *montaña,* or mountain jungle. Bananas are grown and gold is panned in this terrain, which flattens out about 180 miles from the eastern foothills.

The Jungle – Stretching from the eastern slopes of the Andes to the Atlantic coast, the vast South American jungle extends through eastern Colombia, Ecuador, Perú, through most of northern and central Brazil, and as far north as French Guiana, Suriname, Guyana, and Venezuela. The Amazon River forms the world's largest river basin and runs 4,000 miles from Perú to the Atlantic, with a network of thousands of tributaries. The Amazon Basin spreads over 2,300,000 square miles. In Venezuela, the Orinoco River flows about 1,600 miles from the Colombia border into the Atlantic. Along one of its tributaries, the Caroní River, near the Guyana Highlands, Angel Falls, the world's highest waterfall, drops a straight 3,200 feet. The Orinoco River plain, or *llanos,* occupies one-third of Venezuela. The major resource of the jungle is oil. Venezuela, Ecuador, Perú, Colombia, and Brazil now produce petroleum. In Perú and Bolivia, the few remaining natural rubber groves in the world yield high-quality rubber for domestic use. In the rivers of the Peruvian jungle, gold is panned during the dry season. The discovery of new deposits of gold has led to a government-sponsored gold rush, with government engineers helping the miners develop more efficient techniques. The entire continental jungle is one of the last strongholds of rare wildlife. Many species are indigenous only to the Latin American continent. In southwestern Brazil, the Mato Grosso is a high, flat, savannah swamp. In February, the southern Mato Grosso floods; the northern Mato Grosso floods in June. In September, the entire Mato Grosso dries out and the area becomes a lush pastureland. The jungle is sparsely populated for good reason: Temperatures soar into the 100s; sudden torrential rains paralyze all transportation. Supplies and medicine are in short supply, and premature death from lack of medical attention is common. Diseases such as malaria are widespread, as are poisonous insects, scorpions, and spiders. For many inhabitants of remote jungle outposts, evening entertainment consists of swatting mosquitoes. (Spray cans of insect repellent have not yet found their way into the depths of the green hell.) However, the South American jungle is one of the most exotic and spellbinding places on earth.

Plains and Pampas – Extend for about 500 miles east of Buenos Aires, Argentina, and cover the entire country of Uruguay. This is gaucho country, land of the famous South American cowboys. Here, world-renowned Argentine cattle graze on the rich grasses of the pampas. The pampas get fewer than 100 days of rain a year. The Paraná River flows through the Paraguayan Chaco, or plains, along the border with Brazil and Argentina through the pampas to Buenos Aires, where it joins the Atlantic Ocean. The Paraguay River feeds into the Paraná at Asunción, Paraguay's capital.

Patagonia – South of the Río Colorado in Argentina, the terrain becomes a rugged, glacially scarred plateau. Covering a large part of both Chile and Argentina, Patagonia reaches from the Andes to the Atlantic and as far south as Tierra del Fuego. It is generally wilderness land, with spectacular scenery, not unlike a wilder Scandinavia, and sometimes just as cold.

When to Go

 Think of South America, and the image of people relaxing on a sunlit beach is probably the first thing that comes to mind. But there is more to South America than sun, sand, and surf. Cosmopolitan capitals such as Rio de Janeiro, São Paulo, Caracas, and Buenos Aires have a complete range of sophisticated cultural facilities: museums, parks, the opera, theater, and a plethora of intriguing restaurants. The ski resorts in Chile, Argentina, and Bolivia are not only set along some of the most spectacular slopes in the world, but have the advantage of being at their peak between June and September, when ski resorts in the Northern Hemisphere have gone to pasture. South America is really a year-round destination; the decision of when to go can be dictated by what you want to do. For a dazzling suntan in the height of a blustery northern winter, choose any South American beach resort (there are dozens) between November and April (remember that Northern and Southern Hemisphere seasons are reversed). The South American autumn, between March and June, is the best time to visit Machu Picchu and other sites in the Andes. The mountains are green after the rainy season, skies are usually blue, and temperatures can hit the 70s and 80s during the day. Anytime between March and October is good for exploring the jungle since this is the drier season. Temperatures average in the 80s and 90s F. Winter temperatures drop into the 20s and 30s F in central and southern Argentina and Chile, and it sometimes snows. The rest of the continent has a mild, desert, or tropical climate along the coast throughout the year.

TOURIST SEASONS: These vary from country to country and from region to region. During Carnival (in February or March) in Rio de Janeiro, Bahía, and Santos, Brazil, hotel rates are higher than at other times during the year. The beach resort season is at its height between November and March throughout South America. Prices tend to be higher at the more chic resorts during this period. High season for ski resorts is between June and September. Although the major South American capitals do not have a tourist season, the best time to visit is in the spring, around October, or in the autumn (around March), before winter.

CLIMATE: The climate of each South American country is described briefly below, along with a climate chart giving average Fahrenheit temperatures. For specific information for each city, see *Climate and Clothes* in each chapter in THE CITIES.

Argentina – A dry, temperate climate prevails throughout most of the country, although the north, around Iguazú Falls, has a tropical climate. Temperatures are considerably cooler in the Andes and in Patagonia. In Buenos Aires, summer temperatures climb into the smoggy 80s; winter temperatures drop to the 40s. The mountain resorts at Bariloche in the Lake District offer fishing and swimming in the summer, skiing in winter.

Bolivia – In the Andes and the altiplano, the dry season is from May to November, but daytime temperatures average in the 60s all year round. The jungle is tropical, with the rainy season beginning in November, and lasting until March or April. Daytime temperatures in the jungle are in the 80s and 90s.

Brazil – The Northeast, the Amazon, and Rio de Janeiro share a tropical climate. Summer, from November through February, is the hottest season, with temperatures climbing into the 90s and even the 100s. São Paulo, at an elevation of approximately 2,700 feet, is cooler and windier. Sometimes it even snows in the winter, although summer temperatures are in the 80s.

A SOUTH AMERICAN CLIMATE CHART (Average Temperature in °F)

Country	Dec.-Feb.	March-May	June-Aug.	Sept.-Nov.
Argentina (B.A.)	83	82	57	66
Bolivia (La Paz)	64	64	62	70
Brazil (Rio)	84	80	76	77
Chile (Santiago)	85	73	60	72
Colombia (Bogotá)	67	67	65	66
Ecuador (Quito)	72	70	72	72
French Guiana	85	86	89	91
Guyana	84	85	86	87
Panamá	88	87	87	86
Paraguay (Asunción)	94	84	75	90
Perú (Lima)	82	78	67	71
Suriname	85	86	88	91
Uruguay (Montevideo)	82	71	59	82
Venezuela (Caracas)	78	80	79	78

Chile – The northern section has an arid, desert climate, with temperatures in the 90s and 100s during the day, dropping into the 50s at night. The central area is in the temperate zone, with temperatures in the 80s in the summer, dropping sometimes as low as the 20s in winter. Southern Chile is rainy in summer, snowy in winter. Between June and September, the ski resorts in the Andes are at their peak.

Colombia – Has two rainy seasons: one in March and April; the other in October and November. The Caribbean coast has an average yearly temperature of 83°. In Bogotá, 8,669 feet above sea level, the average temperature is between 64° and 70° throughout the year.

Ecuador – The climate varies considerably, depending on the elevation. The equatorial lowlands along the coast and the Galápagos Islands have an average daytime temperature of 83 throughout the year. During the rainy season, temperatures are hotter. In the Central Valley, Quito has an average yearly temperature of 59°. The climate in the Ecuadorian Andes is gentler than in the Peruvian and Bolivian Andes.

French Guiana – Similar to Guyana, with temperatures in the humid 80s and 90s throughout the year. The rainy season is from April to July.

Guyana – Hot and humid throughout the year, with temperatures in the 80s all year.

Panamá – Hot and humid, with temperatures in the 80s and 90s throughout the year. The Chiriqui highlands, on the other hand, are comfortably temperate. Summer (December through March) is the dry season. It rains at least once a day the rest of the year.

Paraguay – Often intolerably sticky during the summer months, Paraguay's subtropical climate is humid and warm throughout the year, without much variation. Daytime temperatures are in the 80s and 90s.

Perú – Along the desert-lined coast, temperatures are in the 80s most of the year. A thick, heavy fog often hangs over Lima, although it is sunny and dry several miles to the east of the capital. Lima's temperatures drop into the damp 50s during the gray, winter months. Summer is clear and warm. The Andes have a dry, temperate climate between April and November with daytime temperatures in the 60s and 70s. Nights are cool, with temperatures in the 40s. In June and July, it drops into the 30s and 20s. Summer (between mid-November and March) is the rainy season. The *montaña* generally has temperatures in the 80s; the *selva,* in the 90s and 100s, particularly during the summer rainy season.

Suriname – Humid, tropical climate, with year-round temperatures in the 80s.

Uruguay – With 200 miles of Atlantic Ocean beach resorts, the Riviera of South America has a warm, temperate climate 9 months of the year, with daytime temperatures in the 80s, cooling off into the 50s at night. In winter, between June and September, the temperature drops to the 40s and fog is frequent.

Venezuela – Most of the country has a steamy, tropical climate, with temperatures in the 80s all year. The rainy season is between May and September. Caracas, at an altitude of 3,500 feet above sea level, has cooler nights, in the 50s, although daytime temperatures are in the 80s.

Traveling by Plane

 Flying is the best way to get to South America, and it is the quickest, most convenient means of travel once you are there. There are many different fares — seasonal, group, family, excursion — and they have different stopover privileges. Therefore, it is important to investigate all the alternatives before buying a ticket.

You should also find out what are the available flight connections between points to which you will be traveling — particularly between the interior, main cities, and onward. Since fares and flight schedules are always changing, it is essential that you check with a travel agent or the airline when you plan your trip and continue reconfirming all the way. Keep in mind that if you plan to travel around Christmas, Easter, or Carnival, you should make reservations well in advance. South Americans are traveling more extensively nowadays, and the planes are also full during summer vacations.

If you decide to fly, you should know what kinds of flights are available; the rules and regulations pertaining to air travel; and the options for special packages offered by airlines and tour operators.

SCHEDULED FLIGHTS: The following are airlines offering regularly scheduled flights to South America, listed with their US gateways:

Aerolíneas Argentinas (Argentina): Los Angeles, Miami, New York
AeroPerú (Perú): Miami, New York
Air Panama (Panamá): Miami
Avensa (Venezuela): Miami, New York
Avianca (Colombia): Los Angeles, Miami, New York
Eastern (US): Los Angeles, Miami, New York (direct connections in Miami from other points in the US)
Ecuatoriana (Ecuador): Los Angeles, Miami, New York
Faucett (Perú): Miami
Guyana Airways Corporation (Guyana): Miami, New York
Japan Air Lines (Japan): Los Angeles
LAB (Bolivia): Miami
LADECO (Chile): Miami
LAN Chile (Chile): Miami, New York
LAP (Paraguay): Miami
Pan American (US): Los Angeles, Miami, New York
Suriname Airways (Suriname): Miami
Varig (Brazil): Los Angeles, Miami, New York
Viasa (Venezuela): Houston, Miami, New York

The major US international lines serving South America are Eastern, which flies to the west coast of the continent, and Pan Am, which serves the east and west coasts.

For most international flights on all carriers to South America, the major US gateways are Miami, New York, and Los Angeles.

There are several international South American carriers whose domestic services can be used on unlimited mileage tickets; for extensive travel in a single country, these tickets are worth considering and must be purchased prior to leaving the US. Aerolíneas Argentinas offers year-round, 30-day, unlimited mileage tickets on its domestic services for $250. Brazilian airlines now have the Brazil Pass I for $330 that is valid all year for unlimited travel for a period of 21 days; Brazil Pass II offers four stops for 14 days for $250. However, these passes can be used on either a combination of Varig and Cruzerio de Sul or on Vasp or Trans Brazil and are not valid on flights between Rio's Santo Dumont Airport and São Paulo. The "Visit Perú" ticket, offered by AeroPerú and Faucett, is $180 for 30 days of unlimited travel; the ticket cannot be used from December 15 to January 15 or from July 15 to August 15. The "Visit Chile" fare is $249 and includes Arica, Iquique, Puerto Montt, and Punta Arenas; the fare including Easter Island is $449. Double-check all prices quoted here; they fluctuate.

National and Intracontinental Airlines – Because of the great distances and rugged topography, air travel is the most efficient way to move around each country and between them. In addition to the airlines mentioned above, the following airlines fly regularly scheduled or commuter routes within each country and between South American destinations. (Note that they do not fly to the US.)

South American Carriers

Aces (Colombia)	LADE (Argentina)
Adsa (Panamá)	LAPA (Argentina)
Aeronorte (Paraguay)	LAV (Venezuela)
Aeroperlas (Panamá)	PLUNA (Uruguay)
Aeropostal (Venezuela)	Rio Sul (Brazil)
Aerosur (Paraguay)	SAETA (Ecuador)
Alas Chiticanas (Panamá)	SAM (Colombia)
Austral (Argentina)	SAN (Ecuador)
Avensa (Venezuela)	Sasa (Panamá)
Cessnica (Colombia)	TAME (Ecuador)
Chitreana (Panamá)	Tasa (Panamá)
Copa (Panamá)	Trans-Brasil (Brazil)
Cruzeiro de Sul (Brazil)	VASP (Brazil)
Helicol (Colombia)	

There are four general categories of fares: first class, business, economy, and excursion. Latin American fares, set by the International Air Transport Association (IATA), are followed by almost all carriers. Some non-IATA carriers, such as LAB Boliviano Airlines and LAP Paraguayan, often have lower ticket fares on their flights from Miami, and Faucett and AeroPerú have a special fare from Miami to which the "Visit Perú" fare can be added for their own inter-Perú flights only.

A first-class ticket is your admission to the special section of the aircraft with larger seats, more leg room, sleeperette seating on some wide-body aircraft, better food (or more elaborately served food, in any case), free drinks, and, above all, lavish attention. First-class fares are about double those of economy, and the vacation traveler should consider the alternatives seriously. Business class is available on a limited number of airlines and flights.

Like first-class passengers, people paying economy fares are entitled to reserve seats, and tickets are sold on an open reservations system. This means that there are no advance booking requirements; you can buy a ticket for a flight up to the time of takeoff if seats are available. If your ticket is round-trip, you can make your return reservation anytime you wish, months before you leave or the day before you return. You are not required to stay at your destination for any specified amount of time (tickets are generally good for a year, after which they must be refunded or reissued if unused).

Excursion fares on South American routes generally differ according to the season and the number of travel days permitted. They are only a bit less flexible than economy tickets and are therefore useful for both business travelers and tourists. On most excursions, reservations can be changed within the prescribed time limits, but don't count on extending a ticket beyond the time of return or staying less time than required. On the other hand, South American flights don't have as many of the complicated advance-purchase requirements now in effect on other US or international routes. (But reserve well ahead for holiday seasons; all of South America seems to take to the air at Christmas, Easter, and at the end of the US school year.) Different airlines may have different regulations concerning the number of stopovers permitted, and sometimes excursion fares are less expensive midweek.

There are also group inclusive tour fares available to many destinations. The requirements vary as to number of travel days, number of stopovers permitted, and number of passengers required for a group. (The last can be as few as five full fares.) The group fare always requires that a specified dollar amount of ground arrangements be purchased in advance with the ticket. No matter what fare you travel on, reconfirm every flight on your ticket as you travel, starting with the first flight in the US. In South America, this is a nuisance because almost everywhere you can't reconfirm at the airport on arrival, but must do so in town at the ticket office. The city ticket office should be the first stop on a city tour, just so you don't forget.

There is another category of fares, called "on line" fares, which can bring considerable savings when you do all your flying to and within South America on one airline. Check with individual carriers (usually the South American companies).

RESERVATIONS: When making plane reservations through a travel agent, ask the agent to give the airline your home phone number as well as a daytime business number. All too often the agent uses the agency number as the official contact for ticket and flight plans. Winter months — prime time for a South American journey — are also prime time for the weather to wreak havoc on flight schedules. And bad weather can occur hundreds (or even thousands) of miles away and still affect your flight. Aircraft are constantly in use, and a plane delayed in the Orient or on the West Coast one day can miss its scheduled flight to Santiago from the East Coast the next morning. Airlines are pretty good about getting news of delays to passengers — if they can reach them; diligence does little good at 6 PM if the airline has only the agency or an office number.

If you look at the back of your ticket, you'll see the need for reconfirmation of return flights stated explicitly. Most return reservations from international destinations are automatically canceled after a required reconfirmation period has passed. Every travel agent or airline ticket office should give every passenger a reminder to reconfirm flights, but this seldom happens, and the responsibility rests with the traveler. Don't be lulled into a false sense of security by the "OK" on your ticket next to the number and time of the return flight. That means only that a reservation has been entered; a reconfirmation is still necessary.

When in South America, reconfirm your next flight on arrival at each stop. Do not count on doing this at the airport, but reconfirm at the city ticket office where flight space control is maintained (generally). Reconfirmation is particularly important when traveling within a country from the capital to the provinces. Airplanes are the primary transport link for most of the continent, and you will find that local flights are almost always fully booked — as in the US — particularly on Fridays, Sundays, Mondays, and holidays.

SEATING: Check in early for South American flights, even with advance seat assignments. You must decide if you want a smoking or nonsmoking section, or plan your seating in relation to a movie screen. Most airlines furnish seating charts, which make choosing a spot much easier, but in general, there are a few basics to consider. Airline representatives claim that most craft are more stable toward the front and midsections, while seats farthest away from the engines are quietest. Passengers with long legs should request a seat in the first row of a desired section or a seat directly behind emergency doors (as seats next to the exits often can be removed). Bear in mind, however, that watching a movie from the first row is difficult and uncomfortable. A window seat protects you from aisle traffic and allows you a view, while an aisle seat enables you to get up and stretch your legs more easily. Middle seats are the least desirable.

Simply reserving an airline seat in advance, however, may actually guarantee very little. Most airlines require that passengers arrive at the departure gate at least 30 minutes (sometimes more) ahead of time to hold a seat reservation. A far better strategy is to visit an airline ticket office (or one of a select group of travel agents) to secure an actual boarding pass for your specific flight. Once this has been issued, airline computers show you as "checked in," and you effectively own the seat you have selected (this is also good insurance against getting bumped from an overbooked flight and is, therefore, an especially valuable tactic at peak holiday times).

US carriers often have clubs for frequent travelers who pay for membership. These are not clubs for first-class passengers. Membership (which by law now requires a fee) entitles the traveler to use the private lounges along their routings, to refreshments served in those lounges, and to check-cashing privileges at most of their counters. Extras include special telephone numbers for individual reservations, embossed luggage tags, and a membership card for identification. Airline club membership is the key to never getting bumped. The US airlines flying to South America that offer membership in such clubs are: Eastern — one family member $105, spouse an additional $20 — and Pan American — one family member $150, spouse an additional $45. However, these companies do not have club facilities in all foreign airports. Lounge privileges are also offered to first-class passengers, and South American airlines, too, have clubs and lounges in many airports.

If you have a weight problem, you may face the prospect of a long flight with special trepidation. Center seats in the alignments of wide-bodied 747s, L1011s, and DC-10s are about 1½ inches wider than those on either side, so heavyweights tend to be more comfortable there.

If you have specific diet requirements (vegetarian, kosher, salt-free), make sure you let the airlines know well before departure time. It is advisable to request special meals when you make your reservations — check-in time is too late. Special meals will probably not be available on flights within South America and definitely not available on domestic flights.

GETTING BUMPED: A special air travel problem is the possibility that an airline will accept more reservations (and sell more tickets) than there are seats on a given flight. This is entirely legal and is done to make up for passengers who don't show up for a flight for which they have reservations. If the airline has oversold the flight and everyone does show up, the airline is subject to stringent rules laid down to protect travelers.

The airline first seeks ticketholders willing to give up their seats voluntarily in return for a negotiable sum of money, or some other inducement such as an offer of upgraded seating on the next flight or a voucher for a free trip at some other time. If there are not enough volunteers, the airline may bump passengers against their wishes. Anyone inconvenienced in this way, however, is entitled to an explanation of the criteria used to determine who does and does not get on the flight, as well as to compensation if the resulting delay exceeds certain limits. If the airline can put the bumped passengers on an alternate flight that gets them to their planned destination within 1 hour of their originally scheduled arrival time, no compensation is owed. If the delay is more than an hour, they must be paid denied-boarding compensation equivalent to the one-way fare to their destination (but not more than $200). If the delay is more than 4 hours on an international flight, the compensation must be doubled. (These rules do *not* apply to charters or to inbound flights from abroad, even on US carriers.) The airline may also offer bumped travelers a voucher for a free flight instead of the denied-boarding compensation. The passenger can choose either the money or the voucher (the dollar value of which may be no less than the monetary compensation to which the passenger would be entitled). The voucher is not a substitute for the bumped passenger's original ticket; the airline continues to honor that as well.

The rules also do not apply if the flight is canceled or delayed, or if a smaller aircraft is substituted due to mechanical problems. In such cases, some airlines provide amenities to stranded passengers, but these are strictly at the individual airline's discretion. Deregulation of the airlines has meant the traveler must find out for himself what he is entitled to receive. A useful booklet, "Fly Rights, A Guide to Air Travel in the US," is available for $1 from the Superintendent of Documents, US Government Printing Office, Washington, DC 20402; stock number 003-006-00513-55.

BAGGAGE: Each passenger is allowed only one carry-on bag. The total combined dimensions of length, width, and breadth must be less than 45 inches. First-class and economy-class passengers are allowed two pieces of checked luggage. However, in first, no bag may exceed a total of 62 inches for length, width, and breadth. In economy, the total dimensions of both bags must not exceed 106 inches, and neither piece may be more than 62 inches. When considering baggage, it is well to remember that many domestic services in South American countries will not take on your full international luggage weight. The popular flight from Lima to Cuzco is a good example of this situation; check-in baggage allowance is 44 pounds. In addition, although two pieces of luggage are permitted from North America to South, on international flights northbound, some carriers will insist on the old baggage rules of 66 pounds for first class, 44 pounds economy. Best bet: Travel with one suitcase.

If your baggage is not in the baggage claim area after your flight has arrived or if it has been damaged, report the problem to the airline immediately. (Some airlines disclaim liability for missing or damaged luggage that is not reported in writing within 4 hours of the arrival of the flight.) If luggage is missing, be sure to give the airline your destination and/or the telephone number where you can be reached. Also take the name and number of the person in charge of recovering lost luggage, and make sure you fill out a claim. In the case of damaged luggage, fill out a claim and be sure to ask the airline's representative to inspect your damaged luggage immediately. There are regulations permitting later filing for unnoticed damages, but claim what's important. By no means should you sign any papers that indicate that you'll accept any offered settlement at that moment. Since the airline is responsible for the value of your bags within certain statutory limits, you should take time to assess the extent of your loss.

Considering the increased incidence of damage to baggage, it's now more than ever a good idea to keep the sales slips that confirm how much you paid for your bags. These are invaluable in establishing the value of damaged baggage and eliminate any arguments. A better way to protect your precious baggage from the luggage-eating conveyers is to try to carry your gear on board wherever possible.

CHARTER FLIGHTS: By booking a block of seats on a specially arranged flight, charter tour operators offer travelers air transportation, often combined with a hotel room, meals, and other arrangements, for a substantial reduction over full economy fare. While charters were once the best bargain around, they are rare nowadays except to Rio. However, there are some very competitive fares now available on scheduled flights.

While charter flights have never made up a large part of the air traffic between the US and South America, when they are offered, there are some things to keep in mind about the charter game:

1. If you are forced to cancel your trip and have no cancellation insurance, you can lose all your money. Trip cancellation insurance is a must (see *Insurance,* GETTING READY TO GO).
2. Charters have little of the flexibility of scheduled flights; if you book a return flight, you must be on it, and if you miss your flight, you lose the flight and the money. You can't simply rebook as you can a scheduled flight.
3. By virtue of the economies of charter flights, your plane will almost always be full; you will fly crowded but not necessarily uncomfortably.

Charters are available to a limited number of South American destinations, primarily Rio de Janeiro during the high (Carnival) season. For the last few years, Vacation Travel Concepts, 133 E 58th St., New York, NY 10020 (phone: 212-888-1860) and Tourlite International, 1 E 42nd St., New York, NY 10165 (phone: 212-599-2727 or 800-223-7605) have been the major charter operators to Rio, with both flights and land programs available December to May.

BOOKING: If you do take a charter, read the contract carefully.

1. Note when you are to pay the deposit and its balance and to whom the check is to be made. Ordinarily, checks are made out to an escrow account, which means the charter company can't spend your money until your flight has safely returned. This provides some protection for you. To ensure the safe handling of your money, make out your check to the escrow account, the number of which must appear by law on the brochure, though all too often it is on the back in fine print. Write the details of the charter, including the destination and dates, on the face of the check; on the back, print "For Deposit Only." Your travel agent may prefer that you make out your check to the agency, saying that it will then pay the tour operator the fee minus commission. It is perfectly legal to write the check as we suggest, however, and if your agent objects too vociferously (he or she should trust the tour operator to send the proper commission), consider taking your business elsewhere. If you don't make your check out to the escrow account, you lose the protection of escrow should the trip be canceled. Furthermore, recent bankruptcies in the travel industry have served to point out that even the protection of escrow may not be enough to safeguard a traveler's investment. More and more, insurance is becoming a necessity (see *Insurance*). The charter company should be bonded (usually by an insurance company), and if you want to file a claim against it, the claim should be sent to the bonding agent. The contract will set a time limit within which any claim must be filed.
2. Note specific stipulations and penalties for cancellations. Most charters allow you to cancel up to 45 days in advance, but some cancellation dates are 50 to 60 days before departure.
3. Note the conditions under which the tour operator has the right to cancel the charter. Remember that if a tour is canceled, your money must be returned immediately, and if an operator can't fly at the specified time or via the designated route, no last-minute substitutions may be made. Under those circumstances, the tour must be canceled and money refunded.

DISCOUNT TRAVEL SOURCES: An excellent source of information on economical travel opportunities is the *Consumer Reports Travel Letter,* published monthly by Consumers Union. It keeps abreast of the scene on a wide variety of fronts, including package tours, rental cars, insurance, and more, but it is especially helpful for its comprehensive coverage of air fares, offering guidance on all the options from scheduled flights on major or low-fare airlines to charters and discount sources. For a year's subscription, send $37 to Consumer Reports Travel Letter, Subscription Dept., Box 5248, Boulder, CO 80322 (phone: 303-447-9330 or 800-525-0643). Another source is

Travel Smart, a monthly newsletter. For a year's subscription, send $37 to Communications House, 40 Beechdale Rd., Dobbs Ferry, NY 10522.

Still another way to take advantage of bargain air fares is open to those who have a flexible schedule. A number of organizations, usually set up as last-minute travel clubs and functioning on a membership basis, routinely keep in touch with travel suppliers to help them dispose of unsold inventory at discounts of between 15% and 60%. A great deal of the inventory consists of complete tour packages and cruises, but some clubs offer air-only charter seats and, occasionally, seats on scheduled flights. Members pay an annual fee and receive the toll-free number of a telephone hot line to call for information on imminent trips. In some cases, they also receive periodic mailings with information on upcoming trips for which there is more advance notice. Despite the suggestive names of the clubs providing these services, last-minute travel does not necessarily mean that you cannot make plans until literally the last minute. Trips can be announced with as little as a few days' or as much as two months' notice, but the average is from one to four weeks before departure. It does mean that your choice at any given time is limited to what is offered and, if your heart is set on a particular destination, you might not find what you want, no matter how attractive the bargains. Among these organizations are:

> *Discount Travel International,* 114 Forest Ave., Suite 205, Narberth, PA 19072 (phone: 215-668 2182). Annual fee: $45.
>
> *Encore Short Notice,* 4501 Forbes Blvd., Lanham, MD 20706 (phone: 301-459-8020 or 800-638-0930). Annual fee: $36 per person.
>
> *Last-Minute Travel Club,* 132 Brookline Ave., Boston, MA 02215 (phone: 617-267-9800) Annual fee: $30 per person or $35 per couple or family.
>
> *Moments Notice,* 40 E 49th St., New York, NY 10017 (phone: in New York State, 212-486-0503; elsewhere, 800-221-4737). Annual fee: $35.
>
> *On Call to Travel,* 11739 SW Beaverton Hwy., Ste. 120, Beaverton, OR 97005 (phone: 503-643-7212 collect). Annual fee: $45.
>
> *Stand Buys Ltd.,* 311 W Superior, Suite 414, Chicago, IL 60610 (phone: in Illinois, 312-943-5737; elsewhere, 800-255-0200). Annual fee: $45.
>
> *Worldwide Discount Travel Club,* 1674 Meridian Ave., Miami Beach, FL 33139 (phone: 305-534-2082). Annual fee: $50.

Net Fare Sources: The newest notion for supplying inexpensive travel services comes from travel agents who offer individual travelers "net" fares. Defined simply, a net fare is the bare minimum amount at which an airline or tour operator will carry a prospective traveler. It doesn't include the amount that would normally be paid to the travel agent as commission. Traditionally, such travel agent commissions amount to 8% or above on international tickets and 10% on domestic fares — not counting significant additions to these commission levels that are payable retroactively when agents sell more than a specific volume of tickets or trips for a single supplier. At press time, at least two travel agencies in the US were offering travelers the opportunity to purchase tickets and/or tours for the net price. Instead of making their income from conventional commissions, these agencies assess a fixed fee for specific services that may or may not provide a bargain for travelers; it requires a little arithmetic to determine whether you're better off with a net travel agent or with one who accepts conventional commissions.

A major net fare agency, *McTravel* (2335 Sanders Rd., Northbrook, IL 60062; phone: 312-498-9390 or 800-331-2941), will make a reservation for a domestic flight of $275 or morefor a fixed fee of $8, will write a domestic ticket for $10, will reserve a seat on an international flight for $20, and will write the international ticket for $20. Based on these fees, operative at press time, any international trip for which the ticket costs more than $400 looks like a good net buy, while the breakeven on domestic tickets is somewhat lower. There's also the opportunity to further economize by making your own airline reservation, then asking *McTravel* only to write/issue your ticket. For travelers who reside outside the Chicago area, business may be transacted by phone, and purchases may be paid by using a credit card.

CONSUMER PROTECTION: Consumers who feel that they have not been dealt with fairly by an airline should make their complaints known. Begin with the customer service representative at the airport where the problem occurs. If he or she cannot resolve your complaint to your satisfaction, write to the airline's consumer office. In a businesslike, typed letter, explain what reservations you held, what happened, the names of the employees involved, and what you expect the airline to do to remedy the situation. Send copies (never the original) of the tickets, receipts, and any other documents that back your claims.

Until December 31, 1984, travelers with problems could also contact the Civil Aeronautics Board, which was responsible for overseeing the airline industry in a number of areas important to passengers. The Airline Deregulation Act of 1978, however, mandated the gradual phasing out of the CAB, though the law that put it out of business did not cancel the consumer protection regulations established by the CAB nor its consumer assistance responsibilities. These responsibilities, along with many former CAB employees, were transferred intact to the Department of Transportation. Passengers with problems such as lost baggage, compensation for getting bumped, smoking rules, charter regulations, or deceptive practices by an airline should now write to the Consumer Affairs Division, Room 10405, Office of Community and Consumer Affairs, Office of Governmental Affairs, US Department of Transportation, 400 Seventh St., SW, Washington, DC 20590, or call the office at 202-366-2220. Nevertheless, consumers should still address their complaints initially to the airline that provoked them.

Touring by Car

DRIVING YOUR OWN CAR: Given unpredictable road conditions, extremely variable weather, as well as a political climate that is unstable at best, driving is not currently a recommended travel option. Still, for those diehards who refuse to abandon their wheels, traveling through South America by car is an unforgettable adventure. But whether you remember the experience with love or with a shudder depends to a great extent on how effectively you prepare for the journey. You should know enough Spanish or Portuguese (if you plan to drive in Brazil) to communicate basic needs. You will be spending most of your time on the road in areas uninhabited by English-speaking people. Not only is it inadvisable, it is downright foolhardy to attempt traveling through South America unless you can speak and understand a modicum of Spanish. It is difficult, if not impossible, to find your way unless you can ask directions and understand people's responses. In many parts of South America the roads are not marked. Even in some major cities, some streets are not marked.

Surprises are inevitable. Not only is the terrain of astounding variety — tropical jungle and desert, Andean mountains and Patagonian wilds — but driving patterns and road practices are a world apart from standard North American highway courtesy. Some Americans enjoy the challenge of adapting to new tactics as well as road conditions. Others frequently wish they had left the driving to someone with a lifetime of experience.

Before setting out, make certain that everything you need is in order. Read about the places you intend to visit and study maps. If at all possible, discuss your intended trip with someone who has already driven the route to find out about road conditions and available services. (For a complete description of major South American driving itineraries, see DIRECTIONS.)

License – To drive in South America, you need an Inter-American Registration and a Driving Permit, issued by the American Automobile Association (AAA) for $5 each. Two photos are required. AAA headquarters are at 8111 Gatehouse Rd., Falls Church, VA 22047 (phone: 703-222-6000; ask for "Foreign Motoring").

Car Permits – The AAA will also provide the Carnet de Passage en Douanes, a document with which cars are allowed through various customs points duty free. Without the *carnet,* you might be asked to pay a tax for "importing" a vehicle even though you are only in transit. The *carnet* costs $85 (which includes an international driving permit and other necessary documents), plus a $200 refundable cash deposit to cover possible charges for cables, telexes (flat rate $10 each), and other special handling. With the *carnet* you are expected to carry a letter of credit worth 150% of the market value of the car. It is good for the entire South American continent except Brazil (if you are entering overland), Perú, Chile, and Argentina; these countries will allow you to bring your car in without a *carnet* for a period of 90 days. If you are entering Brazil by sea, you will need a *carnet* and a letter of credit for an amount based on the weight of the car.

You will save time at borders if you prepare a sheet of paper with the following information listed clearly in Spanish: name, address, nationality, age, place and date of birth, sex, passport number and place of issue, destination, point of departure, profession, driver's license number, *carnet* number, owner of car, auto registration number, serial number, license plate number, make, year, and model of car, as well as a checklist including the number of spare tires, radio, tape deck, heater, air conditioning, number and color of seats. You will encounter many military checkpoints along country roads as well as at entrances to cities that require this information. Generally, major borders between countries will speed you through in about 15 minutes, but there are innumerable smaller road stations where the process is less efficient. It's not a bad idea to carry an inventory of your possessions written in Spanish and notarized by US customs before you leave home. It can save endless hassles.

Car Insurance – US policies are not valid in South America. It is therefore necessary to buy special policies for the countries of South America, and this can present some difficulties because few US insurance companies are authorized to issue foreign insurance, and at least one South American country — Ecuador — doesn't recognize insurance issued in another country. (Neither does Costa Rica, in Central America.) Your choices are to go to a US company that can issue a foreign policy (AAA's underwriters, discussed below, are one of the largest), being fully prepared to purchase additional local insurance where it is required, or to go from country to country getting local policies. The pervasive problem is always the rapidity with which South American insurance laws change, and the difficulty for any agent — even those for South American companies — to stay abreast of the latest developments. If you decide to go the route of single, country-by-country policies, you will discover that often no insurance is available at the border and that you will be forced to drive to the nearest large town before purchasing insurance, leaving you virtually unprotected on the interim journey. For this reason, we advise contacting AAA about the varieties of pan–South American insurance available, recognizing that even such a policy may prove inadequate in the eyes of local authorities when you reach South America.

AAA has two kinds of Latin American policies, one providing full coverage (comprehensive, collision, fire, and theft), another offering limited liability. Rates are determined by the number of months you will be driving in South America and the book value of your car. (It is a good idea to get a comprehensive policy that covers theft and vandalism.) For more information, contact your local AAA office (you don't have to be a member to buy a policy); the national office at 8111 Gatehouse Rd., Falls Church,

VA 22042 (phone: 703-222-6000); or the AAA agent at American International Underwriters, Automobile Underwriters' Department, 99 John St., New York, NY 10038 (phone: 212-770-7000 or 770-9741 for South American information). American International Underwriters maintains offices staffed by English-speaking people in the following locations in South America:

Argentina: American International Underwriters Para Representación y Mandatos en La Argentina, Av. Roque, Saenz Pena, 648, Planta Baja, 1 y 2 pisos, Buenos Aires (phone: 33-30-47-16)

Brazil: American International Underwriters, Representcoes, Caix Postal 1893-2c-00, or Rua Senador Dantas 74/70, Rio de Janeiro (phone: 52-21-20); Praça de República 497, 5° andar, São Paulo (phone: 36-01-98); Rua Uruguay 335, S/71, Pôrto Alegre (phone: 25-20-61)

Colombia: American International Underwriters de Colombia, Calle 78 No. 9-57, Bogotá (phone: 255-9700)

Uruguay: American International Underwriters, Calle Rincón 467, Montevideo (phone: 80-92-6)

Venezuela: C. A. de Seguros American International, Av. Fco. de Miranda, Ed. Seguros Venezuela, Apdo. 61320 Chacaeo, Caracas 106 (phone: 33-43-31/2/4/5)

Automobile Clubs – In addition to being able to provide fine road maps, AAA can help you plan your route and offers full reciprocity with automobile clubs in Chile and Venezuela. They have limited reciprocal agreements with clubs in Argentina, Bolivia, Brazil, Colombia, Ecuador, Paraguay, Perú, and Uruguay. You can join the AAA through local chapters (listed in the telephone book under "Automobile Club of . . ."). For information, contact the AAA national office, noted above. Other large clubs in the US are:

Allstate Motor Club: Run by Allstate Insurance; join through any Allstate agency. Ask for information from the club, 30 Allstate Plaza, Northbrook, IL 60062 (phone: 312-291-5000 or 800-323-6282).

Amoco Motor Club: Join through any Amoco dealer or the national office, PO Box 9049, Des Moines, IA 50366 (phone: 800-334-3300).

Montgomery Ward Auto Club: Open to people with a Montgomery Ward charge account. Join through any Montgomery Ward store; ask for information from the national office, 250 E Carpenter Fwy., Irving, TX 75062 (phone: 214-348-5058 or 800-621-5151).

United States Auto Club Motoring Division: Ask for information from the national office, 1700 Mishawaka Ave., South Bend, IN 46624 (phone: 219-236-3700).

The following are automobile clubs in Latin American countries:

Argentina: Automóvil Club Argentino, Av. del Libertador 1850, Buenos Aires (phone: 802-6061)

Bolivia: Automóvil Club Boliviano, Av. 6 de Agosto 2993, (San Jorge) La Paz (phone: 3-51667)

Brazil: Automovel Club do Brasil, 90 Rua do Passeio, 90, ZC-06 Rio de Janeiro (phone: 297-4455); *Touring Club do Brasil,* Praça, Maua-Estaçao, Maritima, (Berilo Neves) Rio de Janeiro (phone: 268-7442)

Chile: Automóvil Club de Chile, Pedro de Valdivia 195, Santiago (phone: 225-7253)

Colombia: Automóvil Club de Colombia, Av. Caracas 14, No. 46-72, Bogotá (phone: 232-7580)

Ecuador: Automóvil Club del Ecuador, Elay Alfaro 218 y Berlin, Quito (phone: 237779)

Guyana: Georgetown Automobile Association, Georgetown

Panamá: Automóvil Club de Panamá, Av. Tivoli 8, Panamá (phone: 62-04-45)

Paraguay: Touring y Automóvil Club Paraguayo, 25 de Mayo y Brasil, Asunción (phone: 97-801)

Perú: Touring y Automóvil Club del Perú, Av. Cesar Vallejo 699, Lince Lima (phone: 40-32-70)

Suriname: Automobilisten Vereniging, Paramaribo

Uruguay: Automóvil Club del Uruguay, Avdas. del Libertador, Brig. Lavelleja & Uruguay, Montevideo (phone: 98-47-0); *Centro Automovilista del Uruguay,* Blvd. Artigas 1773, Montevideo (phone: 412528)

Venezuela: Touring y Automóvil Club de Venezuela, Edificio Auto Comercial, Plaza Sur de Altamira, Caracas (phone: 926373)

Maps – Automobile clubs are the best source of maps. You can also obtain maps from the Exxon Touring Service, 1251 Ave. of the Americas, New York, NY 10019 (phone: 212-398-3000). There is a chart of mileage, altitude, and road conditions for the complete Pan-American Highway and alternate routes in the *Latin America Travel Guide and Pan-American Highway Guide,* by Ernst A. Jahn. Although this book is out of print, you may be able to find it in some bookstores or at the library.

Preparing Your Car – Before getting on the road, always make certain your car is in excellent condition. Have it inspected very carefully, and be sure that your brakes and spare tire are functional. It is a good idea to use six-ply tires with inner tubes. Tire repair shops (*vulcanizadores*) can be found in small towns and large cities. They are generally reliable and will often be able to supply used tires. New tires cost almost twice as much in South America as they do in North America. Make sure you bring extra inner tubes, a tube repair kit, valves, a hand air pump, a gauge, and a couple of aerosol inflators in case you get a flat on a long, empty stretch of road.

1. In addition to the tire repair kit, gauge, and aerosol inflators, bring the following equipment: a flashlight, jack, wrench, two wooden blocks; an extra set of keys; a first-aid kit; jumper cables; gloves; a white towel (useful for signaling for help as well as for wiping the car).

   Make sure, too, that you carry a couple of extra fan belts, distributor points, a fuel pump replacement kit, a container of water for the radiator, and a steel container of gasoline. (Plastic containers tend to break when the car is bouncing over rocky roads. This, in turn, creates the danger of fire should the gasoline ignite from a static electricity spark. Plastic containers also tend to burst at high altitude.)

   In Venezuela, in order to carry gasoline, you must have a police permit — which can only be obtained after you pay a fine for having run out of gas. Otherwise, you can be fined for breaking the laws against transporting gasoline.

   Bring condensers and spark plugs. If you are driving at a high altitude, you should change cold spark plugs for hot and advance the spark to prevent the engine from stalling. It is essential that you carry all spare parts, as many Latin American towns do not stock them, especially for foreign cars. This will save your spending a week or more waiting for spare parts to arrive from the capital.

2. You will find that Latin American mechanics are just as efficient as those at home. If you have the parts, they are quite capable of repairing your car.

3. When you fill your tank, make sure the attendant moves the counter back to zero. It is also a good idea to carry at least 2½ gallons of reserve gas because many areas experience frequent shortages. The price of gasoline varies considerably from country to country; be prepared to pay for it with cash.

   In many rural areas, the gasoline is diluted with water or kerosene. If your car stops after you have just filled up, it could be due to impure gasoline. Sometimes dirt gets into the fuel line, so it is a good idea to have an in-line fuel filter.

4. Take it easy your first few days on the road. Try not to drive more than 6 or 7 hours a day, if possible. Stop to rest when you are tired. It is very important to be alert.

Breakdowns – If you have a breakdown on the road, immediate emergency procedure is to pull off the road, raise the hood to signal that help is needed, and tie a white rag to your radio antenna or door handle. Don't leave the car unattended.

Unlike in Mexico, where the Green Angel emergency service fleet patrols the road, most of Latin America has no such service. However, people are very helpful, and someone will stop to help you. Truck drivers are usually very good mechanics since they have to be able to repair their own vehicles when they break down in out-of-the-way places.

Car Care – Shell Oil publishes a series of pamphlets on car care, obtainable from Shell gas stations in the US or by writing to Shell Oil at PO Box 80, Tulsa, OK 74102 (phone: 800-331-3703). It helps to have some idea of what might be wrong with your car and to know something about standard maintenance.

1. A car needs its oil changed about every 3,000 miles; a tune-up every 12,000 miles (24,000 for transistorized ignition cars); spark plugs every 25,000 miles; fan and air-conditioning belts every 5,000 miles.
2. Recognize warning signals:
   - Fluid leaks: Spread paper and look for the following: brown or black fluid, *oil leak;* pink fluid near wheel, *leaking brake fluid;* pink or reddish fluid, *automatic transmission seal leak;* colorless or greenish fluid near front, *radiator or hose leak.*
   - Car has trouble starting: May be vapor lock caused by hot weather; a cold, wet rag on the fuel line and pump may help.
   - Engine missing after quick acceleration: Could be a fleck of carbon lodged between the electrodes of a spark plug. Clean plug.
   - Rattle in rear: Loose muffler or tailpipe.
   - Rattling noise: Bent fan blade or loose pulley.
   - Loud squealing noise when wheel turns: Low power steering fluid.

Road Safety and Highway Conditions – The Pan-American Highway is not a well-surfaced superhighway. In many cases, it is only a two-lane gravel road. In Perú and Chile, it is a two- and occasionally a three-lane paved road in good condition. In the Andes, roads are generally gravel. In the rainy season, landslides often make it impossible to pass. Make sure you have enough gasoline and supplies should you have to turn back. If you have to stop on the road, make sure you get all the way off.

Be particularly careful about the following:

1. Don't drive after dark. The fields are not fenced in, and you never know when a llama or a cow will decide to see what's on the other side of the road. (Even in the daytime, they sometimes stand in the middle of the road and stare you down.) Bicycles and other vehicles without lights are also nighttime road hazards, as are pedestrians.
2. You will occasionally encounter one-lane bridges on two-lane highways. The driver who flashes his or her lights first is supposed to cross the bridge first. This is standard procedure both day and night. Make sure you slow down as you get to the bridge and take it slowly as you cross.
3. Obey speed limits and traffic regulations, especially driving through towns and cities. As there are very few bypass roads, you will have to slow down going through populated centers. Speeds are always given in kilometers, and most countries use international symbols on highway signs. They are easy to understand.

RENTING A CAR: The better alternative to driving your own car is renting one in South America. Both Hertz and Avis maintain offices in the major cities, and car rental desks are often found in big hotels. However, car rentals are very expensive on a per-day basis, and with mileage rates and the long distances between points in South America, the total cost can be astounding. Gas, however, in a few places such as Ecuador, may seem reasonable. Cars often can be rented on a weekly basis — which is still not inexpensive. The minimum age for renting a car is 25 in Brazil and Argentina, 21 elsewhere. Also in Brazil, local restrictions require payment in cash. Otherwise, credit will usually be extended to holders of American Express, Diners Club, MasterCard, and Visa. Generally, South America finds Visa and Diners Club most acceptable.

Other considerations when renting a car:

1. International driving permits are required for Brazil and Uruguay; in other countries, your US license will be accepted.
2. If you plan to cross an international border, check with the rental company in advance. Most local offices will permit their cars to be driven out of the country and will give you a letter of border authorization. Other government papers may also be required. You will probably have to return the car to the location — thus the country — where it was rented.
3. Be sure you know the phone number of your rental office for any auto-related problems that come up once you are on the road.
4. If you get a traffic ticket, follow police instructions and don't argue. You can report any unfair treatment later, but don't expect any quick resolutions of problems that arise far from major cities.

Hertz has 126 South American offices. Avis has 74 South American offices. Budget Rent-a-Car has offices in 7 countries. In addition, there are reliable, local car rental firms. (See the *Getting Around* entry in each city report in THE CITIES.)

Touring by Ship

Travel by ship is leisurely and romantic. If you are not susceptible to seasickness, a cruise is a thoroughly delightful social experience. Although such travel used to be the province of the wealthy classes, today cruises are priced so that middle-class people can afford them, too. Some cruises are expensive by median-income standards, but a good many are reasonably priced. Most of them last 2 weeks or longer and include frequent stops at interesting ports.

Very few visitors to South America choose sea travel alone as a means of transport. It is slow, service is infrequent to most places, and, compared to air travel, quite costly. Generally, people take a cruise ship to South America for the sheer pleasure of it, because it's part of a Caribbean cruise, or because of a special interest in a particular area that is best visited by sea.

CABINS: The most important factor in determining the price of a cruise is the cabin. Cabin prices are set according to size and location. On older ships, cabin sizes can differ considerably. On recently modernized vessels or newer ships, cabins have less variation. Some of the most modern ships have uniform cabins.

Shipboard accommodations have the same pricing pattern as hotels. Suites, which consist of a sitting room–bedroom combination and occasionally a private small deck that could be compared to a patio, cost the most. Prices for other cabins (or staterooms) are usually more expensive on the upper passenger decks, less expensive on lower decks. The outside cabins with portholes facing the water cost more than inside cabins without views and are generally preferred. As in all forms of travel, accommodations are more expensive for single travelers. If you are traveling on your own but want to share a double cabin to reduce the cost, you have to wait until the ship line finds someone of the same sex willing to share quarters. Then your reservation can be confirmed. If the cabin has a bathtub instead of a shower, the price will probably be increased.

The brochure provided by the cruise line includes a deck plan for each ship, with the exact location of each cabin and a list of rates for any scheduled cruise. It is advisable to book your reservation as soon as possible after the cruise is announced. When you book your passage you can select your cabin, but if it is not available, you must wait to be informed of alternate spaces that are closest in price, room size, and location to your original request.

When considering the cost of the cruise, it is important to remember that all food expenses on board are included. The meals are usually excellent.

CRUISE LINES: South American ports of call are visited most frequently in combination with Caribbean cruises and by ships cruising through the Panamá Canal. These include Costa, Cunard, Epirotiki, Holland America, Home Lines, Paquet, Princess, Royal Caribbean, Royal Cruise Lines, Royal Viking, Sitmar, and Sun Line; sailings are both east- and westbound through the Canal, but check with cruise lines for exact dates.

Delta Lines, long the major cruise company in South America, no longer carries passengers. However, Cunard/Norwegian American's *Vistafjord* sails annually to Rio, with stops at Devil's Island, Belém, Recife, and Salvador. Sun Line's *Stella Solaris* makes the Rio cruise with an east coast routing for Carnival and has other winter departures from Miami. Epirotiki's MV *Jason* also sails this route and other South America regional sectors. Both programs offer Amazon River cruises, which include one way by air and one by sea. Allegro Cruises uses the *Boheme* for sailings through the Caribbean and down to Rio.

Occasionally, steamship freighter lines also carry passengers. The Lykes Bros. Steamship Company (Lykes Center, 300 Poydras St., New Orleans, LA 70130; phone: 504-523-6611) has ships that carry 12 passengers and sail from the US to Cartagena, through the Canal to Guayaquil, Valparaíso, and Callao (the port for Lima). Ivaran Lines (phone: 212-442-8989) has two ships, each with a pool and capacity for 12 passengers, that have routings to Mexico, Barbados, Puerto Rico, Brazil, Uruguay, and Argentina.

Panamá is the cruising ground for the *Great Rivers Explorer,* which stops at small ports of call (Darien Jungle, Portobelo, San Blas Islands) on both the Atlantic and Pacific sides of the Canal. For 5- and 6-day-cruise information, contact Exploration Cruise Lines, 1500 Metropolitan Park Bldg., Seattle, WA 98101 (phone: 206-625-9600).

Some of the most fascinating waterbound trips originate in South America and offer such exotic destinations as the Galápagos Islands off Ecuador, the river system of the Amazon Basin, and Antarctica.

Galápagos Cruises, which is affiliated with Metropolitan Touring of Quito, has a year-round cruise ship and yacht program in the islands. The company's 90-passenger *Santa Cruz* offers 3-, 4-, 5-, and 7-night itineraries, and its *Amigo I* yacht, accommodating 14 passengers, sails on week-long cruises. In addition, the company has motor sailing yachts for charter that accommodate from 4 to 16 passengers; itineraries are somewhat flexible. For information, contact the US representative in Dallas, Adventure Associates, 13150 Coit Rd., Dallas, TX 75240 (phone: 214-907-0414 or 800-527-2500).

The *Buccaneer* also carries 90 passengers to the Galápagos on 3-, 4-, 5-, and 7-night cruises. Reservations in the US from Galápagos, Inc., 7800 Red Rd., South Miami, FL 33143 (phone: 305-371-3386 or 800-327-9854).

Both Galápagos cruise ships are air conditioned and sail with naturalist guides who lead the shore expeditions and lecture on wildlife and conservation. (See *Ecuador,* DIRECTIONS, for details.)

The *Society Explorer* and *World Discoverer* of Society Expeditions sail, via the

Falkland Islands, to Antarctica from Buenos Aires; the itinerary includes nature reserves on the Valdez Peninsula and stops along the Antarctic shore. In addition, the ship offers an Amazon program from Belém and Manaus to Leticia, Colombia, and Iquitos, Perú. Naturalist guides are on board, and small riverboats provide tributary exploration. For information, contact Society Expeditions, 3131 Elliott Ave., Seattle, WA 98123 (phone: 206-285-9400 or 800-426-7794). The Allegro's *Boheme* heads south from Rio, stopping at Montevideo and Buenos Aires, with a routing around Cape Hope and to the ports of Punta Arenas, Chile, and Ushuaia, Argentina. Two Costa Line ships, the *Enrico* and the *Eugenio,* combine Caribbean ports, Brazil coast cruises, and a route south to Buenos Aires; the ports of call are Santos and Angra dos Reis in Brazil and Montevideo, Uruguay. The *Sea Goddess II,* a deluxe 58-cabin cruiser, also follows a southern continent routing between Rio and Buenos Aires during November and December, but can stop at many smaller ports because of her more diminutive size. For the exact itinerary, check with Sea Goddess Cruises, now owned by the Cunard Line (phone: 800-458-9000).

Flotel Orellana carries passengers very comfortably on the Napo River, an Amazon tributary in Ecuador. Eastern and Ecuatoriana airlines have tour programs using the *Flotel* on 4- and 5-day cruises that include jungle walks, visits to Indian villages, and small-craft rides to interior lakes. More rugged excursions to Pañacocha are available by motor launch. For information on this Metropolitan Touring excursion, call Adventure Associates at 800-527-2500.

Amazon River travel is coming into its own from Brazil, with new options now available between Belém and Manaus. Perhaps the most important addition will be the *Stella Solaris,* flagship of Sun Line's fleet, sailing up the big river on its gala Christmas cruise. For information, call 212-397-6400 in New York or 800-223-5760 elsewhere. Epirotiki's *World Renaissance* also sails along the Amazon from December to March (phone: 212-599-1750 in New York or 800-221-2470 elsewhere). Astor United Cruises, a new company with a 600-passenger ship, in January will begin sailing from Rio to Bahía, Belém, and Manaus; from Manaus, back along the Amazon, north to Cayenne and Port of Spain. For information, contact the line at PO Box 13140, Port Everglades St., Fort Lauderdale, FL 33316 (phone: 800-327-8152). Two smaller ships have been built specially for Amazon cruising: the *Victoria dos Palmares,* departing Fridays from Manaus and returning there on Mondays, and the *Para* (of the ENASA line), which will cruise between Belém and Manaus. Making 3- and 6-day circuits from Manaus is the *Tuna,* a small and comfortable expedition craft with a naturalist guide aboard. On the Peruvian Amazon, there are 5-night cruises of the MV *Margarita,* a classic riverboat accommodating 12 passengers on a circuit from Iquitos. For information on these specialized trips, contact Ladatco, 2220 Coral Way, Miami, FL 33145 (phone: 800-327-6162 or, in Florida, 800-432-3881).

SHIP SANITATION: Much has been made recently of the sanitary — or in many cases unsanitary — conditions of the world's cruise ships. The US Public Health Service currently inspects all passenger vessels calling at US ports, so very precise information is available on which ships meet the Public Health Service requirements and which do not. The further requirement that ships immediately report illness that occurs on board adds to the available data.

So the problem for a prospective cruise passenger is to determine whether the ship on which he or she plans to sail has met the official sanitary standard. New (1986) regulations require the PHS to publish actual grades for the ships inspected — rather than the old pass or fail designation — so it's now easy to determine any cruise ship's sanitary status. Nearly 1,000 travel agents receive a copy of each monthly ship sanitation summary, though a random sampling of travel agents indicated that few had any idea what this ship inspection program is all about. Perhaps the best advice is that you deal with a travel agent who specializes in cruise ships and cruise bookings, for he or she is most likely to have the latest information on the sanitary conditions of all cruise ships. To receive a copy of the most recent summary, write to Mr. John Yashuk, Public Health Service, 1015 N America Way, Room 107, Miami, FL 33132.

Touring by Train

Whether you enjoy efficient, air-conditioned train rides along well-maintained tracks or like the nostalgic wheezing of steam locomotives, you'll be able to find a railway to suit you somewhere in South America. Rail service varies considerably from one section of the continent to the other. Generally, trains in the southern part of South America are more efficient, comfortable, and modern than those in the northern sections. In Argentina, Brazil, and Chile, railway service remains relatively punctual and fairly smooth. However, in Ecuador, Bolivia, and Perú, trains tend to be considerably more ramshackle on rail lines originally built to connect the coastal cities and inland mountain settlements close to the mines. Although the scenery in the Andean countries is among the world's most spectacular, one prerequisite for traveling by train is indomitable patience, a good sense of humor, and a tolerance for spending long hours jammed in a rickety wooden seat in a passenger car filled with people and an occasional chicken. It is well worth the discomfort.

Another factor to keep in mind when considering a train trip through South America is the time involved. In addition to long distances, there are innumerable mechanical delays, flooding during the rainy season, and often rugged terrain to cross, all of which combine to stretch a distance of some 200 or 300 miles into a 10- to 15-hour trip.

ACCOMMODATIONS AND FARES: The quality of train accommodations varies considerably in different countries as well as within each country. Argentina's trains have air conditioning, Pullman cars, overnight sleeping compartments, and diners. Some of Brazil's trains, in the state of São Paulo, have air conditioning, Pullman cars, and buffets. On the other end of the scale, the Quito-Riobamba train in Ecuador provides neither heat nor food. The "tourist train" from Cuzco to Machu Picchu in Perú has comfortable seats, whereas the "Indian train" along the same route is generally "standing room only." The Uyuni-Pulcayo Railway in Bolivia uses old-fashioned steam engines, as does the railway system in central Paraguay. The overnight train from Santiago to Puerto Montt, Chile, has air conditioning, sleeping cars, and a restaurant.

As in the US, fares are assessed according to the type of accommodations. Some trains have first-class and second-class cars. First class will generally be less crowded. Train travel anywhere in South America is unbelievably inexpensive compared to that in the US. There is no way to generalize about train fares.

BOOKING: Tickets can be purchased at train stations in each country. There is an unlimited-mileage rail ticket called AMERAILPASS that is issued locally in Argentina, Bolivia, Brazil, Chile, Paraguay, and Uruguay. It can be used only in these countries and can be purchased only by an international transit passenger with a passport. Passes are available for one-, two-, and three-month periods; currently the cost starts at $90; but rates are expected to increase, so for up-to-date information write to Asociación Latino Americano de Ferrocarilles, Florida 783, Buenos Aires. Since short-run South American train tickets come at bargain travel prices, the passes are useful only to those traveling extensively by rail.

SERVICES: While it is extremely difficult to generalize about the quality of South American train services, a rule of thumb might be that they are fairly good in the southern zone (Chile and Argentina) as well as in parts of Brazil. Elsewhere on the continent, the trains seem more appropriate for carrying cargo, not passengers. Generally, trains called *ferrobus* are the best. You may take as much baggage as you can carry onto a South American train; many people drag their entire worldly possessions along with them. Most stations have porters who will carry your baggage; a minimum tip of 50¢ is greatly appreciated. On board, keep constant track of your belongings.

RAILWAY OFFICES: The major railway offices in South America are:

Argentina – Argentine Railways (Ferrocarriles Argentinos [FA]), Av. Ramos Mejia 1302, Buenos Aires. The Argentine railways have 27,000 miles of track. Formerly a British-owned rail system, it has diesel-drawn engines, new dining cars, and sleepers built by an Argentine subsidiary of Fiat. Two of the most popular routes are the Buenos Aires–San Carlos de Bariloche in the Lake District, a 30-hour trip, and the Buenos Aires–Mendoza route, which is 14 hours minimum.

Bolivia – National Railway Company (Empresa Nacional de Ferrocarriles [ENFE]), Estación Central, Casilla 428, La Paz (phone: 352510 or 353510). This 1,400-mile system of railway tracks is divided into an eastern and a western region. A mixed Argentine-Bolivian railroad commission is constructing a railroad from Santa Cruz, Bolivia, to Río Mamore, Argentina. Other railway systems are: Machacamarca-Uncia Railway (Ferrocarril Machacamarca-Uncia), Machacamarca; and Uyuni-Pulcayo Railway (Empresa Minera Pulcayo), Pulcayo. With five steam engines, this is the oldest railway in Bolivia.

Brazil – With 23,125 miles of track, Brazil's railways are divided into 22 government-owned divisions that in turn are organized into four regional systems. The Rede Ferroviaria Federal, SA (RFFSA)'s regional offices are: *Northeast:* Rua D. María Cesar, 170, 3rd floor, Recife (phone: 24-32-62; 24-05-35; 24-51-68). *Central:* Ed. D. Pedro 11, Praça Cristiano Otoni, 4th floor, Rio de Janeiro (phone: 242-0648). The central region's most popular train is the Rio–São Paulo Cruzeiro do Sul express, a 7-hour trip. Trains have sleeping cars. *Central South:* Praça da Luz, Caixa Postal 8061, ZP-01120, São Paulo (227-7222). The dramatic, 30-mile trip from Santos to São Paulo takes 1½ hours in a comfortable, air-conditioned train with buffet food service. *South:* Largo Visc. de Cairu, 17, 3rd floor, Pôrto Alegre (phone: 24-18-61). Other Brazilian railways include: São Paulo Railways (Ferrovia Paulista, SA [FEPASA]), Rua Libero Badaro 39, 01009, São Paulo (phone: 239-0022); Amapa Railways (Estrada de Ferro de Amapa), Pôrto Santana, Macapa, PO Box 396, Belém, 66000; and Victória a Minas (Cia Vale do Rio Doce), Caixa Postal 155, Victória Espirito Santo.

Chile – Chilean State Railways (Ferrocarriles del Estado), Casilla 134-D, Santiago (phone: 89-116). Most of Chile's 5,200 miles of track run north-south. The British-owned Antofagasta (Chile) and Bolivia Railroad maintains headquarters at 1 Broad St. Pl., London EC2 M7EL (phone: 588-7456). Trains run east from Antofagasta through the northern Atacama Desert and across the Andes into Bolivia. The Trans-Andine train, pulled by a Swiss engine, travels through a 10,900-foot pass within sight of Mt. Aconcagua, the highest peak in the Andes, to Las Cuevas. The Trans-Andine trip takes about 12 hours. The Arica–La Paz Railway, Casilla 9D, Arica, provides rail service across the Atacama Desert to La Paz. The 278-mile trip takes 10 hours.

Colombia – National Railways of Colombia (Ferrocarriles Nacional de Colombia), Calle 13, No. 18-24, Bogotá (phone: 775-577). The 2,300 miles of Colombian rail track are served by trains varying from rather comfortable to certainly usable. The better trains have restaurant facilities, and many routes go through such scenic territory that the slow pace and rather rundown equipment are secondary travel elements.

Ecuador – Ecuadorian State Railways (Empresa de Nacional Ferrocarriles del Estado), Carrera Bolívar 443, Quito (phone: 21-61-80). The 288-mile Quito-Guayaquil railway, completed in 1908, was severely damaged by floods a few years ago, and only the sector between Quito and Riobamba is fully operative on a daily basis. The train, however, travels through terrific mountain scenery, a ride of about 5 hours. In addition, on this track is a single-car autoferro, which operates daily except Sundays.

French Guiana – No railways.

Guyana – There is minimal service around Georgetown.

Panamá – While rail service is minimal in Panamá, there is one very interesting ride from the capital to Colón. There are half a dozen runs each day and the routing roughly parallels the Canal, with window views of both the ship movements and the jungle.

Paraguay – President Carlos Antonio López Railway (Ferrocarril Presidente Carlos Antonio López), PO Box 453, Calle México, Asunción. One of the oldest railways in South America, the 217-mile Paraguayan system dates from 1861 and has 21 steam locomotives. The Paraguay Northern Railway (Ferrocarril del Norte), Villa Concepción, extends 35 miles from Villa Concepción to Horqueta. It was built in 1910 to transport employees, supplies, and products related to the sawmill industry.

Perú – Peruvian National Railroad (Empresa Nacional de Ferrocarriles del Perú [ENAFER]), PO Box 1379, Ancash 207, Lima. The 2,214-mile Peruvian railway system includes the world's highest standard-gauge railway from Lima to La Oroya, which reaches a height of 15,688 feet. The Lima–Huancayo–Huancavelica train is recommended; leave Saturday to be in Huancayo for the Sunday market. Daily trains for Machu Picchu leave Cuzco early in the morning. The other Peruvian railway is Mining Company of Central Perú Railway Division (Empresa Minera del Centro del Perú Division Ferrocarriles), August N. Wiese 81, Lima (phone: 275-210). Formerly the train servicing the Cerro de Pasco mines, it takes passengers into the Andes.

Suriname – Paramaribo Government Railway, Onverwacht, Paramaribo. This 134-mile track leads from Paramaribo to the interior. The Suriname Bauxite Railway is now in the planning stages.

Uruguay – Uruguay State Railways (Administración de Ferrocarriles del Estado), Calle La Paz 1095, Casilla de Correo 519, Montevideo (phone: Montevideo 8-95-51; 8-58-66). The system links all parts of the country.

Venezuela – Venezuela National Railways (Ferrocarriles Nacional de Venezuela), Estación Caño Amarillo, Apdo. 146, Caracas (phone: 41-61-41). A poor railway system of 102 miles connects Guanta Naricual and Puerto Cabello with Barquisimeto. Railways are not given high priority as a transportation system in Venezuela; the government favors developing sophisticated highways and airports. The Encanto Historical Railway (Empresa del Ferrocarriles Histórico del Encanto), Caracas y Valencia, Caracas, takes passengers along an 8-mile track. This is for tourists only.

Touring by Bus

 The immense distances and the uncertainty of connections make it difficult to be enthusiastic about bus travel to South America from North America, but it is possible. From the US, both Greyhound and Trailways serve Laredo, Texas, where you can pick up a Mexican bus for the journey to and through Mexico City to points south. However, within South America, buses are inexpensive, frequent, relatively reliable (albeit often dilapidated), and a viable transportation alternative as long as you have time to spare for long delays due to bad roads and poor equipment. Bus travel is best in Brazil, Chile, and Venezuela.

Buses link nearly all areas of Central and South America, and many South American stations accommodate several private companies. It is fair to say that wherever a road exists (be it gravel or two-lane asphalt), you will find a bus route. Not only do buses run between major cities, they also travel between out-of-the-way towns and villages. (You will find that buses serve almost all the routes outlined in DIRECTIONS.)

Most people in South America depend on buses for transportation, so this is a good place to communicate with them. If you are lucky, you might make the acquaintance of a llama herder, teacher, health worker, farmer, labor union organizer, miner, doctor, missionary, or the lady whose goat may be riding on top of the bus.

ACCOMMODATIONS AND FARES: Four basic kinds of buses service South America: those with air conditioning and standard toilets; those with air conditioning and pull-down toilets; those with air conditioning without toilets; and the most common, called regular buses, without air conditioning or toilets, which can be found everywhere. In rural sections of the continent, they offer the only bus service available, and though crowded, cramped, and renowned for infrequent and some desperately needed "pit stops," they do the donkey work of public conveyance in South America. If you do any extensive traveling, you will undoubtedly ride one at some point.

Nonetheless, for obvious reasons you will be more comfortable on the better grades of "plush," or air-conditioned, first-class buses. These buses are clearly marked at the stations throughout South America, and you will pay a bit more for a ticket, though fares are so inexpensive across the continent in comparison to fares in the US that the difference between a regular and a first-class bus will seem quite small to most tourists.

BOOKING: Purchase tickets at the station. Because many bus companies oversell tickets, it is a good idea to buy your ticket early and get to the station in plenty of time to be among the first to board. The addresses of the major bus stations are listed in the *Getting Around* entry in the individual city reports in THE CITIES.

SERVICES: One caustic traveler called South American bus schedules "the best Latin American fiction since the Inca legends"; nonetheless, they provide extremely inexpensive long-distance transportation that is usually no more than a few hours off schedule. Beyond that very basic service, you will have to fend for yourself. Long-distance buses do stop at roadside cafés for food, but most North Americans will be more comfortable providing their own sustenance.

Package Tours

 Tour programs offer a combination of travel options for one price, and only one booking is necessary. Air or sea transportation, ground transfer from airport to hotel, ground accommodations, several meals, and sightseeing can be purchased as one unit for considerably less than if each element were bought separately. A package tour provides more than economy and convenience: It releases the traveler from having to make individual arrangements for each separate section of the tour.

As South America has come into its own as a travel destination, more and more package tours have become available. Airlines and travel agencies are offering a wide range of general sightseeing tours to major cities and exotic, remote destinations. Nearly all package tours include transportation, hotel accommodations, some meals, and a local tour of the major sites of interest. Sometimes the transportation part of the package is booked on a group air fare that costs less than economy fares; this lowers the cost of the package even further. Another economical way to travel is to buy a package or tour for land arrangements. For specific information on package tours, ask a travel agent. Below are many tour operators specializing in package tours to South America. Although you can contact them directly, we recommend booking through a travel agent.

Tour programs generally can be divided into two categories — "escorted" and "independent" — depending on arrangements offered. An escorted tour means that a guide will accompany the group from the US and through to return; a locally hosted tour means that the group will be met upon arrival in each country and have a different local host in each country. On independent tours, you generally have a choice of hotels, meal plans, and sightseeing trips in each city as well as excursions around each country. The independent plan is for people who do not want a set itinerary but who prefer confirmed reservations. Usually, US tour operators have corresponding local agents who are available to give additional assistance or make other arrangements on the spot. If you travel independently, be sure to take along the names of your travel agent's or US tour operator's contact in each country.

There are also a number of very precise and specific questions that you should ask a travel agent about an operator whose tour is being recommended. Among these are: Have you ever used the packages provided by this tour or charter operator in the past? How long has the tour operator been in business? And if you're talking about a charter package, make sure you find out if there is an escrow account in which deposits will be held, and find out the name of the bank in which the account has been placed.

Be sure, too, that you take the time to read the brochure *carefully.* Keep in mind that travel brochures are written to entice you into signing up for a package tour. Often the language is deceptive and devious. For example, a brochure may quote the lowest prices for a package tour based on facilities that are unavailable during the off-season, undesirable at any season, or just plain nonexistent. Information such as "breakfast included" (and it usually is on Brazil packages) or taxes (which can add up) are important items to note. Look for other special notes such as "locally hosted" tour, which means that you will have a new leader in each country, or "fully escorted," which means that one person will be along for the duration of the entire tour. "FIT" tours mean that you will be sightseeing with other people put together from all over; an escorted tour will generally begin and end with the same group.

If you are single, remember that prices quoted in brochures are based on double occupancy (two people traveling together). There is a single surcharge for people who travel alone. Whether you intend to travel alone or with a companion, keep in mind that the price of the package tour is based on one point of departure. If you do not live there, the cost of transportation to and from there should be added to the cost of the package.

As you study the brochure describing the package, keep a mental checklist of questions that relate to your priorities:

1. What kind of services do you require (air fare, other transportation, sightseeing, meals, and so on)? Does this package provide these services?
2. If the brochure indicates that "some meals" are included, does this mean welcoming and farewell dinners, two breakfasts, or every evening meal?
3. What classes of hotels are offered?
4. Do you get a refund if you cancel? If not, be sure to obtain cancellation insurance.
5. Can the tour operator cancel if too few people join?

Read the responsibility clause on the back page. Here, the tour operator usually reserves the right to change services or schedules as long as you are offered equivalent service; this clause also absolves the operator of responsibility for circumstances beyond human control, such as floods, famines, or injury to you or your property.

Following is a list of many of the major US operators who provide escorted or independent tours to Latin America. All tours are either deluxe or first class; none is economy, because there is no reliable economy hotel structure on the continent. Some offer AP (all meals), others MAP (breakfast and one main meal), and a few just breakfast or no meals. All these tours have several departure dates, depending on length of tour and countries visited.

Abreu Tours, 60 E 42nd St., New York, NY 10165 (phone: in New York, 212-661-0555; elsewhere, 800-223-1580). Specializes in independent tours, to Argentina or Brazil, for example.

Amazon Explorers, Rte. 9, Parlin, NJ 08859 (phone: in New Jersey, 201-721-2929; elsewhere, 800-631-5650). Colombia, Perú, and Brazil, with a focus on Amazon locales and safaris.

American Express, American Express Tower, 16 Executive Park Dr. NE, Atlanta, GA 30329 (phone: in Georgia, 404-320-5850; elsewhere, 800-241-1700). A full range of escorted regional and around–South America tours, as well as "freelance" programs of city-by-city and countryside touring of one country by independent travelers.

Andes International Tours, 85-06 Roosevelt Ave., Jackson Heights, NY 11372 (phone: in New York, 718-651-9444; elsewhere, 800-221-0464). Colombia.

Victor Emanuel Nature Tours, PO Box 33008, Austin, TX 78764 (phone: 512-477-5091). Specializes in bird-watching tours.

Four Winds Travel, 175 Fifth Ave., New York, NY 10010 (phone: in New York, 212-505-0901; elsewhere, 800-248-4444). Regional and around–South America 2- and 3-week escorted, deluxe tours.

Holbrook Travel, 3540 NW 13th St., Gainesville, FL 32609 (phone: 904-377-7111 or 800-451-7111). Imaginative, well-run natural history and special interest expeditions.

Ipanema Tours, 9911 W Pico Blvd., Los Angeles, CA 90035 (phone: in California, 213-272-2162 or 800-252-0681; elsewhere, 800-421-4200). Escorted tours around South America or country-by-country packages for independent travelers. Special air/sea programs.

Kuoni Travel, 10880 Wilshire Blvd., Los Angeles, CA 90024 (phone: in California, 213-475-5865 or 800-352-6581; elsewhere, 800-421-6616). Escorted tours around South America.

Ladatco Tours, 2220 Coral Way, Miami, FL 33145 (phone: in Florida, 305-854-8422 or 800-432-3881; elsewhere, 800-327-6162). Locally hosted Latin American tours; country-by-country and/or city packages; a variety of South American cruises.

Lindblad Travel, 1 Sylvan Rd. N, Westport, CT 06881 (phone: in Connecticut, 203-226-8531; elsewhere, 800-243-5657). Deluxe, escorted South America tours, including Easter Island, the Galápagos Islands, and the Amazon.

Maupintour, PO Box 807, Lawrence, KS (phone: in Kansas, 913-843-1211; elsewhere, 800-255-4266). A deluxe, escorted tour includes Ecuador, a Galápagos Islands cruise, and Perú.

Melia International, 1501 Broadway, New York, NY 10036 (phone: in New York, 212-719-3604; elsehwere, 800-223-7177). Regional South America tours with an accent on Brazil.

Mountain Travel, 1398 Solano Ave., Albany, CA 94706 (phone: in California, 415-527-8100; elsewhere, 800-227-2384). Adventure-travel tours and trekking and mountaineering expeditions.

Nature Expeditions International, 474 Willamette St., Eugene, OR 97440 (phone: 503-484-6529). Nature programs in Ecuador and the Galapagos Islands.

Nova World Tours, 444 Brickell Ave., Miami, FL 33131 (phone: in Florida, 305-864-1555; elsewhere, 800-327-7736). First-class, independent, 1- and 2-week tours of several countries (various combinations).

Olson Travelworld, PO Box 92734, Los Angeles, CA 90009 (phone: in California, 213-670-7100; elsewhere, 800-421-2255). Top-of-the-line deluxe and all-inclusive tours, from 17 to 30 days.

Portuguese Tours, 321 Rahway Ave., Elizabeth, NJ 07202 (phone: in New Jersey, 201-352-6112; elsewhere, 800-526-4047). Brazil.

Questers Tours & Travel, 257 Park Ave. S, New York, NY 10010 (phone: 212-673-3120). An extensive program of nature tours.

The Right Way Travel Corp., 16030 Ventura Blvd., Suite 250, Encino, CA 91436 (phone: in California, 818-906-1141 or 800-252-2085; elsewhere, 800-491-9100). Escorted and locally hosted regional tours around the continent.

See & Sea Travel, 50 Francisco St., San Francisco, CA 94133 (phone: in California, 415-771-0077 and 415-434-3400; elsewhere, 800-348-9778). Specializes in programs featuring scuba diving, sailing, and other water sports.

Sobek Expeditions, PO Box 1089, Angels Camp, CA 95222 (phone: in California, 209-736-4524; elsewhere, 800-344-3284). Adventure trips to Chile and Perú (including whitewater rafting), Ecuador (the Galápagos), and Brazil (national parks).

Society Expeditions, 3131 Elliott Ave., Seattle WA 98123 (phone: in Washington, 206-285-9400; elsewhere, 800-426-7794). Top-of-the-line (in price and operation) expeditions; travel with experts in nature and archaeology to the Amazon and Antarctica aboard the *World Discoverer* and *Society Explorer* and to Easter Island.

Tara Tours, 6595 NW 36th St., Miami Springs, FL 33166 (phone: in Florida, 305-871-1246; elsewhere, 800-327-0080). Group and independent travel in Perú; regional tours.

Tourlite International, 1 E 42nd St., New York, NY 10017 (phone: in New York, 212-599-2727; elsewhere, 800-272-7600). 1- and 2-week charters and city packages to Rio.

Travcoa, 400 MacArthur Blvd., Newport Beach, CA 92660 (phone: in California, 714-476-2800 or 800-992-2004; elsewhere, 800-992-2003). Deluxe programs around the continent, with good itineraries and escorts.

Traveluxe, 11 Broadway, New York, NY 10038 (phone: 212-233-6580). "Gourmet" tours; independent tours around South America and ski tours of Chile.

Vacation Travel Concepts, 57 W 57th St., New York, NY 10019 (phone: in New York, 212-888-1860; elsewhere, 800-221-4462). Charter flights to Brazil and/or Buenos Aires with Pan American and with Tower Airways.

Wilderness Travel, 1760 Solano Ave., Berkeley, CA 94707 (phone: in California, 415-524-5111; elsewhere, 800-247-6700). Specialists in outdoor adventure vacations, trekking, river trips, overland travel, and nature tours.

Tours are generally offered by operators in cooperation with one or more airlines, and you or your travel agent can request brochures from either. The airlines include Aerolíneas Argentinas, AeroPerú, Air Panamá, Avianca, Eastern, Ecuatoriana, Faucett, LAN Chile, LADECO, Pan American, Varig, Viasa.

Preparing

Calculating Costs

$ Estimating the cost of travel expenses in South America depends on what part of the continent you plan to visit, how long you will stay there and, in some cases, what time of the year you plan to travel. In addition to the basics of transportation, hotels, meals, and sightseeing, you have to take into account seasonal price changes that apply on certain air routings and at certain resorts; the comfort and style you want; and the inflation and, recently, currency devaluation factors in each country. While the price guidelines in this book will probably remain useful, costs for both facilities and services may have changed in the months since publication.

Generally speaking, it is still less expensive to travel in South America than in Europe. In capitals and major resorts, the cost difference between the two continents may be narrowing for hotel accommodations; however, meals, services, and local transportation (except car rentals) still cost far less in South America. According to tourism surveys by the United Nations, Caracas is ranked as one of the most expensive urban centers in the world, although the dollar is now so strong in most of South America that few of its cities will seem expensive to American travelers.

On the other hand, services, facilities, and meals are either substantially less expensive than New York, or even just plain reasonable, in Bogotá, Quito, Panamá City, Paramaribo, Lima, La Paz, Asunción and Montevideo. One example of the difference in price between city and resort is Montevideo, where the cost of staying is half that of the beach area of Punta del Este. It should be noted that this is an extreme price difference, but the basic premise can also be illustrated by Panamá City and Contadora Island in Panamá or Buenos Aires and Mar del Plata (in season) in Argentina.

Throughout South America, you will find a great divergence in prices between city and countryside, with rural areas offering some of the best travel bargains in the hemisphere. Haciendas in Colombia and Ecuador, lakeside lodges in Chile, small hotels near pre-Columbian sites in Perú and in colonial centers in Bolivia have comfortable accommodations and fair to fine local cuisine. In addition to their price-is-right feature, they are also right in or near places you will want to see. The only drawback to planning to stay a while in the countryside is the limited number of rooms available; this means that trips have to be planned ahead, especially to well-known areas.

When calculating costs for South American travel, start with the basics, but don't forget such extras as fees to museums, tips, local transportation, and shopping. The reasonable cost of these items is a positive surprise in your budget; such extras as drinks served with imported liquors and airport departure taxes are definite negatives. For specific guidance on what is worth budgeting for where, see the *Best in Town* sections of THE CITIES and the *Best en Route* suggestions of DIRECTIONS.

ACCOMMODATIONS: There is a wide range of choice and a vast difference in quality between the expensive, moderate, and inexpensive South American hotels. Generally all hotels of international chains in a given city are priced about equally. In

Brazil's major tourist centers, Caracas, or Buenos Aires, this can be from $65 to over $100 for a double (with Brazilian hotels, this usually includes breakfast); in Bogotá and Lima, $55 and $75. There is a big jump from these international-class hotels to those in the moderate category in the same cities, and accommodations will generally be about $15 to $20 less per night. Inexpensive, yet acceptable, hotels charge about $20 for a double room. In almost any small city or town, you can get a decent hotel room for about $15 a night. When inquiring about hotel rates, be certain to ask if they include local taxes and service charges.

Caribbean and other beach resorts charge about $50 to $80 a night for a double room at expensive hotels; $35 to $45 in those labeled moderate; and $20 or less in the inexpensive price range. In the last-named, you will probably not find guests or staff speaking much English.

FOOD: Compared to New York or Los Angeles, a meal at a lavish restaurant in most large South American cities is not expensive. Whereas it's easy to spend between $40 and $50 for a meal for two in a major US city, a similar meal in a top-quality restaurant in most urban centers below the equator should not come to more than $35, excluding drinks, wine, or tips. A typical twosome can dine well at a comfortable, moderately priced restaurant for less than $20, for less than $10 at an inexpensive restaurant. Prices are much lower outside the cities, but you have to take care because sanitary conditions sometimes are not up to US standards. The best food bargains in South America are local produce — fruit, vegetables, bread, beer, sausage — that are great for picnics and snacks on long journeys through rural areas where restaurants are hard to find.

GETTING AROUND: Bus and train transport is very inexpensive. If you are driving, you will find that gas prices vary considerably. It is least expensive in Ecuador, probably most expensive in Chile.

Planning a Trip

123 Travelers fall into two categories: those who make lists and those who do not. Some people prefer to plot the course of their trip to the finest detail, with contingency plans and alternatives at the ready. For others, the joy of a voyage is its spontaneity; exhaustive planning only lessens the thrill of anticipation and the sense of freedom.

Neither approach works perfectly in South America. It is an area that requires considerable preparation; internal flights often run only once or twice a week, and an advance booking can mean the difference between continuing to a new city or cooling your heels for several days awaiting another flight. On the other hand, fanatic planners will have to live with a degree of improvisation; some of the most exciting tours — into jungles, along rivers, to South America's fantastic natural wonders — can be arranged from nearby cities after your arrival. And whether you consider yourself a planner or a free spirit, you still have to decide certain basics at the very start: where to go, what to do, how much to spend. These decisions require a certain amount of forethought, consideration, and planning. Even perennial gypsies and anarchistic wanderers have to take into account the time-consuming logistics of getting around South America, and even with minimal baggage, they need to think about packing. So before rigorously planning specific travel-related details, you might want to establish your general travel objectives:

1. How much time do you have for the entire trip, and how much of it do you want to spend traveling?
2. What interests and activities do you want to pursue while on vacation?

3. At what time of year do you want to go?
4. What kind of geography or climate would you like?
5. How much money can you spend for the entire vacation?
6. Would you like a group or an independent tour?

Obviously, your answers will be determined by your personal tastes and life-style. These will condition the degree of comfort you require; whether you will select a tour or opt for total independence; and how much responsibility you want to take for your own arrangements (or whether you want everything arranged for you, with the kind of services provided in a comprehensive package trip).

You will not find a great deal of background and/or current information on travel in South America other than what is updated yearly in reliable travel guides. There are only a few South American countries with tourist offices in the US, and neither they nor their US consulates are known for replying punctually (or at all) to written requests for information on tourist facilities or activities. The local tourist offices listed under *Sources and Resources* in each city report in THE CITIES cannot be counted on to mail materials either; however, they can be very helpful when you arrive in a country. In the US a visit or phone call to the sales office of an airline with extensive routes on the continent will probably be more useful. In addition, a good travel agent (one who knows whom to ask if he or she doesn't know) can supply information on hotels and rates, air fares, and organized tours and packages. Motor clubs can often be a good source for brochures and maps, but, in general, there are few good descriptive tourist brochures for South America. (Colombia's are probably the best.) On the other hand, there are good little city and country guides available in English in many cities on the continent.

Make your travel plans early if you want to benefit from special fares or if you intend to visit popular destinations. Often, you are required to book reservations for charter flights as far ahead as 3 months. During the high season (December through February), beach resorts in Panamá, Brazil, Uruguay, Argentina, Chile, and Perú require reservations months in advance. If you plan to attend Carnival in Rio de Janeiro or anywhere else, be prepared to book as far ahead as 10 months to a year at one of the big hotels, and expect to pay considerably more than you would for the same accommodations any other time. Some hotels require deposits before they guarantee reservations, but most reputable hotels are flexible and will honor your reservation when you arrive. Make sure you have a receipt for any deposit and, preferably, some written confirmation of your reservation if you booked it yourself. If you plan to visit a particular country on a national holiday or during Easter week, it is also a good idea to book your hotel well in advance.

If you know ahead of time that you will be traveling to South America, you should consider learning some basic Spanish and/or Portuguese. Your trip will be much more rewarding and enjoyable if you can communicate with the people who live in the countries you will be visiting and, if you care, order from menus. South Americans do not frown on or criticize beginners' attempts at speaking their language; rather, they enthusiastically encourage you to continue fumbling your way through prepositional phrases by smiling and profusely assuring you that *"Ud. habla bien el castellano"* or *"Voce fala bom portugues"* ("you speak Spanish well" or "you speak good Portuguese"). You will find that having taken the time to learn a few extra words really will help when you are in South America — where English is far from the lingua franca. Most adult education centers offer courses in basic Spanish, and a good many teach Portuguese, too. Berlitz, among others, has a series of teach-yourself language courses on records or audio cassette tapes. These enable you to listen to phrases and repeat them. If you are shy about faltering phonetically in front of other people, these home study courses enable you to practice speaking in private. And a phrase book brought from home is always helpful.

Before you leave, make sure you attend to the following household details:

1. Arrange for your mail to be held by the post office or picked up daily at your home. Someone should check your door occasionally to pick up any unexpected deliveries. Piles of leaflets, circulars, packages, or brochures announce to thieves that no one is home.
2. Cancel all deliveries (newspapers, milk, and so on).
3. Arrange for the lawn to be mowed and plants to be watered at regular times.
4. Arrange for care of pets.
5. Etch your social security number in a prominent place on all appliances (television, radios, stereo, cameras, kitchen appliances). This considerably reduces their appeal to thieves and facilitates identification.
6. Leave a house key, your itinerary, and your automobile license number (if you are driving your own car) with a relative or friend, and notify the police, the building manager, or a neighbor that you are leaving and tell them who has the key and your itinerary.
7. Empty the refrigerator and lower your thermostat.
8. Immediately before leaving, check that all doors, windows, and garage doors are securely locked.

To discourage thieves further, it is wise to set up several variable timers around the house so that lights and even the television go on and off several times in different rooms of the house each night.

Make a list of any valuable items you are carrying with you, including your credit card numbers and the serial numbers of your traveler's checks, as well as a photocopy of your passport. Put copies in your luggage, purse, or pocket, and leave copies at home. Put a label with your name and home address on the inside of your luggage to facilitate identification in case of loss. Put your name, but not your address (or a business address only), on a label on the outside of your luggage.

Review your travel documents. Be sure you have your passport with necessary visas and/or tourist cards; an international driver's license, available for a small fee from the AAA (see *Touring by Car*, GETTING READY TO GO); and your tickets. If you are traveling by air, check to see that your plane ticket has been correctly filled in. The left side of the ticket should have a list of each stop you intend to make, even if you are only stopping to change planes, beginning with your departure point. Be sure that the list is correct, and count the number of coupons to make sure that you have one for each flight. If you have confirmed reservations, be sure that the column marked Status has "OK" beside each flight. Have with you vouchers or proofs of payment for any reservation paid in advance. This includes hotels, transfers to and from the airport, sightseeing, car rentals, special events, and so on.

If you are driving, be sure that, in addition to your driver's license, you have your car title, auto registration, proof of insurance, maps, books, flashlight, batteries, emergency flasher, first-aid kit, extra car keys, sunglasses, and extra water container. Take your jack and spare tire. When you get to the border, you will be issued a car permit, for which you must present your car registration. (For more information on preparing your car, see *Touring by Car*, GETTING READY TO GO.)

If you are traveling by plane, call to reconfirm your flight 72 hours before departure, both going and returning. This will not prevent you from getting bumped in case the flight is overbooked (see *Traveling by Plane*, GETTING READY TO GO). Reconfirmation applies to point-to-point flights in South America.

Finally, you should always bear in mind that despite the most careful plans, things do not always occur on schedule, especially in South America, where *ahora* ("now") means anytime between today and tomorrow, and *ahorita* ("right now") means anytime within the next 3 hours, so be prepared. If you maintain a flexible attitude at all times, shrug cheerfully in the face of postponements and cancellations, you will enjoy yourself a lot more. Because more and more transportation companies and hotels throughout South America are operating efficient, punctual services, delays are much less frequent than they were even a few years ago.

Entry Requirements and Documents

However you choose to travel to South America, American citizens will need a valid passport and, for most countries, an ongoing or round-trip ticket. You no longer need an international vaccination certificate. You can apply for a US passport at designated county court houses and post offices and the US Passport Agency nearest you (Boston, Chicago, New Orleans, Philadelphia, Honolulu, Houston, San Francisco, Los Angeles, Washington, D.C., Miami and Stamford). The New York City office is at 630 Fifth Ave., New York, NY 10020 (phone: 212-541-7700). To obtain a passport, you must bring proof of citizenship: either a birth certificate, naturalization certificate, or a previous passport. A driver's license, credit card, or military papers are not acceptable, although you should bring these or similar identification with your current description and signature in addition to proof of citizenship. You will also need two color photographs, 2 inches square, taken against a plain white background. Passport officials are very fussy about these pictures, and photographers charge about $5 to produce a pair of acceptable passport photos. Passport photographers maintain studios near the agency. The passport itself will cost $42, and a renewal, $35; it is valid for 10 years. It is easier, though more time-consuming, to write for an application and complete the entire process by mail. You must allow at least 2 weeks for delivery, even when submitting your application in person.

The entry requirements of each country are listed in FACTS IN BRIEF. While some countries ask for only a valid passport and proof of onward transportation, tourist cards or visas are required by five countries: Argentina, Brazil, Colombia, Panamá, and Venezuela. For Argentina, a passport must be delivered or mailed to the nearest consulate and left for 5 working days for processing. The Brazilian visa also must be obtained from the consulate, but there is no waiting time if delivered personally. Colombia requires that visitors have tourist cards, which may be obtained from the government tourist office in New York, any consulate, or any airline serving Colombia; cards are issued immediately, but passports must be accompanied by two passport-size photos. The Venezuelan consulate or the airlines and ships that serve the country issue this tourist card. For the above countries, tourist cards and visas are issued free of charge. Airlines and ship lines charge $2 for a Panamanian tourist card; the consulates call the same paper a visa and issue it free.

While traveling, carry your passport with you at all times — except in Colombia, Perú, and Brazil, where it is safer to leave it in the hotel safe and carry a copy of the pertinent pages. If you lose your passport, report it immediately to the nearest US consulate or embassy. (For a complete listing, see *Medical and Legal Aid,* GETTING READY TO GO.)

Generally, entering South American countries by air is a routine matter. Customs and immigration officials at airports tend to be fairly easygoing and will usually process anyone who looks reasonable in a few minutes without any hassle. South Americans love to travel around the continent, and the procedures involved in crossing from one country to another have been improved to accommodate the flow of traffic. Some countries require that you fill in an embarkation-disembarkation card. At major international airports, such as Rio de Janeiro, São Paulo, Buenos Aires, and Santiago, sophisticated computer technology enables immigration agents to punch in your passport number and obtain clearance in seconds. (It goes without saying that if you are wanted for a civil or political offense in these countries, the computer will inform the immigration authorities accordingly.)

How to Pack

 No one can provide a completely foolproof list of precisely what to pack, so it's best to let common sense, space, and comfort guide you. Keep one maxim in mind: Less is more. You simply won't need as much clothing as you think, and though there is nothing more frustrating than arriving at your destination without just that item that in its absence becomes crucial, you are far more likely to need a forgotten accessory — or a needle and thread or scissors — than a particular piece of clothing.

As with almost anything relating to travel, a little advance planning can go a long way. There are specific things to consider before you open the first drawer or fold the first pair of underwear:

1. Where are you going (city, country, or both)?
2. How many total days will you be gone?
3. What's the average temperature likely to be during your stay?

A few degrees can make all the difference between being comfortably attired and very real suffering. You will find climate information in each city entry in THE CITIES. Airlines and travel agents can provide weather facts, too.

Far and away the best source of accurate, complete information on climate, the clothes you will need, and sanitary conditions is the "World Climate Chart for South America," available free from the International Association for Medical Assistance to Travelers (IAMAT), 736 Center St., Lewiston, NY 14092 (phone: 716-754-4883). This thoroughly useful pamphlet contains a month-by-month chart of peak and low temperatures, in Fahrenheit and Celsius; altitude, in meters and feet; humidity; recommendations on the type of clothing to bring for each month; and advice on water, milk, and food. (For a general discussion of seasons in South America, see *What's Where* and *When to Go,* GETTING READY TO GO.)

Keeping temperature and climate in mind, consider the problem of luggage. Plan on one suitcase per person (and in a pinch, remember that it's always easier to carry two small suitcases than to schlepp one roughly the size of the *QE2*). Standard 26-inch suitcases can be made to work for one week or one month, and unless you are going for no more than a weekend, never cram wardrobes for two people into one suitcase. Young travelers might do well to remember that there is a distinct prejudice among South American border officials against backpacks; you'll have less hassle with a traditional suitcase or a duffel bag.

Women should figure on a maximum of five daytime and three late afternoon–evening changes. Whether you are going to be gone for a week or a month, this number should be enough. Before packing, lay out every piece of clothing you think you might want to take. Eliminate items that don't mix, match, or interchange. If you can't wear it in at least two distinct incarnations, leave it home. Try to stick with a single color scheme to minimize accessories.

Accessorize everything beforehand so you know exactly what you will be wearing with what. Perishable clothes — pure cotton and linen — are the hard-to-keep-up fabrics and should be left behind. Man-made fabrics, such as jerseys and knits, make the best traveling companions, although in very hot climates cotton clothing may be most comfortable.

Men will find that color coordination is crucial. Solid colors coordinate best, and a sport jacket that also goes with a pair of pants from a suit provides an added option. Hanging bags are best for suits and jackets, and shirts should be chosen that can be used for both daytime and evening wear. Double-duty shoes are also preferable. Latin Americans are appearance conscious, and although styles vary from place to place, certain standards apply throughout the major cities. For daytime, bring informal, comfortable clothes. Blue jeans are acceptable, although khakis or polyesters are preferable. At night, dress depends upon the formality of the place you are visiting. Generally speaking, anything that is clean, comfortable, and that looks presentable is acceptable everywhere but the most elegant restaurants and nightclubs. In beach resorts and Rio de Janeiro, bathing suits are acceptable anywhere near the water. Men often wear shirts over their trunks; women, skimpy sundresses at beach cafés. At night, trousers replace bathing trunks. Women's attire may remain pretty much the same, although dresses are often dressier after dark. In other cities, beachwear is not acceptable beyond the immediate vicinity of a hotel's swimming pool. Men rarely wear ties except for business and more formal evenings out.

Pack clothes that have a lot of pockets for traveler's checks, documents, and tickets. If your bag gets lost or stolen, you will retain possession of the essentials. It is a good idea to wear loose-fitting, lightweight clothes that can be rinsed in Woolite or a similar cold-water detergent and hung to drip dry. And be sure to have comfortable shoes. Pack lightweight sandals for beach and evening wear. It is permissible to wear your most comfortable shoes almost everywhere.

Your carry-on luggage should contain a survival kit with the basic things you will need in case your luggage gets lost or stolen: a toothbrush, toothpaste, medication, a sweater, nightclothes, and a change of underwear. With all of your essential items at hand at all times, you will be prepared for any sudden, unexpected occurrence that separates you from your suitcase. If you have many one- or two-nighters, you can live out of your survival case without having to unpack completely at each hotel.

The basic idea of packing is to get everything into the suitcase and out again with as few wrinkles as possible. Simple, casual clothes — shirts, jeans and slacks, permanent-press skirts — can be rolled into neat, tight sausages that keep other suitcase items in place and leave the clothes themselves amazingly unwrinkled. The rolled clothes can be retrieved, shaken out, and hung up at your destination. However, for items that are too bulky or too delicate for even careful rolling, a suitcase can be packed from bottom up to ensure the most protection for everything. Put heavy items on the bottom toward the hinges so that they do not wrinkle other clothes. Candidates for the bottom layer include shoes (stuff them with small items to save space), a toiletry kit, handbags (stuff them to help keep their shape), and an alarm clock. Fill out this layer with things that will not wrinkle or will not matter if they do, such as sweaters, socks, a bathing suit, gloves, and underwear.

If you get this first, heavy layer as smooth as possible with the fill-ins, you will have a shelf for the next layer, or the most easily wrinkled items, like slacks, jackets, shirts, dresses, and skirts. These should be buttoned and zipped and laid along the whole width of the suitcase with as little folding as possible. When you do need to make a fold, do it on a crease (as with pants), along a seam in the fabric, or where it will not show, such as shirttails. Alternate each piece of clothing, using one side of the suitcase, then the other, to make the layers as flat as possible. On the top layer put the things you will want at once: nightclothes, an umbrella or raincoat, and a sweater.

With men's two-suiter suitcases, follow the same procedure. Then place jackets on hangers, straighten them out, and leave them unbuttoned. If they are too wide for the suitcase, fold them lengthwise down the middle, straighten the shoulders, and fold the sleeves in along the seam.

SOME PACKING HINTS: Put liquids and cosmetics in plastic bottles wrapped in plastic bags and tied, and take what you will need; cosmetics are expensive. Otherwise, and in general, take less than you think you will need. You will acquire souvenirs, pamphlets, and other items as you travel, and you will appreciate having space for them.

For more information on packing clothes, send your request with a #10 stamped, self-addressed envelope to Samsonite Travel Advisory Service (PO Box 39609, Denver, CO 80239) for its free booklet, "Getting a Handle on Luggage."

How to Use a Travel Agent

To make the most intelligent use of a travel agent's time and expertise, you should know something of the economics of the industry. In most cases, you pay nothing for the services performed by the agent — from the booking of hotels to general advice on the best hunting lodges. Money that the travel agent makes on the time spent arranging an itinerary — booking hotels, resorts, or flights or suggesting activities — comes from commissions paid by the principals who provide these services — the airlines, hotels, and so on. These commissions currently average 10%, but can range from 7% to 15% — not so much considering the amount of time a good agent can spend arranging for your trip.

This tradition may be changing, so that in some cases a travel agent may ask you to pay a fee for services that do not include making reservations, but at the moment it is standard operating procedure for most agents across the country.

This commission system implies two things about your relationship with any agent:

1. You will get better service if you arrive at the agent's desk with your basic itinerary already planned. Know roughly where you want to go and what you want to do. Use the agent to make bookings for you (which pay commissions) and to advise you on facilities, activities, and alternatives within the limits of the basic itinerary you have chosen. You get the best service when you are requesting commissionable items. There are few commissions on camping or driving-camping tours; an agent is unlikely to be very enthusiastic about helping to plan one. The more vague your plans, the less direction you can expect from most agents. If you walk into an agency and say, "I have two weeks in June; what shall I do?" you will most likely walk out with nothing more than a handful of brochures. Do your homework.

2. There is always the danger that an incompetent or unethical agent will send you to a place offering the best commission rather than the best facilities. The only way to be sure you are getting the best service is to pick a good, reliable travel agent, one who knows where to go for information if he or she is unfamiliar with an area. To most agents, South America is an unfamiliar area.

You should choose a travel agent with the same care with which you choose a lawyer or a doctor. You will be spending a good deal of money on the basis of the agent's judgment, and you have a right to expect that judgment to be mature, informed, and interested. At the moment, unfortunately, there are no real standards within the industry itself, and the quality of individual agents varies enormously. Several states are toying with the idea of licensing agents (at press time only Rhode Island does so), which might help ensure that anyone acting as a travel agent is honest, if not necessarily competent. While there are as yet no laws regulating travel agencies, there is an industry organization, the American Society of Travel Agents (ASTA), which guarantees that any member agency belongs to the International Airline Travel Agent Network (IATAN) or is accredited by the Airlines Reporting Corp. Any travel agent who has completed the 18-month course at the Institute of Certified Travel Agents of Wellesley, Massachusetts, will carry the title Certified Travel Counselor (CTC). This certification guarantees a certain level of expertise.

For a list of ASTA members, write to the American Society of Travel Agents, 4400 MacArthur Blvd., Washington, DC 20007. ASTA has about 12,000 retail agent and tour operator members nationwide. The Association of Retail Travel Agents (ARTA), although much smaller, emphasizes consumer rights. It maintains an ethics board so that clients can present complaints and grievances. Its 3,200 members must attend educational programs on the travel business. For more information, write to ARTA, 25 S Riverside Ave., Croton-on-Hudson, NY 10520.

A number of banks own travel agencies, too. These provide the same services as other accredited commercial travel bureaus. Anyone can become a client, not only the bank's customers. You can find out more about these agencies, which belong to the Association of Bank Travel Bureaus, by inquiring at your bank or looking in the Yellow Pages. The US Travel Service publishes a free pamphlet, "The Benefits of Using a Travel Agent," which you can obtain by writing to Consumer Information, US Travel Service, US Department of Commerce, Washington, DC 20230 (phone: 202-377-2000).

Perhaps the best way to find a travel agent is by word of mouth. If the agent (or agency) has done a good job for friends over a period of time, it indicates a level of commitment and concern in your favor. Always ask for the name of the specific agent within an agency; it is the individual who serves you. There are some superb travel agents in the business, and they can facilitate vacation or business arrangements.

Once you've made an initial selection from those recommended, be entirely frank and candid with the agent. Budget considerations rank at the top of the candor list, and there's no sense in wasting the agent's (or your) time poring over prospective itineraries you know you can't afford. Similarly, if you like a fair degree of comfort, that fact should not be kept secret from your travel agent, who may assume that you wish to travel on a tight budget even if that's not the case.

In the past few years, South America has been moving up in the travel business as a more popular destination. A number of excellent package tours (see *Package Tours,* GETTING READY TO GO) have made booking less complicated for the agent. Arranging the itineraries of independent travelers takes more time than selling a package; therefore, you should be as specific as possible when consulting your agent. More and more travel agents are recommending South America as a travel destination.

Insurance

 For the most part, insurance is an option rather than a necessity when you travel. It is a good idea to consider different types of coverage, depending on your present homeowner's and medical policies. You may be insured against theft or illness in a foreign country as well as at home. But because as a traveler you will incur different risks, your insurance should provide you with specific coverage in case of accident, theft, injury, illness, or flight cancellation while you are out of the country. What follows are some suggestions about various types of insurance to consider before embarking on your trip to South America.

KINDS OF INSURANCE: Your decisions about the amount and type of travel insurance you need are primarily determined by your method of transport (US auto insurance is not valid in South America, and anyone traveling on a package tour should have cancellation insurance), the policies you hold already, and your attitudes toward travel. As a traveler, there are five basic types of insurance to consider:

1. Baggage and personal effects insurance
2. Personal accident and sickness insurance
3. Automobile insurance
4. Trip cancellation insurance
5. Flight insurance

Baggage and Personal Effects Insurance – Ask your agent if baggage and personal effects are covered by your current homeowner's policy, regardless of where you lose them in South America. If you are not covered, you will have to decide whether you need more protection than is automatically included in an airline ticket. (If you intend to drive, make sure you discuss full coverage for property damage and theft with your agent. See *Touring by Car,* GETTING READY TO GO.) The insurance offered by most airline companies includes only limited protection against loss or damage of luggage. The fine print on every ticket for an international flight specifies the limits of airline liability for luggage and contents at a maximum of $9.07 a pound or $560 per suitcase. These payments are assessed on the value of your baggage and its contents. They are not automatic payments. (It is a good idea to keep the sales receipts of baggage in your files.)

If you intend to bring goods of a greater value than the maximum protection designated on your ticket, you should consider excess value insurance, available from the airlines for about 50¢ per $100 of protection. You can purchase this excess value insurance at the ticket counter when you check in at the airport. *Note:* Be sure you read the fine print involving any excess value or baggage insurance policy. Often specific items, such as money, tickets, furs, gold and silver objects, art, and antiques, are excluded. Also remember that insurance companies usually pay the depreciated rather than the replacement value of the goods. As an extra precautionary measure, take photographs of valuables that will be traveling in your luggage and keep a record of all serial numbers of such items as cameras, typewriters, radios, and the like to verify your ownership of the objects. If your baggage disappears en route or is damaged, report it immediately at the airport, train station, or point of arrival. If an airline loses your luggage, you will be asked to fill out a Property Irregularity Report before you leave the airport. (You will probably have to wait until you return to the US for the actual payment on your declared losses.) If your property disappears elsewhere, report it to the police immediately.

Personal Accident and Sickness Insurance – Medical insurance covers your costs in case of illness during your trip or death in an accident. Most policies insure you for hospital and doctor's expenses. Most life and health insurance policies include this as a standard component, but such coverage does not necessarily apply to accidents and sickness occurring in foreign countries. Find out if your current medical policy covers you in foreign countries. If not, you can take out a separate vacation accident policy or an entire vacation insurance policy that includes health and life coverage.

Car Insurance – US policies are not recognized in South America, and you must have a special policy (issued in the US primarily by AAA) for driving in Latin American countries. Some South American countries recognize only locally issued policies; others recognize policies issued in the US. For a complete discussion of this confusing situation, see the insurance section of *Touring by Car,* GETTING READY TO GO.

Trip Cancellation Insurance – Although modern public charters have eliminated many of the old advance booking requirements, most charter and package tour passengers still pay for their travel well in advance of departure. The disappointment of having to miss a vacation because of illness or any other reason pales before the awful prospect that not all (and sometimes none) of the money paid in advance might be returned. So cancellation insurance for any package tour is a must. It is available from travel agents and tour operators in two forms: as part of a short-term, all-purpose travel insurance package (sold by the travel agent); or as specific cancellation insurance designed by the tour operator for a specific charter tour. A free brochure, "How to Select a Package Tour," is available from the US Tour Operators Association (USTOA), 211 E 51st. St., New York, NY 10022. Generally, tour operators' policies are less expensive, but also less inclusive. Cancellation insurance is also available directly from insurance companies or their agents as part of a short-term, all-inclusive travel insurance policy.

Before you decide which policy you want, read each one carefully. (Either can be purchased from a travel agent when you book the charter or package tour.) Be certain that the policy you select includes enough coverage to pay your fare from the farthest destination on your itinerary should you have to miss the charter flight. Also, be sure to check the fine print for stipulations concerning "family members" and "pre-existing medical conditions," as well as allowance for living expenses if you must delay your return due to bodily injury or illness.

Default and/or Bankruptcy Insurance – Although trip cancellation insurance usually protects you if you are unable to complete — or depart on — your trip, a fairly recent innovation is coverage in the event of default and/or bankruptcy on the part of the tour operator, airline, or other travel supplier. Some travel insurance policies now have this additional feature, and it is worth considering since it is no longer a remote possibility given estimates that some 50 commercial passenger airlines of all sorts have ceased operations since the advent of airline deregulation in 1978.

Should this type of coverage be unavailable to you (state insurance regulations vary, there is a wide variation in price, and so on), the best bet is to pay for airline tickets and tour packages with a credit card. The federal Fair Credit Billing Act permits purchasers to refuse payment for credit card charges where services have not been delivered, so the potential onus of dealing with a receiver for a bankrupt airline falls on the credit card company. Do not assume that another airline will automatically honor the ticket you're holding on a bankrupt airline, since the days when virtually all major carriers subscribed to a default protection program are long gone. Some airlines may voluntarily step forward to accommodate stranded passengers, but this is now an entirely altruistic act.

Flight Insurance – US and South American carriers alike have carefully established limits of liability for the death or injury of passengers. But these limits of liability are not the same as insurance policies. They usually only state the *maximum* an airline will pay in case of death or injury, and every penny is often the subject of a legal battle. This may make you feel inadequately protected, but before you buy last-minute flight insurance from an airport vending machine, consider the purchase in light of your total existing insurance coverage. A careful review of your current policies may reveal that you are already amply covered for accidental death, sometimes up to three times the amount provided for by the flight insurance offered at the airport.

Be aware that airport insurance, the kind you typically buy at a counter or from a vending machine, is among the least economical forms of life insurance available, and that even within a single airport, rates for approximately the same coverage vary widely. Often the vending machine policies are simply more expensive than coverage sold over the counter, even when the policies are with the same national company.

If you buy your plane ticket with an American Express, Diners Club, or Carte Blanche credit card, you are automatically issued life and accident insurance at no extra cost. American Express automatically provides $100,000 insurance; Carte Blanche, $150,000; Diners Club, $650,000. American Express offers additional coverage at extremely reasonable prices if you sign up for it in advance: $4 per ticket buys $250,000 worth of insurance and $6.50 buys $500,000 worth; $13 purchases $1 million worth of coverage.

Combination Policies – Short-term insurance policies, which include personal accident and medical coverage, trip cancellation insurance, and baggage and personal effects insurance, are available through insurance agencies, automobile clubs, and many travel agents. These combination policies are designed to cover you for the duration of a single trip.

Hints for Handicapped Travelers

 Although for many years the needs of seriously handicapped people were generally ignored, in recent years a series of imaginative, inter-American programs aimed at improving facilities and services for the handicapped in Latin America have been initiated. Chief among these is Partners of the Americas, which coordinates joint projects of special teams from US states working in various Latin American cities. In Minas Gerais, Brazil, for example, a Colorado team has been conducting a pilot project to develop technology to benefit disabled people. For more information, write to 2001 S St. NW, Washington, DC 20009. Partners of the Americas maintains an extensive library with information on this and similar programs throughout Central and South America.

Despite this relatively recent effort to develop special facilities for the disabled, handicapped travelers face pretty much the same problems in South America as in other parts of the world. Rural areas have no facilities. Cities have some, but there is no consistency, and data on services and facilities are fairly sparse throughout the continent.

PLANNING: The best way to find out if your intended destination can accommodate a handicapped traveler is to write or phone the tourist authority or hotel and ask specific questions. If you require a corridor of a certain width to maneuver a wheelchair or if you need handles on the bathroom walls for support, ask the hotel manager (some large chain hotels, such as the *Brasilton Hotel* in São Paulo, Brazil, have bathroom wall grips). A travel agent can be particularly helpful by getting this information for you (see *How to Use a Travel Agent,* GETTING READY TO GO). The following sources offer general information on access:

Access Travel: A Guide to the Accessibility of Airport Terminals, published by the Airport Operators Council International (1700 K St. NW, Washington, DC 20006; free). More than 400 airports in 42 countries are rated according to 70 features, including accessibility to bathrooms, corridor width, and parking spaces.

Access to the World, by Louise Weiss (Facts on File, 460 Park Ave. S, NY 10016; $14.95)

A List of Guidebooks for Handicapped Travelers, President's Committee on Employment of the Handicapped, 1111 20th and L sts., NW, Vanguard Bldg., Washington, DC 20210 (free; published September 1975)

Mobility International/USA (MIUSA), the US branch of Mobility International, a nonprofit British-based organization with affiliates in some 25 countries, offers advice and assistance to disabled travelers — including information on accommodations, access guides, and study tours. Among its publications are a quarterly newsletter and a comprehensive sourcebook, *World of Options, A Guide to International Educational Exchange, Community Service, and Travel for Persons with Disabilities.* Individual membership is $20 a year. For more information, contact MIUSA, PO Box 3551, Eugene, OR 97403 (phone: 503-343-1294, voice and TTY).

Travel Tips for the Handicapped, published by the US Travel Service. This free pamphlet can be ordered as part of the Consumer's Guide to Travel Information or by writing USTS, US Department of Commerce, Washington, DC 20230.

Moss Rehabilitation Hospital has a Travel Information Service (12th St. and Tabor Rd., Philadelphia, PA 19141; phone: 215-329-5715, ext. 2468), which will help plan a trip by providing details on hotels, restaurants, and other particulars. The service is free.

The Information Center for Individuals with Disabilities (20 Park Plaza, Room 330, Boston, MA 02116; phone: 617-727-5540) publishes information on tour operators, travel agents, and travel resources.

TOURS: Several organizations plan group tours for handicapped and disabled persons. Most will also arrange overseas itineraries for foreign independent travelers (FITs). They are:

Society for the Advancement of Travel for the Handicapped (SATH), Penthouse, 26 Court St., Brooklyn, NY 11242 (phone: 718-858-5483). To keep you abreast of developments in travel for the handicapped as they occur, you may want to join SATH, a nonprofit organization whose members include travel agents, tour operators, and other travel suppliers, as well as consumers. Membership costs $40 ($20 for students) and the fee is tax deductible. SATH publishes a quarterly newsletter and can provide information on travel agents or tour operators in the US and overseas who have experience or an interest in travel for the handicapped. Send a stamped, self-addressed envelope to SATH.

Mobility Tours, division of All State Tours, 26 Court St., Suite 1110, Brooklyn, NY 11242 (phone: 718-858-6021). Custom-designed tours arranged for individuals and for groups of 10 or more.

Pro Med International, Airport Square, 1200 W 73rd Ave., Ste. 606, Vancouver, BC, Canada V6P 6G5 (phone: 604-536-0209). Will provide RN's to accompany tour groups.

Travel Horizons Unlimited, 11 E 44th St., New York, NY 10017 (phone: 212-687-5121). For kidney dialysis patients. Custom-designed tours for indviduals.

Whole Person Tours, PO Box 1084, Bayonne, NJ 07002 (phone: 201-858-3400). Also publishes *The Itinerary,* a bimonthly newsletter for disabled travelers; a one-year subscription costs $9.

Wings on Wheels, Evergreen Travel Service, 19505 44th Ave. W, Lynwood, WA 98036 (phone: 206-776-1184; within Washington, 800-562-9298; elsewhere, 800-435-2288).

BY PLANE: Advise the airline that you are handicapped when you book your flight. The Federal Aviation Authority (FAA) has ruled that US airlines must accept disabled and handicapped passengers as long as the airline has advance notice and the passenger represents no insurmountable problem in the emergency evacuation procedures. As a matter of course, American airlines were pretty good about helping handicapped passengers even before the ruling, although each airline has somewhat different procedures. Ask for specifics when you book your flight.

However, the FAA has no authority over foreign carriers on South American routes, and you should make some effort to discover the regulations, attitudes, and facilities of any South American airline you are using. In most cases, the US offices of these firms will provide the information you need.

Some US and foreign airlines will provide wheelchairs if you tell them you require one. It is a good idea to arrive at the airport about an hour before departure time. If you are bringing your own wheelchair, you must get a baggage tag for it. For a partial rundown of some airlines' facilities and regulations, see *Access to the World,* by Louise Weiss.

BY TRAIN: There are no special facilities for handicapped travelers on Latin American trains. However, people are usually quite helpful and will go out of their way to assist disabled people.

BY BUS: Bus travel in Latin America is generally not recommended for handicapped people.

BY SHIP: Some cruise ships cannot accommodate handicapped travelers because of their many sets of narrow steps, which are less convenient than wide ramps.

Hints for Traveling with Children

 By and large, South Americans are very fond of children and enjoy having them around; in fact, they generally have larger families than North Americans. No matter where you travel in the southern hemisphere, you will encounter parents with infants and youngsters. South American kids are generally considered quite well behaved by North American standards. They do not cry, complain noisily, or fight in public. They are unobtrusive travelers. It is also common for older children to care for younger ones while their parents are working.

Children are treated with affectionate warmth in most hotels and restaurants. They are generally fussed over, smiled at, and given extra little treats. However, it is up to the parents to ensure that children are entertained during their travels. Here are several hints for making a trip with children easy and fun:

1. Children should be part of the planning of the trip, and preparations should begin about a month before you leave, using maps, atlases, magazines, and books to make clear exactly where you are going and how far away it is. Part of the excitement of the journey will be associating the tiny dots on the map with the very real places the children visit a few weeks later. You can show pictures of streets and scenes in which they will stand within a month. Don't shirk history lessons, but don't burden them with dates. Make history light, anecdotal, and pertinent.

2. Children should be in on planning the itinerary, and where you go and what you do should reflect some of their ideas. If they already know enough about architecture and geography, they will have the excitement of recognition when they arrive.

3. Before you leave, eat some traditional South American foods. This will familiarize the children and interest them in what is to come. They may be surprised by the differences in the same dishes prepared absolutely authentically.

4. Learn the language with your children — a few basics like "hello," "good-bye," and "thank you." Thus armed, your children will delight South Americans and help break the ice wherever you go.

5. Give children specific responsibilities. For example, they can carry their own flight bags and look after their own personal things.

Make sure to pack clothes that can be easily washed and are preferably stain and wrinkle resistant. Have children take along a couple of their favorite small toys or games. Children become restless during long waiting periods, and the game plus a small snack, such as a box of raisins or crackers, will help keep them quiet. It is also a good idea to carry tissues, Band-Aids, a pocket medicine kit, and premoistened washcloths. Pace your day with the children in mind — break the trip into activity time and travel time. Try not to spend more than 5 or 6 hours traveling.

BY CAR: Without a doubt, a car is the most flexible means of transportation. Driving allows you complete independence in arranging your schedule and itinerary. If you are driving your own car, bring an ice chest and a grill so that you can picnic along the way. As soon as you leave the boundaries of any major South American city, you will find yourself in a rural or wilderness environment. There are plenty of places to pull over and have a meal. Keep your car supplied with dried fruits, crackers, candy bars, bottled water, and facial tissue and/or toilet paper. Many American kids are not satisfied with foreign dishes and yearn for hot dogs and hamburgers. All the large cities, resorts, and big hotels serve American-style food, but you will have to settle for the local cuisine everywhere else. Fortunately, you'll find Coca-Cola everywhere, along with popular soft drinks such as Inca Kola in Perú or Guaraná in Brazil.

BY PLANE: Children under 2 can fly for free if they travel on the lap of an obliging adult. However, as many flights to South America last 8 hours or more, this is not comfortable. Children between the ages of 2 and 12 can travel for half the adult fare. Most flights to South America are overnight flights, which means that when you arrive you will be tired and not really up for sightseeing. The best thing to do when you disembark from a long night flight is to head for your hotel, shower, have a snack, and take a nap. If your children are too excited to sleep, give them some toys to play with while you rest. With any luck, there will be empty seats on the plane so that you and the children can get some sleep. Make sure your baby is nursing or is sucking a bottle, pacifier, or a thumb when the plane takes off and lands. This sucking will make the child swallow and help to clear stopped ears. A piece of hard candy will do the same thing for an older child.

When you make your reservations, let the airlines know that you are traveling with a child and request a bulkhead seat, especially for infants who may be provided with a bassinet. The international airlines often stock baby food as well as games.

Note: Newborn babies, whose lungs may not be able to adjust to the altitude, should not be taken aboard an airplane. And some airlines may refuse to allow a pregnant woman in her eighth or ninth month aboard, for fear that something could go wrong with an in-flight birth. Check with the airline ahead of time and carry a letter from your doctor stating that you are fit to travel and indicating the estimated date of birth.

THINGS TO DO: Obviously, the number of special programs in English for children is bound to be limited in South America. But throughout the continent you will find splendid activities that children will love with no language barrier. In addition to swimming pools and beach activities, most large resorts have babysitting services (though, generally, sitters speak little English). And there are plenty of things to do in the big cities. In Rio de Janeiro, children will enjoy the Flamengo Park puppet theater, Lagoa Rodrigo de Freitas and Tivoli amusement parks, H. Stern's English-language tour of a gem factory, the planetarium, and the zoo. The famous cable car ride up Sugarloaf (Pão de Açucar) Mountain delights everyone. Why don't you picnic near the top? São Paulo's biggest draw is the Butantan Institute, where poisonous snakes are milked for their antitoxins. The Museum of Contemporary Art (Museu de Arte Contemporanes) has its modern paintings mounted on clear plastic stands instead of hanging on walls. Among children's favorite places in Caracas are: Parque del Este, where there are a zoo and the Humboldt Planetarium; the Transport Museum (Museo del Transporte); the Macuto cable car; El Conde amusement park; and ice skating at Mucubaji rink and Mt. Avila. Lima's oceanfront Parque Miraflores has terrific balloon-sellers permanently posted along the promenade facing the Pacific Ocean; Parque de las Leyendas features natural habitat exhibits on Perú's three main geographic sections: coast, mountain, and jungle. Parque Barranco has a pond with kid-sized rowboats. In Buenos Aires, children will enjoy the National Railroad Museum (Museo Nacional Ferroviario), the zoo, and the planetarium. Santiago has a funicular railroad up San Cristóbal mountain and an interesting zoo. The district of Maipú, just a few miles from the center of town, looks like a set from *Bonnie and Clyde,* with dusty streets, old cars, cottages, eucalyptus trees, and uniquely Chilean horse-drawn carts driven by farmers who till the neighboring fields. The witches' market in La Paz and the boat trip from Copacabana to the Island of the Sun in the middle of Lake Titicaca are glorious adventures for children. Fiestas and Carnival (celebrated before Lent throughout Latin America) provide colorful, free-for-all entertainment for older children. Carnival festivities vary from Rio de Janeiro's incredible samba parades to the gargantuan devil dancers of La Paz. (For a complete description, see *Special Places* and *Special Events* in each city report in THE CITIES.)

Hints for Single Travelers

By and large, the travel industry is not prepared to deal fairly with people traveling by themselves. People traveling alone almost invariably end up paying more than individuals traveling together in pairs. Most package tours, hotel deals, resort packages, and cruises are priced according to *double occupancy* rates, which means the per-person price is offered on the basis of two people traveling together who fill a double room (which means they will each spend a good deal more on meals and extras). The single traveler must pay a surcharge, called a single supplement, for exactly the same package. In extreme cases, this can add as much as 30% or 50% to the basic per-person rate. As far as the travel industry is concerned, single travel has not yet come into its own.

There are, however, countless thousands of individuals who *do* travel alone. Inevitably, their greatest obstacle is the single supplement charge, which prevents them from cashing in on travel bargains available to anyone traveling as part of a pair. The obvious, most effective alternative is to find a traveling companion. Even special "singles' tours" that promise no supplements are based on people sharing double rooms. If you are interested in finding another single traveler to help share the cost, consider contacting the travel agents listed below. Some charge fees; others are free.

Gender-Blender: Serves men and women, primarily ages 21-55. At your request, the agency will match you with a member of the opposite sex. It arranges its own tours, on which each individual is matched with a roommate (of desired sex) at no charge; it also places clients on existing tours. One-time membership fee, $5. 27 N Prince St., Lancaster, PA 17603 (phone: 717-299-3691).

Travel Mates: Will try to arrange shares on existing package tours for men and women of any age. The agency will also organize group tours for its own clients. Annual membership fee, $15. 49 W 44th St., New York, NY 10036 (phone: 212-221-6565).

Womantour: Run by feminist Estilita Grimaldo. As its name implies, this agency puts together group and individual travel programs for women exclusively. 5314 N Figueroa St., Los Angeles, CA 90042 (phone: 213-255-1115).

A book called *A Guide for Solo Travel,* written by Eleanor Adams Baxel and published by the Berkshire Traveller Press, offers information on how to avoid paying supplementary charges, how to pick the right travel agent, and much more. The book is out of print now, but may be found in a public library.

WOMEN ALONE: A single man can travel easily and unobtrusively around South America; a single woman is bound to arouse more than the usual share of attention (by North American standards). This, more than any other single factor, can demoralize a woman on her own. However, exploring South America can be terrifically exciting. Most places are quite safe, and people will go out of their way to be helpful. Once the sense of being foreign wears off, a woman traveler can feel at home in most out-of-the-way places, desert and jungle included. A single woman traveler is such a rarity that in many villages people consider it a privilege to meet one and will invite her to visit their families.

Still, a first-time visitor who speaks no Spanish is advised to join a tour of some kind; and even well-prepared or seasoned women travelers in South America invariably describe the experience with ambivalent feelings. Although there is little danger of physical harm if you apply common-sense guidelines (as you would if you were traveling in the US or Europe), any woman considering a trip to South America on her own must be prepared to encounter psychological discomfort if she minds being whistled at occasionally or if she is self-conscious about traveling alone in a male-dominated, family-oriented society.

But despite some inevitable problems, women are choosing to travel everywhere, including South America, on their own. It is still exotic and strikingly beautiful.

Here are some suggestions for handling difficult situations:

1. Try to take even an abbreviated language course before setting out, and carry a dictionary or phrase book so that you can better communicate with people en route. A little intelligent discourse will go a long way to help you maneuver from place to place with fewer problems. A foreign woman who does not speak the language well enough to handle basic questions and answers may well find herself persistently hounded by impertinent and unpleasant characters.

2. Know where you are going. When you are walking in the street, have some idea of your destination — whether market, museum, bus station, or hotel. Ignore whistles, jeers, and remarks.

3. Wherever possible, ask women residents of a particular region or city the districts they consider safe. Do not wander into unsafe neighborhoods.

4. Do not walk alone at night. This applies to the countryside as well as to the city.

5. Bus and railway stations and airports are the areas in which women are approached by offensive individuals most frequently. A single woman waiting for transport can reduce that likelihood by joining a group of women travelers or a family. They will usually be pleased to have you sit with them and may even accept you as part of their group within a short time.

6. In most cases, men who approach women on their own are not dangerous, merely annoying. If ignoring the masher doesn't work, a harsh look and a sharp command (*Váyase* — "Go away" or *Un poco de respeto, por favor* — "A little respect, please") tends to discourage unwelcome advances. In the last resort, approach a policeman for help or, if the incident occurs in a public facility, as is often the case, retreat to the women's room.

7. Never open a hotel room door to anyone you do not know.

8. Rest when you are tired; your psychological resistance is lowered and you are less able to care for yourself in a potentially troublesome situation.

Hints for Older Travelers

Older travelers have the great blessing of time; no longer limited by 2-week vacations and the demands of a full-time job, they can travel during the seasons when the most visited places are free from large tour groups, their atmosphere more relaxed, and their facilities less crowded and less expensive. There are some distinct disadvantages to South America as a destination for older travelers, however. Few of the senior citizen discounts so prevalent in North America exist in South American countries. This is mitigated by the fact that most facilities — accommodations, restaurants, and so on — are so much less expensive in South America in the first place; discounts are less of a necessity.

The greatest obstacles to travel throughout South America are the climate, terrain, and altitudes involved. The average pan–South American tour involves sudden changes from high mountain countries to jungle lowlands. These pose some danger for anyone with heart or breathing problems. In cities like La Paz, everyone has trouble breathing, even the most fit. When planning a visit, prepare your itinerary with one eye on your own physical condition and the other on a topographical map.

PACKAGE PROGRAMS: Only one organization plans tours to South America specifically for older travelers, the American Association of Retired Persons. With 10 million members, the association is open to anyone 55 or older. Membership costs $5, from Membership Processing Dept., PO Box 729, Long Beach, CA 90801 (phone: 213-432-8701).

Gadabout Tours, 700 E Tahquitz, McCallum Way, Palm Springs, CA 92262-6761 (phone: 619-325-5556), arranges tours for people age 55 and older.

Other organizations for mature Americans are:

National Association of Mature People: This is a relatively new organization, in the South and Midwest, for people age 55 or older; yearly dues are $9.95. 2212 NW 50th, PO Box 26792, Oklahoma City, OK 73126 (phone: 405-752-0703). It also books individual tours for senior citizens.

National Council of Senior Citizens: Membership costs $10 per person, $14 per couple, from the council at 925 15th St., NW, Washington, DC 20005 (phone: 202-347-8800). It does not arrange group tours to South America, but its travel service does book individual tours anywhere for members (no minimum age requirement for membership).

HEALTH: If you have specific medical problems, bring prescriptions on your trip; also carry a "medical file" with these items:

1. A summary of medical history; current diagnosis
2. A list of drugs to which you are allergic
3. Your most recent electrocardiogram if you have heart problems
4. Your doctor's name, address, and phone number

For a complete discussion of health for older travelers, Rosalind Massow's excellent *Now It's Your Turn to Travel* (Collier Books; $10.95) has a chapter on medical problems. It is out of print but available in libraries, Also, see *Medical and Legal Aid,* GETTING READY TO GO.

On the Road

Medical and Legal Aid and US Consular Services

MEDICAL AND LEGAL AID: Nothing ruins a vacation or business trip more effectively than sudden injury or illness. You can have an accident anytime, but travelers to South America are especially vulnerable to certain illnesses. The change in climate, altitude, and eating habits; the tension of finding yourself in strange places; and the presence of new, unfamiliar bacteria contribute to lower your resistance to disease. No matter where you travel, you should carry an all-purpose identification card listing your name, home address, social security number, blood type, drug allergies, chronic health problems, health insurance numbers, and whom to contact in case of emergency. It's also a good idea to pack a compact personal medical kit that includes Band-Aids, antiseptic, nose drops, insect repellent, aspirin, an extra pair of prescription glasses or sunglasses, over-the-counter remedies for diarrhea, indigestion, and motion sickness, a thermometer, and a supply of the prescription medicines you take regularly. In a corner of your kit, keep a list of all the drugs you have brought and their purpose as well as duplicate copies of your doctor's prescriptions (or an equivalent note from your doctor). These copies could come in handy if you are ever questioned by police or airport authorities about any drugs you are carrying; they also are necessary to refill any prescriptions in the event of loss. When you register at a hotel, it's not a bad idea to include your home address; this will facilitate the process of notifying friends, relatives, or your own doctor in case of an emergency.

Insurance policies designed for travelers include medical and life insurance, but before you take out additional insurance coverage check your current policy; it most likely includes coverage that will protect you on a journey. (For a complete discussion, see *Insurance*, GETTING READY TO GO.) Before you leave home, you can get up-to-date information about health conditions in South America and worldwide plus pretravel medical service at reasonable rates at the International Health Care Service, which is affiliated with New York Hospital at 440 E 69th St., New York, NY 10021 (phone: 212-472-4284).

There are several international organizations whose specific purpose is to provide emergency medical care and advice to the traveler. It might be a good idea to investigate their services and facilities before you leave home — particularly if you have a chronic medical problem or are traveling with small children.

Assist-Card is sold only through its office and provides a number to call — 24 hours a day, 365 days a year — through which complete emergency medical assistance can be arranged, including ambulance or air transportation to the proper treatment facilities, local lawyers for a case that is the by-product of an accident, and up to $5,000 in bail bonds for a judicial proceeding that is the result of an accident. It will also arrange for a flight home if the traveler is unable to complete his or her trip, and will pay any fare differential that may be required. Fees for the Assist-Card vary according to the length of the trip. The published schedule of fees calls for charges from $30 per card for a trip of only 5 days to a $220 fee for a 90-day itinerary. Contact: Assist-Card Corporation of Florida, 444 Brickell Ave., Suite M130, Miami, FL 33131 (phone: 800-372-1646).

Intermedic, a division of Executive Health Examiners, provides access to a directory of English-speaking physicians in 170 cities in over 90 countries. The fee is $6 per year for an individual and $10 a year for a family. Each physician listed has provided Intermedic with data on his or her medical education, professional experience, and hospital affiliation; and each has indicated a willingness to respond promptly to calls from traveling Intermedic members. They have also agreed in writing to a ceiling on fees for any initial visit. Contact: Intermedic, 777 Third Ave., New York, NY 10017 (phone: 212-486-8900).

International Association of Medical Assistance to Travelers (IAMAT) publishes a booklet listing its participating doctors around the world as well as the clinics and hospitals in various cities. A nonprofit organization, IAMAT appreciates donations, with a suggested minimum of $5; for $20, a set of worldwide climate charts detailing weather and sanitary conditions will be included. Delivery can take up to 5 weeks, so plan ahead. Contact: IAMAT, 736 Center St., Lewiston, NY 14092 (phone: 716-754-4883).

The International Health Care Service provides information about health conditions in various foreign countries, advice on immunizations recommended, and treatment if necessary. A pre-travel counseling and immunization package costs $155 for the first family member, $135 for each additional member; a post-travel screening is $75; lab work extra. Appointments are required for all services. Contact: International Health Care Service, which is affiliated with New York Hospital, at 440 E 69th St., New York, NY 10021 (phone: 212-472-4284).

International SOS Assistance provides a medical service program that covers medical emergencies while traveling. Again, members are provided with telephone access — 24 hours a day, 365 days a year — to a worldwide monitored multilingual network of medical centers. A phone call brings assistance ranging from telephone consultation to transportation home by ambulance or aircraft and, in some cases, transportation of a family member to the place of hospitalization to assist in treatment or care. The service can be purchased for a week, a month, or a year, and fees depend on the time period being covered. Formerly available only on a corporate basis, the service is now being offered to individuals. For information contact: International SOS Assistance, Inc., PO Box 11568, Philadelphia, PA 19116 (phone: in Pennsylvania, 215-244-1500; elsewhere, 800-523-8930).

Medic Alert sells identification tags that specify that the wearer has a medical condition not readily apparent to a casual observer. A heart condition, diabetes, epilepsy, or severe allergies are the sorts of things that these badges were developed to communicate — they are conditions that, if unrecognized at a time when emergency treatment is necessary (a time, incidentally, when you may be unable to speak for yourself), can result in tragic treatment errors. In addition to the identification emblems, a central file is maintained (with the telephone number clearly inscribed on the ID badge) where your complete medical history is available 24 hours a day via a telephone call. Collect calls from South America are accepted in an emergency. The one-time membership fee of $20 is tax deductible, and the cost of the ID depends on what sort of metal you select: steel, $20; silver, $30; gold, $38. Contact: Medic Alert, PO Box 1009, Turlock, CA 95381 (phone: 209-668-3333 or 800-ID-ALERT).

QUALITY OF CARE: The type of medical care available in South America varies considerably from place to place. In the capitals you will find thorough, well-trained specialists in all fields; clinics (including Anglo-American ones); hospitals (both private and government); pharmacies; drugstores; dentists; optometrists; and most drugs found in the US, many of which are available without prescriptions at a lower price than in the US. However, if you go to a hospital, it is preferable to check into one that is private rather than government-owned. American and British hospitals are invariably staffed with English-speaking doctors who were trained in the US or the United Kingdom. In addition, a private medical facility is more likely to give you the kind of assurance you need to feel comfortable if you do not speak the language.

MEDICAL PROBLEMS: Certain health risks are endemic to South America. Hepatitis (nicknamed the Big H by gringos) is frequently caused by dirty hypodermic needles, a risk even in hospitals. (One Peace Corps worker in Perú came down with hepatitis in Cuzco after donating blood to help a sick friend!) If you are a diabetic or require regular injections for any other condition, carry disposable plastic hypodermic syringes. And any traveler should consider a gamma globulin injection to help immunize against hepatitis before leaving the US.

Without a doubt, a traveler's most serious complaint in South America is dysentery or diarrhea, accompanied by severe intestinal pain and a foul taste in the mouth. As with the other diseases discussed above, prevention is the best cure. Do not drink or eat raw milk, unpasteurized or uncooked dairy products, unpurified water, unpeeled fruit or fruit washed in unsterilized water, or uncooked vegetables. Do not take ice in your drinks. Stay away from tempting-looking alcoholic concoctions served in coconuts or pineapples. Do not buy food from the picturesque vendors in markets and street fairs. Do not eat anything garnished with fresh vegetables — the shredded lettuce and tomatoes can play havoc with your gastrointestinal system the morning after. The *New England Journal of Medicine,* volume 298, recommends a daily 100-mg tablet of Doxycline, an antibiotic, as a prophylactic against dysentery. Start taking it a week before your trip actually begins. Ask your doctor for recommendations, and be sure to get a prescription for an antidysentery medication at the same time. Some people find Lomotil or Diodiquin to be effective; they're both rather mild potions. If you are stricken with diarrhea and have no medication with you, call a doctor or visit the nearest pharmacy. Pharmacists in Latin America can generally give you an over-the-counter drug to quell the pangs and concomitant bowel problems. When you get back to your hotel, order manzanilla tea. It is an old, favored South American remedy.

If you intend to travel into the jungle, where malaria is prevalent, pick up some antimalarial tablets in a pharmacy in a city before you fly into the bush. These very inexpensive tablets are available everywhere. (Malaria is called *paludismo* in Spanish; ask for *medicina contra paludismo.*) Presently, a yellow fever inoculation and prophylactic medication against malaria are recommended and, in many cases, mandatory for travel in many of the interior tropic and subtropic regions of South America, particularly for visitors making extensive trips in the Amazon basin. Check specifically with the Travelers Health Activity, Center for Disease Control, at the main office in Atlanta, GA (404-329-2572). Vitamin B-1 or thiamine tablets will help immunize you against ordinary but irritating mosquito bites, a terrific nuisance, especially on jungle expeditions. Ask for Tiamina in any pharmacy. The aftereffects of Vitamin B-1 are truly extraordinary. If you are at all susceptible to mosquito bites, you will be amazed at how quickly the vitamins work. Otherwise, take along Cutters repellent.

One illness for which there is no known preventative is altitude sickness (*soroche*). Travelers disembarking from planes at El Alto airport in La Paz (or Cuzco) more often than not feel the effect of *soroche* during their first steps across the tarmac to the customs desk. It arrives in the form of a wave of dizziness, frequently accompanied by a minor spasm in the chest. Occasionally, you may feel you are going to faint. (In some ways, *soroche* feels like motion sickness, only the ground below is not moving.) Sit down immediately or, if possible, lie down and take deep breaths. The only cure for *soroche* is acclimatization. (Old Andean hands claim it takes a month to get fully acclimated.) Do not exert yourself. If you must walk, walk slowly. Ask someone to carry your luggage. Rest often. You will probably find that when you fall asleep, you wake up wanting more air, with breathing difficulties similar to symptoms of the common cold. This occurs because your breathing involuntarily slows down when you sleep and you are unable to take in the extra air you need. It usually takes a few days for the first stages of *soroche* to pass, during which time you may also have headaches and eyestrain. Many hotels and some tourist trains provide *soroche* sufferers with oxygen, which helps to clear the head. You can try coca tea, but better to buy Coramina, made by CIBA-Geigy and available in highland pharmacies without prescription. If you have any kind of medical problem affected by altitude, discuss the problem with your doctor. For most people, *soroche* is a discomfort but not a vital health hazard. For more information, read *Mountain Sickness: Prevention, Recognition, and Treatment,* by Peter Hackett, MD (available from Mountain Travel, 1398 Solano Ave., Albany, CA 94706; $5.50, including postage and handling).

For more information on protection from malaria and other diseases, contact IAMAT (International Association for Medical Assistance to Travelers), 417 Center St., Lewiston, NY 14092 (phone: 716-754-4883) or write to the US Government Printing Office, Washington, DC 20402, for the US Public Health Service's booklet "Health Information for International Travel" (HEW Publication CDC-86-8280; enclose check or money order for $4.75 payable to Superintendent of Documents). For general information on pretrip health preparations, see *Travelers' Health Guide,* by Patrick J. Doyle and James E. Banta (Acropolis Books; $$9.95).

LEGAL PROBLEMS AND CONSULAR SERVICES: The American embassy or consulate is the best place to turn to should you require legal aid for anything ranging from a traffic incident to a drug bust. (Do not expect US foreign service officials to be sympathetic if you are picked up for any drug-related offense, however. Chances are, they will notify a lawyer and your family, and that's about all.) As in Mexico, justice in South America is based on the Napoleonic Code, which assumes the defendant to be guilty. This makes any encounter with the police highly uncomfortable. The system of legal rights and requirements that protect citizens in the US is highly capricious or simply nonexistent in most South American countries. Remember, in most cases you are not dealing with democratic authority. By treaty, police are required to inform the US consul if an American citizen is arrested, but the degree of respect that is shown your person will depend to a frightening degree upon the crime you are accused of and how the police view you. Well-dressed American tourists involved in mundane legal problems will most likely be hassled very little; a young person traveling with a backpack who is accused of carrying drugs can expect more trouble. Americans accused of drug offenses or political crimes have been physically abused in South American jails. Be respectful, have documentation of your status, and be firm. To add "be shorn and shaven" should indicate some of the problems of any confrontation with South American authority.

In the case of minor traffic accidents, it is most expedient to settle the matter before the police get involved. If the police do get involved in minor accidents or violations, try to establish a fine on the spot and pay it. If you speak the language and feel competent, you can try to bargain the fine; but wisdom declares that you do what is necessary to get the matter settled on the spot. There are few experiences more horrible than being hauled off to a South American jail. For questions about Americans arrested abroad and how to get money to them, call the Office of Special Consular Services in Washington, DC (phone: 202-647-3712).

The US Department of State in Washington insists that any American citizen who is arrested in South America has the right to contact the US embassy or consulate "immediately," but it may be a long time before you are given permission to use a phone. Keep in mind, too, that the consulate cannot act as an arbitrator or ombudsman on an American citizen's behalf. The consul has no power, authorized or otherwise, to subvert, alter, or contravene the legal processes, however unfair, of the country in which he serves. Nor can he oil the machinery of a foreign bureaucracy or provide legal advice. The consul's responsibilities do include providing a list of English-speaking lawyers, giving information on local sources of legal aid, assigning an interpreter if the police have none, informing relatives in the US, and organizing and administering any defense monies sent from home. If a case is tried unfairly or the punishment seems unusually severe, the consul can make a formal complaint to the authorities. In case of what is called "legitimate and proven poverty," the consul will contact sources of money (such as family or friends in the US), apply for aid to agencies in foreign countries, and, in the last resort, arrange for repatriation at government expense.

Do not expect the consulate to help with trivial difficulties such as canceled reservations or lost baggage. The consulate is primarily concerned with the day-to-day administration of services such as issuing passports and visas; providing notarial services; distributing VA, social security, and civil service benefits to resident Americans; depositions; extradition cases; and reporting to Washington the births, deaths, and marriages of US citizens living within the consulate's domain.

We hope that none of the information in this section will be necessary on your travels through South America. If you can avoid legal hassles altogether, you will have a much more pleasant trip. If you become involved in an imbroglio, the local authorities may spare you legal complications if you make clear your tourist status. Do not get into fights with residents, no matter how belligerent or provocative they are in a given situation. Whenever possible, walk away from a confrontation.

Below is a list of all the US embassies and consulates in South America. If you are not in any of the cities listed when a problem arises, contact the nearest office. If you are not a citizen of the US, contact your own nation's consulate.

Argentina: 4300 Colombia, 1425, Buenos Aires (phone: 774-8811; 774-9911).

Bolivia: Edificio Tobás, 2 Piso, Calle Posoti, esq. Colón (phone: 32-049-4).

Brazil: Av. das Nacoes, Lot #3, Brasília, DF (phone: 223-0120); Av. Presidente Wilson 147, Rio de Janeiro (phone: 292-7117); Edificio Conjunto Nacional, Rua Padre João Manuel 933, São Paulo (phone: 881-6511).

Chile: Cordina Bldg., 1343 Agustinas, Santiago (phone: 710-133).

Colombia: Calle 37 No. 8-40, Bogotá (phone: 232-9100); Edificio Pielroja Carerra 3 11-55, Cali (phone: 88-11-36/7); Edificio Seguros Tequendama, Calle 34 44-63, Baranquilla (phone: 457-705; 457-624).

Ecuador: 120 Av. Patria, Quito (phone: 238-498); 9 de Octubre Garcia Moreno, Guayaquil (phone: 511570).

French Guiana: Consular District of Martinique, FWI, 14 rue Blenac, Boîte Postal 561, Fort de France 97206 (phone: 71-93-01).

Guyana: 31 Main St., Georgetown (phone: 54900).

Panamá: Av. Balboa E, Calle 38, Panamá City (phone: 27-1777).

Paraguay: 1776 Mariscal López, Asunción (phone: 201-041).

Perú: Grimaldo del Solar 346, Miraflores, Lima (phone: 44-36-21).

Suriname: Dr. Sophie Redmondstraat 129, PO Box 1821, Paramaribo (phone: 72900).

Uruguay: H. Abadie Santos 808, Montevideo (phone: 40-90-51).

Venezuela: Av. Francisco de Miranda and Av. Principal de la Floresta, Caracas (phone: 284-7111); Edificio Matema, 1 Piso, Av. 15 Calle 78, Maracaibo (phone: 516506/7).

Credit and Currency

 FOREIGN EXCHANGE: All South American currencies are based on the decimal system; like the US dollar, each subdivides into 100 smaller units, usually called centavos or cents. Like all currencies, their values in relation to the dollar fluctuate daily, affected by a wide variety of phenomena. Check with your own bank, any American Express office, or International Inc. (phone: in Illinois, 800-972-2192; elsewhere, 800-621-0666) for the location nearest you. In general, the dollar is strong in South America, and the continent offers many destinations that are travel bargains.

Currency is issued in paper bills and coins, often large and heavy, even when denoting small denominations. Remember that many South American nations use what North Americans recognize as a dollar sign ($) as the symbol of the local currency. More than one uninitiated traveler has been stunned to receive a check of $34 for coffee and rolls before realizing it did not mean 34 US dollars.

Exchange – Every country has an official rate of exchange, posted in banks, airports, exchange houses (*casas de cambio*), and hotels. In some places, a slight variation exists between the rates offered in banks and those in hotels, with banks usually paying more for dollars. The convenience of cashing money in your hotel (sometimes on a 24-hour basis) usually makes up for any minor difference in the exchange rate; anyone who has ever stood in line in a South American bank for 2 hours can attest to this. Don't try to bargain in banks or hotels — no one will change the rates for you.

In many countries, an unofficial rate of exchange (the "black market") buys US dollars at a significantly higher rate of exchange than banks and exchange houses. Changing money on the black market is not usually recommended in most countries, nor is buying local currency from street vendors waving bills around. However, at this writing, a few South American countries have an unofficial (but officially recognized) and legal "parallel" rate of exchange. In Argentina and Brazil, the *cambios*, or exchange houses, and even some stores use this new exchange device, and the bonuses in local currency are considerable. Your rate of exchange, by the way, will be far better in Buenos Aires and Rio than in smaller towns, and because you are changing dollars for local currency at a technically unofficial rate, do not count on reconverting to dollars on departure from the country. In other words, plan to convert only what you anticipate spending.

Travel agencies and exchange houses all around Buenos Aires (Rio de Janeiro, too) offer convenient alternate-exchange-rate access, providing convenient assistance in paying as many local bills as possible in cash. Remember, these are two South American countries where paying hotel, restaurant, and retail shop bills with credit cards is a definite no-no. Remember that purchases paid for with plastic are ultimately transacted at the *official* exchange rate, which can mean paying as much as 100% more for goods and services than is absolutely necessary.

You can also change money legally at the main airports, but these facilities are not open 24 hours a day in all countries. If you plan to fly from one South American country to another after regular business hours, you should change enough dollars into the currency of your next destination so that you can take a cab or bus when you arrive (though, in a pinch, dollars may be accepted). However, when open, airports have bank-rate exchanges.

TRAVELER'S CHECKS: It's advisable to carry traveler's checks with you instead of (or in addition to) cash. And it is recommended that traveler's checks be in denominations of $50 or less, since greater amounts are hard to cash anyplace other than at banks.

In addition, this will remind you not to get stuck with large amounts of South American currencies, which may be hard to convert back to dollars on departure. Note that it is often difficult to redeem traveler's checks — or even use them as currency — outside big towns, and small hotels may find exchanging large-denomination traveler's checks (or even cash in large bills) difficult, particularly on weekends. Keep track of the serial numbers or receipts of traveler's checks should you need to redeem lost checks; ideally, keep these records separate from the checks themselves.

Every type of traveler's check is legal tender in banks around the world, and each company guarantees full replacement if checks are lost or stolen. After that the similarity ends. Some charge a fee for purchase, others are free; some are available by mail; and, most important, each differs in its refund policy — the amount refunded immediately, the accessibility of refund locations, and the availability of a 24-hour emergency refund. Here's a rundown of the major traveler's checks:

> *American Express:* To report lost or stolen checks in the continental US, call 800-221-7282; in Alaska and Hawaii, call 800-221-4950; outside the US, call the nearest American Express office, or 801-968-8300, collect.
>
> *Bank of America:* To report lost or stolen checks in the US, including Hawaii and Alaska, call 800-227-3460; outside the US, call 415-622-3800, collect.
>
> *Citicorp:* To report lost or stolen checks in the US, including Alaska and Hawaii, call 800-645-6556. Outside the US, call 813-623-1709, collect.
>
> *MasterCard:* To report lost or stolen checks in the US, including Alaska and Hawaii, call 800-223-9920; from outside the US, call 212-974-5696, collect.
>
> *Visa:* To report lost or stolen checks in the US, including Alaska and Hawaii, call 800-227-6811; outside the US, call 415-574-7111, collect.

CREDIT CARDS: Essentially, two different kinds of credit cards are available to American consumers, and travelers must select the type that best serves their interests. "Convenience" or "travel and entertainment" cards — American Express, Diners Club, and Carte Blanche — are the most widely accepted. They cost the cardholder a basic annual membership fee ($35 to $40 for these three) but put no limit on the amount that may be charged on the card in any month. However, the entire balance must be paid in full at the end of each billing period (usually a month), so the cardholder is not actually extended any long-term credit.

"Bank" cards are also rarely issued free these days, with the one exception of Sears' DiscoverCard, and certain services they provide (check cashing, for example) can cost extra. But they are *real* credit cards in the sense that the cardholder has the privilege of paying a small amount (1/36 is typical) of the total outstanding balance in each billing period. For this privilege, the cardholder is charged a high annual interest rate (currently three to four times the going bank passbook savings rate) on the balance owed. Many banks now charge interest from the purchase date, not from the first billing date as they used to do; consider this when you are calculating the actual cost of a purchase. There is also a maximum set on the total amount the cardholder can charge to the card, which represents the limit of credit the bank is willing to extend. Major "bank" cards are Visa (formerly Bank Americard) and MasterCard.

Also, remember that paying with plastic in South America can be an expensive convenience. Since credit card charges are converted to US dollars at the "official" exchange rate — often only half the rate offered on the "alternate" currency market — you may be doubling the cost of South American travel services. Check carefully on the local scene before deciding whether to settle bills by charging or paying cash.

> *American Express:* Emergency personal check cashing at American Express or representatives' offices (up to $200 cash in local currency, $800 in traveler's checks); emergency personal check cashing for guests at participating hotels

and, for holders of airline tickets, at participating airlines in the US (up to $50). Extended payment plan for cruises, tours, and airline tickets. $100,000 free travel accident insurance on plane, train, bus, and ship if the ticket was charged to your card; up to $1,000,000 additional low-cost flight insurance available. Contact: American Express Card, PO Box 39, Church St. Station, New York, NY 10008 (phone: 800-528-4800).

Carte Blanche: Emergency personal check cashing for guests at participating hotels (up to $250 per stay). Extended payment plan for airline tickets. $150,000 free travel accident insurance on plane, train, and ship if the ticket was charged to your card. Contact: Carte Blanche, PO Box 17193, Denver, CO 80217 (phone: 800-525-9135).

Diners Club: Emergency personal check cashing worldwide; emergency personal check cashing for guests at participating hotels (up to $250 per stay). Qualified card members are eligible for extended payment plan. $650,000 free travel accident insurance on plane, train, and ship if the ticket was charged to your card. Contact: Diners Club, PO Box 17193, Denver, CO 80217 (phone: 800-525-9135).

DiscoverCard: Launched in early 1986 by Sears, Roebuck and Co., it provides the holder with cash advances at more than 500 locations nationwide and offers revolving credit line for purchases at a wide range of service establishments. Other deposit, lending, and investment services are also available. At this time, its broad acceptance in South America is not very likely. For information, phone: 800-858-5588.

MasterCard: Cash advance at participating banks worldwide and revolving credit line for purchases at a wide range of service establishments. Interest charge on unpaid balance and other details are set by issuing bank. Check with your bank for information.

Visa: Cash advance at participating banks worldwide and revolving credit line for purchases at a wide range of service establishments. Interest charge on unpaid balance and other details are set by issuing bank. Check with your bank for information.

You should always find out the prices and rates charged for money being changed or any goods and services. Prices are generally posted in hotels and restaurants, but if they are not, ask. People expect this.

Carry your money carefully. You might consider carrying your money (cash and checks) in several places. Never put money in a back pocket or in an open purse. Money is best kept in a buttoned front pocket or in a money purse pinned inside your shirt or blouse. It may be quaint and old-fashioned, but it works.

A note on credit card charges: The exchange rate that is applied to a foreign purchase made on your credit card may have nothing to do with the exchange rate in effect on the day you bought the goods. This is because card companies calculate costs at the exchange rate in effect on the day your charge arrives at the company's financial office from the individual hotel, restaurant, or retailer, not at the rate in effect when the transaction was originally made. And most companies give retailers as much as a year before they must send in bills. Contemplate this for a moment: It means that charges against your account with the credit card company can vary widely — and rarely in your favor nowadays — from the cost you *thought* you were paying when you made the purchases. The only mitigating factor is that if you really get stuck — if in the intervening weeks or months the dollar drops radically in relation to the currency in which you made the purchase — you can call your card company and ask for some kind of relief. At their discretion they may agree.

Dining Out

 Although it is a good idea to select restaurants with care to minimize the risk of gastrointestinal infections caused by unsanitary utensils and food preparation, there is no dearth of fine restaurants in all price categories. South Americans love to dine out, and even in small towns you can usually find a couple of unexpectedly good little restaurants or cafés (*confiterías*). The trick to avoiding dysentery is not so much where you eat as what you eat. Meat, fish, and vegetables that are thoroughly cooked should not cause problems. The restaurants that we recommend are listed in the *Best in Town* sections of THE CITIES. South American food is discussed in PERSPECTIVES.

Throughout South America, dinner begins after 7 PM and can go on for hours. Dinner parties that begin at 9 PM and meander through the dessert, coffee, and liqueur 'round about midnight are not uncommon, especially in Chile and Argentina. (In rural areas, though, evening meals are served earlier than in the cities.) People fill up on sandwiches, pastries, and coffee or tea around 5 or 5:30 PM. South Americans enjoy dressing up to go to restaurants. Older men wear business suits or dinner jackets in the larger cities; younger men prefer flashier suits with splashy, fitted, open-neck shirts and white or cream-colored jackets and pants. (Remember John Travolta in *Saturday Night Fever*? That's the look.) It is customary for men to leave the top three of four buttons of their shirt open. At resorts, menswear is universally casual, and no one wears a tie. Women get dressed up for dinner no matter where they are. In summer, low-cut, frilly dresses or pants suits are popular. In winter, sweaters over blouse-and-pants combinations or knit dresses are worn. Cashmere and suede combinations are worn by men and women in Chile and Argentina. Blue jeans are only acceptable in discos that cater to a young clientele.

Dinners are lengthy by American standards, and you will have to look for American-style drive-ins or fast-food chains for snacks. In Bogotá, the most popular chain is *Riki Rice;* in Brazil, it's *Bob's. McDonald's* intends to plant its golden arches in Brazil within a couple of years. Good snack foods available throughout South America are meat pies (*empanadas*) and roast chicken with french fries (*pollos a la brasa*). Most international hotels and resorts have coffee shops that serve club and BLT sandwiches, hamburgers, chicken soup, ice cream concoctions, and breakfasts as well as expensive restaurants specializing in the best regional cuisine with some Continental dishes. At beach resorts as well as in the cities, you will invariably find pleasant cafés and spanking-clean ice cream parlors. Many have outdoor tables so you can munch away in the open air, day or night.

These cafés and American-style restaurants offer the best bets for quick bites between meals. They are safer than eating from the ubiquitous street vendors and marketplaces, where tempting smells can mask an invitation to digestive disaster.

You will certainly want to sample regional specialties. In Argentina, Uruguay, and Paraguay, barbecued steak is served with fried eggs (*bife a caballo*) or with pieces of sausage (*chorizo*) in a mixed grill (*parrillada*). In Chile, Uruguay, and Venezuela, different varieties of seafood are prepared in a seafood stew (*chupe de mariscos*), broiled, or served raw with lemon. Brazil is a good place to sample shrimp or fish stew (*vatapa*) and the intimidating-looking, bubbling black bean, pork, and sausage national dish (*feijoada*). Spicy, marinated fish (*ceviche*), a Peruvian specialty, can also be found in Colombia and Ecuador. Bolivia's Lake Titicaca trout (*trucha*) and Paraguay's freshwater river fish (*pescados*) are justifiably renowned, as are the shrimp (*camarones*) retrieved from Panamanian waters. Guyana, French Guiana, and Suriname have excellent game (for the adventurous eater) and fish as well as Indonesian-Dutch *rijsttafel* and some French dishes. A multiethnic continent, South America has innumerable Chinese (*Chifa*), Italian, German, and Japanese restaurants. São Paulo has an Arab quarter, and, south of São Paulo, the city of Curitiba has Polish and Eastern European restaurants, reflecting the cuisine of its large community of settlers. Contrary to the stereotype, food is not highly seasoned. But watch out for that little dish of green sauce served with your meal. A dainty dab is enough to burn your tongue, and it takes some getting used to. A word of advice: Beware when you order anything *picante* (very spicy) or cooked with *ají* (extra hot pepper). Depending on your personal taste, you can safely order dishes cooked with garlic (*ajo*). (Be sure to read *Food and Drink* in PERSPECTIVES to familiarize yourself with the full spectrum of South American food, spices, and cuisine.)

RESERVATIONS: Most places do not require reservations. Exceptions, as noted in the *Eating Out* entries in the city reports, are the more expensive, chic establishments, restaurant-nightclubs offering prime entertainment, or places where a particular dish is served on one night only. Ask at your hotel if the restaurant you would like to visit requires reservations. If you do not speak Spanish or Portuguese, someone at the hotel will phone for you. (The listings in *Best in Town* include telephone numbers.)

If you plan to eat in your hotel, find out the scheduled serving times. These are usually noted on a card describing the hotel's services in your room. At the larger, modern hotels, restaurants usually have set meal times, whereas coffee shops and room service operate more flexibly.

A service charge, generally about 12%, is added to all bills so that it is not necessary to leave a tip. However, waiters work hard, and they always appreciate a few extra pesos. (Note that Argentina recently eliminated automatic service charges so that now clients should leave a tip of about 10%.) Remember, too, that some South American countries use what North Americans interpret as a dollar sign ($) to indicate local currency. So don't blanch when your tab runs into four or more digits. You can expect meals to be about 20% to 40% less expensive than an equivalent meal in a major US city. Detailed price information is included in restaurant listings in the city reports.

Accommodations

 The remarkable increase in the flow of visitors to South America during the 1970s was responsible for the development and construction of dozens of new hotels and resorts. Despite this burgeoning of beds, however, it's said that there are still fewer hotel rooms in the entire 13-nation South American continent than in Austria. And Austria is only half the size of Uruguay, one of the smaller South American countries!

However, the popular beach resorts, such as Rio de Janeiro, Salvador (Bahía), Guarujá, the Venezuelan/Colombian Caribbean, Contadora Island, Punta del Este, and Viña del Mar, are famous — not always justifiably — for their hotels and settings. The major cities — Caracas, Buenos Aires, Santiago, and São Paulo — have excellent accommodations with every possible amenity and the same conveniences you would find in any European or North American metropolis. Many of these are operated by well-known international hotels. Some examples: Inter-Continental has 10 hotels in Brazil, Colombia, Ecuador, and Venezuela. Hilton has opened its eleventh property in Belém for a total of 3 in Brazil, 2 in Colombia, 4 in Venezuela, and 1 in Panamá. Sheraton has 7 hotels, in the capitals of Argentina, Bolivia, Brazil, Chile, and Perú, and also beachside in Brazil (Rio) and Venezuela (Macuto). Holiday Inn (also Holiday Inn

Crowne Plaza, the deluxe model) is represented by 9 hotels in Bolivia, Brazil, Chile, Panamá, Perú, and Venezuela, and new hotels are being built in Santos, Brazil, and in Cuzco, Perú. Meridién, a French chain, operates 2 good hotels, one in Rio and the other in Salvador (Bahía). Hyatt International has 1 hotel in Panamá, and Executive House has 1 hotel in Suriname. Though rates vary from city to city in South America, they can be as much as 40% lower than those of their sister hotels in Europe.

A number of South American chains are also active and should not be overlooked. Othon, the largest, has 16 hotels in Brazil, and HORSA, another Brazilian chain, has 7. Tropical, a 10-hotel chain; Monte, a 5-hotel chain; Gandara, a 7-hotel chain; and the 2-hotel chains of Plaza and Delphin, a luxury chain, complete the major Brazilian hotel chains. Although not quite as luxurious as the Hiltons and Sheratons, these hotels are aesthetically pleasing, well maintained, and comfortable. Panamericana, a Chilean hotel chain, has a total of 5 hotels in Paraguay, Brazil, and Chile. Within the same country, there is little price difference between South American–owned hotels and those owned by international firms.

In addition to chains, the growth of tourism has spawned diversified accommodations for economy-minded travelers. Throughout South America, you will find a variety of small *pensiones,* converted haciendas and mansions, thermal spas, gambling centers, ski lodges, jungle lodges, and resorts that offer something special in the way of atmosphere and experience (see *Best in Town* in THE CITIES, *Best en Route* in DIRECTIONS, and *Resorts and Spas* in DIVERSIONS). Many South American countries have some sort of government-run hotel or hostel program, such as the Tourist Hotels in Perú.

You will not find large budget hotels in South America, but there are innumerable clean, inexpensive hotels of all descriptions — modern, colonial, secluded, centrally located, or on the road — that offer basic amenities. Don't expect air conditioning, nightclubs, fancy bars, discos, swimming pools, or TV in rustic, out-of-the-way places. Here, the charm consists of a genuine welcome, personal hospitality, incredibly gorgeous scenery, and privacy. Some of these places offer guided trips into the surrounding countryside; some have natural mineral water spas. In almost every case such hostelries — simple or luxurious — will cost much less than their equivalents in the US.

RESERVATIONS: It is always advisable to book accommodations in advance in South America; in the cities it can be crucial. This is made easier in urban centers by the computerized reservations systems of the national and international chains, to which there is access by phone from the US (all hotel, inn, and lodge listings in the *Best in Town* sections of the city reports include addresses and phone numbers for reservations; where they exist, phone numbers are included in hotel listings in the *Best en Route* sections of DIRECTIONS). In the country, reservations are complicated by erratic communications, and you will probably be doing business by mail. The only compensation is that in remote areas, inns and hotels treat such arrangements with some flexibility, and if you arrive a day early or a day late, you will most likely find a room waiting.

Experienced travelers in South America learn quickly that no matter where they go in this hospitable and friendly continent, there is a place to stay come nightfall. If your journey takes you to a region without *pensiones* or public facilities to accommodate travelers, someone in town will invariably offer to put you up. Such occurrences are not so rare in South America, and they account for many people's addiction to off-the-beaten-track travel in this part of the world. *Note:* Carnival, the festival that begins on Ash Wednesday to mark the commencement of Lent, is celebrated madly in all South American countries. If you plan to travel at this time, make reservations at least 6 months in advance. Christmas, New Year's Day, and Easter week are heavily booked, too. If you plan to visit any of the beach resorts at Christmas, book at least 3 months ahead.

OVERBOOKING: Although the problem is not unique to South America, the international travel boom has brought with it some abuses in the hotel trade that are pretty much standard operating procedure in any industry facing a demand that outstrips the supply. Hotels overbook rooms on the assumption that a certain percentage of no-shows are inevitable. When cancellations don't occur and everyone with a reservation arrives, you can find yourself holding a valid reservation for which no room exists.

There's no sure way to avoid the pitfalls of hotel overbooking, but there *are* some ways to minimize the risks. First, always carry evidence of your confirmed reservation. To have the greatest impact, this evidence should be a direct communication from the hotel to you or your travel agent. A letter or computer reservation slip should specify the exact dates and duration of your stay and the price of your accommodations. Make sure your travel agent passes on to you any official information received from the hotel. The weakest form of confirmation is the voucher slip a travel agent routinely issues, since it carries no official indication that the hotel has verified your reservations.

Even better is the increasing opportunity to guarantee hotel reservations, and this is becoming the only practice to ensure that a room will be held for you. This guarantee is accomplished by giving the hotel (or its reservation system) the number of your American Express, Diners Club, MasterCard, or Visa credit card, and agreeing that the hotel is authorized to charge you for that room no matter what. Even with a guaranteed reservation, it's still possible to cancel if you do so before 6 PM of the day of your reservation (sometimes 4 PM in resort areas). But when you do cancel under this arrangement, make sure you get a cancellation number to protect you from being erroneously billed.

If all these precautions fail and you are left standing at the front desk with a reservation that the clerk won't honor, you have a last resort: Yell as long and as loudly as necessary to get satisfaction. The person who makes the most noise gets the last room in the house.

What if you can't get reservations in the first place? This is a problem that hassles business people who can't plan months ahead. The word from savvy travelers is that a bit of currency (perhaps attached discreetly to a business card) often increases your chances with recalcitrant desk clerks. There are less venal ways of improving your odds, however. If you are making reservations for business, ask an associate at your destination to make reservations for you.

There is a good reason to do this above and beyond the very real point that a resident has the broadest knowledge of local hotels. Often a hotel will appear sold out on the international computer when in fact a few rooms are available. The proliferation of computerized reservations has made it unwise for a hotel to indicate that it suddenly has five rooms available (from cancellations) when there might be 30 or 40 travel agents lined up in the computer waiting for them. That small a number of vacancies is much more likely to be held by the hotel for its own sale, so a local associate is an invaluable conduit to these otherwise inaccessible rooms.

Tipping and Shopping

 TIPPING: Although a service charge of between 10% and 25% is levied on most restaurant and hotel bills throughout South America, tipping is still standard practice. Since waiters, waitresses, porters, and bellhops do not receive salaries that are in any way comparable to those in the US, a few extra pesos help them considerably without putting undue financial burden on the customers. By and large, tips constitute a sizable part of service employees' livelihood.

In restaurants, tip up to 10% of the bill where a service charge is included. A tip of 15% is expected where there is no service charge added. Whenever possible, tips should be left in cash, not charged on a credit card; this is because tips indicated on credit card receipts are rarely given over to the help.

Porters should be tipped the equivalent of 50¢ per bag in local currency. If you get off the plane without any foreign coins, tip in US money, preferably a dollar since quarters and other American coins are often not readily convertible. When in doubt, it is preferable to tip (in any denomination or currency) than not to tip.

Taxi drivers do not expect tips except in Uruguay, where 10% of the fare is an acceptable minimum. In Brazil, rounding out the fare to the nearest 100 cruzeiros takes the place of tipping. If the fare is 2,900 cruzeiros, pay 3,000, for example.

As a general rule, tip chambermaids and porters about $1 per person per day per room — at least $5 a week. Ask the clerk at your hotel for guidance if you feel uncomfortable. Bellboys usually get 50¢ a bag.

Throughout South America, young children in the street offer to watch cars or clean windows. Many of these children behave aggressively, jumping onto cars to wipe windows with dirty rags. In such cases, the most expedient thing to do is to give the kid a peso (or cruzeiro) and tell him to go away (*Váyase!*). Very often children will open the door of your car in an attempt to help you get out. You must tell them no immediately. Otherwise they will probably station themselves against your car, allegedly guarding it, until your return. If they insist on "protecting" your car, the wisest recourse is to give them a couple of coins. But first check that everything in the car is as you left it. Arriving and departing from airline terminals can turn into a royal battle with youngsters over carrying your luggage. Be firm! Choose one.

Parking lot and garage attendants expect a small tip, as do ushers in movie houses and theaters and museum guides. Customs officials do not expect to be tipped. In many South American countries, any procedure that requires an official signature or stamp involves tipping. If you need to secure a police report of a robbery, you may have to file your request for such a report on special paper that can often be purchased from street vendors outside the police station or from banks. These papers have to be written in a specialized language. Someone in the police station will write it for you; tip the scribe the equivalent of $4 or $5. In most South American countries, lawyers take care of the complicated transactions involving documents and tips to government officials.

SHOPPING: South America is a good place to purchase handicrafts, weavings, suede, and leather. Brazil has great buys in semiprecious stones (amethyst and topaz are the two most popular), and Colombia's emeralds are renowned. Buy jewelry or expensive stones only from reputable dealers. Street vendors rarely deliver what they promise. The Indian markets in the Andean countries — Ecuador, Bolivia, and Perú — are the best places to pick up ponchos, woolen hats, sweaters, and other textiles and woven goods. If you shop in the central market (*mercado central*), you will find much better deals than in hotel shops, the airport, or in any tourist shops. The markets do not accept credit cards, but prices will be lower. Bring small change.

Indian merchants do not always like to bargain with tourists, contrary to popular belief. You will probably strike a better deal if you speak Spanish (even better, Quechua or Aymará); often haggling only antagonizes the seller. He or she probably assumes that if you are rich enough to afford a trip to South America, you can spend a few extra pesos for your blanket. Unless you can cajole pleasantly, do not expect a reduction in price. By and large, prices are standardized in each market. You will usually find the same merchandise at more or less the same prices at each stall in any given market.

Argentina, Uruguay, and Chile offer the best buys in suede and leather; in Colombia, the leather goods are very good and reasonably priced. For specific suggestions on where to shop, look under *Shopping* in each city report in THE CITIES.

Time Zones, Business Hours, and Bank Holidays

It usually surprises North Americans to discover that South America's west coast is roughly due south of the eastern coast of the US. This means that Panamá, Colombia, Ecuador, and Perú are on Eastern Standard Time all year (only Chile observes Daylight Saving Time). When it is noon in any of these countries, it is noon in New York. Countries to the east — Chile, Bolivia, Paraguay, most of Brazil (which has four time zones), and Venezuela are one hour ahead, with their clocks at 1 PM when it is noon in New York. Eastern Brazil, that fat proboscis of land that juts far into the Atlantic and includes the major cities Salvador, Rio, and São Paulo, is 1 hour ahead of the rest of Brazil; in this same time zone are Uruguay, Argentina, Guyana, and French Guiana, all 2 hours ahead of New York. Suriname is 1½ hours ahead of eastern US.

Throughout South America, a 24-hour timetable is used for public transport schedules. By this method, midnight is recorded as 2400, 1 PM as 1300, 6 PM as 1800, and so on.

Many South Americans have a more flexible concept of time than people in the US. When you make an appointment or receive an invitation for a specific time, it is generally understood that you are actually expected to meet about an hour later. If you invite friends for dinner at 8 PM, do not expect them until 9 PM. If they have not arrived by 10 PM, you can assume that something came up. This is not intended as a personal insult nor should you think of yourself as having been stood up. Punctuality and social responsibility are generally perceived in a loose framework in southern countries, and it is not an offense for someone to fail to keep a social engagement. (This is much less likely to happen in a business situation, in which appointments are kept punctually.) One of the fascinating differences between the residents of Rio de Janeiro and those of São Paulo, Brazil, is their attitude towards time. In Rio, pleasure-oriented Cariocas affectionately and exuberantly promise to meet friends later or tomorrow, then disappear until a chance encounter at a future date. Sober, work-oriented Paulistas are more sincere in keeping their appointments; if they are more than an hour late, they apologize for the inconvenience and explain the reason for the delay.

In the jungle, time as we know it does not exist. There is no point in worrying how long it will take to travel from one point to another because there are innumerable unpredictable variables: sudden storms, surprise visits by the driver's long-lost cousins, mishaps, accidents, and general procrastination and sloth. Jungle guides, aware that gringos like to know how long expeditions are likely to take, are fond of giving estimated times. If a guide tells you a trip will take 3 hours, do not be surprised if it takes at least twice that long.

Most transport systems, such as major airlines, buses, and collective taxis, keep fairly regular schedules, weather permitting. Ask your hotel concierge to call the airport a few hours before your international flight to make sure there are no long delays. People who provide services to tourists, such as tour escorts and cabdrivers, can be relied upon.

If you bear in mind that, as in Mexico, South Americans say *ahora* (now) when they mean anytime today or tomorrow, *ahorita* (right now) when they mean anytime within the next 3 or 4 hours, and *en seguida* (immediately) when they mean within the hour, you will be spared a lot of anxious waiting. If you adopt a southern attitude toward time during your trip through South America, you will find everything more enjoyable.

BUSINESS HOURS: In smaller cities and towns, people follow the natural rhythm of day and night; bank hours, for instance, are more definite than commercial hours. Farmers and fishermen start work at dawn, and businesspeople open shops, cafés, and markets around 8 AM. In Cuzco, Perú, and La Paz, Bolivia, as well as in other Andean cities, shops and some offices open at 8:30 or 8:45 AM, close at noon for long lunches (until 4 PM), then reopen until 6 or 7 PM. Shops that cater to tourists stay open later, until 8 or 9 PM. Below is a list of business hours in South America. For bank hours, see the country-by-country listings in FACTS IN BRIEF.

Argentina: 9 AM to 7:30 PM, Mondays through Fridays; 9 AM to 1 PM, Saturdays

Bolivia: 9 AM to noon, 2 to 6 PM, Mondays through Fridays; 9 AM to 1 PM, Saturdays

Brazil: 9 AM to 6:30 PM, Mondays through Fridays; 9 AM to 1 PM, Saturdays

Chile: 10 AM to 7 PM, Mondays through Fridays; 10 AM to 2 PM, Saturdays

Colombia: 8:30 or 9 AM to 6:30 or 7 PM, Mondays through Saturdays

Ecuador: 8:30 AM to noon, 3 to 7 PM, Mondays through Fridays; 8:30 AM to noon, Saturdays

French Guiana: Erratic, midmorning to late afternoon, Mondays through Saturdays

Guyana: 7:30 AM to 4 PM, Mondays through Thursdays; 7:30 AM to 6 PM, Fridays; 8 AM to noon, Saturdays

Panamá: 9 AM to noon, 2 to 6 PM, Mondays through Saturdays

Paraguay: 7 to 11:30 AM, 3 to 7 PM, Mondays through Saturdays

Perú: 9:30 or 11:30 AM to 4 or 7 PM, Mondays through Saturdays

Suriname: 7 AM to 1 PM, 4 to 6 PM, Mondays through Fridays; 7 AM to 1 PM, 4 to 7 PM, Saturdays

Uruguay: 9 AM to 7 PM, Mondays through Fridays; 9 AM to 12:30 PM, Saturdays

Venezuela: 8:30 AM to noon, 2:30 to 6:30 or 7 PM, Mondays through Saturdays

South American business establishments are universally closed on Sundays.

BANK HOLIDAYS: Government offices, banks, and stores are closed on national holidays, many of which are Roman Catholic celebrations. For each country's independence day and other holidays, see *Special Events* section in each city section in THE CITIES. The following holidays are celebrated in all South American countries (in many cases, the day preceding and the day following each holiday are nonbusiness days): New Year's Day; Epiphany, January 6; Pre-Lent Carnival; Holy Thursday; Good Friday; Independence Day (varies in each country); Assumption, August 15; All Saints' Day, November 1; Christmas.

Some countries also celebrate Corpus Christi Day, June 9; Columbus Day, October 12; and Bolívar's birthday, July 24.

Mail, Telephone, and Electricity

MAIL: Although much improved in recent years, mail service in South America is not all it could be. An airmail letter from the US takes a week to 10 days to reach one of the capital cities; mail to any of the smaller cities takes anywhere from 2 weeks to forever. Letters from South America to the US have been known to arrive in as short a time as 5 days, but it is a good idea to allow 10 days for delivery in either direction. (If you must contact someone in a hurry, send a cable or telegram through a private — not government-run — telecommunications firm such as All-America ITT or Cables West Coast, both of which have bureaus throughout the southern continent.) Ecuador and Venezuela reputedly have the least reliable postal services. Anything to either of these countries should be sent airmail. Even so, expect delivery in somewhat under 2 weeks. In most South American countries, internal surface mail service is highly irregular, and it is worth the few extra centavos to send letters airmail between cities in any country.

You can send postcards and letters from your hotel with reasonably secure odds of their safe arrival, but it is not a good idea to put anything in a mailbox and expect it to arrive at its destination. Experienced travelers use the central post office (*correo central*) for the most reliable service. If you want something registered (*certificado*), the central post office can take care of this more efficiently than a branch. Generally, all mail that leaves any country goes through the central post office, so you can be sure of the most efficient service. Packages should never be sent surface mail, which is totally unreliable; carry what you can or air freight it.

There are several ways to route mail; the most reliable way is to have letters sent to your hotel, clearly marked "Hold for Arrival," with the date of your reservation. If you are a client of American Express, you can have mail sent to any of its South American offices. Central post offices will hold mail addressed to you if it is marked: c/o Lista de Correos (care of General Delivery). However, as South Americans have more than one surname, your mail could be mis-sorted.

To avoid confusion, do not use middle names when sending mail to South America. South American surnames, especially those of Spanish origin, often begin in the middle. It is only a problem when mail is alphabetized if you have included anything more than a first and last name. Ask the post office clerk to look for it under the first letter of your first or middle name should there be nothing under the first letter of your last name. Remember, too, that in small towns, separate sets of post office boxes are segregated into *señors* and *señoras.* Your letter may not have landed in the correct sexual category. If you plan to remain in one place for more than a month, consider renting a post office box (*cajón postal, casilla, apartado*) in the central post office to eliminate the chance of mail getting lost in local delivery. If you are expecting documents or important papers, the US Embassy or consulate will hold mail for US citizens. (The consulate will not handle trivial mail.)

TELEPHONE: In many areas of South America, telephone service is so unreliable that it is simply not an effective means of communication, and, even in some major cities, people prefer to drop in on friends unannounced rather than try to phone. Recently, however, telephone service has greatly improved in many big cities, especially for international calls. Where new systems have been introduced, there are generally all new telephone numbers, so if you have a lot of trouble with local calls, ask the hotel operator for assistance. The Brazilian telephone system has been totally overhauled, with city code dialing between state capitals and direct overseas dialing to many countries, including the US. In most countries, however, it is still easier to call South America from the States than vice versa. And as with elsewhere in the world, it's usually easier to get through on an international call either before or after business hours, when the trunk lines are less busy.

Listings in THE CITIES include phone numbers, but you may experience some frustration trying to use them, and they change often. If at all possible, get someone at your hotel to make calls for you.

In Brazil, Argentina, and Chile, tokens are needed for public telephones. You can buy them at hotel desks, post offices, and at some stores.

ELECTRICITY: Power failures are not as frequent as they were several years ago, but thunderstorms can produce temporary blackouts. All hotels supply candles. Neither electrical circuits nor plugs and sockets are standardized in South America, and in many countries they differ from those in the US. The American chain hotels have

US-style sockets for electric razors, although larger appliances, such as hair dryers, should not be plugged in to these outlets. For the most part, US-made electrical items are useless in South America without some kind of adapter plug or convertor.

The voltages used in South America are:

Argentina: 220 volts AC
Bolivia: 110–220 volts AC, La Paz; 110 volts AC, Potosí; 220 volts AC elsewhere
Brazil: 110 volts AC, Rio de Janeiro and São Paulo; 220 volts AC, Brasília; 127 volts AC, Salvador (Bahía), Manaus, and Curitiba
Chile: 220 volts AC
Colombia: 150 volts AC, Bogotá; 110 volts AC elsewhere
Ecuador: 110 volts AC
French Guiana: 110 and 220 volts AC
Guyana: 110 and 220 volts AC
Panamá: 110 volts AC
Paraguay: 220 volts AC
Perú: 220 volts AC
Suriname: 127 volts AC
Uruguay: 220 volts AC
Venezuela: 110 volts AC

Drinking and Drug Laws

 DRINKING: There are few cultural or legal restrictions on drinking in South America; a person must look extremely young before being denied a drink in a public place. In general public drunkenness is not a legal offense, and car accidents caused by drunken drivers are depressingly common, as are bar fights.

That is only a small part of the story, though, and innumerable South American fiestas, at which drinking is an important but not immoderate part, provide wonderful opportunities to get to know and enjoy South Americans. Each country has its own national alcoholic beverage, worth sampling at least once. Argentina's wines and beers are among the finest in South America. Bolivia and Perú are known for *pisco* (a potent grape brandy) and *chicha* (fermented corn beer). Brazil's *cachaça* (sugarcane liquor) is usually mixed with fruit juice in a blender to form a mixed drink known as a *batida.* Brazil's best beers are Pilsner, Brahma, and Antarctica. In addition to fine *pisco,* Chile manufactures fiery *aguardiente,* a brandy, and magnificent wines (Santa Carolina, Cousiñol Macul, and Undurraga are recommended white wines; Tarapaca is considered among the finest burgundies). Escudo is Chile's most popular beer; Club Colonia is Colombia's. Colombia's most popular rums are Ron Caldas and Ron Medellín. *Guarapo,* a local sugarcane liquor, is wickedly potent. Ecuador is known for its Pilsner and Club beers. In French Guiana, rum is the national drink, as it is in neighboring Guyana. Guyana's British heritage is reflected in one of its alcoholic products: Diamond Club whiskey. Panamá is a good place to sample inexpensive imported liqueurs, rum, and a variety of beers: Balboa, Atlas, Panamá, and Cristal. Paraguay's *caña* is an exceptionally powerful sugarcane rum. In Suriname, people drink whiskey; Uruguay's *grappa* (grape brandy), *caña,* and beers, both *rubia* (light) and *negra* (dark), are favorite brews. Local wines are exceptional, particularly Santa Rosa Cabernet (red) and Mil Botellas Chablis (white). Venezuela's Cardenal, Polar Zulia, and Solera beers are all good, but local rum is the specialty. Try *ponche crema,* a rum punch made with milk or cream. Tequila, the Mexican beverage, is not commonly found in South America.

DRUGS: Famous throughout the world (the straight world as well as the underworld), Colombian cocaine can be obtained at a costly and dangerous price, the most obvious of which is imprisonment (see *Medical and Legal Aid,* GETTING READY TO GO). Drug dealing itself is a vicious business, even without the illegality. One American who has lived in South America for many years reports that cocaine dealers have a nasty habit of supplying *gringos* with substances ranging from relatively harmless powders to ground glass.

Marijuana is available in most large cities. Colombian grass is reported to be the best, with Ecuadorian rating the nickname *lechuga* ("lettuce") because it is comparatively weak. Prices fluctuate depending on the availability of the crop, influenced by such factors as the duration and strength of the rainy season in the Andes. As with cocaine, the main drawback to buying marijuana is the inherent risk of getting locked up. US embassies and consulates do not react sympathetically when they learn of young American drug users or dealers languishing in the clink, so you cannot count on any but the most perfunctory assistance from them. The best advice we can give you about drugs in South America is: AVOID THEM!

Customs and Returning to the US

 Upon entering the US from any South American destination, you will have to pass through US customs. You must declare to the official at the point of entry everything you have bought or acquired during your sojourn on the southern continent. Customs procedures are usually perfunctory, though you can experience delays if the agents have any suspicions. Keep all receipts handy and pack souvenirs and acquisitions together in an accessible part of your suitcase. Most customs agents are looking for drugs and fresh fruit and vegetables, although in the Andean countries (particularly in Perú), they watch for antiquities, which require official export permits. Customs checks are a prerequisite for entering the US no matter how you arrive — by air, overland, or through a seaport.

DUTY-FREE ARTICLES: US citizens returning from a journey overseas are entitled to bring home $400 worth of purchases duty-free. This limit includes items used or worn while abroad, souvenirs, and gifts to be given to others, as well as gifts you have received during the trip. Beyond the duty-free limit, returnees are required to pay a flat fee of 10% of the retail value of purchases ranging from $400 to $1400. Keep in mind that the duty you might pay is far less than the penalty (forfeiture of the articles, a fine, or imprisonment) for failing to declare an article or misrepresenting its value. Families and/or traveling companions may combine duty-free allowances: A family of four, for example, may bring back $1600 worth of goods before any duty is assessed on their foreign purchases.

Certain articles are duty free. These include up to 100 cigars, one quart of liquor, and foreign-made articles taken abroad, such as cameras or jewelry. These last items should be registered with the customs bureau nearest your home before your departure so that you will not have to pay duty twice on a particular item.

DUTY-FREE CRAFT ITEMS: In order to help developing nations improve their economy through export, the US has adopted a Generalized System of Preferences (GSP). In effect since 1976, the GSP entitles US citizens to bring home 2,800 items duty-free as long as they are manufactured in one of the developing countries. In South America, these nations are Argentina, Bolivia, Brazil, Chile, Colombia, Ecuador, Guyana, Panamá, Paraguay, Perú, Suriname, Uruguay, and Venezuela. The GSP enables you to bring in products worth more than the $600 duty-free exemption discussed above. The list of goods eligible for this status includes candy, bone and other china, cigarette lighters, cork, earthen tableware or stoneware (except sets), china figurines, furs, wood or plastic furniture, games, ivory, jewelry of precious metal or stones, musical instruments, perfume, printed matter, records and tapes, silverware, toys, weavings, and wood carvings. Clothing, rugs, and many leather items are not included.

If you have any questions about the GSP status of a particular item, check with the nearest customs office or at the US Embassy (for a list of US embassies and consulates in South America, see *Medical and Legal Aid,* GETTING READY TO GO). For more information on any aspect of US customs regulations, write to the US Customs Service, 1301 Constitution Ave. NW, Washington, DC 20229, and ask for the booklet "Know Before You Go."

MAILING GOODS HOME: Although we do not recommend that you send any packages through the notoriously unreliable South American postal systems, you are entitled to send up to $50 worth of goods to the US duty-free. Be sure to mark each package "Unsolicited Gift — Value under $50."

FORBIDDEN IMPORTS: Narcotics, plants, and many kinds of food are not allowed to enter the US. Organic matter that is admitted includes dried bamboo, baked goods, beads made of seeds other than Jequirity beans, candy, fully cured cheese, coconuts without husks, canned or processed fruit, herbs, dried insects, jams, jellies, lichens, mushrooms, nuts, seeds, shamrocks, seashells, spices, straw articles, truffles, canned or processed vegetables, and some plants.

If you ship your car back to the US, it must be cleaned to remove all traces of potentially bacteria-laden foreign oil at your own expense before entering the US. This does not apply if you are entering through Mexico.

For more information, write to *Quarantines,* US Department of Agriculture, Federal Bldg., Hyattsville, MD 20782, or get in touch with the Animal and Plant Health Inspection Service office nearest your home (check under the US Department of Agriculture listings in your telephone book).

The Department of the Treasury, US Customs Service, Washington, DC 20229, publishes a free kit of pamphlets with this year's customs information. It includes "Pets"; "Wildlife"; "Traveler's Tips on Bringing Food, Plant, and Animal Products into the United States"; "GSP"; "Pocket Hints"; "US Customs Hints for Visitors (Nonresidents)"; "Customs Highlights for Government Personnel/Civilian and Military"; "Currency Reporting"; "Buying a Car Overseas"; "Trademark Information for Travelers"; and "Rates of Duty". These pamphlets tell you everything you always wanted to know about US customs but were afraid to ask, and then some. They are great pretrip briefing material.

Crime in South America

 South American countries, like anywhere else in the world, have their share of pickpockets and thieves working the tourist areas (camera thefts have become especially common in recent years). Don't let them spoil your trip. Exercise the normal common-sense precautions you would observe at home, and be particularly careful in crowded markets, airports, and stations. The US embassy recommends the following precautions:

1. Do not keep your passport, extra traveler's checks, cash, onward tickets, ID, credit cards, or other valuables in your purse or outside pockets. Carry only what you will need and leave the rest locked in your hotel safe. In addition, do not wear valuable earrings, necklaces, rings, or watches.

2. If you must carry your passport, it is safer fastened in an inner pocket than in a purse.

3. Keep your ID cards separate from your passport because a replacement cannot be issued without some form of identification. Better yet, carry a separate photocopy of your passport (and also photocopy the visa pages for the countries to be visited). If you lose a passport, make it known at once to the nearest police station. Ask for a copy of the resultant police report; you will need it for a new passport, which can be issued by a US consul section only during office hours.

Sources and Resources

South American Embassies and Consulates in the US

 Below is a list of South American embassies and consulates in the US. They can issue tourist cards or visas needed to visit Panamá, Venezuela, and Brazil and legalize official documents, such as commercial and residence visas. Embassies and consulates sometimes provide maps and some travel literature, although in general the selection of brochures is sparse compared to those obtainable from airlines and travel agents. They can also provide lists of accommodations and some information on tours. Offices are usually open Mondays through Fridays.

The best places to get tourist information in each South American country are listed under *Sources and Resources* in each city report in THE CITIES.

Embassies

Argentina: 1600 New Hampshire Ave., NW, Washington, DC 20009 (phone: 202-969-6400)

Bolivia: 3014 Massachusetts Ave., NW, Washington, DC 20008 (phone: 202-483-4410)

Brazil: 3006 Massachusetts Ave., NW, Washington, DC 20008 (phone: 202-745-2700)

Chile: 1732 Massachusetts Ave., NW, Washington, DC 20036 (phone: 202-785-1746)

Colombia: 2118 Leroy Pl., NW, Washington, DC 20008 (phone: 202-387-8366)

Ecuador: 2535 15th St., NW, Washington, DC 20009 (phone: 202-234-7200)

French Guiana: French Embassy, 2535 Belmont Rd., NW, Washington, DC 20009 (phone: 202-234-0990)

Guyana: 2490 Tracy Pl., NW, Washington, DC 20008 (phone: 202-265-6900)

Panamá: 2862 McGill Terrace, NW, Washington, DC 20008 (phone: 202-483-1407)

Paraguay: 2400 Massachusetts Ave., NW, Washington, DC 20008 (phone: 202-483-6960)

Perú: 1700 Massachusetts Ave., NW, Washington, DC 20036 (phone: 202-833-9860)

Suriname: Watergate Office Bldg., Suite 711, 2600 Virginia Ave., NW, Washington, DC 20037 (phone: 202-338-6980)

Uruguay: 1918 F St., NW, Washington, DC 20006 (phone: 202-331-1313)

Venezuela: 2445 Massachusetts Ave., NW, Washington, DC 20008 (phone: 202-797-3800)

Consulates

Argentina: 350 S Figueroa, Los Angeles, CA 90071 (phone: 213-687-8884); 12 W 56th St., New York, NY 10019 (phone: 212-603-0400); 25 SE 2nd Ave., Ste. 722, Miami, FL 33131 (phone: 305-373-7794)

Bolivia: 211 E 43rd St., New York, NY 10017 (phone: 212-687-0530); 25 SE 2nd Ave., Ste. 700, Miami, FL 33131 (phone: 305-358-3450)

Brazil: 3810 Wilshire Blvd., Los Angeles, CA 90010 (phone: 213-382-3133); 630 Fifth Ave., New York, NY 10011 (phone: 212-757-3085); 777 Brickell Ave., Miami, FL 33131 (phone: 305-377-1735)

Chile: 619 S Olive St., Los Angeles, CA 90014 (phone: 213-624-6357); 866 UN Plaza, New York, NY 10017 (phone: 212-980-3366); 25 SE 2nd Ave., Ste. 803, Miami, FL 33131 (phone: 305-373-8623)

Colombia: 3600 Wilshire Blvd., Ste. 1712, Los Angeles, CA 90010 (phone: 213-382-1136); 10 E 46th St., New York, NY 10017 (phone: 212-949-9898); 14 NE 1st Ave., Miami, FL 33132 (phone: 305-373-3087)

Ecuador: 548 S Spring St., Los Angeles, CA 90013 (phone: 213-628-3014); 18 E 41st St., New York, NY 10017 (phone: 212-683-7555); 25 SE 2nd Ave., 5th Floor, Miami, FL 33131 (phone: 305-371-8366)

French Guiana: French Consulate, 8350 Wilshire Blvd., Ste. 310, Beverly Hills, CA 90211 (phone: 213-272-5452); 934 Fifth Ave., New York, NY 10021 (phone: 212-535-0100)

Guyana: 611 S Wilton Pl., Los Angeles, CA 90005 (phone: 213-627-9139); 622 Third Ave., New York, NY 10017 (phone: 212-953-0920)

Panamá: 548 S Spring St., Los Angeles, CA 90013 (phone: 213-627-9139); 1270 Ave. of the Americas, New York, NY 10019 (phone: 212-246-3771); 150 SE 3rd Ave., Miami, FL 33131 (phone: 305-379-7280)

Paraguay: 8322 Seaport Dr., Huntington Beach, CA 92646 (phone: 714-969-2955); 1 World Trade Center, Ste. 1947, New York, NY 10048 (phone: 212-432-0733); 2901 Ponce de Leon Blvd., Coral Gables, FL 33134 (phone: 305-444-8250)

Perú: 805 Third Ave., New York, NY 10022 (phone: 212-644-2850); 2490 Coral Way, Ste. 201-202, Miami, FL 33143 (phone: 305-856-1355)

Suriname: 6555 NW 36th St., Miami, FL 33166 (phone: 305-871-2790)

Uruguay: 747 Third Ave., New York, NY 10017 (phone: 212-753-8193); 25 SE 2nd Ave., Ste. 337, Miami, FL 33131 (phone: 305-358-9350)

Venezuela: 870 Market St., Ste. 665, San Francisco, CA 94101 (phone: 415-421-5172); 7 E 51st St., New York, NY 10022 (phone: 212-826-1660); 2655 Le June Rd., Ste. 614, Coral Gables, FL 33134 (phone: 305-446-2851)

Recommended Reading

The following list of suggested titles is far from comprehensive, but it does give a sampling of many books — most in print, others in libraries — that may be useful and interesting background reading or delightful companions on the road. There is at least one good bookstore in every major South American capital, and it is worthwhile to visit it in search of the occasional good locally published guide, which often will be carried in hotel shops as well. Imported books are very expensive, however, and guidebooks in particular will probably be out of date.

General

Ancient Arts of the Americas by G. H. S. Bushnell (Praeger, 1967)
Andean Culture History by Junius Bird (Natural History Press, 1964)
The Book of Latin American Cooking by Elizabeth Ortiz (Knopf, 1979)
The Conquest of the Incas by John Hemming (London: Macmillan, 1970)
Cut Stones & Crossroads by Ronald Wright (Viking, 1984)

Galápagos Islands, Lost in Time by Tui De Roy-Moore (Viking, 1980)

Galápagos Pacific by Luis Robles Maldonado (Paris: Editions DS, 1982)

The Golden Man, the Quest for El Dorado by Victor Von Hagen (London: Book Club Association, 1974)

History of the Conquest of Peru by William Prescott (Heritage Press, 1957)

The Incredible Incas & Their Timeless Land by Loren McIntyre (National Geographic Society, 1975)

Indian Art in South America by Frederick Dockstader (New York Graphic Society, 1967)

In Patagonia by Bruce Chatwin (Simon & Schuster, 1978)

Latin-American Spanish for Travelers, with a 60-minute cassette also available (Berlitz)

The Origin (a biography of Charles Darwin) by Irving Stone (New American Library, 1982)

Passage through El Dorado by Jonathan Kandell (Morrow, 1984)

Voyage of the Beagle by Charles Darwin (Bantam, 1972)

The Whispering Land by Gerald Durrell (Penguin, 1982)

The Outdoors – These books are guides to outdoor South America, published by Bradt Enterprises (95 Harvey St., Cambridge, MA 02140). They can generally be found in the travel section in bookstores and are useful to sojourners in the great outdoors.

Backpacking in Chile, Argentina plus Falkland Islands, 1980

Backpacking in Venezuela, Colombia & Ecuador, 1979

Backpacking and Trekking in Peru & Bolivia, 1980

Climbing & Hiking in Ecuador, 1984

South America River Trips (Colombia, Ecuador, Perú, Brazil, Chile), 1981

South America River Trips II (Suriname, Venezuela, Perú), 1982

Fiction

At Play in the Fields of the Lord by Peter Matthiessen (Bantam, 1981)

Aunt Julia and the Scriptwriter by Mario Vargas Llosa (Avon, 1982)

Bridge of San Luis Rey by Thornton Wilder (Avon, 1976)

Doña Flor and Her Two Husbands (1977) and *Gabriela, Clove & Cinnamon* (1978) by Jorge Amada (Avon)

Emperor of the Amazon by Marcio Souza (Avon, 1980)

Green Mansions by W. H. Hudson (Airmont, 1965)

One Hundred Years of Solitude by Gabriel García Márquez (Avon, 1971)

Weights and Measures

The countries of South America, like most of the world, use the metric system. The tables below should give all the information necessary to translate metric into US units of measure.

CONVERSION TABLES METRIC TO US MEASUREMENTS		
Multiply	**by**	**to convert to**
LENGTH		
millimeters	.04	inches
meters	3.3	feet
meters	1.1	yards
kilometers	.6	miles
CAPACITY		
liters	2.11	pints (liquid)
liters	1.06	quarts (liquid)
liters	.26	gallons (liquid)
WEIGHT		
grams	.04	ounces (avoir.)
kilograms	2.2	pounds (avoir.)
US TO METRIC MEASUREMENTS		
LENGTH		
inches	25.	millimeters
feet	.3	meters
yards	.9	meters
miles	1.6	kilometers
CAPACITY		
pints	.47	liters
quarts	.95	liters
gallons	3.8	liters
WEIGHT		
ounces	28.	grams
pounds	.45	kilograms
TEMPERATURE		
$°F = (°C \times 9/5) + 32 \qquad °C = (°F - 32) \times 5/9$		

Camera and Equipment

 Vacations are everybody's favorite time for taking pictures. After all, most of us want to remember the places we visit — and show them off to others — through spectacular photographs. Here are a few suggestions to help you get the best results from your travel picture-taking.

BEFORE THE TRIP: If you're just taking your camera out after a long period in mothballs, or have just bought a new one, check it thoroughly before you leave to prevent unexpected breakdowns and disappointing pictures.

1. Shoot at least one test roll, using the kind of film you plan to take along with you. Use all the shutter speeds and f/stops on your camera, and vary the focus to make sure everything is in order. Do this well in advance of your departure so there will be time to have the film developed and to make repairs, if they are necessary.
2. Clean your camera thoroughly, inside and out. Dust and dirt can jam camera mechanisms, spoil pictures, and scratch film. Remove surface dust from lenses and camera body with a soft camel's hair brush. Next, use at least two layers of crumpled lens tissue and your breath to clean lenses and filters. Don't rub hard and don't use compressed air on lenses or filters because they are so easily damaged. Persistent stains can be removed by using a Q-tip moistened with liquid lens cleaner. Anything that doesn't come off easily needs professional attention. Once your lens is clean, protect it from dirt and damage with an inexpensive skylight or ultra-violet filter.
3. Check the batteries in the light meter, and take along extra ones just in case yours wear out during the trip.

EQUIPMENT TO TAKE ALONG: Keep your gear light and compact. Items that are too heavy or bulky to be carried with you will likely stay in your hotel room.

1. Most single-lens reflex (SLR) cameras come with a 50mm, or "normal," lens, a general-purpose lens that frames subjects within an approximately average angle of view. This is good for street scenes taken at a distance of 25 feet or more and for full-length portraits shot at 8 to 12 feet. You can expand your photographic options with a wide-angle lens such as a 35mm, 28mm, or 24mm. These give a broader than normal angle of view and greater than normal "depth of field," that is, sharp focus from foreground to background. They are especially handy for panoramas, cityscapes, and for large buildings or statuary from which you can't step back. For extreme close-ups, a macro lens is best, but a screw-on magnifying lens is an inexpensive alternative. Telephoto lenses, 65mm to 1000mm, are good for shooting details from a distance (as in animal photography), but since they tend to be heavy and bulky, unless you anticipate a frequent need for them, omit them from vacation photography equipment. (However, many Indians do not like having their pictures taken, so either keep your distance or respect their wishes.) A zoom, which is a big lens but relatively light, has a variable angle of view so it gives a range of options. Try a 35mm to 80mm; beware of inexpensive models that give poor quality photographs. Protect all lenses with skylight or ultraviolet filters, which should be removed for cleaning only. A polarizing filter helps to eliminate glare and reflection, and to achieve fully saturated colors in very bright sunlight. Take along a couple of extra lens caps (they're the first things to get lost) or buy an inexpensive lens cap "leash."

2. Travel photographs work best in color. Good slide films are Kodachrome 64 and Fujichrome 50, both moderate- to slow-speed films that provide saturated colors and work well in most outdoor lighting situations. For very bright conditions, try slower film like Kodachrome 25. If the weather is cloudy, or you're indoors with only natural light, use a faster film, such as Kodachrome or Ektachrome 200 or 400. These can be "pushed" to higher speeds. Recently there are even faster films on the market for low-light situations. The result may be pictures with whiter, colder tones and a grainier image, but high-speed films open up picture possibilities that slower films cannot handle.

Films tend to render color in slightly different ways. Kodachrome brings out reds and oranges. Fujichrome is noted for its yellows, greens, and whites. Agfachrome mutes bright tones, producing fine browns, yellows, and whites. Anticipate what you are likely to see, and take along whichever types of film will enhance your results. You might test films as yuo test your camera (see above).

If you choose film that develops into prints rather than slides, try Kodacolor 100 or 400 for most lighting situations. Vericolor is a professional film that gives excellent results, especially in skin tones, but suffers shifts in color when subjected to temperature extremes; take it along for proplr photography *if* you're sure you can protect it from heat and cold. All lens and filter information applies equally to print and slide films.

How much film should you take? If you are serious about your photography, pack one roll of film (36 exposures) for each day of your trip. Film is especially expensive abroad, and any leftovers can be bartered away or brought home and safely stored in your refrigerator. Processing is also more expensive abroad and not as safe as at home. If you are concerned about airport-security X-rays damaging your undeveloped film (X-rays do not affect processed film), store it in lead-lined bags sold in camera shops. This possibility is not as much of a threat as it used to be, however. In the US, incidents of X-ray damage to unprocessed film (exposed or unexposed) are minimal because low-dosage X-ray equipment is used virtually everywhere. As a rule of thumb, photo industry sources say that film with speeds up to ASA 400 can go through security machinery in the US five times without any noticeable effect. Overseas, the situation varies from country to country, but at least in Western Europe the trend is also toward equipment that delivers less and less radiation. While it is doubtful that one exposure would ruin your pictures, if you're traveling without a protective bag you may want to ask to have your photo equipment inspected by hand, especially on a prolonged trip with repeated security checks. (Naturally, this is possible only if you're carrying your film and camera on board with you; it's a good idea anyway, because it helps to preclude loss or theft or the possibility at some airports that checked baggage will be X-rayed more heavily than hand baggage.) In the US, Federal Aviation Administration regulations require that if you request a hand inspection, you get it. But overseas the response may depend on the humor of the inspector. One type of film that should never be subjected to X-rays, even in the US, is the new, very high-speed film with an ASA rating of 1000. If you are taking some of this overseas, note that there are lead-lined bags made especially for it. Finally, the walk-through metal detector devices at airports do not affect film, though the film cartridges will set them off.

3. A small battery-powered electronic flash unit, or "strobe," is handy for very dim light or at night, but only if the subject is at a distance of 15 feet or less. Flash units cannot illuminate an entire scene, and many museums do not permit flash photography, so take such a unit only if you know you will need it. If your camera does not have a hot-shoe, you will need a PC cord to synchronize the flash with your shutter. Be sure to take along extra batteries.

4. Invest in a broad camera strap if you now have a thin one. It will make carrying the camera much more comfortable and considerably more thief-proof.

5. A sturdy canvas or leather camera bag, preferably with padded pockets — not an airline bag — will keep equipment organized and easy to find.

6. For cleaning, bring along a camel's-hair brush that retracts into a rubber squeeze bulb. Also, take plenty of lens tissue and plastic bags to protect equipment from dust.

7. For Amazon or other excursions where darkness and dampness might be a problem, use ASA 200 film as well as a plastic bag to protect the camera.

SOME TIPS: For better pictures, remember the following pointers:

1. *Get close.* Move in to get your subject to fill the frame.

2. *Vary your angle.* Shoot from above or below — look for unusual perspectives.

3. *Pay attention to backgrounds.* Keep it simple or blur it out.

4. *Look for details.* Not just a whole building, but a decorative element; not just an entire street scene, but a single remarkable face.

5. *Don't be lazy.* Always carry your camera gear with you, loaded and ready for those unexpected moments.

FACTS IN BRIEF

Argentina

Tourist Information – Argentine Embassy: 1600 New Hampshire Ave., NW, Washington, DC 20009 (phone: 202-969-6400). Consulates: 350 S Figueroa, Los Angeles, CA 90071 (phone: 213-687-8884); 12 W 56th St., New York, NY 10019 (phone: 212-603-0400). US Embassy and Consulate in Argentina: Colombia 4300, Buenos Aires 1425, (phone: 774-8811, 774-9911).

Entry Requirements and Customs – American citizens require a valid US passport and tourist visas, issued by any Argentine consulate office. Passports must be delivered or sent (with a self-addressed, stamped envelope) and left with the consulate for 5 working days. No photos or fee required. Travelers can enter Argentina with cigarettes, liquor, and personal effects other than clothing of a total maximum value of $500.

Climate and Clothes – Dry, temperate climate prevails throughout most of the country. The area around Iguazú Falls has year-round tropical temperatures. The Andes, Patagonia, and Tierra del Fuego are considerably cooler. Seasons are reversed; the Northern Hemisphere's winter (December-March) is Argentina's summer. Buenos Aires temperatures are in the 80s F in summer but drop into the 30s and 20s F in winter, with occasional snow. Clothing is casual in the rural areas; blue jeans are acceptable anywhere. Buenos Aires residents are more fashion conscious and formal: Evening attire is recommended for elegant restaurants.

Money – Austral. Banks are open from 9 AM to 4 PM, Mondays through Fridays. Note that the austral has replaced the peso as the unit of Argentine currency. The old peso notes are worthless, except perhaps to collectors.

Language – Spanish.

Getting There/Getting Around – Main entrance points are Buenos Aires and Mendoza. Airlines serving Argentina on direct flights from the US are Aerolíneas Argentinas, Eastern, and Pan Am. Aerolíneas now also flies once a week from Miami to Jujuy in Argentina. Domestic airlines provide the fastest, most efficient way of covering vast distances, but Argentina has excellent roads linking different sections of the country.

Calculating Costs – Hotel prices range from $75 up in the expensive bracket for a double; $30 to $60, moderate; under $30, inexpensive. (Note that a 20% room tax must be added to these rates.) Steak is inexpensive and plentiful; so is Argentine wine. The inflation rate in Argentina has in recent years been one of the world's highest.

Holidays – New Year's Day, Epiphany (Jan. 6), Carnival (pre-Lent), Holy Thursday, Good Friday, Easter, Independence Day (July 9), Anniversary of San Martín's Death (Aug. 17), Christmas.

Sports – Soccer, polo, and *pato,* a gaucho ball game played on horseback.

Shopping and Tipping – Leather, suede, some furs, and local wine are the best buys, and are now reasonable. Tip 10% in restaurants; 15% if no service charge is billed. Cab drivers get 10% of the fare; porters get 50¢ per piece of luggage. Washroom attendants should be tipped 20¢. Movie and theater ushers should be tipped 20¢.

Airport Departure Tax – Domestic $1; regional (surrounding countries) $3; international $10.

Bolivia

Tourist Information – Bolivian Embassy: 3014 Massachusetts Ave., NW, Washington, DC 20008 (phone: 202-483-4410). Consulate: 211 E 43rd St., New York, NY 10017 (phone: 212-687-0530). US Embassy in Bolivia: Edificio Tobías, 2 Piso, Calle Potosí, esq. Colón, La Paz (phone: 320494).

Entry Requirements and Customs – US citizens require only a valid US passport. Business travelers and tourists staying longer than 6 months must obtain a visa and pay a $50 fee. Travelers are allowed to bring in one bottle of liquor and one carton of cigarettes.

Climate and Clothes – Daytime temperatures in the Andes are generally in the 40s F in the dry season, between May and November, and in the 50s and 60s F in the rainy season, from mid-November to April. The jungle's climate is tropical all year.

Money – Bolivian Peso. Banks are open from 8:30 to 11:30 AM, and 2:30 to 4:30 PM, Mondays through Fridays. Hotels have foreign exchange desks.

Language – Spanish is the official language and is spoken by 36% of total population; Quechua is spoken in one part of the high plateau and valleys, by 37%; Aymará is spoken in almost all of the high plateau, by 25%; and Guaraní is spoken in the south of Bolivia by 2.5%. Itonama, Yara, Siriono, and other dialects are used by people of the jungle in the eastern part of Bolivia.

Getting There/Getting Around – The main entrance points are La Paz and Santa Cruz by air, and by land at the Bolivia/Perú checkpoint on Lake Titicaca. Eastern and LAB serve Bolivia direct from Miami, connecting with Santa Cruz as well as La Paz. Although bus and truck routes connect most towns, long distances are best traveled by plane. Domestic air service is frequent and pretty reliable. Railroad buffs will love Bolivia's trains — they're antiques on rails.

Calculating Costs – Expect to pay anywhere between $30 and $90 a night for a double room in La Paz. Costs are lower in other parts of the country except Santa Cruz. Meals also cost more in La Paz than elsewhere in Bolivia — $15 to $35 for two.

Holidays – Carnival (pre-Lent), Independence Day (Aug. 6), Easter, Christmas.

Sports – Soccer (*fútbol*), mountain climbing, skiing (world's highest run), golf, and tennis.

Shopping and Tipping – Ponchos, weavings, colored knit hats (*chullos*) and playful items — miniature reed boats, airplanes, and magic charms. Tip 10% in restaurants. Porters get 3 pesos; taxi drivers are not tipped. Look for *artesanía* beyond the tourist shops and visit the market behind Bogotá's San Francisco Cathedral.

Airport Departure Tax – $10 for international.

Brazil

Tourist Information – Embratur, 551 Fifth Ave., Ste. 421, New York, NY 10176 (phone: 212-286-9600), Brazilian Embassy: 3006 Massachusetts Ave., NW, Washington, DC 20008 (phone: 202-745-2700). Consulates: 3810 Wilshire Blvd., Los Angeles, CA 90036 (phone: 213-382-3133); 630 Fifth Ave., New York, NY 10111 (phone: 212-757-3085). US Embassy in Brazil: Av. das Nacoes, Lot #3, 70403 Brasília, DF (phone: 223-0120). US Consulates in Brazil: Edificio Conjunto, Presidente Wilson 147, 20030 Rio de Janeiro, RJ (phone: 292-7117); Edificio Conjunto Nacional, Rua Padre João Manuel 933, 01000 São Paulo, SP (phone: 881-6511).

Entry Requirements and Customs – US citizens require a valid passport and visa, issued free, but requiring one photo. Note that US passports must be valid for 6 months beyond the end of a trip. Visas are valid for 90 days and may be renewed once. Acquiring a business visa in the US can be a nightmare of red tape; it's suggested that even if you're traveling on business, apply for a tourist visa. Travelers are allowed to bring in two cartons of cigarettes, two quarts of liquor, two quarts of champagne, and three quarts of wine.

Climate and Clothes – The Northeast, the Amazon, and Rio de Janeiro have a tropical climate (80s F most of the year). In summer the mercury climbs into the 90s and 100s. São Paulo is hot and muggy in the summer, in the 50s F in the winter.

Money – Cruzado, which at press time had just replaced the old, familiar cruzeiro. Banks are open weekdays from 11:30 AM to 4:30 PM.

Language – Portuguese.

Getting There/Getting Around – The main entrance points are Rio de Janeiro and São Paulo. From the US, Varig and LAB have direct services to Manaus; Varig to Salvador, Recife, and Belém. Airlines serving Brazil from the US include Varig, Pan Am, Japan Air Lines (from Los Angeles only), and Aerolíneas Argentinas. Excellent domestic air service links the major cities as well as remote jungle settlements. Amazon cruises and exploratory expeditions along its tributaries are exciting travel experiences. Roads vary from the rugged Trans-Amazon Highway to the sleeker network of highways connecting Rio de Janeiro, São Paulo, Pôrto Alegre, and the Uruguay-Argentina frontiers.

Calculating Costs – At the moment, Brazil is a particularly good buy for North American visitors, due to the significant economic problems existing in the country. Double rooms in Rio and São Paulo start at $100 a night at the more deluxe hotels, but visitors can find a very comfortable beachfront room in Rio for about $60. The quality of hotels in both cities has been improving as the country puts more emphasis on tourism. Restaurants usually tack on a 10% service charge to the bill, and some charge $1 or $2 for a "couvert" — a spread of bread, olives, and other tidbits served before the meal — which is optional but will appear on the bill if you don't specifically decline it. An expensive meal will run $30 and up; moderate, $15 to $20; and inexpensive, under $15. Outside major cities, both accommodations and meals cost the same as or less than they do in the centers of Rio and São Paulo.

Holidays – Rio de Janeiro's Carnival, 4 days before Lent, is perhaps the most famous special event in the world. Other carnivals are held in Salvador (Bahía), Santos, Belém, and Guarujá. Other holidays are New Year's Day, Good Friday, Labor Day (May 1), Independence Day (Sept. 7), Republic Day (Nov. 15), and Christmas.

Sports – Three-time winner of the World Cup, Brazil is a country of soccer fanatics. Swimming, sailing, and fishing draw enthusiasts from all over the world.

Shopping and Tipping – Brazilian semiprecious stones — amethyst, topaz, and opal — can be purchased at gem factories around the country. Other good buys are rosewood (*jacaranda*) carvings, Amazonian dolls, leather goods, and sexy bikinis (*tangas*). A 5% tip is customary, although a service charge is included on a restaurant bill. Taxi drivers are not tipped, but the usual practice is to round the fare to the next cruziero. Tip porters the equivalent of 50¢ per piece of luggage; chambermaids, $1 per day. Cloakroom attendants and museum guides are also tipped.

Airport Departure Tax – International tax is 124 cruzados ($9 at press time), depending on the airport; domestic taxes also vary according to airport but are generally less than $1 (10 cruzados).

Chile

Tourist Information – Chilean Tourist Board (at LAN Chile Airlines), 630 Fifth Ave., New York, NY 10111 (phone: 212-582-3250). Chilean Embassy: 1732 Massachusetts Ave., NW, Washington, DC 20036 (phone: 202-785-1746). Consulates: 619 S Olive St., Los Angeles, CA 90013 (phone: 213-624-6357); 866 UN Plaza, New York, NY 10017 (phone: 212-980-3366). US Embassy and Consulate in Chile: Cordina Bldg., Agustinas 1343, Santiago (phone: 7-10133).

Entry Requirements and Customs – US citizens require a valid passport. Travelers are allowed to bring in two cartons of cigarettes and two liters of liquor.

Climate and Clothes – Arid desert in the north; moderate in the central valley, with temperatures in the 80s F in summer, dropping into the 20s F in winter. Southern regions are rainy and cool in the summer (temperatures in the 60s F), snowy in winter. The Andes' ski resorts are at their peak between June and September.

Money – Peso. Banks are open from 9 AM to 2 PM, Mondays through Fridays.

Language – Spanish.

Getting There/Getting Around – The main entrance points are Santiago, Valparaíso, and Arica. Airlines serving Santiago directly from the US are: Eastern, LAN Chile, Ladeco, and Pan Am. The Pan-American Highway runs the length of Chile from the Peruvian frontier at Arica to Puerto Montt, where the land breaks into rugged fjords and glaciers. The Pan-American is in good repair. Trains run frequently. A railroad trip through the Andes is unforgettable; so is a boat trip through the southern fjords. For quick transport between long distances, use domestic airlines and air taxis.

Calculating Costs – Throughout most of Chile, expect to pay $70 and up for a double room in an international-class hotel and $30 and up for an expensively classed meal. Easter Island runs about $10 above the norm for accommodations and food, and if you hit Portillo's ski resorts, prices can skyrocket to $150 per night for a double. Robinson Crusoe Island is also a relatively expensive resort area, with prices from $50 to $60 a night.

Holidays – New Year's Day, Good Friday, Labor Day (May 1), Battle of Iquique Day (May 21), Assumption Day (Aug. 15), Independence Day (Sept. 18–19), Columbus Day (Oct. 12), Immaculate Conception (Dec. 8), Christmas.

Sports – Soccer is the most popular spectator sport. Skiing (downhill and cross-country) at world-famous Portillo draws skiers from all over the globe. Deep-sea fishing off the Chilean coast and trout fishing in the Lake District attract anglers.

Shopping and Tipping – Weavings, ceramics, lapis lazuli, copper enamel goblets and cutlery, suede, leather, and excellent wine are available at good prices. For crafts, try the government CEMA cooperatives. Avoid inexpensive copper ashtrays in downtown Santiago souvenir shops. Seek out small shops in Providencia for unusual ceramics and finely crafted wooden objects. Tip 10% in restaurants. Porters get 50¢ per bag. Taxi drivers do not get tips.

Airport Departure Tax – $12.

Colombia

Tourist Information – Colombian Government Tourist Office, 140 E 57 St., New York, NY 10022 (phone: 212-688-0151). Colombian Embassy: 2118 Leroy Pl., NW, Washington, DC 20008 (phone: 202-387-8366). Consulates: 3600 Wilshire Blvd., Ste.

1712, Los Angeles, CA 90010 (phone: 213-382-1136); 10 E 46th St., New York, NY 10017 (phone: 212-949-9898). Corporación Nacional de Turismo: Calle 28, No. 13A-15, Bogotá (phone: 283-9466); also at Bogotá airport. US Embassy in Colombia: Calle 38, No. 8-61, Bogotá (phone: 85-13-00). US consulates: Calle 77 and Carrera 68, Centro Comercial Mayorista, Baranquilla (phone: 459-464).

Entry Requirements and Customs – US citizens require a valid passport and tourist card, valid for one entry and a stay of 90 days. Passport, proof of onbound transportation, and two passport photos must be presented to the Colombian Government Tourist Office, 140 E 57th St., New York, NY 10022, or any consulate or airline serving Colombia. When applying by mail, you must request tourist card forms in advance and submit them with the above documents. There is no fee. Travelers are allowed one carton of cigarettes and 3 liters of liquor.

Climate and Clothes – The Caribbean coast averages a year-round temperature of about 80°F. Bogotá, 8,669 feet above sea level, ranges from the mid 50s to the 70s F throughout the year. Colombia has two rainy seasons: one in March and April, the other in October and November.

Money – Peso. Banks in Bogotá are open from 9 AM to 3 PM, Mondays through Fridays.

Language – Spanish.

Getting There/Getting Around – The main entrance points are Bogotá, Baranquilla, Cartagena, Medellín, and Cali. Airlines serving Colombia from the US are: Avianca, Aerolíneas Argentinas, Eastern, and Ladeco. Roads are in fair condition and trains are not well maintained, so the best bet for getting around in Colombia is by air. A number of domestic airlines service the interior, coast, and capital.

Calculating Costs – The highest hotel rates in Colombia are in Bogotá and Cartagena, ranging from $60 and up to as low as $15 a night for a double. Other areas can be very inexpensive, with rates going from $30 down to $15 per night for a double. Bogotá also has the highest priced meals in the country. Here, an expensive dinner runs from $35 up; moderately priced, $15 to $30; and inexpensive, $10 to $15.

Holidays – New Year's Day, Epiphany (Jan. 6), St. Joseph (Mar. 19), Holy Week (before Easter), Labor Day (May 1), Sacred Heart (June 14), Corpus Christi (May 24), Peter and Paul (June 29), Independence Day (July 20), Battle of Boyacá (Aug. 7), Columbus Day (Oct. 12), Immaculate Conception (Dec. 8), and Christmas.

Sports – Soccer, deep-sea fishing, and mountain climbing are most popular.

Shopping and Tipping – Woolen ponchos (*ruanas*), leather goods, artisan products, and weavings can be purchased at the government-run Artesanías de Colombia. Emeralds mined here are among the world's finest. There are several famous dealers, and the Tequendama and Hilton hotels in Bogotá have reliable gems. Do not purchase gems from street vendors and do not purchase cocaine or marijuana. In restaurants, tip 10% if no service charge is added to the bill; 5%, if a service charge is included. Porters get 50 pesos per bag; washroom attendants, 25 pesos.

Airport Departure Tax – International tax is $15; domestic tax varies according to airport.

Ecuador

Tourist Information – Ecuadorian Embassy: 2535 15th St., NW, Washington, DC 20009 (phone: 202-234-7200). Consulates: 548 S Spring St., Los Angeles, CA 90013 (phone: 213-628-3014); 18 E 41st St., New York, NY 10017 (phone: 212-683-7555). US Embassy in Ecuador: 120 Av. Patria, Quito (phone: 561-698). Consulate: 9 de Octubre y García Moreno, Guayaquil (phone: 323-570).

Entry Requirements and Customs – US citizens must present a valid US passport and an ongoing ticket. Tourists may stay 90 days.

Climate and Clothes – The coastal lowlands and Galápagos Islands have a year-round equatorial climate in the humid 80s F. During the rainy season, November through May, temperatures are hotter. Quito has a temperate, Andean climate, with an average yearly temperature in the 50s F. The dry season runs from April through November; June and July are the coolest months, but also the clearest in the highlands.

Money – Sucre. Banks are open from 9 AM to 1:30 PM, Mondays through Fridays.

Language – Spanish; Quechua.

Getting There/Getting Around – The main entrance points are Quito and Guayaquil. Airlines serving Ecuador from the US are: Aerolíneas Argentinas, AeroPerú, Eastern, Ecuatoriana, LADECO, and Pan Am. The train ride from Quito to Riobamba, a half-day roller-coaster ride through the Andes, is quite spectacular and well worth it if you have the time. Buses make the run from Quito to Guayaquil in 10 hours; airplanes, in 35 minutes. Air service is recommended for trips to the interior. The Galápagos Islands can only be toured by cruise ship or yacht, the Amazon by Flotel cruises.

Calculating Costs – A double room at the highest priced hotels in Quito ranges from $60 to $70; in Guayaquil, from $70 up. More moderately priced accommodations are available for between $30 and $40. Meal costs generally coincide with hotel rates: expensive, $33, moderate, $15 to $30, and inexpensive, $13 and under. The best food bargain is the lobster and other shellfish in Quito. Outside the cities, travelers can find very inexpensive accommodations ($10 to $12 a night), but the rooms slant toward the primitive in comparison to US standards. There are several very nice country inns.

Holidays – New Year's Day, Carnival (pre-Lent), Good Friday, Labor Day (May 1), Battle of Pichincha (May 24), Bolívar's Birthday (July 24), Independence Day (Aug. 10), Anniversary of Guayacuíl (Oct. 9), Columbus Day (Oct. 12), Independence of Cuenca (Nov. 3), Founding of Quito (Dec. 6), and Christmas.

Sports – Soccer, bullfighting, horse racing, fishing, mountain climbing, and hunting are Ecuador's favorites.

Shopping and Tipping – The market at Otavalo is the best place to buy hand-made weaving, as Otavalo residents have been fine weavers for generations. The market, a colorful pageant, is active all week, although it reaches its peak on Saturdays. By all means bargain, but don't expect much of a break — prices are fairly standard, even in the markets. Ponchos, weavings, and straw items, including the famous Panama hat, can be found at OCEPA — Artesanías del Ecuador craft shops in Quito.

In restaurants, tip 10% if there is no service charge; otherwise, 5%. Porters should get 5 or 10 sucres per bag.

Airport Departure Tax – $20.

French Guiana

Tourist Information – French Embassy: 4101 Reservoir Rd., NW, Washington, DC 20007 (phone: 202-944-6000); French Government Tourist Office, 610 Fifth Ave., New York, NY 10020 (phone: 212-757-1125). In French Guiana: US Consular District of Martinique, FWI, 14 Rue Blenac, Boîte Postal 561, Fort de France 97206 (phone: 71-93-01).

Entry Requirements and Customs – US citizens require a valid passport, a visa, an ongoing ticket, and a yellow fever inoculation certificate for stays longer than 2 weeks. Travelers may bring two cartons of cigarettes and one liter of liquor.

Climate and Clothes – Tropical climate throughout the year, with temperatures in the 80s F.

Money – French franc. Banks are open from 7:15 to 11:45 AM and 2:30 to 5 PM, Mondays through Fridays, except Wednesdays, when they are open from 7 AM to noon.

Language – French.

Getting There/Getting Around – The main entrance points are Cayenne and St. Laurent. There are no direct flights from the US. The easiest way to get there is by taking American Airlines to either Martinique or Guadeloupe and making a connection to French Guiana via Air France. River trips from Cayenne to the Suriname border at St. Laurent are among the most exciting expeditions in South America. As there are no roads to speak of, overland travel is nonexistent.

Calculating Costs – Hotels here are small, quiet, comfortable, and few. A double room in the most deluxe hotel in Cayenne would run approximately $70.

Holidays – New Year's Day, Mardi Gras, Good Friday, Easter Monday, Labor Day (May 1), National Day (July 14), Assumption (Aug. 15), Armistice Day (Nov. 11), and Christmas.

Sports – Fishing and hunting.

Shopping and Tipping – Since French Guiana is a department of France, most goods are imported from France and are very expensive. There are some local crafts, but they are not of as high quality as those in neighboring Suriname. In restaurants, tip 10% of the check. Porters get 1 franc per item of luggage. Taxi drivers are not tipped.

Airport Departure Tax – None.

Guyana

Tourist Information – Guyanese Embassy: 2490 Tracy Pl., NW, Washington, DC 20008 (phone: 202-265-6900). Consulates: Embassy of the Republic of Guyana, 611 Wilton Pl., Los Angeles, CA 90005 (phone: 213-389-7565); 622 Third Ave., New York, NY 10017 (phone: 212-953-0920). US Embassy in Guyana: 31 Main St., Georgetown (phone: 54900).

Entry Requirements and Customs – US citizens require a valid passport, an outward-bound ticket, and a tourist visa, which requires 3 forms and 3 photos, issued by the consulate before arrival. Travelers are allowed to bring one carton of cigarettes and 32 ounces of liquor. If you plan to hunt, be sure to register your weapon at the Ministry of Home Affairs, Georgetown.

Climate and Clothes – Tropical climate throughout the year, with temperatures in the humid 80s F.

Money – Guyana dollar. Banks are open from 8 AM to noon, Mondays through Fridays; 8 to 11 AM, Saturdays.

Language – English.

Getting There/Getting Around – The main entrance point is Georgetown. Airlines serving Guyana from the US and the Caribbean are BWIA, Guyana Airways, and Tropical Airways (except from New York). Auto traffic follows the English system, with drivers keeping to the left. Bus service connects the main coastal cities. Boats travel the major rivers. Domestic air service is the best way to get to the interior.

Calculating Costs – Guyana is mainly a tropical jungle, and accommodations are fairly primitive. Overnight rates are surprisingly expensive considering the conditions, and a top double room in the capital can run $100. Expect to pay between $25 and $50 a night for an average hotel room — some with outhouses.

Holidays – New Year's Day, Youman Nabi (Feb. 21), Republic Day (Feb. 23), Phagwah (Mar. 25), Good Friday, Easter Monday, Labor Day (May 10), Caribbean

Community Day (first Monday in July), Freedom Day (first Monday in August), Deepavali (Oct. 31), Eid-ul-Ahza (Nov. 11), Christmas, and Boxing Day (Dec. 26).

Sports – Cricket is played in Georgetown. Soccer is another popular spectator sport. At Easter, there is an annual rodeo at the Rupunini savannah ranches. Fishing, hunting, and tennis are the main participant sports.

Shopping and Tipping – Native crafts — beads, wood carvings, blowpipes, and straw weavings — can be purchased at reasonable prices at Staebroek Market, Georgetown. Be sure to bargain. Guyanese diamonds are another good buy. Enachu Diamond Traders, Ltd., in Georgetown is a reputable dealer. In restaurants, tip 10% of the check. Porters get 25¢ (US) per item of luggage. Taxi drivers are not tipped.

Airport Departure Tax – Approximately $11.50.

Panamá

Tourist Information – Panama Government Tourist Bureau: 2355 Salzedo St., Ste. 201, Coral Gables, FL 33134 (phone: 305-442-2313). Panamanian Embassy: 2862 McGill Terrace, NW, Washington, DC 20008 (phone: 202-483-1407). Consulates: 548 S Spring St., Los Angeles, CA 90013 (phone: 213-627-9139); 1270 Ave. of the Americas, New York, NY 10020 (phone: 212-246-3771). US Embassy in Panamá: Av. Balboa E, Calle 38 (phone: 27-1777).

Entry Requirements and Customs – US citizens must produce a valid passport and a tourist card, which can be purchased for $2 from any of the airlines serving Panamá or obtained at no cost from the Panamanian Consulate. You may bring in three and a half cartons of cigarettes and three bottles of liquor.

Climate and Clothes – Hot, muggy, tropical climate throughout the year, with temperatures in the 80s and 90s F; cool and pleasant in the highlands.

Money – US dollars. The Balboa coins are for collectors only. Banks are open from 8 AM to 1:30 PM, Mondays through Fridays; Saturdays, 9 AM to 1 PM.

Language – Spanish.

Getting There/Getting Around – The main entrance point is Panamá City. Airlines serving Panamá from the US are: Eastern, Pan Am, Air Panamá, LAN Chile, and Ecuatoriana. Flamboyant buses connect the major cities; some are ramshackle, others are air conditioned. Domestic airlines fly to Contadora and San Blas Islands and some interior destinations. Many cruise ships takes the Panama Canal on Caribbean sailings.

Calculating Costs – Most hotel rooms in Panamá are in the moderate range, between $40 and $70 for a double room per night. Accommodations are slightly higher in Panamá City; Expensive rooms go from $90 on up. Some hotels around Panamá get as low as $30 for a double.

Holidays – New Year's Day, Day of the Martyrs (Jan. 9), Carnival Tuesday (pre-Lent), Good Friday, Labor Day (May 1), Revolution Day (Oct. 11), Memorial Day (Nov. 2), Independence from Colombia (Nov. 3), Flag Day (Nov. 4), Mothers Day (Dec. 8), and Christmas.

Sports – Horse racing, cockfights, basketball, baseball, soccer, boxing, and car racing are the most popular spectator sports. Deep-sea fishermen adore the marlin-filled Pacific and Caribbean waters. Freshwater fishing in the rivers and lakes is good, too.

Shopping and Tipping – Famous around the world for bargains in high-quality imported items, Panamá's best buys are cameras, small electronic goods, watches, perfumes, and luxury items — Irish crystal, Oriental jade, and silk. Local handicrafts include appliqué cloth (*molas*) and bead necklaces (*chaquiras*). For Panamanian crafts, visit Artesanía Nacional in the old city or Salsipuedes Market. There is a duty-free shop at the Panamá City airport. In restaurants, tip 15%. Porters get 25 Panamian cents per bag. Taxi drivers are not tipped.

Airport Departure Tax – $15.

Paraguay

Tourist Information – Paraguayan Embassy: 2400 Massachusetts Ave., NW, Washington DC 20008 (phone: 202-483-6960). Consulates: 8322 Seaport Dr., Huntington Beach, CA 92646 (phone: 714-969-2955); 1 World Trade Center, Ste. 1947, New York, NY 10048 (phone: 212-432-0733). US Embassy in Paraguay: Mariscal López 1776, Asunción (phone: 201-041).

Entry Requirements and Customs – US citizens require a tourist card ($1), a US passport and onbound tickets. Travelers may bring in any amount of cigarettes and liquor for personal use.

Climate and Clothes – Humid and warm throughout the year, without much variation. Daytime temperatures are generally in the 80s and 90s F.

Money – Guaraní. Banks are open from 7 AM to noon, Mondays through Fridays; exchange houses (*casas de cambio*), from 7 AM to noon and 4 to 7 PM.

Language – Spanish, Guaraní.

Getting There/Getting Around – The main entrance points are Asunción, Iguazú, and Encarnación. Two airlines serve Paraguay from the US: Líneas Aéreas Paraguayas (LAP) and Eastern, from Miami only. Domestic air service is the best way of getting to remote sections of the country. Boat traffic plies the Paraguay and Paraná rivers. It is possible to travel to Buenos Aires, Argentina, on the Paraná River from Asunción.

Calculating Costs – Basically, Paraguay is moderately priced when it comes to hotel rates and is relatively inexpensive for eating out. In Asunción, an expensive hotel will run $50 and up for a double; moderate rates are from $20 to $30; and inexpensive, from $12 to $20. The most expensive stay in the country is around Iguazú Falls, where hotel rates go as high as $85 a night for a double. Meals classed in the expensive range run $18 and up, moderate meals, from $10 to $18, and inexpensive, $10 and under.

Holidays – New Year's Day, San Blas Day (Feb. 3), Heroes' Day (Mar. 1), Maundy Thursday, Good Friday, Labor Day (May 1), Independence Day (May 14 and 15), Chaco Peace Day (June 12), Corpus Christi (May 24), Foundation of Asunción Day (Aug. 15), Constitution Day (Aug. 25), Battle of Boqueron Day (Sept. 29), Día de la Raza (Oct. 12), Immaculate Conception (Dec. 8), and Christmas.

Sports – Soccer and hunting safaris in the jungle are Paraguay's most popular sports.

Shopping and Tipping – Ñandutí lace is sold in front of the cathedral in Asunción. Linen (Aó Po'i) clothing, rugs, ceramics, gourds for drinking *maté,* silver puzzle rings, and other crafts can be purchased in Pettirossi Market, Asunción, and at markets throughout Paraguay. In restaurants tip 15%. Porters get 100 guaranís per piece of luggage. Taxi drivers are tipped 10%.

Airport Departure Tax – $5 for all international flights.

Perú

Tourist Information – Peruvian Embassy: 1700 Massachusetts Ave., NW, Washington, DC 20036 (phone: 202-833-9860). Perú Tourist Office (FOPTUR), 50 Biscayne Blvd., Ste. 123, Miami, FL 33132 (phone: 305-374-0023). Consulate: 805 Third Ave., New York, NY 10022 (phone: 212-644-2850). US Embassy and Consulate in Perú: Av. Wilson 1400, Lima (phone: 33-8000); Grimaldo del Solar 346, Miraflores, Lima (phone: 44-36-21).

Entry Requirements and Customs – US citizens require a valid US passport. Travelers may bring in an unspecified amount of cigarettes and liquor for personal use.

Climate and Clothes – A thick, heavy fog hangs over Lima in winter. Summers tend to be somewhat clearer, with temperatures in the 80s F. Winter temperatures are in the 50s F. Several miles east of the capital, a dry, warm desert climate prevails year round. The Andes' dry season runs between April and November, with daytime temperatures in the 60s and 70s F. In June and July, the mercury does drop below freezing, and it occasionally snows. Summer (between mid-November and March) is the rainy season in the Andes and in the jungle. *Montaña* jungle, along the hilly eastern slopes of the Andes, generally has a daytime temperature in the 80s F; the flat jungle (*selva*) frequently gets as hot as the high 90s, low 100s F.

Money – Inti. Banks are open from 9:15 AM to 12:45 PM and 4:30 to 6:30 PM, Mondays through Fridays.

Language – Spanish/Quechua.

Getting There/Getting Around – The main entrance points are Lima, the port of Callao, and Iquitos. Airlines serving Perú from the US include LAN Chile, Eastern, AeroPerú, Faucett, and others. The Pan-American Highway, paved but narrow, is clogged with trucks, buses, and frenetic drivers. Since distances between Peruvian cities are long, domestic air service is the best way to get around. Train rides through the Andes are scenic but slow. River trips through the jungle in dugout canoes are great for watching wildlife — and in some areas offer the only transportation — but be prepared to spend days in transit.

Calculating Costs – As Lima's tourist trade has increased, so has its number of hotel rooms. Although a double room in a top Lima hotel starts at $60, most accommodations run between $25 and $40. An overnight stay in the Cuzco area will run from $25 to $60. Other areas of Perú are less expensive, with the common cost for a room a mere $14. Good food is important to Peruvians, so eating virtually anywhere is a pleasure — and the bill won't spoil your appetite. On the average, a dinner for two runs between $15 and $25 in Lima.

Holidays – New Year's Day, Good Friday, Labor Day (May 1), St. Peter and St. Paul (June 29), Independence Day (July 28 and 29), Santa Rosa Day (Aug. 30), National Dignity Day (Oct. 9), Immaculate Conception (Dec. 8), and Christmas (Dec. 24 and 25).

Sports – Soccer, bullfighting, cockfighting, polo, and horse racing are Perú's most popular spectator sports. The Andes attract climbers and trekkers from all over the world. Lima's beaches have a loyal crowd of surfers.

Shopping and Tipping – Peruvian handicrafts — weavings, ponchos, woolen hats, and carvings — should be purchased in Cuzco or an Andean market rather than in one of the Lima tourist shops, where the same goods are three or four times more expensive. The quality of woolen items is not quite as fine as in Bolivia. Again, bargaining is more of a social pastime than an effective method of reducing prices unless you're fluent in Quechua. Lima's jewelry shops sell excellent hand-wrought gold and silver jewelry in Inca motifs, but check the silver items to make sure they have been carefully soldered or they may soon fall apart. A 10% service charge as well as meal tax is added to the check; tip from 5% to 10% on top of that, depending on service.

Airport Departure Tax – $10.

Suriname

Tourist Information – Suriname Airways, Miami International Airport, Concourse E, PO Box 59-5039, Miami, FL 33159 (phone: 305-871-2602 or 800-321-6864). Suriname Consulate, Suriname Embassy, 2600 Virginia Ave. NW, Ste. 711, Washington,

DC 20037 (phone: 202-338-6980). Consulate: 6555 NW 36th St., Ste. 201, Miami, FL 33166 (phone: 305-871-2790). US Embassy in Suriname: Dr. Sophie Redmondstraat 129, PO Box 1821, Paramaribo (phone: 72900).

Entry Requirements and Customs – US citizens require a valid passport, visa, and an outward-bound ticket. A tourist visa costs $17.50 and requires two photos. Also required is a form, available through the Suriname Consulate. Handling charge is $5. The visa can also be obtained through the consulate and takes at least two weeks to issue. Travelers may bring in an unspecified amount of cigarettes and tobacco for personal use.

Climate and Clothes – Hot, humid, tropical climate with temperatures in the 80s F throughout the year.

Money – Suriname guilder. Banks are open from 7:30 AM to 1 PM, Mondays through Fridays; 7:30 to 11 AM, Saturdays.

Language – Dutch.

Getting There/Getting Around – The main entrance points are Paramaribo, Albina, and Nickerie. Arrow and Suriname Airways fly directly from Miami to Paramaribo. A coastal road connects Paramaribo with the borders of French Guiana and Guyana, but there are no roads to the interior. Domestic air service and boats along the rivers are the best alternatives.

Calculating Costs – Accommodations that Americans will find most appealing in terms of creature comforts are expensive in Suriname. Expensive rates in tourist-styled resorts run anywhere from $35 to $60 a night; more moderate ones are $21 to $34. Inexpensive accommodations are available in fairly primitive guesthouses.

Holidays – New Year's Day, Carnival (pre-Lent), Phagwah Day (Mar. 1), Good Friday, Easter Monday, Labor Day (May 1), Freedom Day (July 1), Independence Day (Nov. 25), and Christmas (Dec. 25 and 26).

Sports – Soccer and basketball are the most popular spectator sports. Fishing and hunting are the leading participant sports.

Shopping and Tipping – Imaginative wood carvings, necklaces, hammocks, and woven fabrics are the best buys in Suriname. It is customary to bargain in the markets. In restaurants, tip 10% unless a service charge has been added to the check. Porters get .50 guilder per item of luggage. Taxi drivers are not tipped.

Airport Departure Tax – Approximately $17.50.

Uruguay

Tourist Information – Uruguayan Embassy: 1918 F St., NW, Washington DC 20006 (phone: 202-331-1313). Consulate: 747 Third Ave., New York, NY 10017 (phone: 212-753-8193). US Embassy in Uruguay: H. Abadie Santos 808, Montevideo (phone: 40-90-51).

Entry Requirements and Customs – US citizens require a valid passport. Travelers are entitled to bring one carton of cigarettes and two bottles of liquor.

Climate and Clothes – Its warm, temperate climate and 200 miles of Atlantic Ocean beaches have earned Uruguay the nickname "the Riviera of South America." Daytime temperatures are in the 80s F, dropping into the 60s F at night. In winter, between June and September, the temperature drops into the 40s F and skies turn foggy.

Money – Peso. Banks are open from noon to 5 PM, Mondays through Fridays. (Varies slightly depending on season, type of bank, and location.)

Language – Spanish.

Getting There/Getting Around – The main entrance points are Montevideo, Río Branco, and Colonia. Airlines serving Uruguay from the US are: Pan Am and Varig. A good network of roads links the interior with the capital. There is ferry and hydrofoil service between Buenos Aires and Colonia. Bus service is reliable. Domestic air service is the fastest way of reaching the interior. Boats travel to a number of ports along the Uruguay River, Carmelo, Mercedes, and Salto.

Calculating Costs – Hotel rates are fairly consistent in Uruguay — in the vicinity of $40 to $60 per night. The coastal resorts are more expensive, however, and can range from $40 to $100 in season for a double room. The bargain in this country is its restaurants. Our expensive classification goes from $20 on up for a three-course meal including wine and coffee. Moderate meals run between $10 and $15; inexpensive ones, under $10.

Holidays – Landing of the Orientales Day (Apr. 19), Battle of Las Piedras (May 18), Don José Gervacio Artigas's Birthday (June 19), Signing of the Constitution (July 18), Independence Day (Aug. 25), Columbus Day (Oct. 12), Immaculate Conception (Dec. 8), and Christmas.

Sports – Soccer, basketball, horse racing, rugby, and polo are the most popular participant sports. During the summer, swimming, surfing, and sailing attract enthusiasts from all over the continent. Deep-sea fishing is good throughout the year.

Shopping and Tipping – Leather clothes and accessories, amethysts, and woolen clothing are good buys. Stroll along Avs. 18 de Julio and 8 de Octubre between Plaza Independencia and Plaza Libertad, where the best shops are located. In restaurants, tip 10% of the check. Tip porters 3 pesos for each item of luggage. Taxi drivers get 10% of the fare.

Airport Departure Tax – $3.50.

Venezuela

Tourist Information – Venezuelan Government Tourist Bureau, 7 E 51st St., New York, NY 10022 (phone: 212-355-1101). Venezuelan Embassy: 2445 Massachusetts Ave., NW, Washington, DC 20008 (phone: 202-797-3800). US Embassy and Consulate in Venezuela: Av. Francisco de Miranda, La Floresta, Caracas (phone: 284-6111); APO MIA 34037, Maracaier, Zulia (phone: 61-84253).

Entry Requirements and Customs – US citizens are required to have a tourist card issued by the Venezuelan tourist office, consulate, or by airlines and steamships serving Venezuela upon presentation of proof of citizenship (a passport, birth certificate, voter's registration card) and an outward-bound ticket. (Do not lose that tourist card, as it must be surrendered upon departure and you'll find it difficult to get through immigration without it. Furthermore, whether your trip is for business or pleasure, it's far easier just to indicate on the card "pleasure.") Travelers are entitled to bring in two cartons of cigarettes and two bottles of liquor.

Climate and Clothes – Tropical along the coast, cooler inland. Caracas, at 3,400 feet above sea level, has a warm spring climate all year. The rainy season is between June and November, but be prepared for sudden tropical downpours at any time. In the Andes, temperatures are in the 60s and 70s F during the day, dropping considerably at night. The rainy season begins in May and lasts until November.

Money – Bolívar. Banks are open from 8:30 to 11:30 AM, and 2 to 4:30 PM, Mondays through Fridays.

Language – Spanish.

Getting There/Getting Around – The main entrance points are Caracas, Maracaibo, Margarita Island, and La Guaria. Airlines serving Venezuela from the US are Pan Am, Viasa, Avensa, Eastern, and Varig (Los Angeles only).

Calculating Costs – Hotel rates here depend on where you are going, but the average is between $40 and $50 a night. East coast beachfront hotels and those on

Margarita Island are more expensive — between $60 and $90 per night. Caracas is just about as high, with rooms from $40 to $60 and up. A meal for two will cost from $20 to $35 and up in expensive restaurants, but good dinners are available for under $20.

Holidays – New Year's Day, Carnival (pre-Lent), Holy Week (after Easter), Declaration of Independence Day (Apr. 18), Labor Day (May 1), Anniversary of the Battle of Carabobo (June 24), Bolívar's Birthday (July 24), Columbus Day (Oct. 12), Anniversary of the Death of Bolívar (Dec. 17), and Christmas.

Sports – Horse racing, bullfights, and baseball are the most popular spectator sports. Swimming, snorkeling, scuba diving, water skiing, and deep-sea fishing lead the list of participatory activities.

Shopping and Tipping – Caracas is now an expensive place to shop, and handicrafts are better purchased in the markets of small towns. Margarita Island has a duty-free zone offering liquor, perfume, gold and silver jewelry, and Margarita pearls. In restaurants, tip 10%. Porters get 2 bolívars. Taxi drivers are not tipped.

Airport Departure Tax – $4 for tourists; $25 for business travelers.

PERSPECTIVES

History

PRE-COLUMBIAN ERA

America began to be populated some 30,000 years ago, when the last glacial advance froze sufficient water to allow a land bridge to form between Asia and Alaska. The peoples who crossed over into what is now North America gradually wandered south in nomadic bands, existing by hunting and occasionally warring among themselves for territory and game. Eventually they occupied even the southernmost regions of the continent. There is evidence that Stone Age hunters occupied parts of Patagonia and highland Perú 20,000 years ago. According to recent archaeological findings of a formative sedentary agricultural community in the central Peruvian Andes, tribes began cultivating seeds for planting squash, corn (which is thought to have been brought from México), beans, and peppers as far back as 5,000 years ago. The llama was domesticated as a draft animal and used as a source of meat and fleece around that time, too. And pottery, the solid clue of a settled culture, may have originated in Venezuela 4,000 years ago, an innovation that was adopted by other nascent civilizations in the Andean region that now forms Ecuador and Perú. In Perú, agricultural and fishing communities evolved into villages. Where food supplies were stable enough to permit expansion and specialization of production, some men became farmers, some became potters, and others, warriors. Perú and Ecuador perhaps have the oldest and most varied history of the continent. The spread of culture and the control of one group by another began early in northern Perú. By 1000 BC, the culture known as Chavín was influencing coastal development.

Chavín highlights two elements that became characteristic among pre-Columbian civilizations: an elaborate religion that usually assigned religious significance to natural phenomena — animals, weather, changes in the sun, moon, and planets — and finely developed artistic skills displayed in metal-working and ceramics and in the design and construction of massive buildings and temples. The influence of Chavín can be seen in many subsequent Peruvian civilizations; for example, the artistic style found in the Nazca culture of the second century AD on Perú's southern coast clearly reflects Chavín.

Several groups that once existed have become known as the "forgotten peoples" of pre-Columbian history. However, certain indigenous tribes have persevered in the Caribbean area to this day. The Cuna tribe in Panamá, for example, was until recent times cut off from contact with neighboring peoples because the isthmus of Panamá itself formed a natural point of cultural separation. To the north, the development of civilization was predominantly influenced by the Central American Olmec cultures (from 1000 to 500 BC) and later by the Mayans. South of the isthmus of Panamá, the Chibcha-speaking people of the Bogotá Valley in Colombia produced remarkable works of gold that led the sixteenth-century Spanish conquistadores to search for El Dorado ("The Golden Man"), the legendary ruler who was ritually bathed in gold. In the Atacama Desert of northern Chile and the area that is now northern Argentina lived a number of pre-Columbian tribes who are now virtually extinct. The indigenous inhabitants of the Colombian and Venezuelan coasts conducted trade with and later migrated to several Caribbean islands.

The extent of communication between these formative cultures and civilizations is still under investigation and the subject of keen debate. Nonetheless, there are sufficient clues — duplication of styles found in early Mexican, Ecuadorian, and Peruvian ceramics; apparent similarities in mythology and worship; and evidence of a seaborne trade from Ecuador — to surmise that social and commercial intercourse was as prevalent and crucial as conflict and conquest.

Yet the heart of the great South American civilization lies in Perú. The dry, overcast, sandy plains that form the coast of Perú experienced a continual refinement of culture. The evolution of Peruvian civilization can be accurately traced through the manifold techniques of ceramics: from the sculpted human likenesses of Mochica pottery (AD 500) found in the northern valley of Moche to the depiction of animals, birds, and fish on the pottery of the later Nazca group. The Nazca civilization — whose mysterious line drawings scratched on the surface of the Peruvian coastal desert have stimulated international speculation about the possibility of communication with outer space visitors — existed from the third to the eighth century AD. There is an abundance of intact specimens of work dating from this period, work that allows scholars to pinpoint accurately separate periods of historical development. Weaving was a special Peruvian art; the finely crafted burial shrouds of the Paracas peninsula south of Lima date back to 500 BC. They are woven of finely spun alpaca wool on the almost universally used backstrap loom. Many examples of this art exist, preserved in the arid soil of the Peruvian coast. The skill of the Peruvian weavers is considered unequaled to this day.

By the ninth century AD, two more complex groups appeared; the Tiahuanaco, on the plains of Bolivia near Lake Titicaca, and the Gran Chimú in Perú. The city built by the Tiahuanaco poses an architectural mystery: The famed stone archway now referred to as "the Gate of the Sun" not only displays faint traces of the earlier Chavín but is clearly a precursor of the Inca. By the eleventh century, the Tiahuanaco civilization somehow disappeared, either by conquest, disease, or by simple attrition. Even the Incas, when questioned by the Spaniards, confessed that they knew nothing of the people who built the stone monoliths of Tiahuanaco except that they were a far older civilization.

The Gran Chimú civilization evolved on the coast of Perú; the Chimú culture was highly developed, more widespread, and more imperial than its forerunners. The Chimú kingdom, with its headquarters in the walled city of Chan-Chan, was artistically the most advanced of the pre-Inca civilizations of Perú, and under Chimú overlords, metalworkers, potters, and jewelers made enormous progress. Again, the pattern of growth and organization was largely hierarchical. Chimú, like previous minor empires, was ordered: A priesthood and local autocracy headed a society divided into functional classes of soldiers, artisans, farmers, and workers.

Despite the presence of the great Chimú culture, it is said that Peruvian history actually begins in about the eleventh century AD, when a small tribe near the valleys north of Lake Titicaca began the conquest of the Andean Sierra. Rapidly achieving dominance in the mountains, this clan, called the Incas, swept down to the coastal regions and subjugated the powerful Chimú kingdom.

The Incas most likely originated from a tribe in the Cuzco area. Their rather self-serving mythology claims that they were commanded by Inti, the sun god, to found a capital where a golden shaft would be swallowed by the earth. This was Cuzco, and from here, divinely inspired and divinely led, they commenced their expansion.

To appreciate the Incas' contribution to South American history, you must understand their attitude toward conquest and government. They believed strongly in the concept of nation, in bringing disparate peoples together under one allegiance and authority. The Incas are often spoken of longingly by contemporary South Americans; an atavistic current still runs through modern South American thought that glorifies the Incas as the "true" South Americans of the past.

The Incas were successful for various reasons, but an administrative genius and a creative eclecticism were of prime importance. Frankly not initiators, the Incas sought to preserve and consolidate the social and technological features of conquered territories that they found useful. Inca generals were magnanimous in victory, and through such policies as the *mitimae,* whereby entire vanquished tribes were transferred from their native lands to colonize and police new areas, the Incas created a vast empire.

The empire and state existed to serve the interests of the Incas, a term that refers to a hereditary class rather than to a people or race. All productive resources, all energies in Inca society, were channeled to serve "the Children of the Sun," as the Incas dubbed themselves, and they in turn provided their subjects with a totally controlled, albeit safe, society. In this sense the state was a religious dictatorship, not a "socialist" society, as some have claimed. It has become fashionable to describe Inca history glowingly in modern terms, but for the individual citizen, life must have been hard, patterned, and predictable. Inca law was apparently unyielding: Flogging and execution were common punishments for theft, sacrilege, and adultery. Agricultural production was strictly controlled; the crops, which consisted mainly of potatoes, corn, and a cereal grain known as *quinoa,* were divided into three portions: one-third for the people, one-third for the Incas, and one-third stored for the sun, the ultimate diety.

As builders, the Incas were unparalleled masters of stone. Roads were constructed between major population centers to speed the progress of armies and messages; they were invariably built high along mountain ridges for reasons of defense. Fortresses were erected at strategic points along the many valleys of their empire, named Tahuantinsuyo ("Empire of the Four Quarters" — the Incas divided their world into four sectors, with the center at Cuzco). Machu Picchu is believed to have been one such fortress.

The Incas were very conscious of the need for good defense; they had many enemies along the rim of their empire, which at its zenith of expansion in the fifteenth century encompassed Ecuador, Perú, Bolivia, and parts of Argentina, and extended as far south as the Maule River in Chile. Beyond the Maule lived the Araucanian Indians, warriors who successfully resisted both the Incas and Spaniards until 1850, when a peace treaty was signed with the Chilean republic.

Inca legend claims that there were fourteen Incas in the ruling dynasty, although the exact number may have been less. The population of Tahuantinsuyo is disputed by authorities, for estimates run from 1½ to more than 12 million. Recent finds indicate that agricultural techniques and irrigation under the Incas were more highly developed than previously thought (and in fact output may have been higher than modern levels). This data supports theories that a population exceeding 8 million may not be inaccurate.

There is much that is not known about South America's pre-Columbian past. The unreliability of historical witnesses and the relative paucity of early records leave many fields open to fruitful study and entertaining speculation. Improvements in dating methods have already prompted researchers to alter some historical eras by hundreds of years by updating or backdating recently found artifacts. The Andean area, in particular, attracts anthropologists and archaeologists eager to sift through the Inca past, although the most important new finds have been made in jungle regions. It is now clear that the Inca civilization that began in the twelfth or thirteenth century was not old or auspiciously long-lasting. In a sense, a whole history stops at the end of the fifteenth century (with the arrival of the Europeans) and another begins.

CONQUEST AND COLONIZATION

In the fifteenth century, European traders and sailors became very interested in finding a new route to the Orient, where they could obtain highly valued spices and other rare commodities. Trade with the Orient was lucrative, but travel there was expensive and time-consuming. Finally, in 1492, the Crown of Spain was convinced by an unknown Genoan named Columbus to underwrite his explorations for a shortcut *west* to the fabled Spice Islands. That the world was round was not in serious dispute in Columbus's time: However, the length of its circumference and the presence of an entire continent between the Orient and Europe were not known. Columbus's initial voyages to the Caribbean and the coast of Venezuela and subsequent missions by Amerigo Vespucci produced glittering, enticing reports of an earthly paradise, a realm of innocence and savagery, and a world of gold and immeasurable riches. The actual discovery of South America was a great accident, a monumental example of serendipity. Even the eventual naming of the continent was accidental: A German cartographer came upon one of Vespucci's many maps and began to call the lands America from Vespucci's Latinized first name, Americus. After a short period of probing and limited exploration, it was evident that the New World was indeed immense, and soon exploration became earnest conquest.

To understand the Spanish conquest, you must first picture sixteenth-century Spain at the moment of America's discovery. It was the most powerful kingdom in Europe, ruling half of Italy and Flanders. Spain's new monarch, Charles I, was concurrently Charles V of the Holy Roman Empire, defender of the faith. As such, he was responsible for preserving, militarily and politically, the realm of Catholic Christendom. Financial and religious reasons merged to compel Spain to take quick advantage in the New World. All discovered lands were considered part of the Spanish Crown. Thus, Vasco Nuñez de Balboa, the early conquistador who crossed the isthmus of Panamá in 1513, claimed the entire Pacific Ocean and all contiguous lands for Spain. A board was established in Seville, the Casa de Contratación, to ensure that only selected Spaniards would be allowed on the new Spanish territory. Hispaniola (now Haiti and the Dominican Republic) was the site of the first Iberian colonies. Cuba and other Caribbean islands were invaded and quickly fell. So rapid was the pace of events that by 1516, a seaborne force of Spaniards was sailing up the Río de la Plata in what is now Argentina.

The pattern of conquest and colonization of America was in many aspects similar to the process used to pacify Spain itself during the medieval struggle to win the country from the Moors. One feature transposed was the founding of strong urban enclaves, a tactic first used in Spain on conquered territory. (King Ferdinand advised Columbus from a siege city founded outside Granada.) This practice soon became widespread in America.

Through another Spanish tradition, individuals who participated in campaigns in the service of the Crown were rewarded with land and servant-retainers from conquered territories. In the New World, this custom engendered the *encomienda* system, whereby soldiers were awarded lands and Indian vassals as a labor force, with the added proviso that each lord (*encomendero*) care for the spiritual health of those assigned to him. Spanish America, then, was originally organized along feudal lines according to an old, yet proven, policy. This assured that settlements were widely separated and extremely personalized — an extension of Spanish custom and character. The bureaucracy created to administer these new territories also reflected the strong desire to centralize administration so as to benefit the Crown. Refinements of this class structure are still evident today.

The conquistadores themselves, the military vanguard, were men capable of great heroic deeds. Many possessed the fabled stamina that permitted feats such as the incredible voyage of Francisco de Orellana, who, with a small band of men, carved a boat with their swords and sailed more than 2,000 miles down the Amazon River. The explorers were often veteran European infantrymen or simply penniless and nameless men lusting for personal recognition and the riches of gold. And to achieve those ends, they were also capable of intolerable cruelties.

The natives of the continent were simply unable to offer effective resistance to the conquistadores, who had the great advantages of armor, cannons, and horses. This last is perhaps the most salient factor in Spanish victories. (Hernando de Soto once actually won a battle by falling off his horse, terrifying the native onlookers, who believed man and mount were one being.) Mounted charges, cannonade, and quick, close combat were usually sufficient to defeat armed opposition, even though native armies often vastly outnumbered the invaders.

On the heels of the conquistadores came the inevitable retinue of priests. The Catholic Church, ubiquitous throughout the conquest and after, was responsible for some of the most accurate chronicles of the era. Its role in spreading Spanish culture almost equaled that of the King. Priests participated in mass baptisms and supervised the construction of churches and schools. In many cases, priests presented an earnest defense of Indian rights, a tradition that continues to this day.

The most important chapter of the conquest began in 1532, when Francisco Pizarro, an earlier comrade of Balboa's in Panamá, landed with 180 men and 27 horses at Tumbes in northern Birú (now Perú) to search for the legendary kingdom of gold. Pizarro was fortunate. The last Inca, Huayna Capac, had decided to split the empire between his true Inca son, Huascar, and his son by a princess of Quito. Upon the death of his father, Atahualpa warred against his half-brother and had him executed. The continuing civil strife that plagued Tahuantinsuyo at the time of Pizarro's arrival was exploited by the conquistador throughout the campaign — a situation and tactic successfully employed by Cortés in Mexico as well. The Spanish and the Incas met in the city of Cajamarca in November 1532. After a violent, quick battle, Atahualpa was captured, and the reign of the divine Children of the Sun ended. Their empire rapidly disintegrated. Cuzco was occupied and plundered the following year; true to Spanish habit, however, Pizarro made his capital — Lima, City of Kings — on the coast.

Later expeditions, by Mendoza to Buenos Aires in 1535 and by Valdivia to Chile in 1540, resulted in the settlement and colonization of those areas. By the middle of the sixteenth century, Spain was secure in South America. Conquest and preliminary colonization were accomplished by no more than 30,000 European immigrants.

Although Spain was the major European influence in South America, Portugal's presence in the New World was secured by the early (1493) Treaty of Tordesillas. This was actually a papal decree granting the Portuguese rights to all lands east of a longitude some 370 leagues from the Cape Verde Islands. The Portuguese exploration and colonization of that area of the continent they called Brazil (from *braza,* or hot coal; the term described a certain tropical tree found on the coast) was sporadic and slow. There were Indian tribes to dominate but no wealthy empires to conquer. It was not until 1540 that the Portuguese Crown began to found settlements in earnest on the coastal areas of Brazil. The territory over which they had theoretical sovereignty was huge. Soon the English, the Dutch, and the French were establishing beachheads on the northeastern shores of the continent. These countries — now called Guyana, Suriname, and French Guiana — became the only non-Iberian enclaves on the continent.

INDEPENDENCE

South America enjoyed (or suffered) colonial status for over 300 years. Spain instituted elaborate systems of management to exploit her territories effectively, dividing the continent into the viceroyalties of New Spain (Mexico); New Granada (Colombia, Venezuela, and Ecuador); Perú; La Plata (Argentina); and Chile. The Spanish king was sovereign, represented by his viceroys; however, local *criollos* (native-born of Spanish blood) authorities were always able to circumvent the maze of royal regulations that limited their activities. They became, in effect, individual barons in their own areas. The Crown's authority was respected but, more often than not, ignored. This was, again, a Spanish tradition that soon became a South American custom, exaggerated by the immense distance between Spain and her colonies.

Spain's long reign was considered peaceful, and few wars or incidents of violence marred the colonial period. Visitors to the colonies would frequently remark that the mail service was surprisingly swift and travel relatively safe. A rather indulgent viceroyal society grew up in those port cities founded by the conquistadores, often in complete isolation from the vast undeveloped hinterlands and in relative isolation from other royal capitals. Lima was considered the historical center of administration and trade, for Perú was the wealthiest and most valued viceroyalty, far richer in precious metals than the others. All trade filtered through Lima. Even products from Argentina were carried through Lima to Panamá for eventual shipment to Seville. The Hispanicized cities flourished culturally and economically, especially the viceroyal cities, but the enormous countryside was largely ignored.

The Europeans' attitude toward the Indians in the rural savannahs and mountain villages was at least partially tempered by the religious conviction that, even though demonstrably inferior, the "childlike" natives did possess immortal souls. Church-inspired lip service, however, did not protect their underlings from enforced labor, disease, and suffering, especially in areas like Potosí in Bolivia, where silver miners spent virtually their entire lives underground. One social development was of critical importance: free intermarriage between the Spanish victors and the vanquished Indian. This was carried out with libertine fervor from the earliest days of the conquest. The mixed offspring — the *mestizo* (literally, "mongrel") — enlarged the population base and produced a cultural melding. As time went on, this offered a basis for the argument that South American society has a unique heritage and that a true Latin American consciousness has emerged through the centuries.

Despite this widespread intermarriage, power remained firmly in the hands of the Spanish and *criollos,* who became the dominating class. This group gradually began to resent Spain's economic control, especially its policy of buying raw materials inexpensively and selling finished goods at dear prices, so that "two cents of Peruvian cotton sent to Spain became a four-dollar handkerchief sold in Buenos Aires." In addition, trade with any country other than Spain was prohibited. Spain was determined to isolate her possessions from the world and keep them subservient. Even those colonials who considered themselves loyal and patriotic Spaniards became estranged, their ambitions curbed by royal control.

Economic reasons for separation from Spain joined other motives, often conflicting in nature. Native merchants and landlords came to mistrust Spanish administration for the surprising reason that it was too liberal; strong laws protecting Indian rights jeopardized the ruling class's social and economic status. In an opposite vein, enlightened thought, born of the American and French revolutions, slowly became somewhat popular in the urban intellectual centers of South America. While the impact of such ideas should not be overstated, there were enough daring individuals who found democracy and federalism romantically appealing. An early example of the contradictory nature of the revolt was the uprising of Tupac Amaru, a Peruvian Indian merchant, in 1780. Although his Indian army was dispersed after a year, his rebellion was carried out in the name of the king to protest the unfair advantages accumulated by the *criollo* minority of his country.

Another development in Europe hastened the movement toward emancipation: the deposition of the Spanish king by Napoleon in 1810 and the installation of his brother as ruler. Here was a situation that all could deplore. War was declared on the French king holding a Spanish throne, and he was condemned as a threatening liberal and a usurper. Patriotism in the name of the mother country was converted to South American nationalism.

Serious attempts at rebellion began in Venezuela in the early nineteenth century. After several preliminary failures against Royalist forces, the Venezuelan patriots, along with some British allies, rallied under the young Colonel Simón Bolívar.

Bolívar was an extraordinary individual — a period Romantic (he was greatly admired by the English poet Byron), a democrat, a well-traveled intellectual. He was all of these, but he was also a shrewd realist who recognized the shortcomings of his countrymen and the difficulties of waging war in America. He managed to lead his little army brilliantly to a series of hard-fought victories in Caracas and Bogotá, eventually advancing to Guayaquil in Ecuador.

At the same moment, General José de San Martín secured Argentina and began preparations for an epic campaign across the Andes to free Chile from Royalist control. San Martín was an accomplished soldier and a meticulous tactician (he had learned his craft in the Spanish army years earlier); he easily defeated the Spanish and Royalist garrison in Chile. He then turned north, taking his army by sea to Lima, and occupied the capital city, which had been abandoned by the Peruvian viceroy and his followers for the safety of the Andean Sierra.

Hitherto, the efforts of the two great patriots were separate and uncoordinated, but it was felt that a unification of forces would be necessary to confront successfully the strong Royalist army encamped in the mountains. A meeting was arranged in 1822 between the Liberator (Bolívar) and the Protector (San Martín). Perhaps it was inevitable, but the two could not agree on postwar policy; San Martín was somewhat of a monarchist, Bolívar, ever the republican. Sorely dejected, San Martín exiled himself to Europe, leaving

Bolívar free to enter Perú and soundly defeat the Royalists at the Battle of Ayacucho in 1824.

The wars for independence ravished many areas of the continent. Venezuela was extremely hard-hit, with bands of armed men looting the countryside, burning villages, and settling regional rivalries and petty jealousies by force. The great conflict was actually a civil war, where a victorious minority "liberated" the majority against their will. The Spanish colonial apparatus holding the territories together was shattered, and with nothing immediate to replace it, so was Bolívar's dream of a great South American union. His postwar travels were telling: Upon his arrival in southern Perú, the entire area seceded from the old viceroyalty and, perhaps in misplaced gratitude, adopted the name Bolivia in honor of the Liberator. Bolívar's own Gran Colombia in the north split into the three sovereign republics of Ecuador, Colombia, and Venezuela. The noblest efforts of great men were insufficient to overcome the centuries of local history, local enmities, and the sudden collapse of common authority. Writing near the end of his life, Bolívar expressed his misgivings and disappointment: "I was in command for twenty years, and during that time came to only a few definite conclusions. (1) I consider that, for us, America is ungovernable; (2) Whosoever works for a revolution is plowing the sea; (3) The most sensible action to take in America is to emigrate; (4) This country will ineluctably fall into the hands of a mob gone wild, later to fall under the domination of obscure small tyrants of every color and race."*

Brazil's experience was substantially different and somewhat more fortunate. Whereas Spanish America was under a relatively tight colonial system, Portuguese America prospered under a more pliant rule. The mother country had other important interests in Africa and in the Far East, so the Brazilians were largely left to themselves. One major factor that hastened Brazilian development was that the port cities were open to shipping with all nations, which allowed a thriving trade with Great Britain. The other was that its independence, which again was in part the result of the Napoleonic invasion of Portugal, was relatively peaceful and orderly.

Dom João, the regent of Portugal, fled his country upon Bonaparte's invasion, transferring his throne to Rio de Janiero. Brazil became the legal seat of the sovereign, equal with Portugal itself. Brazilians welcomed Dom João's arrival and even lamented his eventual departure to recapture his throne, which meant that Brazil would again become a colonial appendage. Dom João, however, left his son, Dom Pedro, behind in Brazil as his regent; he was quickly elevated to be Emperor Dom Pedro I of an independent Brazil. The transition from colony to monarchy under the continuity of a single royal house was accompanied by the transfer of an intact colonial administration to national hands. Free from the disasters of combat, Brazil enjoyed qualitative advantages over its continental neighbors during its period of national infancy.

Any hopes for a union of the fledgling republics were soon dashed after the

*Carlos Rangel, *The Latin Americans* (New York: Harcourt Brace Jovanovich, 1977), p. 6.

failure of the 1826 Conference of Panamá, which Bolívar called to unite the republics by treaty and mutual agreements on trade and foreign policy. Only four nations sent representatives. Instead of concentrating their efforts on items of common interest and hemispheric solidarity, the new nations attempted to resolve their individual problems of reconstruction and eagerly defend their newly perceived self-interests and responsibilities or, conversely, defend historic claims.

The first 60 years of independence were marked by internal disorder, war, and a constant change of government. The familiar pyramid social structure of South America, the obvious legacy of the colonial era, was more firmly entrenched by the political behavior it inspired. Most of the republics fashioned constitutions similar to the US document (Argentina's was so like the US Constitution that Argentine jurists frequently quoted US legal precedent). In most cases, however, the *criollo* caste easily dominated national congresses and executive branches through deliberately limited suffrage. In practice, politics became *caudillismo,* strong man regimes, where the powerful and influential would seize the government and rule alone, couching their decrees in vague ideological terms. In many cases, the wars of independence created a military caste system, the armed forces being the symbol of nationhood and often the only instrument available to preserve order. Perú's political history has developed along such lines, divided between *militaristas* and *civilistas.* By 1879, Chile had a navy superior to the US fleet of the time and was able to defeat Perú and Bolivia handily in the War of the Pacific. And, in perhaps the saddest example of military adventurism, Paraguay, desiring primacy in the Río de la Plata region, challenged Uruguay, Argentina, and Brazil in the War of the Triple Alliance (1865–1870). In that encounter, Paraguay almost lost its entire male population.

The Roman Catholic Church was one institution that survived and prospered after emancipation, and in several cases it was constitutionally the only legally permitted faith. From the beginning, the Church dominated all education and was actively involved in formulating social policies (the *encomienda,* for example). No political activity was possible without the assent of the ecclesiastics. The canonical attitude of Catholicism meshed with Spanish legalistic tradition to form an inherently strict, conservative factor in Spanish-American society.

Independence also thrust the republics into the arena of overseas foreign policy. Great Britain was the first nation to recognize the South American nations. With the opening of the ports to British vessels, a long, profitable period of British economic ascendency was under way. Argentina was the major beneficiary of British investment; by 1890, one-quarter of Argentina's population was foreign-born. Buenos Aires grew into a European-style capital, her upper classes very "English." By the same year, the British had built almost 6,000 miles of railroad to transport grain and refrigerated beef to the coast for shipment to Europe. Chile's early years were similar. While immigration to Chile was not as voluminous, a European-style society based on large farms and nitrate mining evolved to make it the second most developed Spanish-speaking country in Latin America.

Brazil, under Emperor Dom Pedro, was following a different course. The

Spanish-speaking countries have always considered Brazil a separate entity with a distinct historical heritage. Brazilians, who happily proclaim that "God is Brazilian," gladly share the opinion. Successive booms in coffee and rubber propelled Brazil to wealth, and São Paulo became one of the largest, most industrial cities in the Southern Hemisphere. Slavery was a particularly Brazilian issue. The practice was not terminated until 1888. The following year, Dom Pedro was forced to abdicate, a republic was proclaimed, and Brazil began to resemble her Latin neighbors more closely.

The reaction of the US to Latin American independence was the 1823 promulgation of the Monroe Doctrine, which declared that the US would not tolerate European interference in hemisphere affairs or attempts at new colonization (which included a feared reconquest by Spain). It also announced, in vague principle, a commonality of interests between the US and the Latin American countries. The Monroe Doctrine certainly did not deter Britain from expanding its direct investments; it continued to dominate Latin American economic growth until the turn of the century. It was, however, an early statement of principle and attitude that the hemisphere was American, north and south, and that the US, from the beginning, rather unilaterally assumed the role of leader and protector, teacher and policeman, on its side of the globe.

THE TWENTIETH CENTURY

The eventual ascendency of the US in hemispheric relations dates from the American victory over Spain in 1898. The US occupied Cuba and Puerto Rico (and, intermittently, Nicaragua and the Dominican Republic). Such open interventions were based on an addendum to the Monroe Doctrine known as the Roosevelt Corollary, which stated that the US assumed the right to intervene in any hemisphere nation where disorder threatened North American interests. The great North American interest was the Panamá Canal, an engineering feat completed in 1914 and accomplished by arranging the creation of the eleventh South American nation, Panamá, which seceded from Colombia under the guns of a US warship. In 1928, US State Department policy shifted, and the Roosevelt Corollary was declared to be inappropriate in terms of the Monroe Doctrine. Franklin Delano Roosevelt's 1933 inaugural address initiated the Good Neighbor Policy, which professed to respect the rights of other nations. This policy was seen as a reflection of government and public disenchantment with the Roosevelt Corollary.

The evolution of US involvement in South American affairs, and US interventionist behavior in particular, was noted with alarm in Latin America. Viewed within the context of the increasing "Americanization" of Latin American society, it demonstrates the often contradictory feelings held by the South toward the North. Latin Americans have always made analytical comparisons between their history and that of Anglo-Saxon Protestant North America, and while greatly admiring and emulating North American society, Latin Americans have not been able to compete, socially and economically, with the US. There have been real grievances in an inherently unequal relationship, yet the concept of a partnership still exists on an emotional and historical level, an affinity based upon all being "American."

By the early decades of this century, the US had eclipsed Great Britain as an influence in Latin America. It was largely US interests and capital that developed Venezuelan petroleum, Chilean copper, and Brazilian coffee. Political *caudillos* became business *caudillos,* and the wealthy class that produced so many leaders had its allegiance split between its nationalism and the world of international business. Latin America began an economic transformation, but investment was invariably in specialized sectors; it was growth but not development.

These same decades were marked by a hitherto muted demand for social and economic change. The European- and American-dominated societies were conservative in nature and reluctant to change long-established custom. But, at the same time, they were open to (or vulnerable to) reforms, and in some cases revolutions, to better the plight of the growing numbers of urban workers and rural peasants who comprised the majority of the population. The demands came from different sectors: In Mexico, the *campesino* ("peasant") wanted land, while in Argentina the middle classes wanted a voice in the political process. In 1928, the Peruvian Haya de la Torre founded the Alliance for the American Revolution (APRA), based on Marxist principles but tailored to the realities of semicolonial societies. APRA has contined to influence South American leftist political theory, for the core of APRA's ideology is an ever popular anti-imperialist stance and a measured, gradual transition to socialism.

In other cases, change was effected through the old tradition of single-handed leadership. In Argentina, for example, the ultimate *personalista,* Juan Domingo Perón, based his political formula on the underclasses, the famous *descamisados* ("shirtless ones"), and his highly individual ideology encompassed terms ranging from communism to fascism. *Caudillismo* remained the most common, and perhaps the most effective, method of promoting or arresting change.

After World War II, which had brought undeniable prosperity to many Latin American countries, US global policy tended to ignore Latin America and concentrate instead on Europe and Asia, where communism presented a security threat. US policy in the Western Hemisphere was aimed toward promoting and strengthening regional organizations compatible with American interests.

Dreams of an effective program of inter-American cooperation remained alive after the ill-fated Panamá conference of 1826. In 1890 the first conference of Latin American diplomats was held in Washington. Successive meetings in Mexico, Buenos Aires, Lima, and Rio de Janiero culminated in the founding of the Organization of American States (OAS) in 1948. Although begun under US auspices, the OAS provided a useful forum for discussion and cooperation in science and culture.

A new, troublesome chapter in hemispheric relations began on January 1, 1959, when the guerrilla army of Fidel Castro entered Havana, toppling the dictatorship of Fulgencio Batista. When it became evident that Castro was an avowed Communist and clearly allied with the Soviet Union, the US reaction was severe enough to prompt an attempted invasion and even the threat of nuclear war. It was one of the very few times a major foreign power gained an ally in the hemisphere, and immediately communism became the dominant theme in inter-American politics.

In order to promote political and economic stability in Latin America, and thereby counter the growing Communist influence, the US upgraded the partnership concept by announcing the Alliance for Progress, a massive program of construction and development. Leaders in most hemisphere nations were at last becoming convinced that poverty and inequality bred dangerous social unrest and placed the economic status quo in jeopardy. The focus of political and economic responsibility began to shift toward ameliorating these long-standing conditions; reform programs and true developmental economic policies won acceptance and legitimacy. This sense of urgency was accompanied by Latin America's demand for continued US leadership and contributions in assisting its development, openly welcoming North American overtures.

The events of the 1960s and 1970s highlight the growing love-hate relationship between Latin America and North America, as well as the inseparability of their histories. As the wealthier, more powerful neighbor, the US is held accountable for much of Latin America's current difficulties; at the same time it is assumed that the US will, by good intentions, examples, and deeds, assist in providing solutions. Expectations are complicated by the diversity of Latin American interests, for the US has had a tendency to treat the continent as a semihomogeneous bloc. New North American policy suggestions, based on country-by-country appraisals, have served to improve relations. The 1978 Panamá Canal Treaty, which grants Panamá sovereignty over the canal by the year 2000, has also been favorably received, for it symbolizes the rectification of an old injustice.

Contemporary Latin America features an ever-widening disparity of interests and levels of culture. The impelling force is nationalism, which shapes and directs the social and political paths Latin American nations follow today. Each nation is keenly aware of its own history and problems and its own heartfelt destiny. The experiences of four major nations illustrate this.

Brazil is clearly the largest, most populous, and one of the most prosperous of the Latin American republics. Brazil's experience has been qualitatively different, but Brazil has periodically taken part in what was once considered a Spanish-American tradition, that of military rule. The same forces of internal disorder — or fear of internal disorder — have caused Brazil to pursue repressive policies to protect its sometimes mighty, sometimes faltering economy. The belief that Brazil is a first-rate power — even a nascent superpower — is strong and has been demonstrated. Brazil sent combat troops to Europe during the World War II and today builds its own jet aircraft. The US has favored Brazil economically and strategically (hence former President Nixon's declaration: "As Brazil goes, so goes South America").

In contrast, its neighbors view Brazil with a mixture of envy and mistrust. The mere fact that all South American nations — except Panamá, Ecuador, and Chile — share a border with Brazil is not overlooked.

Argentina is a nation with frustrated historical ambitions and presumptions of rather great proportion. Argentina's European society is more homogeneous, more highly cultured, than those of its sister republics, and Argentines have felt that their nation could have become the Colossus of the South, matching the US in wealth and prestige; its failure to do so has led Argentina to the most sophisticated anti-Americanism. Argentine foreign policy has been unpredictably independent: Only under great prodding did Argentina declare war on Germany during the last war. Several decades later, despite its advanced society, Argentina participated in several Third World causes, such as the 1978 United Nations conference on technical cooperation among developing countries. What the future politics will be in post–Falkland War circumstances remains to be seen; but meanwhile, the 1984 return of civilian government to Argentina by popular election was cause for cheering both here and abroad. For the first time, Argentina and Brazil have taken steps toward economic cooperation — a recent development considered by many to be a direct result of civilian control in both countries.

Chile had enjoyed many decades of almost uninterrupted republicanism and prosperity. Many years of oligarchic rule ended in 1970, when Chile became one of the few nations to elect peacefully a self-proclaimed Marxist as president, Salvador Allende. His government faced immense economic problems, many of which were induced by US intervention. Chile's troubles continued to mount and finally resulted in a *golpe de estado* (coup) in 1973 and the subsequent founding of yet another military *caudillismo*. This political situation is common for Latin America but rare for Chile. To this day, many Chileans' response to the military government's repressive policies is: "We never thought it could happen here." International censure directed at human rights violations by the regime, and continuing economic malaise, have isolated Chile from several of its allies. General Augusto Pinochet became president in a 1980 election and is slated to serve until 1989.

Perú is the heart of the empire of Tahuantinsuyo; it has, therefore, the largest Indian population among the various countries. This demographic group has not been integrated socially or economically with the cosmopolitan coast. Perú has always been a country of extremes. Even today, desert, jungle, and wealthy cities lie below a mountain "nation" still in the sixteenth century. Lima and other urban centers have become clogged with people migrating from the bleak Sierra in search of jobs and a better future. Faced with a duality of cultures, the problem confronting Peruvians is: Which is the real Perú? Many feel that the Spanish-European influence has been alien and corrupting and would prefer to go back to the Inca past, recreating Inca "socialism" in a contemporary form. Meanwhile, the democratically run election of 1984 ended the long reign of Perú's military regime, and despite the burden of enormous economic problems, the present civilian government continues to survive.

With some 300 million faithful followers, the Catholic Church remains the most important enduring institution in Latin America, and in recent years, it has become increasingly active in such temporal affairs as human rights and agrarian reform — largely through the efforts of such orders as the Jesuits and the Maryknolls. Although historically conservative, this new "Church of the people" may yet play a significant role in shaping the future for many South American countries.

The South American nations are undeniably mature members of the greater family of nations and participate in a variety of international organizations and endeavors. Many countries have become active in Third World affairs, often participating in the underdeveloped countries' voting bloc in the UN. Prominent South Americans, such as the Argentine economist Raúl Prebisch, have long been leaders in Third World research. Venezuela was a leader in the formation of the Organization of Petroleum Exporting Nations (OPEC), later joined by Ecuador. Intracontinental cooperation has grown: The republics of Venezuela, Colombia, Ecuador, Perú, and Bolivia have formed the Andean Common Market to coordinate trade and foreign investment policy, and the OAS has amplified its activities into creating training programs, export promotion, and the like.

Increasing international exposure and more sophisticated monitoring of internal affairs do place new pressures on South American governments. Through their political processes, several nations in the past and Chile in the present have not been able to deal constructively with dissent and have been accused of repeated human rights violations. On this count, major advances have been made in Argentina and Uruguay since civilians were elected to lead these countries.

THE SOUTH AMERICAN FUTURE

A large Pan American middle class has been expanding for some time between the traditionally rich and the traditionally poor. Economic growth has led to increased mobility in most Latin American societies, and while the old families still tenaciously influence events, the consumer-oriented middle classes comprise new bases of political power and new sources of fashion and taste. But this phenomenon has also had its spiritual price. Latin Americans often harbor deep feelings based upon what they perceive as the tragedy of their history and the difficulties of modernizing their societies, where old and established habits coexist uneasily with new social practices.

Latin Americans often feel insecure about their future, sensing that real progress in narrowing the gap between rich and poor classes, and rich and poor nations, is in fact slowing down. Economies still geared to the production of raw materials, coupled with global events beyond their control, have resulted in rates of inflation that would be intolerable for North Americans — and that are becoming unbearable in many South American countries. Indeed, overextended bank loans, bearing interest rates that the debtor countries are unable to repay, have created both national and international crises of confidence. It is an uphill struggle for the newly elected governments that replaced former military regimes to meet even the basic needs of their people.

Yet the generally unharried pace of life seems to indicate that Latin Americans will continue to live their lives along predictable lines. The discomfort of altering expectations has been tempered by a long history of phlegmatic acceptance and justifiable pride in the many cultural achievements of Latin America. The pre-Columbian nations and their monuments are now appreciated more, and Indian culture, still sometimes a source of embarrassment to some, is undergoing a more respectful evaluation. Colonial art and architecture, the poems of Argentine Jorge Luis Borges, and the contemporary novels of the Colombian Gabriel García Márquez and the Peruvian Mario Vargas Llosa, whose works are popular in North America and Europe, attest to the richness of the Latin American experience. George Pendle makes perhaps the most concise and accurate appraisal: "The world will hardly look to the Latin American for leadership in democracy, in organization, in business, in science, in rigid moral values. On the other hand, Latin America has something to contribute to an industrialized and mechanistic world concerning the value of the individual, the place of friendship, the use of leisure, the art of conversation, the attractions of the intellectual life, the equality of races, the juridical basis of international life, the place of suffering and contemplation, the value of the impractical, the importance of people over things and rules."*

*George Pendle, *A History of Latin America,* 2nd rev. ed. (Pelican Original, 1971), p. 225. © George Pendle, 1963, 1969, 1971. Reprinted by permission of Penguin Books Ltd.

Religion

Ever since South America was claimed for the Spanish and Portuguese Crowns, the continent has been officially Roman Catholic. Although historians tend to play down this fact, the new lands were claimed first for God, then for the king. The Spanish and Portuguese were every bit as zealous in their desire to save the souls of the pagan Indians as they were in any of their other endeavors. Ironically, it was a Spanish missionary, Bartolomé de las Casas, who wrote the first work in defense of the Indian, *Brevísima Relación de la Destrucción de las Indias (Short History of the Destruction of the Indies)*. This work unleashed the *leyenda negra* ("black legend") that has plagued the Spanish in South America ever since, for it relates the familiar account of the Spaniards' greed and their mistreatment of the Indians. It has been used by many to justify a hatred of the Spaniards and all things Spanish.

The widespread conversion of the Indians may have been misguided, but it was in large part sincere. The Spaniards had to be sincere to last long in the Andes mountains and the Amazon jungle of 500 years ago. The missionaries were convinced that God saved only Catholic souls. They considered themselves members of a more enlightened race and felt it their responsibility to teach the Indians the true religion and to make them follow it. This enabled the Spanish and Portuguese to justify their conquest of the Indians through their feeling of religious superiority.

At any rate, the missionaries must never have heard the maxim about leading a horse to water. They may have gotten the Indians to convert by threatening, punishing, and beating them, but no one knows how many Indians today really believe in Catholicism or how many are just trying to avoid conflict or lessen the number of visits by the clergy. The same holds true for the African slaves converted by the Portuguese. How many of their descendants are sincere Catholics and how many still believe in the African cults is anybody's guess. To this day, there are Catholic missionaries out in the jungle attempting to contact and convert the remaining "pagan" Indians; at the same time, Protestant missionaries all over the continent are trying to reconvert Catholics to Protestantism. The 500-year struggle for lost souls thus continues. Despite all this, most South Americans say they're Catholic.

Unlike Spain and Portugal until just recently, the South American countries have allowed some form of religious freedom and separation of church and state ever since independence, so you will find people of almost every conceivable religion in all the South American nations. If you belong to any one of the major Western religions, you should have no trouble finding a place to worship in any of the larger cities. Many smaller religions are represented as well; but since the tragedy in Jonestown, Guyana, most governments are keeping a close watch on obscure cults, especially those from the outside.

Although the separation of church and state is more theoretical in some areas than in others, it does exist. South Americans tend to be anticlerical, for a number of historical reasons. Most North Americans have trouble understanding this concept and more difficulty in accepting it. South Americans themselves have no problem at all in balancing anticlericalism with a staunch faith in the Mother Church. But it's best to avoid a discussion of the subject. Try to visit churches and cathedrals when mass is not being said. Most likely no one will say anything to you if you interrupt the prayers, but it is one of the reasons for a dislike of tourists.

Whether or not you agree with the philosophy and methodology of the early missionaries, you will come across their influence almost everywhere you go in South America. No one denies their impact on art, architecture, literature, and history, either through their own works or through those of their Indian and African pupils. Jesuits, Dominicans, Franciscans, and others taught the natives and the slaves to read, write, sing, and compose church music. They also showed them how to play European musical instruments, paint on canvas, use new tools, and develop new forms of folk art, clothing, and architecture. A significant number of these students and apprentices went on to enjoy a certain amount of fame and respect.

The Indians, however, did not abandon their old ways immediately; in fact, they never completely gave them up. They rejected some Spanish and Portuguese customs and adopted others, just as the Africans did later.

When the Spanish and Portuguese first came into contact with the jungle Indians, they were horrified. The Jívaro Indians practiced their now infamous head-shrinking; many other tribes carried trophy heads and ate their enemies. Human sacrifices and torture were apparently fairly common, although reports of these practices have probably been exaggerated to emphasize how savage and beyond salvation the Indians were. How many of these practices had religious significance is not known. At least some of the sacrifices must have been made to the supernatural spirits in an effort to ensure plentiful fish and game and to banish disease and natural disasters.

Although head-shrinking is now illegal, the laws against it are probably not enforced in the jungle. Supposedly, most cannibalistic tribes have died out or have been subdued or converted to Christianity and are now living on missions. What has not been eliminated is the tendency to use hallucinogenic drugs to contact the spirits and supernatural forces. Neither has the dependency on shamans and magic been abandoned. The rites and rituals of most of the jungle tribes have not been organized into a formal cult. Almost everything centers around the magic of the shaman, who avails himself of a variety of herbs and drugs to produce different results. There are many small tribes, each with slightly varying rites and beliefs. If you find Carlos Castañeda's works on the Yaqui Indians interesting, you will be absolutely entranced (pun intended) by the South American Indians and their beliefs. The early Spaniards and Portuguese finally gave up most of their attempts to convert the jungle tribes, and many of the Indian practices survive almost unchanged to this day.

There were many Andean and coastal tribes prior to the Incas. Today we can at least partially reconstruct their religions through the myths and legends that have come down to us and through artifacts found at various archaeological sites. The vast number of burial sites in the Andean countries supports the theory that most of the tribes believed in an afterlife, since the bodies were all buried with their possessions to take to the next world.

The coastal tribes apparently worshiped the moon as their ruling deity because it controls the tides of the all-important sea. The sea itself must have had a guiding spirit, celebrated by certain rituals.

Several of the Andean tribes believed in a creator-god, Viracocha, who was later adopted by the conquering Incas. In general, when the Incas defeated another people, they did not try to destroy their religion. The Incas realized that this would cause no end of hatred and hostility — a lesson learned the hard way by the European conquerors. Instead, they incorporated the local deities into the state system of religion and allowed the defeated peoples to maintain their own temples. The most important temples were at Pachacamac, near Lima, and at Chan-Chan, near Trujillo, Perú. The Incas did require that a shrine also be built to Inti, the sun god, near any shrine dedicated to a local god.

It was Inti that the Inca were worshiping when the conquistadors arrived, hence the name Kingdom of the Sun given to their empire. (Contrary to a popular belief, Inca civilization wasn't called this because of the sunny climate of the Andes; the region has a very wet rainy season.) The Incas were as systematic about their religion as they were about everything else. Their subjects were organized into groups called *ayllus,* a sort of tribal arrangement based on kinship. Although each *ayllu* had its own sacred object, or *huaca,* to worship, all *ayllus* also paid tribute to both Inti and a special *huaca* at Huanacauri, near Cuzco. This special *huaca* has since disappeared or been overgrown with vegetation like Machu Picchu. A *huaca* could be almost anything as long as the members of a particular *ayllu* all agreed that it was sacred. *Huaca* also means burial ground, an obviously sacred site. Some Indians preserved the bodies of ancestors (*mallquis*) in stone towers called *chullpas.* Some *chullpas* are still standing in the Puno–Lake Titicaca region.

An *ayllu* could choose the god or spirit of a nearby lake, river, cave, or other natural formation as its *huaca.* All natural formations were believed to be inhabited by spirits, who also caused natural disasters. An earthquake meant that Pachamama ("Earth Mother") was angry. Avalanches, rainstorms, and floods brought about by melting snows were the work of the angry Apus and Aukis who lived on the mountain peaks. (These spirits are called Achachilas by Bolivian Aymarás.) Ccoa, a feline spirit, was believed to inhabit the Ausangate peak in Perú. In fact, all mountains and volcanoes had great religious significance for the Indians, and each had residing spirits. Ccoa caused lightning and hail to ruin Peruvian crops. Knuno, the god of snow, did the same in Bolivia. This animistic system allowed — and still allows — the Indians to believe that they had some control over their destiny. All they had to do to avoid natural disasters was to make offerings to keep the gods and spirits happy. Some of the offerings developed into formal communal rituals such as those held in Inti Raymi (June 22–July 22), the first month of the Inca calendar.

While the Incas did occasionally practice human sacrifice, especially of young virgins and children, the llama was a far more popular sacrificial item. The missionaries and conquistadors put an end to human sacrifice, but llamas are still offered up in Inti Raymi. Now, however, the festival is celebrated on St. John's Day, and the masks used in the Diablada dance have the horns of the Christian devil.

The Indians have held to almost all their other beliefs, whether openly or in secret. Llama fetuses are used as sacred offerings. No Quechua or Aymará Indian would think of building a new house without burying a llama fetus under the cornerstone to ensure a happy and prosperous life. In fact, you can buy a llama fetus in almost any Indian market.

Another way to appease the gods is to offer them some drink. Before any Indian partakes of his *chicha* (home brew), he faithfully sprinkles a few drops on the ground for Pachamama. If no *chicha* is available, he can make an offering of the ubiquitous coca. Coca can be used by diviners to foretell the sex of a baby and a number of other facts. Most Indians also believe in diviners, oracles, and omens. Superstition seems to be stronger in Bolivia than in Perú and Ecuador, but the farther you get from the urban centers and the white Catholic influence in any of these countries, the more ancient rituals you will observe. In the most remote areas, the priest comes through only once a year to marry couples, give communion, and bless the deceased.

By worshiping both the Christian God and the pagan gods, the Indians have it both ways. Before you dismiss them as religious hypocrites, however, think of the last time you threw salt over your shoulder, cried over a broken mirror, or crossed a street to avoid a black cat. The Indians reconcile their different religious beliefs just as we do. The missionaries made it easy by placing their cross on the mountain peaks also inhabited by the Apus or Achachilas. This mixture of witchcraft, native religion, and Catholicism is a complex, fascinating subject.

The blacks of Brazil have learned that their native African cults have commercial value among the tourists, and the Andean Indians are starting to find this out about their festivals. The *candomblés* of Bahía (West African in origin) and the *macumba* rites of Rio (from Angola and the Congo) are often arranged and practiced in advance, and tourist agencies sell tours that include a visit to one or the other. The blacks distinguish clearly between *candomblé* and *macumba,* but most whites think of them both as voodoo. A third type of ritual, *caboclo,* has been strongly influenced by native Indian cults and is looked down upon by practitioners of the other two. By all means go to these services if you have the chance. Each is slightly different, but they are all equally interesting.

You should bear in mind that the more sincere of these rituals are never performed when outsiders, especially whites, are present. As a result, what you will see is often more theater than religion. This is not to say that there is no sincerity in a staged rite; even there, a participant can feel a spiritual force, causing him or her to fall to the ground and writhe in ecstasy.

There are many more spiritualistic cults all over Brazil, whose members generally come from the lower classes of society. Most of these people also go to mass and worship as Catholics. All cult gods have two names, an African one and a Catholic equivalent. Like the Andean Indians, the black spiritualists have no trouble reconciling the two different beliefs. One helps them function in a Catholic-dominated world; the other allows them to maintain ties with their African heritage and be true to their roots.

If you are a very religious person, try to approach the black and Indian religions with an open mind. If you are black, you already have the advantage of understanding the historical background on which these cults are based. But attending a ceremony for the purpose of reaffirming a preexisting prejudice does no one any good. These native religions have survived almost 500 years of persecution and are obviously necessary and vital to their followers. As such, they deserve tolerance and understanding.

Legends and Literature

 The most interesting aspects of South American literature are the traditional legends and the works of modern authors. The few masterpieces in the intervening 300 years stand out like pine trees in the Atacama Desert. Even so, there's enough good reading to keep you busy for quite some time.

Although the pre-Columbian tribes had no written language, a rich oral tradition of myths, legends, and folklore was carefully handed down from one generation to the next. Only certain members of each tribe were entrusted with the knowledge of this tradition, which they then committed to memory. The Incas were so systematic about this that, when a noble died, the *amautas* (wise men) met to decide which facts about his life would make it into the "official" Inca history. An ingenious device called a *quipu* was used as an aid to memory. It consisted of a series of knots on strings. The color, size, and way in which each knot was tied indicated something to the *quiposcamayo* (*quipu* reader). The Spaniards never bothered to write down the code of the knots, and the Indians stopped using the system. Why transmit a history of defeat, humiliation, and slavery? So, while *quipus* are displayed in several museums in both North and South America, no one knows how to read them. Much oral literature embodied in the *quipus* has thus been lost forever.

A few of the early legends were preserved by the Spanish chroniclers in their letters and books. Most were either ignored or scorned as the work of the devil. The Spanish scribes claim to have preserved the few surviving legends just as the Indians told them. The problem is that the Spaniards already had started teaching Catholicism to the Indians. So by the time the stories were copied, the originals had probably been influenced by Church teachings.

The Indians may also have altered a legend or two to fit what they thought the Spaniards wanted to hear. The story of Atahualpa indicates that this would have been a wise course of action. According to the story, when Pizarro told Atahualpa that the Bible was the Word of God, the Inca chief put the book up to his ear. When he didn't hear anything, he disgustedly threw it to the ground. If it was the Word of God, why couldn't he hear it? This so angered a Spanish priest that he insisted on the chief's death.

Besides the legends rescued from oblivion by the chroniclers, countless others are still told whose origins are unknown. Experts surmise that all the South American tribes had myths about nature gods, especially the gods of the sun and the moon. There were also stories about supreme creator gods, but none of the tribes had a pantheon as organized as that of the Greek gods of Mt. Olympus. The functions of the gods in South American legends are confused by an overlapping of their names and deeds, so it's often hard to determine which god did what.

If you want to go to the source, the best chroniclers are Pedro de Cieza de León, *History of Perú;* Cristóbal de Molina, *Conquest and Settlement of Perú;* and, above all, Garcilaso de la Vega, *The Florida of the Inca* and *The Royal Commentaries of the Incas.* Garcilaso was the son of an Inca princess and a Spaniard, and he should not be confused with a famous Spanish poet of the same name who was a relative of the chronicler.

All the tribes had legends that explained their origins. When the Incas conquered another tribe, they borrowed or changed local legends to prove Inca supremacy. According to the Incas, the sun god Inti felt sorry for man when he saw people living in a barbaric, primitive state. Inti sent his own two children, Manco Capac and Mama Occlo, to earth to teach man all the arts of civilization. They landed on an island in Lake Titicaca, and from there they were to travel until they found the place where the long golden rod they were carrying would sink easily into the soil. (This is significant because the Incas depended almost entirely on agriculture.) The rod sank into the ground at Cuzco, so Manco Capac and Mama Occlo founded their capital there. They taught civilization to the natives and converted them to the religion of the sun. As the direct descendants of the chiidren of a god, the Incas believed they had the right to conquer and rule others.

The Tiahuanaco people lived near Lake Titicaca in Bolivia before the Incas came, but almost nothing is known about them. They did leave behind huge, carved stone monoliths over 6 feet high. According to the Incas, these huge statues were originally people who had disobeyed the laws of the creator god Viracocha. Angry at having been disobeyed, Viracocha turned them to stone. (Shades of Lot's wife and pillars of salt?) This same legend is supposed to explain stone statues at other South American sites. A different story states that these monoliths were Viracocha's mock-ups for the peoples he was planning to create.

Viracocha is a rather confusing god (or gods, since he appears in many places with slightly different names and guises). Among other legends describing a great flood are a number of Viracocha stories that are usually called the Deluge myths. At some long-forgotten time, man was evil and lived in sin. This upset Viracocha, so he sent a great deluge to destroy man. Only a select few survived. Viracocha, a white god with a beard, told these men he would return someday. This is supposed to account for the lack of resistance the Indians put up against the white-skinned, bearded Spaniards. In fact, many Indians called their Spanish overseers on the haciendas by the name Viracocha, an equivalent of the "my lord" used by medieval British serfs.

Some tribes claim their origin from these survivors of the Great Deluge. Others claim to be descendants of lakes or mountains or other nature gods. When you are in the La Paz, Bolivia, region, be sure to take a good look at Illimani or the other great Andean peaks. Natural sites worshiped by the Aymará Indians are called *achachilas,* and these peaks fit into that category. Illimani was supposedly Viracocha's favorite. This is understandable, since it is the most beautiful mountain overlooking La Paz. When the nearby peak Mururata complained to Viracocha that he was jealous of Illimani, Viracocha punished him by breaking off his top, so now he is flat. (Mountains are either male or female, according to Indian beliefs. Two peaks that are close together are usually one of each.) Most residents can point out the peaks to you, but it is the Indians who know the legends.

Since before the Inca conquest, Andean Indians have believed that chewing coca leaves enables them to endure cold, hunger, and long hours of work. Supposedly, the Incas reserved the privilege of chewing coca leaves for their nobility. Coca leaves also have medicinal and, the Indians believe, magical powers, and they are used extensively in rituals. The origin of the use of coca, like other important aspects of Indian life, is explained in a legend. A long, long time ago, the Indians of the Lake Titicaca region moved to new areas in the Yungas, the valleys and foothills of the Andes. When they burned the vegetation to clear the land for planting, the smoke rose and contaminated the mountain peaks. The god of snow, Khuno, woke up and saw what had happened. In anger he flooded the Yungas and destroyed the Indians' homes. When the waters subsided the Indians could find nothing to eat. After much searching they came across a plant with bright green leaves. They discovered that chewing the leaves produced a sudden feeling of well-being. They returned to Tiahuanaco with the news of this wonderful plant, and Indians have chewed coca leaves ever since.

Legends of the Chibcha Indians of Colombia also have survived in one form or another. The creation of the beautiful Tequendama Falls near Bogotá is explained by the myth of Bochica, the chief of the gods. This time it was the god Chibchacum (the name varies) who was angry with the peoples of the Bogotá plateau and flooded their land. (No wonder South America has so many rivers and lakes.) The desperate people appealed to Bochica for help. He appeared in a rainbow, sent the sun to dry up the water, and opened a deep cleft in the rocks to allow the waters to recede. The Tequendama Falls still pour over this split in the cliffs.

The most famous legends of all concern El Dorado. One version appears to have been a Chibcha legend based on an annual ritual. Once a year, the body of a young Indian male would be entirely covered with gold dust. Placed on a raft laden with offerings of silver, gold, and precious stones, he would float into the middle of Lake Guatavita in Colombia. There he would throw the offerings overboard, then jump into the lake to wash off the gold dust. A piece of gold sculpture in the Museo de Oro in Bogotá seems to represent this ritual. It depicts a raft with an Indian in the center surrounded by offerings for the god of the lake. Don't miss it when you are in Bogotá.

Gold was plentiful all over central and northern South America, and it seems that every tribe had a legend of a golden city or a golden people. Also, the fame of the Inca empire, based on its enormous wealth, had spread all over the continent, giving rise to several El Dorado–type stories. Even so, the beauty of the metal itself and its representation as the sun god's rays were enough to inspire myths. It has also been suggested that the Indians repeated and embellished the legends just to watch the greedy Spaniards go trekking off into the dangerous mountains and jungles on a wild goose chase. There are to this day dreamers who go off to South America in search of El Dorado, and there have been several fairly recent attempts to drain Lake Guatavita to recover the loot that is supposed to be there.

The Spanish and Portuguese brought several hundred European legends with them, mostly stories of the Virgin Mary and the saints. Once the missionaries discovered that the Indians already had a fondness for this kind of storytelling, they used the legends to help in conversion. The Indians' sensibilities seemed to be especially attuned to Mary because of the many stories of her miraculous appearances. Most European légends have undergone Americanization, though a few are told in the original version. Others have simply served as inspiration for an American counterpart.

When the black slaves were brought over from Africa, they carried their legends with them. In the area around Bahía, where the African influence is strongest, many of the legends have remained intact since the days of slavery. The others were added to or combined with the large body of oral literature already in existence in South America.

South America's history itself often reads like a legend. The battles of the conquest, the Indian and slave rebellions, and the wars of independence all furnished heroes and other material for stories. Among the more colorful figures are the *bandeirantes* of the Brazilian *sertão* and the gauchos of the pampas of Argentina, Uruguay, and the Rio Grande do Sul of Brazil. These men and occasional women loom so much larger than life, it is hard to believe they could ever have really existed. Yet it is with them that life, legend, and literature come together. Many of their names can be found in the history books, poems, novels, and legends time and time again.

The pampas of Argentina are a vast desert of thorny bushes, containing a number of trees and animals found nowhere else. The *sertão* is similar in its vastness, but life there is even harsher because the region is one of the most drought-plagued in the world. The origins of the gauchos and the *bandeirantes* — mestizos of Spanish and Indian blood — are not clear, but they certainly have been out on the pampas and *sertão* since the late 1700s. These cowboys and hunters were social outcasts with little or no formal education, no organized religion, and their own limited concept of law: an eye for an eye and survival of the fittest. It is easy to see how such men and women became the stuff of which legends are made. You had to be strong to survive.

In the case of the gauchos, the reverse was also true: Literature became life. The Argentine poem "Martín Fierro" (1872) was a literary creation of José Hernández, an educated man who had lived among the gauchos and admired them very much. This work is a classic of South American literature, and Argentine students still have to memorize portions of it for school. It is *the* gaucho epic: the story of Martín Fierro and his life out on the pampas, his time in the army during the wars of independence, and his desire for freedom. The poem also deals with the problems this desire causes him with the police and society in general. "Martín Fierro" became very popular and was recited frequently to the illiterate gauchos around their campfires and at their festivals and dances. This hero was so real to them that they began to believe in his existence, and many more legends grew up around his name.

Domingo Faustino Sarmiento's *Civilization and Barbarism: The Life of Juan Facundo Quiroga* is an excellent study of the gauchos and another South American classic. The book is a biography of sorts, but if you are interested in the gaucho, it is the place to start. The work is filled with the author's passion for his subject.

In Brazil, Euclydes da Cunha wrote *The Sertões* (1902), an equivalent study of the *bandeirantes* and their descendants. Unlike Sarmiento's book, da Cunha's is a novel, yet it lacks the personal passion that makes *Facundo* so readable. Da Cunha subscribed to the French naturalist school of thought and, like Émile Zola, thought that a novel should be a scientific study of man's behavior.

Gaucho and *bandeirante* legends have been around almost as long as the people themselves. But the people of these regions are not the only subject. The flora and fauna also have their own stories explaining their origins or unusual characteristics. The *ombú,* for example, is a tree that exists only in the pampas. It is a wonderful shade tree, a necessary shelter in a hot, dry climate, but its wood is of very little use. A myth tells that in the beginning all trees were alike. One day God was in a particularly good mood, and He decided to visit earth to give each tree its wish. He talked to the pine, the oak, and all the other trees; they all wanted to be tall, straight, beautiful, and have hard wood so they could not be cut down easily. Then God came to the *ombú* and asked what it wanted. The *ombú* answered that it wanted to be big so it could give shade to man, but it wanted soft, weak wood. God granted the request, but he was puzzled by it, so He asked the *ombú* why it didn't want to be strong. The *ombú* answered that it never wanted its wood to be used as a cross for the sacrifice of a saint. Ever since then, the *ombú* has had soft, weak wood, and no one bothers to cut it down.

Bandeirante and gaucho authors almost inevitably include legends in their works. It is well-nigh impossible to portray a believable gaucho or *bandeirante* without his guitar, his songs, and his stories. So you get two for the price of one: a good novel or poem and myths and legends as well. Because of the disappearance of gauchos, fewer works are being written about them and their life-style, and the gaucho is no longer the major theme in Argentine literature. The *bandeirante* held on a bit longer in Brazil, but he too is being replaced by other subjects.

The two outstanding authors of gaucho novels are Benito Lynch and Ricardo Güiraldes. In *Raquela, El inglés de los güesos (The Englishman of the Bones), The Romance of a Gaucho,* and *Los Caranchos de la Florida (The Carrion Hawks),* Benito Lynch has captured the language and customs of a dying breed. The epitome of the gaucho novel is *Don Segundo Sombra.* Güiraldes's hero, Don Segundo, is the ideal gaucho. He is a symbol, as his name *sombra* ("shadow") implies. The story really has no plot, but is a series of vignettes of gaucho life. The moment Don Segundo must take leave of his young apprentice is especially touching.

The inhabitants of the *sertão* — from the *bandeirantes* of the past to the present *sertanejo* — have been the subject of many novels.

José de Alencar introduced the *sertanejo* to the world in 1870 with *The Gaucho.* (This figure isn't limited to Argentina's literature; he also shows up frequently in Uruguayan literature.) Since then, most of Brazil's leading authors have written about the *sertão.* Da Cunha's novel *The Sertões* (also known as *Revolt in the Backlands*) has already been mentioned. Writing about the same time, José Pereira de Graça Aranha produced *Canà,* a novel with much local color and particularly beautiful descriptions.

José Américo de Almeida started a true literary rebirth in Brazil (the birth had taken place in the early 1800s, just after independence) with his novel *A Bagaceira (Cane Trash,* 1928). The author was born in the *sertão,* so the problems he describes are based on firsthand knowledge.

Graciliano Ramos spent his youth in the *sertão.* He became a staunch defender of the poor and spent time in jail for his leftist views. *Vidas sêcas (Parched Lives,* 1938) is the study of a poor, uneducated man (the typical *sertanejo*) and his family during two periods of drought. Character development is traced with a very skillful hand.

Rachel de Queirós is not only a regional writer of the *sertão,* but also one of South America's rare feminist authors, and her novels deal with the position of women in Brazilian society and the need for women's rights. De Queirós herself is a strong character. In a land dominated by *machismo* (while the term is Spanish, the Brazilians understand it well), she published her first novel at the age of 18. *O Quinze (The Year Fifteen,* 1930) tells of the *sertanejos'* struggle for survival during the terrible drought of 1915. It is a strong, sober novel. She has since written the better-known *The Three Marys.*

João Guimarães Rosa wrote only one novel, but it is a masterpiece. Not unexpectedly, the subject is the *sertão.* Unjustly overlooked in its English translation, *The Devil to Pay in the Backlands, Grande Sertão: Veredas* (1956) is fully appreciated in South America. It is a long monologue in which the bandit Riobaldo looks back on his life in the *sertão.* He is convinced that he is a good man who sold his soul to the devil and, as a result, evil forces have plagued him all his life. But in the end he comes to realize that the devil is no more than his own instincts. As a psychological study, this novel is not easily surpassed, and it is still one of Brazil's leading novels.

Then there is Erico Veríssimo, the novelist of the city, whose books are set in places like boarding schools and hospitals, where people are drawn together by circumstances and then separated. Veríssimo shows the influence of John Dos Passos or perhaps Aldous Huxley in his cross-sectional views of life. Some of his more famous works are *A Place in the Sun* (1936), *Behold the Lilies of the Field* (1938), and *Saga* (1940).

One of Brazil's greatest authors, Machado de Assiz, was also an urban writer. (His full name is Joaquim Maria Machado de Assiz, but he is so well known by his last name that no one remembers the first two.) All of his works have been translated into English and many other languages. The best known are *Memórias Póstumas de Braz Cubas (Epitaph of a Small Winner), The Heritage of Quincas Borba* (1890), and *Dom Casmurro* (1900). Machado was a cynic with an ironic sense of humor, and character development is his strongest feature. Some critics considered him Brazil's foremost psychological novelist.

Until recently, most great South American novels were regional in character. Two other giants of Brazilian literature are also regional authors: José Lins do Rêgo wrote of the northeastern sugar plantations near the *sertão.* He published what is still considered to be one of the greatest twentieth-century South American works, *The Sugar Cane Cycle,* begun in 1932 with *Menino de Engenho (Plantation Lad)* and followed by *Doidinho (Little Fool,* 1933), *Bangüe* (1934), *O Moleque Ricardo* (1935), and *Usina (Factory,* 1936). Lins do Rêgo was raised on a sugarcane plantation and, like the other writers, knew his material well. With *O Moleque Ricardo,* Lins do Rêgo also produced what is perhaps the most interesting study of a black man to be found anywhere in Brazilian literature. The novel avoids all the clichés and stereotypes: Ricardo is not an exotic creature to be studied for his picturesque speech or African customs. He is an average Brazilian who happens to have black skin.

Lins do Rêgo's writing has a light touch, and his love of life shows through in his pages. It is his own childhood and youth that he is describing, and he obviously enjoys sharing it with us. Even such scenes as the young boys' discovery of sex in the barn with the cows are handled in such a way that we feel amused rather than scandalized.

This same sensual approach to life shows up in the works of Jorge Amado, the best-known contemporary Brazilian writer. Although his books are deeply rooted in the Salvador (Bahía) region, they have been translated into many languages. One of his novels, *Dona Flor e Seus Dois Maridos (Dona Flor and Her Two Husbands),* was recently made into a delightfully erotic film that earned itself an "X" rating in some US cities. Filmed in Salvador (Bahía), the photography alone makes it worth seeing.

Amado also created Gabriela, the most popular female character in Brazilian literature. The heroine of *Gabriela, Cravo e Canela (Gabriela, Clove and Cinnamon)* is a charming, barefooted, free-loving spirit. Before he discovered the commercial value of sex in fiction, Amado wrote some of the best social protest work to come out of South America. He described the lives of the street urchins who eke out a living through petty theft and other crimes in *Capitães de Areia (Beach Waifs).* He then turned his attention to the plight of the workers on the cocoa plantations in *Cacau* and *Terras de Sem Fim (Lands Without End)* and to that of the wretched slum dwellers in *Suor (Sweat).* No one has captured the people and life of his native Salvador (Bahía) better than Amado.

In the Andean countries, the regional and social protest novels were known alternately as Indianist or indigenist. The Indian novel was first written from a point of view outside Indian culture by whites and mestizos. Under the guise of social protest, many of the earlier examples of this genre stressed the Indian's exotic and picturesque elements, which made him a curiosity to outsiders. The first writer to denounce openly the mistreatment of the natives was a woman, Clorinda Matto de Turner, the wife of an English hacienda owner. Although *Aves Sin Nido (Birds Without a Nest,* 1889) was no masterpiece, it did pave the way for what became the main Andean theme for quite some time. In Bolivia, Alcides Arguedas's *Raza de Bronce* is the leading novel of this type; in Ecuador it is Jorge Icaza's *Huasipungo.* While all three novels are noble attempts to awaken their societies to the plight of the Indian, none of them shows any real understanding of the Indians themselves. These writers were merely interested and accurate observers of behavior.

The principal Indianist writers, Ciro Alegría and José María Arguedas, are both Peruvians. Alegría's *Ancho y Ajeno es el Mundo (Broad and Alien Is the World)* and Arguedas's *Los Ríos Profundos (Deep Rivers)* are masterpieces of Peruvian literature. Arguedas pointed out that since Alegría was writing about the northern Quechua Indians and he about the southern, there was no basis of comparison between them. Although Alegría brings us closer to the Indian than any of his predecessors, it is Arguedas who finally takes us inside the Indian culture. He spent his childhood living among the Quechuas, and Quechua was his first language. As far as Arguedas was concerned, the Indians were his people. His works are highly autobiographical, and several of his narrators are thinly disguised versions of himself. Arguedas became something of a martyr after he committed suicide in 1969, claiming that he could no longer help himself or the Indian because he could no longer write. He included pages from his suicide diary in his last, incomplete novel, *El Zorro de Arriba y el Zorro de Abajo (The Fox from Above and the Fox from Below)*, referred to by most critics as *The Foxes*.

After Alegría and Arguedas, the Indian seems to have disappeared as an Andean literary subject, much as the Argentine gaucho did earlier. This is to be lamented for at least one reason: The literature included Indian legends and myths. (As an anthropologist and ethnologist, Arguedas had been especially active in collecting and preserving Indian legends.)

Lacking a common theme, the novels of the other South American countries were until recently grouped under the broad category of rural or regional novel. The most famous and still the most popular romantic novel of Colombia (and all of South America) is *María,* by Jorge Isaacs. The plot would make a good opera. Ephraim, the hero, falls in love with his young, orphaned cousin María, an epileptic. When Ephraim is sent to medical school in Europe, María's condition worsens, and she is dying. Ephraim is sent for. Will he arrive in time? There lies the suspense of the novel.

Despite the idyllic setting of *María,* all was not well in the countryside. In *Dona Bárbara,* Romulo Gallego's novel of the Venezuelan *llanos* (plains), nature is okay, but man is ugly. Dona Bárbara, having been betrayed and savagely raped as a girl, declares vengeance on all men and becomes the most powerful figure of the region by committing all manner of crimes. When Santos (saint) Luzardo moves to the area, Bárbara (barbarian) falls in love and repents her evil ways. Alas, Santos is not interested in her at all, but in her illegitimate daughter. This is the crux of the final conflict. Gallego's psychological study of Bárbara is one of the high points of the novel. *Dona Bárbara* was made first into a film and later into an opera; it is Venezuela's best-known novel.

La Vorágine (The Vortex), by José Eustasio Rivera of Colombia, is the jungle novel par excellence. Rivera describes the effects of the jungle on man's mind and body in great detail. Quicksand awaits the unwary, snakes hang from trees, and parasites are everywhere. Those who go in rarely come out. Rivera was himself lost for a time in the Colombian jungle, and he was unhealthy for quite a while after he did manage to get out. And, as if the jungle weren't enough to contend with, he describes the cruel and inhuman exploitation of the workers on the old rubber plantations deep in the jungles. These plantations no longer exist, but Rivera's novel is still compelling as a strong indictment of man's inhumanity to man.

Things are no better in today's cities if we are to judge by current works. Uruguay's two most prominent novelists, Juan Carlos Onetti and Mario

Benedetti, write about life in Montevideo although they are in exile. Onetti's themes stress modern man's inability to communicate. In *Tan Triste Como Ella (As Sad as She Was)*, *Los Adioses (The Goodbyes)*, *El Astillero (The Shipyard)*, and *La Vida Breve (The Brief Life)*, his characters lead despairing lives. Man goes through the motions of living but never really succeeds at life. Benedetti's work stresses the impersonality of the modern city. The opening of *Gracias por el Fuego (Thanks for the Light)* is set in New York, but the emphasis is on the problems of Uruguayan society and on the inability of his own generation to remedy the situation.

Augusto Roa Bastos is Paraguay's foremost novelist, although he, too, is in exile. His *Hijo de Hombre (Son of Man)* is based on Paraguayan history, including the peasant uprisings of 1912 and the Chaco War of the 1930s. It tells the familiar South American story of the oppressed struggling against the ruling elite and is replete with Christian symbolism, myth, legend, and poetic effects. Paraguay is a place that few outsiders know anything about and even fewer visit, yet Roa Bastos's work has created a new interest in the country.

Current Peruvian fiction is dominated by Mario Vargas Llosa, a novelist of international stature whose works have been translated into several languages. *La Ciudad y los Perros (The City and the Dogs)* is set in a Lima military academy — the "dogs" are the cadets. The academy is a microcosm of society's dishonesty, betrayal, violence, torture, and bestiality. *La Casa Verde (The Green House)* is set in both the jungle and a brothel in Piura. Vargas Llosa constantly shifts back and forth in time, breaking off a train of thought and picking it up later, thus destroying chronology. The lives of the main characters come together, crisscross, separate, and run parallel, as in life. *Conversation in the Cathedral* is an interesting, complicated series of intertwining conversations. There is a lighter side to Vargas Llosa. His *Pantaleón and the Visiting Service* is a very funny satire on a "service" that the Peruvian government provided for the workers in the jungle oil fields. Vargas Llosa carries his idea to its ludicrous extreme. The hero is originally in charge of a small house with a few prostitutes. As the service grows until he is the biggest pimp in South America, his military superiors must disguise and deny the whole operation.

José Donoso leads the field in Chile, and his works are now being translated almost as soon as they are published. *Coronation* deals with the impotence of a ruling class that has outlived its usefulness. Chilean life now belongs to the young and to the working classes, not to the degenerate aristocracy. *The Obscene Bird of Night* deals with physical deformity, insanity, and similar subjects. The sexual scenes are ludicrous, repelling, and anything but erotic. Some of the technical effects are original, and Donoso has an active imagination and a macabre view of life.

Argentina has produced a great number of top-notch modern writers, among them the urban and urbane Jorge Luis Borges and Ernesto Sábato. Borges was one of the first writers to put South America on the map of world literature. His works are intellectual games played with his readers. Most of his writings are short story–essays that he calls fictions. Two of his favorite themes are labyrinths and mathematics. He enjoys destroying our concepts of time, space, infinity, and truth, using personal friends and other people as fictional characters and quoting actual reference works to back up his invented theories. His mystery stories are especially enjoyable, as they take you through the whole process of solving a crime. For the skeptical Borges, life is tragic because it is limited by time and is irreversible, but we can relieve the tragedy by constructing games to distract ourselves. Borges's friend Adolfo Bioy Casares, who shows up as a character in some of the fictions, also uses the detective story as a game. You occasionally get the impression that the two of them are trying to outdo each other and that the reader is just incidental to the process.

Ernesto Sábato's works are not fun and games. While his masterpiece, *About Heroes and Tombs,* deals with a large segment of Argentine history, it stresses the twenties and thirties and pre-Perón Argentina. The heroine Alejandra is one of the most powerfully drawn women in South American literature. As the novel begins, Alejandra (who symbolizes Argentina itself) has just killed herself and her father and set fire to the house. Then we learn the history of her unusual family. Buenos Aires, with its corruption, lies, and violence, is the real villain.

Julio Cortázar and Manuel Puig are the best of the younger Argentines, but keep your eye on Eduardo Gudiño Kiefer, whose popularity is rising. Cortázar, another game player, sets the tone in his titles: *End of the Game, Hopscotch, The Prizes, A Novel to Put Together. Hopscotch* is a series of episodes, dialogues, and monologues. Each section has two numbers. You can read the novel consecutively and get one story, or you can read the sections according to the second set of numbers, which skip around in a different order. Sometimes you jump forward and sometimes backward (as in hopscotch), thereby getting a different story. This technique is part of Cortázar's rebellion against literary convention. Characters invent their own games; Buenos Aires and Paris are interchangeable; anarchy abounds. *A Novel to Put Together* is, just as it says, a do-it-yourself kit for a novel.

Manuel Puig has written three novels that have received critical acclaim and commercial success: *The Buenos Aires Affair, Boquitas Pintadas (Painted Mouths),* and *The Betrayal of Rita Hayworth.* Movies and novels are more real for Puig's characters than their own humdrum existence.

The most famous and popular contemporary South American writer is the Colombian Nobel Prize winner Gabriel García Márquez, author of the international best-seller *A Hundred Years of Solitude.* For South Americans the story of Macondo and the Buendía family is an allegory of their continent. For others it is just an extreme pleasure to read, with all manner of strange happenings repeating themselves in defiance of all laws. García Márquez takes us through seven generations of this family. The author has a very offbeat sense of humor, allowing him to describe deaths and tragedies without upsetting the reader. The reader is compelled to move on to each unexpected event to see how the Buendía family copes with it. Equally funny and macabre is the more recent *Autumn of the Patriarch,* the story of a dictator who dies several times. But does he really die? He's been in the presidential palace so long that no one remembers when he wasn't. *No One Writes to the Colonel* is an earlier work that is definitely worth reading. If you know Spanish, be sure to read García Márquez in the original. His style and use of language are incomparable.

The commercial and critical emergence of Latin American literature has continued into the 1980s with names both familiar and new. The following are among the current works that represent the best of this genre: García Márquez's latest novella, *Chronicle of a Death Foretold,* a tale of murder in his native Colombia; *We All Loved Glenda So Much,* a collection of short stories by the Argentine writer Julio Cortázar; and Peruvian Mario Vargas Llosa's satirical novel, *Aunt Julia and the Scriptwriter.* And two female Latin American writers have recently emerged in American publishing: Luisa Valenzuela, the Argentine short story writer whose book, *The Lizard's Tail,* has appeared on best-seller lists in the US; and Chilean poet Maria Luisa Bombal, who has finally achieved recognition here not for poetry, but for short stories, in a collection entitled *New Islands.*

In the mid-1980s, Latin American literature continues to thrive in several genres, especially in the novel. Among those well-established authors who recently have published new works are the Peruvian Mario Vargas Llosa, with his gigantic novel *The War at the End of the World,* and the Chilean exile José Donoso, with *A House in the Country.* In addition, the highly censored 1976 novel, *Kiss of the Spider Woman,* by Argentine Manuel Puig, was made into a daring film by the Brazilian director Hector Babenco, followed by the 1986 publication of the English translation of Puig's critically acclaimed novel, *Pubis Angelical,* under the title *Angel Hair.* In 1986 a highly unusual novel reminiscent of Raymond Chandler's detective fiction of the 1940's came from Brazil. Translated from the Portuguese, *High Art* presents a stark portrait of urban Brazilian society.

With a distinguished political heritage conferred by her name and by her status as a Chilean exile living in Venezuela, a new female writer also has taken a well-deserved place among the few women novelists of Latin America. She is Isabel de Allende, and her novel, *House of the Spirits,* is a fascinating work that offers many insights into the overthrow of the Allende government of the mid-1970s.

If your real love is poetry, South America has plenty to offer you. Even when no good novels were being produced, South America had an abundance of excellent poetry. Pablo Neruda and Gabriela Mistral, both Chileans, are Nobel Prize recipients. And several anthologies of South American poetry are available in English.

South American literature now ranks with the world's best. Once you get to a big city in South America, check out the best-seller lists or talk to a book dealer to find out who the promising young authors are. Then, even after you are back in the US, keep an eye out for translations or watch for imports if you read Spanish or Portuguese.

Music and Dance

 South Americans come by their love of music naturally. With a triple heritage of Indian, Iberian, and African influences, they have a terrifically varied background upon which to draw. Thus, each ethnic group has contributed its own rhythms, scales, and instruments to new musical forms that exist nowhere else.

And for almost every song there is a dance. So closely related are the two that the Quechua Indians of the Peruvian Andes have only one word, *taqui,* for both. South Americans are among the world's most graceful dancers — men as well as women. Indeed, unlike some North American men, South American men need no coaxing to get them on the dance floor. They rank dancing with eating, drinking, and lovemaking (not necessarily in that order). After watching the sensual movements of some of the dances, you will realize that for them dancing *is* a form of lovemaking. (Back in the days of watchful chaperones, a dance was the only excuse for having physical contact with one's fiancée.)

Music has always been an important part of South American life. The early missionaries succeeded in wiping out most of the indigenous music, but Spanish chroniclers state that the Indians used drums, flutes, and rattles, especially in their religious ceremonies. (It has been said that some Indians carved their flutes from the legbone of a particularly hated enemy.) The Incas, who had the highest musical development among the Indians, played complex panpipes, some with as many as 36 tones. Such instruments are still used in the Andes, as is the basic five-tone (pentatonic) scale used by many primitive tribes.

The Spanish and Portuguese colonists brought the stringed instruments — the guitar, harp, mandolin, and violin — as well as the seven-tone scale and their own rich musical heritage. The Indians were quick to adopt the European instruments and to adapt them to their own tastes. The use of an armadillo shell as a sounding box resulted in the *charango,* a small, ukelele-like instrument that helps give Andean music its distinctive sound. The Andean harp, with only 36 strings, produces a rather strident pitch, but the Indians wanted the harp to be portable for their parades and street festivals, of which there are literally thousands. In the mountains all events, both pagan and Christian, are observed, usually with a curious compromise between the two traditions. The Indians appease both God and the gods with their music, just in case. And music helps them cope with the harsh realities of Andean life.

Since many Indian dances are symbolic, at major festivals each dance is performed in a different costume, the splendor of which will amaze you. Elaborately worked papier-mâché masks top outfits of neon colors with intricate sequin, bead, embroidery, and lace designs. The huge, carved-wood heads used in the Diablada (devil) dance would scare anyone. Two festivals to be considered are Inti Raymi (the festival of the sun god Inti, in Cuzco, Perú, June 24, which has become rather touristy) and the Virgen de Candelaria (Lake Titicaca area, February 2-10). The Diablada is performed at Oruro Carnival in Bolivia, the Saturday before Ash Wednesday. (Be warned that any Indian festival is accompanied by much drinking. The Indians will sing, drink, and dance until they pass out. Since there is no taboo against it, the women get as drunk as the men. After a few glasses of home brew, the normally reserved Indians may want you to dance with them. Since a drunken person is always unpredictable, handle these situations with as much tact and grace as you can muster.) Regardless, the festivals are well worth attending for the music, the spectacle, and for the interest in a people that has for over 500 years struggled to maintain its traditions in the face of tremendous adversity. Unfortunately, as the Indians come into contact with twentieth-century civilization, the typical Andean band of flutes, panpipes, violin, harp, drum, and *charango* is slowly being replaced by the noisier brass band common to all North America.

In the highlands of Perú and Bolivia the *yaraví* and *huayno* are the most common songs. The *yaraví* or *haraví* (Quechua for "lament") is a ballad-like piece about death, lost love, or other unhappy themes. It can be sung or just played on a flute. Many aficionados feel that it is the truest expression of the melancholy Indian spirit. More popular is the *huayno,* which is both a song and a dance. The *huayno* begins with a slow *triste* (sad song) and ends with a quick-paced *fuga* (flight). The dance consists of small, quick steps executed close to one's partner but with little contact. Like unfamiliar food, the *huayno* is an acquired taste, for it is often sung with a whining quality. In Ecuador, a variation of the *huayno,* the *sanjuanito* (named for St. John, the patron saint of Ecuador) is the national song and dance. Andean music is also found in southwestern Colombia and northern Chile and Argentina with slight regional adaptations.

Admittedly, Andean music is not for everyone. Don't let internationally acclaimed vocalist Ima Sumac's highly touted five-octave range scare you off. Her voice is definitely unique, but she is a trained professional and in no way typifies folk singers. If you start with the hauntingly melodic flute music, then progress to the male vocalists, you should soon be ready for the higher-pitched wailing sounds of the female singers. Simon and Garfunkel's *El Condor Paso* notwithstanding, excellent artists are now interpreting Indian music. Americans who develop an appreciation of Andean music become lifelong devotees.

In Paraguay, Jesuit missionaries taught the Guaraní Indians to sing religious music and to play the harp. The Guaranís, like the Quechuas, quickly adopted the instrument. Paraguayan music, however, is almost always gay and lilting. Many songs imitate bird calls, falling rain, and other sounds from nature. Add to this the melodious cadences of the Guaraní language and you have a combination that makes for pleasant listening.

The *canción* (*purajhei* in Guaraní) is sung in Guaraní. The *galope* (gallop) and the *polka paraguaya* (Paraguayan polka), while sometimes sung in Guaraní, are really European in origin with a tropical touch added. They cannot be considered Indian in the same way a *huayno* or *yaraví* is. Even the popular *guaranía,* a ballad with a waltzlike beat, was created by professional composers who wanted to return to native melodies. The authentic Guaraní music, apparently slower and more melancholy in nature, was destroyed long ago.

Traditional Indian melodies have nevertheless inspired much of the protest music coming out of South America. This movement, which calls itself the *nueva canción latinoamericana* (new Latin American song), had its origins in southern South America and Chile, where it flourished under the Allende regime in the early 1970s. It rapidly became international, especially after the military junta executed or exiled most of the protest musicians in 1974. One of the most famous singers of Chilean protest songs, Victor Jara, was shot to death in the National Stadium, where he was ordered to sing before thousands of people. Many political composers and singers are aware of the value of South America's Indian heritage and do not wish to see it destroyed in the name of progress. Their songs represent a fusion of the new and the old similar to our folk revival of the 60s. These young, highly skilled musicians have produced some of the most creative and dynamic South American music around. (*Quilapayun* and *Inti-illimani* are the best known in the US today.)

Creole (*criollo*) music did not look to the Indian for its inspiration. Though born in South America, all *criollos* originally shared a southern European (mostly Iberian) heritage, and their music tended to cross national boundaries easily. First popular in colonial Lima, Perú, the *zambacueca,* with its name shortened to *cueca,* became the national dance of Chile. Once the *cueca* was firmly established as Chilean, the Peruvians changed the name of their *cueca* to *marinera* to avoid any reference to its rival to the south. In Argentina, the *zambacueca* gave rise to two dances, the *zamba* and the *cueca,* each slightly different. These dances are fun to watch because of the graceful, flirtatious waving of handkerchiefs and the playful, coquettish movements of the couples. Despite the increasing popularity of rock and disco in South America, the *cueca* and the *marinera* are still very much alive. Since those of white European stock live mostly along the coastlines, *criollo* music has been subject to various outside influences. This has led to the creation of some rather amusing combinations such as the *foxtrot incaico* (Inca foxtrot), which has nothing of the Inca in it.

No one, including leading ethnomusicologists, seems to have sorted out all the origins and influences found in *criollo* music. The musical crisscrossing of borders has only confused the issue. In Argentina, people simply ascribed all creole music, with the exception of the urban *milonga* and *tango,* to a romantic gaucho figure, the colorful *payador* (wandering ballad singer) of the pampa. He has now been replaced by radio and television. With him went the *contrapunto* (counterpoint), the last vestige of the troubador's art in South America. (If you scour the pampa of Argentina or the *sertão* of Brazil, you might be lucky enough to find a lone troubador still entertaining the people of the remoter regions.)

Many other creole songs and dances, whether gaucho or not, have been saved from oblivion in nightclubs, called *peñas,* which offer folklore shows (see *Nightclubs and Nightlife,* THE CITIES). The *vidala* or *vidalita* (my life), the *triste* (sad song), and the *estilo* (style) are slow, sentimental songs that describe life on the pampa or relate some event of national or regional importance. A *triste* is often a love song for one who is far away. The *gato* (cat) and the *pericón* (large fan) are very lively country dances that were extremely popular with the gauchos. They were frequently accompanied by songs of varied content, some of which were quite humorous. The *tamer cielito* (little heaven) and *cuando* (when) resemble a waltz and a minuet respectively.

The music of rural Uruguay is similar to that of Argentina because this, too, is gaucho country. Like the American cowboy of the Far West, the gaucho sings to keep himself company while riding herd. Since this folklore is not written down, we have no idea how many gaucho songs there really are.

The urban music of Buenos Aires and Montevideo has little in common with the songs of the rural plains. When it was first introduced, the famous Argentine tango — which is Andalusian, not Italian, in origin — was considered very naughty. It even caused a scandal because, for the first time, men and women danced with their entire bodies touching! Before the tango, most dances were done in lines or circles, and physical contact was limited. Even in a waltz the partner had been kept at arm's length. With the advent of disco dancing, Buenos Aires has become one of the disco capitals of South America. Consequently, even the tango finds itself relegated to the realm of folklore. But a tango well done is still a thing of beauty and grace (see *Buenos Aires,* THE CITIES).

As in Argentina, the music of Colombia and Venezuela is predominantly Spanish in style, but unlike Argentina, there are regions where the African influence is strong. Along the northern coastline the blacks have contributed more complex, syncopated rhythms to the popular music. Their influence is especially evident in the lively Colombian *bambuco* and *cumbia* and in the Venezuelan *joropo*. The *cuatro* (four-stringed guitar) and the *tiple* (five-stringed guitar) are played in both countries. Their peculiar sound, similar to that of the *charango,* may take a bit of getting used to. Despite this, Colombian and Venezuelan music is usually lively and lots of fun to dance to.

In any of the aforementioned countries, you can find clubs that offer flamenco and other elements of Spanish folklore should you want a taste of the mother country. The mother country of Brazil is Portugal, which offers not flamenco but *fados,* very sad, haunting melodies about homesickness or lost love. It is difficult to believe after seeing the bubbly craziness of the Brazilians that these melancholy, beautiful songs are part of their heritage.

Brazilians are the most musically oriented people in South America, and at no time does this stand out more than during Carnival. There is no spectacle like it anywhere else on the continent. The *samba* is the predominant dance of Carnival, and the costumes of the *samba* schools have to be seen to be believed, they are so incredibly ornate. Incredible also is the energy of the people, who sing and dance for 4 days and nights, literally nonstop. It is impossible to walk down the street without getting caught up in the rhythm and vitality of it all.

When you think Carnival, don't just think Rio. Salvador (Bahía) and other cities in the north have Carnivals that are not as jammed with tourists and commercialized. In fact, the *samba* was started in the *favelas* (slums) of Rio by blacks who had originally emigrated from the north. Although by no means the only one, the *samba* is the South American dance most frequently associated with blacks, and Carnival is really their festival.

The *samba* is only one dance performed at Carnival. The *marcha* and the *frêvo* can also be seen, although they are becoming increasingly overshadowed by the *samba*. There are numerous other Brazilian songs and dances. After you recover from your Carnival hangover, you can begin to discover them for yourself, one at a time. There is also special music that accompanies the various types of *macumba* (secret religious rites). (See *Festivals,* DIVERSIONS; *Rio de Janeiro* and *Salvador (Bahía),* THE CITIES.)

If you prefer some culture with your revelry, South America has many excellent symphony orchestras that often perform the works of South American composers. In Lima, *zarzuelas* (operettas à la Gilbert and Sullivan) imported from Spain are performed. The Teatro Colón in Buenos Aires, one of the world's great old opera houses, features regular concert, opera, and dance performances by such groups as the orchestras and ballet companies of São Paulo, Brazil, and Caracas, Venezuela, which are generally considered to be the most sophisticated on the continent.

There is enough music in South America to keep your toes tapping and your hands clapping for the better part of your trip. When you find something you love, spread the word back home. South American music has been overlooked for far too long.

Crafts

As South America slowly becomes more familiar and accessible, travelers are beginning to discover and delight in its remarkably varied handicrafts — historic, colorful, fine, crude, amusing, traditional, first- and second-rate. In many countries these hand-made items embody artistic links to pre-Columbian and Hispanic heritages. And even if you were never before interested in handicrafts per se, seeing them on location may add a special dimension. A poncho will no longer be an ethnic item seen in fall fashion shows, but rather an essential garment to protect the wearer against the Andean cold. Cloth made of llama, alpaca, and vicuña wool somehow feels warmer once you've seen the animals grazing and the weavers weaving.

In Latin America vital folk art traditions flourished centuries before the arrival of the Europeans and, despite the laments of scholars and purists, not all local skills are dying or dead. Certain crafts can perhaps be called "endangered species," compromised by synthetic fibers, machine looms, and plastic materials. But there is hope for others as governments and private citizens become aware of the cultural and economic value of handicraft production. That hope will not be fulfilled, however, until the continent's tradition of exploiting the workers is revised so that they can make a living wage and function as independent craftspeople.

Some ancient skills are now being revived; many craftspeople remain faithful to tradition while others are updating their products. The mixing of past and present can yield amusing results, as it did during the hot pants craze in the late 1960s. Indian women, dressed in their traditional layers of full-skirted *polleras,* busily knitted alpaca hot pants decorated with Inca motifs to sell to tourists.

Such novelties aside, the truly South American items will attract your attention with their bright colors, fine workmanship, and mysterious and/or primitive designs. Before you look around urban artisan centers or country markets, it is always interesting to visit local folk art museums. There are many very fine ones — in Quito, Recife, and Bogotá, for example — where costumes, utensils, and musical instruments are displayed by region and clearly and imaginatively demonstrate what is most important about handicrafts: their utilitarian or spiritual function.

Folk art reflects the variety of influences on the local artisan; the most dramatic change in South America came with the arrival of the Spanish and the introduction of Christianity. Indian artistic skills and imagination quickly took to the baroque trappings and awe-inspiring pageantry of the Catholic church. Even today, Indian handicrafts continue to interpret Christian themes with local dramatis personae: a cross, a bird-god, and a political figure may all appear on a Cuna Indian *mola* appliqué from Panamá; Inca suns emblazon frames of colonial-style mirrors made in Perú; and llamas may guard the manger of Jesus in a nativity scene etched around an Ecuadorian gourd.

The most basic change between ancient and contemporary crafts is the separation of function and decoration. Isolated Amazon tribes, who were not part of either the Inca or Spanish conquest, continue to make objects — baskets, pottery, hunting weapons, and musical instruments — for practical purposes and decorate them in a traditional way. Objects that we call artistic, the tribesman would call useful. However, items crafted by artisans who *have* been exposed to colonial and modern influences may now be either utilitarian or ornamental.

Without doubt, all South American countries are not equally endowed with treasuries of superb folk arts. Historically, the finest come from the Andean centers of pre-Columbian cultures whose craftspeople excelled in weaving, pottery-making, and gold- and silver-smithing. Creativity was never simply applied to art for art's sake, but was devoted to enhancing things that were used in daily life and religious ritual. For these peoples, design and embellishment celebrated the close association between themselves and nature, between man and god. Folk art — ancient and modern — remains intrinsically linked with life, as you will see in the objects that continue to bloom in Colombia, Ecuador, Perú, and Bolivia.

In Argentina, Chile, and Uruguay the same folk art principle applies, yet it is the gaucho who has influenced the regional *artesanía.* Silver is used to decorate the harness and saddle trappings of his horse as well as his own costume. Watch for other gaucho paraphernalia: heavy belts fashioned from silver coins and chains (worn only by old-timers) and the silver gourd and *bombilla* (drinking straw) that are basic to making and taking tea on the range. Gaucho countries are also noted for their leatherwork. The hide of an unborn calf is most highly valued, but horsehide, kid, and snakeskin are also used in making clothing and furniture. These leatherwork skills have transferred easily into good workmanship on fur clothing.

Centuries ago, the Spanish and Portuguese nuns taught the Indian women embroidery and lacemaking and, in most countries, rich needlework patterns adorn women's and men's clothing. The delicate *ñandutí* lace and the Aó Po'i embroidery of Paraguay are among the finest on the continent, and the patterns of sequins, beadwork, and stitching on costumes for religious and folk ceremonies in Brazil, Bolivia, Ecuador, and Perú absolutely defy description.

Generally, the best places to find high-quality handicrafts are often the government stores, which serve as cooperative centers for marketing and distribution. These are headquartered mostly in capitals and major towns. Here also, from time to time, you will find the gallery of a contemporary craftsperson whose specialty is using ancient materials (such as beads and textile pieces found in pre-Columbian graves or colonial embroideries and metal religious objects) to fashion modern jewelry, clothing, or collages.

Yet nothing can beat the country market as a source for particular crafts. There you will find not only a wider selection of certain objects, but also lower prices. Bargaining is accepted, but haggling over pennies is certainly poor form when you consider the seller's time, effort, and annual income. Above all, in a village market, you can watch a craft emerging from the skilled hands of its creator.

Each South American country offers a handicraft specialty, although the best folk arts and crafts are concentrated in some half-dozen areas. We have focused on the leading craft countries, listing city centers and village markets where handwork is found and/or produced. The latter are particularly fascinating and colorful in the Andean regions — here you should make an effort to adjust your travel itinerary to accommodate the weekly market schedule. (The same is true for the annual festival, where the finest items are worn or displayed in their appropriate functional/decorative framework.) For the location of and transportation to a town or village, you may want to refer to each country's DIRECTIONS section.

BOLIVIA: After you've caught your breath in La Paz, your next problem is to decide what to see first in this city of dramatic Andean peaks and fascinating, somber people. Make your first stop the Museum of National Ethnography and Folklore, a repository of folk arts — musical instruments, which are still played beautifully and frequently in local restaurants; contemporary costumes; and the masks of the Diablada (devil) dance. Then head for the city markets — the Artisans Market off Plaza San Francisco, the Mercado Negro (Black Market), and the food market on Av. Camacho — which are always open for business. The best known is the Witches Market, where you may or may not want to buy sheep or llama fetuses, believed to bring fertility or good luck to new enterprises. At all these markets you'll recognize the sellers (female) by their black *boina* hats. Favorite purchases in the city are ponchos; *chuspas* (coca pouches) decorated in interesting figurative and geometric patterns; wonderfully dressed dolls; and musical instruments, ranging from unusual strings to all kinds of pipes.

Many fine weavings — tapestries, rugs, and blankets — can be found in Cochabamba, Bolivia's third-largest city. This is the home of Fotrama Cooperative, founded by a Maryknoll priest from the US, where the Indian women are taught advanced weaving and knitting skills. The nearby valley town of Villa Rivero produces the only tapestry weaving in Bolivia. In the area around Cochabamba many village markets are held, mostly on Sundays.

Sixty miles by rail or road from La Paz is Oruro, where the region's big social event — the Wednesday markets — takes place. Oruro's annual Diablada performances held during Carnival are probably the best in the country and the masks and costumes are among the most fascinating examples of folkloric arts.

BRAZIL: The best crafts found in the major visitor centers — Rio de Janeiro and São Paulo — come from another part of Brazil. This doesn't mean that you won't find good-quality crafts in Rio's specialty stores or at its Hippie Market, or at the Sunday market in the Praça de República in São Paulo. In fact the latter has good crafts from every region of the country, particularly leather bags and jackets from the immediate area. But the major arts and handicrafts center is Salvador (Bahía), whose wildly decorative arts allude to both Portuguese and African influences.

Go to Bahía's Museu da Cidade to see life-size models dressed in the opulent old Bahian costumes and headdresses — the ultimate in layered, embroidered fashion. The silver jewelry on display is probably close in quality to what you will find in the Mercado Modelo (Model Market). Other regional crafts that can be found in Bahía range from bejeweled dolls dressed as lavishly as the museum models to Bahian rug tapestries with primitive scenes woven in the warmest Gauguinesque colors. Oil painting is done in this same folkloric style, and both have rightly attracted the attention of international art collectors — prices have risen accordingly. Tilework, rendered in the more formal patterns and colors of Portuguese ceramics, is also good here.

The influence of the Africans who were brought to Brazil as slaves is most apparent in Bahía, and a common purchase is the *figa*, a charm bringing fertility or good luck and once worn by the slaves. Shaped as a clenched fist, the *figa* can be made of jacaranda wood and silver, solid silver, or colored quartz. Other charms are collected into a *penca* (bunch) and worn as a cluster on a neck chain or bracelet.

Brazil is also known for fine baskets and hammocks (the bed used most frequently in the tropics). At Fortaleza in the northeast, you'll find some of the most intricate, beautifully woven hammocks at the Centro de Turismo, the Tourist Handicraft Center, housed in an old prison whose cells are now little shops. Delicate Brazilian lace is sold in the vast São José Market in Recife, as are skillful woodcarvings — masks, statues, and utilitarian objects such as bowls, eating utensils, and platters — made from Amazon mahogany and jacaranda. In the Minas Geras area, between Rio and Salvador, is a major craft center that specializes in pewter reproductions of antique vessels, such as tea and coffee pots, mugs, and pitchers.

CHILE: Chile is a country rich in high-quality raw materials from which many folkcrafts are fashioned — wool, leather, wood, copper, and even lapis lazuli. Small crafts centers have sprung up from top to bottom of this long thin country; in *Chile,* DIRECTIONS, we have noted those towns and villages that have their own specialties.

In large cities such as Santiago, you will find a variety of crafts at the Galerías Artensale CEMA, a government-initiated project founded to help women earn household money. CEMA (Centro de Madres, or Mother's Center) basically distributes and markets artisan goods from all over the countryside. From Arica come ceramics modeled after the artifacts of the pre-Inca Diaguitas Indian culture; from the Central Valley come *boradores de Isla Negra,* fabric panels embroidered with scenes of rural Chilean life, as well as vicuña and alpaca garments — ponchos, sweaters, and jackets. From towns near Santiago come baskets, pottery, blankets, capes, and shawls and a variety of leatherwork and cowboy accessories such as ornamental stirrups. From the southern Lake District and the island of Chiloe off Puerto Montt come thick woolen knits, mostly sweaters, in muted shades of brown, white, and tan. CEMA also carries copperware, but the more interesting lapis jewelry is found in Santiago's specialty stores.

COLOMBIA: Bogotá, Colombia's capital, is a gem of a city for the folk arts lover; almost everything you find here is as good — although perhaps not as inexpensive — as it is in the place of manufacture. Craft traditions are rather well looked after and supported by the Artesanías de Colombia Cooperative, with a shop across from the Tequendama hotel in Bogotá. The main store is in the colonial convent of Las Aguas church, Carrera No. 18-60 (phone: 283-4211). Other branches are in Cartagena and Popayán. The store offers a wide variety: traditional ponchos; *ruanas* — Colombian ponchos, which wrap like capes and come in wonderful single and mixed colors; straw baskets of every imaginable shape and woven design; rugs; and leather. The Artesanías was instrumental in encouraging the pursuit of fine appliqué work done in the coastal regions; whether window or wall size, these colorful depictions of local scenes are a joy.

The gift shop of the Museum of Popular Arts and Traditions near the Presidential Palace also sells fine textiles, basketry, ceramics, and wood carvings. The museum, which occupies a former monastery, has one of the finest permanent folk art exhibitions on the continent, with emphasis on how people live in various regions and the household objects they use. As a visit to the Gold Museum will show, goldsmithing is an ancient Indian skill and, although it has gone far beyond folk art, the goldwork now produced in *galerías* that specialize in copies of pre-Columbian pieces is superb. Galería Cano in Bogotá, at Carrera 13, No. 2798, is a pioneer in this craft, and there are branches in Cartagena and at Bloomingdale's in New York.

In Cartagena itself, the craft center is said to be in the stalls of the Bovedas (restored dungeons in the fortifications), but the quality of the products is better in stores off the old city square. An hour from the coast is the city of San Jacinto, an important center for bags, hats, baskets, cotton weaving, and hammocks. Some years ago Peace Corps workers in this area originated cotton string wall hangings called *divisorios;* they were an overnight success and are now found everywhere, executed in two or more colors and geometric designs. Some are more interesting than others, so don't buy the first one you see.

The province of Boyacá is the leading crafts-producing area of Colombia and, if you don't want to stay in one of its charming colonial inns, at least take a day's excursion from Bogotá. Tunja, the provincial capital, has a lively daily market and is a good place to buy fine *ruanas;* rugs; *bolsas* (knitted bags); esparto grass baskets and hats; and *fique* (fiber from the century plant) items such as placemats, toy animals, large bags, and purses. From Tunja it is not far to Duitama, a furniture-making center, from which reproductions of colonial pieces can be shipped. Other more portable and traditional Duitama woodcrafts are hand-carved plates, bowls, trays, and spoons. The pottery produced in the small town Raquira is famous, fragile, and fun: Clay birds can be blown as whistles, clay frogs make another kind of peep, and ceramic vessels are covered with all sorts of fanciful figures. The market in Duitama is held on Tuesdays; in nearby Villa de Leyva on Saturdays; and in Raquira on Sundays.

En route to Boyacá is the Cocontá Monday market, known for its fine leatherwork, primarily found on horsemen's gear. Beautiful woolen shawls (*panolones*) with 3-foot macramé fringes also come from this area. In Chiquinquirá, local craftspeople make handsome guitars and tambourines inlaid with shell designs.

ECUADOR: Quito is probably one of the best craft-shopping capitals on the continent. Here you'll find everything from straw mats and hats to elegant little dolls, Indian beadwork, ceremonial drums and flutes, weavings, embroideries, jewelry, baskets, wooden statues, and bread sculpture. Be sure to pay a visit to the Folklore Gallery (Av. Colón 260, Quito; phone: 23-17-67), which has a variety of goods to see and buy. Olga Fisch, grande dame of Ecuadorian folk art, designs rugs, and her daughter-in-law, clothing and jewelry; both women incorporate regional material and motifs into their lovely patterns. They also carry crafts from all over the country, as does the government center OCEPA (Exportation of Ecuadorian Artisan Products) at Washington 752 and at the excellent La Bodega at Av. Juan León Mera 614. Quito is the home of many other contemporary South American artists; their galleries — open to the public on request — are worth seeing and their work (particularly paintings) is internationally recognized.

With its large Indian population, Ecuador has an almost unending spectacle of markets, some three dozen from one end of the country to the other. You should leave enough time to visit either Otavalo or Ambato, both crafts markets, as well as a produce market such as Saquisili or Pujili.

Otavalo's big day is Saturday. Reserve well ahead through your travel agent or a local tour operator so that you can go on Friday and secure one of a limited supply of rooms in the area. Only in this way can you be up and in the marketplace at sunrise when the distinctively dressed *otavaleños* begin to sell their ponchos, wall hangings, thick wool sweaters, baskets, decorative woven pouches called *shigras,* rugs, blankets, and thick ropes of gilt and red glass beads that they themselves wear. En route to or from Otavalo, stop in Calderon where the flamboyant bread-dough figures are shaped, baked, and painted and in the woodcarving center of San Antonio de Ibarra.

The *otavaleños* also carry their weavings to Ambato, but keep your eyes open here for locally made rugs and for tapestries made by the Salasaca Indians. This area produces fine leatherwork, and multicolored, woven belts — some with different patterns on each side. And, since the Ambato market is close to the Amazon jungle region, you will also find baskets and pottery.

At the Saquisili market (held on Thursdays), the emphasis is on supplying what the local people need, not what visitors want, so on sale here are fine baskets and mats made from Totora reeds. Pujili (Wednesdays and Sundays) is also a local supply market and one where you will see llamas. Other markets within easy reach of Quito are Latacunga (Tuesdays), Machachi, and Salcedo (Sundays).

The Canari people, famous artisans for centuries, live in the Cuenca region. They are weavers and leatherworkers; for the tourist trade they produce fine and interesting woven belts and macrame. There are other things to buy in Cuenca, including pottery and the misnamed Panama hat — you can watch both in production right in the city. Finally, there is an OCEPA craft store off the central plaza, and a good display of regional artifacts in the Municipal Museum.

PANAMÁ: The best selection of Panamanian crafts is the Artesanías Nacionales in Old Panamá (City). The displays here include straw hats and bags, leatherwork, and ceramic and wood items. But nothing is more quintessentially Panamanian than the national costume; for women, this is the *pollera,* and for men, the *montuno.* The *pollera* is a wonderful multilayered dress with intricate embroidery that gives it a delicate lacy look. The *montuno* is a loose-fitting overshirt, also of finely embroidered cotton.

Another Panamanian specialty is the beautifully beaded collars worn and made by the Guaymi Indians who live in the central part of the country, about 4 hours from the capital. (The best buys are found on location.) The most famous handicraft from Panamá, the *mola,* is an appliquéd square made by the Cuna Indians of the San Blas Islands. Set into the front and back of a woman's blouse, a good *mola* is made of four or five layers of colored cloth through which the pattern is cut. (This is different from conventional appliqués, in which layers are stitched one atop another.) The *mola* designs are pure fancy — taken from nature, from good and bad "spirits," even from patterns seen on food labels! Look carefully when you buy. Panamá is now deluged with *mola*-style objects, from wall hangings to aprons, pocketbooks, sun hats, and men's shirts and sport jackets. They are generally second-rate in workmanship; special attention and creativity is usually reserved for a woman's own apparel, which later may be bought by a visitor to the San Blas or an art collector. And certainly, in the islands, *molas* are *never* worn by men!

Another fanciful Indian craft is the birdcage made of the *piruli* reed by the people of the Chiriquí Highlands. Cages may be shaped like a bird, a plane, or their own *bohío* (thatched hut). Sunday is market day in that region.

PERÚ: Perú's artisans may produce the most interesting and varied crafts on the continent — indeed, some of the finest in the world. The official center is Artesanías del Perú, which has stores in Cuzco, Arequipa, and Iquitos. Some popular items are ponchos of various designs; woven belts from different regions; decorative woolen pillow cases and wall hangings; woven shoulder bags; copies of colonial knickknacks such as mirrors and altar candleholders; *tupos* (shawl pins, and try to find the old ones); and alpaca fur everything, from slippers to rugs. (The slippers are patterned in brown and white, and you will be lucky if they last a year in a centrally heated home.) Lima's Museo Nacional de la Cultura Perúana has a fair collection of handicrafts, but to really understand why the country is the leading handicraft center, go to study pre-Columbian history at the Museum of Anthropology and Archaeology; ceramics at the Larco Herrera Museum; and textiles at the Amano Museum (by appointment).

Lima stores offer a wide selection of merchandise from throughout the country, but it is always fun to buy items where they are produced at prices that can be considerably lower. So, if you can, try to include the following places on your itinerary; each trip alone is worth consideration.

Most travelers to Cuzco go dashing off to Machu Picchu on a 2- or 3-day excursion and don't leave enough time to see the surrounding region or the former Inca capital. Cuzco is full of big and little treasures, including colonial antiques, which simply require browsing time to find. Crafts come to Cuzco from all over the highlands, but the most local items are *chuspas;* wonderfully carved wooden locks; and all kinds of pottery. At the Sunday market in nearby Pisac, the plaza is filled with ponchos, blankets, highland woolen hats and slippers, and *varas,* processional staffs decorated with silver. Less of a craft market but more of an all-Indian gathering is the Sunday market at Chinchero, where people come to Mass and then picnic.

The very fine Ayacucho ceramic bulls, the carved gourds, and the famous *retablos* — miniature to grand in size, gaily decorated portable altars with doors that open into a divided scene of secular and religious carved figures — have become hard to find here, but keep looking; the price will be right. With the political problems of this region, the best bulls and *retablos* are probably in Lima's better craft stores. (Try Artesanías Huamanqaqa on Av. Jirón Union in Lima, as well as the Los Alamos gallery in the Urbanización Zarate district.) Near Ayacucho is the mountain village of Quinua, famous for its folkloric pottery.

If you take the train from Cuzco to Puno, make at least a fast stop at Pucara, famous for its charming pottery bulls. The Puno area itself is a knitting center, and the price is absolutely right for sweaters, vests, stocking caps, ponchos, and wonderful little, knitted, stuffed animals called *animalitos.* Saturday is the big market day in Puno, Thursday in nearby Juli, and Sunday and Monday in Juliaca. The Lake Titicaca region in general is an excellent center for craft and festival folklore.

Huancayo, a wild and fascinating train ride from Lima, is another remarkable craft town, with market days on Sundays. Gourds are also made here and the region is famous for rugs, blankets, tapestries, and knitted goods. For life and people, this is the most interesting market in Perú, but leave time to get used to the altitude.

SURINAME: At the indoor market in Paramaribo, sellers greet buyers in Dutch, Hindi, Sranang Tongo, Chinese, and Javanese. It is the linguistic chorus of a nation whose citizens hail from around the world. In the same market, you will find a variety of imported merchandise from those foreign shores, from Javanese bamboo and Indonesian batik prints to Indian saris and Dutch cheeses.

But this is also the central market source for local crafts made by the skilled hands of the Bushnegroes, descendants of the 17th- and 18th-century slaves, whose own African roots are reflected in their arts. Their finest work is woodcarving, and geometric designs cover tabletops, wall panels, stools, water containers, shields, and paddles. These items are less expensive when purchased in the local village markets along the banks of the jungle rivers, but if you're not going into the interior, you'll find the quality in the capital just as good.

Also locally made — and to be watched for — are native necklaces of seeds and kernels; bauxite jewelry; carefully woven straw baskets and mats; and the Suriname square nickel coins, which are mounted for charm bracelets.

VENEZUELA: When compared to many other countries on the continent, Venezuela is not a place where the serious handicrafts collector will be happiest. However, a representative selection of what is made — ceramics, baskets, pottery, and woolens — is housed in Caracas at the Artesanía Venezolana. The blankets, rugs, *ruanas,* and ceramics generally come from the highland regions; from the western area, you will find sisal products, seed necklaces, woodcarvings, and finely woven hammocks.

Venezuela shares the traditional Diablada ceremonies with Perú and Bolivia, and the home for this annual event on Corpus Christi Day is San Francisco de Yare. In June, the villagers dress as little Lucifers and dance in the streets, wearing grotesque masks that are intricately carved and exuberantly decorated. Masks can be purchased at the little shops in town or sometimes in the craftspeople's homes.

Food and Drink

 Few Americans have sampled authentic South American cuisine in the US. Each country has its specialities, which vary from region to region. Depending upon the ethnic background(s) of the people and upon the crops, tastes range from bland to hellishly hot.

Most Americans already know that Argentina has as many cows as Texas. A natural — and correct — assumption, then, is that Argentines eat a lot of beef. Don't pass up any opportunity to attend an Argentine *asado* (outdoor barbecue), at which the entire cow is roasted in the hide and literally everything but the hide gets eaten. Should you have any nonreligious prejudices about which animals or which parts of the animal are edible, put them aside and try everything once. You will be pleasantly surprised more often than not.

A favorite restaurant meal is the *parillada mixta* (mixed grill), consisting of steak, *chorizo* (spicy pork sausage), *morcilla* (blood sausage), and *mollejas* (sweetbreads). This last is especially worth trying. So is *bife a caballo* (beef on horseback) — a fried egg "riding" atop a steak. The plate may be garnished with *papas fritas* (french fries) or with slices of lettuce, tomato, onion, ham, and fried bananas.

Argentines are also fond of lamb and chicken, whether baked, roasted, broiled, or in stews (*pucheros*). *Pucheros* can have a corn, bean, or potato base, to which sausages and cuts of meat or chicken are added. A *puchero* is often a meal in itself.

Argentina produces quality wines. By all means sample any variety not readily available back home. Exercise some caution when you try *grappa,* a potent grape brandy brought over by the Italians.

South American coffee is excellent but strong. You can get *café americano* (American-style coffee) or Nescafé in the larger cities should you desire a weaker variety, one that does not keep you going all day. The national drink of Argentina, however, is *yerba maté,* a somewhat bitter herbal tea. Go easy on it at first. *Maté* has been known to give even the gauchos a mild case of *turista.* In spite of this minor inconvenience, *maté* is an acquired taste for many. It is not, as some advertisements suggest, an aphrodisiac.

Uruguay and southern Brazil are also beef-producing regions. Menus here are similar to Argentina's, although there are a few regional dishes not found elsewhere. In Uruguay, order a *carbonada,* a dish made with rice and fruit — usually raisins, pears, and peaches. The inhabitants of these areas also drink *maté* and *grappa.*

In Chile, the beef is of a slightly inferior quality but still worth ordering. When you tire of *churrascos* (braised beef), try a famous Chilean *empanada* (pastry turnover), filled with ground beef, eggs, olives, and spices, or a *pastel de choclo* (corn pie), a meal similar to shepherd's pie with a flavorful corn mush replacing the mashed potatoes.

If you prefer seafood, Chilean menus offer great variety. *Chupe de mariscos* (seafood stew) is a favorite. The thin broth is full of *camarones* (shrimp), *langostinos* (crayfish), *jaibas* (crabs), *almejas* (mussels), whatever fresh fish is available, and chunks of potato and *choclo* (corn on the cob). In many port towns you can wander down to the docks to sample the latest catch, raw, with a few squirts of lemon juice to enhance the flavor. *Erizos* (sea urchins) are particularly in demand. If *caldillo de congrio* (conger eel soup) sounds too adventurous, choose a dish made from the more conventional *corvina* (sea bass).

Chileans and Argentines observe teatime (*té completo* in Argentina, *onces* in Chile) should your sweet tooth crave *galletas* (cookies) and *pasteles* (pastries). Little round cakes called *alfajores* are considered the national dessert of Chile.

While Chilean beer is good, be sure to try the excellent wines, the best in South America. Red and white varieties are of equally high quality. Undurraga and Macul are among the best labels.

In the countries to the north, different ethnic groups — Indian, African, Chinese, Dutch, Indonesian, and French — have made significant contributions to their respective national cuisines. Dishes in the north tend to be spicier (hotter) than those in the south. If past experience has told you that you cannot handle lots of chili pepper, now is the time to learn the important phrase *"No muy picante, por favor"* ("Not too hot, please").

Indian and African dishes tend to be both hot and starchy, with lots of beans, potatoes, rice, and corn. They are also interesting and not to be overlooked. The Andean Indians know more ways to serve potatoes than anyone else in the world. *Chuño,* a boiled dinner of *chuño* (black balls of dehydrated potato), eggs, meat or fish, and cheese is perhaps one of the more intriguing.

Since Bolivia is landlocked, fish is not abundant, but chicken and beef usually are. In Copacabana and other towns along Lake Titicaca, you can get freshly caught *trucha* (trout). Giant frog's legs from the lake are exported to France. Try a *picante de pollo* (chicken in *ají,* a very strong chili). Bolivians snack on *empanadas salteñas,* spicy pastry turnovers of beef, eggs, olives, peas, potatos, onions, and peppers. In La Paz try a *plato paceño* (the La Paz plate), a meal of corn, potatoes, beans, and cheese guaranteed to fill you for the rest of the day. For curiosity, sample a glass of *chicha blanca* (white *chicha*), the home brew made from sugarcane. This potent drink accompanies every Indian festival from birth through death. It is not served in better restaurants.

In Perú there is also a nonalcoholic *chicha morada* (purple *chicha*) made from maize. Be sure to specify which *chicha* you want or you could be unpleasantly surprised. Perú also produces a soft drink called, of all things, Inca Kola. It is touted as having *el sabor nacional* (the national flavor). It has a yellowish color and a distinctive taste you will not confuse with anything else.

Perú has perhaps the most varied cuisine in South America. *Cebiche* (fish soaked in a spicy lemon marinade) and *anticuchos* (marinated, grilled beef hearts, livers, or whatever) are both a must. Peruvians know how to prepare fish literally hundreds of ways, all delicious. *Corvina* is the most common fish, either stuffed with seafood (*almejas, choros, machos*), smothered in a sauce, or both. *Ocopa* (boiled potatoes or eggs in a spicy, condensed milk sauce) and *ají de gallina* (shredded chicken in a chili and cheese sauce) are two hot items (*muy picante*) to try. Try anything prepared *a la chiclayana;* the cuisine of the Chiclayo region is generally acknowledged to be the best in Perú. *Chifas* are Chinese restaurants, and Lima has some of the best outside Asia. Don't be disappointed if the dish you order is not exactly what you are used to. Chinese food in Perú has not been Westernized to the extent that it has in the US, and it is actually more authentic. For the cocktail hour, *pisco* sours are an absolute must. *Pisco* (grape brandy) is also used in the popular *chilcanos* (with ginger ale) and *algarrobinas* (with carob syrup).

Quechua Indian dishes are rarely found in tourist restaurants. If you come across them, try *tacu-tacu* (mashed rice and garbanzo patties), *cau-cau* (spiced tripe, potatoes, peppers, and rice), or *cuy* (guinea pig).

In Ecuador the national drink is nonalcoholic. Start your day with a glass of frothy *naranjilla* (green oranges) juice — it's indescribably delicious. Indeed, the availability of fresh tropical fruits is one of the greatest pleasures of South American eating. Papayas, mangoes, *guanábanas* (custard apple), *lúcuma* (egg fruit), and many, many more are served all over South America in one form or another. *Dulce de membrillo* (quince sweet) and *pasta de guayaba* (guava paste) are frequent dessert items, best eaten with a piece of white cheese to balance the almost excessive sweetness of the fruit jelly.

While in Ecuador, sample *humitas* (similar to Mexican tamales), *locro* (a corn or potato and cheese soup, sometimes served with avocado), or the popular *llapingachos* (an omelette of cheese and fried potatoes with an egg on top). *Cebiche* is as common here as in Perú, but the spices in the Ecuadorian version are slightly different.

Fish is abundant in Colombia as well, but residents tend to prefer meat and chicken. *Arroz con pollo* (chicken with rice) is found on most menus. Be sure to try a *piquete* (meat, potatoes, and vegetables in *ají*). Two hearty soups are the *cuchuco* (a thick barley and meat soup seasoned with peppercorns) and *mazamorra* (a similar soup thickened with a pap of ground maize). (To add to the confusion, in Perú *mazamorra* is a dessert made with the same maize pap and fruit.) No Colombian goes through a day without *arepas* (a corn-meal pancake often eaten in place of bread) or that great Colombian coffee. The local brew is called *aguardiente* (literally, "fire water") and should be approached with caution.

Neighboring Venezuela serves the sweeter and milder *ponche crema* (egg nog) all year. You do not have to wait until Christmas to drink it. Sweeter still is the dessert with the catchy name *bien me sabe* (it tastes good to me), made from coconut custard on cake and topped with meringue. Although Caracas is one of the most Americanized cities in South America, its menus rarely resemble ours. Try *mondongo* (tripe with lots of vegetables). Order a *sancocho* (meat stew with squash, sweet potatoes, and plantain) or a *pastel de maracay* (a turtle meat pie). Other favorites are *pabellón criollo* (shredded beef in spiced tomato sauce served with fried bananas, white rice, and black beans) and *cazuela de mariscos* (similar to Chilean *chupe de mariscos*).

In Brazil, Portuguese and African dishes will replace the Spanish and Indian meals of the other countries. The black influence is strongest in the region around Salvador (Bahía). One of the local specialties is *vatapá*, a peppery fish or chicken and shrimp stew seasoned with coconut milk, peanut and palm oils and served with manioc or rice powder. The Brazilian national dish, *feijoada*, carried to its ultimate complexity, can have some 20 or more different kinds of sausage and cuts of meat — tongue, pig's feet, or *chorizo* (sausage) — added to a black bean soup that is also served with the ever-present manioc powder. Be warned that a spoonful of moist manioc powder sticks to the roof of your mouth like peanut butter. (Best mix it in with the *feijoada*.) The variety of spicy sauces is what makes a *picadinha* (hash) worth ordering. The *comidas criollas* (Creole cooking) are Portuguese in origin and tend to be bland. A *cozido* (stew) is a transplanted Portuguese dish of boiled meat and vegetables. It is identical to the *cocido* found in the Spanish-speaking countries.

Wash down your meal with *cachaça* (home-made whiskey) if you dare, but no Brazilian considers a meal complete without a *cafezinho*, a demitasse of pure coffee extract almost strong enough to stand your spoon in. These are served in coffee bars, where you drink standing up. Brazilian beer is perhaps the best in South America, but Brazilians drink a lot of *batidas*, a potent drink of *cachaça* and fruit juice. One of the best is a *caipirinha* — *cachaça*, sugar, and lime. It's very potent. In Spanish, *batida* (sometimes *batido*) means an ice cream or fruit shake. (Don't confuse the two.)

In Paraguay, the local moonshine is *caña*, a rum made from sugarcane or honey. The national meal is *so'o-yosopy* (a Guaraní word), a meat soup. Try also *sopa paraguaya* (Paraguayan soup), which is more of a soufflé made from mashed corn, cheese, milk, eggs, and onions. The *surubí* fish is a delicacy prepared in a number of ways.

Paraguay and all the other northern countries have jungle regions. Should you venture off the usual tourist routes, you will be faced with armadillo, snake, monkey, and various other unidentifiable meats. People will tell you that you are eating meat or bird. If it tastes good, don't ask any more. Try any and all of these dishes as long as they are well cooked. Do not watch them roast a monkey on a spit or you may lose your appetite. A jungle diet otherwise consists of fruits and starches (plantain, potatos, rice, lots of yucca and manioc). Tortoise egg omelettes are very good, although the consistency is rather spongy compared to those made with chicken eggs.

The Guianas are usually the least known, most overlooked countries of South America, but dining there can be an amazing experience because of the additional ethnic backgrounds. In French Guiana, old-style French cooking still predominates, while in Guyana you can order roast beef and Yorkshire pudding. Suriname offers a choice of Dutch, Indonesian, and Chinese meals. *Nasi goring* or *bami goring* (rice or noodles tossed with various cuts of meat) are both Indonesian in origin. All three countries offer some native Indian or black dishes as well.

The capitals and a few of the larger cities have restaurants that serve international cuisine. This usually means French or Italian dishes, but occasionally you can find German, Japanese, Greek, and other foreign establishments as well. Imported vodkas, gins, and whiskeys are served in all the better bars, but they are very expensive. Why not enjoy what is uniquely South American instead?

You will not have any unpleasant experiences with food or drink if you follow a few simple rules. The water supplies in the larger cities are fairly safe, but when in doubt, remember the two B's: boiled or bottled. Peel fruits before eating them, and avoid any with severely damaged skin. Anything that has been thoroughly cooked is safe so you need not worry if you find you just ate armadillo stew by mistake. The biggest danger is overeating and drinking too much at the higher altitudes. *Soroche* (mountain fever) is not fatal unless you suffer from severe heart problems, but no one will be able to convince you otherwise when you are feeling its effects. To help avoid *soroche,* eat *very* lightly your first day or two in the mountains. Tea and toast or chicken broth is highly recommended. Do not drink anything alcoholic unless you want to be higher than the Andes themselves. One *pisco* sour in Cuzco will have the same effect as three or four in Lima. After a day or two of taking it easy, you should be able to eat normally with no side effects. But always take care with alcohol.

We have included information on specific restaurants in the *Best in Town* section of each city report in THE CITIES. As South Americans say before a meal, *Buen provecho!* (May it benefit you!)

THE CITIES

ASUNCIÓN

The capital of Paraguay is one of the best-kept tourist secrets in South America. With a population of 650,000 — one-fifth the national total — Asunción is small, clean, and provincial enough to have retained the charm of a South American colonial town, yet it has all the amenities for the most demanding American tourist.

Life still centers around the plaza with its many flowers, trees, fountains, box camera photographers, shoeshine men with elaborate chairs, lace vendors, and a mixed crowd of businessmen, schoolchildren in white uniforms, and a few Macá Indians. Spending just a few minutes on its four city blocks will give you a feeling of how life used to be in the bigger cities of South America and how it still is in most small cities and towns. Surrounding the plaza are modern government buildings, shops, and restaurants. The most important business here is government, but the city is also a valuable port, and many light industries are on the outer fringe of town. The business section covers about 20 square blocks, but since there are no zoning regulations, the high-rise buildings blend with the low, stucco residential districts. The downtown area is not yet choked with cars and pollution; trolley cars and buses are the main form of municipal transportation. Many flowering trees and palms line the streets. Gardens bloom with giant orchids and poinsettias. Although not a glamorous, exciting metropolis, Asunción's quaintness gives it a subtle appeal.

The people's work habits have evolved in response to the hot, humid climate. With hardly an exception, everyone wakes up early and goes to work before it gets hot. Everything shuts down tight at noon, and siesta is not over until 3 or 4 PM. Shops and some public buildings open again until 6:30 or 7 PM. The siesta is responsible for Asunción's four rush hours rather than the usual two. At 7 AM and noon, and again at 3:30 and 7 PM, the streets are jammed with cars and buses. Since everyone has a siesta, people dine late and generally don't go to bed until well past midnight, when it finally begins to cool off.

Situated on a series of seven small, rolling hills on the east bank of the Río Paraguay, part of the Río de la Plata system that flows into the Atlantic at Buenos Aires, Asunción is practically in the center of South America, nearly equidistant from the Atlantic and the Andes. The city stands at an altitude of about 250 feet and covers about 45 square miles. Paraguay itself is about the same size as Montana, covering 150,000 square miles of rugged scrubland and jungle. Because it is remote and quite undeveloped, it is often called the last frontier of the Americas (see *Paraguay*, DIRECTIONS).

The first permanent settlement in southern South America, Asunción was founded in 1537 by Spanish explorers seeking lost cities paved with gold. They named it Nuestra Señora Santa María de la Asunción (Our Lady Saint Mary of the Ascension). The early Spanish settlers mixed readily with the native Guaraní Indians, and even today, most of the city's population is of mixed background and is bilingual in Spanish and Guaraní. Two years after its founding — still more than 60 years before Captain John Smith sailed up the James River in Virginia — Spain designated Asunción as the capital of its entire southern South American empire.

Independence was granted in 1811 without violence. The Spanish government was replaced by a supreme junta headed by a supreme dictator, José Gaspar Rodríguez de Francia. Despite his autocratic title, Rodríguez held Paraguay together peacefully for the first 20 years. But the country has known much turmoil and war. In the course of two major wars, the country twice lost more than half of its adult male population. In the 1860s it put up a gallant fight against Brazil, Uruguay, and Argentina in the War of the Triple Alliance. In that war, Paraguay's greatest hero, Marshal Francisco Solano López, died with his Irish mistress at his side in a decisive battle near the border of present Brazil. In the 1930s, the country fought Bolivia in a stalemate war in the inhospitable Chaco region of western Paraguay. To this day, women outnumber men in Paraguay, and male visitors generally find that it's not too difficult to socialize with members of the opposite sex. It is the aggressive woman who usually gets her man. True, until recently respectable single women were never seen out in the evening without a chaperone. But times have changed, and single women now go out alone or in groups without fear of social stigma or harassment.

Asunción is one of the safest cities in the world, day or night, thanks to the warmth and friendliness of its residents. Progress takes the form of paved streets and relatively modern American and European cars. These indicators of the twentieth century have been among the positive factors attributable to the reign of President Alfredo Stroessner, Paraguay's supreme dictator in fact if not in actual title. He has been in power since 1954, and posters lining the streets of Asunción laud: "Peace, work, and well-being with Stroessner." But human rights organizations claim that many people have disappeared or are reported dead after forcible arrest by Paraguayan authorities. In response to such criticism, President Stroessner called human rights "a Trojan horse of international communism." Despite continuing political pressure from the US administrations, Asunción residents tend to be kindly disposed toward Americans. The American community numbers about 1,000, most of whom are embassy personnel and Protestant missionaries of various denominations.

And speaking of various denominations, money flows freely in Asunción's *casas de cambio* (exchange houses), where you can obtain greenbacks for your traveler's checks, if you wish. The exchange houses will probably even take your personal check. Change your money at the *casas de cambio* rather than at the bank or your hotel, for they offer several more *guaranís* (600 guaranis = $1 US at press time) for your dollar, and it is all legal. If you are going on to Brazil, you can also pick up some *cruzados* here. Asunción is full of Brazilian tourists who fill up the *casas* with *cruzados,* so they are only too glad to have you take some off their hands, especially if you have dollar traveler's checks.

And one more thing: Bring your bathing suit for a swim in a hotel pool. Asunción is hot, hot, hot, except during the winter months of June, July, and August, when it is only somewhat cooler.

ASUNCIÓN AT-A-GLANCE

SEEING THE CITY: The best place to start your tour of Asunción is at the top of the *Hotel Guaraní* on the main plaza. From the 13th-floor lookout, you can see most of the city and Río Paraguay beyond. It is not difficult to imagine why the first settlers chose this high spot as the location for Asunción, with its natural vantage point over the low-lying flatland bordering the river to the north and south of the city. Take the elevator at the rear of the hotel to reach the 13th floor, which has an outdoor walkway completely around the building. At times, this floor is used for private receptions and may be closed to the public, but if you speak to the man behind the reception desk, he will probably have the door at the top unlocked for you.

SPECIAL PLACES: You can see almost all the special places in Asunción on a walking tour beginning at the main plaza. The downtown streets are laid out in a neat and orderly grid. As you stand in front of the *Hotel Guaraní* with the main plaza in front of you, you are on Calle Oliva. The next street down, crossing the heart of the plaza, is Calle Estrella, and the street at the bottom of the plaza is Calle Palma. Oliva, Estrella, and Palma — the olive, the star, and the palm — are the three symbols on the Paraguayan flag. The official title of the upper two square blocks of the plaza is the Plaza de la Independencia and the lower two blocks is the Plaza de los Héroes. However, local folks refer to the whole place as the main plaza and so will we.

The Pantheon (El Panteón) – In the lower corner of the main plaza sits the Pantheon where Paraguay's military heroes lie enshrined. It is a replica of Les Invalides, Napoleon's tomb in Paris. As you pass the smartly uniformed guards beneath the pillars, you enter a large rotunda. Below, in the center, is the tomb of the unknown soldier, commemorating the many Paraguayans who gave their lives for their country. On all sides are vaults containing the remains of national heroes, including Francisco Solano López, hero of the Triple Alliance War, and José Félix Estigarribia, hero of the Chaco War. On the upper walls are numerous plaques, gifts of friendly foreign governments. At the far side of the rotunda is a statue of the Virgin Mary, patron saint of Asunción. It is said that she holds the rank of marshal in the Paraguayan army. Open daily from 6 AM until 6 PM. No admission charge. At the main plaza, corner of Calle Palma and Calle Chile.

Independence House (Casa de la Independencia) – Here the Paraguayan revolutionaries plotted to overthrow the Spanish in 1811. Independence House is one of the few authentic colonial buildings still standing, and it has recently been fully restored. Be sure to visit the room at the back, where the revolutionaries declared independence on the night of May 14, 1811. Open from 7:30 to 11:30 AM and from 3 to 6 PM except on Saturday afternoons. Closed Sundays. No admission charge. Calle 14 de Mayo just below Calle Palma.

The Port – For centuries before a road connected Asunción with Brazil, Asunción was literally Paraguay's lifeline to the rest of the world. Here oceangoing freighters dock to unload manufactured goods and to load Paraguay's agricultural surplus: cotton, soybeans, tobacco, wood, and meat products. The port is also the point of embarkation for overnight river cruises or the 4-day trip to Buenos Aires. There are, however, no short boat tours of the Bay of Asunción and the adjoining river. To reach the port, walk through the Customs Building, across the street at the end of Calle Colón, onto the dock. In front of you is the Bay of Asunción. Río Paraguay lies out of sight behind a peninsula that forms the far shore of the bay.

The Government Palace (Palacio del Gobierno) – If you see what looks like a whole truckload of soldiers in front of the Government Palace, you can be sure the president is at his desk. If you only see one or two guards around, you can be sure the president is elsewhere. The palace was constructed more than 100 years ago for Francisco Solano López by his father and was intended to be his private residence, but the Triple Alliance War intervened, costing young López his life. The building became the offices of the president and the Ministry of Foreign Affairs. Open Mondays through Fridays 8 AM to noon and Saturdays 8 to 10 AM. Free. Calle El Paraguayo Independiente between Calle 15 de Agosto and Calle O'Leary.

Constitution Square (Plaza Constitución) – The city's original plaza is almost on the waterfront, just down Calle Palma from the Pantheon. Take a seat on one of the plaza's gaily colored bleachers and just let the world go by. The plaza is surrounded by important buildings and contains several statues in honor of Paraguay's heroes. But by far the most interesting item is the small tank that was captured from the Bolivians during the Chaco War in the 1930s. As you face the river, the Legislative Palace lies in front of you, the former military school is to your left, the cathedral to your right. Behind you are the main post office and police headquarters. On the low land between the plaza and the river, notice the amusement park — you can hardly miss it with the super slide rising out of the mud behind the Legislative Palace. This area, called Chacarita, is where the poor people live, but it is by no means a slum. Asunción's relatively small population of 650,000, aided by migration to Brazil and Argentina and the government's successful voluntary rural colonization schemes, have helped to prevent the growth of slums that plague so many South American capitals. Plaza Constitución covers the two-block area between Calle Chile and Calle Independencia Nacional on the river.

The Cathedral (Catedral) – The Catholic metropolitan cathedral is neither exceptionally large nor ornate by Latin American standards. Built in the 19th century, it is rather plain inside. Of note is the intricate carving of the altar, which contrasts with the edifice itself. Most people who attend church go to neighborhood churches scattered around the city. While there is complete freedom of religion and many Protestant churches in Asunción, the overwhelming majority of Paraguayans are at least nominally Roman Catholic. Open daily. Free. Calle Independencia Nacional and Calle Coronel Bogado.

The Ethnological and Archaeological Museum (Museo Etnológico y Arqueológico) – If you want to know more about the Indians who roamed Paraguay before the Europeans colonized it, this museum has excellent collections of Indian artifacts and historical exhibits. The Guaraní dominated an area far greater than today's Paraguay. Iguazú and Itaipú are two of many Guaraní Indian words in use today. (The Guaraní words are easy to recognize, as the accent is usually on the last syllable.) The museum also has an excellent library. Open Mondays through Saturdays 8 to 11 AM and Wednesdays 3 to 6 PM. Closed Sundays. Calle España 217. It's about a 15-minute walk from the main plaza or a quick trip on the Las Mercedes trolley line (phone: 20-575).

Villa Morra – Asunción is not quite large enough to have suburbs as we think of them, but it does have interesting neighborhoods. To see Villa Morra, the best of these, take the Villa Morra trolley along Avenida Mariscal López. The street is lined with homes of some of Asunción's finest families interspersed with embassies. At the crest of the hill of this *jacarandá* tree–lined avenue, about a dozen blocks from its start, is the Department of Defense (Departmento de Defensa), which houses the Military and History Museum (Museo Militario y Histórico). On the right a few blocks farther on is the US Embassy, at the corner of Avenida Kubitschek and Avenida Mariscal López. In the middle of the next block on the right, behind the big fence and all the shrubbery, is the president's residence. A bit farther is the imposing edifice of the embassy of Japan, also on the right, followed shortly by the Recoleta Church and Cemetery. You will soon reach Avenida Argentina, where you may wish to turn around and head back to the city center. Before you start back, try a visit to a Paraguayan supermarket, with products from all over the world crammed into a small, air-conditioned building. *Supermercado Villa Morra* is on Avenida Argentina just two blocks to the right of Avenida Mariscal López. The trolley goes right by the door. Next door is the *Amandau* ice cream parlor. The ice cream is excellent, and there are several flavors you may never have tasted, such as prune and chocolate bariloche, a delicious chocolate with raisins.

The Recoleta Church and Cemetery (Iglesia Recoleta y Cementerio) – Here the well-to-do bury their dead, though, in fact, the dead remain aboveground in caskets on the shelves of each family's mausoleum. You may wander freely among the mausoleums, many as large as small houses. On All Saints' Day, November 1, and other religious holidays, thousands of people descend on the cemetery. Wealthy residents arrive early with folding lawn chairs, throw open the doors and windows of the mausoleums, and sit and fan themselves as the mourners stream past. Immediately to the left of the church is the memorial to Madame Lynch, Francisco Solano López's Irish mistress. There are also many modest gravesites with simple tombstones. In front of the Recoleta Church is a flower market, where the mourners purchase small bouquets to place in vases before the mausoleums. Open daily. Free. Av. Santísimo Sacramento and Av. Mariscal López. Take the Villa Morra trolley, only a 10-minute ride from downtown.

The Botanical Garden (Jardín Botánico) – If the old saying "getting there is half the fun" has any truth, here is the proof. Asunción's Botanical Gardens are a somewhat rundown park sprawling over many acres, with two museums, a zoo, stables, and a golf course. Taken all together, it makes a visit worthwhile, but the chief attraction is getting there — if you can catch the train. The old wood burner leaves from the station on the Plaza Uruguaya near the city center for the Botanical Gardens and points south Mondays, Wednesdays, and Fridays at 1 PM, Paraguayan time (*muy* flexible). You can take a taxi or bus back. Check the train schedule before you set out (phone: 46-789). Open daily. Small admission charge. At the corner of Av. General Artigas and Av. Santísimo Sacramento in the Trinidad neighborhood.

The Macá Indians – A tour of the Macá Indian village — on an island in the Paraguay River not far from Asunción — can be arranged through any local tourist agency. These Indians never integrated with the Guaranís, and you will see them selling their wares on the main plaza. They are wise to tourists, and you will have to pay if you want to snap pictures. (The women quickly remove their blouses when tourists approach to get a better price when they pose, so that pictures you may see of them bare-breasted don't reflect the customs of the tribe.)

■**EXTRA SPECIAL:** The estate where Marshal López kept his mistress, Eliza Lynch, is now the *Gran Hotel del Paraguay*. The old estate, with its lush gardens and tropical vegetation, remains much as it must have been 100 years ago. The dining room with its hand-painted ceiling was the madame's theater. In the garden behind the hotel is a small zoo with native species, including monkeys and large parrots. Calle de la Residencia and Calle Triunvirato, about a 15-minute walk from the city center.

SOURCES AND RESOURCES

 TOURIST INFORMATION: For general information and tours, your best bet is Inter-Express, a tourist agency whose personnel speak English and which offers a fleet of buses and private cars with drivers. Inter-Express can arrange tours of the city and its environs, as well as of neighboring Brazil and Argentina. Yegros 690 (phone 90-111/12/13/14/15). At the government's National Tourism Office, on the ground floor at the corner of Calle Oliva and Calle Alberdi, you may find some useful information on current and upcoming events, but rarely is there anyone in attendance who speaks English.

Land of Lace and Legend (American Women's Club of Asunción; $2.75) is the best guide in English to the city and the country. Copies may be obtained by writing to Las Amigas Norteamericanas del Paraguay, c/o Embajada Americana, Av. Mariscal López 1776, Asunción. Enclose a check for $3.25, which includes the cost of postage, payable to Las Amigas Norteamericanas del Paraguay. In Asunción, you can buy it at *Librería Hotel Guaraní,* in the galería, *Hotel Guaraní; Librería Universal,* Calle Palma 519; and at the International Airport magazine and book stand. Or call the American Embassy (phone: 201-041/9).

Local Coverage – The *Buenos Aires Herald* and the *Brazil Herald* are the only English-language newspapers available in Asunción. You can pick them up, along with the fortnightly English magazine *Guaraní News,* one day after publication at major newspaper stands (for example, those at the corner of Chile and Estrella, the *Guaraní* hotel, and the airport.

The municipality of Asunción puts out an adequate city map, which (when it is not out of print) is available at most stationery stores, called *librerías. Land of Lace and Legend* contains two maps of the city, one with a key to major points of interest.

Food – There is no food guide to Asunción in English. Paraguayan food consists of beef, beef, and more beef. Meals usually include the indigenous soup — *sopa Paraguaya* — a tasty variation of cornbread mash.

 CLIMATE AND CLOTHES: Asunción is hot except during the winter, June through August, when the weather is warm, though winter temperatures may dip into the low 50s F (around 10°C) during a cold snap. It is also rather humid, so light clothes and air-conditioned hotel rooms are recommended. Evenings are delightful, and much evening dining and entertainment takes place under the stars.

GETTING AROUND: Bus – Virtually everything downtown is close enough to walk to. Avoid the buses if you can.

Taxi – For trips outside the city center, taxis are available at taxi stands. Cabdrivers do not cruise the streets in their aging US-made gas guzzlers with the price of gasoline over $2 a gallon. Considering the cost of fuel, the price of a cab ride as listed on the meter plus a small tip is not expensive.

Car Rental – If you want to drive, try *Rent-a-Car,* Calle Palma 503 (phone: 92-731/33).

Trolley – Trolleys are fun to ride and cost only a dime or so. There are two lines: One runs along Calle España to Las Mercedes suburb; the other runs along Avenida Mariscal López past the embassies to Villa Morra suburb (see *Special Places*). Avoid the trolleys during rush hours. Unfortunately, they do not run in the evenings, Saturday afternoons, Sundays, or when it rains.

MUSEUMS: Independence House (Casa Independencia) and the Ethnological and Archaeological Museum (Museo Etnológico y Arqueológico) are described in *Special Places*. Other museums of interest include:

Military and Historical Museum (Museo Militar y Histórico) – Ministerio de Defensa, Av. Mariscal López and Calle General Santos.

National Museum of Art (Museo Nacional de Bellas Artes) – Calle Mariscal Estigarribia and Calle Iturbe (phone: 91-208).

Archbishop Monsignor Juan S. Bogarin Museum of Paraguayan History (Museo Bogarin) – Metropolitan Seminary, Calle Kubitschek and Calle Azara (phone: 200-723).

SHOPPING: Asunción is tops for special souvenirs. Paraguayan lace is beautiful, lightweight, and fits easily into even overloaded suitcases. Craftspeople make rainbow-hued spiderweb lace called *ñandutí* into beautiful doilies, placemats, tablecloths, coasters, and other household items. Just as popular is *Aó Po'i*, embroidery work done on cotton cloth that is made into shirts, blouses, dresses, tablecloths, napkins, neckties, and breadwarmers. These items wash well and will not fade, though they may require ironing. There are also locally made leather items and straw and rattan goods as well as pottery and ceramics. But nothing compares with the lace. If you take home a dozen *ñandutí* doilies and half a dozen *Aó Po'i* breadwarmers, you will not regret it. You will never see the likes of it elsewhere, and the prices are low, especially for handmade goods. If you have the opportunity, visit the town of Itagua, 30 minutes from Asunción, where much of the lace is made.

In Asunción, several shops along Calle Colón near the port carry a wide assortment of *ñandutí* and *Aó Po'i*. You can also make your purchases at the airport, where prices are only slightly higher, or from itinerant merchants at the main plaza.

Confecciones Catedral is the best store of all. Here, you can have a shirt or blouse made to order in 24 hours if you don't see anything that strikes your fancy. Three blocks from the main plaza at Calle Presidente Eligio Ayala 189.

SPECIAL EVENTS: Religious processions are held on *Good Friday* and on August 15, the anniversary of the founding of the city; check locally for details if you are there on either date. June 24 is *St. John's Day,* commemorating the patron saint of fire. On the evening of June 23, bonfires are built and barefoot men and some women run across the hot bed of coals when the fire burns down. This ritual takes place at many locations; check locally. July and August are folk festival months, when many concerts, exhibits, and parades are held in towns in the interior. On September 21, the spring festival is celebrated with a parade and flowers everywhere. The most special event is December 8 (*Feast of the Immaculate Conception*); on this day it seems as though the whole city walks or rides (the president flies by helicopter) 30 miles (48 km) to the shrine at Caacupé. Thousands go on foot, leaving after work on the seventh, arriving in Caacupé about sunrise, in time for the first mass at the large church with the blue Virgin over the altar.

SPORTS: Fishing – The fishing in the Río Paraguay and its tributaries is excellent. The problem is getting there. The only area developed for fishing is at Villa Florida, on the road to Encarnación, a 2-hour drive from Asunción. See the tourist agencies for more information.

Gambling – There's a complete gambling casino that's open 7 nights a week at the *Itá Enramada* hotel, Calle Cacique Lambaré and Rivera del Río Paraguay (phone: 33-041/9).

Golf – Asunción has two golf courses: the 18-hole *Asunción Golf Club* at the Botanic Garden, and the 9-hole *Yacht y Golf Club Paraguayo* in the suburb of Lambaré.

Hunting – Hunting has been temporarily outlawed in Paraguay because of overhunting in the recent past.

Soccer – Soccer is the national sport year-round — people passionately play, watch, and follow the game on the radio. Professional soccer matches take place every Sunday afternoon. If you are going on to Brazil, Uruguay, or Argentina, you may want to wait until you get there to see soccer at its very best.

Tennis – If you want to play tennis, stay at the *Itá Enramada* hotel, which has several good lighted clay courts.

 THEATER: Several theater companies perform at the *Asunción Municipal Theater (Teatro Municipal), Teatro Arlequin,* and *Teatro de las Americas.* Check the newspapers to see what's playing, if anything. Most presentations are in Spanish; the rest, in Guaraní.

 MUSIC: Don't miss the Paraguayan folk music. You can hear it live over dinner at many fine restaurants. Typically, groups of three — two guitarists and a harpist — sing in Spanish and Guaraní. A record of Paraguayan folk music makes a nice souvenir; they're available at all record stores and at the airport.

 NIGHTCLUBS AND NIGHTLIFE: Asunción's nightlife consists mostly of shows at restaurants that go past midnight (see *Best in Town,* below). There is a nightclub with dancing and entertainment at the gambling casino at the *Boite "Yasy"* of the *Itá Enramada* hotel. The "in" place for the younger crowd is the *Caracol Discotèque,* about 20 minutes from downtown on the road to Itá Enramada.

 SINS: Hugh Hefner's old-fashioned "Look, but don't touch" rule does not apply at Asunción's *Playboy Club.* Needless to say, it's got nothing to do with the magazine empire, and you won't need a key to get in. But if you are not really looking for some action, perhaps it's better to stay away. Open every night. Calle Catorce de Mayo and Calle Oliva. Helpful hint or fair warning: The difference between a bar and a *whiskería* is that ladies of the evening frequent the latter.

BEST IN TOWN

 CHECKING IN: There is a wide range, but limited choice, of hotels in Asunción, from the out-of-town *Itá Enramada* hotel to family-style *pensiones.* All entries have air-conditioned rooms with private baths. Hotel prices are relatively modest in Asunción. Expect to pay up to $100 for a double in those places listed as expensive; between $30 and $50 in those hotels in the moderate category; and under $20 (and as little as $12) in inexpensive hostelries.

Itá Enramada – This is Paraguay's outstanding hotel, set on 15 sprawling acres on the banks of the Río Paraguay, about 15 minutes south of the city. Facilities include a gambling casino, nightclub, bar, restaurant, coffee shop, sauna, tennis courts, playground, and two gorgeous swimming pools. There are 150 rooms, each with a direct-dial phone, color TV, and wet bar. The drawback is the distance from downtown, but free shuttle buses go back and forth to the *Chaco* hotel downtown at regular intervals. Calle Cacique Lambaré and Ribera del Río Paraguay (phone: 33-041/49). Expensive.

Yacht y Golf Club Paraguayo – Asunción's newest, modern resort hotel, just outside of town near the *Itá Enramada* on the shores of the Paraguay River. Rooms range from comfortable doubles to deluxe suites. There is a dining room, the *Salon Verde,* and a 9-hole golf course. 15 minutes from town in the suburb of Lambaré (phone: 36-117 to 135). Expensive.

Chaco – Among the newer hotels, run by the same people who run the *Itá Enramada.* The *Chaco* has a fine reputation, based on its excellent restaurant and outstanding service. It must be doing something right since it is always full and reservations are a must. The rooms and indoor swimming pool are small. Everything looks quite modern. Av. Mariscal Estigarribia and Calle Caballero (phone: 92-066). Expensive.

Excelsior – A new and very good 123-room hotel, with a pool and a good restaurant. Chile 980 (phone: 95-632). Expensive.

Cecilia – A well-recommended, reasonable hotel, with a popular restaurant. Estados Unidos 341 (phone: 91-271). Moderate.

Guaraní – This imposing, 13-story structure, with its angular lines, dominates the plaza. Recently totally renovated and reopened under new management, it can be counted on for a comfortable stay. Visiting chiefs of state always stay at this government-run hotel. With rooms somewhat larger than those of the *Chaco,* it also has a restaurant and swimming pool. Reservations are required. Calle Oliva and Calle Independencia Nacional (phone: 91-131). Moderate.

Gran Hotel del Paraguay – If you want to relive Asunción's past — and get away from modern, boxlike hotel rooms — this is for you. This was Madame Lynch's home 100 years ago. It is surrounded by beautiful grounds, an outdoor pool, and even a mini-zoo with wild animals and birds native to Paraguay. It is about 1 mile from the downtown area — guests can walk or take a trolley or taxi. Calle de la Residencia and Calle Triunvirato (phone: 203-981). Moderate.

Paraná – Just up the street from the *Chaco,* it is similar, but somewhat drab. If the *Chaco*'s full, try this place. No pool. No reservations needed. Calle Caballero and Calle Veinticinco de Mayo (phone: 44-543). Moderate.

Pension Lapacho – The translation of *pension* is usually "boarding house," which would be an injustice to this place. The *Lapacho* is a house in a residential neighborhood with a dining room, patio, pool, garden, lots of grass, and some 15 air-conditioned rooms. There are two rates: one with complete board and one without it. Reservations are a must. Many Americans stay here, as it is close to the US Embassy. Especially recommended for visitors with children, it is about 15 minutes from downtown just off Av. Mariscal López where the Villa Morra trolley passes. Av. Kubitschek 158 (phone: 20-721). Inexpensive.

EATING OUT: Paraguayans eat late, often under the stars, and with live entertainment. All restaurants are open every day, except where noted. The restaurants with shows do not start serving dinner before 9 PM; shows start at 10 PM. Other restaurants serve dinner from about 7 PM. Lunch counters are an option for those who prefer to eat earlier. An increasing number of the better restaurants are taking Diners Club and American Express credit cards. To pay with a credit card, it is best to check beforehand to make sure it will be accepted. Restaurant prices are reasonable. Expect to pay about $20 at restaurants in our expensive category; between $10 and $18 in the moderate range; under $10 at places classified as inexpensive. Prices are for dinner for two, not including drinks, wine, or tips.

Talleyrand – Considered by many to be Asunción's finest, and probably its most expensive. The food is good; French cuisine is a specialty. The atmosphere is cozy if a bit formal. Reservations a must. Av. Mariscal Estigarribia 932 (phone: 41-163). Expensive.

Tayi Poty – A fine new dining spot in the casino of the *Itá Enramada* that features live music for dancing and typical Paraguayan music daily except Sundays. Calle Cacique Lambaré and Ribera del Río Paraguay (phone: 33-041/9). Expensive.

La Preferida – Typical Paraguayan food, featuring beef and freshwater fish. The decor is plain and there is no entertainment. Reservations recommended in the evening. Calle 25 de Mayo 1005 (phone: 91-126). Expensive.

Hermitage – This is the place to dine under the stars, beside swaying palm trees. The food is good; the show is better. Watch for the bottle dance. Reservations recommended, but if you get there before 9 PM you will very likely be the first to be assured of a table with a good view of the show. Closed Sundays. Calle Quince de Agosto and Calle Primera Proyectada (phone: 41-001). Expensive.

Yguazú – Similar to the *Hermitage* but a bit more of a tourist trap. The food is also better at the *Hermitage*. Furthermore, the amplifiers here are often turned up too high, and it's about 10 minutes by taxi from the city center. Having said all that, this is still a good bet for a first-rate show with your dinner. Dining is outside unless it rains. Reservations recommended. Calle Choferes del Chaco 1334 (phone: 61-008). Expensive.

Gran Hotel del Paraguay – Even if you don't stay in this hotel, at least take the time for a meal in its colonial dining room. Although the usual fare is international cuisine, the curry — the Wednesday night special — is recommended. Entertainment and dancing Wednesday nights as well. Reservations recommended for Wednesday nights only. Calle de la Residenta and Calle Triunvirato (phone: 200-051). Expensive.

Chaco – The restaurant on the second floor of this hotel serves very good international cuisine. Reservations recommended in the evening, unless you arrive early or are staying at the hotel. Av. Mariscal Estigarribia and Calle Caballero (phone: 92-066). Expensive.

Confiteria Imagen – How about a "*Gone With the Wind*" or a "*Grand Prix*" sandwich? Fancy creations with fancy names for a trendy crowd are available at any hour here. This is a good spot for a light lunch or supper or a sweet cake or tart for tea. No reservations. Presidente Franco and Quince de Agosto (phone: 91-580). Moderate.

El Caballito Blanco – Good German food; however, the decor is nothing special and the service can be slow. Reservations not required. Closed Sundays. Calle Alberdi 631 (phone: 44-560). Moderate.

La Pergola del Bolsi – Commonly called the *Bolsi*, it has a popular lunch counter with an adjoining dining room. It is a favorite of businesspeople who lunch at noon; it's less crowded in the evening. The typical Paraguayan bill of fare features especially good fish. Reservations recommended for lunch, but a table is usually available after a short wait. Calle Estrella and Calle Alberti (phone: 91-841). Dining room, moderate; lunch counter, inexpensive.

The Lido Bar – Nice for a light meal or snack, this place calls itself the crossroads of South America. That may be a bit of an exaggeration, but it is without a doubt at the crossroads of Asunción. Right on the main plaza across from the Pantheon, it's usually wall-to-wall people. Try their soup of the day or the *empanadas* (meat pies). (If it is too full and all you want is a filling bite, it's just two blocks to the *Bolsi*'s lunch counter. Prices are even lower at the *Lido* than at the *Bolsi*.) No reservations. Calle Chile and Calle Palma (phone: 46-171). Inexpensive.

Shakespeare Pub – Most informal (and least expensive) place in town, and a prime meeting place for English-speaking people. Open daily, except Sundays, after 6:30 PM. No meals. Calle Chile 750.

BOGOTÁ

Long before the Spaniards' quest for gold led them to hunt on the plateau on which the present city of Bogotá now rests, the Muisca (or Chibcha) Indians worshiped the fabulous, sun-colored metal with such intensity that they actually coated themselves with it as part of their rituals. Was it any wonder that the Spanish conquistadores believed they had finally arrived at the fabled land of El Dorado (The Gilded Man) in the early sixteenth century, when 166 members of what had originally been an 800-man exploratory expedition found themselves among the gold-loving Muisca?

The Spanish found their El Dorado hidden above the tropical forests and rivers of the South American continent, above the clouded ramparts of the Andes, on the high mountain plateau where Bogotá now raises its elegant modern buildings to the sky. And a traveler approaching the city by jet today may feel touched by some of their ancient awe and excitement as the plane rises to avoid the steep, craggy slopes that gather protectively around the city and emerges into the crystal sunlight of the plain surrounding the city. The "descent" into Bogotá's Eldorado Airport — named for the legend to which this modern capital owes its existence — is hardly a descent, since the city sits on a plateau 8,640 feet above sea level.

Indian gold, "the sweat of the sun," proved, paradoxically, to be a curse. It led to the extermination of the Indian cultures and eventually undermined Spain's control of the continent. When most of Europe was learning how to produce, Spain knew only how to consume, and when the gold ran out, so did its prosperity. Yet strangely enough, gold is not native to Bogotá's fertile highland basin, the savannah. In this and in other ways, Bogotá is a city of historical and cultural paradox.

Not the least of these paradoxes is the continual contrast of the city's obvious prosperity with its oppressive poverty. Bogotá has everything one might expect in a modern and exceptionally beautiful capital: lavish hotels, ultramodern offices and business facilities, fascinating shops, excellent restaurants, diverse cultural activities, and a varied nightlife. A magnificently situated city, nature's work has been enhanced by the judicious placement of parks and elegant residential areas. A broad avenue links the airport to the city; as drivers approach the downtown area, modern skyscrapers — glistening brightly in beautiful white stone and glass facades — stand out against the dark mammoth peaks of the Andes in the background. A system of bridges and underpasses whisks traffic into various parts of the city. And yet, in the city's most luxurious centers, you will meet Bogotá's ubiquitous, impish "gamines," the street urchins of the city. Bogotá has between ten and twenty thousand homeless children living in its streets. Every skyscraper overlooks a shantytown; overpasses are often cluttered with impossibly derelict cars;

and even after 150 years of constitutional government, guards stand watch over public buildings and recreational complexes.

Covering 111 square miles, Bogotá occupies an unusual geographical position for a South American capital. Although Colombia is the only country that can claim both a Pacific and an Atlantic (Caribbean) coast, its capital remains securely nestled on an inland plateau called the *sabana de Bogotá* (Bogotá savannah), about 150 miles wide and 30 miles long in the Cordillera Oriental (eastern range) of the Andes. Most South American capitals are closer to the sea. Colombia's 439,500 square miles contain three Andean ranges: the Cordillera Occidental (western range), the Cordillera Central (central range), and the Cordillera Oriental (eastern range). The Sierra Nevada de Santa Marta, a mountain chain independent of the Andean system, stands along the Caribbean coast. The eastern slopes of the Andes consist of jungle, which follows the contour of hilly land in the region called *montaña.* Farther east, the land flattens and the jungle becomes the *selva* of Colombia's Oriente (the east), which occupies about two-thirds of the country's land, although barely 2% of the nation's population of 28 million live there. Apart from the Amazon port of Leticia, few people venture into the region, although the Colombian government has been involved in a number of projects aimed at resettling inhabitants from the overcrowded shantytowns in the capital to roomy but rugged frontier developments.

Bogotá runs along a north-south axis at the foot of the mountains. To the north, the city stretches elegantly out into the country, its houses ever more luxurious, more spacious, more extravagant. Downtown, the business and colonial centers snuggle side by side — the modern muscles of a dynamic metropolis and the sedate charm of neighborhoods that have seen years pass like the water trickling in their patios. To the west, away from the mountains, are the serried ranks of industrial plants, factories, and warehouses. And to the south, as far as the eye can see, dusty, dirty, shabby, and engaged in a mortal struggle for survival, is the great melting pot of the poor.

Bogotá has nearly 6½ million inhabitants, expected to grow to over 10 million before the end of the century. The conglomeration of industrial and agricultural technology here since the century began has made Bogotá Colombia's main industrial center, and it has attracted people from all over the country in an ever-increasing torrent. Perhaps the most dynamic sector of industry is construction, yet the problems of a city expanding at this rate are many. There is a great variety of industry — though Bogotá is not associated with any one sector of production in particular — and the dynamism generated has also attracted foreign interests and personnel. These residents are joined by the personnel of diplomatic missions and those of numerous international organizations, many of which have regional offices in Bogotá because of its importance and its strategic geographical position. These foreign communities — of which the North American (*gringo*) community is the largest — contribute to the city's thoroughly cosmopolitan atmosphere.

When the Spaniards reached the *sabana de Bogotá,* they were above all impressed with the numbers of Indians living in the palisaded villages of wood and thatch houses, rich with cultivation and crafts and splendid temples. The Muisca Indians had developed agriculture, salt and emerald mining, and textile production as well as a flourishing trade in which these products were exchanged with neighboring tribes for gold and other luxuries. Their advanced political and social organization included a class of serfs ripe for slave labor under the Spaniards, unlike the less advanced, more isolated Indian groups from other parts of Colombia, who resisted conquest and were exterminated or driven into the jungles and mountains. The Muisca ruling class lived in large, well-constructed "palaces" and were carried about in gold-covered litters. The Muisca religion centered on a sun cult, in which especially valiant prisoners were sacrificed, the belief being that the bravery of the conquered would be passed on to the victors. Caves, hilltops, and most particularly lakes were considered sacred places, and no lake was more sacred than Guatavita, the circular lake about 50 miles (80 km) from Bogotá, gouged in the top of a mountain by a huge meteorite. Juan Rodríguez Fresle, in his chronicle of the conquest, explained the significance of Guatavita. After the future chief of the Muisca had fasted and abstained from women for six years in a cave, he was taken to Lake Guatavita, where his nude body was covered from head to foot in gold dust. So prepared, he was rowed in a rushraft along with four braziers and four plumed nobles to the middle of the lake. To a great clamor of drums, flutes, and rattles from the lake's shore, where a vast host of Indians filled the mountain crater to its very brink, the future chief dove into the lake, giving his offering of gold and emeralds to the waters of the sacred lake.

The word Bogotá, and the names of the surrounding towns of Zipaquirá, Facatativá, and Fusagasugá, are Indian, but Bogotá is not an Indian city. Its temple was razed by the Spanish and replaced by a cathedral. The Indian rulers gave the Spanish all their gold to be melted down and were tortured to death when they could give no more. Their serfs became slaves of the Spaniards, and as time passed they mixed with their masters and lost their language and their culture. Only in the museums do Bogotá's Indian history and culture come alive in all its human and creative splendor.

The Spanish tradition is more apparent, from the language itself, the magnificent sixteenth-, seventeenth-, and eighteenth-century churches in the city's colonial center, the Andalusian-style houses with their secluded patios, to the lifestyle of flamboyant *machísmo.*

The Spanish history of Bogotá began in 1538 when the expedition of Gonzalo Jiménez de Quesada arrived on the savannah after spending months in the debilitating jungles of the Magdalena River valley. Curiously enough, two other conquistadores arrived on the same spot in the same year: Nicolás de Federmann, who crossed the grass plains (*llanos*) to the east from what is now Venezuela, and Sebastián de Belalcázar, who came from Perú in the south. Fortunately, Quesada, who arrived first, also had the largest troop, so an armed conflict between the three was avoided. The town founded near the Muisca capital of Bacatá was given a name both Spanish and Indian, Santa Fé de Bogotá, after Jiménez de Quesada's home town, Santa Fé de Granada, Spain. For 281 years it was referred to as Santafé. The city's Spanish era came to a tumultuous end in 1819 after a long struggle for independence. By then, Bogotá had already become what it is today — an essentially mestizo city, in which Spanish blood and culture are mixed with Indian and transformed and regenerated. Witness the "Creole" elements in Spanish churches — the Indian and Negro features of many figures and the representation of native flora and fauna. The lavish decorative use of gold, mirrors, and sun symbols, related to the preconquest suncult, draw subtle attention to the Indian heritage. Witness also the free mixing of the artistic styles and tendencies of Renaissance and post-Renaissance Europe — mannerist, baroque, rococo, neoclassical — which in Spain were much more clearly defined.

At the beginning of the twentieth century, Bogotá earned itself the name Athens of South America because of the refinement of its customs and culture. More than anything else, this was due to a tradition common among the old established families — those who refer to themselves as *santafereños* rather than *bogotanos* — of writing, reciting, and occasionally improvising poetry. Bogotá became a town of amateur poets that stimulated such fine talents as Guillermo Valencia and León de Greiff, and even today, if you are invited to such a gathering, you are likely to hear a recitation after lunch or dinner. Gabriel García Márquez, Nobel Prize winner and author of *Cien Años de Soledad (One Hundred Years of Solitude),* the contemporary epic that is universally acclaimed as Latin America's greatest modern classic, has returned from Mexico City to live in Bogotá, where he has recently published yet another bestseller, *El Amor en los Tiempos del Cólera (Love in the Time of Cholera).*

The city's aristocracy also created a culinary tradition that enlivens Bogotá's kitchens to this day. Recipes served with special pride include *chocolate santafereño* (rich cocoa with cheese floating on top, accompanied by *pan de yuca,* yucca bread); *mazato santafereño* (a fermented drink made from maize or rice, eaten with a special brown bun); *tamales* (spiced chicken and chopped vegetables in a steaming maize mixture wrapped in, and flavored by, a plantain leaf); and *ajiaco* (a corn and potato soup served with shredded chicken, avocados, and capers).

Indian, but not Indian; prosperous, but dogged by intransigent poverty; a sophisticated modern city surrounded by the immutable power of ancient traditions and ageless mountains — Bogotá is something of a primer in modern South America, a glittering introduction to the joys and frustrations of this multifarious continent. It is, in all ways, the starting point.

BOGOTÁ AT-A-GLANCE

SEEING THE CITY: High above a sheer cliff of Monserrate, the mountain that stands behind the city like a drop curtain, is the shrine of Monserrate. It can be reached easily from the city center in a cable car or by funicular, and the ride up is as exhilarating as the view from the top is superb. All of Bogotá lies at your feet: the skyscrapers thrusting up ambitiously, the colonial quarter with its neat white walls and tiled roofs, and the rest of the city expanding exuberantly in every direction. Beyond, the magnificent, many-toned plateau is fringed by distant mountains. On a clear evening you may have a breathtaking vision of two snow-clad volcanoes of the Cordillera Central, some 74 miles (120 km) away. One of these, the Nevado del Tolima, is a perfect cone, like Japan's Fujiyama.

On Sundays, thousands of *bogotanos* swarm up Monserrate Mountain to "keep a promise" (*"pagar una promesa"*) to the Fallen Christ, a colonial figure sculpted by Pedro de Lugo y Albarracín, to whom the church is dedicated. Some carry crosses or climb on their knees; other visitors will find an amusement park, pleasant shops, cafeterias, and an excellent restaurant, the *San Isidro,* from which to savor the view.

On your way up or down, stop at the Quinta de Bolívar museum at the base of the cable car. You will enjoy the atmosphere of this fine country house, which was given to the Liberator by a rich Spanish merchant in 1820 and is now a splendid museum of Bolívar exhibits. Closed Mondays. Calle 20, No. 2-23 E (284-6819).

 SPECIAL PLACES: The city is laid out according to a familiar grid system, so you should not have difficulty finding your way around. *Carreras* (roads) run north-south, parallel to the mountains. *Calles* (streets) run east-west, toward the mountains, with numbers increasing as you move north from the city center. *Calles* and *carreras* intersect at right angles. The best bet for transportation is a taxi, preferably one of the green and white tourist taxis that stand in front of the main hotels and have English-speaking drivers who also conduct tours of the city on request. Buses and microbuses are comfortable when they are not too crowded, and you will learn the major routes quickly. A warning: Bogotá is known as a pickpockets' city. So infamous is its reputation that groups of New York police come here to get advice from the more experienced Bogotá police. By day you should have no trouble in the areas discussed below, but it is a wise precaution to leave jewelry at home (or at the very least in your hotel's safe); at night be wary of people "accidentally" bumping into or touching you.

DOWNTOWN

The Gold Museum (Museo del Oro) – To step from the bustle of modern Bogotá into the almost religious atmosphere of this extraordinary museum is to bridge centuries, break the barriers of cultural distance, and discover the enormous relevance and dignity of the Quimbaya, Tairona, and Muisca Indian civilizations that have all but disappeared except for these sensitive displays. These exhibits of the largest gold collection in the world are presented to give you a clear idea of their precise origin, sociocultural context, and method of production. For you, the legend of El Dorado will become not a curse but a real and meaningful blessing. Closed Mondays and Sunday afternoons. Admission charge. Films in English at 10 AM and 2:30 PM. Calle 16, No. 5-41 (phone: 281-3065).

San Francisco, La Veracruz, La Tercera Churches (Las Inglesias de San Francisco, La Veracruz, La Tercera) – Three magnificent colonial churches stand opposite the Gold Museum, reminding us that Spain's conquest was largely due to the devastating moral and physical power of her Church.

Built in 1567, San Francisco is the oldest and most beautiful of all. Its somber interior is lit by the countless candles of the faithful. By their light, you can see some of the fine sculpted figures that are venerated. The gilded wooden altarpiece (*retablo*) of the main altar is a rococo masterpiece by Ignacio de Ascucha built over an earlier work in the baroque style of the rest of the ornamentation. The San José altar is particularly splendid; the carved ceiling is also of great beauty; and there are paintings by Gregorio Vázquez, Gaspar de Figueroa, and others. Open daily. Free. Av. Jiménez and Carrera 7. La Veracruz and La Tercera both have rococo ornamentation. The latter is built on the site where the mass celebrating the foundation of the city was sung by Bartolomé de Las Casas, the famous bishop who denounced the atrocities committed against the Indian peoples. Open daily. Free. Carrera 7 and Calle 16.

Jiménez Avenue (Avenida Jiménez) – Located between Carrera 10 and the mountains, this is the business and financial center of the city. Colonial architecture like that of San Francisco and of the Plazoleta del Rosario contrasts with tall modern buildings such as the Bank of the Republic and the Banco Ganadero.

Seventh Avenue (La Carrera Séptima) – Running the entire length of the city parallel to the mountains, this road joins the colonial district to the downtown areas, the international sector, and the north. It is the *bogotanos'* favorite street, along which the traditional *paseo,* or stroll, may extend from the Plaza Bolívar as far as the international sector. This entire stretch is alive with commerce, cafés, and restaurants as well as the bustle and noise of countless street vendors.

Nineteenth Avenue (La Avenida Diécinueve) – Between Carrera Séptima and the mountains is an elegant commercial center that has many shops of special interest, selling ethnic and craft wares, leather goods, and jewelry (especially Colombia's famed emeralds). A pleasant walk to the top of the avenue will take you past the Colombian American Center to the delightful little church of Las Aguas (Carrera 3, No. 18-66). Flanking this church is a lovely cloister that houses the arts and crafts shop of *Artesanías de Colombia,* containing an extensive assortment of ethnic and craft wares from all over the country; another branch of the store is located in front of the *Hotel Tequendama* (Carrera 10, No. 26-50). In the same building is one of the best restaurants for Creole cooking, the *Casa Vieja del Claustro* (Carrera 8, No. 18-60; phone: 284-3484).

THE COLONIAL CENTER — LA CANDELARIA

Take your time and your camera to wander around the well-preserved colonial neighborhood of La Candelaria, with its delightful old houses nestling quietly around flowered patios in the old Moorish style. Much of the planning and plotting that shaped Colombia's history occurred behind these broad adobe walls and under these graceful tiled roofs. You may come across some interesting antique shops, too, and can have the best Creole food in this same setting. Calles 7 to 13 and Carreras 1 to 8.

The Archaeological Museum (Museo Arqueológico), in the House of the Marquis of St. George (Casa del Marqués de San Jorge) – The finest and most interesting of the stately colonial houses of old Bogotá — built in the 17th and 18th centuries and admirably restored in recent years — is the setting of one of Latin America's most important collections of pre-Columbian pottery from Mexico, Colombia, Ecuador, and Perú. The exhibits are beautifully presented, and you will be totally enchanted as you wander through the whitewashed rooms — each with green woodwork and wooden floors, yet each different from the next — along corridors, onto balconies, and out into the typically Moorish patios with cool fountains and fresh plants. It's a perfect introduction to the old center of Bogotá. Also on the premises is a good and inexpensive restaurant, serving lunch only. Museum open Tuesdays through Saturdays, 10 AM to 5 PM; Sundays and holidays, until 1 PM. Admission charge. Carrera 6, No. 7-43 (phone: 282-0740).

Church of San Agustín (Iglesia de San Agustín) – Just below the House of the Marquis of St. George you will come across the austere façade of the Church of San Agustín, first constructed in 1575 and remodeled in 1748 after an earthquake. The interior has fine baroque decoration, and among the more important pictures and wooden sculptures you will find a *Flight from Egypt* by Vázquez and the statue of Jesus of Nazareth by Pedro de Lugo. Open daily. Free. Calle 7 and Carrera 7.

Presidential Palace (Casa de Nariño) – Standing opposite San Agustín, this imposing edifice, reconstructed in 1979, is again the seat of government. Built in 1906, it was gutted by a mob in 1948, after the assassination of populist Liberal leader Jorge Eliecer Gaitán. This incident sparked off a bitter civil war that lasted nearly a decade. This bitter chapter in Colombia's predominantly peaceful history is appropriately known as La Violencia ("the violence"). The changing of the Presidential Guard every afternoon at 5 is well worth a visit. Open to the public Saturdays, Sundays, and holidays. Calle 8 between Carreras 7 and 8 (phone: 284-3300).

Museum of Popular Art and Tradition (Museo de Artes y Tradiciones Populares) – Displayed here is a marvelous variety of craftwork produced in different regions of the country. Some have been made by inhabitants of remote sections of the interior. In an old monastery, the museum has a restaurant and a shop that sells ethnic items and crafts. Closed Mondays and Saturdays; the fine craft shop stays open Mondays. Admission charge. Carrera 8, No. 7-21 (phone: 281-5319).

Monastery of Santa Clara (El Monasterio de Santa Clara) – If you walk two blocks north along the Carrera 8, passing the neoclassical Observatorio Astronómico, with its shroud of colonial and republican history, you come to the Monastery of Santa Clara. Part of this colonial church and monastery has been converted to a museum that houses interesting religious art. The monastery is open daily; the museum is closed Mondays. No admission charge for the monastery; small admission charge for the museum. Calle 9, No. 8-72 (phone: 258-7669).

Plaza Bolívar – One block farther north is Bogotá's main square, named after the Liberator. Three sides of the square are indeed republican — the fine Greek classical capitol, the Town Hall (Alcaldía Mayor), and the modern Palace of Justice (Palacio de Justicia), the last of which was tragically burned in November 1985 by an insurgent group (the M-19) and is currently being reconstructed.

The Cathedral and the Sanctuary Chapel (Capilla del Sagrario) on the fourth side already existed in Bolívar's time. The cathedral stands on the site of an early Muisca temple, where the first Christian church of Bogotá was built in 1565. The present neoclassical church was designed at the beginning of the 18th century by Fray Domingo de Petrés and contains some of the woodwork from the earlier church. In one of the side chapels is the tomb of Bogotá's founder, Gonzalo Jiménez de Quesada. The Sanctuary Chapel can be reached from inside the cathedral, though it actually predates the cathedral and has an impressive baroque screen and many of the paintings of Gregorio Vázquez Arce y Ceballos, the finest Colombian painter of the 17th century. Open daily. Free. Carrera 7 with Calle 10.

The Twentieth of July Museum (Museo 20 de Julio) – Occupying a colonial house on the corner of the plaza next to the cathedral, it was here, on the twentieth of July, 1810, that an insignificant incident sparked rebellion among the Creoles. The Spanish merchant José González Llorente reportedly insulted the Creole family of one Francisco Morales, whose supporters rioted. The ensuing Act of the Twentieth of July called for an independent Colombian constitution and denounced the Spanish viceroy. The site of this historic argument, which eventually cost Spain half her colonial provinces in the Americas, contains many paintings and relics of those who participated in the events. Open Tuesdays through Saturdays, 9:30 AM to 6 PM; Sundays and holidays, noon to 5 PM. Admission charge. Calle 11, No. 6-94 (phone: 234-4150).

Church of San Ignacio (Iglesia de San Ignacio) – Just off the other end of the Plaza Bolívar, opposite the beautiful Plazuela de San Carlos, stands the Jesuit Church of San Ignacio, which contrasts architecturally with the more rustic structures of the other churches of the same period (early 17th century). Inside are magnificent baroque altarpieces some of which are attributed to Juan de Cabrera, many remarkable wood sculptures by the great Pedro Laboria, others by Pedro de Lugo and lesser artists, and some fine paintings by Gregorio Vázquez. If you're lucky enough to be in town on the saint's name day (October 23), you'll have the special opportunity to see a very special gold chalice, so encrusted with huge emeralds that it is affectionately known as La Lechuga (The Head of Lettuce). Calle 10 with Carrera 6.

The Museum of Colonial Art (Museo de Arte Colonial) – This building, just up the street from San Ignacio, was originally built to serve as a Jesuit university. After the expulsion of the Jesuits in 1768, it served successively as a national congress, a prison, a national library, a school, a natural sciences museum, a court of justice, and finally as the Ministry of Education before being converted to its present use. In the sober splendor of its halls and two-storied colonnade are the finest paintings, drawings, sculptures, carvings, furniture, and silverwork of the colonial period, including 160 paintings and drawings by Gregorio Vázquez Arce y Ceballos. Closed Saturdays, Sundays, and Mondays. Admission free. Carrera 6, No. 9-77 (phone: 241-6017).

San Carlos Palace (Palacio San Carlos) – Until recently the presidential palace, this is known as the House of the Liberator (Casa del Libertador) because none other than Simón Bolívar himself resided here. In the garden is a tree that he allegedly planted. Exhibits pertaining to Bolívar's life are on display. Carrera 6 and Calle 10 (phone: 281-7811).

Colón Theater (Teatro Colón) – A landmark in its own right, this elaborate 19th-century building is still *the* place for theater, opera, and ballet in Bogotá. It is the home of Colombia's National Symphony, and hosts visiting touring companies. Open during performances only. Across the street from San Carlos. Calle 10, No. 5-32 (phone: 241-6141).

National Theater (Teatro Nacional) – Mostly Spanish-language plays are presented here, along with occasional concerts or mime performances. Calle 71, No. 10-25 (phone: 212-5930).

Alzate Avendaño Foundation (Fundación Alzate Avendaño) – As you leave the Colón, stroll along Carrera 5 toward Calle 9, a picturesque colonial street. Head up cobblestoned Calle 9 toward Calle 10. If you feel like some refreshment in a delightful setting, stop at the Alzate Avendaño Foundation cafeteria. The foundation houses an art gallery featuring works by painters living in La Candelaria. Calle 10, No. 3-16 (phone: 242-5375).

Bogotá Urban Development Museum (Museo de Desarrollo Urbano de Bogotá) – Inside this colonial house are stunning old photographs, paintings, and exhibits concerning the city's early life. If your walk through contemporary and colonial Bogotá has aroused your curiosity about the old days, be sure to spend some time browsing here. Closed Sundays. Admission charge. Calle 10, No. 4-21 (phone: 284-5353).

Royal Mint (Casa de la Moneda) – Here gold was coined for the first time in Latin America. Its beautiful buildings (built in 1627) now contain the Numismatics Museum, with a complete collection of all the money coined to date, and the Museum of Plastic Arts. Closed Sundays and holidays. Free. Calle 11 below Carrera 4 (phone: 234-3200).

THE INTERNATIONAL SECTOR

The tallest skyscrapers, the most elegant hotels, the best restaurants and cinemas, some of the most exclusive shops and night spots, and every kind of tourist and business facility are concentrated in the international sector, which is close to Bogotá's center. Among its many other attractions is one of the city's best coffee shops, *Café Oma* (Carrera 10, No. 27-91), an excellent place to sample exquisite Colombian coffee and to buy coffee beans. The northern branch of this establishment (Carrera 15, No. 82-60; phone: 256-4086) also has a magnificent bookshop.

The National Museum (Museo Nacional) – Established in the old city prison, this complex includes an excellent anthropological museum as well as interesting national history and fine arts museums. Closed Mondays. Admission charge, except Thursdays. Carrera 7, No. 28-66 (phone: 242-5925).

The Church of San Diego (Iglesia de San Diego) – This is a pleasant example of early 17th-century colonial architecture with a fine altarpiece. Especially interesting is the Lady Chapel, dedicated to Our Lady of the Fields. Open daily. Free. Calle 26 with Carrera 7.

The Natural History Museum and the Santa Fe de Bogotá Gallery (Museo de Historia Natural and Galería Santa Fe de Bogotá) – Both occupy part of the building of the District Planetarium (Planetario Distrital), which stands next to the bullring (plaza de toros). Few countries have as many varieties of flora and fauna as Colombia, so there are some fascinating exhibits. The Santa Fe de Bogotá's temporary exhibitions are invariably interesting, and the stars never lose their magic. Closed Mondays. Parque de la Independencia on Calle 26 at Carrera 7 (phone: 284-7396).

Museum of Modern Art (Museo de Arte Moderno) – Just across the bridge from the Planetarium, this museum was founded in 1981 by Colcultura, and is the country's principal modern art museum. There is a fine restaurant on the premises. Closed Mondays. Calle 26, No. 6-05 (phone: 283-5845).

THE NORTH

Carrera 15 – From Calle 72 to Calle 100, this road is Bogotá's elegant busy commercial axis, with businesses and shops.

Chicó Museum (Museo del Chicó) – Formerly the home of the distinguished Doña Mercedes Sierra de Peréz, it now houses a chock-a-block collection of objets d'art amassed by the late matron during her world travels. Closed Saturdays and Sundays. Free. Carrera 7, No. 94-17 (phone: 236-7285).

Unicentro – This futuristic, highly exclusive shopping center has about 300 boutiques and services under one roof. If you get homesick for shopping malls, this is Colombia's snazziest. Carrera 15 and Calle 123 (phone: 213-8800).

Chapinero – Bogotá's traditional center of commerce is still fairly active if not quite as glamorous as Carrera 15. Carrera 13 between Calles 48 and 68.

ENVIRONS

Salt Cathedral of Zipaquirá (Catedral de Sal) – The Muisca Indians mined salt as well as gold. The mines of Zipaquirá ("the town of the chief") were producing salt long before the Spaniards arrived and they are being mined today. In the heart of this vast mountain of salt is a unique cathedral with four aisles and a capacity of 8,000. Open daily. Admission charge. On Carreterra Libertador, 31 miles (50 km) north of Bogotá.

Tequendama Falls (Salto del Tequendama) – The magnificence of this 448-foot waterfall and its extraordinary rock canyon surrounded by mists clinging to the Andean jungle make this an exciting, romantic place to visit. (For information on excursions from Bogotá, see *Getting Around, Sources and Resources.*) On the road to Mesitas del Colegio, 17 miles (28 km) from Bogotá.

Villa de Leyva – It's a longish drive, but you will never forget the scenery. Nor will you forget this perfect colonial town that has managed to preserve its beauty so perfectly. We suggest booking a hotel room from Bogotá and spending the night in one of the first-class hotels: *Molino de Mesopotamia, Duruelo,* or *Mesón de la Plaza Mayor.* About 86 miles (140 km) north of Bogotá near Tunja.

Sasaima – If you drive east, over the brink of the savannah, then wind down the eastern slopes of the Andes, the vegetation changes as you descend to this tropical mountain resort. Soon you will be stripping off layers of clothing. There is nothing more restful than dozing at the edge of a swimming pool in the warmth of the tropics. About 50 miles (80 km) from Bogotá.

The Eastern Prairies (Llanos Orientales) – This is another longish drive, winding for 2½ hours down an impressive gorge, but the view from the final escarpment before you reach Villavicencio is like looking out to sea from a high cliff. And Villavicencio is just like a port, except that the sailors ride in on horseback after the long cattle drive and blow their money riotously on wine, women, and song in true cowboy tradition. The climate is warm and breezy, with all the fragrance and body of the tropics and none of its oppressiveness. There is good hunting in most areas and excellent fishing on some rivers. Villavicencio has some good hotels: the *Hotel del Llano, Hotel Centauros,* and the *Hotel Inambú.*

■**EXTRA SPECIAL:** If you are beguiled by the myth of El Dorado, discover for yourself the lake where it all reportedly occurred. Torn from the top of a mountain by a giant meteorite, its great depths filled with emerald waters, Lake Guatavita perches at the top of an Andes peak. About 75 miles (121 km) from the capital, it has lost none of its mystery. Legend claims its fathomless bottom still retains its treasure. To get to the lake, go by Jeep or hire horses near the new town of Guatavita la Nueva, and ride up to the lake's shores as did the Spanish, whose half-man, half-animal appearance so terrified the Muiscas. It will take an hour each way, and the trip will be more pleasurable if you carry a picnic to enjoy at the top. Or plan to eat at Guatavita la Nueva upon your return. The old town of Guatavita was flooded in 1967 by an artificial lake, Lago Tominé, on whose banks stands a delightful modern town built entirely in colonial style, complete with church, cobblestoned streets, and bullring. The taverns are excellent; the countryside, enchanting.

SOURCES AND RESOURCES

 TOURIST INFORMATION: General information, brochures, and maps can be obtained from the Corporación Nacional de Turismo, on the first floor of the Edificio del Centro de Comercio Internacional (Calle 28, No. 13A-15; phone: 283-9466), or from the Instituto Distrital del Turismo de Bogotá (Carrera 8, No. 10-65; phone: 281-8400). You will probably find a free copy of the bilingual *Guía de Bogotá* in your hotel room. A slightly more detailed guide, *Bogotá for the Visitor*, can be bought at stalls, where you will also find the Cartur Map of Bogotá. For historical information, we recommend *Historical Dictionary of Colombia*, by Robert H. Davis (The Scarecrow Press; $11).

The American Embassy is at Calle 38, No. 8-61 (phone: 285-1300); the British Embassy is at Calle 38, No. 13-35 (phone: 287-8100).

 CLIMATE AND CLOTHES: Bogotá is almost on the equator — but then, it is 8,640 feet above sea level, too, so you will feel the height more than the heat. Don't drink alcohol for the first 24 hours and you will adjust more comfortably. Days are springlike, with an average year-round temperature in the 50s and 60s F; the sun is prickly hot when it's shining, but the shade is always cold and nights are nippy. The only variation of climate is when it rains (and an *aguacero,* or cloudburst, can be as violent as it is short-lived!). It can rain anytime, but there is a rainy season between May and November. It rains somewhat less frequently during the summer, from December through March.

Casual city clothes are appropriate for daytime. *Bogotános* enjoy dressing up for a night out, so bring evening wear. Be sure to have a warm sweater for evenings.

GETTING AROUND: Bus – Only take buses that are relatively empty.

Taxi – The best service is offered by the green and white tourism taxis that stand outside all major hotels (phone: 282-0151). Taxis are a real bargain here; the fare from the airport to your hotel should be around $6. The drivers speak a little English and will take you on tours of the city or surrounding sights at fixed hourly prices. Check current prices in the *Guía de Bogotá.* Other taxis are easy to hail in the street, or you can call Radio Real (phone: 243-0580) or Radio-Taxi (phone: 285-7600).

Car Rental – *Hertz — Hotel Tequendama,* Carrera 10, No. 26-21 (phone: 284-1080); *Hilton International Bogotá,* Carrera 7, No. 32-16 (phone: 285-6020); *La Fontana* hotel, Av. 127, No. 21-10 (phone: 274-9490); El Dorado Airport (phone: 266-9200); El Dorado Airport Shuttle Terminal (phone: 263-1779). *Dollar Rent-a-Car —* Carrera 13, No. 82-28 (phone: 218-4011); El Dorado Airport (phone: 268-7670); El Dorado Airport Shuttle Terminal (phone: 263-2945).

Excursions – *All Colombia,* Calle 29, No. 6-58 (phone: 232-4550); *Granturismo,* Carrera 10, No. 27-51, No. 207 (phone: 296-8001); *Lowrie Travel Service,* Carrera 7, No. 19-29 (phone: 243-2546/7).

 MUSEUMS: The Gold Museum, Twentieth of July Museum, Museum of Popular Art and Tradition, Museum of Colonial Art, Numismatics Museum, the National Museum, Bogotá Urban Development Museum, and the National History and Modern Art museums are all described in *Special Places.* Others include the *Coffee Growers' Cultural Foundation (Fondo Cultural Cafetero),* Carrera 8, No. 7-93 (phone: 281-6480); the *Military Museum (Museo Militar),* Calle 10, No. 4-92 (phone: 281-3086); and the excellent *Museum of Religious Art,* Calle 12, No. 4-31 (phone: 81-0556). All museums are closed on Mondays.

 SHOPPING: Main shopping areas are mentioned in *Special Places,* above. Visit the *Galería Cano* for pre-Columbian gold ornaments and pottery. *Cano* sells perfect gold-dip replicas of the figures you saw in the Gold Museum, produced by the same techniques, international sector Carrera 13, No. 27-98, Torre B (phone: 284-4801), and *Hilton Hotel. Artesanías de Colombia* (handicrafts and ethnic wares) has shops in the international sector (Almacén San Diego, Carrera 10 No. 26-50), downtown (Almacén Las Aguas, Carrera 3, No. 18-60). At these shops you will find very attractive woolen goods — knit purses, sweaters, embroidered folk tapestries, the traditional woolen *ruana,* or Colombian poncho — basketwork, hats, rustic and original pottery, leather, and the beautiful flowing gowns of the Guajira Indians called *mantas.* For emeralds go to *Greenfire* (shops in the *Tequendama* hotel and the Bavaria Bldg., international sector), *Stern* (shops in the *Tequendama* and *Hilton* hotels and at El Dorado Airport), *Muzo (Hotel Tequendama),* or *Sterling Joyeros (Hotel Tequendama, Hotel Bogotá,* and *Unicentro).* Even better, visit the *Sterling* factory (Calle 11, No. 68B-37; phone: 260-3860) for lower prices and a tour of the factory, where you will see the entire operation, from design through gold smelting and gem faceting to the finished product. Wonderful leather can be found all over town; try *Boots 'n Bags (Hotel Tequendama* and Calle 19, No. 5-35), *Colombian Bags (Hotel Tequendama* and Carrera 15, No. 93-03), or *Land Leather* (Calle 23, No. 22-52; phone: 268-1747; and Carrera 14-A, No. 82-26; phone: 256-6570). Special places for knitted, handwoven, and traditional Colombian goods of all kinds are *TAB* (Carrera 14, No. 79-60) and *Tibabuyes* (Calle 33, No. 6-15). Silverware is inexpensive but good in the small shops along Carrera 6 between Calles 12 and 13 and along Calle 12 between Carreras 6 and 7. There is a value added tax of 15% on all luxury goods.

 SPECIAL EVENTS: *Día de la Raza* (October 12) commemorates Columbus's discovery of America and the subsequent fusion of races; parades include Indians from tribes all over the country, folk dancers, and theater groups. In July and December, an excellent crafts fair is held in the Parque Nacional, Carrera 7 and Calle 36. July 20 is *Independence Day.* On even-numbered years, you can visit the *Commercial Fair (Feria Exposición Internacional),* Centro Nariño, from July 10 to 25. On Sundays and holidays, you can browse at *El Mercado de San Alejo (Flea Market),* where you just might find that very special *bibelot* you've been looking everywhere for. Open 8 AM to 5 PM. Carrera 3 from Calle 19 to 24.

 SPORTS: Auto Racing – Mostly local competition and karting on Bogotá's circuit. Sundays and holidays. *Autódromo,* Autopista del Norte, about 15 km out of town.

    Basketball – Club championships are held at the *Coliseo El Salitre.*
Boxing – Most tournaments also share the *Coliseo El Salitre.*
Bullfighting – Bogotá has a fine bullring in the international sector, and excellent

programs are held Saturdays and Sundays in season. The festivals are in December and February. Plaza Santamaría.

Fishing – There's good trout fishing north of Bogotá at Lake Neusa, Lake Sisga, and Lake Tominé and at Lake Tota in the State of Boyacá.

Football – Soccer (*fútbol*) is one of Colombia's most popular sports and can be watched Sundays at *El Campín Stadium,* Calle 57 and Carrera 37 (phone: 235-6044).

Golf – The best courses are those of the *Country Club* (phone: 258-3300) and the *Los Lagartos Club* (phone: 253-0077).

Horse Racing – Meetings at the sophisticated *Los Andes* track on Saturdays and Sundays.

Sailing – Neusa, Muña, and Tominé lakes are the main sailing centers.

Tennis – Any number of good courts can be found in Bogotá's elegant clubs. If you want a game before or after business, the *America Tennis Club* is close to the city center (Calle 51 No. 4-06; phone: 245-0608).

Water Skiing – *Los Lagartos Club* has top facilities on its spacious lakes (phone: 253-0077).

 THEATER: There's no national theater company but plenty of experimental theater. Check the papers to see what's on (almost always in Spanish). Visiting companies stop mainly at the *Teatro Colón,* Calle 11, No. 5-32 (phone: 241-0475). An amateur English-speaking theatrical group, *Community Players of Bogotá,* offers something like six plays a year. Check the local press. Variety theater on the lines of café-concert is listed under *Nightlife.* Movies are shown in their original language, usually with Spanish subtitles.

 MUSIC: The National Symphony Orchestra plays weekly at the opera-style *Teatro Colón* (phone: 241-0475), alternating with visiting orchestras. Top-rank soloists and chamber groups appear at the beautiful *Concert Hall of the Luis Angel Arango Library* (phone: 243-9100). Another remarkable hall is that of the National University, which sometimes presents fine programs. Check the local paper for what's going on at the newly opened *Colsubsido Theater* at Calle 26, No. 25-40 (phone: 285-0100).

 NIGHTCLUBS AND NIGHTLIFE: Some of the restaurants we recommend offer the opportunity of enjoying indigenous food and music at the same time. *Los Sauces, Tierra Colombiana,* and *El Zaguan de Las Aguas* specialize in Creole cuisine and dancing; *Doña Barbara* (Calle 81, No. 11-86; phone: 257-3876) has excellent guitar music. At the *Restaurante Colonial* in the *Bacatá Hotel* you can dance to Plinio's orchestra (phone: 283-8300). Or, if you like something faster, there are discos all over town. The "in" discos these days are *Keops Club* (Calle 96, No. 10-54; phone: 218-2258) and *Stardust Club* (Darrera 7, No. 133-95; phone: 274-1652). For members only, they will nonetheless welcome you if you flash your foreign passport. Also try *Unicorn* (Calle 94, No. 7-75; phone: 236-2641) or *Topsi* (Av. 116, No. 25-36; phone: 259-8707). The *Casa Colombia* (Carrera 5, No. 26A-40, phone: 243-3562) is a super place for dancing to live Colombian folk rhythms. The *Galería Club* has blackjack and a good bar (Carrera 10, No. 27-27; phone: 234-3526). If your Spanish is up to it, you may enjoy cabaret shows at *La Gata Caliente* (Calle 100 and Carrera 15; phone: 256-8496); and at *La Casa del Gordo* (Calle 90, No. 15-51; phone: 218-1147).

SINS: Bogotá's *pride* is the largest gold collection in the world at the Gold Museum (Museo del Oro), Calle 16, No. 5-41 (phone: 281-3600). If gazing at the magnificent display arouses your *envy* or possibly even *greed,* there are gold-dipped replicas of many of the items on display in the museum that are for sale at *Galería Cano. Galería Errazuriz* in the lobby of the *Tequendama* hotel offers authentic pre-Columbian artifacts, mostly necklaces and ceramics, complete with certificates of authenticity. You can also purchase emeralds at several local stores (see *Shopping*).

BEST IN TOWN

CHECKING IN: Two hotels with very different styles have shared the scene since the 1950s: the *Continental,* in the heart of the business world, overlooking the colonial center, and the *Tequendama,* which pioneered the international sector. Quite recently, the lead has been taken by the *Hilton,* the *Bogotá Plaza,* the *Cosmos 100,* and the brand-new *Bogotá Royal.* In addition to these, we have listed some more modest establishments in order to provide as wide a range as possible from which to choose. Expect to pay $110 and up for a double in the *Hilton;* $85 to $95 at other deluxe establishments; between $40 and $60 for hotels in the moderate category; and under $32 (and as low as $18) in inexpensive places. A 15% value added tax is now in effect for accommodations and meals in the expensive category.

Hilton International – Certainly the most elegant and luxurious hotel in town, and also the only one to have a heated swimming pool and a gymnasium. Its 195 rooms all have remarkable views, and the vista from *Le Toit* restaurant (on the 42nd floor) is unbeatable. (*Le Toit* also offers very good French cooking.) Downstairs are quaint cafeterias, another restaurant, attractive lounges, and three spacious conference halls, as well as a number of very useful shops and agencies. International sector, Carrera 7, No. 32-16 (phone: 285-6020). Expensive.

Tequendama – More centrally located than the *Hilton* and inhabited by better shops, the address is at the core of the international sector. Its restaurants and cafeterias are very reasonably priced. The *Salón Monserrate* on the 17th floor has the most fashionable nightclub in town and a good orchestra and guest performers in the evenings. The 721 rooms all have attractive views over this part of the city and up toward the mountains. Calle 26, No. 10-42 (phone: 286-1111). Expensive.

Bogotá Royal – Opened in 1986, this impressive 80-room hotel, in Bogotá's World Trade Center, is an ideal choice for business travelers. There is an informal restaurant, the *Café Royal,* and *El Estudio,* a very inviting bar that includes a string quartet and looks more like a library than a drinking establishment. Av. 100, No. 8-01 (phone: 218-3261). Expensive.

La Fontana – A new five-star property in the North Bogotá area, in front of the Unicentro shopping mall. With elegant suites and well-equipped meeting and conference rooms, it caters mostly to business travelers. Av. 127, No. 21-10 (phone: 274-0200). Expensive.

Cosmos 100 – In the northern residential area, with 128 very large rooms, three restaurants, two bars, and a sauna. All rooms have color TV and mini-bar. Calle 100, No. 21A-41 (phone: 257-9200). Expensive.

Charleston – It offers 32 sophisticated suites, each with bar and TV, as well as a restaurant. Reservations necessary. Carrera 13, No. 85-46 (phone: 257-1100). Expensive.

Bogotá Plaza – This very modern hotel is in a smart residential area well away from the city center, but it's easily accessible from the airport. This, and its excellent service, elegance, and comfort, make it an ideal stopover. Calle 100, No. 18A-03 (phone: 257-2200). Expensive to moderate.

Continental – The elegance of this extremely comfortable hotel is subdued and a little old-fashioned, but both its restaurant and cafeteria are favorite meeting places for businesspeople downtown. In part that's because it's so convenient, standing at the top of Avenida Jiménez, Bogotá's main street, overlooking the Parque de los Periodistas and the colonial neighborhood. Shops and services are good and include a sauna bath. Av. Jiménez 4-16 (phone: 282-1100). Moderate.

Bacatá – Also in a busy part of town, this very comfortable modern hotel has 230 rooms and very good service. At night guests can dine in the *Restaurante Colonial* and dance to the music of Plinio's orchestra. Calle 19, No. 5-20 (phone: 283-8300). Moderate.

Dann – Literally surrounded by some of the best shops downtown, it has much of the ambience and service of a luxury hotel at a much more modest price. The lobby and lounge are modern and distinguished. Rooms are very comfortable and all have TV. Calle 19, No. 5-72 (phone: 284-0100). Moderate.

Presidente – Situated between the international sector and downtown, this new hotel has 150 agreeable and spacious rooms, a pleasant restaurant, a cafeteria, and a good bar. TV is optional in single rooms. Calle 23, No. 9-45 (phone: 284-1100). Moderate.

Tundama – Still quite comfortable and well attended though somewhat past its prime, the address is central, and the staff offers the same tourist and business facilities as the other moderately priced hotels. TV optional in its 70 rooms. Calle 21, No. 8-81 (phone: 241-4132). Inexpensive.

Del Duc – A small modern hotel with quite spacious and agreeable rooms, a welcoming restaurant, and a bar and cozy lounges, it is central and gives excellent value for a reduced cost. TV optional. Reservations recommended. Calle 23, No. 9-38 (phone: 234-0080). Inexpensive.

San Diego – This small hotel in the international sector offers many advantages, the most prominent of which is that it is very inexpensive. The restaurant is undistinguished, but the 34 pleasant rooms all have a view. TV in the lounge only. Reservations recommended. Carrera 13, No. 24-82 (phone: 284-2100). Inexpensive.

Dann Colonial – This 80-room hotel provides an air of local charm, not to mention a good and inexpensive dining room. It's located in the Colonial section. Calle 14, No. 4-21 (phone: 241-1680). Inexpensive.

Hostería La Candelaria – A delightful, restful 10-room hostelry in three restored colonial mansions; convenient to theaters, museums, and concert halls. Calle 9, No. 3-11 (phone: 282-7724). Inexpensive.

 EATING OUT: There is some excellent French and international food in town, but we recommend trying the creole (*criollo*) food as well. The term *criollo* stems from the colonial era and refers to people of Spanish ancestry born in Colombia. Creole restaurants usually include a particularly attractive colonial atmosphere, and several offer dance shows that are entertaining. Unless otherwise noted, reservations are not necessary. Expect to pay $55 and up for a meal for two in those restaurants in our expensive category; $20 to $50 in those listed as moderate; and between $12 and $18 in those noted as inexpensive. Prices do not include drinks, wine, tips.

Casa San Isidro – The sun sets over the savannah, the city lights shimmer in the twilight, and the distant mountains appear silhouetted against the blood red of the dying day — that is supper at *San Isidro,* on a cliff on the peak of Monserrate Mountain. If one forgets the very respectable French menu in contemplation of the view, the waiter will call attention to it. *San Isidro* is open for lunch every day except Sunday, and for dinner on Fridays and Saturdays, when there's a fire to warm this large old colonial house. Reservations necessary. Major credit cards. Teleférico (phone: 284-5700). Expensive.

La Fragata – If seafood is your druther, there is no better place in town. A fleet of fishing boats keeps this group of restaurants — and their sister operation in Cartagena — in fresh seafood, rushed from the coast every day. Main courses are complemented by excellent wines and good service. The decor is so nautical that diners don't know whether they're on land or at sea, but surely frigates were never this attractive or luxurious. Open daily. Major credit cards. There are three restaurants in different parts of town. Baravia Bldg., Carrera 13, No. 27-98 (phone: 243-2959); Calle 77, No. 15-36, Int. 1 (phone: 236-3243); and Diagonal 127A, No. 20-36 (phone: 274-6684). Expensive.

Le Toit – On the roof of the *Hilton* — the tallest and most elegant hotel in town — this is a French restaurant in the grand style. It has a magical ambience, impeccable service, a magnificent wine list, and the most varied French menu in Bogotá. Open daily. Reservations recommended. Major credit cards. Carrera 7, No. 32-16 (phone: 285-6020). Expensive.

Chez Stefan – With a limited, but carefully selected, menu featuring French food only, this is the "in" place to eat in Bogotá. Chef and owner Stefan personally takes individual orders and helps in the selection of the proper wine to accompany dinner choices. Closed Mondays. Major credit cards. Carrera 18, No. 82-10 (phone: 236-1082). Expensive.

Saint Simon – Posh decor, excellent food, and impeccable service punctuate lunch or dinner Mondays through Fridays, or dinner only on Saturday nights. Major credit cards. Calle 82, No. 12-51 (phone: 257-3508). Expensive.

Tramonti – Thanks to its location high above the city, diners can enjoy a spectacular view while savoring the excellent Italian cuisine. Carrera 1, No. 93-50 (phone: 218-2400). Expensive.

Limón y Menta – All kinds of international food are served here, as well as an endless list of complicated drinks using every exotic liquor imaginable. "Busy" is the word for the decor, which dazzles with hanging plants, waterfalls, light shows, and more. Closed Sundays. Calle 82, No. 13-35 (phone: 256-6670). Expensive.

La Casa Vieja – Colombian creole cooking is far from exotic. On the whole, it consists of very simple meals delicately flavored with herbs — good, wholesome combinations that always have something especially delicious to remember them by. There is a saying in Colombia: *La comida entra por los ojos* ("The meal enters through the eyes"). It all looks so appetizing — food, earthenware dishes and pots, the large wooden ladles for serving — and the four branches of *La Casa Vieja* prepare it better than any other restaurant in the city. As an appetizer, Colombians have a fruit juice. If you want to do things right, have a *sorbete de curuba* before eating. A local fruit, *curuba* is really good news and grows nowhere in the world outside the savannah. Aperitifs are based on rum; excellent Chilean wines can accompany your meals, and the traditional *canelazo* (warm and anise-flavored) goes very well with dessert. We recommend the *ajiaco bogotáno,* to begin. It will serve to acquaint you with the full flavor and dimension of this cuisine. Ingredients could not be more simple: three varieties of potato, chicken, and a corn cob. But there's some Muisca magic here, which may be the herb *guasca* or the thick cream, capers, and avocado. The *viudo* fish soup, the *sobrebarriga,* and *puchero* stew are also excellent. The oldest of the four restaurants, on the Avenida Jiménez, is on the fringe of La Candelaria and is a quaint little house in which everything is curiously asymmetrical, down to the antique furniture and colorful decorations. Open daily. Major credit cards. Av. Jiménez 3-73 (phone: 234-6171). The *Casa Vieja del Claustro* nearby puts life and movement into the colonial cloister of Las Aguas, which it shares with the handicrafts and ethnic wares of *Artesanías de*

Colombia. Closed Sundays. Carrera 3, No. 18-60 (phone: 284-3484). The *Casa Vieja de San Diego* is just opposite the *Hotel Tequendama* in the international sector, occupying another cloister, that of the Church of San Diego (Carrera 10, No. 26-50; phone: 284-7359). Open daily. *The Casa Vieja del Norte* is in the northern residential area, Carrera 11, No. 89-08 (phone: 236-3421).

Le Grand Vatel – For decades this has been one of the city's best French restaurants, and glamour still clings to the classical old house like the ivy of its façade. The food is excellent and the price very reasonable. Open daily. Major credit cards. Carrera 7, No. 70-40 (phone: 255-8142). Moderate.

Los Sauces – This may well be your choice for a lively night out, for few night spots are more fun than this restaurant. Even at lunchtime it has plenty of show to it, and if you are new to Colombian food and customs, they will be presented to you in all their succulence and charm. Folk dancers provide the entertainment. Open daily. Major credit cards. Carrera 16A, No. 76-38 (phone: 256-2769). Moderate.

El Taller de Clemont – A limited menu, but uniformly high quality. To suggest this restaurant's local status, it's the only eatery in town where diners absolutely must have reservations. Major credit cards. Closed Sundays. Carrera 7A, No. 84-45 (phone: 236-8165). Moderate.

Pueblito de Yerbabuena – If your Sunday is free and you want to change the city scene, this is a charming little village that turns out once a week to become virtually a village-wide restaurant, serving excellent creole food. Sundays and holidays only. Kilometer 24 on the Carretera a Tunja. Moderate.

El Portico – On the outskirts of town, this beautiful old farmhouse in the savannah is surrounded by attractive parks and playgrounds and has a horse-drawn carriage and an ox-drawn cart to take you around. This is another restaurant that combines delicious creole food with a thoroughly bucolic setting. There's even a bullring for those who want to fight with calves and a real *trapiche* — a sugarcane press — that you can see at work. We recommend the *carne a la Fragua,* a delicious grilled fillet served with potatoes called *papas chorreadas.* Open daily. Major credit cards. Carretera Central del Norte, Kilometer 16 (phone: 255-7841). Moderate.

El Teatro – Just beyond the bull ring and, as its name suggests, a favorite of Bogotá's show biz community. Take time from gathering autographs to try to the chicken in mustard sauce — the house specialty (phone: 234-7726). Moderate.

Tierra Colombiana – This restaurant, in the elegant international sector, offers a lively folk show and light music as well as both creole and international dishes. Closed Sundays. Major credit cards. Carrera 10, No. 27-27 (phone: 234-9525). Moderate.

Noches de Colombia – Authentic Colombian cuisine accompanies an excellent Afro-Colombian folklore show. Carrera 15, No. 97-65 (phone: 236-4865). Moderate.

Litani – It features Middle Eastern food, with tasty Lebanese dishes its specialty. Open daily, but reservations are a must. Major credit cards. Carrera 15, No. 93-37 (phone: 236-1980). Moderate.

Giuseppe Verdi – The decor isn't much to speak of, but the menu — some of the best Italian food in town — more than makes up for it. Closed Sundays. Major credit cards. Calle 58, No. 5-35 (phone: 249-5368). Moderate.

Pescadero del Sur – Saltwater fish, freshwater fish — practically anything that swims is the specialty here, and you know it's fresh because you choose it live when you walk in. Decor is nil, service is spotty, and the restaurant is in a low-income southern suburb, but the trip's worth it, for lunch or dinner, Mondays through Saturdays. Colombian credit cards only. Carrera 19, No. 24-69 Sur (phone: 239-0064). Moderate.

Café de Rosita – The best buy in town, it's in a restored house in the colonial sector of La Candelaria. The fixed menu changes daily, and each day improves on the day before. No reservations or credit cards. Calle 9, No. 3-11 (phone: 282-7724). Moderate.

Pavo Real – Every day is Thanksgiving in this place, which serves only turkey. Centrally located, right across the street from the *Presidente* hotel, and two doors from *Hotel del Duc.* Open daily. Calle 23, No. 9-64 (phone: 243-3197). Moderate.

La Teja Corrida – The name roughly translates as "The Screw Loose," and it is a rather crazy place, serving creole food and drinks made from the local firewater. Music, especially on weekends, is mostly Colombian; however, if you feel a song coming on — in any language — just tell the waiter and suddenly the spotlight is on *you!* Downtown, just across the way from the bullring. Closed Mondays. Carrera 5, No. 26A-54 (phone: 242-4783). Moderate.

Refugio Alpino – Small, cozy, and with very friendly service, this place specializes in European food. Afternoons you'll find locals taking business lunches that tend to be very long and very liquid. Closed Sundays. Major credit cards. Reservations are highly recommended. Calle 23, No. 7-49 (phone: 284-6515). Moderate.

El Integral – For vegetarians, this is the place. Carrera 11, No. 95-10 (phone: 256-0899). Moderate.

El Zaguán de Las Aguas – A fair variety of good creole dishes and folk dancing in the evening are the main attractions of this very central restaurant. Try the *jaiba al Zaguán,* a giant crab done au gratin with a tasty cognac sauce. Open daily. Major credit cards. Calle 19, No. 5-62 (phone: 241-2336). Inexpensive.

Hong Kong – If you are in the mood for Chinese food, it's good and varied at the *Hong Kong's* two locations, with competent service. Closed Sundays. Major credit cards. Carrera 11, No. 92-51 (phone: 236-2758) and Calle 23, No. 5-98 (phone: 242-7304). Inexpensive.

Crema y Lujuria – Any restaurant called "Cream and Lust" can't be all bad. This is a place to indulge in mouth-watering pastries and ice cream concoctions. Open daily. Two locations: one in the Unicentro shopping mall, the other on Calle 124, No. 6-47 (phone: 213-5074 and 213-5286, respectively). Inexpensive.

Nankin – This offers a limited selection of well-prepared Chinese dishes at very reasonable prices. Decor is distinctly drab. Open daily. No reservations or credit cards. Calle 23, No. 5-35 (phone: 241-2089). Inexpensive.

La Parrilla de Oro – Although not even moderately comfortable, its excellent churrasco has made it highly popular. Many delicious preparations of the less refined Creole cuisine are also offered at unbeatable prices. Open daily. No reservations or credit cards. Carrera 4, No. 17-94 (phone: 243-9587). Inexpensive.

Bodegón Cartagenero – If you're not going to Cartagena but want to try *costeño* food, this is the place. The second-floor boutique is an added touch that features exclusive designs by the owner at unbeatable prices. In other words, chop and shop. Colombian credit cards only. Calle 90, No. 13A-31 (phone: 256-4699). Inexpensive.

Brasa Brazil – Enjoy an almost unlimited array of meat dishes, all for a set price. Daily except Sundays from noon to midnight, and if there's a good-size crowd, closing time usually stretches a bit. Major credit cards. Av. 19 and Calle 118 (phone: 214-8064). Inexpensive.

Donde Canta la Rana – Translated, the name of this place becomes *Where the Frog Sings,* and it's a must for the truly adventurous diner questing for the most authentic native delicacies. Among the most notable items on the menu is a barbecue of "liver and lights," including cow's udder and bull's testicles. Anything but elegant, it is a real culinary experience. Carrera 24C, No. 20-10S (phone: 239-1870).

Las Acacias – Pop in at one of the 15 branches of this ubiquitous restaurant chain for typical Colombian food. For a list of their locations and a coupon for free dinner, phone the main office (212-9187). Inexpensive.

BUENOS AIRES

Acclaimed by both residents and travelers as the Paris of South America, Buenos Aires is one of the most haunting and attractive destinations on the continent. The city shares a considerable number of architectural elements with its French nicknamesake: wide boulevards, flowers and foliage, large parks, and ornate, gray buildings dating from the 1930s with rococo and baroque decorations. Some Spanish colonial elements are detectable — most notably, the many government and religious buildings around the Plaza de Mayo — but the Parisian influence predominates. Just as Paris has its Eiffel Tower, B.A. (as Buenos Aires is called by English-speaking residents) has its own picture-postcard landmark: the towering obelisk in the center of the plaza where Avenida Corrientes intersects Avenida Nueve de Julio, the boulevard that city officials claim is the world's widest. The city's 40-mile Avenida Rivadavia, stretching from the Plaza de Mayo to the suburbs, is frequently referred to as the world's longest street, although a metropolis of such grand dimensions hardly needs grandiose hyperbole.

Bordered on the northeast by the Río de la Plata (River Plate), the city sprawls inland across 76 square miles. The Río de la Plata is not really a river, but a deep, wide estuary that receives the waters of both the Río Paraná, which begins in Brazil and flows south through Paraguay to northern Argentina, and the Río Uruguay, which flows south from the southern Brazil–northern Argentina border. Along the waterfront stretches one of the city's most famous neighborhoods, La Boca (the Mouth), where costumed, singing waiters serve generous Italian meals in colorful *cantinas*. As in Paris, each neighborhood is distinctive, with its own shops, restaurants, *confiterías* (cafés), and *ferias* (public food markets). The neighborhood of San Telmo is the site of numerous tango parlors. The luxurious Barrio Norte (North District) is renowned locally for its "fat ladies," who spend the afternoon in fashionable cafés stuffing themselves with tea and rich pastries.

The capital's lifestyle takes its rhythm from Paris, too. Restaurants, theaters, cabarets, shops, and art galleries line the ground floors of many buildings, few of which exceed six and seven stories. The Teatro Colón (Colón Theater), one of the world's premier opera houses and concert halls, draws many international artists. More than 100 movie theaters present films ranging from Bergman's heavy dramas to grade B Italian sex comedies. There are several first-rate, if controversial, Argentine filmmakers, such as Leopoldo Torre Nilsson, who produced *Boquitas Pintadas (Little Painted Mouth)* in 1974, and Raul de la Torre, with *Crónica de una Señora (Chronicle of a Lady)* in 1971. Overall, Argentina's literacy rate of 92% ensures a lively cultural atmosphere.

The strong presence of the legitimate arts is enhanced by a proliferation of nightclubs, cabarets, and music halls that are responsible for B.A.'s reputation as "the city that never sleeps." A paradise for insomniacs, the downtown streets are busy practically 24 hours a day. Restaurants are accustomed to serving diners emerging from shows after midnight. Nighttime is devoted to window shopping or taking leisurely breaks over espresso at favorite *confiterías*. On weekends, groups of friends carouse until dawn, then stop for coffee and pastries called *media lunas* (half moons) before retiring. There is nightlife for all tastes. And the streets are safe after dark, well lit all night, and usually busy with pedestrian traffic. Violent street crime is minimal. Unlike in Bogotá, Colombia, it isn't necessary to remove jewelry before leaving your hotel. While it is perfectly acceptable and safe for women to go to restaurants, *confiterías*, and movies without a male escort or chaperone, women customarily go out in groups.

Fueling this restive energy is Argentina's abundant beef, touted as the tastiest in the world; Argentines devour more than 176 pounds of beef per capita annually. Because it is so plentiful, beef is relatively inexpensive compared with other meats and fish, as a stroll through a *feria* (market) readily reveals. In fact, Argentina claims to have 1½ head of cattle for each of its 28.7 million inhabitants. In addition to beef, Argentina produces a vast array of other foodstuffs, and is a major exporter of fruit, vegetables, and grain. Unlike many other South American countries, Argentina is well-fed and comfortable: The country produces enough food to feed its large population, provides free education and medical treatment, and supplies 90% of its own petroleum.

Most of Argentina's exports are shipped through Buenos Aires, which has become the country's main port and commercial center. The city struggled to reach this dominance. When first settled by Pedro de Mendoza in 1536, it was barely a dot on the map of the Spanish Empire. The first five years of its existence were less than auspicious, as the settlement was constantly under Indian attack. When the Indians finally succeeded in burning it down in 1541, the Spaniards simply left, and the first permanent settlement was founded by another Spaniard, Juan de Garay, in 1580. The town grew slowly. By the mid-seventeenth century, the population barely reached 1,000. In that era, Spanish colonial life was controlled from the headquarters of the Spanish viceroy in Lima, Perú, the city founded by Francisco Pizarro. Conquistador Pizarro bore the primary responsibility for Spain's conquest of South America. Eventually, the Spanish colonies became too large to be controlled from one site, and in response to pressures from independent-minded Buenos Aires, a separate viceroyalty of the Río de la Plata was formed in 1776, headquartered in B.A.

The viceroyalty did not last long. By the beginning of the nineteenth century, the winds of revolution were whipping through Latin America. On May 25, 1810, a cautious Buenos Aires declared independence from the viceroy but wisely pledged continued loyalty to the Spanish crown. This forced the viceroy's resignation, resulting in the formation of a local government without the violence of a revolution. Full independence from Spain was declared on July 9, 1816, in the city of Tucumán in Argentina's interior. This event provoked a long battle between B.A.'s political leaders and those from the provinces who feared centralized control from B.A. as much as from

Spain. A bitterly divided Argentina suffered a series of civil wars in which rival political leaders fought for national control. Buenos Aires did not become the permanent capital of the country until 1880.

For the next 50 years, the city developed as an important shipping center, but nothing of major significance occurred. The first waves of immigrants from Italy, Spain, and Eastern Europe began arriving around the turn of the century, lured by the Argentine government's offer of economic opportunity in a rich, new world. (Today, Italian immigrants and their descendants form the biggest ethnic block, about 40% of the population. And England — which forged strong economic and political ties with the country after Argentine independence — is regarded as a cultural model.) In the 1930s, the city's population swelled when thousands upon thousands of rural migrant workers poured into the capital in search of more profitable work.

These *descamisados* (shirtless ones) were the foundation of Juan Domingo Perón's formidable political base. Just one of a group of colonels who seized power from the elected Republican government in 1943, Perón was appointed labor minister. By endorsing the demands of the labor unions, Perón accumulated a broad and loyal political following, which later enthusiastically supported him for president. His totalitarian regime remained strong until the early 1950s, when it was seriously weakened by local economic conditions and the death of Eva ("Evita"), his wildly popular second wife. Perón himself soon disintegrated psychologically and refused to resist a military takeover, preferring exile in Spain to a battle for power. While outside the country, Perón encouraged his supporters to aggressively confront the government, which had banned the Peronist labor unions and political parties.

Juan Domingo Perón became leader of Argentina for a second time when President Hector Campora stepped down in 1973. But his regime lasted only three chaotic years. Perón died in 1974 and was succeeded by his third wife, María Estela de Perón, known as Isabelita. Whereas Eva Perón's dedication to the *descamisados* had won her folk-heroine adulation, Isabelita lacked any comparable following. In fact, her dependence on the minister of social welfare, José Lopez-Rega, was said to be so great that the presidency was actually in his control. The military finally forced her to resign in early 1976, and seized power directly. In the seven years of military rule that followed, Argentina's economic and political conditions deteriorated precipitously. Inflation reached a phenomenal high of 300 percent in May 1976. Terrorist assassinations were followed by government-sanctioned "disappearances" of social and political opponents, in the course of which an estimated 20,000 people were detained for questioning and simply never returned.

The junta's defeat in the ill-advised Falkland Islands war against Great Britain in 1982 ultimately forced the downfall of the military government. General elections were held in October 1983, and Raul Alfonsin, a lawyer and human rights advocate, was elected president. Today, few vestiges of the past turmoil are visible, though significant economic problems remain. The social climate of the country has changed drastically, however, and seemingly overnight. Military police are no longer a major political force; press censorship has eased; exiled artists, film directors, and actors have returned; and for a week following the elections, risqué magazines even appeared on newsstands. Americans will find the Argentines buoyantly optimistic about their new democracy, though visitors would still do well to refer to the Falklands by their Spanish name, Las Malvinas.

One of the major issues that continues to preoccupy the Argentines is the inflation rate and currency (no longer the *peso* but the *Austral*) devaluation. For the moment, however, Buenos Aires is not in the sky-high-capitals category, but it is no longer the bargain, especially for shopping, that is has been in recent years.

The tension between the *porteño's* indulgent lifestyle and political and economic realities seems to result in an air of sadness, a vein of melancholia in their vision of life. *Porteños* have an uncanny knack for expressing the dark side of life between healthy mouthfuls of steak and potatoes, washing down the bitterness in mellow red wine. Some people attribute the *porteños'* stormy nature to the rains that dowse the city through much of the year; others theorize that the widespread melancholia is part of a middle-class syndrome of people whose physical needs are abundantly filled and who brood incessantly over every emotional and personal setback. Yet another hypothesis is that *porteños,* caught in the crossfire of various national and ethnic heritages, are still in search of an identity. *Porteños* are often described as Italians who speak Spanish and think they are English. Whatever the reason, a *porteño* (or *porteña*) can dramatize a personal problem, such as a broken love affair, into a social tragedy. Nothing expresses this more eloquently than the tango.

As inextricably bound to B.A. as Dixieland jazz is to New Orleans, the tango was born at the turn of the century, the musical expression of the poor black population. But the music was adopted by successive waves of working-class Europeans who had immigrated to Argentina to make their fortunes. The lyrics were a social barometer of their desires and aspirations. In the 1920s, optimistic tangos reflected a hopeful political situation. In the 1930s, after a populist party failed, tango lyrics mourned the desperate hardship of the Depression. Argentina became exceptionally prosperous immediately after World War II by providing food for Europe. This minimized economic problems, increased the ranks of the middle class, and saw the evolution of a new style of tango that bewailed the frustrations of modern life. One of the most famous tangos, *Cambalache* (*Bazaar*), evokes a powerful, nihilistic image of the twentieth century as a big bazaar where values are bartered:

> Everything is the same.
> Nothing is better.
> A mule is equal with a great professor.

The song complains that today's heroes are those crooks, robbers, and swindlers who get away with it. The lyrics of another song lament:

> I know a city called Buenos Aires
> A city where my love was born.
> For the two of us along the city's solitary streets
> Love was born during a winter that had flowers in bloom.

After the love affair ends, the song grows bitter:

> This city doesn't exist anymore.
> It doesn't have streets for walking.
> It doesn't have homes to share happiness.

A natural for throaty female torch singers capable of squeezing tragedy and despair into their facial expressions, the tango also lends itself well to deep male voices expressing the pathos of unfaithful love. Lyrics are often written in *lunfardo,* the *porteño* slang that intertwines Spanish and Italian to form a third language full of twists and tricks. The key instrument of the tango is the *bandoneón,* similar to a concertina but slightly larger, with piano and violin accompaniment. The tango is a way of life in Buenos Aires, and tangos outsell the latest hits from the US and Europe. Carlos Gardel, who died in 1935, is still the most popular tango singer. His records are played regularly on radio stations, and street vendors hawk his picture along with national flags, pennants, and banners at public events.

The *porteños'* heavy reliance on nostalgia for the past may be a sign of their discontent with the present, but it could also be only the sincere expression of their love for the city and its traditions. Despite decades of turmoil, Buenos Aires has retained its grace and dignity. When Pedro de Mendoza founded his settlement, he called it Nuestra Señora de la Santísima Trinidad de los Buenos Aires (Our Lady of the Blessed Trinity of Good Airs). Since the Spanish explorer planted his conqueror's cross, the settlement has grown tremendously and the name has shortened considerably. But throughout its growth (and despite its growing pains), this city has always retained something of its good air.

BUENOS AIRES AT-A-GLANCE

SEEING THE CITY: The sheer vastness of Buenos Aires makes a sweeping, panoramic view from any one spot difficult to find. Since the city lacks true skyscrapers, getting a glimpse of even a significant section is not easy, either. For the best view of the downtown area, try the cocktail lounge on the top floor of the *Sheraton Hotel.* To the east, you can see the docks and the shimmering waters of the Río de la Plata, which shines iridescent-silver under the full moon. To the west, you can get a good look at the tree- and flower-lined Plaza San Martín linked to a network of narrow, grid-webbed streets. It is courteous to order a drink while enjoying the view. However, no one will stop you from walking in, taking a look, and leaving. Open daily until 2 AM. San Martín 1225 (phone: 311-6310).

SPECIAL PLACES: Walking through the downtown area is easy: Streets are laid out in an orderly grid, and the 32-square-block heart of downtown is restricted to private traffic between the hours of 10 AM and 7 PM, weekdays. Alternate streets are designated as either pedestrian or public transport thoroughfares, so, with every other street free of vehicular traffic, you can wander comfortably. When you are tired, just meander one block to pick up a bus or taxi. After 7 PM, private cars can drive along those streets that are limited to public transport during the day. Taxis are plentiful, inexpensive, and can be hailed on the street. If you do not speak Spanish, write the address of your destination on a slip of paper and present it to the taxi driver.

May Plaza (Plaza de Mayo) – One block wide and two blocks long, the city's principal square is surrounded by government and religious buildings. It was named to commemorate the date of independence from the Spanish viceroy — May 25, 1810. A center of political activity during its various postcolonial incarnations, the plaza was the scene of huge demonstrations during the populist governments of Juan Perón (1946–55, 1973–76), when as many as 100,000 people jammed the square to hear their leader. In those days, the plaza was practically bare, with only a few trees, one statue, and a flagpole. After the overthrow of the Peronists in March 1976, flower gardens were planted and fountains placed throughout the plaza. Av. de Mayo and Calle San Martín.

Pink House (Casa Rosada) – Named for its color, this huge building facing the eastern side of the Plaza de Mayo houses the office of Argentina's president. A fortress in colonial days, it was constructed to protect the city from sea invasion via the Río de la Plata, which once lapped at its back door. The roof is equipped with a helicopter pad, numerous radar scanners, and large communications antennas, but the interior retains its original Spanish atmosphere, with courtyards full of flowers, fountains, and statuary. The courtyards, once open to the sky, are now enclosed. It is from the balcony of this building that Eva Perón once delivered her stirring rhetoric to the Argentine masses. The Casa Rosada does not have regular public visiting hours. For permission to visit — sometimes granted, often not — contact the National Tourism Office, Santa Fe 883 (phone: 312-22-32). Balcarce 50 (phone: 30-3050).

Government House Museum (Museo de la Casa del Gobierno) – This small museum in the basement of the Casa Rosada contains historical mementos of ex-presidents. (The side entrance of the Casa Rosada belongs to the museum.) Closed at press time. Hipolito Irigoyen 219 (phone: 30-3050).

The Council House (El Cabildo) – The house of the Spanish viceroys' counselors, this was where the counselors declared independence in 1810, running from the building to shout their jubilation in Plaza de Mayo. In 1940, the Council House was declared a national monument, redecorated, and converted into a museum containing mementos of the 1810 uprising. As is the Casa Rosada, the Cabildo is guarded by soldiers in red and dark blue 19th-century ceremonial uniforms, complete with sword and feathered top hat. Open from 3 to 7 PM, Tuesdays through Fridays and Sundays. Bolívar 65 (phone: 30-1782).

The Cathedral (La Catedral) – On the site of the first church built in Buenos Aires (ca. 1620), this Greek-façaded, gray structure has gone through many renovations, the last of which took place after the cathedral and other Catholic churches were severely burned on June 16, 1955, by rampaging Peronists, who felt the Church was a center of opposition to their government. The cathedral contains the tomb of General José de San Martín, the Argentine who, with Simón Bolívar, led the South American wars of independence from Spain in the 19th century. The cathedral also houses the Chair of Rivadavia, a symbol of the Argentine presidency. The chair belonged to Bernardino Rivadavia, the nation's first president, and is used when the current president attends official ceremonies at the cathedral. This occurs fairly frequently, as Catholicism is the state religion and the Constitution stipulates that the Argentine president must be a practicing Catholic. Often, on important national and religious holidays, the president and his ministers parade the two blocks to the cathedral, which fronts the Plaza de Mayo on the north, to attend services. Open daily. Free. Rivadavia 450.

National Congress Building (Edificio del Congreso Nacional) – More a tourist attraction than a center of national debate in recent years, the building houses the nation's bicameral legislature. It is a square, block-long, white Greco-Roman structure at the end of Avenida de Mayo, the street that starts at Plaza de Mayo and ends a little more than a half mile away at the plaza in front of the Congress Building. Visits have to be arranged in advance by calling 47-3081. Entre Ríos 53.

San Telmo – The tango is alive and well in San Telmo, with music seven days a week. A pocket of urban antiquity, it has retained its cobblestoned streets, colonial houses that formerly housed cattle barons, and passageways too narrow for modern cars. Antique shops are concentrated around Plaza Dorrego, at the corner of Calle Humberto 1° and Calle Defensa, the scene of a giant flea market on Sundays and holidays, where you can buy anything from a copper milking pail to a rare edition of an out-of-print *porteño* magazine. Bargaining is requisite. At night, San Telmo metamorphoses into a string of brightly lit tango bars and cabarets, with musical renditions so sensual they would make Rudolph Valentino blush. If you speak enough Spanish to feel comfortable on your own, be sure to stop in at *El Viejo Almacén* (*The Old Grocery Store*), at one time an old grocery store. It offers what amounts to a crash course in the tango, with songs, dances, and instrumentals. At the corner of Calle Balcarce and Esquina Independencia (phone: 362-1453). *Casa Rosada,* Chile 318 (phone: 361-8822), also has a good tango show and folk music. Tours of San Telmo that include nightclub stops can be arranged through most hotels. The district is several blocks south of the Plaza de Mayo.

The Obelisk (El Obelisco) – Jokingly nicknamed "the Argentine monument to the suppository" by bus drivers, this 70-foot structure stands in the heart of town. The most frequently photographed symbol of the city, it reminds some visitors of the Washington Monument. It marks the intersection of Avenida Nueve de Julio and Calle Corrientes, an active nightlife street.

July Ninth Avenue (Avenida Nuevede Julio) – One city block wide, this thoroughfare measures 425 feet across, which *porteños* claim make it the world's widest street. The boulevard has grassy squares in its center, each sectioned off and named after different provinces. It was built by tearing down square block after square block of downtown apartment and office buildings. Presently 26 blocks long, the avenue is still growing, and city planners seem determined that it fulfill some urban manifest destiny by cutting a swath through the city until it reaches the Río de la Plata. In addition to the obelisk, the avenue has two huge fountains with special lighting effects that can be seen for several blocks at night. An ideal place for strolling and people watching, the *confitería*-lined avenue has some terrific places to have tea, coffee, cocktails, and sandwiches while you watch the parade. The *Exedra,* at the intersection with Calle Córdoba, is one of the more fashionable sidewalk *confiterías*.

Colón Theater (Teatro Colón) – Filling almost one square block, this majestic building about three blocks from the obelisk is the center of the city's classical music life. One of the world's major opera houses, it hosts concerts and ballets as well as works by its own ballet troupe, opera company, and symphony orchestra, whose repertoires are enhanced by frequent guest appearances of international artists. Underneath the theater, a maze of rehearsal halls, carpentry shops, tailor shops, and work areas are devoted to the vast number of tasks involved in launching any performance. The theater's main entrance is on Plaza Lavalle, a large tree-filled park whose fountain, decorated with statues of ballet dancers, commemorates an Argentine ballet troupe that died in a plane crash en route to Montevideo, Uruguay, in the 1960s. The rear of the building and its stage entrance overlook spacious Avenida Nueve de Julio. Along one side of the theater Calle Toscanini, a tiny street named after the world-famous symphony conductor, passes the entrance to the upper balconies. The highest balcony is called El Paraíso (Paradise) because it sits so close to the heavens. It is also paradise for students and other music lovers of humble means because the seats here are least expensive. Although dress codes are no longer strictly enforced, men customarily attend performances in jacket and tie. The concert season runs from March through November. Tours of the Colón and its underground complex are available throughout the year. Open daily. There's an admission charge for tours and performances. Tucumán 1161 (phone: 35-54-14).

Cervantes Theater (Teatro Cervantes) – Its venerable wood-paneled interior reeking of ages of glossy polish, this is the house of tried and true classical drama. Foreign companies on tour play the Cervantes stage. English-language programs with principals such as Sir Michael Redgrave have performed here in recent years. Spanish translations of the works of Shakespeare, Brecht, and other dramatists are also staged. Although the main season runs from March through November, it often has limited summer engagements. Open daily. Libertad 815 (phone: 45-4224).

San Martín Plaza (Plaza San Martín) – Named after Argentine liberator General José de San Martín, this park has a huge statue of its namesake at its western end. The statue is a favorite spot for visitors from other parts of Argentina to take photographs of each other. Over a square block in size, the plaza is a popular gathering place for downtown residents. Youngsters play in a section with swings and slides while senior citizens read newspapers and exchange gossip on the benches under the plaza's many shade trees. It is the center of the city's most fashionable area, and Calle Florida and Av. Santa Fe will lead you from the plaza to some of B.A.'s most elegant shops.

Palermo Park – When in Buenos Aires, do as the *porteños* do and head for the park — 1,100 acres of lakes, lawns, forests, and formal gardens — which, like the Bois de Boulogne in Paris, is within the city itself. Sports-loving Argentines flock to its golf courses and tennis courts, as well as to the racetrack, polo fields, and riding and walking trails. On Sundays, families come to picnic, grilling steaks on portable stoves and taking long siestas. The park can be reached via the D line subway.

La Boca – The old port area of the city faces the point at which the Río Riachuelo empties into the Río de la Plata. La Boca is the Italian district, many of whose inhabitants trace their ancestry to the northern Italian port of Genoa. Like any waterfront area, it has plenty of sleazy bars and nightclubs, but it also has gaily decorated homes and art galleries, as La Boca has long been favored by Argentine painters. There is a daily open-air exhibition of paintings portraying tango in the Caminito section. (There is also a gallery of contemporary arts, featuring an open-air rooftop exhibit of modern sculpture, in the school museum at Calle Pedro de Mendoza 1835.) It is perfectly safe to stroll through this neighborhood alone during the day; at night, you would be well advised to travel with a group and stick to the well-lit main streets. It is difficult to get to know the residents of La Boca. They form a closely knit, independent, and somewhat insular community within the larger city. In fact, they half jokingly refer to their neighborhood as the Independent Republic of La Boca. Tourists and inhabitants meet in the Italian *cantinas*, family-style restaurants that feature singing and dancing waiters who spend more time clowning with the customers than serving meals. Every meal has the atmosphere of an Italian wedding, with loud bands and masters of ceremony exhorting customers to dance and sing. Haphazard seating arrangements, along long benches and tables, add to the sense of a cheerful, cacophonous free-for-all. Menus are fixed and usually consist of all the fish, spaghetti, chicken, and dessert you can eat and copious quantities of wine. Although *cantinas* were formerly patronized by residents from other sections of town, in recent years they have become popular with tourists, and prices have gone up a bit. While a meal should not cost more than $15 per person for entertainment and food, there are places where it's easy to get ripped off. Be sure to ask the price before sitting down to eat. Tours of La Boca, including a dinner at a *cantina*, can best be arranged through one of the travel agencies with desks at the major hotels. The most famous *cantina* is *Spadavecchia*, Necochea 1180 (phone: 21-49-77). Stay away from *La Cueva de Zingarella*, which has the reputation among *porteños* as a grossly overpriced tourist trap.

France Plaza (Plaza Francia) – Particularly lively during spring and summer, this favorite park lures *porteños* to sunbathe, picnic, and nap. Students use it as a place to study and young lovers, as a site for trysts. About twice as big as Plaza San Martín, Plaza Francia has enough grass for children to play soccer. Situated on a long, sloping hill, its asphalt walkways make handy speedways for skateboards and go-carts, so be wary. Vendors sell popcorn, candies, coffee, and ice cream. Also on the plaza is a new and very attractive Cultural Center, or Centro Cultural (Junín 1930; phone: 824-1041), housed in a building once occupied by a home for the aged. Nearby, plenty of *confiterías* and restaurants provide comfortable roosts for surveying the scene. The plaza is on the 1300 block of Av. Libertador.

National Gallery of the Fine Arts (Museo de Bellas Artes) – Across the street from Plaza Francia is Argentina's finest art gallery, with a very strong collection of modern Argentine painters and sculpted wooden artifacts from the interior. Its collections of classical paintings and sculpture are poor in comparison to those found in major US and European museums. One of the greatest honors for a living Argentine artist is to have his or her work exhibited in the gallery, even for a brief time. Open Tuesdays through Saturdays. Admission charge. Av. Libertador 1473 (phone: 83-8814).

Recoleta Cemetery (Cementerio Recoleta) – If you liked Forest Lawn in Los Angeles, you'll adore this place. About half a block from Plaza Francia on Calle Junín, this mausoleum is a venerated necropolis — a city of the dead — and *the* place to be buried in Argentina. The final resting place of patriarchs, presidents, and poets, no common graves are allowed — only crypts housing generations of famous families. Arranged neatly along walkways, the crypts range from the simple to the ostentatious, with architecture in every style from Arabian and Moorish to Greco-Roman, decorated with little pyramids, banks, and war memorials. The central lane of the cemetery, extending from the main Doric entrance, is lined with cypress trees. At the far end stands a bronze statue of the Resurrection. Every day fresh flowers are sold outside the cemetery walls for visitors to place on the graves. For a bit of history, stroll over to the crypt of former President Pedro Aramburu, from which a left-wing group stole his remains in the early 1970s as a political protest. Also pay a visit to the crypt of Eva Peron ("Evita"), a big attraction; it's fun to watch the "pilgrims" come in (most of whom, today, are North American theatergoers). Open daily. Free. Calle Junín.

Rural Society Fairgrounds (Sociedad Rural) – The fairgrounds are the pride and joy of Argentine cattlemen, who take the annual national fair and rodeo, held for three weeks at the end of July, very seriously indeed. The Rural Society, the major cattlemen's association, holds competitions during the fair to determine Argentina's best bull, cow, horse, sheep, and pig. The grounds runneth over with meat on the hoof and on the plate as fairground restaurants spring up to feed hungry cattlemen and cattlewatchers. The most popular event is the gaucho bronco-busting competition, in which these famous Argentine cowboys, dressed in their leather trappings, baggy pants, and boots, ride bucking broncs — it's just like rodeos back home. The fairgrounds' exhibition halls serve as promotional centers for various companies' products — wineries, meat-packing houses, textile handicrafts, leather, and hand-carved bone. At other times, the fairgrounds host exhibitions ranging from dog shows to toy fairs. For information on the fair, check the newspapers or look for posters — it is advertised all around town. Av. Santa Fe 3001, Palermo (phone: 771-6080).

Botanical Gardens (Jardín Botánico) – A municipally run garden containing flowers from around the world, its plants are arranged in orderly rows with labels. One section specializes in Argentinian flora. Plenty of benches line the walkway, so you can sit and breathe the floral-scented air. The gardens are a good place to relax or read outdoors, and many *porteños* come here to do just that. Across from the fairgrounds at Av. Santa Fe 3951.

Argentine Racetrack (Hipodromo Argentino) – With a wooden clubhouse and grandstands that seat around 45,000 spectators, this racetrack is practically a functioning museum piece. Since Argentina is a major producer of thoroughbred horses, the

Hipodromo is the site of most big races, including the National Prize (El Premio Nacional), Argentina's equivalent of the Kentucky Derby, held every year around October. It also is the site of premier international races for horses from other parts of Latin America. Meets take place throughout most of the year. In Palermo, the racetrack can be reached by a 10-minute suburban train ride from Retiro Station downtown. Get off at the stop called Tres de Febrero. Av. Libertador just off Parque Tres de Febrero, Palermo. (phone: 772-6022).

Presidential Residence (Residencia del Presidente) – Covering more than two square blocks, the grounds of this giant mansion are surrounded by a high brick wall with manned sentry posts. Roads lined with shrubs and plants wind through the gardens, where several interesting guesthouses stand. During the last Peronist government, it was possible to visit the chapel where the coffin of Juan Perón, who died in 1974, and the preserved body of his second wife Evita, who died in 1952, were on display. Take a suburban train for a 30-minute ride, from Retiro to Olivos. Calle Maipú, Olivos.

■**EXTRA SPECIAL:** A well-loved Argentine town, *Luján* stands on the spot where a miracle occurred almost 350 years ago when the wagon carrying the statue of the Virgin from one regional church to another suddenly stopped on the road and would not budge for man or beast. Taking this as a sign, the people built a chapel to the Virgin on this site, and the town grew up around it. Every year, more than four million pilgrims worship at the shrine of the Virgin of Luján. In addition to its religious interest, Luján has some great antique automobiles, campsites, and recreational areas with swimming pools. Ancient trees line the banks of the Río Luján, inviting you to lie down in the shade. The Basilica of the Virgin of Luján has become a monumental gothic structure, which you won't be able to miss once you hit town. Along the main street, Calle Constitución, stands the Colonial and Historical Museum of Enrique Udaondo (Museo Colonial e Histórico Enrique Udaondo). It contains reconstructed rooms with period furniture, some dating from the era of Napoleon III, historic carriages, and other archaic vehicles. The museum attracts history buffs from all over Argentina. Also worth a look is the Town Council's prison (carcel de Cabildo), no longer in use. Its list of former occupants include such notables as Bartolomé Mitre, later president of Argentina. To get to Luján, take Avenida Rivadavia west to Route 7 for about 43 miles (71 km). After you cross the white bridge in Luján, you will be on Calle Constitución. You can also take a train from Buenos Aires, the Ferrocarril Sarmiento.

SOURCES AND RESOURCES

TOURIST INFORMATION: For general information, brochures, and maps, contact the National Tourism Office, Av. Santa Fe 883 (phone: 312-2232). Open from 8 AM to 8 PM, Mondays through Fridays. It also has a price list of all major hotels in Buenos Aires and the other major Argentine cities. The Buenos Aires City Tourism Board has information stands at Calle Florida 800 and Calle Florida 100, staffed with some English-speaking employees, where you can pick up their monthly guide for tourists.

Most hotels and tourist agencies provide free maps of the downtown area. Maps of Greater Buenos Aires, including subway and suburban train lines, are available at newsstands for around $2.

Don't expect much from the overloaded telephone system that has not been able to expand fast enough to meet the needs of the rapidly growing city. Also, seepage from the heavy rains frequently causes short circuits in underground cables. Telephone numbers change often, and by the time the telephone book comes out, a staggering proportion of the numbers are already out of date. Telephone numbers are included with addresses in this chapter, but it is only fair to caution you. It is generally faster to visit someone rather than to try to contact them by phone. If the person is not in, you can leave a note. (Dropping in is socially acceptable.) On the other hand, international direct dialing is available in some homes, offices, and hotels.

Local Coverage – The *Buenos Aires Herald,* an excellent English-language morning daily, provides local and international news. It also contains a restaurant and shopping guide, movie listings, and schedules of major cultural events, including performances at the Teatro Colón. *Where,* a monthly publication that includes listings of places to dine, can be found at many new kiosks or in hotel bookstores.

Food – The *Buenos Aires Herald* reviews restaurants and publishes a list of those popular with tourists.

CLIMATE AND CLOTHES: Keep in mind that Buenos Aires lies south of the equator, and its seasons are reversed in relation to those in the Northern Hemisphere.

When it is winter in the US, it is summer in Argentina. B.A.'s winter runs from June to September, with temperatures generally dropping into the 40s F. Rarely does it get colder. The average temperature during July, the coldest month, is 49°F. During the summer, from December to March, temperatures climb into the 80s F, accompanied by high humidity. The mean annual temperature is 61°F. The average yearly rainfall is 38 inches, with the principal rainy season during the winter. Due to the city's proximity to the spot where the 275-mile-wide Río de la Plata meets the Atlantic Ocean, marking the largest coming together of fresh and salt water in the world, Buenos Aires experiences heavy rains. A raincoat or umbrella always comes in handy. In the fall and winter, carry sweaters as further protection against penetrating cold and dampness. Pack dressy clothes for evening wear if you intend to dine at the city's better restaurants or visit nightclubs. During the daytime, informal city dress (not shorts) is appropriate.

GETTING AROUND: Bus – If you arrive at Ezeiza International Airport, you can take a bus to any of the major downtown hotels. Purchase a ticket at the tourist booth just beyond the customs area. The fare is approximately $4.50. Getting around Buenos Aires by bus is easy because of the city's well-organized grid system. Buses pass frequently, about every 5 to 10 minutes, but during rush hours, buses are overcrowded and slow-moving. Fares are based on distance and range from about $1 to $2.50. When you get on the bus, tell the driver your destination and he will tell you the correct fare. Exact change is not required, although drivers are reluctant to change big bills. There is a fairly new bus terminal next to Retiro Station, for city as well as countrywide service. City buses generally do not run between midnight or 1 and 5 AM.

Taxi – You can hire a chauffeured car at the airport for the trip downtown. Because of the country's high inflation, the fares increase frequently. The meter will display a number indicating a fare on an official list displayed in the taxi; a small tip, about 10%, is expected. A trip from the airport to downtown should cost around $30, but an airport bus takes passengers to most hotels for $4.50. In Buenos Aires, taxis are plentiful, inexpensive, and easy to hail in the street anytime. Cabs are metered. Taxi rides around the 32-square-block downtown area cost around $2. If you do not speak Spanish, it is advisable to write the address of your destination for the driver. Taxis are black with a yellow roof. When available, they have a red flag visible in the windshield.

Car Rental – Major international firms are represented. *Hertz,* Av. Corrientes 6122 (phone: 854-8015; *Avis,* Suipacha 268 (phone: 45-19-43 or 311-8882). Other car rental agencies are: *Cars Express SCA,* Marcelo T. Alvear 678 (phone: 311-8563); *Rent-a-Car International,* Marcelo T. Alvear 680 (phone: 312-9475); and *National,* Esmeralda 1084 (phone: 311-3583 or 312-4318).

Subway – Buenos Aires has an antiquated, but serviceable, subway system, outlined on most street maps. It consists of five lines, with one line crossing the others as a transfer line. Four of the lines meet at Plaza de Mayo. A suburban train system, outlined on most street maps, connects downtown with outlying residential areas. The trains leave from four major stations, each heading in a different direction. There are no formal street addresses for these four stations. Any taxi or bus driver will be able to find them by name. You can try to telephone for information, but the phone lines are as busy as Amtrak information in the US. It might be less frustrating to go to the Railway Information Center (CIFA) at Galería Pacífico, Calle Florida 729-53 (phone: 311-6411). The four major train stations are: Retiro (phone: 312-6596); General Belgrano (phone: 311-5287); Constitución (phone: 23-20-01); and Once (phone: 87-00-41).

Plane – Aerolíneas Argentinas offers unlimited travel in Argentina for about $300, good for a period of 30 days. You must buy your ticket in the US, but you do not have to select an itinerary until you arrive in Argentina. You cannot visit any destination on this ticket more than once. This fare is subject to currency changes, so contact Aerolíneas Argentinas, 9 Rockefeller Plaza, New York, NY 10020 (phone: 212-974-3370).

 MUSEUMS: In addition to the National Gallery of Fine Arts (Museo de Bellas Artes), Council House (El Cabildo), and Government House Museum (Museo de la Casa de Gobierno), mentioned in *Special Places,* Buenos Aires has a number of interesting museums:

Museum of Decorative Arts (Museo de Arte Decorativo) and Museum of Oriental Art (Museo de Arte Oriental) – Av. Libertador 1902 (phone: 802-0914).

National Historical Museum (Museo Histórico Nacional) – Contains General José de San Martín's uniforms and furniture. Defensa 1600 (phone: 27-47-67).

Ricardo Rojas Museum and Library (Museo y Biblioteca Ricardo Rojas) – A colonial home dedicated to a famous Argentine man of letters, it contains his library, books, and souvenirs of his travels. Charcas 2837 (phone: 824-4039).

Mitre Museum (Museo Mitre) – In the former home of 19th-century Argentine President Bartolomé Mitre, who was also the founder of *La Nación* newspaper, it contains his manuscripts and documents. Calle San Martín 336 (phone: 394-8240).

Hispanic-American Art Museum (Museo Municipal de Arte Hispano Americano) – In a lovely reproduction of a colonial mansion, this museum specializes in colonial artifacts and silver. Suipacha 1422 (phone: 393-5899).

Natural Science Museum (Museo de Ciencias Naturales) – Contains zoological, marine, botanical, and mineralogical exhibits. Av. Angel Gallardo 490 (phone: 812-5243).

José Hernandez Museum (Museo José Hernandez) – Specializes in the culture of the gauchos, Argentina's fabled cowboys. José Hernandez is the 19th-century writer who immortalized gaucho life in his classic, *Martín Fierro.* Av. Libertador 2373 (phone: 802-9967).

 SHOPPING: Traditionally, Buenos Aires has been a good place to buy leather goods. All those cows that provide good eating also provide good tanning. Fine-quality leather is again inexpensive compared to prices for leather of comparable quality available in the US and Europe. When shopping, remember not to confuse the currency, called australes. On June 15, 1985, the Argentine peso, up till then legal tender, was changed for the austral. One austral is equivalent to 1,000 Argentine pesos. You can change money at banks from 10 AM to 1 PM and at exchange houses, which are located primarily along Calle San Martín between Corrientes and Cangallo (Mondays through Fridays from 10 AM to 3 PM; one or two exchange houses are open on Saturday mornings, on a rotating basis, from 9 AM to noon). Be sure to carry your passport when changing traveler's checks.

The most expensive shops can be found on Calle Florida and along Av. Santa Fe off Plaza San Martín. *López* is one of the best places to purchase quality leather. There is a branch in the *Sheraton* hotel, San Martín 1225 (phone: 311-6310) and another in the *Plaza* hotel, Florida 1005 (phone: 311-5011). Be sure to check the thread on leather goods and clothes. As a cost-cutting measure, low-quality thread, which breaks easily, has been used. The *Pullman* chain of shops is another good choice for leather goods; Esmeralda 321, Florida 350, Florida 985 (phone: 46-41-11). Also noteworthy is *Lofty's* at M. T. de Alvear 519. *Rossi y Caruso,* Av. Santa Fe 1601 (phone: 41-19-65), has traditional leather goods. As does *Welcome* at the corner of San Martín and M. T. de Alvear.

Folk crafts in leather or wool from the Argentine provinces are available at *Artesanías Argentinas,* Montevideo 1386 (phone: 44-26-50), and *Carpinchería,* Galería del Este, Calle Florida at San Martín Plaza (no phone).

Harrods, Buenos Aires's largest, exclusive department store, stocks leather goods, toys, cutlery, and a range of products similar in quality to its high-class London namesake (though they are not related). Florida 877 (phone: 312-4411).

For the best buys in suede over-the-calf boots (*botas saltenas*) for men and women, hunt along Calle Carlos Pellegrini, which runs parallel to Avenida 9 de Julio. Prices here are less expensive than along Florida.

For bargains in clothing, check out the piles of merchandise in the bargain-basement stores of the Once (Eleven) district, starting around Corrientes 2400. In clutter, friendly noise, and rock-bottom prices, the atmosphere is similar to that of New York's Lower East Side. But be patient: It takes determined hunting to locate better-quality goods in the piles of merchandise.

SPECIAL EVENTS: Argentina's two independence days, May 25 and July 9, are national holidays celebrated with religious services at the cathedral, and special performances at the Teatro Colón. The *Rural Society Fair (Feria de la Sociedad Rural),* around the end of July, is the occasion for mass family outings at the fairgrounds. *Tradition Day (Día de la Tradición),* November 10, honors the gaucho. It is celebrated with folkloric and cultural activities, especially in the town of San Antonio de Areco, an hour's drive west of the capital. The *Feast of Our Lady of Lujan (Fiesta de Nuestra Señora de Lujan),* a major religious celebration on December 8, is marked by a pilgrimage to Lujan from Buenos Aires, with the pilgrims accompanied by colonial-style oxcarts and gauchos in rustic costumes on horseback.

SPORTS: By far the most popular spectator and participant sport, soccer (*fútbol*) generates fevered passion among Argentines. Auto racing, *pato* — a unique Argentine combination of polo and soccer on horseback — and polo have large followings, too. For information on sports events, consult the listings in the *Buenos Aires Herald.*

Golf – Golf remains the domain of the privileged classes. The *Sheraton, Claridge,* and the *Plaza* hotels can arrange for guest passes to private clubs.

Pato – A combination of polo and soccer, *pato* is played on horseback. The object is to throw a soccer-sized ball through the opponent's goal. Handles are attached to the ball so it can be passed from horseman to horseman. Allegedly the game got its name, which means "duck," because where it originated in the Argentine interior a live duck was used rather than a ball. The best time to see *pato* is during the national championships, held in November and December at the Campo de Mayo, San Isidro, and Palermo sports fields just outside B.A.

Polo – This is one of the more pronounced Anglicisms in Argentine life. Some of the world's best polo players can be found on Argentine teams, competing in international tournaments. The season runs from August through November and consists of a series of tournaments in which teams compete according to their handicap. The season climaxes in November with the Open Championship at the Palermo Polo Fields. For information, see the *Buenos Aires Herald*.

Racing – Around the second week in January, Buenos Aires hosts the opening race of the annual world Grand Prix championship, at the Autodrome (Autodromo), General La Paz and Puerto Ocho, Parque Almirante Brown (phone: 601-5590). National Races are held throughout the year. The major horse racing event, the National Prize (El Premio Nacional), is run around September or October, at the Hippodrome (Hipodromo), Av. Libertador, 3 de Febrero, Palermo. International races for horses from other parts of Latin America take place throughout the year.

Soccer – Greater Buenos Aires has about ten major league teams that create innumerable crosstown rivalries, similar to those in London, England. The strongest rivalry is between *Boca Juniors* and *River Plate*. To celebrate victories, their fanatical fans drive around the city all night, blowing car horns and waving their team's pennants. In addition to the major leagues, some form of soccer tournament is going on all year long. The soccer fever is heightened by government-sponsored gambling. Weekly soccer pools offer *porteños* the chance to become rich overnight if they guess the winning teams that week. If you plan to attend a soccer match for the first time while in the city, bear in mind that the fans often become rowdy. The most frenzied game of all took place in 1978, when Argentina first won the World Cup, the symbol of international soccer supremacy, in a round-robin competition against the top teams from 15 other nations. Victory was especially sweet since the championships were held in Argentina, with B.A. the site of the deciding match. Since winning the World Cup for a second time in Mexico in 1986, the Argentines have become, if anything, even more fanatical. A word of advice to first-timers: When in doubt, root for the home team.

Tennis – Since Guillermo Vilas, an Argentine, became a US Open winner and one of the world's top tennis players, tennis (*tenís*) has started to gain popularity with the public. The *Sheraton* hotel has tennis courts, and there are public courts at Centro de Deportes de la Boca, Costanera (no phone), where anyone can play for a fee.

 THEATER: The few English-language productions, staged mostly by amateur groups, are listed in the *Buenos Aires Herald*. Occasionally professional English-language touring groups pass through town, performing at *Teatro Cervantes,* Libertad 815 (phone: 45-42-24). If you are comfortable with your Spanish, by all means, go to see an Argentinian play. The acting is generally good, the staging excellent and imaginative. Argentina has produced its own theatrical form, "the theater of the grotesque," so called because many of its characters are physically ugly or deformed as a symbol of their tortured lives and souls. Similar to the early tangos, the basic themes of these *obras grotescas* (grotesque works) are the social aspirations and subsequent frustrations of the poor and working classes. From time to time, theaters stage excellent Spanish adaptations of famous plays from other languages. For modern, lighter plays, visit the *Teatro Regina,* Av. Santa Fe 1235 (phone: 41-57-09). New, experimental plays can be seen at *Teatro Payro,* San Martín 766 (phone: 312-5922). The best places for Spanish adaptations of foreign-language plays are *Teatro Cervantes* (address and phone above) and *Teatro San Martín,* Av. Corrientes 1530 (phone: 46-8611 or 40-01-11). Complete theater listings are published daily in *La Nación, Clarín, La Prensa,* and *La Razón.*

MUSIC: Classical music and tangos dominate the music scene. Local jazz and rock groups of rather unexceptional quality proliferate. B.A.'s excellent chamber music group, *Camarata Bariloche,* performs regularly during the winter and fall season at *Teatro Coliseo,* Marcelo T. Alvear 1119 (phone: 393-7115). Opera is strictly the domain of the *Teatro Colón.* Although performances are not up to European standards, they are generally the best in Latin America. B.A.'s foremost tango musicians, singer Susana Rinaldi and bandoneón player-composer Astor Piazzola, perform at various clubs during the fall and winter. Piazzola has modernized tango music by adapting it to electronic instruments. A classic spot for tango is *El Viejo Almacén,* in the San Telmo district, at Av. Independencia and Balcarce. Visitors may not understand the jokes, but the art form speaks a universal language. Outside San Telmo the best tango parlor is *Caño 14,* Talcahuano 975 (phone: 393-4626). The clown princes of Argentine music, the group *Les Luthiers,* zanily spoof everything from opera to travelogue background music. They specialize in playing unusual, funny instruments — slide trombones made from vacuum cleaners and violins made from giant ham tins. To fully enjoy it though, you need a working knowledge of Spanish. Although their musical high jinks and sight gags need no translation, many sketches depend on dialogue. Complete listings of Les Luthiers' scheduled engagements and other musical performances are found in the Spanish-language dailies with selected entries in the *Buenos Aires Herald* and *Que Hacemos.*

 NIGHTCLUBS AND NIGHTLIFE: The downtown area is practically one big nightclub. *Michelangelo,* a reconverted old warehouse, serves dinner and has a show at Balcarce 433 (phone: 33-53-92). Other well-known nightclubs are *Karim,* Carlos Pellegrini 1143 (phone: 393-9609); *King's,* Córdoba 937 (phone: 392-0499); *Karina,* Corrientes 636 (phone: 40-17-08); and *Maison Doree,* Viamonte 548 (phone: 312-1152). *Karim* is noted for its *coperas* (cup bearers), overly friendly hostesses who spend most of the evening enticing men to buy them expensive drinks. The come-on is accompanied by a vague promise that the hostess might be willing to walk the man home. If a man can stay sober and not spend all his money during the show, a *copera* might even keep her promise. For disco, try *Le Club* at Quintana 1111 and the *Mau-Mau* at Arroyo 866. For tango dancing (go escorted) and a tango show, try *Taconeando,* which opens at 11 PM.

Vaudeville is alive and well in Buenos Aires. Known as *revistas,* these music hall revues of scantily clad women, double-entendre skits, and stand-up comics are exceptionally popular with *porteños.* Tickets should be reserved in advance. One of the most popular *revista* music halls is *Teatro Maipo,* Esmeralda 443 (phone: 392-4882). If you are looking for an intimate, softer bar, try *Cristóbal Colón,* Las Heras 2435 (phone: 825-3666), and *Bar-Baro,* Tres Sargentos 475.

Nightclubs exclusively featuring folk music from the provinces are *El Palo Boracho,* Av. Corrientes 2166 (phone: 941-0164) and *El Chalchalero,* Cuba 2290 (phone: 785-8124).

SINS: If you want to indulge in *gluttony,* try any restaurant in B.A. *Porteños* are natural gluttons. To satisfy any *lust*ful cravings, stroll along Veinticinco de Mayo between Viamonte and Córdoba. This three-block-long honky-tonk string of bars and dives caters primarily to merchant sailors, so watch out: The cost of penicillin to combat the effects of a quick fling here can up the price of your lustful jaunt from around $30 to something considerably higher. At *Karim* (see *Nightclubs and Nightlife,* above), an evening with a *copera* will cost a bit more than a trip through Reconquista; expect to pay between $25 and $40 for favors rendered. The *porteños'* rabid enthusiasm for soccer is always a source of *pride,* whether they win or lose.

BEST IN TOWN

 CHECKING IN: Buenos Aires has downtown hotels aplenty for every pocketbook. However, the city's top-quality establishments are not exactly inexpensive; those bargain prices that proliferated a couple of years ago have climbed the stairs. Expect to pay at least $85 a day for a double room in hotels we've classed as very expensive, $75 in expensive, about $50 in hotels rated moderate, and between $15 and $25 for hotels in the inexpensive category.

Plaza – This long-time favorite of locals and foreigners alike is centrally located, across the street from tree-filled Plaza San Martín. The public rooms have been lovingly refurbished, as have the guestrooms overlooking the plaza. Nothing is new about the *Plaza*'s reputation as the place to have high tea. Both the *Grill* restaurant and the hotel's bar are popular spots in town. Florida 1005 (phone: 311-5011). Very expensive.

Sheraton – Contemporary comfort in a self-contained hotel environment makes this exceptionally popular with conventions and package tour groups from the US. En route to the restaurants, cocktail lounges, coffee shop, boutiques, wine and cheese bar, heated swimming pool, tennis courts, or sauna, you can expect to encounter groups of conventioneers shuttling from guestrooms to meeting halls. The lobby is busy, too. The hotel offers chauffeured limousine service, tour agencies, and a shopping arcade. San Martín 1225 (phone: 311-6311). Very expensive.

Claridge – The most venerable of Buenos Aires hotels, with some visitors it will always be tops. English elegance prevails, from the wood paneling and high ceilings to the prim uniformed maids (in starched caps) parading around the floors. The hotel has its own chauffeured limousine service, with English-speaking drivers available (at prices substantially higher than taxi fares; rates are quoted in advance for trips to specific parts of town). Guestrooms are equipped with refrigerators stocked with soft drinks, beer, snacks, ice cubes, and liquor. You are charged for what you consume. The restaurant is one of the best in town, and high tea here is a delicious tradition. There is also an outdoor swimming pool. Tucumán 535 (phone: 393-7212). Expensive.

Elevage – The most deluxe establishment in town, though service isn't always first rate. The hotel is small (86 rooms and 12 suites), with an outdoor patio and pool, bars, nightclub, and the *L'Escoffier* restaurant. Just off Calle Florida and the Plaza San Martín. Maipu 960 (phone: 393-2882). Expensive.

Bauen – A modern hotel not far from the San Martín theater/cultural center. The restaurant boasts reasonably priced good meals and the nightclub attracts some of the most popular local and international entertainment. Callao 360 (phone: 393-2210). Expensive.

Libertador – This hotel has 212 rooms; two fine restaurants, *El Portal* and *La Pergola*. Facilities include rooftop swimming pool and solarium, sauna, and gym. Av. Córdoba 664 (phone: 392-2095). Expensive.

Panamericano – A fairly new hotel almost opposite the obelisk, it has 225 rooms and 25 suites, all with color TV and a refrigerator. There are also three bars, a restaurant, and a basement pool. Carlos Pellegrini 525 (phone: 393-6017). Expensive.

De Las Américas – First class and centrally located, off Avenida 9 de Julio and not far from the Colón Theater, with 175 fully air-conditioned rooms, sauna, beauty salon, snack bar, restaurant, and auditorium. Libertad 1020 (phone: 393-3432). Moderate.

Lancaster – This is one of the best moderately priced hotels. Although the rooms are not very big, they are comfortable and well furnished. A spacious reading room set behind the small lobby is stocked with daily newspapers. A cozy breakfast room and bar behind the reading room serves breakfast, snacks, and drinks most of the day. There is a small, excellent restaurant. Av. Córdoba 405 (phone: 311-3021). Moderate.

Gran Hotel Buenos Aires – Just off Plaza San Martín, it offers comfort and efficiency without luxury. It is big, conveniently located, and usually has rooms available. No restaurant, but a small breakfast room. Marcelo T. Alvear 767 (phone: 312-3001). Moderate.

Liberty – Ideally situated on Avenida Corrientes around the corner from Calle Florida, this modest hotel features a small but popular bar that seems to be frequented by friends of the hotel's guests. Be sure to secure a room away from Corrientes or else the noise of the city that never sleeps will prevent you from catching even a few winks. Corrientes 626-32 (phone: 46-0261). Moderate.

Regidor – Conveniently and centrally located, this hotel offers the additional advantage of not being on a street that is heavily traveled at night. If you are sensitive to noise, it is a better choice than the other downtown hotels in this category. Tucumán 451 (phone: 393-9615). Moderate.

Carsson – Although not well known, this tastefully decorated, wood-paneled downtown hotel often has rooms available for travelers arriving, baggage in hand. It also has a nice tea room that serves cocktails and a central location. Viamonte 650 (phone: 392-3551). Moderate.

City – If you are traveling on a budget but still want to experience the heritage of old-style elegance for which the grander hotels are famous, this is the place. Near San Telmo, the tango district, this old building has big rooms, spacious, old-fashioned bathtubs, and noisy radiators. At one time among the foremost hotels in town, the *City* retains the character of the old days, although the polish, snap, and performance of its former era of luxury are gone. Bolívar 160 (phone: 34-6481). Moderate.

San Antonio – Another place for the budget-conscious traveler, with neat, clean rooms with sparse but serviceable furnishings. There's a small, comfortable breakfast room that also serves short-order lunches and dinners. Paraguay 372 (phone: 312-5381). Inexpensive.

King's – Across the street from the *Liberty,* this place has more of an English flavor than its neighbor. The small, cozy cocktail lounge and tea room are worth visiting even if you do not stay at the hotel, but don't confuse it with *King's* nightclub (see *Nightclubs and Nightlife*). Corrientes 623 (phone: 392-8161). Inexpensive.

Mendoza – Excellent if you're planning to stay in town for a long time, this place comes highly recommended by experienced South American travelers. In the center of town, it is clean, friendly, and modestly priced. There are no private baths, but lots of hot water. Calle 25 de Mayo 674 (phone: 311-3305). Inexpensive.

Plaza Francia – If you want to stay out of the commercial district, this hotel is within walking distance of Plaza Francia and the elegant shops at Av. Alvear. Eduardo Schiaffino 2189 (phone: 441-7223). Inexpensive.

 EATING OUT: As dedicated night people, *porteños* love to eat out. Argentine food is abundant and tasty, and visitors have no trouble finding places to eat well that are relatively inexpensive. The main dish is beefsteak, usually accompanied by salad, wine, potatoes, dessert, and espresso. In fact, the all-pervasive aroma of beef led one Egyptian journalist to comment that B.A. smelled like a steakhouse. Although Argentina has excellent fish, most *porteños* prefer beef, and most of the restaurants do not prepare fish very well, except in specialty houses so advertised. The dinner hour is late by US standards; most restaurants do not start serving the evening meal until 8 PM. For those unwilling to wait, try a *confitería* or pizzeria. Remember, too, that restaurants do not serve light soup and sandwich lunches as they do commonly in the US. In most places, the lunch menu is the same as the dinner menu. *Confiterías* are the best bet for light lunches and for cocktails. Restaurants serve cocktails, but do not specialize in mixed drinks. Argentines drink wine with dinner.

Unless specified, there's no need for reservations at any of the restaurants listed below. Because of inflation and the current devaluation, restaurant prices have been fluctuating considerably in the past few years. Expect to pay around $40 to $50 for dinner for two at the restaurants we've noted as expensive; between $10 and $20 at those places noted as moderate; about $10, inexpensive. Prices do not include drinks, wine, or tips.

Claridge – One of the best restaurants in town because of its excellent cuisine, service, and elegant atmosphere. As you enter, you pass the portable cold buffet table of appetizers — salads, marinated fish, and cold meats. Waiters deftly maneuver the sumptuous, felt-cushioned wooden armchairs so that you fit snugly around the tables. In addition to the ubiquitous steak, the *Claridge* serves a variety of other beef dishes — pepper steak, sliced steak, and other cuts smothered in a variety of mushroom and wine sauces. One of the best dishes, pressed duck, appears regularly on its international menu. The wine list includes an impressive, expensive selection of imported vintages. This is the restaurant chosen by wealthy *porteños* for grand celebrations. Open daily from noon until 3 PM and from 8 PM until midnight. Reservations are not required. Major credit cards accepted. Tucumán 535 (phone: 393-7212). Expensive.

Plaza Grill – Alternating with the *Claridge* as the "in" restaurant of B.A., it still advertises such exotic dishes as wild boar. You will probably be better off sticking to steaks, casseroles, and fish in wine sauces — all well prepared. Service is a little slow here, and getting the attention of your waiter can be trying. Open from noon to 4 PM and from 8 PM to midnight. Reservations are not necessary. Major credit cards accepted. Florida 1005 (phone: 311-5011). Expensive.

El Aljibe – This restaurant of the *Sheraton* hotel offers good American cuisine and is a pleasant alternative to local and international menus of the standard B.A. restaurants. Grilled salmon and stuffed turkey are among the specialties. Open daily from noon to 3 PM and from 8 PM to 1 AM. Major credit cards accepted. San Martín 1225 (phone: 311-6311). Expensive.

El Recodo – As you settle into one of the high, delicate, straight-backed chairs, you can expect luscious international food and personal service. Meals are often preceded by complimentary sherry, but don't let it go to your head — you'll want to appreciate the appetizers of salads and cold meats that are wheeled to your table. We suggest you follow the starters with seafood. Smoked trout and salmon are the house specialties. Open daily except Sundays from noon to 4 PM and from 8 PM to 1 AM. Diners Club only. Lavalle 130 (phone: 312-2453). Expensive.

Pedemonte – This elegant restaurant is where the leaders of the business community meet for lunch and where visiting celebrities frequently dine in the evenings. Typical Argentine dishes as well as international favorites are featured on the menu. Av. de Mayo 676 (phone: 34-4633). Expensive.

Hostal del Lago – At this beautiful restaurant in the park area of Palermo, there's music and dancing and international cuisine. During the summer, cocktails are served on the terrace under the trees. Av. Figueroa Alcorta 6400 (phone: 783-8760). Expensive.

Clark's I – *The* hangout for the jet set. A window filled with colorful exotic birds sets the style for lively dining. The food is quite good, though expensive. One offshoot of this restaurant, *Clark's II,* is in the heart of the downtown business district, and is patronized by the city's leading businessmen. *Clark's I* is at Junín 1777 (phone: 801-9502), and *Clark's II,* at Sarmiento 645 (phone: 45-1960). Expensive.

Catalinas – Ramiro Rodriguez Pardo, formerly of *Clark's,* has taken over *Catalinas* and is doing a beautiful job. Excellent international cuisine has made it very popular among *porteños.* Reconquista 875 (phone: 313-0182). Expensive.

Tomo I – An excellent, family-run, French restaurant in an elegant turn-of-the-century house. Credit cards accepted. Las Heras 3766 (phone: 801-6253). Expensive.

London Grill – An English chop house popular with journalists and businesspeople, the *Grill* fills very quickly at lunchtime, when it is wise to reserve in advance. No reservations are necessary in the evening. Besides serving mountains of meat, it offers an excellent chicken casserole and trout in black butter. Open daily. No credit cards. Reconquista 455 (phone: 311-2223). Moderate.

La Cabaña – One of the city's most famous steak houses, it specializes in huge *bola de lomo,* a tender filet. It also serves Argentine *parrillada,* a mixed barbecue of sausage, blood sausage, and parts of the cow not normally eaten in the US — intestines and brains, for instance. The off-cuts taste a lot better then they sound, so don't be squeamish about trying them. Another specialty is *matambre* — a generous slice of rolled veal stuffed with hard-boiled eggs, olives, pepper, salt, onion, garlic, and chili. As you enter, you will see rows of refrigerated cuts of meat available for you to select. Open daily. Major credit cards accepted. Entre Ríos 436 (phone: 38-2373). Moderate.

Tropezón – Another fine steakhouse with an additional house specialty called *puchero mixto,* a casserole of boiled slices of beef, pork, and chicken with vegetables. Open daily. No credit cards. Callao 248 (phone: 45-6453). Moderate.

La Estancia – In the heart of downtown, near the movie and hotel district, this place features eye-catching cooks dressed as gauchos who roast steak, chicken, goat, and pig. Try the roasted goat (*chivito*) and suckling pig (*lechon*). The *parrillada* and steaks are good, too. Open daily. Major credit cards accepted. Lavalle 941 (phone: 35-0336). Moderate.

Felix – In business for over 20 years, this is a good spot to sample seafood. The fish filet al roquefort (*pescado con roquefort*) is covered with a rich, thick, and creamy sauce. If you are feeling adventurous, order the Italian squid dishes (*calamaretti*) or frog (*rana*). Codfish (*bacalao*) is popular with the regulars, too. Closed Sundays. Open from noon to 4 PM and 7 PM to 2 AM the rest of the week. Diners Club accepted. Ecuador 794, Avellaneda (phone: 208-2539). Moderate.

Subito – This sleek new Northern Italian restaurant, on the second floor of an elegant shopping gallery, was modeled after *Pronto* in New York. Like its prototype, it features an airy, multi-level dining room, a chic crowd, and a pasta chef who churns out spectacular tagliatelle and fettuccine. Open from noon to 4 PM and 8:30 PM to midnight. Closed Sundays. Diners Club and American Express accepted. Paraguay 640 (phone: 313-6125). Moderate.

Cantina Norte – A small restaurant serving excellent steaks and a limited international menu, it numbers among its foremost patrons B.A.'s most distinguished author, Jorge Luis Borges. The simple, folksy decor consists of hams hanging from the ceiling and shelves of wine lining the walls. To retrieve wine from the top shelves, the waiters tip the bottle with a pole and then catch it as it falls. They rarely miss. Stuffed pasta, meat pies (*empanadas*), and seafood round out the culinary repertoire. Major credit cards accepted. Open daily from noon to 3 PM and from 8 PM to midnight. Marcelo T. Alvear 786 (phone: 312-8778). Moderate.

El Caldero – This medieval banquet hall allows you to serve yourself all you can eat from huge cauldrons of soups, casseroles, goulash, vegetables, and garnished meats. Musicians perform medieval songs. Open from 9:30 PM to 2 AM. Closed Sundays and Mondays. Reservations required. Major credit cards accepted. Gorriti 3972 (phone: 89-2335). Moderate.

Kalispera – Greek and Middle Eastern food are served to the accompaniment of Greek and Armenian music with dancers. The atmosphere is pleasant and offers an enjoyable change from the usual. Closed Mondays. Open from 11 PM to 4 AM the rest of the week. Diners Club accepted. Montevideo 779 (no phone). Moderate.

El Palo Borracho – Folklore nightclub entertainment is offered with meals featuring a hot, spicy meat, a corn casserole (*locro*) from rural Argentina, and an assortment of goat cheeses (*quesos de cabra*). Closed Mondays. Open from 9 PM to 3 AM the rest of the week. The show starts at 11 PM. Reservations are advisable. Diners Club accepted. Corrientes 2166 (phone: 941-0164). Moderate.

Edelweiss – As its name suggests, this is a good place to sample decent German cooking (or a good steak, if you prefer). Its wide assortment of cold appetizers include pickled vegetables and marinated fish. The service is good and the waiters, friendly; popular with artists. Closed Sundays. Open 24 hours a day the rest of the week. Libertad 431 (phone: 35-33-51). Moderate.

La Mosca Blanca – Don't let the name ("the white fly") turn you off. This is an excellent, comfortably priced steak house specializing in portions big enough for two hungry people (you can order half-portions). In addition to steak, the menu offers pork chops, seafood, pasta, breaded beef cutlet stuffed with ham and cheese — enough to feed four people. Another hearty filler is the boiled meat and vegetable stew (*puchero*). The major drawback here is the restaurant's location between two major railroad stations, which makes for a noisy background. Open daily from noon to 3 PM and from 8 PM to midnight. Dr. J. M. Ramos Mejía 1430 (phone: 313-4890). Moderate.

Don Luis – One of the premier homemade pasta restaurants, this is the best place in town for macaroni topped with spicy sauces and ample shavings of grated cheese. Try *capelettis caruso* — macaroni covered with a thick tomato, meat, and mushroom sauce. Paella, the Spanish rice dish, is another good choice. Although no reservations are needed, the place is jammed at lunch. By 1 PM, all tables are full. In the evening, seating is no problem. Open daily from noon to 2:30 PM and from 8 to 11:30 PM. Diners Club accepted. Viamonte 1169 (phone: 46-18-06). Moderate.

L'Eau Vive – About 42 miles (about 68 km) from B.A. in the small town of Lujan, an odd combination of cuisine from Haiti, Algeria, black Africa, and the South Seas is the specialty here. You can order chicken, Algerian style; rabbit prepared in any number of different national dishes; and Caribbean meats covered with juicy, sweet tropical fruit. The restaurant is operated by an organization of Roman Catholic laywomen with members from Third World countries around the world dressed in native clothing. The women also serve meals and cook. Closed Sundays and Mondays. Open the rest of the week from noon to 4 PM and from 8:30 PM to midnight. Reservations are required. No credit cards. Constitutión 2105, Lujan (phone: 0323-2-1774). Moderate.

La Bodega – Aptly named "the wine cellar," the long, narrow interior is lined with wine bottles. Homemade pastas and steaks cooked in a variety of sauces and spices are the house specialties. In this male-dominated society, this restaurant observes the unusual practice of employing waitresses only. No reservations are necessary, but as the restaurant seats only about 100 people, it fills quickly for both lunch and dinner. Closed Sundays. Open from noon to 3 PM and from 8:30 PM to 12:30 AM. No credit cards. Bartolomé Mitre 1286 (phone: 38-9955). Inexpensive.

El Mundo – Although it offers little variety outside of steak, salad, antipasto, and vegetables, the food and service are good and the portions, hefty. Excellent value. Closed Sundays; open from 11 AM to 4 PM and from 7 to 10 PM. No credit cards. Maipú 550 (phone: 392-2397). Inexpensive.

El Globo – This quaint Spanish restaurant with light brown wood paneling and huge fans hanging from the ceiling serves terrific paella — rice and peas heaped with meat and fish. It also serves a tasty seafood casserole in rich, dark gravy (*cazuela de mariscos*). Open daily from noon to 4 PM and from 8 PM to 1 AM. No credit cards. Hipólito Yrigoyen 1199 (phone: 38-3926). Inexpensive.

La Payanca – A rustic, bilevel restaurant with a large bar–service counter downstairs and a family dining room upstairs. Bartenders clang a huge bell every time they are tipped. Upstairs is somewhat more subdued, but it's still not the place for a quiet meal. However, it is the best place in the city to taste northern Argentine cuisine, generally spicier than the food in Buenos Aires. The corn or wheat casserole with chopped meat and hot pepper (*locro*) is very good. Closed Sundays. No credit cards. Suipacha 1015 (phone: 312-5209). Inexpensive.

Confiterías – No section on eating out in Buenos Aires would be complete without mentioning these cathedrals for the worship of teatime pastries. Many are located in huge, old buildings with high ceilings. Inside are display cases of bread, sweet rolls, cream puffs, eclairs, cakes, and pies in abundance. Although *confiterías* specialize in afternoon tea, they also serve excellent sandwiches and are popular for quick lunches. As in Paris cafés, *confiterías* rather than bars are frequented by businesspeople stopping in for a drink after work. Cocktails are served with delicious snacks that are a meal in themselves. *Confiterías* are open from breakfast through midnight snack. Some of the best are: *Periplo,* an elegant pub opposite the *Plaza,* M. T. de Alvear (phone: 311-2885); *Richmond,* Florida 468 (phone: 392-1341); *Ideal,* Suipacha 384 (phone: 35-1515); *Petit Colón,* Libertad 505 (phone: 35-7306); *Queen Bess,* Santa Fe 868 (phone: 311-3885); *Florida Garden,* corner of Florida and Paraguay (phone: 312-7902); *Petit Café,* Santa Fe 1818 (phone: 41-6325); and *Tortoni,* Av. de Mayo 825 (phone: 34-4328).

Los Carritos de la Costanera – Costanera is a broad avenue that winds alongside the Río de la Plata, and the word *carritos* refers to the modern, almost identical beef barbecue restaurants lining the side of the road. The restaurants are so named because years ago men with pushcarts (*carritos*) containing grills used to barbecue meat for hungry railway and dock workers' lunches. The pushcarts have long since disappeared, but *los carritos* now serve the same fare. If you stroll along the Costanera, you will see about 20 such restaurants of varying quality. They have names, but are often referred to by number. During the summer, you can sit outdoors under a pavilion. Open daily. Some accept credit cards. Costanera. Moderate to inexpensive.

CARACAS

The capital of Venezuela — the richest nation in Latin America and one of the world's largest producers of oil — is a contemporary, cosmopolitan city with chronic growing pains. New buildings are going up all the time. Businesspeople from all over the world pass through town, and many take up residence for periods of years. Yet despite the sleek sophistication for which it is renowned, *caraqueños* (as residents are called) are frequently unable to praise their city at the same time they express affection for it. Raucous Caracas is one of those places that grows on you, they say. It's not a city you're likely to fall in love with at first sight, if at all.

But inhabitants of any city are generally too immersed in its day-to-day rhythms to be able to perceive it with the openness of a first-timer. They become accustomed to wrestling with the problems of traveling to and from offices, working, and raising families. Yet Caracas is, in a strange way, extremely well suited to tourism. And visitors are able to sample its best without succumbing to the frustrations that *caraqueños* gripe about.

A city of about 4 million people (probably many more if you count illegal aliens), Caracas occupies a long, narrow, 9-mile valley that follows the east-west course of the Río Guaire. The Guaire rises about 20 miles (32 km) west of Caracas in El Junquito, flowing southeast through the city into the Río Tuy, which in turn flows into the sea. Covering about 45 square miles, the city stands about 12 miles (19 km) south of the Caribbean coast, with a forested mountain, Mt. Avila (7,380 feet above sea level at its peak), separating it from the sea. The uniform greenness of Avila contrasts with the unrelenting "forest" of cement and steel girders of downtown Caracas. The city's elevation of about 3,000 feet gives the place a springlike climate, with an average yearly temperature of 77°F (25°C). Unquestionably, the mountain, linked to the city by a *teleférico* (cable car), and the mellow weather are what *caraqueños* like best about the place.

A glittering valley at night, Caracas tends to be a hectic, traffic-clogged, polluted nightmare during the middle of the day, and despite all cars having to spend one day a week off the road, traffic jams are a continuous hazard. (However, the first stage of the city's subway, which has now been in operation for two years, has facilitated west-east travel as far as Chacaito. The next stage, through to Petare in the west, is eagerly awaited.) Afternoons are more chaotic, especially during the rainy season from May through December. Then, the so-called Ciudad de las Autopistas (City of Highways) becomes a frenzied, soggy mess.

Because of the incredible wealth that has poured into Caracas from the oil revenues, it has sometimes been compared to Dallas or Houston. "I'm sure Texas runs a lot better," one resident observed with wry good humor. "Actually, it's more like Nigeria or Saudi Arabia. In spite of the profusion of

Mercedes-Benzes and other big foreign cars, the rampant construction, and all other indications of modern-day progress, Caracas suffers from an overloaded phone system, poor drainage in the streets, lousy garbage collection, and occasionally even water shortages. The city has grown too quickly in the past few decades; just 40 years ago it was less than one-fourth its present official size. As in many developing countries, services have not kept pace with the people's needs." Vast improvements have been made in recent years, though the pace of urban development has slowed as the recent glut of oil (and a diminution of revenues) has grown.

Although oil was first discovered in Venezuela's Lake Maracaibo in 1917, Caracas began to be profoundly affected by the impact of the expanding petroleum industry only after World War II. From the postwar years until the present, Caracas has absorbed more than one million immigrants, mostly from Italy, Spain, Portugal, and the rest of Latin America. Many entered the country illegally from Colombia and Ecuador, lured by the prospect of employment in the oil fields; a smaller number of people arrived from the US, Northern and Western Europe, and the Orient. But current lack of employment has stemmed the flow and even reversed it in some cases, with people returning to their home countries. Caracas is still flooded with immigrants from the Venezuelan interior, many of whom have settled in the red huts dubbed *ranchos* that cover the western part of the city and the slopes of the eastern hills. Although many *ranchos'* floors are dusty ground rather than shiny linoleum and bathrooms are little more than washbasins or holes in the floor, plasterless walls are lined with posters of the latest rock and cinema stars, and intricate antennas adorn many roofs — a testament to the presence of brand-new TVs, attained by means legal and illegal.

Lining the valley, between these ramshackle shelters of the poor who comprise more than 50% of Caracas's population, are the business section (El Centro) and the affluent eastern residential area (El Este), where you need an income of over $50,000 a year in order to live. Even a house without a golden toilet or an oil well in the garden can cost as much as $300,000 in El Este. Most of the snazzy shopping malls and private schools are concentrated here, as are office buildings that strive to outdazzle each other with marble decorations and spacious penthouse executive suites. El Centro, the oldest section of the city, contains most of the city's colonial buildings, historical monuments, museums, and old churches. But, unfortunately, these picturesque remnants of old Caracas are being methodically swallowed up by office buildings, replaced by government projects and retail centers, and eaten away by automobile exhaust. Sadly, only a few of the older buildings in La Candelaria and La Pastora sections of town have been preserved and restored. El Centro is dominated by the two skyscrapers of Centro Símon Bolívar and the government-subsidized residential city of Parque Central: five high-rise buildings equipped with standard modern comforts, yet from time to time lacking such essential services as water, electricity, and elevators that function. Looking into the city from either of these two busy complexes at midday offers a more realistic idea of what life is like for most *caraqueños* than the wide-angle, long-distance view from Mt. Avila. Long lines of bumper-to-bumper cars interlaced with motorcycles give the streets the appearance of multicolored placards. Columns of people march up and down the sidewalks and buses whose drivers seem depraved zigzag like ambulances through streets plastered with sexual graffiti–adorned commercial and political posters. Most residents go to El Centro only when necessary, although the subway has made it a much easier journey and is now the favored way of getting there. As one Caracas lawyer fumed, "Hell is having an important business appointment and attempting to find a parking space in El Centro's limited facilities."

Although Caracas is in the Federal District and is headed by a governor, the eastern part of the city is under separate jurisdiction and is ruled by a municipal council. Although El Este's neighborhoods remain the enclaves of the privileged, with splendid greenery, tropical flowers, and singing birds, recent municipal councils have failed to enforce zoning violations, a failure that has resulted in a rash of construction projects that conflict with the architectural integrity of the suburbs, such as Country Club, Altamira, and La Castellana. Novelty shops, restaurants, clubs, bars, discotheques, and *areperas* (corn meal snack stands that are Venezuela's equivalent of hot dog counters) are steadily encroaching. And, although some members of former municipal councils have actually been jailed for accepting payoffs and violating zoning codes, the residents of these districts are only beginning to form cohesive community organizations that could effectively halt commercial development. However, in the center and southern parts of the city, neighborhood groups have been somewhat more successful in stemming the seemingly inevitable tide of shops and businesses.

In this rush to high-rise, nothing remains of the original settlement, founded in 1567 by Diego de Losada, a Spanish conquistador who found the remarkable green valley inhabited by the Caracas Indian tribe. With the arrival of Spanish colonists, the settlement remained essentially tranquil until the War of Independence between 1803 and 1824. Venezuela's victory over Spain was attributable, in no small part, to the courage and leadership of Símon Bolívar, who was born in Caracas in 1783. The Liberator, as Bolívar was called, is revered throughout the city, where monuments, streets, buildings, and plazas bear his name. (Even the Venezuelan monetary unit is called the bolívar.) Although Símon Bolívar dreamed of a united Latin America, he found it impossible to realize, and he died, disenchanted, in Colombia in 1830 (see *History,* PERSPECTIVES).

During the nineteenth century, life in the "city of red roofs," as Caracas became known, unfolded drowsily and happily among a conservative Catholic population that emulated the European elite. At the end of the nineteenth century, President Guzmán Blanco banned the Roman Catholic church from Venezuela, shutting monasteries and convents when he found himself in conflict with the conservative religious hierarchy. During this period of authorized secularism, many social patterns began to loosen up. Compared to other South American countries, Venezuela (especially Caracas) has been considered relatively progressive for many years. Although family life is not as unstructured as in the US, *caraqueños* do not adhere to family relationships as formally structured as in other parts of South America. It is not uncommon for men to have mistresses as well as wives and to father children (whom they may or may not acknowledge) by a number of different women. It is also common to find people with one surname, indicative of their having been born out of wedlock. This in itself is a sign that having children outside of marriage is accepted in the society rather than something of which to be ashamed.

Since 1959, with the election of Rómulo Betancourt as president, Caracas has been the seat of a popularly elected, democratic national government. In 1975, under the presidency of Carlos Andrés Pérez, Venezuela's oil reserves were nationalized. Oil accounts for more than 95% of the country's foreign exchange earnings, and while the Pérez administration channeled a large part of the money (reported to be about $10 billion) into the construction of steel plants, electrical power plants, shipyards, and the development of agro-industry designed to increase the country's self-sufficiency so that it can cut down its food imports, the public became dissatisfied with reports of kickbacks being taken by high government officials, especially those in the Ministry of Defense. Pérez himself was implicated in some of the charges involving arms purchase deals. In December 1978, Luis Herrera Campins was elected president for a 5-year term, replaced in February 1984 by Jaime Lusinchi of the opposing Acción Democratica party, who is still carrying on a campaign against the corruption of the previous administration.

But the vicissitudes of politics will more than likely be the last thing on your mind if you ascend Mt. Avila at dusk. At that time the capital, to the south, is just commencing its softer evening rhythm, a gentle glow of light shining from the valley. To the north, the turquoise Caribbean acquires a special, rich sheen. As the sea wind blends with the scent of tropical flowers, the reality of Caracas takes a different form. It becomes more of a vision, an enchanting place you once imagined but never thought you would find in real life.

CARACAS AT-A-GLANCE

SEEING THE CITY: From one side of the 7,380-foot summit of Avila Mountain, now designated a National Park, you can see all of Caracas; from the other, the choppy waves of the Caribbean Sea. There is a road going up, and a cable car (*teleférico*) that operates daily, except Mondays, from the city to the summit and back (but no longer back down to the coast, as it used to). The *teleférico* (approximately $1.70 US) is very crowded on weekends and holidays. The vegetation on Avila ranges from tropical to temperate, with crystal-clear cascades flowing through its interior. On top of the mountain, there is a former hotel school for Venezuelan students and a recreation center with a restaurant, bar, cafeteria, dance hall, ice skating rink, shops, and very fine views. This used to be a place for mass weekend gatherings of local people, but its popularity has lessened without the cable ride. The views are still very fine, however. Surveying the city is also a pleasure from the public and guestrooms of the *Tamanaco Inter-Continental.*

Another spectacular, more urban view of the city can be observed from the restaurant-nightclub *Cota 880* on the top floor of the *Hilton* hotel. Open daily. El Conde (phone: 571-2322).

SPECIAL PLACES: As mentioned in the essay, eastern Caracas (El Este) is far and away the swankest section of the city. The historic district, El Silencio, stands to the west of the busiest commercial sector, El Centro. It's important to keep in mind that *caraqueños* do not use street addresses in the formal sense that we are accustomed to in the US. Each site is referred to by district, then (if necessary) by the main street and, occasionally, the nearest cross street. Every district has a main street called Avenida Principal. La Calle (literally, "the street") refers to the first street intersecting the Avenida Principal in a particular district. Street names are not always marked, and they change without notice. This makes driving very difficult for someone unfamiliar with its difficult address designations.

Plaza Bolívar – This is the meeting place for old-fashioned *caraqueños*. Smack in the middle is a statue of the Liberator on horseback. Perched on his squat shoulders are a handful of pigeons, and beneath his stirrups are shoeshine boys, beggars, and blind lottery salesmen. Surrounding this informal pageant of Venezuelan street life are the bastions of Venezuelan government — the National Congress, the governor's office, the Ministry of Foreign Affairs — and the local parish headquarters. Open daily. Free. El Silencio.

The Cathedral (La Catedral) – Built in 1595, this masterfully constructed church was rebuilt in 1637 and soon thereafter consecrated as a cathedral. Totally demolished by the earthquakes early in the 19th century, the cathedral wasn't rebuilt until 1876, and since that time no major structural changes have occurred. It is a colonial-style temple with a sober but artistically decorated interior. The fine wood carvings and the curved altar are adorned with paintings by Rubens and Arturo Michelena. Open daily. Free. Just east of Plaza Bolívar.

Santa Teresa Basilica (Basilica de Santa Teresa) – Probably the most popular and venerated church in Caracas, it harbors the Nazareno de San Pablo, the oldest image of Christ in Venezuela. He is dressed in a purple velvet robe trimmed with gold embroidery and carrying a cross. The basilica (actually a double church with a central altar serving the congregations of Santa Ana and Santa Teresa) is known as the Church of the Miracles (Iglesia de los Milagros). According to legend, during a period of epidemic, the statue was being carried in a procession. The cross caught in a lemon tree, and when people began eating the lemons, they were cured. It is believed that every year the statue bends farther under the cross's weight. The most devout followers attend 4 AM mass every Holy Thursday to give thanks for favors granted. Open daily. Free. Centro Simón Bolívar.

The Capitol (El Capitolio) – This landmark is the home of the National Congress, inaugurated in 1873. Its gilded dome makes it one of the most attractive sights in the city. Inside, the elliptical room displays 52 oil paintings of Venezuelan patriots. The dome's ceiling is covered with scenes from the Battle of Carabobo, perhaps the most crucial event in the War of Independence from Spain. Virtually all of the paintings are the works of Martín Tovar y Tovar (1827–1902), one of Caracas's most extraordinary artists. Closed Mondays. Free. Plaza Bolívar (phone: 483-3644).

Raul Santana's Museum of the Criollo Way of Life (Museo Criollo Raul Santana) – This institution, whose title reads more like a short story than a museum, depicts the traditions and ways of life of Caracas's past. There are houses and street scenes, reduced to miniature, in wood and other materials. Both city and rural life are masterfully recreated in three-dimensional, full-scale replicas. Closed Mondays. Free. In City Hall (Consejo Municipal) at the Los Naranjos corner of Plaza Bolívar (phone: 545-8688).

Bolívar's Birthplace (Casa Natal de Simón Bolívar) – Not only is the Liberator's home one of the most outstanding examples of colonial architecture in Caracas, it is also one of the most charming, well-laid-out sites in the country. In its rooms, patios, and gardens, you can visualize the day-by-day life of the colonial aristocracy. The house contains memorabilia of the Liberator's childhood, and many of his early possessions can be related to his turbulent career as a politician, political and social theorist, and warrior. The halls are adorned with a variety of portraits and paintings, all of which depict the key personalities of the colonial and independence period. The central patio is where Bolívar was baptized, and the other rooms are associated with innumerable incidents of his youth. Closed Mondays. Free. One block east of Raul Santana Museum on Calle Traposos at Calle San Jacinto (phone: 545-7693).

Bolívar Museum (Museo Bolivariano) – The documents, arms, and personal belongings of Bolívar are kept in this nationally renowned museum. The historical collection includes the gold medallion awarded to the Liberator and a lock of his hair (and one of George Washington's, as well). Closed Mondays. Open on national holidays, most of which, in one way or another, commemorate Bolívar. Closed Mondays. Free. Next door to Bolívar's birthplace, on Calle Traposos and the corner of Calle San Jacinto (phone: 545-9828).

San Francisco Church (Iglesia de San Francisco) – Here Simón Bolívar was given the title of Liberator. Of more immediate interest are its delightful grounds, relics, sculptures, and luxurious tapestries. Open daily. Free. Av. Universidad at the corner of Calle San Francisco.

National Pantheon (Panteón) – The site of Jimmy Carter's proclamations in Spanish to the Venezuelan people, this monument, built in 1874, is the tomb of Simón Bolívar. The front is sober and somewhat grim; the interior, luxuriously adorned marble. Closed Mondays. Free. Av. Norte, Plaza del Panteón (phone: 82-15-18).

Simón Bolívar Center (Centro Simón Bolívar) – These twin towers are the home of most Venezuelan ministries and agencies. The towers are pathetically outdated as modern architecture; the boutiques and bars on the lower levels, run-down. All in all, these buildings only deserve a quick peek. Two blocks north of San Francisco Church.

Los Caobos Park (Parque Los Caobos) – This is Caracas's artistic hangout, home of the few real bohemians in this glittering, money-conscious town. It also happens to be one of the few places downtown where the smell of bus exhaust is not pervasive, thanks to its breathtaking foliage and cool lawns. In the open areas, people ride bicycles, roller-skate, skate-board to their heart's content, and even jog. The park adjoins the new Theatrical Arts Center, the Arts and Science Museum, and the National Cinematographic Library. Peace and art fill the air. Open daily. Free. Teresa Carreño and Paseo Colón (phone: 571-0421).

Museum of Natural Sciences (Museo de Las Ciencias Naturales) – This museum contains a varied collection of stuffed animals from Venezuela and many other parts of the world. Reptiles, insects, and birds adorn the corridors, interspersed with pre-Columbian archaeological exhibitions and Neolithic and Miocene fossils. Closed Mondays. Free. At the end of Av. Mexico in Parque Los Caobos (phone: 571-1265).

The Lofty (Los Proceres) – Caracas's Central Park, named for the fathers of Venezuelan independence, is actually a promenade and knoll adorned with fountains, statues, and plaques honoring many Venezuelan patriots. Highlighting the promenade are two parallel, monumental marble walls surrounded by gardens and floral wreathes. A walk through this park is nothing less than a stroll through Venezuela's history. The home of the annual North American Association picnic and the site of various Venezuelan university graduations and spectacles, it is also the parade grounds of the nation. Open daily. Free. Av. Los Proceres, Santa Mónica.

El Pinar Park (Parque El Pinar) – What makes this park unique is that it is the only real, species-varied zoo in town *and* that it is practically impossible to find without a special guided tour. Just getting here is an adventure. Closed Mondays. Admission charge. Av. Guzmán Blanco, El Paraiso (phone: 461-7794).

Fine Arts Museum (Museo de Bellas Artes) – Here is the city's best sampling of the work of Venezuela's creative artists as well as an attractive collection of Oriental ceramics and carvings of wood and marble. European art is well represented. The museum is a meeting place for Caracas's art lovers. The building also houses the *Cinematica*. Closed Mondays. Free. Opposite the Natural Science Museum, adjoining Parque Los Caobos (phone: 571-1813).

Contemporary Art Museum (Museo de Arte Contemporareo) – Entirely dedicated to channeling the currents of international modern art toward Caracas, its
exhibits represent most of the recent trends and schools of art. Guided tours for foreign
groups and students can be arranged in advance. Closed Mondays. Free. Parque
Central (phone: 573-4602).

Children's Museum (Museo de Los Niños) – Recently opened and internationally
acclaimed as a must for adults and children alike. Closed Mondays and Tuesdays.
Admission charge. Parque Central (phone: 573-1056).

Colonial Arts Museum – Perhaps the most pleasant and refreshing place one can
visit in Caracas. A beautifully kept colonial house, it offers not only a handsome
collection of period furniture, a coach house, and a blacksmith's forge, but also a
delightful garden whose tranquillity provides a welcome escape from the bustle of the
city. Admission charge. Av. Panteón, San Bernadino (phone: 51-85-17).

East Park (Parque del Este) – Home of the joggers, a recreation center for the
children, magnet of the humble, watering hole for the athlete, this park has a little
something for everybody. As its name suggests, it's in the eastern part of the city and
covers more than 494 acres. A choo-choo train chugs around the grounds carrying
jovial passengers past families picnicking near an artificial lagoon in which floats a
replica of Columbus's ship, the *Santa María.* (Yes, you can board the ship.) Another
special feature of the park, not yet well known to most *caraqueños,* is the terrarium
— a congregation of snakes, turtles, and lizards displayed in cabinets of thick glass. The
park also includes a domed planetarium, a parrot cage, and a band shell. Puppet shows
are performed regularly, and political speakers hold forth on Sundays. Closed Mondays. Admission charge. Between Av. Francisco de Miranda, Autopista Francisco
Fajardo, and La Carlota Military Airport and Aeroclub (phone: 284-3022).

Los Chorros Park (Parque Los Chorros) – A gift from former President Caldera,
this beautiful park is in the lush, eastern neighborhood of Los Chorros. Its freshwater
cascades, streams, tropical vegetation, and cool breezes more than compensate for
weariness of the soles acquired on any long ramble through the park. Closed Mondays.
Open other days until 5:30 PM. Admission charge. Although the grandparents of
today's youngsters used to come here by then-existent railways, now they reach the
park by following Av. Boyocá or by winding up the mountain from Av. Francisco
Miranda (phone: 36-17-79).

President's House (La Casona) – Formerly a colonial cacao plantation, this
modern mansion was restored in 1966 as the residence of the Venezuelan chief of state
and the first lady. Various paintings and other works of art have been gathered here
amid the gardens and fountains of this villa-estate. With an information center for
tourists, an adjacent parking lot, and guides, La Casona is between the La Carlota and
Santa Cecilia districts. Open Tuesday afternoons by prior arrangement; phone in
advance. Free. You can get there by following Av. Principal of La Carlota or by taking
the Santa Cecilia exit of the Autopista Francisco Fajardo (phone: 36-12-61).

■**EXTRA SPECIAL:** Thanks to the Caracas–La Guaira Freeway (although your
thanks will be short-lived if you get caught in a traffic jam), it takes only half an
hour (without traffic) to reach the sunny central coast beaches (*el litoral central*)
perched on the Caribbean shore behind Mt. Avila. The best ones (although they
are by no means Venezuela's finest) are part of private clubs: Playa Grande, Playa
Azul, Puerto Azul, and Camuri Chico. All of the remaining beaches are public,
culminating in the vacation city of Los Caracas, conceived as a utopia for
Venezuela's working class. However well equipped the apartments are, the rocky,
dirty beaches and muddy streams are no one's idea of a Caribbean paradise. But
just a bit to the east, you can find unspoiled beaches inhabited by blacks, who rely
on fishing and gardening for their living. (You can find traces of African tradition

in the Barlovento region, as this area is called.) The beaches here are quite worth the trip. Among the best are La Sabana, Todasana, Caruao, Chuspa, and Higuerote. To get here you will need a Jeep, as the roads are very dusty. To the west, Cata, Choroni, and the keys of Morrocoy National Park beg to be visited.

SOURCES AND RESOURCES

TOURIST INFORMATION: The Venezuelan Government Tourist Office, Venezuelan Consulate, 7 E 51st St., 2nd floor, New York, NY 10022 (phone: 212-355-1101), has English-language brochures on special attractions and facilities for travelers. In Caracas, the following places have helpful tourist information: Venezuelan Tourism Corp. (Corpoturismo), Plaza Venezuela, Capriles Center, Ground floor (phone: 781-8311); Venezuelan Airlines Association (ALAV), Galerías Bolívar, Building A, 1st floor, Office 11A, Av. F. Solano, opposite the *Tampa* hotel (phone: 72-85-51 or 71-54-61); National Association of Hotels (ANAHOVEN), Av. Libertador, Res. Crillon, P-H1 (phone: 72-22-45); Venezuelan Association of Tourist Travel Agencies (AVAVIT), of Av. Lincoln and Av. Las Acacias, Torre Lincoln, 6th floor, Office E (phone: 781-2310). The best city maps are available at CVP gas stations.

Local Coverage – The *Caracas Daily Journal* is the city's English-language newspaper.

Food – The *Caracas Daily Journal* has restaurant listings.

CLIMATE AND CLOTHES: With an annual average daily temperature in the 70s F (20s C), Caracas's elevation of 3,000 feet accounts for its delightful climate. You will hardly ever need a sweater in the daytime, although in the evenings the temperature can drop to as low as the 50s F (between 10° and 16°C). Like most tropical locations, Caracas's two seasons are dry and rainy. The former generally runs from December through May. The remaining months are humid and rainy, although in lucky years the rain arrives and stops before the day has truly begun and often doesn't recommence until well into the afternoon.

As a general rule, the lighter the clothing the better. Blue jeans and American T-shirts are common attire for the young and the young at heart for sightseeing around town. Yet the cosmopolitan atmosphere that pervades Caracas makes it more formal than sporty. Venezuelans take pride in their appearance, and in the city you are expected to be well dressed, day or evening. If you are staying at the beach, you can get away with casual resort attire.

GETTING AROUND: Bus – Unfortunately, the Caracas buses have been stereotyped as the working-class mode of transport, but new minibuses and the metro have gradually been driving them to extinction. Minibuses are inexpensive and tend to run along most east-west and some north-south courses. Routes are not well marked, and visitors who speak only English will have trouble negotiating the system. The intercity bus services are efficient.

Taxi – Taxi meters have finally arrived. The problem now faced by travelers is convincing drivers that the trip is worth it; they are frequently unwilling to take a job even if the price is right. This — and the disorganization of the taxi lines in front of hotels and public places — can be very frustrating. (*Note:* Many *taxistas,* or drivers, are not from Caracas and don't know their way around, so be prepared with good instructions on how to get where. A 10% surcharge is levied on Sundays, holidays, and late at night.) To call a cab, dial *Tele-Taxi,* 752-9122, or *Taxi Tour,* 74-94-11.

Por Puestos – As a step above the buses and as an alternative to walking, there are collective cars and minibuses, called *por puestos.* The same or sometimes twice the price of a bus but still a fraction that of a taxi, these cars have been getting larger as buses become fewer. Both driver and client must be extremely agile in order to coordinate the many pickup and drop-off points that are not already designated.

Car Rental – If you're not sufficiently frightened by the traffic and want to get behind the wheel yourself, you'll find ample rental facilities. The major car rental agencies are: *ACO,* the ACO Building, Las Mercedes (phone: 91-81-45); *Avis,* Av. Casanova and Av. Guaicaipuro, El Rosal (phone: 71-94-51); *Budget,* 50 Av. Luis Roche, Altamira (phone: 284-5023); *Fiesta,* Av. Venezuela, El Rosal (phone: 33-31-21); *Hertz,* Av. Principal El Bosque, Centro Commercial Chacaito (phone: 72-73-09); and *National,* Edificio Polar, Plaza Venezuela (phone: 718-1011).

Subway – The city has completed the first stage of its subway, which is beautiful but limited in range; it operates from 6 AM to 9 PM. The second stage of building continues to cause upheaval in the eastern part of the city. The development of the metro has not been all negative, however, with the whole of Sabana Grande being transformed into an attractive pedestrian zone and its businesses revitalized. New cafés have sprung up beside the traditional meeting place, *El Grand Café,* and the area is now an important social meeting place for anyone from writers to families with young children, even chess enthusiasts, who can learn or challenge the experts at the many tables on the promenade. Even the chaos of Chacaito has given over to a large pedestrian square, Plaza Brion, dominated by a giant chess board painted into the square.

MUSEUMS: In addition to the Raul Santana Museum of the Criollo Way of Life (Museo Criollo Raul Santana), Bolívar Museum (Museo Bolivariano), Museum of Natural Sciences (Museo de Las Ciencias Naturales), Fine Arts Museum (Museo de Bellas Artes), Contemporary Art Museum (Museo de Arte Contemporareo), described in *Special Places,* other museums of note include:

Arturo Michelena Museum (Museo Arturo Michelena) – A traditional 19th-century home open to the public. Closed Mondays and Fridays. La Pastora (phone: 82-58-53).

Bolívar Home (La Cuadra Bolívar) – The country home of the Liberator's family is an enchanting escape from the rigors of modern city life into the tranquillity of the past. Closed Mondays. Free. Piedras a Barcenas (phone: 283-3971).

La Rinconada Art Museum (Museo de Arte La Rinconada) – This striking new building houses a permanent exhibition of paintings, sculptures, pre-Columbian pieces, and ceramics by Venezuelan artists in addition to temporary international shows. Closed Mondays. Av. Intercomunal del Valle, La Rinconada (phone: 606-6702).

Transport Museum (Museo de Transporte) – On view are old cars and locomotives and scale models of Caracas as it was 100 years ago. Open Wednesdays and weekends. Admission charge. Parque del Este, near Urbanización Santa Cecilia (phone: 34-22-34).

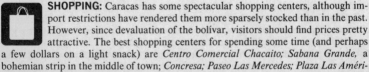

SHOPPING: Caracas has some spectacular shopping centers, although import restrictions have rendered them more sparsely stocked than in the past. However, since devaluation of the bolívar, visitors should find prices pretty attractive. The best shopping centers for spending some time (and perhaps a few dollars on a light snack) are *Centro Comercial Chacaito; Sabana Grande,* a bohemian strip in the middle of town; *Concresa; Paseo Las Mercedes; Plaza Las Américas; Centro Plaza;* and the biggest to date, *Centro Comercial Tamanaco.* The Avenida Urdaneta shopping district downtown has a more Latin flavor but is unappealing for its head-splitting pollution.

For good buys in food, visit the open-air markets at *Quinta Crespo, Chacao, El Junquito,* and *Guaicapuro.*

 SPECIAL EVENTS: The two days and nights before *Ash Wednesday,* when *Carnival* is celebrated, Caracas and the rest of the country close down. The same is true during *Semana Santa (Holy Week),* the week before *Easter.* In addition to Roman Catholic holidays, Venezuela observes *Independence Day* (July 5), *Labor Day* (May 1), the *Anniversary of the Battle of Carabobo* (June 24), *Bolívar's Birthday* (July 24), and *Columbus Day* (October 12).

SPORTS: Unlike in the rest of South America, baseball rather than soccer is the major spectator sport. The nearby Caribbean beaches are perfect for water sports. Many say Morrocoy is the best.

Baseball – Venezuelan players David Concepción, Marcano Trillo, Luis Aparicio, Vic Davalillo, and Antonio Armas have been stars in the US major leagues. Upcoming Venezuelan stars and athletes imported from the US get together in the winter leagues in Caracas to keep in shape. The local teams are quite colorful, and although the "raw" quality of play has declined somewhat in recent years, the color and spirit of the games never wane. Especially fascinating are the Little League World Series and the Series of the Caribbean, where teams from the region, mostly Spanish-speaking, vie for the number one slot. All games in Caracas are played at the Central University campus (phone: 61-98-11). The Venezuelan season runs from October through February; most games are played at night, except for Saturdays and Sundays, when afternoon games are held. For information, check the sports pages of the *Caracas Daily Journal.*

Bowling – Another import. Caracas has closely followed the leads of this popular stateside spectator sport, which is becoming very popular although the largest, most active bowling alley, *Bowling del Este,* in La Castellana just burned down.

Boxing – You can see aspiring hopefuls, some of whom are fighting their way to greater success in the next Olympics, at the *Poliedro,* next door to La Rinconada racetrack.

Bullfighting – Depending on whether your sympathies lie with the man or the bull, you'll find these contests challenging or sickening. Superior performances and more elaborate displays can be found in other Venezuelan cities, but Caracas has its own bullring. (A word of caution: watch your wallet.) Bullfights take place on Sunday afternoons at *Plaza de Toros,* Nuevo Circo. San Martín at the corner of San Roque. Maracay and Valencia have their own rings and the same fighters as Caracas.

Deep-Sea Fishing – You can charter a boat with tackle, gear, and crew (lunch and drinks included) from the *Macuto Sheraton* marina.

Golf – Ask your hotel to arrange privileges at the *Altamira, Junko, Lagunita,* or *Caracas* country clubs. The *Macuto Sheraton* offers guests playing privileges at the 9-hole *Caraballeda Golf Course,* and the *Tamanaco* can arrange for guests to play at the 18-hole *Valle Arriba Golf Course,* but only at certain hours.

Horse Racing – Millions of the billions of bolívares floating around Venezuela are spent weekly on the horses, both off the track (at the betting game known as the *Cinco y Seis*) and at *La Rinconada Hipodromo* itself. Surrounded by a green, rising plain, *La Rinconada* is considered one of the best in Latin America and seats a capacity crowd of 30,000. Jackets and ties are required dress for gentlemen, and ladies must wear skirts or dresses in the clubhouse. Races are run every Saturday and Sunday and in Valencia the first Thursday of each month throughout the year. La Rinconada, El Valle.

Sailing – Rent a sailboat or cruiser from the *Macuto Sheraton* marina.

Snorkeling and Scuba – Rent scuba equipment with a boat and guide from the

Macuto Sheraton. Other hotels along the Caribbean rent flippers and masks for a small fee.

Swimming – The Litoral coast has some terrific (and not so terrific) beaches. For a complete description, see *Extra Special,* above.

Tennis – Guests have first choice at the *Caracas Hilton, Macuto Sheraton,* and *Tamanaco,* but nonguests can play for a small fee.

 THEATER: In addition to the spectacular Teresa Carreño dramatic arts center, which recently opened, there are countless other theaters for live dramatic productions, all of which are in Spanish. Consult the *Caracas Daily Journal* or the Spanish press (*El Universal, El Nacional,* and *El Diario de Caracas*) for schedules and details. The *Caracas Theater Club* presents plays in English. Calle Chivacoa, San Román (phone: 91-13-11).

 MUSIC: All sorts of musical productions are presented in Caracas, from the Korean National Dance Group to Beverly Sills. The best concerts are given at the Teresa Carreño Center's *Sala Rios Reina,* opposite the *Caracas Hilton,* but whether the locale is here, the *Aula Magna* auditorium of the Universidad Central (phone: 61-98-11), or the *Teatro Municipal,* home of the Caracas Symphony Orchestra, this is a musical town. *Teatro Municipal* is near the south side of Centro Simón Bolívar, one block east of Av. Baralt (phone: 41-53-84). Pop stars from the States and other countries usually perform at the *Poliedro,* next door to La Rinconada. Concerts are usually well publicized in the newspapers.

 NIGHTCLUBS AND NIGHTLIFE: Whatever else you might think or say about Caracas, it is certainly ideal at night. The city is full of bright lights and gaiety, with everything from sophisticated midnight shows to raunchy "welcome bars," where ladies of the evening ply their trade. The numerous discotheques play top American rock and Latin soul music. Some of the more exclusive discos have their own bands and occasionally offer a top international group. In El Este, there are two kinds of discos: those conducive to romantic interests exclusively and those that provide quieter areas, where you can hold a conversation without having to scream. Piano bars are also extremely popular. Even on weeknights, you'll find Caracas vibrant at midnight. This is often perplexing to foreigners, who wonder how these same night owls can party so late, then spend a hard day at work. *Naiguatá* at the *Tamanaco* (phone: 91-45-55) puts on the best show in town, and on Mondays the *Caracas Hilton* stages "Noches Caraqueñas" for guests. The most popular discos are *New York, New York,* Centro Comercial Concresa, Plaza Bolívar 1 (phone: 979-1886 or 979-7778); *Winners,* Centro Comercial Ciudad Tamanaco, Nivel C-1 Chuao (phone: 91-78-71 or 92-79-91); *Le Club,* Centro Comercial Chacaito, Sotano (phone: 72-48-14 or 72-39-27); *1900 My Way,* Centro Comercial Ciudad Tamanaco, Nivel C-2 (phone: 92-22-56); *Memories,* Av. Venezuela, El Rosal (phone: 33-89-84); *Reflections,* Plaza Venezuela, Phelps Tower Mezzanine (phone: 782-6457); *The Flower,* Plaza La Castellaña, Av. Francisco de Miranda (phone: 33-30-13); *Rainbow,* Centro Comercial Bello Campo (phone: 31-60-88). The finest piano bars are *Number Two,* Av. Principal, La Castellana (phone: 31-51-13); *Juan Sebastian Bar,* Av. Venezuela, El Rosal (phone: 32-42-29); *Crystal Club,* Av. Principal, La Castellana (phone: 31-49-73); *Duke's Pub,* Centro Comercial Chacaito (phone: 72-98-34); *Gypsy,* Paseo Las Mercedes, Nivel Trasmocho (phone: 91-29-90); *Magic,* Calle Madrid, Las Mercedes (phone: 92-87-04); and *Gala,* Calle Madrid, Las Mercedes (phone: 91-67-82). Also very enjoyable is the British atmosphere of the *Dog and Fox Pub,* Av. Rio de Janeiro, Las Mercedes (phone: 91-73-19). The *Crazy Discoteque* in Centro Comercial Bello Campo is a lively gay haunt, as is the *Ice Palace* in Altamira Sur — both frequented by straights as well. Other gay bars can be found in the Sabana Grande area.

Young, attractive women traveling alone in Caracas can expect to be accosted with rude remarks, sneers, and lip-smacking noises during the day; the problem is exacerbated at night. *Caraqueñas* and women from other parts of the country suffer the same fate in the city. It is annoying but rarely dangerous, and usually by simply ignoring the provocation it is possible to avoid confrontations. Men generally assume that women out alone at night are looking for pickups; at the worst, they assume such lone travelers to be prostitutes. A woman who goes to a restaurant, bar, or nightclub can expect to be approached; unaccompanied women are often refused entry to bars, clubs, and discos. However, there are many cafés, especially in Sabana Grande and the commercial centers, where such sexist treatment is not the case. One of these exceptions is *Café Margana* in Centro Plaza (phone: 284-6590).

SINS: For those looking for carnal entertainment, Plaza Sur Altamira, Chacaito, and Sabana Grande are the principal areas where bars harboring prostitutes are found. Along the Av. Libertador, in the vicinity of the *Hotel Crillon,* is another possible source should you not want to waste time and money on the preliminaries of drinking at a bar. If these spots don't satisfy your requirements, try the *Palacio Imperial.*

BEST IN TOWN

CHECKING IN: While finding an empty hotel room has been a pretty tough chore in the past, several new hotels have recently sprung up, alleviating the pressure. At the most expensive end of the range, some judicious tipping might be necessary to find an empty bed, but even that might not do the trick on the spur of the moment. The best insurance, obviously, is to book well in advance and be sure you have some confirmation in writing. There is a hotel reservation center at the airport for those who land without a reservation (phone: 031-552-747; or 031-552-599). Expect to pay about $50 to $75 for a double room in the hotels listed below as expensive; about $20 to $30 at those places listed as moderate; less than $20, inexpensive.

Caracas Hilton International – Favored by businesspeople, this 908-room hotel has ballrooms, conference rooms, and a lounge on each of the top six executive floors of the tower, plus good business services. The food is excellent, and the 15th-floor restaurant-nightclub, *La Cota 880,* offers continuous dancing and a spectacular view of the city. The downtown location is convenient to the neighboring cultural complex, the Parque Central complex for shopping, and the Contemporary Art Museum. Credit cards accepted. El Conde (phone: 571-2322). Expensive.

CCCT – This new hotel offers swimming pool, tennis, sauna, and gym, as well as a restaurant and bars. Centro Ciudad Comercial Tamanaco, Entrance Sotano 1 (phone: 92-61-22). Expensive.

Macuto Sheraton – A natural choice for beach lovers who prefer to visit Caracas proper at night, its complete range of aquatic sports facilities includes 2 swimming pools, sailboat rental, fishing, scuba diving, water skiing, and the beach. There are tennis courts, lighted for night play, and a bowling alley of sorts on the premises; golf privileges entitle you to play at a nearby course. The rooms, however, have none of the sparkle of the sporting areas and need renovation. The expected *Sheraton* accoutrements are all present in force: restaurant, disco, nightclub, gift shop, bookstore, beauty salon, and travel agencies. It is 20 miles (32 km) from Caracas. Macuto Beach (phone: 031-918-01). Expensive.

Melia Caribe – Owned and run by a Spanish chain, this is a tough, newer competitor of the *Sheraton*. It has beautiful and sophisticated architecture, gardens, a disco, and a wide variety of restaurants and bars. Facilities include a gym, tennis courts, marina, pool and poolside bar, band, and buffet. Credit cards accepted. Macuto Beach (phone: 031-924-01). Expensive.

Residencias Anauco Hilton – In Parque Central, the *Anauco* has 262 suites and 55 twin guestrooms. Most have balconies, but ask for a room on the "quiet side." Suite accommodations (with a living room, dining room, and 2 to 4 bedrooms) are available for both long and short stays. Amenities include pool, sauna, tennis courts, gym, and a good choice of restaurants. The complex also has shops and a supermarket. Parque Central (phone: 573-4111). Expensive.

Tamanaco Inter-Continental – A favorite with visitors, and recently redecorated, it offers above-average dining, a great swimming pool and gym, a spectacular view of Caracas, shows, shops, and genuine Latin soul. Credit cards accepted. Av. Principal, Las Mercedes (phone: 91-45-55). Expensive.

Holiday Inn – Pocketed in one of Caracas's finest shopping centers, it has no facilities for recreation, but it is within walking distance of the *Tamanaco* and provides guests with golf privileges nearby. Service is competent, as you would expect. Credit cards accepted. Av. Principal, Las Mercedes (phone: 91-04-44). Expensive to moderate.

Avila – Pleasantly situated on a hill overlooking the city, this gracious, older hotel has plenty of original Venezuelan charm. Meals can be enjoyed alongside the swimming pool, while listening to the chatter of birds (instead of the perennial hum of traffic). There is a pleasant piano bar and an English- and Spanish-language newsstand in the lobby. It's the perfect alternative to supermodern, international-class hotels, although it lacks one of the features that's taken for granted in contemporary buildings: air conditioning. Most nights are cool enough for comfortable sleeping, however. Credit cards accepted. Av. Jorge Washington, San Bernardino (phone: 51-51-55). Moderate.

Continental Altamira – Well situated in Altamira, it features a swimming pool, restaurant, and bar. Credit cards accepted. Av. San Juan Bosco, Altamira (phone: 283-8511). Moderate.

Crillon – Neither as classy as the *Tamanaco* nor as flashy as the *Hilton,* this is a substantial, comfortable, modern (but not too modern) establishment near the Sabana Grande shopping district. Most of the accommodations are 2-room suites, complete with refrigerator and television. Almost all have terraces. Try the excellent Swiss restaurant, *El Chalet.* Credit cards accepted. Av. Libertador and Av. Las Acacias (phone: 71-44-11). Moderate.

El Marqués – Someone finally invested money in a "middle of the road" hotel and is making money. In an unlikely residential area of the city, it is charming and well run. Credit cards accepted. Av. El Saman and Calle Yuruari, El Marqués (phone: 239-3211). Moderate.

Tampa – Near Plaza Venezuela and the Sabana Grande shopping district, this hotel's location and reasonable prices make it a good bet. Av. Fco. Solano López, Sabana Grande (phone: 72-37-71). Moderate.

El Condor – With a convenient location in Chacaito, near the subway, this new hotel is fast becoming popular. It also has a restaurant and bar. Av. Las Delicias de Sabana Grande (phone: 72-99-11). Moderate to inexpensive.

Kursaal – Our first choice in the money-saving category, it's not in the same class as the hotels listed above, but it does have clean, decent rooms and a restaurant and bar. Credit cards accepted. Av. Casanova, Calle El Colegio (phone: 72-18-24). Inexpensive.

Tanausu – Another money-saver. This one, too, has adequate rooms, some with terraces. It has no recreational facilities, restaurant, or bar, but it is close to the Sabana Grande shopping district. Av. Las Acacias, at the corner of Av. Casanova, Sabana Grande (phone: 782-6177). Inexpensive.

 EATING OUT: As far as food is concerned, *caraqueños* need not suffer any inferiority complex. The main problem with eating out in Caracas is the existential anguish of deciding which among so many restaurants to visit first. Most of the best restaurants are found in the east, and a proliferation of new eateries, especially in Las Mercedes and El Rosal, makes choosing even more problematic. On weekdays, the majority of diners are prosperous businesspeople, but on weekends all *caraqueños* come out in force. Caracas restaurants are relatively expensive, but for inexpensive eating there is an abundance of soda fountains, snack bars, and fast-food chains. One can also eat informally and well in any of the many Spanish *tascas* (taverns) in La Candelaria or the Sabana Grande areas. If you wish to "dine out" with a three-course meal, expect to pay $25 to $30 for two at the restaurants listed below as expensive and $15 in the moderate range. Prices do not include drinks, wine, or tips. (Wine is unbelievably expensive in Caracas, and not normally of the best quality.)

Gazebo – Prepare to dress for this very formal Continental restaurant. According to David Brown, the producer of *Jaws,* this is one of the best restaurants in the world. Gourmands in Caracas's French community say the food — and prices — are as impressive as Paris's best. If you are going to Caracas on business, this is a good place to impress a client. Closed Saturdays at lunchtime and Sundays. Reservations recommended. Dress is formal. Major credit cards accepted. Av. Rio de Janeiro, Las Mercedes (phone: 92-95-02). Expensive.

La Atarraya – One of the few really classy restaurants in the center of town, it serves traditional *criollo* dishes — *natilla,* cheeses from Coro with *arepas* (corn cakes), *cazón* (ground shark meat), and *pabellon* (a typical meat-and-bean plate). Government big shots abound, and the sangría is very good. Credit cards accepted. Esquina de San Jacinto (phone: 545-8235). Expensive.

La Belle Époque – This remains one of Caracas's finest French restaurants. Delicious asparagus and artichoke appetizers serve as a prelude to the main course. The trout here is particularly succulent. Enjoy the romantic atmosphere and lively music at night. Open daily. Reservations recommended. Jackets preferred. Major credit cards. Closed Sundays. In Edificio Century on Av. Leonardo da Vinci, Colinas de Bello Monte (phone: 752-1342). Expensive.

Cota 880 – The refined dishes (mostly French and northern Italian), cosmopolitan atmosphere, panoramic view, excellent entertainment, and dancing to live music make this one of the best choices in Caracas. Buffets are served on Sunday evenings, and a jacket is required in the evenings. Closed Mondays. Reservations recommended. On the top floor of the *Caracas Hilton,* El Conde (phone: 571-2322). Expensive.

Da Emore – A very special, reasonable menu of assorted Italian dishes is offered here. There are only prix fixe menus. Closed Mondays. Reservations recommended. Major credit cards. In Concresa Commercial Center (phone: 979-3242). Expensive.

El Francesito – A highly popular French restaurant with unpretentious decor. Closed Saturdays midday and Sundays. Calles Madrid and Trinidad, Las Mercedes (phone: 91-23-20). Expensive.

Mayfair Station – A high-quality restaurant with an international menu; frequented by businesspeople. Jackets required. Major credit cards accepted. Av. Ppl. Bello Campo (phone: 32-30-72). Expensive.

Patrick's – Excellently prepared French specialties are served at one of Caracas' best new restaurants. It has already become quite popular. Calle Trinidad, Las Mercedes (phone: 91-66-42 or 92-55-79). Expensive.

Porta Romana – This small and elegant Italian restaurant, also serving international specialties, is rapidly building a stellar reputation. Major credit cards accepted. Closed Saturdays midday and Sundays. Calle New York, Las Mercedes (phone: 91-48-18). Expensive.

El Barquero – Since its recent redecoration, this restaurant has become even more popular and is worthy of its reputation as one of the finest seafood establishments in Caracas. Open daily. Major credit cards accepted. Av. Luis Roche, Esq. 5th Transversal, Altamira (phone: 262-1412 or 261-4645). Expensive to moderate.

Bogavante – Decorated as a fishing boat, this restaurant specializes in lobster, crab, shrimp, and fish filets. The Italian and Spanish wine list is quite good. Open daily. Reservations recommended. Major credit cards accepted. Av. Venezuela, El Rosal (phone: 71-86-24). Expensive to moderate.

Casa Juancho – A popular restaurant in a garden setting, with a high-quality Spanish menu. Open daily. Major credit cards accepted. Av. San Juan Bosco, Altamira (phone: 33-46-14). Expensive to moderate.

La Cigogne – This restaurant continues to command esteem — even though the decor has declined. Its pâtés are superior, and other French dishes are worth a taste. Open daily until midnight. Reservations recommended. Major credit cards accepted. Closed Sundays. Off Av. Principal, Colinas de Bello Monte (phone: 751-3313). Expensive to moderate.

El Dragon Verde – Superlative Chinese food at one of the oldest Chinese restaurants in Caracas. Edificio Chine Paris, La Campiña (phone: 71-84-04 or 72-59-11). Expensive to moderate.

La Estancia – A converted colonial-style house and covered terrace make this a refreshing and tranquil spot to enjoy excellent steaks and traditional *criollo* cuisine. The proximity of the garden completes the escape from the bustle of the city. Closed Sundays. Major credit cards accepted. Av. Principal, La Castellana (phone: 32-24-19). Expensive to moderate.

Hereford Grill – This fine steak house does prime meats to perfection. *Medallón de lomito al oporto* (steak in port), and *pollo deshuesado Hereford* (boned chicken) are special. Calle Madrid (phone: 92-51-27). Expensive to moderate.

El Hostal de la Castellana – Don Quixote and Sancho Panza stand guard at the portals of this Spanish stronghold lined with conquistador souvenirs and audible Flamenco overtones (the music starts at 8:30 PM). The gazpacho, paella, and *pierna cordero castellana* (leg of lamb) are all commendable. Av. Principal at Plaza Castellana (phone: 33-42-60). Expensive to moderate.

Il Padrino – Billed as the most beautiful restaurant in the world, it is certainly the most beautiful in Caracas. Originally designed as a Russian restaurant, its basic decor features vaulted ceilings. A few years ago, it was converted to a Sicilian restaurant, and Italian hardwood furniture and lamps from Toledo, Spain, were added. Distinguished by its incomparable salad bar and antipasto (virtually a meal in itself), it has music for dancing, accordion-playing waiters, and wandering photographers. Don't go expecting a quiet, romantic evening. Open daily. Reservations recommended. Major credit cards accepted. At the bottom of Plaza Altamira (phone: 32-76-84). Expensive to moderate.

El Portón – The owners claim that no important person who comes to Venezuela ever leaves without first tasting a *criollo* meal here. With *criollo* scenes painted all over the wall and the excellent food, you walk away feeling as though you've just had an especially delicious lesson in Venezuelan culture. This is one of the best *criollo* restaurants in the city. A band plays in the evenings. Open daily. Reservations recommended. Major credit cards accepted. Av. Pichincha No. 18, Esquina Calle Quaicalpuro, El Rosal (phone: 71-60-71). Expensive to moderate.

Comilona – Conveniently located for the *Tamanaco* or the *Holiday Inn* at the end of Av. Ppl. Las Mercedes, it offers an Italian menu in a friendly atmosphere. Open daily. Major credit cards accepted. Opposite Paseo Las Mercedes (phone: 92-12-31). Moderate.

La Era de Acuario – This vegetarian and macrobiotic restaurant offers pleasant, informal surroundings and an extensive menu, from whole wheat pizzas to salads to fish. Open daily from noon to 11 PM. Major credit cards accepted. Calle Madrid, Las Mercedes (phone: 91-32-57). Moderate.

Jardín des Crêpes – Handsomely filled crêpes, both sweet and savory, plus meat and fish dishes tempt palates here. Sit at the open, plant-filled balcony, then drop by the bar for live music. Major credit cards accepted. Calle Madrid, Las Mercedes (phone: 91-41-93). Moderate.

Lee Hamilton Steak House – If you're homesick for hamburgers or steak, this is your place. Recently revamped, it's known for basic American fare. Open daily. Reservations not required. Major credit cards accepted. Av. San Felipe, La Castellana (phone: 32-52-27). Moderate.

LA PAZ

The highest city in the world, at an altitude of 12,500 feet, La Paz, Bolivia, is also one of the most exceptional. How well you respond to the place will depend most on your ability to adjust physically to the altitude and psychologically to the extraordinary human pageant that passes by every day. Its combination of Indian and Spanish cultures, the extreme effect of its altitude, and its rather astonishing location in a shallow bowl between mountains make it a city even visitors familiar with other South American cities view with wonder. "Why go to the moon when you can go to La Paz?" a former UPI bureau chief for Perú used to ask adventure-hungry travelers. Why indeed? You'll only know by going.

From the moment your plane lands at El Alto Airport — another "world's highest" title-holder at 13,450 feet — you will be aware of something different in the air. Or, to be more accurate, something *not* in the air — namely, oxygen. This atmospheric thinness partially accounts for the moderately bumpy landings on El Alto's 2½-mile (4-km) airstrip. (Irregular paving is another factor.) When you emerge from the airplane, you will undoubtedly feel lightheaded, somewhat breathless, and sometimes cold. While these sensations can be invigorating initially, they also produce a weird, sudden fatigue, much as if the air was being sucked from your head by a giant, invisible vacuum cleaner. If you take the time to catch your breath (literally), this first flash of *soroche* (altitude sickness) will soon go away. (Smoking is not recommended.)

The original site of the La Paz settlement was, like the present airport, on the flatlands of the altiplano, a barren, windswept plateau fenced in by the Andes. But the Spanish conquistadores, arriving in 1548, found it too windy and moved it down into the valley below the tableland. A modern highway now connects the old site and present city and winds down some 1,600 feet from the airport into La Paz.

The road is dotted with playful billboards. One, advertising hydrofoil service across nearby Lake Titicaca — yet another global altitude champion at 12,500 feet — has a life-size replica of a traditional reed boat paddled by an Aymará Indian wearing a brightly colored *chullo* (woolen hat) and poncho. Just before the road comes to the city, it joins a concrete freeway interchange that links La Paz with the mysterious ruins at Tiahuanaco (see *Bolivia*, DIRECTIONS). Unlike most other cities, where the highest stretches of land become the mansion-lined residential districts of the wealthy, the higher neighborhoods of La Paz belong to the poor. In recent years, the *barrio* (neighborhood) of El Alto has become one of the most politically active in La Paz, with residents demanding improved roads, housing, sewage, and other municipal services. As if in response to some of their demands, a brand-new, reddish-brown prefab housing project spreads beside a hill on the side of the road edging the city. As you look to your right, the flat altiplano (Andean mountain plain) suddenly drops away. Below, inside a huge crater, stands the city of La Paz, the sky above it a clean, icy blue. The rectangular tin roofs of Aymará huts cling to the crater's inner walls, glittering in the sun like spangles on a dancer's costume. About 1,000 feet below, near the bottom of the crater, stand high-rise apartment buildings and skyscrapers. (At night, the approach to La Paz is even more dramatic. Unlike most cities, which seem to rise in front of you, La Paz looks like a bowlful of shimmering smoky topaz and glowing sapphire lights.)

The road winds through a eucalyptus grove, spiraling down at angles of between 50° and 80°, passing the small, chunky Aymará men and women whose colorful clothing contrasts with their plaintive faces. The men favor red and maroon sweaters, leaving peacockery to the thick-waisted women, who wear as many as seven cheerful *polleras* (petticoats) and skirts, striped or embroidered shawls in infinite rainbow pinks, blue, reds, and yellows, topped by either bowlers or white top hats. (These incongruous hats were introduced by an English merchant before the turn of the century.) All Aymará women wear their shining black hair in long, thick braids. Almost all seem to be carrying babies, each tied in an ingenious bundle of striped blanket on their backs. As you circle down the mountain, you will see busy throngs conducting commerce at numerous street stalls, hopping onto crowded, colorful microbuses, and bustling along steep, winding, cobbled thoroughfares. You will see tiny *cargardores* (porters) practically buried (except for their jogging legs) under what looks like a household of furniture or enough brick to build a school, and men in white coats carry large ice cream boxes strapped to their backs. Dust-covered Aymará newspaper women sit practically in the path of buses on noisy, jammed street corners, chanting *"El Diario!"* (one of La Paz's daily newspapers) into the din. In the evenings, the streets are equally packed as *paceños* (La Paz residents) gather to discuss the day's events or the results of a soccer match, generating the mad excitement of a block party on just about every street.

As you descend to the modern sector, the crowd becomes more cosmopolitan: engineers from the US and Australia, upper-middle-class mestizo Bolivians, visitors from other South American countries, and tourists from Germany, France, England, and Japan intermingle with the Aymará. Nobody stops to stare at foreigners here. Nobody is out of place.

This is an ideal spot from which to get your bearings. Looking up, you will see the city surrounded by snowcapped mountains, the Cordillera Real (Royal Range). And you will understand why *paceños* affectionately call their city *El Hueco* (the Hole). The lowest point of the city is the confluence of rivers known as Calacoto. The Calacoto district contains elegant neighborhoods, residences of US embassy personnel, and the homes of aristocratic Bolivian families. Then the city rises again toward the Cordillera Real. As the altitude increases, the population decreases, but the city is spreading to the mountains at a surprisingly rapid rate. The city's present population of one million (out of a national total of 5.6 million) is expected to double by the year 2010. La Paz itself, geographically spreading across barely 10 square miles at present (compared to Bolivia's 424,200 square miles), is already starting to absorb some of the world's most rugged, spectacular scenery. Like Denver, Colorado, one of La Paz's finest features is its proximity to gorgeous mountain wilderness with extraordinary wildlife, especially birds. Southeast of La Paz stands the incomparable Mt. Illimani, the 21,100-foot sentinel that can be seen from almost any point in La Paz. In 1961, according to local legend, the mayor of La Paz led an expedition up Mt. Illimani by Jeep, donkey, and foot to an Indian hut at an elevation of 19,800 feet in search of bear. Instead of bear, they found "a human footprint, eleven or twelve inches long," as described by one expedition member. The natives described "a fearful, two-legged creature between 10 and 11 feet high with tons of hair who sometimes came for food, chickens, sheep, and crops." This little-known Andean equivalent of the Himalayan Abominable Snowman has yet to be better documented.

Archaeologists, anthropologists, historians, and sociologists have long pondered the origins of the lost Tiahuanaco civilization that disappeared from the shores of Lake Titicaca (see *Exploring Bolivia,* DIRECTIONS) around AD 900. But succeeding Aymará and Quechua communities settled in the natural shelter carved by the Río Choqueapu in what is now the city, using the valley to cultivate those sturdier varieties of potato and corn that the cold, dry, windy, rocky altiplano allows to survive. They were living there on October 20, 1548, when Captain Alonso de Mendoza founded La Paz after a long quest for gold. It soon grew to a mining camp of 20,000 Europeans. By the turn of the seventeenth century, around the time Jamestown, Virginia, was settled, La Paz had grown tremendously due to its unique geographical position between the gold and silver mines in the Oruro-Potosí area and the seaports in Perú. Upon entering the nineteenth century, La Paz became the national capital of the emerging nation of Bolivia, rivaling the "official" capital of Sucre. Bolivia began its lengthy war of independence in 1809. The Spanish did not easily surrender the colony that, they claimed, had given them enough silver to build a bridge of the precious metal between themselves and their colony.

Fifteen years later La Paz, now part of a newly independent Bolivia, began another phase of what developed into a confusing, violent history. In 1879, Chile went to war with Bolivia (which was allied with Perú), only to cease hostilities in 1883 after Bolivia lost its entire coastline, the factor that, more than any other, has determined the country's underdevelopment and retarded its modernization in the twentieth century. Even today, the spine of the La Paz phone book sports the slogan *"Bolivia Demanda su Derecho de Salida al Mar"* (Bolivia demands her right of access to the sea), referring to Antofagasta, the vital port on the Pacific that now belongs to Chile. When the 1983 expiration of the Hundred Year Treaty of the War of the Pacific was looming on the political horizon, many Bolivians thought there would be an attempt to recapture their corridor to the sea. "It is part of the Bolivian mentality," a chauffeur in La Paz explained. "We cannot rest until we have our port back again."

However, Bolivian politics are rife with rumor. At one time during the 1970s, newspaper headlines in La Paz declared: BRAZIL PREPARES TROOPS TO INVADE BOLIVIA as *paceños* strolled past newsstands as unperturbed as

New Yorkers glancing at a headline reading MASS MURDER IN QUEENS. *Paceños* intuitively know they can't believe anything until it happens. Although the city's name means "the Peace," La Paz has been ironically singled out as the site of more than 160 revolutions, coups (violent and bloodless), and various overthrows of government, thus 60 different presidents have served since Bolivia's independence in 1825. And despite the fact that Aymará and Quechua Indians outnumber the mestizo and white residents by approximately four to one, it is a city suffering from racial disunity and prejudice. Neither World War I nor World War II touched Bolivia, but a strong German migration after 1945 noticeably increased the presence of blond heads and blue eyes in La Paz. This migration has shaped the sociopolitical arena — subtly at first, more overtly in the 1970s. It is no secret that former Nazis — among them SS Colonel Klaus Altmann Barbie, "the hangman of Lyons" — have made their homes in the Bolivian capital. However, under a new government, Barbie was arrested and deported to France despite the fact that no extradition treaty exists between the two countries.

Although the city is almost entirely confined to its huge hole in the altiplano and its disadvantageous geophysical location would seem to preclude further development, the master plan for the future of La Paz projects an expansion in all directions: toward the Cordillera Real, into the valleys, to the shores of Lake Titicaca, across the altiplano, and downriver to the agricultural areas. Due to economic uncertainties, the construction of several new downtown buildings has been halted in mid-stream. But in spite of the chaotic, fragmented quality of its political life, the highest city in the world continues to reign as the undisputed queen of the Andes.

LA PAZ AT-A-GLANCE

SEEING THE CITY: The road from El Alto Airport takes you to the edge of the altiplano, where the city below fills every level and most inclined pieces of land. At night, these layers of light increase the unreality of this already unbelievable scene. You will be able to trace one main artery of lights. From the new highway, it becomes Avenida Montes, then changes its name to Plaza Pérez Velasco, Avenida Mariscal Santa Cruz, El Prado or Avenida 16 de Julio, Avenida Villazón, and Avenida Arce, continuing down hundreds of feet to become the main street of the Obrajes and Calacoto districts. The Cordillera Real is visible just a few miles from the center of the city. The northern approach to the city, coming from El Alto, is called Ceja del Alto ("the eyebrow," or edge of the altiplano). Behind this sprawling suburb, the altiplano stretches to the north, south, and west until it meets the western Cordillera Occidental (western range) about 80 miles (129 km) away, that extends from north to south, dividing Bolivia from Chile and Perú. On clear days, you can see this and much more. During the rainy season, you can observe the awesome altiplano storms approaching from as far as 150 miles away.

SPECIAL PLACES: The downtown (centro) section has a sloping diameter that can be covered on foot in about half an hour (going downhill). It is bordered by the San Francisco Church on the northwest, Plaza Murillo to the northeast, the *Sheraton* hotel to the southeast, and Avenida Buenos

Aires to the southwest. It is difficult to get really lost since you can always walk or climb to a higher spot and see where you are.

DOWNTOWN

El Prado – This three-block-long stretch of the main avenue has a central divider of flowers, benches, fountains, and statues. Considered the center of La Paz, it is lined with trees and increasingly tall buildings. It's the international sector of the city and contains many of its higher-priced shops. Although, relative to other large cities, nothing is expensive in La Paz (except rent, cars, and real estate), there is a big gap between tourist trap prices and those in other parts of the city. Browse here, by all means, but spend your money in other sections of town, where you'll be sure to get better value. There are several neat cafés along this stretch. Try the *Gargantua Snack,* a place where tourists and locals gather for good, fast-service food on Av. 16 de Julio.

National Archaeological Museum of Tiwanaco (Museo Nacional Arqueológico de Tiwanaku) – Whether you are planning a day trip to the ruins or have just come to town via a long trek around Lake Titicaca and its environs, stop in for a good look at the artifacts and implements excavated from the site of the lost city. Ceramics, bronze items, and jewelry of copper and silver are on display. Now open again after a 3-year renovation.

Camacho Market (Mercado Camacho) – An unobtrusive gate marks the entrance to the city's central produce market. As you make your way past the Indians sitting on the ground selling cheese *empanadas,* you'll file down a narrow set of steps lined with stalls displaying steel wool, canned goods, powdered soup, pickled onions, green and black olives, lard, yogurt, Brazil nuts, wooden doors, garlic, sponges, toilet paper, Horniman's tea, bananas, grapefruit, lemons, macaroni, powdered milk, cans of Nescafé, cheese, and sausages. And that's just the beginning! Indoors, a covered market sprawls under a tin roof where vegetables and straw baskets are piled high and rotund Aymará women, grinning mouthfuls of gold teeth, hack off sections of meat to order. Behind the market, a stream flows through rocky banks. One word of advice: Don't buy vegetables, fruit, or meat at the market. The residents are immune to the local bacteria but you aren't. Open daily. Free. Av. Camacho and Calle Bueno.

Plaza Sucre – A charming plaza floored with black and white tile patterns framed in red, this is a meeting place for shy schoolchildren and older citizens. Crews of laborers trim the lawn and manicure the plaza's hedges with machetes. Along the fringes of the plaza, photographers with brightly decorated old-fashioned box cameras vie for business. The photographers are happy to kid around with gringo amateurs, but shy at being photographed themselves, as are most other *paceños* who make this their home away from home. (You should have at least a 105-mm lens.)

Indian Witches' Markets (Calle Sagárnaga) – Probably the most incredible street in the world, Sagárnaga begins at San Francisco Church and ascends up a steep, cobblestoned hill to the southwest. At the bottom of the hill are little stores selling lovely ponchos, weavings, and appliquéd wall hangings with Tiahuanaco motifs. But beyond this tourist market a dazzling variety of Indian markets awaits. Past the tourist shops, a right turn onto Calle Linares (an almost 2-hour walk) will bring you to a line of shriveled women selling magic charms, herbs, and paraphernalia for all purposes. They will not sell to gringos, and many will refuse to explain what their wares are meant to do. Those brightly colored squares that look like cookies with patterns — cows, tables, a skull and crossbones — are stamped with blocks of incense meant to be burned at particular times. If you want your cattle to be healthy, burn a few squares with cows on them. A table-decorated charm will ensure plenty of food; the skull and crossbones will protect against the angel of death. You will see plenty of grotesque, dried fetuses of llamas. These question-mark-shaped skeletons are buried under the foundations of new houses to protect them. (There is some question whether US customs will allow you to bring one of these bizarre-looking items back into the country, should you manage to prevail upon its owner to sell it to you.) Calle Sagárnaga from Av. Mariscal Santa Cruz to Segurola.

Calle Illampu Market (Illampu Street) – On another fascinating back street, off Sagárnaga, this daily market has artfully arranged displays of purple onions, glowing red plums, carrots, and other fresh produce. Each enterprise is presided over by a dignified Aymará woman in voluminous skirts and bowler hat. On Avenida Marisal Santa Cruz, also off this part of Sagárnaga, there are stalls selling hardware, shoes, and other practical goods.

The Black Market (Mercado Negro) – The name is legitimate. This section of town is dedicated to the sale of contraband and, later in the evening, stolen goods. Only the Bolivian mining industry nets more than imported and exported contraband, so the black market is only regulated theatrically — that is, for show. Any imported contraband is freely accessible. Among the hot items are Peruvian toilet paper and American canned goods. Stay away from exportable contraband. It's handled by a well-organized, tightly knit monopoly — La Paz's equivalent of the Mafia. At the black market you can easily and safely fill a shopping basket with Brazilian, Argentinian, and American necessities for a lower price than you'll find in most American cities. Open daily. Calle Max Paredes and Graneros.

Plaza Murillo – This square park is the center of government activity, with a large section devoted to commerce. The presidential and legislative palaces overlook the plaza and occupy the upper corners. (Remember, everything slants in La Paz — up and down are literal directions.) The Cathedral of La Paz, one of the most beautiful churches in the city, also stands on the plaza. As much the property of pigeons as of humans, Plaza Murillo stubbornly maintains its uniquely *paceño* architectural heritage while outside, but close to the plaza, the tall buildings creep ever closer.

El Montículo – At the southern edge of the area we consider "downtown," there is a hill that juts into La Paz. The park, a small church, and an observatory (*mirador*) provide a beautiful view and a quiet respite from the nearby hustle of the city. Calle Lisimaco Gutierres and Calle Presbitero Medina. Take the "M" microbus from Av. 6 de Agosto.

SUBURBS

Valley of the Moon and Cactus Garden (Valle de la Luna and Mallasilla) – "Why go to the moon when you can go to La Paz?" And well you might ask. Intriguing beige and red spires of earth and rock sculpted by wind and water surround you, reaching for the sky. Between them lie gorges, dangerous drops, and narrow, steep paths connecting different parts of the valley. If you visit before sunset, you'll see a dazzling burst of light and color. Just around a bend in the road from the Valley of the Moon, at a slightly lower elevation, the municipal cactus garden contains a fascinating concentration of regional flora. Erosion is a real threat here, and the garden was planted as a land reclamation project. Open daily. Free. Follow Av. José Ballivían in Calacoto to Mallasilla (about 30 minutes) or take the No. 130 microbus to Mallasa.

The Devil's Molar (La Muela del Diablo) – If you have come to the Andes to sample the offerings of nature, this is a fruitful place to spend a day. Climbing this strange volcanic cap that divides the downriver section, where the city is expected to spread, from the southern neighborhoods of Calacoto and San Miguel, you will see many kinds of geological formations, birds, and plants. On the weekends, many *paceños* and visitors hike along this trail. It's best to ask the way, since the volcanic cap cannot be seen for the first 90 minutes of the hike. At the bottom of the hill, beside the road, you'll find several restaurants, including *La Pergola,* a favorite with *paceños.* From Av. 6 de Agosto, take the "Ñ" microbus to Cota Cota.

Achocalla – This is actually another huge hole in the altiplano, rather like the one that cradles La Paz. It provides even better views of the mountains than you'll find within the city itself. At present, there are no high-quality restaurants here, but it is a rapidly growing area. There are tennis courts, horseback riding, and boating facilities. You can rent a taxi for the day, for about $35 or $40, round trip. Or take the main avenue uphill to El Alto and follow the signs to the Oruro road. Then, after about 10 minutes, take the turnoff to Koritambo.

Chacaltaya – The world's highest ski slope, at 17,716 feet, it is a 1½-hour drive from El Alto on a rugged road that is definitely not for the fainthearted. Four-wheel-drive vehicles are the best way to get here, as the rocky, pitted, twisting, hairpin-turning, mind-blowing road will destroy a normal car (and a city-trained driver's nerves). The scenery en route is simply dazzling: splendid panoramic views of the city nestled in its crater, getting smaller and smaller as you ascend; tiny stone shacks inhabited by God-knows-who clinging to the mountains near running streams (ideal when your radiator water evaporates at the high altitude). Just before you arrive at the rudimentary ski hook tow lift and restaurant hanging on the edge of precipice, you will pass the Bolivian Institute of Cosmic Physics, operated by the Bolivian Institute for Atomic Energy, a complex of white buildings high on a ledge, overlooking some weird instruments set among the black rocks to measure ultraviolet radiation and a shrine to the Virgin Mary. If you enjoy the challenge of driving on empty, tough roads, the trip is definitely worth it even if you're not a hard-core downhill skier. If you are, and can handle the very fast, steep runs here, contact the Club Andino, Calle México 1638 (phone: 32-46-82), for information. The ski season runs from October through April — the rainy season (at lower elevations) — after that, it's too cold. The lift fee for one day is about $2; equipment is about $10. By the way, even if you're accustomed to the altitude in La Paz, be prepared for some dizziness and *soroche* at Chacaltaya. You need to be in top physical condition to ski here. Take the road to Tiwanaco at El Alto, then turn right on Avenida Chacaltaya (avenida is a euphemism) and continue until you come to a stone indicator at a fork in the road, where you bear right. Chacaltaya is about 19 miles (30 km) from La Paz. They're guaranteed to be among the most unforgettable 19 miles you'll ever ride.

■**EXTRA SPECIAL:** After you've seen Chacaltaya, you'll probably find yourself irresistibly drawn to the majestic group of mountains in the background: the Cordillera Real. Bounded by Mt. Illiamani to the south and Mt. Illampu to the north, the mountains contain a number of rich mines and attract serious climbers from all over the world. For outstanding photography and some of the cleanest air in the world, however, you don't have to climb them. Dirt roads permit vehicular traffic to approach to about 16,500 feet — the off-season snow line. The Zongo pass, between 20,000-foot Huayna Potosí (where daredevils ski down glaciers) and Chacaltaya, reveals jungles behind the white mountains. To reach the Zongo pass, take the road to Chacaltaya and bear left where the road forks beyond the power station. The road climbs past still lakes, where you can catch sumptuous catfish and trout, through thatched adobe villages where Aymará Indians live as they have for thousands of years, and past herds of llamas; then it descends from 15,167 feet to 5,904 feet, into tropical terrain.

SOURCES AND RESOURCES

TOURIST INFORMATION: For general information, brochures, and maps, contact the Instituto Boliviano de Turismo, Plaza Venezuela, Edificio (Bldg.) Herrmann, fourth floor, or write Casilla 1868, La Paz (phone: 36-74-42 or 36-74-63/4), or visit the Tourist Information Center at the end of

El Prado. You can get a free city map from the Tourist Information Center, but the Center keeps erratic hours. A better city map, published by Cicerone, is available in bookstores.

English-language tour books are few and far between. *Los Amigos del Libro* bookstore, on Calle Mercado and in the *Sheraton* hotel, has a wide range of books on Bolivia in Spanish. For encyclopedic coverage of Bolivia in Spanish, we recommend *Bolivia Mágica,* by Hugo Boero Rojo. A cultural guide to the city that includes addresses and hours of operation for museums and theaters is available at *Casa Municipal de la Cultura,* across from the San Francisco Cathedral, and at some museums, but it is also in Spanish.

Local Coverage – *Presencia* and *El Diario* (both morning dailies) are the two top newspapers. *Selecciones Librería, El Mundo del Santa Cruz,* and *Amigos del Libro* sell *Time, Newsweek,* the *Miami Herald,* and the *Latin American Daily Post,* published daily in São Paulo, Brazil. Everything arrives from the States several weeks late. If you are addicted to hard news, you will find La Paz a frustrating place to visit. The Centro Boliviano-Americano has the best English-language library. Playa Zenon Iturralde 121 (phone: 35-16-27 or 34-25-82).

 CLIMATE AND CLOTHES: Although we have discussed altitude sickness in passing in the essay, above, and in *Medical and Legal Aid,* GETTING READY TO GO, be aware that this is an inevitable factor to consider when planning a trip. Altitude and overall human health is a relatively ignored subject. One important component of those symptoms attributable to high altitude is psychosomatic, but there is definitely an important physical element. People who have come from sea level or lower altitudes to live in La Paz attest to a physical accommodation period that ranges from six months to a year. It takes about that long for the red blood cell count to double. Since there is less air pressure at 12,000 feet, the altitude of Plaza Murillo, less oxygen enters the bloodstream, water boils at a lower temperature, and the atmosphere is drier and more electric. If you intend to explore the city and neighboring countryside, you should practice lung-enlarging exercises before your trip. Some heart accelerants are sold in La Paz, but these should only be used in emergencies. Most hotels supply *coca* tea (ask for *maté de coca*) to perk you up. If you have severe respiratory or heart disorders, you should avoid La Paz. As a rule, the better your physical health, the more thorough and enjoyable your visit will be. Note, however, that travelers coming from Cuzco, Perú (via the train to Puno and across Lake Titicaca — a popular routing), will be acclimated to the altitude and should have little discomfort, if any, in La Paz and environs.

The temperature throughout the year ranges from 30°F (− 1°C) to 70°F (22°C), with about a 20°F (7°C) difference between sun and shade. Evenings are cold enough to require a sweater almost every night of the year. It is perceptibly chillier at El Alto than in the city itself. You will need much warmer clothing from May through August. The winter months, June through September, are very cold and clear, with June and July the coldest. The climate in the mountains is comparable to that of the Arctic. High-altitude sun exposure, windburn, and snow blindness occur frequently, so bring sunscreen and sunglasses. The meteorological conditions do not follow the patterns you are accustomed to at sea level. The rainy season starts a month after the beginning of spring (in September) and lasts until the middle of March, with torrential, cold downpours and chilling fog throughout the season. Although storms are generally brief, weather changes are sudden so be sure to take a sweater and rain gear if you go out on a touring expedition. Spring temperatures are more moderate than those of the autumn and winter months, but La Paz can be uncomfortably cool if you are not prepared. The most beautiful days are generally in April and May and, if you don't mind the cold, June and July.

GETTING AROUND: Bus – The least expensive form of transport, buses fall into two categories: micros and the larger colectivos. Try to avoid colectivos, especially during the lunchtime rush hour, around noon. Neither micros nor colectivos run after midnight, officially, but it is unlikely you will find one after 10 PM.

Taxi – There are two kinds of taxis: *trufis,* which run along an established route, stopping to discharge and pick up passengers so that the car remains full, and taxis. Sometimes a taxi driver will stop to pick up another fare while someone is in the car, but he will drop the first passenger at his or her destination first. *Trufis* cost about five pesos more than micros. They are easily distinguishable by the colored flags they display on their front bumpers. Taxis have red license plates. Bargain with the driver before hiring him. La Paz's cab drivers can be pretty fierce when it comes to over-charging gringos. Check with the Tourist Information Desk at El Alto Airport (phone: 37-12-20/1) to find out the going rate for a trip into town. If possible, have someone who works at the airport negotiate the fare (about $25) for you before stepping into the cab. A trip to Tiahuanaco will cost about $45 per half day. You can leave and return at your convenience. You can also call *Taxi Service,* Av. Mariscal Santa Cruz 1289 (phone: 35-83-36) or Av. Manco Capac 337 at the corner of Calle Viacha (phone: 35-78-22), for car service to anywhere in the city or environs. *Taxi Service* connects with a Peruvian car service that travels regularly to Puno, on the Peruvian shores of Lake Titicaca. Daily tours by car to Tiahuanaco are $40 per person, to Lake Titicaca, $45, and can be booked through your hotel. You can also make arrangements with local agents, such as *Crillon Tours* (phone: 350-363) or *Turismo Balsa* (phone: 354-049).

Car Rental – A Jeep or equivalent four-wheel-drive vehicle is essential when tackling Bolivian roads. *Oscar Crespo Maurice Rent-a-Car,* Plaza España, can provide you with Toyota Land Cruisers, Toyota or Datsun sedans, Volkswagens, and other types of autos. *Kolla Motors,* Calle R. Gutierrez (phone: 35-17-01), rents Jeeps. For more information on car rentals, contact Automóvil Club Boliviano, Av. 6 de Agosto (phone: 37-21-39 or 34-20-74). *Rent a Car* is at Av. Simón Bolívar 1865 (phone: 350-974). Current Jeep prices are about $75 and up a day; cars, $20 plus mileage.

Train – Riding a train through the Andes is an unbelievable experience. Although it is not by any means the fastest way to travel long distances, a train is probably the best way to get a leisurely look at the countryside and people. Don't expect to get where you're going on time, either. If you arrive on the same day, consider yourself fortunate. (See *Touring by Rail,* GETTING READY TO GO.) Railroads link most parts of Bolivia, Perú, and Chile. For information, contact *Estación Central,* Av. Manco Capac (phone: 35-25-10). There is a spectacular ride from La Paz to Antofagasta through the Uyuni Desert. *Ferrocarril Antofagasta–Bolivia* sells tickets at Estación Central. A different train goes to the northern frontier of Chile. *Ferrocaril Arica–La Paz.* Information and tickets are available at the main station.

MUSEUMS: Among La Paz's many fine museums is the *Tiahuanaco Archaeological Museum* (*Museo Arqueológico de Tiahuanaco*), a building reminiscent of the ancient pyramids, which displays a good collection of pre-Columbian artifacts. You enter at the foot of a flight of stairs by the María Auxiliadora church off the Prado. The *National Museum of Art* (*Museo Nacional del Arte*), in the former palace of the Count of Arana (perhaps the finest old building in La Paz), contains beautifully furnished rooms and galleries with a fine display of colonial and modern Bolivian paintings. Open Tuesdays through Fridays from 1 to 7 PM and weekends from 10 AM to 12:30 PM. Plaza Murillo at the corner of Calle Socabaya (phone: 34-34-22). Nearby, the *Casa Murillo* at Calle Jaén (phone: 32-60-40) houses restored colonial furniture in salon settings, colonial religious art, and exhibitions on folk medicine and music. Also worth a visit is the *Museo de Costumbres,* with ceramic figurines set in tableaux portraying scenes of Bolivian history and culture, as well as the *National Museum of Ethnography and Folklore.* The latter, occupying the former Villaverde Palace, offers a premier course in local folk arts and crafts, especially the room of masks and ceremonial costumes worn at different fiestas. Calle Ingavi 916.

Generally, museum hours in La Paz are 9:30 AM to noon and 2 to 6:30 PM. However, there are variations, so check with your hotel concierge.

SHOPPING: La Paz has terrific selections of well-made ponchos, *chullos* (woolen hats), wall hangings, knitted alpaca sweaters and gloves, and other textile products at very reasonable prices. The craftsmanship is superior to that of goods of similar style and fabric found in neighboring Perú, and the prices are better. As mentioned in *Special Places,* the best streets for shopping are Calle Sagárnaga and Calle Illampu. Toiletries, cosmetics, and packaged goods should be purchased in the *Mercado Negro* (Black Market), Calle Max Paredes and Calle Graneros. One particularly good crafts store, though not inexpensive, is *Tiendas Bolivianas,* at Plaza Avaroa.

Generally, it is a good idea to stay away from imported items — electrical goods, china, clothing made of synthetics.

SPORTS: The most popular sport is definitely soccer (*fútbol*). The world's highest golf course and tennis courts are here, too.

Fishing – Great trout and catfish live in the lakes of the Negruni-Chacapa region of the Cordillera Real and in Lake Titicaca. You will need a fishing license, valid for 1 year, from the Ministry of Agriculture, Av. Camacho, or from the US Embassy. Bring two photographs, around passport size, for the license.

Golf – *Golf Club Mallasilla* has the world's highest 18-hole course. Be careful on your drives — there's less air resistance here and it's easy to overshoot. On the road to Valle de la Luna, through two tunnels, then bear right at the fork. Av. Montes 725, Malasilla (phone: 34-1581).

Horseback Riding – You can rent horses from the stables at *Club Sargentos,* Calle 9, Obrajes (phone: 78-4899).

Hunting – Again, you need a license from the US Embassy or the Ministry of Agriculture. If you want to meet other hunters and anglers, go to the building in front of the Golf Club in Manzanilla, which houses the *Hunting and Fishing Club* (*Club de Caza y Pesca*) (no phone).

Mountain Climbing – Many expeditions leave for Huayna Condoriri and Mt. Illimani. The other mountains require more time and are not as popular. For information, contact the *Club Andino Boliviano,* Calle México 1638 (phone: 32-46-82). They can also give you hints on hiking and camping.

Sailing – When the weather's good, the world's highest lake has brisk winds and cobalt blue waters. There is a yacht club in the town of Huatajata on Lake Titicaca (phone: 32-41-59).

Skiing – The world's highest slope, at Mt. Chacaltaya, is the only one in Bolivia with a lift. It is primitive, but preferable to walking up. (See *Special Places,* above.) A new ski station is planned for Mt. Mururata, which is an hour from La Paz and has a 9-month season. For information: *Club Andino Boliviano* (phone 32-46-82).

Soccer – The Estadio Hernando Siles hosts the best games in Bolivia. Miraflores (phone: 36-5644).

Swimming – Mountain lakes, such as Titicaca, are not recommended because the water is always icy cold. *Mallasilla Golf Club* also has the world's highest pool. The *Automóvil Club,* Av. Ballivián at the corner of Calle 12, Calacoto (phone: 38-21-26), has a pool. *The German Club* (*Club Alemán*) has a pool, tennis courts, riding stables, and a soccer field. It's in Calacoto, near Calle 23, but you'd best call for directions (phone: 32-43-97).

Tennis – Excellent for people with hearty lungs who prefer running after balls to hanging off cliffs, this sport is gaining in popularity, with a number of clubs now in operation. The world's highest is *Club Tenís La Paz,* Av. Florida, La Florida (phone: 79-25-90). Also, *Sucre Tennis Club,* Av. Busch 1001 (phone: 32-44-83).

THEATER: Daily newspapers carry listings of performances. The *Municipal Theater (Teatro Municipal)* presents operas and, occasionally, very good performances in Spanish. Calle Jenaro Sanjines (phone: 35-08-38). *House of Culture (Casa de la Cultura),* Plaza San Francisco (phone: 32-67-47), has good local talent appearing in plays and concerts. It also has changing displays of art and handicrafts.

MUSIC: The *peñas* offer the best regional music. Reservations are necessary for what is usually a very rewarding night at *Peña Naira,* Sagárnaga 161 (phone: 32-57-36), or at *Marka Tambo,* Calle Jaén 710 (phone: 34-04-16 or 34-36-83). Another good place for folk music is *Casa del Corregidor,* Calle Murillo 104 (phone: 36-36-33).

NIGHTCLUBS AND NIGHTLIFE: The nightclub scene in La Paz is definitely disco, with clubs moving in and out of favor and existence at a fast clip. Current top nightspots are *Baccara,* Av. 20 de Octubre 1824 (phone: 32-40-39); *Disco Studio,* Av. 6 de Agosto; *Packa,* Av. 6 de Agosto, Edificio Santa Teresa (phone: 35-07-45); *Exclusivo Bar,* Av. Sanchez Lima 2237 (phone: 36-25-44); *Candilejas,* Calle Capitan Castrillo 458 (phone: 37-69-25). Visitors staying at hotels have the benefit of gathering places such as the nightclubs at the *Sheraton,* Av. Arce (phone: 35-69-50), and the skytop lounge at the *Plaza,* Paseo de Prado (phone: 37-83-11).

Coffee shops serve good food and anything to drink short of hard liquor. They are the best places for meeting people and making friends. Popular places include the *Sucre* in the *Sucre Palace,* on El Prado (phone: 35-50-80); *Confitería La Paz,* across the street from the former *La Paz* hotel on Av. Camacho (phone: 35-52-92); and *Marilyn,* Calle Potosí 1106 (phone: 34-12-13).

SINS: Unquestionably the *pride* of La Paz is its title, "the highest city in the world." Other "highests" include: lake, golf course, tennis court, and swimming pool. Concomitant with the altitude is a paucity of oxygen, which has the initial effect of inhibiting sex drive and hunger. *Soroche* is, in fact, as effective an appetite-suppressant as amphetamines. It is unlikely you will feel much like indulging in *gluttony* or *lust,* at least for the first few days.

BEST IN TOWN

CHECKING IN: Until a few years ago, La Paz suffered from a frightful shortage of hotel rooms. But the opening of the *Sheraton* and the *Plaza* in the last 5 years has given a considerable boost to the city's list of accommodations. Expect to pay between $50 and $90 for a double room in those hotels we've classified as expensive; between $25 and $40 at places in the moderate category; under $20 in inexpensive places. Add 20% to 27% for service and taxes.

Plaza – This is the newest and most expensive hotel in town, and a lovely one indeed.

It has 200 well-appointed rooms and suites with central heating, private bath, and phone. Facilities include Turkish baths and sauna, plus heated swimming pool. There's a good choice of bars and restaurants, including those with top-floor views, and a shopping mall downstairs. The service is said to be just about the best in town. Paseo del Prado (phone: 37-83-11). Expensive.

Sheraton – An elegant high-rise hotel with a lobby full of shops, newsstands, a travel agency, foreign exchange desk, postal desk, cable office, and snazzy bar. The austere ground-floor decor has astonishing polished red granite that was cut in Italy and a $78,000 chandelier made in Vienna and then assembled in Bolivia that is a twin to the one hanging in New York's Lincoln Center. The upstairs rooms have great views of the city and Mt. Illimani. It's lovely to breakfast on croissants and coffee in your room, gazing at the view. Although the hotel is well kept, service can be erratic. A fine new fitness center, the *Joy Club,* has facilities that include a pool and sauna. Av. Arce (phone: 35-69-50; 35-69-66). Expensive.

Crillon – In the same class as the *Sucre* (below), this one still maintains its high quality. The lobby's polished floor and mirrored walls give it an inviting feel. The staff at the front desk is extremely helpful, pleasant, and speaks good English. The restaurant is good. Plaza Isabel Católica (phone: 35-21-21). Moderate.

El Dorado – Across the street from the main university, San Andres, this offers comfort and a convenient location at fair prices. It's named for the legendary Inca man of gold. Av. Villazón (phone: 36-34-03; 36-33-55; 36-34-08). Moderate.

Gloria – Across the street from the House of Culture (see *Theaters,* above), this has a flashy, uninviting lobby, but with attractive, well-kept rooms (all with bath) and a top-floor restaurant with a lovely view of the Plaza San Francisco this is a very good value. Calle Potosí at the corner of Calle Jenaro Sanjinez (phone: 37-00-10). Moderate.

Libertador – The best of the new, moderate hotels, it is well located in the commercial center. If you are looking for a downtown location, it leaves little to be desired. Calle Obispo Cardenas (phone: 34-33-60). Moderate.

Sagárnaga – A relatively new establishment, this is a good bet in the Aymará quarter. It has an attractive lobby decorated with bright Inca motifs and a small restaurant. Some rooms have baths but none have heat. Calle Sagárnaga 326 (phone: 32-02-52; 35-87-57). Moderate.

Sucre Palace – More Bolivian than American in decor, this older, mellower establishment in the center of El Prado was for many years the best in La Paz. The furniture in guestrooms is comfortably faded, the beds are soft, and the telephones, heavy and old-fashioned. Downstairs, the lobby and café are decorated in a medley of white stucco and Tiwanaku designs. Unfortunately, there have been some complaints about the hotel lately. Av. 16 de Julio 1636 (phone: 35-50-80). Moderate.

Residencial La Hostería – As the name suggests, this is a house that has been partly transformed into a hotel. It is the best in its class: clean accommodations with communal baths and no frills. Calle Bueno 138 (phone: 32-49-79). Inexpensive.

 EATING OUT: Even though La Paz has not been a small town for some time, it has, until very recently, been the kind of place where most people ate at home. But with more travelers and businesspeople heading here, the range of eating establishments has widened considerably, and *paceños* are eating out more and more. Not only are new restaurants opening, old ones are improving. Many restaurants tend to imitate Argentinian cuisine, and delicious barbecued *parrillada* can be found almost everywhere. Expect to pay between $20 and $40 for dinner for two at those restaurants we've classified as expensive; between $10 and $20 at those places in the moderate range; under $10, inexpensive. Many of our restaurant selections do not accept credit cards, and because of anticipated currency fluctuations, those that presently honor them may not in the future.

Pabellon Alaya – A handsome supper club atop the *La Paz Sheraton,* it offers an international menu, good service, and dancing far into the night. Also on the top floor is a lovely sunken bar, and from every side, the vistas are dazzling. Service and the quality of the food are uneven. Av. Arce (phone: 35-58-91). Expensive.

Arcón de Oro – The *Plaza's* top-quality dining room, and one of the two best bets in town for a meal in the Continental tradition. The rich, deep-red walls and carpet create an atmosphere of luxury, and if you order the trout from Lake Titicaca, it's possible to experience the best of the European and South American cuisines in one dish. Plaza Hotel, Paseo del Prado (phone: 37-83-11). Expensive.

Dominique – The menu is international at this sophisticated bistro. Reservations required. Calle Capital Ravelo 2123 (phone: 37-71-73). Expensive.

El Refugio – A cozy place for international cuisine. Especially good are the meat and fish selections. Reservations required. Av. 20 de Octubre 2458 (phone: 35-56-51). Expensive.

La Suisse – As the name suggests, this restaurant, on the corner opposite the *Sheraton,* serves good Swiss cuisine, including fondue. Reservations required. Av. Arce (phone: 35-31-50). Expensive.

Club Alemán – Not to be confused with the private club of the same name, *Club Alemán* is located right behind the *Plaza* hotel. The extensive menu offers everything from Lake Titicaca trout to sauerkraut and rye bread, but don't be surprised if the preparation is a bit heavy-handed. The clublike dining room is a popular lunch spot. Calle Carlos Bravo (phone: 32-43-97). Expensive to moderate.

La Carreta – One of several popular Argentine-style grill restaurants. The *parrillada* keeps coming and coming, served on wooden planks. Salad is wheeled to your table on a cart so you can choose what you like. Bring your appetite. Reservations are not needed. Calle Batallón Colorados 32 (phone: 35-58-91). Expensive to moderate.

Utama – This dining room on the top floor of the new *Plaza* hotel offers more spectacular views of the city. The menu specializes in Bolivian dishes and there's a salad bar that rivals the best in the States. Paseo del Prado (phone: 37-83-11). Expensive to moderate.

La Cabaña del Nono – Those looking for barbecue served outdoors will want to try this place. Av. Ballivían 387 (phone: 79-21-92). Moderate.

Casa del Corregidor – In one of the oldest colonial houses of La Paz, this is a favorite place to come for European cuisine and not too heavily spiced local dishes. It's also nice for listening to folk music. Murillo 1040 (phone: 36-36-33). Moderate.

Chingo – Said to serve the best American-style hamburgers in La Paz. Plaza Isabel La Católica, by the *Crillon* hotel. Moderate.

Giorgíssimo – One of the more popular lunchtime restaurants, it caters to an international clientele, resident and traveling. Calle Loayza at the corner of Av. Camacho (phone: 32-44-50). Moderate.

Naira – Considered by many to be the most typically Bolivian restaurant in La Paz. The atmosphere is almost medieval — family-style dining at long wooden tables set with locally made pottery. Bolivian cuisine features Andean potatoes and corn in a variety of soups and casseroles. The food itself is bland; the sauces, *piquante* (very hot). *Escabeche,* a boiled chicken dish, will not harm your palate. After dinner, take a walk next door to the *peña,* featuring a dazzling variety of folk music and dance groups. Reservations recommended. Calle Sagárnaga 161 (phone: 32-57-36). Moderate.

Sucre – Recommended by *paceños* for sampling the local cuisine. Don't try walking here from the center of town until you've adjusted to the altitude: It's a practically vertical half-hour hike. Reservations advised. Corner of Calle Ecuador and Pedro Salazar (phone: 32-29-12). Moderate.

Eli's – It's a simple, hearty café in which Bolivian food is served to a lively clientele of *paceños* and tourists. Steak with an egg on top, hamburgers, and even chicken soup are available. If you want to meet the locals, make this the stop for your Sunday midday meal. Av. 16 de Julio 1497 (phone: 32-51-59). Inexpensive.

La Fontana – This is the coffee shop in the *Plaza* hotel. Bright and cheerful, and overlooking a bubbling fountain, it's a good place for sandwiches and other light fare at any time of day. Paseo del Prado (phone: 37-83-11). Inexpensive.

Marilyn – A large, boisterous restaurant and tea shop, it offers hamburgers, hot dogs, and pastries, in addition to some more substantial fare. Calle Potosí 1106 (phone: 34-12-13). Inexpensive.

Verona – Caters to a local clientele. It's not as fancy as *Naira* but serves essentially the same cuisine at much lower prices. No reservations. Calle Colón at the corner of Av. Mariscal Santa Cruz (phone: 32-11-59). Inexpensive.

LIMA

For those fortunate enough to circle Lima's Jorge Chávez International Airport on a clear day, the first view of Perú's Pacific coast has the same purity and power that attracted the original Spanish settlers more than 400 years ago: white Pacific breakers buffeting desert sand beaches; an arm of the Andes reaching so far into the sea that its final peaks form the chain of islands of Frontón, San Lorenzo, and the Palominos; and some seven miles inland, in the lush oases of the Rimac Valley, Lima itself, dominating this panorama of sea, desert, and mountain just as it did when it was the capital of Spain's South American empire.

In 1621, when the Pilgrims were sitting down to their first Thanksgiving dinner, Lima had been the most important city in the Western Hemisphere for 80 years. Known originally as the City of Kings — because conquistador Francisco Pizarro established the site of the new city on January 6, 1535, Epiphany, or Day of the Kings — it was the center of Spain's viceregency from its founding until independence swept across the continent at the beginning of the nineteenth century. It picked up the name Lima soon after its founding by virtue of a mistake. The city was laid out along a river and a valley known to the Indians as Rimac; the Spanish misunderstood the word as Limac, and before they corrected the error it was shortened to Lima.

The name was just about the only mistake Pizarro and his conquistadores made in planning the city. The sketch he drew with his pikestaff in the fertile fields around Río Rímac indicated a city built slightly inland from the coast served by an efficient port (Lima's seaport, Callao, is still one of the busiest in South America), surrounded by wide plains with plenty of space for growth (modern Lima covers 27 square miles and is still growing, unimpeded by natural obstacles), at a point midway along Perú's 1,400-mile coast (Lima is not only the crossroads for Perú, but for much of the north-south air traffic between the continent's major cities). The city that emerged from these ambitious plans was protected, beautifully situated, and regally proud — one of the finest products of colonial culture in South America. Pizarro designed a city to stand for the ages.

Such foresight was fortuitous, for Lima has never ceased to be a capital even as the fortunes of the colony, and later the country, have risen and fallen. When contemporary *limeños* claim with great pride *"Lima es Perú,"* compatriots in provincial cities such as Cuzco, Trujillo, Puno, and Arequipa are forced ruefully to agree. Everything — government, finance, industry, education, newspapers, and magazines — is centralized in the capital. And increasingly it is the center of the nation's population as well. For the last two decades, the sons and daughters of Indian farmers in the mountains have left their villages to move to the coast in the hopes of bettering their lives. All the coastal cities have been affected by this population upheaval, but none quite so much as Lima. In 1940, Lima had 500,000 inhabitants. Today, Greater Lima has approximately 7 million people, at least one-quarter of the entire population of Perú, and demographers are predicting a population of more than 10 million by the end of this century.

The pressure of this precipitous increase in population is felt everywhere in the city. *Pueblos jóvenes* (young towns) of ramshackle homes made of cardboard, oil drums, and adobe have sprung up on the sides of hills and beside the airport. Peddlers of all kinds, called *ambulantes,* line the major downtown streets selling anything from razor blades to handicrafts. Fiscal mismanagement by Perú's military government pushed the country close to bankruptcy by the spring of 1978, and underemployment affects almost half of the working population, although the general economy has improved somewhat under the civilian government elected in 1985. In January 1986, the inti, a new, revalued monetary unit, was introduced into circulation. At present, the inti-dollar exchange rate is frozen and government controlled. All money exchange must be made through official, government-approved exchange offices.

But troubled times are hardly new to *limeños,* and Peruvians are a peaceful people by nature. They disarm adversity with humor, as when the government declared 1978 "the Year of Austerity" and residents joked that 1979 would undoubtedly be "the Year of the Survivors."

The patience of Lima residents has been further taxed recently by terrorist attacks spurred on by the violent Maoist antigovernment group that calls itself "The Shining Path." Begun in the Andes, this dissident movement has lately made its presence felt in Perú's cities as well. Still, the threat is not yet very severe, and for *limeños,* life goes on as usual.

And perhaps residents are schooled in patience by Lima's frankly peculiar winter weather. On the face of it, the city would seem to be especially blessed in its climate. Although Lima is close to the equator, it enjoys a temperate climate, owing to the cold Humboldt Current that flows north from Chile to Ecuador. Because of the juxtaposition of the Andes range, almost hugging the ocean, and the cold Humboldt Current racing northward, it rarely rains in Lima. However, between July and October, rare, too, are sunny days. Winter skies are depressingly gray, and at times a mistlike rain makes the days even more overcast. Peruvians call the fog bank that hangs over the capital *garúa.* When the sun shines through the *garúa* unexpectedly on a winter day, the very pace of life on the streets quickens; people appear in bright clothes, and at least for a moment the city casts off its dreary garb of winter gray.

What makes the *garúa* worth it is the city itself: the city center, a very South American combination of modern and colonial architecture; the mountains in the distance; and the string of beautiful, carefully maintained suburbs along the Pacific coast. Visitors should not limit their explorations to the old city (which is very much the new and modern city as well), for Lima's peaceful suburbs are a delight. The palm-lined streets, stately mansions, and modern, clean, high-rise apartment buildings contrast with the Spanish colonial and office-block gray of downtown. In the wealthier suburbs, the contemporary architecture contains certain colonial features — balconies, red tiles, latticework, and sculptured wood. Miraflores, the beachfront community that sits on a long cliff overlooking the Pacific, has an atmosphere similar to that of a resort town, with sidewalk cafés, boutiques, first-class restaurants, cinemas, and surfers. Because the principal streets of Miraflores are well lit, more and more *limeños* go there to shop, to eat out, and to kick up their heels at night.

Bordering Miraflores are the group of beaches known as the Costa Verde. In the summertime they are packed with people, particularly on weekends. The best time to use the beach is between Mondays and Fridays, but for swimming, stick to beaches from La Herradura on south. Closer to Lima the water is somewhat polluted, though strolling is still very fine here. The Costa Verde, linked to downtown Lima by a modern expressway, is less than a half-hour drive away.

Almost 450 years old, Lima has lived through earthquakes and invasions, seen many changes of government, and experienced immense wealth and widespread poverty. It is a city striving to catch up with the twentieth century to prepare for the twenty-first. In this race against time, the odds and the obstacles are large, but so is the will to prevail. And there is a sense that in many ways, Lima is still the fulcrum of the continent; where it goes, so goes South America.

LIMA AT-A-GLANCE

 SEEING THE CITY: From the spacious windows of the elegantly decorated dining rooms of the fine Chinese restaurant *El Dorado,* on the 20th floor of the building of the same name, you get a wide-angle view of the entire city. Also known for their panoramas are *La Terraza* and the *Sky Room* at the *Crillón* hotel, La Colmena 589 (phone: 28-32-90), and *La Azotea Bar* at *Cesar's* hotel, corner of La Paz and Diez Canseco in Miraflores (phone: 44-12-12). At all of these places you will have to order something in order to savor the view.

 SPECIAL PLACES: You will need a minimum of three days to visit Lima's special places. The first day could be spent in getting to know the heart of colonial Lima, starting with its main square, the Plaza de Armas, where you will find the Presidential Palace, the cathedral, the Archbishop's Palace, and city hall. Near the Plaza de Armas, you can easily walk to a number of colonial churches and convents, such as Santo Domingo, San Agustín, La Merced, San Pedro, and San Francisco (the largest church and convent complex remaining from earliest colonial times) as well as visit some authentically viceregal homes, Torre Tagle Palace, and the original seat of the Inquisition. Crossing the Rimac River by one of its four bridges, you can easily get to the District of Rimac, known popularly as Bajo el Puente (Beneath the Bridge). Among the noteworthy sights are La Quinta de Presa, the home of the famous Perricholi whose life has been immortalized in Offenbach's lovely operetta *La Perrichole,* the Alameda y Convento de los Descalzos, and the famed Bullring of Acho.

The second day could be spent visiting museums, of which there are some 21 scattered throughout the city and suburbs.

You could reserve the third day for visiting archaeological sites or one of Lima's fine beach resorts (see *Perú,* DIRECTIONS). Or for a respite, you might want to escape to

Chosica, a small sunny city a bit upland where well-to-do *limeños* have winter homes (see *Extra Special,* below).

Summer and winter hours often vary; so before setting out on a walking tour, check schedules in the *Perú Guide,* available in all major hotels and free to tourists.

CENTER

Armaments Plaza (Plaza de Armas) – The governmental center of viceregal and republican Lima was planned by Pizarro in 1535 to include the buildings of the principal colonial institutions. It is worthwhile to time your arrival or return to the Plaza de Armas so that it coincides with the changing of the presidential Guard of Honor, the Hussars of Junín, at 1 PM.

The Cathedral (Catedral) – On the spot designated for the building of the first cathedral by Pizarro, the present building was begun in 1746 after the first edifice was destroyed in one of Lima's many earthquakes. The carved choir stalls were a gift of Charles V to the first cathedral of Perú. On the right-hand side of the cathedral, as you enter, is the chapel where Pizarro's remains are kept in a glass casket. There is some dispute as to whether or not these really are his bones. The cathedral is open to visitors daily from 10 AM to 1 PM and 2 to 5 PM, as is the Museum of Religious Art. Plaza de Armas.

Union Street (Jirón de la Unión) – Connects the Plaza de Armas with the other important square of central Lima, the Plaza de San Martín. This was Lima's elite shopping street before the flowering of the suburban Miraflores shopping area. Recently, the entire 5-block area has been repaved and turned into a pedestrian mall, with several large shopping galleries that include good *artesanía* shops and interesting restaurants. If you would like to try typical Peruvian *criolla* food for lunch, go to *Raimondi.* It has excellent fare and good service. Jirón Antonio Miró Quesada 110, behind La Merced Church (phone: 27-79-33).

Church and Monastery of Santo Domingo (Iglesia y Monasterio de Santo Domingo) – One block west of the Plaza de Armas are the church and monastery of the Dominican friars, built in 1549. Here South America's oldest university, San Marcos, was founded in 1551. It is a fine example of colonial architecture. The church is open daily from 7 AM to 1 PM and 4 to 8 PM. The monastery and tombs are open Mondays through Saturdays from 9:30 AM to 12:30 PM and 3:30 to 5:30 PM. Sundays and holidays, they are open in the morning only. Jirón Camaná 170, Plazuela Santo Domingo.

Oquendo's House (Casa de Oquendo) – After leaving Santo Domingo, walk along Calle Superunda to this magnificent late-18th-century mansion, where General José San Martín stayed after proclaiming Perú's independence from Spain in 1821. The mansion has recently been restored and is now open to the public. Calle Conde de Superunda 298.

Church of San Agustín (Iglesia de San Agustín) – From the corner of Camaná and Superunda, turn left on Camaná and go down to Ica, where you will find this lovely church, which unfortunately was quite badly damaged in the earthquake of 1974. Although it is presently undergoing repairs, you can appreciate its gracefully carved stone facade. Open daily, 8:30 AM to noon and 3:30 to 5:30 PM. Free. Jirón Ica 225.

Church of La Merced (Iglesia de La Merced) – From the corner of Ica and Union walk one block to this famed church, with its great facade carved from granite brought from Panamá. Open from 7 AM to 12:30 PM and 4 to 8 PM; the convent hours are from 8 AM to noon and 3 to 5:30 PM. Free. Jirón de la Unión 621.

Torre Tagle Palace (Palacio Torre Tagle) – A few blocks from La Merced Church stands this priceless example of elegant Spanish colonial architecture. Basically Sevillian in style, the palace shows a strong Moorish influence. Built in 1735 and restored in 1958, it is rightly considered one of the most outstanding architectural relics of Spanish America, especially of colonial Lima. Today it is used as the Ministry of Foreign Relations. You can stand in the first patio and look in, but tours are not allowed. Jirón Ucayali 363 (phone: 27-67-50).

Church of San Pedro (Iglesia de San Pedro) – Half a block from the Torre Tagle Palace, this baroque church was built by the Jesuits in the early 1600s. Its dome is a small replica of the great dome of St. Peter's Basilica in Rome. But most striking are its many wooden altars covered with gold. Open daily, 7 AM to 12:30 PM and 6 to 8 PM. Free. Jirón Ucayali 300.

The Church and Monastery of St. Francis (Iglesia y Monasterio de San Francisco) – The brethren of St. Francis of Assisi were one of the first Catholic missionary groups to arrive in Lima. The present church of St. Francis, built on the site of the first one, constructed in 1546, was completed in 1674. Baroque and Andalusian architectural styles influenced its design. Both the church and monastery complex deserve a prolonged visit, for they have a great deal to offer: 15 chapels, elaborately carved choir stalls from cedar imported from Panamá, beautiful ceilings, and the catacombs, a surprising bit of architecture, with galleries of three floors below the earth where once were buried the bodies of thousands. Open daily, 10 AM to 1 PM and 3 to 6 PM. Admission charge for the catacombs. Visits to the monastery and the catacombs by guided tour only. The last groups start daily at 12:45 and 5:45 PM. Jirón Ancash 300.

Promenade of the Barefoot Friars (La Alameda de los Descalzos) – Inaugurated in 1606 by the viceroy, the Marquis de Montesclaro, the Alameda was the "in" place for fashionable *limeños* of the 17th century. Here elegantly dressed, well-chaperoned young upper-class society women promenaded to look at one another and to be perused by young gentlemen. While promenading yourself, you might want to visit Los Descalzos, the church run by Carmelite friars. The monastery has recently been opened to the public and provides a wonderful look at colonial monastery life, including a pharmacy, library, and lovely inner courtyards. Around 9 AM is the best time for savoring the peace and beauty of this typical 17th-century *limeñan* monastery. The Alameda can be found behind the Palacio de Gobierno on the other side of the river, in the district of Rimac. Cross the bridge at the end of Jirón de la Unión.

Acho Bullring (Plaza de Toros de Acho) – Not far from the Alameda, you will find the bullring in the Plaza de Acho, north of Balta Bridge. It is the oldest ring in South America, built by Viceroy Amat in 1764 and restored in 1945, with its original façade preserved and protected. The first bullfights in newly established Lima took place in 1540. (Pizarro himself took part.) From that time until the present, the bullfighting season has always brought together all that is traditional, colorful, and lively in Lima. It is the one time of the year when social distinctions disappear and all of Lima gives itself over to its two great passions — the October processions of the venerated image of the Lord of the Miracles and the bullfights. The big season is October and November, when world-renowned toreadors come to Acho to compete for the prized Gold Scapular of the Lord of the Miracles. The cost of tickets is relatively high these days, and the best seats are reserved for those with season passes. Ask for seats in the shade — *sombra*. The bullfights take place on all Sundays and holidays during October and November at 3 PM. A number of hotels, including the *Lima Sheraton* and the *Crillon*, offer "*criollo*" buffet lunches before the fights and transportation to and from the Plaza de Acho ring. Ticket sales: Jirón Huancavelica 278 (no phone).

The Museum of the Inquisition (Museo de la Inquisición) – Leaving Acho by crossing the Balta Bridge (Puente de Balta), you will come to Avenida Abancay and Plaza Bolívar, formerly known as the Plaza de la Inquisición (Inquisition Plaza). Here stands the Congress Building (Palacio del Congreso). To the right as you face the

Congress is the building that houses the Museum of the Inquisition. The Tribune of the Inquisition of Lima was established in 1569 to "protect" the Catholic religion in the jurisdiction of the new viceroyalty. It endured until 1813 when it was abolished by royal decree, at which time *limeños* happily vandalized the building, destroying records and instruments of torture. In contrast to its grisly purpose is the building itself, with some of the most beautiful wood carving in Lima. The ceiling of Audience Hall is an exceptional piece of work; it dates from the 18th century. You can also visit the prisoners' galleries and cells on the subterranean levels. Open Mondays through Fridays from 9 AM to 7:30 PM and from 9 AM to 4:30 PM on Saturdays. Free. Jirón Junín 548 at Plaza Bolívar (phone: 28-79-80).

Museum of Anthropology and Archaeology (Museo de Antropología y Arqueología) – This museum has exhibits of rare pottery, weavings, and mummies. The unique tapestries from Paracas and Nazca (where mysterious line drawings in the desert have stimulated worldwide controversy about possible communication with extraterrestrial beings) are works of art in their own right, as are the images and vessels in gold and silver. Open daily, 10 AM to 6 PM. Admission charge. Plaza Bolívar in Pueblo Libre (phone: 63-50-70).

Larco Herrera Archaeological Museum (Museo Arqueológico Larco Herrera) – When this part of Lima was still farm country, this building used to be a hacienda. Now it has been transformed into a museum housing the famed Larco Herrera collection of pottery, most of it from cultures on the northern coast of Perú. These ceramics date back to the so-called fluorescent era of Peruvian culture, which lasted from AD 200 to 600. Open Mondays through Saturdays from 9 AM to 1 PM and 3 to 6 PM and from 9 AM to 1 PM on Sundays. Admission charge. Av. Bolívar 1515 (phone: 61-13-12).

Museum of Art (Museo de Arte) – Collections of pottery, tapestries, gold and silver objects, weavings, mummies, and paintings illuminate Perú's 2,500 years of culture according to its different historical epochs: pre-Inca, Inca, colonial, and republican. A newly opened cinema also offers some interesting film features. Open Tuesdays through Sundays from 9 AM to 6 PM. Admission charge. Down the street from the *Sheraton* hotel at Paseo Colón 125 (phone: 23-47-32).

Gold Museum (Museo del Oro) – Approximately 6,500 pieces of worked gold — images, bowls, cups, plates, and ceremonial objects — are found here. One awe-inspiring glimpse of such wealth and you will undoubtedly regret that European greed melted down, indiscriminately, other great works of art, such as the gold and silver garden in the Temple of the Sun in Cuzco. What remained — the pieces collected here — was what were small enough to be overlooked. Open daily from noon to 7 PM. Admission charge. Av. Alonso de Molina 1100, Monterrico (phone: 35-29-17).

Chinatown (Barrio Chino) – For many years, this exotic little district around the Plaza de Armas was a lively area of shops selling products imported from China, around 30 *chifas* serving diverse platters of Cantonese cuisine, and tea parlors offering exquisite pastries. Most of the restaurants have moved to fancier suburbs, though three excellent ones remain: *San Joy Lao,* founded in 1938, *Chung Kuo,* and *Tay Kum.* They are as alike as three peas in a pod; customers sit in booths separated from the rest of the restaurant by swinging wooden doors. Still, you should wander along Calle Capón, where a giant gate of carved wooden columns and marble dragon's heads marks the entrance to Chinatown. On a foggy night Chinatown could be the perfect setting for a mystery movie. Lima's Chinese population numbers around 500,000 descendants of the original immigrants of 1872 and 10,000 who have come more recently. The majority of Chino-Peruanos do not speak Chinese. Calle Capón and the other Chinatown streets are snuggled among Av. Abancay, Jirón Huallaga, Jirón Paruro, and Jirón Ancash.

SUBURBS

A word of explanation. Strictly speaking, Lima as a municipal entity is pretty much restricted to the area that we have been calling the center of Lima. Metropolitan Lima is made up of various districts of which Lima proper is one. In American terms, we can speak of the city of Lima, the county of Lima, and the state of Lima. Metropolitan Lima is under the jurisdiction (especially financial) of the county of Lima, which is actually governed by the mayor of Lima. Thus, when we speak of suburbs, we are actually speaking of the various districts of the province (county) of the state of Lima.

Leaving the center of Lima, you can take the Via Expresa, a modern, six-lane expressway uniting the center of Lima with Chorrillos and the beaches of the Costa Verde. Chorrillos, 7 miles (12 km) from the Plaza de Armas, is one of downtown Lima's original summer resorts, beautifully placed on bluffs high above the Pacific Ocean. In between are some residential areas of Greater Lima: the working-class neighborhoods of La Victoria and Lince, and the middle-class and wealthier areas of Jesús María, Surquillo, Miraflores, San Isidro, and Barranco. Surrounding these enclaves are the massive "young towns," a euphemism that describes those many square kilometers of shantytowns where new, mainly poor immigrants from the hinterlands of Perú live.

Miraflores – Without a doubt the loveliest part of Lima, this suburb along the Pacific embraces contemporary and earlier architectural styles. Actually, it is a small, elegant city in itself. By comparison, the center of Lima is run-down, indeed. Miraflores's central shopping street, Avenida Larco, ends in a pleasant little park (Parque de Salazar) overlooking the ocean where balloon-sellers decorate the sky with large balloons shaped like Mickey Mouse and other cartoon characters. The park is actually a landscaped section of a steep cliff, below which stretches a narrow strand of public beach. The beachfront road, called the *malecón,* is lined with very expensive apartment buildings and occasional grand colonial mansions. (Most of the truly splendid homes have been torn down to make way for more profitable apartment houses, but as you head farther north along the shore, you will come upon more houses.) Miraflores is spotted with many surprising little flowery parks. The best time to see Miraflores is after 4 PM, when the shops have reopened after the long lunch break and residents come in their best casual attire to shop and meet friends in the cafés. Often in the summer, Miraflores can be disappointingly misty, but if you are a hard-core surfer, you will find waves worth tackling along its shore. You can get to Miraflores along 60-block-long Avenida Arequipa, a lovely tree-lined street that becomes Avenida Larco. San Isidro, a suburb between Lima and Miraflores, is the most elegant residential district in the greater Lima area and has some wonderful shops and restaurants.

Barranco – Two miles (3 km) south of Miraflores, Barranco is a pocket of splendid old mansions built by the "beautiful people" of the Republican era. Note the many fanciful balconies, gables, and other English architectural touches that give Barranco an unusual charm. Many of the mansions have been divided into smaller apartments. Although it was *the* summer resort 80 or 90 years ago, it is now part of metropolitan Lima, and is no longer secluded enough to qualify as truly chic. However, an afternoon spent wandering among its quiet, well-planned parks, trees, flowers, and the Bridge of Sighs will refresh you. In the summertime, Barranco is an enchanting, cool place to be. To get to Barranco, turn left at the end of Avenida Larco and continue along the oceanfront road or take Paseo de la República to Avenida José María Egurén. The ocean is to your right.

Costa Verde – This handsome circuit of beaches is better for looking than for swimming. The water is polluted, the undertow here is strong, and a prolific community of jellyfish takes up residence at different times of the year. Still, it is very popular with residents, especially on weekends. If you visit, do so during the week, and bring a picnic lunch. There are numerous restaurants and food stands along the beaches, but their hygiene is questionable, especially for visitors' stomachs, unfamiliar with local food. Both the *Restaurant Costa Verde* and the *Rosa Nautica* are relatively new additions and are elegant spots with international standards in food and hygiene. Costa Verde extends from the northern border of Miraflores at Avenida Brasil and the *malecón* to Barranco.

La Herradura Beach – Just south of the Costa Verde, this beach tends to be less crowded, although it's not deserted. Its name, "horseshoe," refers to the shape of the bay, in which some people practice surf casting. Here, too, you'll find food stands and restaurants along the shore. The new *El Salto de Fraile* is worth a visit. No matter which beach you go to, be sure you leave all valuables in your hotel. Esplanada, Chorrillos.

Park of the Legends (Parque de Las Leyendas) – This small zoo has, as its central motif, the presentation of the three principal geographical regions of Perú: the desert coast, the Andes, and the Amazon jungle. Worth visiting if you're traveling with small children, for whom it provides a vivid picture of geography. Closed Mondays. Admission charge. Av. La Marina, San Miguel (phone: 52-69-13).

■ **EXTRA SPECIAL:** One of the most popular day trips from Lima, especially during the gray winter months, is the excursion to the mountain resort town of *Chosica,* 25 miles (40 km) from the center of town on the Central Highway (Carretera Central). About 19 miles (31 km) from Lima you will pass through Chaclacayo, a town of approximately 23,000 inhabitants, where the sun shines at least 350 days a year. It has a number of fine, modern houses, but it's not much to look at from the road. Chosica is a city of 150,000 that was Lima's select winter resort 80 years ago, attested to by its Victorian houses. In those days, access to Chosica was easy because it was only an hour away by train. However, as more indigenous people settled in and around the town, its desirability as an exclusive winter resort lessened drastically, and the old families built new houses in Chaclacayo, down the road. Although Chosica is a bit faded, it remains a charming city. Its very large plaza is surrounded by many shady, impressive palm trees. Because it is 600 feet higher than Chaclacayo, its climate is even better. It has clearer air and brighter winter sunshine. However, it is more susceptible to the summer rainstorms that come swirling down from Cerro de Pasco and Huancayo in the Andes. It is worthwhile visiting the public market to get an idea of how mountain markets function in the daily lives of the people. Mention Chosica or Chaclacayo to most *limeños,* and they'll immediately say *"La Granja Azul,"* a lovely country restaurant that specializes in exotic drinks and delicious grilled chicken. Next door is the *Pueblo Inn,* a delightful restaurant-resort complex in Santa Clara, which has two golf courses, a pool, and pleasant rooms. It's ideal for an overnight rest. Reservations accepted. Carretera Central, Chosica, (phone: 35-07-77). Expensive.

SOURCES AND RESOURCES

TOURIST INFORMATION: General tourist information in the form of pamphlets, brochures, and maps are available from the Government Tourist Information Office, Belén 1066 (phone: 72-19-28). There is also a government-sponsored information bureau before the customs check in the airport and a privately run kiosk at the exit for international passengers. The government hotel chain is ENTUR Perú. Its offices at Javier Prado 1358 (phone: 40-46-30) will book state hotels in over two dozen towns in Perú, but these can be reserved perhaps even more easily through any local travel agency. One of the most efficient is *Lima Tours,* Belén

1040 (phone: 27-66-24), with branches in Miraflores, San Isidro, and at the *Lima Sheraton* hotel.

Lima and Environs and *Guide to Perú,* both written by Gonzalo de Reparaz, are two of the best books that are locally available for a historical and cultural overview of Lima and Perú; they also have good maps. *Perú Guide,* the country's monthly tourist guide, is distributed for free at the airport, tourist information office, *Lima Tours,* and all the better hotels.

Local Coverage – *Lima Times,* published weekly in English, contains local news, restaurant and film reviews, and a listing of the week's cultural events in Lima.

Food – *Perú Guide* has a thorough listing of Lima's restaurants, categorized by specialty.

CLIMATE AND CLOTHES: Lima's climate is moderate, with seasons the opposite of those in the US and Europe. Clothes that you would wear during the spring and fall in the Northern Hemisphere are suitable for Lima's winter (June through October). Light clothing is the rule for the summer months, but shorts of any description for men or women are not acceptable streetwear in Peruvian cities. Bring a sweater for summer evenings, just in case, and don't forget to pack a bathing suit. Lima's climate is similar to that of Los Angeles.

GETTING AROUND: Bus – There are plenty of buses, both publicly and privately owned. The public buses usually offer better service. Known as *bussing* (pronounced *boo-*sing), public bus lines reach all of the important parts of the city. Buses are not really recommended unless you speak Spanish. Lima is a large city, and it's easy to get lost by taking the wrong bus.

Taxi – The best and easiest way to get around. There is a new program to install meters in all Lima taxis, and many cabs now have them. In those that don't, determine the price of your trip in advance. Ask the people at the reception desk in your hotel about the going rate to your destination. The best hotels offer a permanent taxi service called *taxis remisse,* but they charge more than taxis hailed in the street (and are usually in better repair). Lima cabdrivers often overcharge foreigners by refusing to honor agreed-upon rates or by refusing to state fares in advance. If you can, ask a *limeño* to negotiate the price in advance. Cabs at the airport charge a fixed fare. Usually each taxi takes more than one passenger into the city and everyone pays the same price. Try to avoid rush hour travel.

Car Rental – All the major hotels have car rental offices near downtown and at the airport: *Avis,* Sheraton Hotel (phone: 32-72-45); *Budget,* Civic Center (phone: 31-47-35); *Hertz,* Ocoña 262 (phone: 28-63-30); *National,* Av. España 449 (phone: 23-25-26).

MUSEUMS: The Museum of Anthropology and Archaeology (Museo de Antropología y Arqueología), the Larco Herrera Archaeological Museum (Museo Arqueológico Larco Herrera), National Museum of Art (Museo de Arte), and the Gold Museum (Museo de Oro) are described in *Special Places.* Other outstanding Lima museums are

Real Felipe Fortress (Fortaleza Real Felipe) – Stands in Callao, the city's port. Built over a 30-year period in the 18th century, the immense pentagonal structure was used to defend the city against attacks by Dutch and English pirates. Closed Mondays and Fridays. Free, but visitors must present identification. Callao (phone: 29-15-05).

Amano Museum (Museo Amano) – Houses a private collection of weavings from Chancay and ceramics from various cultures, and is the best museum to visit if you have only a short time in Lima. Tours by appointment only, 2 to 5 PM Mondays through Fridays. Calle Retiro 160, Miraflores (phone: 41-29-09).

National Museum of Peruvian Culture (Museo Nacional de Arte) – Exhibits include a fine collection of folk arts, costumes, and ceramics from all periods. Open weekdays from 10 AM to 5 PM, Saturdays from 9 AM to 5 PM. Admission charge. Av. Alfonso Ugarte 650 (phone: 23-58-92).

Museum of Contemporary Peruvian Folk Art (Museo Nacional Contemporane de Arte Folklórico) – On display is an excellent private collection, mostly of ceramics, from all parts of the country. Closed Sundays. Donation suggested. Saco Oliveros 163 (phone: 31-65-63). Call for an appointment.

 SHOPPING: Of greatest appeal are items of silver, gold, leather, and wood as well as pottery, textiles, tapestries, and alpaca rugs and sweaters. The center of Lima is filled with *artesanía* (artisan) shops of all kinds. One of the main shopping streets is Av. Nicolás de Piérola, better known as La Colmena, and Av. Belén is even better.

On the way to the airport, in the tenth block of Avenida La Marina, are a group of Indian Markets offering handcrafted products from various regions of Perú. There are many good buys. These shops are open daily till around 7 PM.

Artisan goods of all kinds can also be found in Artesanías del Perú, formerly called EPPAPERU, now a private organization dedicated to the development and sales of native handicrafts. Its principal store is on Jorge Basadre 610, San Isidro (phone: 22-88-74).

Other fine shops are

Los Alamos Gallery – The owner has fine, old pieces in ceramic, gourds, weavings, and wood. The gallery, at Av. Luriganche 991, Zaraté (82-91-42), is hard to find. Take a taxi and ask the driver to wait.

Alda – Excellent leather products. At El Alamo shopping center, La Paz and Diez Canseco, Miraflores; and Centro Camino Real, San Isidro (phone: 45-74-46).

Antisuyo – This store specializes in high-quality jungle handicrafts, beautiful Chulucanas ceramics, and weavings from Taquile, Pomata, and Cajamarca. Tacna 460, Miraflores (phone: 47-25-57).

Artesanías Huamanqaqa – Perhaps the best crafts store in Lima, with especially good tapestries and *retablos* (portable altars decorated with religious or secular scenes). On Jirón Unión, between the *Gran Bolívar* and *Sheraton* hotels.

Cabuchon – An elegant shop specializing in gold and silver goods, excellent jewelry, and some expensive artisan goods. In the Libertadores shopping center. 532 Libertadores, San Isidro (phone: 40-90-63).

Camusso – If you speak Spanish fluently, you can buy gold and silver objects from the factory. *Camusso* has two outlets: Av. Colonial 679 (phone: 27-61-70) and Las Magnolias 788, San Isidro (phone: 42-03-40).

Casa Más – One of the better gold and silver dealers. Jirón de la Unión 814 (phone: 27-75-61).

Casa Welsch – Down the block from *Casa Más,* this shop offers essentially the same wares. Prices run about the same at both places, but it's a good idea to do some comparison shopping. Jirón de la Unión 498 (phone: 27-61-53).

Conquistadores – A wide selection of fine handicrafts, particularly tapestries. In the lobby of *Cesar's* hotel, La Paz 463, Miraflores. (phone: 44-12-12).

La Gringa – This craft shop, run by an American woman, features a fine selection from around the country. In the Alamo shopping center, across from *Cesar's* hotel in Miraflores. La Paz 522.

Helen Hamann – Fashionable, high-quality alpaca and cotton knit sweaters. Expensive, but less so than in the US. The factory store is at Tacna 370, Miraflores (phone: 46-86-09). There is also a shop at the Gold Museum, Av. Alonso de Molina 1100, Monterrico.

Murguía – Gold and silver items. Jirón de la Unión 553 (phone: 27-59-55).

Las Pallas – This new shop in Barranco features selected crafts from around Perú and has very much the same goods as at *Los Alamos,* but at a more accessible address. The quality of artisan works here is probably, overall, the highest in the Lima area. Cajamarca 212, Barranco (no phone).

Silvania Prints – Sophisticated contemporary textiles, incorporating ancient Peruvian designs, are sold by the meter or made into scarves, dresses, and handbags. This is an expensive shop, but everything is well made and quite stunning. Three locations: Av. Nicolás de Piérola 714 (phone: 24-39-26); Conquistadores 902, San Isidro (phone: 22-64-40); and in *Cesar's* hotel, Miraflores (phone: 44-12-12).

H. Stern – Fine gold and silver jewelry with exclusive Peruvian designs. Things are expensive but backed by an international guarantee of credit or exchange. Main lobby of *Lima Sheraton* (phone: 32-90-50, ext. 4105).

Vicky's – Objects of glass and metal with pre-Columbian designs. The sets of cocktail, wine, and water glasses are conversation stoppers. Again, this is an expensive shop where the prices are worth the quality. Three locations: Av. Nicolás de Piérola 783 (phone 28-19-56); and Ocoña 160, and La Paz 640 in Miraflores.

 SPECIAL EVENTS: From January through March, the *Summer Festival of Ancón,* Lima's Nice on the Pacific, is celebrated with choreographed sea spectaculars, a song festival, art expositions, and world surfing championships (see *Perú,* DIRECTIONS). In April and November, the *Official National Competition of Peruvian Pacer Horses* takes place at Mamacona, south of Lima. The modern Peruvian *caballo de paso* is a descendant of the horses that the first Spaniards brought to Perú. They are noted for their fine lines, arrogant natures, and the graceful, dancing rhythm with which they walk. They are generally ridden by skilled jockeys called *chalanes,* who ride dressed all in white with straw hats and flowing ponchos.

In October, *Señor de los Milagros* festivals honor Our Lord of the Miracles. A painting of the crucified Christ, which was supposedly done on an adobe wall of the slaves' meeting place in the 1600s, has survived all of the great earthquakes in Lima (those of 1655 and 1746 being the worst) and thus is considered by the *limeños* their special patron. Formerly, the Christ in the painting was called the Lord of the Abandoned, probably because it was primarily an object of devotion of the blacks. But today, tens of thousands of *limeños* take part in the three great ritual processions that wind through the streets of Lima on October 18, 19, and 28. Throughout October you will see many people either dressed in purple or with some touch of purple on their clothes to show that they are devotees of the Lord of the Miracles. At the same time, the secular side of the feast is celebrated with the Golden Scapular bullfights in honor of the Lord of the Miracles. It is very impressive. Every November, *Fería Internacional del Pacífico* (the *International Pacific Fair*) takes place at its own special fairgrounds, devoted primarily to the exposition of the industrial products and technical developments of the participating countries. Many bars and restaurants offer the typical food and drink of the participating nations. Av. de la Marina (phone: 52-81-40).

 SPORTS: The most popular sports in Lima are soccer (*fútbol*), bullfighting, and surfing.

Bullfighting – One of the major rings in Latin America, the *Plaza de Toros de Acho,* is described in *Special Places.* The major bullfighting season is October and November on Sundays and holidays. Ticket sales: Jirón Huanacavelica 278 (no phone).

Cockfighting – This "sport" has been outlawed in the US but is practiced in Lima on Wednesdays, Fridays, Saturdays, and Sundays at 8:30 PM at Coliseo Sandia, Calle Sandia 150 (phone: 28-12-04).

Cricket – Aristocratic Anglo-Peruvians play cricket at the *Lima Cricket and Foot-*

ball Club, Av. León de la Fuente 151, Orrantia (phone: 61-0080). There are no regularly scheduled matches; check *The Lima Times.*

Fishing – You can surf-cast at La Herradura Beach or travel to Pucusana 39 miles (62 km) south of Lima on the Pan-American Highway. You can rent boats with local fisherman as guides. Fishing boats can also be rented at Ancón (see *Perú,* DIRECTIONS).

Golf – As this is the sport of Perú's elite, there are no public golf courses. The two main private clubs are *Lima Golf Club,* Camino Real, 7th block (phone: 22-78-00), and *Los Incas Golf Club,* Av. Golf (phone: 35-20-46). These clubs make their courses available to nonmembers on weekdays; arrangements should be made through your hotel or travel agent. If you are really hankering for 18 holes and can't get into either club, take a trip to the *Pueblo Inn,* Carretera Central, km 17 (phone: 35-07-77), or *Huampaní Golf Club,* Carretera Central, km 26 (phone: 91-03-42).

Horse Racing – Races are held on Tuesdays, Thursdays, Saturdays, and Sundays at the *Hipódromo Monterrico.* Av. Javier Prado (phone: 35-10-35). Check at the reception desk in your hotel or consult the morning newspaper for race schedules. On Fridays and Saturdays, you can place bets on the winners in Sunday's La Polla sweepstakes. The betting office is near Plaza San Martín, Jirón Tambo de Belén 175 (phone: 23-80-41).

Polo – Horses can be rented at the *Lima Polo and Hunt Club* (phone: 37-30-66), Monterrico, near *Los Incas Country Club.*

Sailing – The regatta season runs from January through March. Four major yacht clubs offer privileges to members of other clubs: *Lima Regattas Club,* Chorrillos (phone: 67-25-45); *Union Regattas Club,* Plaza Galvez, La Punta (phone: 29-02-86); *Yacht Club Peruano,* Muelle Darsena, Callao (phone: 29-07-75); and *Yacht Club de Ancón.*

Soccer – Lima's three best teams are *Universitario, Alianza Lima,* and *Sporting Cristal.* Major games are played at the National Stadium (Estadio Nacional), Calle General Diaz (phone: 32-91-77).

Surfing – You can see surfers in the waves along the Costa Verde beaches throughout the year, sun or fog. International competitions are held in Lima from time to time. For information, contact *Waikiki Club,* Bajada Baños de Miraflores (phone: 45-11-49). The best surfing beaches are La Herradura, Macaja, Punta Rica, and Ancón.

Swimming – Good surfing beaches are not always best for swimming because the waves are pretty rough. There are swimming pools at the *Lima Sheraton,* Paseo de la República (phone: 32-90-50); *Lima Country Club,* Los Eucaliptos, San Isidro (phone: 40-40-60); *El Pardo,* Pardo 420, Miraflores (phone: 47-02-83); *María Angola,* Av. La Paz 610, Miraflores (phone: 44-12-80); *Miraflores Cesar's Hotel,* La Paz 463, Miraflores (phone: 44-12-12); *El Bosque Country Club,* Carretera Central, km 33, Chaclacayo (phone: 91-06-82); *Los Condores Country Club,* Chaclacayo (phone: 91-00-58); and *Villa Country Club,* Chorrillos, just off the Pan-American Hwy. S, km 22 (phone: 67-08-51).

Tennis – In addition to the country clubs and golf clubs listed above, there are courts at the *Lawn Tennis Club,* Av. 28 de Julio 744 (phone: 24-71-50), which also has a swimming pool, and at the *Club Tenís Las Terrazas, malecón* 28 de Julio, Miraflores (phone: 45-29-97).

Water Skiing – Ancón is the best place in Perú for water skiing. Contact the *Yacht Club de Ancón* for details. *Malecón* de Ancón (no phone).

 THEATER: There's no professional English-language theater in Lima, but there is a fine amateur company, *The Good Companions* (phone: 47-9760). See the *Lima Times* for listings of English-language productions. If you know Spanish, you might enjoy many theatrical productions. The daily newspaper *El Comercio* gives all theater listings in its cultural section. The principal theaters in the center of Lima are: *Segura,* Jirón Huancavelica 255 (phone: 27-74-37), and the *Municipal,* Jirón Ica 355 (phone: 28-23-03). The latter presents concerts, ballet, and folklore spectaculars, both Peruvian and from other nations.

 NIGHTCLUBS AND NIGHTLIFE: There are plenty of nightclubs and lots of nightlife, especially on the weekends, but not in the center of Lima unless you want to stay in your hotel: If it's the *Crillón,* you can go to the *Sky Room;* the *Lima-Sheraton* has the *Koricancha; Cesar's* nightclub is *El Lúcumo.*

The better discotheques are *Ebony 56,* Las Magnolias 841, San Isidro (phone: 42-46-95); *Las Rocas,* Las Magnolias 821, San Isidro (phone: 42-09-06); and *Percy's,* Los Tulipanes 125 (phone: 72-45-68). They are jammed full of people and are noisy, colorful, and expensive — very North American in style. Bring your passport for admission to these clubs. *Satchmo Jazz Bar,* a recent addition to the Miraflores scene, offers national and international jazz names in an elegant, New Orleans–style setting. Drinks and hors d'oeuvres are served, and reservations are a must. Cover charge about $15. La Paz 538, Miraflores (phone: 44-17-53).

There are two elegant dinner/discos in Miraflores: *La Miel,* Pardo 120 (phone: 45-03-22), and *Privilege,* beneath the *El Condado* hotel at Alcanfores 469 (phone: 47-46-57).

Lima is a great city for *peñas* — either *criolla,* or coastal music, or folklore, mainly music from the highlands. There are *peñas* all over the city, including some larger ones on the Av. del Ejército that have become largely tourist traps. We recommend: *ABBA* (criolla), Schell 168, Miraflores (phone: 44-30-15); *El Buho Pub* (criolla), Sucre 315, Barranco (right next door to the *El Otro Sitio* restaurant); *La Casa de Edith Barr* (criolla), Ignacio Merino 250, Miraflores (phone: 41-06-12); *La Estación de Barranco* (folklore and criollo), Pedro de Osma 112, Barranco; *Karamanduka* (criolla), Benavides 621, Miraflores (phone: 44-30-10); *Hatuchay* (folklore), Trujillo 228, Rimac. Most *peñas* are open Friday and Saturday nights only, from about 10 PM until the last reveler decides to go home.

If you have had a long day of touring and don't feel much like anything except a quiet drink in relaxing surroundings, try the *Johann Sebastian* bar, Schell 369, Miraflores (phone: 46-52-53), and enjoy taped classical music in a lovely Tudor building that is in itself a piece of classical European art.

If you're in the mood for a drink or for some light food and people watching, try one of the popular outdoor cafés, all right in the heart of Miraflores: *Haiti,* Benavides 160 (phone: 47-50-52); *La Sueca,* Larco 759 (phone: 45-97-33); *La Tiendecita Blanca,* Larco 111 (phone: 45-97-97); and *Vivaldi,* R. Palma 258 (phone: 47-16-36).

There are no singles bars in Lima, and if a woman is traveling alone and knows no one locally, she is somewhat restricted in her choice of nightlife. If she insists on going alone to a club or café-theater, she had better be prepared to accept leers and remarks. Men or women are ill advised to go alone into the bars called *cantinas,* of which there are a number in the center of the city. It is much safer to go out with others at night since the crime rate has been increasing rapidly.

 SINS: *Machismo.* As in many Latin countries, women alone or in small groups are considered by a certain class of male to be an open invitation to whistles, hisses, and muttered obscenities. Intelligent women will do exactly what they do anywhere in the world when confronted with this type of situation — ignore it and keep on walking.

BEST IN TOWN

CHECKING IN: Since the early 1970s, Perú has become an international tourist destination. People come from Japan, Germany, France, Italy, New Zealand, the US, and England at great cost to appreciate both pre-Columbian and colonial Perú. As a result, the major cities on the prime tourist route — Lima, Cuzco, and more recently Arequipa — have built several new hotels and hostels of all categories. In Lima, expect to pay as much as $100 for a double room at those hotels we've classified as expensive; between $30 and $50 at hotels in the moderate category.

Cesar's – One of Lima's newest and most luxurious hotels, in the elegant suburb of Miraflores. The rooms are spacious, air conditioned, and handsomely furnished with replicas of the furniture that graced the fine mansions of colonial Lima. One of the bars, *La Estación,* is decorated like a first-class coach car on one of the early English trains brought to Perú almost a century ago; there's lovely wood paneling and silver adornments — very British-Peruvian. The tea room, *La Reja,* or the cafeteria-bar, *La Vereda,* have excellent Peruvian pastries and sandwiches. The hotel's elegant restaurant, *El Lúcumo,* offers both Peruvian and international menus. Or, if you want to see Miraflores from above, go up to the restaurant with a view, *La Azotea.* The hotel has its own drugstore, flower shop, barber and beauty shops, an open-air swimming pool, small stores, and parking. Reservations are necessary. Major credit cards accepted. Av. La Paz and Av. Diez Canseco (phone: 44-12-12). Expensive.

El Condado – One of Miraflores' newest and most elegant properties, with 50 rooms, 27 suites, 2 good restaurants, and a bar. In the chic El Suche shopping center, it is within walking distance of virtually all of the better Miraflores eating and drinking spots. Alcanfores 465 (phone: 44-36-14). Expensive.

Crillón – This first truly modern hotel in Lima is on the Colmena, one of the principal streets. Twenty-two stories high, its comfortable rooms and suites are all air conditioned. Its roof garden restaurant has an excellent smorgasbørd Mondays through Fridays from noon to 3 PM, from January through March, with a sumptuous spread of both Peruvian Creole and international food. In the evenings, the *Sky Room* on the 22nd story offers a view with its live entertainment. You should try colonial Perú's unique contribution to the world's alcoholic beverages, the pisco sour, in the *Bar Galeón.* Downstairs, *La Baica* restaurant serves some of the best local and international food in downtown Lima. Room reservations required. Major credit cards accepted. Av. Nicolás de Piérola 589 (phone: 28-32-90). Expensive.

Gran Hotel Bolívar – The name is Spanish but the influence is all British, for whom the Peruvians have a cultural affinity that dates from independence in 1821. An enduring and endearing custom is tea served with dainty petit fours by white-gloved waiters in the glass-domed rotunda every afternoon. The hotel bar is a popular meeting place and serves possibly the best *pisco* sours in the capital; the dining room serves fine Peruvian fare. Public and guestrooms have been recently refurbished and the *Bolívar* has its old shine back. Pass up a room overlooking the picturesque plaza in favor of a quieter one facing inside. Conveniently located at Plaza San Martín (phone: 27-64-00). Expensive.

Lima Sheraton – This addition to the Sheraton chain has few surprises as far as architectural design and rooms are concerned. However, its 20-story lobby is enlivened by striking sculptures by Delfín, one of Perú's best-known artists. Also very striking are the magnified copies of Nazca and Paracas tapestries, which decorate all of the public rooms as well as the far end of the lobby. On weekends, the *Koricancha* restaurant-nightclub presents a supershow with internationally known Latin American stars. Reservations are necessary. The main dining room is furnished with colonial-style tables and chairs and decorated with some fine pieces of 17th- and 18th-century viceregal art. Dinner is always served by candle-light. The coffee shop, open 24 hours a day, serves American food. The BLT and club sandwiches are decent. You should make reservations for rooms. Credit cards accepted. Paseo de la República 170 (phone: 32-86-76). Expensive.

María Angola – Another new addition to Miraflores, right down the street from both *El Condado* and *Cesar's*. A medium-sized hotel with good service, it has both a rooftop pool and *Los Faisanes* restaurant, now one of Lima's finest. La Paz 610 (phone: 44-12-80). Expensive.

El Pardo – Another of Miraflores' convenient lodging places, the *El Pardo* boasts a fine restaurant and rooftop swimming pool and caters mainly to business people. Av. Pardo 420 (phone: 47-02-83). Expensive.

El Pueblo Inn – Formerly called the *Granja Azul Inn* by its Swiss founders, its name, which means "the village," really reflects the physical nature of this hotel: It's constructed like a typical Andean village (were the typical Andean village to have such beautiful antiques and carved doors and ornate, wrought-iron grillwork). Truly impressive, comfortable and more Peruvian in flavor than any of the city's luxury hotels, it is outside the city in the Rimac Valley, only 25 minutes from the airport. Surrounded by the low peaks of this part of the Andes chain, *El Pueblo Inn* enjoys sun almost every day of the year, making especially attractive its 18-hole golf course, horseback riding facilities, several pools, and other activities. Besides rooms, there are 34 bungalows, 3 restaurants, a bread and pastry store, tearoom, cinema, billiard parlor, bowling alleys, Turkish baths, and a sauna. A few steps away is the well-known *Granja Azul* restaurant. Carretera Central, km 14 (phone: 35-07-77), or write Casilla 2585, Lima 100. Expensive.

Hostal Ariosto – In the heart of Miraflores, the *Ariosto* is a pleasant, medium-sized hostel, offering room and laundry service, car rental, and telex. A small *criollo* restaurant is open daily, and *La Pergola Bar* serves drinks and hors d'oeuvres. Av. La Paz 769 (phone: 44-14-16). Moderate.

Hostal Beech – This small, pink house has a lovely little garden and serves breakfast and light snacks. In the heart of San Isidro, it is owned by an American, James Plunkett. Los Libertadores 165 (phone: 40-55-95). Moderate.

Country Club – Until a few years ago, this was one of the most booked-up hotels in Lima, sought after by visitors who wanted to enjoy tranquillity and the lovely green parks of San Isidro, one of Lima's most exclusive residential districts. Although the *Country Club* can no longer be considered a luxury hotel, it still offers its own golf links in front of the hotel, tennis courts, and a swimming pool. Los Eucaliptos (phone: 40-40-60). Moderate.

Libertador Lima – Formerly the *Hotel Suites de Golf,* this very pleasant 52-room hostelry is right next to the *Country Club,* overlooking the golf course, where guests can arrange to play. Los Eucaliptos 550, San Isidro (41-64-92). Moderate.

Hostal Miraflores – This very economical, modern, and comfortable hostel just one block from the center of Miraflores has carpeted rooms with bath and telephone, a cafeteria, and parking. Av. Petit Thouars 5444 (phone: 45-87-45). Moderate.

El Plaza – Only steps away from Plaza San Martín, it's a small, new, first-class hostelry with a cozy cocktail lounge called *Don Eduardo* and a small restaurant, *La Placita.* The bedrooms, decorated in pure modern, are all air conditioned. Av. Nicolas de Pierola 850 (phone: 28-6270). Moderate.

Riviera – This modern hotel is close to the geographical center of Lima, with comfortable, clean rooms, a restaurant, and cafeteria service. It's comparable to a typical medium-sized American hotel. Reservations recommended. Av. Garcilaso de la Vega 981 (phone: 28-94-60). Moderate.

 EATING OUT: Judged on its restaurants alone, Lima would have to pass as a very cosmopolitan city. Peruvians consider food an important part of life, and this attitude has influenced the development of restaurants in the capital, where a broad spectrum of cuisines spill out of kitchens around the city. The most pervasive is native Peruvian cooking, called *criolla,* a combination of Spanish and Indian cooking which is the child of the first mating of those two disparate cultures. There are hundreds of *criolla* restaurants in Lima, and though atmosphere and quality vary widely among them, the basic ingredients of native spices and vegetables are the same in all. Lima also has good German, Arab, French, Spanish, Italian, Argentinian, Mexican, Swiss, Jewish, Japanese, Chinese, and vegetarian restaurants.

Expect to pay $25 to $35 for a dinner for two at those restaurants in the expensive category; between $15 and $20 at those places we've classified as moderate; under $15, inexpensive. Prices do not include drinks, wine, tip, or tax.

Carlin – This Miraflorino restaurant has an interesting international menu, but it is most famous in the neighborhood as the best purveyor of a very good *pisco* sour, the Peruvian national drink. It is in *El Suche Galleries,* where you can browse through the exhibits of handicrafts. Open daily. Reservations recommended. Major credit cards. Av. La Paz 646 (phone: 44-41-34). Expensive.

Los Condes de San Isidro – If you'd like to relive the grace and charm of the colonial days and sample traditional Peruvian dishes at the same time, this is the place to go. The lovely mansion-restaurant has elegant dining in the main room or outside on the terrace by the garden. Open daily. Reservations not necessary. Major credit cards accepted. Paz Soldan 290, San Isidro (phone: 22-25-57). Expensive.

La Costa Verde – Many say that this is the best of all Lima's fine seafood restaurants. Right on the beach, *La Costa Verde* is perfect for a relaxing lunch at a beachside table with one of the excellent piña coladas, or the ideal setting for a romantic dinner outdoors. Open daily. Reservations necessary. Major credit cards accepted. Barranquito Beach, Barranco (phone: 67-82-18). Expensive.

Los Faisanes – Very elegant atmosphere with good, and sometimes excellent, French cuisine. Downstairs in the *María Angola* hotel, La Paz 610, Miraflores (phone: 44-12-80). Expensive.

La Granja Azul – A must for anyone spending a few days in Lima who is looking for something different in the way of a restaurant. For one price, you can eat your fill of charcoal-broiled chicken, with plenty of hot sauce at hand if you like your bird spicy. Homemade bread is served hot from adobe ovens that you can see in the restaurant. In addition to good bar service, on weekends an orchestra plays, and there is dancing nightly. Open daily. Reservations are necessary. Major credit cards accepted. At km 11 of Carretera Central (phone: 35-07-77). Expensive.

Pabellón de Caza – One of Lima's luxury restaurants, a few yards from the Gold Museum in Monterrico. The chef is French, and venison and other game (in season) are specialties of the house. The *Bwana Grill,* the latest addition to the *Pabellón* complex, offers excellent grilled meats, a salad bar, and fine wines by either the bottle or the glass. Open daily. Reservations not necessary. Major credit cards accepted. Alonso de Molino 1196 (phone: 36-95-40). Expensive.

Rosa Nautica – This currently popular Miraflores spot is built over an ocean breakwater and provides a view of the ongoing parade of surfers. Seafood, international, and Peruvian dishes are featured at lunch and dinner; there's also brunch on Sundays. Open daily. *Malecón* Costa Verde SN (phone: 47-00-57 or 45-01-49). Expensive.

Tambo de Oro – Once upon a time the native Peruvian dishes served here were wonderful and the decor dazzling. Nowadays, however, the decor — 19th-century colonial — is still lovely, but the food is disappointing. At least go for a drink and a look. Belén 1066 (phone: 31-00-46). Expensive.

Las Trece Monedas – In the center of Lima, this illustrious colonial mansion built in 1787 now houses one of the best truly Peruvian restaurants. The coat of arms over the main entrance contains 13 coins, from which comes the restaurant's name. The atmosphere is unexcelled, and the *criolla* food, superb. The international selections on the menu are also well prepared. Closed Sundays. Reservations are necessary. Major credit cards accepted. Jirón Ancash 536 (phone: 27-65-47). Expensive.

Valentino – A charming Italian-Peruvian eating place in San Isidro popular with both Peruvians and resident foreigners, it offers simple and delicious Italian fare with a Peruvian touch. Reservations recommended. Manuel Bañon 215 (phone: 41-61-74). Expensive.

Blue Moon – The restaurant has an unlikely name and an unlikely setting — the largely residential district of Lince. Once inside, though, you're in for a treat. The highlight of the decor is the ceiling — completely covered with more than 5,000 bottles of wines and liquors. The owners are Italian, so the pastas are tasty and you can get real Italian ices as well. Open daily. Reservations not necessary. Major credit cards accepted. Pumacahua 2526 (phone: 71-13-89). Moderate.

Casa Vasca – Particularly to be recommended in this Basque restaurant is *ceviche,* a Peruvian specialty made with raw fish marinated in lemon juice and hot pepper and served with onions and corn on the cob. Reservations recommended. Major credit cards accepted. Av. Nicolás de Piérola 734 (phone: 23-66-90). Moderate.

Chalet Suisse – The decor is high "Swiss kitsch," but the food is in the best of taste, with specialties from Swiss and Viennese cuisine. Open daily. Reservations recommended. Credit cards accepted. Av. Nicolás de Piérola 560 (phone: 31-29-85). Moderate.

El Cortijo – Specializes in Argentine food, primarily baby beef charcoal-broiled with large salads served with a carafe of wine. Broiled chicken is on the menu, too. A pleasant, somewhat rustic spot quite a distance from the center of Lima. Open daily. Reservations are not needed. No credit cards. Av. Panamericana 675, Barranco (phone: 45-44-81). Moderate.

Giannino – Solid, plain Italian dishes. The downstairs decor is plain; upstairs, schmaltzy elegant, but the food is of high quality and ample quantity on both floors. Closed Sundays and holidays. Jirón Rufino Torrico 899 (phone: 31-49-78). Moderate.

José Antonio – For some of the best in *criolla* food and music, try this little jewel of a restaurant, tucked away in San Isidro. The atmosphere is colonial and the weekend crowds are lively. Open daily. Reservations not necessary. Major credit cards accepted. Monteagudo 200 (phone: 61-99-23). Moderate.

El Otro Sitio – If you're out for a moonlight stroll through the picturesque Barranco and over the Bridge of Sighs, stop here for a good *criolla* dinner. Closed Sundays. Reservations not necessary. Major credit cards accepted. Sucre 317, Barranco (phone: 67-89-72). Moderate.

La Pizzeria – Currently one of Miraflores' most popular night spots, offering international, Italian, and Peruvian cuisine at very reasonable prices. Great people watching, too. Benavides 322 (phone: 46-77-93). Moderate.

Rincón Gaucho – Perched on a cliff overlooking the Pacific at the end of Avenida

Larco, this spectacular Argentine restaurant serves terrific *parrillada* and steaks. Be prepared for long lines, especially around 8:30 and 9 PM. It's jammed on weekends, too, and reservations are not accepted. Open daily. No credit cards. Parque Salazar, Miraflores (phone: 47-47-78). Moderate.

El Dorado – Very good Peruvian-Chinese fare with a spectacular view of Lima. Try the crab claws (*uñas de cangrejo*). No reservations necessary. Arequipa 2450, San Isidro (phone: 22-10-80). Moderate to inexpensive.

Lung Fung – With private dining rooms and indoor gardens, it is the most dramatic of Lima's *chifas,* or Chinese restaurants. The wontons are good as is the shrimp "cristal," light, deep-fried shrimp served with a piquant lemon sauce. No reservations necessary. Av. República de Panamá 3165, San Isidro (phone: 22-63-82). Moderate to inexpensive.

Matsuei – Excellent Japanese cuisine. Reservations recommended. Canada 236, La Victoria (phone: 72-22-82). Moderate to inexpensive.

Rosita Ríos – In one of the oldest parts of Lima, the district of Rimac (across the river and behind the Presidential Palace), is this truly representative Peruvian coastal restaurant, with a large variety of pretty spicy dishes. Along with your meal, you are served a heaping portion of all kinds of Peruvian music. A delightful place. Closed Mondays. Best to make reservations. No credit cards. Cajatambo 100, La Florida (phone: 81-41-05). Moderate to inexpensive.

Bircher Benner – Installed in a charming old house, this vegetarian restaurant offers good meatless dishes, fresh juices, herb teas, and very good natural ice cream sundaes, all at very reasonable prices. There is also a natural foods store on the premises. Closed Sundays. Reservations not necessary. No credit cards. Schell 598, Miraflores (phone: 47-71-18). Inexpensive.

MONTEVIDEO

Residents of Montevideo are fond of referring to their home as a place hardly anyone knows. The capital of the Oriental Republic of Uruguay (the name means "purple land," a reference to the ubiquitous verbena that grows in the surrounding hills), Montevideo shares South America's Atlantic coast with Rio, and the River Plate with Buenos Aires, but it is frankly overshadowed by Buenos Aires to the west and São Paulo to the north.

Uruguay is a land of low hills and rolling grassy plains with abundant pastureland and a temperate climate on the eastern bank of the Río Uruguay, its frontier with Argentina. This river, in turn, flows into the great estuary of the Río de la Plata, whose wide shores are shared by Buenos Aires and Montevideo. With an area of 71,060 square miles, Uruguay is one of the smallest countries in South America. Its population of about 2.8 million inhabitants is very unevenly distributed: 1.4 million people make their home in the capital; the remainder live in the cities in the interior and in the countryside.

If residents of the city and citizens of the country are sanguine about the relative obscurity of city and state, wedged between the trailing tail of Brazil and Argentina's overweening bulk, it may be because in the life-style sweepstakes they are doing quite well. The country is predominantly middle class, and its people are extremely well nourished by international standards. Uruguayans are well educated, with a literacy rate of 85%, second only to Argentina's in South America. Life expectancy is 69 years, and there is a low infant mortality rate.

The first European to step on Uruguayan soil was Juan Díaz de Solís, who arrived in 1516. The Spanish explorer was sailing southward along the eastern coast of South America, seeking a strait leading to the other side of the New World; as soon as they landed, he and his party were attacked and killed by the Charrúas (Uruguayan Indians). Four years later, the Portuguese discovered the area. Captain Ferdinand Magellan, whose crew first circumnavigated the globe, sailed cautiously into the Río de la Plata. A sailor posted as lookout saw the hill that today's *montevideanos* call the *cerro* (see *Extra Special*) and called out *"Monte vide eu"* ("I see a mountain").

From those days of Solís and Magellan to the coming of the British (who occupied the city for a brief seven months in 1807), and the independence from Spain soon thereafter, the Banda Oriental del Uruguay (as it was then called) served as a natural arena of conflict between the Spanish and Portuguese empires.

Finally in 1828, with Great Britain's intervention, both Brazil and Argentina recognized Uruguay as an independent nation, a buffer state between two large and jealous neighbors. Despite the fact that independence had been secured, the gaucho spirit, which played godfather to the political philosophy of independence in the 1820s, continued as a strong factor in the Uruguayan way of life. Although its constitution was promulgated on July 18, 1830, the early history of the republic was confused by civil war between rival presidents.

The pattern for the country's political development in the twentieth century was set in 1903, when José Batlle y Ordóñez, known as the Father of Modern Uruguay, was elected president. Batlle advocated political and social reforms, extensive welfare measures, and government participation in many sectors of the economy. These reforms were still in evidence in 1970. Founder of the newspaper *El Día,* he believed in a democratic form of government with constitutional procedures, and he promoted measures designed to protect the country against the emergence of dictatorships. But this admirable tradition of democracy ended in the early 1970s, when Montevideo became the center of activity for a left-wing guerrilla group called the Movimiento de Liberación Nacional (Movement for National Liberation), better known as the Tupamaros. In 1973, the military seized control of the government, dissolved the parliament, and began an intensive crackdown on the Tupamaros, their friends, relatives, and associates. However, military rule ended in 1985 with the first popular election, and a civilian government now runs the country.

Foreigners are always well received in Montevideo. *Montevideanos* are renowned for their warmth, friendliness, and hospitality. Tourism is one of the country's most important industries and the capital is a safe city; a single woman can travel without being made to feel uncomfortable. During the day, the Ciudad Vieja — the district between the main plaza and the port — is the center of business activity. You will find it a compact, walkable area of old and new buildings. The Avenida 18 de Julio is rapidly becoming a chic commercial street. Surrounding the heart of the city are three major residential areas: to the north, the Prado, where in the late nineteenth century the well-to-do raised enormous families in equally enormous mansions; to the east, along the Rambla Pocitos, the high-rise center of the city; and farther east, residential, fresh-aired Carrasco.

But most crucial to life in the city are its beaches, from Pocitos Beach to Carrasco (which, being river-water beaches, are not representative of the ocean-blue beaches farther east), on which residents study, play, and strut. The Rambla (riverfront drive), which borders these city beaches and which runs from the port to Carrasco (the last metropolitan area), comes to life as *montevideanos* promenade during summer evenings and winter afternoons. And a long walk along a quiet beach in the middle of the afternoon says more about the quality of life here and the attitude of its residents than a thousand pictures.

MONTEVIDEO AT-A-GLANCE

 SEEING THE CITY: The best place to get a view of Montevideo is from the Mirador (Lookout Tower) on top of the Intendencia Muncipal (Town Hall). It includes a tea room and a recently inaugurated fine restaurant (see *Eating Out*). 18 de Julio, the main downtown avenue and shopping center, runs directly below you. Ten blocks to your left along 18 de Julio is the Plaza Independencia with its bronze statue of national hero José Gervasio Artigas. On the other side of the plaza is the Ciudad Vieja (Old City), which constituted the heart of the colonial city. Today it is the business and banking center of the country, where you will find the Banco República (the government commercial import-export bank), the Stock Exchange (Bolsa de Valores), the Central Post Office, the Customs House, the Central Bank, most of the foreign banks' central offices, and the shipping center.

 SPECIAL PLACES: There is one main street in downtown Montevideo (18 de Julio). Since the streets are laid out in an orderly way, it will be easy for you to find your way around. The Uruguayan person-on-the-street is very helpful, so do not hesitate to ask anyone for directions. The streets you will use most (described as if you were standing at Plaza Independencia facing Avenida 18 de Julio) are Colonia, running parallel to and left of 18 de Julio, and San José, to its right. Quite a few side streets cross 18 de Julio between the plaza and Ejido (some 11 blocks from the main plaza). Behind you, Sarandí, which would be the continuation of 18 de Julio on the other side of the plaza, runs through the Ciudad Vieja and down to the port.

DOWNTOWN

Mausoleum of José Gervasio Artigas (Mausoleo de José Gervasio Artigas) – Under the equestrian statue in the center of the main plaza, this mausoleum, dedicated to Uruguay's national hero, is made entirely of marble and granite. Artigas became the leader of the gaucho movement between 1811 and 1821 that fought both the Spanish and the Portuguese to maintain Uruguayan independence. He is considered the father of Uruguayan nationhood and is credited with keeping alive the spirit of freedom during the darkest days of foreign dominance. Its different date inscriptions depict various stages of the hero's life and participation in the country's liberation. Open daily, except the first Monday of every month. Free. Plaza Independencia.

Town Hall (Cabildo) – An interesting exhibition of old Montevideo, from early Indian days until present times, with a brief résumé of the country's history, complemented by slides and recordings, and a display of paintings, antique pieces of furniture, costumes, and even a replica of the old Montevideo bastion. Open Tuesdays through Sundays from 2 to 8 PM. Small admission charge. Plaza Cabildo, Sarandí and J. C. Gómez (phone: 98-28-26).

Montevideo Cathedral (Catedral de Montevideo) – Roman Catholicism is the national religion of Uruguay, although churches of various other denominations exist. Since the days of Batlle in the early 1900s, there has been total separation between church and state. This large, ornate cathedral was built between 1790 and 1804. Open daily. Free. Plaza Cabildo, Sarandí and Ituzaingó.

Legislative Palace (Palacio Legislativo) – This superb piece of architecture is built on a rise on Agraciada, 15 blocks north of 18 de Julio. Designed by the distinguished Italian architect Gaetano Moretti and inaugurated in 1925, this building combines 45 varieties of marble and granite in its mosaic floors and walls. Its stained-glass windows depict historic events and are extraordinarily beautiful. The building cost approximately $17 million, an exorbitant figure 54 years ago! Open daily. Free. Av. Libertador Lavalleja and D. Fernández Crespo (phone: 29-70-26).

The Obelisk (El Obelisco) – Sculpted by Uruguayan Zorrilla de San Martín, it commemorates the signers of the country's first constitution. 18 de Julio and Bulevar Artigas.

La Carreta Statue – Blending into the landscape above a reflecting pool in the José Batlle y Ordóñez Park, this bronze monument to the pioneers of Uruguay takes the form of three yokes of oxen drawing a covered wagon and a bearded gaucho. José Batlle y Ordóñez Park, Av. Italia and Las Heras (no phone).

Soccer Stadium (Estadio Centenario) – If you hear that an important soccer match is to be played while you are visiting, don't miss it. It will be one of the best opportunities to see Uruguayans at their most passionate public moments. The largest stadium in the country, with a seating capacity of 70,000, it was built in 1930 to commemorate the nation's 100th anniversary and to host the World Football Championship, which took place that same year. José Batlle y Ordóñez Park, Av. Italia and Las Heras (phone: 78-42-70).

Rodó Park (Parque Rodó) – Children will enjoy this amusement park on the Rambla, with rides, an open-air summer theater, an artificial lake, and ponies for rent. This is one of the places where you can taste the typical *chorizos al pan* (very good sausages) and *churros* filled with *dulce de leche* (fried round pastry with a sweet filling). Open daily in the afternoon. Admission charge. Parque Rodó, Rambla M. Gandhi.

Zoological Gardens (Jardínes Zoológicos) – Leo, the first South American–born elephant, was born here in 1974, and on these same grounds you'll find one of the best planetariums in South America. Closed Mondays and Tuesdays. Admission charge. Av. Rivera 3275 (phone: 78-06-42).

Rural Association of Uruguay (Asociación Rural del Uruguay) – This is where horse-breaking competitions are held during Easter Week (*Semana Criolla*); other activities include exhibitions of typical dances and folklore music contests led by real gauchos. The other important event here is the Cattle Show (*Exposición Rural*), in August. As Uruguay is a cattle-breeding country, this event is of great importance to all breeders, and only the very best animals are brought to this show. The show is enlivened in the evening with folklore singers, dancers, and ever-present *parrilladas* (South American barbecues). Lucas Obes 96 in Parque Prado (phone: 39-36-16).

Tristán Narvaja Market (Feria de Tristán Narvaja) – This flea market, about ten blocks long, convenes every Sunday morning from 7 AM until noon. Here you can find anything and everything from live house pets to meat, vegetables, automobile spare parts, and priceless antiques. Sundays only. Free. Tristán Narvaja between 18 de Julio and La Paz.

Solís Theater (Teatro Solís) – This beautiful piece of architecture is the center of the city's regularly scheduled concerts and cultural activities. Open daily. Free. Buenos Aires 678, just off Plaza Independencia (phone: 91-64-88).

Natural History Museum (Museo de Historia Natural) – Designed especially for children and young students, it has a good display of archaeological objects, fossils, and Uruguayan flora and fauna. Call to check the schedule. Usually open daily. Free. On the ground floor of the Solís Theater. Buenos Aires 652 (phone: 90-41-14).

National Pre-Columbian and Colonial Art Museum (Museo Nacional) – An excellent exhibition of original art collections from the pre-Columbian and colonial periods, including religious paintings of the 17th and 18th centuries. Closed Mondays. Admission charge. Ejido and 18 de Julio, beside the Post Office in the Municipality Bldg. (phone: 90-55-56).

Fortaleza General Artigas – This is a great place to get a good look at Montevideo, except that it is slightly out of the way. Once a fort, this building stands on the *cerro* (hill) for which Montevideo was named. It is now a military museum with a good display of Spanish uniforms, guns, and artifacts dating from the era of the battle for independence. Closed Mondays. Admission charge. About a 30-minute ride from downtown. Camino del la Fortaleza s/n (phone: 31-11-54).

Museum of Contemporary Art (Museo de Arte Contemporáneo) – Recently opened, this art gallery has changing national and international exhibits. Plaza Cagancha 1168.

SUBURBS

Carrasco – Take a cab or drive along the Rambla to the Carrasco area, once the summer resort of Montevideo's most wealthy residents. Some five blocks after the *Carrasco* hotel, turn off the Rambla into the residential area and take a good look at the contrast and variety of the old, elegant houses and the luxurious newer homes. Then treat yourself to an ice icream at *Las Delicias* at the corner of Arocena and Dr. Schroeder.

■ **EXTRA SPECIAL:** *Mercado del Puerto* (Port Market) is very old and not especially impressive at first sight, but it has terrific personality and bubbles with life. It is across the street from the Customs Building, and over the years it has become the lunch site for the businesspeople in the Ciudad Vieja. It consists of many small delicatessen stands and *parrilladas.* After having a glass of *medio y medio* white wine at the Roldós stand, try a *chorizo* (sausage) and *pulpa* or *entrecot* (delicious cuts of meat) at a *parrillada* (South American barbecue). There is also a sit-down restaurant, *El Palenque,* if you are not pressed for time. Open daily. Free. Perez Castellano 1579-85 (phone: 95-47-04). *Parador del Cerro,* a restaurant-disco on the side of the hill, looks out over the city lights. At midnight, there is usually a nightclub show with singing and dancing. Open nightly. Reservations required. Camino de la Fortaleza (phone: 31-13-14).

SOURCES AND RESOURCES

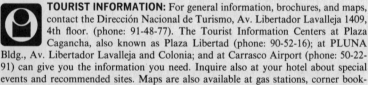

TOURIST INFORMATION: For general information, brochures, and maps, contact the Dirección Nacional de Turismo, Av. Libertador Lavalleja 1409, 4th floor. (phone: 91-48-77). The Tourist Information Centers at Plaza Cagancha, also known as Plaza Libertad (phone: 90-52-16); at PLUNA Bldg., Av. Libertador Lavalleja and Colonia; and at Carrasco Airport (phone: 50-22-91) can give you the information you need. Inquire also at your hotel about special events and recommended sites. Maps are also available at gas stations, corner bookstands, and bookstores. By dialing 214, you can contact the Central Bureau of Information for an update on events and schedules. They will also answer your queries. There are two English-speaking travel agencies, *Viajes Bueme's,* at Colonia 979, and *Turisport Ltd.,* at Mercedes 924; the latter represents American Express in Uruguay.

Local Coverage – The only English-language newspaper is the *Buenos Aires Herald.* Available at most newsstands, it will not give you much information on Montevideo. *La Manaña, El País,* and *El Día* (all Spanish-language morning dailies) contain entertainment schedules.

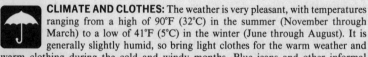

CLIMATE AND CLOTHES: The weather is very pleasant, with temperatures ranging from a high of 90°F (32°C) in the summer (November through March) to a low of 41°F (5°C) in the winter (June through August). It is generally slightly humid, so bring light clothes for the warm weather and warm clothing during the cold and windy months. Blue jeans and other informal clothes are suitable. A light raincoat and umbrella are handy in winter.

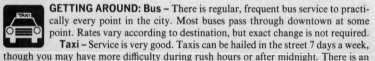

GETTING AROUND: Bus – There is regular, frequent bus service to practically every point in the city. Most buses pass through downtown at some point. Rates vary according to destination, but exact change is not required.
   Taxi – Service is very good. Taxis can be hailed in the street 7 days a week, though you may have more difficulty during rush hours or after midnight. There is an

efficient *Radio Taxi* service (phone: 58-91-92, 58-77-75) that is not expensive. Taxi drivers expect a 10% tip.

Car Rental – Besides *Avis* (Rambla Rep. de México 6333; phone: 50-4602, 50-8129) and *Hertz* (Colonia 813; phone: 90-7957, 98-5756), there is *Auto Rent* (Yaguarón 1683; phone: 90-87-78/82). The minimum age is 23 years old, and a $100 deposit is required. Most major credit cards are accepted.

 MUSEUMS: In addition to the Natural History Museum (Museo de Historia Natural), the National Museum (Museo Nacional), the military museum at Fortaleza del Cerro, the Museum of Contemporary Art, and the Town Hall (Cabildo) exhibit described in *Special Places,* the following are worth a visit:

Oceanographic and Fish Museum (Museo Oceanografico) – Rambla República de Chile 4215 Puerto Buceo (phone: 79-53-12).

National Art Gallery (Galería Nacional de Arte) – Parque Rodó (phone: 41-63-17).

National Historical Museum (Museo Histórico Nacional) – Rincón 437 and Zabala 1469 (phone: 95-10-51 and 95-10-28).

Don José Batlle y Ordóñez's House (Casa de Don José Batlle y Ordóñez) – Teniente Rinaldi 3870 (phone: 22-36-00).

Fernando Garcia Museum (Museo de Transporte) – Camino Carrasco 6003 (no phone).

House of Juan Zorrilla de San Martín – Author of major Uruguayan literary works, Ellauri 96 (phone: 70-18-18).

National Museum of Plastic Arts/Juan Manuel Blanes (Museo Nacional de Artes Plasticas Juan Manuel Blanes) – Official painter of the republic, Av. Millán and Arroyo Miguelete (phone: 38-54-20).

 SHOPPING: Uruguay has an extensive textile industry, and the fabrics it produces are inexpensive, of excellent quality, and can be found in most downtown stores. Uruguayan nutria (a fur-bearing mammal) is one of the best of the breed in the world, with longer, thicker, softer hair and better color than can be found elsewhere. Nor is the fur expensive. The best shops for nutria are *Peletería Pendola,* San José 1087, and *Peletería Holandesa,* Colonia 892.

A large shopping center with more than 100 shops has recently opened at Carrañala and Veíntiseis de Marzo. Besides clothing, leather, and souvenirs, there are restaurants, a supermarket, and a cinema.

Beware of street vendors offering you watches, electric appliances, and perfumes. It is preferable to pay more and buy these goods at a shop. Shops are normally open from 9 AM until 6 PM. Other fine Uruguayan bargains are

Agates and Amethysts – *Amatistas del Uruguay* (Sarandi and J. C. Goméz) carries an extensive selection of key rings, pendants, ashtrays, and rare cuts. Several other new shops selling agates and amethysts have sprung up along Sarandi (between Plaza Independencia and Ituzaingó).

Leather – Excellent shoes, purses, and wallets of high-quality leather can be found throughout Montevideo. For women's shoes, visit *Arbiter,* 18 de Julio 943; for wallets and belts, *Taborelli,* 18 de Julio 1184; for purses: *Sagali,* in Galería Polvorín and Galería Libertad (downtown).

Souvenirs – *Puccio* shops, on Río Negro and Galicia, and *Casa Schiavo,* Uruguay 1050, have the best selection.

Woolen goods – *Manos del Uruguay* stocks high-quality, pure hand-woven wool products from all parts of the country — sweaters, rugs, ponchos, curtains, and modern tapestries. The main shop is on the corner of J. C. Gómez and Reconquista and another has opened at San Jose 1111.

SPECIAL EVENTS: During *Carnival Week,* before Ash Wednesday, do not miss the Las Llamadas parade. An interesting display of color, music, and rhythm, it takes place in the Barrio Palermo, where, along the narrow streets of Carlos Gardel and La Cumparsita, the dancing and the drums continue until the early morning hours. The *Cattle Show* takes place in August at the Asociación Rural del Uruguay, Lucas Obes 96, in Parque Prado.

SPORTS: Soccer (*fútbol*) is the national sport and games take place year round. Try to see a *clásico* between the two most popular teams and traditional rivals, *Nacional* and *Peñarol.* Any hotel clerk or person on the street can tell you if a match is coming up.

Basketball – This sport has become almost as popular as soccer. Final and championship games are played either at the *Cilindro Municipal* (phone: 58-51-69) or at the *Palacio Peñarol* (phone: 40-20-16).

Gambling – You can try your luck at roulette and blackjack or even bingo in either of the two informal casinos in town: the *Parque Hotel,* Rambla M. Gandhi s/n (phone: 49-71-11), and *Hotel Casino Carrasco,* Rambla Republica de México s/n (phone: 50-12-61).

Golf – Can be played at the *Punta Carretas Golf Club,* Bulevar Artigas 379 (phone: 70-17-21/25) or at the *Club de Golf del Cerro,* Punta de Lobos s/n (phone: 31-13-05). Both offer a fantastic view of the city.

Horse Racing – The *Hipodromo de Maronas* has races on Thursdays, Saturdays, and Sundays. It's about 20 minutes from downtown by taxi. J. M. Guerra s/n (phone: 58-88-61).

Rugby – Between April and September, this British sport is played throughout the city. Consult the newspapers for schedules.

Soccer – Professional matches are played every weekend in the afternoons. You will undoubtedly see people playing it, especially in the residential areas, on any and every day of the week. The main stadium is *Estadio Centerario,* Parque José Batlle y Ordóñez, Av. Italia and Las Heras (phone: 78-42-70).

Swimming – Carrasco's beach is the best; Playa Honda and Playa Malvin are next best. The finest of all are found at Punta del Este (see *Uruguay,* DIRECTIONS).

Tennis – No hotel in the city has tennis courts. However, if you want to watch some good matches (often featuring international players), try the *Carrasco Lawn Tennis Club,* Dr. Eduardo J. Couture 6401 (phone: 50-43-12); the *Círculo de Tenís de Montevideo,* Buschental s/n (phone: 39-35-00), or the *Club Biguá,* José Vázquez Ledesma s/n (phone: 70-24-85), all of which have brick-dust courts. Tennis matches are publicized in the newspapers.

THEATER: Acting in Uruguay is very good, but almost all performances are in Spanish. If there is any visiting international performance, it will take place at the *Teatro Solís,* Buenos Aires 678 (phone: 91-64-88). The Comedia Nacional (National Theater Group), the resident company of the *Teatro Solís,* is very good. The *Millington Drake Theater* sometimes presents an English-speaking acting group, The Montevideo Players. *Teatro del Notariado, Teatro Circular,* and *Sala 18 de Mayo* are some of the theaters that present Spanish works.

Modern films are shown at downtown theaters, and you will often find replays of good old films. The films are always shown in their original language. The newspapers list what's showing.

MUSIC: Don't miss tangos and Uruguayan folk music. You will find the tangos at the *Tanguería del 40* on the ground floor of the *Columbia Palace Hotel,* Reconquista 468 (phone: 95-30-22), and in the taverns on Carlos Gardel Street. You will get folkloric music at some of the local restaurants, but if there is any special show on at the time of your visit, don't miss it. For classical music, the Official Radio Broadcasting Services Orchestra (SODRE), inaugurated in 1931, has become the National Symphony Orchestra and now plays at the *Solís*.

NIGHTCLUBS AND NIGHTLIFE: Montevideo has a few good discotheques, known as *boites,* that admit couples only. Among the most popular are *Zum Zum,* Rambla Armenia 1647 (phone: 78-12-06); *Lancelot,* an old French castle in Carrasco, Friburgo 5817 (phone: 50-41-24), on weekends only; and *Ton-Ton Metek,* beside a Carrasco lake, Oficial B 9635 (phone: 50-17-54). There are dinner and dancing at *Makao del Hotel Oceanía* (from which you get a beautiful view), Mar Artico 1227 (phone: 50-04-44); *Portofino,* Belastiqui 1325 (phone: 50-03-23); *La Cantina,* Carlos Crocker 2531 (phone: 58-93-36). If you plan to go to any of these on a Friday or Saturday night, make a reservation first.

SINS: The *Cubilete,* Gabriel Pereyra 3106 (phone: 78-21-21), is a nightclub where there are always some very thirsty young ladies. If you are looking for action, try the port area, but take care. The best place to indulge rampant *sloth*fulness is on Carrasco beach, the *pride* of Montevideo.

BEST IN TOWN

CHECKING IN: There is quite a variety of hostelries in Montevideo, from air-conditioned luxury hotels to family-style *pensiones*. All hotels listed here have private baths. Reservations are essential during the summer months. Expect to pay $60 to $85 and up for a double in those places we've classed as expensive; between $35 and $50 at places in the moderate category; under $30, inexpensive. Rates include breakfast but not the 20% value added tax.

Cottage – This hotel has been renovated, enlarged (though still not too big), and generally restored to first-class condition. In front of Carrasco beach, on the Rambla. Miraflores 1360 (phone: 50-08-67). Expensive.

Hostería del Lago – Only a 5-minute drive from Carrasco or 15 minutes from downtown, this new, luxurious lakeside establishment offers its guests tennis courts, a pool, watersports, and convention facilities. Expensive.

Victoria Plaza – This 18-floor high-rise in front of the main plaza is air conditioned, with good service and an excellent view from its rooftop restaurant. On Friday nights, there is entertainment in the lobby. Plaza Independencia 759 (phone: 98-95-65). Expensive.

Casino Carrasco – On the Rambla in Carrasco, 20 minutes from downtown, the beach is just across the road. Inaugurated in 1921, it has been renovated and has very spacious rooms. The casino, restaurant, and cocktail lounge are on the ground floor. Rambla República de México s/n (phone: 50-12-61). Moderate.

Columbia Palace – Newer than the *Victoria Plaza* (the other top hotel in town), some rooms face the Rambla and on a windy day offer an exciting view of the rough river water hitting its walls. Its rooms are comfortable. It also has an international restaurant and a *tanguería* downstairs that is worth a visit. Reconquista 468 (phone: 98-93-64). Moderate.

Embajador – Basic but comfortable downtown establishment. San José 1212 (phone: 981-622). Moderate.

Internacional – New, with good downtown location and air conditioning; offers full board. Colonia 823 (phone: 90-70-00). Moderate.

Lancaster – Downtown, with smallish rooms. There is a good cocktail lounge, *La Vela,* downstairs. Plaza Cagancha 1334 (phone: 98-46-21). Moderate.

London Palace – Not luxurious but very relaxing and excellently located in the middle of downtown; with a cocktail lounge and garage. Río Negro 1278 (phone: 98-94-20). Moderate.

Parque – This older luxury hotel, recently renovated and remodeled, is very comfortable. Unless you have a car, it is not too conveniently located. Rambla M. Gandhi s/n (phone: 49-71-11). Moderate.

Balfer – Very modest, but clean. Breakfast included. Cuareim 1328 (phone: 98-55-64). Inexpensive.

Ermitage – For a beach stay that is closer to town than the beaches at Carrasco, this is your best bet. It is one block up from the Pocitos Beach, 10 minutes from downtown. Request a room facing the sea; the view of Pocitos Bay in the evening is enchanting. J. B. Blanco 783 (phone: 70-40-21). Inexpensive.

Klee – One of the newest hotels in Montevideo, comfortable but not luxurious. Breakfast included. Yaguarón 1306 (phone: 91-06-71). Inexpensive.

Oxford – The same kind of relaxing but not luxurious hotel as the *Lancaster* and *Klee,* it is also well located and has air conditioning. Breakfast included. Paraguay 1286 (phone: 98-94-65). Inexpensive.

Presidente – This is the perfect place for shopping forays, with an entrance in *Galería Madrileña.* 18 de Julio 1038 (phone: 98-21-65). Inexpensive.

EATING OUT: Restaurants are a bargain. Special meat cuts are reserved for restaurants, so the very best *entrecôtes* and *pulpas* can be sampled. Besides the restaurants listed here, a healthy, good, economical lunch or dinner is available at any sidewalk café along the main street or downtown. Dinner is never served before 8 PM. Although most major credit cards are now accepted, you should still check beforehand. Expect to pay $30 or more at restaurants in our expensive category, between $15 and $25 in the moderate range, and under $12 at places noted as inexpensive. These prices are for two, for a three-course meal (with meat), wine, and coffee. They do not include drinks, tip, or 20% value added tax.

El Aguila – An old and traditional restaurant beside the *Teatro Solís.* If you have a sweet tooth, order the omelette surprise. Open daily. Reservations accepted. Buenos Aires 694 (phone: 98-37-42). Expensive.

Bungalow Suizo – Has two locations, one downtown and one in Carrasco. Try the Carrasco branch, which, although slightly out of the way, is built in Swiss-chalet style, with a very warm, cozy atmosphere and excellent food. The specialties are cheese fondue, smoked pork chop (an excellent choice), and Swiss potatoes. Open daily, but closed December through March. Reservations accepted. Two locations: Sol 150, Carrasco (phone: 51-10-73); and downtown at Andes 1427 (phone: 90-12-40). Expensive.

La Camargue – Very small establishment serving well-prepared French cuisine. Mercedes 1133. Expensive.

Cantón Chino – The ever-present Chinese restaurant is alive and well in Montevideo. Although not up to international standards, the spring rolls and sweet and sour pork dishes are very good. Open daily. Reservations not necessary. 8 de Octubre 2611 (phone: 40-22-88). Expensive.

Club Alemán – The place in itself isn't too welcoming, but the German food they serve is first class. Open daily. Reservations advisable. Paysandú 935 (phone: 91-74-96). Expensive.

Doña Flor – The newest and most expensive restaurant in town, the *Doña* offers a very limited but excellent menu. Open for lunch and dinner, but closed Sundays and January through February. In front of the Faculty of Architecture, Bulevar Artigas 1034 (phone: 78-57-51). Expensive.

Emerson Unlimited Salad Bar – Excellent international cuisine. Open daily for dinner and at midday on Sundays. Costa Rica at Rivera (phone: 50-48-86). Expensive.

Golf Club – A 10-minute ride from downtown will get you to this luxurious club with a wide variety of dishes, a buffet, and dessert table. If you decide to go at midday, watch the golfers play right outside the French windows. Open daily for lunch only; members only on Sundays. Reservations advised. Bulevar Artigas 379 (phone: 70-17-21). Expensive.

Hawaii – The excellent *parrillada* is worth the trip to the Carrasco suburbs. Murillo 6608 (phone: 506-311). Expensive.

Panorámico Municipal – At the top of the Lookout Tower downtown, this restaurant offers an international menu. Open at midday and at night. Reservations accepted. Soriano, corner Ejido (phone: 98-46-47). Expensive.

Morini – A very large restaurant on top of the *Mercado Central.* The seafood is extra special here. Open daily. Reservations not required. Ciudadela 1229 (phone: 90-05-45). Expensive to moderate.

Catari – If you feel like eating Italian food, this is your best choice. Try the lasagna with mushroom sauce — it's excellent. Open daily. Reservations not required. San José 935 (phone: 90-57-43). Moderate.

Otto – Whether it's cocktails, lunch, tea, dinner, or a quick snack, the food is tasty and the service friendly at this small and cozy restaurant. Good German-style pastries. Rio Negro at the corner of San José (phone: 90-19-94). Moderate.

La Azotea – This *parrillada* is very good. It's on the Rambla in Pocitos Bay. No reservations necessary. Rambla República del Perú 1063, Pocitos (phone: 79-67-14). Moderate to inexpensive.

El Entrevero – An absolute must if you want to try a typical Uruguayan place. The *parrillada* has particularly delicious meat. Open daily. No reservations required. 21 de Setiembre 2774, Pocitos (phone: 70-04-81). Moderate to inexpensive.

Balón de Oro – A small but welcoming place, where you can get a good and fast *milanesa* or equal. 18 de Julio 1616 (phone: 40-60-04). Inexpensive.

El Chivito de Oro – A *chivito* here is a mouth-watering experience. It consists of a hot steak sandwich with whatever you choose to have on it. The grilled ham and cheese sandwiches (*sandwich caliente*) and the mixed cold sandwiches (*olímpicos*) are filling and succulent here, too. Open daily. No reservations. 18 de Julio 1251 (phone: 90-51-60). Inexpensive.

Conaprole – If you stay at one of the Carrasco-suburb hotels, this will be a convenient place to eat. It has a lovely location in a park and serves full meals (steaks, *"chivitos,"* omelettes), as well as breakfast and afternoon tea. Eduardo Couture, corner Av. Arocena Carrasco (phone: 50-00-47). Inexpensive.

Hispano Bar – Quite simply the best pizza place in Montevideo. Open daily. Reservations not required. San José and Río Negro (no phone). Inexpensive.

Oro del Rhin – Do not leave Montevideo without having had breakfast or tea at this *confitería.* The sandwiches and German-style cakes and pastries are the pride of all Uruguay. Ask for a *te completo* (which consists of toast, marmelade, grilled sandwiches, cakes, pastries, and tea or coffee) or choose your own sandwiches and cakes from the front counter. Closed Mondays. No reservations. Colonia 897 at Coronel Latorre (phone: 90-28-33). Inexpensive.

Soko's – If you are looking for a place to have a cocktail before a meal, this elegant new place serves tables full of excellent appetizers. Handy hint: Imported whiskey is very expensive; the local one, not anywhere near as good, is half the price. Closed Mondays. No reservations. 18 de Julio 1250. Inexpensive.

PANAMÁ CITY

During the 1880s, when the French were in the midst of a doomed attempt to cut a sea-level canal across the steaming Isthmus of Panamá, an outraged missionary described Panamá City as a "hideous dung heap of moral and physical abomination." It was a place where the definition of a good time was as broad as the ocean the city overlooked, and tomorrow was a day whose arrival could not be expected with certainty.

While Panamá City has grown from the striking collection of shacks and moldering colonial structures of a century ago to become one of the most exciting and cosmopolitan metropolises of Latin America, one thing has not changed — it is still a city dedicated to the pursuit of pleasure. Whether a visitor's tastes are high-brow or low-rent, classy cabaret or strip joint, hotel or flophouse, racetrack or bullring, seafood or honky-tonk junk food, casino or bingo hall, it's possible to indulge them in Panamá City, where "gambling is not only a cornerstone of the country's economy, but a way of life."

At the more hospitable end of the world's most important nautical short cut, Panamá City is home to almost one-half million persons — just over one-third of the entire population of Panamá. The majority of the city's residents are *mestizo,* a mixture of Spanish and Indian. There is also a sizable black population, living primarily in an area called Caledonia, an important minority of highly enterprising Chinese, and many western Europeans. Although the Canal Zone ceased to exist as an American-governed enclave on October 1, 1979, thousands of *norteamericanos* continue to live there in the tropical equivalent of suburbia.

Large numbers of Panamanians still live in ramshackle tenements, teeming with humanity and humanity's laundry, scattered throughout the city, but these are gradually being replaced by new, concrete, government-built tenements. In either case, they contrast starkly with the sleek glass and concrete high-rise office buildings, condominiums, banks, and hotels that dominate the city's skyline.

The present city is the second Panamá City. The first was founded in 1519, 4 miles east of the present site, 18 years after the Atlantic coast of Panamá was discovered by Columbus. The city's founder was Pedro Arias Dávila, known as Pedrarias the Cruel, who murdered Vasco Nuñez de Balboa, who discovered the Pacific Ocean at Darién in 1513. Pedrarias also began the grisly work that eradicated all but three of Panamá's 60 indigenous Indian tribes during Spain's 300-year tenure. In 1524, the conquistador Francisco Pizarro began the plunder of the Inca empire from Panamá City. The city became a storage terminal for the incredible golden treasures of the Incas and 200,000 tons of Bolivian silver, which were then taken across the Isthmus by heavily guarded mule trains to be shipped to Spain. Although strongly garrisoned, the city was not built in a particularly defensible location. So after resisting several earlier attempts, the city was sacked and burned in 1671 by an archetypically bloodthirsty horde of buccaneers led by Henry Morgan.

The city was rebuilt within a year, behind stout walls, at the tip of the peninsula that forms Panamá Bay. It was never taken by force again. Panamá was granted independence from Spain without violence in 1821 and joined the Republic of Greater Colombia, a federation of the countries that today forms Colombia and Venezuela. Panamá separated from Colombia in 1903, with the help of the US, when Panamá signed the Hay–Buneau–Varilla Treaty granting the use of the 10-mile-wide and 51-mile-long Canal Zone to the US permanently and exclusively. "Permanently" has turned out to mean "until 1979".

The more than 300-year-old Spanish colonial town of stucco, wrought-iron grillwork, and balconies overlooking narrow cobblestoned streets is the core of modern Panamá City. The peninsula on which the city stands extends south into the Pacific Ocean, with the bay to the east and the Canal to the west. The city extends northeast across the peninsula and overflows into progressively newer and less frenetically crowded urban districts. The newest section, which includes a *Dairy Queen* and a high-rise luxury *Holiday Inn,* lines a sleek boulevard and looks west across the placid bay toward the walls and spires of the colonial city.

Although the Canal Zone is no longer officially American sovereign soil, the enclave still contrasts sharply with the rest of Panamá City. On one side of a six-lane boulevard are expansive lawns framing split-level homes, before which air-conditioned Detroit monsters sit in paved driveways. On the other side of the street are tenements and crowded streets jammed with battered taxis, litter, and the most flamboyantly decorated buses in South America. In the former Canal Zone, Americanisms and Americans still prevail: Protestant churches, supermarkets, and the most southerly lodge of the Benevolent and Protective Order of Elks.

The gringos and their condescending ways were long a source of irritation to the Panamanians and the 15 years preceding adoption of the new canal treaties were marked by periodic episodes of violence. Except for anti-American demonstrations late in 1979, when Panamá gave refuge to the deposed Shah of Iran, the mood of the Panamanian public toward the US has softened during the past 5 years. The Americans, or Zonians, however, greeted the pacts with belligerent dismay and displays of jingoistic patriotism, brought about by the realization that their unique tropical paradise was finally coming to an end.

The pact, which has left most Panamanians pleased, and which elevated former US President Carter to a level of esteem uncommon even in his own country, gives Panamá sovereign rights to the Canal in exchange for Panamá's establishing it as a neutral zone through which all vessels will have equal rights of passage. Traffic between the Atlantic and the Pacific continues as always. The interesting year will be 1999, when all foreigners are supposed to be out of the canal control room.

Despite any residual anti-American sentiment, Panamá City continues to encourage tourism. Many travelers take advantage of the city's freewheeling nightlife and duty-free bargains and, regardless of politics, tourists are always welcome. English is taught in the schools and a visitor who doesn't speak Spanish will have no problems.

Panamá has always been a way station on a trade route traversed by adventurers, seafarers, soldiers of fortune, merchants, and gold seekers who came because it was one end of the shortest distance between the world's two great oceans. It has seen conquistadores and pirates, American '49ers rushing to California gold fields, French canal builders, and American engineers, who finally conquered the jungle, malaria, and yellow fever to complete the Canal in 1914.

Panamá has never really controlled its own affairs. Even today, its internal affairs are strongly influenced by the US Government, by giant multinational corporations like United Brands (formerly United Fruit), and by more than 100 banks from more than two dozen countries.

As in any large city where great affluence and poverty live side by side, unwary travelers in Panamá City may soon be separated from their possessions. Although it is not as rife with petty crime as Bogotá or Cartagena, Colombia, or Caracas, Venezuela, theft is a pretty serious problem. Like any Latin American city, it is no place for a lone woman who does not like to be whistled at more than occasionally.

But these negative aspects should not inhibit anyone's enjoyment of Panamá City. A few simple precautions will keep a traveler out of harm's way. Prices should always be agreed upon before a service is rendered. Bags and belongings should be held securely and never left unattended. Cameras should be kept out of sight, except when being used. Jewelry should be left at home. (Even eyeglasses with expensive frames have been stolen from people's faces in crowds.) As in any big city, the odds are against becoming a victim of crime, but the danger is there and should be recognized.

Panamá City is a city on the make, a city that hustles. As long as the Canal is an important trade route, it will have a captive audience for the bazaar-like open-air markets, the sleek boutiques, the phantasmagorical discos, the bars, and casinos. Now that the end of the foreign occupation of the Canal Zone is in sight, it is a city full of a new sense of identity and a determination to grow into the grandiloquent sobriquet bestowed on it by the Institute of Tourism: "Heart of the Universe."

PANAMÁ CITY AT-A-GLANCE

SEEING THE CITY: There is a superb view of Panamá City looking west across the bay toward the heart of the city, from the *Belvedere* rooftop lounge of the *Holiday Inn Panamá;* it is especially impressive at night. Open until 3 AM. Vía Italia and Winston Churchill at Punta Paitilla (phone: 69-1122).

SPECIAL PLACES: It would take the instincts of a lovelorn bloodhound to overcome the haphazard asymmetry of Panamá City's streets. The Canal can be found to the west of the city proper. Most of the streets of the major shopping district run east-west near Panamá Bay. Many of the streets (*calles*) run along a north-south axis and are numbered; other streets have recently been renamed, and some addresses given here may be under their former names.

France Plaza (Plaza de Francia) – At the southernmost tip of the peninsula on which the city is built, this is the heart of the old colonial section and a logical place to begin a walking tour. Shaded by red-flowering trees, the square contains monuments to Finlay, the conqueror of yellow fever, and former Panamanian President Pablo Arosemena and an obelisk dedicated to the French canal builders, who started work before the Americans. The Palace of Justice, where the Supreme Court meets, and a number of colonial buildings line the square. At the end of Calle C-1.

Promenade of the Dungeons (Paseo de las Bóvedas) – This lovers' walk atop the old city wall is reportedly not only for lovers these days, but pickpockets too — so beware! It can be reached by stone stairs from the Plaza de Francia and affords a good view of the bay and offshore islands. Beneath the wall are the old dungeons that give the promenade its name. Behind the Plaza de Francia.

Church of Santo Domingo (Iglesia de Santo Domingo) – Not far from the Paseo de las Bóvedas, this church, now in ruins, contains a flat archway, more than 350 years old, made of brick and mortar that stands without any internal support. The archway's durability was taken as proof that Panamá was not endangered by earthquakes and was a conclusive argument for building the Canal here instead of in Nicaragua. Av. A.

Presidential Palace (La Presidencia) – The president's palace is the most striking building in Panamá City. Its main attractions are the gardens and fountains in its internal courtyard, where a flock of heron holds court for visitors. Tours of the palace are available. Av. Norte.

Indian Market (Mercado de los Indios) – An open-air market full of color, with handcrafted articles of all descriptions, including the distinctive appliquéd *mola* shirts made by the Cuna Indians of the San Blas Islands. Weavings, leatherwork, and jewelry can be purchased here, too. Bargaining is expected and is usually fun. Nearby are the fishermen's wharves. It's a fine place to go with a camera. Av. Norte.

Independence Plaza (Plaza Independencia) – This main square of colonial Panamá City is the site of the cathedral that, with its mother-of-pearl twin towers, took 108 years to complete. The Archbishop's Palace, now a university, and the Central Post Office, headquarters for the French attempt to cut a canal through the Isthmus, also front the square. Av. Central.

Church of San José (Iglesia de San José) – This church houses one of the greatest treasures of Panamá and of all Central America — its magnificently convoluted gold baroque altar, the only gold in the first Panamá City (Panamá Viejo, or Old Panamá) that escaped the pirate horde of Henry Morgan in 1671. It was saved by a monk, who painted it black, and by the citizenry, who protected the ruse. Calle 8a, just beyond the cathedral.

Salsipuedes District – This section, whose name means "get out if you can," is an area of narrow streets crammed with vendors who will sell you anything, including a deed to the Canal. It is just outside colonial Panamá in the older commercial section, where the Panamanians do their shopping. This is a particularly good place to visit at lunchtime, for it has many good Chinese restaurants of unassuming decor, moderate price, and excellent quality. Just off Av. Central. The largest camera and electronics stores are along Central Ave. and President Kennedy Ave.

Balboa Monument – In suitably heroic style, this marble monument depicts the discovery of the Pacific Ocean by Balboa in 1513. Then he stood "silent upon a peak in Darien." Now he stands just as silently upon a globe supported by representatives of the four races of man. The monument also offers a good view of the bay. Av. Balboa.

Museum of the Panamanian Man – Pre-Columbian gold, relics of the Spanish occupation, displays covering archaeology and ethnography of the many tribes that inhabited the isthmus. Best museum in town. Open Tuesdays to Saturdays, 10 AM to

3:30 PM and Sundays 3 to 6 PM; closed Mondays. Plaza 5 de Mayo at Av. 7 Central (phone: 62-0415).

Bridge of the Americas (Puente de las Américas) – Honors the American engineer George Washington Goethals, who is also commemorated in the steel latticework of the Goethals Bridge connecting New Jersey to Staten Island, this mile-long span joins the Pacific end of the Panamá Canal. From it, there is a great view of the Canal, the Canal Zone, Panamá City, and the offshore staging area where ships await their turn to make the 8-hour voyage to the Atlantic Ocean. If asked, taxi drivers will stop at scenic overlooks at either end of the span. Av. Amador.

CANAL ZONE

Panamá Canal – It is unthinkable to visit Panamá City without seeing the "Big Ditch," one of the certifiable wonders of the modern world. First suggested by the Spanish in 1524, the Canal remained a dream for almost four centuries. It was first attempted by the French hero of the Suez Canal, Ferdinand Marie de Lesseps. Two decades and tens of thousands of lives later, de Lesseps gave up in the wake of a political scandal that rocked France. It was the Americans in the era of Theodore Roosevelt's Big Stick diplomacy who finally joined the oceans with a 57-mile (90-km) canal that rises and descends 85 feet through six sets of locks to cross the rocky backbone of the Americas. In the course of building the Canal, the scourges of the tropics, malaria and yellow fever, were also conquered. The Canal and the 5-mile (8-km) strip on each side of it were ceded to the US "in perpetuity" by the 1903 treaty under which it was built. In the year 2000, the Canal will revert to Panamá.

There are a number of ways to see the Canal, including a package tour, rental car, railroad, and boat. In the 1920s, one man swam it. It cost him 36¢ in tolls, which are based on weight. The railroad was completed in 1855 to carry '49ers to California and was the first "transcontinental" rail link. It leaves from the Frangipani Street Station, takes 90 minutes to cross the isthmus, and costs $2, a considerable comedown from the 1855 fare of $25. Buses cost 40¢ and leave frequently from the bus terminal at Shaler Plaza. It's a 15-minute walk from the bus stop to the Miraflores locks, where bleachers have been set up for spectators. Otherwise, rent a car or check with your hotel desk. Every tourist hotel offers transportation to the Canal. A tour boat trip takes 8 hours one way.

Balboa – The chief city of the former Canal Zone, Balboa is not so much a city as an American suburb, homogenized, manicured, air-conditioned, and all but hermetically sealed from the Latin disorder and passion that seethes along its borders. Although no longer strictly American property, it retains its character and most of its gringo population. If you have been too long on the road and need a fix of supermarkets and stainless steel cafeterias, Balboa is a good stop. Or ask for the army base and Balboa Yacht Club, underneath which is a wonderfully lazy gringo bar filled with characters straight out of Jimmy Buffet lyrics. Av. de los Martires and Av. Balboa.

Taboga – This would be an unspoiled island paradise except for the heavy tourist traffic, for there are no cars and no pollution. It does have fragrant blossoms (Taboga is also called the "Island of Flowers"); beautiful beaches; good snorkeling, skin diving, and water skiing; delicious, juicy, ripe mangoes (best eaten in a bathtub or while wearing a raincoat) and pineapples; and *ceviche* (corvina, or sea bass, marinated in lime juice), a perfect accompaniment to a cold brew. There are two hotels, the *Taboga* (phone: 23-8521) and the *Chu* (phone: Taboga 35), both inexpensive and small. Water taxis called *pangas* provide transportation around the island. Boats leave from Pier 18 in the Canal Zone. There is a regular daily schedule except on Wednesdays, and the fare is $2 each way. For a tour, call *Argo Tours,* Calle 53 (phone 23-72-79). *Panamá Tours* runs a launch that leaves daily at 7:30 AM from Pier 18 (phone: 64-7433). For more information, contact the tourist office (phone: 26-7000).

OUT OF TOWN

Old Panamá (Panamá Viejo) – This is the original city founded in 1519 by Pedrarias the Cruel, who moved the provincial capital here from the Atlantic coast because of the drier, healthier climate. It was destroyed in 1671 by as ruthless a band of pirates as ever swashed a buckle. The city was rebuilt on a more defensible location farther west. What is left are the moss-covered remains of churches and residences, including the old Church of San José, which contained the golden altar now in colonial Panamá's church of the same name. There are a stone bell tower and the ruins of the city's cathedral along with what is left of treasury houses and government buildings. The King's Bridge, which was the beginning of the mission trail known as El Camino Real, a muddy track that crossed the Isthmus and was the most important road in the Spanish empire, still stands. Over this bridge marched the gold- and silver-laden mule trains and their escorts of halberd-clad Spanish soldiers. You can also see the dungeons built low in the city walls, where rising tides drowned prisoners. The area has been restored to a state of studied, moss-enshrouded ruin by the Panamá Tourist Authority. A taxi will take you there for about $2. For a little extra, the cabbie will stop en route at the Justo Arosemena Institute Zoo and at La Cresta, a hill that offers a good view of the ocean and the bay. Vía Cincuentenario.

Pacific Beaches – So many people get intoxicated by the gambling and nightlife of Panamá City that the beaches are still relatively uncrowded and unspoiled. Your best bet is to rent a car from one of the agencies and get a map from the Institute of Tourism in the *El Panamá Hilton,* Vía España (phone: 64-4000). Several hotels and clubs on the ocean open their facilities to day tourists — these have the best beaches. The loveliest of all is the *Coronado Beach,* with a golf course, restaurant, and villas. Call ahead and you will be welcomed (phone: 23-1342). Other beachfront hotels are the *Su Lin* in Campana (phone: 62-0372); *Motel Punta Chame* in Punta Chame (phone: 23-1747); and the *El Palmar* (phone: 23-7685) and *Río Mar* (phone: 64-2272) in San Carlos.

■**EXTRA SPECIAL:** The Pearl Island archipelago 35 miles south of Panamá City was Balboa's base for his explorations of the Pacific coast. Once the source of a wealth of pearls, the islands now offer excellent snorkeling, water skiing, sailing, skin diving, and fishing. There are more than 300 islands in the chain, and you can get to the principal ones by a 20-minute flight from Paitilla Airport or by tour boat. The gem of the Pearls is Contadora (which means "cashier" or "numberer"), where pearls were counted before being shipped to the king of Spain. This island paradise was the retreat of the late Shah of Iran and most recently the site of the Contadora peace conference. It is 2 miles square and is the home of the *Contadora Resort & Casino,* which includes 210 rooms, golf course, tennis courts, restaurants, and bars. The island has 13 beaches, all of them free of clutter, human and otherwise. Round-trip air fare is about $30, and boat excursions run about $15. For air information, call Aerolíneas Islas de Las Perlas (phone: 64-2906); air departures are from Paitilla Airport.

SOURCES AND RESOURCES

TOURIST INFORMATION: The Panamá Institute of Tourism, in the Convention Center (ATLAPA) across from the *Marriott* on Via España (phone: 26-7000), has excellent city maps and the best English-language guides. Basic information is provided at the information stand at Tocumen Airport.

Open from 9 AM to 4 PM daily except Sundays. *Focus on Panamá* and *Panama 2000,* available from the Institute of Tourism, are the best English-language guides.

Local Coverage – The *Panamá American* and the *Panamá Star Herald,* both morning dailies, contain English-language news and are available at hotel desks.

Food – An updated listing of restaurants is supplied by the Institute of Tourism. It does not list prices.

CLIMATE AND CLOTHES: Tourist literature advertises the climate as "pleasantly tropical . . . from 73° to 81°F (22° to 35°C) in coastal areas. Nights are generally cool." Don't bet on it. Panamá City's weather runs hot and muggy, with temperatures into the 90s F (30s C), which matches the humidity during the rainy season (from April to December), when it rains daily, but usually for brief periods (annual precipitation of 65 inches). The dry season is hot but uniformly sunny and generally comfortable. Dress for the tropics, casually, and in light cottons. In the rainy season, bring along a raincoat and umbrella. Synthetics are fashionable but will be uncomfortable in the outdoor heat. At night, casual is the rule, although a tie and jacket is appropriate in the best restaurants. Neither ties nor jackets are required in casinos. Women may find a sweater or shawl a good way to fight the air conditioning in theaters, restaurants, and nightclubs in the evening.

GETTING AROUND: Bus – Latin America's most picturesque — gaudily painted, hung with fringe, wrapped with Day-Glo vinyl, armed with air horns, and festooned with windshields that look like a cross between a religious gift store and a naughty postcard stand. More crowded than the winner's locker room after the Super Bowl, they would give claustrophobia to all but veterans of the Tokyo subways. Good fun for the adventurous and well worth the unbelievably low price of admission for those addicted to the best in local color, but definitely not for the fainthearted. The bus system goes everywhere.

Taxi – The best bets for getting from place to place are the flocks of battered taxis with no meters that roam the streets and hover around hotel entrances. Fares start at $1 and are governed by a zone system. There are two brands of taxi: big taxis and little taxis. They are priced according to the taxi's size and zone and are very reasonable. You can get most places in the city for $5. Cabbies almost universally speak English and will gladly hire out by the day. They are also a good source of information on nightclubs and know every prostitute in the city. Getting to outlying tourist attractions is easiest by taxi. An hourly rate is negotiable. Because of street crime, it is unwise to walk the streets at night, particularly downtown.

Most people enter Panamá at Omar Torrijos Airport, a modern facility 18 miles (29 km) from downtown. It is a 50¢ bus ride, $10 by cab. If you are willing to share a ride, the fare can go down to $5.

Car Rental – Driving in Panamá City can be fun for the daring or torture for the timid. *Avis* (phone: 66-2360), *Budget* (phone: 66-7527), *Dollar* (phone: 20-0663), *Hertz* (phone: 66-1896), and *National* (phone: 66-0144) are represented at the airport and in the lobbies of the major hotels.

MUSEUMS: The Museum of Panamanian Man and the ruins of Old Panamá are described in *Special Places.* Other interesting museums are:

Panamá History Museum (Museo Historia de Panamá) – Plaza de la Independencia Antiguo Palacio Municipal (phone: 22-1353).

Museum of Contemporary Art (Museo de Arte Contemporaneo) – Features exhibits by 20th-century artists. In the former Canal Zone.

Museum of Colonial Religious Art (Museo de Arte Religiosa Colonial) – At the ruins of Santo Domingo Church, Av. A (phone: 22-8154).

SHOPPING: Panamá City is called "the Hong Kong of North America." Prices are no lower than in other free ports, such as the US Virgin Islands, but they're no higher either. Camera prices are actually higher than at discount outlets in New York City. Still, if only for the number of stores and the quantity and variety of merchandise, it is a good shopping stop. Duty-free goods must be paid for at the store and picked up at the airport on your way out of the country. Regulations do not allow you to open your purchases until you and they are on the airplane; however, the head of customs in the airport will allow you to open and reseal any packages in his presence to make sure you got what you bought. Free port shops are extremely honest and reliable in making deliveries.

The main articles of trade are perfumes, cameras, projectors, electronic goods, radios, lace, watches, china, chess and backgammon sets, and Oriental art. The main shopping area is along the Vía España. Other stores, especially camera and electronics stores, can be found along Avenida Central and Avenida de los Martires. All the major hotels have shopping areas, too. You can bargain in most places.

For distinctive shirts, weavings, baskets, wicker, soapstone figures, necklaces, beaded collars, leather goods, straw, wooden figurines, ceramics, and the distinctive appliquéd *mola* fabrics, visit the *Public Market* (*Mercado Público*) on Avenida Norte at the waterfront and the *Salsipuedes* open-air bazaar off Avenida Central (see *Special Places*). Offer half the stated price and try to meet somewhere in the middle. Those who want to purchase an authentic Panama hat will be disappointed. What we've come to know as a Panama hat is actually made in Ecuador, though the Panamanians make a very durable straw hat of their own, called a *pintado.*

Handicrafts of a more uniform quality, with predictably higher prices, can be purchased from *Artesanías Nacionales,* the government-run cooperatives for native artisans.

Major US credit cards are cheerfully accepted everywhere except in the open-air markets.

 SPECIAL EVENTS: *Carnival* begins the Friday before Lent and ends on Ash Wednesday. There is dancing in the streets, colorful costumes, all-night parties, and general revelry. The *Folkloric Ballet* features native folk dances and costumes and performs during February and March at Panamá Viejo. Panamá's *Independence Day Festival* is August 15. The *Underwater Fishing Tournament* takes place every year in April or May. The *International Fishing Tournament* draws anglers from all over the world and generally produces a world record or two during its August–October run. Check with your hotel or the Institute of Tourism.

 SPORTS: Panamá has just about every major outdoor athletic activity — from baseball and soccer to deep-sea fishing.

Baseball – Panamá's representatives to major league baseball include Rod Carew, Omar Moreno, and Manny Sanguillen. A lively Winter League runs from December through February, drawing its participants from US major and minor leagues and local talent. It's like watching spring training. Games are played at *Estadio Juan de Arosemena,* Curundu section.

Boxing – Panamá has given the world as many as four international champions. They mix it up regularly at the *Gimnasio Nuevo Panamá,* a huge outdoor stadium near the airport (no phone).

Cockfights – Take place every Saturday and Sunday from May through November at the *Club Gallistico,* Vía España. Monday fights are added for the main tourist season, from December through April.

Fishing – Panamá is an Indian name meaning "place where many fish are taken" and is the black marlin capital of the world. More than 40 world records have been taken in Panamá's waters. Boat charters can be arranged through your hotel. Also, try *Club Pacifico* on Coiba Island (phone: 64-5010) or *Tropic Star Lodge* at Piñas Bay in southeastern Panamá (phone: 64-6793). Lists of boats for hire are available at the Institute of Tourism, Vía España 124 (phone: 64-4000), or at the branch office in the *El Panamá Hilton.*.

Golf – At the *Panamá Golf Course,* Caraquilla (phone: 24-9969), and at the *Coronado Beach Golf Club* (phone: 23-3175). There is a nine-hole par-three course at the *Contadora* hotel (phone: 25-16-40). International tournaments are played at *Club de Golf de Panamá,* Cerro Viento (phone: 66-7777).

Horse Racing – Many of the world's top jockeys were either born or trained in Panamá, so the citizens take the sport seriously. Races take place on Saturdays, Sundays, and holidays at the *Hipodromo Presidente Ramón,* Vía José A. Arango (phone: 24-1600). Pari-mutuel betting is available.

Hunting – Wild boar, tapir, jaguar, and puma can be hunted in the interior. Contact *Tropic Star* (phone: 64-6793).

Snorkeling and Scuba – Scuba diving excursions can be arranged through *Isla Grande Resort* in the San Blas Islands. Bring your own regulator and vest (phone: 64-5010). Snorkeling, skin diving, and water skiing are available at Taboga Island and Contadora Island.

Soccer – Played at *Estadio Revolución,* near the airport. The game in the stands is sometimes more exciting than the one on the field. Check at your hotel for a schedule.

Swimming – Most hotels have swimming pools, and there are plenty of beaches.

Tennis – At most major hotels.

 THEATER: The wonderfully neoclassical *National Theater,* in Colonial Panamá, periodically hosts performances — although odds are that unless it's the *Folkloric Ballet,* it is not really worth the time. Check with the tourist office for events. Calle 2a (cq) (phone: 22-2302). The newspapers contain addresses of the movie theaters. All English movies are shown with Spanish subtitles.

 MUSIC: The *National Symphony* is best left to itself. Outdoor concerts are held in Plaza Santa Ana on Thursdays and on Sundays, in Parque Cathedral. There are outdoor dances and folkloric music shows at Panamá Viejo's ruins during February and March. Check at your hotel for schedules or ask at the tourist office.

 NIGHTCLUBS AND NIGHTLIFE: This is Panamá City's specialty; the beat goes on all night. There are dancing and floor shows at the following: *El Continental* hotel, where a mighty Wurlitzer organ accompanies a light show nightly in the *El Sótano* nightclub, Vía España (phone: 64-6666); *Las Tinajas,* where women turned out in festival dress, dripping with gold combs and jewelry, and men topped with a straw hat (a *pintado*) perform *el punto,* the traditional Panamanian dance, Calle 51, Bella Vista (phone: 63-7890); *Holiday Inn,* Vía Italia and Winston Churchill at Punta Paitilla (phone: 69-1122); *Club Windsor,* Av. Nacional (no phone); *21 Club,* Vía España (no phone); *Playboy Club,* Calle 55 (no phone); *El Bon Ton,* Río Abajo (no phone); *El Criollo,* Villa María, Juan Diaz (phone: 21-1282); *Maxim's,* Calle 48 Sur, near Vía España (phone: 64-9047); and *Camelot,* Río Abajo (no phone). Discotheques are an ephemeral breed that go boom and bust, so check local listings, but some to look for are: *Cactus,* Vía El Dorado; *Las Molas,* Los Angeles section C-41, near the Chase Manhattan Bank (phone: 60-2291); and *La Fiesta,* in a beached cruise boat next to the *Holiday Inn* (phone: 69-1122).

Casinos are government-operated and honest. There is a $1 minimum bet and no tax on winnings. Slot machines, roulette, poker, blackjack, baccarat, craps, and a spin-the-wheel game called jackpot are available. There are casinos in the following hotels: *Holiday Inn, Continental, Granada, Monteserin, Gran Lux, Soloy,* and at the airport.

 SINS: If you're male, there's usually local talent hanging around the hotel lobby; if not, take a walk on the Vía España at night; sin will find you. (If you're female, you can find a companion just about anywhere.) If you want the latest and the hottest of sin bins, ask your cabbie and pay him a little extra to wait around outside for you. Try whetting your *lust* at one of the strip-tease joints: *Ancón Inn,* Av. 4 de Julio, Calle 5, and Av. de los Martires (phone: 62-0451) or *Taverna Don Quixote,* Av. 7 España, Vía Porres (phone: 23-7036). *Slothfully* sun yourself on the nearby beaches and be sure to visit the *pride* of Panamá: the Canal.

BEST IN TOWN

 CHECKING IN: Panamá City has always been a place to spend the night and have a drink or two, and there is no shortage of places in which to do that, although hotel rooms have become very costly. The city has more than 3,000 hotel rooms — as many as Atlanta, Georgia, and more than other Latin American cities twice its size.

Panamá City is one of the most expensive cities in Latin America. Expect to pay $90 and up for a double room in hotels rated expensive; from $40 to $70 in moderate; and under $30 in inexpensive. Major credit cards are accepted in all but the most inexpensive hotels.

Contadora Resort and Casino – There are 150 rooms and 60 cabanas in this sleek, rustic get-away in the Pearl Island archipelago. Only 20 air minutes from Panamá City's Paitilla Airport are 13 hassle-free beaches, Sunfish sailboats, deep-sea fishing, tennis, a par-3 golf course, swimming pools, a casino, bars, and restaurants. Contadora Island (phone: 27-0033). Expensive.

El Continental – It has 240 rooms, a shopping arcade, a bar, six dining rooms, lounges, international shows, a casino, and a terrazzo lobby. Vía España (phone: 64-6666). Expensive.

El Ejecutivo – A 96-room hotel catering to business people, it is well priced and suitable for travelers without expense accounts. It has a pool, sundeck, and bar but no casino. Rooms have direct-dial phones, divan beds, and desks with swivel chairs. Calles 52 and Aquilino de la Guardia (phone: 64-3333). Expensive.

Granada – A nice, medium-sized, 165-room hotel with a small pool, casino, intimate bar, coffee shop, and a location from which you can safely walk to the diversions of the more expensive hostelries nearby without paying their room rates. Calle Eusebio A. Morales, one block off the Vía España (phone: 64-4900). Expensive.

Marriott Caesar Park – Adjoining the ATLAPA Convention Center, this new 18-story hotel has 400 rooms near the ocean, a good view from the top-floor restaurant-lounge, and fine interior décor. It also has a casino, pool, tennis courts, and several choices of restaurants. Vía Israel (phone: 26-4077). Expensive.

Panamá Holiday Inn – The only oceanfront hotel in the city proper, this 20-story, 274-room, round tower has a lofty vista of the bay and Panamá City. Ask for a bayside room, however, or you may end up with a stunning view of the *Dairy Queen* and technical high school. It is vintage *Holiday Inn,* except for the mirrored casino-in-the-round, with its incredibly massive chandelier, a frivolity rarely found stateside. All rooms are air conditioned and have phones. Features include a pool, tennis courts, a lobby coffee shop, and the roof-top restaurant, *Belvedere.* Vía Italia and Winston Churchill at Punta Paitilla (phone: 69-1122). Expensive.

Caribe – Probably the best of the budget hotels, it has 163 air-conditioned rooms, a good dining room, and a lounge. It also has good service and is excellently located for shoppers. Av. Perú and Calle 28 (phone: 25-0404). Moderate.

Gran Hotel Soloy – This well-situated, 200-room tower has direct-dial telephones and color TV in every room. It also has a bar, restaurants, casino, and a really fine view of the city and the Canal from the top floor. One of the better bets in the city. Av. Perú and Calle 30 (phone: 27-1133). Moderate.

Central – The city's funkiest and architecturally most interesting hotel. What this 143-room relic lacks in convenience it makes up for in charm. In the heart of the colonial city, it has a restaurant, bar, and coffee shop. A good choice for the budget traveler. Plaza Independencia (phone: 22-6068). Inexpensive.

Colonial – Another old hotel in the colonial city with the bare essentials, great prices, and a good personality, it does have a pool, a bar, and a restaurant, although not of the luxurious variety. Plaza Bolívar (phone: 22-9311). Inexpensive.

EATING OUT: Panamá is a polyglot city with a hedonistic atmosphere, and eating out is almost a national pastime. Meals range from the simplicity, tang, and culinary adventure of pushcart vendors (scenic but rarely sanitary) to elaborate candlelit dining rooms. The quality is generally good, particularly in the moderate-price range, where competition is keenest. Seafood, the national specialty, reflects the Spanish influence and is usually excellent. The melting-pot nature of the city is reflected in good Italian, French, Chinese, and other cuisines. Although it is hard to find the really cheap meals that characterize other Latin American cities, the average meal still costs less than its US equivalent. A bill of fare is ordinarily posted at the door. For a gastronomic adventure, try walking into a restaurant that looks as if it would never be listed in a travel guide and ask for the specialty of the house. You will probably be pleasantly surprised. Panamanian beers — Panamá or Soberna (both light), or the hearty Balboa — are very good. Avoid the local rum. Instead, try Haitian Barbancourt or Dominican Bermudez, both among the best rums made.

It costs more than $30 for dinner for two in those restaurants we've classified as expensive, including those in the top hotels. Expect to pay between $20 and $30 at those places in the moderate category; under $20, inexpensive. Prices do not include drinks, wine, or tips. Major US credit cards are honored at all but the inexpensive restaurants.

Sarti – This piece of Italy in the tropics has a pleasing atmosphere, good food, and fine service. Try the *fettucine al pesto* or any of the excellent veal dishes. Open daily. Reservations a must. Calle Ricardo Arias (phone: 23-8275). Expensive.

Le Trianon – The best restaurant in town, with a fine international menu. In the *Marriott Caesar Park* next door to the ATLAPA Convention Center. Via Israel (phone: 69-1122). Expensive.

Bohio Turístico – Serves both Continental and local specialties, with an emphasis on seafood. There is live music every evening. Next to the Morelos statue in Old Panamá. Via Cuncuentenario (phone: 26-5166). Moderate.

La Casa del Marisco – Seafood cooked Panamanian style; try the eel and squid. Open daily. No reservations. Av. Balboa (phone: 23-7755). Moderate.

Granada – The Spanish decor looks as if it came out of a bottle, but the food is reasonably priced and the restaurant is very popular with locals. Open daily. Reservations advised. Calle Eusebia A. Morales (phone: 64-4900). Moderate.

Gran China – Despite the paper lanterns and embossed felt wallpaper, the food is exceptionally good and the service fine. Open daily. No reservations. Av. Balboa (phone 25-0533). Moderate.

Matsuei – Long a stronghold of Chinese cuisine, several Japanese restaurants have recently opened in Panamá City. This one is patronized by local Japanese businessmen and specializes in Japanese fish dishes. Reservations recommended. Av. Eusebio A. Morales A-12 (phone: 64-9547). Moderate.

El Pez de Oro – "The Golden Fish" serves seafood Peruvian style in a pleasant atmosphere. Try the red snapper. Open daily. No reservations. No credit cards. Via Italia Punta Paitilla, Centro Commercial, Bal Harbor (phone: 64-9528). Moderate.

Las Tinajas – The place to experience both typical Panamanian fare and the country's lively folkloric dancing. Appetizers like *carimañolas* (yucca croquets), *patacones* (green mashed plantains), *bollo* (corn timbals), and *ceviche,* are followed by plates piled high with chicken and pork, seafood and shellfish. Several nights a week elegant ladies and dashing gentlemen perform the traditional *punto* on a tiny stage to the delight of all. Calle 51, Bella Vista (phone: 63-7890). Moderate.

Palacio Rey Kung – A new addition to the city's long list of Chinese eateries. Go for the *dim sum.* Open daily. Vía España (phone: 69-0956). Moderate to inexpensive.

El Dragón de Oro – As you would expect from the name, this is a Chinese restaurant where meals are filling, plentiful, and cheap. It is one of the city's best food values. Open daily. No reservations. No credit cards. Vía España (phone: 23-5719). Inexpensive.

Napoli – Not strictly Italian, but definitely one of the better bargains in Panamá City. Food is plentiful, good, and the owner is said to have a pathological dislike for raising his prices. Calle Estudiante (no phone). Inexpensive.

Panamar – Serves very good Panamanian seafood specialties in a pleasant, open-air dockside setting. Ask for whatever was caught fresh that day prepared in the local style. Open daily. No reservations. No credit cards. Calle 50 (phone: 26-0892). Inexpensive.

VFW – In the Canal Zone, this place serves three hot dogs (stadium variety) smothered in sauerkraut with pickles, relish, mustard, a bag of gringo potato chips, and three or four frosty mugs of draft beer for under $4. You can eat in shaded indolence while watching the ships glide through the mouth of the Panamá Canal. Open daily. No reservations. No credit cards. On the US Army Base, Balboa (no phone). Inexpensive.

QUITO

When the Spanish conquistadores arrived in the heart of Ecuador's Central Valley in the beginning of the sixteenth century, they discovered Quito, today the capital, then the seat of government of the northern half of the Inca empire, governed by Atahualpa. When Atahualpa was killed by Francisco Pizarro in the land south of present Ecuador that is now Perú, Atahualpa's general, Rumiñahui (whose name meant "face of stone") continued the battle and literally razed Quito in 1534. After destroying the last vestiges of Inca resistance, the Spanish rebuilt the city, constructing homes over Inca foundations and building resplendent colonial cathedrals in the stubborn, inhospitable Andes.

Although Quito retains many Spanish colonial buildings and considers itself the center of aristocratic Hispanic culture in Ecuador to this day, its roots go even deeper into the past than the relatively recent Inca civilization. And the pattern of destruction and reconstruction by both man-made and natural forces recurs throughout its recorded history.

More than 5,000 years ago, primitive hunters settled in a sheltered nook of the Andes at the foot of Pichincha volcano, on the site of what is today a modern housing development not far from Quito's Mariscal Sucre International Airport. It was the beginning of one of South America's earliest and most successful civilizations, the Cotocollao kingdom, which survived in the same area for the next 2,000 years, only to be replaced by successive Indian communities that culminated in the fabulous Inca empire. The Incas were discovered, defeated, and then destroyed by the Spanish, who in 1563 made the rebuilt city of Quito the seat of the royal audiencia, a judicial subdivision of colonial rule. But colonial rule proved no more secure than any of the earlier civilizations, and in August 1809 the first sparks of the anti-Spanish rebellion were struck in Quito. Some 13 years later, the final battle of the Independence War, the Battle of Pichincha, was fought on the mountain's slopes. Marshal Antonio Sucre led the fight, defeating General Melchor Aymerich on May 24, 1822, a date that has since become a national holiday.

Culturally and physically, modern Quito is a product of the eighteenth century, when the city reigned as a colonial capital. Now, 200 years later, the heart of colonial Quito is still largely untouched, with dignified colonial buildings, superb religious art, and beautiful Spanish architecture. It has been called "the Florence of the Americas," and its colonial treasures of art and architecture earned Quito a place on the UNESCO list of World Cultural Heritage Sites. Modern development is contained by strict conservation laws aimed at preserving the rich legacy of the past.

Standing at 13' south of the equator (about 15 miles) and at an altitude of 9,350 feet, Quito's incomparable position between the only two Andean mountain ranges in Ecuador (the Cordillera Central and Cordillera Occidental) has been the major factor in its independence and self-determination. In the distance glow the snow-covered peaks of the Andes — of Cotopaxi, the world's highest active volcano (at 19,347 feet), and Cayambe, both of which are usually visible from the city on a clear, bright, day, especially during the mornings. It is easy to understand the religious awe in which the conquistadores held this part of the world, where mountains are sculpted into vast panoramas and the very air seems to give objects far and near an animation slightly supernatural.

Quito has a population of over a million, about an eighth of Ecuador's national total, and though it is the capital, it is not the largest or the richest city in the country. That honor belongs to Guayaquil, on the Pacific coast, an astounding 12-hour train ride (or 30-minute flight) from Quito. While the city may lack industrial clout, it has so far held most of the political reins and certainly, in its mountain isolation, is one of the continent's loveliest cities.

With adequate room to grow, the heritage of different ages and cultures coexists in Quito without noticeable strain. You will find supermarket chains and dawn street markets. Color televisions carry US network news, but Quechua, the language of the Incas, is heard in the streets. Since 1972, the Ecuadorian economy began booming a bit because of the oil discovery that brought a concomitant expansion of the middle class. The wealthier sectors of Quito are steadily expanding northward, and a contemporary Andean architecture has developed, using plenty of airy arches, big windows, open patios, and split-levels in homes designed for affluent *quiteño* families.

Between the newer residential districts and the old city spreads a mixed area, surrounding the El Ejido and Alameda parks and the Avenida Amazonas shopping district. Its pretty nineteenth- and early-twentieth-century houses stand beside modern office and apartment blocks, hotels, stores, and restaurants. Smaller houses, painted pink and blue, are scattered across encircling hillsides.

Along with other Latin American countries, Ecuador now has a heavy foreign debt, a huge budget deficit, and lots of other economic problems. There is poverty in Quito, but there are few of the rambling shantytowns common to so many South American cities. For now, the city lacks many of the social and political tensions that tend to breed violence, and the scene remains safe and conservative on the surface. While walking at night on the Panecillo Hill is not recommended, it probably would never occur to a visitor to do so.

So if you follow common-sense guidelines, you'll find this a comfortable, relaxed city with squares and parks that sparkle with flowers. The *quiteños'* town pride reaches a climax during the November *Minga,* a tradition dating from Inca times, when everyone joins in a day of weeding, painting, scrubbing, dirt-clearing, and general cleaning in preparation for the annual fiestas. The first week of December is a time of fireworks, masks, parades, partying from bar to bar, and bullfights. Drinking and dancing in the streets culminate in the *Amazonazo,* a packed procession of mad dancers and bands along Avenida Amazonas that lasts through the night and leaves most participants in a state of total collapse the next day. It is a time when friendships can be made more spontaneously than usual because the *quiteños'* normal reserve toward foreigners dissolves in the general merriment. But the 2 or 3 weeks before the pre-Lent Carnival tend to be more chaotic than enjoyable, with buckets and balloons full of icy water occasionally hurling down on unsuspecting pedestrians from passing cars and second-floor windows with infuriating accuracy.

However, Quito is a lovely city to visit almost any time. The residents complain of the telephone and postal service (with reason), and the bureaucracy operates with expected inefficiency. If you find yourself getting impatient, remember that different ages come together in Quito, and the twentieth is not the dominant century here. You will enjoy the atmosphere and visual pleasures of bygone times — particularly well preserved in this city that takes care to preserve its heritage. It is a place to be explored at a leisurely pace, a place to experience colonial South America and the ghosts of Indian civilizations.

QUITO AT-A-GLANCE

SEEING THE CITY: The Panecillo (Breadloaf) Hill, on the southern side of the old city, offers a sweeping view of the red roofs, cobbled plazas, and winding streets below and the rugged Andes ranges surrounding Quito. On a clear day, you can see the volcano Cotopaxi. Now topped by an unappealing statue of the Virgen de Quito, the Panecillo Hill is thought to have been reshaped by the Incas as a monument to the sun god. The bus marked Mitad del Mundo–Panecillo will take you to the top. On the hill, the *Panecillo* restaurant has a good terrace from which you can watch the daytime bustle of the town and a panoramic window through which the city lights glitter at night. Restaurant hours are erratic, so it's best to call in advance; the food is mediocre (phone: 51-72-77).

SPECIAL PLACES: At the foot of the Panecillo spread some of the oldest streets of the city. Crossing the Avenida Veinticuatro (24) de Mayo, with its open-air markets where red crabs and roast guinea-pig are among the snacks sold from stalls, you come to Calle Morales, known as La Ronda because the rounds of singers and serenaders used to gather here. Through a half-closed eye it still seems to be the 1500s: Flower-laden balconies almost meet overhead, and the soft light from old iron lamps makes you expect the sounds of spurs and hoofs on the cobblestones.

THE OLD CITY

Plaza San Francisco – Three blocks from La Ronda stands the wide Plaza San Francisco, named for the magnificent San Francisco Church and Convent. Founded in 1536, the church is the oldest in South America and is considered one of the world's masterpieces of baroque art. Every inch of wall and ceiling is painted or covered with gold leaf. Its ornate altars are especially sumptuous. But its richness of decoration is only surpassed by La Compañía Church, two blocks east. The museum in the convent is packed with art from the 16th to the 18th century. Paintings, sculpture, and more outstanding carvings can be seen in the Cantuna Chapel (*capilla*). Open daily. Free. Calles Cuenca, Bolívar, Benalcazar, and Sucre.

Plaza Santo Domingo – Head east along Calle Bolívar and you will come to this busy square, named for another of Quito's 86 exquisite churches filled with fine religious sculpture. The road to the southeast has a carved stone arch that really does join the houses over your head. Calles Rocafuerte, Flores, Bolívar, and Guayaquil.

Plaza Independencia – The real center of the old city, this square is flanked by the Presidential Palace on the west; the Cathedral, to the south. The new city administration building, completed in 1978 to replace one that was irreparably crumbling, has been designed to blend with the surrounding architecture. Careful restorations have been made on the archbishop's palace on the north side. A small shopping precinct has been included in the tasteful modernization. The Presidential Palace is, itself, another odd mixture of architectural forms: The palace guard's 18th-century blue, red, and gold shakoes and uniforms obviously contrast with their modern automatic rifles, put to good use in repelling an attempted coup in September 1976. Most battle scars were repaired immediately, but a few bullet pockmarks are still visible on the cathedral walls. Built into the basement level of the palace is a row of small stores selling carvings, Panama hats, postcards, and handicrafts. Calles Espejo, Venezuela, Chile, and Garcia Moreno.

St. Augustine Church and Monastery (Iglesia y Monasterio de San Agustín) – The only way to enjoy the center of Quito is by walking (parking is impossible in the narrow streets). A one-block stroll along Calle Chile from Plaza Independencia brings you to the San Agustín Church and its monastery. Inside is a silent, flower-filled patio and colonnaded cloisters, with robed monks pacing between oils by master painter Miguel de Santiago, who spent most of his life in the monastery illustrating the life of St. Augustine. The third floor of one wing is now occupied by the restoration workshops of the Cultural Heritage Institute. Open daily except Mondays. Free. Calles Chile and Guayaquil.

La Compañía – Richly ornate both outside and in, this 16th-century cathedral is a masterpiece of Baroque and *Quiteño*-colonial art. In fact, it is one of the most splendid churches in Latin America. Open daily, 10 to 11 AM and 1 to 6 PM. Calle García Moreno, one block from Plaza Independencia.

San Diego Convent – A newly restored Franciscan convent of the 17th century, now serving as a museum while remaining a cloister. Open Tuesdays through Sundays, 9 AM to 1 PM and 2 to 5 PM.

THE NEW CITY

Central Bank Museum (Museo del Banco Central) – Actually, the Central Bank has two museums. Their most valuable treasure is a painting with a frame of precious stones and gold valued at more than $10 million. It rarely leaves the deepest vault. But you will find a well-laid-out display of the finest items of pre-Columbian art on the fifth floor. Remember, as you gaze, that these items have been selected from the tens of thousands of pieces stored in the basements. Clay figures from coastal cultures more than 2,000 years old show strong character and witty observation of personality. Some of the delicately ornamented double-bellied jugs have spouts with air holes worked to whistle as water is poured out. Multilingual guides and display cards give clear histories and explanations, but artistically, the items speak admirably for themselves. A sixth-floor collection contains religious and colonial painting, with examples from all the great painters of the School of Quito. Whenever archaeologists discover and excavate an important site, the museum puts on a new display and presents public lectures. Open Tuesdays through Fridays, 2:30 to 5:30 PM; Saturdays and Sundays, 10:30 AM to 2 PM. Small admission fee. Av. 10 de Agosto, near the corner of Alameda Park (phone: 510-302).

Jijón y Caamaño Museum – The Catholic University houses this collection, donated in 1963 by the family of Jacinto Jijón y Caamaño, a scholarly aristocrat whose life's work digging, analyzing, and classifying pre-Columbian remains provided the basic knowledge of Ecuador's different tribes and civilizations. His own books are now valuable rarities, though new editions of some are planned. Other departments of the university provide language courses for foreigners; Quechua is taught using audiovisual labs. Open Mondays through Fridays. Small admission fee. Catholic University, Av. 12 de Octubre and Calle Robles (phone: 529-240).

Amazonas Avenue (Avenida Amazonas) – Green and cool under the tropical midday sun, El Ejido Park (Parque El Ejido) usually has dozens of Otavalo Indian families shyly picnicking under the trees. Trays on their heads, sellers of chocolate-covered doughnuts stroll around and Indian women sell *fritada, papas, y mote* — small portions of meat, potatoes, and maize. For a snack or meal without the sanitary worry, the sidewalk cafés of Avenida Amazonas start just off the north side of the park, past the city's largest hotel, the *Colón Internacional. La Fuente* and *Manolo's Churreria* are popular spots for meeting friends, sipping cold beer, or watching the passing world. The half-mile of Amazonas, now a pedestrian mall, and the surrounding streets contain some of the most useful and best-quality stores, services, and meeting and eating places in town: bookstores; international banks; travel agencies; airlines; fashion, antique, and craft stores; as well as art galleries. During the Quito Festival in December, Avenida Amazonas becomes one big open-air ballroom.

Central University (Universidad Central) – The left-wing politics of the student body here do not engender anti-American sentiment as violently as in many South American colleges. Except when some issue has boiled over into a labor strike, everyone is welcome at some conferences and at University Cinema (Cine Universitario), where films are changed frequently (sometimes, even daily). Close by, the Santa Clara market (Mercado Santa Clara) sells the best fruit, vegetables, and herbs for *quiteños* in the northern sector of the city. Six blocks from Av. Amazonas on the lower slopes of Mt. Pichincha.

SUBURBS

Hotel Inter-Continental Quito Ridge – On the other side of the city from Pichincha is the mountain pass used by Francisco de Orellana in 1542 for his expedition into the jungles that led to the discovery of the headwaters of the Amazon on his way to the Atlantic and then to Spain. (In 1977, an expedition led by another Spaniard reenacted the trek.) Orellana's road passes right by some of the choicest home sites, looking eastward to the next range and westward across the city from the ridge. The *Inter-Continental Quito* hotel is in the best spot. Opposite it are an English pub, bar, and a Chinese restaurant. Several other small clubs and restaurants are within easy walking distance. Just over the ridge and down the hill is Guapulo, a village cluster of houses and the late-17th-century Guapulo church, built by Indian slaves. Its pulpit, by the sculptor Menacho, is famed as the finest piece of carving in Quito.

Iñaquito Shopping Center (Centro Comercial Iñaquito) – Quito's answer to the American urban shopping complex is, by local standards, large and luxurious, but Lilliputian to anyone who knows the real thing. Still, the range of goods on its two floors is good: European and American tobaccos, pipes, and rolling papers at the *Admiral Nelson Smokers' Shop,* a branch of the *Favorita Supermarket; McDonald's* and other fast-food outlets; and shops selling books, clothes, toys, car accessories, records, health food, plants, and pets. The nearby *Cine Iñaquito* often has good US movies. Two other shopping centers, the *Caracol El Basque* and the *Naciones Unidas,* have joined *Iñaquito* at the same crossroads. *Dimpy* cafeterias in all the centers provide excellent coffee and good sandwiches. Av. Naciones Unidas and Av. Amazonas.

Middle of the World Marker (Mitad del Mundo) – The equator passes 15 miles (24 km) north of Quito, and a few commuters cross from one hemisphere to the other twice a day. There is a small monument commemorating this line on the road to Otavalo and another on the road going out to the large new ethnographic museum complex in the village of San Antonio. The area is exciting to explore, with volcanic craters and the ruins of Rumicucho, the site of a pre-Incan fortification. Take a tour car from any of the hotels or the bus marked Panecillo–Mitad del Mundo.

Mt. Cotopaxi – In the early Indian legends, the mountains are gods and goddesses, quarrelsome but revered. Mt. Cotopaxi's power to inspire reverence is unabated, as it majestically rears through the clouds. The mountain and surrounding stark *paramo* (moor) are now respected enough to have gained the status of a protected national park. Rent a car and head south on the Pan-American Highway; about one kilometer beyond the former NASA-station turnoff is a signposted road to Cotopaxi that leads right up to the mountain refuge. At the gates to the national park administration office are the stables for a breeding herd of llamas. Some 150 can usually be spotted at the 11,000- to 12,000-foot level. If they have very new young, the mothers scurry them away and the old males spit defensively. Otherwise, they are friendly and elegant animals. Wild horses can sometimes be seen galloping across the horizon in the distance. Car engines often give up well below the snow level, and human lungs have to work hard to take you any higher, but the cold, desolate splendor is worth it. A mountaineers' refuge just above the snow line serves as a base camp for serious climbers. Combine the drive with a trip to Saquisilí village, a half-hour away, where one of the prettiest Ecuadorian Indian markets takes place on Thursdays.

■**EXTRA SPECIAL:** There is a totally different market in Otavalo, 2 to 2½ hours north of the center of town by a speedy microbus that you can pick up at the corner of Avenida Patria and Avenida 10 de Agosto. Otavalo is a town at the center of a group of Indian villages with strong textile traditions whose work is now sold all over the continent and as far away as Europe. In addition to the well-known Saturday morning market, where you can purchase weavings (they have gotten very commercial, unfortunately, but good stuff can still be rooted out), there are squares selling food and animals. On one corner you can see dealers haggling over sacks of squeaking *cuyes,* the ubiquitous Andean guinea pigs. Watch for sellers of coral-colored beads worn by Otavalo women. Sometimes you can find bargains in fine, antique corals (see *Ecuador,* DIRECTIONS). Since the market starts before dawn on Saturdays, it is easiest to spend Friday night in Otavalo in a local hotel or hacienda (see *Ecuador,* DIRECTIONS). Advance reservations are essential.

SOURCES AND RESOURCES

TOURIST INFORMATION: For general travel assistance, the National Tourist Board, DITURIS, on the corner of Avenida Reina Victoria and Avenida Roca (phone: 239-044) is extremely helpful. Maps, guidebooks, information packets, and lists of registered guides are all free. The people in the office make great efforts to help with most unusual queries. Detailed, large-scale maps can be purchased at the Instituto Geográfico-Militar, Calle Paz y Miño (phone: 522-066).

Libri Mundi, at Calle Juan León Mera 851, and in the *Colón* hotel shopping arcade, carries virtually every publication in print on Ecuador. Outdoors people are strongly recommended to obtain *The Fool's Climbing Guide to Ecuador and Peru,* Michael Koerner (504 Willets Hill, Birmingham, MI 48009; $2) and *Backpacking in Venezuela, Colombia and Ecuador,* by Hilary and George Bradt (54 Dudley St., Cambridge, MA 02140).

Local Coverage – The *Miami Herald* (a day late) and the *New York Times* (a few days late) are available at the *Colón Internacional* and *Inter-Continental Quito* hotels. Spanish dailies include *El Comercio* (morning daily), *Hoy* (a new morning daily),

Últimas Noticias (afternoon daily), and *El Periódico* (afternoon daily). *El Comercio* lists all cultural and social events; *Hoy* is the most modern newspaper in layout and is fast catching up to *El Comercio* in content.

CLIMATE AND CLOTHES: Ecuador's proximity to the equator wipes out expected seasonal changes. In the dry season, roughly May through October, and sometimes in November and December, people with sensitive skin need a sunscreen to protect them from the ultraviolet rays that are so much stronger at this elevation. Even during the rainy seasons during the rest of the year, the sun is often very strong in the morning. Nights can be cold enough to require a thick sweater or poncho, but daytime temperatures rarely stray from the upper 60s F (20°C). A lightweight waterproof jacket or collapsible umbrella is essential. Give yourself enough time to adapt to the altitude. Get plenty of rest, especially when you feel a headache beginning. (See *Medical and Legal Aid,* GETTING READY TO GO.)

GETTING AROUND: Bus – Buses are inexpensive and cover all of the city, but they are crowded, uncomfortable, and few run after 9:30 PM. A useful route is the Colón-Camal, which runs along Av. Colón and Av. 10 de Agosto to the center of the old city. The Amazonas line — with modern, double-decker blue and white buses — runs from the center of Quito at El Ejido Park all along Av. Amazonas to the airport and back. It is a good, safe, and comfortable way to travel.

Taxi – There are meters in all authorized cabs, and the fares around town and to the airport are inexpensive. Cab ranks are scattered at the obvious places: supermarkets, hotels, Plaza Independencia, Universidad Central. They also cruise for passengers. To phone for a cab, just select the nearest of the fifty or so cab cooperatives listed in the Quito telephone directory.

Car Rental – *Avis* and *Hertz* both have representatives at the airport; *Hertz* also has an office at Edificio Volkswagen, Plaza Sebastián de Benalcazar (phone: 241-733). *Ecuacar,* Av. Colón 1280 and Av. Amazonas, offers cars, Jeeps, and trucks (phone: 523-673). Local agencies provide vehicles of varying quality at varying prices. Check with care.

MUSEUMS: Many of the city's art and archaeology displays are described in *Special Places:* San Francisco Church's museum, San Agustín Church and Monastery, Central Bank Museum, and Jijón y Caamaño Museum. Also worth visiting are the Museum of Colonial Art, Av. Espejo 1147 and Av. Benalcazar (phone: 210-863), and the Ethnographic Museum in the Colegio Mejía, with exhibitions on Ecuador's different racial groups and Indian tribes. Open Tuesdays through Saturdays, 8 AM to noon. Av. Venezuela and Av. Antonio Ante (phone: 230-257). Casa de la Cultura Ecuatoriana, on Av. 12 de Octubre and Av. Patria (across from the US embassy), houses some very interesting museums: the Natural Science Museum (open weekdays), Museum of Musical Instruments, Museum of Contemporary Art, and National Library.

SHOPPING: As mentioned in *Extra Special,* Ecuador has very, very fine crafts to buy. Highly recommended stores include *Folklore* (also known as *Olga Fisch's Folklore Gallery*), 260 Colón (with branches at the *Colón Internacional* and *Inter-Continental Quito* hotels), and *La Bodega,* Calle Juan León Mera 641, a few blocks from the *Colón Internacional,* for an intriguing selection of antiques, textiles, and Indian craft products, including blowpipes and fish traps. Also worth a visit is *Galería Latina,* Calle Juan León Mera, next door to *Libri Mundi,* specializing in balsa wood carvings and jungle crafts; *La Guaragua,* at Jorge

Washington 614, which carries antiques such as musical instruments, jewelry, ceramics, and colonial artifacts; *OCEPA,* at Carrion 13-36, (and branches at Av. Amazonas and Av. Jorge Washington, and near the *Quito* hotel), the government center for Ecuadorean handcrafted goods from around the country. Across the street from *La Bodega,* you will receive friendly attention from the multilingual staff of *Libri Mundi,* a bookstore with a wide selection of books in Spanish, English, French, and German — everything from fiction through science and history, plus its own photo book on the Galápagos. Calle Juan León Mera 851.

SPECIAL EVENTS: The *Quito Festival,* the first week in December, is the biggest fiesta of the year, but not the only one. From December 28 through January 2 is the week for costumes and masks, with an effigy representing the previous year (usually bearing a remarkable resemblance to some unpopular politician) burned on New Year's Eve at hundreds of sidewalk parties. In San Rafael, near Quito, January 6 is a day of costumed processions celebrating the *Day of Three Kings (Epiphany).* Quito and the surrounding Andean countryside hold giant parades during *Holy Week (Semana Santa),* the week before Easter. This is a better time to visit than during the pre-Lenten carnivals. In August and September, Otavalo holds *El Yamor,* an annual harvest festival dating from pre-Columbian times. The festival culminates in the arrival of a *coraza* — a triumphant horseman whose face is covered with golden tinsel and who wears plumed, sequined, and fringed regalia.

SPORTS: Soccer is Quito's favorite sport, with seasonal bullfighting running second. Ecuador's marlin fishing is legendary among anglers.

Bullfighting – The December fiestas attract big-name *toreros* from Spain and other Latin countries. Tickets should be bought well before the big *corridas* (bullfights). There are a few bullfights earlier in the year and in other towns. At village fiestas, where bulls are caped but not killed, aficionados are sometimes allowed to try their skills. *Plaza de Toros,* Av. Amazonas and Av. Cofanes (no phone).

Fishing – Good-sized trout can be caught in nearby mountain lakes and some rivers, especially south of Cuenca. Boats can be hired in Salinas for deep-sea excursions in pursuit of big marlin and swordfish in the Pacific. *Pescatours* has six boats for hire and bungalow accommodations (phone: in Guayaquil, 343-365; or in Salinas, 772-391).

Golf – The *Quito Tennis and Golf Club* has an 18-hole course at "El Condado," Av. Occidental, north of Quito, (phone: 533-809). Ask your hotel concierge for information.

Horseback Riding – Horses can be hired from the *Cusín* hotel, near the San Pablo Lake, 1½ hours north of Quito, and from the excellent *Hostería Chorlavi,* on the Pan-American Highway, near Ibarra (phone: 950-777).

Mountain Climbing – Climbing in Ecuador is excellent, with several local clubs and equipment available for hire. One of the continent's best-known mountaineers, Marco Cruz, leads climbs and treks; a complete description of those programs is available from *Metropolitan Touring,* Box 2542, in Quito, or from *Adventure Associates,* 13150 Coit Rd., Dallas, TX 75240.

Soccer – Matches take place Sundays at the *Estadio Olímpico Atahualpa* (Olympic Atahualpa Stadium), which is also used for athletic meets. Av. 6 de Diciembre and Av. Naciones Unidas (no phone).

Swimming – In addition to the *Quito Tennis and Golf Club,* the *Inter-Continental Quito* hotel, Av. Gonzalez Suarez 2500 (phone: 230-300), and *Colón Internacional* hotel, Av. Patria and Av. Amazonas (phone: 561-333), have swimming pools.

Tennis – The *Quito Tennis and Golf Club* has nine clay courts. Temporary membership is expensive but worth it for use of the swimming pool and the social life (phone: 533-809). *Club Municipal Quito Tennis* has six courts and an expensive membership fee. Av. Atahualpa and Av. 10 de Agosto (phone: 242-918). *Ecuador Tennis Club* has four courts at lower cost. At the top of Av. La Gasca (phone: 237-666).

THEATER: The Pichincha Playhouse, a good amateur English-language group, puts on several productions a year. US and British embassies and *La Favorita* supermarkets usually carry their playbills. Other theaters are *Teatro Nacional Sucre,* Calle Flores and Calle Manabí (phone: 216-668), and *Teatro Prometeo,* Casa de la Cultura, Av. 6 de Diciembre 794 (phone: 231-142). Quito's two universities — *Universidad Central,* Av. America (phone: 521-590), and *Universidad Católica,* Av. 12 de Octubre and Calle Robles (phone: 529-240) — often provide biting, witty political theater.

MUSIC: Visiting symphonies and opera companies play at *Teatro Nacional Sucre* and in the *Casa de la Cultura* and the *Conservatorio Nacional de la Música,* Madrid 1159 (phone: 544-883). Traditional Andean music can be found in the *peñas,* an important part of a rather limited city nightlife. You will hear songs played on instruments like the *charango* — a member of the guitar family that has an armadillo shell for its body — and the *rondador,* the South American pan pipes. *Peñas* tend to sprout up, then wither quickly. The most popular and best is probably *Pachamama,* but there are others such as *Nuestra America* (Zñaquito 149, Amazonas) and *El Chucaro* (Calle Reina Victoria 1335). Most *peñas* serve as normal bars do, but some restaurants have good Spanish-American and Indian music to accompany the fine Pacific seafood. Andean music fills the streets during the December fiestas. Radio Músical, a medium-wave pop station, occasionally gives news of rock concerts.

NIGHTCLUBS AND NIGHTLIFE: Discos spring up in Quito only to vanish as swiftly. The best are still the oldest. *La Licorne* at the *Colón Internacional* hotel has sufficient light and flash to come sporadically into fashion with high-society youth. *Pims,* Calle Calama 413 (phone: 524-346), is a small, relaxed bar with an international flavor to the drinks and the company. *Bambu Bar,* La Pradera 167 (phone: 231-648) has a nice atmosphere, good drinks, and music, and is popular with young people. *Quito Jazz Club,* Av. de la República 176 (phone: 239-666) also has very good music and an appealing atmosphere. A warning note: Alcohol has swift and powerful effects at this altitude. That's something to remember when you're offered strong local brandies — *pisco* and anise-flavored *paico.* Oxygen tanks are sometimes needed for first-timers' hangovers. The *Hotel Colón* serves the traditional restorative, *caldo de patas* (pig trotter broth), for suffering revelers at dawn. Gambling is popular and legal, with casinos presently at the *Colón, Inter-Continental, Chalet Suisse,* and *Tambo Real* hotels.

SINS: It is hard to think of Quito as a major sin city, for in demeanor, at least, the Ecuadorian capital is notably conservative. But there are two temptations to avoid. One is the purchase of antiquities for export without a license. Some very fine artifacts are available (new treasures continue to turn up, sometimes on private estates and in unpatrolled areas of the country), but if the visitor is discovered with unauthorized antiquities when he or she leaves the country, there will be an enormous problem with local customs. Increasingly, also, unauthorized pieces will be confiscated by US customs. Drugs of any kind are another sin in the eyes of the local law. Carelessness in pursuit of illicit euphoria can mean years of jail (and that's simply for possession), a predicament with which the US embassy is unable, and unwilling, to help.

BEST IN TOWN

CHECKING IN: Not only has an aggressive tourism policy made Ecuador a major travel destination, but since the early 1970s, Quito has become a center for international meetings and conferences, putting pressure on room space. DITURIS plans to double the number of first-class rooms to over 2,000; incentives include cancellation of revenue payments for 10 years and low-interest credit. The first fruit was the attractive 250-room extension to the *Colón Internacional,* and the newest is the *Alameda Real,* a good hotel in a good location, reasonably priced. Several new, smaller hotels are in the planning or building stage, while there are plans to modernize and upgrade others. But the growth rate is slow, and failure to book well ahead can result in having to settle for a hotel in a less desirable category. Quito offers good value for the money and some pleasant surprises in the moderate price range. Expect to pay $70 to $90 (plus 20% tax) for a double room at those places we've bracketed as expensive; $35 to $60 at those places bracketed as moderate; under $30 and as low as $15 for a clean, simple room in the inexpensive category.

Alameda Real – New to Quito, this hotel has 150 rooms, featuring 2-room-suite accommodations, 2 restaurants, and a piano bar. Roca 653 and Amazonas (phone: 562-345). Expensive.

Chalet Suisse – An elegant, Swiss-managed, 50-room hotel offering good atmosphere and excellent service, especially in its first-class restaurant. Features casino and entertainment (frequent musical shows). Av. Reina Victoria and Av. Calma (phone: 562-700). Expensive.

Colón Internacional – A new extension has turned this from a pleasant 200-room hotel into an efficient, international-class 450-room hotel. An intimate quality has been lost, but new facilities include a modern conference center and an arcade of stores, lounges, restaurants, and galleries. The extra bar and restaurant space has been kept to small units with attentive service. With the food of the older *El Conquistador* restaurant, the Sunday buffet lunch (around $6), the casino, and the disco beneath it, this remains one of Quito's major social centers. Major credit cards. Av. Amazonas and Av. Patria (phone: 561-333). Expensive.

Quito Inter-Continental – High on the ridge over the village of Guapulo, this building is sometimes bathed in low clouds, sometimes in scorching sun. A casino, *La Llama* nightclub, a steakhouse, a large conference center, ballrooms, and the elegant rooftop *El Techo del Mundo (The Roof of the World)* restaurant put it in the luxury class. Regular guests swear that what brings them back is the palm-shaded pool looking across the valley. Be forewarned, however, that although the view is superb, the service sometimes isn't. Av. Gonzalez Suárez 2500 (phone: 230-300). Expensive.

Tambo Real – The 70 rooms at this hotel, across from the/US embassy, are well-furnished and comfortable. This and *Chalet Suisse* are the next best choices after *Colón, Quito,* and *Alameda.* Restaurant, cafeteria, casino, and shopping. Av. 12 de Octubre and Av. Patria (phone: 524-260). Expensive to moderate.

Auca Continental – A small, modern hotel, near the center of the city, this is a useful, well-situated base from which to explore old Quito. It also has an economical café-restaurant. Calle Venezuela and Calle Sucre (phone: 512-240). Moderate.

Embajador – In the Amazonas district, this is an unpretentious, pleasant bargain. Rather small, with only 37 rooms, it has parking facilities and a restaurant, but no swimming pool or frills. Prices include breakfast. Av. Colón and Av. 9 de Octubre (phone: 230-040). Moderate.

Embassy – Especially pleasant for families. Some of the suites are self-contained units with motel-style parking. It has an adequate restaurant and a good location. Calle Wilson 439 (phone: 561-990). Moderate.

Majestic – This new hotel, near the busy Santa Clara market, is a good value. There are just 36 rooms and a small restaurant and cafeteria. Calle Mercadillo 366 and Calle Versailles (phone: 543-182). Moderate.

República – A modern hotel in the residential section near Av. Amazonas and Av. República, a new and fast developing business and shopping area. Comfortable, pleasant, and efficient, it is one of the best choices in this range. Av. República and Av. Azuay (phone: 450-075). Moderate.

Residencia Cumbres – Tucked into a quiet street at the heart of the Amazonas district, the *Cumbres* is, as its name suggests, a residential hotel. The dining room is only for residents. Calle Baquedaño 148 (phone: 527-633). Moderate.

Savoy Inn – Not far from the airport, with its own travel bureau. Three conference rooms make it a popular choice for business meetings, and the 100-seat restaurant is good enough to attract people from the other side of town. It has a small billiard and card room and disco nearby. It appears to be coming up in the world. Calle Yasuní (phone: 247-222). Moderate.

Royal Inn – Small (13 rooms) and comfortable, of a type similar to the *Embajador,* but with better service and facilities. 6 de Diciembre 2751 and Av. República (phone: 238-260). Moderate to inexpensive.

Viena Internacional – In the heart of colonial Quito, this is the best choice of its category still remaining in the old section. The rooms all have private facilities. Well managed, clean, and friendly, with telephone, TV, and a small restaurant. Flores 610 and Av. Chile (phone: 519-611). Inexpensive.

 EATING OUT: National policies on fishing rights and frequent seasonal bans on lobster exports mean that seafood finds its way onto local tables at reasonable prices, and Quito eating places make extensive use of shellfish and crustaceans, although many restaurateurs still complain that they never get enough lobster to meet the demand. Traditional highland dishes provide some delicious lower-priced surprises, especially *llapingachos con hornado* — fried potato and cheese cakes with crackling roast pork. Expect to pay around $30 for a dinner for two in those restaurants we've bracketed as expensive; between $15 and $20 in the moderate category; under $10, inexpensive. Prices do not include drinks, wine, tips, and taxes.

La Belle Époque – Fine French food and a range of Chilean, Argentine, and French wines, with attentive but not annoying service. The lobster is delicious, as are the *profiterolles.* Reservations weekends. Closed Sundays. Major credit cards. Calle Whimper 925 and Av. 6 de Diciembre (phone: 233-163). Expensive.

Chalet Suisse – Some of the best Continental food in Quito is elegantly served in a pleasant atmosphere for serious food lovers. A subdued piano and small casino in the adjoining hotel add to its popularity with diplomats and lovers. Closed Sundays. Reservations advisable. Major credit cards. Calle Calama and Calle Reina Victoria (phone: 563-908 or 230-686). Expensive.

El Conquistador – Colonial Spain inspired the decor and the old world charm of this fine restaurant with a menu that highlights international cuisine as well as some tasty local dishes; every meal benefits from the country's fresh fruits, vegetables, and splendid fish and meat. A popular spot with the local people. Reservations recommended. Major credit cards accepted. Hotel Colón Internacional, Av. Amazonas (phone: 560-666). Expensive.

Costa Vasca – Splendid Spanish food, with especially good prawns and *calamares* flavored liberally with garlic. Open daily. Diners Club accepted. Calle Reina Victoria 836 (phone: 234-846). Expensive.

Flandes – Serving delicious mussels and other seafood, it has a good, lively atmosphere with well-chosen music on weekends. Among the French dishes that are definitely not for weight-watchers, try the Russian crêpe with vodka, chocolate sauce, and whipped cream. Evening reservations advisable. Closed Sundays. Major credit cards. Av. Santa María 431 and Av. Amazonas (phone: 232-308). Expensive to moderate, depending on your self-control.

La Gritta – Elegant European decor, fireplace, and good atmosphere in what is probably the best Italian restaurant in Quito. The pasta dishes are superb, and the wine list is commendable. Reservations suggested. Major credit cards. Av. Santa María and Av. Reina Victoria (phone: 230-566). Expensive.

La Marmite – Another elegant, well-appointed restaurant, very popular with businesspeople, local VIPs, and tourists. The cuisine is international but basically French, with especially tasty seafood and meat dishes and excellent desserts. Reservations. Major credit cards. Mariano Aguilera 287 (phone: 237-751). Expensive.

Le Peché Mignon – One of the best restaurants in Quito, specializing in French cuisine, it is small, cozy, and tastefully decorated. Very pleasant atmosphere. Reservations recommended. Major credit cards. Belo Horizonte 338, next door to *La Ronda* (phone: 230-709). Expensive.

El Techo del Mundo – The *Inter-Continental Quito's* so-called *Roof of the World* is so high on the ridge over the city that diners are sometimes surprised to see aircraft almost level with the windows as they make the turn to land. Seating 110, it is quietly elegant with unobtrusive music. European chefs prepare *langostinos estragon* that would do justice to many a Paris restaurant. Open daily. Reservations advisable on weekends or for groups of more than four. Major credit cards. Hotel Inter-Continental Quito, Av. Gonzalez Suárez 2500 (phone: 230-300). Expensive.

La Terraza del Tartaro – This penthouse restaurant offers fine views of the city and, if you're lucky, the distant snow peaks as well. The varied menu is strong on good seafood and steak dishes. Closed Sundays. Reservations are advisable at dinner. No credit cards. Calle Veintemilla 926 and Av. Amazonas (phone: 527-987). Expensive.

La Vieja Castilla – One of Quito's best Spanish restaurants, with a very nice atmosphere in which to enjoy the excellent dishes that emerge from its kitchen. Reservations. Major credit cards. Almagro 1011 and Av. Santa María (phone: 230-916). Expensive.

Rincón de Francia – Excellent French food in a family atmosphere — the owner cooks, and his wife takes the orders. They offer a different specialty each day, all of them worth trying. Closed Sundays. Reservations are recommended. Major credit cards. Av. General Roca and Av. 9 de Octubre (phone: 232-053). Expensive to moderate.

La Taberna Piemonte – Decorated in a rather rustic, but tasteful, Italian country style, this is a good eatery serving excellent antipasto and Northern Italian specialties. Good Italian wines. Reservations aren't really necessary. No credit cards. Eloy Alfaro 2286 (phone: 242-474). Expensive to moderate.

La Casa de Mi Abuela – The best meat in Quito, and such generous helpings that diners tend to stagger out. Closed Sundays. Reservations advisable on weekends. No credit cards. Av. Juan León Mera 1649 (phone: 521-922). Moderate.

La Choza – A good place to sample local dishes in a pretty Quito setting. Start with *empanadas de morocho,* drink some *chicha,* and try the *llapingachos con fritada* — pork with potato cakes and an avocado salad. Open daily; Saturdays and Sundays, lunch only. Reservations accepted. Major credit cards. Av. 12 de Octubre 1821 (phone: 230-839). Moderate.

Churrasquería El Tropeiro – A small and informal steakhouse serving excellent meats and *churrascos,* abundant and tasty. Veintimilla 546 (phone: 548-012). Moderate.

Pekin – This small, unpretentious restaurant serves the best Chinese food in Quito. It ain't Beijing, but it's good. There's carry-out service, too. Closed Monday lunch. Reservations unnecessary. No credit cards. Calle Bello Horizonte 197 (phone: 520-841). Moderate.

La Ronda – Another good spot for local fare as well as Andean music. Open daily; Saturdays and Sundays, lunch only. Reservations accepted. Major credit cards. Bello Horizonte and Diego de Almagro (phone: 540-459). Moderate.

Chantilly – An ideal place for coffee and a mouth-watering pastry. Lunches are served as well. Pastries and sweets are also on sale at the shop downstairs. Closed Sundays. No credit cards. Calle General Roca 736 and Av. Amazonas (phone: 528-226). Inexpensive.

Manolo's Churrería – This sidewalk café serves excellent snacks, sandwiches, and fruit juices. It's one of the few places in Quito where you can be sure of getting a good cup of coffee. Open daily. No reservations. No credit cards. Av. Amazonas and Calle Robles (no phone). Inexpensive.

Las Redes – *Ceviche* (marinated seafood) is served in many Quito restaurants, but here it is particularly tasty. Try mussel *ceviche,* accompanied by toasted corn and an ice cold pilsner beer. Also good are the bouillabaise and the mixed seafood grill. Open daily. Reservations unnecessary. Major credit cards. Av. Amazonas and Av. Veintimilla. Inexpensive.

La Taberna Quiteña – Both branches of this restaurant, in cellar-like tavern settings, specialize in Ecuadorian food and draft beer. The Manabí branch is new. Live music in the evenings. Closed Mondays. No reservations. Major credit cards. Av. Amazonas 1259 and Calle Luis Cordero (phone: 545-098); Calle Manabí 535 and Calle Luis Vargas (phone: 213-102). Inexpensive.

RIO DE JANEIRO

Cariocas (as residents of Rio de Janeiro are called) say that one of the six days God needed to create the world was devoted to making Rio. No one yet has complained that the time was ill spent. Just under the brow of Brazil's long Atlantic coast, Rio washes inland on a tide of tawny beaches across the graceful valleys and hillsides of the tropical mountains that dot its 15-mile section of coast. Above the city, on Corcovado Mountain, the world-famous sculpture of Christ the Redeemer spreads its arms in an open embrace of the city and the sea beyond. The sentiment of the gesture — the radiant accept-ance of something almost miraculous in its beauty — touches even the most casual first-time visitor. Mention Rio to a recently returned traveler and you are practically guaranteed a smile and a deep sigh of pleasure: "Ah, Rio!" It's a universal response.

Brasília is the capital of Brazil (at least since 1960; for the preceding 137 years that honor belonged to Rio); São Paulo is the country's conscience and keeper of its work ethic; but Rio is its soul, undisputed master of its heart. If *cariocas* sometimes seem giddy with pleasure and pleasure-seeking, be more sympathetic than censorious. Rio is not an easy city in which to be serious — or at least serious about anything except beauty. In a town so utterly devoted to and so generously endowed with glamour, the business of being beautiful is taken very seriously.

The site of Rio de Janeiro — River of January — was discovered on Guanabara Bay by Portuguese sailors in January 1502, just two years after the first Portuguese incursions into northern Brazil at Salvador de Bahía. Though the Portuguese established settlements at Bahía, Rio was actually settled by the French, and only after numerous bloody battles during which the city changed hands several times did it become Portuguese in 1567. Salvador and many other settlements in early Brazil flourished by raising sugarcane, then tapping rubber, and by mining gold and gemstones. Coffee plantations were established in the area as well. In 1763 Rio replaced Bahía as capital of the colony.

The Portuguese ruled from Europe for 300 years until Napoleon invaded Portugal in 1807 and the royal family fled to Rio for refuge. When Napoleon was defeated, King João VI returned to Portugal and left his son Pedro as regent. In 1822 Pedro, following the behests of the wealthy plantation owners, declared Brazil independent and named himself Emperor Dom Pedro I. An unpopular monarch, he had to return to Portugal to take the crown as Pedro IV, leaving his 5-year-old son, Dom Pedro II, whose 58-year reign was known as Brazil's golden era. Dom Pedro II fostered land reforms, encouraged mass education, and opened Brazil to immigration. In 1888 he abolished slavery, an act so unpopular with his wealthy supporters that he was forced to flee Brazil for Paris, where he died shortly after. Many years later his body was returned for reburial in the Cathedral of Petropolis. In 1889, Brazil was declared a republic; Rio remained its capital. It was a boom time for Brazil, with coffee in high demand and the discovery of rubber in the Amazon bringing untold wealth into the country. Immigrants from Japan and Europe poured to Rio and São Paulo, bringing with them the creativity and industry of all immigrant peoples, and successive discoveries of a vast array of natural resources continued to fuel economic progress. Brazil's economic miracle did not divide the spoils equally among its citizens, however, and the recent 21-year military regime (1964–1985) did not resolve problems of unemployment, poverty, the largest foreign debt of any developing nation, and rampant inflation. Rising prices have now affected everyone — rich, poor, and tourist alike. Nevertheless, the happy-go-lucky atmosphere is not gone.

Certainly, Rio never seems to stop growing. Today the city has more than 5 million residents (9 million in the greater metropolitan area) in beach communities and inland suburbs that stretch for miles around the downtown commercial center of Guanabara Bay, the site of the original Rio settlement. The city's incessant growth has been primarily to the south, where the beaches lie, and has been fed in part by Rio's position as the number one tourist destination in South America and in part by the *cariocas'* native craving for fine strands, as one after another of these small beach communities have become part of Rio's overall urban plan. During the 1940s, Copacabana Beach was the center of Rio's chic sun-worshiping life; today eight beach communities, of different styles and degrees of development, are all part of Rio.

These communities stretch south of the bustling, noisy downtown area like beads on a string. That image is more than apt, in fact, because much of the city is connected by 13 tunnels, the quickest way to negotiate the mountains around which the city is splashed like paint from a profligate artist. Clinging precariously to the sides of these mountains are small homes made of wood and hammered tin. Although they appear gaily painted and picturesque, these *favelas* are actually the slum dwellings in which poor *cariocas* live. Celebrated in song and in the haunting film *Black Orpheus,* the people who live here are a lot tougher and less glamorous in real life than on screen. Many *favelados* have emigrated from other parts of Brazil in order to support destitute relatives, and life is hard. Thefts, stabbings, the drug traffic, and contraband trade are all too common in the *favelas;* and, all too often, street crime overflows *favela* borders.

Rio's downtown area is bustling, hectic, and noisy, and though it has a number of hotels, restaurants, shops, and night spots, the really chic establishments are concentrated in the more fashionable beach communities. Downtown is devoted to business, where modern high-rises abut traditional Brazilian public buildings. Since most residents live outside the downtown area, traffic on weekdays is always heavy.

Adjacent to the downtown area are the beach communities of Flamengo and Botafogo, whose beaches face Guanabara Bay. Both areas are primarily residential, although they have some good older hotels and restaurants. During the 1930s and 1940s, they were the center of Rio's resort area. From time to time, Guanabara Bay has been closed for swimming due to pollution, so swim elsewhere.

Passing through the Botafogo tunnel, you come to the Leme-Copacabana Beach strip, the "grande dame" and heart of Rio's resort area. World-renowned Copacabana is popular with *cariocas* from all walks of life and all age groups. The wide, black and white mosaic sidewalk lines Avenida Atlântica, site of the majority of Rio's fine hotels, excellent restaurants, sidewalk cafés, and nightclubs. Visitors inevitably spend a good part of their time in this area.

Through the next tunnel is Ipanema, prime rival for popularity with Copacabana, and now considered more fashionable. Acclaimed in the hit song *The Girl from Ipanema,* it is quieter than Copacabana, with fewer hotels, but is very popular with Rio's chic young crowd. It has the city's finest restaurants, boutiques, and a Sunday flea market. A modest beachfront apartment in either Copacabana or Ipanema rents for $2,000 a month; prices escalate to $3,000 to $3,500 per month for grander establishments. During Carnival, even a modest apartment can cost several thousand dollars for a month or less.

Next along the Atlantic strip, primarily residential Leblon is the home of many wealthy Rio residents. Posh apartment buildings facing the ocean along Avenida Delfim Moreira and Avenida Vieira Souto have duplex and triplex apartments, penthouses, and rooftop swimming pools.

Ten years ago, the long beach at São Conrado was inhabited mostly by waterfowl and driftwood. As tourists poured into Rio during the early 1970s, the need for luxury accommodations became acute, and within a few months of one another, three resort hotels opened their doors on Avenida Niemeyer in 1971. These three — the *Sheraton, Inter-Continental,* and *Nacional Rio* — led the building boom that has made São Conrado Rio's newest fully developed beach community. Its skyline is littered with high-rises and the streets, lined with shopping centers and recreational areas. Rio's development isn't over, however. The story of São Conrado is now being repeated in Barra da Tijuca, even farther from the downtown area. Until recently, Barra was no more than a 10-mile strip of beach, honky-tonk bars, a few seafood restaurants, and various campgrounds. Now it is being developed as a major residential site, as Rio grows relentlessly southward.

As you stroll through these communities trying restaurants and browsing in the boutiques, art galleries, and antique shops, you will savor the special rhythm, sound, and smell of each. Perhaps you will be drawn to one section above the others: Copacabana, with lithe sunbathers and soccer players; the sweet pineapples hacked apart by a machete; graceful papagallo kites soaring over the sand and water; or Ipanema, where the beach and streets are less crowded and even traffic jams are tamer, but the bathers younger, more beautiful, less inhibited.

And despite the recent development of the area, some say Rio's best beach can still be found in São Conrado, which is isolated from the rest of the city by a long oceanside cliff. Here you can watch hang gliders soar from the rocky heights as you sip the milk of chilled coconuts sold on the beach.

Rio is truly a multiracial society in which the color of a citizen's skin is relatively unimportant and people of all shades live together in apparent harmony. Discrimination exists, but it is different than the blatant racism of the US, and Brazilians have not experienced the racial disturbances that mark our recent history. Though the majority of *favela* dwellers are black and poor, among the growing middle class in Brazil are blacks, whites, mulattos, and Orientals. Most Brazilians are mulatto, descendants of the black slaves, Indian tribes, and Portuguese, Dutch, and Spanish settlers. The opening of Brazil to immigration in the early twentieth century and after both world wars brought large numbers of Eastern Europeans, Italians, and Japanese. There are large numbers of Europeans in Rio's business centers, shops, and restaurants, and a huge Japanese sector in São Paulo.

As in the rest of Brazil, Portuguese is Rio's native language. But the *cariocas'* dialect, more closely akin to that of Portugal, is distinct from that of São Paulo's *paulistas,* which was influenced by the past immigration of Italians. Surrounded by Spanish-speaking neighbors, you would expect Spanish to be the second language here, but, surprisingly, English is more widely spoken. (A distant second to be sure, but English is taught in secondary schools, and many *cariocas* study it privately.) Hotels, better restaurants, and shops invariably have English-speaking personnel. If you speak some Spanish, try using it in a pinch, since *cariocas* in the tourist business deal with many Spanish-speaking visitors and the languages are similar. And, if you are fluent in Spanish, don't be surprised to find yourself gesticulating and trying to lip-read in an attempt to understand the lilting inflection of the unfamiliar-sounding Portuguese words. It is easier for Brazilians to understand Spanish than for Spanish speakers to understand Brazilian Portuguese. Both are Romance languages, with similar grammatical structures and many words are much the same, but pronunciations are quite different. Don't believe people who tell you that Portuguese and Spanish are identical. They are similar, yes; but it takes time and patience to learn the essential phonetic distinctions that will allow you to communicate effectively.

Much of the *cariocas'* leisure time is spent in pursuit of *la dolce vita,* Brazilian style, their enthusiasm for the pleasures rather than the responsibilities of life no less earnest for the country's current economic problems. From dawn until dusk the easily accessible beaches are a kaleidoscope of color and activity, with men and women in brightly hued tangas and bikinis sunning, swimming, surfing, dancing, singing, and playing soccer, bongos, and guitars — it's a beehive of hedonistic activity.

The residents' incessant pursuit of pleasure makes Rio an easy place to meet people of the same or opposite sex. On the beaches, in sidewalk cafés, and in discotheques, people are busily engaged in the business of meeting people. The image of a young woman out on a date with a grim-faced chaperone two paces behind is not a picture of Rio. Young people here are free to enjoy themselves as they choose. In addition to the discotheques that cater to the young, pizza parlors and sidewalk cafés serve as meeting places. Flirtatious and frivolous, *cariocas* seem to have an innate sense of how to flatter and charm, quickly accepting newcomers into their circle of friends or family.

Although there is not a strong women's movement in Rio, both men and women are sexually liberated. The women of Rio are known for their beauty, and they are quite open about their sexuality. Sex is readily available for anyone looking for it, male or female. A single woman will find more acceptance in Rio than anywhere else in Latin America, and attention from men, on the beach or in a café, is usually friendly; it can be accepted or rejected. The only stumbling blocks for single women are in nightclubs. Many clubs do not permit single women to enter, and it is unusual for a woman to go to a club or bar unescorted. However, clubs usually allow female tourists to enter to see the show, especially in the big hotels.

Another of Rio's special features is the home-grown cult, *macumba.* While ostensibly Roman Catholic, many *cariocas* follow the rituals and practices of this sect, which is rather like voodoo. Its houses of worship, called *terreiros,* can be found throughout the city, and services are held nightly. Macumbistas believe that spirits affect all aspects of life and that there are good and evil spirits. They employ a medium to call down the good spirits to assist them. You should definitely visit a *terreiro* during your stay in Rio; the ceremony is fascinating. Macumba festivals are held at other times during the year. The most important one, the Feast of Iemanjá, takes place on the beach on December 31, New Year's Eve, when, at midnight, gifts are placed along the shore and flowers thrown into the water as offerings to the goddess of the sea.

Soccer provides a different outlet for many people, who enjoy the sport as both participants and spectators. Every beach, most parks, and all school yards have soccer goal posts. They are constantly in use in impromptu as well as organized league games. Many are lighted for night play. These games are hard-fought, which you will sense immediately by the ferocity of the play. The hysteria of the fans at Maracaña Stadium during professional matches far surpasses that of Super Bowl and World Series crowds. The noise is deafening, the betting fierce, and the enjoyment contagious.

The most important event in Rio is Carnival. While it is true that this pre-Lenten celebration lasts only for the 5 days preceding Ash Wednesday, some pre-Carnival activities start as early as November, when costumes are designed and made, parties are planned, and nightclubs begin samba contests. All business comes to a halt as Carnival begins. The entire city is festooned with colorful streamers and lights, and bandstands are set up for street dancing that lasts from dusk till dawn. Traditional Carnival events take place downtown in the Sambódromo, a wide boulevard edged by permanent bleacher seats, constructed by the government to promote and establish Carnival as part of the Brazilian culture. During the year, classes are held in the bleachers and musical concerts in the square at the end of the boulevard. The Carnival parade is now held on both Sunday and Monday evenings and is a spectacle worthy of Cecil B. De Mille. Samba schools consisting of several thousand members strut, glide, dance, and samba down the avenue in elaborate costumes to original musical accompaniments, singing lyrics written by club members around an assigned theme. The multitude of spectators take an active part by singing and clapping. Carnival is also the time for costume balls held at local social clubs, nightclubs, and fashionable hotels. The costumes range from whatever you have to gorgeous, opulent displays of feathers, bangles, and glitter. Sometimes costume competitions feature outfits costing hundreds of dollars, feasts for the eyes; otherwise, and especially at small clubs, celebrants dress as they wish — but always with a mask. Rio's high society attends these balls in either costume or formal attire.

Words can describe a museum filled with marvelous paintings or an ancient ruin, but Rio de Janeiro is an experience that enchants mind, soul, and body. The bubbly sensuality of the *cariocas;* the splendid colors of sea and mountains playing against the colorful crowds moving gracefully along the streets; the mingled scent of ocean and tropical flowers: These are all part of the elixir called Rio. It is a dynamic collage playing on all senses. It is alive; to be there, life-giving.

RIO DE JANEIRO AT-A-GLANCE

SEEING THE CITY: *Cariocas* adore their city. They take pleasure in looking at it themselves and pride in showing it to visitors. There are several natural viewing points, as well as a number of man-made ones. Pão de Açúcar (Sugar Loaf), jutting into Guanabara Bay, and the peak of Corcovado (Hunchback) Mountain, farther inland, offer the most spectacular views and are Rio's major tourist attractions (see *Special Places,* below). The road leading up Corcovado has two viewpoints: The Vista Chinesa (Chinese View) at 1,300 feet, overlooking the lovely lagoon (*lagoa*) section, Ipanema, and Leblon; and, at 1,500 feet, the Mesa do Imperador (Emperor's Table). Both provide excellent panoramas for photographs. Many of the city's newest hotels have cleverly positioned nightclubs, first-class restaurants, or quiet piano bars on their top floors. What better decor than a view of Guanabara Bay at sunset, the purple-hued mountain range, or the city's skyline? Visit the *St. Honoré Restaurant* on the 37th floor of the *Hotel Méridien,* Av. Atlântica, Copacabana (phone: 275-9922), and the *Skylab* nightclub, on the 30th floor of the *Rio Othon Palace Hotel,* Av. Atlântica, Copacabana (phone: 255-8812). *La Tour,* downtown, is a revolving restaurant that makes its rounds once an hour. The view pans from Pão de Açúcar to Corcovado and the beach areas. Rua Santa Luzia (phone: 240-5795). Another restaurant with a stunning view of the downtown skyline and harbor is *Cota 200* on Urca Hill, adjoining Sugar Loaf. It's accessible by cable car from Av. Pasteur.

SPECIAL PLACES: Rio has warm weather nearly all year, with hot, hot weather in the summer (December to March) months and a number of the best beaches in the world, so you are bound to spend a good deal of your visit supine, playing footsies with the Atlantic's fine sands. But there is much else to see and do in Rio.

Sugar Loaf Mountain (Pão de Açúcar) – Rio's number one tourist stop is a brown gumdrop-shaped mountain at the entrance to Guanabara Bay. Standing at 1,325 feet, its summit is reached via two cable cars. Glass-enclosed and large enough to hold 70 people, the first car carries you from Praia Vermelha station to Urca, a sister peak 650 feet high. The ride takes only 5 minutes and the views of the bay area are lovely. At its peak, Urca is larger than Pão de Açúcar and is a popular picnic spot. It also has a small restaurant, a museum of primitive sculpture (see *Museums*), featuring wood carvings by Antônio de Olveira, a playground, and an open-air theater with bleacher seats and a dance floor. It's used for Carnival balls, New Year's Eve parties, and samba or popular music shows throughout the year. On the second leg of the journey, the cable car from Urca to Pão de Açúcar seems to rise vertically before swinging out over the water. Although the peak is small, the views are nothing less than stunning — on one side, the harbor and downtown skyline; on another, the mountain range, with Rio's fabulous white beaches spread along the shore; still another, Corcovado Mountain and its famous Christ the Redeemer statue. On a clear day, you will swear you can almost see forever. Bus 511 from Copacabana (15 minutes) or 107 from downtown

(25 minutes) will drop you at Praia Vermelha station. The cable car runs every half hour from 8 AM to 10 PM daily; it's crowded on weekends. Admission charge. Praia Vermelha station, Av. Pasteur, Botafogo (phone: 541-3737).

Hunchback Mountain (Corcovado) – Rivaling Pão de Açúcar in popularity, this is the mountain on which stands the 120-foot statue of Christ the Redeemer. If you are familiar with Antônio Carlos Jobim's evocative jazz composition *Corcovado,* you will undoubtedly place this higher than Pão de Açúcar on your itinerary. Built in the late 1920s with money raised in churches throughout Brazil, the statue is visible from most parts of the city, especially when illuminated at night. The views of the city from its 2,400-foot peak are perfect for photographers. The beach areas, Guanabara Bay with Pão de Açúcar beside it, Rio's lagoon, modern buildings, and huge ships are all within lens' view. By the way, wear comfortable shoes; there is a steep climb from the parking lot to the statue peak that's arduous but worth every huff and puff. To reach the statue the easy way, you can hop a 30-minute ride on a railroad that leaves from Cosme Velho station every half hour from 8 AM to 8 PM, making several stops along the way at residential stations. Bus 583 from Copacabana; 422, 108, or 498 from downtown to Cosme Velho station. Admission charge.

It is worthwhile to explore the mountain as well as the statue, which you can do if you rent a car, cab, or come via tour bus. There is a good road up the mountain, with several lookout and picnic points along the way. As mentioned above, the two most popular lookout points are the Vista Chinesa (Chinese View) and the Mesa do Emperador (Emperor's Table). The Vista Chinesa is marked by a green pagoda with ferocious dragon heads. The Mesa do Imperador was a favorite picnic area of Emperor Dom Pedro II. Both overlook the city and you get better views than from the peak. Also on the way up is Largo do Boticario, a cluster of five lovely historic colonial houses. Open daily. Free. Cosme Velho station, Corcovado (phone: 285-2533).

Paquetá Island (Ilha Paquetá) – For a different view of Rio, set aside one day and hop a motor launch for a relaxing ride through Guanabara Bay. The launch leaves from a downtown marina and heads into the bay beside the Pão de Açúcar mountain chain under the new Niteroi suspension bridge, giving you a completely different perspective of the city. As you near Paquetá, you will see fishing boats, water skiers, and snorkelers. Easily the most picturesque island of the 84 in Rio's bay, it has a population of 2,300, most of whom are fishermen. Some of the more fashionable homes belong to *cariocas,* who come on weekends. Since no cars are allowed on the island, the best way to get around is to rent a bicycle from one of the several rental offices near the dock. It costs about $2 for the day. A more relaxing, albeit slightly more expensive, way to see the island is to rent a horse-drawn carriage. The going rate is $5 per hour. Stop for a swim at the island's main beach, José Bonifacio. You can bring a picnic or have a filling seafood lunch at *La Fragata* hotel (no phone). *La Fragata* and the *Lido Hotel* (phone: 397-0377) are modest but clean and comfortable enough for an overnight stay. Try to schedule your visit on a weekday since weekends are quite crowded. The launch leaves from Praça 15 de Novembro (downtown) near the *Alba Mar* restaurant (see *Eating Out*) Mondays through Saturdays, 5:30 AM to 11 PM; Sundays, 7:10 AM to 11 PM. Returning boats leave Paquetá from 5:30 AM until 8:30 PM. The trip takes 1¼ hours (phone: 231-0396). You can also visit Paquetá and other islands on the special *Bateau Mouche* ferry. *Bateau Mouche* has several day cruises as well as an evening cruise, with both first- and tourist-class accommodations. The daily schedule is available from any hotel desk. Admission charge. *Bateau Mouche,* adjacent to Rio Yacht Club, Botafogo (phone: 295-1997).

Tijuca Forest (Floresta de Tijuca) – Only 20 minutes from downtown, Tijuca gives city folk a perfect opportunity to stroll through a tropical forest along a road shaded by towering trees and lined with flowers. Tijuca was cleared as a coffee plantation, but Mother Nature has reasserted herself here, and the forest has returned to its natural state. There are many types of trees, small waterfalls, narrow paths winding through the woods, picnic grounds, a hiking path, and even a 3,000-foot peak (Pico da Tijuca) to conquer. You enter the forest at Alto de Boa Vista, and the road winds past Taunay Waterfall (Cascatinha Taunay), whose waters are used to produce Brahma Chopps Beer; the Mayrink Chapel; and *A Floresta* and *Os Esquilos* restaurants, the latter of which has the decor of a colonial housefireplace, lace curtains, and a garden where drinks are served. The area of the forest called Bom Retiro (good retreat) at the end of the road is a good picnic spot and also the starting point of the 2-hour hike to the peak. A cab from Copacabana costs about $8. Bus 415 and 416 from Avenida Copacabana will drop you at Usina da Tijuca, where you take Bus 221 (destination: Alto de Boa Vista), which drops you near the Taunay Waterfall. All city tours include a visit to Tijuca. Alto de Boa Vista, Tijuca Forest.

Art Fair (Feirarte) – Formerly the "Hippie Market," Feirarte has outgrown its jeans-and-sandals image. This is the *carioca* version of a flea market, but you will be able to find a multitude of items ranging from the frivolous to the first-rate. Held every Sunday in Ipanema, the market draws enthusiastic shoppers, bargain hunters, and the curious. The vendors imaginatively display their wares in makeshift stalls, on rugs on the ground, and even on tree branches. Very popular are copper wall plates and mirrors, tapestries, hand-tooled leathers — bags, belts, sandals, and wallets — trays, and wood carvings. Silver jewelry, gaily painted ceramics, and kitchen utensils make excellent gifts. The market provides a gallery for the work of a number of very talented young artists not yet well known to command real gallery space but whose oil paintings — ranging from primitive to modern — are available at extremely reasonable prices and just could be valuable investments. Prices range from a few dollars to more than a hundred; what you pay will in large part depend on your ability to bargain. Nobody pays the first price here or the second. Bargain like crazy. The fair takes place on Sundays from 8 AM to 6 PM, Praça General Osório, Ipanema.

Gemstone Tour – Brazil is to gemstones what Saudi Arabia is to oil. This mammoth nation produces 90% of the world's supply of colorful minerals — aquamarine, topaz, amethyst, opal, turquoise, agate, and coral, to name a few. Take a guided tour through several workshops to learn how and why Brazil sparkles. A real show is that of *H. Stern*, Rio's largest gemstone dealer and, with more than 100 shops in Latin America, the US, Europe, Asia, and the Caribbean, one of the world's largest jewelers as well. The very modern tour uses headphones, slides, and views of workers behind glass; it lasts about 30 minutes. It begins with an exhibit of a gemstone in its raw state, embedded in rock. Then you are shown the cutting, shaping, polishing, faceting, and the gem in its final form, ready to be set in a piece of jewelry. You'll learn how stones are graded and how new designs are planned in design workshops. Unless you are a jeweler, you'll probably be surprised to discover that not all amethysts are purple nor all tourmalines green. The tour is interesting even if you don't plan to buy any jewelry (there is no pressure to do so); if you do, it will give you some insights toward making an intelligent purchase. And you can't beat the price. Free. Closed Sundays. Rua Visconde de Pirajá 490, 3rd floor, Ipanema (phone: 259-7442).

DOWNTOWN AND FLAMENGO BEACH

Avenida Rio Branco – This is the major street of commercial Rio. During the day, the black-and-white-tiled sidewalks are filled with people rushing to work in the offices, banks, and public buildings. Traffic is heavy and so is pollution. At night, this street is very quiet. From its northernmost point in the Praça Mauá dock area, it runs south several miles to Avenida Beira Mar, near Flamengo Beach.

Mauá Square (Praça Mauá) – The older dock area is interesting to stroll through because the older, ornate gray architecture of the nearby streets is so different from that of modern Rio. Ocean liners dock nearby. The area is full of local color, bordering on the seamy and sleazy.

Monastery of São Bento (Mosteiro do São Bento) – Not far from Praça Mauá, this delightful religious complex contains one of the most beautiful baroque golden chapels in Brazil. Open daily 6 AM to 6 PM (until 5 PM on Sundays). Free. Rua Dom Gerardo 68, Ladeira de São Bento (phone: 291-7122).

Calendaria Church (Igreja Calendaria) – Built in the early 18th century, the church stands in the plaza that for many years was the starting point for the samba school paraders during Carnival. The back entrance of the church faces the main street; the front doors open onto Guanabara Bay. The original church was built by mariners in the early 17th century after they had witnessed a shipwreck, and many of the paintings inside depict this terrible scene. Praça Pio X, Av. Presidente Vargas, and Av. Rio Branco.

Praça XV – This is the oldest square in Rio, ringed by little 16th-century churches and pastel-colored buildings.

Downtown Shopping District – Rio's major shopping area embraces several streets: Rua Ouvidor, Rua Goncalves Dias, Rua Buenos Aires, and Rua Uruguaiana. The main flower market, Praça Olavo Bilac, is here, too. Shops specialize in handcrafts, *macumba* items, leather goods, records, and home furnishings of wood and stone. In the last year, several fashionable boutiques have opened in this area. (Also see *Shopping* section.) Rua Gonçalves Dias is a mall and good for browsing. The few streets that cross the shopping area are rather narrow. Drop in for a snack at *Confeiteria Colombo,* Rua Gonçalves Dias 32 (phone: 231-9650).

Carioca Square (Largo da Carioca) – This small concrete plaza near the shopping center area has benches to rest on, shoeshiners and faith healers plying their trades, and street vendors selling everything from candy to folk art. The nearby St. Antonio Convent and Church (Convento e Igreja de São Antônio) is one of Rio's oldest, dating from the early 17th century. It has interesting blue tile work, indicating Portugal's influence, and some early paintings. Open daily. Free. Adjoining San Antonio.

The Church of St. Francis of the Penitence (Igreja de São Francisco da Penitencia) – Don't be discouraged by the uninspiring exterior of this church. Inside are carved altars and ceiling paintings by José de Oliveira, one of Brazil's outstanding artists. Rua Uruguiana and Carioca.

Metropolitan Cathedral (Catedral Metropolitana) – Rio's avant-garde cathedral was under construction for 15 years. The structure is conical, angular, and its only gesture to traditional design is the presence of four enormous stained-glass windows. Services are held on Sundays at 10 AM, daily at noon. Free. Near Largo de Carioca on Av. Chile (phone: 240-2869).

Municipal Theater (Teatro Municipal) – Modeled after the Paris Opera House, the Municipal Theater was built over an underground lake. Since it opened in 1909, it has been home to Brazil's best artists as well as visiting companies from North America and Europe. Opera, ballet, and concerts are performed here regularly. Performances are advertised in the *Brazil Herald,* the daily leisure supplement to the English-language newspaper, the *Latin America Daily Post.* The theater has undergone a major renovation in the last 4 years and its interior has been completely modernized. You'll recognize the building on the skyline by the eagle on its bronze roof. Av. Rio Branco at Praça Marechal Floriano (phone: 262-6322).

Museum of Fine Arts (Museu de Belas Artes) – This impressive building houses over 800 paintings and other works of art. Many of the works are reproductions of well-known artists. Closed Mondays. Admission charge. Av. Rio Branco 199 (phone: 240-0160).

Cinelândia – This is Rio's crowded downtown entertainment center, very busy every night. Clustered in this area are several large movie theaters, restaurants, hotels, pickup bars both straight and gay, and nightclubs. The main street, Rua Senador Dantas, begins at Praça Mahatma Gandhi and runs for several blocks.

Flamengo Park (Parque Flamengo) – Built in 1965, on the 400th anniversary of

Rio's founding, this bustling park has children's areas with playgrounds, a puppet theater, soccer fields, volleyball and basketball courts. A small tractor-pulled train takes you from place to place. Also in Flamengo Park are the Museum of Modern Art, the National War Memorial, and the Military Museum. The park stretches along Flamengo's shore.

The Museum of Modern Art (Museu de Arte Moderna) – This museum is Rio's finest. The building, designed by A. E. Reidy, a well-known Brazilian architect, is as modern as the works it houses. Although ground-floor exhibits are changed continuously, the second floor has the works of Brazilian and world masters. Ceramic and metal sculptures are also exhibited. This museum was partially destroyed by fire in 1978 and was closed to the public, but has recently reopened. Closed Mondays. Admission charge. Av. Beira Mar, Flamengo Park, Flamengo (phone: 220-3622, 240-6351).

National War Memorial (Monumento dos Mortos da II Guerra) – Two 150-foot pillars supporting a curved bowl with an eternal flame mark the war memorial. Three statues of servicemen, one from each branch of the military, guard this flame and the crypt beneath it. Inside is the Tomb of the Unknown Soldier and remains of Brazilian soldiers killed during World War II, in which Brazil fought with the Allies. These soldiers were killed and buried in Italy until reinterred here. Closed Mondays. Free. Flamengo Park, Flamengo.

Military Museum (Museu Militar) – Near the memorial stands a small military museum with memorabilia from World War II, including touching photographs, captured weapons, and murals. Closed Mondays. Admission charge. Flamengo Park, Flamengo (no phone).

Museum of the Republic (Museu da República) – This historical museum is in the Catete Palace, which was designed by a German architect and built between 1858 and 1866. In its checkered career it has served as a bank and hotel before it became the home of Brazil's presidents for 63 years. In 1960, when Brasília became the capital, Catete Palace became a museum. The inlaid wood mosaic floors are so highly polished you can see your reflection in them. Visitors are given slippers to wear in the museum. One room is the bedroom of former President Getulio Vargas; another, a huge banquet hall; a third, the former game room. The palace grounds are stunning. The garden has a series of royal palm trees, some as tall as 150 feet. Closed Mondays. Free. Rua do Catete 179, Catete (phone: 225-4302).

BEACH COMMUNITIES

With eight beaches at your disposal, you can visit a different one each day. Each has a distinct atmosphere and rhythm. Closest to downtown are Flamengo and Botafogo. You can swim in the calm waters of Guanabara Bay, but it is not advised because of pollution. Farther south are Leme, Copacabana, Ipanema, Leblon, São Conrado, and Barra da Tijuca, where you will be swimming in the Atlantic Ocean. It is best to swim in the morning and use your afternoons and early evenings to visit Rio's other "mustsee" attractions. Leave all valuables in your hotel when you come to the beach. Brazil's crime rate increases dramatically during the tourist-filled summer months, and it's asking for trouble to take cameras, watches, passports, and more than pocket money to the beach.

Copacabana – The heart of Rio's resort area, this community actually combines Leme and Copacabana beaches. The beach area is the longest and widest in the city. This is where the action is on sunny weekends all year. Avenida Atlântica, the wide, mosaic-tiled beachfront street, is lined with many fine hotels, excellent restaurants, sidewalk cafés, and elegant shops as well as fashionable apartment buildings. The area's major street however, Avenida N. S. da Copacabana, is one block from the beach. Here you will find somewhat less expensive but chic hotels, shops, cinemas, and art galleries. It is always crowded with people. Barata Ribeiro, two blocks from the beach, is a tree-lined street with take-out food stalls, antique shops, and private homes. At some points, Copacabana is only four blocks wide due to an encroaching mountain range.

Ipanema – The crown princess of beach areas is chic Ipanema. Slightly narrower and less crowded than Copacabana, it draws young bongo players, singles, college students, and upper-class *cariocas* with homes nearby. Avenida Vieira Souto, the beachfront street, has some good hotels and restaurants but is primarily residential. Rua Visconde de Piraja, two blocks from the beach, is the chicest shopping area of the city. The five-block stretch from Praça General Osório to Praça Nossa Senhora de Paz is lined with zany boutiques, shopping arcades, and small restaurants. Check out this area before buying anything, especially clothing. The Feirarte (see *Special Places,* above) is held in Praça Osório every Sunday at 8 AM. Rua Maria Quitéria is an important cross street of boutiques, night spots, and restaurants.

Leblon – Avenida Delfim Moreira, the oceanfront street, is lined with duplex and triplex apartment buildings in which many of Rio's wealthiest families live. Leblon is no longer the quietest of Rio's beaches, since several restaurants have opened on Avenida Ataulfo de Paiva, two blocks from the beach.

São Conrado – Until 10 years ago, São Conrado had a lovely beach, a golf club, and wide open spaces. Then the *Sheraton, Inter-Continental,* and *Nacional Rio* hotels went up along the São Conrado beaches. Soon apartment complexes, shopping areas, restaurants, night spots, schools, and supermarkets were built, and a new area of the city was developed. Avenida Niemeyer, which runs along the beach, is easily accessible by buses that run frequently from Copacabana. You can use the tennis facilities, nightclubs, and excellent restaurants at these three hotels (see *Checking In*).

Barra da Tijuca – Rio continues to expand in a southerly direction, and Barra is the newest area undergoing rapid growth. The city fathers are making a concerted effort to develop this area in a controlled manner to avoid overcrowding. New residential complexes under construction are already changing the Barra skyline, and hotels are also on the increase here. Barra's beach is very long and very narrow, and camping is permitted. Several unimposing restaurants serving superb seafood are right off the beach. A favorite is *Dinabar* (no phone), where the shrimp dishes are highly recommended. Although Barra is accessible by bus, a recent spate of bus crimes in the area — holdups and even murder — makes this a dangerous choice of transportation. Take a taxi.

SUBURBS

Santa Teresa – A visit to this picturesque area of the city, high up on a hill, will give you some idea of what Rio de Janeiro was like in colonial times. The narrow, winding streets are lined with lovely old buildings and homes, very different from the modern glass structures found downtown and on the beaches. The delightful tree-lined streets contain excellent examples of 19th-century architecture. You get a bonus when visiting this area: a chance to ride one of Rio's last trolleys. Take Bus 433 or 464 from Copacabana to Avenida Chile, where you get the trolley. Take off watches and hold on tightly to bags because thieves spot tourists easily and strike quickly, jumping off the moving trolley with their loot.

Chácara do Céu – This museum, whose name means "small farm of heaven," occupies a lovely old mansion. Its major emphasis is on modern and impressionistic works by Brazilian artists, although it exhibits Picassos, Monets, and Modiglianis from time to time and some metal sculptures, as well. The rooms of the mansion are elegantly appointed; the grounds, impeccably groomed; and the views of Botafogo from the rear garden, striking. After you take bus 433 or 464 from Copacabana to Avenida Chile and hop on the trolley, ask to be dropped at the museum. Closed Mondays. Admission charge. Rua Martinho Nobre 93, Santa Teresa (phone: 224-8981).

National Museum (Museu Nacional) – Set in a huge park, this museum, formerly the residence of Brazil's emperors, focuses on archaeology, anthropology, and the natural sciences, with exhibits like that of the Bendego meteorite, one of the largest ever found on earth. Particularly interesting are the displays of Amazon Indian tribes' weapons, clothing, and tools. Brazil's Amazon region has an astonishing variety of butterflies and birds, which are also on display. Closed Mondays. Admission charge. Buses 138 and 299 from downtown, 472 from Flamengo and 474 from Copacabana will drop you at the Quinta. Quinta da Boa Vista, São Cristóvão (phone: 264-8262).

Zoological Garden (Jardim Zoológico) – The zoo occupies part of the Quinta da Boa Vista and has the usual assortment of tigers, lions, and gorillas as well as several rarer species, especially in its bird and reptile collections. It's worth a look, particularly if you visit the National Museum. Closed Mondays. Admission charge. Quinta da Boa Vista, São Cristóvão (phone: 254-2024).

Botanical Gardens (Jardim Botânico) – A serene oasis in the middle of this big city where huge water lilies float in still ponds and you can find over 7,000 varieties of tropical plants, cacti, orchids, and banana plants. The paths are delineated by towering royal palm trees, and the aroma of the flowers is almost overpowering. The Kuhlmann Botanical Museum (phone: 294-9348), on the grounds, has exhibits explaining the types of vegetation found in different areas of Brazil. It also houses a part of the Palma Mater, an original palm planted in 1808, when the gardens opened, by Portuguese King Dom João VI. The palm was struck by lightning in 1973 and had to be cut down. Open daily. Admission charge. Bus 573 from Botafogo, 574 from Copacabana, and 172 from downtown will drop you at the garden. Botanical Gardens, Corcovado (phone: 274-4897).

Planetarium (Planetario) – This stop is worthwhile primarily to see the different constellations in the southern sky, of which the Southern Cross (Cruzeiro do Sul) is the best known. Open weekends only from 3 to 10 PM; there are sky shows from 3 until 9 PM. Admission charge. Take Bus 591 or 592 from from Copacabana or Botafogo. Rua Padre Leonel Franca, Gávea (phone: 274-0096).

Tivoli Amusement Park – More like an American amusement park than its namesake in Copenhagen, Tivoli has a hair-raising assortment of rides for adults and children. On the lagoon, there are some snack shops and fast-food counters. Fun to visit. Closed Mondays. Open 3 until 10 PM. Admission charge. Rides extra. Lagoa, near Jockey Club (phone: 274-1846).

■**EXTRA SPECIAL:** If you want to get away from Rio's crowded beaches without leaving the shore, head east on Route 101 and continue past the town of Niterói, with its 8-mile bridge. Niterói's beaches — Saco de São Francisco, Adão e Eva, and Icaraí — are popular weekend spots for *cariocas.* Historic sites include the 16th-century forts of Santa Cruz and Barão do Rio Branco. Continue east along the coast to Saquarema, a town with a boating and fishing lake as well as spectacular beaches. For a super view of the town, climb to the 17th-century church of Senhora de Nazaré. Cabo Frio, 100 miles (161 km) from Rio de Janeiro, at the easternmost tip of this stretch of shore appropriately named the Sun Coast (Costa do Sol), is one of the most popular resort areas in the state of Rio. About 14 miles (23 km) to the east, Armacão dos Búzios, known locally as Búzios, is the hideway of wealthy *cariocas,* jet-set millionaires, and visiting celebrities. Its beaches — Brava, João Fernandes, Ossos, Tamoios, and Rasa — are justifiably famed. The *Pousada dos Hibiscos,* in the center of town on Ossos beach, has a swimming pool, restaurant, and bar in addition to an ideal location. (For reservations, phone 274-4225 in Rio de Janeiro.) Just outside of town, on Praia Bahía Formosa, is *Auberge de l'Hermitage,* another excellent pousada. If you're looking for clean, modest accommodations, try *Estalgem Repouso do Guerreiro* on the main drag in town, Rua José Bento Ribeiro Dantas (phone: 2243; in Rio de Janeiro, phone 246-0455). On the same street are two charming, good restaurants, *Le Streghe*

Búzios and *Au Cheval Blanc.* Armação dos Búzios is a fishing village filled with restaurants specializing in seafood and fish. *Capelinha* and *Cabañas* on the beach are two of the best.

Or go south from Rio on the Santos highway to discover what the Brazilians know — the Frade hotels. Composing this charming trio are the *Portogalo,* high on a hill overlooking Ilha Grade Bay (phone: 65-1022); the *Hotel do Frade,* on its own beach on Angra Bay (phone: 65-1212, 65-1343); and the *Pousada D. João,* a restored colonial inn in the historic landmark town of Paratí. The first two are expensive and offer all the best of the sea; the third is moderately priced and one of several pousadas in this dream town. Paratí is the farthest down the road, 3 hours by car from Rio.

SOURCES AND RESOURCES

TOURIST INFORMATION: The English-language guidebook, *Rio Alive,* by Arnold and Harriet Greenberg, is available for $4.95 from Alive Publications (11 Park Pl., New York, NY 10007). *The Insiders Guide to Rio de Janeiro,* by the British journalist Christopher Pickard, who has lived in Rio for several years, offers a detailed rundown of the city and its goings-on as well as good maps; the book is sold in hotel bookstores in Rio, as well as in a few bookstores in the US, for about $7. *The Rio Visitor* (with map), *This Week in Rio,* and *Tourist Calendar Rio* are provided (free) by many hotels. You can pick up English-language pamphlets from RIOTUR, Rua São José 90, 8th floor (phone: 232-4320), or at its information booths at Corcovado station, Galeão Airport, and on Av. Atlântica, Copacabana. *Embratur,* Rua Matriz e Barros 13 (phone: 273-2212), has English-speaking staff members and an office in New York City at 551 Fifth Ave. (phone: 212-916-3206). *H. Stern* jewelers (see *Special Places*) produces a good map of Rio, available free at many hotels and on larger beach streets. *Schaeffer Guide* is also available at newsstands and hotel bookstores in Rio.

Local Coverage – The *Latin America Daily Post,* the South American equivalent of the *International Herald Tribune,* is published daily except Mondays in Rio and is distributed to newsstands in all the major South American cities. In Brazil, it contains the supplement, the *Brazil Herald,* which was formerly Rio's English-language newspaper. Check the *Herald* supplement for local events. The new editions of *Time* and *Newsweek* magazines arrive on Wednesdays. In the bookstores of major hotels you can buy the *New York Times, Miami Herald,* and the *International Herald Tribune.*

Food – *Rio Alive* contains excellent information on where to eat. *The Rio Visitor* has listings, too. Unless you speak fluent Portuguese, it is a good idea to ask someone at your hotel to phone for reservations when you need them. Once a disaster, the telephone system in Rio de Janeiro is gradually improving; but telephone numbers change frequently, and chances are you will reach as many wrong numbers as correct ones. Modernistic phone booths are on most street corners, if you are masochistic enough to insist. Use a *ficha,* or token, which you can buy at newsstands.

CLIMATE AND CLOTHES: Roughly on the same latitude as Puerto Rico but south of the equator, Rio de Janeiro has a tropical climate. Spring and summer, between October and March, have average temperatures of between 85° and 95°F (between 29° and 39°C). It does get much hotter, and it is sometimes very humid. Evenings are usually cool, with breezes sweeping in from the bay and ocean. Heavy rains start and stop quickly and frequently during the summer. Fall and winter, between April and October, are cooler, with temperatures falling into the high 70s F (around 22°C) and occasionally as low as the 60s F (around 16°C). In winter, it is less humid and rains less often. You can swim and sunbathe all year, although *cariocas* do not really consider October warm enough for the beach.

Brazilians have a flair for fashion and are well dressed. As in most tropical climates, informality is the key, but you will not feel out of place if you dress up. People feel free to dress to suit their mood, much as they do in New York. Bring comfortable, lightweight, colorful clothing. Most hotels have laundry service, but wash-and-wear clothing will prove much less expensive. Bring comfortable walking shoes for sightseeing. Some of the posher restaurants require jackets and ties, so tuck a tie in your pocket just in case.

GETTING AROUND: Bus – Plentiful and the least expensive mode of transportation. Always crowded, they are sometimes air-conditioned. Buses go from all parts of the city to outlying beaches and parks. Bus stops are marked Onibus; you enter through the rear door. Two bus lines, the Alvorada and São Conradorantes, link the Galeão International Airport with hotels in the downtown beach areas.

Taxi – Ubiquitous and, except for peak hours, easy to hail. Most are VW bugs with the front seat removed and meters installed. There is a surcharge after 10 PM. Rio cab drivers make breaking wild horses seem like a tame ride. Sit back and hang on. To check your fare, look at the table glued on the back window; Brazilian inflation has outpaced the meters in digits, and prices change every few months. Two reliable radio taxis at the airport are *Cootramo* and *Transcopass;* you prepay at the airport.

Car Rental – *Hertz* and *Avis* have offices at both Galeão and Santos Dumont airports. Rates start at $20 a day plus mileage for a Volkswagen. Larger cars are more expensive. Gasoline costs about $2.25 a gallon. Remember that there is a national ban on selling gasoline on Sundays, so tank up early and take enough extra gas so that you don't get stranded in some out-of-the-way place. *Hertz*'s main office is at Av. Princesa Isabel 334-B, Copacabana (phone: 275-4996); *Avis,* Av. Princesa Isabel 150 (phone: 542-4249).

Trolley – Rio has a few trolley lines that are fun to ride. The most interesting is from Avenida Chile to the Santa Teresa section (see *Special Places,* above).

MUSEUMS: The Museum of Modern Art, the Military Museum, the Museum of the Republic, the National Museum, and the Kuhlman Botanical Museum (Botanical Gardens) are described in *Special Places.* Other museums of special interest include:

Carmen Miranda Museum – Filled with photographs from the motion pictures of the popular star of the 1940s. Her famous pineapple turbans and extraordinarily high sandals are on exhibit along with costumes and jewelry. Open Tuesday through Friday, 11 AM to 5 PM, and Saturday and Sunday, 1 to 5 PM. Av. Rui Barbosa 560, Flamengo Park, Flamengo (phone: 551-2597).

Antônio de Oliveira Museum – A tribute to Brazil's famous sculptor, it contains more than 1,200 wood carvings depicting scenes from Brazilian life in colonial times, early Carnivals, and folk dances. On Urca Mountain, the first stop in the cable-car link to the summit of Pão de Açúcar.

Pharmacy Museum – Contains old pharmaceutical equipment, apothecary jars, containers, scales, and an antique music box that plays eight different tunes. Rua Santa Lúzia 206 (phone: 297-6611).

Police Academy Museum – A mini-version of the FBI Museum in Washington, with exhibits on ballistics, fingerprinting, and forging equipment. Don't ask pointed questions about human rights violations or police items not on display. Rua Frei Caneca 162 (phone: 224-6058).

Indian Museum (Museu do Indio) – Reopened in its new building, the museum contains articles and scenes of contemporary Indian life in Brazil's Amazon region. Ceramics, utensils carved of jatoba wood, clay dolls, baskets, and religious articles still used by these primitive tribes are on display. Rua das Palmeiras, 55 Botafogo (phone: 286-8799).

SHOPPING: Brazil is the world's leading exporter of gems, and they are easily the best buy here. Often referred to as semiprecious stones, they have become increasingly popular in recent years with both men and women. High-quality gems are set in 18-karat gold; less expensive ones, in silver. Designs are innovative and trendy. Bracelets, pendants, earrings, and rings in a multitude of colors sparkle in the windows of elegant shops. The most popular stones used in fine jewelry are aquamarine, in various shades of blue; the tourmaline, of which the green are most popular; purple amethyst; and gold-yellow or brown topaz. Stones are classified by color as well as by size and degree of perfection. Turquoise, cat's-eye opal, and lapis lazuli are the gemstones most often set in popular silver costume jewelry.

Brazil's rich folk traditions are expressed in primitive paintings, woven wall tapestries, batiks, wood carvings, and masks. These colorful items are not yet well known in the US and make interesting home decorations. Other good buys are salad bowl sets, ashtrays, bookends, and serving platters made of Brazilian rosewood (*jacarandá*). Ashtrays and paperweights of chunks of rock with low-grade stones imbedded in them are good gift items. Bikinis and *tangas* (micro-bikinis), T-shirts, leather shoes, and handbags are also highly prized Rio catches. The prices of these items are comparable to US prices, but the quality is good and the styles are Brazilian. No one should leave Rio without a *figa,* the Brazilian good luck charm — a clenched fist with a raised thumb. They come in any number of colored stones, carved in wood and even gold and silver, and make inexpensive, yet thoughtful, purely Brazilian gifts.

Boutiques and shops are scattered throughout downtown and the beach areas. However, three clusters of shops give you an easy way to browse and compare. The finest boutiques for clothing and accessories are on Rua Visconde de Pirajá, the main street of Ipanema, and its side streets. Small shopping arcades jut off the main street as well. Avenida Copacabana, one block from the beach, is the major shopping area of Copacabana, with native crafts stores, art galleries, and costume jewelry shops. The area near the old Copacabana Palace is thronged with shoppers in search of folklore items, *jacarandá* wood, and Indian artifacts (see *Special Places*). Prices here are slightly lower than in the other streets mentioned.

Stores open at 9 AM and often stay open until 6 or 7 PM. Most are open on Saturday until 1 PM. What follows is a list of leading shops. Undoubtedly, you will discover more as you browse.

Copacabana Couros e Artesanatos – A small shop with a variety of leather items: lampshades, folding chairs, beanbag chairs, desk sets, briefcases, and footrests are the best-selling items. Belts, wallets, and handbags are close behind. Everything in the shop is made on the premises. Rua Fernando Mendes 45A, Copacabana.

Feirarte I – Formerly the Hippie Market, this is held every Sunday from 9 AM to 6 PM; it's as much an institution as Corcovado Mountain. Original oil paintings in modern and primitive styles, hand-tooled leather belts, handbags, sandals, wallets, carved wood statues, bowls, gaily painted ceramic planters, wooden boxes of all sizes, kitchen utensils, handmade aprons, potholders are all yours for the bargaining (see *Special Places,* above). Praça General Osório, Ipanema.

Feira de São Sebastião (or Feirarte II) – A smaller version of Feirarte I, it's held in one of Rio's most historical sections, downtown. Although you can get handicrafts of metal, leather, and straw, it is best known for its large selection of antiques, coins, and stamps. Open Thursdays and Fridays from 9 AM to 7 PM. Praça XV de Novembro, downtown.

Folklore – Costume jewelry and folklore items are sold together in this highly successful shop, with a lot of merchandise crammed into a small space: *figas,* charms, and Indian artifacts, along with silver jewelry set with opal, cat's eye, and agate. If you are looking for a great gift for a young child, consider a set of small, polished gemstones sold with the raw material from which they came. It is also a good place to find eye-catching palm bark wall masks and papagallo kites. Av. Atlântica 1782, Copacabana.

Forum de Ipanema – This new, modern arcade of small boutiques specializes in sportswear, bikinis, even briefer *tangas,* and T-shirts. Creative store windows depict the latest trends. Rua Visconde de Pirajá, in front of the Square Nossa Senhora da Paz, Ipanema.

Galeria 444 – Another shopping arcade with boutiques jam-packed with blue jeans, T-shirts, and *tangas.* Rua Visconde de Pirajá, Ipanema.

H. Stern – Brazil's largest gemstone retailer, and the first stop if you are interested in buying jewelry. The classy new showroom staffed by multilingual personnel contains private viewing areas where tray upon tray of bracelets, rings, pins, or whatever your heart and pocketbook desire is presented for your appraisal. *H. Stern* jewelry has extremely contemporary as well as traditional settings. There is no hard sell, but the gems are hard to resist. Prices start at $50 and go way up. Gems are set in 18-karat yellow gold, white gold, or platinum. You are issued a written guarantee, and your jewelry can be returned to any *H. Stern* outlet within 1 year of purchase. Since there are more than 100 shops worldwide, including one in New York, it is easy to have repairs done or stones matched. *H. Stern* maintains shops and service desks in virtually every hotel in Rio, but the main showroom is at Visconde de Pirajá 490, 3rd Floor, Ipanema (phone: 259-7442). If you are not interested in buying gems, at least take the free workshop tour (see *Special Places,* above).

Northeastern Fair – Those who can't get to the northeast of Brazil should stop in for a taste of its regional food (typical cheeses and *carne-de-sol,* a meat dish with beans), its music (an interesting combination of accordion, triangle, and drum — live), and its flea market mania (hammocks and leather goods proliferate). Open Sundays from 6 AM to 1 PM. Campo de São Cristorão.

Rio Design Center – This ultra-modern shopping center fills three floors with Rio's most chic home (and office) furnishings stores. It also has a variety of art galleries and restaurants and is a good place to browse when it rains. Av. Ataulfo de Paiva 270, Leblon.

Rio Sul – Another shopping center, it features just about every Brazilian store worth visiting and a smattering of typical tourist boutiques as well. Free bus transportation available along Av. Atlântico. Just a hop, skip, and jump from the bustling Copacabana.

São Conrado Fashion Mall – Close to the *Intercontinental Rio* and *Nacional Rio* hotels, this shopping mall gears its merchandise to the tourist. Exhibitions on Brazilian culture are presented regularly on the top floor. São Conrado.

Sidi – Carries items made of jacarandá, or rosewood, such as salad bowls and trays, as well as souvenir items, including stones. *Sidi* has two locations: Av. Atlântica 1536-A and at Shopping Cassino Atlântica, Av. Atlântica 4240, loja 205, Copacabana.

Zuhause – For more unusual local crafts as well as interesting dehydrated plants, visit one of this company's two shops in Copacabana. Rua Barata Ribeiro 303-A or 458.

 SPECIAL EVENTS: *Carnival,* Rio-style, is the granddaddy of all special events and the standard by which all others are measured. If you've ever been to Mardi Gras in New Orleans or other pre-Lent celebrations in the Caribbean, multiply the excitement by 1,000 and you'll just be coming close to what happens here! It's as if the outside world fades away and nothing exists except the samba beat and the will to be part of unrestrained joy. People who've never danced before find themselves caught up in the tremendous outpouring of rhythm and gaiety. Carnival (Cahr-nah-val) officially takes place on the five days that precede Ash Wednesday, but the Carnival spirit starts early in November, when preparations go into high gear at social clubs all over Rio. These clubs each sponsor a samba school — a huge group of singers, dancers, and musicians that will strut through the Sambódromo downtown on Sunday and Monday of Carnival in frenzied competition with other outstanding clubs. Club members painstakingly create original lyrics, samba music, dance steps, and fantastic costumes around a theme chosen by each individual school. Each club has fans and admirers in the more than 500,000 onlookers sitting in bleacher seats along the street or standing on the sidewalks. They sing, clap, cheer, stamp their feet, whistle, and dance along with their favorites. You, too, will become involved very quickly. The refrains are repeated frequently, and since a school can have between 2,000 and 3,000 marchers, it can take 45 minutes for a group to pass you. The parades begin at 6 PM Sunday and Monday and may continue (with waits of up to an hour between groups) until noon the following day. The entire city is decorated with colored lights and streamers. Bandstands are erected on street corners to allow dancing in the streets. On those corners without bandstands, impromptu combos play. People in very skimpy costumes dance gaily through the streets on all 5 nights of Carnival. Everywhere — from on the buses to on the beaches — samba is king. Business comes to a halt for the duration of the frenetic holiday in which *cariocas* welcome the world to participate with them.

Another exotic aspect of Carnival is the fabulous balls held in *Canecão Nightclub* and major club ballrooms. A few of the best are the *Vermelho e Preto* ball at the Flamengo football club; the Yacht Club Ball, a week before Carnival; and *Baile de Pão de Açúcar* at Sugar Loaf. Wealthy and socially prominent *cariocas* attend in formal attire or fantastic costumes. Elaborate silk gowns, gem-encrusted tiaras, and even powdered wigs make this an incredible sight. If you plan to attend a ball, formal attire or a costume is suggested, although Brazilian ball-goers often dress informally: men wear anything from T-shirts and gym shorts to caftans; women tend to be more festive, with feathers and plenty of glitter. In any event, dress coolly — the balls are crowded and hot. (Note: Ball tickets, bleacher seats for the samba schools' parades, and hotel accommodations require reservations months in advance.) Since ball tickets can run $50 and up, you may prefer to spend the night club-hopping. Many clubs have all-night samba shows in which the audience participates. On Tuesday night, the street dancing winds down, and when dawn breaks on Ash Wednesday, the city is strangely quiet. Another Carnival is history.

Cariocas in exile can get accustomed to living without beaches, warm weather, and *feijoada,* but they cannot survive without celebrating Carnival. Every year, the Brazilian community in the US and Canada flocks to the Grand Ballroom of the Waldorf-Astoria in New York for a wild evening of samba schools, costume contests, and a leading Carnival band imported from Rio de Janeiro. In fact, the pageantry of the northern Carnival has become an attraction in its own right, with some *cariocas* traveling from Brazil to participate. ("After all," they claim, "we've seen Carnival in Rio for so many years.")

If you are going to be in Rio anytime between November and Carnival, you should visit a samba school rehearsal for an inkling of what the main event is like. Samba schools are really social clubs; they can be found throughout Rio and are especially common in low-income areas and *favelas.* There are a great many of them and they are ranked. The top 14 clubs take part in the major Carnival parade, while those with lower ranks dance in other parts of the city. Every August, each school chooses its own theme. The goal is to be judged best on Carnival night. Winning means money for the club and, occasionally, fame for the top performers. Starting in November, rehearsals are well organized enough to permit visitors. While the costumes are not completed, the music, lyrics, and enthusiasm of the several hundred participants are contagious, and you'll soon be moving to the samba beat yourself. Many of these clubs have been taking part in Carnivals for over 100 years and are rich in tradition. The practice halls are far from Copacabana, unfortunately, but some can be reached in 30 minutes by car. Mangueira, one of the oldest clubs and a frequent prizewinner, practices Friday, Saturday, and Sunday nights from around 10 PM at the *Palacio do Samba,* Rua Visconde de Niterói 1072, Mangueira (phone: 234-4129). Beija-Flor, winner of four recent Carnivals, has rehearsals on Friday, Saturday, and Sunday nights at 11 PM at *Quadra de Nilopolis,* Rua Pracinha Wallace Paes Leme 1652, Nilopolis (phone: 791-1571). Salgueiro rehearses Saturdays at 10 PM at Rua Silva Teles 104, Andarai (no phone). In addition, Beija-Flor and Portela samba schools hold rehearsals in Botafogo, which is more convenient for tourists to attend. Check your hotel for schedules.

Macumba is the ritual practiced by some ten million Brazilians. Loosely related to voodoo and based on African and Indian rituals, *macumba* draws most of its followers from descendants of African slaves but has adherents in all levels of society. *Macumb eiros* believe that spirits affect all aspects of our lives for both good and evil. *Macumba* rituals allay the evil spirits and encourage good ones. A medium (called *cavalo,* meaning "horse") is used to call on the spirits to assist individuals in need. When the slaves tried to practice their own faith, slave owners and the Catholic Church suppressed it, forcing the slaves to conduct secret ceremonies in the forests and on the beaches. To appear more orthodox, many *macumba* gods and goddesses were renamed Christian Biblical names. Over the years, African ritual intermingled with the Indian traditions, so *macumba* as practiced today is not akin to any African religion but to other regional religions such as voodoo. You can attend a *macumba* rite in houses of worship called *terreiros.* Outside each *terreiro* is a small house where the evil spirit (Exu) is held captive. Lighted candles placed outside the house are designed to keep Exu imprisoned during the ceremony. The *terreiro* itself is usually a large room dimly lit by candles. An altar in the center holds a crucifix as well as statuettes of Oxala (the major god, comparable to Jesus), Iemanjá (the goddess of the sea, comparable to the Virgin Mary), and other figures. The ceremony opens with singing, interrupted by the white-robed *cavalos* (mediums). They grunt, grimace, and roll on the ground, speaking in strange tongues. By observing this business, adherents can tell which spirit has possessed the *cavalo.* As the *cavalos* position themselves around the *terreiro,* worshipers queue up to speak to the spirit guide from whom they need assistance. A cleansing ritual, chanting, and some herbal medicines are involved. The ceremony goes on for hours. *Pai Jeronimo* (Rua Barão de Uba 423, Praça da Bandeira, Zona Norte), a 20-minute cab ride from Copacabana, is a *terreiro* that permits visitors at its 10 PM ceremony. Wear white, sit quietly, and don't cross your arms or legs, as this is believed to interfere with the arriving spirits. Leave your camera in the hotel — no photographs are allowed.

Other *terreiros* that permit visitors are *Tenda Espirita Mirim* (597 Av. Marechal Rondon, São Francisco Xavier) on Wednesday and Friday evenings at 8 PM, and *Yansa Egum Nitã* (152 Rua Santa Ifigenia, Jacarepaguá) on Saturday evenings at 10 PM.

The Feast of Iemanjá, a major and highly visible *macumba* festival, occurs on December 31, when thousands of *macumbeiros* come to Rio's beaches, starting at sunset and continuing until dawn. Lace cloths are spread along the tide line, and offerings of fruits, perfumes, colorful ribbons, and flowers are laid on them by the worshipers. Drums keep up a hypnotic beat as frenzied dancing begins. Candles placed on small mounds of sand flicker eerily. At midnight Iemanja, goddess of the sea, sends a huge wave that either accepts (carries out to sea) or rejects the offering. The dancing and rituals go on until dawn. If you face Copacabana Beach, you have the best "seat." Also at midnight, spectacular fireworks explode over Copacabana Beach and from atop the *Rio Othon Palace* home.

SPORTS: Bicycling – Bicycles can be rented on Paquetá Island (see *Special Places,* above). Avoid biking in Rio, where traffic is heavy.

Fishing – Marlin, bass, shark, and codfish are among Atlantic catches. Make arrangements with *Bateau Mouche,* Av. Nestor Moreira II, Botafogo (phone: 295-1997).

Golf – Most golf courses in Rio are part of private clubs and closed to nonmembers. The best course open to the public is the *Gávea Golf Club,* opposite the *Nacional* hotel. You can play 18 holes on a lovely course for $35 in greens fees plus $5 for the caddy. One catch — you can only play weekdays. Hotels can make a starting-time reservation for you. Estrada de Gávea 800, São Conrado (phone: 399-4141).

Sailing – The two big annual sailing regattas are from Rio de Janeiro to Buenos Aires in February, and from Rio to Santos in November. For information, contact the yacht club: *Iate Club do Rio de Janeiro,* Av. Pasteur (phone: 295-0048). Rio de Janeiro has been a harbor in round-the-world sailing races in recent years.

Soccer – On every beach in Rio, soccer (*futebol*) goal posts are in continuous use. In parks, plazas, and on quiet neighborhood streets, young boys are playing soccer, often with a ball so worn that it is barely recognizable. Brazil has an illustrious name in soccer lore, having won the World Cup in three competitions. This enabled it to keep the trophy in the country. The culmination of hard-fought matches played all over the world during a 2-year span, the cup is awarded every 4 years. The site of the championship competition changes each time. Brazil has many outstanding players. Some play on professional teams in Brazil; others, in foreign countries. The man acclaimed as the greatest soccer player ever, Pelé, hails from Santos, Brazil. The world's best-known and highest-paid athlete, Pelé led Brazil to victory in three World Cup finals. Recently he played for the New York Cosmos, leading them to their league championship and helping to popularize soccer in the US. The pro soccer clubs of Rio and visiting national and international teams play matches at *Maracanã Estádio* (Stadium), São Cristovão (phone: 264-9962). It holds 200,000 spectators and has six tiers. The team's aficionados wave banners, stamp their feet, hoot at the referees, and cheer their team. This is an exciting introduction to high-level soccer. Matches are held Saturday evening at 9 PM and Sundays at 5 PM. Bus 443 from Copacabana or 442 from Flamengo will whisk you there. Amateur but highly skilled players compete in league games at Parque do Flamengo on weekends.

Swimming and Surfing – Take your pick of ocean beaches, but remember that the Atlantic Ocean waves pound the shore in the afternoon. That's good for surfing, and you'll see any number of surfers along Ipanema Beach. If you are a serious swimmer who prefers to swim laps in calm water, you will do better at one of the large hotels' swimming pools. *The Sheraton,* Av. Niemeyer, Vidigal (phone: 274-1122), and the *Inter-Continental,* São Conrado (phone: 322-2200), have gorgeous pools in which you can easily spend hours. The pool is open to the public for a fee. In fact, wealthy *cariocas* use the *Sheraton*'s swimming pool, poolside bar–restaurants, and tennis courts as a country club.

Track – The *Jockey Club,* Rio's racetrack, has quite a setting, more like a park than a track. It has towering palms, colorful plants, flowers, and even a small lagoon in the center. Races are held on Saturdays and Sundays at 2 PM and on Monday and Thursday evenings at 7:45 PM. You can bet as little as $1 or as much as $20. "Win" windows are called *vencedor* and "place" are called *place.* There is no "show" bet. Admission is about $1 in the stands. Bus 574 from Copacabana or 438 and 172 from downtown will take you there. Praça Santos Dumont (phone: 274-0055).

Tennis – The *Inter-Continental* and *Sheraton* hotels have tennis courts that can be rented for an hour by nonguests. Call the hotel to make arrangements. *Inter-Continental,* São Conrado (phone: 322-2200), or *Sheraton,* Vidigal (phone: 274-1122). There are six illuminated courts at *LOB,* which has English-speaking teachers. Rua Stefan Zweig

290 Laranjeiras (phone: 225-0329 for reservations). There are also courts at Parque Flamengo, but they are difficult to reserve.

 THEATER: The *Escola Americana,* Estrada da Gávea, Gávea (phone: 322-0825), is one theater in Rio where English-language plays are presented regularly. Most of the plays are scaled-down versions of Broadway dramas and musicals. It is an amateur theater company, not professional, but the shows are enthusiastically done. *The Players* theater presents Shakespeare and other English-language productions several times a year. Rua Real Grandeza, 99 Botafogo (phone: 226-0564). Tickets for both run around $5. Check the *Brazil Herald* for scheduling.

 MUSIC: The 2,000-seat Municipal Theater (Teatro Municipal) is Rio's Carnegie Hall, presenting operas, ballets, and concerts. Often the performance features a touring company from the US or Europe. Ticket prices start at $5 and run as high as $30. Check the *Brazil Herald* or the Caderno B entertainment section of the Portuguese-language daily *Jornal do Brasil* for current attractions. Av. Rio Branco at Praça Floriano (phone: 262-6322). Chamber music is played at the *Sala Cecilia Meireless,* Rua da Lapa 47 (phone: 232-9714), and at the *Sala Nicolau Copernico* in the *Planetarium.* Rua Padre Leonel Franca 240, Gávea (phone: 274-0096).

 NIGHTCLUBS AND NIGHTLIFE: Rio's nightlife is world-renowned. There are plenty of night spots of all kinds, and since dinner is rarely started before 9 PM, most clubs don't get going until 11 PM and stay open until the last guest staggers out. Feel like dancing? Try a frenetic discotheque. Enjoy watching? Visit a club featuring a sex-charged samba show. Like your drinks with a stiff upper lip and darts? Drop into an English pub. The list and variety of clubs goes on and on — ranging from posh supper clubs to far-out discotheques to piano bars, gay and hetero pickup bars, and even a German beer hall or two. Rio has a surprisingly large number of clubs that have remained jammed on weekends for over 10 years. It also has clubs that are very "in" for a short time and very "out" soon after.

Dress is informal, except at some supper clubs. In clubs with shows, there is a cover charge — usually $8, sometimes more. Often, there is a two-drink minimum as well. By the way, Scotch is extremely expensive in Brazil, so stick to rum, gin, or vodka.

As in much of Latin America, nightclubs admit couples only. Single women are rarely admitted by the doormen, who zealously guard the entrances. Sometimes single men are admitted. Still, the times they are a changin', and some clubs, particularly those with shows, will admit women if they are tourists.

Popular nightclubs with shows include *Canecão,* which is large enough to hold 2,000 people. *Canecão* maintains its status as Rio's top club by delivering top Brazilian and foreign entertainers as well as continuous dance music, both Latin and rock. Reservations are important on weekends. Shows are at 9:30 PM on Wednesdays and Thursdays, 10:15 PM on Fridays and Saturdays, and 6:30 PM on Sundays. Open daily from 8:30 PM to 4 AM; the cover charge is about $6. Av. Venceslau Braz 215, Botafogo (phone: 295-3044). And if it's sheer luxury you're after, be sure to see the show at *Scala-Rio;* one of the newest and largest (1,500-person capacity) nightclubs, it provides a first-rate Las Vegas–style show with Brazilian flair — lots of nudity and samba. Dining and dancing are also on the agenda; reservations suggested. Av. Afrânio de Melo Franco 296, Leblon (phone: 239-4448).

Oba Oba's famous show features majestic mulatto showgirls in a variety of skimpy outfits as well as samba dancers. Shows start at 11 PM, with an additional show at midnight on Friday and Saturday nights; closed Mondays. Rua Humaita 110, Humaita.

Phone 286-9848 for reservations on weekends (a must). Better yet is *Plataforma I,* whose samba show is at 11 PM nightly. Rua Adalberto Ferreira 32, Leblon (phone: 274-4022).

Regine's, a branch of the very exclusive French *boîte,* is a membership club but frequently admits tourists. Expensive but very attractive, at the *Méridien* hotel, ground floor (separate entrance), Av. Princesa Isabel at Av. Atlântica, Copacabana (phone: 275-9922). Two other popular private clubs that might let you in are *Hippopotamus,* Praça Nossa Senhora da Paz, and the *Palace Club* at the *Rio Palace* hotel, Av. Atlântica 4240 (several hotels in Rio will, on request, provide their patrons with cards that allow entry to *Hippopotamus*). *Alô-Alô,* a dimly lit, sophisticated piano bar next door to the *Hippo,* shares the same owner and attracts a classy but more relaxed crowd than its neighbor; Rua Barão da Torre 368, Ipanema (phone: 047-7178). *Mikonos,* a club in a private house, features jazz for listening upstairs, music to dance to downstairs. Open from 10 PM to 4 AM nightly. Av. Bartolomeu Mitre 366, Leblon (phone: 294-2298). *Sobre os Ondas,* a club with live music on the second floor, which overlooks the Copacabana street scene, is quiet and pleasant for listening or for dancing; Av. Atlântica 3432 (phone: 287-6144). The discotheque with the best location in town has to be *Noites Cariocas,* atop Urca adjoining Sugar Loaf Mountain, where you'll see the most avant-garde steps in town. Open Friday and Saturday evenings at 10. Cable car. Praia Vermelha Station, Av. Pasteur, Botafogo. *Circus Disco* is a swinging spot popular with the young Ipanema beach crowd. It's right above the *Bella-Blu Pizza Parlor,* Av. General Urquiza 102, Leblon (phone: 274-7895). *Cassino Royale,* a two-story building overlooking São Conrado Beach, lets patrons choose among disco dancing, soft music, video games, even bowling. On the Estrada do Joá, São Conrado (phone: 399-3311). Rio's newest disco, *Help,* on the busy Copacabana stretch, draws a young crowd; its flashing lights can't be missed. Av. Atlântica 3432 (phone: 521-1296). For those who want to experience the special beat of the Northeast, there's *Forró da Lapa;* the regional music — played with accordion, triangle, tambourine, and drum — has its own skippy dance step and is considered Brazil's version of country-and-western music. It opens at 9 PM; Rua Riachuelo 19 (phone: 242-6586).

Couples of all ages flock to *gafieiras* on weekends. These large dance halls offer live music for good old twosome dancing. Two traditional *gafieiras* are *Elite,* upstairs on Rua Frei Caneca 4, Centro (phone: 232-3217) and nearby *Estudantina,* which draws a younger crowd. Praça Tiradentes 79, Centro (phone: 232-1149). The newest and most sophisticated *gafieira* is *Asa Branca.* Besides its large dance floor, this club also features shows with some of the country's best singers. Av. Mem de Sá 17, Lapa (phone: 252-4428).

Not a club devotee? You have plenty of other choices: English-language cinemas, sidewalk cafés with live music for only a small donation, *macumba* services, samba school rehearsals, sporting and cultural events of all kinds, and moonlight to do with what you wish. If you're alone, it's easy to find someone to share the moonlight with. What more can you ask for? *Lord Jim Pub* is a popular meeting spot for English-speaking people living in Rio. It is more of a Swiss chalet than a pub, but with bars on both floors, darts, and steak and kidney pie on the upstairs restaurant menu, the feeling is strictly British. Rua Paul Redfern 63, Ipanema (phone: 259-3047).

 SINS: As befits a cosmopolitan city, Rio has its share of raunchy clubs that cater to indiscriminate *lust* (primarily male). In addition, some night spots feature erotic shows and nude dancers and one club draws guys, gals, and hookers. Erotic shows are the draw at *Assyrius,* Av. Rio Branco 277 (phone: 220-1998), and *Erotika* at Av. Prado Junior 63, Copacabana (phone: 237-9390). Both clubs are attractive and offer late-night shows and women eager to join unattached men for a drink. Many couples come here for the show, which includes simulated sex and nude dancing. The majority of pickup clubs cater to unattached men. *Bolero* and *Holiday* on Avenida Atlântica in Copacabana are institutions, having been around for years. The bar area sprawls with unattached females ready to join paying customers for a drink or two (at the least).

The sin spots along Rua Belfort-Roxo in Copacabana, between Avenida Copacabana and Avenida Atlântica, sport names like *Pussycat Bar*. One block over on Avenida Princesa Isabel, such spots as *Barbarella, Funky,* and *New Scotch* offer more raunchy entertainment.

Streetwalkers are hard to avoid, and unescorted men will be approached on most parts of Avenida Atlântica, Copacabana; on the beachfront avenue, Defim Moreira, at the beginning of Leblon; and on Rua Senador Dantas, downtown. Most of the women have apartments for their enterprise; the minority frequent small hotels.

BEST IN TOWN

CHECKING IN: Rio has hotels to suit any taste or pocketbook. A visitor can select a downtown hotel but would probably enjoy a nearby beach community more, a far cry from the hotel-upon-hotel scene of such places as Miami Beach or Honolulu. No hotel in Rio is directly on the beach. The majority of hotels on Copacabana Beach are discernible from the adjoining apartment buildings only by their lobbies. They offer beachfront accommodations and comfortable surroundings. It was less than a decade ago that resort-style hotels opened in Rio. Designed by Brazil's foremost architects, they were built on newly developed São Conrado and have swimming pools, tennis courts, beautifully landscaped grounds, boutiques, several restaurants, and nightspots. Although the areas around them have become more residential, these hotels still offer some measure of isolation, yet they're only minutes from the heart of Copacabana.

Choosing a hotel just a block or two off the beach can save a considerable amount of money and still assure clean, pleasant surroundings. All rooms are air conditioned and have private baths, unlike the small European hotels with communal bathrooms. An added bonus: Hotel rates usually include a delicious breakfast that is often served in your room. Breakfasts range from Continental style (juice, rolls, and coffee) to complete meals, with fresh fruit, cheese, warm rolls, and coffee.

Hotel rates have risen here as they have everywhere, but compared to those of resort hotels in the Caribbean, the prices are moderate. Our expensive choices cost from $100 to about $140 for a double room; moderate, $65 to $90; inexpensive, under $60 (and as low as $40) nightly.

Caesar Park – Newly opened, and already a favorite, this is Ipanema's first true luxury hotel. A tall, ultra-contemporary structure with a small swimming pool, its rooms are all luxuriously decorated, with conveniences like stocked refrigerators. It prides itself on excellent service, and the *feijoada* meal on Saturdays is an event. Prices are high. Av. Viera Souto, Ipanema (phone: 287-3122). Expensive.

Copacabana Palace – To get an idea of luxury 1920s style, walk through the lobbies and public rooms of Rio's dowager queen of a hotel. This grand establishment occupies the entire block from Avenida Atlântica to Avenida Copacabana, and its 145 rooms have 14-foot ceilings and terraces facing the beach. The *Palace* has its own following, who return every year. It has a pool, very elegant restaurants, and an English-language bookstore. Fortunately, plans to replace this lovely building with an apartment house fell though, and it has been recently renovated instead. Av. Atlântica 1702, Copacabana (phone: 257-1818). Expensive.

Inter-Continental Rio – Part of the superior worldwide hotel chain, the Rio branch holds up very well, its only drawback being that it's a bit far from the center of things. Its well-kept grounds include the best of Rio hotel recreational facilities: two tennis courts (lighted for night play), a jogging path along its beach, and a double pool with a bar forming the island between. Rooms are furnished in contemporary Brazilian style. All have balconies, facing either the ocean or the grounds. It's particularly lovely at dusk. The hotel has its own shops, airline offices, beauty salons, and restaurants. The *Papillon* discotheque is very popular with young *cariocas*. Av. Litorânea 222, São Conrado (phone: 322-2200). Expensive.

Marina Palace – Not to be confused with its sister resort, *Marina Rio,* it is also subdued and elegant, with a very good restaurant on the second floor, overlooking the beach. It's one of the few beachfront hotels in Leblon with a view. Av. Delfim Moreira 630, Leblon (phone: 259-5212). Expensive.

Marina Rio – With only 70 rooms and set on Rio's most subdued beach, Leblon, this is the place to go for a quiet retreat in elegant, understated surroundings. Even the music at the piano bar is muted, and waiters in the fine Continental restaurant speak in hushed tones. Not everyone's idea of Rio, but it may be yours. Av. Delfim Moreira 696, Leblon (phone: 239-8844). Expensive.

Méridien Copacabana – The outstanding French chain has built on a major Copacabana thoroughfare. The *Café de la Paix* on the main floor could settle in amid the brasseries of the Champs-Élysées, and Paul Bocuse's *Le St. Honoré* on the 37th floor serves classic haute cuisine. Rooms are elegantly appointed, and the decor of the entire hotel is particularly stylish. The swimming pool on the fourth floor is edged by a comfortable sun deck and well-stocked bar. Rooms have radio, TV, and refrigerators. Av. Atlântica 1020 at Av. Princessa Isabel, Copacabana (phone: 275-9922). Expensive.

Nacional – Oscar Niemeyer, the renowned Brazilian architect who created Brasília and designed the UN building in New York, is responsible for this hotel. It is a round, glass, 26-story structure that blends perfectly into the surrounding area of mountains and pulsating Atlantic waves washing onto the beach. With huge convention halls and banquet rooms, the lobby is always buzzing with many languages. Two pools, a nearby golf course, and a nightclub featuring a raunchy samba show make this a popular stop. Unfortunately, however, the rooms have become rather musty recently. Av. Niemeyer 796, São Conrado (phone: 322-1000). Expensive.

Rio Othon Palace – Not to be confused with the sleek *Rio Palace* (see above), this has been a popular Rio stopping place since 1976. From the rooftop pool and solarium to the *Patio Tropical,* this hotel was designed for easy living. The rooms are large and many have ocean views. All are air conditioned, with TVs and small refrigerators. The *Estancia* restaurant is known for its gaucho-style barbecued beef. The colorful coffee shop is open late. Av. Atlântica 3264, Copacabana (phone: 255-8812). Expensive.

Rio Palace – The newest hotel in town is destined to be the center of attention for a long time. Its location at the junction of Copacabana and Ipanema beaches is excellent, and the 415 richly decorated rooms have individual balconies overlooking the beach. Duplex apartments are available for long-term rentals. An external glass elevator whisks you from the lobby to the sixth floor's two swimming pools, bar, health club, and tea room. There are also several restaurants, including Gaston Lenôtre's *Le Pré-Catalan,* a shopping center, a large convention center, and a parking garage. The decor is very modern, using Brazilian woods and fabrics especially designed for it. It's quite a place. Av. Atlântica 4240, Copacabana (phone: 521-3232). Expensive.

Rio Sheraton – It's possible to enjoy a terrific vacation and never leave the grounds here. Dramatically perched on a lovely (but narrow) private swimming beach, it also has two swimming pools with restaurants and bars, tennis courts, sauna and health club, elegant shops, chic boutiques, a nightclub, discotheque, excellent restaurants, a late-night coffee shop, and even a small antique museum. The lobby is as busy as Galeão Airport. The 617 rooms are brightly decorated and modern. All have air conditioning, radio, TV, and a small refrigerator. Many rooms have terraces with spectacular views of Ipanema. The road outside is very noisy at night. Av. Niemeyer 121, São Conrado (phone: 274-1122). Expensive.

Everest Rio – This 23-story building stands on a quiet street in Ipanema, but it is only a few minutes' walk to the action and the price is lower than for beachfront accommodations. There is a pool on the 23rd floor as well as a bar and coffee shop. Rooms are comfortable if undistinguished in decor, with air conditioning, TV, and refrigerator. A good choice. Rua Prudente de Morais 1117, Ipanema (phone: 287-8282). Moderate.

Leme Palace – In a quieter section of Copacabana, this 17-story hotel looks like a modern apartment building. It has only a small lobby, but it crams a lot into the small area. The 194 rooms (all air-conditioned) are large, and the furnishings, modern and attractive. The small refrigerator in each room is stocked with liquor and mixers as well as snacks. You pay for what you consume. The top-floor nightclub has a great view and the restaurant is highly regarded. Av. Atlântica 656, Leme (phone: 275-8080). Moderate.

Ouro Verde – Considered the class hotel in its price range, this place is so spotless it could make it in Zürich. Everything is meticulous, including the white gloves of the elevator operators. Service is impeccable, and the Continental restaurant is highly respected. A small sitting area in one part of the lobby is always stocked with international newspapers. You can relax in a leather armchair and catch up with the news. All 64 rooms are air conditioned and have radios and telephones. Av. Atlântica 1456, Copacabana (phone: 542-1887). Moderate.

Sol Ipanema – Opened in 1973, this hotel uses Brazil's natural resources in a stunning blend of color and good taste. Lustrous *jacarandá* furniture is set off by colorful upholstery; Bahian tapestries provide the finishing touches. A small pool and a roof solarium are available for those who like their swimming *sans* sand. The hotel has 90 rooms spread over 15 floors. All have air conditioning, TV, and radios. Av. Viera Souto 320, Ipanema (phone: 227-0060). Moderate.

Bandeirantes Othon – A new hotel, opened in 1978, its spotless 90 rooms all have air conditioning and TVs. On a quiet street two blocks from Avenida Atlântica, it is surrounded by apartment buildings, small restaurants, and antique stores. Rua Barata Ribeiro 548, Copacabana (phone: 255-6252). Moderate to inexpensive.

Castro Alves – A charter member of the Othon hotel chain, this one is a block from the beach, so it's slightly less expensive than equivalent hotels on the shoreline. The 75 rooms are a good size and are furnished in motel-style modern. All have air conditioning, TVs, and stocked refrigerators. Av. Copacabana 552, Copacabana (phone: 257-1800). Moderate to inexpensive.

Debret – Once a modern apartment house, this hostelry became a hotel in 1972 and has provided pleasant accommodations ever since. The lobby, tastefully decorated with works of sculpture and good paintings, is a cozy spot to sit in. The area of Avenida Atlântica on either side has sidewalk cafés that are popular hangouts for young people at night. Rua Almirante Gonçalves, Copacabana (phone: 521-3332). Moderate to inexpensive.

Lancaster – A small, 74-room hotel, converted from an apartment house, this is a comfortable stop for people not concerned with luxurious atmosphere. Many of the large rooms have separate sitting areas, and those rooms facing Avenida Atlântica have terraces. All are air conditioned and have TVs. Its friendly service and good location bring people back time and time again. Av. Atlântica 1470, Copacabana (phone: 541-1887). Moderate to inexpensive.

Luxor – This 123-room, 11-floor hotel uses *jacarandá* wood on the walls, in the furniture, and even in the headboards of the beds. The rich warm tone sets off the vibrant colors of the ultramodern lamps and furnishings. With a terrace restaurant and beachfront location, this, too, is an excellent choice. Av. Atlântica 2554, Copacabana (phone: 257-1940). Moderate to inexpensive.

Trocadero – The key word is convenient. Walk across the street and you are in the center of the Copacabana Beach strip, only one block from the major shopping section of Avenida Copacabana. Yet this 120-room hotel stands as a quiet oasis in Copacabana's pulsating heart. Rooms are large, comfortably furnished, and have refrigerators. The *Moenda,* one of Rio's finest Bahian restaurants, is in the hotel. Its sidewalk café-bar is very popular at sunset. Av. Atlântica 2064, Copacabana (phone: 257-1834). Moderate to inexpensive.

Vermont – A small 38-room hotel, right on the main street of Ipanema, the building is marked by a red and white canopy over the door. All rooms are carpeted, air conditioned, and while not exactly large, they are comfortable. Breakfast is served in your room. Rua Visconde Pirajá 254, Ipanema (phone: 247-6100). Moderate to inexpensive.

Ambassador – In the heart of the Cinelândia theater district, this is splendid for people who enjoy being in the center of things. A short walk brings you to the Municipal Theater, the downtown shopping center, and Flamengo Park. The 130-room hotel opened in 1949 and was a favorite of businessmen for many years. There's lots of traffic noise, so get a back room. Rua Senador Dantas 25 (phone: 297-7181). Inexpensive.

Canada – A nonluxury choice in the midst of posh Copacabana Beach, the 63 rooms with brightly colored bedspreads, drapes, and large, tiled bathrooms are on ten floors. Ask for a back room to avoid traffic noise if you are a late sleeper. Av. Copacabana 67, Copacabana (phone: 257-1864). Inexpensive.

Florida – Another acceptable choice in the Flamengo section. The 200 rooms are large with parquet floors and big, tiled bathrooms. The furniture is undistinguished, but the rooms are bright and the hotel, clean and well cared for. Rua Ferreira Viani 81, Flamengo (phone: 245-8160). Inexpensive.

Novo Mundo – In the Flamengo section, this hotel has 200 air-conditioned rooms, all with TVs. An outstanding hotel when it opened in 1950, its views of Guanabara Bay and Pão de Açúcar are still stunning. The main disadvantage is that you must walk to Flamengo Beach or take a bus to an Atlantic Ocean beach. The furnishings are well worn, but spit-and-polish is evident in the care they receive. Praia do Flamengo 20, Flamengo (phone: 225-7366). Inexpensive.

The newest alternative to the traditional hotel in Rio is the rental of unique one-bedroom, furnished apartments with kitchen as well as customary hotel services such as maid, laundry, front desk, and room service. Nicknamed "apartotels," some have swimming pools and saunas, and all are in modern, new buildings. In the expensive-to-moderate price range, they have become a great option during peak seasons, when the hotels are full. Try *Apart Hotel,* Rua Barata Ribeiro 370, Copacabana (phone: 256-2633); *Copacabana Hotel Residencia,* Rua Barata Ribeiro 222, Copacabana (phone: 256-2610); or *Rio Flat Service,* Rua Almirante Guilhem 332, Leblon (phone: 274-7222).

 EATING OUT: Brazilians revel in the good life, and eating out is a major part of that. Visitors cannot fail to be impressed at the sheer quantity of restaurants in Rio, all crowded with people enjoying themselves. The sophistication of the population is reflected in the variety of restaurants: Chinese,

German, Japanese, French, Italian, and Swiss are just a small sample. Many have English menus. Typical Brazilian restaurants serve tasty, unusual dishes.

Called Bahian, the local cuisine was created by slaves in the Bahía province of Brazil, north of Rio. Because beef was scarce, the dishes use seafood, poultry, nuts, fruits, coconuts, and milk. *Feijoada,* the national dish, consists of black beans and rice. *Feijoada completa,* traditionally served on Saturdays, adds sausage and pork to the beans and rice. *Xinxim de galinha* is another popular dish, featuring pieces of chicken in a white sauce. *Vatapa* is a creamy dish of shrimp or fish in coconut milk. *Siri* is a spicy and delicious stuffed crab appetizer. *Frango con arroz* is Brazil's version of chicken and rice. Have a *batida* cocktail while you wait for your main course to arrive. *Batidas* are mixed drinks based on *cachaça,* a strong cane liquor, and fruit. Order a *caipirinha,* made with *cachaça,* sugar, and lime. Brazilian fruits are superb on their own: *abacaxi* (pineapple), mamão (papaya), and *goiaba* (guava). And be sure to sample Brazil's national soft drink, *Guaraná.* Very sweet, it's made from the seeds of a fruit that grows in the Amazon jungle. It's reported to be effective in combatting diarrhea because of the tannin it contains. *Churrascarías* are Argentine-like barbecue restaurants where excellent beef, lamb, and sausages are charcoal grilled.

Most restaurants have a cover charge (*couvert*), which covers bread, butter, a cold vegetable platter, and tiny quail eggs that are ubiquitous as side dishes. *Churrascarías* include sausages. *Couverts* range from $1 to $3 and are optional.

While fast-food and counter restaurants are open continuously, most sit-down restaurants serve lunch from noon until 3 PM. Dinner is rarely eaten before 9 PM, and most kitchens remain open till 2 or 3 AM. Expect to pay over $50 to $60 for restaurants in the expensive category; $35 to $40 in the moderate category; under $25, inexpensive. Prices are for dinner for two, without drinks, wine, or tips.

IN TOWN

Antiquarius – It's a very pleasant restaurant decorated with antiques. The bar area is small but comfortable, a nice place to sip a drink while waiting for your table. The Portuguese codfish dishes are quite good. It gets crowded here, so reservations are suggested. Open daily until 2 AM. Major credit cards accepted. Rua Aristides Espinola 19, Leblon (phone: 294-1049). Expensive.

Le Bec Fin – Many *cariocas* would choose this as the best French restaurant in Rio. The lobster is unmatchable and the *canard* (duck) dishes run a close second. The horseshoe-shaped dining room doesn't allow for much privacy and the decor is unimpressive, but you definitely need reservations here. Major credit cards accepted. Open daily for dinner only. Av. Copacabana 178A, Copacabana (phone: 542-4097). Expensive.

Café do Teatro – This lunch-only choice in the newly refurnished Municipal Theater is open from noon to 3 PM, Mondays through Fridays. The international cuisine and the Assyrian mosaic walls and lovely decor make it an excellent place to while away a few leisurely hours. Closed Saturdays and Sundays. No reservations. No credit cards. Av. Rio Branco at Praça Floriano (phone: 262-4164). Expensive.

Castelo da Lagoa – The name of this restaurant, "Castle on the Lagoon," says it all. Set in a large private home overlooking the lagoon, the attractive indoor dining room has brown leather chairs and gold tablecloths. If weather permits, try for a table in the garden, and after dinner, move next door to *Chico's Bar,* where the Brazilian music is live and good. Open from noon to 4 AM daily. Major credit cards accepted. Av. Epitacio Passoa 1560, Lagoa (phone: 287-3514). Expensive.

Grottamare – One of Rio's most popular and crowded seafood restaurants, this place draws a chic crowd. Recommended are fish served right off the grill, as well as the fresh green salads and pasta dishes. Open for dinner Tuesdays through

Sundays, lunch on Sundays and holidays. Diners Club credit cards accepted. Rua Gomes Carneiro 132, Ipanema (phone: 287-1596). Expensive.

Michel – An intimate restaurant, consistently listed among Rio's finest French restaurants, its patrons return again and again — the most faithful have one of the restaurant's wall signs engraved with their names. Among its regulars are many of Rio's "beautiful people." Rua Fernando Mendes 25, Copacabana (phone: 235-2127). Expensive.

Ouro Verde – There are few restaurants in Rio with a better reputation than this long-time favorite on the second floor of the hotel of the same name. It doesn't need neon signs — the French food prepared perfectly, the unobtrusive service, and quiet ambience are justly famous. Try the châteaubriand or a veal dish in wine sauce. And try to get a table overlooking the beach. You can't miss. Open daily from noon to midnight. American Express cards are accepted. *Hotel Ouro Verde,* Av. Atlântica 1456, Copacabana (phone: 542-1887). Expensive.

Le Pre Catelan – This charming restaurant, at the *Rio Palace* hotel, is known for its light French cuisine. French chef Gaston LeNôtre reviews the menu every two months. Open for dinner only, 7:30 PM to 1:30 AM daily. Reservations suggested. Major credit cards accepted. *Hotel Rio Palace,* Av. Atlântica 4240, Copacabana (phone: 521-3232). Expensive.

Le Saint Honoré – On the 37th floor of the *Méridien* hotel, the *Saint Honoré* is considered one of the finest restaurants in town and the best of hotel dining. The food is French, with many dishes created by Paul Bocuse. Pâté de caneton and shellfish in delicious light sauces are recommended. Lovely views of the city and music at dinner add the right atmosphere to complement the delectable fare. Closed Sundays. Reservations necessary. Major credit cards accepted. Av. Atlântica 1020 at Av. Princessa Isabel, Copacabana (phone: 275-9922). Expensive.

La Tour – The only restaurant in Rio where you can have your appetizer while gazing at Pão de Açúcar, your entrée under the outstretched arms of Christ the Redeemer high atop Corcovado, and dessert facing the downtown skyline. The restaurant, on the 37th floor of an office building, revolves once every hour. The extensive menu lists Italian, French, and German dishes side by side. At night, roving musicians play Latin melodies as you dine. Open daily for lunch and dinner. Major credit cards accepted. Rua Santa Lúzia 651 (phone: 242-3221; 242-2221). Expensive.

Antonio's – Perhaps because it caters to Rio's artists, writers, and actors, this place is reminiscent of Greenwich Village restaurants. Wood-paneled walls lined with wine racks and framed posters, a dining terrace, and a very popular bar contribute to the feeling. The menu is in Portuguese, but some items don't need translations: fettuccine Alfredo, scaloppine marsala, and filet mignon a pizzaiola come highly recommended. The maître d' speaks some English and can help you decide. Jackets are common, but ties are not required. Reservations are a must on weekends. Major credit cards accepted. Open noon to midnight every day. Av. Bartolomeu Mitre 297, Leblon (phone: 294-2699). Expensive to moderate.

Café de la Paix – On the ground floor of the *Méridien* hotel, this French brasserie with comfortable booths and tables loaded with Gallic charm offers a varied menu, good wines, pâtés, omelettes of all kinds, and absolutely scrumptious pastries. Open daily for lunch from noon to 3 PM and for dinner from 7 to 11 PM. Major credit cards accepted. Av. Atlântica 1020, Copacabana (phone: 275-9922). Expensive to moderate.

Enotria – This small restaurant, considered the best in Rio for Italian food, has only nine tables, albeit elegantly decorated ones. The same owner runs a fine food shop next door for those who wish to take a snack back to the hotel. Rua Constante Ramos 115, Copacabana (phone: 237-6705). Expensive to moderate.

Moenda – While in Brazil, you should definitely sample Brazilian food. This is one of Rio's finest Bahian restaurants. On the second floor of the *Trocadero* hotel, overlooking Copacabana Beach, it is first class in style and service. Fresh flowers on every table, hanging plants, comfortable high-backed chairs, and low-beamed ceilings create an inviting feeling. The friendly, traditionally clad waitresses will offer you a fruit punch of *cachaça* to start your meal. The maître d' speaks English and will gladly explain the special features of each dish. Open daily until 1:30 AM. Reservations are recommended on weekends. American Express accepted. *Hotel Trocadero*, Av. Atlântica 2064, Copacabana (phone: 257-1834). Expensive to moderate.

Alba Mar – What better location for a seafood restaurant than overlooking the water? The circular building with a turret roof in the downtown dock area was once the municipal market but has since been converted into a two-level restaurant serving some of the best seafood in town. Many of the dishes are prepared Bahian style, but if these don't suit your palate, you can stick to shrimp, crab, oyster, and fish dishes prepared in more familiar fashion. The main dining room is on the second floor. Closed Sundays. Reservations are recommended. American Express cards accepted. Praça 15 de Novembro (phone: 240-8378 or 240-8428). Moderate.

Arataca – If you can't make the trip to the northern Amazon, at least try some of the regional cooking at *Arataca*. The restaurant serves fish typically found in the Amazon, a duck dish called *pata de tucupi,* and *carne-de-sol,* a meat dish with beans. Ask about regional fruits, such as *cupuaçu, açai,* and *graviola;* they make great *batidas,* juices, or ice cream. Two locations, at Rua Dias Ferreira 135-A, Leblon (phone: 259-5846), and Rua Figueiredo Magalhães 28 AB, Copacabana (phone: 255-7448). Moderate.

Bella Blu – In the same genre of good Italian restaurants serving pizza and pasta, fish, chicken, and veal in attractive surroundings, this place has not yet made it big on the tourist trail. Open daily. No reservations. No credit cards. Three locations: Rua Siqueira Campos 107, Copacabana (phone: 257-2041); Rua da Passagem 44, Botafogo (phone: 295-9493); and Rua General Urquiza 102, Leblon (phone: 274-7895). Moderate.

Centro China – One of Rio's best Chinese restaurants, this two-story establishment is on Lagoa Rodrigo de Freitas and has a few tables with views of the lagoon. Try the duck with hot sauce. Av. Epitácio Pessoa 1164, Leblon (phone: 287-3947). Moderate.

Chale – Another excellent place to sample Bahian specialties. Set in a converted private house built in 1884, it has three small dining rooms and an exceptionally pleasant atmosphere. Attractive waitresses clad in native Bahian attire (wide skirts, flowered turbans, and highly visible costume jewelry) bounce through the rooms carrying bubbling *siri* (stuffed crab appetizers) or *moqueca* (seafood stew). Sample several dishes, if possible. Desserts are sweet and delicious. Strolling musicians play at dinner. Open daily until 12:30 AM. Reservations are recommended. Major credit cards accepted. Rua da Matriz 54, Botafogo (phone: 286-0897). Moderate.

El Faro and Rio Jerez – Like Tweedledum and Tweedledee, these adjoining restaurants serve reasonably priced Spanish food. They both have indoor dining rooms, but the al fresco tables are always the most crowded. Start with gazpacho, then try some paella or *zarzuela de pescado* (fish stew). The sangria is a good buy. Open until 3 AM daily. Reservations are not required. Diners Club accepted. Av. Atlântica 3806, Copacabana. El Faro (phone: 267-1128); Rio Jerez (phone: 267-5644). Moderate.

Lagoa Charlie's – Why eat Mexican food in Rio? Because *Lagoa Charlie's* is here. The outdoor dining room is particularly gorgeous under a full moon and starry sky. You can gaze across the lovely lagoon. The trilingual menu is fun to decipher and so are the strolling mariachi players. But above all, *Charlie's* serves very good Mexican food. Chili con carne (hot), spicy guacamole, and enchiladas (chicken and cheese) are just a few of the familiar names. If you have room, by all means order a crêpe cajeta (a hot pancake with ice cream and caramel) for dessert. Open for dinner only until 2 AM daily. Very informal. No reservations needed. No credit cards. Rua Maria Quitéria 136, Lagoa (phone: 287-0335). Moderate.

Lucas – Rio would never be mistaken for Munich, but this restaurant makes the effort. The indoor dining room is rather austere, but the outdoor terrace (just covered by a roof) is very relaxed. Sausages and wine bottles dangle everywhere, and the aroma of wurst (*salsichas*), beer, and the salty ocean air will give you an appetite. A favorite dish is wiener schnitzel (a fried, breaded veal cutlet) served with an egg on top, home-fried potatoes, and salad. Steak Leipzig is also fine. Home-baked brown bread and butter are the *couvert.* Open daily. Reservations are recommended. No credit cards. Av. Atlântica 3744, Copacabana (phone: 247-1606). Moderate.

Pizza Palace – One of the most popular meeting places in Rio, this is a particular favorite of late-night revelers. Open from 11:30 AM until 6:30 AM daily. Next door to the fashionable disco *Hippopotamus,* at Rua Barão da Torre 340, Ipanema (phone: 267-8346). Moderate.

Rincão Gaucho – One of Rio's best Argentine restaurants, with music from 8:30 each evening continuing until 1 AM weeknights, 3 AM on weekends. The food is well prepared, and the sight of the meats grilling over large charcoal fires will make you hungry. Baby beef and filet mignon are house specialties. The *couvert* is a meal in itself, consisting of a huge platter with pâté, olives, quail eggs, sausage, tomato and onion salad, hearts of palm, plus bread and butter. The cowhide rugs and wagon wheels on the walls and the aviary in the rear give the place the atmosphere of an Argentine ranch. *Gaucho* is very large, with seating for more than 1,000 people. Open daily; live music, dancing, and a midnight show on weekends. Reservations recommended. No credit cards. Rua Marquez de Valencia 83, Tijuca (phone: 264-6659). Moderate.

Catina La Fiorentina – A casual, boisterous, show biz crowd's hangout, this place is jammed with after-theater revelers. The decor consists of Chianti bottles, posters, and signed photographs of the famous and not so famous. The menu is partially in English. The pizza is fair, but shrimp and pasta dishes are excellent. The dining room on the terrace is cozier than the indoor dining room. Open from noon until 5 AM daily. Major credit cards accepted. Av. Atlântica 458, Leme (phone: 275-7548). Moderate to inexpensive.

Churrascaria Copacabana – Easy to find, this is one of the most pleasant, informal beef restaurants in town. Filet mignon and other juicy cuts are sizzled and brought to you by gaucho-costumed waiters. On Wednesdays and Saturdays, traditional *feijoada* is served. You get a good view of the comings and goings on one of Copacabana's most active streets. Open daily. Reservations are not required. American Express cards accepted. Av. Copacabana 1144, Copacabana (phone: 267-1497). Inexpensive.

Churrascaria Jardim – The charcoal pits are on the left as you enter this barbecue restaurant. The decor amounts to plain tables on bare floors with some tables outdoors; others are under a tin roof. Choose beef steaks, lamb, or pork — all are superb. They are brought to your table on small ovens where they cook and stay hot till the final bite. French fries and tomato-onion salad are the typical side dishes. Open until 1 AM daily. Reservations are recommended. Major credit cards accepted. Rua República do Perú 225, Copacabana (phone: 235-3263). Inexpensive.

Colombo – An institution in this part of the world, this is a "must" stop for at least one lunch during your stay. Head for the fast-food counter, where you can select tiny breaded chicken drumsticks or large breaded shrimp-stuffed crab goodies, meat or cheese pies, and many other delicacies. Take your lunch and a soft drink (Guaraná, perhaps?) and head for the nearest greenery to munch. The *Colombo* also offers afternoon tea, a time to sit and relax in the beautiful, authentic Art Nouveau atmosphere. Open Mondays through Fridays. No reservations. No credit cards. Rua Gonçalves Dias 32 (phone: 231-9650) or Av. Copacabana 890, Copacabana (phone: 257-8960). Inexpensive.

Garota de Ipanema – Among the many sidewalk cafés around the beach areas, this one stands out because here the hit tune *The Girl from Ipanema* was composed. If it's too crowded, wander over to Avenida Viera Souto, where *Barril 18* offers a good alternative. Sidewalk cafés are almost always open, thanks to Rio's superb weather. They are most frequently jammed in the early evening and again late at night. Open daily. No reservations. No credit cards. Corner of Prudente de Morais and Vinicius de Morais (which used to be Rua Montenegro but was renamed for the co-composer of *The Girl from Ipanema*), Ipanema (no phone). Inexpensive.

Helsingor – Sandwiches are the specialty, making this a perfect choice for a late-night snack or light lunch or dinner. You would be amazed at what the chef can fit into a roll or bun. Filet mignon with sour cream and potato tastes better than it sounds. Roast beef and turkey are also excellent. Cold platters are available, too. Red-and-white-checked tablecloths and pretty posters of Denmark add a cheerful touch to the two indoor dining rooms and outdoor terrace. Open from noon until 2 AM daily except Sundays. No reservations. No credit cards. Rua General San Martín 983, Ipanema (phone: 294-0347). Inexpensive.

Mariu's – This is one of the few *churrascarías*, or barbeque houses, on the beach-front. The modern decor features lots of mirrors, and the view of Leme Beach is a delight. This is the place to stuff yourself on beef, pork, or chicken that has been grilled on a spit. The meat comes with salad, rice, and other trimmings. Open from 11 AM to 2 AM daily. Accepts major credit cards. Av. Atlântica 290-B, Leme (phone: 542-2393). Inexpensive.

Oriento – If you have a very large appetite or a very low budget, make a beeline for this budget restaurant. Not only are the portions huge, but the food is well prepared. The egg drop soup is full of peppers, eggs, and mushrooms. The beef with green pepper and diced chicken with bean sprouts are delicious. Anything you order will be large enough for sharing. Chinese lanterns provide the decor. Open until midnight nightly. No reservations. Major credit cards accepted. Rua Bolívar 64 and Av. Copacabana, Copacabana (phone: 257-8765). Inexpensive.

Oxalá – This counter-only eatery downtown, on one of Cinelandia's narrow streets, has the best Bahian food in Rio. It packs in the natives at lunchtime. Specialties include delicious *vatapa, frigideiras* six inches high and generously stuffed with shrimp, *moqueca* (fish, oyster, or crab), and *carurú*. For dessert, don't pass up the *pudin,* a milk pudding you'll never forget. Rua Francisco Serrador 2, Lojas I and J (phone: 220-3035). Inexpensive.

IN THE SUBURBS

If you're willing to travel for good food, consider a day trip to Pedra de Guaratiba, a fishing town on the outskirts of greater Rio. This is the home of delicious fresh seafood, and the two restaurants listed are among the best in Rio and its environs. To get there, make taxi arrangements or catch the bus marked "Santa Cruz" on Avenida Atlântica in town.

Candido's – Ask to be seated on the terrace; then settle back and watch the sunset as you dine on the daily catch. The owner of this popular restaurant is a woman named Doña Carmen. Whether you make reservations through Carmen or an assistant, make them you must or you'll never get seated. Open from 11 AM until 11 PM daily, in January and February until 7 PM. Rua Barros Alarcão 352 (phone: 395-1630). Expensive.

Quatro Sete Meia – A neighbor to *Candido's,* this place is much smaller and just as popular. Its setting is a house and garden overlooking the sea; you can watch the local fishermen bring in their catch. The menu is limited to a few well-prepared dishes, mostly seafood. Try a *batida,* a drink made with *cachaça* (Brazilian rum), fruit juice or coconut milk, and honey. Open weekends only, from noon until 11 PM. Reservations are a must. No credit cards. Rua Barros Alarcão 476 (phone: 395-2716). Expensive.

SALVADOR
(BAHÍA)

The sign at the airport says it all: "Smile — You're Arriving in Bahía!" And, indeed, there's a lot to smile about. Picture a fat thumb of land tapering southward from Brazil's northern Atlantic coast some 30 miles into the inky blue Atlantic. Along the eastern shoreline stretches mile after mile of golden sand beaches lined with tall coconut palms, while on the other side lies a vast bright blue bay studded with islands. And perched on the narrow tip of the peninsula, where 365 days a year the sea breezes blow from the ocean to the bay, is one of the loveliest cities in the world: Salvador da Bahía de Todos os Santos, known affectionately as Bahía or simply Salvador.

If Rio is the heart of Brazil and São Paulo its brain, Salvador is its spirit, for it was here that Brazil cut its first painful teeth and grew to potent young nationhood. And it was here in 1549 that the Portuguese founded the capital city and chief port of their new colony — and just in time, too, for in the next half century the young colony was attacked by the stubbornly persistent Dutch, who didn't make peace until 1647. Meanwhile, the city prospered, as Bahían cacao fed the European rage for chocolate. Vast fortunes were made with slave labor, both native American and African, and much of the shameful slave trade was transacted here. The Americans often preferred death to enslavement, but the resilient Africans endured and outlived it. Today Salvador's colonial heritage remains alive not only in its glorious old buildings, but also in its beautiful brown-skinned citizens, with their unique mix of native American fortitude and European civility, both charged with the exuberance and sensual grace of Africa.

Bahians are infinitely hospitable, accepting with smiling patience all sorts of foreign intrusions and influences; but whatever comes to Bahía — human being or social institution — undergoes an almost imperceptible transformation, a very gradual and profound process of Bahianization. Witness the Roman Catholic Church: Since the very beginning, the Church has strewn its cathedrals, convents, monasteries, churches, and chapels all over the Bahian landscape; today there are more than 300, many of them breathtaking examples of gold-encrusted baroque extravagance. Yet for every church there are several *terreiros* dedicated to the ancient African gods, here known as *candomblé*. During *candomblé* ceremonies, devotees dance hypnotically to the specific drumbeat of each African god in turn, until the god being invoked suddenly "descends" into the body of his devotee, triggering, in some cases, a spectacular spasmodic reaction. Naturally the Church frowned on all this for a long time, but Afro-Bahians, who were delighted to accept the Christian God and His Son (and especially the Son's mother and grandmother), have clung to both faiths; today they coexist so amicably that the African gods and goddesses have been completely syncretized with the Christian saints and are worshiped under both names. With this potent blend of historical and cultural riches to draw on, it's no wonder that Salvador inspires so much of Brazil's first-rate art. Internationally acclaimed writers Jorge Amado and João Ubaldo Ribeiro live here, as do such highly gifted musicians and graphic artists as Carybé, Mario Cravo, Jr., and Jenner Augusto.

Although nowhere nearly as large as Rio de Janeiro, some 664 miles (1,691 km) south, Bahía is a hard-working, modern metropolis. With the recent discovery of oil nearby and the founding of the $3 billion Camaçari petro-chemical complex, the city is growing northward at a galloping rate, and the new network of highways can barely keep up with the traffic. Between 1965 and 1980, Salvador grew from a cozy 400,000 to a very crowded 1,500,000, and there's no end in sight.

To get a sense of the city's layout, imagine that you are driving in from the airport along the beach road. You pass the pleasant beaches of Itapoã, Piatã, and Boca de Rio, each with its cluster of fishermen's houses and its scattering of luxurious summer villas; then come the middle-class residential neighbor-hoods of Rio Vermelho, Pituba, and Amaralina, where little pink and blue and yellow houses snuggle up against newer white apartment buildings; then comes Ondina, where the new luxury hotels stare proudly over the ocean. Finally, at the squared-off point of the peninsula, is the elegant residential neighborhood of Barra, with expensive boutiques, hip discos, and pretty little urban beaches. At this point the playful beach road curves around to the right, becoming the dignified Avenida Sete (7) de Setembro, which begins its grad-ual climb to the Upper City. Here it takes on the splendid trappings of colonial decor: great Portuguese palaces set in formal gardens, baroque churches, and carefully laid out parks and plazas. This stretch of broad avenue hugs the edge of the cliff overlooking the Bay of All the Saints, rewarding you with sudden, dazzling views between old mansions and new apartment houses. At the Campo Grande (a sort of tropical Central Park bordered by the very imposing Cardinal's Palace and the ultramodern theater Castro Alves) it turns right, then left, and abruptly plunges into narrow streets crammed with modern banks, shops, and offices. All traffic inches along at a painful pace for several blocks, finally breaking free at the main plaza, Praça da Sé, where most bus routes end. Like Lisbon, the city on which it was modeled, Salvador is built into a cliff.

From Praça Municipal, the giant, public Lacerda Elevator carries you down to the Lower City in a few thrilling seconds, and you emerge onto a scene of frenetic activity: a thriving jumble of contemporary buildings and colorful open-air markets poised on the edge of a spectacularly beautiful harbor. In the streets of this area, you may catch an impromptu demonstra-tion of *capoeira,* the ancient art of footfighting that the African slaves (who were forbidden to fight by their Portuguese owners) cleverly disguised as a ritual dance. You're sure to see Bahian women dressed in traditional layers of brightly printed skirts and snowy, lace-trimmed blouses selling *acarajé:* plump crispy fritters of ground beans, fried in the bright gold oil of the *dendê* palm, and stuffed with *vatapá* — a paste of manioc flour, dried shrimp and spices, studded with fresh shrimp, and spiked, if you ask for it, with hot pepper sauce. And this is just the beginning, for in Salvador you can explore one of the world's most remarkable cuisines. Invented by African slaves, it combines European cooking techniques with the rich oils and fragrant spices of Africa as well as with the vegetables and seasonings indigenous to the New World. Be sure to try a *moqueca,* freshly caught fish (or shellfish) simmered in golden *dendê* oil with what Bahians call "all the seasonings": sweet peppers, onions, scallions, tomatoes, garlic, parsley, cumin, and fresh coriander. Like most Bahian dishes, your *moqueca* will arrive with a side dish of rice. If you like spicy food, ask for the hot pepper sauce (*molho de pimenta*) — but watch out; this stuff is *hot.* If you'd prefer to try the same seafood poached in fresh coconut milk (with the same seasonings), ask for an *ensopado.* Two other tasty Bahian dishes are *galinha ao molho pardo,* freshkilled chicken in a savory brown sauce enriched with the chicken's own blood, and *ximxim de galinha* (pronounced sheen-sheen), chicken in a thick tasty sauce of ground peanuts or cashews, plus "all the seasonings." And for dessert, don't fail to order *quindin* (keen-jeen), a jewellike custard of egg yolks, sugar, and coconut; or *papo-de-anjo,* which is the same thing without the coconut; or the rich coconut candies known as *cocadas.*

Not only are the food and layout of Bahía remarkable; even more so are *baianos* themselves. Their effervescence is not an act — it's for real. When someone from Bahía is feeling sad, his or her friends admonish cheerfully, "Why be depressed? Let's go dance a samba!" It works every time.

SALVADOR AT-A-GLANCE

SEEING THE CITY: Because Salvador sprawls over so many different levels of terrain, there's no single vantage point that will give you a bird's-eye view of the whole city. But you can get a panorama of the Upper City from the *St. Honoré* restaurant atop the *Hotel Méridien,* Rua Fonte do Boi 216 (phone: 248-8011); and from the Lacerda Elevator you'll get a fine view of the Lower City and the bay. Best of all is the terrific sight of the city's western face from Mont'Serrat (see below), especially in the late afternoon.

SPECIAL PLACES: A unique split-level city on a peninsula, Salvador is divided into Upper and Lower, with beaches on three sides. Catch a bus marked *Itapoã* or hire a car and driver and head for Bahía's 44 miles of golden beaches. (A word of caution: when the buses get packed, they turn into a haven for pickpockets.) You can stop and swim at any of the beaches, but watch out for undertows; it's best to swim only where you find Bahians. The two furthest beaches, *Piatã* and *Itapoã,* are probably the most beautiful and the longest, respectively; both offer plenty of restaurants where you can picnic royally on cooked crabs, lobster, shrimp, and the like. After *Itapoã,* the Metropolitan Region of Salvador begins. The Estrada do Côco, an asphalt road, runs parallel with the coast and connects most of the small towns with beaches. Here are a few to watch for: *Ipitanga,* km 2; *Buraquinho,* km 6; *Jauá,* km 15; *Arembepe,* km 26; *Barra do Jacuípe,* km 37; *Guarajuba,* km 42 (good camping here also); and *Itacimirim,* km 49 (has some hotels and restaurants).

UPPER CITY (CIDADE ALTA)

Church of St. Francis (Igreja da São Francisco) – *Baianos* joke that they have a church for every day of the year, but the total number is only 76. And some of them are tremendously impressive. Two blocks from the Praça da Sé (walk past the whole line of buses and turn right) is one of the most famous 18th-century baroque churches in the world. Built by Franciscans with Portuguese stone, it's best known for the dazzling expanse of gold leaf that covers the interior. There are also some fine examples of hand-carved Brazilian rosewood and some charming scenes from the life of St. Francis in blue and white Portuguese tiles. The adjacent monastery has a very pretty tiled courtyard, which women may see only by peering through the door; men are welcome to tour the inner sanctum, accompanied by one of the Franciscans, from 8 to 11 AM and from 2 to 5 PM, except Sunday afternoons. The same hours apply for the church, although you may also attend mass before or after visiting hours. Closed Sunday afternoons. Free. Praça Pe. Anchieta 1 (phone: 243-2367).

Church of the Third Order of St. Francis (Igreja de Ordem Terceira de São Francisco) – Next door to the Church of St. Francis, this smaller church was completed in 1703; its façade, built of squared gray stone, is of the plateresque baroque style — the only such building in Brazil. Open from 8 to 11:30 AM and 2 to 5 PM, Saturdays from 8:30 to 11:30 AM (phone: 242-7046). Largo de São Francisco.

The Cathedral (Catedral Basilica) – Walk back from the Church of St. Francis through the Terreiro de Jesus, where on Sundays there's an open-air handicrafts market known as the Hippie Fair. There you can pick up primitive paintings by Bahian artists that some critics predict will soar in value (as did Haitian art about 20 years ago). The massive church at the far end of the square is the cathedral, built from 1657 to 1672 by the Jesuits, who then lost it to the local archdiocese in 1759, when they were kicked out of Brazil. Here, too, is some splendid gold leaf, especially the high altar. Open daily from 8 to 11 AM and from 2 to 6 PM. Closed Mondays. Free. Terreiro de Jesus (phone: 243-4573).

Pillory Hill (Ladeira do Pelourinho) – From the cathedral, it's just a short walk down Rua Alfredo de Brito, Pelourinho, a wonderful old neighborhood of gaily colored colonial houses jammed together on steeply twisting cobbled streets. A couple of centuries ago, the respectable ladies of the district would while away long afternoons on these pretty little balconies, observing the agonies of the disobedient slaves and other miscreants who were pilloried in the square below. Today these colorful streets harbor more than one juvenile pickpocket, and the ladies of Pelourinho are reputed to be not so respectable (some women might not feel entirely comfortable walking here alone, though they would certainly be in no actual danger). The government authorities, in an attempt to uplift the moral character of the neighborhood, are encouraging writers and artists to live and work here. You should stop briefly at the Museum of the City (Museu da Cidade) to see its interesting collection of *candomblé* artifacts, among other things. Open 8 AM to midnight and 2 to 6 PM, except Sundays; Largo do Pelourinho 3 (phone: 242-8773).

Carmo Convent Museum (Museu do Convento do Carmo) – From the bottom of Pelourinho, it's a short but steep walk up the Ladeira do Carmo to the Church of Passo (Igreja do Passo). Climb this impressive flight of steps and continue to the top of the hill. Here you'll find a beautiful Carmelite church, founded in 1585, with a delightful little museum containing many dolls in religious costumes; ceremonial objects in silver, gold, and precious stones; and a colorful exhibit explaining the syncretism of *candomblé* gods with Christian saints. Do step into the next-door *Luxor Hotel,* which occupies (without violating its essential character) the original convent itself. If you're here at mealtime, the *Forno o Fogão* restaurant downstairs is an excellent place to try Bahian food. Convent open daily. Admission charge. Largo de Carmo (phone: 242-0182).

Carlos Costa Pinto Foundation Museum (Fundaçao Museu Carlos Costa Pinto) – This little jewel of a museum gives you a great way to see how the other half lives (or used to live). The descendants of Costa Pinto have built a showcase for the family's collection of 17th- and 18th-century furniture, Chinese porcelain, Baccarat crystal, dazzling jewelry, and a wonderful collection of silver *balangandãs* (fruit clusters). Closed Tuesdays. Admission charge. Av. 7 de Setembro 2490 (phone: 247-6081). Open from 1 to 7 PM.

Church and Convent of Saint Teresa (Igreja e Convento de Santa Tereza) – This compound was built in the 17th century for the Shoeless Carmelite's Order of Saint Teresa. The Federal University of Bahía has restored the church and convent and installed the Museum of Sacred Art (Museu de Arte Sacra). This is the most impressive of Bahía's museums, with an immensely valuable collection of religious art in various media: tiles, sculptures, paintings, and silver artifacts. Open from 10 to 11:30 AM and 2 to 5:30 PM. Closed Sundays and Mondays. Admission charge. Rua do Sodré 25 (phone: 243-6310).

Church and Monastery of Our Lady of Grace (Igreja e Mosteiro de Nossa Senhora da Graça) – Considered the oldest church in Bahía, this 18th-century structure includes part of a 15th-century monastery. The sacristy houses a fine collection of famous paintings. Open daily from 9 AM to noon and 2 to 5 PM. Closed Sundays. Largo da Graça (phone: 247-4670).

Fort of St. Anthony of Barra (Forte de Santo Antonio da Barra) – Known locally as the "Lighthouse of Barra" ("Farol da Barra"), it's the oldest and most picturesque fort of Salvador. Recently the Hidrographical Museum was installed in it. Open from 11 AM to 5 PM, closed Sundays, Mondays, and Thursdays. Free. Av. Oceanica, Porto da Barra.

Administrative Center of Bahía (Centro Administrativo da Bahía) – Originally constructed to encourage the growth of a new urban area of Salvador, this stark modern building is accented with sculptures and murals by Bahía's artists. The CAB was designed by Lúcio Costa and landscaped by Burle Marx, both of whom were involved in the development of Brasília. Av. Pararela.

LOWER CITY (CIDADE BAIXA)

Church of Our Lady of Immaculate Conception at the Beach (Igreja de Nossa Senhora da Conçeicão da Praia) – As you exit from the Lacerda Elevator in the Lower City, turn left past a row of small shops and snack bars (the Brazilian soccer shirts in the sporting goods stores make nice presents for Yankee soccer fans) and you'll come to Conçeicão da Praia, a magnificent Portuguese baroque church built by a Portuguese nobleman in honor of his daughter's wedding in 1739. Bahians also worship the sea goddess Iemanjá here. Open daily. Free. Largo de Conçeicão da Praia (phone: 242-0545).

Bonfim – About 5 miles (8 km) from downtown Salvador, on a little hill overlooking the bay, is the most popular of all Bahía's churches, the Church of Our Lord of the Good Ending (Igreja de Nosso Senhor do Bonfim). For Bahians, Our Lord of Heaven (Jesus of Nazareth) is identical with Oxalá, the father of the *candomblé* gods and goddesses. Worshipers often come here wearing the traditional costumes of that faith, especially in white and silver, Oxalá's colors. Bonfim has none of the gilded splendor of the powerful city churches, but there are beautiful scenes done in blue and white tiles. In the far right-hand rear corner is a tiny room full of grisly but touching mementos of "miraculous" cures brought about by the guiding spirit of the place: Wax castings of innumerable feet, hands, limbs and organs, once mutilated or otherwise distressed, are now completely recovered. The front steps look out over the city and bay. Open daily. Free. Adro do Bonfim (phone: 226-0196).

São Joaquim Market (Feira de São Joaquim) – This is the largest market in Salvador, a vast sprawl of tiny stands crammed with strange, vivid fruits, vegetables, herbs, roots, and everything necessary to Bahian life. There are terrific bargains here on clay pots (some of them glazed on the inside for easy cleaning) and very funny little figurines from Maragogipe. Stop here on your way to or from Bonfim or come by taxi. The market is open from 6 AM to 6 PM daily, 6 AM to 1 PM on Sundays. Free. Av. Jequitaia.

Mont'Serrat Church (Igreja do Mont'Serrat) – This church is just a few blocks away from Bonfim. The road winds past some lovely old hospitals and the Fort of Mont'Serrat (closed to the public), ending on a little point of land that juts out into the bay, where there is a sweeping view of the entire shoreline all the way to Barra, at the tip of Salvador's peninsula. Here, too, is the simple, 16th-century chapel of Mont'Serrat, with its rough wooden benches and handsome Portuguese tiles. A few blocks away is the beach of Boa Viagem, where on Sundays (after mass at the Church of Bonfim) happy crowds gather to eat crabs and drink beer. Open daily. Free. Ponta de Itapajipe.

■**EXTRA SPECIAL:** If you'd like to spend a cool and restful day away from the city, consider an excursion to the island of Itaparica. Through your hotel or travel agent you may arrange a day's ferry cruise to several small islands, stopping in Itaparica for sightseeing, swimming, and lunch before returning to Salvador. The town of Itaparica is a sleepy little place, untouched by the galloping economic boom of the mainland. Be sure to visit the Fonte da Bica, a public garden in the heart of town where you can drink from a natural spring of mineral water. Pleasant beaches are within walking distance, and several modest hostelries offer excellent fresh seafood. There is also a fine Club Med on the island. Or you can cruise the bay on giant schooners (spelled *escuna* in Portuguese). They make the all-day trip to Itaparica, just as the ferries do; and they also make shorter cruises along the Salvador shoreline. Consult Bahiatursa or any of the other tourist agencies.

SOURCES AND RESOURCES

TOURIST INFORMATION: Bahiatursa, the official state tourist agency, has its main office on Belvedere da Sé off Praça da Sé. It's tricky to find. As you enter into Praça da Sé, on the left-hand side of the Palácio Arquiebiscopal building there's a sort of paved patio; descend the stairway at the far right-hand corner and you'll find Bahiatursa tucked into the hillside, with a nice view of the Lower City and the bay. This agency has just recently geared up for foreign tourists, and provides several pamphlets that include maps and a schedule of events (though only one is in English). The enthusiastic young staff members speak some English and are eager to help travelers arrange guided or unguided tours and plan excursions. A map of the city is available for about $1. Open daily. Belvedere da Sé, off Praça da Sé (phone: 241-4333). Bahiatursa has several other locations around town including stands at the airport (phone: 249-2468), the city bus station (phone: 231-2831), and the square, Praça Avevedo Fernandes.

It's possible, though not probable, that your hotel clerk will be able to give you up-to-date schedules for such events as concerts, folklore shows, and *candomblé* ceremonies. He can certainly put you in touch with tourist agencies accustomed to guiding *norteamericaños* around town.

Local Coverage – Salvador has no English-language newspaper, but you can get the *Latin America Daily Post* at the airport and at newsstands near the Lacerda Elevator. *Time* and *Newsweek* are also available in major hotels and newsstands.

 CLIMATE AND CLOTHES: Thanks to the blissful coincidence of tropical sun and constant sea breezes, Salvador has balmy weather throughout the year, with highs usually in the 80s F (around 29°C), lows in the 70s F (20s C). During the summer (December through February), temperatures can climb into the 90s F (30s C), but this is fine, clear summer heat, never the sticky sultry air that can be so oppressive in Rio. During these months, too, there are occasional fierce but brief rains — to be on the safe side, bring an umbrella. From June through September, the rains are more frequent, gentler, and longer-lasting.

Baianos place a high premium on a neat and elegant appearance. No shorts, please. You'll see middle- and upper-class women in the very latest European styles, either imported or cleverly copied on home sewing machines. American jeans and French T-shirts are also popular, worn with high-heeled sandals and lots of jewelry so there's no mistake about the wearer's gender. Women travelers will be most comfortable in cotton-blend sundresses or summer pants outfits, with a light sweater or jacket for cool evenings and sturdy, flat-heeled sandals for steep, cobbled streets. Men can go virtually anywhere in lightweight pants and sport shirts, although Brazilian men of the upper classes often wear close-fitting dark suits (never sport coats) to restaurants and the theater. For the beach, men and women alike wear the most brief of bikinis; and women often wrap themselves in long swatches of cotton in bright tropical prints, known as *kanga;* these do triple duty as long skirts, sarongs, and beach blankets.

 GETTING AROUND: Bus – If you don't mind circuitous travel at breathtaking speeds, you won't mind the buses. They go virtually everywhere and cost very little. Fares depend on the routes, which are marked on the windshield. On most buses, you get on at the rear, pay at the turnstile, and exit at the front. (They will not change large notes on buses, so bring plenty of small change.) On air-conditioned, deluxe buses, called *seletivos,* you board at the front and take a seat; a ticket-seller collects the fare, generally about $1, en route. Most routes terminate at the Praça da Sé, where you'll see long lines of Bahians patiently waiting their turn to climb aboard with a restraint unknown in New York.

Taxi – The best way to get around town, cabs are inexpensive and plentiful; and drivers can sometimes be persuaded to drive at less than murderous speeds, which is not true of Bahian bus drivers. After 11 PM and on holidays, the rate goes up by a fixed percentage, which the driver charges by raising the #2 flag on the meter. For longer trips — along the beach road or to the Church of Bonfim — arrange a fixed price in advance; otherwise, pay only what's on the meter or official price table that represents recent rate increases.

Car Rental – Don't. Streets are rarely marked and traffic is impossible. However, if you insist, *Avis-Lokarbras* has an office on Av. 7 de Setembro 1796 (phone: 237-0154) and in the airport (phone: 249-2550).

 MUSEUMS: In addition to the Museum of the City and the Carmo Convent Museum, mentioned in Special Places, Salvador's major museums are:

Museum of Bahian Art (Museu de Arte da Bahía) – A restored colonial mansion houses 18th-century tiles, furniture, ceramics, silver, and paintings from Europe as well as Bahía. Open from 2 to 6 PM. Closed Mondays. Av. 7 de Setembro 2340, Vitoria (phone: 235-9492).

Museum of Modern Art (Museu de Arte Moderna) – Open from 11 AM to 5 PM, weekends from 1 to 5 PM. Closed Mondays. Ave. de Contorno, Solardo Unhão (phone: 243-6174).

Technology and Science Museum – Exhibits on human biology, energy, and industry. Open from 11 AM to 6 PM Tuesdays through Fridays and 3 to 6 PM weekends and holidays. Av. Vale do Cascão, Parque de Pituaçu, Boca do Rio (phone: 231-9368).

Estácio de Lima – Cultural anthropology, African culture, and criminology. Open daily from 8 to 11 AM and 2 to 5 PM except Sundays. Av. Vale dos Barris, near the police station, or Policía Técnico (phone: 245-4917).

Afro-Brazilian Museum (Museu Afro-Brasileiro) – A historical portrayal of African influence on Brazilian society, including clothing, musical instruments, and photography. Open from 9 to 11:30 AM and 2 to 5 PM. Closed Sundays and Mondays. In the old School of Medicine, Terreiro de Jesus (phone: 243-0384).

 SHOPPING: Good buys are silver jewelry, hand-carved rosewood, and (especially useful if your suitcases are stuffed to capacity) leather bags of all sizes and shapes.Bahía is also the home of many interesting artists. Among the galleries you might want to check are: *Acervo,* Rua Almirante Marquis de Leão 39 (phone: 247-2540); *Art Boulevard,* Rua Anisio Teixeira 161 (phone: 248-1524); *Epoca,* Rua João Goures 246 (phone: 245-5541).

Gerson Shops – For silver of reliable quality at fixed prices, outside the chaos and bargaining of the market, these establishments may suit you better. *Gerson* has branches in all the luxury hotels, in the Carmen Convent Museum, and on the third floor of the *Iguatemi Shopping Center,* on the road to the airport.

Iguatemi Shopping Center – Bahians are very excited about this very big, very American shopping center. It even has a *Big Burger* restaurant on the ground floor, and every store in town has an outlet in it somewhere. Most shops are open from 9 AM to 7 PM on Tuesdays and Wednesdays, and until 10 PM on Thursdays and Fridays. On Mondays, they're open from 1 to 7 PM. Closed Sundays.

Instituto Mauá – This nonprofit organization is dedicated to preserving traditional arts and crafts of the Brazilian interior: embroidery, weaving, lacemaking, potting. It has branches at Porto da Barra (phone: 235-5440). Closed Sundays.

Itaijara Shopping Center – Another modern, American-style shopping mall, it has three levels filled with shops. Not far from Iguatemi Shopping Center, on Av. Antonio Carlos Magalhães, Pituba.

Mercado Modelo – Destroyed by fire in 1984 and now reopened, it is the best place to stock up on silver or rosewood figas for all your friends and relatives, to protect them from the evil eye. The smallest ones can be found for less than $1 apiece. Or you may want to harvest a collection of the lovely silver fruits known as *balagandãs,* which you see everywhere hanging in clusters from silver brackets (*pencas*). In colonial days, Portuguese swains gave these as tokens of appreciation to the slave women whose favors they enjoyed, and the women wore them at their waists as readily convertible assets, much the way some women today sport diamond rings. Be careful not to mistake acrylic for rosewood (*jacarandá*); or silverplate (*banhada de prata*) for real silver (*prata legítima, prata noventa*). There are also a couple of silver alloys widely sold in the market, known as prata sessenta and alpaca; these have the advantage of not corroding, and also cost less than real silver, but they don't much look like real silver, either. On Praça Cairu, in the Lower City.

SPECIAL EVENTS: You're welcome to witness the colorful *candomblé* ceremonies at some of the major *terreiros.* Please remember that, despite the vivid costumes and spirited dancing, these are religious ceremonies. Dress conservatively, and don't take your camera. Men will be asked to sit on one side of the room, women on the other. Don't be nervous. This is a very friendly, humanistic religion, and all the participants are Roman Catholics as well. Remember to leave a donation in the collection dish at the drummer's feet after the ceremony. If you prefer to go with a guide, check with any of the tourist agencies, which regularly sponsor evenings of *candomblé*. Try to arrive by 7:30 PM to get a seat. Most ceremonies begin around 8:30 PM and end between 11 PM and midnight. Arrange return transportation to your hotel in advance. To go on your own, call Bahiatursa for a list of current ceremonies (phone: 241-4333).

You'll see demonstrations of *capoeira*, an ancient and agile footfight-turned-ballet in any of the folklore shows (at the SENAC building, A Moenda, A Tenda dos Milagres); but if you get hooked on it, you can see more complete exhibitions (or even sign up for a course) at one of the official *capoeira* schools. Call Bahiatursa (phone: 241-4333) for up-to-date schedules.

Bahians celebrate every conceivable Roman Catholic and/or patriotic occasion with unbelievable enthusiasm. On these dates (which seem to occur every ten days or so until December, and then go nonstop through *Carnival*) it becomes impossible to find a taxi, and buses are very infrequent. Try to allow a lot of time for getting around town; or just relax and let the full flood of Latin *alegría* flow over you. Besides *Carnival* (the four days preceding Ash Wednesday), the most outstanding festivals include:

January 1, *Boa Viagem,* when a procession of boats carries the image of Our Lady of the Sailors across the bay to the beach at Boa Viagem, where the sailors carry her tenderly to her little church. Thousands of people eat, drink, and make merry.

On the Thursday before the third Sunday in January, *Bonfim,* costumed Bahian women wash the steps of the most popular church in the city. This ritual is followed by feasting, as above. The feasting is repeated on the following Sunday (and fairly continuously in between).

On February 2, the feast *Iemanjá* is celebrated. To win the goodwill of the goddess of the sea and to bribe her not to swallow up their fishermen husbands, brothers, and fathers, Bahian women in traditional lace costumes assemble at the water's edge in Rio Vermelho and send little gifts of pretty cakes and scented soaps floating out to sea. General feasting goes on all day.

June 24 and June 29 are *St. John's* and *St. Peter's* days. The saints in this case provide slender excuses for what are really harvest festivals, with bonfires, fireworks, and traditional dishes of *canjica* (a firm pudding made of sweet corn and coconut milk) and homemade fruit liqueurs.

On September 27, *Saints Cosme* and *Damian* are revered. Everybody feasts enthusiastically, and a lot of *caruru* (stewed okra) is consumed.

On December 8, *Conceição da Praia,* a religious procession to the church of that name, is preceded and followed by immoderate eating, drinking, and merriment in the area surrounding the *Mercado Modelo.*

 SPORTS: Salvador is just one soccer-mad city in a *futebol*-mad country.

Soccer – Don't miss a chance to attend a soccer match in the *Estádio Otávio Mangabeira,* which is as memorable for the passionate delight of the spectators as for the brilliant performances of the players. Games start at 4 PM on Sundays and at 9 PM, Wednesdays. Arrive an hour ahead of time, earlier for championships or other really big events, and pay the extra few cents for seats in the section marked NUMERADAS. You won't be allowed to bring glass bottles with you. Beer and snacks are sold by vendors throughout the game. Fonte Nova (phone: 243-7507).

Swimming – In addition to the beaches mentioned in *Special Places,* there are swimming pools at most of the better hotels listed in *Checking In,* below. Remember that the tropical sun is very strong, especially when reflected off sand and water. Unless you're already tanned when you arrive, you won't be able to spend more than a few minutes a day on the beach anyhow.

Tennis – There are courts at the *Hotel Méridien,* Rua Fonte do Boi 216 (phone: 248-8011); *Hotel Vela Branca* (Av. Antonio Carlos Magalhães, s/n, Pituba (phone: 248-7022); and *Hotel Quatro Rodas,* Rua Pasárgada, Farol de Itapoa, Km. 28 (phone: 249-9611).

 THEATER: The largest and most important theater is *Teatro Castro Alves,* Praça Dois de Julho, Campo Grande (phone: 235-7616), in the Upper City, which seats 1,700 people in air-conditioned comfort. You can almost always get tickets for plays and concerts at the last minute. If you want to buy them in advance, the box office is open from 9 AM until noon and from 2 PM until the performance.

 MUSIC: Among Brazil's best-known musicians, such internationally acclaimed Bahian music-makers as Caetano Veloso, Maria Bethânia, and Gilberto Gil perform annually in Salvador; they pack the *Teatro Castro Alves* to overflowing. Check at your hotel to find out if any major Brazilian artists are appearing during your visit.

 NIGHTCLUBS AND NIGHTLIFE: As throughout most of South America, disco has taken over the nightclub scene in Salvador. You're as likely to hear American rock as you are bossa nova in the most swinging discos. At the present, these are: *Le Zodiaque, Méridien* hotel, Rua Fonte do Boi 216 (phone: 248-8011, ext. 574); *Hippopotamus, Bahía Othon Palace* hotel, Av. Presidente Vargas 2456 (phone: 247-1044, ext. 1518); *Champagne, Salvador Praia* hotel, Av. Presidente Vargas 2338, Ondina (phone: 245-5033); *Canoa, Méridien* hotel, Rua Fonte do Boi 216, Rio Vermelho (phone: 248-8011); *Churrascaría Roda Viva,* Av. Otávio Mangabeira, Jardim dos Namorados (phone: 248-3499); Av. Otávio Mangabeira 54, Pituba (phone: 248-7063); *Bual Amour,* Av. Otávio Mangabeira, Corsário (phone: 231-9775).

 SINS: After dark, you'll find all the juicier types of *lust* flourishing in the general neighborhood of Pelourinho. Keep an eye on your wallet here. If you prefer a less professional ambience, complete with semiprofessional and even amateur co-sinners, try *Holliday,* at Rua Chile 29. Also in the downtown area, check out *Number 1,* at Rua Carlos Gomez 89, or *Palace Pigalle,* at Rua Rui Barboza 17.

BEST IN TOWN

 CHECKING IN: By American standards, Salvador's hotels tend to be pretty expensive for the level of service they provide. Here, as elsewhere, you pay considerably more for a beachfront address than for similar comfort elsewhere in the city. And you may not use the beach enough to make the difference worthwhile. Furthermore, real beach enthusiasts won't want to limit themselves to the small urban beaches of the big hotels, with much more spectacular beaches a few minutes down the road.

All the hotels listed here are air conditioned unless otherwise specified. All provide complimentary breakfasts of fruit, coffee, and bread. All but the inexpensive ones accept American Express, Diners Club, and Visa. Of the four best hotels in town, three are very big, very new, right on the beach, and expensive. Expect to pay $60 and up for a double room in hotels we list as expensive; between $30 and $55 at those in the moderate category; and under $15 in the inexpensive range.

Méridien Bahía – Just up the beach from the *Othon,* the *Méridien* provides the same degree of luxury on a much larger and jazzier scale, with a beach, pools, boutiques, a sauna, a solarium, tennis courts, a marina, a couple of restaurants, bars, and a super disco, *Regine's* (see *Nightclubs and Nightlife,* above), part of the sleek international chain. The ocean view from the top floor is terrific. Rua Fonte do Boi 216 (phone: 248-8011). Very expensive.

Bahía Othon Palace – Palace is a good word for this sumptuous new member of the Othon chain. Completely modern and elegantly appointed, it has nonetheless managed to incorporate into its architecture and decor many traditional elements of Bahía's urban landscape: the soaring stone arches of its cathedrals, beautiful ceramic tiles, pale rattans, polished woods, and vivid textiles. Perched on a hill at the edge of the sea, it offers a smallish beach, an immense pool, a legitimate massage parlor, several boutiques, a coffee shop, the excellent *Lampião* restaurant, a couple of bars, and a nightclub. Each room has an ocean view. Av. Presidente Vargas 2456 (phone: 247-1044). Expensive.

Hotel da Bahía – The newest of the Tropical Hotel chain and the best property now in the downtown area, it is tailored more to the businessperson than to the resort seeker. There are 282 rooms and very attractive public areas. Major credit cards accepted. Praço Dois de Julho 2, Salvador-Bahía (phone: 237-3699). Expensive.

Quatro Rodas – This newest of Salvador's deluxe establishments is on Itapoã Beach, about a 40-minute drive from town. In addition to 206 rooms, the hotel has a pool, tennis, and sand and sea out front. Praia de Itapoã, Salvador (phone: 249-9611). Expensive.

Salvador Praia – Right next to the *Othon* on the Ondina beach, this one is smaller but only slightly less expensive. Its comfortable rooms overlook the ocean and swimming pool. You'll find the predictable services: boutiques, beauty parlor, coffee shop, restaurant, bar, and nightclub. Av. Presidente Vargas 2338 (phone: 245-5033). Expensive.

Bahía do Sol – Close to the *Vila Velha,* this smallish hotel has a pleasant ambience, reasonable prices, and services, with a bar, coffee shop, and restaurant. Av. 7 de Setembro 2009 (phone: 247-7211). Moderate.

Hotel do Farol – A walk across the street from this hotel will take you to the Farol do Barra beach, where a lighthouse (*farol*) at the far point makes for a lovely view at sunset. Fashionable boutiques and lots of pizza parlors make this a fun and popular neighborhood, and the hotel itself has a restaurant, bar, and pool. Av. Presidente Vargas 68, Barra (phone: 247-7611). Moderate.

Grande Hotel da Barra – Also on Avenida 7 de Setembro, but all the way down the hill where it meets the sea in a posh residential section, this place has a split personality. There is the older, street side of the hotel, where rooms are less expensive but also shabbier and noisier; and there is the ocean side. Here, the attractive newer rooms have balconies overlooking either the adjacent beach, which is fine though crowded, or the inner courtyard and pool. Each side has its own reception desk, but guests in any of the rooms may use the various hotel services — pool, bars, or restaurant. By all means pay the extra $5 or so for a newer room. Little English is spoken. Av. 7 de Setembro 3564 (phone: 247-6011). Moderate.

Luxor Convento do Carmo – By far the most charming of Salvador's hotels and probably the most tranquil, it occupies a convent built in 1580 and now preserved by the National Historic Patrimony. Here you sleep in the actual white-painted cells once occupied by the nuns of the order (though they never enjoyed the comforts of modern plumbing and air conditioning now available, not to mention the color TVs and the refrigerator-bars). There's a lovely central courtyard with a large pool. Downstairs, the outstanding *Forno e Fogão* restaurant serves Bahian and European specialties. The *Luxor*'s only defect is that it's not very convenient to any of the beaches. Largo do Carmo 1 (phone: 242-3111). Moderate.

Ondina Praia – This is the budget version of the three big beach hotels. It sits across from the *Bahia Othon Palace* and the *Salvador Praia* on the other side of the perilous Avenida Presidente Vargas, which guests must cross to get to the beach. Small, pleasant, and ultramodern, it, too, has a pool, coffee shop, and gift shop. Av. Oceânica 2225 (phone: 247-1033). Moderate.

Praiamar – Next door to the *Grande Hotel da Barra,* just a few steps removed from the beach, the *Praiamar* is very new and aggressively modern in decor. It, too, has a pool, bar, restaurant, and shops. Av. 7 de Setembro 3577 (phone: 247-7011). Moderate.

Vela Branca – This one feels more like an American motel than a Bahian hotel. A few minutes farther out of town than the more expensive beach hotels, it does have quite a good beach as well as a pool, restaurant, and bar. Av. Carlos Magalhães, Pituba (phone: 248-7022). Moderate.

Vila Velha – A few doors down from the *Plaza* and a bit less expensive, this attractive little hotel is popular with American families. No pool or beach, but a friendly ambience and all the necessary services. Av. 7 de Setembro 1971 (phone: 247-8722). Moderate.

Anglo-Americano – Another reconverted house offering no-frills accommodations at no-nonsense prices. Again, no credit cards or air conditioning. Av. 7 de Setembro 1838 (phone: 247-7681). Inexpensive.

Camping Club do Brasil – If you are prepared to camp on the beach and prefer the convenience of campsites, the area has room for 350 tents, several caravan sites, showers and washing facilities, toilets, and a store. On Praia do Flamengo, about 50 miles (31 km) from town (phone: 249-2001). Inexpensive.

Caramuru – If you are traveling on a budget, you'll be able to find a single room without a private bath for as low as $7 in this 12-room house. Doubles with baths can be rented for as low as $8 a night. No credit cards. Av. 7 de Setembro 2125 (phone: 247-9951). Inexpensive.

EATING OUT: To savor the full glory of Bahian cooking, your best bets are the modest restaurants popular with Bahians themselves; these include *Yemanjá* out on the beach road and the *SENAC* restaurant in Pelourinho. Among the more elegant establishments, *Forno e Fogão* and *Lampião* also serve excellent local specialties. Alas, certain international restaurants tend to adulterate Bahía's brilliant sauces with canned condensed milk and, in a misguided effort to imitate European cuisine, garnish honest cuts of meat with limp, tasteless, canned vegetables.

Lunch is usually served from noon until 3 PM, dinner from 7 until 10 PM, although all such hours in Bahía are approximate and variable. Except for major tourist stops, most places are closed on Mondays. You don't need a reservation or a necktie, although upper-class Bahian men usually wear the latter to the fancier restaurants.

There's only one menu for both lunch and dinner. Bahians traditionally eat their big meal at noon. Portions are hefty; you probably won't need a first course. Besides, first courses can cost almost as much as entrées, since only tourists order them. Beware, too, of ordering drinks containing imported booze: they often cost $8 or more. Brazilian beer is excellent with Bahian food.

Expect to pay $30 and up for a meal for two at those restaurants we've categorized as expensive; between $10 and $20 for a meal at restaurants in the moderate category;

under $10, inexpensive. This does not include appetizers, drinks, wine, or tips. Imported booze is *very* expensive.

Casa da Gamboa – In an old colonial house with lace curtains and antique furniture, its atmosphere evokes a past era. Bahian specialties are served up by waitresses dressed in typical regional costume. Open for lunch from 12 to 3 PM and for dinner until 11:30 PM. Closed Sundays. Rua Gamboa de Cima 51, Aflitos (phone: 245-9777). Expensive.

Chez Bernard – This intimate little room feels more European than Brazilian. Prized by local cognoscenti for its consistently good French food, it also offers a spectacular view of the bay. Open for dinner only, 7 PM to midnight; closed Sundays. Major credit cards. Rua Nilton Prado 11 (phone: 245-9402). Expensive.

Lampião – Named for the Robin Hood of the Brazilian northeast, this handsome, bright red restaurant in the *Bahía Othon Palace* features delicious Bahian food beautifully presented. Try any of the *moquecas* here. It's too bad *Lampião* isn't open for lunch, because it looks out on a nice stretch of ocean. Dinner is served from 7 PM until midnight daily. Major credit cards. Av. Presidente Vargas 2456 (phone: 247-1044). Expensive.

St. Honoré – You get an impressive view of the city from up here on top of the *Hotel Méridien,* and the French food is pretty good by local standards, but you'll certainly pay top dollar for it. Open for dinner from 7 PM to midnight daily. Major credit cards. Rua Fonte do Boi 216 (phone: 248-8011). Expensive.

Solar do Unhão – Here you dine in a wonderful old sugarcane processing factory, where the waves of the Bay of All the Saints literally lap at the thick, hand-built stone walls. Elegant and comfortable, this place is a popular rendezvous for Bahian politicians and jetsetters. Stick to the simpler dishes on the international menu. If you come at lunchtime, be sure to visit the adjoining museum and art gallery. Closed Sundays. Major credit cards. Av. do Contorno (phone: 245-5551). Expensive.

A Moenda – Definitely on the tourist route, but worth a visit nonetheless, this place serves a wider variety of Bahian dishes than most of the fancier spots in town. Furthermore, if you linger after your dinner until 11 PM and pay about $5 per person, you can see a lively floor show of traditional dances and sambas. Closed Mondays. No credit cards. Jardim Armação (phone: 248-7469). Moderate.

Baby Beef – Owned by the Paes Mendonça chain, this sophisticated *churrascaría* (barbecue place) and its sister establishment, *Baby Beef Hereford,* offer tempting meat dishes for those who've had enough of Salvador's seafood. *Baby Beef* is at Av. Carlos Antonio Magalhães, Pituba; *Baby Beef Hereford,* at Av. Otávio Mangabeira, Jardim dos Namorados. Both moderate.

Forno e Fogão – This serene and lovely restaurant occupies the refectory of the 16th-century Convento do Carmo. Dark blue table linens and pewter service plates enhance the beauty of the convent's ancient stone walls, lofty arches, and hand-hewn beams. Both Bahian and international dishes are excellent here; some of them cost less than $5. Be sure to save room for self-indulgence when the dessert cart rolls around: The *quindins* are sublime. Open from noon to midnight every day. Major credit cards. Largo do Carmo (phone: 242-3111). Moderate.

Tenda dos Milagres – Similar to *A Moenda,* except that the show starts at 9 PM, and you pay about $5 more for it, which gives you the right to one *batida* and one *acarajé.* The dance based on the pulling in of the fishing nets is worth the price of admission all by itself. No credit cards. Closed Mondays. Av. Amaralina 553 (phone: 248-6058). Moderate.

Yemanjá – Also on the shore road, an excellent choice for both seafood and typical Bahian dishes. Here too you will find a lot of local color, though it's off the main tourist route. Open from noon to 4 PM for lunch, 7 PM to midnight for dinner.

Closed for dinner Sundays and for lunch on Mondays. No credit cards. Av. Otávio Mangabeira at Jardim Armação (phone: 231-5069). Moderate.

Restaurante do SENAC – This is one of the best deals in town and should be one of your first stops. Sponsored by the Center for Professional Training in Tourism and Hospitality, it's a self-service cafeteria in an attractive colonial dining room. Here you pay about $5 for all the Bahian food you can shovel onto your plate from a buffet that contains some forty items, all of them labeled so that you can make a note of the things you want to seek out at other restaurants. As an added attraction, downstairs there are free folkloric shows every night at 8 PM, including exhibitions of *candomblé, capoeira,* and *samba* as well as frequent productions of plays by local playwrights. Open for lunch from noon to 3 PM and for dinner from 7 to 10:30 PM; from 5 to 8 PM there is also a *seia* — coffee or hot chocolate served with a variety of typical Bahian sweets, costing less than $2. Closed Sundays. Major credit cards. Largo do Pelourinho 13/19 (phone: 242-5503). Inexpensive.

Paes Mendonça – When your schedule, budget, or appetite dictates a light lunch or a quick snack, head for the nearest *Paes Mendonça.* These are a chain of formica-tiled fast-food places with all the charm of *McDonald's,* but they're efficient, clean, and very inexpensive. Here you can get a decent grilled cheese sandwich (*queijo quente,* pronounced kã' zhoo ken' chee) for about 50¢ as well as hot dogs, hamburgers, miniature (and not very Italian) pizzas, hot fudge sundaes, and assorted junk food. One of the better sandwiches is the Americano: ham, cheese, sliced tomato, and fried egg. There are also special daily dinners for about $6, including meat, rice or potato salad, a little vegetable garnish, and a slice of bread. You have to know the procedure: Decide what you want, pay for it at the cashier, then take a seat and order it, presenting your receipt. *Paes Mendonças* are highly visible in virtually all the major plazas and are open from 7:30 AM to 11:30 PM. Closed Mondays. No credit cards. Perhaps most convenient for travelers are the *Paes Mendonça* directly across the street from the *Mercado Modelo* and the one facing the beach in Barra (no phones). Inexpensive.

At the following places, you can have a good meal (international or Bahian cuisine), as well as enjoy some fine music.

Berro d'Agua – The "in" gathering spot for young *baianos* to talk and mingle. Av. Barão de Sergy 27-A, Porta da Barra (phone: 235-2961).

Bristô Do Luis – Piano. Rua Conselheiro Pedro Luis 369, Rio Vermelho (phone: 247-5900).

Dose Dupla – Discotheque for the young. Rua Bravlio Xavier 2, Vitoria (no phone).

Nino's Bar – Popular nightspot for dancing. Rua Greenfeld 168, Barra (phone: 235-4807).

O Vagão – Jazz and *forró* (Brazilian country music). Rua Almirante Barroso 46, Rio Vermelho (phone: 237-1227).

Uauá – *Forró* and *caipira* on Fridays and Saturdays. Av. Otávio Mangabeira 46, Itapuan (phone: 249-9579).

SANTIAGO

On crossing the border into Chile, having braved all the hazards of the Pan-American Highway from California through mountains and jungles, washed-out mud tracks, and plagues of tropical insects, drivers have been known to exclaim in relief, "Good Lord! We're in civilization." Because in spite of the frankly insane geography of this country — narrow as a leaf and 2,600 miles long (like a blade, Henry Kissinger once pointed out, "pointed at the heart of Antarctica"), with every conceivable kind of geography from the surreal orange Atacama Desert in the north to the icy green fjords and powder blue glaciers of Tierra del Fuego in the south — it is custom-made for the Pan-American Highway, the spinal column through which 11 million Chileans interact, and an unusually reliable way of seeing at least three-quarters of this diverse country. And near its center, in a region known as the Central Valley, lies the dynamic heart of activity — Santiago.

This splendid architectural collage of Northern European elegance, North American suburbia, and South American imagination and culture is the home of four million *santiaguinos,* as residents are called. The city covers an area 40 miles from north to south and 20 miles east to west, surrounded by some of the most productive farmland in the nation and flanked on two sides by an overwhelming range of the Andes called the Cordillera.

Santiago owes its existence to a half-starved Spanish soldier-of-fortune who, under the sponsorship of King Charles III, staggered into a rich, fertile valley and grandly proclaimed the founding of Santiago del Nuevo Extremo on February 12, 1541. Its beginning was not without setbacks. Indians living along the Mapocho River did not take kindly to founding father Pedro de Valdivia and his motley group of armor-clad soldiers. They burned down the budding future capital of Chile twice. No sooner was it reconstructed and well on its way to becoming a permanent settlement than it was leveled in a savage earthquake in 1674. But the descendants of the early Spanish adventurers and the other Europeans who joined them in this New World did not give up easily, and by 1800 the city had become a major South American capital.

As in so many South American cities, contemporary Santiago is a confused jumble of colonial buildings in the grandest style competing for space and attention with modern corporate architecture. It is not just the surrounding mountains that make Santiago's high-rises seem not so high. Like all areas that circle the Pacific Ocean, Chile is an earthquake zone, and the height of buildings is carefully controlled to make them somewhat earthquake-proof. The city's highest building is only 23 stories high. The urban sprawl of Greater Santiago might remind you of one of the newer American cities west of the Mississippi, except for the shantytowns (*poblaciones*) in the northern and southern parts of town. Although compared with similar settlements in neighboring Latin American cities, Santiago's are relatively sturdy (some even have television antennas), there has been an attempt to block them from sight by constructing five- and ten-story housing projects.

Like most North American cities, Santiago is primarily middle class, with a high proportion of university-educated adults. Cosmopolitan and articulate, *santiaguinos* genuinely welcome foreigners. You will not see quaint Indian markets here. The government-sponsored CEMA-Chile has many shops in town where you can buy the best traditional and modern handicrafts from all over the country. The native population — or *araucanos,* as the Spanish called them — were still fighting long after their counterparts in other areas of the continent were either dominated or driven to such remote regions that the conquering population ceased to worry about them. In Chile the battle lasted 300 years, which explains the reduced number of the original inhabitants. Nevertheless, the majority of Chileans are dark-haired, and many bear the wide cheekbones that speak of diluted Indian blood. You will also encounter many Chileans who are tall, with light hair and eyes. You might even mistake them for Swedish tourists until you get close enough to hear them chirping away in Spanish. Early migrations of British, Germans, Yugoslavs, French, and — to a lesser extent — Italians have combined with the *criollo* (Spaniard born in Chile) and *mestizo* (mixture of Spanish and Indian) to produce a diversified and unusually attractive people. Chilean men and women take great pride in extolling the beauty of their women. Chilean pin-up girls in skimpy bikinis adorn most Chilean travel brochures and posters, and Chilean men aren't bad looking, either. And although *machismo* is a Spanish word that still applies to Chileans, the men are generally more polite and considerate toward foreign women than in other South American cities. By the way, no offense should be taken if you hear someone call you gringo or gringa. Chileans love to invent nicknames, and gringo usually refers to anyone with light hair, foreign or native. If you are a black American, you may feel somewhat uneasy, as black people are rare in this part of the world and often become objects of curiosity.

Chileans are fond of calling their country "the end of the world," and this vision has given them all, and especially *santiaguinos,* an outgoing frontier spirit. Like pioneers of the American West, they go out of their way to extend themselves to foreigners who have traveled thousands of miles to get here. What always impresses travelers is the genuine graciousness with which they are welcomed. This is what endures, and it is the reason why many visitors fall in love with Santiago.

SANTIAGO AT-A-GLANCE

SEEING THE CITY: At 1,145 feet above Santiago, at the crest of San Cristóbal Hill (Cerro San Cristóbal), stands a beautiful statue of the Virgin, her arms open to the city below. South of her feet lie the modern buildings of the downtown area, and on a clear day you can easily distinguish the nearest peaks of the Andes to the east and the more undulating slopes of the coastal mountain range to the west. Unfortunately, in the summer (November through April), a thick, yellow pall of pollution often obscures the view. The principal entrance to this terraced park is at the end of Calle Pio Nono, from which you can either drive up or take the funicular. Cable cars carry you atop the hill for a bird's-eye view of all the attractions the Parque Metropolitano has to offer: the city's zoo, with 2,000 different species; two lovely hilltop swimming pools, the Tupahue and Antilén; picnic grounds; hiking paths; and the Enoteca, a modern building constructed in the traditional Spanish colonial style, where you can taste the best and most famous Chilean wines, eat at its restaurant, see a folkloric show, or snack in its tea room. Restaurant open daily; reservations not required. Visa credit cards accepted. Parque Metropolitano (phone: 77-96-15). The park is open daily, and the zoo, Tuesdays to Sundays; small admission charge. The pools are open daily in season; admission charge.

 SPECIAL PLACES: The axis of the city lies along the Avenida Libertador O'Higgins (called Alameda by residents), the city's chief artery, from the Plaza Baquedano (known as the Plaza Italia) to the Plaza Bulnes, about 15 blocks away. The best place to begin a walking tour of the city is at the Plaza de Armas at Calle Catedral, Paseo Ahumada, Calle Estado, and Calle Merced.

Plaza de Armas – The oldest plaza in Santiago contains the monument *Liberty of America,* celebrating liberation from colonial rule. On the northeast corner stands a bronze statue of Pedro de Valdivia, the city's founder. At the corners of Calle Catedral, Paseo Ahumada, Calle Estado, and Calle Merced.

Ahumada Passage (Paseo Ahumada) – Since 1977 this street has been open exclusively to pedestrians. Along its cobblestoned walkway are flower gardens, fountains, some of the nicest downtown shops, and Santiago's biggest department store, *Falabella.* It is also the center of the banking district and a great place for people-watching. Paseo Ahumada extends for five blocks south of the Plaza de Armas, crossing the recently inaugurated Paseo Huerfanos, Santiago's second pedestrian street.

Cathedral – Dates from 1780, when it was built on the original site that the conquistadores planned as the center of the city in 1541. In the main altar lie the remains of various prominent figures of Chilean history. Open daily. Free. On the Plaza de Armas at Calle Catedral.

National Congress (Congreso Nacional) – A short distance from the Plaza de Armas, you'll notice the white columns of the National Congress building. It was constructed on the site left by the Compañía Church, which was leveled by a fire that cost some 2,000 lives. A statue of the Virgin in its gardens commemorates this tragic event. The Congress has been dissolved since 1973, but the library (*biblioteca*) is open. You cannot tour the interior of the Congress building, but you can visit the library. Closed Saturdays and Sundays. Free. On Calle Bandera between Calle Catedral and Compañía (phone: 71-53-31).

Supreme Court (Tribunales de Justicia) – The Supreme Court building, across the street from the National Congress, was designed by French architect Emile Dovère, and built in 1905. On Calle Compañía between Calle Bandera and Calle Morandé (phone: 71-71-23).

Colored House (Casa Colorada) – This national monument, a colonial relic, served as the 1810 residence of the first president of the Junta Nacional de Gobierno, Don Mateo de Toro y Zambrano, the Count of the Conquest. The building has just been restored. Closed Sundays and Mondays. Free. Calle Merced (no phone).

Presidential Palace (Palacio de la Moneda) – Initially designed by Italian architect Joaquin Toesca as the national treasury, the building was begun in 1743 using exclusively Chilean materials: wood from the southern forest, brick, cut stone, and lime. Since the middle of the last century, it served as the center of government and often as the official residence of ruling Chilean presidents. The last to have his office here was President Allende; the Moneda was bombed on September 11, 1973, during the coup that deposed him. General Pinochet is now installed in his offices in this historic palace.

Inside visits by the general public are not allowed. Calle Moneda and Calle Teatinos (phone: 71-41-03).

Diego Portales – This modern construction of steel, copper, aluminum, and glass was initially built in record time for the United Nations Commission on Trade and Development, which explains why many residents still call it the UNCTAD. But since 1973, it has housed the offices of the military government. Visitors are not allowed inside unless on special business, and if you would like to take a picture, don't let anyone see you. (The law prohibits the photographing of all military and government installations.) Av. Libertador O'Higgins (phone: 222-1202).

University of Chile (Universidad de Chile) – One of the foremost institutions of higher learning in South America, its headquarters can be found on the Alameda near Plaza Bulnes, a busy intersection where people stage demonstrations from time to time. Av. Libertador O'Higgins at Calle Morandé.

San Francisco Church and Museum of Colonial Art (Iglesia San Francisco y Museo del Arte Colonial) – Originally constructed in the middle of the 16th century, this church was rebuilt in 1853, conserving its original style. It is now a national monument, and in 1969 the cloisters of the adjoining Convent of San Francisco were converted to house the colonial art museum. In its age-old corridors are valuable colonial paintings, sacred ornaments, and what appears to be an infinite variety of colonial pieces. Church open daily. Free. Museum closed Mondays. Free. Av. Libertador O'Higgins 834 at Calle San Francisco (phone: 39-87-37).

National Historical Museum (Museo Histórico Nacional) – This museum houses an exhibit of Chile's great men, including portraits, personal effects, period furniture, and a complete collection of firearms. At its front door stands the National Library (Biblioteca Nacional). Closed Mondays. Small admission charge. Plaza de Armas 951 (phone: 38-14-11).

Santa Lucía Hill (Cerro Santa Lucía) – This lovely park is sometimes referred to as "the lungs of Santiago" because of its oxygen-producing greenery. Above the grand fountains that mark its entrance is a winding road that takes you past trees and flowers in bloom, past a little chapel built by the great Chilean historian and statesman Vicuña Mackenna, to the summit overlooking downtown. There stands a fantasy of a fortress that looks like it could have come from a storybook. Open daily. Free. Av. Libertador O'Higgins and Calle Santa Lucía.

American Museum of Popular Art (Museo del Arte Popular Americano) – Contains a wide selection of Chilean and South American handicrafts and artisan items. Closed Mondays. Small admission charge. On top of Cerro Santa Lucía, it can best be reached from the Calle Merced entrance to the hill (phone: 33-01-38).

Forestal Park (Parque Forestal) – The huge old trees lining the embankment along the banks of the Río Mapocho provide plenty of shade for joggers. Its flowering plants and trees are known to hide young lovers. As you stroll, you'll also run across a playground for small children and an occasional gypsy who will tell your fortunes for a price. This is the most Parisian part of Santiago, with older, dignified apartment houses facing the trees. A long, romantic, leisurely, or even melancholy promenade is sure to bring to mind images of the Seine. The park runs from the beginning of Av. Libertador O'Higgins along the water to the Mapocho station (Estación Mapocho).

Fine Arts Museum (Museo de Bellas Artes) – A beautiful palace rivaling the best Parisian architecture, this is one of the most respected fine art museums on the American continent. It has a large collection of work by both Chilean and foreign artists as well as by traveling exhibits. Closed Mondays. Small admission charge. Parque Forestal and the corner of Calle José Miguel de la Barra (phone: 33-06-55).

Pre-Columbian Museum (Museo Precolombino) – This new museum has one of the most complete collections of early South American artifacts. It is next to the Plaza de Armas, at Bandera and Compañía (phone: 71-70-10).

Central Market (Mercado Central) – This market is not a place for finding Indians weaving rugs or selling strange-looking fruits, but if you are a seafood enthusiast, it is the best spot in town to have a quick snack of raw shellfish to "recharge your batteries," as one of the attendants puts it. Whatever comes out of the Chilean sea you will be sure to find here, at the end of the Parque Forestal on the corner of Calle 21 de Mayo and Calle Ismael Valdés Vergara.

La Vega Market (Mercado La Vega) – If you want something a little more earthy, more "authentic," the real guts of the city are across the river in the extensive market-place that supplies all Santiago with everything from used shoes to filet mignon. Vegetables, meat, and seafood arrive daily in trucks and horse-drawn carts. Watch out for the *cargadores* (porters): They are so heavily burdened by their loads that they can't look out for you. Open daily. Free. Calle Andres Bello and Calle Salas.

Fantasilandia – As its name implies, this is Santiago's version of Disneyland. The most modern amusement park in Latin America, it has mechanical rides, an artificial lake, and green surroundings. It is a great place for children of all ages. Open daily. Admission charge. To get there, take Line 2 of the Metro from the station Los Héroes on Avenida Libertador O'Higgins to the station called El Parque. It is in Parque O'Higgins on the corner of Calle Tupper and Calle Beauchef (phone: 93-03-5).

Providencia – This is the center of the most exclusive shopping area in town. Elegant boutiques and shops built around spiral walkways called *caracoles* (snails) are filled with the very best that Chile has to offer. They also sport such international names as Christian Dior and Pierre Cardin. Chilean women of means are among the best dressed of Latin America and the tasteful decor and quality goods of the shops reflect their cosmopolitan style. Men will find the clothing shops equally interesting. There are an enormous number of imports: the latest color TVs, stereos, and electronic equipment and Japanese motorcycles. About 2 miles east of downtown, Avenida Providencia is the continuation of Avenida Libertador O'Higgins; the best shops are concentrated between Calle Pedro de Valdivia and Avenida Tobalaba.

SUBURBS

Barrio Alto – Farther east from Providencia are the swanky residential areas of Vitacura, Las Condes, and Los Dominicos, the home of many of the American residents, diplomats, and well-to-do Chileans. The *barrio alto* — or "high neighborhood," as it is called — reaches about 15 miles (24 km) east of the city to the foothills of the Andes. It derives its name from two factors: First, being closer to the Andes foothills, it is more elevated than the rest of town, which means cleaner air and a more refreshing breeze after the sun goes down. Second, this is where the upper class lives and shops. The *barrio alto* begins to the east of Calle Tobalaba and extends along Avenida Apoquindo, the extension of Avenida Providencia.

Los Dominicos – Along the Camino del Alba, beyond the twin spires of an old Dominican mission, lies one of the most beautiful residential areas of Greater Santiago. Along its winding streets you can see the immaculate, manicured gardens with their fruit trees and sweet-smelling flowers that hide the homes of Santiago's elite. Sundays at noon, artisans gather here to sell ornamental clay figures. East of the city on Camino del Alba.

Cerro Lo Curro – At night the street lights of this exclusive neighborhood meander around the hill like the twinkling lights on a Christmas tree. Most of the homes here are relatively new, and their bold angles of glass, wood, and stone display some of the imagination of contemporary Chilean architecture. Northeast of the city on Costanera Norte.

■**EXTRA SPECIAL:** The occasional view of a horse-drawn cart bringing produce to market is a reminder that Santiago is the center of one of the most fertile valleys of Chile. It is surrounded by vineyards, fruit groves, *fundos* (ranches), and small farms. The city gives way on three sides to enchanting scenery of dry, undulating hills set among cultivated patchwork farms. The fields are often divided by a line of poplar trees, and there is hardly an irrigation ditch without its company of weeping willows. Eucalyptus groves populate unused areas, and in the spring, wild flowers color the roadside in bright yellow, blue, and red. The town of Melipilla, with its tree-lined streets, is renowned for its fruit, which is both exported and eaten at home. It has numerous markets and is one of the most popular sites for the Chilean Independence Day celebration on September 18. Public transportation leaves from a bus terminal next to the Estación Central, the major train station, and the ride takes about 1 hour. Pomaire, a neighbor of Melipilla, is best known for its potters, who use sticks and stones to model red clay. You can find Donald Duck and Mickey Mouse among more traditional figures. About 15 miles (24 km) southeast of Santiago, the river valley called Cajón del Maipo contains some pleasant towns facing the mountains; and northeast of Santiago, hundreds of sleepy little towns nestle in the tucks and folds at the base of the Andes.

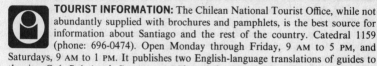

SOURCES AND RESOURCES

TOURIST INFORMATION: The Chilean National Tourist Office, while not abundantly supplied with brochures and pamphlets, is the best source for information about Santiago and the rest of the country. Catedral 1159 (phone: 696-0474). Open Monday through Friday, 9 AM to 5 PM, and Saturdays, 9 AM to 1 PM. It publishes two English-language translations of guides to the city: *Guía Práctica de Santiago* and *Plano de la Capital.* There is a scarcity of good information in English. A monthly publication called the *Calendario de Eventos* (*Calendar of Events*) lists exhibits and cultural events all over Chile. The booklet is available — free of charge — from most airlines and travel agencies.

Local Coverage – *El Mercurio* (morning daily), *La Tercera* (morning daily), *La Nación* (morning daily), and *La Segunda* (afternoon daily) provide coverage in Spanish. Every Friday *El Mercurio* publishes a weekend section with suggestions of what to see and where to eat.

CLIMATE AND CLOTHES: Santiago's climate tends to be sunny and warm throughout most of the year, with daytime temperatures ranging from the 30s F (around 3°C) in winter (June through September); into the 80s F (around 29°C) in summer (December through March). Winter rarely brings snow, but be prepared to get wet and bring sweaters and heavy clothing. You will need to wear sweaters indoors, since most Chilean heating leaves much to be desired, mostly heat. In summer, the smog and lack of air conditioning can make the city seem hotter than it is, but you should bring a light jacket or sweater for the evening. Occasional showers are common in fall, winter, and spring, so bring rain gear.

GETTING AROUND: Bus – There is service within walking distance of almost any street in town. Buses are generally crowded and slow, and should be avoided during rush hours. Multiple signs in bus windows make it difficult to discern the route; people often board in the middle of the street.

Taxi – Widespread unemployment has caused a general plague of taxis. You can find one almost anywhere. Most radio taxis listed in the Yellow Pages have a post-curfew service for emergencies or late night trips to the airport. Call 225-1733 during the day; from 9 PM to 6 AM, phone 40-10-4. Collective taxis (*colectivos*), which carry up to five passengers, follow a fixed route and will leave you anywhere along that route for a set price. The fare from the international airport to your hotel will be about $12.

Car Rental – *Hertz* has an office at Calle Costanera 1469, Providencia (phone: 225-9328). *Avis* has two: Av. Libertador O'Higgins 136 (phone: 39-22-68); and *Sheraton San Cristóbal,* Av. Santa María 1742 (phone: 74-76-21).

Metro – Santiago's clean, modern subway system provides rapid crosstown transportation until 10:30 PM. Since only two lines have been completed, it's impossible to get lost. The *Pajaritos–Las Condes* line runs under the Av. Libertador O'Higgins–Providencia–Av. Apoquindo artery and is the fastest way to whiz under traffic jams at rush hour. There's also a southern spur from the central station, *Los Heroes.* In each station is a map of the city to help you find your way.

 MUSEUMS: Santiago could be nicknamed "the City of Museums." Among its treasures are the Museum of Colonial Art, the Museum of Fine Arts, the National Museum of History, the Pre-Columbian Museum, and the Popular Art Museum (see *Special Places.*)

 SHOPPING: Although Providencia has the best shops in Santiago, there are a couple of government-run stores sponsored by CEMA-Chile, that are worth looking into. CEMA brings together women from different parts of the country and instructs them in the art of creating handicrafts. Their shops sell traditional and modern artisan products. CEMA's main display can be found at Av. Portugal 351; a women's exchange near this entrance is also good for handmade items. CEMA's outlet at Plaza Palmas, off Av. Providencia, offers a nice selection of clothing. *Morita Gil,* a boutique near the *Sheraton San Cristóbal,* specializes in things made of stone — carvings and original jewelry with precious metals and stones such as lapis lazuli, onyx, and turquoise. All the work here is custom designed at reasonable prices. The boutique is in a residential area, at Los Misioneros 1991, and also has a branch at the airport.

A bonus in Santiago is the superb tailoring and beautiful locally produced wool and alpaca for men's suits. A recommended tailor, or *sastre,* is Sr. Hector Villarroel, at Estado 115, Office 304 (phone: 39-14-27).

 SPECIAL EVENTS: September 18 is the *Chilean Fourth of July,* celebrated with rodeos in San Bernardo and Melipilla (see *Extra Special*) as well as *fondas* — stalls where *huasos* (Chilean cowboys or farmworkers) dance the national dance (called the *cueca*) and drink both wine and the fresh grape or apple cider called *chicha. Fondas* appear all over Santiago, but the best — since Chile's national tradition has its roots in the rural population — are in the little farming towns along the Central Valley. This event is followed by a military parade in Santiago's Parque O'Higgins on September 19. All major Catholic holidays are celebrated, too.

SPORTS: The national sport of Chile is soccer (*fútbol*), as in most South American countries.

Car Racing – The *Autodromo Las Vizcachas* has an international track 1 mile long for all kinds of car racing. It is 14 miles (23 km) from Santiago on the road to El Volcán (phone: 74-10-25).

Fishing – The Laguna de Aculeo, about 40 miles (64 km) from Santiago, is a good place to fish for mackerel. It's near the coastal mountain range and offers a chance to breathe clean mountain air. Buses leave from the first block of Avenida San Alfonso. Take any one marked Santiago-Aculeo. The Embalse del Yeso, an artificial lake 60 miles (97 km) from the city in the Cajón del Maipo, is ideal for trout fishing, but you must ask permission in person 72 hours in advance from the Guarnición Militar de

Puente Alto. Private transportation is the only way to get there. On the road to El Volcán. There is marvelous fishing in the south (see *Fishing,* DIVERSIONS).

Golf – *The Prince of Wales Country Club,* Av. Ossa and Av. Francisco Bilbao and the *Club de Golf* (Av. Ossa and Av. Presidente Kennedy) have private golf courses. Ask your hotel manager to arrange greens privileges.

Horse Racing – Santiago has two racetracks: the *Hipodromo* and the *Club Hípico.* The *Hipodromo* races are run on Saturdays from 2 to 9 PM in the evening. Av. Vivaceta and Av. Hipodromo Chile (phone: 37-42-78). The *Club Hípico* has Wednesday afternoon races on alternate weeks with the *Hipodromo,* and on Sundays between 2 and 9 PM. Av. Blanco Encalada and Av. Molina (phone: 91-757 or 96-113).

Skiing – The season begins in June and lasts until September, which makes Chile a favorite with professional skiers from the Northern Hemisphere. Thirty very winding miles (48 km) from Santiago, at 6,700 feet, *Farellones* can be reached in about 2 hours. Take Avenida Providencia east, then Avenida Apoquindo and Avenida Las Condes. After the turnoff to Barnechea, you will see a road sign to *Farellones. La Parva,* another ski resort, is just 3 miles (5 km) farther. There are also ski runs at *Lagunillas,* about 10 miles (16 km) from San José de Maipo in the Cajón del Maipo. You can spend the day skiing at any of these places and return to the city at night.

Soccer – Santiago is the home of numerous professional soccer clubs. Games are held each Sunday in the *Estadio Nacional* (*National Stadium*) at 4 PM in winter and a bit later during the summer, when it is somewhat cooler. For information, consult the publications listed above. Av. Grecia at Campos de Deportes (phone: 49-75-12).

Swimming – The pool at the *Carrera* hotel is okay for a quick dip, as is the terrace pool at the *Tupahue* hotel, Calle San Antonio 477 (phone: 38-38-10 or 39-52-40). The pool at the *Sheraton San Cristóbal* is the nicest in town, and there are two public pools at Parque Metropolitana, mentioned in *Seeing the City,* above. For ocean swimming, go to Viña del Mar (see *Chile,* DIRECTIONS), Santiago's plush seaside resort.

Tennis – The *Sheraton San Cristóbal* has tennis courts where visitors can play for a fee. Av. Santa María 1742 (phone: 74-50-00).

THEATER: Check the newspapers for a complete listing of all cultural events and schedules. One of the most interesting theater groups is the Ictus, whose pieces are usually a collective creation. They play at *La Comedia,* Calle Merced 349 (phone: 39-21-01). The Grupo Imagen is best known for their productions of plays written by young Chilean authors, presented in the *Teatro Bulnes,* Av. Bulnes 188 (phone: 72-73-33). The Comediantes put on both modern and traditional productions of foreign and national playwrights. They perform in the *Teatro Del Angel,* at Huerfanos 786 (phone: 33-36-05). Plays are staged almost exclusively in Spanish. Most films are shown in their original language — if you can figure out what that might be from the Spanish titles, which bear little resemblance to the original.

MUSIC: Santiago has everything from classical to burlesque and from folklore to disco. The *Teatro Municipal (Municipal Theater)* is the queen of serious music, concerts, opera, and ballet. Calle San Antonio 149 (phone: 32-80-4).

For folkloric music that combines the traditional with contemporary rhythms, try the *Casona San Isidro* on Av. España 115 or the *Casa Folklórica Doña Javiera* in San Diego 847. The show starts at about 10 PM on Fridays and Saturdays only. Food and drinks are served, but a small entrance fee allows you to see the show without extra expense.

Also visit the old, quaint suburb of Barrio Bellavista, which has been turned into a bohemian quarter, with good restaurants, lots of interesting shops, art galleries, old book stores, and little cafés with folkloric, jazz, and modern music all featured. Turn-of-the-century houses have been restored, and there is a special ambience here during the second half of January, when the barrio holds a festival.

NIGHTCLUBS AND NIGHTLIFE: Music is such an integral part of Latin American life that you simply have to choose which kind you most enjoy. At *Fausto — the* place to go after dark — you can have a drink in the piano bar, a good moderately priced meal in the restaurant, or dance in the underground disco. It's a favorite with *santiaguinos,* both gay and straight (Av. Santa Maria 823; phone: 77-10-41). Dixieland is going strong at the *Club de Jazz de Santiago,* open Fridays and Saturdays around 9 PM, on Av. Jose Alessandri 85 (called Macul by most residents). Small entrance fee. You'll find the cream of the *barrio alto's* unattached improvising steps to the hot, loud disco at the popular *Eve;* closed Mondays, couples only (Av. Vitacura 5480; phone: 48-63-41). The supermarket of dancing, *Maxim,* promises lots of flash and loads of people (Av. Matta 533, phone: 222-7946). But if you didn't come to Santiago to listen to music imported from north of the border, try *La Sirena,* which offers live music (usually two bands a night) playing Latin beats: cumbias, tangos, bossa nova. They also have a nightclub show that features a rather prudent striptease that isn't liable to offend anyone and generally a comic act that might. It opens at 9 PM on Calle Irarrázaval 27 (phone: 22-47-02).

Santiago has several restaurants that also offer dancing and a show. One of the bigger ones, the *Alero de Los de Ramón,* serves many typical Chilean dishes, the most common of which is *parrillada,* an assortment of beef cuts sizzling on a brazier. They also have a folkloric show with singing and dancing usually tied into a skit, plus an orchestra for after-dinner dancing. It is a tourist attraction, but you get what you pay for. Av. Las Condes 9889 (phone: 220-1069). Also try *Los Adobes de Argomedo,* which has the best folk show in town, dancing, and Chilean specialties (Corner Lira and Argomedo; phone: 222-2104); reservations recommended. Also offering good entertainment is the *Bali-Hai,* with Easter Island and Polynesian atmosphere (Av. Colón 5146; phone: 228-8273).

SINS: *Lust* has been raised to a fine art in Santiago. With many couples following the traditional pattern of living at home with their families until marriage, hotels specifically for couples have developed, with greater or lesser extravagance. The *Valdivia* hotel, the sophisticated Chilean's answer to the lack of private apartments, is a palace of love with a selection of rooms designed to encourage and abet indulgence in any secret fantasy. As in most sex emporiums in the US, singles are not allowed. Each couple is privately escorted to the room of their choice with the utmost discretion. Reservations are recommended, especially on weekends. Calle García Valenzuela 45 (phone: 222-6644 or 222-2504). If you don't have a partner, you're sure to find one during an evening stroll down Providencia.

Your *greed* will undoubtedly come to the surface when you see the thousands of exquisite goods for sale in the Providencia boutiques and the gorgeous homes and gardens in the *barrio alto.* If you want to get away from the urge to possess everything in sight, head for Cajón del Maipo or one of the other towns described above in *Extra Special* and spend a *slothful* afternoon reclining in a field drinking superb wine.

BEST IN TOWN

CHECKING IN: One of the most pleasant aspects of Santiago's hotel scene is the range of alternatives: from modern, snazzy buildings to old-fashioned, pretty hotels that remind you of romantic Paris. Expect to pay $75 up to $120 for a double room at those places we've classified as expensive; between

$35 and $55 at hotels in the moderate category; under $25, inexpensive. For local taxes, add another 20%. Breakfast is often included in room prices.

Carrera – For many years this was *the* hotel. In fact, journalists covering the 1973 coup used it as headquarters and filed stories to news organizations around the world from its telex desk in the lobby. It remains a top establishment, a landmark bordered by the Presidential Palace and still a favorite with many international business people who like being at the center of the action. The hotel has just been refurbished from top to bottom; it offers restaurants, a coffee shop, a popular bar, and a terrace swimming pool. Calle Teatinos 180 (phone: 698-2011). Expensive.

Galerias – Also very new, and within walking distance of the business and banking center. The hotel has 162 rooms, plus a pool and patio, as well as bars and restaurants. Av. Moneda and San Antonio (phone: 38-40-11). Expensive.

Holiday Inn Crowne Plaza – The newest hotel in the city, with 300 ultramodern rooms and special facilities that include a sauna, a pool under a glass dome, and a tennis court. Hotel service (common to Chile) is very good, and there is a choice of bars, boites, and restaurants. Av. Libertador O'Higgins 136 (phone: 46-51-58; 38-10-42). Expensive.

Sheraton San Cristóbal – This hotel is now considered the best in town. At the foot of San Cristóbal Hill, its rooms overlook the hotel's private swimming pool and tennis courts on one side, the Mapocho River on the other. While somewhat removed from the bustle of downtown, it is only minutes away by taxi. Av. Santa María 1742 (phone: 74-50-00). Expensive.

El Conquistador – Yet another modern hotel with all essential comforts. Pleasant, with a tasteful, sober interior, it is in the center of town, on one of Santiago's many pedestrian passageways. M. Cruchaga 920 (phone: 39-62-31). Moderate.

Don Tito – A very good choice for those desiring a small (25 rooms), intimate, first-class hotel. The service, overseen by the English-speaking owner, is excellent. Centrally located, one block from Santa Lucía Hill. Huerfanos 578 (phone: 38-10-24). Moderate.

Foresta – On the quiet end of the Santa Lucía Hill. Although small, each room has its own separate sitting room. The little reception area and its restaurant on the top floor are both tastefully decorated with antiques. This genteel quality gives the hotel a character all its own. Most rooms look out to the greenery below, as does the restaurant. Av. Victoria Subercaseaux 353 (phone: 39-62-61). Moderate.

Santa Lucía – Meets international travelers' needs, without unnecessary frills. It does have a telex service in the building itself, which is helpful if you need to keep in touch with the office during your stay. Calle Huérfanos 779 (phone: 39-82-01). Moderate.

Tupahue – This deluxe hotel combines a central location with a striking modern interior of bright, bold color. Although the reception area is on the first floor, the hotel's restaurant, snack bar, and lobby are all located on the third floor along with the terrace swimming pool and a piano bar called *Chiloé*. Calle San Antonio 477 (phone: 38-38-10). Moderate.

Libertador – An old hotel with a more local atmosphere than most; refurbished a few years ago. Av. Libertador O'Higgins 853 (phone: 39-42-11). Inexpensive.

Metropoli – A small, quiet, centrally located establishment with very good personal service. Calle Dr. Sotero del Rio 465 (phone: 72-39-87). Inexpensive.

Montecarlo – Recently constructed on the quiet side of Santa Lucía Hill, the *Montecarlo* provides most creature comforts. Although it has no restaurant, there is 24-hour room service and drinks are served in its arched-ceilinged lobby–sitting room. Victoria Subercaseaux 209. (phone: 39-29-45). Inexpensive.

Orly – As its name implies, this intimate hotel, a block from the exclusive Providencia shopping area, has a certain Parisian charm. Av. Pedro de Valdivia 27 (phone: 231-8068, 232-8225). Inexpensive.

Riviera – Although this tiny but endearing hotel has no real restaurant, its rooms are comfortable. Calle Miraflores 106 (phone: 33-11-76). Inexpensive.

São Paulo – This older establishment has the air of a provincial place that has been spruced up. Calle San Antonio 357 (phone: 39-80-31). Inexpensive.

 EATING OUT: In the downtown area, most shops and offices stay open for lunch, but you may find it difficult to find anyone there since many people go home for lunch. In other parts of town, businesses close from 1 to 4 PM. Most Chileans believe in a good, hearty lunch of several courses. If you feel like having something light, try *lomito,* the local version of the hamburger, the basis of which is roast pork. It is served in all the soda fountains that pepper the city center. Many of these little cafés also serve a more substantial menu at lunchtime for around $3. Chileans tend to dine at each other's homes rather than at restaurants unless it is a special occasion. Dinner starts around 9 or 9:30 PM. Chileans are rather informal, so you do not have to wear evening clothes at restaurants or nightclubs.

Be sure to try *locos* (abalone), any *mariscos* (seafood), and *empanadas* (meat pies). *Cousino* and *undurraga* wines are superb. No matter what you order, you'll find Chilean food terrific — especially at the restaurants listed below. Expect to pay $40 and up at those places we've listed as expensive; between $20 and $30 at restaurants in the moderate range; under $20, inexpensive. Prices are for two and do not include drinks, wine, and tips.

Aqui Está CoCo – A stone's throw from Providencia, this is a fine choice for seafood. Plenty of it, and all sorts, are prepared in any number of delicious ways. Open daily. Reservations not required. Major credit cards accepted. Calle La Concepción 236 (phone: 46-59-85). Expensive.

Maistral – A small, intimate restaurant that serves fine haute cuisine. Closed Sundays. Reservations recommended. Mosqueto 485 (phone: 3-0870). Expensive.

Martin Carrera – Considered one of the very finest restaurants in Chile, its cuisine is international *nouvelle.* In the past two years, Señor Carrera, the chef, has won quite a few gastronomic contest prizes, thereby invigorating the city's haute cuisine world. His wife, María Gloria, is his partner in the business, which is located in one of Santiago's prettiest suburbs. Reservations recommended. Isidora Goyenechea 3471 (phone: 231-2798). Expensive.

Caleta Los Leones – Cozy, with pleasant ambience and a good selection of Chile's famed seafood. Av. Los Leones 195 (phone: 232-5110). Moderate.

Da Carla – Very good Italian food served in a setting replete with checkered tablecloths and an occasional exclamation in Italian from the direction of the kitchen. MacIver 577 (phone: 33-37-39). Moderate.

Chez Henry – This is really three distinct places: take-out store, a restaurant, and a nightclub with nonstop dancing to a Latin beat. The restaurant is generally crowded at any time of day and any day of the week. Open daily. Reservations recommended. Diners Club cards accepted. Entrance is through the store, under the archways that surround the Plaza de Armas. Portal Fernandez Concha 962 (phone: 696-6612). Moderate.

Hostería Las Delicias – Set in the foothills of the Andes, this is one of the best places to find authentic Chilean cuisine and atmosphere. Live Chilean music is common on weekends. Puente San Enrique, El Arrayán (phone: 47-13-86). Moderate.

Mesón del Arzobispo – In this rustic setting, you'll find some of the best Spanish country cooking. Ask for the *picoteo* to accompany cocktails, or try the *conejo escabechado* (marinated rabbit) or *liebre civet* (wild hare). Watch out for the hot peppers in *gambas a la Española.* Bellavista 601 (phone: 77-88-65). Moderate.

La Pensión No Me Olvides – This is *the* place for typical Chilean food. Don't miss the *pastel de choclo* (a casserole of chicken, onions, and raisins with a crusty ground-corn topping) when in season. You'll leave this eatery — decorated with national handicrafts and warmed by Chilean hospitality — feeling as though a friend had invited you home to meet the family. Closed Mondays. On San Enrique 148080 in Arrayán, first block on the right from the cutoff to Farellones (phone: 47-28-37). Moderate.

Pinpilinpausha – *The* Basque restaurant of Santiago, *Pinpilinpausha*'s bistro atmosphere and tasty Spanish dishes make it a favorite of many international visitors as well as foreign residents. Centrally located in downtown Santiago at Matias Cousiño 62 (phone: 696-1835). Moderate.

La Pizza Nostra – Both branches of this restaurant serve good Italian food. One is at Av. Providencia and Pedro de Valdivia (phone: 223-5351); the other, at Av. Las Condes 6757 (phone: 229-7321). Moderate.

Yie Kung – Here you'll find some of the best Chinese food in town, particularly its fried Chinese ravioli (*wonton frito*). Dinner is served in a roofed-in garden. Near Providencia at La Concepción 62 (phone: 223-3535). Moderate.

Los Buenos Muchachos – Chilean food — *empanadas, mariscos* — in a Chilean environment, with the music of guitars and the Chilean harp. Closed Sundays, but open Sunday evenings only in the summer. Reservations not required. Major credit cards accepted. Calle Ricardo Cumming 1083 (phone: 698-0112). Inexpensive.

Naturista – This is the place for vegetarians, featuring a wide selection of omelettes. You can ask for your own concoctions if they aren't too complicated. No matter your taste preference, you will enjoy a drink in the juice bar. Closed Sundays. Reservations not required. Visa accepted. Calle Moneda 846 (phone: 698-4122). Inexpensive.

Tavelli – A delightful ice cream parlor and coffee shop in Providencia. Andres de Fuenzalida 36 (phone: 231-9862). Inexpensive.

Venezia – This restaurant sits in a lovely older neighborhood of quiet, tree-lined streets below San Cristóbal Hill. Abundant platters of beef, lamb, and pork and reasonable prices make *Venezia* a favorite of artists who live in the area. Visa accepted. Pio Nono 200 (phone: 37-09-00). Inexpensive.

SÃO PAULO

A surprisingly humble site for an event as important as the proclamation of Brazilian independence in 1822, the city of São Paulo has since come to embody and celebrate the bold spirit of that action. In its 150-year transition from backwoods outpost to South America's largest city, São Paulo has cultivated its stubborn independence, held on to its brash pioneer tradition, and shed any semblance of humility. As recently as 1932, the city led a serious secessionist revolt. It continues to surprise and challenge just about everyone, from the national leaders in Brasília, who would like to tame this unruly dynamo, to the visitors, who must somehow reconcile the fact of a skyscraper jungle with their previous visions of Brazil as a country of silent Amazonian waterways and sensuous Rio de Janeiro sambas.

São Paulo defies both the silent and sensuous stereotypes. It is, instead, a roaring tumult of a city, an often-polluted perpetual motion machine of over 12 million *paulistas* (officially, *paulistanos*) who never seem to stop hurrying, honking, or building. With their impatience and unabashed materialism, the *paulistas* drive the economic locomotive that has pulled Brazil to its current place as the world's eighth largest economy. In their state capital, they have joined the agricultural importance of a Chicago with the industrial might of a Detroit to create a commercial center that they proudly call "South America's second country." Within the city's 580 square miles (approximately ten times the area of Washington, DC), they make up almost 10% of the country's population.

The reward for all this urban concentration and bustle: One of South America's highest standards of living, some of the best restaurants on the continent, and an active cultural and night life that many foreigners rate far superior to that of more famous Rio.

From the very beginning, when Jesuit Padre Anchieta climbed to the 2,400-foot Piratininga plateau to found his São Paulo Indian mission in 1554, the city has been different from the rest of Brazil. Instead of hugging the coast like the sugar planters of Rio, Recife, and Salvador, the São Paulo pioneers, the *bandeirantes,* penetrated the inhospitable frontier. And slowly they pushed the evangelizing Jesuits south into Paraguay, for they had their own uses for the Indian population — they married the women, sold the men into slavery, and adopted such tongue-twisting Tupí-Guaraní place names as Anhangabaú (An-han-gab-ah-*oo*) and Itapetininga (*Ee*-tap-ay-tee-*neen*-gaa) for their streets and towns. For almost three centuries the *bandeirantes* had the region to themselves. The Portuguese crown profited first from the coastal sugar plantations and then the gold mines of Minas Gerais, but not until 1850 did São Paulo play its economic trump card — coffee.

Coffee built São Paulo. To grow it, southern Europeans immigrated by the hundreds of thousands. To transport it, Englishmen built two railroads to the coast, the Santos-Jundiaí and the Sorocabana, then managed the warehouses and docks of the port of Santos. To enjoy its financial rewards, the now-wealthy *bandeirantes* divided their time between the state's immense plantations and Paris's elegant salons.

The twentieth century brought a new wave of immigrants — Japanese, and Syrian and Lebanese Arabs — for whom trade and commerce were a far more palatable means of support than plantation life. King coffee had a competitor. While the Japanese continued the rural immigration pattern, the Arabs settled in the city, where industrial São Paulo was just emerging. Instead of allowing their rivers to flow south unimpeded over the 2,500 miles to Buenos Aires, São Paulo engineers dammed two of them during the 1920s, installed generating plants, and set São Paulo on its industrial path. Volkswagen and the Big Three American auto producers (Ford, General Motors, and Chrysler) have since set up shop in São Paulo, where they too are perpetuating the city's brash *bandeirante* spirit by pioneering the production of alcohol-driven cars. It is estimated that Brazil now has more than a million cars that burn alcohol instead of gas on the road. Besides saving money for petroleum-poor Brazil, the alcohol craze has also changed exhaust smells on the street. Multinational chemical corporations have chosen suburban Mauá, and innumerable manufacturers are in the city itself. In fact, 75% of Brazil's electrical goods, rubber, and machinery are produced within the city limits — all in all, a staggering 50% of the total industrial output of the nation. Greater São Paulo, easily acknowledged as the largest industrial region in Latin America, absorbs 75% of foreign investment. São Paulo state produces most of the coffee from which Brazil supplies two-thirds of the world's need. Coffee futures and other commodities are traded in São Paulo. Tons of agricultural produce are shipped through the city and Santos, its port.

Billed as the world's fastest growing city, São Paulo increases by about 300,000 inhabitants per year, 70% of whom migrate from other parts of Brazil. Although accurate statistics are hard to come by, the city has more than doubled in size from 1960, when it had 3.8 million residents compared to Rio de Janeiro's 3,307,000. (Rio is 272 miles — 435 km — north of São Paulo.) In 1970, there were six million *paulistas* and four million *cariocas* (residents of Rio de Janeiro). By 1980, Brazilian census takers had become somewhat more sophisticated, separating the population of the city of São Paulo (eight million) from that of Greater São Paulo (10,040,000), which includes Osasco, Santo Andre, São Bernardo, and São Caetano. That's quite a change from 1872, when São Paulo numbered only 32,000 inhabitants.

With more than 3.5 million workers, São Paulo has a strong labor movement and outspoken and often courageous political leaders. Since May 1978 when some 400,000 São Paulo workers held the country's first strike in 10 years, work stoppages have once again become legal and have spread to other cities such as Rio, Belo Horizonte, and Porto Alegre. Strikes, which had been declared illegal when the former military government was in power, are an important way in which São Paulo pushed more political freedom throughout the country.

A fearless spirit is part of the city's twentieth-century history. The coffee aristocracy that built splendid mansions along then-residential Avenida Paulista had to make way for empire-building immigrants — Italians like the millionaire Matarazzo family, Arabs such as São Paulo congressman Paulo Salim Maluf, and Japanese like artist Manabu Mabe. A typical rags-to-riches hero, Mabe labored on a coffee plantation as a young man and now sells paintings for up to $30,000 to international collectors, among whom are numbered the late Nelson Rockefeller.

São Paulo has not managed to escape entirely the pervasive South American problem of widespread poverty. It has its poor, like every city on this continent, and some one million *paulistas* crowd into homemade shacks in shantytowns called *favelas*. Less than half of the city's inhabitants are connected with the sewage system; 72% having running water. Half the city's population earns less than $200 per month and the average yearly income in the state is somewhere between $2,000 and $3,000. These figures are all the more staggering when contrasted with the exorbitantly high rents in modern apartment buildings — as much as $800 a month for a two-bedroom apartment without furniture. (Who can afford it? Americans and other foreigners whose companies pay for housing, which, one resident commented, "has the unfortunate effect of giving landlords the idea they can get away with it, which in turn forces prices to skyrocket even higher.")

Surrounded by upward-mobility success stories on every side, it is no wonder that *paulistas* are obsessed with movement. A visitor who would be sprinting among the relaxed saunterers of Rio de Janeiro quickly gets overtaken by São Paulo's determined, jostling crowds. The difference in the two cities' tempos and life-styles is immediately apparent, even to a first-timer. In Rio de Janeiro, *cariocas* (men *and* women) often lounge around like juicy centerfolds awaiting a photographer. In São Paulo, everybody looks as if he or she were late for work. In contrast to the shirts unbuttoned to the navel that are everyday street attire in Rio, *paulistas* wear business suits and ties, even on oppressively humid, hot afternoons. Occasionally a man will wear the top two buttons of his shirt open. Women wear skirts and blouses, demure in contrast to the low-cut shifts and *tanga* bikinis of Rio. In São Paulo, people walk around absorbed in their own thoughts, sometimes tired, sometimes lonely, sometimes annoyed. In contrast to the seductive, playful *cariocas, paulistas* look very real. A first-time visitor coming from another section of Brazil is also bound to notice that the ever-present *cafezinho,* sipped and savored in other parts of the country, gets gulped in São Paulo at a stand-up bar. And all those people carrying books (rather than surfboards)? Most are headed for an English class or a professional course for an evening of study after a full day's work. One *paulista* eloquently summed up both cities: "In Rio, it's women, samba, and *cachaça* [cane liquor]. In São Paulo, it's work, work, work 48 hours a day. No wonder the people are crazy!"

Returning to the city itself, a semblance of order does reign among the residential areas that ring the south and west of downtown, although business activity continually encroaches. On hills reminiscent of those of San Francisco, apartment buildings and chic boutiques start at Avenida Paulista and give way to the quiet lanes of the residential neighborhoods, called *jardins* (gardens), before commerce returns at Avenida Faria Lima. Farther south, in the Zona Sul, *paulistas* have built suburbs on the American model —

Morumbí, Santo Amaro, and Chácara Flora. However, they, too, are getting surrounded by commerce, as has already happened to the *jardins* and to the western suburbs such as Pinheiros, Pacaembú, and Sumaré.

This growing city will never be voted one of the planet's most attractive. Although it does have mosaic sidewalks with curved patterns laid into wide pedestrian walkways, palm trees, and grand boulevards, it is overpoweringly noisy, hectic, and anonymously modern. And the predominant color is gray from top to bottom: sky melting into buildings melting into concrete. Even the most photographed site — the spectacular S-shaped Copan apartment building designed by Oscar Niemeyer curving sinuously across the street from the cylindrical tower of the *São Paulo Hilton* — can lose its dramatic appeal in the washed-out, unattractive daylight. Like the majority of industrial cities around the world, São Paulo's appeal has nothing to do with its physical appearance; rather, its most impressive quality is the human energy that built it and keeps it moving. It's a city with heart. People love it despite its ugliness, which seems to go endlessly in office building after office building, apartment house after apartment house, and factory after factory. You can drive through São Paulo for one hour and be convinced that you are in the same part of town in which you started out, so identical are the sections of unrelieved urban landscape. Which makes it even more surprising when you get to the edge of the city and find a tropical forest with mist clinging to flower-filled gorges. Then you understand the triumphant, mammoth undertaking that has become São Paulo: It is a city hacked from jungle!

In the evening, *paulistas* head home to pockets of relative tranquility to recuperate among traditionally tight-knit families. Except for an occasional late dinner, play, or concert at the magnificent Municipal Theater (never before 9 or 10 PM), *paulistas* abandon downtown to the city's poorer (and tougher) population at night. Similarly, on weekends the affluent flee to beach houses or country homes while the majority spend time among family or fellow soccer fans. Those who remain crowd the city's restaurants on Sunday — maid's day off. But beware the long weekend. At the slightest excuse, *paulistas* will descend to the coast en masse, creating 10- to 12-hour traffic jams when they return on Sunday night.

This very private and family-centered social life frustrates both the city's estimated 12,000 resident Americans and foreign visitors. The 550 American firms that have personnel scattered throughout the city and the state try to solve the problem as wealthy *paulistas* do: They buy memberships in the city's many expensive sports clubs. Public recreational facilities do not exist.

A more viable alternative for tourists seeking casual but respectable encounters are evenings at what one American calls São Paulo's "California-type bars." (Less respectable encounters are well advertised for traveling businessmen in the hotel tourist pamphlets.) The action at these bars starts late, after 10 PM, and reflects traditional São Paulo society. The bars are away from downtown, and socializing most often takes place in groups.

This paradoxical mix of modern business and traditional social customs is just one example of São Paulo's growing pains. Spectacular growth has also caused plenty of physical problems. Winter rains annually force thousands from their homes. Residents who enjoy an extensive public telephone system (tokens, called *fichas,* are sold at newsstands and lunch counters) may find it difficult to obtain a private line. And everyday concrete replaces more of the city's precious trees.

Yet São Paulo remains undaunted. Even with predictions of a population of 20 million by AD 2000, *paulistas* face the future with optimism and confidence — *bandeirantes* to the end.

SÃO PAULO AT-A-GLANCE

 SEEING THE CITY: Although only a plane can provide a complete view of the sprawl that is São Paulo, the top floors of the downtown Edifício Itália offer a good substitute. The city's hills swallow the suburbs, but at your feet lies the labyrinth of downtown streets, and to the southwest you should be able to spy the huge Itaú time and temperature sign that marks Avenida Paulista. A combination of two elevators will whisk you up to the 41st floor. From there you can choose the free and often windy view from the balcony, a soft drink or costly but scenic meal at one of the two restaurants, or a drink at the bar. The best time to go is at night, when everything sparkles. Reservations not needed. Open daily until 2 AM. Av. Ipiranga 344 (phone: 257-6566).

 SPECIAL PLACES: With its tortuous traffic patterns and pedestrian malls, downtown São Paulo is best explored on foot. Wear sensible shoes and be prepared for the construction that can turn any sidewalk into an obstacle course. You'll do well to remember that the city is divided into named neighborhoods (downtown being *centro*) and that streets frequently change names — for example, Rua Augusta becomes Rua Colómbia, then Rua Europa, and finally Rua Cidade Jardim before expiring at the river. Trust your map rather than generous but often uninformed residents, and don't forget that most museums open only in the afternoon and are closed Mondays. One final note: Don't wear valuable jewelry or carry large amounts of cash while walking around the city. Street assaults are rampant, especially downtown.

DOWNTOWN

Tea Viaduct (Viaduto do Chá) – Here is the nonstop heart of nonstop São Paulo. It is people, people everywhere. Bustling Brazilians overflow from the sidewalks onto the already bus-and taxi-jammed streets. Vendors and beggers, bankers and delivery boys, are all fellow companions on the Viaduto do Chá. Linking the two major squares Praça da Patriarca and Praça Ramos de Azevedo, it provides the primary downtown reference point. The Praça da Patriarca and the malls of São Paulo's lucrative financial district, the Old City, lie to the east. To the west, the Praça Ramos de Azevedo, the ornate Municipal Theater, and *Mappin* department store mark the beginning of the New City and the downtown shopping area. The viaduct spans the 18-lane Anhangabaú traffic artery.

Cathedral Plaza (Praça da Sé) – Rebuilt in 1977 and inaugurated in 1978, the Praça da Sé is dominated above by South America's largest cathedral and below by the city's major subway station. Contiguous to the financial district, both the fountains of the square itself and the vaulting coolness of the gothic cathedral that holds 8,000 people offer a quiet interlude. The city's second subway line, partially functioning now and due for completion before 1990, will meet the north-south subway line here. The subway entrance is to the left of the cathedral, and the 20¢ ride will provide ample demonstration of the vastness of the city. Wall maps at the entrance indicate the subway route; just watch the *paulistas* to learn how the computerized gates work. Two points of interest, Bairro Oriental (Liberdade) and the Sacred Art Museum, can be reached by subway. Two blocks east of Praça da Patriarca on Rua Direita.

Bairro Oriental (Liberdade) – Treats galore lie beyond the welcoming red lacquer gates of São Paulo's Oriental district: tranquil rock gardens perched above the traffic din; herb stores stocked with mysterious remedies; and numerous Japanese, Chinese, and Korean restaurants that come alive under the glow of the district's Japanese lantern street lights. São Paulo state boasts the largest Japanese population outside of Japan and Liberdade is its urban hub. Besides curio shops that sell both Brazilian and Oriental souvenirs, numerous little shops feature delicate, hand-painted kimonos. The nearby Japanese Immigration in Brazil Museum (Museu da Imigração Japonesa no Brasil) recounts the interesting 75-year story that has given the country some 800,000 Japanese-Brazilian citizens. Rua São Joaquím 381, open Tuesdays through Sundays, 1:30 to 5:30 PM (phone: 279-5233). A handicraft fair fills the local square on Sunday afternoons. South of Praça da Sé along Praça da Liberdade and Rua Galvão Bueno.

Sacred Art Museum (Museu de Arte Sacra) – Locals claim that this museum, housed in the colonial Convent of the Light (Mosteiro da Luz), has the largest collection of religious art outside the Vatican. Carved wooden altars, statues, and several rooms of gold altarpieces are exhibited around an interior courtyard. If you call ahead, you may be able to arrange for an English-speaking guide. Open Tuesdays through Sundays, 1 to 5 PM. Small admission charge. Across from Tiradentes subway station on Av. Tiradentes 676 (phone: 227-7694).

Republic Plaza (Praça da República) – This lovely square is full of exotic tropical plants and shaded by palm tree. You'll find many pleasant tourist shops around the edge and along the two nearby pedestrian shopping streets, Barão de Itapetininga and 24 de Maio. *H. Stern* sells exotic gems right across the street. In the nearby *Galería California,* at Av. Barão de Itapetininga 222, more than a dozen souvenir shops offer typical items. If you're in town on a Sunday, don't miss the morning Hippie Fair. Leather craftsmen and local artists exhibit beside wizened coin and stamp collectors. Be cautious with the regional snacks sold by the *baianas* — the sauces can be pretty fiery for an uninitiated stomach. Never wander here at night. Av. Ipiranga and Av. Barão de Itapetininga.

São Paulo Art Museum (Museu de Arte de São Paulo — MASP) – Balanced dramatically on four concrete pylons, this museum displays South America's most complete permanent collection of Western art — a Rembrandt, a Raphael, and a sampling of French Impressionist works. There are also examples of contemporary Brazilian art and frequent excellent traveling exhibitions. All paintings are mounted on plastic stands instead of hung on walls so that they appear to be floating. After taking in the galleries, enjoy the greenery of the Trianon Park across the street and then stroll along Avenida Paulista — once the avenue of stately mansions but quickly becoming a second financial district of adventurous, impressive contemporary architecture. Open Tuesdays through Sundays, 1 to 5 PM. Free. Av. Paulista 1578 (phone: 251-5644).

Pacaembú Market (Feira de Pacaembú) – This market offers everything from orchids to octopus, with luscious tropical fruits and vegetables in between. (You may wonder why none of this produce appears on local menus; it's because Brazilians feel that vegetables aren't "classy" enough to serve to guests in the home or in restaurants. However, if you ask, most restaurants can come up with a cooked mixed-vegetable platter — *panache de legumes* — even if it's not included on the menu.) Held Tuesdays, Thursdays, Fridays, and Saturdays in Pacaembú Stadium at Praça Charles Miller.

SUBURBS

Rua Augusta and the Jardins – You'll see *paulistas* at one of their favorite occupations — shopping — as you descend the rather steep Rua Augusta from Avenida Paulista. Side streets such as Alamedas Tietê, Lorena, and Oscar Freire are filled with boutiques, native art stores, art galleries, informal lunch counters, and several good restaurants. Try the *Cantina de Piero* at the corner of Rua Bela Cintra and Alameda Oscar Freire or the ever-popular *Churrascaría Rodeio* at Rua Haddock Lobo 1498. Cross Avenida Estados Unidos at Rua Bela Cintra to wander among the lush vegetation and modest mansions that mark the beginning of the residential *jardins* area.

Ibirapuera Park (Parque Ibirapuera) – After a morning of dodging the traffic and elbowing the downtown crowds, the willow-bordered lakes and eucalyptus groves of Ibirapuera Park provide a welcome respite. The park was designed by Oscar Niemeyer, architect of Brasília's most impressive buildings, and because it is such a large place (400 acres) you might take a taxi to a specific place — the Contemporary Art Museum (phone: 571-9818) or the Japanese Pavilion (Pavilhão o Japonesa), a reconstruction of Japan's Katura Palace. Then, with an ice cream purchased from a vendor, meander across the lawns to one of the museums or to the planetarium (nightly shows during the week; afternoons on weekends and holidays). Try the roads that have been closed to traffic or, if you stay along the main thoroughfares, watch out for the motorcyclists. They are as enamored of this oasis as pedestrians — but they go a lot faster. Open daily. Free. Parque Ibirapuera.

Butantã Institute (Instituto Butantã) – Snakes are the specialty here: live ones that are "milked" for medicinal purposes and stuffed specimens of poisonous snakes, spiders, and scorpions that are displayed for educational ends. The important snakes, though, are the live ones that sun themselves and slither around the open pits. Well protected by high leather boots, researchers extract venom from these fellows six times a day (10, 10:30, and 11 AM, and 3, 3:30, and 4 PM), and they delight in showing their fangs and darting tongues to the crowd. Walk behind the museum parking lot to get a view of the city horizon. Open daily, 8 AM to 4 PM. Small admission charge. Bring small change; attendants will not change large notes. Av. Vital Brasil 1500 (phone: 211-8211).

Pioneer House (Casa do Bandeirante) – Within walking distance from Butantã, you can see how the *bandeirantes* lived. As this oversize reconstruction of an 18th-century pioneer home shows, they led a spartan, nomadic existence. These pioneers used uncomfortable but portable rope hammocks for beds and substituted well-traveled trunks for the chests and buffets of more settled city life. Scattered around the grounds, you'll discover the unwieldly ox carts still used in Brazil's less-developed regions and three mills: one for sugarcane, another for corn, and one primitive, all-purpose mill. If you ask, the caretaker will turn on the water to show how this mill worked. Open Tuesdays through Saturdays noon to 5 PM; Sundays 9 AM to 5 PM; closed Mondays. Free. Praça Monteiro Lobato (phone: 211-0920).

Brazilian Home Museum (Museu da Casa Brasileira) – In an imposing residence that was built in 1945 in 1800s neo-classical style, this museum offers a good overview of how Brazil's elite has lived during the past 400 years. Excellent photographs of elegant Victorian drawing rooms and enlargements of 16th- and 17th-century sketches augment the museum's large furniture collection. Fashioned from beautiful native woods, you'll notice their immense size and the preponderance of religious pieces. English-speaking guides available. Open Tuesdays through Sundays 1 to 5 PM; closed Mondays. Free. Av. Brig. Faria Lima 774 (phone: 210-3727).

Zoo (Jardim Zoológico) – A great source of pride for residents and a required stop for anyone remotely interested in tropical animals, the São Paulo Zoo is perhaps the best substitute for a trip up the Amazon. There are anteaters, sloths, tapirs, and cage after cage of spectacular birds: toucans, parrots, and macaws (always paired, the macaws scream incessantly and vary from brilliant blue to bright red). The scattered signs *Não Pise na Grama,* by the way, mean "Don't Walk on the Grass." Be sure to pick up the useful map the ticket seller gives you. Open daily. Small admission charge. Av. Miguel Stefano, Água Funda (phone: 276-0811).

Ipiranga Park and Paulista Museum (Parque Ipiranga e Museu Paulista) – There's a little of everything for history buffs here. The Paulista Museum, a converted palace, displays old maps, coins, firearms, colonial furniture, and art. Fountains and statuary dot the grounds, and you can walk through the preserved mud house where Dom Pedro I spent the night before giving the Cry of Ipiranga, the Brazilian Proclamation of Independence. Open daily, 9:30 AM to 5 PM. Small admission charge. Parque Ipiranga (phone: 215-4588).

Wholesale Markets (CEAGESP and CEASA) – Beware the trucks that rumble into São Paulo's wholesale produce market, CEAGESP, about midnight. The drivers are bringing food to Latin America's largest food distribution center. You'll see fruits and vegetables you've never heard of. On either a Tuesday or a Friday midmorning visit to the adjoining wholesale flower market, CEASA, you'll see hundreds of delicate ferns and exotic birds of paradise. The CEAGESP restaurant serves hearty, typical Brazilian meals. Open daily. Marginal do Rio Pinheiros.

Interlagos and Guarapiranga Reservoir – About 8 miles (13 km) south of the city along Avenida Atlântica, the reservoir affords a quick escape from the urban environment. The beaches and restaurants fill up on weekends, but most facilities are open all week long. Besides pleasure boats and sailboats for rent, there are hydroplane rides and pony trots for the kids. The *Interlagos Restaurant* is a good place for a meal or just a beer. The Brazilian Grand Prix is held at the nearby Interlagos Raceway. Estrada de Interlagos (phone: 240-6290).

Embu – This colonial town about a half-hour drive from downtown has a well-attended Sunday artisan fair and permanent shops that are open all week. At midafternoon on Sundays, the local oompah band serenades shoppers and townsfolk from the central bandstand. Restaurants along the main square serve snacks or lunch on rustic tables. About 16 miles (26 km) west on Rte. BR-116.

Itú – After someone made a joke about the size of things in Itú several years ago, the city adopted the idea and now uses it as a successful tourist gimmick. An immense telephone booth towers over the heads of visitors in the main square, restaurants sell meter-long hot dogs, and all souvenirs come in gargantuan sizes. The narrow cobblestone streets and antique stores provide plenty of interest. Eat at the *Bar do Alemão,* Rua Paulo Souza 575 (phone: 482-4284). About 75 miles (120 km) or 2 hours west on the Castelo Branco Highway.

■ **EXTRA SPECIAL:** When *paulistas* want to escape to the shore, they don't have to go as far as Rio de Janeiro: The resorts of Guarujá, Santos, and São Vicente lie 43 miles (70 km) to the southeast. The road winds through hills of purple flowers and jungle vegetation, with fog and clouds rising steamily from the gorges. Santos, Brazil's largest port, is a frayed, seamy, tough Latin waterfront town with huge container ports, mechanics' shops, and storefront merchants selling tired little bananas. However, don't get too depressed as you travel through this part of town, for soon you will reach Gonzaga — a beachfront of white apartment buildings, with cafés like those in Rio de Janeiro and a long grassy plaza along the water, good for walking along or eating beside, but not for swimming. Guarujá, across the channel, is considerably more elegant. Nicknamed "the Miami Beach of Brazil," its nucleus of ubiquitous white high-rises contains well-tended cafés, restaurants, promenades, and surf shops. At the far end of a long road is a section of hillside villas clinging to cliffs that offer views as good as any at Big Sur. Halfway in between lies one of the ultimate, consummate resorts in the Americas: *Casa Grande.* A converted ivy-covered hacienda replete with white Victorian wooden verandahs, palm trees, alcoves with bird cages, and a palm-lined swimming pool, it faces a wide, clean, white beach with palms to shade you from an overly hot sun. *Casa Grande*'s restaurants include a spanking new luncheonette featuring ingenious sandwiches on pita bread and a superb French restaurant that serves giant lobster in a hollowed-out pineapple. Pelé, the world's most famous athlete, is a habitué of *Casa Grande*'s disco. American companies based in São Paulo hold conventions here, too. Av. Miguel Estefno 999, Praia da Enseada (phone: 86-2223). In São Paulo, you can make reservations at the *Casa Grande* office, Av. Europa 571 (phone: 282-4277). If you are not up for driving (traffic jams are awful during the summer), there is frequent bus service from the city to Santos and Guarujá. Better yet, take an Expresso Luxo chauffeured car. Expresso Luxo cars carry five passengers; the trip takes about 2 hours. Cars leave as soon as they're full throughout the day until midnight. Expresso Luxo offices, Av. Ipiranga 932 and Rua 7 de Abril, across the street from the Praça da República (phone: 222-7325; 223-5161). To get to Santos from Guarujá, take the number 8 or 94 bus to the old blue and white wooden ferry. The terminal is near the small amusement park, but if you ask the driver for "el ferry," he will tell you when to get off. The ride across the channel, past multicolored fishing boats, sculling crews practicing rowing, and giant freighters, takes about 10 picturesque minutes. If you are driving, take the Anchieta or Imigrantes highway to Santos and follow signs to Guarujá.

SOURCES AND RESOURCES

 TOURIST INFORMATION: The State Secretary of Sports and Tourism maintains information offices at Av. São Luiz 115 (phone: 257-7248), open weekdays from 8 AM to 6 PM; and Praça Antonio Prado, sixth floor (phone: 229-3011, ext. 418), open weekdays from 9 AM to 5 PM. Both offices have helpful, multilingual staffs. The São Paulo city information office at Praça da República 154 (phone: 259-2200) has maps and information on the city's attractions, and recommends guided tours. Ask for the English-language pamphlet *São Paulo Is All.* A number of brochures on São Paulo state's spas and resort facilities are available, too. Congonhas Airport maintains a reception and information center (phone: 240-1108 or 542-5681). The American Consulate can provide some help to travelers at Rua Padre João Manuel 927 (phone: 881-6511). (Remember, some São Paulo telephone numbers have six digits; others have seven).

Quatro Rodas Guia de São Paulo is the best local guide and and has the most complete map of the city. Available for about $2 at most newsstands, the guide is written in both English and Portuguese. Probably the most handy map, though incomplete, comes with the tourist office's monthly *São Paulo* pamphlet.

Local Coverage – Brazil has a single English language daily: the *Latin American Daily Post,* which is published Tuesdays through Sundays in Rio and sold in all major cities. Two São Paulo morning papers, *O Estado de São Paulo* and *Folha de São Paulo,* cover the news and contain complete events listings. A freebie at most hotel reception desks, the "Este Mês em São Paulo" pamphlet in Portuguese and English includes the most comprehensive monthly calendar of the city's cultural offerings.

Major foreign newspapers are available in the big hotels as well as at newsstands at the corner of Avenida Ipiranga and Avenida São Luis and on Avenida Paulista near

Rua Augusta. Newsstands throughout the city sell both *Time* and *Newsweek*. Available mid-week, the Sunday *New York Times* costs $14.

CLIMATE AND CLOTHES: Located on the Tropic of Capricorn, São Paulo has a pleasantly moderate climate. The average summer temperature (December through March) is 75°F (23°C) and the average winter temperature (June through September) is only 10° lower at 65°F (around 17°C), but the thermometer can swing drastically and quickly. In general, it's best to wear fairly light clothing and always carry a warm sweater or jacket. The lack of central heating can make the humid winter seem colder than the thermometer indicates. An umbrella is a must for the torrential rains that fall from October through March, and plastic boots also come in handy. For day, casual city attire is appropriate. Men generally wear business suits with ties, although sport shirts and slacks are all right for sightseeing.

GETTING AROUND: Bus – Not recommended except as an adventure in itself or as a test for those who expect to be reincarnated as sardines. The *Executive Buses,* fancy blue and white coaches, are an exception. Catch one at Praça da Patriarca or hail one along the street — the line has no set stops — and ride as far as you like. The main bus station, Estaçao Rodoviária, is at Av. Cruzeiro do Sul 1777, subway station Tietê (phone: 235-0322).

Subway – Again, an adventure rather than a useful mode of transportation. The supermodern 15-mile-long subway merits a ride — get on at the Praça da Sé and go north, south, or both ways — but it won't really get you to many of the places you want to go.

Taxi – The best bet for travel within the city. All taxis have meters, but with triple-digit inflation, taxis are granted hefty fare increases so often that the meters are usually set on old rates. Fare are calculated using a table of prices, called a *tabela,* which gives the new price for any amount shown on the meter. The omnipresent Volkswagens start at about 3 cruzados (according to the updated price table posted in the window, not the meter reading). The orange and white cabs (phone: 251-1733) start at 2 cruzados. The large Ford Specials (phone: 258-2896 or 258-2885; drivers are multilingual) charge only by the hour: 20 cruzados an hour for a minimum of three hours. Volkswagens will balk at carrying more than two passengers, and if a cabbie passes you by, he's probably off to eat or returning the cab to the company. Little flags that indicate a 20% fare raise go up on the taxi meter after 11 PM and on Sundays and holidays. It costs about 10 cruzados to get from Congonhas Airport or the newer International Airport to the center of town in the medium-priced cabs. Tips are not expected but are greatly appreciated. Cab drivers have to spend long hours in the grueling traffic.

Car Rental – Try *Hertz* at Av. Consolação 301 (phone: 256-9722; at the airport, 531-6275). If you plan to travel on a weekend, be sure you have enough gas for Sunday, when gas stations are closed.

MUSEUMS: Most museums in São Paulo are open only in the afternoon and are closed Mondays. The Sacred Art Museum, the São Paulo Art Museum, the Brazilian Home Museum, Pioneer House, and Paulista Museum are all described in *Special Places.* On its grounds, Ibirapuera Park (Parque Ibirapuera) also has a Folklore Museum (Museu de Folclore) (phone: 544-4212); Modern Art Museum (Museu de Arte Moderna) (phone: 571-9818); an Aviation Museum (Museu de Aeronãutica) (phone: 570-3915); Crèche Museum (Museu do Presépio; phone: 544-1329), where nativity dioramas are on display; and the Planetarium (Planetario) (phone: 544-4606).

SHOPPING: Although São Paulo is the nation's major shopping city, Rio is really the place for tourist trinkets. Visit the *Shopping Center Iguatemi,* Av. Brigadeiro Faria Lima 1.191, or the fancier *Shopping Center Ibirapuera,* Av. Ibirapuera 3100, the *Eldorado Shopping Center* on the Marginal Rio Pinheiros, or the new *Shopping Center Morumbi* on the Marginal Rio Pinheiros, near Morumbi Bridge, which have a variety of goods; check out the Sunday artisan fairs at Praça da República, Embú, and Liberdade described in *Special Places.* São Paulo housewives still buy their produce at colorful outdoor markets that set up on different streets each day; one of the largest is held four mornings a week in the Pacaembú Stadium parking lot not far from downtown. Praça Charles Miller. (See *Special Places*).

Leather continues to be one of Brazil's best exports and one of the best buys in the country. Remember that most São Paulo shops are open from 9 AM to 6 PM weekdays and closed Saturday afternoons; shopping malls, however, are open all day on Saturdays. No stores are open on Sundays.

São Paulo's sophisticated boutiques line Rua Augusta. Two shopping centers — Conjunto Nacional and Center 3 — on the 2000 block of Avenida Paulista contain movie theaters, cafés, and a plethora of intriguing shops.

The most stylish fashions for the young can be found along Rua Clodomiro Amazonas, Rua Joaquim Floriano, and Rua João Cachoeira. For bargains in shoes, purses, and other leather items, go to Rua do Arouche, close to Lago de Arouche. In eastern São Paulo, Rua 25 de Março in the Jewish-Arab district offers bargain hunters a chance to get cut-rate merchandise of all kinds: toys, clothing, and cloth by the meter. Budget-conscious shoppers should also check out Rua José Paulino, near Luz Railroad Station and Rua Oriente, where wares are similar to those found in 25 de Março.

Other specialty shops include:

Arte Nativa Aplicada – Indian designs are incorporated into the design of contemporary yard goods — scarves, shawls, and pillows. Rua Mario Ferraz 339, Jardim Europa (phone: 813-4359; 211-9780).

Casa de Amazonas – Quite a complete collection of Amazonian objects, the rare pieces only for display and the more common items for sale. Near the Ibirapuera Shopping Center at Alameda dos Arapanas 1456 (no phone).

El Dorado Shopping Center – An ultra-modern emporium with glass elevators and slick chrome design, it houses some of São Paulo's finest boutiques. Visiting here can turn into a whole day's outing. Av. Rebouças 3970, Pinheiros (phone: 815-7066).

Galería Jacques Ardies – Run by an English-speaking Frenchman, this gallery specializes in Brazilian primitive art. Near Ibirapuera Park at Rua do Livramento 221 (phone: 884-2916).

Mimosa Presentes – A large selection of souvenirs at good prices and at two locations; Rua Augusta 1917 (phone: 853-1715) and Rua Joaquim Nabuco 304 (phone: 61-6705).

The Pewter Shop – Hand-wrought pewter, a far cry from the mass-produced pieces generally available, is the specialty here. Rua da Consolação 2973 (phone: 282-6108).

Pororocal – Run by people who specialize in handicrafts from Brazil's northeast, they also carry Indian crafts. Rua Consolação and Av. Oscar Freire.

H. Stern – The gem king of Brazil, *H. Stern* shops offer the classiest objects of silver and precious stones. One large store can be found on Av. Ipiranga and Rua 24 de Maio, a pedestrian shopping mall open till 10 PM weekdays, across the street from Praça de República (phone: 258-1222). Other *H. Stern* shops: Rua Augusta 2340 (phone: 853-9290), Shopping Center Iguatemi (phone: 210-0826), and Shopping Center Ibirapuera (phone: 543-7194).

Supercouros – Fine leather clothing and accessories. Rua Augusta 2607.

Veruska – Another good leather boutique, selling fashionable gear. Rua do Arouche 84 (phone: 220-1204).

SPECIAL EVENTS: In keeping with its industrial character, the city's most spectacular events are often the trade shows held periodically at the huge Parque Anhembi Exposition Center, north of downtown. Newspapers and the "Este Mês em São Paulo" pamphlet will give particulars on current trade fairs. Although nowhere nearly as spectacular a show as in Rio de Janeiro, *Carnival* is celebrated with aplomb in Santos and Guarujá just before Lent, and the São Paulo *Carnival* gets bigger and better every year.

 SPORTS: As in most of Brazil, soccer — or *futebol* as Brazilians label it — is the city's sport. The teams seem always to be battling through a state or national championship, and on weekend afternoons, fans drive the city streets waving huge, homemade team flags that flap beautifully in the breeze. Pelé's home team, *Santos,* plays in São Paulo from time to time. Informal beach leagues compete on the beaches of Santos every Sunday, with a big soccer festival every Christmas. For information on soccer and other sports, call the Sports and Tourism Secretary's Office (phone: 257-7248).

Car Racing – Brazil's *Formula One Grand Prix* takes place in March at the *Interlagos Raceway,* south of the city. Most weekend afternoons throughout the year, there are races to be enjoyed. Estrada de Parelheiros 315 (phone: 521-9911). "Este Mês em São Paulo" lists schedules.

Chess – Time championships on Saturday afternoons and Friday evenings at the *São Paulo Chess Club,* Rua Araújo 154 (phone: 259-6442). Open 2 PM to 2 AM.

Golf – São Paulo has few golf clubs. However, you might try the *São Paulo Golf Club,* Praça Dom Francisco de Souza, 540 (phone: 521-9255).

Horse Racing – Thoroughbreds run on Monday and Thursday nights; Saturday and Sunday afternoons at the *Jockey Club de São Paulo,* Av. Lineu de P. Machado, 1263 (phone: 211-4011). A well-attended track with a modern, computerized electronic scoreboard, the *Jockey Club* also sports an elegant restaurant where you can dine and bet at the same time.

Soccer – São Paulo has three stadiums and 3 days of *futebol* each week — Wednesday nights and Saturday and Sunday afternoons. *Morumbi Stadium,* in the southern part of the city, is the third largest private stadium in the world and can hold 120,000 spectators. Av. Giovanni Gronchi (phone: 814-3377). *Pacaembú Stadium* is the most centrally located. Praça Charles Miller (phone: 256-9111). *Antarctica Stadium* is in the Água Branca neighborhood (phone: 263-6344). Check the newspapers for times.

Surfing – If the beaches of Guarujá and Santos are any indication, surfing is quite popular with local lads. There is a surf shop across the street from the beach in the center of Guarujá, near the Expresso Luxo station.

Swimming – You will find pools at the *Hilton* and *Brasilton* hotels, both under Hilton management. The *São Paulo Hilton,* Av. Ipiranga 165 (phone: 256-0033); *Brasilton,* Rua Martins Fontes 330 (phone: 258-5811). There are also pools at the *Caesar Park,* Rua Augusta 1508 (phone: 285-6622); at the *Maksoud Plaza,* Alameda Campinas 150 (phone: 251-2233); and at the *Mofarrej Sheraton,* Alameda Santos 1437 (phone: 284-5544). Obviously, the best place to swim is in the Atlantic Ocean at Guarujá (see *Extra Special*). One advantage to swimming in the city is the pools' proximity to saunas. *Paulistas* have recently developed an affection for saunas, but men and women have to sweat separately. The *Maksoud Plaza, Caesar Park, Brasilton,* and *Hilton* hotels all have saunas. Other saunas are: *Araxá,* Rua Antonio Carlos 394 (phone: 288-3070); *Magna Vita Center,* Rua Groenlandia 513 (phone: 852-8228).

Tennis – The racket rage has hit São Paulo in a big way. Court time usually costs from $15 (dollars) up and you get the luxury of ballboys, who should be tipped at about 50¢ per hour. *Hobby Sports* has courts in four locations: Marginal de Pinheiros 16111 (phone: 246-6990); Rua João Lourenço 463, Parque Ibirapuera (phone: 241-1094); Av.

Santo Amaro 5104, Brooklin (phone: 542-5674); and Av. Morumbi 5759, Morumbi (phone: 240-4214). *Tennis SESC* has courts at Rua Lopes Neto 89 (phone: 212-6454).

THEATER: Check the English-language paper for the occasional English presentations and the local papers for plays in Portuguese. Generally, tickets must be purchased at the theater in advance, but the larger hotels can sometimes make arrangements for guests. The *Municipal Theater* (*Teatro Municipal*) in the Praça Ramos de Azevedo often has first-class traveling opera, ballet, and other entertainment (phone: 222-8698).

MUSIC: São Paulo offers the music lover a little bit of everything — from classical to samba to Sunday afternoon improvisations. The São Paulo Symphony Orchestra and the Municipal Symphony Orchestra provide most of the classical music. The Municipal Symphony has free Sunday morning (10 AM) concerts at the *Municipal Theater,* Praça Ramos de Azevedo (phone: 222-8698). Various musical events take place at the São Bento Subway Station at 3 PM on Sundays. For samba information, see *Nightclubs and Nightlife.*

NIGHTCLUBS AND NIGHTLIFE: São Paulo nightlife, without question the liveliest in South America, could as appropriately be called morninglife, since few places hit their stride before midnight. A cover charge that may or may not include drinks is common. Warning: Brazilian whiskey (always scotch and never bourbon) is fairly poor quality, and you pay astronomical prices for the imported stuff. Too often nightclubs will pour local brew into an imported bottle; then both you and your pocketbook suffer. The safest bet is to stick with beer, gin, or vodka drinks.

Sambas can be melodic, snazzy, or frenetic. But whatever the tempo, the rhythm of the samba is unquestionably the heartbeat of Brazil. Samba *shows* are actually nightclub entertainment. Samba *houses* are dance halls — and they're jammed with working people on weekends. One of the best shows in São Paulo is at *O Beco,* where a Brazilian orchestra and female mulatto dancers perform and the first of four nightly shows starts at 11 PM; Rua Bela Cintra 306 (phone: 259-3377). Another spot for live samba and good music and dancing is *A Vila 1,* Av. Ibirapuera 2461, Moema (phone: 543-2764). Dick Farney, Brazil's Frank Sinatra, sings nightly at *Regine*'s, Rua Bela Cintra 1951 (phone: 883-0163).

Less chic than the places listed above, the samba houses are less expensive, less sophisticated, and more spontaneous. If you can't be in Rio for Carnival, these are the places to samba: *Moema Samba,* closed Mondays, Av. Ibirapuera 2124 (phone: 549-3744) and *República do Samba,* closed Sundays, Rua Santo Antonia 1025, Bela Vista.

Several bars, some with live Latin American music, have sprouted along the Rua Henrique Schaumann: *Latino-Americano,* No. 185 (no phone); *Quincas Borba,* No. 170 (phone: 282-6667); and *Barravento,* No. 311 (phone: 64-3329). Other casual evening spots are along the Rua 13 de Maio and Rua Santo Antonio in the somewhat bohemian area of Bexiga: Try the *Cafe do Bexiga,* Rua 13 de Maio 76 (no phone), or the *Carbono 14,* a punk rock bar at Rua 13 de Maio 363 (phone: 34-7591). *Clube do Choro* is a good choice for listening to typical Brazilian music, called *choro,* where the instruments include a ukulele, tambourine, flute, guitar, and a Brazilian instrument called a *reco-reco* that sounds like a washboard; nightly performances, Rua João Maura 763, Pinheiros (phone: 883-3511).

The hangouts of *paulistas* from 18 to 35, these California-type bars often have a short life. *L'Absinthe,* open nightly, Rua Bela Cintra 1862 (phone: 853-7212); *The Victoria,* open nightly, Av. Lorena 1604 (phone: 853-3967); *The Queen's Legs,* open nightly, Rua Dr. Melo Alves 490 (phone: 64-5319); *London Tavern,* at the *Hilton Hotel,* open nightly, Av. Ipiranga 165 (phone: 256-0033).

São Paulo's most elegant discotheque is the *Gallery,* Rua Haddock Lobo 1626, Jardin Paulista (phone: 881-3291). You can also dance at the *Hippopotamus,* which draws a young crowd, Av. 9 de Julha 5872, Jardin Paulista (phone: 881-2403).

SINS: You can gorge yourself until your stomach has had its fill of *gluttony* at any number of São Paulo's restaurants. *Bolinha*'s *feijoada, Maria Fulo*'s complete dinner, or *Churrascaría Eduardo*'s barbecues should do for starters. *Paulistas* take great *pride* in their industriousness — whereas Buenos Aires is the city that never stops, São Paulo is the city that never stops *working.* The flipside of the workaholic coin is *sloth,* and while many *paulistas* would never admit they indulge, they are probably just the ones who slip away to the beach at Guarujá, where every slothful whim can be catered to at the *Casa Grande.*

BEST IN TOWN

CHECKING IN: Because business is São Paulo's business, the city's hotels cater to the men in gray flannel suits and to their expense accounts. As a result, travelers can pick and choose from comfortable but rather pricey hostelries, where a few extra dollars often provide the luxury of adequate soundproofing from the 24-hour traffic din. All prices include a Continental breakfast (sometimes served in your room), and most also cover the traditional 10% service charge. Doubles at the expensive hotels start at $85, while the moderate rates fall in the $50 to $75 range; the inexpensive hotels run less than $35.

Two American credit cards are known by their Brazilian counterparts: MasterCard is called Passaporte and Visa doubles as Cartão Elo.

Cá D'Oro – Besides two swimming pools, two tennis courts (just for guests), Ping-Pong, a pool table, and an exercise room, the hotel also has a dog kennel. Rooms in the brand-new addition cost more, but you can request accommodations in the old wing. Try the excellent restaurant. A drawback: The *Cá D'Oro* accepts only American Express credit cards or cash. Rua Augusta 129 (phone: 256-8011). Expensive.

Caesar Park – Lush vegetation at the entrance and an elegantly subdued lobby greet a guest to this lovely and serene hotel. There are 200 rooms and the efficient, multilingual staff provides excellent service. You can pick up free copies of the local papers or buy the most recent *New York Times* or *Wall Street Journal* to peruse over breakfast fruits beside a small garden. The coffee shop offers a lunch buffet, and at night there's live music at the rooftop bar. Rua Augusta 1508 (phone: 285-6622). Expensive.

Maksoud Plaza – Without a doubt, this is São Paulo's "most" hotel — most luxurious, most recent (opened in 1979), most architecturally daring, most security-conscious, and most expensive. Some 420 rooms and indoor gardens surround its 22-story atrium and a one-ton, 40-meter suspended stainless steel sculpture by Brazilian artist Toyota. You can choose from one of eight restaurants, including a 24-hour coffee shop, a Scandinavian smorgasbørd, and the excellent *La Cuisine du Soleil.* For recreation, the hotel offers a swimming pool, sauna, shuffleboard, and even two rooftop squash courts (for emergencies, a doctor is on duty at all times). There are also mezzanine-level offices available for short term rental. Rooms on the top two floors have butler, maid, and valet service. Alameda Campinas, 150 (phone: 251-2233). Expensive.

Mofarrej Sheraton – A 330-room deluxe property close by the *Caesar Park* that offers its guests the conveniences of a solarium, coffee shop, restaurant, drugstore, and jewelers. Alameda Santos 1437 (phone: 284-5544). Expensive.

São Paulo Hilton – The red plush lobby beneath the *Hilton*'s 32-story tower bustles with tour groups and with local gatherings that use the hotel's convention facilities. Geared to tourist traffic, the hotel has several nice shops on the ground floor and a sauna and swimming pool on the tenth floor. There is also a rooftop restaurant with a good view of downtown. The hotel's location at the beginning of the city's red-light and gay district discourages evening strolls. Av. Ipiranga 165 (phone: 256-0033). Expensive.

Brasilton – Known as "the other Hilton," this is a member of the international chain's more moderately priced hotels. About three blocks from the older *Hilton,* it offers tastefully subdued decor with a fairly complete wet bar and refrigerator in its 251 guestrooms. The bathtubs have handles on the wall for the handicapped. All rooms have color TVs. There's a swimming pool on the roof, and a sauna, masseuse, and an impressive program of activities for guests. *O Braseiro* restaurant features Brazilian grilled *churrasco* dishes. Everyone here, from doormen to telephone operators, is friendly. Rua Martins Fontes 300 (phone: 258-5811). Moderate.

El Dorado Higienópolis – Near downtown in the tree-lined residential neighborhood of Higienópolis, this is certainly the quietest of the moderately priced hotels. It boasts a lovely pool and an informal poolside restaurant. Rua Marquês de Itú 836 (phone: 222-3422). Moderate.

Nikkey Palace – One of the nicest hotels in the Japanese section (called Liberdade), it's known for its restaurant, serving, and, needless to say, Japanese food. Av. Galvao Bueno 425, Liberdade (phone: 270-8511). Moderate.

San Raphael – Clean and comfortable, this hotel has 252 rooms. Its location in the downtown area makes for convenient shopping. Av. São João 1173 (phone: 220-6633). Moderate.

Cambridge – Long a gathering place for cost-conscious travelers, the *Cambridge* has an international clientele and a central location. Av. 9 de Julho 216 (phone: 239-0399). Inexpensive.

Novotel – In the upper-class suburb of Morumbi, minutes away from the big industries, this is a convenient choice for the business traveler. Rua Ministro Nelson Hungria 450 (phone: 542-1244). Inexpensive.

Samambaia – More frequented by Brazilian travelers than foreign tourists, this 70-room hotel is right off the Praça da República. Rua 7 de Abril 422 (phone: 231-1333). Inexpensive.

São Paulo Center – In the bustling heart of the city, this family-run hotel has 110 rooms decorated in a very Brazilian modern style. A complimentary breakfast includes every available tropical fruit and a selection of fresh pastries and sweet breads. Largo Santa Efigênia, 40 (phone: 228-6033). Inexpensive.

EATING OUT: Drawing on its diverse ethnic cuisines, São Paulo has become the unchallenged culinary capital of Brazil — perhaps of all South America, as some people claim. From barbariously generous barbecues (*churrascos*) to small but succulent *sukiyaki,* you can hardly go wrong. In fact, only the pseudo-American restaurants disappoint. Restaurants routinely provide a $1 to $2 *couvert* (bread, butter, and nibbles) that you can refuse if you like, and most include a 10% service charge on your bill. Imported liquor (*whiskey escocés* or *importado* instead of *whiskey nacional,* the Brazilian product) will swell your bill immediately. *Paulistas* generally dine after 9:30 or 10 PM. For dinner, dessert, and a Brazilian drink apiece, a meal for two at an expensive restaurant will come to at least $50. Expect to pay between $20 and $40 for two at those places we've listed as moderate; less than $20, inexpensive. Prices don't include drinks or tips.

La Colombe d'Or – An excellent French restaurant that is handy for visitors who find themselves near Avenida Paulista at lunchtime or dinnertime. Open for lunch and dinner Mondays through Fridays, for dinner on Saturdays. Closed Sundays. Reservations. Major credit cards. Rua Alameda Santos 1165 (phone: 287-2431). Expensive.

Marcel's – Chef Jean Durand displays his friend Paul Bocuse's portrait in this tiny restaurant with pride and justification. For 10 years Chef Jean has been serving the very finest French cuisine in the city. Shrimp dishes and delicate desserts are among the specialties. It's superb food in a simple setting. Open for lunch and dinner Mondays through Fridays, for dinner on Saturdays. Closed Sundays. Lunch reservations required. No credit cards accepted. Across from the *São Paulo Hilton,* Rua Epitácio Pessôa 98 (phone: 257-6968). Expensive.

Maria Fulô – Originally a slave in Dom Pedro II's household, Maria Fulô won her freedom because of her extraordinary culinary talents, and the owners of her namesake restaurant offer a six-course meal of Brazilian fare in 19th-century regal style. A *baiana* waitress will first serve you *acarajé* (a bean and shrimp appetizer) in the entrance garden. Then comes the soup course followed by two fish courses, fowl, meat, and more desserts than you've ever imagined. Try the traditional sweets with such unusual names as *papos de anjo* (angel's double chins), *baba de moça* (maiden's delight), and *beijos de coca — cocadas* (coconut kisses). Coconut and *dendê* oil are the two essentials of Bahía's spicy cuisine. There is no menu — the food just keeps coming, and it alone will run $40 for two. A second location has opened up closer to town at Av. Rebouças 2320 (phone: 853-6287). The original is in a hidden suburban location so have your hotel doorman find a cabbie who already knows the way. Open for dinner Mondays through Saturdays and for lunch on weekends. Reservations required. Major credit cards. Rua São José 563, Alto de Boa Vista (phone: 247-0951). Expensive.

Paddock Jardim – Good service and a limited but well-prepared menu of international dishes make this a favorite restaurant of São Paulo's elite. Comfortable with music after 9 PM. Closed Sundays. Reservations required. Major credit cards. Inside Cal Center Shopping Center on Av. Faria Lima 1541 (phone: 814-3582) and downtown in the Zarvos building at Av. São Luiz 258 (257-4768). Expensive.

Bolinha – In Brazil, Saturdays mean *feijoada,* a tasty concoction of black beans and all cuts of pork. *Feijoada* is the country's national dish, and *Bolinha* serves an excellent one. You'll find a long line between 2 and 4 PM on Saturday. Just give your name to the maître d', order a *caipirinha* at the bar, and watch the bustle. Open daily for lunch and dinner. No reservations accepted. Major credit cards. Av. Cidade Jardim, 53 Jardim Europa (phone: 852-9526). Moderate.

Churrascaría Eduardo's – While *feijoada* comes from the coast, the *churrasco* has a southern history. *Eduardo's* serves *churrasco à rodízio.* Waiters who circulate with huge hunks of meat that are sliced directly onto your plate will offer nine cuts of meat. You can choose from 14 salads at the salad bar. Open daily 24 hours a day. Reservations advised. Major credit cards. Rua Nestor Pestana 80 (phone: 257-0500). Moderate.

Colonna – Here you'll find São Paulo's lightest homemade pasta — *fettucine verdi al pesto, ravioli alla parmegiana, capelletti al triplo burro.* The *cassata* (an ice-cream pie topped with walnuts) should not be missed. Open daily for lunch and dinner. Reservations recommended in the evening. Major credit cards. Rua Maranhão 540 (phone: 67-05-47). Moderate.

Suntory – A lovely rock garden beside the bar rivals the fine food as the main attraction at this popular Japanese restaurant. You can either call ahead for reservations in one of the restaurant's three rooms — *teppan-yaki, sukiyaki,* and *sushi* — or you can come unannounced to enjoy a drink and then take whatever table becomes available. Open for lunch and dinner Mondays through Saturdays.

Closed Sundays. Reservations recommended. American Express and Visa accepted. Av. Campinas 600 (phone: 283-2455). Moderate.

Almanara – If Japanese food doesn't tempt you but you still want something different, try this busy Arabic restaurant off the Praça da República. It serves generous portions of hummus, stuffed grape leaves, and various sorts of *kibbe* (ground beef) at good prices. Near the bar, you order each dish separately while past the partition you pay a set price and watch the delicacies appear and reappear. Open for lunch and dinner daily except Christmas. No reservations. Visa and Diners Club. Rua Basilio da Gama 70 (phone: 257-7580); Av. Brig. Faria Lima 1191, Iguatemi Shopping Center (phone: 212-6990); and Rua Oscar Freire 523, Cerqueira César (phone: 280-2724). Inexpensive.

Ao Guanabara – This surprisingly large, crowded, noisy dining room with the atmosphere of a train station serves terrific barbecued fish, shrimp, and beef. It's very popular with businessmen who work in or around the central post office (*correo central*). Closed Sundays. No reservations. No credit cards. Av. São João 128 (phone: 228-0958). There is another branch at Rua São Bento 514 (phone: 239-0187). Inexpensive.

Cantina d'Amico Piolin – After midnight, you'll find half the city's actors and actresses here, fortifying themselves on homemade pastas and the house specialty, Tom Payne chicken. Open daily until 4 AM. Reservations advised. Major credit cards. Rua Augusta 89 (phone: 256-9356). Inexpensive.

Clyde's – If you've been traveling long enough to yearn for a charcoal-grilled hamburger, onion rings, and a fudge brownie, this is the place for you. Modeled after the Washington, DC, *Clyde's*, it's a favorite of both the local American community and young *paulistas*. Sunday brunch is a specialty. Open for lunch and dinner daily. Reservations recommended in the evening. Major credit cards. Rua de Mata 70; tell your taxi driver that it's a cross street at Av. 9 de Julho 5345 (phone: 852-1383). Moderate.

Eno Moto – Set behind a small Oriental rock garden on Liberdade's main street, this Japanese restaurant is one of São Paulo's best bargains. Raw fish fans will want to try the counter in back, while those who stick to *sukiyaki* and *teriyaki* should wait for a front table. Open for lunch and dinner daily except the tenth, twentieth, and thirtieth of each month. No reservations. No credit cards. Rua Galvão Bueno 54, Liberdade (phone: 279-0198). Inexpensive.

Genghis Khan – Although the city's Chinese restaurants generally can't compare with the Japanese establishments, this is one exception. On the second floor you can try a Chinese barbecue (*churrasco*). Open for lunch and dinner daily. Reservations. Visa. Av. Rebouças 3241, Pinheiros (phone: 212-8951). Inexpensive.

Jucalemão – This little German restaurant is best-known for its *kassler* (pork chops with a large serving of homemade sauerkraut) and paprika schnitzel (pork tenderloin in paprika sauce). Dessert is a highly recommended apple strudel. There are five suburban locations: Alameda Lorena 527 (phone: 283-2934); Rua Ministro José Gullotti 134, Brooklyn (phone: 61-65-20); Av. Santo Amaro 594, Santo Amaro (phone: 853-4436); Rua Nhuguassu 303, Campo Belo (phone: 531-4747). Inexpensive.

Mexilhão – Almost lost among the many pizzerias of the Italian district, this serves excellent seafood. Like garlic? Try the *camarão á paulista* (*paulista* shrimp). Open daily from 11:30 AM to 2:30 AM. Reservations advised. Visa. Rua 13 de Maio 626, Bela Vista (phone: 288-2485). Inexpensive.

Rodeio – The "in" *churrascaría* of discriminating *paulistas*, this is a meat lover's delight. Try *picanha na brasa* — São Paulo's best beef grilled right at the table. The hot *pão de queijo* that arrives automatically is a specialty of Minas Gerais State. To avoid a long wait, get there before 1 PM for lunch and before 8:30 PM for dinner. No reservations. No credit cards. Rua Haddock Lobo 1468 (phone: 883-2322). Moderate.

Rubaiyat Churrascarías – Another chain that boasts of its "baby beef." Open daily for lunch and dinner. No reservations. Major credit cards. Downtown: Dr. Vieira de Carvalho 116 (phone: 222-8333). Near Av. Paulista: Rua Alameda Santos 86 (phone: 289-6366); and Jardim Europa: Av. Brigadeiro Faria Lima 533 (phone: 813-2703). Moderate.

Vegetariano Sattva – This simple restaurant boasts a daily special although most regulars seem to always order the special salad — with a superb fruit dressing. Open for lunch only, Mondays through Saturdays. No reservations. No credit cards. Rua da Consolação, 3140 (phone: 852-5807). Inexpensive.

DIVERSIONS

DIVERSIONS

Introduction

For many travelers today, the point of a trip is not merely to visit someplace new but to participate in something special once they get there. Whether it's athletic, sybaritic, or educational — playing a new golf course, lolling on a beach, or examining ruins with an experienced guide — activity-oriented vacations are becoming increasingly popular.

South America is an old yet still relatively young continent. Its cities were settled by the Spanish almost a century before the English landed on Plymouth Rock, and its colonial architecture and traditions predate those of the US. But the South American colonists preferred to remain along the continent's coastlines, and to this day most of the interior still remains lightly explored and open for settlement and development. Populations are clustered in cosmopolitan centers hemmed in by dramatic topography — towering mountains, vast deserts, and lush rain forests. The visitor is confronted immediately by the juxtapositions of environment — modern urban and ancient rural cultures, deluxe and basic facilities. In South America, expect to find astounding diversity.

Which is not to say that all countries on this continent are equally endowed with natural wonders or tourist facilities. South America is a Third World continent, and many of its nations are only beginning to recognize the inherent value of their abundant natural resources as tourist attractions; other countries are in the process of developing tourist services, and still others, long familiar with the international traveler, have facilities as finely tuned as any in the world. Resort cities in Colombia, Venezuela, and Brazil offer golf, tennis, swimming, diving, and fishing with luxurious accommodations and a full complement of sophisticated *après* activities. And unparalleled wilderness experiences — at the top of the world or in the heart of a rain forest — are open to anyone willing to rough it through the lesser-known spots of Ecuador, Chile, Argentina, Perú, and other countries. It is just this choice — the variety of experience available in any single visit to the continent — that makes South America so appealing to the adventurous traveler. And wherever you go there is Latin cordiality.

Combining the right activity with the right place is something of an art, and most difficult in so diverse a continent as South America. The pertinent question is, "Where is the quality of experience highest?" In the following pages, we attempt to answer it by suggesting the best places in South America to pursue 17 different activities. Certainly the emphasis is on uniquely Latin American experiences — Carnival or jungle excursions, wilderness trekking and exploring the continent's incredible Indian ruins — but not on these solely. With each section is all the information you need to organize a trip, including the names of organizations that offer special interest package tours to South America. Whether you want to climb mountains, fish in the Pacific, hike through Andean mountain villages, or observe wildlife in the jungle, the number of group tours to South America oriented around these activities is growing rapidly. Formerly out-of-reach, exotic parts of the continent are now being made accessible to travelers.

Joining a group ensures that reservations and facilities are arranged in advance. A package tour will also guarantee that at least one member, the tour escort, will speak Spanish, an important consideration when traveling out of the major city centers and off the beaten path. In addition, a tour devoted to a particular activity enables you to travel with a group of people who share your interests.

If you plan to travel on your own, you might still want to consult a special interest travel organization when planning your trip. Each one is usually staffed with experts who know the field in which you are interested, and they can advise you of the range of services and accommodations available. (See *How to Use a Travel Agent* and *Package Tours,* GETTING READY TO GO.)

Whether you travel independently or with a group, on a budget or with unlimited funds, it is important to remember that the diversions of South America are as varied as its topography, its individual countries, its ancient cultures, its different paces of modernization. Above all, no matter what sport or activity you pursue, South American diversions will seldom fail to provide new adventures and experiences. Herewith, those places throughout the continent where you can expect to find the highest quality of experience.

For the Body

Sinfully Sensuous Beaches

 Whether you are used to the sharp cliffs dropping into the Pacific on the Oregon coast, the muscle beaches of Southern California, the boardwalk madness of New Jersey's Atlantic shore, or the serenity of the Outer Banks off the Carolina coast, South America is bound to radically change your perceptions of a beach. Somewhere, whether on the Atlantic, Pacific, or Caribbean coasts, visitors are likely to find a beach that's just right for sunning, swimming, body surfing, riding a surfboard, floating lazily, gathering shells, or playing Robinson Crusoe.

By and large, the climates and waters of Perú and Ecuador (on the Pacific), Colombia (Pacific and Caribbean), Venezuela (Caribbean), and Brazil (Atlantic) from Rio de Janeiro north are warm enough for most North Americans to bask and bathe in all year, although many South Americans insist that the winter months are just too cold for jumping into the water. (Even hedonistic *cariocas* — residents of Rio de Janeiro — shudder at the thought of plunging their much-cared-for tans into the shimmering Atlantic in October, when the thermometer still hugs the mid-80s.) Except for the northern desert beaches around Arica and Iquique, Chile's coastal waters are chilled by the icy Humboldt Current that sweeps north from Antarctica. Here, as in Argentina, Uruguay, and southern Brazil, visitors need to plan their visits around the warmer spring and summer months (late October through March). Remember that not all of South America is sunny and tropical. (For a full description of climate and terrain, see *What's Where* and *When to Go*, GETTING READY TO GO.)

There are innumerable varieties of beach topography — white, gray, black, yellow, fine grain and coarse grain sand, and foliage (especially coconut palms). Remember that the sun is particularly strong near the equator. Bring plenty of sunscreen to protect you from the ultraviolet rays.

Listed below are some of the choice spots on the continent. Some are very popular; others, more private. They are by no means the only beaches. If you have a taste for adventure, ask some questions and use many of the following spots as jumping-off points for sniffing out new beache sites, often just beyond that next cove.

ARGENTINA

Mar del Plata – December through March are the warmest and driest months at this world-famous resort of tree- and flower-filled plazas that is truly the center of Argentina's beach life. About 240 miles (386 km) south of Buenos Aires, its population of 550,000 easily triples during peak season, so make reservations well in advance, whether you plan to bed down in luxurious hotels or less expensive boarding houses. The 5 miles of clean, sandy beaches — including fashionable Playa Grande (playground of the rich), Playa Perla, and Punta Iglesia — can get crowded at times, but it's always easy to find a more secluded spot by walking a bit.

Atlantida Coast – North of Mar del Plata, and considerably less crowded, the beaches still offer plenty of conveniences, good fishing, and swimming. Best along this stretch are Villa Gesell, with beautiful dunes, pine forests, and friendly, small hotels; Pinamar, rapidly becoming a fashionable resort town with casinos; Miramar, to the south, another fast-paced vacation center with high-rise hotels, golf courses, and casinos; and Necochea, with about 15 miles of the best and cleanest beachfront.

Pehuen-Co – Not far from Bahía Blanca, this is just one of many spots on a huge stretch of an isolated, undeveloped shore, with pine trees and space to camp.

BRAZIL

With almost 4,450 miles of coastline, the climate affecting Brazil's beach life exhibits a bit of variability. In the south, the hottest months (January to March) are also the wettest, and while the rain is never extreme, the heat can rise to well over 100°F (37°C) around Rio. This is the period when the beaches are most crowded. July and August are a bit cooler — not too cold for gringos, but cool enough to keep Brazilians home and the beaches fairly empty. Along more northerly coasts, the temperatures are invariably even hotter throughout the year, so visits do not need to be planned around a calendar. Rain is intense when it comes, but its duration is generally short.

Rio de Janeiro – Copacabana and Ipanema are probably the best-known stretches of sand in the world. They are crowded in midsummer (December through February), and quite a few residents head for the more secluded beaches at Cabo Frio, Búzios, and Angra dos Reis. For a complete description of Rio's beaches and Cabo Frio, see *Rio de Janeiro,* THE CITIES.

Itaipauaçú – About 25 miles (40 km) north of Rio's Niterói Bridge, it has lots of empty, open, sandy beaches, good for camping. Swimming can be dangerous, as the surf is quite rough, but there are some great rocks from which to dive. There are a couple of little restaurants, but no hotels.

Saquarema – Seventy miles (112 km) north of Rio de Janeiro, this is *the* surfing beach, where international competitions are often held. The gigantic waves break on huge, wide, white beaches, where visitors can camp. The *Panorama* is the leading hotel, with a restaurant and bar. Av. Saquarema 1680 (no phone). There are a number of smaller hotels and restaurants, too.

Florianópolis – This island state capital, about 433 miles (699 km) south of São Paulo, is full of serene bays and shores. Get to Praixa Inglês on the far side of the island for greater privacy and good camping.

Armação dos Búzios – Cross over the Niteroi Bridge from Rio de Janeiro to reach this beach, where well-heeled Rio residents come to get away from it all. There are few hotels, so divers, snorkelers, water skiers, and sun worshipers have miles of sea and sand to themselves. Among the informal inns here are *Pousada Casteja, Pousada dos Ossos, Casas Brancas Pousadas,* and *Pousada nas Rocas.*

São Sebastião – Heading north from Santos, São Paulo's seaport, on the superb Rio-Santos highway, are plenty of unpopulated beaches where the tropical mountains meet the sea. São Sebastião, a small fishing village about 125 miles (201 km) north of Santos, is one of the prettiest along the route. Hotels on the route are modest. *Recanto dos Passaros* has a swimming pool, sauna, and a restaurant. Av. Guarda-Mor Lobo Viana 822 (phone: 52-15-36).

Angra dos Reis – About 102 miles (163 km) south of Rio, this lovely spot is to become the site of a nuclear power plant, much to the dismay of local beach lovers. In addition to plenty of smaller bays with quiet beaches, the large bay on which the town is situated is full of wonderful islands, easily reached by boat. The main hotel is the *Do Frade,* a splendid property that permits its guests to walk right out on the beach or into their boats parked in the yacht basin. An excursion boat is available to guests for cruises among the islands, as well as tennis, golf, horseback riding, windsurfing, and scuba. For reservations: Frade Hoteis, Rua Joaquim Nabuco 161 (phone: 021-267-7375).

Salvador (Bahía) – Terrific tawny sands surround the city. (See *Salvador (Bahía)*, THE CITIES.)

Porto Seguro – This beach, 440 miles (704 km) south of Salvador (Bahía), has become *the* spot for Brazilian young people. It is an old colonial town, with miles and miles of empty beaches and lodgings in all price ranges. Two coral reefs keep the light blue water very calm and warm. Camping is possible almost everywhere, but there's maximum privacy out of town toward Santa Cruz Cabrália. The Franciscan Monastery school puts up people for free when classes are not in session.

Leave town in the opposite direction and cross the bay to find more beautiful, uninhabited, white, sandy beaches below the bluffs of Nossa Senhora de Ajuda, an old, quaint place with great views of the ocean below and full of fishermen.

Trancoso – Hike another 11 miles (18 km) down deserted beaches, past red cliffs and up the bluff, to reach this splendid little fishing village with a population of just a few hundred. No lodgings, electricity, or restaurants, just a tiny store, some marvelous residents, gentle waves, and a jungle environment that's fine for camping. It is a good place for relaxing and learning how simply some people can live. Carry supplies with you so you can continue on to more isolated sands.

Itamaracá – Near Recife, this is a somewhat touristy little fishing island town, with a few hotels and restaurants serving very good seafood. Weekend houses of the wealthy stand beside fishermen's shacks. A great reef beyond the horizon keeps the water placid along the narrow, but not particularly clean, beach. Camping is permitted anywhere, but for wider, cleaner beaches (and much more privacy), walk to the end of the island opposite the fort and look for a dirt road that heads up a bluff through the trees beyond the last house. This leads to a bay where, during the day, a ferryman carries workers from the coconut grove back and forth across the water in his canoe. Carry supplies you will need and ride his canoe to the other side, where you can camp under the coconut palms or in an empty hut. There are miles of gloriously empty beaches to walk down and plenty of coconuts to eat and drink.

Natal – Some of the most unusual sand formations in the country are near this city. Huge dunes, just right for rolling down, have been formed by the wind.

Canoa Quebrada – This tiny fishing town, between Natal and Fortaleza, is known for its outstanding blue waters and friendly natives, who are happy to take in guests and show them a bit of their way of life.

Alcântara – Another small fishing village, it is best reached by ferry from São Luís. Outside town is some of the best beachcombing in Brazil. Little shacks belonging to the fishermen can be rented for next to nothing. Old Portuguese ruins nearby provide something to focus on when the sun begins to fall.

Ilha do Mosqueiro – This fantastic, jungle-covered island near Belém has tiny hotels, some villas, and plenty of clean, sandy beaches.

CHILE

Viña del Mar – Not only is this the foremost beach resort in Chile, but it is one of the very best in all of South America, a refuge for thousands of tourists, both Chilean and international, during the summer (October through March). A graceful town of flowers, trees, parks, and palaces, mixed with modern buildings, Viña also hosts many cultural events. There is a casino, and hotels in every price range. Steep bluffs rise behind the city, and its 10-mile stretch of sandy shoreline includes the gray, sandy beaches of El Recreo and Caleta Abraca, crowded in spots, but with enough open space to move around.

Santiago Province – All the beaches here have wonderful climates in the summer and, like the rest of Chile, waters cooled by the Humboldt Current. Most are popular with Chilean vacationers and can get pretty crowded at the height of the season. At San Sebastián, Cartagena, Las Cruces, Isla Negra, El Tabo, and El Quisco, the sand ranges from gray to yellow to white. Another beach, Algarrobo, is exceptionally peaceful, and its waters are quite good for snorkeling and skiing.

COLOMBIA

Parque Tairona, near Santa Marta – The equatorial climate does not vary too much during the course of the year. December through April and July through September are the driest months on the Pacific as well as on the Caribbean coast. Parque Tairona is a national park on the jungle-bordered Caribbean coast in the shadow of the Sierra Nevada. Its many beaches are filled with little warm coves. Cañaverales Beach has freshwater showers, palm trees, and dangerous currents. Next door, Punta de la Concha offers some of the best snorkeling in the Caribbean. From Cañaverales visitors can hike for 2 hours through the humid jungle and arrive at Finca Martínez, a private beach with crystal Caribbean waters. Huts with hammocks and meals are available, and it's also possible to pitch a tent under the coconut palms. It is not the cleanest place in the world, but it's a good starting point for a hike along the coast to some really fine isolated beaches.

Tolú – This small fishing town south of Cartagena is on the magnificent Caribbean Gulf of Morroquillo. Its miles of white sand and warm, blue waters are perfect for fishing and swimming. It is an out-of-the-way spot with some decent accommodations.

San Andrés and Providencia – Both of these Caribbean islands are far from any part of Colombia. There are direct flights from Colombia and the US to San Andrés, where the most beautiful beaches are on the cays. Fine beaches, such as those on Johnny Key, are reached by a short launch trip. To reach tiny Providencia, 50 miles (80 km) north, there is daily commercial air service or boat charters. Make certain of return arrangements as well as the presence of supplies on the island.

ECUADOR

San Jacinto and San Clemente – These two remote fishing villages can be reached by bus from Portoviejo. Although they do not coax much from the tourist trade, there are a few camping sites and rustic hotels. Adela Guerrero, a former New York City resident, will accept guests at her half-finished motel for a fair price. Pigs and chickens roam the gray, sandy beaches. This town provides a peek at a good slice of down-home Ecuadorian life. Walk south from San Jacinto, cross a river, and you're alone on a miles-long stretch of sparkling white sand. Unfortunately, unfriendly encounters on the beach have been reported recently.

Atacames – In the north, not far from Esmeraldas and the nearest hotels, this beach is popular with young people. Camping is easy under the palms, but somewhat crowded on the weekends. But it's always possible to move farther down the beach for more privacy. The surf is often good and the local seafood dishes are tasty.

PERÚ

Beaches in Perú range from a few chic resorts to wild stretches of beautiful sand, perfect for camping. Punta Sal, the country's most popular resort, is located near Tumbes in the north. There are individual beachhouses to rent, and the hotel restaurant serves fresh fish daily. Reservations should be made well in advance through a local Lima agency and should include round-trip air travel to and from Tumbes, plus a resort transfer car on arrival. Extremely popular with *limeños* is Ancon, one hour north of Lima. On weekends, day-trippers jam the public-access beaches here, so those who prize private relaxation should stick to weekdays. An hour south of Lima is the Santa María Beach Club, a fine day trip. More convenient are El Silencio or Punta Hermosa, with modest (but good) oceanside restaurants. Further south, the Paracas Wildlife Reserve has a lovely small hotel with a pool. Lovely white sand beaches are a short drive away, and transporation is available on request.

URUGUAY

Montevideo – This city has many tranquil beaches, of which Carrasco is the trendiest. Montevideo's best beach weather occurs between December and April. (See *Montevideo,* THE CITIES.)

Atlántida – To the east of the capital, surrounded by magnificent pine and eucalyptus forests, this tranquil water resort has casinos, a golf course, and fine fishing. Las Toscas and Parque de la Plata are its two best beaches.

Piriápolis – To the east of Atlántida, set around a horseshoe bay near some pleasant hills and rock gardens, this town has good restaurants, a golf course, and comfortable facilities.

Punta del Este – The internationally famous resort stands on a peninsula, with picturesque pine and eucalyptus trees shading white sand. The calm waters of Playa Mansa (on the bay) are excellent for swimming. Playa Brava (on the ocean) is good for surfing. From here, explore the coast north to Brazil. (See *Luxury Resorts and Special Havens,* DIVERSIONS, and *Uruguay,* DIRECTIONS.)

VENEZUELA

El Litoral, near Caracas – The Macuto area, closest to the city, has a fine stretch of beach. Drive west to the chain of beaches called El Litoral, with some great places for sunning and swimming. Caraballeda, Catia La Mar, La Bahía, and Chichiriviche are the best. Weekend traffic jams along the Litoral coast are legendary: It can take hours to inch a couple of miles.

Margarita Island – Smooth Caribbean shores at their most seductive bring Venezuelans here by the thousands. The big draw is the unique combination of white-on-white beach, mangrove lagoons, and duty-free port status. The most isolated sections can be found in the north: in the mangrove lagoons along the Macanao Peninsula to the west (watch for scarlet ibis and exotic seashells); and in the Porlamar resort center to the southwest. Although the climate does not vary much, expect some rain from May through December. (See *Venezuela,* DIRECTIONS.)

Best Depths: Snorkeling and Scuba

The clearest, warmest waters can be found off South America's northern coast, abutting the Caribbean Sea. Here are abundant coral reefs and tropical fish, as well as some intriguing shipwrecks, especially off the Colombian and Venezuelan shores.

Diving equipment is available for rent at resorts in Colombia, Venezuela, and Panamá, but such facilities are nonexistent in some of the key diving spots, so be prepared to bring your own gear. Snorkeling (a much simpler affair) requires only a mask, flippers, and snorkel. Remember to wear rubber-soled shoes if you plan to roam around shallow-water coral reefs.

Since scuba diving requires skill and knowledge to use high-pressure cylinders of compressed air and regulators that control the flow of oxygen during descent and ascent, reputable diving shops and expedition leaders require proof of the successful completion of a diver's certification course, upon the conclusion of which a C card is issued. It's easy to find a 6-week course, 1 or 2 nights a week, in the US. For information, contact: the *National Association of Underwater Instructors* (NAUI), 4650 Arrow Hwy., PO Box 14650, Montclair, CA 91763 (phone: 714-621-5801); the *Professional Association of Diving Instructors* (PADI), 1243 E Warner Ave., Santa Ana, CA 92705 (phone: 714-540-7234); or your *YMCA.*

ARGENTINA: The only place where organized scuba diving is practiced is Puerto Madryn, in the heart of the Welsh country in southern Argentina. During the first week of February, a diving and underwater fishing championship is held here. Equipment can be purchased in Buenos Aires at *Subacuo,* Montevideo 264 (phone: 35-77-45), and at the *Casa del Buceador,* Córdoba 1859 (phone: 41-17-66). As mentioned above, bringing your own gear is preferable. In Argentina, steep inflation rates can make purchase prices prohibitive.

BRAZIL: Scuba is popular along the resort-studded coastline north and south of Rio de Janeiro, from Cabo Frio, 90 miles (145 km) north, to Angra dos Reis, 120 miles (193 km) south. The main spots are Búzios and Cabo Frio, about 4 hours by bus or car from Rio, and Saquarema, about 2 hours from Rio. Bring your own equipment.

In northern Brazil, there's good diving and surfing off the island of Fernando de Noronha. Fly there from Recife, João Pessoa, or Natal for a day's outing, or stay overnight in the *Pousada da Esmeralda* (phone: 134), a small hotel on the island. *TransBrasil,* one of Brazil's domestic airlines, acts as an agent for the hotel. Its office in Rio de Janeiro is at Av. Santa Luzia 651 (phone: 221-3722).

COLOMBIA: Cartagena, the walled city from which the Spanish colonials shipped precious metals home to the royal court, was a prime target for pirates. Eight miles offshore, there's a sunken Spanish supply ship with cannon still aboard. *Jim Buttgen* runs tours, rents equipment, and provides supplies. Contact CaribeTours at 42966 or 41221.

San Andrés and Providencia, two tiny Colombian islands in the Caribbean that are closer to the Caribbean coast of Nicaragua, have palm-studded beaches and turquoise waters. San Andrés has great snorkeling. Nearby Johnny Key is known for lots of splendidly hued fish, and Haines Key for sea urchins. (Be sure to wear rubber-soled shoes for protection against reefs and wrecks.)

Conditions on the island can be primitive, but *Bahía Marina* can supply craft and equipment. Write to *Bahía Marina,* PO Box 597, San Andrés, Colombia. The island is only 8 miles long and 2 miles wide, so what few hotels exist get booked ahead. Reservations are essential for visits in December, January, Easter Week, July, or August. The *Royal Abacoa* and the *Eldorado* hotels both have small casinos and some air-conditioned rooms. Providencia is much farther out and requires an additional flight from San Andrés, but it's worth the ride for beautiful scuba diving. The one hotel here, the *Aury,* has 14 rooms.

ECUADOR: The Pacific waters contain the breeding and feeding grounds of hundreds of species of fish, undersea archaeological sites, and several wrecks from the days when the Galápagos Islands were a pirate stronghold. Guayaquil and Salinas are headquarters for all water sports. For information, contact *Club Naútico del Salado,* Malecón de Salado, Ciudadela Ferroviaria, Guayaquil (phone: 39-10-71). *See and Sea Travel Service* organizes an 18-day diving trip to the Galápagos Islands. Escorted by a naturalist, divers explore coral reefs, pinnacles, and caves where starfish, conch, anemone, whale, sunfish, and sea lion live. The expedition includes visits to the Darwin Station Research Center. The price includes some equipment. For information, contact *See and Sea Travel Service,* 50 Francisco St., San Francisco, CA 94133 (phone: 415-434-3400). Yachts are also for hire in the Galápagos for week-long diving trips.

PANAMÁ: There are coral reefs and shipwrecks off the San Blas Islands, where diving is not currently very well organized. However, if you bring your own tanks filled, plus regulator and vest, you will be able to make arrangements on Porvenir Island and on Wichub Wala. There is also excellent historic wreck-diving in the old Spanish Main off Portobelo.

There's also scuba at Taboga Island and Contadora Island. The main resort hotel on Contadora Island is the *Casino Contadora* (phone 27-00-33), 20 minutes by air from Panamá City's Portilla Airport in the Pearl Island archipelago.

VENEZUELA: Margarita Island is known for its excellent reefs. Arrangements to dive can be made through the *Margarita Concorde* hotel in Porlamar (phone: 3-21-01), which rents equipment as well. The 800-room hotel has five tennis courts, a yacht dock, three outdoor swimming pools, and an ample marina where arrangements can be made not only for scuba, but for snorkeling, sailing, skiing, and deep-sea fishing.

In Caracas, the *Hilton* arranges scuba excursions on the coast and currently lists the price as $125 per half day. Av. Libertador on the corner of Sur 25, Caracas (phone: 571-2322). Write: Aptdo. 6380.

Los Roques, a tiny atoll in the Caribbean, can be reached by boat from La Guaira, around 65 miles south, or by air from Macuto, outside Caracas. There is a small hotel.

The Morrocoy Reef at Tucacas, a dirty little town off the central coast, has hundreds of reefs, tiny islands with palm trees, and very clean lagoons. Although not one of the more developed resort areas, it is an enclave for the wealthy, many of whom maintain homes here. Off the shore of Boca Grande are the coral islands, of which Cayo Sombrero is the most splendid. There's good diving among lobster, squid, barracuda, sunfish, and colored fish. Boat transport is available from shore. Nearby, Chichiriviche has similar reefs with more tourist facilities.

Sailing

 Opportunities for chartering yachts are somewhat limited in South America compared to Mexico and the Caribbean islands. The most extensive facilities are on the Caribbean coast, where tourism is more fully developed. But the prime lure of sailing in these waters is that it allows travel at a very leisurely pace into open blue sea, anchorages alongside tiny, palm-filled islands, and exploration of the coasts from an entirely personal perspective.

Keep in mind that during peak season (November through March), chartering a boat at any of the major resorts is going to be more expensive than in the off-season. However, in Argentina, southern Brazil, and Uruguay, the fall and winter months offer far from optimum sailing conditions.

ARGENTINA: It is possible to rent small sailboats in Bariloche for trips on the larger lakes, such as Nahuel Huapi. For information, contact the *National Tourism Office,* Santa Fe 833, Buenos Aires (phone: 32-22-32). The *Club Naútico* (phone: 80-03-23), in the superplush seaside resort of Mar del Plata, rents yachts and sailboats.

BOLIVIA: There are two ways to sail the world's highest navigable lake, Lake Titicaca. One is to bring your own boat, as did Welsh sailor Tristam Jones in 1974. (He sailed up the Amazon, then hauled the boat by road to the Peruvian side of the lake, where he launched it — to the great wonder of the Quechua Indian population.) Unless you have many free months, this is not a very feasible plan. But boats may be chartered (with a skipper-guide who knows the inlets and islands of the lake) at Copacabana. Stroll down to the dock and ask around. There is a yacht club in the town of Huatajata (no phone).

BRAZIL: The renowned *Iate Club do Rio (Rio Yacht Club)* is in the heart of the city, directly beneath Pão de Açucar (Sugarloaf Mountain) in the Botafogo Inlet. Sailboats can be chartered for cruises south to Angra dos Reis and the so-called green coast, which is speckled with dozens of small islands, of which Ilha Grande is the best known. Av. Pasteur (phone: 226-4549). At Cabo Frio, the weekend resort for wealthy *cariocas,* charter boats are found at Búzios. Contact the *Strelitzia Travel Agency,* Praça Dom Pedro II, loja 2, for information or wander down to the docks at Rua Jonas Garcia. About 6 miles (10 km) out of town, there is a marina at *Arraial do Cabo* on Anjos Beach and *Armacão de Búzios.* At Interlagos, outside São Paulo, boats may be rented at the marina at *Parque de Guarapiranga* (no phone).

In Salvador (Bahía), no individual rentals are available, but a tour of the bay, on large schooners that carry between 20 and 30 passengers, can be arranged. Contact *Bahiatursa,* Belvedere da Sé off Praça da Sé (phone: 243-0282).

Sailing and wind surfing are two of the many sports enjoyed at *Club Med*'s new resort on Itaparica Island opposite Salvador. One- and two-week vacations, *Club Med* style, can be booked by calling the US toll-free number 800-528-3100.

COLOMBIA: Sailing is popular in Colombia's Caribbean waters, and there are a number of spots where boats can be rented. At San Andrés, the small island far off the northwest coast, all sorts of charters and equipment can be rented from *Bahía Marina Resort,* PO Box 597, San Andrés, Colombia. Then cruise to Bolívar Key, about 45 miles (72 km) northwest of San Andrés and Albuquerque Key, 15 miles (24 km) east. In Cartagena, sailboats of all sizes are for rent. From Cali, sailing and motorboat tours on the Cauca River, where egrets and other birds come to nest at sunset, are popular. The *Club Naútico* in Cali sponsors this; arrange a tour through your hotel or travel agent. There are also facilities for sailing at the Calima Reservoir, near Cali. Lake Tomine, at Guatavita, about an hour's drive from Bogotá, has sailboats for rent at its marina.

ECUADOR: For races, regattas, fishing, cruising, and simply enjoying the company of the yachting crowd, the only place in Guayaquil is the *Yacht Club* at Malecón and Illingworth (phone: 51-52-25). The *Miramar* hotel in Salinas (phone: 77-21-15) caters to sailors. The *Punta Carnero* hotel in Salinas (phone: 75-22-68) has a fleet of sunfish, cruisers, and fishing boats.

Private yachts that carry between 5 and 16 passengers can be chartered to tour the Galápagos Islands, 600 miles (966 km) west of the Ecuadorian coast. These special wildlife tours combine hiking and sailing with experienced naturalists who specialize in the Galápagos. *Oceanic Society Expeditions,* 240 Fort Mason, San Francisco, CA 94123 (phone: 415-441-1106) is one of several companies offering these trips. *Betchart Expeditions,* 10485 Phar Lap Dr., Cupertino, CA 95014 (phone: 408-245-9517) and *Inca Floats,* 1606 Juanita Ln., Tiburon, CA 94920 (phone: 415-435-4622) are two others. Other yachts — the *Encantada, Sulidae, Bronzewing, Amigo,* and *Charles Darwin* (the former research vessel of the Darwin Station) can be reserved through *Adventure Associates,* 13150 Coit Rd., Dallas, TX 75240 (phone: 800-527-2500).

PANAMÁ: Sunfish sailboats can be rented at Contadora Island's *Casino Contadora* hotel (phone: 27-00-33).

In the San Blas Islands, there are *cayucos* (Indian canoes) for rent at small island hotels for short day trips.

PERÚ: Guest privileges are extended to members of other sailing clubs at *Lima Regatta Club,* Chorrillos, Lima (phone: 45-25-45); *Union Regattas Club,* Plaza Galvez, La Punta (phone: 29-06-56); *Yacht Club Peruano,* Muelle Darsena, Callao (phone: 29-07-75); and *Yacht Club de Ancón,* Malecón de Ancón (phone: 28-70-51).

URUGUAY: Sailboats are for rent at the *Punta del Este Yacht Club.* For information, contact the information center at Liga de Fomento, Punta del Este.

VENEZUELA: Sailboats are for rent at the *Margarita Concorde,* the luxury hotel at Porlamar on Margarita Island. Write: Apdo. 570, Porlamar (phone: 32-10-1). The *Macuto-Sheraton,* in Caraballeda, just outside Caracas, has a complete marina where a Sunfish or catamaran can be rented (phone: 319-1801). The *Hilton* hotel, El Conde, Caracas (phone: 571-2322), will arrange boat rentals upon request.

There are smaller marinas at Morrocoy, Chichiriviche, and Maracaibo. Morrocoy has delightful lagoons and tropical scenery.

Tennis

 Tennis courts, ranging from adequate to excellent, can be found in all of South America's major cities and luxury resorts. This sport is not as popular in South America as it is in the US, and there are very few package tours to South America designed specifically for serious tennis players. But if you regard travel as an opportunity to sample different courts in different settings, there is enough of a selection around South America to justify taking along a tennis racquet.

ARGENTINA: There are no commercial tennis courts in Argentina, and courts at private clubs are for members and their guests only. Buenos Aires's *Sheraton* hotel at San Martín 1225 (phone: 311-65-65) has courts, and municipal courts are available in B.A. at Centro de Deportes de la Boca, Costanero.

BOLIVIA: For players in truly excellent physical shape, the challenge of the world's highest court awaits in La Paz: *Club Tenís La Paz,* Av. Florida, La Florida (phone: 38-25-89). Other tennis facilities in La Paz are: *Sucre Tennis Club,* Av. Busch 1001 (phone: 32-44-83), and *Club Tenís Ferrovario,* Pasaje Loa, Av. Vasquez (phone: 35-25-62).

BRAZIL: Two hotels in Rio de Janeiro have tennis courts: the *Inter-Continental Rio,* Praia da Gávea 222 (phone: 399-2200), and the *Sheraton,* 121 Av. Niemeyer (phone: 274-1122). Both hotels' courts overlook the Atlantic Ocean and are lighted for night play. For those not staying at these hotels, ask for permission to play at the *Rio Country Club,* the *Caiçaras* in Ipanema, or the *Paissandu Club* in Leblon.

In São Paulo, two hotels have tennis facilities: the *Caesar Park,* Rua Augusta 1508 (phone: 285-6622), and the *Ca d'Oro,* Rua Augusta 129 (phone: 256-8011). The *Maksoud Plaza* has squash, Alameda Campinas 150 (phone: 251-2233).

In São Paulo, commercial courts are a booming business. Court time usually costs $15 and up per hour. Ballboys should be tipped the equivalent of about $1 per hour. *Hobby Sports* has courts in four locations: Rua Luis Correa de Melo 225, Granja Julietta (phone: 246-6990); Rua João Lourenço 463, Parque Ibirapuera (phone: 241-1094); Av. Santo Amaro 5104, Brooklin; and Av. Angelica 634, Higienopolis (phone: 826-8411). There's also the *Academia Paulista de Tenís,* Rua Lopes Neto 89 (phone: 212-6454), *Tennis Center,* Rua Tenete Negrão 114 and 166 (phone: 853-4471; 853-6488), and *Tennis Place,* Rua Borges de Figueiredo 1325 (phone: 274-6799). Professional instruction is available at all the São Paulo courts but not always in English.

At *Club Med Itaparica,* on an island off Salvador (Bahía), there are 12 tennis courts for guests, as well as 2 paddle tennis courts. Tennis lessons are free. The deluxe *Méridien Bahía* hotel also has tennis facilities, as does the equally deluxe *Tropical Hotel Manaus,* on the Rio Negro tributary of the Amazon. There is also riverside tennis at the *Das Cataratas* hotel at Iguaçu Falls.

The *Casa Grande* resort hotel in Guarujá, outside São Paulo, also has tennis courts. Av. Miguel Estefno 999 (phone: 9-19-00).

In Recife, there are fine courts at the beachfront resort property of the *Quatro-Rodas* hotel, Av. Jose Augusta Moreira 2200 (phone: 081-431-2955).

In Brasília, the *Centro Deportivo Presidente Medici,* Setor Diversoes Norte (phone: 223-5834), has spectacular courts designed for tournaments (phone: 223-5834).

CHILE: Courts at private clubs in Chile are only for members and their guests, but travelers can rent one of the three courts at the *Rancho Mellink,* Camino Las Flores 11020 (phone: 20-03-16), in the Las Condes district of Santiago. Courts rent for about

$10 per hour during the day, $12 per hour in the evening until 10 PM, and about $14 per hour from 10 PM until midnight. There are racquets for rent. Call ahead to reserve courts. The *Sheraton San Cristóbal* hotel, set on a grassy hilltop overlooking Santiago, has two courts lighted for night play, Av. Santa Maria 1742 (phone: 74-50-00), and the *Holiday Inn Crowne Plaza* in town also offers tennis.

COLOMBIA: Arrangements to play tennis at most private clubs can usually be made by securing guest cards from a hotel, airline, or tour operator. Bogotá's main clubs are *Los Logartos* (phone: 253-0077), *Country Club* (phone: 258-3300), and the *American Tennis Club* (phone: 245-0608).

In Cartagena, there are three tennis courts at the *Cartegena Hilton.* Your hotel can arrange guest privileges at the *Country Club,* the *Club Cartagena,* and the *Club Naval.*

Clay courts are open for playing at the *Gaira Golf Club* and the *Irotama Hotel* (phone: 40-59) in Santa Marta.

On San Andrés Island, there are four public courts at the *Tennis Club,* near the *Isleno* hotel, on the Avenida de la Playa. They are open to all for a nominal fee.

In Cali, there are courts at the *Country Club, San Fernando Club,* and the *Tennis Club;* in Cucuta at the *Tennis Club;* in Medellín at *El Rodeo,* the *Country Club,* the *Llanogrande, La Raza,* and *La Macarena* hotels. In Medellín, there are also public courts available at the *Inter-Continental* hotel, at the *Club de Tenís de la Sociedad de Mejoras Publicas,* and at the *CONFAMA* recreation center in Copacabana. The *Lagomar El Peñon* resort complex in Giradot and the *El Prado* hotel in Barranquilla have courts.

ECUADOR: It's possible to purchase an expensive temporary membership at the *Quito Tennis and Golf Club* that will provide access to the nine clay courts and the swimming pool. Av. Brasil (phone: 24-19-18). For a fee, play is permitted at the *Quito Municipal Tennis Club*'s six courts on the corner of Av. Atahualpa and Av. 10 de Agosto; or, for a lower price, at the *Ecuador Tennis Club* at the top of Av. La Gasca. For guest cards for tennis clubs, ask at your hotel in Quito.

PANAMÁ: Most major hotels have tennis courts. The best are at the *Casino Contadora* hotel on Contadora Island (phone: 27-00-33) and in Panamá City at *El Panamá Hilton,* Vía España (phone: 23-16-60).

PARAGUAY: There are composition courts at the *Ita Enramada,* a luxury hotel 25 miles (40 km) south of Asunción. The hotel will arrange a tennis partner if you need one. (For reservations from the US, call 800-327-9471, nationwide except Florida, where the phone numbers are 305-949-4581 and 305-565-1828.) Near the *Itá Enramada,* there is also tennis and squash at the new *Hotel del Yacht & Golf Club Paraguayo* (phone: 36-121/30).

PERÚ: There are tennis courts in Lima at *Lima Cricket and Football Club,* Av. Leon de la Fuente 151, Orrantia (phone: 61-90-80); *Lawn Tennis Club,* Av. 28 de Julio 744 (phone: 28-46-95). Elsewhere in the country: *Club Tenís las Terrazas,* Malecón 28 de Julio, Miraflores (phone: 45-29-97); *Country Club,* Los Eucaliptos, San Isidro (phone: 40-40-60); and *El Pueblo Hotel,* Carraterra Central, km 17, near Chosica (phone: 27-94-64).

SURINAME: The *River Club Hotel/Motel* (phone: 74-52-9), 7 minutes by car from Paramaribo near the mouth of the river, has tennis courts.

URUGUAY: In Montevideo there are courts at *Carrasco Lawn Tennis Club,* Punta del Lotos (phone: 31-13-05); *Círculo de Tenís de Montevideo* (phone: 39-35-00); and *Club Bigúa* (phone: 70-24-85).

In Dayman, near Salto, there are a number of public tennis courts. Punta del Este's best courts are at *Cantegril Country Club* and, in Atlantida, at the *Country Club.*

VENEZUELA: For a nominal fee, nonguests may play on the three courts of the *Tamanaco Inter-Continental Hotel,* which have night lighting, Av. Principal, Las Mercedes (phone: 91-45-55); the *Caracas Hilton*'s one court, Sur 25 (phone: 57-23-22);

or the *Macuto-Sheraton*'s two courts, Caraballeda (phone: 031-918-01). Hotel guests are given preference.

The mammoth *Margarita Concorde* hotel on Margarita Island has five tennis courts (phone: 3-21-01). The *Melia* hotel in Puerto la Cruz, overlooking the Caribbean, has tennis facilities, too. Write: Apdo. 4522 Paseo Colón, Puerto la Cruz, Venezuela (phone: 081-69-13-11; or, to make reservations from the US, phone: 212-575-0080). Tennis is also available at the *Inter-Continental del Lagos* in Maracaibo.

Great Golf

 For any one of the thousands of Americans who cheerfully lug heavy bags full of clubs to airports in anticipation of trying new golf courses, it will be a delight to discover that it's easy to play your way around South America, teeing off in nearly every major city. But keep in mind that courses range in quality from luscious, hilly, 18-hole tournament-class courses — such as the *Club de Golf de Panamá* — to simple 9-holers that most serious golfers would not consider enough of a challenge to be worth teeing up for.

To most South Americans, golf remains a sport exclusively for the wealthy, and the supremely manicured greens, fairways, and surroundings form an important part of the privileged realm in which most South American golfers circulate. Membership in private clubs is extremely expensive — *Altamira* in Caracas charges a $30,000 initiation fee — but your hotel, travel agent, or airline can usually arrange guest privileges for a fee.

ARGENTINA: For golfers lacking a friend at one of Buenos Aires's private country clubs, the choice is B.A.'s *Palermo Municipal Golf Course,* in the Palermo District, on the corner of Calle La Pampa and Calle Figueroa Alcorta, right near the Lisandro de la Torre railroad station. This course is open to everyone. Most golf clubs in the provinces are connected with the military or on military bases. With an official handicap card from your own club and a letter from the club's pro or president, guest privileges can usually be arranged.

BOLIVIA: Not far from the heart of the world's highest capital, La Paz, stands *Golf Club Mallasilla,* which claims to be the world's highest course. But don't even attempt to play its 18 holes unless you are in truly excellent physical condition. And even if you are, be sure to allow a couple of days rest after arriving in La Paz to acclimate to the altitude. When teeing off, remember that the air is thinner, the ball sails farther, and overshooting a target is a fairly common problem. The golf course is on the road to Valle de la Luna, through two tunnels. Bear right at the fork. Av. Mallasilla (phone: 35-33-27). Several thousand feet lower, at Santa Cruz, there is a good 18-hole golf course at the *Los Tajibos* hotel.

BRAZIL: The *Gávea Golf Club* outside Rio de Janeiro overlooks the Atlantic Ocean near the *Inter-Continental, Nacional,* and *Sheraton* hotels. Special guest privileges are available on a fee-per-day basis, plus a caddy fee. (There are no carts.)

Outside São Paulo, in Guarujá, the luxury *Casa Grande* hotel has a modest course, open daily except weekends. Av. Miguel Estefno 999 (phone: 9-19-00).

CHILE: It's necessary to know a club member to get to play Chile's private golf courses unless you stay at the *Sheraton San Cristóbal* hotel in Santiago (phone: 74-50-00). The hotel will try to arrange a tee-off time at the *Los Leones, Sport Français,* or *Country Club* courses, but nonmembers are not permitted to play on weekends.

COLOMBIA: Golf courses are part of private clubs, but guest cards are generally available from your hotel, tour operator, or airline. In Bogotá, there's the *Lagartos*

Club; about an hour out of town is the country's highest course, the *San Andrés Golf Course.* Barranquilla has two 18-hole courses, one at the *Country Club* in the city and the other at the *Club Lagos de Cavrajal,* a short distance from town. The country club at Cartagena has a 9-hole course.

Medellín has four clubs with courses; the *Club La Macarena,* the *El Rodeo Club* (both 18-hole courses), and the 9-hole country club and *Club Llanogrande* courses. The Colombian Tourist Bureau recommends making arrangements through your home club by asking for exchange privileges on Medellín courses.

At Santa Marta, there's the 9-hole *Gaira Golf Club* course, a short drive from the *Irotama* resort hotel. Foreign visitors can play here without arranging for exchange membership privileges. There are also 18-hole courses in Cali at the country club, in Manizales near Medellín, and in Bucaramanga near Barbosa.

ECUADOR: The *Quito Tennis and Golf Club* has an 18-hole course to the leeward side of Mt. Pichincha. The thin Andean air makes 9 holes sufficient for most visitors, but those brisk few hours are usually enough to pick up a tan. Av. Brasil (phone: 24-19-18).

PANAMÁ: The *Casino Contadora* hotel on Contadora Island (phone: 27-00-33) has a par-3 9-hole course. More centrally located are the *Club de Golf de Panamá,* Cerro Viento (phone: 66-77-77), where international tournaments are played; the *Coronado Beach Golf Course* (phone: 23-13-42); and the *Panamá Golf Course,* Caraquilla (phone: 24-99-69) — all in Panamá City.

PARAGUAY: There is a new 9-hole course at the *Hotel del Yacht and Golf Club Paraguayo* (phone: 36-121/130). The *Asunción Golf Club,* Jardín Botánico (phone: 29-02-51), is a public course, open from March through November. It's not that great, but it's the only one in town and it's worth playing, if only for the social coup of being able to tell your friends that you birdied the fifth in Asunción.

PERÚ: In Lima, the most popular course is the somewhat flat, 18-holer at the *Country Club,* Los Eucaliptos, San Isidro (phone: 40-40-60). Many travelers take a trip to *El Pueblo Hyatt,* another 18-hole course, at Carreterra Central, km 17, Chosica (phone: 27-94-64). There are private courses at *Lima Golf Club,* Camino Real, 7th block (phone: 22-78-00), and at *Huampaní,* Carreterra Central, Km 26, Chosica (phone: 91-03-42).

URUGUAY: There's a good golf course in Parque Rodo on the ocean near the casino in downtown Montevideo. Guest cards are also available at the *Montevideo Country Club* (par 73) and at the *Cerro Golf Club* (also par 73). Both courses are lovely.

Golf is also excellent in Punta del Este at the *Cantegril Country Club* for those staying at the Club's hotel facilities and at the *Punta del Este Golf Club.*

VENEZUELA: The better hotels in Caracas can sometimes arrange for guests to play at the private courses at *Junko, Lagunita,* and the *Caracas* country clubs. The greens fees are stiff; caddies and club rental are extra. Guests at the *Tamanaco Inter-Continental* hotel (phone: 91-45-55) can play at the 18-hole *Valle Arriba Golf Club.* Note: Private club playing has become more difficult to arrange in Caracas.

Guests at the *Macuto-Sheraton* (phone: 031-918-01) can use the facilities of the *Caraballeda Golf and Yacht Club*'s 9-hole course, about 5 minutes from the hotel. Nonmembers are not permitted to play at the *Caraballeda* on weekends and holidays. On weekdays there are no restrictions, and tee-off times are easy to arrange. The *Hilton* hotel in Caracas (phone: 57-23-22) can arrange play on any of the 18-hole courses in the city or on the 9-hole *Caraballeda* course, Mondays through Fridays. Prices at the time of writing were listed as $16.50 for greens fees, $9.50 for club rental, and $7 for caddie service (required).

Nonmembers can play at the *Junko Golf Club,* on a mountainside outside Caracas, but on weekends and holidays golfers must tee off on the back nine.

There is a small golf course, as well as an 18-hole course, overlooking the Caribbean on the grounds of the *Melia* hotel in Puerto La Cruz (phone: 081-69-13-11; in the US, 212-575-0080).

Fishing

 South America offers unbelievably varied fishing grounds: from the deep-sea Caribbean waters off the shores of Venezuela, Colombia, Suriname, French Guiana, Guyana, and Panamá, to the sparkling mountain lakes of Chile and Argentina and the exotic rivers of the interior. And the entire South American continent is bordered by thousands of miles of Pacific and Atlantic Ocean, just swimming with countless numbers of fish.

Whether planning a fishing tour on your own or purchasing a package, check to find out where a particular species is running during the regular fishing season. When chartering a boat, make sure to fully discuss all of the following points: price; what the captain of the boat will provide (tackle, bait, food, drink); what fish are running; how the catch will be divided; and cancellation terms.

For advance planning, consult *The PanAngler,* a monthly newsletter updating the fishing scene in South America (and other parts of the world), issued by specialists in arranging fishing expeditions. The subscription rate is $15 per year or $26 for two years. Contact *PanAngling Travel Service,* 180 N Michigan Ave., Room 730, Chicago, IL 60601 (phone: 312-263-0328).

ARGENTINA: There are three main fishing areas. In the northern rivers, the prime catch is *dorado,* the strongest freshwater game fish in South America. The season runs from July through October. In the Lake District, there are trout, salmon, and perch waiting to be caught. The trout season runs from November 15 through April 15; January and February are the most outstanding months in Patagonia and Tierra del Fuego. In the Atlantic Ocean off the coast of Mar del Plata, Argentina's biggest seaside resort, anglers can catch hake (*merluza*), sea bass (*corvina*), and shark (*tiburón*). The best month for deep-sea fishing is October.

The southern lakes and rivers have salmon and rainbow, brown, and brook trout. The largest rainbow trout caught in Argentine waters weighed almost 28 pounds, and the largest brown trout about 35 pounds. The best trout fishing centers around the Bariloche area. One of the best current programs is a tour for wade fishing with fly or spinning tackle to Bariloche, operated by *Laddie Buchanan,* Las Heras 2948, Apt. 4H, 1425 Buenos Aires (phone: 45-67-21 and 45-72-49). Arrangements for fishing trips with Buchanan can also be made through *PanAngling Travel Service,* 180 N Michigan Ave., Chicago, IL 60601 (phone: 312-263-0328). Arrangements for fishing excursions to Bariloche and San Martín de los Andes can also be made through *Alun-Co Turismo,* Bartolomé Mitre 22, Bariloche (phone: 2-2283). The company works with some good guides and can arrange trips to the Huaculaufquén, Urrhue, Tromen, Traful, and Esquel Huaculaufquén lakes, as well as the Chimehuin, ColonCura, and Malleo rivers, depending on fishing conditions. *Aerolineas Argentinas* runs sport fishing tours to the Bariloche–San Martín de los Andes area through *Sport Fishing Tours,* PO Box 83, Califon, NJ 07830 (201-832-2173). Contact *Aerolíneas Argentinas*'s tour and group information desk, 9 Rockefeller Plaza, New York, NY 10020 (phone: 212-554-5142).

Trout fishing tours to Patagonia (season: November 15 to April 30) and to Tierra del Fuego (season: mid-January through March) are operated by *Laddie Buchanan,* Las Heras 2948, Apt. 4H, Buenos Aires (phone: 45-67-21, 45-72-49). *Safari Outfitters* goes to Patagonia, *Buchanan* to Tierra del Fuego. Up the Paraná River lives the *dorado,* a real fighter that can reach 60 pounds or more. Known in Argentina as the "Tiger of the Paraná," it can be fished from the provinces north of Buenos Aires — Corrientes, Missiones, and Entre Ríos — between the beginning of August and the end of October. (For a description of this region and a list of hotels along the river, see *Argentina,* DIRECTIONS.) *Laddie Buchanan* runs a *dorado* fishing tour on the Paraná.

In the Mar de Ajó, near Buenos Aires, red and black sea bass (*corvina*) can be caught. The best time to go is the beginning of October, when an annual fishing championship is held. Prize catches of up to 101 pounds have been hauled from these waters. In Mar del Plata, *Club Naútico* (phone: 80-03-23) arranges private charters for shark fishing. The lakes around Puerto Madryn and the Valdez Peninsula coast in Chubut have good freshwater and saltwater fishing.

Fishing in the Río de la Plata around Buenos Aires is prohibited because of pollution.

BOLIVIA: Trout fishing in Lake Titicaca has been getting mixed reports lately. Some people claim the fish are just not biting these days; others claim the catch is still good. There are plenty of mountain lakes outside La Paz, on the road to Chacaltayo, where fishing for catfish, trout, and perch is reportedly excellent. Near Cochabamba, around the Corani Dam, trout fishing is also good.

BRAZIL: Whether you prefer deep-sea fishing or the challenge of exotic rivers, Brazil has it all. Along the coastline of the states of Rio de Janeiro and Espiritú Santo, north of Rio, underwater and deep-sea fishing for marlin, swordfish, and other big-game fish is excellent. Underwater fishing championships are frequently held at Cabo Frio. Other good spots are the Ilha Grande, Angra dos Reis, Itacuraca, Itacoatiara, Saquarema, Armacão dos Búzios, and Macae.

During the first half of January, a national deep-sea fishing tournament is held off the coast of the state of Espiritú Santo. The best places for deep-sea fishing in this state are Jacaraipe, Nova Almeida, and Santa Cruz.

Surf casting is excellent off the shores of Salvador (Bahía). Fortaleza and João Pessoa, in the northeast, are the country's major commercial fishing areas. The catch includes shrimp as well as ocean fish. Boats can be chartered for day excursions at the docks.

In the southeast, Ilhabela is popular with surf casters. Squid is quite plentiful. Cassino, an Atlantic resort town near Rio Grande do Sul, has good deep-sea fishing. Charters are available.

Giant catfish and *dorado* can be caught in the Amazon. For rare tropical species, however, it's hard to beat the Araguaia River, near Aruana in the Mato Grosso. Standing along the banks of the river at dawn or sunset should yield any number of unusual fish: *tucanarés* (a rare catfish), dogfish, the one-eyed *soia, poraque* (an electric fish), *tambarana* (a fighting fish), *pacu,* and *pitarucú.* (They have no English names because these fish are found only in the South American interior.)

For information on charters and licenses, check with *Embratur,* Praça Mauá 7, 11th floor, Rio de Janeiro (phone: 233-1537); and *Riotur,* Rua São Jose 90, 8th floor, Rio de Janeiro (phone: 263-9122).

CHILE: With its 2,600-mile (4,186-km) coastline and its extensive southern lake region, Chile provides anglers with many different options: deep-sea fishing, beach fishing, surf casting, underwater fishing, dry-fly and wet-fly casting, and trolling. The lake district has some of the most outstanding trout fishing in the hemisphere. The first stop for anglers in Chile should be the local office of the *Servicio Agricola y Ganadero,* better known as *SAG,* for the required permit to fish. Police make regular spot checks of anglers for permits, as well as for minimum-size and catch-limit violations. There are special month-long licenses for tourists, or there is a season license. The *SAG* office in Santiago is at Pedro de Valdívia 942 (phone: 46-03-78). There are 32 *SAG* offices in Chile; every major town and city has one. *SAG* can advise on local variations on the inland fishing season, which generally runs from November 16 through April 15. The season varies in certain districts, and for certain species of fish. There's also a 10-fish or 44-pound catch limit. The minimum size depends on the species. Be sure to check with *SAG*.

The ocean is open all year; there is no season for deep-sea and coastal fishing. Deep-sea fishing is most common in the north of Chile, where anglers bag swordfish, long-finned and big-eyed tuna, bonito, and shark. World records have been broken at both Iquique and Tocopilla, the Chileans claim. Despite the fishing potential of the area, there is not yet an adequate infrastructure to promote fishing tourism in the north. The State Development Corporation (CORFO) and the national tourist office (SER-NATUR) are working on a plan to acquire boats with fighting seats. Northern deep-sea fishing is best from April to September.

Surf casting and beach fishing are common from La Serena, at the fringe of the northern Atacama Desert, along the coast as far south as Concepción. Ocean and river mouths in the central area have sea bass (*corvina*), sole, perch, tunny, and scad. Los Choros beach, near La Serena, is famous for scad fishing. Other popular beach fishing spots are Tongoy, Los Vilos, Papudo, Quintero, Algarrobo, El Tabo, Cartagena, Las Cruces, Rocas de Santo Domingo, Navidad, Pichilemu, Cahuil, Bucalemu, Llico, Iloca, Constitución, Curanipe, Colquecura, Dichato, and Concepción. In the central region's inland streams, pools, and rivers, there are carp, trout, and various other species.

The focus of the Chilean fishing tourist trade is the lake region of Chile, beginning at Lake Villarrica, just south of Temuco. A relatively uninhabited region of impressive scenery, southern Chile always seems to offer yet another lake, river, or stream to the adventurous angler in search of brown, rainbow, brook, and perch trout. The best fishing is in November and December and April and May. Showers are frequent even during the December to February summer months and are almost constant during the cold winter months of June through August — when few but the hardiest even think of fishing. Popular spots are in the Toltén River flowing into Lake Villarrica, Lake Panguipulli, Lake Ranco, Llifén, and Lake Calafquén. There are ample modest and first-class hotels in the lake district, although reservations are almost always needed during the summer season, from December through February. All hotels have a list of locals who act as guides and boatmen. For information on fishing in all waters of Chile, contact *Turismo Cocha,* PO Box 1001, Santiago.

Adrian Duffloq also runs a superb lodge that offers stream and river fishing for trophy brown and rainbow trout on the Cumilahue River. The lodge is small (10 guests at a time) and well run, according to American tastes. Inquiries in the US can be made through *PanAngling Travel Service* in Chicago (phone: 312-263-0328). In addition to the Cumilahue, other rivers within a short car ride can be fished and experienced; English-speaking guides are available to guests.

For those seeking a combination raft and fishing trip, check into *Sobek Worldwide Wilderness Expeditions and Tours'* rafting trip along the Bío-Bío River in southern Chile. In between shooting whitewater rapids, it's possible to cast for brown and rainbow trout. PO Box 761, Angels Camp, CA 95222 (phone: 209-736-2661). For fishing trip information, also contact the tour desk of LAN Chile in New York City (phone: 212-582-3250) or LAORCO Airlines in Miami (phone: 305-371-2799 or 800-328-1003).

COLOMBIA: Both ocean and river game fishing are possible. At the upper reaches of the Amazon and its tributaries around Leticia you can go after giant, spotted and yellow catfish, *pirarucú, tucunaré,* and native species similar to bass, trout, tarpon, and amberjack. Fishing in the Caribbean off the eastern coastline will usually net marlin, wahoo, kingfish, grouper, amberjack, and red snapper.

There's no off-season for fishing in the Caribbean, but conditions are better during the spring and summer seasons. In the deep-sea waters off Cartagena, there are sailfish, tuna, wahoo, mackerel, and the dolphin-like *dorado*. In the shallower waters, barracuda, pompano, tarpon, and bonefish swim.

Caribbean fishing can be arranged in Cartagena, Santa Marta, and on San Andrés Island. San Andrés has very deep waters just 3 miles (5 km) off its shores, but there is limited hotel space — the two main hotels are the *Royal Abacoa* and the *Eldorado* — so reserve well ahead for December, January, Easter week, July, and August. In the deep waters are marlin, sailfish, wahoo, bonito, amberjack, and dolphin; in the reefs around the island, grouper, jewfish, and red snapper. In the flats there are large bonefish. Fishing charters generally run about $125 a day and can be arranged through the *Bahía Marina Resort,* PO Box 597, San Andrés.

For Caribbean fishing in Cartagena, book charters through the *Club de Pesca* in the San Sebastian fortress or through *Pepino Mogollón* (phone: 42-96-6). Mogollón captains a Bertram 31 with two diesel engines and radiotelephone, and has fished Colombian waters for years. His rates run about $100 per day, including bait, tackle, and ice. Rent a boat for cruising and fishing for about $10 an hour from *Acuatur,* next door to the *Caribe* hotel.

In Santa Marta, go to El Rodadero Beach and ask for the office of *Captain "Pancho" Ospina,* who charters a variety of crafts at a variety of prices. He'll arrange for ocean game fishing or river fishing for tarpon, snook, and *mojara.* (When arranging charters in Colombia, as anywhere, be sure to know in advance exactly what you're paying for and that you and the captain agree.)

For surf casting in Santa Marta, try Rodadero Beach or Irotama Beach. There's also surf casting off the *Tairona National Park*'s Arrecifes beach. The park begins about 20 miles (32 km) east of Santa Marta and stretches along the Caribbean coastline almost to Taganga, spreading inland to cover 37,500 acres. It's open from 8 AM to 5 PM, although it's possible to camp at the park with the permission of *INDERENA,* the government agency in charge of national resources, which has an office at the entrance gate. There are public restrooms with showers for campers. Access to the beach is by horseback or foot, however, as cars are not allowed in the park. Bring your own gear. For information, write the *Corporación Nacional de Turismo,* Carrera 2 No. 16-44, Edificio del Claustro del Seminario, Santa Marta (phone: 33-41-8 or 35-77-3).

The inland fishing scene really centers around the Orinoco drainage, and many rivers make up this system. In the last few years, the Orinoco has proven to be the best provider of exotic fishing in the world, with many world-record *pavon* and *payara* taken here — some far larger than even experienced world anglers thought existed. The local operator is Erland von Sneidern; the US representative is *PanAngling Travel,* 180 N Michigan Ave., Chicago, IL 60601 (phone: 312-263-0328). At present, von Sneidern's headquarters are at a small, exclusive hotel in Puerto Carreno, on the eastern coast of Colombia. Excellent *tucarnare* (or peacock, butterfly, and speckled *pavon*) fishing is available within a short run of the hotel. In addition, anglers can catch near-world-record-class *payara,* which can tip the scales at up to 30 pounds, plus *arawana, pacu, sardinita,* and *giant catfish,* among other species. The best fishing months are June to December; bring your own heavy- and medium-weight tackle and equipment.

ECUADOR: Renowned for exceptional ocean fishing for marlin, swordfish, big-eyed tuna, and *dorado,* its inland lakes and rivers also have ample trout. One of the continent's best fishing resorts used to be the *Punta Carnero* hotel, on the coast north of Guayaquil. Experts report that something happened — an underground earthquake, shifts in the current, or some such calamity — to seriously deplete the fishing here. Recently it has come back for good striped marlin fishing, but it is still a shadow of its former self. For those with a sense of adventure, it's worth a shot. Contact *Pesca Tours* near the *Punta Canero,* which has a fleet of boats and equipment for rent. Deep-sea fishing reaches its peak in this area from January through May, although

November through April are best for striped marlin, and April to June for black marlin.

There are jungle safaris to the tropical Oriente region. Fish here include peacock bass, piranha, *dorado,* and giant catfish that weigh up to 300 pounds. Bring your own gear. The local operator is *Sam Hogan Safaris,* Casilla A-122, Quito (phone: 45-02-42), who runs superb jungle safaris for the adventuresome who can live off the land with a skilled guide (Hogan). There is fast fishing and exotic wildlife in the area. These trips can be booked in the US through *PanAngling Travel* (phone: 312-263-0238) in Chicago. Trout fishing is best in the rivers and brooks near Mt. Cotopaxi and Chimborazo.

To fish in Ecuador, it's necessary to get a license from the Ministry of Industry. Consult your tour operator about obtaining one.

PANAMÁ: In a local Indian tongue, Panamá literally means "place where many fish are taken." In contemporary English, it is known as the black marlin capital of the world. And any number of other species of big-game fish can be found off its shores, too. World records are frequently set during the July through September *International Fishing Tournament.* In April and May, the *Underwater Fishing Tournament* is held. Boat charters can generally be arranged through your hotel.

Roosterfish, sailfish, amberjack, cubera snapper, wahoo, and marlin swim off Cioba Island in the Pacific Ocean. The main fishing resort on the island is the air-conditioned *Club Pacífico,* which has a tackle store, equipment rental, and a small bar. A 23-foot diesel-powered open boat takes anglers to sea. The best season is the period from late December through mid-April; inclusive packages are offered on a weekly basis only. Contact the club's reservations office at 517 W 49th St., Hialeah, FL 33012 (phone: 305-823-8292 or 800-327-5662).

There's another special fishing tour to the *Tropic Star Lodge* in southeastern Panamá (*Tropic Star Lodge,* 693 N Orange Ave., Orlando, FL 32801; phone: 305-843-0124; local phone: 64-67-93). The lodge's air-conditioned bungalows, fleet of diesel-powered, 31-foot Bertrams for charter, and heavy and light tackle for rent are on Pinas Bay, 150 miles (240 km) south of Panamá City, where black marlin, striped marlin, sailfish, roosterfish, amberjack, wahoo, snook, dolphin, and rainbow runners can be caught. The season runs from early December through April, and weekly packages, including charters, run from Panamá City to camp.

The luxurious *Casino Contadora* resort, 20 minutes by air from Panamá City, is on the 220-acre island Contadora in the Pearl Island archipelago. The 150-room hotel has a 24-foot open diesel-powered boat for fishing marlin, sailfish, amberjack, wahoo, barracuda, and cubera snapper. Spear-fishing equipment can be rented on Taboga or Contadora Island, but on the other islands it's necessary to bring your own gear.

There are now fishing tours to Lake Gatun, the lake formed by the Panamá Canal, which has an abundant population of peacock pavon that run from 2 to 5 pounds. Day trips can be arranged from Panamá City to Gatun, and boats/guides are provided as part of the package.

For Pacifico and Tropic Star fishing trips, *PanAngler Travel* is the most productive agent for both properties.

Lists of boats for hire throughout Panamá can be obtained from the Institute of Tourism, on the ground floor of the *El Panamá Hilton,* Vía España, Panamá City (phone: 23-16-60).

PARAGUAY: Although it's a landlocked country, Paraguay offers good fishing in the Paraguay, Paraná, and Tebicuary rivers. Anglers here go after *dorado,* which average 20 pounds but can weigh as much as 60, catfish (*surubí*), of comparable size or much larger, and salmon. The *dorado* is usually found in fast waters and below waterfalls. Many anglers head for *Villa Florida,*)on the Tebicuary River 100 miles (160 km) from Asunción. The Tebicuary has other lodges and motels as well. Boats can be rented from the *Villa Florida;* make advance reservations for weekends.

There are year-round possibilities for fishing, but the best are available from August through March. *PanAngler Travel* advises that it is using a new operator who offers excellent freshwater *dorado* trips, with catches in the 20-pound (and larger) range possible. The operator uses float planes, 4 x 4 vehicles, and whatever else is required to get anglers to the best fishing grounds. Tours operate out of Ascención and include four days of fishing, although longer periods are available as required.

PERÚ: There's sport fishing in Perú in the Tambopata Wildlife Preserve at Puerto Maldonado, a 45-minute flight from Cuzco. The waters here have catfish (*surubí*), *dorado*, piranha, and peacock bass. There is a tour to the *Explorer's Inn,* which provides decent accommodations in simple cottages, and boats for fishing and exploration. The local operator is *Peruvian Safaris S.A.,* Garcilaso de la Vega 1334, Lima (phone: 31-30-47). Mailing address: PO Box 10088, Lima.

SURINAME: Fishing is good in the inland waters, where the most popular catch is a swamp fish called *kwie-kwie.* The best season runs from July 16 to March. There is little offshore sport fishing. Suriname has a minimum catch size of 12 centimeters for all species and other special minimums depending on the species, ranging from 10 centimeters for crobia to 32 centimeters for tarpon. The legal minimums shouldn't bother anyone, since travelers are inevitably after the big ones, such as the record 7-foot-3-inch, 240-pound tarpon caught in Suriname waters. Native Ojuka (Bushnegro) guides, who are skillful in white water with their dugout canoes, are necessary if you want to go after the most adventurous fishing that Suriname has to offer.

For further information, contact *Suriname Airways,* 6501 NW 36th St., Miami, FL 33166 (phone: 305-871-3602), and the Suriname Tourist Development Board, Kerkplein 10, Paramaribo, Suriname.

URUGUAY: The inland rivers provide excellent freshwater fishing for *dorado, pacu, pejerrey* (kingfish), *surubí* (catfish), and others. Particularly good spots are the Río Negro, Rincón del Bonete, Salto Grande, Nueva Palmira, Río Cuareim, Río Uruguay, and Fray Bentos. Seasons vary according to the species, but the Dirección Nacional de Turismo (National Tourist Office) can provide a chart. Its main office is at Av. Agraciada 1409, 5th and 6th floors, Montevideo (phone: 91-43-40).

Surf casting off Uruguay's Atlantic coastline, and in the Río de la Plata from Montevideo north to the Brazilian border, yields sea bass, conger eel, pompano, bonito, and many other species. The best beach fishing spots are Atlantida, Punta Negra and Punta Rosa near Piriápolis, Punta Ballena at Punta del Este, the mouth of the Río Arroyo, La Paloma, and La Coronilla. The *Yacht Club* at Buceo Port, Montevideo (phone: 78-04-15), arranges charters for deep-sea excursions.

VENEZUELA: White marlin, especially during August and September, and other big-game fish can be tackled in the Caribbean. There are any number of places along Venezuela's 1,800-mile coast where boats can be chartered. The best-known ones are the marina at the *Macuto-Sheraton,* Caraballeda (phone: 031-918-01); *Margarita Concorde* hotel, Porlamar, Margarita Island (phone: 3-21-01); and *Melia* hotel, Puerto La Cruz (phone: 081-69-13-11; in the US, 212-575-0080). In many places, a less expensive price can be negotiated at the local docks than at the luxury hotels. Some of the best marlin and big-game fish can be caught off the atolls of Los Roques.

The high streams of the Andes and the western *llanos* have superb *pavon* and some trout fishing, especially around Santo Domingo and Mérida. So do the Caroní and Paraguay rivers in the state of Guiana, in the Gran Sabana. Smaller freshwater fish (catfish, perch, and several local species) can be found in the streams of Barrinas and Portugesa states. Watch out for piranha, although they are more likely to go after your catch than any part of you. Poisonous stingrays inhabit some rivers.

The fishing season runs from March 16 through September 30. Licenses are issued by the *Ministry of Agriculture,* Torre Norte, Centro Simón Bolívar, Caracas (phone: 483-2458). The ministry, however, can be sticky about letting anglers into unexplored regions for fishing, and the red tape can be long.

Because It's There:
Mountain Climbing

 For those hearty souls who cannot bear to see a mountain just standing there, minding its own business, without contemplating an assault on its summit, the Andes of South America are an irrestible magnet. A 4,500-mile ridge of some of the world's most glorious mountains, the Andean chain is commonly referred to as the backbone or spinal column of the southern hemisphere.

While the Andes are indeed challenging, there are all grades of climbing in South America. Naturally, the level of personal expertise will determine whether you sign on for a simple afternoon climb or a difficult high-altitude expedition that lasts for weeks. Keep in mind that most climbing in the Andes is ice, rather than rock, climbing and requires knowing how to use ropes, ice axes, crampons, pitons, nuts, and chocks. In fact, there is very little actual rock climbing, and even a so-called easy climb is likely to be well beyond the skills of a novice.

Whether you choose an organized expedition or prefer to arrange one with friends, be sure to bring along a comfortable pair of mountaineering boots that are already broken in. As far as other equipment is concerned, check with each outfitter when inquiring about climbing trips to find out what kind of gear is included in the cost of a trip. If you plan to form your own group, the *American Alpine Club,* 113 E 90th St., New York, NY 10028 (phone: 212-722-1628), will cheerfully recommend equipment and establish contact with other mountaineers. Another good source for South American climbing is *Mountain Travel,* 1398 Solano Ave., Albany, CA 94706 (phone: 415-527-8100, 800-227-2384), which runs expeditions from Ecuador to Chile.

The center of mountaineering in South America is the Cordillera Blanca in Perú. The town of Huaráz serves as the Chamonix of the area, for it is here that climbers meet, exchange information on conditions, and form expeditionary teams. June and July are considered the best (driest) months. In comparison to the Himalayas, the Andes have more reliable weather during the dry season (June through October). When fair weather arrives, it normally lasts for weeks at a time. There is also less danger of storms and avalanches than in the Himalayas.

Experienced climbers are most likely to find others of similar skill in Huaráz. (It is possible to travel to the Andes alone and be fairly certain of encountering climbing mates.) It is less expensive to form your own team than to sign on with one of the many operators in the mountaineering business, but again, you should be truly expert to attempt it.

Below is a list of climbing associations, outfitters, and peaks.

ARGENTINA: The highest peak in the Western Hemisphere, Mt. Aconcagua, at 22,834 feet, has challenged mountaineers from all over the world. At press time, none of the mountain climbing trip operators had a program for Aconcagua or the Argentine ranges. However, there are frequent locally organized expeditions (usually during January), although climbing permits are not easily obtained. Contact the *Club Andinesta Mendoza,* Calles Pardo and Ruben Lemos, Mendoza, Argentina (phone: 24-18-40), for information, and leave plenty of time for them to reply.

BOLIVIA: The most popular climbing trips from La Paz are to Huaya Potosí, at 19,975 feet, and to 21,100-foot Mt. Illimani. *Club Andino Boliviano,* Av. 16 de Julio

1473 (phone: 31-46-82), puts climbers in contact with one another and arranges expeditions. The two major US outfitters that organize trips to Bolivia are *SOBEK Expeditions,* PO Box 1089, Angels Camp, CA 95222 (phone: 209-736-4524 or 800-344-3284), and *North Cascades Alpine School/Mt. Baker Guide Service,* 1212 24th St., Bellingham, WA 98225 (phone: 206-671-1505).

BRAZIL: Although not in a class with the Andes, Brazil's mountains attract some climbers. Mountaineering is not an industry here, so it's usually necessary to bring your own gear. The mountains, such as they are, can be found in the Serra dos Orgãos Park region around Teresópolis, halfway between Rio de Janeiro and São Paulo in Parque Itatiaia, and at Nova Friburgo, where the 7,575-foot Pica da Caledônia stands.

CHILE: Although the southern Andean peaks are as dramatic as any in the entire chain, climbing is neither as well organized nor as popular as in neighboring Perú, Argentina, or Bolivia. Parque Nacional Torres del Paine has challenging peaks. For information on mountain climbing, the best bet is to contact the *Club Andino de Chile,* Ahumada 47, Departamento 208, Santiago (phone: 28-54-49), or write Casilla 1823, Santiago. An American firm, *Mountain Travel,* has a 23-day trip that includes the Paine Towers National Park and crosses the Patagonian icecap (known as Hielo Continental). Contact *Mountain Travel,* 1398 Solano Ave., Albany, CA 94706 (phone: 415-527-8100, 800-227-2384).

ECUADOR: The snowcapped Ecuadorian ranges offer everything from scrambles to climbing volcanoes. Mt. Cotopaxi, at 19,342 feet, is the world's highest active volcano. The highest peak in Ecuador is 20,561-foot Mt. Chimborazo. The tropical eastern slopes of the mountains endure abrupt changes in weather conditions. It's wise to get a licensed guide or travel with a local climbing group or organized expedition. For further information, contact *DITURIS,* Reina Victoria and Roca, Quito (phone: 23-90-44). Mountaineers leave messages on the bulletin board at the *Hojas de Hierba* restaurant, Av. 6 de Diciembre 1536, Quito (phone: 54-01-52), and at the *Libri Mundi* bookstore, Calle Juan León Mera 851. One of the best climbers and guides on the continent is Marco Cruz, whose expeditions are represented in the US by *Adventure Associates,* 13150 Coit Rd., Dallas, TX 75240 (phone: in Texas, 214-907-0414, or 800-527-2500 elsewhere). Also contact *North Cascades Alpine School,* 1212 24th St., Bellingham, WA 98225 (phone: 206-671-1505).

PERÚ: The most active mountaineering center in South America is the Cordillera Blanca near Huaráz, where more than 30 peaks reach heights of more than 20,000 feet. Mt. Huascarán, at 22,134 feet, is the nation's tallest. The major US organizations that conduct trips to the Cordillera Blanca and the nearby Cordillera Vilcanota are: *SOBEK Expeditions,* PO Box 1089, Angels Camp, CA 95222 (phone: 209-736-4524 or 800-344-3284); *North Cascades Alpine School/Mt. Baker Guide Service,* 1212 24th St., Bellingham, WA 98225 (phone: 206-671-1505); *Mountain Travel,* 1398 Solano Ave., Albany, CA 94706 (phone: 415-527-8100, 800-227-2384); and *Iowa Mountaineers,* 30 Prospect Pl., PO Box 163, Iowa City, IA 52240 (phone: 319-337-7163).

VENEZUELA: Although not an organized sport, mountain climbing is acquiring numbers of participants in Venezuela. Mt. Avila, the 8,000-foot mountain right in Caracas, is emminently climbable. Visitors driving along the Cota Mil in Caracas often see climbers practicing on a certain limestone face beside the road. They are usually friendly and helpful. There is some snow climbing in the Sierra Nevada de Mérida. Many of the 1,000-foot *tepuyes* (vertical cliffs) in the Gran Sabana are unclimbed, but there is as yet no great interest in the region.

The Wild Continent:
Hiking, Backpacking, and Camping

South America is indeed a wild continent: from the coastal deserts to the perpetually ice-glazed faces of the Andean chain's southern tip in Chile and Argentina, to the snowcapped cones of Bolivia's and Ecuador's volcanoes, to the thousands of square miles of jungle, to the walls of the Patagonian glaciers.

The fact that all this wilderness exists on a developing continent has advantages and disadvantages that should be realistically appraised while planning a trip. One thing that is immediately apparent is how easy it is to lose the urban crowds if you really want to. Quite simply, there are far fewer people climbing around in the South American hills or floating down its rivers than is the case in the US. Campsites littered with beer cans are few and far between, although popular routes, like the Inca Trail, are beginning to show the effects of increased gringo traffic.

It is primarily this remoteness that can make traveling difficult, unless a four-wheel-drive vehicle is available. Transportation is not always available or frequent, and it's rarely punctual. But the *campesinos* (rural peasants) scattered throughout the small villages that dot the countryside do have to get to the markets in the larger towns, so it's usually possible to find a bus, train, or boat to drop you somewhere near a good spot to begin a jungle hike or volcano climb. The train may not leave on the precise day you prefer (or even that week), but in South America travelers quickly learn that adaptability is their most useful piece of luggage. And whether traveling in your own Land Rover or using public transportation, the road will inevitably be rocky, dusty, bumpy, and fascinating.

Some other things to keep in mind:

1. Bring all your own gear. Good camping and climbing equipment is very hard to come by in South America. And even when it is available, it is at least two or three times the US price. It's seldom wrong to bring what may seem like too much gear. What you don't need or can't carry can always be sold for more than it cost, and you'll still be doing a favor for the person to whom you sell it.

2. A lightweight tent provides maximum camping-out flexibility. Shelters are rare, and the rainy seasons often long. But the *campesinos* are often friendly and may offer not only a floor on which to throw a sleeping bag but also a look into a type of life thought only to exist in the novels of South American authors like Gabriel García Márquez or Jorge Amado.

3. A small backpacking cook stove, such as a Svea 123 or Mountain Safety Research (MSR), is definitely useful. The MSR is especially recommended because, unlike most stoves that run only on white gas (available in very limited supply in South America), it also works with kerosene, alcohol, or *cachaça,* the Brazilian national drink. A stove helps out when you're knee-deep in the mud of the rainy season, and it's a great way to help stretch limited funds. (A stove also lets you cook that brown rice you were saving when the local meat begins to taste just a bit too much like your hiking boots.)

4. Do not expect to find much dehydrated or freeze-dried food. Dried soups, cheese, rice, beans, honey, seeds, oats, and some dried fruits are, however, often available.

5. Maps of most areas are generally available from the military, but marked trails,

both on the maps and in the mountains, are not as complete as those the American Forest Service issues. Markers range from very poor to nonexistent, so be prepared to get lost more than once, even with a compass.

The wilderness travel business is now a multimillion-dollar industry. Organized backpacking and camping trips enable travelers to meet in the US and travel through one of the South American wilderness areas with experienced, English-speaking guides. Whether you want to hike around the base of Mt. Aconcagua, camp along the shores of an Amazon tributary, or walk in the footsteps of the Incas, there's probably a North American outfitter who has just the trip. Some of the best practical information is found in the South America backpacking guides done by Bradt Enterprises (95 Harvey St., Cambridge, MA 02140). The guides cover Venezuela, Colombia, and Ecuador, Perú and Bolivia, and Chile and Argentina. This company also publishes two guides for South America river trips.

When considering a package tour to the wilderness, be sure to find out if equipment is included and what individual participants are required to bring — down parkas, heavy sleeping bags, cooking stoves, tents. If you plan to spend a lot of time in the mountains, find out if the group's itinerary includes time to acclimatize. Some of the schedules are much too rigorous, even for people who are in excellent health and physical condition at sea level. Don't underestimate the demands placed on your body by sudden shifts in altitude and climate. They are exceedingly wearing and, if you push yourself too hard, can result in severe exhaustion and related illnesses. (See *Medical and Legal Aid,* GETTING READY TO GO.)

The major US wilderness travel organizations that conduct trips to South America include: *SOBEK Expeditions,* PO Box 1089, Angels Camp, CA 95222 (phone: 209-736-4524 or 800-344-3284); *North Cascades Alpine School/Mt. Baker Guide Service,* 1212 24th St., Bellingham, WA 98225 (phone: 206-671-1505); *Mountain Travel,* 1398 Solano Ave., Albany, CA 94706 (phone: 415-527-8100 or 800-227-2384); and *CanoAndes Expeditions,* 310 Madison Ave., New York, NY 10017 (phone: in New York, 212-286-9415; elsewhere, 800-242-5554).

Whether you plan to travel with an organized group, with friends, or on your own, what follows is a list of South America's prime wildernesses:

ARGENTINA

Both the southern Andean *cordillera* and the Lake District border on Argentina and Chile.

Glacier National Park (Parque Nacional de los Glaciares) – The park contains Lake Argentino, and at the far end of the lake, the huge Perito Moreno Glacier, one of the few on the planet that's still advancing. With a thunderous sound, walls of ice "calve," or break off from the glacier, every half hour or so, crashing into the lake and creating enormous waves. The glacier is also famous for the ice bridge it builds every 3 or 4 years, sealing off one end of the lake from the other, until the pressure becomes so great that a cataclysmic explosion of ice and water occurs, uniting the two halves of the lake once again. The park can be reached from the town of Calafate by bus. See park headquarters there for more information.

Moving east from the mountains into the heart of Argentina's Patagonia, geographic similarities with Chile fade. The weather here is often blustery and cold even during the somewhat drier summer months; the fjords, channels, and islands seem to transform into a barren, flat, gray, and desolate plain. Transportation can be difficult without your own vehicle. Bus service is limited but relatively inexpensive. Travel along the coast is the most intriguing route.

Valdés Peninsula and Camarones – Thousands of Magellanic penguins harbor here on the Patagonian coast until the end of March, when they head south for the winter. Colonies of sea lions continuously perform their antics on the rocks of the *loberia* (sea lion refuge), unless a hungry killer whale is cruising the area. Blubbery sea elephants waddle their way in and out of the bone-chilling sea. See park officials at Valdés for more information about camping. The *Automóvil Club de Argentina,* with offices in larger cities, supplies information and maps.

The Lake District – Farther north and deeper into the mountains, this area full of lakes and forests is popular with tourists, but it's easy to slip away from the crowds into some amazing countryside. Much of the region is devoted to a national park. Snowcapped peaks surround the trout-filled lakes: Nahuel Huapi, Correntoso, Guitierrez, Mascardi, and Guillelmo. Lake Futulafquen in Las Alceres National Park is an especially good fishing spot. Lanín Park, outside of San Martín de los Andes, contains the Lanín Volcano (12,000 ft.). Visit the *Club Andino de Bariloche* in Bariloche for more information, including maps of hiking trails. It is also possible to go by boat, bus, or train to the Chilean lake district.

Quebrada de Huahuaca and Quebrada del Toro – These two vast mountain valleys, ranging between 11,000 and 15,000 feet high, have some 16th-century Dominican and Franciscan chapels near Salta.

The Chaco – North and east of Salta are swamps, very deep forests, grasslands, some of the hottest temperatures on the continent, lots of birds, and unusual vegetation. Visitors usually arrive from the east via the Río Paraná or from the west via Tucumán.

BOLIVIA

Here, where the Andes are their widest and road transportation is possibly the worst on the continent — only 300 miles (483 km) of Bolivian roads are paved — the topography can be exceptionally strange and fascinating.

Altiplano – Lake Titicaca – at 12,500 feet, the world's highest navigable lake — must be visited (see *Bolivia,* DIRECTIONS). But the lake is only one feature of the stark, seemingly endless altiplano. A long, bleak, windswept plain cutting through the Peruvian and Bolivian Andes, the altiplano is inhabited by sheep, red fox, llama, alpaca, vicuña, chinchilla, and some hardy Quechua (Peruvian) and Aymará (Bolivian) Indians. Travel from Cuzco, Perú, by bus, train, or *collectivo* to the shores of the lake and from there to the Bolivian capital (see *La Paz,* THE CITIES). Then take a train from La Paz to Antofagasta, Chile. The track traverses the altiplano, passing the snowcapped mountains that form its border. With a four-wheel-drive vehicle, it's possible to visit many traditional Indian villages. The mountains are driest and coldest between April and November. June through August are the clearest (but chilliest) months. The lowlands receive their heaviest rains from November through March. The *Club Andino Boliviano,* on Calle México just behind the *Sucre* hotel, can provide hiking information.

La Cumbre to Coroico – This is a different type of hike, leading from the cold, upper reaches of La Cumbre pass, at 14,000 feet, downhill into the semitropical Yungas Valley. Trekkers walk along an Inca or pre-Inca stone road, pass several ruins, and see plenty of Indian towns. The first day of this 3- or 4-day trek is spent crossing the snowy pass to a super view of the eastern slopes, with lots of bright birds and butterflies.

Train from Santa Cruz to Corumba, Brazil – The Death Train, as it is fondly nicknamed by those who regularly ride on it, rolls through some of the wildest parts of Bolivia. Jungle birdlife abounds along this 400-mile (644-km) ride through a frontier region that has only recently been vacated by Indians. Train service has improved of late, and derailments now occur with far less frequency than was once common.

River Trip to Trinidad – Perhaps one of the most exotic regions in South America, the jungle lowlands of Bolivia are called "the forgotten corners" by the residents themselves. Clouds of brightly colored butterflies shimmer in the clear light; villagers gather to welcome travelers; and utterly exotic species of wildlife — wild boar, armadillo, giant tortoise — sun themselves on the banks of the rivers. Travel from Cochabamba to Puerto Chipiriri by road, a distance of about 120 miles (193 km). From there, it is about 4 days' journey up the Río Grande to Trinidad. Bring a sleeping bag and plenty of mosquito repellent. It's also possible to travel by *peque-peque* (motorized dugout canoe) along the Río Madre de Dios from Perú into Bolivia (see *Perú* and *Bolivia* in DIRECTIONS).

BRAZIL

Although this is one of the few South American countries in which the Andes do not crowd the horizon, one-third of Brazil (whose landmass occupies almost half of the southern continent) is part of the Amazon basin. In fact, 1979 was declared the International Year of the Amazon by a group of Brazilian environmentalists and journalists. About 15% to 20% of the total Amazon jungle — an area larger than Holland — has been deforested for development projects. Ecologists and conservationists from all over the world are drawing attention to the increasing destruction of wildlife, foliage, and human habitation patterns.

The vast Amazon River system has been the main transportation route for people living in the world's largest rain forest since humans first settled the region, and it is still the most practical route of passage. Today, deluxe boat trips on the Amazon are almost as easy to book as Caribbean cruises. Airlines, such as *Varig* and *Pan Am,* run tours to the Amazon region, all of which include time spent on the river but do not usually include camping. These trips can be arranged through a travel agent (see *How to Use a Travel Agent,* GETTING READY TO GO). For a complete description of Amazon travel, see *Brazil,* DIRECTIONS.

Any real exploration of the region requires a trip up the tributaries of the river. It's possible to set up individual day trips by hiring a guide in Manaus who has his own *peque-peque.* Another inexpensive way to scout the area is to go on a milkboat that leaves daily around 5 AM, stops at several villages accessible only by water, and returns to Manaus in the afternoon. It's also possible to stay overnight at one of the villages.

Travelers with a bit of gumption can take a ferry through the Wedding of the Waters, where the brown Amazon meets the black Rio Negro, and continue by bus to Manacapurú, a small fishing village on the Rio Negro. Go to the dock area and ask among the fishermen for one who lives deeper into the interior. More than likely, he will be pleased to provide a lift farther upstream into the wilds, for a nominal fee. Carry everything you need with you — from there you are on your own.

São Francisco River, from Pirapora in Minas Gerais to Juazeiro in Bahía, is another beautiful river trip. Bring a hammock and prepare to relax for 4 or 5 days as you float through some inspirational countryside. November to April is the best time. (Other routes into the Brazilian interior are described in *Brazil,* DIRECTIONS.)

CHILE

In the course of winding your way down this elongated country, some of the topography will already be familiar if you have explored the more northern countries. There are also many altogether new formations. In the north, there is rainless desert devoid of vegetation. Moving south and into the mountains, the Andes build to a height that peaks at over 20,000 feet and then begins tapering down as the trail leads into the more active volcanoes of the stunning, forested lake district south of Santiago. Still farther south is a maze of dense forests, glaciers, islands, fjords, channels, and the Straits of Magellan, finally arriving at the blustery, raw, often stormy tip of the continent, Tierra del Fuego, where the heavily glaciated Andes come to an end.

Tierra del Fuego Region – A popular way to see Chilean Patagonia, the area between Puerto Montt and Tierra del Fuego, is to take the monthly *Empresa Marítima del Estado* ship from Puerto Montt on a 4-day journey to Punta Arenas in the south. It is a good idea to make advance reservations with the company in Santiago for first or second class to guarantee a place on the voyage. Bring along a copy of Darwin's *The Voyage of the Beagle* to get real insight into the region, plenty of warm clothes, and enough food so that you won't have to buy all your meals on the ship. The mildest months for the journey are between November and March. Another way to follow the same routing, but in greater comfort (though at greater cost), is aboard the *Skorpios,* with 38 cabins for 78 passengers. Sailings are scheduled for Saturdays, September through April, from Puerto Montt. Check with Eastern Airlines or LAN Chile tour desks for US tour operators through whom you can book (see *Package Tours,* GETTING READY TO GO).

Parque Nacional Torres del Paine – Accessible from Puerto Natales (reachable by bus from Punta Arenas), the park has mini icebergs; abrupt rock escarpments; *guanacos* (similar to llamas); *avestruz* (ostrich-like birds); red and gray fox; some pink flamingos; and the huge Gray Glacier, an awesome, gnarled mass of rock and ice dropping 150 feet into the water. Rock and ice climbing can be attempted on the Torres del Paine Mountains. Visitors who arrive after the tourist season (December through February) may have to finagle a bit to find transportation out to the park. But check with park headquarters in town. They are very helpful and can supply some maps, and usually a lift on a supply truck that heads to the park once or twice a week.

The Island of Tierra del Fuego – Half owned by Chile, half by Argentina, the fjords, glaciers, waterfalls, mountains, and sea lions here are most easily explored from the Argentine city of Ushuaia, the second most southerly town in the world (after nearby Puerto Williams). Ushuaia is served by plane or bus. Go to the *Club Andino de Ushuaia* for more information.

COLOMBIA

Generally more developed than the other countries in the Andean group, Colombia has better roads, buses, and more extensive tourist information. Here, at the northeast end of the continental landmass, the Andes split into three mountain ranges. A climber can move from the *tierra fría* (cold country) of the mountains to the *tierra caliente* (hot country) of the valleys in a matter of hours. (For those heading south on an overland trip through South America, Colombia offers the first opportunity to enter the Amazon basin.) The mountains are driest and clearest from December through March, which is the jungle's rainiest season. The jungle usually gets some rain every day, no matter what time of year. *Rana Tour Operators,* Carrera 8 No. 15-73 (phone: 282-3377), arranges trips to La Guajira, the Amazon, the Sierra Nevada, and San Agustín, which, at this writing, are not the safest parts of the country.

San Agustín – From this little town, famous for its archaeological sites and leather-work, backpackers can hike or ride horseback in almost any direction and find something special. See Tomás Palacio (or write to him at San Agustín) in the market. He can arrange horses and a guide for a 5-day journey up the steep and lovely Magdalena River valley — past mountain vegetation, an emerald lake, waterfalls, and archaeological sites. *Hospedaje* (food and lodging) can usually be found in little villages along the way. Tomás will do his best to strike a fair deal as far as price is concerned.

The Llanos – The great grassland is the intermediary zone between Colombia's mountains and the eastern jungle. Poisonous snakes, alligators, pumas, and jaguars are all part of the landscape. Trips start from Villavicencio.

Leticia – Where the borders of Colombia, Perú, and Brazil meet is one of the best jumping-off points for trips into the Amazon jungle. *Avianca* and *Intercontinental de Aviación* both fly there.

To see how the Indians live and get to know some of the world's most exotic wildlife, it's necessary to travel into one of the tributaries of the Amazon River with someone who knows the Indians well. There are regular trips to Monkey Island and to Tacuna and Yagua Indian villages, but even more isolated areas can be reached with the right guide. Guide service tends to be less expensive here than in the Manaus region of Brazil — about $30 per day, with a group, compared to $60. Ask at the *Parador Ticuna* or *Anaconda* hotel for someone to lead your trip, or check with Earl Hanks, manager of *Lowrie Travel Service,* Carrera 7, No. 19-29, Bogotá (phone: 243-2546/7).

ECUADOR

A mountain climber's and alpine hiker's haven, this country has more than 30 huge, volcanic peaks, not all of which are dormant. The equatorial latitude affects the climate at higher altitudes, so it's possible to travel through the Andes without encountering weather changes as severe as those in the south, where the sun's rays are less direct. May through September are filled with crisp, dry days. Late November and December are often pleasant, too. Good maps are available at the *Instituto Geográfico Militar,* Calle Paz and Calle Mino (phone: 52-20-66).

Mt. Cotopaxi – This snow-covered cone last erupted during the 1940s. A visitor can see where the mass of lava and melted ice washed away the tiny village that lay below. If you have your own vehicle, you can drive to 13,000 feet; otherwise take a bus from Quito that stops at the entrance of Parque Nacional Cotopaxi. Hiking and climbing are not technically difficult, but the lack of oxygen is. Acclimatize in Quito for a week or so before attempting any strenuous activity.

The Oriente – Ecuador is not all mountain. The Oriente is very accessible, and there are possible river trips that do not require guides. The gateway to this region is the ramshackle town of Misahualli, on the Río Napo, reached by bus from Tena. There is motorized canoe service downriver to the muddy town of Coca every few days. From there, it's necessary to ask around in the port for someone continuing downstream. By traveling in this manner, there is a good chance of spending a few nights with a family living in a bamboo hut along the riverbank. Carry your own supplies.

Three hours down the Río Napo from Coca is Limoncocha, home to the Amazon Research Station, where regional plants and animals are studied. Nearby is Limoncocha's alligator- and piranha-inhabited lake. Cofan and Secoya Indian tribes are not far away, either.

Other excursions begin in Misahualli. To see this primitive area in relative comfort, talk to Señor Jorge R. Hurtado M. of *Natura Turismo* in Tena. He will describe how to contact Douglas Clark, a gringo (in name only) guide on Anaconda Island, about an hour downstream from Misahualli. Clark's tours include meals, and nights are spent in huts with flush toilets. He will also take you to meet a *bruja* (witch), drink *chicha de yucca* (the local firewater), or to eat guavas with the Alama Indians. He knows the jungle well and can point out the spectacular vegetation and wildlife.

Douglas or one of the other guides in Misahualli can also act as a guide on a rigorous 4-day hike to an Auca Indian village. These people have only recently begun to accept white people in their territory. It is a demanding trip up and down what is often mucky countryside. But, as always, it's necessary to get off the well-trodden paths to see what is most unusual.

There is a good 5-day escorted tour to this area overland from Quito. Travel is by motorized dugout; visitors stay at jungle lodges and get to explore rain-forest trails. Contact *Adventure Associates,* 13150 Coit Rd., Dallas, TX 75240 (phone: 214-907-0414, 800-527-2500). Also ask them about Marco Cruz's trekking expeditions.

PERÚ

In contrast to the rather solitary volcanoes scattered across the face of Ecuador, the Peruvian Andes are arranged in formations more favorable to backpacking trips of several days' duration rather than single mountain climbs. The highly organized Inca Empire carved a road network into the mountains, which makes Perú one of the best backpacking areas in South America. Trails formerly used by the Inca are now the well-tramped routes of international hikers. For extensive information, see *Backpacking in Perú and Bolivia,* by Hilary and George Bradt (Bradt Enterprises, 54 Dudley St., Cambridge, MA 02140; $8.95). *Note:* As of press time, warnings issued by the US Department of State in response to recent urban terrorist activity as well as incidents in southern Perú, including parts of the Inca Trail, were still in effect. Caution is advised.

The Inca Trail – This well-worn path is still one of the world's greatest. It skirts several Inca ruins along the way, culminating with the hiker entering the grandeur of Machu Picchu through the same stone archway the Inca used 500 years ago. Take the "Indian train" from Cuzco and ask to be let off at Km 88. From there it is a 3- to 6-day hike, depending on your own pace, and how much time is spent dawdling along the Inca highland trails.

Bring a tent and cook stove. May and June are the best months to do it, but don't forget — it is a popular route, so there's little chance of being alone. Hiking in the less crowded rainy season has its advantages, but dry socks is not one of them. Pick up a copy of *Journey Through the Clouds* in Cuzco or Lima for more details and a good map. The tourist bureau in Cuzco also issues a map, but it is not very good. It is available at all hotels, too. Take along all the reference material available because so many people have gone the wrong way that the incorrect path is often better detailed than the right one. Stock up on dried bananas, oranges, and D'Onofrio chocolates from the *supermercado* on the plaza in Cuzco.

To tread a section of the Inca Trail that allows hikers to sleep at an abandoned temple beside a waterfall, climb to the guardhouse at the top of Machu Picchu and follow the track along the ridge overlooking the sacred Urubamba River to the Inca gate. Looking back, notice how the lost city has diminished in size. Once through the Inca gate, the descent leads down a set of slimy, irregular steps carved into the cliff. These end right in the middle of a green rain forest with climbing vines and leaves bigger than a human head. The trail is very hard to follow since it is overgrown with tangled vegetation, but turn right at the bottom of the steps and keep going to eventually emerge onto a dry trail similar to the one connecting Machu Picchu to the Inca gate. Take this path over the ridge to Huiña y Huayna, a most remarkable set of ruins. Here is the place to recover from the 8-hour trek, pitch a tent, and spend the night. Bring plenty of mosquito repellent, and don't litter at any campsite or anywhere along the trail. Recently, tours have been organized just to clean up this historic highway.

Colca Canyon – Just outside Arequipa is Colca Canyon, one of the continent's most dramatic areas. Cut by the Colca River, it is twice as deep as the mighty Grand Canyon. Like the early Indians, today's travelers walk through this moonscape region in the shadows of the Misti and Chachani volcanoes. There are ancient Inca aqueducts and rock drawings here, and *CanoAndes* runs a series of rafting and hiking trips in the area. A member of this organization was the first person to travel the whole Amazon River — from its source north of Colca to the Atlantic — by kayak. Contact *CanoAndes,* 310 Madison Ave., New York, NY 10017 (phone: 212-268-9415 or 800-242-5554).

Parque Nacional Huascarán – In the north of Perú are many spectacular hikes through the Cordillera Blanca, of which Mt. Huascarán, at 22,205 feet, is the highest. The hikes, which cover between 8 and 40 miles, can last from 1 to 6 days and venture as high as 15,000 feet. All trails start at the Callejón de Huaylas Valley.

One favorite hike, from Yunguy to Caras via Calcabamba, leads past Mt. Huascarán and Lake Llanganuco, which has great camping and trout fishing. It is the base camp for expeditions to the surrounding peaks. The trek will take about 6 days (not recommended for beginners). The remnants of the brutal 1970 earthquake are visible, as are tiny mountain villages, and there are few gringos. Additional information and maps are available at Huascarán Park headquarters in Huaráz.

Iquitos – Follow the route of the Amazon explorer Francisco de Orellaña to the

Explorama Lodge, 50 miles downriver from Iquitos, and then along the tributary of the Napo to *Explornapo Camp.* Accommodations at this base camp are hammock- or floor-mat-style in elevated, thatched-roof huts without walls. *Explorama* operates a basic 5-day circuit jungle itinerary, but arrangements can be tailored to group needs. Guides accompany all expeditions into these Amazon backwaters and jungle trails. For information, contact *Explorama Tours,* Box 446, Iquitos, Perú.

Madre de Dios – A rough, mountainous jungle region with sparkling rivers and unusual trees, butterflies, and wildlife, Madre de Dios is accessible by airplane or truck from Cuzco (see *Perú,* DIRECTIONS). The best way to see the area is via the river. Arrange transportation at the dock in Puerto Maldonado. The *American River Touring Association,* 445 High St., Oakland, CA 94601 (phone: 415-465-9355), runs camping trips to Madre de Dios.

VENEZUELA

Some of the last, really wild frontier on the continent can be found in the Venezuelan interior.

Orinoco Jungle – Actually part of Amazonas Territory, the trackless Orinoco Jungle is a sparsely inhabited area, full of rivers, falls, plateaus, and Indians. The upper Orinoco can be navigated by small craft. There is a camp for travelers in Yutajé. For information, contact Coredes Turismo in Caracas (phone: 33-57-33/74).

The Gran Sabana – Also known as the highlands of Guyana, this is another relatively unexplored area of more than half-million square miles. The topography consists of pink massifs, jungle, and sandstone mountains called *tepuyes.* It's about a 10- or 12-hour drive from Caracas to Upata, on the edge of the Gran Sabana (see *Venezuela,* DIRECTIONS).

Parrots, Penguins, Piranhas:
Wildlife Expeditions

More and more people are traveling around the world specifically to observe wildlife in its natural environment. Wildlife tours, which take bird- and animal-watchers to sanctuaries, preserves, and wilderness areas, are becoming increasingly popular. The eminent ornithologist Dr. Roger Tory Peterson attributes the evolution of this special interest branch of the travel industry to "hard-core birdism." Those bird-watchers who spend half the year traveling in search of new species constitute a new kind of traveler. "If you're obsessed with natural history, you want to keep seeing different species," he observes.

Although preparations for a bird-watching or nature expedition vary with the destination, certain factors are common to all such trips. Whether you plan to observe iguana in the Galápagos, penguins in the Falkland Islands, or monkeys in the Amazon, consider the following:

1. Choose binoculars with care. For most trips, binoculars of 7 × 30 or 8 × 40 are good. Steadier hands can manage a 10- or 12-power. Zeiss, Leitz, and Nikon are best.

2. Carry a field guide. Although some of the more remote sections of South America have not yet been covered, many favorite bird-watching areas have been catalogued. Contact the *National Audubon Society,* 950 Third Ave., New York, NY 10022 (phone: 212-832-3200), for a list of books.

3. Travel with someone who knows the area. Tours are escorted through the area by

guides who know the local species. Throughout South America, there are knowledgeable natives and long-term foreign residents who can help.
4. Study records and cassettes of birdsong. Familiarize yourself with the sounds
before leaving home or carry a small tape recorder. Bird records and cassettes are
available from the *National Audubon Society.*
5. Carry a camera. Although not necessary for sighting birds, a camera enhances the
enjoyment of any expedition. Unless you plan to construct a blind and wait for
a close-up, you should have a 300-mm or 400-mm lens and a tripod. Penguins are
the one exception. It's possible to get very close to them because they don't seem
to be afraid of people.

Although wildlife tourism is not as developed in South America as in Africa, a
number of organizations offer well-planned tours to different parts of the continent.
Listings of some of these are included in *The Adventure Book,* an Arthur Frommer
publication (Simon & Schuster; $14.95); *Adventure Travel Abroad,* by Pat Dickerman
(Henry Holt & Co., $12.95); and *Finding Birds Around the World,* by Peter Alden and
John Gooders (Houghton Mifflin; $17.95). Some of the major travel agencies specializ-
ing in wildlife tours include: *Nature Expeditions International,* 474 Williamette St.,
Eugene, OR 97440 (phone: 503-484-6529); *Holbrook Travel,* 3520 NW 13th St.,
Gainesville, FL 32601 (phone: 904-377-7111); *Questers Tours and Travel,* 257 Park
Ave., New York, NY 10010 (phone: 212-673-3120); *Victor Emanuel Nature Tours,* Box
33008, Austin, TX 78764 (phone: 512-477-5091); *Society Expeditions,* 3131 Elliott
Ave., Seattle, WA 98123 (phone: 206-285-9400 or 800-426-7794); *South American
Wilderness Adventures,* 1760 Solano Ave., Berkeley, CA 94707 (phone: 415-524-5111).
Below is a list of the best areas for wildlife expeditions in South America.

ARGENTINA: It's possible to observe the sea lions, sea elephants, and Magellanic
penguins on and around the Valdez Peninsula. Unlike the Galápagos Islands, however,
wildlife is fenced in. The *World Discoverer* and *Society Explorer* cruise from here to
Antarctica with *Society Expeditions,* 3131 Elliott Ave., Seattle, WA 98123 (phone: in
Washington, 206-285-9400; elsewhere, 800-426-7794). A land program in Argentine
and Chilean Patagonia, plus a stay at Lt. Marsh base in Antarctica, is offered by
Travcoa, 4000 MacArthur Blvd., Newport Beach, CA 92660 (phone: 714-975-1152 or
800-992-2003).
BRAZIL: There are some exceptional wildlife specimens visible in the extensive
Amazon jungle. Tourist agencies in Belém and Manaus can arrange expeditions. Daily
flights from Belém or Manaus, on Cruzeiro do Sul, TransBrasil, and Varig Airlines,
go to some 52 towns in the Amazon.
From Manaus, there are boat excursions to Parrots Island, where thousands of
parrots flock at sunset. Longer trips can be taken to bird-rich Oriole Island and up the
Rio Negro from Manaus. The Rio Negro is a black tributary of the brown Amazon,
and both colors are visible where the two rivers flow separately into the same riverbed,
along whose banks live alligators, kingfishers, butterflies, and parrots.
From Belém, there are excursions by air (30 minutes) and Enasa Line riverboats (5
hours) to Marajó Island, where there are jaguars, monkeys, anteaters, sloths, ocelots,
parrots, giant armadillos, and tropical birds by the thousands. There are a few water
buffalo ranches (*fadenzas*) that accept guests for one or more nights. Inquire at a travel
agency in Belém. Travel to Jaguar Island is also possible by boat from Belém, along
the Pará River.
Even more exotic than the Amazon is the less well known Mato Grosso, where
thousands of rare animals live, including the hoatzin (a bird that can only fly for short
stretches) and porpoises. For information on tours, contact Embratur, 551 Fifth Ave.,
New York, NY 10176 (phone: 212-916-3206).

COLOMBIA: The jungle areas and eastern prairies are home to jaguars, tigers, wildcats, ocelots, tapirs, pumas, black panthers, leopards, deer, beavers, possum, several types of monkey, parrots, alligators, armadillos, iguanas, turtles, anacondas, boar, ducks, and pigeons.

The Amazon town of Leticia is one of the best bird-watching areas, with 1,500 species (120 of which are hummingbirds). The *Turamazonas* tourist agency runs bird-watching tours and trips to *Monkey Island Lodge,* a monkey preserve of 1,000 acres where there are also thousands of green parrots. Contact the agency through the *Parador Ticuna* or ask Earl Hanks at *Lowrie Travel Service,* Carrera 7, No. 19-29, Bogotá (phone: 243-2546/7).

There are a number of observatories for watching wildlife in Tairona National Park, which runs east from Santa Marta for about 20 miles (32 km) along the Caribbean coastline almost to Taganga, ending at the mouth of the Piedras River. Sea turtles can be glimpsed off Playabrava and Mayuey points. The park is closed to vehicles, so it's necessary to walk or ride horseback to the observatories. For information, write the *Corporación Nacional de Turismo,* Carrera 2 No. 16-44, Edificio del Claustro del Seminario, Santa Marta (phone: 33-41-8 or 35-77-3).

ECUADOR: Ecuador's Galápagos Islands, where Darwin formulated his "survival of the fittest" theory, is a dream trip for most nature lovers. Giant tortoises, weighing over 500 pounds and perhaps more than 100 years old, land iguanas, marine iguanas, penguins, cormorants, sea lions, and fur seals are part of the pageant of fauna inhabiting the archipelago's 13 largest islands. Galápagos means "giant turtles," although few have survived on the islands, which have both 40-foot cacti in dry, coastal desert areas and creepers and ferns in dense rain forests a few miles inland. The islands are a national park area.

Several boats ply the waters around the islands, stopping for nature observation in accordance with national park laws. The newest is the MV *Santa Cruz,* specially built for Galápagos cruising; it accommodates 90 passengers. Of comparable comfort and capacity is the MV *Buccaneer.* Both boats have lecture programs to prepare visitors for the shore visits; each has a 7-night tour that either combines flying to the islands and then sailing, or sailing one way to or from Guayaquil. The *Santa Cruz* also has 3- and 4-night programs. To book the *Buccaneer,* contact *Galápagos, Inc.,* 7800 Red Rd., South Miami, FL 33143 (phone: 800-327-7732). Eastern and Ecuatoriana Airlines with *Adventure Associates,* 13150 Coit Rd., Dallas, TX 75240 (phone: 214-907-0414 or 800-527-2500), have tour programs on the *Santa Cruz,* and on the *Amigo* yacht, a cruiser that accommodates 14 passengers on 7-day cruises, as well as charters for 5 to 10 persons on the yachts *Encantada, Sulidae, Bronze Wing,* and *Charles Darwin.*

Ecuador's Amazon region is also good for wildlife trips. The *Flotel Orellana,* a comfortable boat-hotel, cruises the Napo River, stopping often for jungle walks and visits to native villages, accompanied by trained naturalist guides. Owned and operated by *Metropolitan Touring* of Quito, the *Flotel Orellana* has first-class food and facilities. *Eastern* sponsors a Flotel Napo River Safari in cooperation with *Adventure Associates.* It's also possible to sign on for another *Eastern* jungle trip to the tropical Oriente region, where participants stay in tent camps and have the chance to do some unusual fishing. The local operator is *Sam Hogan Safaris,* Casilla S-122, Quito (phone: 45-02-42).

PERÚ: In Perú's eastern areas, part of the Amazon River basin, there are tropical birds, monkeys, deer, peccaries, capybaras, tapirs, and other animals. Among the tours to the Amazon region is one by *Peruvian Safaris,* Garcilaso de la Vega 1334, PO Box 10088, Lima (phone: 31-30-47), which takes you to the Tambopata Wildlife Preserve from Puerto Maldonado. Also, Victor Yohamona (Calle Cajamarca s/n, Lado Hospital, Puerto Maldonado) has been recommended as a fine guide who makes arrangements locally. In addition, contact *Eastern, Aero Perú,* or *Faucett* airlines in Miami for tours of the Iquitos Amazon area, with day excursions by river cruiser and canoe expeditions to see nocturnal animals. From the *Explorama Lodge,* which is 50 miles downriver from Iquitos, guides take groups for more rugged exploring to the Explornapo Camp. (See *Perú,* DIRECTIONS.) Closer to town is the *Amazon Safari Camp,* where guests usually stay for one or two nights. This is the departure point for Amazon River cruises aboard the MV *Margarita,* which sails between Iquitos and Leticia, Colombia. These Amazon programs can be booked through US tour operators.

SURINAME: Suriname has five nature preserves administered by the *Foundation for Nature Preservation in Suriname (STINASU).* Four of the preserves have basic accommodations, from hammocks to bungalows, where visitors may stay while observing the wildlife. *STINASU* makes a real effort to see that each trip is educational. It has published nature guides to the reserves and provides field trips, films, and lectures. A trip can be self-service or organized, as desired, simply by arranging to cook food in bungalow kitchenettes or going on a completely catered tour. For information, write *STINASU,* C. Jongbawstraat 10, PO Box 436, Paramaribo (phone: 75-85-4). You can also consult *Suriname Airways,* 6501 NW 36th St., Miami, FL 33166 (phone: 305-871-3602).

The 14,820-acre Brownsberg Reserve is 90 miles (145 km) south of Paramaribo and can be reached by car in 2½ hours. It stands at an elevation of 1,500 feet on the Mazaroni plateau. There are brocket deer, agoutis, peccaries, large gray-winged trumpeters, black curassows, and many other birds, giant toads, communal spiders, and seven species of monkey and jaguar.

At an elevation of 375 feet above the jungle, the Voltzberg Reserve can be reached only after a 3-hour trek on foot up to the top of a granite mountain. There are monkeys, trumpeter birds, and crickets living amid the surrounding rock slopes and granite plateaus.

Set among rivers, rapids, and waterfalls are the 149,000 acres of the Raleigh Falls Reserve, on the upper Coppename River. The reserve's headquarters and guest lodge are on Foengoe Island, a site replete with many birds. Travelers get to the Raleigh Falls Reserve by a 1-hour flight from Paramaribo or a 120-mile drive through savannah and jungle, followed by a 4-hour boat trip in a motorized dugout canoe.

There are two lodges on the 90,000-acre Wia-Wia Reserve, one at the mouth of the Matapica Canal and the other, Krofajapasi, on the west side of the reserve. These can be reached by a 2½-hour *STINASU* boat trip from Paramaribo or by road with a short boat trip. This reserve is home to scarlet ibis, egrets, herons, woodstorks, black skimmers, and thousands of migratory birds: roseate spoonbills, herons, storks, kites, terns, and crab-eating hawks, among others. Giant turtles also nest on the beaches.

Giant turtles are the attraction at the 10,000-acre Galibi Reserve. There are lodges at Galibi and nearby Babosensanti. This reserve is accessible by a 2-hour boat trip from Albina that passes by several Amerindian villages. As many as 500 Olive Ridley sea turtles were seen one night nesting on the Eilante Beach in the reserve. At both the Wia-Wia and Galibi reserves, the turtles come ashore to lay their eggs between February and July, but they can best be seen from March through June.

Prices at the reserves' lodges are moderate, but in some places it's necessary to bring along bedding. (Bedding costs extra.) At some places, you must also bring your own food. Transport in Suriname is fairly inexpensive; however, at this writing, travel through the interior is not very safe.

VENEZUELA: A jungle resort recently developed in the Canaima National Park can be reached only by air. Excursions arranged by the local *AVENSA* Airlines fly over the 3,212-foot Angel Falls. The guest lodge is rustic but comfortable, with space for 150 guests on a per-bed basis. The food is good, and there is swimming at the riverside beach by the lodge. There's an opportunity to see jungle wildlife on a variety of excursions run by local tour operators, ranging from a few hours to more than a week. These can be short river trips, one full-day trip in a motorized dugout canoe to Orchid Island, or a week-long trip on foot, by Jeep, and in dugout canoe to Angel Falls. In the US, contact the Venezuelan national airlines, *VIASA* (tour desk), 18 E 48th St., New York, NY 10017 (phone: 212-486-4370). In Miami, the AVENSA reservations number is 305-381-8001, and in Caracas, offices are at Av. Urduneta, corner of Platanal, in the Banco de Construcción y de Oriente building.

Downhill Skiing

 When it's sweltering at home and the favorite North American slopes have long turned green, it is peak ski season in South America. Whether dedicated skiers want to iron out the kinks so that they look like pros when winter comes back home, or whether the main appeal is merely the novelty of it all, it's great fun to ski in South America during July, August, and September. What's more, it's a snap to combine a sightseeing trip to Buenos Aires, Argentina, or Santiago, Chile, with a side trip to an Andean ski resort.

Mention South American skiing to anyone even vaguely knowledgeable about it, and two places come immediately to mind: Portillo, Chile, and Bariloche, Argentina (see *Chile* and *Argentina* in DIRECTIONS). Although these are far and away the best-known ski resorts, there are a number of others, mostly in the southern Andean region known as the Switzerland of South America or the Lake District.

There are slopes for skiers of all levels of expertise. Novice, intermediate, and once-a-year skiers will do well at San Martín de los Andes and Esquel in Argentina and at some of the smaller Chilean resorts. Ski bums, intermediate, and expert skiers rave about Portillo, especially the extremely difficult Roca Jack slope. And the most exciting new resort, *Valle de Las Leñas,* now offers world-class skiing near Mendoza, Argentina. There are other challenging runs at Bariloche and San Martín de los Andes. Families prefer the more organized facilities at Portillo, Bariloche, and San Martín de los Andes. Experts and hard-core downhill enthusiasts in search of a challenge even tackle the glaciers at Chacaltoy, Bolivia, the world's highest ski slope at 17,500 feet, or near Mérida, Venezuela, at 14,400 feet (see *Venezuela,* DIRECTIONS).

Officially, the season at most South American resorts opens in early July. But some places have better snow conditions later in the season. Portillo's light, deep powder is reputedly among the finest anywhere, especially in early July. San Martín de los Andes and Esquel, Argentina, have better spring skiing in September and sometimes October. Argentina has granular powder snow. The best time to ski Chacaltayo is July; Mérida, in July and August.

Facilities range from ultra-luxurious to downright rustic. Portillo's hotel is the most lavish and expensive, with the Bariloche resorts running a close second. Comfortable, clean accommodations can also be found near the slopes in other parts of Chile and Argentina. Most resorts are accessible by car, on pretty good roads. Others are close enough to major cities to be suitable for a day trip. Most ski areas have ski patrols, first-aid stations, and instructors who speak English, Spanish, and German.

To ski at the larger, better-organized places in Chile or Argentina, it's unnecessary to weigh yourself down with excess equipment. Just pack a parka, heavy sweater, and ski pants or warm-ups. All equipment, from skis to boots, can be rented right at the mountain. Professional skiers from the US report that some Andean resorts (particularly Portillo) have a nasty habit of overcharging on rentals, and you should keep a close eye on anything you do own, as equipment and clothing often get ripped off. There are no rental facilities in Bolivia, Venezuela, or at the smaller Chilean and Argentine resorts.

Inflation and currency fluctuation make it difficult to provide accurate prices for lift tickets or rental fees. Argentina's prices are generally the highest; expect to pay between $20 and $30 there, and about $10 a day at Chacaltayo.

Ski tours can be booked in the US through *Aerolíneas Argentinas'* offices and the group information desk at 9 Rockefeller Plaza, New York, NY 10020 (phone: 212-554-5142); brochures available. *Ladatco Tours* has several ski packages to Portillo, which include 7 nights at the resort and 3 nights in Santiago. 2220 Coral Way, Miami, FL 33145 (phone: 800-327-6162). Travel agents in Buenos Aires and Santiago can also arrange ski trips. *Austral Airlines,* a domestic Argentine carrier, operates *Sol Jet* tours to Bariloche.

ARGENTINA

Bariloche – A Swiss-like village perched on the southern shore of Lake Nahuel Huapi in the Argentine Andes, this resort is exceptionally crowded during the peak season. The Cerro Catedral slopes are about 12 miles (19 km) from town and are easily reached on good, paved roads. The Cerro (hill) derives its name from the natural formation of rock, which resembles a cathedral. The peak itself stands 6,888 feet above sea level, with a range of ski runs from novice to expert that cover almost 15½ miles. Facilities include a cable car with a 25-person capacity, 4 double chairs, and 3 T-bars with a total capacity of 5,000 people per hour. The longest run, about 2½ miles, will keep even an expert skier happy.

The official ski season opens on July 9 every year and continues through September, snow conditions permitting. Cerro Catedral is frequently the site of national and international competitions. The colorful Fiesta de la Nieve snow carnival takes place in August and should not be missed. Bear in mind that because Bariloche has become so popular with Argentines and other South Americans, interminable hours can be wasted waiting in lift lines during July and early August. However, restaurants and refuges midway down the slopes are refreshing places to stop, refuel, and avoid the crowded lines at the base of the mountain. Argentine and Austrian ski instructors give classes in Spanish, English, and German.

The *Catedral Ski* hotel, at the base of the lifts, is adequate and offers *après-ski* nightclub entertainment. There is also a hostel at Punta Condores, on the side of the mountain. During July and August, accommodations are scarce, so book ahead. For other hotels in Bariloche, see *Argentina,* DIRECTIONS.

Cerro Chapelco, near San Martín de los Andes – Smaller than Cerro Catedral and much less crowded, Chapelco has good spring skiing through September and offers a variety of slopes for novice, intermediate, and once-a-year skiers, with veritably no wait in any lift line. From the top of Chapelco (which means "water of chapel plant" in the Mapuche Indian dialect), it's possible to see the Lanín Volcano and Lake Lacar, which cross the Chilean border a few kilometers away.

Skiers can reach the 6,396-foot slopes by a triple chair lift, double chair lift, a T-bar, and poma lifts. The longest run, some 3.8 miles, is wide and gentle in most parts. There are smaller, more difficult offshoots to test even expert skiers.

Projects are under way to expand the mountain resort and add chalets and hotels around the base lodge, but there are still no hotels at the slopes. The town of San Martín de los Andes is only about 7 miles (11 km) down the mountain, snuggled at its base along the shores of Lake Lacar. There are comfortable lodgings here, some with meals, at very reasonable rates. Bungalow communities rent cabins with complete kitchens (including utensils), which can sleep as many as eight people for less than $50 per day. *Cabañas Lacar,* two blocks from the lake, is one of the best. *Los Pinos,* across the street, is also popular with skiers. It has clean, inexpensive rooms and good food.

The *Manolo* refuge, halfway down the main ski run, serves hearty lunches and snacks, so it's unnecessary to go all the way back to the base lodge. The cafeteria at the base serves decent, inexpensive meals. The *Jockey Club* restaurant, behind the central bank in San Martín de los Andes, offers a buffet: all you can eat for around $6.

In contrast to Bariloche's active nightlife, San Martín closes early, but the *Sol Jet* hotel (used primarily by *Sol Jet* ski tours) has a casino and nightclub. It's on a hill on the road to Cerro Chapelco.

Chapelco regulars recommend avoiding late July and early August — during school vacation break — unless you're coming for the annual Fiesta de la Montaña snow festival on August 5.

Ski equipment can be rented at the mountain's base lodge or at any of the ski shops along the main street of San Martín. If you don't speak Spanish, ask a resident to help you negotiate a price so that you are not overcharged. Ski students can take lessons from English-, Spanish-, or German-speaking Argentine or Austrian instructors.

Las Hoyas, Esquel – Much less well known, and certainly less jammed than either Chapelco or Catedral, these slopes are popular with learners, intermediate skiers, and infrequent skiers. The slopes are about 9 miles (15 km) from Esquel, which is about 155 miles (250 km) south of Bariloche. They have limited skiing, with a chair lift and T-bar to carry skiers up the slopes.

Las Hoyas' southern location makes it ideal for spring skiing; in fact, the season lasts through October. Many spring skiers, finding no snow at Catedral or Chapelco, make their way to Las Hoyas to finish the season. Equipment can be rented at the mountain and at Esquel. The Argentine instructors are quite good.

The best of several reasonably priced, clean hotels in Esquel are the *Vascongada* and *Ski Residencial.* The *Teluche* hotel, at the corner of Belgrano and 9 de Julio, is also good and serves some of the best meals in town. The *Mari-Mari* and *La Cabana* are popular restaurants, too, and are in the center of town.

Las Leñas – South of Mendoza and near the Chilean border, this new, 15,000-acre ski complex has all the potential to become the premiere ski resort of South America and is presently being used for training by French, Swiss, and American Olympic ski teams. It already has a ski school and equipment shops and will eventually include restaurants, shopping malls, and other attractions to complement the three existing hotels — *Escorpio, Acuario,* and *Geminis* — at the base of the lifts, which travel from a base elevation of 7,382 feet to 11,253 feet. Prime time is June through October. For reservations, contact Valle de Las Leñas, Suipacha 238, 1008 Buenos Aires (phone: 35-9921/5). For information and reservations in the US, phone 305-864-7545.

For more information about skiing in Argentina, write directly to the ski resorts or to the *Federación Argentina de Ski,* Viamonte 1560, Buenos Aires (phone: 40-71-27). In Buenos Aires, Bariloche, or Neuquen, check with any travel agent.

BOLIVIA

Chacaltaya, near La Paz – After skiing Chacaltaya, everything else is tame. Billed as the "world's highest ski slope," the glacial run at 17,500 feet is only for very accomplished skiers in peak condition. Relatively undiscovered, the slope is about a 2-hour drive from the world's highest capital (La Paz), on difficult, empty roads that challenge the brave and instill terror in anyone with even a mild fear of heights. The road is actually dangerous, with mind-bending hairpin turns twisting around sheer green shale cliffs that drop thousands of feet. Those who survive the ride, and do not succumb to altitude sickness, will probably find the spartan restaurant and ski hut next to the Bolivian Institute for Cosmic Physics complex a fascinating change from more sophisticated resorts. There are now two hook tows which take skiers from the edge of a cliff to the top of the Chacaltaya Glacier to begin the descent. The best times to ski are January through April (when the snow is cold and there is a good powder) and October and November. Later in the season, it gets too windy and icy. The tow fee is about $5. Bring your own equipment, since the ski rental shop is open only on weekends. Contact Ricardo Ramos (372-920). For more information on skiing, contact the *Club Andino Boliviano*, Calle México, La Paz.

CHILE

Portillo – Probably the best-known South American ski resort, this is also the toughest. Many national and international competitions have been held here, including World Cup Ski Championships. The world's speed record, 124 mph, was set here by American Steve McKinney in 1978.

Some 93 miles (150 km) northeast of Santiago in the Cordillera de los Andes, 9,348 feet above sea level, Portillo's granular powder slopes have challenged skiers for more than 40 years. The seven main runs are reached by seven lifts, including a double chair, T-bars, and tows. Lift lines are shorter than at Bariloche. Although the season runs from May through October, depending on snow conditions, expert skiers agree that the period from July to early August is best.

But it's not necessary to be a dynamite skier to try the slopes. Beginners can start on an 861-foot run along a 305-foot slope served by a tow lift, graduating to the Plateau, a 2,736-foot run with a 981-foot slope served by a ski chair. Juncalillo, the longest and best intermediate slope, is a run of 4,595 feet with a slope of 1,105 feet. Other slopes are Enlace, 1,040 feet with a 266-foot slope, and Nido de Condores, 1,170 feet with a 513-foot slope. The most challenging slope of all is Roca Jack, 2,760 feet, of which 1,000 feet are vertical. For those who have never skied, there's a bunny hill of 845 feet and a 211-foot slope. Siggi Grottendorfer, an Austrian, operates a ski school where there are private or group lessons in beginning, intermediate, and advanced skiing. The Roca Jack and Plateau runs come together at the bottom, forming a V.

Despite its glamorous reputation as a jet-set resort, Portillo is becoming more popular with Argentines and Chileans than with Europeans and Americans, although foreign teams from the north do come to Portillo to train during the off season. Professional US skiers have been openly expressing disappointment about the way skiers are overcharged for renting skis and for using the facilities at the one hotel. They also caution that theft of clothing and equipment is now a big problem. So keep your eye on everything that's yours, and don't leave anything lying around.

Robert Purcell, an investment banker whose New York holding company took financial control of Portillo in 1963, now runs the entire mountain-hotel resort complex. The 650-bed *Portillo* hotel on the shores of the blue glacier lake, Laguna del Inca, has a cinema, nightclub, swimming pool, sauna, and medical station. Reservations can be made at its office in Santiago, Calle Don Carlos 3227, Departamento C (phone: 28-65-01). Or in the US contact LAN Chile Airlines (phone: 800-327-3614) for ski package information and reservations. (For a full description of Portillo, see *Chile*, DIRECTIONS.)

Farellones, near Santiago – About a 1-hour drive from downtown, this is an ideal day trip, and thousands of Chileans descend on the place on winter weekends. There are three easy runs (good for beginners and intermediates), the longest of which is 5,576 feet. All can be reached by a T-bar and tow lift. Reservations can be made at the *Farellones* hotel by telephoning 250 in San Francisco de las Condes.

La Parva, near Santiago – Another very popular weekend ski area, its five runs (beginner and intermediate) have about 1,640 feet of vertical drop.

El Colorado, near Santiago – Actually, it's between Farellones and La Parva. There are four slopes reached by a chair lift and a T-bar; the longest is 6,560 feet.

Lagunillas, near Santiago – This small ski station, only 6,560 feet above sea level, 37 miles east of the city, is relatively new. Only two slopes have currently been prepared for skiing. The road to Lagunillas winds around the Cajón del Maipu, one of the most enchanting valleys in Chile (see *Santiago,* THE CITIES.) The *Club Andino de Chile* runs a clean, inexpensive refuge. For reservations, contact the club at Calle Foster 29, Santiago.

Chillán, near Santiago – About 50 miles (80.5 km) southeast of the capital, at 6,232 feet above sea level, this small ski area has two runs about 980 feet long.

Antuco, near Concepción – Three slopes run down the side of an inactive volcano, the Volcán Antuco, 9,790 feet above sea level. All can be reached by a T-bar. There are university-sponsored cabins and a small refuge. Reservations can be made at the University of Concepción or in the village of Los Angeles, 115 miles (184 km) southwest of Antuco. Although a road goes to the ski station, it's also possible to fly in by small plane. The nearest airport is only about 4 miles away.

Llaima, near Temuco – Another spot recommended for beginners. The highest of the two slopes is 5,904 feet above sea level.

Villarrica, near Pucon – Several short, easy runs reached by chair lift and T-bar.

Antillanca, near Bariloche, Argentina – Nowhere as large as the resorts across the border, this ski area has three medium-length runs serviced by T-bars.

VENEZUELA

Mérida – Not far from this Andean town, at an elevation of 14,400 feet, there is glacial skiing for the utterly determined. Bring your own equipment and be prepared to do about 2 hours of hiking and climbing to get to the top of the Timoncito Glacier after a cable car ride from Mérida. There are no lifts, and unless you hire your own helicopter in Caracas, no other means of transport. There are no facilities en route other than totally spartan mountaineers' huts. Some people do attempt it between June and September, but skiing is not very popular here.

Hunting

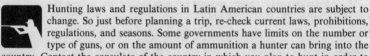

Hunting laws and regulations in Latin American countries are subject to change. So just before planning a trip, re-check current laws, prohibitions, regulations, and seasons. Some governments have limits on the number or type of guns, or on the amount of ammunition a hunter can bring into the country. Contact the consulate of the country in which you plan to hunt in order to arrange to bring your weapons along with you. You will probably be asked to supply information on the make, model, caliber, and serial number of your arms, as well as your passport number, home address, addresses in the country you are visiting, arrival and departure dates, and the places you plan to hunt. Check with the consulate to see whether you must register with local police or other organizations once you get into the country. If the consulate doesn't know, try other sources — hunting organizations or travel agents — and by all means, check again once you get into the country.

Note that United States federal law prohibits the import of any animal or bird considered an endangered species. For a list, write the US Department of the Interior, Fish and Wildlife Service, PO Box 28006, Washington, DC 20005.

ARGENTINA: Hunting is permitted for deer, puma, wild boar, peccary, partridge, duck, and wild turkey. Although jaguar and tapir exist, hunting them is now prohibited. Deer hunting season runs from March through April in Neuquén, the southern lake district, La Pampa, and along the Atlantic coast. The black buck can be hunted all year south of Santa Fe and in Buenos Aires province. Wild boar can be hunted all year in La Pampa and along the coast of the province of Buenos Aires and Bahía Blanca; puma, throughout the year, everywhere it is found. Puma hunting is best in

La Pampa, Río Negro, and Neuquén. Peccaries are hunted all year in the northern provinces of Salta, Santiago del Estero, and Formosa.

Partridge season runs from June through August. The bird is found all over the country. Duck can be hunted during the spring season in Santa Fe and Buenos Aires province; wild turkey, during May through July in Chubut province, especially in Trevelin. There are limits on hunting partridge and wild turkey.

Red deer does with their young cannot be taken, or red deer with less than twelve points, and a hunter is not allowed to bag more than two red deer per season.

Firearms must be registered with the *Registro Nacional de Armas* (Figueroa Alcorta 3301, Buenos Aires 1425) before a hunter enters the country. Be sure to secure a permit from this office. Send your name, nationality, passport number, and home address; temporary address in Argentina; length of stay; where and how (plane, train, bus) you will enter the country; the type, model, caliber, and serial number of your arms; and type, caliber, and quantity of ammunition. A hunter is allowed to bring two big-game, two small-game, and one hand gun into Argentina.

To secure hunting permits, go to the National Park Service if you wish to hunt in a national park or to the provincial tourist office in the province in which you wish to hunt. The provincial tourist office can also help you locate a hunting guide. If you want a guide in the San Martín de los Andes area, go to the National Park Service, the *intendencia* of the Lanín National Park, or the tourist information office.

The National Park Service is at Santa Fe 690, Buenos Aires, and the tourist information office, at Santa Fe 883, Buenos Aires.

April through July, there is a waterfowl hunting tour to the southern lake district around Esquel. Contact *Safari Outfitters,* 8 S Michigan Ave., Chicago, IL 60603 (phone: 312-346-9631).

BOLIVIA: Hunting or fishing in Bolivia is permitted with a license, good for one calendar year, available from the US Embassy or the Ministry of Agriculture. You need two small photographs and must pay a nominal fee. If you want to meet other hunters, visit the *Club de Caza y Pesca (Hunting and Fishing Club)* in front of the golf club in Malasilla.

BRAZIL: Guides are available for hunting water buffalo, birds, and animals on the Island of Marajó, at the mouth of the Amazon, and nearby in Macupá.

COLOMBIA: The list of game animals and birds in Colombia is extensive and ranges from water to prairie to jungle fauna: jaguar, tiger, wildcat, ocelot, tapir, puma, black panther, leopard, deer, beaver, possum, several types of monkey, parrot, alligator, armadillo, iguana, turtle, anaconda, boa, duck, goose, dove, partridge, and wild pig. Hunting jaguar, tiger, and monkey is prohibited.

In the swamps and prairies around Cartagena are duck, geese, deer, and wild pig. To hunt this area, contact Jaime Borda (phone: 47-93-7, 41-97-9). Jaime speaks English, has gear, and knows the best hunting spots. For safaris into the Sierra Nevada, contact Captain "Pancho" Ospina at his office on El Rodadero Beach in Santa Marta.

Around Cali, there is small-game hunting for duck, dove, and partridge. Contact *La Rivera Club* through your hotel for assistance. *Safari World Adventures Travels (SWAT),* 10152 Jefferson Hwy., New Orleans, LA 70123 (phone: 504-738-9816), runs a dove-hunting tour around Cali. *SWAT* will provide a hunting license, 12- and 20-gauge Remington automatics, and accommodations in the *Inter-Continental Cali* hotel for the non-hunting part of the tour.

Another dove-hunting tour in the Cauca Valley, around Cali, is sponsored by *Safari de Colombia,* Box 777, Cali (phone: 64-17-49 or 86-18-06). A hunter can rent guns and purchase shells locally. The 5-day tour runs throughout the year, as there is open season on doves. *Safari de Colombia* also offers a duck-shooting tour at Cienega Grande, near Santa Marta, the wintering ground for teal, widgeon, scaup, pintail, shoveler, and other duck.

ECUADOR: There's pigeon shooting near Quito, partridge and deer hunting in the highlands. During the dry season (September through March), for a jungle safari in the Oriente to hunt capybara, paca, peccary, and tapir, contact *Sam Hogan Safaris,* Casilla A-122, Quito (phone: 45-02-42).

To hunt in Ecuador, get a permit from the *Dirección de Parques Forestales,* Ministerio de Agricultura, 5th floor, Guayaquil 1740 (phone: 51-72-00).

SURINAME: Tapir, deer, wild boar (*pingo*), capybara, jaguar, and a genus of crocodile called cayman live in Suriname. The season for most big game is May 1 through December 31, although jaguar and cayman can be hunted all year (except for black cayman, which is a protected group). There's also hunting for waterfowl, jungle cats, and howler monkeys. The hunting season for wild duck runs from September 1 through March 31; for the Amazon parrot, from June 1 through December 31. The hunting season for most birds is September 1 through April 30, except for the wild dove, which can be hunted all year. The hunting of flamingos and ibises is prohibited, as is the killing of most types of turtle. No hunting is permitted in nature reserves.

Big-game hunting parties can be arranged with the help of local tour operators. For a referral list, contact the *Suriname Airways,* 6501 NW 36th St., Miami, FL 33166 (phone: 305-871-3602), or the *Suriname Tourist Development Board,* Kerkplein 10, Paramaribo. The Development Board issues forms for hunting licenses for a small fee. Send your name, the make and caliber of your guns, and the number of cartridges you plan to carry when writing for a license application. Shotguns can be provided by tour operators, or you can bring your own into the country free of charge for up to 3 months. No rifles or sidearms are permitted.

For the Mind

Lost Worlds: The Archaeological Heritage of South America

Even more fabulous than the legends of Golden Empires that lured the Spanish and Portuguese to South America in the 15th and 16th centuries were the indigenous civilizations that flourished at that time and earlier.

The mystery of pre-Columbian history can best be appreciated by visiting any one of the archaeological sites scattered throughout the Southern Hemisphere. Massive stonework, intricately carved into dazzling shapes by unknown masons, stand piled in patterned formation. Some are in areas so remote and sparsely settled that it's an authentic mystery how anyone ever decided to build there.

The fascination about the lives of the people who actually built and lived in the complex structures of these vanished civilizations draws thousands upon thousands of visitors to South America every year. The archaeological site with biggest box office appeal is Machu Picchu, a terraced complex of stairways, temples, and mazes on a mountainside not far from the Andean city of Cuzco. Machu Picchu is one of many archaeological sites with competently guided tours of its ruins, and in Perú in particular — and the Andean countries in general — the guides employed by tour operators are, for the most part, well trained and knowledgeable. Read about the places you plan to visit before your arrival, since there is very little (if any) historical information distributed at the sites. Generally, they are very far off the beaten path. Whenever possible, spend a day in the capital visiting the archaeological museums for background, and consider taking along an English-Spanish dictionary since exhibits are generally described in Spanish. Check the bookstores for locally published guides; some are very good.

Other major sites are at Tiahuanaco, near La Paz, Bolivia; San Agustín in Colombia; the Nazca Desert line drawings in southern Perú; and Easter Island, off the coast of Chile. But there are dozens of smaller ruins, many of which are still being excavated — and more that have not yet been discovered. This is the place where the really adventurous have actually come upon previously undiscovered lost worlds. The site of Gran Pajaten, for example, was recently discovered (in 1985) by a couple of Colorado doctors who mounted their own expedition.

ARGENTINA

Although not the first stop on an archaeological itinerary, Argentina does have some notable pre-Columbian and colonial ruins.

INCAHUASI: Some 4 miles (about 6 km) northeast of the Ingeniero Mauri Railroad Station in Salta, it has extensive remains of a stone Inca fortress.

TASTIL: In the Quebrada del Toro area, near Puerta de Tastil, about 54 miles (87 km) northwest of Salta, are the remains of an ancient Indian dwelling.

MOROHUASI: These ruins of old pre-Columbian dwellings, Inca roads, walls, and art are about 3 miles (5 km) south of the Quebrada del Toro and 7 miles (11 km) northeast of the Diego de Almagro Station in Salta.

TOLOMBON: About 131 miles (210 km) from Salta, in the valley of Santa Maria, some pre-Hispanic ruins are scattered to the east of town. The best way to get there is to walk.

TILCARA: About 50 miles (81 km) north of San Salvador de Jujuy, are some partially restored pre-Columbian ruins — chambers, stairways, tombs, and terraces.

UQUIA: A small town in the Quebrada de Humahuaca, in the state of Jujuy, the remains of Inca ruins are still visible at Peñas Blancas, 3 miles (5 km) from Uquia.

CAYASTA: About 52 miles (84 km) northeast from Santa Fe stands the city founded by Juan de Garay in 1573 to serve as a stopover between Asunción and the kingdoms of Perú. The city became quite developed for its time, but because of the attacks from Indians and the floods from the Paraná River, it was transplanted a century later and became what today is Santa Fe.

ACONQUIJA: About 20 miles (32 km) from Concepción, in the state of Tucumán, at an elevation of 13,448 feet, are some small dwellings and ancient roads.

BOLIVIA

TIAHUANACO: The capital of a civilization believed to be anywhere between 1,000 and 3,000 years old, this 50-acre site — Bolivia's most impressive archaeological zone — has yet to be fully excavated. The center of the pre-Inca Aymará empire, it reached its peak between AD 600 and 900. The major sections are the Gateway of the Sun, a massive doorway carved from a single piece of stone; the Great Idol of Tiahuanaco, a sandstone block with square figures surrounding a central figure said to represent the god Viracocha; some stone monoliths between 9 and 12 feet high; and the ruins of Kalasasaya Palace, a 442-by-426-foot rectangular plaza marked by 20-foot-high perpendicular stones. Nearby stands the Acapaña pyramid. About 42 miles (68 km) from La Paz, Tiahuanaco is accessible by a rugged road (see *Bolivia,* DIRECTIONS).

THE ISLANDS OF THE MOON AND THE SUN, LAKE TITICACA: According to Inca legend, Inti, the sun god, created two children, a boy and a girl named Manco Capac and Mama Occlo, whom he placed on the Island of the Sun. Then he gave them a golden staff, commanding them to found an empire on the spot where the staff would vanish into the earth. In the course of their journey, Manco Capac and Mama Occlo came upon a valley where the staff disappeared. This became the city of Cuzco. The Island of the Moon, or Coati, in the lake, was consecrated by the Incas to their deities, with priestesses (ñustas) in charge of ceremonies of worship. The ruins of the Palace of the Vestal Virgins and a temple to the Moon Mother can also be found on the Island of the Moon. About 100 feet below the surface of the water, divers have found submerged stone walls, believed to be the original Inca city.

CHILE

PUCARA DE LASANA: This pre-Inca fort, to the east of Chuquicamata, has been declared a national monument.

CHIU-CHIU: About 21 miles (34 km) northeast of Calama stands an Indian fortress, a cave with rock etchings, and an archaeological museum.

SAN PEDRO DE ATACAMA: The highlight of Chilean archaeological sites, this town, 60 miles (96 km) southeast of Calama, houses an archaeological museum of mummies, skeletons, and artifacts excavated from the Atacama Desert. Originally inhabited by the Cunzas or Atacamenian Indians, the town was conquered by Don Diego de Almagro in 1536. About 20 miles (32 km) south of San Pedro de Atacama, at Toconao, is a section of the original Inca Highway.

GUAIQUIVILO: Not far from Parral, at an elevation of 9,840 feet, stand the so-called talking stones. Actually huge chunks of rock from the Andean Cordillera, carved with symbols, their markings have not yet been deciphered.

EASTER ISLAND (RAPA NUI): About 1,000 giant stone gods called moais, each between 30 and 40 feet high, are scattered all over the island. They are covered with unintelligible inscriptions, and the mystery as to how and when they were moved continues to puzzle anthropologists, archaeologists, and laypeople. Some evidence dates human presence on the island as early as 530 BC. Carbon 14 dating methods give a reading of AD 386. The biggest ones, measuring around 150 feet in height, can be found in Vinapu and Tongariki. Other stone constructions, ancient tombs, and funeral monuments can be found in other parts of the island (see Chile, DIRECTIONS).

COLOMBIA

SAN AGUSTÍN ARCHAEOLOGICAL PARK: The most elaborate stone carvings in South America are found here, in the Valley of the Statues, about 145 miles (233 km) from Neiva. A few hundred stone figures of men, animals, and gods are scattered over 14 widely separated sites. Many appear to bear strong similarities to the Tiahuanaco carvings. According to Carbon 14 dating methods, the earliest section of San Agustín is Alto de Lavapatas, which dates back to 555 BC. The Lavapatas, or footwashing fountain, is a series of small water ducts carved in the face of a huge, relatively flat rock about 550 square feet in area. The ducts carried water from a stream into terraced pools. It takes about 3 or 4 days to see the most important sites and statues. The archaeological zone is accessible only by four-wheel-drive vehicle or horse (see *Colombia,* DIRECTIONS).

TIERRADENTRO: From either starting point, Neiva or Popayán, the road is rough to San Andrés and the burial caves of Tierradentro. But the scenic trip is worth every bump, the cave paintings are fantastic; bring a flashlight for viewing. Area artifacts are housed in the small San Andrés Museum where it's possible to camp out or stay in the nearby tourist hotel (see *Colombia,* DIRECTIONS).

TAYRONA NATIONAL PARK: To prevent looting, the Colombia government has sealed off one of the largest ancient lost cities ever found. Reliable sources working at the excavation report that the pre-Columbian center was once populated by hundreds of thousands of people. Aviatur, a Bogotá tour operator, has excursions to this "lost city." Check with the Colombian Government Tourist Office in New York City (212-688-0151) for booking information.

ECUADOR

INGAPIRCA: About 43 miles (70 km) from Cuenca, in the province of Canar, stands a castle built by Huayna Capac, the last Inca, during the 15th century. Reachable by car or bus, the ruins are positioned along the Inca road network in the midst of rough, impressive Andean scenery. Its fortlike design, uniquely fashioned chambers, and strange bathtub carvings in stone cliffs far from water are all being excavated by scientists and studied. Not far from Cuenca, archaeologists have uncovered golden crowns, breastplates, and weapons (see *Ecuador,* DIRECTIONS).

RUMICUCHO: Outside Quito, near the Equator Monument at San Antonio de Pichincha, are the ruins of the Temple of Rumicucho, which is one of the largest pre-Columbian sites in the country. A museum at the site is planned.

PANAMÁ

PUNTA ESCOSÉS: In the hot, steamy jungles of Darién Gap, a group of explorers led by Lieutenant-Colonel John Blashford-Snell and Vincent Martinelli of New York's Explorers Club have recently uncovered a remarkable set of ruins. In 1978, they discovered the remains of Fort St. Andrews, the site of an ancient Scottish colony founded in 1698 on the northern coast of eastern Panamá. Keen to know more about the ill-fated colony that ended with the death of some 2,000 men, the expedition members explored deeper into the Isthmus and discovered what are believed to be the first remains of the lost city of Acla, founded by Balboa around 1509, prior to his discovery of the Pacific. Defying schools of barracudas and inquisitive sharks, the expedition's divers also found traces of sunken vessels in the area. Other finds included a fort's moat, a lookout and defensive position built out of coral blocks cut from nearby reefs, a cannonball of the type used in Scotland in the late 17th century, pieces of glazed pottery, and fragments of glass. A complete excavation of the site has been impossible because it is so overgrown by the jungle. One hypothesis of the Fort St. Andrews saga suggests that some of the colonists survived, intermarried with the Cuna Indians, and sired a unique, now lost tribe of red-haired, blue-eyed, dusky Scottish Indians.

PERÚ

Unquestionably the South American nation with the richest archaeological heritage, Perú is the home of the incomparable lost city of the Incas, Machu Picchu, one of the most visited destinations on the continent. But the discovery of lost cities has not ended in Perú, and new sites are uncovered yearly, such as a "sister city" to Machu Picchu which encompasses agricultural terraces and irrigation systems, plus a ritual center with 30 tombs. Or the new sites of the Chanca culture which were found in the Chicah Valley north of Cuzco. And then, in the northern province of San Martín, the newest of the old lost cities, Gran Pajaten, occupied by an unknown people from AD 500 to 1500. Presently, this newly discovered site is under excavation and is closed to visitors.

When Pizarro and his conquistadores arrived in Perú in 1527, the Inca empire, Tahuantinsuyo, stretched along the Pacific coast, through the Andes, as far north as the present northern border of Ecuador and as far south as the Maule River in central Chile.

Though the most famous, the Inca civilization was only the latest of the early South American cultures, reaching its height between AD 1100 and 1500. Around 1470, the Incas conquered the Chimú Indians, whose central city, Chan-Chan, still stands. Predating both groups, the Paracas and Nazca Indians flourished in the deserts of southern Perú 3,000 and 4,000 years ago. Their pottery, mysterious line drawings, and mummies can still be seen (see *Perú,* DIRECTIONS).

MACHU PICCHU: Accessible by train or a 4- or 5-day hike, this incredible complex of temples, houses, baths, hundreds of stairways, and a guardhouse rises 2,000 feet above the valley of the Río Urubamba, the sacred river of the Incas. Discovered in 1911 by American Hiram Bingham, it has more than 100 acres of hard granite block buildings, walls, and plazas. Dr. Bingham separated the city into three distinct sections: the Ingenuity Group, so called because of ingeniously constructed houses set on giant rocks at 45° angles and linked by numerous stairways; the Princess Group, which includes the circular tower built into a rock, a sundial in a cave under the tower, and several stairways; and the Religious Group, containing the Temple of the Three Windows and the priest's house. Recently discovered finds, dating from the 15th and 16th centuries, include agricultural terraces and a ritual center with 30 tombs.

HUAYNA PICCHU: For the best view of the whole city of Machu Picchu, hike up this steep mountain. The strenuous exercise is well worth the effort. At its summit, there are stairways that date from Inca times, stonework, and three small caves.

HUIÑA Y HUAYNA: An 8-hour hike from Machu Picchu, this smaller, abandoned Inca city, whose name means "growing boy," is set on a hillside next to a waterfall, in superb isolation. Overgrown with jungle vegetation, Huiña Y Huayna consists of stone buildings, arches, doorways, and stairs (see Perú, *The Wild Continent: Hiking, Backpacking, and Camping,* DIRECTIONS).

OLLANTAYTAMBO: About halfway between Machu Picchu and Cuzco, this giant fortress stands on a hill overlooking the valley. The remains of circular defense towers guard the lower slopes. But the most unusual section is a wall formed by six huge polished slabs set upright with stone wedges in between. The boulders are said to come from quarries on the opposite side of the mountain.

SACSAHUAMÁN: This impressive fortress, with three gateways and the remains of three towers, stands on a hill overlooking Cuzco. To the east, the Inca temple of Kenko consists of a large boulder set upright on a platform in front of a group of other boulders, with many steps cut from the stone. About 1 mile (1.6 km) beyond Kenko, the small fort of Puca-Pucara dominates two valleys, where there are entrances to tunnels that are said to be connected to Sacsahuaman and Cuzco. According to legend, at least one of the Inca tunnels went all the way to Ecuador.

PISAC FORTRESS CITY: The largest of the fortified cities that guarded Inca Cuzco, the stone complex sits high above Pisac. A road leads about 7 miles (11 km) to the foot of the multiterraced ruins that include a sun temple, baths, guard towers, royal dwellings, and a cliff-burial cemetery. The site is called Intihuatana.

PUCARA: On km 285 of the Cuzco-Puno highway, this was the ceremonial center of another lost city. Artifacts resembling those of Tiahuanaco were discovered in May 1976. Carved rocks, pyramids, and streets cover an area of 2½ square miles at an altitude of 12,792 feet. Several monoliths, one 4½ feet high, stand around the area. Archaeologists believe they were sacred symbols. A temple of carved red rocks, 115 feet in diameter, has also been unearthed.

SILLUSTANI: Heading north from Puno on the shores of Lake Titicaca, follow the turnoff to Lake Umayo. About 15 miles (24 km) from Puno stand the *chulpas* (pre-Columbian funeral towers) of Sillustani, a puzzling sight. Don't miss it.

PARACAS: South of Lima, Paracas is the center and burial place of an Indian culture that flourished more than 3,000 years ago. In the cemetery, Paracas Necropolis, mummies buried in elaborate textiles have been discovered. There's a good museum here.

TAMBO COLORADO: Between Pisco and Paracas lies one of the best-preserved palace complexes of pre-Columbian Perú; some of the original wall paintings remain. This is a worthwhile detour off the coastal road south from Lima.

NAZCA: The famous Peruvian line drawings are in the desert plains between Nazca and Palpa. The Pan-American Highway goes through the heart of the area, but visitors will not be able to see anything from the road. Contact *Aero Condor,* with flights to and over Nazca, at the *Sheraton* hotel, Paseo de la República, Lima (phone: 32-90-50). The designs are believed to have been made as long as 3,000 or 4,000 years ago. The purpose of the lines is subject of constant speculation: Some say they could have served as a calendar or as stellar images. Straight lines, huge triangles, animals, and spiral forms can be seen over the entire area. For guests staying at the *Las Dunas* hotel in Ica, AeroCondor runs a flight over the Nazca drawings; the plane departs from the hotel's landing strip. (See *Perú,* DIRECTIONS.)

CHAN-CHAN: Near Trujillo, the adobe ruins of Chan-Chan cover 11 square miles. Formerly the center of the Chimú empire that stretched from Guayaquil, Ecuador, to the south of Perú, this walled city contained reservoirs, temples, and gardens for its 50,000 inhabitants. It reached its height around AD 1300. The city was discovered by the Incas around 1470, but was ultimately destroyed by the Spanish, who also stole the silver and gold ornaments. Today, the deteriorated city walls contain remains of gardens, houses, canals, and temples. To the north of Chan-Chan, at the mouth of the Chicama River, Huaca Prieta contains subterranean houses lined with stone and roofed with earth.

CHAVÍN: The stone carvings found at the site of this Indian temple are believed to be 3,000 years old. The Chavín civilization appeared at almost the same time as the Olmec civilization in Mexico, and their architecture, sculpture, and carved ceramics were similar. The temple is about 38 miles from Huaráz, on the road to Recuay.

PARAMONGA: About 114 miles (184 km) north of Lima, past the town of Pativilca, this imposing structure was the scene of the Chimús' final, desperate resistance to the advancing Incas in the mid-15th century. Archaeologists disagree about its basic purpose — was it a fortress or a religious ceremonial center?

PACHACÁMAC: About 20 miles (32 km) from Lima, this complex contains contains a pyramid built around the 1300s, the Temple of Pachacamac, the Inca Temple of the Sun, and the House of the Virgins of the Moon.

Memorable Museums

Compared to Europe, South America has a rather limited selection of excellent museums. There are, however, some notable collections. The gold museums in Bogotá and Lima are among the most famous in the world, and Brazil has several unusually fine art museums. Where available, buy English-language guides, particularly for the archaeological museums.

BRAZIL

EMILIO GOELDI MUSEUM: For those who venture no farther up the Amazon than its mouth, this collection of Amazonian Indian relics and exhibits on Amazon life and history (adjoining a zoo with animals from the region) provides an idea of what the interior is like. Av. Magalhães Barata 518, Belém (phone: 222-1544).

ARCHDIOCESE MUSEUM (ARQUIDIOCESANO MUSEU): The works of Brazil's foremost colonial sculptor, Antonio Francisco Lisboa — known as Aleijadinho or "the little cripple" — and of his contemporary, painter João Ataide, can be found here along with Portuguese silverware and religious art. The museum is in Mariana, a few miles from Ouro Preto, on Rua Frei Durao.

OURO PRETO: The center of the Brazilian revolution against the Portuguese in 1922, Ouro Preto is so densely packed with colonial history and art that the entire town has been declared a national monument. Many of Aleijadinho's works are found in the São Francisco de Assisi Church, most notably the altar and carvings. Others can be found in the Carmel, São Jose, and All Souls churches. The *Teatro Municipal,* actually an opera house, is the oldest theater in Brazil. Rua Brig, Mosqueira. The Casa dos Contos, built in 1782, is one of the best examples of Brazilian colonial architecture. The Museum of the School of Mines (Centro de Estudos do Ciclo do Ouro) contains 1,500 different types of stones from all over the country. Rua São Jose 12. (For a complete description of Ouro Preto, see *Brazil,* DIRECTIONS.)

GOLD MUSEUM (MUSEU DO OURO): One of Brazil's richest museums stands in Sabará, about 12 miles (19 km) from Belo Horizonte, a town founded by the *bandeirantes* (pioneers) who were one of the largest suppliers of gold to Portugal. In a house built in 1730, it contains a complete collection of relics and documents from the gold rush era, as well as gold bars imprinted with the Portuguese royal seal. Rua da Intendencia, Sabará.

IMPERIAL MUSEUM (MUSEU IMPERIAL): The summer home of the former royal family houses the Imperial Crown and other items from the royal era. There are also a library and extensive park grounds. Av. 7 de Setembro, Petropolis. Closed Mondays.

MUSEUM OF ANTHROPOLOGY OF NORTHEASTERN MAN: A complex of superb exhibitions, with excellent displays of the costumes, folklore, music, and general lifestyles of the different peoples settled in this Brazilian region. In addition, there is the Sugar Museum, which traces the industry from the days of the colonial mills and slave labor to more modern modes of production. Av. 17 de Agosto 2187, Recife (phone: 268-2000).

BOTANICAL GARDENS (JARDIM BOTÂNICO): This outdoor nature museum has hundreds of varieties of plants and trees. The Victoria Regia water lilies that grow up to 6 feet in diameter are white the first day they bloom; pink on the second day; red, the third. Open daily. Free. Rua Jardim Botanico, Rio de Janeiro.

CARMEN MIRANDA MUSEUM: This quirky, charming place is filled with exotic mementos of the woman who made high-wedged shoes and fancy headpieces her trademark. Closed Mondays. Small admission charge. Parque Flamengo, Rio de Janeiro (phone: 226-2767).

SACRED ART MUSEUM (MUSEU DE ARTE SACRO): This important collection of religious paintings, sculpture, furniture, and objects wrought of gold is housed in the monastery and church of Santa Teresa. Some items were brought from the Old World; others were made nearby. Closed Sundays and Mondays. Admission charge. Rua do Sodre 25, Salvador (Bahía) (phone: 243-6310).

THE CARMO CONVENT MUSEUM (MUSEU DO CONVENTO DO CARMO): A beautiful Carmelite church on top of a hill has dolls in religious costumes, ceremonial objects of gold, silver, and precious stones, and an exhibit on the relationships between *candomblé* gods and Christian saints. Open daily. Free. Largo de Carmo, Salvador (Bahía) (phone: 3-04-29).

Contemporary Bahian art, among the most distinctive in Brazil, can be found in many art galleries in the upper city. See *Salvador (Bahía),* THE CITIES.

THE SÃO PAULO ART MUSEUM (MASP): Known as one of the best art museums on the continent, this extensive collection contains works from the Middle Ages to the present. Works by Rembrandt, Toulouse-Lautrec, Renoir, El Greco, Cézanne, Van Gogh, Modigliani, and several modern Brazilian painters are mounted on plastic stands rather than hung on the walls. Closed Mondays. Free. Av. Paulista 1578, São Paulo (phone: 289-1408).

PAULISTA MUSEUM: A converted palace, this museum contains old maps, coins, firearms, colonial furniture, and art. It's set in Ipiranga Park, where graceful fountains and statues stand amid the foliage. A sound and light show is presented in the evenings. Closed Mondays. Small admission charge. Parque Ipiranga, São Paulo (phone: 63-11-24).

CASA DO BANDEIRANTE MUSEUM: A large, reconstructed 18th-century *bandeirante* home, it has rope hammocks, trunks, and authentic furniture. Oxcarts are scattered throughout the museum grounds, along with three old-fashioned mills. The *bandeirantes* were the first settlers in the São Paulo region. Closed Mondays. Free. Praça Monteiro Lobato, São Paulo (phone: 211-0920).

SACRED ART MUSEUM (MUSEU DE ARTE SACRO): Paulistas claim that this convent-turned-museum houses the largest collection of altars, statues, and altarpieces outside the Vatican. English-speaking guides can be reserved in advance. Closed Mondays. Small admission charge. Av. Tiradentes 676, São Paulo (phone: 228-4063).

COLOMBIA

THE GOLD MUSEUM (MUSEO DEL ORO): This is one of the "must" sights that any trip to South America should include. More than 15,000 pieces of pre-Columbian goldwork from the Calima, Tolima, and Muisca cultures, worth tens of millions of dollars, are housed in the three-story museum. Objects in the form of frogs, insects, animals, serpents, birds, masks, armor, shields, human figures, and instruments are carefully displayed for maximum impact. The choicest items are kept in an intricately illuminated special vault. All the items are carefully labeled, with additional synopses on Indian culture providing background. For a thorough lesson in pre-Columbian culture and art, plan to spend at least a few hours in this museum. Open daily. Free. Calle 16 No. 4-41, Bogotá (phone: 281-3600).

ARCHAEOLOGICAL MUSEUM: A restored 17th–18th-century home is the setting for one of Latin America's most stunning collections of pre-Columbian ceramics from Colombia, Ecuador, Perú, and Mexico. Closed Mondays. Admission charge. Carrera No. 7-43, Bogotá (phone: 282-0940).

MUSEUM OF POPULAR ART AND TRADITION (MUSEO DE ARTES Y TRADIC-IONES POPULARES): The best place to sample the many different styles of craftwork produced in many regions of the country, the museum has a shop selling ethnic items and crafts. Closed Mondays and Saturdays. Admission charge. Carrera 8 No. 7-21, Bogotá (phone: 281-0295).

COLONIAL ART MUSEUM: Originally a 17th-century Jesuit university, this is where Colombia's first president was proclaimed and the country's first constitution was written. The collection of Spanish and native arts and crafts includes 300 pieces of furniture and carvings. Closed Mondays. Admission charge. Carrera 6 No. 9-77, Bogotá (phone: 241-6017).

ECUADOR

ARCHAEOLOGICAL MUSEUM OF THE CENTRAL BANK (MUSEO DEL BANCO CENTRAL): Archaeological pieces from prehistoric times to the Spanish conquest are on display. The collection is quite extensive. Closed Mondays. Free. Av. 10 de Agosto near Parque Alameda, Quito (phone: 510-3002). Guided tours in English.

JIJÓN Y CAAMAÑO MUSEUM: The Catholic University houses the work of Jijón y Caamano, a 20th-century explorer and anthropologist who spent his life studying Ecuadorian Indians. The collection can be visited by appointment only. Catholic University, at the corner of Av. 12 de Octubre and Calle Robles, Quito (phone: 52-92-40).

ETHNOGRAPHIC MUSEUM (MUSEO DE ETNOGRAFÍA): This is another interesting anthropological collection of Indian artifacts. Closed Mondays and Tuesdays. Free. Colegio Mejía, Av. Venezuela and Av. Antonio Ante, Quito (phone: 21-34-18).

MUSEUM OF RELIGIOUS ART (MUSEO DE ARTE RELIGIOSO): Housed in the Convent of the Sisters of the Conception in the city of Riobamba, this collection of paintings, sculpture, and goldwork is outstanding. The convent and gardens have been completely restored. Closed Sundays and holidays. Admission charge. In Riobamba.

PERÚ

PERUVIAN GOLD MUSEUM (MIGUEL MUJICA GALLO MUSEUM): Displayed here are golden treasures from the earliest Peruvian civilizations, as well as splendid feather costumes and objects, all housed in a subterranean museum. (Part of this collection is at the Gold Museum at the *Gran Hotel Bolívar* in Lima.) Closed Sundays and holidays. Admission charge. Outside Lima in Montricco.

MUSEUM OF ART: This extensive collection includes paintings from the Cuzco School (17th and 18th centuries), hand-carved furniture, ivory, silk, and lace collections, plus oil paintings and watercolors by Peruvian artists. Closed Mondays. Admission charge. Paseo Colón 125, Lima (phone: 32-62-42).

RAFAEL LARCO HERRERA MUSEUM: Popularly known as the museum of primitive erotic art, it actually houses one of the first collections of ceramics and other items from the pre-Hispanic coastal cultures of northern Perú. About 44,000 items are on exhibit. Closed Sundays. Admission charge. Av. Bolívar 1515, Lima (phone: 23-43-33).

MUSEUM OF ANTHROPOLOGY AND ARCHAEOLOGY: This is one of the foremost archaeological museums in South America. More than 80,000 objects — rock sculptures, ceramics, basketry, wool and cotton woven goods, jewels, tools, weapons and gold, silver and copper items with precious stones — are on display. Closed Mondays. Admission charge. Plaza Bolívar, Pueblo Libre Lima (phone: 2-32-82).

YOSHIRO AMANO COLLECTION: A private collection of woven fabric from the Chancay Valley north of Lima and ceramic objects from pre-Hispanic Peruvian cultures, it can be visited Mondays through Fridays by appointment only. Call a day ahead to arrange a visit. Calle Retiro 1 60, Miraflores, Lima (phone: 41-29-09).

VENEZUELA

SIMÓN BOLÍVAR'S BIRTHPLACE (CASA NATAL): Mementos from Bolívar's youth and military career are preserved here. Murals depict scenes from the Liberator's life, and the inner courtyard is a fine example of colonial architecture. Closed Mondays. Free. Calle Traposos and the corner of Calle San Jacinto, Caracas (phone: 45-98-28).

CATHEDRAL (CATEDRAL): The cathedral, built between 1665 and 1674 contains three notable paintings: *The Resurrection* by Rubens, *The Presentation of the Virgin at the Temple* by the Spanish painter Murillo, and *The Last Supper* by Venezuelan painter Arturo Michelena. Open daily. Free. One block east of Plaza Bolívar, Caracas.

THE GALLERY OF NATIONAL ART: One of the few museums in Latin America deliberately established to foster national cultural identity, it was opened in May 1976 by the National Board of Culture. Works by more than 40 Venezuelan painters are displayed in the contemporary and popular arts sections. The older Museum of Fine Arts (Museo de Bellas Artes), containing an international collection, adjoins the gallery. Closed Mondays. Admission charge. Parque Los Caobos, Caracas (phone: 571-1110).

JESÚS SOTO MUSEUM OF MODERN ART: Tucked away in a very small city, in the middle of the jungle in the state of Guayana, this extremely attractive museum consists of six rooms surrounding a central patio designed for its function and light. Plastic interpretations of notable kinetic artists are on display. Ciudad Bolívar.

For the Experience

Luxury Resorts and Special Havens

 As we have noted elsewhere, South America offers the traveler an extraordinary spectrum of experiences and pleasures. The range of accommodations possibilities is as varied as the landscape — indeed, in some cases, irrevocably linked to the landscape.

The choice of a vacation retreat is very personal. The places listed below include many of our particular favorites, as well as a few that have earned their stars through popular acclaim. Some are large hotels in famous resort areas that have a long-standing reputation for fine facilities and service. Others are small, one-of-a-kind places in unusually appealing surroundings. Most offer their rooms on the European Plan (no meals), but many include one or more meals. While many are expensive — in the $75-plus per night category — others offer some very attractive bargains. Without exception, both large and small vacation resorts should be booked far in advance, and be sure to leave additional time for reservations requested by mail.

In South America, whether your choice is a big hotel or a small inn, genuine hospitality and personal attention are the rule. Hotel managers are generally accessible and members of their staffs regularly extend their help in arranging sightseeing itineraries; recommending restaurants; and organizing fishing trips, boat rentals, or guest privileges at nearby golf courses and tennis courts. Guests will not, however, always find (either with hotel staffs or with fellow guests) that English is the lingua franca, as travelers from the US have come to assume. Still, there is a pervasive sense that people sincerely want you to feel welcome and will go to great lengths to make sure you do. Just the fact that you have come such a long way makes you a very special guest.

In keeping with our view of a multifaceted South America, our special havens are grouped not by country, but by physical environment and special interest.

SEASIDE SWELLS

INTER-CONTINENTAL RIO, Rio de Janeiro, Brazil: This 15-story structure on Gávea Beach, in the resort area of a resort city, has a spectacular setting beside a white sand beach that stretches for several miles and a backdrop of towering peaks. It also overlooks the 18-hole Gávea Golf Course. The hotel's layout provides all rooms with a view of the ocean and the hills, and the interior decor — with local wood and stone materials and native crafts — maintains the Brazilian atmosphere. Guest facilities include a swimming pool with its own swim-up bar, tennis courts lit for night play, the *Papillon* discotheque for night dancing, and the remarkable beach. Continental food is served in the *Monseigneur Restaurant,* with other eateries reserved for lighter meals and barbecues. Hotel service here is among the best in Brazil. Twenty minutes by car and shuttle bus from Copacabana Beach. Reservations: Inter-Continental offices in the US or Av. Litorânea 222 (phone: 399-2200).

COPACABANA PALACE, Rio de Janeiro, Brazil: For anyone with a penchant for the past, the newly upgraded *Palace* is a triumph of preservation and restoration. In the oldest part of the building, which was erected in 1923, remains a restored Beaux-Arts façade, white marble lobby and staircases, ballroom-size hallways, soaring ceilings, and bedrooms facing the sea; to these, add ample art deco, including painted glass walls in the public areas, such as the *Bife Ouro* (*Golden Beef*) restaurant, and a pervading tropical look. In the 11-story annex, built in 1949, the bedrooms are the size of suites, with antique and Empire furnishings, and the *Bar de Copa* is done in varying tones of brown. Outside, a huge, glamorous pool lies waiting. Conveniently located on Copacabana Beach on Av. Atlântica 1702 (phone: 237-3271). Reservations may be made in the US through Loews International (phone: 212-841-1111).

DO FRADE, Angra dos Reis, Brazil: Getting here is almost half the fun, for the beautiful 2-hour drive loops up and down between the coastal hills and the sea. There are 104 rooms in all, including chalets and suites, and guests can step directly onto the broad beach and into the calmest and bluest of waters, dotted with dozens of tiny islands and framed by rugged green mountains. This fashionable getaway for the Rio set has two restaurants, two pools, tennis, golf, fishing, scuba diving, windsurfing, horseback riding, plus its own schooner for day or overnight cruises. Make an excursion from here to colonial Paratí, a national monument and a gem, and even spend a night at the *Pousada Dom João,* a tiny historic inn also owned by the Do Frade company. Bus service is available from Rio to Do Frade. On Frade Beach, Rio/Santos Highway (phone: in Rio, 021-267-7375; or make reservations through Loews International, 212-841-1111).

CASA GRANDE, Guarujá, São Paulo, Brazil: *Paulistas* say that they never need to go as far as rival Rio de Janeiro because they have their own beach resort at Guarujá, only 55 miles (88 km) away. On an island of white high-rises, this former hacienda, facing the Atlantic, provides a more intimate and sumptuous retreat. Landscaped with tropical flowers and palms, the grounds have a swimming pool with terrace bar, sauna, tennis courts, golf links, and a heliport. The main restaurant serves spectacular lobster thermidor in a hollowed-out pineapple, and superathlete Pelé comes from his home in nearby Santos to dance at the hotel disco. There's a piano bar with more mellow music, too. Manager Hans Schadler goes out of his way to make certain that each guest is very well cared for. Although he speaks perfect English, do not count on the same from everyone at the hotel. Reservations — a must for weekends and during the peak season of December through March — are made through *Casa Grande*'s São Paulo office at Av. Europa 571 (phone: 282-2228). In Guarujá, the hotel address is Av. Miguel Estefno 999 (phone: 9-1900).

QUATRO RODAS, Recife, Brazil: Of all of the northeastern Brazil hotels, this property comes closest to being a self-contained resort — and one where English is widely understood. Its rooms are large, with balcony views of the ocean and beautiful gardens. Daytime activity centers around a nice big pool, served by a thatch-roofed snack bar with exotic fruit cocktails on tap. The hotel beach is the take-off point for sailors and windsurfers, and for the hardy, the hotel has illuminated tennis courts for night play. There are several restaurant and bar settings, including the *Rilla d'Olinda* for international dishes and regional specialties, and the *Piano* bar and *Panoramic* restaurant for weekend dining and dancing. Two additional bonusus: boutiques well stocked with crafts, and proximity to Olinda — an architectural gem of a colonial town — just minutes away. Reservations: Av. José Augusto Moreira 2200, Recife 5300 (Olinda), Pernambuco, Brazil (phone: 081-431-2955).

POUSADA NAS ROCAS, Armação dos Búzios, Brazil: Part of a relaxed resort that attracts high-living guests, this small-scale hotel is located just offshore on its own island, and is reached by a 7-minute boat ride. Landscaping here is lush; facilities include a main lounge with restaurant and veranda overlooking the pool, a snack bar by the bay beach, and lovely double rooms and suites in *casita* or bungalow units. There is waterskiing, windsurfing, sailing, and fishing, and, on the mainland, there are many choice small beaches to explore. Nightlife on the mainland in town is equally laid back, and there are several good restaurants from which to choose when you venture off-island. Búzios is a 3-hour drive from Rio or a short flight via small aircraft. Reservations: In Armação dos Búzios, write the hotel at Ilha nas Rocas (phone: 2203).

CARTAGENA HILTON INTERNATIONAL, Cartagena, Colombia: Cartagena finally has a hotel with a beach. Even though it's a small one, the sand is soft and white — a luxury in a hard-sand resort area. In the El Laguito section of Bocagrande, this 300-room hotel is surrounded by water on three sides, and every room has a balcony with a view of the Caribbean. In typical Hilton style, there is a choice of dining rooms and lounges, a grand swimming pool with swim-up bar, three lighted tennis courts, and the wonderful beach. This section of Cartagena also has good restaurants, and the walled city and its massive fortifications are not far away. Reservations: Hilton offices in the US or Box 1774, Cartagena (phone: 959-50660).

IROTAMA, Santa Marta, Colombia: Take the setting here (sea out front, sierra behind), a simple, sybaritic lifestyle, and imagine the Caribbean of 20 years ago. Add modern, air-conditioned, individual bungalows surrounded by tropical vegetation, clear blue water, and wide, clean beaches, and you've described this fine seaside retreat. There are several restaurant choices — open-air terrace dining; air-conditioned, closed-in comfort; and beachside service — as well as a full range of facilities for sailing, diving, snorkeling, and deep-sea fishing. Day excursions to the neighboring Tairoma National Park (with even more beautiful sandy coves) or into the hills to visit a coffee plantation are also possibilities. Reservations: PO Box 598, Santa Marta (phone: 7-642/3).

LUXOR CONVENTO DO CARMO, Salvador da Bahía, Brazil: A 400-year-old building that's been converted from a convent into a luxury hotel, it is the most evocative hostelry in this most Brazilian of Brazilian cities. Off its cavernous corridors, the 70 rooms — once cells for the nuns who dwelt here — have white stucco walls, some adorned with antique Portuguese tiles; jacaranda-wood colonial beds, which some North Americans find too narrow; and dark chests. The colonnaded courtyard is now a sunny public area, with a circular pool, chaise lounges, sculptures, and lush potted plants, and the refectory is a restaurant, *Forno e Fogão* (oven and fire), one of the better places in the city to sample spicy Bahían cuisine. Guests can take an occasional break from history, however, to visit the good, not great, beaches that run north and south of the city. Salvador da Bahía.

SOLANA DEL MAR, Punta Ballena, Uruguay: In a lovely resort area — quieter and prettier than its better-known neighbor at Punta del Este — this is a good vacation choice, especially for North Americans. The hotel is modern, comfortable, and wonderfully decorated, and occupies a superb setting, with a pine forest behind and the ocean and beach below. The food is excellent — important, because meals are MAP. However, it would be hard to imagine being here for long without a car to take an occasional run to Punta del Este for a night at the casino or to the yacht races in season. Other delightful excursions could include a day's boat ride to Lobos Island, with its colonies of sea lions, or to the fine beach (and ex–pirate hangout) on Gorriti Island. The whole coast here is jumping from Christmas to Easter, nearly deserted the rest of the year. But even in the off-season the weather can be good and the golf and tennis facilities not booked. Punta Ballena.

MELIA, Puerto La Cruz, Venezuela: About 9 miles (14 km) from the international airport at Barcelona, this is a smaller, though deluxe, version of the resort hotels near Caracas. It has a full complement of facilities: sauna, gym, Turkish bath, nightclub, bridge and gamerooms, bars, tennis courts, swimming pool, golf, mini-golf, nautical sports, and a shopping center, as well as a fine beach. The hotel will organize a cruise to Caribbean islands or a safari to the Venezuelan jungle. Reservations can be made directly from the US with Melia offices; in Venezuela contact Melia Venezuela, Centro Profesional del Este, Calle Villaflor, Sabana Grande (phone: 72-73-54, or 72-41-90).

CUMANAGOTO, Cumaná, Venezuela: Neighboring Puerto La Cruz and offshore Margarita Island (connected here by ferry service) are better known than historic Cumaná, but the latter is our choice for a vacation in Venezuela. This 80-room, first-class hotel is bordered by wonderful beaches, and the resort also has a super swimming pool surrounded by lovely grounds. Oceanside facilities include waterskiing and fishing boats. It is a short ride to town, the oldest city on the continent, and its sightseeing attractions include a Spanish fort and colonial churches. Cumaná also enjoys a lively Carnival season, although those who have been say an even finer example is 80 miles farther east on the coast, at Carúpano. Cumaná.

ISLAND IDYLLS

AURY, Providencia Island, Colombia: This island is popular with scuba divers and snorkelers who know about the fantasia of submarine life off Providencia's reefs. With just 14 rooms, this is the island's largest inn, although there is also a rooming house that accommodates 6. Built by the sea (the windows face inland however), the hotel is clean, comfortable, fun, and — with or without all meals — reasonable. Providencia is reached on daily small-plane flights from San Andrés Island, and if you're lucky, either the man with the bicycles or the man with the horses will be on hand when you land to provide transportation to town — and it is a lovely town, even if you have to walk the half-mile from the airport. Also within walking distance is the neighboring island of Santa Catalina. Like the cows that go there to graze every day, just wait for the tide to go out and cross the sand. For information, call the Colombia Tourist Office in New York City (phone: 212-688-0151) and ask Jorge Ortiz for help in making reservations.

CLUB PACÍFICO, Coiba Island, Panamá: On the tropical island of Coiba (200 miles from Panamá City), the *Club* has long been a favorite with saltwater fishermen since record catches of black marlin and wahoo are common during the January to April season. Now owner Bob Griffin has extended the season (December to September) to offer the advantages of scuba, snorkeling, and the simple attractions of fine sand and warm sea. Accommodations are in bungalows, each with private facilities and air conditioning. Meals, featuring seafood and local fruits and vegetables, are served in the main dining room-cum-bar. The living is very simple and a lot of the action is underwater, with reefs full of fish and pearl-bearing oysters. Divers can also look for the various wrecks of ships said to have gone down with their gold and silver cargoes in days of yore. For nondivers, there are long stretches of beach, nature trails, and numerous nearby islands to explore. Access to Coiba is by charter flight from Panamá City. Reservations through *Club Pacífico*, 517 W 49th St., Hialeah, FL 33012 (phone: in Florida, 305-823-8282; elsewhere, 800-327-5662).

ISLA ESTEVES, Lake Titicaca, Puno, Perú: Until now, mediocre accommodations made Lake Titicaca merely a region to transit by hydrofoil between Perú and Bolivia. But the Lake Titicaca area finally has a hotel that brings comfort to the great experience of staying in this scenic and historic region. The hotel is on the island of Esteves, just offshore from the port town of Puno, and has central heating (a first here), air conditioning, first-class rooms, and lounge areas. For those especially interested in the Indian culture and with a taste for visiting archaeological sites or attending some of the most colorful weekly markets and Indian festivals on the continent, then this inn perched close to the most sacred lake in Incan mythology is likely to prove perfect. Reservations: South America Reps (phone: in California, 213-246-4816; elsewhere, 800-423-2791).

HISTORIC HOSTELRIES

POUSO CHICO REI, Ouro Preto (Minas Gerais), Brazil: For those able to get a reservation at this lovely inn, it may well be the highlight of their visit to Brazil. (If you can't, try the *Pousada Ouro Preto* for a similar living-history experience.) The *Pouso Chico Rei* is an elegant old home furnished with colonial antiques and charm.

There are no tennis courts and swimming pools here, but the inn is a perfect home base for a visit to this very historic town and art center of Ouro Preto — declared a national monument by the government. Spend several days exploring the town's churches, walking its cobbled streets and stairways, and plan at least one excursion through the beautiful countryside to other art centers of nearby Marina and Sabara. Reservations: Rua Brigadeiro, Mosqueira 90, Ouro Preto.

LA POSTA DEL CANGREJO, Punta del Este, Uruguay: Between the wave-capped Atlantic and the silent-flowing Río de la Plata is Punta del Este, just a 45-minute flight from Buenos Aires and a playground for rich, young Argentines. Out of the fray, in the nearby town of Barra de Maldonado, is this very low-key Mediterranean-style inn, with comfortable and airy rooms overlooking its gardens and the beautiful, powdery sand beaches beyond. Guests relax and socialize in the sun-drenched, tile-floored public rooms and feast on excellent cuisine, under the supervision of co-proprietor Ana María Moya, once a student of Paul Bocuse. There is tennis and, for high rollers, gambling at the nearby *San Rafael* casino after midnight. Punta del Este.

HACIENDA LOS LINGUES, San Fernando, Chile: This beautiful estate, an elegantly restored manor house on a working farm, is the first Relais et Châteaux property in South America — and with good reason. From the furnishings in the vast living room and lounges to the silver used for candlelit dining, the hacienda is full of splendid antiques. Thirty colonial-style rooms face a central patio, where there is a chapel with its own artworks. Stables provide mounts for riding into the hills as well as breeding stock for horse shows and rodeos. Other amenities include a pool, gameroom, hunting, nature walks, and the very personal attention of the owners. Los Lingues is about an hour from Santiago. For reservations, contact the owner, German Claro Lyon, Hacienda Los Lingues, Providencia 1100 T. Tajamar C, Of. 205, Santiago.

HOSTERÍA DEL MOLINO DE MESOPOTAMIA, Villa de Leyva, Colombia: In the province of Boyacá and a 3-hour drive from Bogotá is Villa de Leyva, a deceptively sleepy-looking town that resembles a stage set from *Don Quixote*. It has been designated a national monument, and this hotel, built in 1568 as a flour mill, is one of its loveliest treasures. The inn, set in lovely gardens with paths leading to private home entrances, is full of antiques such as decorative wooden canopied beds. Modern facilities include a pool; stables with horses for guests to take out on long country rides; a bar set in a cave; and a large dining room where the centerpiece is the original millstone. The dining room staff is dressed in period costume and the meals are delicious. Rates are very reasonable, as are prices at the regional market held on Saturdays in the vast cobbled town square. Reservations: Calle del Silencio, Villa de Leyva, Colombia (phone: 35).

PARADOR CUSIN, San Pablo del Lago, Ecuador: Just a 15-minute drive from Ecuador's bustling Otavalo Indian market, guests can relax at this manor house of a working hacienda. The original farmhouse, built about 100 years ago, is incorporated into a new two-story addition surrounding the cobbled central courtyard. The hotel specializes in country elegance and family hospitality. Spacious guestrooms lead off a second-floor balcony overlooking flowers and fountain; bedroom windows frame peaceful views of the surrounding countryside — gardens, fields, and mountains. Furnishings are a mix of antiques and Ecuadorian handicrafts. Cocktails are served in the high-ceilinged central salon, which is dominated by a huge fireplace; dinners (prepared with home-grown produce) are taken in the adjoining dining room. Guests can also relax in a separate bar which resembles an intimate English pub. Bougainvillea and hibiscus bloom everywhere, and in the rear gardens there are several llamas in residence. A stable of horses is available for guest use. Reservations: PO Box 2542, Quito, Ecuador.

HOSTERÍA LA CIENEGA, Lasso, Ecuador: Some 45 miles south of Quito, Ecuador's oldest colonial estate has opened its historic doors as a country inn. The original manor house, built in the mid-17th century for the Marquis de Maenza, remains an elegant stone structure with cobbled patios, Moorish fountains, and grand windows with views of the snow-capped volcanoes of Cotopaxi province. Many original accessories decorate the mansion, and the estate even boasts its own church. Guest accommodations are in 8 double rooms and 3 suites, all with private bath; there are 4 dining rooms, bars, and sports activities, including riding and tennis. Also available are excursions to the wildlife area of Cotopaxi National Park and mountain expeditions up the Cotopaxi peak. Lively weekly markets are plentiful in the area. Minimum 2-day programs with meals and private car from Quito can be booked through Metropolitan Touring, Av. Amazonas, Quito (phone: 524-400) or through Adventure Associates, 5925 Maple, Dallas, TX (phone: in Texas, 214-357-6187; elsewhere, 800-527-2500).

LIBERTADOR, Cuzco, Perú: Everyone knows that Cuzco is the gateway city to Machu Picchu, but few visitors linger long enough to see other ruins and the weekly markets in the area — or to really get to know this former capital of the Inca Empire. It's worth the time, especially when it's possible to stay in a building that was the 16th-century home of the Spanish conquistador Francisco Pizarro. The second floor of the original mansion has 18 large, grand, high-ceilinged suites. Try to arrange to rent one of these — although the newer rooms are also comfortable, modern, and decorated in lively Peruvian fabrics and crafts. The lobby–sitting room, restaurant, and bar all have nice colonial touches, but the restaurant service and food have declined badly. The optimum time to visit is during a Cuzco regional festival (see *Festivals*), but arrangements must be made months ahead. For reservations from the US, call Latin American Reservations Center (phone: in California, 415-974-5138; elsewhere, 800-227-3006). Or write 400 San Augustín, Cuzco (phone: 3482 or 3022).

LAS DUNAS, Ica, Perú: Hang your poncho and sombrero in any one of the 120 rooms at this desert oasis, built like a small Moorish town around a twisting lagoon. There is no shortage of fresh water here — as dramatically demonstrated by the complex's 2 large swimming pools and abundant palm-studded acreage. The air-conditioned rooms have separate dressing and bathing areas, and look out on Spanish patios and the landscaped gardens and dunelands beyond. Guests dine buffet-style, with open-grill cooking, or in a more intimate dining room decorated as a wine cellar. (The latter is appropriate since Ica is Perú's wine center; tours can be arranged to regional vineyards and caves.) In addition to its 2 pools, there are 2 tennis courts, a 9-hole pitch-and-putt golf course, horseback riding, sauna, and health club. Some 150 miles from Lima down the Pan-American Highway, the hotel is in the middle of a major archaeological zone, and guests can fly directly from the hotel's landing strip to the famous Nazca line drawings or drive to Paracas (another ancient center) on the Pacific Ocean for fishing, swimming, snorkeling, and wildlife viewing. Reservations: Latin American Reservations Center (phone: in California, 415-974-5138; elsewhere, 800-227-3006); PO Box 4410, Lima, Perú (the hotel sales office), or Av. La Augostura, Ica, Perú (phone: 40-41-80).

EL PUEBLO, Monterrico, Perú: Just 9 miles from the outskirts of Lima, the sun shines year-round on the *El Pueblo,* a resort complex that resembles an Andean village, complete with gardens, fruit groves, 3 pools, and a golf course. Guests live in balconied, air-conditioned bungalows or in hilltop, white-stuccoed villas — some with private pools — reached by a funicular. The "town" is laced with hibiscus-lined paths and cobbled, lantern-lit streets; no cars are allowed. Everything is right here: a replica bank, post office, shops, bars, cafés, restaurants, a church, a bakery, a discotheque — all tailored to a small village atmosphere. For recreation, there are saunas, a gym, massage, bowling alleys, cinema, tennis and squash courts, and riding. And just down the road is one of Perú's best-known restaurants, the *Granja Azul,* whose specialty is chicken-on-the-spit, salad, and homemade bread. Buses shuttle guests to and from Lima, and the pre-Incan city sites in the valley can be explored by private car or on an organized tour. There is Cajamarquilla, a maze of crumbling adobe walls, and Puruchuco, a reconstructed palace of a former nobleman. On the latter site is also a historical museum and, during the summer months, a folklore festival. Reservations from the US from Latin American Reservations Center in New York City (phone: in California, 415-974-5138; elsewhere, 800-227-3006).

LAKESIDE LODGES

EL CASCO, San Carlos de Bariloche, Argentina: The only area in South America as beautiful as the Chilean Lake District is the Argentine Lake District. The town of Bariloche is an alpine gem hidden among Argentina's lovely lakes and mountains; *El Casco* is its deluxe-plus hotel. A simple white stucco building gives way to 21 elegant guestrooms with lavish antique furnishings and individual sun terraces. Excellent food is served in the restaurant overlooking Lake Llao-Llao and landscaped woodlands stretch down to the beach. Guests may work out at the health spa on the premises, play golf and tennis nearby, or fish practically off the front lawn. In winter, there is skiing at the country's leading center, Cerro Catedral, 15 minutes away. This is an expensive hotel, one that is booked far ahead (and closed in June) but is well worth the price. Reservations: PO Box 634, San Carlos de Bariloche (phone: 2-2532 or 2-3083).

ANTUMALAL, Pucón, Chile: The Chilean Lake District, so scenic and relaxing, has its own special havens. Among the choice inns available, we like this year-round resort that is perched on a hill overlooking Villarrica Lake and surrounded by thick forests and snowcapped mountains. All 22 rooms have baths, central heating, picture windows, and fireplaces. During the summer season, there is boating, sailing, waterskiing; for those who wish, fishing and hunting trips can be arranged. In winter, the hotel transports guests to the Villarrica Volcano ski area. Reservations: PO Box 6-D, Pucón (phone: Pucón 2).

RALÚN, Reloncaví Estuary, Chile: In the heart of the Lake District, surrounded by grand forests and snow-capped mountains, this is one of the loveliest retreats anywhere on the continent. The main lodge sits on a hillside overlooking the point where ocean waters meet lakes. The hotel has stunning public rooms, all paneled in wood, with picture-window views. Luxury suites and double rooms in the lodge face gardens and water; separate cabins have a living room, kitchen, fireplace, and terrace. Come to enjoy swimming, sea- and freshwater fishing, skiing, horseback riding, and nature itself. The hotel is an hour from Puerto Montt. For reservations, contact Hotel Ralún, Casilla 9391, Santiago.

SPAS AND SPORTS SPOTS

SOCHAGOTA, Paipa, Colombia: Treat yourself to a long weekend (or a few midweek days) outside of Bogotá to "take the waters" here. Hot mineral springs erupt in Paipa and are piped into the baths of this Boyacá spa. Each of the hotel's connecting villas has its own private atrium with plunge pool; other diversions include horseback riding, tennis, or the natural Lake Sochagota. Guests can also use the hot springs treatment and stay half a mile away at the *Casona del Salitre,* a 17th-century hacienda used by Simón Bolívar during one of his campaigns. The hacienda has been carefully restored and modernized. Both are managed by *Morales Hotels,* a reliable and reasonable hospitality group. Reservations: in the US: Golden Tulips World Wide Hotels, 432 Madison Ave., New York, NY 10022 (phone: 212-247-7950); phone at *Sochagota Hotel:* 2114.

PORTILLO, Portillo, Chile: South America's most prestigious ski resort stands in a valley at 9,233 feet above sea level, surrounded by peaks laden with the finest deep-powder snow on the southern continent. International skiing champions practice here from June through September. They train on the most challenging of all South American slopes, the incredible Roca Jack (see *Skiing*). Other less demanding slopes serve intermediates and beginners. Lessons are available, and the hotel stocks Rossignol skis and Head and Nordic boots for rent. Guests also can rent ice skates for a glide across the frozen lake that's just a few steps from the hotel's back door. Year-round facilities include a sundeck, sauna, heated outdoor swimming pool, billiards, Ping-Pong, movies, a discotheque, and a cozy bar. Hotel accommodations range from chalets and suites to rooms with bath and dormitory-style sleeping. There are 650 beds, and reservations are at a premium in any price category. No matter when you plan to visit — although particularly in winter — bookings must be made almost a year in advance. Reservations in Santiago: Don Carlos 3227, Office C (phone: 28-65-01).

PUNTA CARNERO, Salinas, Ecuador: The cool Humboldt and the warm Equatorial currents meet around Salinas, north of Guayaquil, and the waters are full of striped marlin year-round. Black marlin, often weighing in at over 1,000 pounds, are in season in November, and the giant tuna are present from January to March. This hotel occupies an oceanside bluff near Salinas, and boasts 40 rooms with balconies, 2 tennis courts, and handsome public rooms. The fish dishes prepared by this kitchen are fresh and delicious. The hotel will arrange cruiser rentals and provide equipment, bait, and box lunch for fishing trips. A package tour called the Salinas Billfish Trip is offered by Adventure Associates of Dallas (phone: 800-527-2500). (*Note:* The package is for 4 days, but rates are available for extra fishing days and for accompanying nonfishermen.)

JUNGLE JUNKETS

TROPICAL HOTEL MANAUS, Manaus, Brazil: This granddaddy of South American resorts is on the Rio Negro, amidst thousands of acres of rain forest in the heart of the Amazon River basin. Despite its remote location, this hotel offers every luxury imaginable. Architecture is colonial, which here in the jungle means wide, spacious hallways, patios of exotic birds, and graceful arches. In addition to air-conditioned rooms, facilities include swimming pools and sauna, tennis courts, a floating river-bar (and other, stationary, cocktail lounges), restaurants, a discotheque, and a casino. Guests may choose from a wide array of sightseeing excursions or fishing expeditions along Amazon tributaries. There is direct air service from the US to Manaus. Reservations from the US: Varig Airlines. In Brazil: Estrada da Ponta Negra, Manaus (phone: 092-234-1165).

FLOTEL ORELLANA, Napo River, Ecuador: This floating hotel offers a moveable feast of jungle experiences — visits to Indian settlements, walks through the primeval rain forest, canoe trips down hidden tributaries. And the living is surprisingly easy in the small, but comfortable, twin-berth cabins with baths. Between guided jungle excursions on foot (or via dugout), guests can lounge in deck chairs in the sunshine or at an umbrella-shaded table. Drinks are served before dinner, and movies and slides about the Amazon flora and fauna are shown after dinner in the large bar-lounge. Try a 5-day cruise. Reservations from the US: Adventure Associates, 5925 Maple, Dallas, TX 75325 (phone: 800-527-2500).

EXPLORAMA LODGE, Iquitos, Perú: For those who prefer hotels built on solid ground but still want to visit the Amazon, this one — located 50 miles downriver from Iquitos and a short ride up the Yanamono tributary — is worth a try. It is a charming and imaginative jungle inn and a miracle of supply and efficiency. Peter Jensen is the majordomo here, presiding over a lodge set among towering hardwood trees intertwined with vines, wild orchids, macaws, parrots, and a resident pet tapir and sloth. The facilities include 8 palm-thatched buildings connected by elevated and covered passageways; there are 3 guest pavilions for sleeping, and separate toilets and showers. Public rooms, like the bar house called La Tuhuaypa (the Swamp), are screened, as is the dining room, where the food is varied and good. Guests can swing in a hammock;

join guided walks along interesting jungle trails; or ride boats to Indian villages, river islands, and inland lakes. They can even leave the lodge comforts for a more rugged camp at *Mazan Nature Reserve*, 45 miles away by boat. Reservations: Explorama Tours, Box 446, Iquitos, Perú.

CANAIMA, Angel Falls, Venezuela: Guests can get to this rustic, but comfortable, cabana resort only by flying over the 3,212-foot Angel Falls, and on a clear day the vista below is spectacular. Set next to a lagoon in a national park, the lodge facilities include a dining room serving good, hearty food at its single seating. With water, water everywhere, there is swimming, sunning, waterskiing, and fishing. Guests may also request a variety of excursions through the jungle on foot or to the splendid Orchid Islands by motorized dugout canoes. Taking a 1-week trip by Jeep, foot, and canoe, it's possible (from May through November) to get right to the base of the falls. Reservations from the US: Viasa Airlines; in Venezuela, Avensa Airlines in Caracas at Av. Urduneta, at the corner of Platanal in the Banco de Construcción y de Oriente (phone: 815-2515-59).

WILDERNESS WHIMSY

ALBATROSS, Ushuaia, Argentina: A travel agent may say that it's a 5-hour flight from the mainland to the southernmost city of Ushuaia (called The End of the World), but count on more flying time, as well as a superb aerial view of glacier country. So plan to spend a week here at this small, comfortable, reasonably priced place, full of interesting people. Hotel guests range from scientists on leave from missions on the Antarctic icecap to ranchers in town on business from their huge sheep farms that spread across the peninsula to ship captains who navigate the dangerous straits between the Pacific and Atlantic oceans. Ushuaia is a frontier town and seaport, not really a city, and the pioneer atmosphere is all-pervasive. Try to visit in January or February, when the days are long and the hotel will arrange drives through the forests of the Tierra del Fuego National Park. Reservations: Maipu and Lasserre Sts., Ushuaia (phone: 9203 or 9251).

PATAGONIAN INN, Dos Lagunas, Chile: Awesome natural wonders are the big draw in this corner of the world, and lodgings often become a secondary concern. However, this inn, in the middle of a sheep ranch, offers comfortable accommodations and good food for 38 guests, and arranges tours of the Paine National Park, probably the most beautiful glacial field anywhere, and a fascinating wildlife preserve as well. (While this is our preferred base, a stay here can be combined with one in Puerto Natales at the *Capitan Eberhard*, a pleasant 45-room inn with a splendid view of fjords. That hotel will also make arrangements for fjord cruises.) From the end of October to March, this tail end of South America cannot be beat for its combination of scenic grandeur and simple comfort. Accommodations are limited, so make plans far in advance. Reservations: *Hotel Cabo de Hornos*, Plaza Munoz G 1025, Punta Arenas, Chile. (They manage the *Patagonian Inn*.)

LOS FRAILES, Santo Domingo, Venezuela: Typically, the mention of Venezuela conjures up images of sparkling beaches and azure waters. While the country does, indeed, have these assets in abundance, it also has an alpine region, with an alpine-style gem of a colonial South American inn (owned by Avensa Airlines). A half-hour above the town of Santo Domingo and 2 hours from Mérida, it is set on a 17th-century monastery site, with the central lodge housing a cozy bar and a fine restaurant. Rooms are connected by covered corridors and are carpeted, heated, and furnished with antiques and reproductions. There are flowers everywhere, and a little brook bounces along its mountain course right through the hotel. The views are grand, and many guests chose horseback riding as the natural way to get out and enjoy the Andean landscape. Especially during holiday season, book well ahead, through Avensa Airlines offices in New York City and Miami.

Great Buys:
Shopping in South America

 South America has great buys in a wide variety of items — handicrafts (*artesanías*), fine quality leather goods, and semiprecious stones. Although only a few countries produce particularly stylish or sophisticated products, each country has its own unique style. Throughout the continent, there are wonderful things to buy.

But visitors should be careful when making a purchase. More than one traveler has bought a handmade wool sweater at an Andean market only to discover later that the sleeves are vastly different lengths. Buying in exclusive, expensive boutiques is not necessarily a guarantee of quality. Even the best shops sell merchandise with flaws that purchasers probably won't notice until they get the item home.

The art of bargaining is still practiced in most of South America. But in some markets the prices are fairly equal, and there are few meaningful bargains obtained by haggling. However, it's worth a try, and the seller may accept a price of about two-thirds to three-fourths of what he or she was originally asking. But at the same time, when dealing with someone who actually made what's for sale, consider the time and labor involved and don't try to shortchange that person. In the big cities and at better stores, bargaining is less common. In some places, when you ask if there is a discount, the merchant willingly marks off between 5% and 10%. But that depends on the individual.

Remember, too, that skins or any article made of animals on the endangered species list cannot be brought back into the US. Get an up-to-date list before leaving from the US Fish and Wildlife Service, Department of the Interior, Washington, DC 20240. Also, check US customs for items on the Generalized System of Preference (GSP) list for items that can be brought into the US duty-free in addition to your $600 allowance. Some gems and handicrafts are on the list.

Below is a list of the best places to shop in South America.

ARGENTINA: There may well be more cattle than people in Argentina, and it may occasionally seem that most of the beasts have "donated" their hides to supply the endless array of shoes, jackets, coats, bags, purses, and luggage for sale in downtown Buenos Aires shops. Leather goods have long been the mainstay of tourist purchases in Buenos Aires, although angora sweaters and fur coats of fox and nutria are traditionally good buys in Argentina.

Whether just browsing or actually planning to purchase, a good place to start a shopping tour is on the mall, La Florida, in downtown Buenos Aires, heading north from Avenida de Mayo (one block from the *Casa Rosada*). The shopping mall extends ten blocks to Plaza San Martín. Along La Florida, there is a great variety of merchandise — from some of Argentina's finest leather boutiques to blue jeans and sneakers shops. The closer to Plaza San Martín, the fancier the shops, but also the better the merchandise and the value. Some of the best purses are found at *Lofty,* on Marcelo T. Alvear right near Plaza San Martín, and *Welcome,* behind the *Plaza* hotel. There's a *Harrods* between Paraguay and Córdoba, but rather than echoing the luxury of its London namesake, it resembles an old Sears store in the US.

Heading west from Plaza San Martín, Santa Fe is one of the city's major shopping streets, with small, exclusive shops close to the plaza. Prices in some of these shops are higher than those in the shops in the arcades of the major hotels around the plaza. Good sturdy purses that are not expensive bear the Suelo Luppi label in *Bazaar Argentina* on Viamonte 701. *Carteras Italianas* on Mercelo T. de Alvear has fine, expensive purses. For cowhide rugs, try shops along Bartolomé Mitre in the 1300 blocks. Leather goods can be bought for less money at the factories in the Once (Eleven) district, near the Plaza Once bus terminal. It takes a good eye and persistence to shop here, however. One successful Once shopper recommends *Majourno Hermanos,* Lavalle 3664.

Fascinating antiques can be found in the small shops around Plaza Dorrego in the San Telmo section. Many stores stock limited collections of very specific items — miniature bronzes, for example. Every Sunday morning and afternoon, at the *San Telmo Fair* in the Plaza Dorrego, dealers put their wares under canvas awnings and sit to hawk and chat. Knickknacks, antique and otherwise, can also be bought in the shops at Vincente López 2102 and Vincente López 2188, near Recoleta Cemetery.

On Saturdays, Sundays, and holidays, artisan fairs are held in Plaza Vincente López, Plaza Britania, and Parque Lezama. Attractive displays of craft items include leather purses and enamel jewelery. Stop in at the Caminito Fair, on the street of the same name in La Boca, for the Friday and Saturday art fair.

Fancy boutiques with exclusive clothing are along the streets between Plaza San Martín and Recoleta Cemetery. Particularly good streets are Esmeralda, Presidente Quintana, Guido, Montevideo, and Avenida Alvear.

Typical items — the maté cup, the silver bombilla straw for sipping maté, gaucho apparel, ponchos, the three-balled bola lasso, onyx ashtrays, and odds and ends — can be found along Paseo Leandro Alem.

BOLIVIA: La Paz has terrific buys on wall hangings, ponchos, alpaca and vicuña sweaters, and jewelry of silver and gold. The most interesting shopping streets are found behind the San Francisco Cathedral, going up on Calle Sagarnaga. About halfway up the steep street, is the so-called "witches' market" (a misnomer), where Aymará Indian women sell wizened llama fetuses (for good luck), herbs, potions, and sundry magic charms. They don't like to sell to foreigners, but it's great fun to browse here. Follow Calle Max Paredes, near Sagarnaga, to the black market (*el mercado negro*), where everything from canned soup to blank audio cassettes can be bought inexpensively. The best shops for handicrafts line the bottom of Calle Sagarnaga, Calle Linares, and Calle Illampu. There are any number of tourist shops in the center of town offering the same goods at much higher prices, as is apparent after even a little comparative pricing.

In addition to the stalls and booths along the streets mentioned above, Indian craftsmen sell their wares from sacks tied to their backs. They are good sources from whom to pick up some rare, excellent weavings at prices lower than those in the shops. There are also some fine things to buy in the provinces in which most specific crafts originate, and the prices for them are right all over the country.

Titikaka, Ltd., on Avenida Sanchez Lima, is a two-story house given over to the display and sale of sweaters, wall hangings, and albums of Bolivian folk music. *Artisanías Bolivianas,* quartered in a restored colonial house, has good regional crafts, including musical instruments. For the finest quality crafts, which are not inexpensive, visit *Tiendas Bolivianas,* at Plaza Avaroa. Fine gold and silver jewelry is displayed at the better hotels. Again, it's wise to price them, then shop around for similar merchandise at lower cost.

BRAZIL: The country is known for its semiprecious stones — tourmalines, amethysts, aquamarines, topazes — and for diamonds and emeralds. Most of the jewels come from the state of Minas Gerais. Semiprecious stones — particularly topaz, aquamarine, and tourmaline — are available at bargain prices. When the stones are purchased already set, the setting is generally 18-karat gold. The best-known dealer, *H. Stern,* offers a free trip from any hotel to its cutting factories. *H. Stern* stores in Rio are on Avenida Pirajá in Ipanema (main store) and in Galeão and Santos Dumont airports and major hotels. *H. Stern* also has branches in São Paulo, Brasília, and other cities. The company offers a one-year guarantee with worldwide service. *Amsterdam and Sauer,* on Avenida Rio Branco 156 in downtown Rio and on Avenida Atlântica in Copacabana, is another top jewelry store chain.

In Rio, the high-fashion shopping district is between the Praça General Osorio and the Praça Nossa Senhora da Paz in Ipanema. A fancy new shopping center in the *Rio Palace* hotel, at the end of Avenida Atlantica, has 188 shops selling a wide variety of Brazilian goods, of which shoes, boots, and bags are the best buys. On the side streets off Avenida Rio Branco, downtown, there are souvenir shops selling leather goods, wood carvings, and dolls. At the Sunday fair in the Praça Osorio, Ipanema, there are all sorts of arts and crafts of varying quality.

In São Paulo, the best shopping streets are Itapetininga, Augusta, and Paulista. There's a fair on Sundays from 9 AM to 1 PM on the Praça da República, where handmade leather, ceramic, silver, and other artisan products are sold.

Salvador (Bahía) is the best place in Brazil to buy silver and art. Practically everything is for sale in the *Mercado Modelo* — rosewood items, silver jewelry, and leather goods are the best buys. The shop in the *Convento do Carmo* also has an extensive line of silver jewelry, as well as Bahian handicrafts. Many Brazilian artists have shops here, but their work is expensive. Handwoven rugs are usually a good buy here.

In Belo Horizonte, there are not only semiprecious stones but pewterware. The town of São João d'el Rei, 110 miles (177 km) from Belo Horizonte, is known for its silver, pewter, leather, and straw goods, as well as hand-loomed bedspreads and tablecloths. Pewterware, wooden goods, and earthenware are also made in Tiradentes, 115 miles (185 km) from Belo Horizonte.

In the state of Ceata, in northeast Brazil, handmade lace is fashioned into various clothing and household articles, and embroidered goods are lovely and inexpensive.

CHILE: Chile's best buys are handsome, diamond-patterned, Mapuche wool rugs that come in all sizes, and jewelry of semiprecious, dark blue lapis lazuli. Unless you are going to Temuco, where the Mapuche rugs are woven, the best buys are found in the government-run *Centro de Madre* (CEMA) stores. In Santiago, they're at Avenida Portugal 351 and Avenida Providencia 1652. There are also CEMA stores in towns throughout the country; these stock handicrafts and artisan works from all over.

Chile is noted for its lapis lazuli jewelry, dark blue stones with minute flecks of mineralization (not spots or streaks) that are often set in silver or made into attractive necklaces. *H. Stern,* at the *Carrera* hotel in town, has a few good pieces on display. There are a number of stores on and near MacIver Street, behind the national library, that sell lapis lazuli. Pieces can be made to order in a few days in *Atelier "Kot"* at Huérfanos 510. Most highly recommended of all is the studio of designer Morita Gil for jewelry and superb stones, at Los Misioneros 1991, near the *Sheraton San Cristóbal* hotel.

Earthenware is another extremely good buy in Chile. It's made in a small town called Pomaire, about an hour outside Santiago, on the road to San Antonio. The entire town is involved in making red clay vases, plates, bowls, casseroles, and knickknacks. There are also a few sidewalk stands in Santiago, one a block off Providencia on Calle Luis Middleton.

Excellent bargains in bolts of fine wool can be found at the end of the winter season (August–September) in downtown Santiago shops. To the north of Santiago, in the town of La Ligua, there are some exceptional buys in alpaca sweaters and cloth at the *La Baltra* factory. Other shops have nice alpaca and vicuña sweaters and ponchos, but unfortunately many are now mixing wool with synthetic fibers.

Chimbarongo, south of Santiago, manufactures wicker furniture and knickknacks. Roadside stands sell items for a song. In Puerto Montt, leave time for shopping for woolen clothing of every description and elaborately carved wooden stirrups in the stalls lining the port at Angelmó.

COLOMBIA: The country is considered the emerald capital of the world. These gems can be purchased at the *Central Bank* and at *H. Stern* shops in Bogotá, but beware the street hawker. *H. Stern* shops can be found in the *Tequendama* and *Hilton* hotels, and at El Dorado Airport. However, the most original jewelry designs, based on pre-Columbian reproductions, are at *Galería Cano's* main store at Carrera 13, No. 27-98, or its branch in the *Bogotá Hilton.* There is also jewelry of superb design at *El Lago,* Avianca Bldg. at Carrera 7.

Colombia's most attractive artisan product is the multicolored *ruana,* or wool poncho, but the country also produces basketry, ceramics, straw goods, leather goods, and coffee. In San Isidro, near Bogotá, there are a number of craft shops where bargains in gold and silver jewelry can be found, as well as reproductions of pre-Columbian artifacts, alligator and snakeskin shoes, belts, and bags. One of the finest craft centers is in the *Museo de Arte y Tradiciones Populares* (*Museum of Popular Art and Traditions*) at Carrera 8, 7-12. The prices are right here and at *Artesanías de Colombia* across the street from the *Tequendama* hotel.

Native handicrafts are a good buy in Cartagena, where there are a number of stalls near Plaza Bolívar, in the Old City. The government-operated *Artesanías de Colombia* has a wide selection of handicrafts at reasonable prices. In the Old City, leather goods and emeralds are also available. *Greenfire Emeralds* has stores in the *Caribe* hotel and the Boca Grande area of Cartagena. Dennis Lynch, a former Peace Corps volunteer from California, runs a handicraft store, *Artexpo,* at the entrance to the Inquisition Palace in Cartagena (but that doesn't mean he'll twist your arm to buy his goods). Other handicraft stores are the *Tropicana* and *Galeria Salomé* in Boca Grande and the *Oriental* in the Old City.

On San Andrés Island, off the Colombian coast, duty-free shops stock Swiss watches, perfume, china, crystal, cameras, and liquor.

ECUADOR: The *Otavalo Indian Market* on Saturday morning sells fine woolen and woven goods and is Ecuador's best-known shopping site. The town is 80 miles (129 km) north of Quito. Get there early in the morning, about daybreak, since the market disperses early. The Otavalo Indian goods are well known, so well known that other Indians will try to pass theirs off as Otavalos in order to get a higher price. About 35 miles (56 km) south of Quito, Saquisili has a *Thursday market,* where fabrics with woven animal designs are sold. The Colorado Indians hold a *Sunday morning market* in Santo Domingo, and there's a *Saturday market* in Riobamba.

Quito is one of the best shopping centers on the continent, and Avenida Amazonas is its main shopping street. However, up the hill at 260 Avenida Colón is *Folklore,* the gallery of Olga Fisch. Ms. Fisch is the grande dame of Ecuadorian crafts. She has not only been instrumental in preserving Indian arts, but she uses their motifs imaginatively in clothing, jewelry, carpets, and decorative accessories. Prices are not low, but the quality is high, and shipping is reliable. Another excellent shop is *La Bodega,* with a wonderful variety of jungle crafts, on Avenida Juan León Mera 614.

Another "don't miss" is the hilltop home-museum-boutique of Ecuador's best-known painter, Oswaldo Guayasamin. His art prices match his reputation, but it's hard to resist his superbly designed jewelry. Every taxi driver knows where he lives.

PANAMÁ: Panamá City is the traditional free port shopping stopover for travelers heading to and from Latin America. Prices are comparable with other Caribbean free ports, though camera prices tend to be higher than those in New York City. But the endless array of perfumes, cameras, projectors, electronic goods, radios, lace, watches, china, chess and backgammon sets, and Oriental art will entrance anyone who enjoys shopping. Camera and electronic stores cluster along the Avenida Central. Other good shopping areas are along the Vía España (in the *El Panamá* neighborhood) and Avenida de los Mártires. All major hotels have shopping areas. You may have success if you try to bargain in stores.

Native handicrafts are found in the *Public Market* on Avenida Norte at the waterfront and at the *Sal Si Puedes* open-air bazaar. Crafts at higher prices, but of more uniform quality, can be bought at *Artesanías Nacionales,* the government cooperative with one shop at the airport and the other at the ruins in Panamá Viejo.

Craft items include shirts, weavings, baskets, wicker goods, necklaces, beaded collars, leather goods, straw and wooden figurines, ceramics, and hand-appliquéd *mola* fabric appliqués. The *molas* are made by the Cuna Indians on the San Blas Islands (where they can also be purchased, as they're exhibited outside every Cuna cottage). The *molas,* with their stylized animals and birds cut through several layers of brightly colored cloth, are one of Latin America's most popular art forms. The *molas* have risen rapidly in price over the past few years, but it's still possible to bargain for a decent price.

When leaving Panamá, duty-free goods will be delivered at the airport. Pick them up on the way out of the country, after paying for them at the time of purchase in the store. Regulations do not allow travelers to open packages until actually aboard the outbound airplane, but the airport customs official allows opening and resealing them *in his presence* to make sure you've received what you bought. Free port shops are extremely honest and reliable in making deliveries. (The airport itself offers no real bargains.)

PARAGUAY: *Ñandutí* (spider web) lacelike weavings for table linen and wall hangings and the *Aó Po'i* embroidered cotton cloth are handsome souvenirs that can be purchased in downtown Asunción. The *ñandutí* is made in Itaguá, a small town near the capital where the *ñandutí* looms stand outside the doorways of the houses along the main street, making it seem as if each home is marked by a distinctive brightly colored giant spider web. The *Aó Po'i* cloth, white or colored, is used to make men's fancy summer shirts and women's dresses, skirts, and slacks. (Don't count on putting anything in a washing machine back home. Dry clean only.) Bright woven belts and sashes, *piri* straw hats, wooden articles, Spanish guitars, and gold or silver jewelry can be purchased at markets in Asunción and in many small towns. The best shops are found along Calle Colón. *Confecciones Catedral* will make a shirt or blouse to order in 24 hours. Calle Presidente Eligio Ayala 189.

PERÚ: Silver, gold, alpaca sweaters and ponchos, and knit and woven goods of llama wool, alpaca, and vicuña are available in Lima. There are moderately priced handicraft stalls at the *Mercado Artesanal* in Pueblo Libre on Avenida de la Marina. Items include knit socks, hats, scarves, blankets, sweaters, rugs, carved wood llamas, llama fur slippers, jackets, and llama rugs. The llama and alpaca sweaters and ponchos have small llama designs woven in. Be careful to check the quality of what you buy.

In Lima, silver and gold trinkets can be found in the shops along the Avenida Nicolas de Pierola, approaching the Plaza San Martín from the *Crillon* hotel and the Jirón Camana. These shops along the Avenida Nicolas de Pierola are also packed with woolen sweaters. Some of the best craft shops, such as the government gallery for Peruvian crafts and the excellent *Huamanqaqa,* are on Avenida Belén, between the *Gran Hotel Bolívar* and the *Sheraton.* This is not an area for bargains, but there are lovely weavings, carved gourds, paintings, embroideries, and other crafts from around Perú. *Los Alamos* gallery is in the Urbanización Zarate district — not a grand neighborhood, but the owner has fine taste. A taxi is needed to get here, and it's best to have the driver wait. Easier to find is *La Gringa,* a fine craft boutique owned and operated by an American in the El Suche section of Miraflores, across from *Cesar's* hotel.

Very nice jewelry can be found at *H. Stern* in the *Gran Hotel Bolívar* on *Plaza San Martín.* Other nice shops line the side street to the left of the hotel facing the plaza.

Handicrafts, particularly rugs and sweaters, can also be bought in stores or from sidewalk vendors in Cuzco and at the Cuzco Indian markets. Prices are almost always lower in Cuzco than in Lima. Puno has well-made, thick ponchos at prices even lower than those found in Cuzco, and the famous Pucara ceramic bulls come from this area.

Lima is where the colorful *retablos* are made. The *retablo* is a gaily painted wooden frame that looks almost like a miniature house with decorated double doors on the front. Inside are religious and secular scenes populated by hand-made ceramic figures.

URUGUAY: Uruguay is known as the country where leather and suede jackets, bags, belts, and shoes can be bought for even less than in Buenos Aires. Whether this will still be true when you arrive depends on the state of each country's currency (and that of the US dollar) at that time, but Montevideo's shops are worth a look. Most of the better shops lie between Plaza Independencia and Plaza Libertad. Very soft leather goods are made from *nonato,* unborn calf. Uruguay also produces soft nutria furs and good-quality amethysts. The best places to purchase nutria are *Peletería Pendola,* San José 1087, and *Peletería Holandesa,* Colonia 892. For agates and amethysts, visit *Amatistas del Uruguay,* Srandi and J. C. Gomez.

VENEZUELA: Once considered the most expensive of South American capitals, Caracas now ranks as more than reasonable. At the moment, items from clothes to cosmetics, imported or well-made locally, offer grand savings over prices in the US. The Island of Margarita is designated as "duty free," and the prices are indeed attractive for perfumes, cigarettes, and shoes; however, on the latter, and on most clothing and jewelry, buyers can do just as well in Caracas.

Caracas's shops and shopping centers are as sophisticated and deluxe as those anywhere in the world. There are any number of snazzy, well-stocked shopping centers offering the same sort of goods found in the US: *Centro Comercial Chacaito, Centro Ciudad Comercial La Florida, Centro Ciudad Comercial Las Mercedes, Centro Comercial Parque Humboldt, Centro Comercial Tamanaco* (especially good), and *Centro Comercial Sabana Grande.* There is a building full of jewelry boutiques (gold glitters everywhere) at the Edificio Francia on Plaza Bolívar.

A variety of handicraft shops cater to tourists, although Venezuela is not well known for highly developed artisan work. The *Palacio de las Industria,* at Avenida Olimpo and Avenida Abraham Lincoln in Sabana Grande, has one of the most complete selections. *Arte Español,* in the Edificio Abril on Avenida Urdaneta between Veroes and Ibarras; *Arte Folklórico,* in the Edificio Askain near the Plaza Chacaito; *Tille's Folklore Shop* in the Edificio Arecuna on Calle El Recreo in Sabana Grande; and *Casa de las Artesanías* on Calle Real de Sabana Grande sell souvenir items and crafts. Crafts shoppers will find woolen ruanas (like ponchos), baskets and hammocks, sisal products, rugs and blankets, masks, and some jungle seed jewelry.

Fabulous Festivals

Splashy, miraculous, colorful, bizarre, intriguing, and musical — a festival anywhere in South America is likely to be an utterly extraordinary human pageant of celebration. Without a doubt, the most famous of all is Carnival, in celebrated Brazilian style. Rio de Janeiro's tops the favorite list, but many aficionados of the mad pre-Lenten festivities insist that Carnival in Salvador (Bahía) is, if anything, more exciting and less commercial.

What most foreigners don't realize is that Carnival is celebrated, in one form or another, for between 3 and 8 days before the beginning of Lent throughout virtually all of South America. In Oruro, Bolivia, masked devil dancers perform the *Diablada,* in which good and evil wrestle for control. In Ecuador and Argentina, however, the main ritual (joyous only for spectators) consists of dropping water-filled balloons on unsuspecting passersby. But whether you prefer to samba in the streets or marvel at the demonic dancers, be sure to make reservations at least 6 months ahead of any Carnival you intend to visit.

Plan ahead for other festivals, too, such as the continent-wide celebration in June of *Corpus Christi,* which, like Carnival, is a moveable feast. When the Spanish priests first came to "civilize" the Indians, they found it expedient to move many of the saints' days nearer to existing local celebrations that had always accompanied planting and harvesting. Today, especially in the Andean countries, fiestas continue to mix Christianity and pre-Hispanic rites, Western and Indian music and pageantry. Celebrations usually include the pomp and circumstance of a procession to Mass at the cathedral, as well as traditional dancing, feasting, and lots and lots of drinking.

For those lucky enough to find a room at festival time, or anywhere in the vicinity of a festival that is about to happen, chances are that it will be impossible to make a telephone call (since none of the operators will be working), buy gasoline (since all stores and shops will be shut), or find local transportation. It's inevitable, however, that every stranger will be invited to dance, drink, feast, and possibly even to marry a member of the opposite sex (be careful of proposals in Brazil, however, since Carnival is a special time for transvestites). Take it all with good cheer and a fine sense of humor. After all, that's what festivals are for.

ARGENTINA: Argentines celebrate everything from wheat and soybean harvests to the founding of cities to a whole string of religious holidays and saints' days. Certain festivals are more important in different provinces. In Puerto Madryn, the new year starts with an *Underwater Fishing Festival;* in Rosario del Tala, in the province of Entre Rios, with a provincial *Tango Festival,* which takes place from January 1 to January 15 on a stage overlooking the Río Gualeguay. In Salta, where *Christmas* festivities begin on December 25 and end on January 15, tableaus and carol singing are staged throughout this period. On January 15, the 2-week *National Folklore Festival* begins in Cosquín, in the province of Córdoba. One of Argentina's most important national events, it attracts artists and musical groups from all over the country. An artisan fair is held at the same time.

In March, the most important *Wheat Festival* in the country is held in Leones (in the province of Córdoba) and features a commercial and industrial exposition, folklore events, and the choosing of a wheat queen. This is followed by a series of other fruit, vegetable, and grain harvest festivals throughout the central crop-growing provinces. The *Vendimia,* one of the country's largest festivals, celebrated in Mendoza during the first week in March, is held in honor of the harvest of the wine grapes. The vines are blessed, there is a parade of floats and antique cars, and a light-and-sound spectacle is held in an amphitheater at the foot of the Cordillera. The city is packed, so be sure to make hotel reservations well in advance.

Carnival is not an official holiday in Argentina, but it is celebrated in some fashion or other in many towns, and most gaily in Corrientes, beginning on the Saturday before Ash Wednesday. In Buenos Aires and other towns, there are a series of balls and parties in hotels and clubs. Throughout most of Argentina, visitors must take care not to be the target of water-filled balloons. In the northern towns near the Bolivian border, *Carnival* festivities begin in Tilcara at the end of January or beginning of February with the *Carnaval de Ablande:* a warm-up for the myriad of festivities that start in February in Humahuaca with a pilgrimage to the Candelaria Virgin supplemented by fireworks, traditional foods, and religious music. In Humahuaca, *Carnival* starts the Friday before Ash Wednesday with a *chicha* festival and altiplano music. If you don't join in the drinking, you'll have to down a large cup in one gulp. In Tilcara, *hermitas* of flowers representing the stations of the cross are hung along the streets, and processions come down from the mountains on Ash Wednesday.

During *Easter Week (Semana Santa)* in Yavi and Abra Pampa, the northern Argentines and southern Bolivians meet to barter and exchange handicrafts and products.

Easter Week is also celebrated with religious events throughout Mendoza province, San Javier in Misiones province, Salta province, and Aimogasta in La Rioja province.

On April 16, there's a *Cultural and Sports Festival* to celebrate the founding of Salta in that city. Corrientes celebrates its *Founding Day* on May 3 with a religious and popular arts festival.

In mid-June, *Semana Salta (Salta Week),* a gaucho festival, commemorates the death of General Martín Miguel de Güemes. Various contests are capped by a parade of *Gauchos de Güemes,* who light a bonfire at the feet of their hero's statue.

St. John's Day is celebrated on June 24 in a number of towns, but the most striking is in Formosa, where the faithful walk barefooted over a bed of hot coals without feeling the burns. During the last two Sundays in October, at the *Manca Fiesta (Festival of the Pot),* the oldest festival of the country in La Quiaca, Argentines from the altiplano and Bolivians from the south of their country come on burros and llamas loaded with merchandise for bartering.

On December 8, in the town of Luján, the festival of *Our Lady of Luján,* the patron saint of the Argentine Republic, is observed. It starts with a pilgrimage in which the devout are followed by old colonial carts and gauchos mounted on decorated horses. The week before, there's a parade of the old coaches from the *Colonial Museum* in Luján, and townsfolk dress in colonial clothing.

The first week in December, the *National Sea Festival* in Mar del Plata is celebrated with sporting events, the blessing of the sea and sea gods, gatherings around bonfires at Laguna de los Padres, and the crowning of a queen. A *Snow Festival* is held in June in Bariloche at the height of the ski season.

An important Argentine event, although not a festival, is the annual *Livestock Exhibition* in July on the grounds of the Argentine Rural Society in the Palmero section of Buenos Aires, where prize cattle, horses, sheep, and pigs are shown and auctioned.

BOLIVIA: In Oruro on *Carnival Sunday,* the *Diablada* (devil's dance) is performed. Dancers representing good and evil, the Indians and the Spaniards, fight it out after a parade and two dramas. This traditional festival kicks off an 8-day *Carnival* celebration.

The *Diabladas* are also performed in La Paz during Carnival, when special days are reserved for water fights. The *Diablada* dancers rarely rest in festival-filled Bolivia, performing also on the *Feast Day of St. Joseph* (March 18); at Lake Titicaca during spring (November) fertility celebrations; and on major saints' days in Oruro.

All Saints' Day and *All Souls' Day* (November 1-2) are occasions for honoring the dead who in pre-Columbian times were buried with many worldly goods and food provisions to sustain themselves in the next world. Bread is still placed on graves, along with special decorations and candles to light the way. At Cochabamba and around the Titicaca area, miniatures of reed boats are offered to ease the passage of souls across the lake. The cemeteries are the place to be.

During the first week of August, the Virgin of Copacabana is elaborately honored in her lakeside hometown and throughout the province. Other honors are bestowed on dogs in San Roque on August 16; on the bakers' patron, *St. Nicholas,* on September 10; on musicians through the good graces of *St. Cecilia* on November 22. There always seems to be cause for celebration anywhere at any time in Bolivia. Other festivities during the year include a Carnival celebration in the town of Tarabuco, near Sucre, in March; the Fiesta of Great Power (Fiesta del Gran Poder) in La Paz in July; and the Fiesta of Urkupiña in Quillacollo, near Cochabamba, in August.

BRAZIL: Brazilians celebrate *New Year's Eve* in Rio de Janeiro on Copacabana Beach by dashing into the ocean carrying offerings — flowers, mirrors, lipsticks, and other items designed to please a woman — letting the waves carry the gifts away to Iemanjá, the goddess of the sea. The celebrations begin a few hours before midnight, when thousands pack the beaches to sing and dance by candlelight.

In Salvador (Bahía), on the Thursday before the third Sunday of January, Bahian women gather on the front steps of the Bonfim Church to wash the steps. This *Lavagem do Bomfim Festival* includes 10 days of dancing and celebrating. On February 2, Bahians celebrate their *Festival to Iemanjá.* Beautifully dressed women put gifts to the sea goddess in boats and launch them from Salvador's Rio Vermelho and Itapoá beaches.

Other important Bahian festivals are the June 24 *Feast of St. John,* with fireworks, bonfires, and dancing; 3 days of festivities beginning December 4 in honor of *St. Barbara;* and the December 8 procession and feast in honor of *Nossa Senhora da Conceição* at the church of that name in the lower city.

Carnival in Brazil, which begins the Saturday before Ash Wednesday, needs no introduction. The days and nights of the parades of the samba "schools" (as Rio's neighborhoods are called) in glittering costumes that Brazilians begin planning a full year in advance make the picture pages of newspapers throughout the world. If you want to join these festivities, make reservations several months ahead; be prepared to pay steep, hiked-up prices for everything; and carry onto the streets only the money and documents you absolutely need — as, among other things, Carnival is a pickpockets' field day. If the exuberant madness of Rio's carnival is a bit overwhelming, consider *Carnival* in Salvador (Bahía) or other northern towns, where street processions, dancing, and the gaiety are equal to Rio's, even if the glitter is not. A seven-day stay is usually required when booking hotel rooms during Carnival.

CHILE: The main festival celebrated throughout Chile is the national holiday, the *Fiestas Patrias,* on September 18 and 19. All over the country, small open huts topped with tree boughs, called *ramadas,* are set up and people gather in the evening to drink the first fermentation of the grapes, *chica,* and dance the traditional dance, the *cueca.* Celebrations reach the highest intensity in and around Rancagua, where there are rodeo competitions between *huasos,* the Chilean cowboys. Chileans also observe a series of religious festivals in the country's small towns. The best known honors the Virgin of Carmen, on July 16 in La Tirana, in northern Chile. Thousands flock to this Atacama Desert town, some walking barefoot or on their knees to repay the *manda* (promise) made to the Virgin for favors granted. There's dancing in traditional Indian costumes and elaborate devil masks.

In the town of Andacollo, southeast of La Serena, a spectacular procession of brightly costumed townsfolk combines Indian and Christian rituals on *Christmas.* This festival, called the *Feast of the Virgin of Andacollo,* is most important in northern mining towns, as Our Lady of the Rosary of Andacollo is the patron saint of miners. Another festival is held on July 26 in Andacollo in honor of the Virgin, when the statue is taken from the cathedral and paraded through the streets. As do many other towns, Andacollo also celebrates the *Day of the Virgin of Carmen* on July 16.

On December 8 (*the Feast of the Immaculate Conception*), an impressive number of people walk barefooted or on their knees from Santiago and Valparaiso to the Lo Vasquez chapel on the road uniting the two cities, asking favors of the Virgin.

On January 20, thousands flock from all over the south to Yumbel, in the province of Concepción, to celebrate the *Festival of San Sebastian.* The center of the festival is a statue of the saint brought to Chile by the Spanish around 1580.

The *Cuasimodo,* a religious procession, takes place in the central zone the Sunday after *Easter.* The priest leaves the church in a horse-drawn carriage, carrying the host to his bedridden parishioners. He is followed by a procession of mounted *huasos* in full dress with decorated horses — and in recent years by bicyclists and motorcyclists. There are numerous processions in localities around Santiago.

A popular annual *Songfest* is held in the beach resort of Viña del Mar during February. Up-and-coming singers (and some who will never arrive) come from all over the world to participate in week-long singing competitions. There's ample entertainment by well-known people to supplement the contestants' singing in the outdoor amphitheater in Quinta Normal Park. To watch the festival, make hotel reservations as far ahead as possible. Even camping space is hard to come by.

COLOMBIA: Among a host of festivals, one of the most colorful is the August *Parade of the Chair Carriers* in Medellín, celebrating Antioquia state's independence from Spain. (Medellín is the state capital.) Hundreds of farmers come down from the hills carrying flower arrangements, including exotic species of orchids. There is a parade of marching bands, horsemen on thoroughbreds, and horse- and oxen-drawn floats. Also in August is the annual *Orchid Show.* Medellín is known as the orchid capital of the world. In February, when the town celebrates the *Feast of the Candelaria,* the city's patron saint day, festivities center around the bullring. Matadors from all over the world come to participate in South America's greatest bullfighting festival.

Holy Week at the end of Lent is a time of religious observance all over Colombia. The most famous is in Popayán where the Indians from the countryside join the city elders in elaborate processions, and life-size saintly statues are taken from the churches and borne through the town. A festival of sacred music is held concurrently. Pre-Lenten Carnival is also important to Colombians who celebrate to the Caribbean rhythms in Barranquilla and Cartagena. The latter now has an annual March festival highlighting Afro-Caribbean music, with visiting combos invited from all around the area. It's exciting music and the scene is lively. Check dates with the Colombian Government Tourist Office (phone: in New York City, 212-688-0151).

During the last 2 weeks of June, Neiva holds its special festival featuring the *bambuco,* the country's national dance. In Ibague, at the end of June, troupes from the highlands, plains, and coast gather for the largest national spectacle of folkloric dances.

ECUADOR: The Indian festivals of Ecuador are important not only for religious reasons but also as social events. Many festivals are highly decorative affairs. An Indian man acquires social prestige by the amount he spends on the festivals and by taking on leadership posts in organizing and supervising them.

On January 6 in San Rafael, near Quito, the *Three Kings Day* procession takes place. The "kings" ride through the streets of the town. In Ambato, there's the *Festival of Flowers and Fruits* sometime during the first part of February, and *Holy Week* in Riobamba and *Corpus Christi* days in June are not to be missed.

In late August or early September, the Otavalo Indians of Imbabura province celebrate their harvest festival, *El Yamor.* This festival is Indian in origin, giving thanks for the harvest, and the Spanish combined it with the *Feast Day of San Luís,* the harvest's patron saint. The arrival of the Inca is reenacted with music and dance. From about June 21 through the beginning of July, highland towns celebrate the feasts of *St. Peter, St. Paul,* and *St. John* with colorful, raucous parades, drinking, and dancing. *St. John's Day,* June 24, coincides with Perú's *Inca Festival,* and both celebrate the Sun God's importance.

In late September, near Cuenca, at the Hermitage of Biblian, a festival honors the Virgin, who saved the people from drought. There are pilgrimages, and giant paper hot-air balloons are released.

PERÚ: In Lima, tens of thousands of worshipers clad in purple robes take part in a procession to honor *Our Lord of the Miracles (Señor de los Milagros)* on October 18, 19, and 28. The festival honors a painting of Christ that, according to legend, has survived all of Perú's worst earthquakes. At the same time, the *Golden Scapular Bullfight Festival* takes place in the Plaza de Acho, Lima's biggest bullring.

In Cuzco, the *Inca Sun Festival (Inti-Raymi)* is celebrated on June 24 at Sacsahuaman, the fortress overlooking the city. Rituals honoring the solstice — singing, dancing, and much drinking of *chicha* (corn beer) — are the order of the day. Although they're colorful, they're no longer very authentic. Make reservations well in advance of your intended time of arrival. (See *Perú,* DIRECTIONS.) (By the way, Cuzco is one of those places where *Carnival* consists of dumping water and other objects on pedestrians, so it's a good time to be somewhere else.)

Before visiting Perú, it is worthwhile to investigate the possibilities of coordinating your stay with the dates of the summer and winter solstices, *All Souls' Day, Corpus Christi,* or any one of the many festival periods celebrated in all Andean countries. Cuzco, Puno, Arequipa, and the Huaras area are major centers for colorful spectacles.

SURINAME: The country's festival calendar reflects its large Asian population of East Indians of the Hindu faith, Indonesians following Islam, and many Chinese. Each group rings in a different New Year. The Hindustanis seem to have more religious holidays than anyone: *Basant Panchami* during Carnival and the harvest time; *Holi Phagwa* marking the beginning of spring; *Deepavali,* the festival of light in the fall. Fireworks and dragon dances are part of Chinese celebrations for their *New Year's Day* and *Nationalist China Holiday* observance. Christians who trace their roots to Holland turn out for the arrival of *St. Nicholas,* who parades in with gifts on December 5.

VENEZUELA: The country celebrates 11 national holidays, in addition to *Easter* and *Christmas,* some of which are religious holidays celebrated in some towns. January 6 is the *Feast of the Magi;* April 19, the *Declaration of Independence;* May 1, *Labor Day;* May 7 (movable), *Asunción Day;* May 28 (movable), *Corpus Christi;* June 29, *Feast of St. Peter and St. Paul;* July 5, *Independence Day;* July 24, *Simón Bolívar's Birthday;* October 12, *Day of the Race;* November 1, *All Saints' Day;* and December 8, *Feast of the Immaculate Conception.*

In January, the *Paradura* (standing up) of the Christ Child is celebrated in Mérida. Peasants take the Infant Jesus statue through the streets to their farms to ask a blessing on the land. They return the statue to its crib, standing up. The procession is accompanied by music and firecrackers.

On February 2, the *Dance of the Vassals of Candelaria* in La Punta celebrates Venezuelan folklore.

Carnival is a wild affair in Caracas, Maracaibo, Barquisimeto, and Cíudad Bolívar, where the fervor rivals that of Brazilian carnivals.

The day before *Corpus Christi,* in the town of San Francisco de Yare, the 2-day *Festival of the Devils* takes place. The townspeople dress in cumbersome red papier-mâché masks depicting grotesque horned creatures. Some of the masks have asses' teeth. The dancers perform in front of the church until fatigued; then drunken revelry ensues.

Casinos Royale

South America's casinos are fewer and smaller than those found in Las Vegas. However, there's a certain cachet in gambling in exotic surroundings — Iquazú Falls, for example. Most of the casinos are in luxury hotels; in many, little English is spoken.

ARGENTINA: All 15 casinos in Argentina are state-owned. The biggest, most modern, luxurious, and best known is the *Central Casino* at Mar del Plata, Maritimo Patricio Peralta 2252 (phone: 2-70-11). Described by one Argentine as a "railroad station for gambling," *Central* has 108 roulette tables, 55 tables for a card game called *punto y banca,* 7 for dice, and 2 for "34." It's open from 3:30 PM to 4 AM all year except for a brief closing for maintenance. The entrance fee is about $3; chips are issued in denominations from $20 to $100. Minimum and maximum bets, depending on the game, run from $1 to $500. The minimum age is 18 and casual dress is allowed. Two other Mar del Plata casinos are annexes of the *Central Casino:* one, at Av. Martínez de Hoz 3545 (phone: 8-40-31; 8-40-32); the other, in the luxurious *Provincial* hotel,

Boulevard Maritimo Patricio Peralta Ramos 2300 (phone: 2-60-95). In the lake district resort San Carlos de Bariloche, the *Bariloche Center* hotel, on the corner of Calle Governador Pagano and Calle San Martín, has roulette and *punto y banca.*

In the *Internacional Cataratas de Iguazú* hotel, on the Argentine side of Iguazú Falls, is a small casino with four roulette tables and two for *punto y banca.*

Other casinos can be found in Miramar, at Calle 9 de Julio 1343; in Necochea at the corner of Calle 4 and Calle 91; in Pinamar in the *Playas* hotel, at the corner of Avenida Arquitecto Jorge Bunge and Calle Las Sirenas; in Alta Gracia at the corner of Velez Sarsfield and Carlos Pellegrini; in La Cumbre at the corner of Velez Sarsfield and Estanislao Olmos de Aguilera; in Paraná at the corner of Costanera Alta and Córdoba; in Resistencia at the international airport; in Puerto Madryn at the corner of Julio A. Roca and Sarmiento; in Comodoro Rivadavia at the corner of 9 de Julio and Rivadavia; and in La Rioja at the corner of Quiroga and Sarmiento.

CHILE: There are three casinos in Chile. The Viña del Mar casino, one of the most outstanding in Latin America, is an elegant building with ample gardens; dress is *very* formal. The casino, right on the bay of Avenida San Martín, is open every night during the summer season from September 15 through March 14 and on weekends during the rest of the year. There are roulette, blackjack, baccarat, and slot machines. To enter the casino, players pay a $1 admission fee, but to enter the gameroom, a membership card for the season, which costs about $2, is necessary. The minimum roulette bet is $1; for blackjack and baccarat it's $10. In Arica, there's a modern, smallish casino at General Velásquez 955. Another small one in Puerto Varas is open only during the summer season.

COLOMBIA: Among the casinos in Colombia, there's an informal one in the *Caribe* hotel in Cartagena, and it's usually crowded until the 3 AM closing time. There are slot machines with chips at 10¢, roulette tables European-style (20 to 30 players long), and blackjack. The *Americano* hotel casino requires coat and tie.

The *Giradot* resort hotel in Lagomar El Peñon has a small casino, as does the *Nutibara* hotel in Medellín. Surprisingly, there are two small casinos on relatively undeveloped San Andrés Island, where the atmosphere is casual, chips start at 30¢, and the casinos are set up for roulette, craps, blackjack, and poker from 9 PM to 3 AM. One is in the *Royal Abacoa* hotel, on the beach near a shopping area. The other, in the *Eldorado* hotel, across the street from the beach.

ECUADOR: The major hotels in Quito, Guayaquil, and Salinas have casinos. Serious crapshooters and blackjack players prefer the atmosphere of Quito's *Colón* hotel casino, where the roulette wheels have two zeros. The hotel, one of Quito's major social centers, is at the corner of Avenidas Amazonas and Patria (phone: 23-13-00). There's also a casino in the *Inter-Continental Quito,* Av. González Suárez 2500 (phone: 23-03-00). A lovely new casino (brightly decorated and where single women would feel welcome) opened at the *Ouro Verde* hotel, 9 de Octubre y García Moreno (phone: 51-02-01).

PANAMÁ: This country's Tourism Institute claims that "gambling is not only a cornerstone of the country's economy, but a way of life." To go native, then, try the popular *El Panamá Hilton* casino, Via España (phone: 23-16-60). In Panamá City, also try the casino at the moderately priced *Soloy* hotel, corner of Av. Perú and Calle 30 (phone: 27-11-33), or *Granada* hotel, Calle Eusebio A. Morales (phone: 64-49-00). On Contadora Island, visit the *Casino Contadora* hotel (phone: 27-11-33). In the Chiriqui Highlands at Volcán, there is a casino at the *Bambito* hotel.

PARAGUAY: Since gambling is outlawed in Brazil, Brazilians who want to outfox fate at the tables cross the border to Paraguay. Right across the line there's a rather basic casino in the *Gran Hotel Casino Acaray,* in Puerto Presidente Stroessner in Alto Paraná. In Asunción, the luxury *Itá Enramada* casino has roulette, baccarat, 21, and slot machines. The address is Cacique Lambares y Ribero del Río (phone: 70-01-4).

SURINAME: There are casinos at two hotels in Paramaribo, the moderate to expensive *Suriname Torarica* and the inexpensive *Suriname Palace.* Make reservations to stay at the *Torarica* by calling 212-247-7950 in New York. In Paramaribo, phone: 71-50-0; 77-43-2. The *Palace* is at 1 Independence Square, facing the president's mansion (phone: 72-81-5; 72-13-1).

URUGUAY: The nine casinos here range from very basic to deluxe. Two of them are in Montevideo; the *Parque Casino* hotel, Playa Ramírez (phone: 40-23-39), and the *Casino Carrasco* hotel near the airport of the same name (phone: 50-19-71). Uruguay's two other fancy casinos are in the seaside resort of Punta del Este: *Nogaró,* at Calle Gorlero and Calle 31, and the *Casino Rafael* hotel, on the Rambla L. Batlle. The beach towns of Atlantida, Carmelo, and La Paloma also have small casinos. There is also one in the *Casino El Mirador* hotel in Colonia (phone: Carmelo 314).

DIRECTIONS

Introduction

The Pan-American Highway is a vast road system running approximately 16,000 miles down the western side of both the North and South American continents. Its road links are of varying quality, with some fine sections and some pretty poor ones. Most of the secondary roads through the mountains and to the jungle are very difficult, and during some seasons they are quite impassable. However, if you especially enjoy driving and prefer to explore the Americas by car, it is possible to drive from Alaska all the way to southern Chile (with a break between Panamá and Colombia where presently the road is unfinished and vehicles must be shipped from Colón or Balboa to ports in Colombia). While the Pan-American is South America's most important highway, and the focal point of the west coast road network, visiting drivers find that there are other good national highway systems on the continent, such as those in Brazil and Argentina, where a through road connects the two via Paraguay.

Although nowhere in South America are there long stretches of six-lane freeways comparable to those at home, you will undoubtedly be impressed that in some of the most out-of-the-way places imaginable roads have been built. Perhaps even more amazing are many of the railway routes that traverse the Andes like a roller coaster. Whether you travel by car (in your own vehicle or one rented locally), by bus (and there are some fine deluxe services, particularly in Chile, Argentina, and Brazil), or by train, you will discover that some of the world's most breathtaking scenery is in South America.

Certainly the easiest way to travel between countries is by air, and along the west coast even the bird's-eye view is spectacular. (A tip on air travel: sit on the left southbound, right northbound.) Flying point to point, you can rent a car in each country to drive where you want, or where the road system will permit. On the other hand, with time, a working knowledge of Spanish, a sturdy car or recreational vehicle, and some thorough research of weather and road conditions, you can indeed start in Boston and get to Buenos Aires.

In the following pages we have outlined driving tours of rural sections of each South American country, including Panamá, which forms the land bridge from Central America to the southern continent. Each tour will generally require several days' travel time, and is designed to direct the traveler to the most interesting areas. From Colombia's sparkling Caribbean coast to the snowcapped volcanoes of the Ecuadorian Andes, to the vast Amazon jungle, to the glaciers of Tierra del Fuego, we have tried to outline tours that start from South America's major cities, with suggested side trips and short journeys. Entries are not comprehensive or exhaustive; they discuss the highlights of the route, including useful suggestions for shopping and dining; in *Best en Route,* they suggest accommodations at the best hotels, inns, and lodges along the way.

Entries are organized by country, with an introduction explaining the routes that follow. Since each country is divided into several routes, it is possible to string them together into longer itineraries if you wish. But if you are pressed for time, by following any single itinerary you will find the most notable spots (and attractive accommodations) in the area.

Argentina

The second largest country in South America, Argentina's 1,078,000 square
miles are wedged into a triangular shape that is wide at the north, then
narrows down to a long skinny tail at the south. On the eastern coast of the
continent, the country is bordered by the Atlantic Ocean and Uruguay to the
east, Paraguay to the northeast, Brazil to the north, Bolivia to the northwest,
Chile to the west, and the Antarctic Ocean to the south. At the southernmost
extreme of the continent, Argentina shares the Tierra del Fuego archipelago
with Chile.

Argentina is separated into four distinct sections. To the east are the white,
sunny coastal beaches; to the west, the snowcapped peaks of the Andes,
including South America's highest, 22,834-foot Mt. Aconcagua. The Lake
District in the west, also known as the Switzerland of South America, is the
most popular skiing and fishing resort area on the southern continent. The
400-mile Río Colorado runs from west to east, cutting the country latitudi-
nally in two, with the humid jungle (the chaco) and fertile plain (pampa) to
the north, and the dry, craggy, infertile cattle fields, small mountains, and
moorlike scenery of Patagonia to the south. The farther south you go, the
starker the land becomes. By the time you reach Tierra del Fuego, across the
Strait of Magellan, the country becomes cold and gray. Daylight rarely
arrives before 9 AM in winter, and the temperature during the summer hardly
ever rises above 52°, just about one-half that found in the northern jungles
(100°). If you continue south to the slice of territory Argentina claims on the
Antarctic continent, you'll find nothing but snow, icebergs, and even colder
subzero weather. The only farmable thing here is the kelp, produced in the
cold Antarctic waters.

Cold or hot, Argentina is a cosmopolitan country. Its 28 million people
— of Spanish, German, Italian, and English descent — are among the most
educated in South America; the literacy rate is over 90%.

Buenos Aires, on the Río de la Plata (actually the mouth of the Río Paraná
and Río Uruguay, which flow into the Atlantic Ocean on this part of the
coast), is Argentina's capital. More than ten million people live in Greater
Buenos Aires. One of the world's largest seaports, it exports tons of fruit,
tanning and leather goods, wool, lumber, paper, rubber goods, iron, steel, oil,
and other manufactured goods. Musically, Buenos Aires is the birthplace of
the graceful, sensuous tango. (For a complete report on Buenos Aires, see THE
CITIES.) Argentina's other major cities are: Córdoba (pop. 2,400,000), Mendoza (pop. 1,000,000), La Plata (pop. 800,000), and Mar del Plata (pop.
500,000).

Discovered in 1516 by Spanish explorer Juan Diaz de Solís (who anchored
in the Río de la Plata), Argentina's first settlement was not founded until
1536, when Pedro de Mendoza came to what is today Buenos Aires. Argen-

tina, like other South American countries, remained under Spanish rule until 1810, when the Spanish viceroy, who had jurisdiction over the Argentine area, was forced by the populace to resign. Independence was declared 6 years later by the Congress of Tucumán, after a fiery, 6-year revolution led by José de San Martín, who went on to liberate Chile and Perú.

Argentina's twentieth-century political course has been fraught with political violence, rebellion, and repression — which continue to erode the country's great economic potential. Juan Domingo Perón, a strong political figure, headed a dictatorial regime from 1946 until his ouster in 1955. His second wife, Eva, was a popular heroine among the large working class that constituted Perón's strongest following. Following a 17-year exile in Spain, Perón returned to Argentina and ruled for a year. When he died in 1974, his third wife, Maria Estela (known as Isabelita) became president of an industrially developed nation whose fortunes continued to slide under her totally inept leadership. She was deposed in 1976 during a military coup headed by General Jorge Rafael Videla whose authoritarian rule neither won applause in world human rights circles nor resolved the country's economic woes. Following the military's attempted takeover of the British-ruled Falkland Islands, Argentina's government fell. Elections held in 1983 put an end to military rule.

Visitors to Argentina are advised to carry their passports and travel documents at all times. Although there is very little threat of actual danger, police frequently ask to see personal documents. If you are driving, be sure you have the proper insurance and that your *carnet* and insurance policy are in order and easily accessible should you have an accident (see *Touring by Car,* GETTING READY TO GO).

The ten routes in this chapter suggest itineraries that will enable you to explore the different areas of Argentina as fully as possible. Although you can drive yourself, it is important to know that distances between towns can be great; if you break down, you may have to wait a very long time for someone to come along to drive you to whatever will be the nearest source for assistance. Touring is often better done via an excellent network of buses, railroads, and domestic airlines that connect even the remote towns and villages.

The first route in this chapter starts in Buenos Aires and heads south on the coastal highway through Mar del Plata, Argentina's largest seaside resort, to Bahía Blanca. The second route takes you from Bahía Blanca west across the Río Colorado valley, where you can see the geological separation between pampas and Patagonian desert, to Bariloche and the Lake District. The Patagonia route runs from Carmen de Patagones south through Santa Cruz to Tierra del Fuego (Land of Fire) and the town of Ushuaia, the self-proclaimed City at the End of the World. From Patagonia you can board a ship heading straight through the Beagle Channel to Antarctica.

If you don't care to rough it, the northern routes offer more comfortable alternatives. The first takes you northeast from Buenos Aires to Mesopotamia, that section of Argentina sandwiched between the Uruguay and Paraná rivers, to Iguazú Falls. From here, you'll return to the capital and continue west, passing through the fertile Mendoza and Córdoba areas, continuing north to historic Tucumán.

Buenos Aires to Bahía Blanca

The 390-mile (600-km) route from Buenos Aires to Bahía Blanca is rich in history, land, and industry. The heartland of Argentina's earliest settlements, the area's natural resources are fully developed: The Río de la Plata, the northeastern river boundary separating Argentina from Uruguay, is the country's chief inland shipping route; the lush, fertile soil of the pampas provides the basis for a thriving farm industry; the Atlantic beaches of Mar del Plata, Miramar, and Necochea are filled seasonally with international and local travelers.

Discovered by Juan Díaz de Solís in 1516, the 550-mile Río de la Plata is the second largest river system in South America (the Amazon ranks first). On the river, Buenos Aires was settled in 1536 by the Spanish conquistador Pedro de Mendoza; it remained the provincial territory capital until federalized as the nation's capital in 1882. La Plata, a coastal city 35 miles (56 km) southeast of Buenos Aires, succeeded as the provincial capital, and today it is a major cultural and import-export center.

The economic growth of Buenos Aires was spurred by two events: the selection of the city as federal capital and the rapid development of the surrounding pampas into farms and ranches. Cattle, horses, and mules were raised on huge *estancias* (ranches) built in the flatland; alfalfa, barley, oats, maize, linseed, and sorghum seed were imported for planting.

More than 68% of the entire Argentine population inhabits the pampas–Buenos Aires area, and the contributing nationalities are diverse: Spanish, Italian, German, Dutch, Portuguese, and Yugoslavian. Sadly, there are few native Argentines, for the colonials literally exterminated the native Indian people. The Campagna del Desierto (1878–1883) was responsible for the founding of most of the cities and towns from Buenos Aires to Bahía Blanca, and many of the large *estancias* originated as spoils of war for victorious military officers.

Pampas towns are usually treeless, yet in the Sierra de Tandil there are pine forests and eucalyptus trees, both imported from Australia.

When you travel to the Atlantic Ocean from the pampas, the landscape changes from browns to greens, from dry to moist, and the beach resorts begin to appear. Mar del Plata — "the happy city," as it is known — has 5 miles of beaches, parks, and campsites. A jaunt on coastal Route 11 north from Mar del Plata takes you to Mar Chiquita, Villa Gesell (a popular youth resort), and Pinamar, resorts that offer fishing, swimming, and sailing. Route 11 south takes you to Chapadmalal and Luna Roja (Red Moon) Beach; Miramar vies with Mar del Plata as a favorite summer retreat.

The city of Bahía Blanca (White Bay) is La Plata's southern counterpart. At the head of a large bay where the Naposta River flows into the Atlantic Ocean, it is the most important town in southern Argentina. Here, a variety of merchandise, from fruits and vegetables to petroleum products, is exported to every part of the world.

Leaving Bahía Blanca, a trip 139 miles (198 km) inland on Route 33 west leads you toward the pampas and a small lake resort area. There, Carhué's 162-acre Lago Epecuen is so heavily mineralized that its salt content is 20 times that of an ocean.

The 240-mile (385-km) path south from Buenos Aires to Mar del Plata on Route 2 is dotted with vacation resorts. For starters, we recommend the stretch that encompasses La Plata and the pampas towns of Chascomus, Dolores, Maipú, and Piran. A side trip from Piran on Route 11 north will lead you to the resorts of Mar Chiquita, Villa Gesell, and Pinamar before you reach Mar del Plata.

Remember, Argentina has more than 100,000 miles of developed highway, mostly paved and modern and good. Road travelers are advised to drop into the Argentine Automobile Club on Avenida del Libertador in Buenos Aires for route maps and road information. As an alternative, the country is equipped with an excellent domestic airline network and more than 27,000 miles of railroad.

LA PLATA: The provincial capital since 1882, La Plata (pop. 800,000) celebrates Foundation Day every November 19. Port Ensenada, 5 miles east of the city on the Río de la Plata, serves as a major eastern seaport for exporting oil, grain, and refrigerated meat. The city is also Argentina's main oil refining center. A 44-mile pipeline runs from the YPF Petroleum refinery to the south dock at Buenos Aires.

La Plata has not always been so named. During his dictatorship, Juan Perón renamed both city and province for his wife Eva. The original name, however, was restored after he was overthrown. A children's village with scaled-down buildings was built during Eva Perón's time in Gonnet, 8 miles before La Plata, near the Yacht Club, Arsenal, and Naval Academy.

A lovely town laid out on a 3-mile-square grid, the city is most famous for its Natural History Museum, with an astonishing collection of skeletons of extinct pre-Pliocene reptiles gathered from the pampas. A part of the University of La Plata (founded 1890), the museum is in Paseo del Bosque, near the zoological gardens and observatory. The cathedral and town hall are on Plaza Moreno, in the city's center. There is also a Garden of Peace, with flowers honoring each nation of the world.

La Plata can be reached by car or by railway and bus from Buenos Aires.

CHASCOMUS: Chascomus is south of La Plata on Route 2. It sits on a 12-acre lake of the same name and its best catch is the pejerrey fish. (Amateur fishing contests are held here during the winter season.) Camping grounds, bathing beaches, and a Regatta Club are at Monte Brown, on the lake's far side, and there is also a gaucho museum.

DOLORES: About 48 miles (76 km) south of Chascomus, Dolores (pop. 30,000) was once famous for its *tribunales* (courts). Today it is a grain and cattle center on the pampas. The town, founded in 1818, was destroyed by Indians 3 years later, then rebuilt.

En Route from Dolores – At this point, you can either continue south to Mar del Plata down coastal Route 8, which leads you through Mar de Ajo, then on to Mar del Plata and as far as Miramar; or continue on Route 2, which will lead you to Maipú and its rural museum. Route 2 is recommended.

MAR DEL PLATA: Argentines call this "the happy city," and well they might. With its 5 miles of beautiful beaches, parks, shopping galleries, and inexpensive products made locally, Mar del Plata is equipped to make people smile. From December through Easter it's a lively resort, where the Argentine elite have met for the last 300 years and where big money can be won — or, unhappily, lost — at the gaming tables of its fabulous casinos.

Originally founded by wealthy Argentines as a retreat from Buenos Aires, Mar del Plata today caters to rich and less rich alike. There are 1,500 hotels in the city, and their prices depend on their proximity to the beach. It's advisable, however, to make your hotel reservations well in advance if you are visiting during the summer season. Hard-core Mar del Plata addicts are exhilarated by the throngs of people who flock here to sit by row after row of colorful beach umbrellas and cabanas, and swing to the frenzied nightlife, particularly in the casinos, theaters, and movies.

The largest gambling establishment in the world is the casino in Bristol Beach, and it rakes in more than $200,000 a night. (Believe it or not, all profits are forwarded to the Welfare Ministry.) The *Provincial* hotel next door has rooms reserved exclusively for high gamblers, and together both places can handle up to 9,000 gamblers at a clip.

There are also convention halls and exhibit halls in Mar del Plata as well as a roller-skating rink and gymnasium. For shoppers, the primary consumer items are sweaters, made in Mar del Plata and sold throughout Argentina. If you notice an abundance of these in sky blue and white, it's no coincidence; Argentines, especially Buenos Aires youth, are partial to sweaters that sport the colors of their flag.

Mar del Plata is also the home of *alfajores,* cookies topped with *dulce de leche* (caramel à la Argentina) and covered with chocolate. Argentines confide that there is a hierarchy of *alfajores;* the best are Havanna brand (nothing to do with Cuba — they're made by a wealthy Greek family); Trassens are very good, too. *Alfajores* are also made in Santa Fe and Córdoba. The Havanna candy factory for *alfajores* is next to La Perla Beach (Av. Constitución).

Too many *alfajores?* Walk them off. Mar del Plata is filled with plazas of trees and flowers. General San Martín and General Arias parks are at elegant Playa Grande, and polo grounds and golf clubs are in the vicinity. Mar del Plata has four 18-hole golf courses. In the extreme north of the city, the sports center of Parque Camet has polo, rugby, and *pato* (the national sport) fields, with ample space for horseback riding. The large new stadium, built for the 1978 World Cup Soccer games, holds 41,500 spectators.

Mar del Plata is also a working port — a bustling, colorful place filled with bright yellow fishing boats with red trim gleaming in the sunlight. The fishing boats return to the harbor daily at 3 PM, followed by herds of seals barking happily and vying for the crews' rejected fish. Bring your camera; on a clear day, this scene makes a beautiful shot.

South of the port, the combination of sand, sea, and rocks continues to the point of Punta Mogotes, whose lighthouse guides ships along the irregular coast.

Some 250 miles (400 km) south of Buenos Aires, Mar del Plata is about 4½ hours by car — a direct route, but driving can become slow, unsafe, and uncomfortable in summer. A 4½-hour train ride on the El Marplatense express from Constitución Station in Buenos Aires ($7) or the 5-hour trip with stops might be preferable. A bus ride (La Costera Criolla is recommended) takes about 5 hours and costs $8.50. The shortest and most expensive trip is the 45-minute plane ride. Mar del Plata's downtown airport is Aeropuerto de Camet, with offices on the *Provincial* hotel's ground floor.

En Route from Mar del Plata – You might want to delay your trip to Bahía Blanca for a few days in order to visit some of the resorts north and inland from Mar del Plata. Take Route 11 north for 25 miles (34 km) to Mar Chiquita. This lagoon, 15 miles long, offers fishing, sailing and saltwater bathing.

Villa Gesell, approximately 78 miles (130 km) from Mar del Plata, was founded and developed by Carlos Gesell in the early 1950s. Today it is becoming one of the more popular youth resorts in the area. It offers a respite from the bustle of other resorts, and its 10-mile beach and woods of cypress, pine, eucalyptus, and acacia provide quiet moments.

Restaurants to try here are *Noa Noa* (Av. 3) and *Don Diego* (Av. 3). About 252 miles (420 km) from Buenos Aires, the resort can be reached by Anton buses departing from the Constitución area or by plane.

Pinamar, another resort, is only 13 miles (22 km) north of Villa Gesell. Like Mar del Plata, it is a summer resort for society families who stay in chalet-type homes. There are plenty of small eating spots for having tea and a meal, including *Status, Catedral,* and the *Cosona del Tío.*

Mar de Ajo, 30 miles (50 km) north of Pinamar on Route 11, is a good place for clamming.

BALCARCE: You can reach Balcarce by following Route 226 northwest from Mar del Plata. Forty miles (68 km) inland from the seaside resort, the small (pop. 20,450) pampas town serves as a good base for hikers who wish to explore the area. An interesting spot to visit is Cinco Cerros, five strangely shaped hills.

TANDIL: Continuing west from Balcarce on Route 226 (or traveling from Mar del Plata directly by train), you reach Tandil. Nestled in hill country, this small town (pop. 65,700) is a leading cheese-producing center in Argentina.

Tandil is the Araucanian Indian term for "high hill." It was settled in 1823 during the Indian Wars when General Martín Rodríguez extended the western frontier as far as Sierra de la Ventana and built Fuerte Independencia (Fort Independence) in Tandil. In the Museo Forte Independencia (4 de Abril 845) are documents, arms, and antique carriages related to Tandil's often bloody history.

From the central Plaza Moreno, follow the avenue that leads down the hill and pass through a stone archway donated by the town's Italian community to commemorate Tandil's 100th anniversary. Beyond the arch, Parque Independencia offers some interesting sights. The stairway leads to a terrace dominated by the statue of General Rodriguez, and there is a good view of the countryside and restaurant atop Castillo Morisco's hill. The side of the hill harbors the John Kennedy amphitheater, accommodating 5,000 spectators.

Tandil's best-known holiday is its spectacular Holy Week Festival held prior to Easter. The predominant religion throughout South America is Roman Catholicism, and during this week, from Palm Sunday to Easter Sunday, thousands of pilgrims flock here for processions to El Cerro Calvari (Calvary Hill), where a 49-foot cross at the summit supports a Christ figure sculpted in French marble. To the left of the cross stands a replica of the Holy Sepulcher and a sculpture representing the Stations of the Cross stands nearby. The hillside itself is covered with groves of eucalyptus and olive trees.

Inaugurated in 1943, Calvary Hill and the sculptures were conceived by Pedro Redolatti, a local businessman, and his cousin, Monsignor Fortunato Devoro, a local priest. You can reach the hill by following Avenida España to Avenida de Calvario.

En Route from Tandil – Leaving Tandil, continue west on Route 226 to Azul, then on Route 3 south; you will arrive at Tres Arroyos, an important wheat and cattle center on the Pampas.

Tres Arroyos is not a major tourist site, but there is good reason to come here if you enjoy fishing. An annual fishing contest, 24 Horas de la Corvina Negra (black bass), is held every February. Information on the event is available from the Club de Cazadores, Calle Velaz Sarsfield 285.

Tres Arroyos is named after three streams that flow into the Río Claromeco, about 46 miles (75 km) north of the town of Claromeco. The three streams — Seco, Orellano, and Del Medio — are popular fishing areas. Regular fishing expeditions are organized, and equipment can be rented in town.

CLAROMECO: This beach resort can be reached by driving south from Tres Arroyos on Provincial Route 73. Claromeco is a favorite with beachgoers because north winds bring balmy weather, and a current from the Brazilian coast keeps the water warmer here than at most other beaches in the area. The dark sands backed by high dunes stretch smooth and soft along the coast. The town is easy to navigate; all streets are numbered and follow each other in logical sequence.

Dining and dancing are Claromeco pastimes. Fresh fish, the local specialty, is served at the *Juanillo* restaurant, *Claromeco* hotel (Calle 7 at 26), and at the *Cabaña de Fermin* (Calle 11 between 7 and 8). The tango haunts include *Don Mateo* (Calle 28 between 21 and 2) and *Claromeco* (Calle 26 between 23 and 2).

A visit to the lighthouse gives you a good view of Claromeco's coast, if you're willing to climb 278 steps for it. If you're not exhausted afterward, cross the bridge that fords Río Claromeco to Dunamar, a forest reserve protecting wildlife.

If you wish to return to the coast and Mar del Plata, retrace your route to Tres Arroyos and pick up Route 226 east. The highway takes you to Mar del Plata and Route 11. Remaining on Route 3 southwest, you go straight to Bahía Blanca.

En Route South from Mar del Plata – Route 11 ends in Miramar, 24 miles (40 km) south of Mar del Plata, but you might want to take coastal Route 8 down through Mar del Sur Necochea.

Before reaching Miramar, however, spend some time in Chapadmalal, halfway between Miramar and Mar del Plata. Though not much more than a general store and some houses, it is a scenic resting spot. Luna Roja (Red Moon) beach curves against cliffs, and purple wild flowers cling to windswept dunes.

Miramar is your first stop south of Chapadmalal. The resort has fewer residents than Mar del Plata, and the beach is markedly less crowded.

Mar del Sur, 10 miles (16 km) south of Miramar on Route 8, has a quiet beach with a fishing lagoon.

Necochea is another 75 miles (120 km) farther south. A popular beach resort (pop. 29,319), it has a new casino that rivals that of Mar del Plata. The beach is 15 miles long and is reportedly one of the best in the country.

From Necochea you can pick up Route 2 and travel south to Bahía Blanca.

BAHÍA BLANCA: The most important city south of Buenos Aires, Bahía Blanca (White Bay) is a modern seaport that sits at the head of a large bay where the Naposta River flows into the Atlantic Ocean. From its five docks — Arroya, Pareja, Ingeniero White, Galvin, and Rosales — fresh produce sails to all ports in the world.

The city was founded in 1828 by Colonel Tomas Estomba and a small band of soldiers, who were searching for a strategic site for a frontier fortress. Today, Bahía Blanca has a population of more than 200,000. Most residents earn their living in port-related employment and at the naval base, Puerto Belgrano. Another major and growing industry in and around the city is petroleum. Argentina, now almost self-sufficient in petroleum production, has two important refineries and a research center in Puerto Galvan.

Bahía Blanca is a cultural center for the southern pampas and Patagonia. The Universidad del Sur and several technological institutes specializing in oceanographic studies are within the city limits. Although Bahía Blanca itself may not offer much in the way of tourist facilities, you might enjoy several excursions to nearby beaches or into the low hills where you can see native flora and fauna, and fish in freshwater streams.

If you stay overnight, take time to visit the History and Natural Science museums, both in the basement of the Municipal Theater, Calle Dorrego 116. Here you can wander through permanent exhibits featuring fossils, maps, and travel diaries relating to Patagonia's past.

The Fine Arts Museum, Calle Alsina 65, displays paintings, sculpture, and drawings of respected Argentine artists, including Sforza, Castagnino, and Quiros. You can visit the museums most days of the week, but check before going, since they do close for local and national holidays.

Outdoors, Bahía Blanca has two major parks, Parque de Mayo and Parque Independencia. In the Parque de Mayo (Av. Alem 1300) you can wander along the banks of lakes fed by the Río Naposta or down paths through 25 acres of gardens. The Parque Independencia, on the outskirts of town, has a zoo on its 40 acres of forest crisscrossed by gravel paths. There are also recreation fields and a municipal swimming pool.

Bahía Blanca has some very good restaurants. *Taberna Baska* (Lavalle 284) has seafood and tasty international cuisine. *Gambrinus* (Arribenos 174) is a popular beer hall. You can't miss at any of the fish *cantinas* along Puerto Ingeniero White. Especially good is *Micho's Cantina,* which also offers Greek specialties.

En Route from Bahía Blanca – If you're not rushing for any destination, plan to stay an extra day or two to explore the countryside around Bahía Blanca, especially Route 3 east and Route 33 north. Sign names signal the Indian origins of most towns and villages in the pampas.

Pehuen-Co, or "pine and water" in the Araucanian dialect, is a stretch of beach dotted by small chalets some 43 miles (69 km) southeast on Route 3. The beach is well shaded by a small grove of pine trees growing near the shore. When you're finished sunning, take a stroll along the Avenida de los Pinos and sample any number of refreshing drinks in the small cafés.

Monte Hermoso is one of several resorts in the small lake district found on provincial Route 78, a detour off Route 33 north. You can rent any fishing or beach equipment needed along the boardwalk extending down Avenida Costanera. Be careful if you go swimming. Jellyfish are known to annoy swimmers during the summer season, even though underwater barriers have been built.

If possible, visit Monte Hermoso near October 15 to be on hand for the Fiesta de la Llanura, complete with fireworks, dancing, and food specialties.

CARHUÉ: The crowning point of this lake district 139 miles (198 km) north of Bahía Blanca, Carhué's Lago Epecuen covers 162 acres and is 20 times saltier than the sea. Its Araucanian name means "almost burning" (*carhué* is Araucanian for "strategic place") and testifies to the water's stinging qualities if accidentally swallowed or rubbed into your eyes. Numerous health spas along the lakefront treat guests for skin problems and rheumatism. At present, much lakefront property remains submerged because of recent, unusually heavy continuous rains, and definite plans to remedy the situation have yet to be implemented.

A replica of a medieval castle, Castillo de Epecuen, sits within a 30-minute walk from the lake.

In Carhué, the cypress-lined streets come alive once a year during the first 2 weeks in March and the annual Folklore Festival. A reconstructed fortress museum 1.2 miles (2 km) from the town's center on Route 78 tells a little of Carhué's history. Fortín Centinela was the sight of a major battle during the Indian Wars of the 1870s. When Colonel Nicolas Lavalle captured Carhué in 1877, he left a small band of soldiers to raise the Argentine flag in a pueblo while he forged westward to expand the frontier. The town's central plaza, which dates back to 1877, bears Lavalle's name.

Both Carhué and Lago Epecuen have fair restaurants. *La Curva* in Carhué has a good assorted grill (*parrillada*) and is less than 1 mile from town on Route 33.

En Route from Carhué – Leaving Carhué, continue northeast on Route 78 to Route 75. This will take you to Reta beach, with its villages of unpaved, sandy streets. Reta, built in 1926, boasts a steady population of 300, which expands to as many as 25,000 in summer.

SIERRA DE LA VENTANA: Driving out of Reta on Route 72 northeast you arrive at Sierra de la Ventana, a small town with a surrounding reserve that offers spectacular views and freshwater fishing. The Ventana peak gets its name from a natural opening in its apex that is shaped like a window, or *ventana*.

You can drive through this cultivated region on good asphalt roads, and there is a variety of inexpensive and free sports facilities in the area: swimming pools, golf courses, horseback riding trails, mountain climbing trails, and trout fishing in the Río Sauce Grande. In Sierra de la Ventana, it's continuous open season on trout and pejerrey fishing, with the exception of the 90-day spawning period, from September 1 to November 30.

BEST EN ROUTE

Hotels in the Bahía Blanca region range from expensive ($25 to $50 per person a night), to moderate ($20–$25), to inexpensive ($10–$20) and provide modern facilities. Travelers, however, are reminded that popular resort areas often raise prices as high as 40% in the summer, so check prices in Mar del Plata, Miramar, and Necochea if you plan to visit at that time.

Your best bet might be one of the many campsites dotting the area. They can cost as little as $5 a night, which nets you a spot, and facilities including hot running water.

CHASCOMUS

Camping grounds are at Monte Brown on the far side of Lago Chascomus, near the beach. Inexpensive.

MAR DEL PLATA

Chateau Frontenac – 80-room hotel, with private baths. Corner of Moreno (phone: 2-7443). Expensive.

Hermitage – 200 rooms with private baths. Av. Peralta Ramos 2657 (phone: 2-3081). Expensive.

Provincial – This 500-room hotel is next to the casino. Blvd. Maritimo 2300 (phone: 2-4081). Expensive.

Flamingo – Near the casino, this hotel has 150 rooms. Moreno 2155. Moderate.

Gran Hotel Dora – This beachfront hotel faces the casino and the sea. Buenos Aires 1841 (phone: 2-5002).

VILLA GESELL

Austral – Moderately priced hotel. Alameda 201.

Hostería Tequendama – This is a good hotel with moderate prices. Paseo 109.

BALCARCE

Balcarce – This new hotel is in the vicinity of Cinco Cerros. Inexpensive.

TANDIL

Ro-Che-Hil – Has a modest but good restaurant. General Rodriguez. Moderate.

TRES ARROYOS

Alfil – In the downtown area. Rivadavia 142 (7001). Expensive.

Catalana – 45-room hotel. Maipú 187. Moderate.

CLAROMECO

Claromeco – Hotel is only open during summer, December through March, and has good restaurant (*Juanillo*) facilities. Expensive.

Residencial La Perla – Hotel is right off the beach. Moderate.

Caravan Park – Camping ground in Dunamar; offers hot running water, cooking and laundry facilities. Inexpensive.

MIRAMAR

Golf Roca – With a golf course and casino.

NECOCHEA

Doble-J Campsite – Less than 1 mile from the wharves with facilities, including hot running water. Inexpensive.
Royal – 210-room hotel.
Atlántico – 80-room hotel.

BAHÍA BLANCA

Austral – 100-room downtown hotel. Calle Colón 159 (20241). Moderate.
Gran Hotel Del Sur – Hotel has 195 rooms and restaurant. Calle Colón 24 (30215). Moderate.
Belgrano – A 100-room hotel with no restaurant. Av. Belgrano 44 (20290). Inexpensive.

MONTE HERMOSO

Residencial Barrio – A 25-room hotel with a restaurant. Av. Dufour (8175). Moderate.
Gran Residencial Romano – This 21-room hotel has no restaurant. Av. Argentina, between Mendoza and Costa (8222). Moderate.

CARHUÉ

Residencial Savoy – Los Pinos 42. Moderate.
Azul – Av. de Mayo 32. Moderate.

SIERRA DE LA VENTANA

Don Diego Caravan Camp – Right on Route 72, this site has all modern conveniences and is a member of the Argentine Automobile Club (8216061). Boasts a natural swimming pool formed by two streams.

Bahía Blanca to Bariloche

The 1,186-mile (1,930-km) cross-country excursion along Route 22 from Bahía Blanca west to Neuquén will be particularly interesting to geographers. It runs parallel to Río Colorado, the boundary between northern and southern Argentina. You'll notice a difference in the terrain of the two areas immediately. To the north stretches the flat lands of the pampas and to the south, the mountainous slopes of northern Patagonia, where the *estancias* are so far from each other that the country resembles a frontier land.

Patagonia is an area whose main distinction is a lack of local color; travelers generally find it boring. The monotony of the countryside ends only at Neuquén, the capital of Patagonia's northernmost province of the same name, which marks the entry into Argentina's Swiss-style Lake District.

Here, at the foot of the Andes near the Chilean border, thousands of *norteamericanos* and Europeans flock every winter (remember that Southern Hemisphere seasons are the opposite of those of the Northern Hemisphere). The district encompasses the western end of Patagonia; south to Lago Argentino and Los Glaciares National Park in Santa Cruz; to Lanín National Park in Neuquén province; and Los Alerces National Park in Chubut province (for more detailed information, see *Patagonia*). The focal point of the district is San Carlos de Bariloche, which sits at the southernmost end of Lake Nahuel Huapi in the national park of the same name.

BARILOCHE: This is the most popular place to ski, particularly at Cerro Catedral, with its 3-mile runs and 3,280-foot incline. The Snow Festival, held annually in August, has become an internationally known sporting, cultural, and social event, but it is only one of the numerous ski championships in the area.

The fishing season in Bariloche lasts from mid-November to mid-March. Lakes and rivers are kept well stocked with brown trout, brook trout, rainbow trout, and salmon. The record catch, a 35-pound salmon, is exhibited at the Nahuel Huapi Fishing and Hunting Association in Bariloche.

In summer, the entire district is overcome with campers, swimmers, anglers, and other outdoors fans, lured to the blue-green lakes, snow-peaked mountains, and clear air. But despite its beauty, or maybe because of it, the Lake District suffers from that one flaw — too many tourists. The year-round popularity of Bariloche, Lake Nahuel Huapi, and Cerro Catedral has produced surplus visitors, and people who know the area well recommend more remote places, like San Martín de los Andes and Junín de los Andes, both north of Bariloche on Route 40.

Experts say it's best to stay away from the large, national highways running through the district and to stick to the local routes. The best map for the area is available from the Río Negro Secretaria de Turismo in the Bariloche office. The Argentine Automobile Club also provides a map with routes in the district. (Local routes, it should be noted, are marked with letters, not numbers.)

Air service is also available to the District via Aerolineas Argentinas and Austral; both connect Bariloche with Buenos Aires by jet in 2 hours. Flights to San Martín de los Andes and Esquel, north and south of Bariloche respectively, are also available. Train service has always been good, with an express run making the 1,472-mile trip in 29 hours. There is a daily bus between these two cities — a 28-hour ride — and other buses serve the route with many stops in between.

NEUQUÉN: Straddling the Neuquén and Lima rivers, the capital of Patagonia's northernmost province (pop. 25,000) is noted for its apples. The Fuder apple factory, 9 miles (14 km) west of the city on Route 22, provides travelers with the opportunity to look at its shipping and packing operations. In town, visitors interested in Patagonian history should stop at the Museo Daniel Gatica (Calle Brown 162), which contains many artifacts pertaining to the province's prehistoric age.

For those who want to buy local souvenirs, the artisan market at San Martín 291 features a moderately priced variety of woven ponchos, spreads, clothing, wood carvings, and sweaters.

Restaurants in Neuquén, moderately priced, include *Rincon Colonial* (Alberdi 110) and the *Del Comuse* (Av. Argentina 387). The *Del Castillo* (Diogonal 9 de Julio 50) is also worth a try. Wherever, try some of the local wine, either Rey del Neuquén or Relmu Lagrim del Limay, and the apple cider.

For diversion, we recommend an interesting side trip to Lago Pellegrini, an artificial lake with camping grounds 9 miles (14 km) north of Neuquén. Cross at Dique Ingeniero Balleste and continue on Route 151 south. When you arrive at the town of Cinco Saltos, follow the road as it bears left. The lake sits beyond the village. You're permitted to swim, water ski, and fish on Lago Pellegrini.

While you're there, take some time and wander into neighboring Cipolletti, a small village just above the lake on Route 151 south. Founded in 1904, Cipolletti boasts a mansion imitating France's Petit Trianon. At the end of Calle Yrigoyen in the midst of a park, it houses a provincial museum containing exhibits and documents about Patagonian history.

Leaving Cipolletti, a ride down Route 151 north to Route 234 south returns you to Neuquén.

En Route from Neuquén – A 115-mile (185-km) jaunt on Route 22 west will take you to Zapala, a major railroad crossing that links the southeastern part of Patagonia with railroads from Bahía Blanca and Buenos Aires. Founded on July 12, 1913, the town has two museums, archaeological and historic. Fortin Regimenteo 21, the town's landmark, was constructed during the Indian Wars.

Leaving Zapala and heading toward Argentina's Lake District you have a choice: You can continue northwest to the Andes and Chilean border or you can head south on Route 40 to the district.

Should you decide to head northwest, don't overlook two sites: Copahue National Reservation, with thermal baths and an extinct volcano; and Laguna Blanca National Park, a haven for animals and birds, particularly flamingos and black-necked swans.

LANÍN NATIONAL PARK: Immense (980,000 acres), with 12 lakes and numerous rivers, this park can be reached by continuing south from Zapala on Route 40, then heading north on Route D. Lago Huechulafquen, the park's largest lake, is a primary fishing area, and divides into two smaller lakes, Paimun and Epulafquen, where camping is available near the Andes Cordillera.

JUNÍN DE LOS ANDES: Twenty miles (33 km) east of Lanín Park and north of San Martín de los Andes on Route D is the tiny fishing village of Junín de los Andes, reputedly the most natural and untouched town in the district. Its biggest attractions are rainbow trout and salmon, caught in Río Chimehuin, the local fishing hole.

A side trip from Junín on Route H will take you 84 miles (135 km) through the Tromen Pass to Lake Villarrica and the city of Pucon in Chile. The high point of the trip is passing the 12,388-foot Lanín Volcano, now extinct.

SAN MARTÍN DE LOS ANDES: Continue 17 miles (27 km) southwest from Junín de los Andes on Route D, and you will arrive at San Martín de los Andes, right on Lago Lacar. Try the skiing at Cerro Chapelco; it has less people and lower prices than Bariloche.

La Raclette, a hostería, has an excellent restaurant that provides a menu as diverse as the tourists' nationalities: dishes borrowed from France, Germany, Switzerland, Italy, China, England, Hungary, and Argentina.

El Barrilite Deo Oro also serves an international menu. As an added touch, Jaime Munoz, the owner, personally attends his clientele. The *Kopper Kettle* offers brownies, lemon pie, cakes, and sandwiches in the afternoon; at night there are cheese *empanadas,* pancakes with cream, fondue, and chocolate and lemon mousse. Travelers aching for pizza, *empanadas,* or a sandwich in the middle of the night can visit *Doscientos 65,* on the main avenue. Homemade candies are sold throughout town, the most delicious being Mamusia chocolate.

Bus service is available to San Martín on a regular basis from Buenos Aires.

NAHUEL HUAPI NATIONAL PARK: Continuing south on Route D, you come to Nahuel Huapi National Park, a sprawling 4,867-square-mile reserve adjacent to Lanín National Park on the Argentina-Chile border. Opened in 1903, the park contains spectacular natural attractions: lakes, glaciers, waterfalls, torrents, rapids, and age-old forests.

Lake Nahuel Huapi, the park's largest lake, stretches 45 miles northwest to southeast and is up to 1,436 feet deep — easily navigable by steamers. The lake divides into eight *brazos,* or arms, that poke into surrounding mountains.

The largest island on the lake is Isla Victoria, which has dense forests, a subsoil of volcanic rock, and cliffs stretching 164 feet into the air on its western side. Large numbers of red deer run free on the 9,259-acre island.

Cruises to Isla Victoria run every day. The boats leave from Puerto Pañuelo (18 miles/30 km north of Bariloche) and dock at Puerto Anchorena on the island in time for lunch. At the *National Hostel,* a restaurant perched atop one of the highest cliffs, you can eat a full dinner or simply sip hot chocolate by the fire. (Note: At press time, the *National Hostel* was closed for renovation; before you embark on the cruise, you may wish to check with the tourist board in Bariloche to see if it has reopened.)

The boat makes a quick stop at the Quetrihue Peninsula, which is thickly covered with *arrayanes* trees. A carefully constructed catwalk, which protects the delicate root systems, winds through the forest, providing a close look at the cinnamon-colored trees. Found only in this area, the *arrayanes'* unusual coloration is said to have so inspired Walt Disney that he featured them in the forests of his movie *Bambi.*

Another side trip is a boat excursion to Puerto Blest, on the eastern arm of Nahuel Huapi, and the waterfall of Los Cantaros. A short drive from the western end of Puerto Blest south on Route H leads you to Laguna Frias, a small lake near the Chilean border. The waters are a striking green, the result of a vein of copper at the lake's bottom. From here, you can see Mt. Tronador, "the thunder maker," a snowcapped mountain, 11,600 feet in altitude.

The base of Mt. Tronador can be reached by taking Route 258 west from Bariloche, which passes Lake Gutiérrez, where there is a grotto to the Virgin of the Snows, and Lake Mascardi. Both lakes are good for fishing.

From Mascardi, take Route 254 west along the lake on to Pampa Linda and the Valley of the Vuriloches to the Black Glaciers, huge blocks of ice in every shade of gray, and the Devil's Gorge, a dare for the mountain climber.

BARILOCHE: On the southern end of Lake Nahuel Huapi, this community of 60,000 people is the heart of the Lake District's resort life. Founded in 1895 by Carlos Wiederhold, travelers are amazed by its resemblance to a European ski village, with its wood and stone chalet-like houses.

The town hall is in the middle of the plaza. Crowds gather for one of Bariloche's daily and most popular events — the noon ringing of the town clock. Four wooden figures emerge from the clock tower and rotate as the hour hand reaches 12. The figures represent the region's people: an Indian, a colonist, a conquistador, and a missionary.

The nearby Patagonian Museum (Av. 12 de Octubre) contains 11 rooms of Indian artifacts and exhibits; housed in the same building is the Domingo Faustino Sarmiento library. The Church of Our Lady of Nahuel Huapi is on Avenida 12 de Octubre at Calle Nicolas Palacios; the Argentine Automobile Club is on Calle Goedeke.

Mountain climbers and hikers can obtain information from Club Andino, behind the Civic Center on Avenida M. Elfiein and E. B. Norales. The provincial tourist office and Aerolineas Argentinas airlines are both on Calle Bartolome Mitre, a few blocks east of the center plaza.

Shoppers should know that Bariloche's most important street is Bartolome Mitre. Boutiques sell wool, leather, and ski jackets called *camperas.* The sweaters and ski coats are unrivaled and cost less here than in Buenos Aires.

Bariloche — "the Switzerland of South America" — is famous for its rich, delicious chocolate. Along Bartolome Mitre are several large stores that sell nothing but. Chocolate lovers will cry with delight as they stroll past floor-to-ceiling glass showcases stocked with all kinds of chocolate. The aroma alone is mouth-watering. Prices are, surprisingly, quite moderate.

Bariloche restaurants are also reasonable and serve good, hearty food to the summer and winter resort crowds. Most feature barbecues, and in season, *El Rincón Patagonia* throws in folk singing with dinner. *El Jabli,* on Av. San Martín, has both venison and trout in season, and *La Casita Suiza* concentrates on Swiss specialties such as fondue. Outside of town, try the *Tres Monedas, La Casona,* or *Dirty Dick's Pub.*

Another point of interest is Bariloche's music camps, where people gather to play outdoors. Here, too, is the home of the Camerata Bariloche, a world-famous chamber music group that performs free during the Snow Festival. Bariloche also claims a one-of-a-kind establishment in South America — the Bernabe Mendez Park Keepers' Training Center.

For skiing, Cerro Catedral is the place to be. With 3-mile runs and a 3,280-foot incline, the slope is internationally famous, and ski competitions are held here throughout the season. Equipped with all modern facilities, chair lifts ferry skiers to the mountain's top, 8,000 feet above sea level.

Club Andino Bariloche, the local ski club, has a lift and station that can be reached by an unpaved road at the mountain's base. Cerro Otto, on the outskirts of Bariloche, and Cerro Colorado, south of Cerro Otto, are also recommended slopes.

Numerous ski tours are offered by various clubs and airlines throughout the season. Check with a travel agent for information. Some tours combine Bariloche and the Chilean ski resort of Portillo. Flying time to Bariloche is 2 hours from Buenos Aires. The Lake District trip (later described in *Exploring Chile*) can be taken starting from Argentina, with boats departing from below the Llao-Llao peninsula. The trip can take 1 or 2 days or longer; however, tour companies usually offer this lake excursion for the 1- or 2-day period, and you travel by boat and bus.

CIRCUITO CHICO and CIRCUITO GRANDE: For travelers who use Bariloche as the base for their visit to the Lake District, there are two highly recommended land excursions. Circuito Chico, or small circuit, provides an afternoon's outing to the village of Llao-Llao. Circuito Grande, or large circuit, is an all-day affair encompassing a northern route through the park. Both circuits begin and end in Bariloche.

For Circuito Chico, follow coastal Route H west to Llao-Llao, at the foot of Cerro Lopez on the peninsula of Lakes Nahuel Huapi and Moreno. It is famous for its trout fishing in the Limay River. Llao-Llao has its own port, Puerto Pañuelo, and a 9-hole golf course. Travelers making the Lake District trip between Argentina and Chile depart and leave from the Llao dock.

Returning to Bariloche, you'll pass Cerro Lopez, a good mountain for beginning skiers on the north shore of Lago Gutierrez, and Cerro Catedral and Punto Panoramico.

Circuito Grande leads north from Bariloche along Route 237, following the winding Limay River. The drive is much more rustic and uncluttered than the route to Llao-Llao. You'll pass the Anfiteatro (Amphitheater), with a wide view of the river, then pass through Valle Encantado (the Enchanted Valley), with its curious limestone rock formations, including the Finger of God and Indian Chief. The Indians believed that the rock shapes were people, frozen long ago by the angry gods.

After passing Valle Encantado, turn left onto Route 1 at the small village of Confluencia. The route will take you north to 20-mile-long Lake Traful, famous for its salmon. Facing the lake at an altitude of 495 feet above the water, you can observe a curious phenomenon: Any light object thrown out over the lake is caught in a strong ascending current of air and returned to its point of origin.

Continuing south on Route H leads you near Lakes Correntoso and Espejo and Villa la Angostura, on the northeast shore of Lake Nahuel Huapi. From there, the road follows the lake to the tip of Brazo Huemul, then reconnects with Route 237 south, returning you to Bariloche.

LOS ALERCES NATIONAL PARK: Continuing south on Route 40 from Bariloche, you reach Los Alerces National Park, a 700,000-acre reservation in the northwest corner of Patagonia's Chubut province. This remote park, obviously a destination for only the most determined traveler, is rife with unspoiled natural wonders — numerous lakes, streams, rapids, and cascades. The gateway to the park is the town of El Bolson, 78 miles (130 km) south of Bariloche, which offers a few small hotels and rooming houses. Fishing in the area is good: Lakes Puelo and Eypuyen are nearby.

Lago Menendez, deep in the park, has two outstanding sights: the high peak of Cerro Torrecillas, with its large glacier ripe for mountain climbing, and forests that contain the 1,000-year-old larches for which the park is named. If these larches are as old as is estimated, they are the second oldest living trees in the world (after California's sequoias).

ESQUEL: This small (15,000-person) village 160 miles (269 km) south of Bariloche on Route 40 was once an offshoot of Welsh settlements in Chubut, 400 miles east on the Patagonian coast. Thirty-six miles (60 km) east of Los Alerces National Park, the town provides no public transportation except boats, but hotel accommodations and restaurants are reasonable. The tourist office, in the bus depot, will give you more detailed information.

BEST EN ROUTE

As in the Bahía Blanca region, hotels and guesthouses range in price per person from expensive ($40–$50), to moderate ($20–$30), to inexpensive ($5–$10). Accommodations are adequate in the larger resort areas, like Bariloche, but be prepared to pay for a room without a private bath anywhere.

Once again, you must make reservations well in advance to stay at a major resort.

Camping is available in all major parks, but check with authorities if you wish to camp in an unofficial camping site: A permit is needed.

NEUQUÉN

Arrayan – 72-room hotel is on Rte. 22. Moderate.
Del Comahue – Rooms for up to 200 guests; a small cafeteria is available. Av. Argentina 377 (phone: 2-2439). Moderate.
Sol-Neuquén – 99-room hotel has private baths and a swimming pool. Moderate.
Europa – Small hotel is opposite the central bus station, with private baths and clean eating facilities. Inexpensive.

LANÍN NATIONAL PARK

Hostería – Hostel in park's southeastern section, near Lago Melinque, is operated by English personnel. Moderate.

JUNÍN DE LOS ANDES

Hostería Chimehun – Hostel near Río Chimehuin is a gathering spot for fishermen. Moderate.

SAN MARTÍN DE LOS ANDES

El Sol de los Andes – Hilltop hotel offers 99 rooms, good food. Expensive.
Los Pinos – German-run hostel offers good food, clean rooms. Moderate.
La Raclette – Hostel provides a multitude of international dishes in its restaurant. Moderate.

NAHUEL HUAPI NATIONAL PARK

Isla Victoria – Small chalet-type, 8-room hotel near forest research station offers lunch for boat tour visitors and a fabulous view of the mountain ridge on the opposite shore.
El Casco – This exclusive, small, 20-room hotel is in the Nahuel Huapi National

Park. Furnished with Spanish colonial antiques, each room is named for the color in which it's decorated (for example, "La Violet"). Every suite or room has its own private sun terrace overlooking the lake. Ruta a Llao-Llao, km 11 (Phone: 2-2532 or 2-3083). Very expensive.

BARILOCHE

Bariloche Ski – This 50-room hotel, with a bar, roof garden, and restaurant, also has ski rentals. In fishing season, guides can be arranged through the hotel. San Martín 352 (phone: 2-2743). Expensive.

Bella Vista – Near the downtown section of Bariloche, this is a good 60-room hotel. Rolando 351 (phone: 2-2182 or 2-2435). Expensive.

Sol-Bariloche – 135-room hotel offers private baths, first-class service. Mitre 212. Expensive.

Tres Reyes – Hotel on lakeshore offers private baths. Av. 12 de Octubre 135 (26121). Expensive to moderate.

Residencia Flamengo – Hotel on Mitre serves breakfast. Moderate.

CERRO CATEDRAL

Catedral Ski – 80-room hotel with baths at foot of ski slope. Moderate.

EL BOLSON

Salinas – This small hotel in town serves as a gateway to Los Alerces National Park. Moderate.

Hostería Steiner – Rooming house is small, but provides adequate services. Moderate.

Patagonia to Antarctica

Southern Patagonia is not a resort center like Bariloche, but a territory for the stalwart adventurer. The northern region of lush forests and numerous lakes gives way to rugged, stark mountains and the drier stony countryside of the southern mountain region. This area is dominated by huge, isolated *estancias,* often covering thousands of acres, populated by English and Welsh immigrants. Travel accommodations are scarce, and not as comfortable and elaborate as those in the Lake District. Backpack camping becomes a requisite for anyone who wishes to enjoy the region at close range.

Patagonia is spread out over 301,158 square miles, from south of the Río Colorado and Bahía Blanca in the northeast to the island territory of Tierra del Fuego in the south. The region also encompasses the provinces of Neuquén in the northwest (for more information, see *Bahía Blanca to Bariloche*), Chubut in the central area, and Río Negro in the northeast. So uninhabited is the area that it has only 400,000 people, most living in the small cities and towns. The largest city is Comodoro Rivadavia, with 120,000 residents. Out of the total Patagonian population, 40% are from Chile, whose laborers cross the border to harvest fruits and crops for wages Argentines find despicable; yet, which are higher than what can be earned in the neighboring country.

Patagonia was discovered by Ferdinand Magellan in 1519, during his voyage around the world. The Strait of Magellan was named after him, for he used the Strait (which separates Tierra del Fuego from both Chile and Argentina) as a corridor between the Atlantic and Pacific oceans. Tierra del Fuego — Land of Fire — received its name from Magellan after he sighted smoke from the Indian campfires along the coast. The natives were nicknamed Patagones, or "people with big feet," and the name stuck. The Indians continued to live on the coast, successfully driving away other settlers and explorers until the Indian Wars 400 years later, when they were all but exterminated. Today, their remaining descendants inhabit Argentina's far north or Tierra del Fuego.

The first Spanish settlement in Patagonia was at Carmen de Patagones in Río Negro on the northeastern coast in the early 1820s. A Welsh settlement followed in 1865 in Puerto Madryn, south of Carmen de Patagones. Additional settlements were established by immigrants from Scotland, Wales, and England from Bahía Blanca southward.

As in the nineteenth century, most Patagonian land is still used for sheep raising; in recent years, however, the discovery of petroleum and the promise of industrial growth encouraged more people to migrate from northern Argentina, transforming Patagonia into a modern, industrial frontier land. The only agriculture to speak of here is in the north, in the Colorado and Río Negro valleys. Irrigation has been very successful in the Río Negro valley, which produces great amounts of fruit, especially apples and pears. The area's alcoholic apple cider is popular throughout the country.

So diverse and, reportedly, so inexpensive is Patagonian produce that Chileans, especially those who live across the border from the Argentine coalmining town of Río Turbio, habitually make the short trip there for groceries. Cross-border buying must be done on government-sanctioned days, however, or the food and other products are held at the border as contraband until the next ordained shopping day. Travelers who want to stock up on food before crossing the border into Chile are therefore advised to inquire with authorities first to be sure they won't lose it at the *aduana,* or customs house.

Allowing Chileans to work and shop in Argentina is ironic in light of the recent heated Argentine-Chilean controversy over three Atlantic islands near the Beagle Channel off Tierra del Fuego (the channel was named after Charles Darwin's *Beagle* expedition in the early nineteenth century). Chile, a Pacific nation, was awarded Lennox, Nueva, and Picton islands through international mediation in 1972, the result of a territorial dispute over Tierra del Fuego. In the nineteenth century, Argentina got control of most of the large island of Tierra del Fuego; Chile was awarded control of the Strait of Magellan; and the other islands remained up for grabs. While Chile has offered to restrict territorial waters around the islands to 12 miles, Argentina still protests. Chile's authority over the three islands expired in 1978, and war nearly erupted over the issue. Pope John Paul II agreed to mediate the dispute, and the resulting recommendation that the islands once again come under Chilean control was agreed to by Argentina.

The weather in Patagonia can be chilly or mild, depending on how near you are to the equator or the Antarctic Circle. Summer temperatures reach as high as 81°F (24°C) in the Río Negro valley; 59°F (15°C) in Santa Cruz; and as low as 52°F (10½°C) in Tierra del Fuego. Travelers in the southernmost regions will be treated to an interesting phenomenon around Río Gallegos: This section of Patagonia is so far south (at the 52° latitude mark) that sunrise occurs at 9 AM.

Not always in top condition, roads in Patagonia have good connections to the north; bad weather conditions, however, can cause even the most direct roads to be closed, and screen windshield protectors are requisite where roads are gravel (protectors are available in Bariloche and Comodoro Rivadavia). The recommended road is Route 3, which extends south from Buenos Aires to Ushuaia. Along it you'll see a wide variety of wildlife roaming freely on the range: guanaco, ostriches, large rabbits, foxes, and, in the Valdes Peninsula, very tame seals, sea elephants, walruses, and penguins. For an unusually perceptive tale of one man's travels through this remote part of the world, read *In Patagonia,* by Bruce Chatwin (Summit Books). Written with consummate grace, it describes his personal odyssey in the 1970s.

There are numerous ways to travel through Patagonia besides by car, however. The Transportes Patagones bus line leaves daily from Buenos Aires for the 50-hour trek through port towns along the coast as far south as Río Gallegos. Buses depart from Estación Terminal de Omnibus in Retiro Square. Flights leave Buenos Aires (city terminal) regularly for all parts of the region, but reserve seats well in advance. Rail service, however, is more limited; it's available in the northwest only, to Neuquén and Bariloche.

Further travel information can be obtained from the Dirección Nacional de Turismo in Buenos Aires, Calle Suipacha 1111 (phone: 311-2745).

Travelers heading for Patagonia should also consider an expedition to Antarctica. A number of excursions are available to the world's Fifth Continent; generally, they are wildlife and scientific expeditions. Tours here are discussed further under Antarctica.

CARMEN DE PATAGONES: On the southern tip of Buenos Aires province, 96 miles (160 km) south of Río Colorado, is the first settlement in Patagonia. It faces the town of Viedma, the capital of Río Negro province, just across the Río Negro. Both towns are irrigated agricultural centers, not of interest to tourists, although you might want to visit Las Mercedes cathedral in Viedma.

A monument on Cerro de la Caballada in Carmen de Patagones commemorates a Brazilian military attack on both towns in 1827.

SAN ANTONIO OESTE: Going west on Route 3 to Route 23 leads you to San Antonio Oeste, a small town on the San Matías Gulf. With only 4,000 people, it is linked with the Río Negro by a canal.

PUERTO MADRYN: Retracing your steps to Route 3 south, drive to Puerto Madryn, 108 miles (173 km) away on the Golfo Nuevo in Chubut province. Founded in 1865 by Welsh immigrants, this small, seaport town has retained Welsh as its official language. A statue of a Welsh woman pays homage to its settlers; it was they who first implemented the irrigation techniques that made the Chubut Valley fertile.

A side trip from Puerto Madryn on Route 256 east leads you to the Valdes Peninsula via Punte Norte, 106 miles (176 km) away. Joined to the mainland by a 5-mile-wide isthmus, the peninsula has thousands of sea elephants, which live and breed here. Travelers should be forewarned, however, that they are generally docile creatures except when their access to the sea is blocked.

The peninsula is a good place to go diving. Large clusters of giant algae and a great variety of sea fauna are found in the waters, which are clear down to 100 feet.

En Route from Puerto Madryn – Returning to the port, continue south on Route 3 and you'll arrive in Rawson, a small (pop. 2,500) port that serves as the capital of Chubut province.

Like Puerto Madryn, Trelew (pop. 18,000), 20 miles (32 km) west of Rawson on Route 25, was founded by Welsh settlers on the Chubut rivers. The highway continues to Gaiman, the most authentic Welsh town in Patagonia today. It has a Welsh museum.

Returning to Route 3 south, those who missed the walruses at the Valdes Peninsula will find them at Camerones. At Punta Tombo is the largest rookery of Magellanic penguins in the world.

COMODORO RIVADAVIA: This small (pop. 100,000) city 249 miles (396 km) south of Rawson on Route 3 is a bustling town. Petroleum was discovered in 1907, and today 28% of Argentina's entire oil supply comes from here. A 1,095-mile pipeline carries natural gas to the federal capital.

This city, on the Gulf of San Jorge, is noted for its frozen meat, ceramics, soap, and lime factories; in addition to oil, wool and hides are exported.

Bus transportation is available to Buenos Aires and Bariloche.

For a side trip, a 119-mile (193-km) drive west on Route 26 to Colonia Sarmiento (between Lakes Musters and Colhué Huapi) leads one to a fascinating forest: a 70,000-year-old petrified forest filled with fallen araucaria trees.

Puerto Aysen in Chile can be reached by continuing west via Paso Río Mayo. The tiny (5,500 people) town is in mountain and fjord country.

En Route from Comodoro Rivadavia – Continuing south on Route 3 leads to Fitz Roy, 68 miles (110 km) away. Here you have a choice of two routes to Tierra del Fuego. If you continue on Route 3's corridor, Route 281, you will reach Puerto Deseado and Río Gallegos; then make a left turn into Punta Delgada. A 40-minute crossing by ENAP oil boats will take you to Punta Espora (check daily schedules for tide changes). From there, the route leads to Río Grande and, finally, Ushuaia.

The alternate route (through Chile) is to take Route 3's corridor Route 282 from Fitz Roy — a short cut that bypasses Puerto Deseado into Río Gallegos, followed by Punta Arenas. Take the regular ferry crossing into Porvenir in Chile, across the Strait of Magellan (make reservations at Transportes Maslov; phone: 2-2056). From Porvenir, the 135-mile (225-km) Route 3 alternate continues into Río Grande in Argentine Tierra del Fuego.

PUERTO DESEADO: Have you ever wondered how the penguin got his name? Well, *pengwyn* is Welsh for "white head"; the name was coined in the 16th century when a member of an English expedition spotted the bird here at Puerto Deseado, southeast of Comodoro Rivadavia. The small town (3,120 people) is of interest for that reason alone.

SANTA CRUZ: Another 282 miles (470 km) south on Route 3, this town has supposedly one of the best harbors in the country at the mouth of the Río Santa Cruz, which flows into Lago Argentino. Bahía Grande, south of the city, was discovered by Magellan during his voyage.

Continuing south, Magellan wintered at San Julian, some 200 miles north of the Magellan Strait. The town marks the 563-mile (925-km) point between Comodoro Rivadavia and Río Gallegos.

RÍO GALLEGOS: The capital of Santa Cruz province, this is the largest city (42,000 persons) south of Puerto Madryn and is known as a primary sheep-raising center, exporting wool, sheepskin, tallow, and processed frozen meat. One of the few developed cities in Patagonia, it has a tourist office (9 de Julio between Alberdi and Avellandoda) and a variety of coffee shops and restaurants in the center of town. A museum sits at the corner of Calle Tucumán and Calle Belgrano, and that is about as interesting as the town gets.

If you remain overnight in Río Gallegos, make hotel reservations in advance. *Chileños* who have moved here have filled up most public houses, but new ones are being constructed to meet the increased demand.

Being so far south, the sun in Río Gallegos usually rises between 8 and 9 AM. Stars this far south are incredible, too, especially the Southern Cross, which rotates on an axial star one complete turn throughout the night; sailors used to depend on it as a guide.

One note: If you're interested in learning about the stars in the Southern Hemisphere, buy a guide before coming to South America. There simply are none to be found once you're here, and people generally aren't knowledgeable about many of the constellations.

   En Route from Río Gallegos – Before descending to Tierra del Fuego — an excursion to be considered only in the summer months (November through February) — you may want to take a side trip to Río Turbio, some 156 miles (260 km) west from Río Gallegos on Route 293. The only two reasons to visit this bleak mining town are: because it is on one of the routes to Lago Argentino; and because by taking Route 3 from here, you cross the border into Chile to Puerto Natales, the gateway to Torres del Paine National Park. This route is impassable in winter.

LAGO ARGENTINO NATIONAL PARK: An icy spectacle highlights the park: the Perito Moreno glacier, 31 miles long and about 2 miles wide at its terminus. The lake contains icebergs, arrestingly blue in color, that have broken off from the glacier, making grumbling, scraping sounds while doing so. *Ventisquero* (glacier) Moreno is unique because it is the one glacier that is increasing in size. It has 0.6 mile frontage on the water and a height of 164 feet.

CALAFATE: A small tourist town on the southern part of Lago Argentino, Calafate, 192 miles (320 km) northwest of Río Gallegos, is the best base for touring the national park because of the availability of accommodations. Calafate is reached via LADE (the air force transport) from Río Gallegos, a 50-minute flight by small craft. Advance arrangements (best made in Buenos Aires) are essential to get a seat on this transport.

The park contains all types of space for outdoor sports. Horses are for hire at *Hostería Kan-Yatun;* the Upsala glacier can be visited by motorboat. Lake Onelli, also in the park, is tranquil, surrounded by snow-covered mountains and beech trees. Cave paintings are 3 miles (5 km) outside of the town. You must request permission to camp from the park rangers. Camping is free, with hot showers provided.

USHUAIA: The southernmost city in the world, the capital of Tierra del Fuego sits at 55° latitude south: a rustic, coastal town set in the midst of waterfalls, glaciers, snowclad mountains, and lenga forests with rich, red foliage. Ushuaia was formerly a Protestant mission town; it was founded in 1884, some 40 years after Charles Darwin's famous expedition on the *Beagle.* Planes make the 1,450-mile trip here from Buenos Aires in 5 hours; ships take 5 days. Sailings around the tip of the continent are scheduled by major cruise lines; ships travel through the strait and dock in Ushuaia.

Ushuaia is a rather desolate town. Houses are painted warm, pastel colors, but the weather is chilly year-round. Winter sports such as cross-country skiing and skating are available. Taxi drivers will take you anywhere you want after much pleading on your part, for they dislike traveling the bad roads at any price. Behind town there is a glacier — a 2½-hour hike away.

The principal industries are sheep raising, timber cutting, fishing, and trapping.

An island itself, Tierra del Fuego encompasses the islands off the Strait of Magellan, though people generally think only of the large island. It divides more or less down the middle, the western part belonging to Chile; the eastern, to Argentina. It is a small island: 250 miles long and 280 miles wide. At the extreme south of the island is Horn Island (Cape Horn).

If you plan to go on to Chile from southern Patagonia (a region called Magallanes in Chile), there is a good road from Río Gallegos to Punta Arenas, as well as bus service. From Punta Arenas you can take a boat to Puerto Montt, which is the gateway for crossing the Lake District to Bariloche. The trip lasts 5 days, with one stopover on the island of Chiloé (where wonderful woolen handmade items are sold at reasonable prices). Third-, second-, and first-class accommodations are available, and there is a good dining room on board.

There is one major drawback to this excursion: The boat leaves once a month, and reservations should be made at least 1 week — preferably more — in advance. For more information, contact Empresa Marítima del Estado in Santiago or Puerto Montt. The trip through the Strait of Magellan is truly like being in another world. As long as you're traveling south, you should consider a trip to Antarctica.

ANTARCTICA: Its summertime temperature never exceeds 40°F (4°C); its winter temperature plummets to −126.9°F (−88°C). Still, the desolate frozen iceland of the Antarctic continent has been an international hotbed of controversy ever since English explorer James Cook discovered it in the late 18th century. The issue: territorial domination of a country of 5,500,000 square miles, with no native human population, but rich in natural resources that include petroleum, minerals, and krill, tiny shrimp that are predicted to be one of the world's largest protein staples in the future.

The 1959 Treaty of Antarctica was signed by 12 nations, including the US, the Soviet Union, Argentina, and Chile. It established the Antarctic as a region to be used "for peaceful purposes, for international cooperation in scientific research, and not the scene or object of international discord."

So far, the treaty has worked pretty well. But with the discovery of offshore oil (potentially greater than the supply in Alaska) and mineral resources, national interests are pushing claims to the cold, southern turf. Environmentalists, however, point to the need for intensive studies before any exploration or exploitation projects are implemented, since the area has a critical influence on global climate, and its ecosystems are highly vulnerable to disturbances. The UN Conference for the Law of the Sea instituted discussions on internationalizing Antarctica so that its resources become available for the common good rather than for the benefit of the few. Third World nations are in accord with this approach and tend to regard the Antarctic Treaty powers as "colonial." With the exception of New Zealand, the signatory nations believe that they have the right to any resources; New Zealand proposes that Antarctica become an international park.

Antarctica's closest neighbors, Argentina and Chile, favor territorializing the continent. Their interests are founded on a papal bull that transpired in 1493, giving all nations west of the 46th meridian to Spain. Argentina itself claims that Antarctic Argentina has been a part of that country since the founding of the Argentine Republic in the 19th century. Formal claims were filed in 1908; these added to original Spanish rights and geographical proximity and affinity support the Argentine argument. Chile bases its claims on 16th-century exploration. Both claims — each totaling one-eighth of the continent — overlap each other between the 80° and 20° latitudes.

Entrance into the Antarctic Circle can be made by boat or plane from Ushuaia through the Beagle Channel into the Drake Passage, and to the Antarctic Peninsula. A trip to the continent is geared only to the serious traveler-explorer interested in environment and wildlife. There are no hotels, no highways, no airports, and no restaurants. Tours must be arranged beforehand; they are usually sponsored by a scientific organization or wildlife-oriented group.

Society Expeditions is the only US organization offering cruises to Antarctica. Groups aboard the *World Explorer* visit glaciers, penguin rookeries, and various research stations, including the American Palmer Station in Admiralty Bay. Contact: Society Expeditions, 723 Broadway E, Seattle, WA 98102.

BEST EN ROUTE

Accommodations in Patagonia are scarce: Camping is allowed in areas such as Lago Argentino National Park, but permits are needed elsewhere.

Any hotels you find will be small and accommodating; often, private homes will lodge travelers for the night. Both hotels and houses are inexpensive, ranging from about $10 to $15 a night per person. Since towns are small, there are rarely street addresses and few telephones, so your safest bet is to make overnight arrangements with a travel agency before your arrival.

Here's a list of recommended hotels:

Carmen de Patagones: *Percaz, Gran Argentina*
Viedma: *Roma, Viedma*
San Antonio Oeste: *Hotel Vasquite*
Puerto Madryn: *Playa, Siguero, Paris, Cantina el Nautico*
Comodoro Rivadavia: *Argentino, Colón, Comercial*
Colonia Sarmiento: *Hotel Americano*
San Julian: *Hotel Londres, Residencial*
Río Gallegos: *Plaza, International, Pension Belgrano*
Calafate: *ACA Motel Calafate* (cabins with kitchens), *Hotel Carlitos*
Ushuaia: *Hotel Albatross* (see *Luxury Resorts and Special Havens,* DIVERSIONS).

The Falkland Islands

Prior to the war between Great Britain and Argentina in the spring of 1982 over the sovereignty of the Falklands, called the Islas Malvinas by the Argentines, it was possible to travel by air via LADE (Argentine Air Force), which provided weekly service from Comodoro Rivadavia to the airstrip behind Port Stanley. At press time this service had been suspended, as had all other inter- and intra-island transportation. It is anticipated that some of these services will resume in time, but no schedule for such resumption is available. Presently, access by air is available only from London. Since conditions remain very unstable, we suggest you double-check the availability of all tours, cruises, and flights mentioned herein.

A group of more than 100 islands 350 miles east of Tierra del Fuego, with a total landmass of 6,500 square miles, the Falkland Islands have an oceanic climate. Extremes here are unknown. Temperatures range from 36°F (2°C) in midwinter to 49°F (9°C) in midsummer. Snow rarely falls, and heat waves and heavy frosts are unheard of. The only catch is the rain. The sky is frequently overcast, and rain falls, usually as a light drizzle, 250 days of the year. November, at the onset of the Falkland summer, is the driest month.

The vista is strongly reminiscent of the western highlands of Scotland or the outer Hebrides Islands. The rolling, windswept hills with their springy turf lure the hiker and explorer; beaches of fine, white sand and the deeply eroded, dramatically shaped cliffs provide superb scenery. The atmosphere is clear and clean; one can often see for vast distances. There is a pervasive spirit of solitude here, broken only by the calls of sea birds and the muttering of the surf. A walk in the Falklands, with a keen wind blowing, is exhilarating and refreshing. The islands are noted for their high winds, which come mostly from the west and south, but fortunately there are many sheltered harbors in the deeply indented coastlines that protect small vessels.

The soil is peat and often spongy, due to an underlying layer of clay. The peat is a vital source of fuel for the islanders. Many ponds and salt lagoons, often of considerable size, support large populations of waterfowl. While there are no native trees, most of the land is covered by grasses, shrubs that rarely reach a height of 5 feet, and a variety of ground plants. Trees planted around the settlements are wind-stunted, but they do provide the shelter essential to keeping land birds on the islands.

A plant of considerable interest is tussock grass, which grows in dense turf as high as 12 feet from its root crowns. From a distance, these clumps look like treetops, which led some early explorers sailing by to report that the islands were densely wooded. Unfortunately, sheep and cattle are very fond of this grass, but although it has been extirpated from some areas, it still grows where the farmers have fenced it in.

Sheep farming is the main industry of the islands; wool is the principal export. Mutton is constantly on the menu, and people say that it is served 364 days of the year — with lamb on Christmas. There is no fishing, although abundant, delicious mussels can be gathered on the tidal rocks. However, few people bother to use them for food or bait.

The total population of the Falklands is only about 1,800. Mainly of Scottish descent, these people are staunchly British and the Falklands have been a British dependency since the early nineteenth century. More than half live in Port Stanley, the only town of any size. The rest of the population is scattered throughout the islands, living in small farm settlements. Since there are no telephones, contact is maintained through radiotelephone, Beaver float seaplane, and small interisland boat traffic. A traveling teacher system provides for the education of small children in the settlements; medical attention can be called for when necessary.

To see wildlife at its best, you should visit the Falklands between November and February, when most of the birds are nesting. Species include the rock-hopper, gentoo, and Magellanic penguins, quaint birds that nest in closely packed colonies. Penguins, however, nest in burrows. The large and handsome king penguin, once exterminated from the islands by seal hunters, is making a comeback, and about 100 birds are now reestablished on East Falkland Island. A fifth penguin type, the Macaroni, can often be found breeding among the rockhoppers. The dignified, black-browed albatross also nests in huge concentrations, and the tame bird can be approached gently within a few feet of its nest without being disturbed.

Despite former persecution by farmers the upland geese are again a common sight here. Three other kinds of geese — the ruddy-headed, ashy-headed, and Kelp — also breed. Of particular interest is the striated caracara, a hawk-like scavenger with long legs and a good stride. It has a strong addiction to shiny articles such as cameras, knives, and binoculars, which should not be left unattended. In addition, up to 17 species of land birds can be found, ranging from the black-throated finch to the long-tailed meadowlark — a striking, red-breasted bird.

Marine mammals are another source of interest. The southern fur seal and southern sea lion are showing signs of recovery from their near-extermination in the 1800s. The sea lion can be seen preying on penguins while they are concentrated in the waters close to their rookeries. And elephant seals bask on the beaches. Although whales are no longer abundant, occasionally they can be seen cruising close to shore, especially the killer whale. The little Peale's and Commerson's dolphins are still plentiful, and they delight in playing around the bows of small vessels.

PORT STANLEY: On the east coast of East Falkland Island, this tiny town (1,000 people) is mostly British. It is the sole town in the island system, the official government seat, and the official port of entry. There are two usable docks on the island; behind them are warehouses operated by the Falkland Islands Company and a small, recently opened museum. There is a large department store and several smaller stores on the main street, which borders the waterfront; the post office and government building lie farther to the right. You can get a feel for local life at one of the many British-style pubs in the area.

Port Stanley is of considerable historical interest. The new museum documents much of the nautical history of the past 150 years while the hulls of several clipper ships end their days along the shoreline. In both World Wars I and II, Port Stanley was involved in major naval battles between British and German forces. Due to the frequent winter gales and the treacherous reefs, hundreds of wrecks are scattered around the coasts. In this connection, much rescuing has been performed by local seamen.

CARCASS ISLAND: Access to this tiny, 4,300-acre island from Port Stanley is either via boat or seaplane. At the northwest end of the system, the island is the bird-watcher's dream spot, the home of several gentoo and Magellanic penguin rookeries close to the shore. Geese, brown pintails, teal, and crested and steamer ducks live in the ponds and along the coast. Brown skuas are so fearless that they will swoop by the heads of intruders when nests are approached; the friendly tussock bird is also very much in evidence.

WEST POINT ISLAND: This 3,100-acre island, only a few miles from Carcass, houses great, noisy rookeries of rockhopper and albatross. These birds are both interesting and very photogenic; they can be approached closely without disturbing them. It is expecially impressive to watch the busy rockhopper traffic in and out of the sea, which breaks heavily on the rocky coast. A favorite vantage point for bird-watching is a rocky promontory known as the Devil's Nose, where you must watch every step to avoid nesting albatrosses.

NEW ISLAND: At the southwest end of the Falkland Islands, this settlement offers the remains of a whaling station and several shipwrecks. A short walk to the windward side brings you to rockhopper rookeries, which are spread up the cliff slopes and far into the surrounding hills. Careful searching will reveal a few pairs of Macaroni penguins, their bright orange head plumes sticking out among the rockhoppers. From the cliffs, sea lions can be watched as they prey upon penguins, seizing them in their jaws and literally shaking them out of their skins. On the northeast side of the island is a rookery of about 1,500 fur seals. Several large gentoo and rockhopper colonies are on the north coast.

KIDNEY AND COCHON ISLANDS: These two small islands, a few miles north of Port Stanley Harbour at the entrance of Berkeley Sound, were declared nature reserves in 1964. In spite of their small size (Kidney is only ¾ mile long and ¼ mile wide), they support an amazing variety of breeding birds. On Kidney, 28 species have been found nesting, including five types of petrel, three shearwaters, three gulls, and six land birds. This high productivity is due to the growth of tussock grass, which covers 90%

of the island, as well as to the absence of predatory animals. The situation on nearby Cochon Island is similar.

Access to these islands, and to the other islands in the area (including Beauchene, Low, the Twins, Middle Islands, Volunteer Point, and Cape Dolphin), is restricted. Requests for permission for serious study and research should be directed to the government in Port Stanley.

BEST EN ROUTE

As we went to press, there were no overnight accommodations available on the Falklands; it may be some time before this area recovers from the war between Great Britain and Argentina and tourism resumes.

Mesopotamia

Like its ancient Asian namesake in the Tigris-Euphrates Valley, Argentina's Mesopotamia is sandwiched between two rivers: the 1,827-mile Paraná and the 1,000-mile Uruguay. The rivers run parallel to each other from Alto Paraná in the north, forming a base southward before flowing into the Río de la Plata, a distance of 690 miles. The distance between the rivers along this route is narrow — only 241 miles in the north to 130 miles near Santa Fe, on the west bank of the Paraná.

High in the northeastern pocket of Argentina, Mesopotamia borders Paraguay, Brazil, and Uruguay. The region encompasses the provinces of Entre Ríos to the south, Corrientes to the northwest, and Misiones to the northeast, where one can gaze at the majestic Iguazú Falls, shared by the three countries.

Topographically, Mesopotamia, like Gaul, is divided into three parts. Tropical jungles fill Misiones; sloping, grassy hills and marshes dominate Corrientes; dry grass and pastures dot the Entre Ríos countryside. Agriculturally, Mesopotamia plays an important role in Argentine citrus production; fruit, linseed, and fowl are also raised here, and rice is grown along the banks of the Río Paraná, between Corrientes and Posadas, the capital of Misiones. Corrientes also produces about nine million head of cattle and sheep annually. Mesopotamian weather is often humid, with little rainfall, and it is hot in the summer, reaching 100°F (37°C) by day, dropping to a cool 70°F (21°C) at night. The Misiones forests are filled with exotic birds and animals: monkeys, tucans, parrots, pumas, and tapirs.

Historically, Mesopotamia plays as important a role in Argentina's settlement as does Tucumán and the northwest region. The importance, however, is more religious than political in nature. Where Tucumán is the site of the declaration of Argentine independence, Mesopotamia is the site of a heavy concentration of Roman Catholic missions, mostly Franciscan and Jesuit, founded by Spanish missionaries in the seventeenth, eighteenth, and nineteenth centuries. The missions had two purposes: to convert the Guaraní Indians (most of whom were exterminated during the nineteenth-century colonial campaign) and to become as a source of spiritual security for explorers and settlers (although several missions were set aflame by marauding

Indians). The ruins of San Ignácio Mini in Misiones are a national monument; this was a Jesuit mission for the Guaranís during the eighteenth century. The mission padres, by the way, were the first producers of *yerba maté* in Argentina; it is still grown in Mesopotamia today.

Traveling north from Buenos Aires, it is possible to take in Mesopotamia by a number of routes. Route 9 runs north up the west bank of the Río Paraná to Rosario (see *Córdoba*) and Santa Fe, then crosses the river by tunnel to the city of Paraná and continues north up the river's eastern bank as Route 12, passing through the river towns of La Paz and Corrientes. At this point the route turns east to Posadas, then continues north to Puerto Iguazú and the falls. Or you can take Route 9 north until it merges with Route 11 north at Rosario, then continue up the Río Paraná's east bank to Resistencia, crossing the river there to Route 12 and Corrientes. Either way, Route 12 will take you into Paraguay and Encarnación, a Guaraní village.

To travel along the Río Uruguay, take Route 9 north from Buenos Aires and cross over at Campana to Route 12 north. This leads to Route 14 and Concepción del Uruguay, an Argentine port. Here, you can cross the river to Uruguay or continue north to Route 126.

If you prefer to explore Mesopotamia by boat, an excursion on the Río Paraná is recommended. The largest river in Argentina, it is a major traffic artery between Buenos Aires and Brazil, Paraguay, and Uruguay. The Río Uruguay, however, is geared more to small boats and vessels, since rapids in midcourse and a lack of navigable tributaries make it difficult to travel.

Tours to Mesopotamia can be booked through Flight Tours in Buenos Aires (Rivadavia 986, 10th floor) or through other Buenos Aires tour operators.

SANTA FE: On the west bank of the Río Paraná on Route 9, the capital of Santa Fe province is not a Mesopotamian city but is linked to Paraná by a 5-mile canal. Founded by Juan de Garay in 1573, Santa Fe was once the center of Jesuit missions and an outpost against the Indians, providing the seat of the constitutional assembly in 1853. The port, actually on Río Salado, is somewhat larger than Paraná.

La Merced Church and San Francisco Church (c. 1680), left from the mission days, are worth a visit. While in Santa Fe, also visit the Museum of Fine Arts, where local artists exhibit, and the Museo Historico Provincial.

En Route from Santa Fe – Before crossing the Río Paraná into Paraná and continuing upriver on Route 12, consider the alternate route: following the river's west bank north, then east into Corrientes.

Barranqueras is 360 miles (600 km) north of Santa Fe on Route 11. A manufacturing and agricultural center, the port ships hardwood and cotton from the Argentine interior.

Resistencia, 4 miles (6 km) northwest of Barranqueras on Route 11, is the capital of El Chaco province and parallels Corrientes on the Paraná's east bank. The railroad junction for the north, this city of 94,000 manufactures tannin and trades in lumber, cotton, and hides. Cattle, quebracho wood (used in tanning), and lead are exported from its port on the Paraná.

Resistencia's international airport has several weekly flights to Salta, Uruguay; check the schedule. Rail and bus service are available to Santa Fe, with train connections available to La Paz and Santa Cruz, Bolivia; full bus service is slated for Posadas, Tucumán, Formosa, Asunción, and Salta.

PARANÁ: Some 80 miles (128 km) north of Rosario and 235 miles (376 km) north-west of Buenos Aires on Route 126, the capital of Entre Ríos province is a shipping center of beef and cattle grain. Founded in 1730, Paraná (pop. 200,000) was the capital of the Argentine confederation from 1853 to 1862.

Find time to stroll around the center of town: Plaza San Martín is full of fountains, and there is a statue of the Liberator.

Paraná can be reached from Santa Fe by taking the connecting tunnel.

CORRIENTES: Continuing north along Route 12 from Paraná takes you to Corrientes, where, it is said, Indians who tried to burn down the cross housed in the pilgrim Church of La Cruz in 1808 were struck by lightning — which appeared, literally, out of a clear, blue sky. Founded in 1588, the capital (pop. 105,000) of Corrientes province is 648 miles (1,036 km) north of Buenos Aires, and 25 miles (40 km) below the merging of the Alto Paraná and Río Uruguay: Passengers en route upriver must change to smaller boats because of the shallow water.

A good time to visit Corrientes is during the pre-Lent Carnival, generally the first or second week in February. Sponsored by wealthy families, the Carnival is patterned after those held in Rio and Bahia. The streets are filled with parades, music, and dancing, and two *scholas* (schools) compete with each other for prizes, their costumes and floats vividly colored.

Directly north of Corrientes, Paso de la Patria provides good waters for dorado fishing.

POSADAS: Continuing north along Route 12, the bend along the Alto Paraná leads to Posadas, the capital of Misiones province, 226 miles (361 km) east of Corrientes. Inhabited by 44,000 persons, this dusty little town is in a *yerba maté–* and tobacco-growing area.

It's possible to take a train from Buenos Aires to Posadas. You can also get here by bus: Be prepared for a 27-hour ride. The bus lines will change your money to *cruzeiros* if you plan to enter Brazil.

If you like dorado fishing, a side trip backtracking toward Corrientes takes you to Paso de la Patria. About 2½ miles (4 km) north of Posadas on Route 12 is the Paraguayan town of Encarnación; Guaraní women come from there to buy and sell wares. Founded in 1862, Encarnación was severely damaged by a tornado in 1926.

SAN IGNÁCIO MINI: Continue on Route 12 north to San Ignácio Mini; a mission first founded in Brazil in 1631, it was reestablished by the Jesuits here to escape Brazilian marauders. By 1731, it had reached the height of its prosperity, swiftly declining by 1767, when the priests were forced to leave the territory under orders from Charles III. No Indians were left by 1810, and the city was burned 7 years later by the troops of Paraguayan dictator Francia. The ruins lay hidden in the jungle until they were discovered in 1897. The Argentine government has maintained the village as a national monument since 1943; it is open to the public, and tours are free of charge (closing time is 5 PM).

The ruins are as spectacular — though certainly in a different way — as Iguazú Falls. The large, open plaza (1,076 square feet), with one lone tree remaining, is flanked by buildings. Constructed from local red and yellow sandstone, the walls take on a bur-nished sheen as the sun sets — a highly recommended time for a visit. A preference for bas-relief is much in evidence. In its heyday, the mission contained 4,356 people; today it stands empty. But the town that took its name has 20,000 people.

Though the roofs disappeared long ago, the walls, some 37 inches thick, are still as high as 30 feet in places. The empty rooms were once classrooms, priests' quarters, workshops, printing shops, barracks, arsenals, one-room dwellings, and storerooms for crops, which included corn, rice, tobacco, *yerba maté,* and citrus fruit. A huge, baroque church on the site dates back to 1724; there is also a cemetery.

Eleven missions were established altogether in Misiones province, but San Ignácio

Mini is the only one that is easily accessible to the traveler. Other Jesuit ruins are São Miguel in Brazil and the Jesus and Trinidad missions of Paraguay. The Subsecretaria de Turismo distributes brochures on other ruins in Misiones.

En Route from San Ignácio Mini – On the way to Puerto Iguazú, stop at Puerto Rico. It has a bus station and a neat little restaurant. If you're traveling by bus, there's no problem in catching another one in a few hours if you decide to stay awhile.

Farther north on Route 12, Puerto Iguazú provides the Argentine doorway to Iguazú Falls.

IGUAZÚ FALLS (LAS CATARATAS DEL IGUAZÚ): A visit to Iguazú is a thrilling and humbling experience, and a trip most easily made from Buenos Aires via one of the daily flights offered by Aerolíneas Argentinas or Austral Airlines. Considered the widest waterfall in the world, Iguazú extends well over 4 miles and claims 275 cataracts. As you approach, you can hear the roar of the falls and can see a huge cloud of mist rising up over the surrounding jungle. A long system of concrete catwalks, built in 1965, winds along the edge of the Río Paraná and skirts the falls, providing a safe perch from which to view (and photograph) the giant cataracts tumbling at your feet. A 2-hour hike will take you past all the falls visible on the Argentine side as well as through the tropical jungle. Brilliant butterflies and birds flutter about — as well as some rather determined mosquitoes. (Swab on repellent before you venture out.) The cataract called Devil's Throat is the most magnificent.

You can take a ferry ride from Puerto Iguazú to Foz do Iguaçu on the Brazilian side. A friendly rivalry exists between the two countries as to whose falls are more beautiful.

Note: If you're planning to visit the falls, do so anytime between August and November; May to July is the area's flood season.

GUALEQUAYCHU: A strange event occurred here one day in 1845: The Italian patriot Giuseppe Garibaldi captured this town for one day during the Uruguayan civil war. Today the town is a meat-packing and tannin producer. Some 11 miles (18 km) west of the Río Uruguay, it is 220 miles (352 km) north of Buenos Aires on Route 12.

CONCORDIA: A thriving city (pop. 56,000) that swaps commercial business with Uruguay, Brazil, and Paraguay, Concordia offers a 9-hole golf course, a motor race course, and Parque Rivadavia along with some waterfalls. On Route 14, a 20-mile (32-km) drive north leads to Salto Grande, the site of a large hydroelectrical plant.

The tourist office at Plaza 25 de Mayo is very helpful.

En Route from Concordia – A small port east of Concordia on Route 3, Monte Caseros faces Bella Union, the Uruguayan town near the Brazilian border.

BEST EN ROUTE

Hotel accommodations in Mesopotamia are small (often lacking single rooms and air conditioning) but adequate; when one finds luxuries, however, one ends up paying for them. For that reason, hotels will cost anywhere from $50 and up (expensive), to $25 to $35 (moderate), to $10 or under (inexpensive). Since many hotels lack telephones or street addresses, it's wise to make arrangements through agencies in advance.

PARANÁ

Mayorazgo – This new hotel has a casino and swimming pool. Moderate.
Gran Hotel Paraná – Here travelers get double rooms. Inexpensive.

POSADAS

De Turismo – This hotel gives you a double room, with bath. Inexpensive.
San Ignácio Mini – Hot showers are included in the room charge. Inexpensive.

IGUAZÚ FALLS

Internacional Iguazú – The falls can be seen from most of the 180 balconied rooms in this elegant new hotel. Other comforts include air conditioning, private baths, pool, disco, casino, and a fine restaurant. Located in Parque Nacional Iguazú (phone: 2748). Reservations can be made in Buenos Aires. Reconquista 585 (phone: 31-47-26). Expensive.

Esturion-Iguazú – Another new hotel in the jungle, the *Esturion* has 118 attractive and air-conditioned rooms, swimming pool, nightclub, and restaurant. (For dinner, order the local specialty, dorado, a fish caught in the waters of the Río Iguazú.) Av. Tres Fronteras 650 (phone: 2020). Reservations can be made in Buenos Aires. Ave. Belgrano 265, 10° piso (phone: 30-49-19 or 34-08-15). Expensive.

Mendoza

The adobe gateway to Mendoza province for travelers arriving from the east bears the slogan: "Bienvenidos a Mendoza, Tierra del Sol y del Buen Vino" ("Welcome to Mendoza, Land of Sun and Good Wine"). There's no more fitting description for the wine-producing center of Argentina, a title shared with San Juan and La Rioja provinces, to the north. And under the warm *mendocino* sun are wonders of nature that beckon mountain climbers, viticulturists (or just plain viticonnoisseurs), hikers, and even convalescents (there are plenty of curative thermal springs). Stark, jagged mountains (among them Aconcagua, the highest peak in the Western Hemisphere) and bountiful, irrigated valleys make this one of the country's loveliest places.

Mendoza (pop. 133,300), 636 miles (1,018 km) northwest of Buenos Aires, is rated among the most beautiful cities in Argentina, second only to the capital. Originally founded in 1561 by a Spanish officer, Mendoza was named for the governor of Chile (not for Pedro de Mendoza, who founded Asunción and the first successful colony of Buenos Aires). Mendoza was destroyed by an earthquake and the ensuing fire 300 years later, and, as protection against possible quakes in the future, the city was rebuilt with one-story office structures. In 1816, General José de San Martín equipped his army of 40,000 men at nearby Potrerillos before crossing the Andes to liberate Chile and Perú. To help him, the women of Mendoza collected their jewelry and presented it to him. The street Patricias Mendocinas was named in commemoration of this event: It means "patriotic women of Mendoza" (*patrician,* or "rich," would also be appropriate).

Today, Mendoza is the largest city in western Argentina. Its outstanding beauty stems from a combination of low buildings on seemingly endless tree-lined streets, with green, artistically designed plazas interspersed throughout. The trees are special: In a given city block, there are ten on each side of the street, often touching overhead. They are unusually tall and full for city trees, due to extensive, open drainage canals that run along the streets, removing excess rainwater and giving the tree roots a good dousing. Because the canals and trees extend to the outskirts of the city, Mendoza hasn't just one pretty part, like most cities; it's all lovely. But be careful when crossing the street in the middle of the block — you can fall into a canal!

Mendoza's surrounding province complements the city. The mineral springs of Cacheuta and Villavicencio to the west are set amid picturesque mountain settings. Puente del Inca (Bridge of the Incas) is grotesque — one imagines trolls hiding under its curved, shadowed arch of rock. To the north, the wine country of San Juan has a dry, Mediterranean climate — excellent for vineyard maintenance.

New to the Mendoza area is Las Leñas, a ski resort recently opened by a French consortium. In season, charter planes take ski buffs from Mendoza to Malargue, where buses complete the trip to Las Leñas. The resort has 1,000 beds and seven lifts, which rise to an altitude of 10,000 feet; it promises to rival that of Portillo in Chile.

Mendoza can be reached by air: Daily jets fly out of Buenos Aires, and Aerolineas Argentinas has flights to Bariloche three times a week. San Martín railway follows a Transandine route from Buenos Aires to Mendoza, but no longer crosses into Chile. Traveling by car, Route 7 west from Buenos Aires goes to Mendoza and straight on to the Chilean border. Route 40 north of Mendoza leads you through the wine country of San Juan and La Rioja provinces.

For further information, contact the tourist offices in Mendoza: Avenida J. V. Zapata (in the main bus station); 11th block, Avenida San Martín; and in the Museum of Modern Art.

MENDOZA: Up to 40% of Mendoza's irrigated land is devoted to grape cultivation, which helps make Argentina the fifth largest producer of wine in the world. The Grape Harvest Festival, Fiesta de la Vandima, is held every March, preceded by a wine festival in mid-February. Some wineries are open to the public and offer informative tours followed by free samples of their products. One of the best *bodegas* (wine cellars) to visit is Arizu — it's also one of the largest in the world. At San Martín 1449 in barrio Godoy Cruz, it's a 10-minute ride on bus 1 or 2 from Plaza 9 de Julio. At the *bodega*, visitors congregate in a room resembling the dining room of a Spanish colonial hacienda, where they meet their guide. Later, they return to toast one another around the wooden table. The tour itself weaves through areas where the grapes are processed, past huge, wooden French vats that line the dimly lit passageways of the earthquake-proof winery. Light streams in from skylights above, and the smell of the wine is heady. The only letdown: The wine is served in plastic cups.

Giol Bodega (or Giol District) also offers tours, but they must be arranged through one of the agencies on Las Heras or Sarmiento streets.

Las Heras, along with Avenida General San Martín, is also a center of shopping activity. Mendoza is famous for additional agricultural products — olives, alfalfa, and fruit. The best place to shop for them is at the central market: It's a wonderland of fresh vegetables, fruit, eggs, cheese, *matambre* (cold cuts), and prepackaged and precooked foods, such as *empanadas* and pizza. A clean store, you can sit and eat your food here.

In the same area, look for good buys on Mendoza sweaters; a lot of shops have them, and they're quite reasonable. Avenida General San Martín has a good selection of *confiterías* (tearooms), too, where you can stroll in and rest after spending your money.

For sightseers, the San Martín museum provides insight into the life and times of the Libertador and into the Mendoza of that period. The Museum of Natural History, at Plaza Independencia, contains items of anthropological interest: It's small, underground, and free.

The *correo central* (main post office), at the junction of San Martín and Avenida Colón (Colón turns into J. V. Zapata), has a well-organized delivery section and is a good place for friends and family to reach you: Have them specify *poste restante.*

One of the most impressive sights in all of Mendoza is the statue atop Cerro de la Gloria (Hill of Glory), which celebrates Argentina's independence from Spain and pays homage to San Martín. Massive yet not overpowering on the forested hilltop, the work portrays the victory in terms of the goddess of liberty, with broken chains dangling from outstretched, forward-thrown arms. Behind her flies a condor; on each side frenzied horses bolt, heads and bodies forward. Bas-reliefs surround the statue's huge stone base; one depicts the women of the city offering their jewels to San Martín. In front of the statue, San Martín sits on his horse, arms crossed over his chest.

Buses travel frequently to Cerro de la Gloria, but you must wait at the base of the hill for another bus to take you up the winding road to the top. Your best bet is to walk down at your own leisure and enjoy the scenery, which includes the soccer stadium built for the 1978 World Cup games.

Mendoza's zoo is at the foot of the mountain. Animals — many surprisingly tame — roam in miniature versions of their own habitats. A trail goes uphill and down and is well marked. You might be standing at the top of an abrupt drop of land only to find yourself eye to eye with a giraffe. Monkeys and bears woo you for a snack, and there are guanaco (part of the llama family), elephants, and North American buffalo. As you arrive at the trail's end, be sure to see the Argentine rabbits, odd-looking little animals with rabbit heads and deerlike bodies. The zoo also has a pet chimpanzee that welcomes visitors and drinks *yerba maté* (stimulating herb tea) like a pro.

You really should take a stroll through Mendoza's parks. Parque General San Martín, ten blocks west of Plaza Independencia, has giant portals, tall palms, winding lanes, and well-kept grounds bespeckled with fountains and statues. Around the man-made lake grow *ceibo* trees, which bear pretty red blossoms that are Argentina's national flower.

One favorite restaurant, *Un Rincón de la Boca* (A Corner of Your Mouth; 500 Las Heras), has the best pizza in town. *Empanadas* are also on the menu, and sidewalk seating is available.

One word about local tours: Agencies offer them for a reasonable price; the guides are young and well informed; and buses will pick you up at your hotel early in the morning. Before leaving, photographers should see that the window is clean — the red dust in the area can create poor visibility on a clear day. If you're driving by yourself, take along a rag for periodic window wipes.

Two interesting side trips from Mendoza lead in opposite directions but reach very similar destinations. Cachueta is 45 miles (75 km) southwest on alternate Route 7. Well known for its therapeutic hot springs, only those with doctor's permission have access to them, so you can look, but not swim.

The mineral springs of Villavicencio are 27 miles (45 km) northwest of Mendoza on alternate Route 7. Nearby is an old amphitheater once used by Indians for rituals.

En Route from Mendoza – By far the best excursion from Mendoza is 96 miles (160 km) west on Route 7 toward the Chilean border and Puente del Inca (Bridge of the Incas). The route follows the Río Mendoza through its valley up into the mountains, climbing from 2,518 feet above sea level to 8,195 feet (bring an extra sweater for the chill and good shoes for walking). If you get a headache, it might be from the height change.

As you get closer to the Chilean border, the mountain range becomes increasingly formidable — a gray, barren beauty. Impressive peaks along the way include 22,310-foot Tupungato, 18,500-foot Tupungatito, and 18,000-foot Los Penitentes.

Aconcagua (Watchman of Rock), near the Chilean border at the Uspallata Pass, is the tallest mountain in the Western Hemisphere. At 22,834 feet with a dazzlingly white blanket of snow, it was first conquered by Matthias Zurbriggen in 1897. The best time for climbers to tackle it is from mid-January to mid-February. For more information, check with the Club Andinista in Mendoza, Calle Pardo y Ruben Lemos.

PUENTE DEL INCA: Among the mountains, this bridge *is* a mountain, carved into a natural bridge 65 feet high, 70 feet long, and 90 feet wide by the Río Mendoza. Mineral springs gurgle out of the earth, making the rocks appear copper and gold tinged with green.

The bridge is set back from Route 7, and must be reached on foot. Over the bridge and up a small hill are the ruins of a community destroyed by a flood. An army base, however, is also there, hindering examination at close range. At the bridge, small figures carved from stone and then bathed in the mineral water for a few days are sold as souvenirs.

From the bridge, you can walk to a number of manmade and natural points of interest. Los Penitentes, the statue *Christ the Redeemer* (also known as *Christ of the Andes*), and Laguna de los Horcones, a green lake at the base of Aconcagua, are each within a 20-minute walk of Puente del Inca.

The work of Mateo Alonso, *Cristo Redentor* (*Christ the Redeemer*) stands on the border of Argentina and Chile, a symbol of peace between the two countries. Erected by Argentine workers, the statue bears the inscription: "These mountains will crumble before the Argentine and Chilean people break the peace sworn by them at the feet of Christ the Redeemer." The statue portrays a beautiful, rugged Christ.

Bad weather often bars access to *Cristo Redentor* except during the summer, and it is virtually impossible to see the statue from the road or train.

Unless you want to go to Chile or visit *Cristo Redentor,* ignore the border town of Las Cuevas, a bleak, barren cluster of about 15 buildings on either side of a narrow road, which is actually Route 7. The orange roofs are a sharp contrast to the surrounding barren land and gaunt mountains. This village, however, is the proposed site of a ski village.

From Las Cuevas, Route 7 continues into Chile. Route 7 branches into two roads; the main road runs along the railway route; the alternate, which is not as modern, goes over La Cumbre Pass. The Transandine railway ends at Los Andes, where connections can be made for Santiago and Valparaíso.

SAN JUAN: Those wishing to see more of Argentina's wine country and to feel more of a dry, Mediterranean climate should take Route 40 north of Mendoza and head toward San Juan province, 106 miles (177 km) away.

An Argentine expression says that when a man is drunk, he is "between San Juan and Mendoza." Besides good wine, San Juan has a paleontological treasure called Moon Valley in the Andean foothills of the Ischigaulasto region. Thirty-six miles long and 9 miles wide, the valley was a lake 100 million years ago. Severe droughts brought subsequent death, and today the remains of former inhabitants — petrified carcasses of enormous reptiles and fossils of gigantic ferns — are strewn about.

Founded in 1562, the city of San Juan (pop. 142,000) was completely destroyed in an earthquake in 1944, but was rebuilt. Domingo Faustino Sarmiento, president of Argentina from 1868 to 1874 and a renowned historian, was born here; his birthplace now houses the Sarmiento Museum.

Regularly scheduled buses and trains travel to San Juan from Buenos Aires 1,297 miles away.

LA RIOJA: The capital of still another wine province is a 6½-hour drive from San Juan — from Route 40 north to Route 607 east (at the village of Jachal), turning onto Route 74 south at Nonogasta, and finally going north on Route 38 at Patquia. Founded in 1591, the city (pop. 45,000) contains a folk museum and the ruins of a Jesuit church. *Pala borracho* (drunken stick) trees are common and unique because of the cotton-like substance that hangs from them (it's used to stuff mattresses); the same tree can be found at Plaza San Martín in Buenos Aires.

An unusual dry wine is produced in the province.

BEST EN ROUTE

Hotels in the Mendoza area are, for the most part, inexpensive (up to $15 per person), but can range from expensive ($50) to moderate ($20–$40). They are clean and comfortable, although they become more rugged and rustic toward the Chilean border. Some are open only in the summer, so you should make reservations through your travel agent or tourist office before taking your trip.

MENDOZA

Aconcague – Modern, air-conditioned hotel with a pool. The best in town. Av. San Lorenzo 545 (phone: 24-2450). Expensive.

Trevi – 120-room hotel with a restaurant. Las Heras 68. Expensive.

Palace – 50-room hotel downtown has clean accommodations. Las Heras 70. Expensive.

Plaza – In the center of town, this 85-room hotel has air-conditioned accommodations, restaurant, bar, and a casino. Chile 1124 (phone: 21-45-60). Expensive.

Sussex – Recommended hotel has a restaurant. Sarmiento 250. Inexpensive.

Pension – The owner, Señora Yolanda Ficarra, is charming and will make you feel at home. Paso de los Andes 236. Inexpensive.

Residencial Mariela – Pleasant downtown hotel. Necochea 359. Inexpensive.

Zamora – Hotel is in a converted house. Perú 1156. Inexpensive.Free camping is available in Mendoza's parks: check with the tourist office first.

VILLAVICENCIO

Termas – Daily lodging offered during the summer only, with full pension. Moderate.

Córdoba

In the heart of Argentina, Córdoba province has maintained its seventeenth-century reputation as an important agricultural center. Founded in 1573 by Don Jeronimo Luis de Cabrera, the province produces port wine, cattle, peanuts, millet, grain sorghum, alfalfa, wheat, birdseed, barley, oats, sunflower, flax, soybean, cotton, tobacco, rye, potatoes, and so on. The list is endless, and much of the produce is shipped to the US, Germany, France, and Belgium.

Industrially, Córdoba is important for one main reason: The first locomotives in South America were built here. There now exists a steadily increasing production of automobiles by IME (Industiras Mecanicas del Estado), Fiat Concord Argentina, and Renault, a good part of which is imported by Uruguay, Brazil, and Chile. The hydroelectric power of the province is also reaching its potential: Up to 19 dams have been built on the province's rivers; the principal thermoelectric plants include Pilar, Dean Funes, Las Playas, Río Cuarto, San Francisco, and Isla Verde.

Geographically, the province is split into two regions. The mountains in the west incorporate three chains: the Sierras Chicas to the east, the Sierras de Pocho (which become the Sierras de Guasampampa) to the west, and the Sierras Grandes, the central chain (they all run parallel to each other, north and south). To the east is the extension of the Argentine pampas.

The Punilla Valley, which stretches between the Sierras Pocho and Grandes, houses a number of rustic mountain towns. There is a large dam at each end of the valley: the San Roque in the south, Cruz del Eje in the north. The tops of the mountain ranges are flat, which earns them the nickname *pampas*.

Córdoba's tourist industry is second only to that of the coastal (Mar del Plata) area, with about three million visitors a year. Outdoor enthusiasts come for the invigorating fresh air and for the swimming, hiking, fishing, camping, and horseback riding, available in the health resorts of La Cumbre, Capilla del Monte, Mina Claveros, and Mar Chiquita. Places like Córdoba and Carlos Pax have a thriving night life as well.

The Traslasierras region, the heart of Córdoba's farming area, centers around Villa Dolores, south of the capital, a small farming town that produces, among other things, peanuts, corn, and tobacco. Neighboring San Javier is a major producer of herbs.

Transportation to Córdoba is no problem: Trains, buses, and planes depart from Buenos Aires and surrounding provinces daily. The tourist office in Córdoba (Blvd. Reconquista, between Blvd. Junín and Calle Corrientes; phone: 33248) has detailed information on routes and sites; airline offices in the city are also accessible, and include Aerolineas Argentinas (Av. Colón 520), Austral (Rosario de Santa Fe 235), and Aero Chaco (27 de Abril 220).

To take in all of Córdoba's tourist attractions, from the northeast to Carlos Pax, Capilla del Monte, and Cruz del Eje down toward Villa Dolores, Río Cuerto, and Alta Gracia, would take about 5 to 7 days. To do this effectively, we recommend a circular route. This takes you, first, northwest of Córdoba on Route 20 to Carlos Paz, continuing north on Route 38, winding your way north, then southwest, from Cruz del Eje to Salsacate and Taninga, continuing south on Route 146 from Yacanto to Route 7 east, then taking Route 8 northeast, coming up north on Route 36 to Río Cuarto and Alta Gracia, and returning, finally, to Córdoba.

While in Córdoba, a possible side trip is to Mar Chiquita.

Although the route starts in Córdoba, one major city cannot be overlooked: Between Córdoba and Buenos Aires lies Rosario, the capital of Santa Fe province.

ROSARIO: With a population of 851,000, Rosario is the second largest city in Argentina. On the west bank of the Río Paraná, it is the major port for exporting produce from the central provinces (including Córdoban products) and plays a major role as a clearinghouse for shipments to Argentina's island territories.

Attractions in Rosario include the Monument of the Flag, a riverbank monument honoring General Belgrano; the Rose Garden in Parque Independencia; and the municipal and provincial museums.

CÓRDOBA: The third largest city in Argentina, Córdoba (pop. 2,400,000) is a

192-mile (307-km) drive from Buenos Aires northwest on Route 9. The capital of Córdoba province, Córdoba was founded in 1573 and is in the center of the country. It became somewhat of a metropolis by the 17th century, an important crossroads and center of religious and intellectual life. The first university in South America, Córdoba Nacional Universidad, was established in 1622 from the roots of a Jesuit seminary. Today, 40,000 students are enrolled here, and the institution retains its reputation as one of the most prominent schools on the continent.

Like other early Argentine settlements, Córdoba was planned on a grid, an easy route for city sightseers. The university is near Plaza San Martín, which, similar to other Argentine plazas, contains a statue of El Libertador. On the western side of the plaza is the cathedral, its 17th-century architecture depicting the Moorish influence on Spanish art at that time. The building, unfortunately, is neither well kept nor always open to the public, so check with the tourist office for details. La Compañía Church (c. 1650) is also near the plaza. East of the church is Casa del Virrey (House of the Viceroy), now the Historical and Colonial Museum (Calle Rosario de Santa Fe). The Natural History section of the Provincial Museum, on the top floor of the *cabildo* (town hall), is beside the cathedral.

Two churches north of Plaza San Martín, La Merced (Calle Rivadavia) and the Church and Convent of Santa Teresa (c. 1770), are colonial institutions worth examining.

At Plaza Velez Sarsfield, a tiny square with a statue honoring the jurist who wrote Argentina's civil code, are the Academy of Fine Arts, Córdoba's theater, and the Olmos School. The Museum of Fine Arts is at Plaza Centenario. East of it is the landscaped Parque Sarmiento, where you can get a good view of the entire city. The Jardín Zoológico is here, and you can pass the afternoon enjoyably among the lions and hippos.

Shoppers will be interested to know that Córdoba was the first Argentine city to turn one of its main streets into a pedestrian mall full of shops and galleries. Prices here are often lower than those in Buenos Aires.

A good, moderately priced restaurant across from Mitre Station is *Romanolo's Clac Clac* (Av. Colón 628), a nice, modern place to have tea and meals; it also serves American breakfasts. Many other good restaurants and *confiterías* (tearooms) are near Plaza San Martín.

Córdoba is only 1 hour from Buenos Aires by air, and flights operate daily: Córdoba's airport is an international one, second in importance only to Buenos Aires's. The Mitre Railroad, which passes through Rosario on the Río Paraná, makes the 434-mile trip in about 12 hours.

A possible side trip is to Jesús Maria, 31 miles (50 km) from the city (north on Route 9 to Route 38 west). Of interest are the national Jesuit Museum, containing more than 15,000 articles of archaeological, historical, and artistic value, and the annual Doma y Folklore Festival the first 2 weeks in January, when there's a lot of native music and horse shows. Along the way, you'll pass Saldan, famous for its mineral waters and the walnut tree that San Martín rested under during his journey to Chile; Río Ceballos, the site of La Quebrada Dam; Candonga, the ranch of Santa Gertrudis, declared a national monument; Ascochinga, a charming township that dates back to colonial times; and Santa Catalina, a former 17th-century Jesuit mission.

Another side trip is the 90-mile (144-km) excursion northeast on Route 9 to Mar Chiquita, a therapeutic saltwater lake, home to thousands of flamingos.

On the way to Mar Chiquita, you'll pass Cerro Colorado, which contains reddish sandstone cave drawings made by primitive Indians who once lived in the area.

En Route From Córdoba – After an outing in Córdoba, you can visit the province's lake resort area by continuing west on Route 20 for about 18 miles (30 km). You will reach the start of the Punilla Valley and the boisterous town of San Roque.

CARLOS PAZ: On the south shore of Lake San Roque (formed by the San Roque Dam), this resort town is noted for its *boites* (nightclubs). It is also called the noise capital of Córdoba. Its main street claims to have the largest cuckoo clock in the world — a boast as yet unchallenged — and crowds gather there on the hour to watch it strike (that is, if their hangovers will let them). A lift up one of the mountains offers grand views of the valley; at the top, a nightclub and tearoom await you.

The folklore festival from January 7 to 14 always attracts large crowds, and many sports, from tennis to golf, boating, and fishing, are offered seasonally. The resort is also a good place to buy such handmade items as bags and pottery.

En Route from Carlos Paz – Continuing north on Route 38 leads you past the health resorts of Bialet Masses, Santa Maria, and Villa Bustos.

Cosquin, 38 miles (61 km) north of Córdoba at the foot of Pan de Azúcar (Sugar Loaf Mountain), is another resort village known for its therapeutic air. Swimming and camping are allowed here, and the village holds a huge Argentine–Latin American Folklore Festival annually during the second 2 weeks in January.

La Pampa de Olean is a tiny village that contains an old chapel and waterfall: It's a picturesque place.

Valle Hermoso, north of La Pampa de Olean, is a cattle-raising center that features the restored chapel of San Antonio. A hydroelectric station is on the Cosquín River.

La Falda, 51 miles (82 km) north of Córdoba, is the site of Córdoba University's holiday center, frequented year-round by students from around the world. The resort is known for its golf and swimming.

Huerta Grande, 2 miles (3 km) north of La Falda (continuing on Route 38), is famous for its medicinal waters; fishing and camping are also allowed.

From here, a right turn onto alternate Route 38 will lead you to the resorts of La Cumbre (with neighboring Cruz Chica) and Los Cocos.

LA CUMBRE: Sixty miles (96 km) north of Córdoba, the village of La Cumbre adjoins the health resort of Cruz Chica, which also has one of the best English boys' schools in the country. Here, trout streams attract fishing enthusiasts from November to April, and swimming, tennis, and golf are major attractions.

Traditionally, La Cumbre has been known as a refuge for writers and the elite. The famous Argentine writer Mujica Laines resides here; he is best known for the novel *La Casa* (*The House*).

LOS COCOS: The next stop on your alternate route, the *Hotel Gran Mansión el Descano,* has a small park containing imitation Roman statues, a honey shop that sells honey goodies (displaying a beehive within glass walls), and a labyrinth made of intertwining hedges. You can wander through the park for a small fee. If you get lost among the hedges, you end up providing free entertainment for other travelers: When a guide leads you to the safety of the cupola, you discover that other people have been watching you and laughing at your self-inflicted misery. Altogether, there are something like 28,000 hotel rooms in the Punilla Valley area. Check with the tourist office in Córdoba for more information.

CAPILLA DEL MONTE: Continuing on alternate Route 38 north leads you to the main route and Capilla del Monte (Mountain Springs), with thermal springs, waterfalls, and grand vistas. Only 64 miles (102 km) from Córdoba, it is in the heart of the Sierras de Córdoba, a line of slopes and hills that rise out of the pampas and contain a wealth of resort activities, including fishing, swimming, camping, and hiking. El Zapato rock offers a wide view of the surrounding area; horseback riding tours are available.

En Route from Capilla del Monte – A left turn northwest takes you onto a small, unmarked, provincial route that connects Capilla del Monte with the San Roque Dam. Here you'll find Ṣan Marcos Sierras. The center of Argentina's honey-producing region, San Marcos is the site of the Honey Festival held every February.

Cruz del Eje, just west of San Marcos Sierras, is the heart of Córdoba's southern olive-growing region and the site of the annual National Olive Festival the last two weeks in July. The nearby Cruz del Eje Dam provides a lake for swimming and fishing; it also marks the end of the Punilla Valley.

From here, Route 38 travels south through Villa de Soto, La Higuera, and San Carlos Minas — not a resort area, but good for hunting and fishing.

Salsacate and Taninga, about 72 miles (115 km) from Cruz del Eje, are in a region of palm trees and dry, tropical air, unlike the sierra resorts.

VILLA CURA BROCHERO: Twenty-seven miles (43 km) south of Taninga on Route 38, Villa Cura Brochero was once the home of Casa de Retiros Espirituales (House of Spiritual Retreat). Now a museum, the house lodges the relics and belongings of José Gabriel Brochero, a legendary priest-goldsmith of the area.

MINA CALVERO: Three miles (5 km) farther south is this popular mountain resort, a charming place where striking rock scenery forms the backdrop. This is a good base for mountain climbing; nearby is lofty Champaquí. There is a casino.

Mina Calvero can also be reached by traveling directly west from Córdoba 84 miles (134 km) by car or bus.

En Route from Mina Calvero – Continuing south on Route 38 takes you farther into Traslasierras Valley, the farming region of Córdoba. Dique la Vina, the first stop, is the highest dam in South America at 335 feet above sea level. Las Rosas, farther south, is the heart of the most important tobacco-growing region in Córdoba.

VILLA DOLORES: Some 116 miles (185 km) southwest of Córdoba, Villa Dolores is the most important town in this region. Despite its small size (pop. 10,000), it is an agricultural center on the Río de Sauces that produces corn, peanuts, wheat, tobacco, and fruit. Wine is another industry here.

SAN JAVIER: Southeast of Villa Dolores on Route 148, San Javier sits on the border of San Luis province and is Argentina's biggest supplier of herbs.

YACANTO: South of San Javier, Yacanto is at the foot of Mt. Champaquí (9,459 feet), the highest peak of the Sierras of Córdoba. You can swim, ride, climb, play tennis, golf, and fish or enjoy the thermal springs.

En Route from Yacanto – A trip down Route 146 south to Route 7 east will lead to Mercedes and the junction of Routes 7 and 8. Take Route 8 north until you reach Río Cuarto; then pass through a series of small villages to Río de los Sauces.

RÍO DE LOS SAUCES: In the Sierras del Sur, this village is laden with willow trees and is a good spot to camp. Nearby Cerro Inti Huasi contains ancient cave drawings.

RÍO TERCERO LAKE: North of Río de los Sauces on Route 36, this lake resort has the country's second electroatomic center on its southern shore. With that in mind, the lake permits fishing and boating.

Villages along the lakeshore include Rumipal, Villa del Dique, and Embalse.

VILLA GENERAL BELGRANO: North of Río Tercero Lake on Route 36, Villa General Belgrano hosts the annual festival popular with Argentina's hops consumers — the National Beer Festival the first two weeks in October.

ALTA GRACIA: Only 29 miles (46 km) southwest of Córdoba, Alta Gracia was once the site of a Jesuit ranch; the colonial church and some dwellings still remain and are open to visitors. Beside the colonial edifices are a casino and numerous nightclubs and coffee houses.

Continuing north on Route 36 will bring you directly into Córdoba.

BEST EN ROUTE

Córdoba province is a favorite with travelers because there are many comfortable and moderate accommodations; most hotels cost no more than $16 per person a night and can run as little as $8. Córdoba city prices are higher; a first-class double room will run about $30 per person. Since access to many hotel addresses and telephone numbers is difficult, we suggest you contact the tourist office in Córdoba for further information and make your reservations early.

CÓRDOBA

Crillon – 120-room hotel provides private baths, excellent service. Rivadavia 85. Expensive.

Gran Hotel Dora – 120-room hotel provides private baths. Expensive.

Dallas – San Jeronimo 339. Moderate.

Claridge – 25 de Mayo 218. Moderate.

Emperado – 25 Mayo 240. Moderate.

MAR CHIQUITA

Miramar – This popular lakeside resort contains more than 3,000 hotel rooms and campgrounds. Contact the Córdoba tourist office for details.

LOS COCOS

Gran Mansion el Descano – This small resort hotel is entertaining: It has Roman statues, a honey shop, and a small park filled with landscaped hedges to get lost in. Moderate.

SAN JAVIER

Yacanto – This small hotel in Traslasierras region has comfortable rooms and excellent service. It's reachable only by car from the Pajas Blancas airport — an attempt on the owners' part to keep it as rustic and removed from the mainstream as possible. Moderate.

ALTA GRACIA

Sierras – This modern hotel has a 9-hole golf course and restaurant. Moderate.

Northwestern Argentina

High near the border of Bolivia, the northwestern section of Argentina is a hodgepodge of diverse topography. The interplay of mountain and plain in El Norte is dramatic: The mountains of Tucumán province are laced by a multitude of fresh streams; mountains wind and plummet through Salta and Jujuy provinces, which are also partly covered with cacti-filled, arid pampas and moist, Scottish-type moors. Toward the Bolivian border, the jagged Quebrada de Humahuaca produces a deep river valley; the mountains range from blue to red to green, the result of their high mineral content. In fact, one town, Maimara, is named after the Coya term for "painter's palette." The region's climate is invigorating; summer days are hot, often reaching up to 100°F (38°C). Nights are a refreshing 70°F (21°C).

Among the earliest provinces to be settled by Spanish explorers traveling south from Bolivia and Perú in the 1500s, Tucumán, Salta, and Jujuy are steeped in colonial history. Churches, government buildings, and houses all remain as they did in the intense, 300-year period of settlement.

Some of the last remaining Indian towns are north of Jujuy, near Bolivia: the Coyas (slang for "Indians") resemble their southern Bolivian neighbors and resent being treated as tourist attractions. A simple people, they are living testament to the will to temper complete Christianization by missionaries, and their Holy Week and Carnival celebrations are vivid, filled with colorful parades and candlelight processions.

The Coyas and some Indian villages in Patagonia and Tierra del Fuego are all that remain of Indians in Argentina, after the colonial exterminations of the 1800s. The villages include Humahuaca, Yavi, Purmamarca, and La Quiaca.

Since the northern region was settled earlier than Buenos Aires, the northwestern region conducted a large trade with Bolivia and Perú during the settlement period. Salta was the heart of commerce, for two rivers, Salado and Dulce, run through its area. Most of the business centered around mules, which grazed in the pampas region near Rosario, Santa Fe, and Córdoba (for detailed information, see *Córdoba*) and were later shipped to the northern mining towns. Maize, alfalfa, and tobacco were also important products.

Tucumán was the seat of the country's sugarcane industry. More than 140 acres of cane were harvested yearly, the land irrigated by the streams of Sierra de Aconquija. Today, some sugar is produced, but the region is better known for harvesting alfalfa and maize for fodder, and it is cattle, not mules, that cross the pampas.

Northwestern Argentina is easily accessible from Buenos Aires. Buses travel as far as Córdoba, with connections made there to Tucumán — a 15-hour trip. The Rayo de Sol and the Estrella de Norte trains offer nightly rides that take about 13 hours.

If you drive, we recommend that you take Route 9 northeast from the capital to reach Tucumán. The route will take you into Salta and Jujuy and eventually straight up into Bolivia. The more scenic way to travel north, however, is to take Route 38 south at Tafi del Valle and continue north on Route 307 to Route 40, which leads you through mountains and valleys, archaeological ruins, and small villages.

The tourist office in Tucumán's main bus station can supply you with maps and brochures.

TUCUMÁN: The largest city in the north, San Miguel de Tucumán sits on the banks of the Río Dulce at the foot of Sierra de Azonquija, whose streams once irrigated more than 141 acres of sugarcane fields. Founded in 1565 by Spanish conquistadores from southwest Perú, the city was moved after the area was hit by a flood in 1580. The existing buildings of the densely populated (400,000 people) province date back as far as the 18th century.

True to its Spanish heritage, the city is laid out on a grid: The main Plaza Independencia is bordered by a cathedral (Calle 24 de Septiembre), Government House (Calle 9 de Julio), and a tourist office (Calle 24 de Septiembre 484; phone: 1-8591). The office distributes maps and brochures on the area. Across the street and one block west is the Provincial Folklore Museum.

Casa Histórica (Calle Congreso 181, between Calles Alvarez and San Lorenzo) is a new museum incorporating the rooms and furniture where the country's declaration of independence from Spain was signed in 1816. The historic event is reenacted each evening with special lighting and recorded music and words in *luz y sonido* (sound and light). The audience stands in each of three enclosed patios of the museum for each part of the presentation. The third patio contains a bas-relief portraying the congressional delegates proclaiming national independence to the people.

There are more sights in downtown Tucumán: Santo Domingo Church, one block west of Casa Historica (Calle 25 de Mayo); the Provincial Museum of Fine Arts (Alvarez and 25 de Mayo); the Museum of Prehistoric Anthropology and Archaeology (25 de Mayo, between San Juan and Santiago); La Merced Church (24 de Septiembre and Rivadavia); and La Casa de Culture (Calle San Martín). The Police Museum is one block east of Avenidas Catamarca and Avellaneda.

Parque Centenario 9 de Julio (Av. Soldati, between Av. Governador del Campo and Benjamin Araoz) contains the house of Bishop Colombres, who introduced sugarcane to Tucumán in the early 1880s. In front of the house is the giant steam press he imported from France in 1883. His first, crude attempt at building his own is in the house.

Any sightseeing trips outside the city can be done on your own. However, local tourist agencies (there are several on 24 de Septiembre, near Plaza Independencia) offer tours, and a guide is always a good idea. Buses also run to tourist attractions, but check if they do so on a daily schedule. The bus station is at Avenidas Benjamin Araoz and Saenz Pena. If you need a map, stop in at the Automobile Club of Argentina office at the corner of Alvarez and Salta.

If you're planning to take a side trip, the resort of Villa Nogues is mandatory. On Route 38 southwest, 1 hour from Tucumán, there is an excellent hostería. North of the villa on Route 341 is Raco, where horseback riding is available. Another good excursion takes you north of Tucumán on Route 9 to Cadillal Dam, about 15 miles (25 km) outside the city. Here you can boat, fish, swim, camp, and browse through a museum. A large amphitheater, canteen, and a modern sculpture of a woman look out over the serene water, formed by the mountains of the sierra. Just beyond Cadillal (the next stop on the local bus) is a favorite picnic-bathing spot for Tucumán residents along a Río Dulce tributary. Tables, barbecue grills, running water, and a bath house (a small fee is charged if you change clothes) are available. No food is sold, so bring your own. The river is refreshing for swimming; the water is cool even on the hottest days, but the current is swift and can be dangerous.

One note about Tucumán province: Be prepared for a lot of holidays. The residents are a festive people, and there's a feast for every occasion. The biggest is July 9, Argentina's Independence Day, but there are a host of local feasts. Craft fairs are held every Saturday morning in Simoca, just south of Tucumán on Route 157. Tafi del Valle holds a cheese festival in midsummer. Amaicha del Valle, on Route 307 in the Valles Calchaquies, hosts the Pachamamna Festival throughout the Carnival season. And, usually in February, Trancas's annual festival (near San Pedro de Colalao on Route 9) is held in the beginning of autumn. Tucumán observes Semana Santa (Holy Week) with processions and holds a music festival every September.

In addition, folk festivals are held in Lules, Monteros, Aquilares, Alberdi, and Tafi Viejo. Inquire in the Tucumán tourist office for their dates and other information.

En Route from Tucumán – Continuing north on Route 9, you come to Salta, some 200 miles (336 km) away. En route you pass San Pedro de Lolalao (left on Route 311 west); horseback riding and camping are available on the banks of the Río Tacanas. Farther north is Rosario de la Frontera, a small resort town with sulfur springs.

Although Route 9 is the most direct way to Salta, the route via Tafi del Valle and Cafayate is more scenic. It is highly recommended, even though the road is unpaved much of the way. The route swoops south (Route 38), then north (Routes 307 and 40) through mountain scenery, then past rolling cattle country and archaeological ruins. If the archaeological aspect interests you, stop in El Mollar, Parque de los Menhires, where there are immense, carved stones; Tafi del Valle;

and Colalao del Valle in the Valle Calchaquies, all on Route 40. The route enters barren, mountainous land, where giant cacti grow beside the road. It isn't unusual to see Indian women weaving or baking bread outdoors in an adobe oven.

If you travel by bus, you'll probably find that the bus driver, having tourists aboard so rarely, will be happy to serve as tour guide.

CAFAYATE: Surrounded by vineyards, this little town is just across the provincial border in Salta (you take Route 38 south, then Route 68 north). Restaurants in the area serve delicious *empanadas*. The craft center, on the northeast side of the main square, contains exhibits, and there are several shops. All attractions are within walking distance.

Professor Rodolfo Bravo, a citizen of Cafayate, maintains a private museum of Calchaqui Indian archaeology in his home; it is open to the public. One room holds artifacts from the surrounding area; Professor Bravo shows a film on the Cayo Indians followed by audience discussion, in another room.

Two *bodegas* (wineries) worth a visit are El Recreo and Michel Torino Hmnos., just north of the town's camping area; tours and samples are available on request, and the vineyard itself is easily seen from the wineries.

En Route from Cafayate – Two miles (3 km) north on Route 40 is San Carlos, which was destroyed four times by Indians. Farther north is Molinas. A church here has become a national monument; it contains the embalmed body of the last royal governor of the province, Colonel Severo Siqueira de Isasmendi y Echalar (d. 1837). A viewing of the mummy must be arranged through the priest.

The country immediately north of Cafayate is arrestingly beautiful; red rock formations in various shapes (including a giant obelisk) are interspersed with sand dunes. Every so often there are rock slides. If you are caught in one, sit back, enjoy the scenery, and wait until the road is cleared. Route 40 continues north through the Valles Calchaquies and the town of Cachi, winds up Cuesta del Obispo, an 11,877-foot mountain, then slopes down into the lush, wooded valley leading to Salta.

SALTA: Founded by Hernando de Lerma in 1582, this city of 260,000 is still very much a colonial city. People build in the style used almost 300 years ago — they get a tax break if they do! Houses with wrought-iron grating in the windows and stately churches are everywhere. Salta, along with Jujuy to the north, is a paradise for people who love to explore historic churches.

Some 775 miles northwest of Buenos Aires (there are regular Aerolineas Argentinas flights), Salta is 140 miles (233 km) north of Tucumán. The province is a center for farming, lumbering, livestock raising, and mining. In fact, Salta is full of minerals — petroleum, iron (Rosario de Larma), and copper (San Antonio de los Cobres) among them. The area is rich with historical significance. It was here that General Manuel Belgrano defeated the Spanish royalists in 1812 and General Martín Miguel de Guemes led the gauchos in seven successful battles against the Spanish in 1814 and 1821.

Salta's first *cabildo* (town hall) was constructed in 1582, followed by a number of others. The present building (Plaza 9 de Julio, Caseros 549) dates to 1783 and has been declared a national monument, housing both the provincial and national museums. If you look closely, you'll notice that the wooden columns on the first and second stories aren't aligned; for some reason, there are 15 on top and only 14 on the bottom.

Other historic buildings are equally interesting. Convento San Bernardo, a national monument, was at one time a hermitage, then a hospital, before housing Carmelite nuns. The massive, wooden double doorway, hand-carved by the Indians, dates from 1762. San Francisco Church has the highest belfry in South America — 174 feet. First built in 1625 (with an addition in 1674), the original church was destroyed by fire in the mid-1750s, after which the present church was built. Inside lie the remains of Don Francisco de Gurruchaga, founder of the Argentine Navy. Declared a national monument in 1941, the church is an easy landmark to spot — not simply because of its belfry, but because the entire building is painted a plum color.

Salta's cathedral, built in 1858, contains the images of Cristo del Milagro (imported from Spain in 1592) and the Virgin Mary, which are paraded through the streets each September in commemoration of a miracle that occurred in 1692, when the same action quelled a large earthquake.

Salta's monument to the Battle of Salta, or 20 de Febrero, sits in the center of Parque 20 de Febrero in remembrance of Belgrano's victory in 1812. The base is made of rock from surrounding mountains and is topped by a bronze statue of a female Victory carrying a laurel branch high above her head.

A monument to Guemes stands at the foot of Cerro San Bernardo. Guemes is portrayed in bronze, dressed in typical gaucho garb. Behind the monument, a steep path leads to the top of Cerro San Bernardo.

The *Internacional* restaurant, near the main plaza, serves entertainment along with food after 10 PM. *La Casa de las Empanadas* (12 de Octubre, near the train station) is noted locally for its *empanadas* and *humitas* (corn tortillas).

If you enjoy shopping, try the Mercado Artesanal (Av. San Martín 2555) — a wonderland of handmade goods — wall hangings, ponchos *salteños,* gloves, socks, leather and woven belts, Indian headbands, pottery, and much more, all reasonably priced. Handmade goods are also sold in shops around and near the main street.

Vino casera, or homemade wine, is sold in the markets for just a little more than the manufactured stock; you might try it before you frequent the *Balderrama,* a renowned *boliche,* or nightclub, where many of Argentina's best-known folk singers started out.

Before beginning your sightseeing, stop at the tourist office at Calles Alvarado and Buenos Aires, one block from Plaza 9 de Julio. An immigration office in town can be of assistance if you have visa problems, and the German consul, who's lived in Salta for many years, is also helpful.

There are some interesting side trips you can take from Salta. San Lorenzo is an idyllic town 8½ miles (14 km) west on provincial Route P. You can swim and camp in the Río San Lorenzo, and there's a rustic bar-café by the river edge.

An excursion to the copper-mining town of San Antonio de los Cobres, 99 miles (158 km) northwest on Route 9, takes you along the Huaytiquina Railroad, which travels from there to Antofagasta in northern Chile.

En Route from Salta – Route 9 leads directly north to Jujuy and to La Quiaca at the Bolivian border, passing the Humahuaca Ravine (Quebrada de Humahuaca). The small towns you pass don't have much in the way of accommodations for travelers, so you may prefer to use Salta as your home base.

JUJUY: Founded in 1593, San Salvador de Jujuy (hoo-hoo-ey) is the capital of Jujuy province, the northernmost province in Argentina and one of the most rural; its population is 120,000, many of them Coyas. Nicknamed the Silver Cup, Jujuy is rich in minerals — many as yet untapped.

Facing Plaza Belgrano, the Government House has the first Argentine flag, which Belgrano created. The cathedral, a colonial structure on the west side of the plaza, has a wooden pulpit carved and painted by the Indians. The doorway to the Lavalle Museum marks the place where General Juan Lavalle, former governor of Buenos Aires province, was killed by an assassin's bullet in 1848 in the campaign against Juan Manuel de Rosas.

Although a number of small shops sell crafts from the area, much of it is too commercial; the best place to buy is in Salta.

The tourist office (Guemes 1632) will provide any information travelers request.

Aerolíneas Argentinas provides daily air service to Jujuy from Buenos Aires. It is also possible to fly from here to Iguazú Falls in northeastern Misiones province (for more information on Iguazú Falls, see *Mesopotamia*). Bus and train service are available to Jujuy from the capital, although not on a daily basis: Frequent flooding makes these routes inaccessible, and you must often be rerouted south to Tucumán, then north.

En Route from Jujuy – The real attraction of the province of Jujuy is not its capital but the northern countryside and small towns that stretch along Route 9 to the Bolivian border.

Termas de Reyes, 5 miles (8 km) north of Jujuy, contains hot springs that supposedly were used during Inca days. Today, the springs pour into a concrete swimming pool.

Quebrada de Humahuaca (Humahuaca Ravine) begins north of Termas de Reyes and continues for about 102 miles (170 km), also along Route 9. A major tourist attraction, the ravine follows a narrow, deep river valley between high mountains that become more and more variegated in color because of a high, diverse mineral content. Along the route, tropical vegetation gets sparse until only shrubs, pygmy herbs, thorny plants, and the local *cardon* (thistle) remain.

Towns along the route are primarily Indian — tiny, with narrow, cobbled streets and adobe houses that gleam white in the sun. Tumbaya, one of these towns, contains some old churches that date from the late 1700s.

As you continue north on Route 9, a montage of mountains of strikingly different hues — red, green, blue, purple, and pink — announces the approach to Purmamarca.

PURMAMARCA: Just beyond Tumbaya, this town is noted for its colorful mountain range. Purmamarca is a well-kept town with a simple church and white houses with orange roofs. Natives sell their wares along the streets for reasonable prices.

MAIMARA: The mountains, like those of neighboring Purmamarca, are fittingly called "the painter's palette." Turn right off Route 9 to enter the town, whose name is derived from the Indian term for "the falling star." A little cemetery on the hillside as you approach the town looks like a small village set against the mountains' backdrop.

TILCARA: A short distance north of Maimara, Tilcara's major attraction is the Pucara, a restored Indian fortress within walking distance of the town. Like the Incas, Coyas lived in stone houses that no longer exist. An excellent archaeological museum on the main square exhibits artifacts found in Pucara as well as those from Bolivia, Perú, and Chile.

Try to plan your trip to the northwestern regions of Argentina around Holy Week. Most festivities, especially those in Tilcara, are beautiful and touching, with many processions and masses throughout the week.

En Route from Tilcara – Two northern villages are noted primarily for their church architecture. Huacalera contains an 18th-century chapel housing the paintings of Marcos Zapaca of the Cuzco School. The chapel is kept locked, but an attendant will open it upon request.

Uquia's church is a well-preserved sample of colonial architecture; its 17th-century paintings show angels dressed as musketeers; they are represented the same, unusual way in the church in Casabindo.

HUMAHUACA: Nestled in the mountains at 9,062 feet, 76 miles (126 km) north of Jujuy on Route 9, Humahuaca's main tourist attraction is a carved, wooden statue of St. Francis that appears daily at noon on the church tower to lift his hand as though blessing the people. The center of town contains a memorial to the Indian, topped by a powerful statue of an Indian brave; a long flight of stone steps leads to the monument.

En Route from Humahuaca – The road to Bolivia (Route 9) continues through tiny villages with colonial churches (there about 20 of these churches throughout Jujuy province). These include La Cueva and Uruya (turn left off the main road), Casabindo (containing "cavalier" angels similar to those in Uquia), and Cochinoca.

Yavi, a tiny town southeast of La Quiaca, has a fine colonial church with an ornate altar. There is a Coya market in town.

LA QUIACA: About 175 miles (280 km) north of Jujuy, La Quiaca is the border town next to Bolivia; a concrete bridge connects it with Villazon, where you can visit for the day and glimpse the Bolivian Indians with their stiff bowler hats.

If you're entering Bolivia, remember to set your watch back 1 hour (Bolivia is in a different time zone) and bring an overcoat, since the high altitude makes the area cool year-round. Rail connections are available from La Quiaca to La Paz, and Argentine pesos and US dollars are both accepted across the border.

BEST EN ROUTE

As far as accommodations go, hotels in northwestern Argentina are small but comfortable; they either supply private baths or they don't for any price. Per person rates are: expensive ($25–$40), moderate ($10–$20), and inexpensive ($10 and under). Camping is available in specified areas.

TUCUMÁN

Gran Hotel Premier – 110-room hotel has private baths, air conditioning. Inexpensive.

VILLA NOGUES

Hostería – With a nine-hole golf course. Inexpensive.

SAN PEDRO DE COLALAO

Hostería – 24 rooms, a dining room, and a swimming pool are provided. Moderate.

CAFAYATE

Cayafate – Small hotel provides clean accommodations. Inexpensive.

SALTA

Salta – Facing the main square, it's a first-class hotel with colonial charm, a pool, and 89 rooms. Calle Buenos Aires 1 (phone: 21-10-11). Expensive.

Huacio – With 75 rooms, this hotel provides good accommodations. Av. Bolivia and Av. Patron Costa (phone: 1-0211). Expensive.

Victoria Plaza – A pleasant, first-class hotel. Zuviria 16 (phone: 1-1222). Expensive to moderate.

JUJUY

Internacional Jujuy – 110-room hotel has air conditioning, private baths. Moderate.

Alto la Vina – A 70-room hotel with private baths and a swimming pool. Moderate.

Provincial de Turismo – In a woodsy setting, with a restaurant. North of town. Moderate.

Bolivia

There is an ever-shrinking club of countries that still qualify as lands for the adventurous traveler. Bolivia remains a charter member and treats visitors to an authentic South American experience of Indian cultures and dramatic, superlative landscapes.

There is no danger of falling into a tourist trap when traveling anywhere in Bolivia. It is not the place to find gaming tables, beaches bathed in eternal sunshine, or historic sites packed with tour groups. What Bolivia is, banal as it sounds, is a country of astounding contrasts. You can get lost in the crowds of the downtown markets of La Paz, or you can stand remote from all earthly things in the stillness of the pre-Columbian monoliths of Tiahuanaco, just 45 miles away. The climate ranges from extreme aridity of the plains of the Chaco in the southeast to the dense humidity of the rain forests of the eastern foothills.

Bolivia is the breathtaking beauty of Lake Titicaca in the north and the brackish lakes and salt beds of Salar de Uyuni in the south. And, while the country has a navigable river system, it is one of the two South American landlocked nations (Paraguay is the other). It borders Brazil on the north and east, Paraguay and Argentina on the south, and Chile and Perú on the west.

Bolivia is a 424,164-square-mile land about the size of Texas and California combined, or twice the size of France, with a population of 5,790,000. While it's the fifth largest South American country, it is one of the continent's most sparsely populated.

The dominant feature is mountains, stretching for just under 400 miles from east to west down the Bolivia/Chile border. Divided into two ranges, the Eastern and Western Cordillera, the Bolivian Andes take in some lofty heights. Among them are Sajama (21,391 feet), Illimani (21,201 feet), and Illampu (20,958 feet).

Between the two ranges lies the heartland of the nation, the 500-mile rust-colored altiplano, a remote, almost unreal plain battered by brutal winds that have swept the land almost bare. But all is not bleak. When the sun hits the altiplano as you travel between Cuzco in Perú and Lake Titicaca, the land, bordering mountains, and spurs are streaked by such a brilliant orange hue that you wonder why you'd ever thought the altiplano was so ugly.

Moving across the altiplano to the Eastern Cordillera, the picture is slightly different. To the northeast, the massive peaks of this range fall away sharply, down toward the Amazon basin's heavily forested slopes, which are indented with fertile valleys known as the Nor Yungas and Sud Yungas (North and South Yungas). In these lush, semitropical valleys drained by the Beni River system, cocoa, sugar, coffee, tropical fruits, and coca — from which cocaine is derived — are grown.

In the river valleys farther south lie the cities of Santa Cruz and Cochabamba, the second and third most important communities in the nation, as well as the large town of Tarija, one of the oldest settlements in Bolivia.

When the Quechua-speaking Incas conquered the Aymará-speaking Indians around Lake Titicaca in the thirteenth century, they found them living among sites of ancient ruins. As archaeologists and historians have pieced the story together, it appears that there was a rich civilization in this area some 600 years or more before the arrival of the Inca, who seem to have appeared during a second phase of Aymará civilization. During this period, they produced extraordinary pottery, textiles, and metalwork as well as massive stone buildings and monolithic monuments.

The Aymará in Bolivia resisted the Inca so fiercely that it took nearly 100 years to subdue them — until the reign of Tupac Yupanqui (1471–93). Even then, the conquest was not total. The Aymarás were allowed to keep their own language and most of their social structures and were permitted to fight for the Inca under their own officers. Only the Inca religious practices were imposed upon them — perhaps more easily than imagined since worship of the sun and natural forces was common to all pre-Columbian cultures. Today Bolivia's population is about 75% Indian, proportionally the largest in South America.

Before visiting Bolivia, keep a couple of things in mind. This is a rugged land — difficult to know well, yet fascinating to see. The altiplano and La Paz altitudes of 12,000 to 13,000 feet (and up) may produce *soroche* (altitude sickness), characterized by dizziness, shortness of breath, or even a first-day headache. Veteran travelers suggest the following: Upon arrival, take time to catch your breath; don't start running around the city. Walk slowly, eat lightly the first day, and go very easy on alcoholic beverages. Carry headache and nausea pills with you and make certain, in advance, that your hotel is equipped with oxygen (most are). Physical orientation takes about 24 hours.

Transportation in Bolivia is limited. Some areas can only be reached by railroad, and the trains are generally old, dirty, and uncomfortable — but "picturesque" and generally the best way to travel overland. All of the major cities and towns are linked by rail, and many by the air services of Lloyd Aereo Boliviano (LAB). Most areas of greatest interest to visitors are accessible by road; the condition of the road, however, is another matter. Only one-sixth of all Bolivia's roads are paved or surfaced with gravel — very rough gravel — and even the popular route from La Paz to Tiahuanaco is a bumpy ride.

The Highlands

The altiplano is, as we have said, an area of paradoxes: agriculturally limited but rich in mineral deposits; plagued with a harsh, cold climate but blessed with bracingly fresh air. The following route winds through the altiplano, west from La Paz to Lake Titicaca, the world-famous site of Tiahuanaco; then south to Oruro; Potosí, once the world's silver capital; Sucre, Bolivia's official capital; and finally Tarija, an isolated farming community in a fertile river valley cut off from the rest of the country by forbidding mountain ranges.

LA PAZ: La Paz is Bolivia's movable capital. Originally it occupied the airport's present location, near Laja, 22 miles up and away. When the conquistadores arrived in 1548, they found the fierce winds of the altiplano too much and moved the settlement down to its present setting in a deep, natural basin. Actually, La Paz is the country's unofficial capital, its center of government and commerce. And in its "capital" role it is the world's highest, at 12,500 feet above sea level.

The city spreads across 10 square miles and has a population of 1 million. Most routes in this section use La Paz as a starting point. For a detailed report on the city, its hotels and restaurants, see *La Paz,* THE CITIES.

TIAHUANACO: Reached by a bone-shattering, 48-mile (72-km) stretch of road — some of it paved, some gullied — Tiahuanaco is Bolivia's crowning glory from the standpoint of pre-Columbian history. It was the center of the Aymará-speaking civilization that is said to date from before AD 600. Archaeological studies indicate that this culture devised a calendar, hieroglyphics, and a method of processing minerals.

There is an incredible loneliness to this site, on the southern end of Lake Titicaca. With its rolling plateau and yellow grass whispering in the wind, you feel you are altogether deserted, alone with the gods of the high Andes. There's a stillness over the air, as if something is there, hanging, waiting to be resolved. Across the street from the ruins is a café that serves coffee, cheese and tomato sandwiches, and other snacks.

Limited excavation (international archaeologists are somewhat miffed that the Bolivian government has reserved all excavation privileges for itself; one contends that the government is making Tiahuanaco its "personal playground") has turned up drainage canals and rectangular stone walls that some experts believe are probably the ruins of dwellings, perhaps of a large city that at one time surrounded the temples.

The best-known symbol of this civilization is the Gate of the Sun, a 10-ton slab of andesite depicting a god figure in the center, 48 attendants approaching him from each side, with a low doorway carved in the center. This is one of the largest single carved blocks (7 feet high, 11 feet wide) in existence. The large relief figure is said to represent the creator-god Viracocha. The Collas (descendants of the Tiahuanaco culture) say that the stone works were built by a race of giants who incurred Viracocha's wrath and were destroyed by him. The god is depicted with cheeks streaked by bands containing tiny circles that look like tears. Heads hang from his belt. In each hand he carries a staff, each ending in a condor's head.

It baffles many that the gate leads to nothing — it just stands there in the midst of the altiplano. One thought is that the gate once led to a palatial structure designed for meetings; another is that it was the entrance to a temple. Some believe it is a religious monument, with figures representing a pre-Inca calendar.

The main ruin is the Kalasasaya ("standing stones") compound, a rectangular earth mound. Its plaza alone runs 442 by 426 feet, squared off at the edges by perpendicular stones about 20 feet high. Other ruins are the two-tiered Akapana pyramid, the top of which has been hollowed out, allegedly by the Spanish conqueror-bandit Pedro de Vargas, who thought it was filled with gold; a subterranean temple in a vast sunken courtyard with scores of prehistoric faces laid in its stone walls; and the Ponce monolith, named for the government archaeologist who found it, a finely carved statue erected on a mound facing the Gate of the Sun. The evidence of the temples and symbolic artifacts unearthed by scientists lead to the conclusion that Tiahuanaco was a great religious center.

A few miles southwest are the ruins of Puma Punku. Its two pyramids are said to be part of a lost city; its massive 100-ton blocks of stone were probably part of a temple.

A taxi to Tiahuanaco from La Paz runs about $45, and entrance costs about 2

Bolivianas. Tours by car are $20 per person and can be arranged through your hotel. The ruins, here and at Puma Punku, close at 5 PM.

LAKE TITICACA: The Incas called Cuzco the navel of the world and Lake Titicaca "the womb of mankind," and lakeside dwellers today regard themselves as the "oldest people in the world." The lake is 110 miles long and 40 miles wide, part of it in Perú. Like many things in Bolivia, it takes another "highest" championship — it is the world's highest navigable lake (12,500 feet). From every part of the shoreline — indented with bays and inlets and covered with farms from waterside to terraced hills — you will see snowcapped Andes in the distance.

The best way to enjoy the Titicaca region is to drive — all the way from La Paz to the first lake port of Huatajata (about 1½ hours). After lunch at the lakeside café, continue to Copacabana via the Strait of Tiquina, which is a ferry boat point for people and produce — a most colorfully chaotic scene. You can stay overnight at Copa, return the same day to La Paz, or, best of all, continue along the western shore to Puno. There are some lovely colonial towns en route as well as Peruvian customs. You can also cross from Huatajata to Copacabana to Juli by hydrofoil — a trip that usually includes a visit to the Island of the Sun — or you can go all the way across the lake by overnight steamer once a week. Arrangements for all lake tours should be made in advance in La Paz.

The best known of Titicaca's islands are those of the Sun and the Moon. The former, dotted with ruins, is the shrine of the early Indians, who believed that when their first emperor, Manco Capac, rose from the island's waters, where he planted his staff would be the center of the empire. According to the Inca, he chose Cuzco. The ruins of the Palace of the Vestal Virgins and of a temple dedicated to the Moon Mother are on Moon Island. The Indians report that you can see a submerged city 100 feet below the surface.

The lake's northern shore holds mysterious, tall (30 feet), round burial towers called *chullpas,* built by the Colla culture. Other pre-Columbian descendants, the Urus, said to be the first Indians to immigrate to South America, live by this part of the lake in rush huts that drift about in the water or are anchored by long taproots. The Urus fish from reed boats or rafts made of rushes and hunt birds with *bolos.* Once they have captured the bird, they kill it, drying the meat to trade with farmers for potatoes, corn, and millet.

Over the centuries, the lake has receded; there is a theory that at one time it flowed up to an ancient city. (By the way, cramming in a visit from La Paz to Tiahuanaco and Lake Titicaca in one day does justice to neither.) While at the lake, you can go to Suriqui, whose islanders built Thor Heyerdahl's raft *Ra II* for his Atlantic crossing, as well as a similar boat for his trip from Iraq to the Red Sea. Natives sell replicas of these craft, which Heyerdahl used to document his theories of ancient world migrations. Boat service to Suriqui Island is available from the new restaurant, *Hostal Balsa,* in Puerto Pérez, about 40 miles (62 km) from La Paz.

COPACABANA: To spend the night in Copacabana, a central Titicaca lakeside resort, there are dozens of little hotels, most of them somewhat spartan. A 3-hour drive from La Paz, you can get here by car, bus, or boat. The people are very friendly and are sure to escort you to a hotel "with running water" the moment you alight from the bus (about $6 to $10 from La Paz, but *colectivo* travel costs only a bit more and is more reliable). The running water may turn out to be in a courtyard of the pension and run only at certain times of the day, but in this crazy little town, it won't matter; you'll be having too much fun to get upset.

There is a tone of gaiety here, and you feel as though you're at a carnival when you encounter these incredibly cheerful people, who actually do have many fiestas. The largest one celebrates the Dark Virgin of the Lake. On August 5, a 3-day festival is held in her honor. Indians travel by foot from all around the Titicaca basin and from as far away as Cuzco to pay homage to her image. The statue is draped in embroidered robes, inlaid with precious stones, and wears a gold crown.

Adding to Copacabana's charm is the brass band that plays every day in the plaza.

YUNGAS VALLEY: Turning northeast from the capital, the road winds down to the warm Yungas Valley provinces 60 miles (97 km) from La Paz, about a 4-hour drive. Natives use this road to bring their crops to the capital, and it's a spectacular trip, traveling over snowcapped Andean peaks before a steep descent of more than 10,000 feet over 50 miles (80 km) to Coroico, the capital of the Nor Yungas region. This is a heavy agricultural area, producing coffee and fruit at 4,500 feet. An hour's drive farther, 80 miles (129 km) from La Paz, is the jungle village of Chulumani, the capital of Sud Yungas and the center of an area rich in citrus fruit and coffee. Between the two capitals is Coripata, the coca-growing center of northern Bolivia.

Returning south to La Paz, you pick up another road at El Alto, on the rim of the crater in which the capital lies. This road takes you to Oruro.

ORURO: Some 100 miles (160 km) south of La Paz, Oruro is set on the slopes of a hill 12,000 feet above sea level. It is the site of Bolivia's first tin smelter, and its population of 110,000 Indians work the area's tin, silver, and tungsten mines. Simón Bolívar's tutor, Simón Rodríguez, founded a boys' school here, and the town also has a university known for its engineering and mining schools.

Oruro's Carnival is the most famous in Bolivia. On the Saturday before Ash Wednesday, all work stops for La Diablada, the parade of the devil dancers who, dressed in wild costumes and grotesque masks, depict the story of the battle between good and evil. La Diablada begins with a salute to the Virgin, continues with the rebellion of the devils, and ends with the victory of Archangel Michael over the devils. Dancers practice the choreography for months before the festival.

This spectacle, which dates from colonial times, is full of the naturalistic elements of a pagan past. Several Diabladas are performed in Oruro during Carnival, starting on the Saturday before Ash Wednesday. Indeed, during the 8 days of Carnival, there are extraordinary displays of dancing night and day.

Seats can be booked for these spectacles at the Oruro town hall, but hotel reservations should be made months in advance.

En Route from Oruro – Two roads lead into southern Bolivia and its three main communities — Potosí, Sucre, and Tarija. The most commonly used road spins off the main paved highway (part of the Pan-American route) east of Oruro, turns south, and divides: One fork leads south to Potosí; the other southeast to Sucre. The second road picks up farther down the main highway, toward Cochabamba, at Epizana, about 85 miles (137 km) from La Paz. The 140-mile (225-km) route to Sucre, like the Oruro road, is stony, dusty, and a tight squeeze in many places. Both are scenic, however, and each will take you about 7 or 8 days. On this roller-coaster journey, the views are spectacular.

POTOSÍ: This is Bolivia's silver city. Founded in 1545 by the Spanish after they had discovered traces of old Indian workings at Cerro Rico (Rich Hill), it was once one of the largest cities on the continent. Even before the Spanish found the silver, the Inca had begun mining. Legend has it that work was called off when the mountain shuddered and a deep voice called, "The Lord guards the treasures for one who will come later." From then on, the mountain was called Potosí, meaning "noise."

When New York City had a population of 150,000, Potosí's numbered 200,000. At an altitude of more than 13,000 feet (higher than La Paz), the climate is often frigid, with nightly temperatures sometimes falling below 0°F during July and August.

Potosí was regarded as Spain's most valuable city in South America in the 17th century, when immense amounts of silver were torn from Cerro Rico, a mountain of 70% silver. For several hundred years silver was shipped to the port of Antofagasta (now in Chile) and on to Spain. Pirates preyed on the ships, waiting for the silver cargo to come around the Horn.

By the 19th century, the lodes began to give out and Potosí's importance decreased, and for two centuries it ranked as no more than a second-rate provincial town. Then, in 1905, Simón Patiño, a mestizo working for a German trading firm, discovered a metal ignored by the Spanish — tin. The rich tin deposits, as well as sizable amounts of copper, lead, and still minable quantities of silver, revived Potosí. Today it is a relatively prosperous community. Tours to a tin mine, usually lasting 3 hours, can be arranged locally.

In its heyday, churches, convents, and palaces were erected that made Potosí one of the most beautiful cities on the continent. Most of it has been preserved, including the Casa de la Moneda (the Royal Mint), first built in 1752 and renovated in 1959; it is now a museum. Open to the public Mondays through Saturdays, 9 AM to noon and 2 to 5 PM, it can only be toured with a guide. The first-floor salon, which is the main art gallery, is so rich and impressive that it overwhelms the paintings it contains. On exhibit are the huge wooden presses that produced the strips of silver from which colonial coins were made; the coin dies themselves; and smelting houses with carved altarpieces from a number of Potosí's churches that fell into ruin. On Calle Chicas at the corner of Ayacucho is the Convent of Santa Teresa (open to the public daily, 1 to 5 PM) and the cathedral. Elsewhere in the city you will also find other fine Baroque churches typical of the Andean or mestizo architecture of the 18th century.

Shopping at the town market and at the merchants' stalls along Calle Bustos is rewarding, particularly for those interested in silverwork — including coins and jewelry — and woven native textiles.

En Route from Potosí – The 4½-hour trip of a little less than 100 miles (175 km) to Sucre is best by train, both for comfort and for the spectacular scenery. By car over a poor road, the trip takes about 4 hours.

SUCRE: Still Bolivia's legal capital, Sucre stands at an altitude of about 9,000 feet. Its climate is mild, averaging 55°F.

In 1825, Bolivia's Declaration of Independence was signed at Sucre, known as the White City because most of its buildings, including private homes, by law must be whitewashed. Its university dates from the 17th century, yet even during the 16th century the town was the cultural center of South America and Spanish families sent their children here to school.

The earliest Spanish settlers were titled families (the titles in those days were purchased from the Vatican), and each represented an order of the Church. Generally, each titled family would build a church dedicated to the saint or order it represented. In one such church is the 17th-century Chapel of the Virgin of Guadaloupe. The statue of the Virgin is staggering — swathed in diamonds, pearls, and rubies. The cost of the statue alone would support the entire economy of Sucre for 3 years. To tour the church, make an appointment with the Padre Tesorero. Visiting hours are daily from 10 AM to noon and from 3 to 5 PM.

Sucre retains an atmosphere of antiquity — a certain quiet, dignified, colonial charm. Its public buildings are impressive. What's more, the recent infusion of money into the community, as a result of the completion of a gas pipeline from the fields at Monteagudo to the southeast, has enabled these buildings to be maintained.

Foremost among the architectural sites is the House of Liberty, or Legislative Palace, where the country's Independence Act was signed — the document itself is in the collection of the Casa de Independencia (Independence House), a museum on the main square.

The Church of San Miguel (St. Michael) is the oldest church in use today in South America. Closed for more than a century, San Miguel is currently being restored to its original state, with carved and painted wooden ceilings, intricate Moorish designs, glistening white walls, and a fine gold and silver altar.

The wealth of Sucre is not kept hidden. During the pre-Lent holidays, church ornaments and tons of silver from the wealthy families of the town are carried by burro in the Parade of Silver to the cathedral to be blessed for the coming year. Another early church worth seeing (like San Miguel, it has carved wooden Moorish ceilings) is San Francisco. To tour these sights, you should arrive early, since most churches in Sucre are closed by 10 AM except on Sundays or holy days.

Other buildings of interest are the Teatro Gran Mariscal Sucre, Junín College, and the more modern Government Palace and Santo Domingo Palace, also known as the Palace of Justice, where Bolivia's federal judiciary, including the Supreme Court, has its seat.

There are a number of museums here: Charcas Museum (Calle Bolívar 401), with fine anthropological and colonial exhibits; the modern art galleries of Sucre University; the Museo de Santa Clara (Calle Oalvo 204); and the Museo de la Recoleta (Calle Pedro de Anzures). On the road to Potosí stands the Glorieta Mansion, a huge pink structure dating from early republican times, which houses a museum as well as a military school. And there are beautiful cloisters and gardens and exquisitely carved wooden choir stalls at the Recoleta Monastery, set on a hill above the town. You'll get some breathtaking views of Sucre and the surrounding countryside from Cerro Churuquilla, which is covered with willowy eucalyptus trees. At its summit stands a statue of Christ, reached by a road bordered by the Stations of the Cross.

Sucre's population of some 90,000 is mostly employed in oil refining and cement manufacturing. A number of shops opposite the Church of San Francisco have interesting handicrafts. On Calle Arenales, at the University Women's Hostel, you can buy alpaca clothing woven at nearby Yotala. Be on the lookout for antique woven items.

En Route from Sucre – It takes 3 hours by taxi to drive to Tarabuco, which has one of the most colorful Sunday Indian markets in South America. Here, in addition to being able to buy ponchos and other typically native garments, you'll see Indian men strolling about playing the *charango,* a stringed instrument that has an armadillo shell for a soundbox. The woven skirts and belts of the women, duplicates of which can be purchased, are among the most unusual in Bolivia. Try to arrive by 9 AM for the opening of the market. Special festival days are March 12 and the first Sunday in October.

TARIJA: This is the last relatively accessible major community of tourist interest in the Sucre-Potosí area (the departure point is Potosí). The 230-mile (370-km) trip south over a bad, all-weather road takes about 10 hours, depending on weather conditions. You can also fly here from La Paz, Cochabamba, Santa Cruz, or Sucre.

Founded in 1574, Tarija (pop. 50,000) is one of the oldest communities in Bolivia, yet the people of Tarija were not officially absorbed into the country until Bolivian Independence in 1825. The people of Tarija declared independence from Spain in 1807 and founded their own little republic. This led to a fierce struggle with colonial powers and ultimately, after the Spanish were defeated, to Tarija's absorption into the new nation. Today, the citizens of this pleasant town are extremely religious and look more like southern Europeans or Levantines than the usual Indian or mestizo Bolivians.

Tarija has a mild climate. At an altitude of about 6,000 feet in the heart of a fertile valley of orchards and vineyards watered by the Río Guadalquivir, the town is the center of a productive agricultural area.

Fall holidays are Tarija's big moment. The most colorful one is the September celebration of San Roque. Bolivia has a patron saint for everything, and San Roque is the protector of dogs. On the first three Sundays of the month, a series of processions carry the saint's statue, clad in ornate vestments, through the streets of the town, led by residents dressed in costumes with cloth turbans and veils; the mutts wear colored ribbons. In another, known as the *niño* (child) processions, women of the town toss flowers from their balconies to carpet the streets. A month later, the feast of the Virgin of Rosario is celebrated with a flower festival on the second Sunday in October.

Tarija is a jumping-off point for road trips to Argentina, which is some 150 miles (242 km) away.

BEST EN ROUTE

Except for those in La Paz, there are few first-rate hotels along this route. In some areas you're in a deluxe accommodation (by Bolivian standards) if running water is available. On occasion you'll come across a property with a pool, tennis courts, and a restaurant, but that's more the exception than the rule. Expect to pay between $15 and $30 for those listed as moderate; and under $15 in those listed as inexpensive.

COPACABANA

Playa Azul – A rustic property, it requires full board. There is no hot water, but you can hear the sounds made by Lake Titicaca's giant frogs. Inexpensive.
La Portenita – Off the main plaza, there is hot water here. Inexpensive.
Ambassador – Full board is also required here, and the hotel has lovely gardens, a pool, and tennis courts. Inexpensive.

COROICO

Prefectural – This pleasant little hotel runs a bus back and forth to La Paz. The food here is good. Inexpensive.

CHULUMANI

San Antonio – By Bolivian standards, this motel is a resort, with new four-room cabins looking out on snowcapped peaks and a swimming pool. Moderate.
San Bartolome – This comfortable, small resort motel is a favorite getaway for La Paz residents and for foreigners. Moderate.

ORURO

Repostero – Probably the best hotel in Oruro; its owners are Germans who offer good service and good food. Singles are available, with or without bath. Inexpensive.
Terminal – A new hotel, by the bus station, this offers private baths and reasonable comfort. Moderate.

POTOSÍ

Turista – Recently renovated, the *Turista* now supplies customers with heat and hot water. The staff will serve you breakfast in bed before you take a hot shower. Moderate.
Hostal Colonial – Built in an old colonial house, this is now considered the best place to stay in town. Rooms have heat, carpeting, and a private bath. Moderate.
Residential America – This place isn't a bad buy, since the cost of a room includes breakfast and all rooms have a private bath. Moderate.

SUCRE

Tajibos Inn – Formerly the Municipal Hotel, this three-star property is now under the management of the *Tajibos Hotel* of Santa Cruz. All rooms have a private bath, and the restaurant and bar are Sucre's best. Moderate.
Londres – A pleasant, clean little hotel near the train station; the price of a room includes breakfast. There's a restaurant on the premises. Moderate.
Hostal Libertad – A comfortable 3-star hotel one block from the principal plaza. Moderate.
Hostal Colonial – In a colonial mansion in the historic government square, this hotel has heat, carpeting, and a private bath in each of its rooms. Breakfast only. Moderate.

Hostal Cruz de Popayan – A charming small hotel with a colonial atmosphere. Rooms have a private bath. Moderate.

Residencial Bolivia – While nothing fancy, at least you can get a hot bath here. Inexpensive.

TARIJA

Victoria – On the main square; this is an old hotel, but comfortable. Moderate.

Asturias – This one has cleanliness going for it in a tastefully furnished setting. Inexpensive.

Residencia Bolívar – A homey, comfortable place; you can get a hot bath here. Inexpensive.

Prefectural – Just outside the city center, it is the newest and largest hotel in Tarifa. All rooms have a private bath, and there is a pool and restaurant. Inexpensive.

Cochabamba and Santa Cruz

The highland landscapes, with their colonial centers and folkloric traditions, may be the Bolivia of picture books, but the lowlands also have great charm and interest. The centers of Cochabamba and Santa Cruz shouldn't be missed, whether you visit by air or road from the easiest departure point, La Paz.

COCHABAMBA: This is the home of the tin king, Simón Patiño, one of the few Bolivian Indians with the cunning to cash in on the area's native resources. But he did it by exploiting his own people and virtually enslaving them in the mines, a tale outlined in Augusto Céspedes's novel *El Metal del Diablo.* The Patiño Foundation is housed in Patiño's former palace, Los Portales, now the sight of cultural events and activities. The palace is open to the public for tours.

Cochabamba is one of Bolivia's garden spots. Vegetation is lush, the climate mild. The best view of the entire area is from the top of San Sebastian Hill on the edge of the city, where a monument commemorates the Bolivian women who fought and died during the War of Independence in the 19th century.

There's great shopping at the Municipal Market and at the retail market at La Cancha, open Wednesdays and Saturdays. The best buys are woolen blankets, ponchos, and carved and painted wood figures of llamas and other animals. Thermal baths are 50 minutes from the city at Liriuni.

This area is Bolivia's biggest producer of grain and fruit. It's also the site of Inca-Llajta, Inca ruins 30 miles from Cochabamba that are seldom visited by outsiders, probably because there's a 2-hour walk up to the mountain site.

En Route from Cochabamba – The 300-mile (483-km) road to Santa Cruz is fairly well paved and skirts the Inca temple ruins of Incallajata, just off the main road, about 65 miles (100 km) from Cochabamba. Back on the road, you climb to the top of Siberia Pass; you'll think you're in the clouds as you watch their formations skim over the surrounding peaks.

From here the road gradually descends over 200 miles (322 km) down to the largely undeveloped plains around Santa Cruz.

SANTA CRUZ: Twenty years ago Santa Cruz looked like a town on the Texas Panhandle — horses roamed the dusty streets, few people could be seen, and about the only noise was that of the howling wind. Then came the discovery of oil and natural gas that has since turned this remote, sleepy outpost into Bolivia's boom town. Its population has grown to 350,000, and it has one of the best hotels in the country, *Los Tajibos,* where American oil engineers stroll about in baseball caps.

Today there are several oil fields — including those at Colpa and Caranda, within 30 miles (48 km) to the north and northwest of the city — and a large gas field at Río Grande, some 25 miles (40 km) southeast, that are being exploited in the department of Santa Cruz. This has led to the construction of a government-run oil refinery in Santa Cruz, accompanied by the extensive development of transportation and communications systems and the improvement of all of the city's facilities.

In addition to access by paved road via Cochabamba, there is domestic and international air service, a railway, and an all-weather road (not recommended) running almost 400 miles (644 km) east to Corumbá on the Río Paraguay. Another rail line extends more than 300 miles (483 km) south to Yacuiba on the Argentine border.

All of these factors have increased integration and altered the population mix of Santa Cruz. At one time, the rural people living here were descendants of the area's first Spanish settlers and are still known as *cambas,* people who live in the tropical lowlands. When the government initiated settlement programs in the sixties, things began to change as land was made available on a first come, first serve basis. Other projects offered houses, schools, potable water, medical care, farming aid, and even long-term loans. The Indians of the altiplano were urged to overcome their fear of the heat and mosquitoes of the lowlands in exchange for a prosperous way of life.

By the seventies, the character of Santa Cruz had undergone a radical transformation. Where once highlanders settled in only for the 3- or 4-month sugarcane harvest, they now came with their entire family. Indians from the highlands were joined in settling Santa Cruz by Mennonites from other parts of South America. Northwest of Santa Cruz, near Montero, there's an Okinawan colony of Japanese. Near Abapó Izozon, 150 German families have immigrated and established a colony that's roughly the size of Holland.

Many of these settlers have entered agricultural enterprises, raising cotton, sugar, rice, and coffee. Cattle ranching and timber processing have also become important. Other mineral deposits, iron ore and magnesium, were found near the Bolivia-Brazil border, bringing even more industry into the region. Along with new discoveries came more settlers, including more highland Indians, who now seem to find Santa Cruz less threatening.

Visitors will find that amusements in Santa Cruz swing to a 20th-century beat. There is swimming and golf at hotels or at the Club Los Palmas, tennis at the tennis club, and horseback riding at the Club Hipico outside town. When the sun goes down, the lights go up nightly at the *Number One, Mermelada,* and *Carly* discotheques.

Shopping is also worthwhile. Although somewhat dirty, Los Pozos market deserves a visit, particularly in the summer, when tropical fruits are on sale, including papaya and pineapple and some local oddities such as *ambaiba,* which looks like a glove (the meat is sucked out of the "fingers"), and *guayperú,* which is like a cherry. More durable buys are leather goods, baskets, hammocks, contraband Brazilian goods, and carvings and furniture made from guayacan and *jacarandá* (rosewood).

BEST EN ROUTE

Since Cochabamba and Santa Cruz are both fairly modern cities, you should have no trouble finding accommodations. Expect to pay $40 or more for a double in the hotels we've listed as expensive; between $15 and $30 for those listed as moderate; and under $15 for those listed as inexpensive.

COCHABAMBA

Gran Hotel Cochabamba – On the outskirts of town amid lush gardens, each of its 50 rooms has a private bath. Suites are available. Facilities include tennis courts, swimming pool, bar, grill, and banquet room. Expensive.

Capitol – Downtown, this 32-room hotel has private baths and room telephones. Suites are available, and there's a restaurant and a bar. Unfortunately, recent reports say the hotel is slipping. Moderate.

Emperador – Small hotel, with 30 comfortable rooms, each with bath; restaurant and bar. Moderate.

Gran Hotel Ambassador – Offers all the comforts of home in a garden setting, plus a central location. Its 70 rooms have private baths, hot water, and telephones; there are tennis courts and a swimming pool on the property. Moderate.

SANTA CRUZ

Los Tajibos – On the outskirts of town, this is a luxurious hotel by local standards, with air-conditioning, a pool, restaurant, bar, sauna, whirlpool, raquetball courts, and meeting rooms. The carpeted rooms have a private bath and telephone. Expensive.

Gran Hotel Santa Cruz – Decorated in "just plain folks" style, this downtown hotel is clean and modern. Each of its 60 rooms has a telephone and some are air-conditioned. Dining rooms are both inside and outside; you can lunch by the pool at the latter. There's a bar and snack service. Moderate.

Cortez – Just on the edge of town, this quiet, unpretentious inn is proud of the food it serves. Even locals come here to eat. There's a swimming pool. Moderate.

Austurias – A solid, clean motel with a pool. Moderate.

Premier – A small, new hotel, kept in first-rate shape. Inexpensive.

Brazil

Covering more than half the continent, Brazil is not only the largest country in South America, but in terms of its people, customs, and physical terrain, it is one of the most diverse countries in the world. Within its boundaries are Indians who have never seen twentieth-century Western men and women; cosmopolitan cities larger than the biggest urban centers in the US; jungles in which the vegetation is so thick that sunlight never reaches the ground; settlements where poverty and starvation exist beside startling examples of ostentatious wealth; and religions that incorporate elements of Catholicism as well as African animism. The country is bordered by the Atlantic on the north and east; Uruguay to the south; Paraguay, Argentina, and Bolivia to the southwest; Perú and Colombia to the west; and Venezuela, Guyana, Surinam, and French Guiana to the north.

Nearly equal in size to the continental US, the bulk of Brazil lies in the tropics, with the equator crossing the country in the north and the Tropic of Capricorn in the southeast. The Amazon Basin contains the world's largest rain forest. It has an equatorial climate, with constant rain and wilting heat. Temperatures climb into the 90s and 100s F. The splendid 4,603-mile Atlantic coast notched with azure bays has some of the most delectable beaches on the continent. Although the seaboard accounts for less than 10% of Brazil's terrain, more than one-third of the population lives here. The cities of Rio de Janeiro, Salvador (Bahía), Santos (the port for São Paulo), Recife, Fortaleza, and Porto Alegre have grown up around natural harbors.

One cannot generalize about a country so large; each region has its own character. Although Brazilians are a complex variety of ethnic types, there is little racial tension because of a tradition of intermarriage started by the Portuguese. Brazil enjoys a homogeneous society, with distinctions based not on race but rather on pride in home states. They like to describe themselves as *paulistas* (from São Paulo); *cariocas* (from Rio); *mineiros* (from Minas Gerais); and *nordestinos* (from the northeast). They are predominately young, with half the population of 131 million under 25.

The country is divided into five geographical regions: the north, northeast, west central, southeast, and south.

In the north, travel through the dense Amazon rain forest is restricted to boats. While a few travel agencies have comfortable excursion boats for tourists, most Amazon travel is by twice-monthly government or private vessel. In this remote region you will find 2,000 species of fish, colorful parrots, and exotic animals such as capybara, crocodile, tapir, and anaconda. The majority of the country's remaining Indian population (120,000) lives in reservations in this area, but generally you cannot visit them for health reasons, as they are terribly susceptible to communicable diseases.

The northeast, with 30% of the national population, is the poorest section of the country. Many of the poor from here migrate to the south. The oldest cities, such as Salvador (Bahía) (pop. 1,500,000), Recife, Natal, and São Luis, contain stunning examples of colonial architecture. Here you will find the origins of Brazil's folklore and customs, such as the spiritualistic religion *macumba,* which is practiced throughout the country by all classes of people. The black population in the northeast has not only retained many African traditions but has also been a profound influence on the rest of the country in terms of art, music, philosophy, and religion. The area has a distinctive cuisine, many deserted beaches, and few foreign tourists.

The west-central (Mato Grosso) region is still a frontier, with savannah grasslands crossed by meandering rivers. There is some cattle farming here, but it is quite rugged. Occasional battles take place between settlers and Indians, and you can still take organized hunting expeditions into the rain forest. The city of Brasília (pop. 500,000), constructed on the edge of the Mato Grosso, became the nation's capital in 1960. (Previously, Rio de Janeiro was the capital.) Also in this region are the mining city of Belo Horizonte and the historic town of Ouro Preto, a national monument.

The heart of industrial, commercial, contemporary Brazil is the southeast, with Brazil's two largest cities, Rio de Janeiro (pop. 5,000,000) and São Paulo (pop. 8,500,000). The most visited destination in South America, Rio is famous for its eight beaches (among them Ipanema and Copacabana), glittering Carnival celebrations, and the statue of Christ the Redeemer on Corcovado Mountain. São Paulo, the largest city in South America, is also one of the world's fastest-growing cities.

In the south are many European settlers. It is an agricultural region of cattle pastures, coffee plantations, and vineyards. You will find picturesque communities such as Curitiba, built for the pedestrian, and Porto Alegre, a modern industrial city that has a slower pace than São Paulo.

When Portuguese explorer Pedro Álvares Cabral first landed in the state of Bahía in 1500, he thought he had found a large tropical island. Portuguese colonists followed over the next hundred years, bringing slaves imported from Africa. They created large sugar and lumber plantations in the northeast as far south as São Paulo, building the cities of Salvador (Bahía) and Recife as monuments to their wealth. Salvador remained the capital for the next 200 years, until population shifts made Rio de Janeiro the country's economic center. With further economic growth, inland cities grew. One was Manaus, strategically placed in the rubber-producing Amazon River basin; Ouro Preto, once a center of gold and diamond mining, and Goiás, another gold-mining area, were two others. The spread of coffee growing and, later, cattle grazing was responsible for the expansion of the region south of São Paulo, now one of the most densely populated areas in the country.

Brazil remained a colony until 1822, when Pedro I, the son of the Portuguese monarch, declared himself the emperor of an independent nation. Due to the abolition of slavery in 1888 and a subsequent financial crisis, the monarchy failed, and the following year the Brazilian Federative Republic was created. The country remained a liberal democracy until 1964, when, after a period of social and economic upheaval, the military took over.

Under the military regime, the country experienced rapid economic growth, known as the Brazilian Miracle. Evidence of that prosperity has been especially prominent in major cities in the south, such as São Paulo and Rio. Brazil has the largest iron ore deposits on earth, ranks third in automobile production, and is a primary supplier of coffee, soybeans, cotton, cocoa, and sugar.

However, while the economic boom brought prosperity to some, 85% of the population continues to struggle for bare economic survival. Unemployment is high, and inflation rates that have lately been more than 200% a year push the cost of staples such as rice and beans almost out of reach. As the poor from the northeast flock to the more prosperous south in search of work, huge *favelas* — slums of cardboard shacks — have grown up on the outskirts of metropolitan areas. The dwindling Indian population, officially protected by a government agency that requires them to live on reservations, consistently resists "citizenship" in a country that does not acknowledge their rights. Ultimately, they face the loss of their land and culture, particularly in the Amazon region, where agriculture and cattle raising are taking hold as major industries.

Military rule in Brazil ended in 1985, some two decades after it had begun. In that period, five army generals led the country, and the last, João Baptista Figueiredo, initiated a gradual return to a democratic government. In 1985, a 686-member electoral college made up of the Chamber of Deputies, the Senate, and delegates from each of Brazil's 23 states elected a civilian, Tancredo Neves, as president. However, he never began his term: The night before his swearing-in ceremony in March, Neves was hospitalized with an intestinal disorder and died soon after. José Sarney, his vice presidential running mate, became president, only to be faced with the continuing overriding problem of inflation, which hit 230% in 1985 and threatened to jump to 500%. Early in 1986, Sarney went on the attack, introducing wage and price freezes and a new currency, the *cruzado,* in place of the *cruzeiro.* (At press time, $1 equals 13 cruzados rather than 13,000 cruzeiros.) Since Neves and Sarney were chosen by an electoral college, with pressure for direct elections mounting, it is unclear how long the new president will remain in office (the Brazilian constitution provides for a 6-year term). Much depends on the success of his economic program.

Still, of all the South American countries, Brazil has the most sophisticated infrastructure for tourists. Quality hotels can be found in most cities and resort areas. An efficient internal air network connects all parts of the country. Whenever large distances are involved, flying is definitely recommended. You can take buses, trains, and freighters into the interior. The southeast has decent paved roads, but in other areas overland travel is considerably more rugged, particularly during the rainy months. Gasoline and service stations are few and far between in remote parts of the country. If you plan to drive the Trans-Amazon Highway, remember that it is in no way comparable to a US road. Be sure to carry the necessary spare parts, and be prepared to make repairs yourself. Check that your insurance papers and *carnet* are in order.

The seven routes in this chapter are: the Amazon, which leads from Belém to Leticia, on the Colombia-Brazil border; the Northeast, from Recife to São Luís; from Rio de Janeiro to Belo Horizonte, which takes you through the mining district and Ouro Preto; from Belo Horizonte to Brasília; from Brasília through the Mato Grosso; from São Paulo to Uruguay, passing through Curitiba, Pôrto Alegre, and Rio Grande do Sul; and Iguaçu Falls.

The Amazon: Belém to Manaus

One of the most exotic and still unexplored regions on earth is the Amazon basin, where the world's largest river and its thousands of tributaries dominate an area of more than 2.3 million square miles, roughly two-thirds the size of the continental US. The area's main feature is its equatorial forest, which creates a landscape of vegetation and wildlife without equal; in some places the foliage is so dense that sunlight never reaches the ground.

The intriguing and romantic notion of anacondas, man-eating piranhas, and species of birds found nowhere else lures many visitors to this area. Such wildlife will probably only be seen in the region's zoos, but the 1,200-mile river excursion from Belém to Manaus still gives one a sample of a part of the earth that remains unconquered by man.

The Amazon River was discovered by the Spaniard Francisco de Orellana, one of Pizarro's lieutenants, in 1592. He had heard reports of a great inland sea that existed on the other side of the Andes. Captains sailing off the coast of Brazil noted fresh brown water mixing with the green ocean as far as 200 miles offshore. Orellana was sent into the jungle from Quito in Ecuador to help Pizarro find the lost city of El Dorado, the mythical Indian community so fabulously wealthy that each night its residents bathed their chief in gold dust. Orellana separated from Pizarro to explore the mighty river and search for the famed warrior women, the Amazons, who were reputed to live there. The explorer's river and jungle adventures, including the battles with the Indians and the hardships that forced the men to eat their shoes and saddles to fight off starvation, were reported by Fray Gaspar de Carvajal, a Dominican priest on the expedition. (His account is available in English through AMS Reprints.) Later groups of adventurers and gold seekers have entered the Amazon basin to explore its riches and mystery and have never been seen again.

The Amazon begins as melted snow high in the Peruvian Andes. Before spilling the brownish-yellow silt into the Atlantic, 4,000 miles away, it is fed by over a thousand tributaries, which make it the world's largest river in terms of water volume. At its mouth, near the city of Belém, the river is 200 miles wide. It provides one-fourth of the world's fresh water and 30% of its oxygen.

The existence of saltwater fish that have adapted themselves to fresh water, such as the Amazon dolphin, supports the theory that before the Andes rose in the west, a salty Mediterranean-like Amazon separated the top third of the South American continent from the rest of its landmass. The jungle, stretching for more than 180 miles along the Atlantic and reaching inland nearly 1,200 miles, has the oldest formation of plant life on earth and is virtually unchanged since the Tertiary Era.

The Amazon region is one of nature's last preserves of wildlife, hosting 2,000 species of fish, 14,000 species of mammals, 15,000 species of insects, and 3,500 birds (including 319 types of hummingbirds). The jungle's more renowned inhabitants — the jaguar, margay, capybara, tapir, wild boar, and anteater; exotic birds such as the mountain cock, morphus eagle, and macaw parrot; reptiles including the anaconda, boa constrictor, alligator (called *caiman*), and turtle; and fish such as river dolphin, tambaqui, piranha and electric eel — are usually unseen by the river traveler, but extensive zoos in Manaus and Belém display much of the wildlife in natural environments.

Although the river and jungle represent one-fourth of Brazil's total area, the region holds only 4% of the country's population. On a river excursion, visitors see occasional homes on stilts or families traveling to nearby towns via dugout canoe. It is not uncommon to find farms as large as 1,235,000 acres where cattle and buffalo are raised. Introduced to Brazil in the late nineteenth century, the buffalo has proved particularly adaptable to the Amazon region due to its resistance to disease and fondness for aquatic vegetation. Here and there, signs of modern technology are creeping into this lazy river scene, and visitors may see mining expeditions in search of iron ore, bauxite, manganese, tin, and oil. The reclusive American billionaire Daniel K. Ludwig made news when he floated a completely self-sufficient factory from Asia up the Amazon to a large tract of the jungle he purchased from the government (and has recently sold back).

Visitors may sample areas that are still unchanged since Orellana's time, but now facilities and transportation are more modern and convenient, and resorts in major cities along the Amazon offer sophisticated comforts.

A voyage up the Amazon sounds exciting and adventurous and is really the only way to see this mighty river at first hand. But the 6-day excursion from Belém to Manaus includes parts of the river that are so wide that you may not even see the shore, not to mention the area's famed wildlife. You can shorten the trip to 4 days by embarking in Manaus and sailing downstream to Belém, but the boats stay in the middle of the river in this direction to take advantage of the swift currents.

A recommended way of going is on the government's twice-monthly ENASA line (Av. Presidente Vargas 41, Belém; phone: 223-3011), diesel passenger boats that also carry some cargo. The ENASA boats have first-class accommodations, which include a stateroom, bed, three meals a day, and access to the upper decks of the ship. Classe Popular passengers must bring a hammock for sleeping (available in Belém for $6) and be prepared to sandwich between bodies swinging on all sides. ENASA also has two new catamaran vessels, the *Para* and the *Amazonas*, offering 138 passengers first-class travel between Belém and Manaus. The 6-day cruises operate year-round, roughly once a month in each direction. The cruise from Belém to Manaus (upriver), however, does not include a day's stop at Marajo Island. Boat facilities include air-conditioned cabins with bath, lounge, snack bar, nightclub, bar, solarium, pool, and sun deck. The boats are comfortable, not luxurious, and the cost is roughly $550 per person for a double cabin. Tour operators handling arrangements are LADATCO, 2220 Coral Way, Miami, FL 33145 (phone: in Florida, 800-432-3881; elsewhere, 800-327-6162) and Tara Tours, 6995 NW

36th St., Miami, FL 33166 (phone: in Florida, 305-871-1246; elsewhere, 800-327-0080).

If you don't want to wait for an ENASA boat, there are sometimes small private boats, such as *Fé em Deus IV* (*Faith in God*), that take passengers upriver. They are found by asking around the Belém docks near the Ver-O-Peso market on Travessa de Breves. These smaller boats will take you as far as Santarém, where there are boats just about daily to Manaus. You can also check with the *capitania do porto* (captain of the port), whose office is just off Av. Presidente Vargas near the ENASA office downtown. This office can tell you about larger freighters that sometimes take passengers upstream. You will need written permission from the *capitania* to gain access to the pier if you care to do your own soliciting of freighter captains, but beware — you will sample Brazilian bureaucracy at its worst. If you are berthing in less than first class, traveling on one of the smaller private boats is usually more pleasant, with more diverse food and eased restrictions. First class on these smaller boats entitles you to put your hammock in a cabin, but many prefer the open deck, with its cool evening breezes. Bugs never seem to be a problem, and if a shower comes along, canvas flaps are dropped to close up the sides of the ship. The private boats are usually less crowded, and the mess chefs may even include a few green vegetables in the day's fare. Also, the smaller private boat usually gives you a better opportunity to mix with the local people, who are very friendly if you extend yourself to them.

No matter what class you're in, the day begins at sunrise with *café da manhã* (breakfast). It will be the meals, no matter how uninspired, that define your day, so after breakfast it is best to occupy your time until lunch with books, magazines, chess, a sketchpad, camera, or whatever you fancy. After lunch, most people pass the hottest part of the day in the famous South American institution of a siesta, an afternoon nap, which is an easy habit to acquire when the only sounds are the steady engine, a few birds, and the Amazon swooshing around the boat. After midafternoon coffee, the most pleasant hours of the day are spent watching the water and sky change color. As the sun lowers toward the horizon and the temperature drops, the jungle colors deepen to a dark greenish gray and the sky becomes a pinkish red. With darkness, the air on open decks can be brisk, so it is best to bring a blanket or sleeping bag for sleeping in hammocks. During the evening, many people form groups for games of dominoes, playing music, drinking, or quiet conversation. By 10 PM most passengers have turned in, and if you are not crowded by nearby hammocks, the gentle swaying of the ship and the Amazon's fresh air provide the perfect sleeping tonic.

During the voyage, the boat will occasionally stop to pick up and discharge passengers. While the ship is never in port long enough for you to go ashore, you will get an opportunity to see a family welcome home a son or daughter from the big city or see a schoolteacher reunited with her students.

A word about health: Although malaria is considered a hazard only for those going into the jungle itself, you still should be taking antimalaria pills as a precaution on a river trip. Aralen is one of the brand names (chloroquine-phosphate, 500 mg) for which you need a prescription. Start taking one pill each week for 5 weeks before entering the area, one every day while you are there, and one each week for 6 weeks after you leave. In this region, as in most of Brazil, do not drink unbottled water, and avoid fruits and vegetables that aren't or can't be peeled, such as lettuce, unpeeled tomatoes, and apples, and don't eat uncooked food. The humid tropical climate is a good breeding ground for hepatitis and dysentery; consult your physician before leaving home.

If you think the complete 5-day ride too much, you can shorten your trip by picking up a boat at Santarém, exactly midway between Belém and Manaus. Santarém, Manaus, and Belém are connected by Cruzeiro do Sul and VASP airlines. If your starting point in Brazil is Manaus, you can fly there directly from North America on Varig or from other Latin American cities by Varig, Air France, Avianca, and Cruzeiro.

BELÉM: At the mouth of the mighty Amazon River, this city of 950,000 is the recipient of all the gifts of the jungle and perhaps the best representative of this area. Eighty miles from the open sea, Belém is on the southern side of the river as it surrounds Ilha de Marajó before pouring into the Atlantic. The Portuguese founded the city a few days after Christmas in 1616 on the feast of Our Lady of Bethlehem. The name Belém is an abbreviated form of Bethlehem in Portuguese.

In the midst of tropical foliage, the city boasts white colonial buildings with red tile roofs, tree-filled public squares, and the leisurely pace characteristic of most towns in the north of Brazil. Only 1½° south of the equator, the heat and the humidity slow most people down, and showers are almost a certainty every day, occurring with such regularity that people in the city often arrange their appointments around the afternoon shower.

Belém is the capital of the state of Pará and the outlet for all the produce from the Amazon. In port you will find freighters loaded with lumber, nuts, dozens of different fruits, jute, fish, cattle, minerals for industry, and orchids. Away from the slow pace of the public plazas, the port is thriving with constant activity as oceangoing vessels pass small fishing boats with multicolored sails. One of the most intriguing sights is the largest outdoor market in Brazil, Ver-O-Peso, on Avenida Castilho França, where stalls four and five deep offer fish and produce, flowers, meat, fruit, and cooked food. There are also hammocks, crocodile teeth, dried boa constrictor heads, sea horses, shell rosaries, handmade clothing, pottery, and charms made by practicioners of *macumba,* Brazil's version of voodoo, guaranteed to solve any love or financial problem. Come early in the morning and plan to spend a good part of the day poking around the blocks of amazing wares, mostly agricultural.

The central plaza, Praça de República, bordered on one side by Av. Presidente Vargas, is shaded by mango trees and dotted with gazebos, lush plants, and flowers. The square is the gathering place for old men sharing stories, young mothers playing with children, lovers strolling, and workers eating during lunch hour. To plan a walking tour from here, contact PARATUR, the regional government tourism bureau, at its new office on Praça Kennedy (phone: 224-9633), for a map of the city and suggested tours; there is also an adjoining craft shop.

One of the relics to survive the rubber boom that boosted this area around the turn of the century is the white marble Teatro Paz on the plaza. This wonderfully restored, interesting theater is one of the largest in Brazil and still hosts classical and folkloric concerts and ballet and visiting theater troupes.

Continuing up Av. Presidente Vargas toward the port, you will find street vendors with interesting and inexpensive specialties of Bahía. There is a delicious shrimp dish called *vatapá* made with coconut milk; *moqueca,* a fish stew cooked in palm oil; and *empadinhas de camarão,* a fried shrimp pastry. At just about every corner, vendors of *sorvete* and *sucos,* ice cream and juices made from the dozens of fruits native to this area, offer a variety of unusual and deliciousconcoctions, such as *bacuri, açai, manga, maracujá, goiaba, graviola, guanabana,* and *cupuaçu.* All these flavors are available at *Cairu,* Av. Catorce de Março.

The Goeldi Anthropology Museum and Zoo (Av. Magalhaes Barata 518; phone: 224-9233) are a must to understand the profusion of wildlife and flora that exists in the Amazon jungle. The museum has an exhibit of Indian clothing, pottery, and weapons and graphic accounts of the various tribes that inhabited the Amazon basin. Next to the zoo, which houses a good selection of jungle animals, is the Paraiso Das Tartarugas, where 3,000 turtles, from hatchlings to old-timers, live in natural environments. The zoo itself houses most of the animals that are hard to catch a glimpse of even when traveling on the river, such as anacondas, tapirs, exotic birds, alligators, and several varieties of monkeys.

Some of the most exotic food in South America is available in the towns along the Amazon, so if you want to sample one of the regional delicacies, such as turtle in its many varieties, the restaurants of Belém are an excellent place to start. There are turtle legs, turtle sauce, minced turtle meat, pancakes made from turtle eggs, and even a dessert made of turtle eggs. *Lá em Casa* (Av. Gov. José Malcher 982; phone: 223-2293) serves several of these regional dishes at reasonable prices. Seafood is particularly good and quite inexpensive in Belém (more so than in the rest of Brazil), and you will find a wide selection at *Marisqueira do Luix* (Av. Sen Lemos 1063; phone: 222-6551).

There are a number of excursions from Belém that shouldn't be missed if you have time. A 5-hour ride on an ENASA boat (Av. Presidente Vargas 41; phone: 223-3011) brings you to the largest island in the Amazon estuary, Switzerland-sized Ilha de Marajó. It is home to great herds of buffalo and zebu, thousands of colorful birds, fishing villages with lovely waterfront homes, and large-scale cattle ranches (*fazendas*). Visit the island during the dry season, July to December, and stay at one of the ranches that accepts guests. One of the nicest is that of Eduardo de Castro Ribeiro, whose family owns *Bonjardim.* He can be reached at Rua Tiradentes 392, Belém, Para, CEP 66000 (phone: 222-1380). The ranch house accommodations are comfortable, and his wife is a superb cook. Both the air taxi from Belém and the boat also land at the town of Soure, which has a very good hotel with pool, *Pousada Marajuara.* Amazon Travel Service (Trav. Pe. Eutiquito 374; phone: 223-1459) runs 8-hour escorted tours by air taxi from Belém that take you to several beaches and restaurants, with prices depending on the number of people going. The small town of Macapa lies directly on the equator, and here you can ride water buffalo with the locals and climb 16th-century Portuguese fortifications that still seem to protect the town. About 3 hours from Belém by bus is Ilha do Mosqueira. Attached to the mainland by a causeway, it is another jungle island with good beaches, but Marajó is more unspoiled.

Salinolopolis, a small city 4 hours by bus from Belém on the Atlantic, is the closest beach of any note, with small beachfront restaurants that feature inexpensive regional specialties.

En Route from Belém – The first 2 days of boat travel from Belém will be the most interesting for those who want an idea of how the river supports and nourishes its people. In this section of the Amazon basin, appropriately called the Narrows, the boat weaves through a labyrinth of tiny islets, passing close to the jungle shore and frequently encountering the small fishing boats that bring their catch to the port of Belém. When the Narrows gives way to the Amazon's full girth, flat-topped mountains appear in the distance, as well as small villages that sit in jungle clearings, such as Monte Alegre. At the point where the clear waters of the Rio Tapajos meet the muddy Amazon, you have reached the exact midpoint of your journey, the town of Santarém. Passengers on the ENASA boat will not have time to disembark, but if you are doing the trip in two or three stages, Santarém is worth a visit.

SANTARÉM: This city of 190,000 was settled in 1865 by residents of South Carolina and Tennessee who fled the Confederacy when slavery was abolished. Brazil permitted slavery for only 23 years after their arrival, but the Southerners still prospered and built a town that has become an important trading center. It now serves as a supply center for miners, gold prospectors, rubber tappers, Brazil nut gatherers, and the jute and lumber industries. Several bars display the Confederate flag, and you still occasionally meet the settlers' descendants, who mixed with the multiracial Brazilians and have names like José Carlos Calhoun.

The city lacks much of the sophistication of Belém and Manaus, but therein lies its charm. Remaining distinctively small-townish with its winding unpaved back streets, friendly slow-paced people, and colonial architecture, Santarém's center is its bustling port, with small fishing boats and dugout canoes delivering a day's catch or produce from one of the interior settlements, both jostling with the large oceangoing cargo ships loading fruit and huge balls of crude gray rubber. Wooden signs and a roving loudspeaker proclaim the next departure for Manaus as vendors shout the lowest prices of bananas and fish. From the port you can look at the river and see the blue, clear waters of the Tapajos, which is 15 miles wide at Santarém, joining the Amazon in a parallel journey before they merge a mile downstream.

You can sail on the tributaries of the clear Tapajos for a breathtaking look at the jungle, which hugs the shore in this area. Your hotel should be able to inform you about boat trips up this river. Prices vary.

Mercado Modelo is the open-air market in the center of town. While not as extensive as the one in Belém, it is still worth a visit to see the local produce and the people socializing. Along the eastern sea wall, a new walkway with benches and flowering shade trees is a good place to relax after lunch during the hottest part of the day.

Restaurants in Santarém are much simpler than those in Belém and Manaus, but you can eat fresh fish at *Mascote* (Rua Lameira Bittencourt 182) and the ever-present barbecue at *Churrascão* (Av. Mendonça Furtado).

En Route from Santarém – On this last 3-day stretch of river travel to Manaus, the ship passes several tiny villages, stopping for 15 to 30 minutes to pick up and discharge passengers. The only city of any note along this route is Obidos, a town of less than 30,000, sitting on the red banks of the Amazon. On the boat's regular schedule, you will pass the town at night (there is not much to see even if you are awake). Finally the boat swings onto the Rio Negro, the largest of the Amazon's tributaries, and docks 10 miles beyond in Manaus.

MANAUS: In the very heart of the Amazon region, this city of 630,000 is in the midst of its second boom. Turn-of-the-century buildings, remnants of the once-lucrative rubber trade, sit beside the modern high-rises indicative of present commercial operations.

Manaus's history is a classic story of a boom-and-bust one-crop economy. Rubber, made from a milky juice that flows from the *Hevea Brasilensis* tree, was known to the explorers accompanying Columbus, who saw Indians playing with hollow rubber balls in Haiti. In the early 1800s, with Charles Macintosh's invention of the raincoat and the development of shoes that could withstand the snows of European winters, rubber became an important Brazilian export. But the rubber boom really began in earnest when Goodyear discovered the process of vulcanization and car and bicycle wheels could be made consistently pliable.

Because the Amazon forest was the only place to get the rubber, foreigners flocked to the area and made enormous fortunes overnight. The residents grew fabulously rich and built a lavish jungle city that competed architecturally and culturally with major European capitals. They brought marble from Italy, tiles from Portugal, and the best china from England and constructed huge mansions in the jungle, a few of which still stand between the skyscrapers in the hilly section of the city. But the greatest remaining monument to this era is the grand, ostentatious opera house, Teatro do Amazonas (Praça São Sebastiao). Dozens of foreign artists and architects were brought to the jungle in 1892 to create a splendid building. Italian marble, English porcelain, French furniture, and wrought iron were imported to adorn the elaborate structure. The ceiling and walls of the lobby were decorated with mirrors and murals of harp-playing angels and Amazon Indians, and the huge dome was painted in gold leaf with green and yellow tiles. Besides the $10 million spent on construction, the city paid exorbitant sums to lure world-famous performers such as Sarah Bernhardt and Pavlova. Opening night in 1896 saw Manaus society at its most resplendent, the ladies dressed in Paris gowns and the men sweltering in woolen tailcoats. Teatro do Amazonas was remodeled in 1962 and again in 1975; it is open to the public Tuesdays through Sundays, 9 AM to 6 PM.

Manaus lost its monopoly on rubber in the early 1900s, when rubber tree seeds were smuggled out of Brazil to Ceylon. The effective cultivation of these trees, lower taxes, a lack of health hazards, and better access to shipping lanes made the Ceylonese rubber a quick success and vastly diminished the Amazon market. Brazil was producing 88% of the world's rubber in 1910, but 3 years later it exported less than half. Fortunes faded, the Europeans left, and the city survived on what could be taken from the river and jungle.

As capital of the state of Amazonas, Manaus has become a major northern center of commerce, exporting Brazil nuts, black pepper, jute, rubber, and lumber. The city's second boom occurred in 1965, when the government decided that if Manaus were to become a thriving city once more, something was needed to encourage industry and money to flow back in. It was decided to turn the city into a free port, with generous tax incentives and duty-free trading. Subsequent years have seen Manaus transformed. There are now hundreds of large and small shops packed with foreign merchandise — televisions, cameras, watches, boats, motorcycles, cars, air conditioners, clothes, and almost anything else you can imagine.

Manaus's harbor is laden with oceangoing vessels that sail up the river some 1,000 miles from the Atlantic, bringing food and other staples for the residents (everything here is very, very expensive due to the high cost of transportation). The city's most fascinating sight is the floating market, where each day people deliver fish, fruit, vegetables, and crafts to the vendors' stalls via dugout canoe. The city also boasts the world's largest floating port, a massive concrete pier constructed in 1906 by British engineers. A few blocks from these floating structures is Mercado Municipal (city market) on Rua do Bares, a remnant of the rubber era. Its entire structural framework was imported from Europe, and architecturally it is one of Brazil's most unusual indoor markets. In an Art Deco setting you see an exotic array of medicinal herbs, caged exotic birds and animals, regional farm produce, arts and crafts, and many varieties of fish. You should come early in the day to see it at its best and plan to spend some time walking around the docks.

The jungle literally creeps up on the city. To get an idea of the plant and animal life around you, plan to explore the museums, botanical gardens, and zoos. The Indian Museum (Av. 7 de Setembro and Duque de Caxis) has authentic Indian costumes, weapons, crafts, and art objects dating from the discovery of Manaus. The CIGS Zoological Garden on the outskirts of town houses 300 animals, including jaguars, tapirs, monkeys, snakes, and varieties of parrots (phone: 232-1094). Turislandia, a 20-minute drive from downtown in the Aleixo District, features groves of Brazil nut trees and cocoa, rubber, and guaraná trees. One of the most natural settings in the Amazon Region in which to observe the ecological system is at Salvadore Lake, where a reserve is open to the public. The reserve, about 5 miles (8 km) from the *Tropical Hotel Manaus* and operated by it, is near the Rio Negro and has an exotic variety of Amazon animals, such as tapirs, jaguars, boars, monkeys, alligators, turtles, snakes, and parrots, which can be seen from floating pavilions. The reserve has a picnic area and hiking along a forest trail about 2 miles (3 km) to the Guedes River narrows. Tours can be arranged through the Tropical Travel Agency at the *Tropical Hotel Manaus* (phone: 238-5757).

You can find some unusual handmade artifacts in Manaus's gift shops. One shop worth visiting is *Casa de Beija-Flor* (*House of the Hummingbird*) on Rua Quinto Bocaiuva 224. The English-speaking owner has stocked his store with Indian weapons, masks, crafts, piranhas, rings, and tropical fish. FUNAI, an Indian organization of the Brazilian government, runs a small store near Praça Adalberto Vale. The store sells handicrafts made by Indians from the interior.

A sight not to be missed is the "Wedding of the Waters" boat trip, one of the most memorable experiences on the Amazon. About 12 miles from the port of Manaus, the Rio Solimões and the blackish Rio Negro, both about 2 miles wide at this point, converge with terrific force, causing whirlpools of black and brown swirling water. These two waters flow side by side for more than 5 miles before mixing, because of their differing velocity and density. Eventually they become a muddy brown, or the *cafe com leite* (coffee with milk) color of the Amazon. Boating excursions can be arranged by contacting your hotel or US travel agency, and overnight trips to the jungle, staying at the *Amazon Lodge* or the *Amazon Village,* can be booked through SELVATUR, Praça Adalberto Valle (phone: 234-8639).

Manaus has the most interesting and best organized hunting and fishing facilities in the Amazon region. Tucanaréare caught by trolling from outboard-powered canoes. Piraiba, pirarara, surubim, and dorado weighing up to 180 pounds require heavy tackle and may be caught in these areas. SELVATUR also has daily 7-hour fishing excursions on the Amazon and Negro rivers; fishing equipment is provided.

There are a few notable dishes in Manaus, such as *mixira* (manatee meat dish); *piracuru* and *tucunare* (river fish); *tacaca,* a snack food prepared with shrimp, tapioca, jambu herb, tucupi sauce; and *manicoba,* similar in taste to the Brazilian favorite *feijoada,* made from pork, calves' feet, animal innards, bacon, sausage fat, vegetables, and beans. Restaurants here are quite expensive, but more plentiful than in Belém or Santarém. *Chapeu de Palha* (Rua Fortaleza 619) specializes in fish from the region, as does *Panorama* restaurant, where you should try the *tucunaré* and *tambagui,* as well as the *creme de cupuaçu,* a tropical fruit dessert. Ask the cab driver for *Panorama* by the river; it has a view, while its sister restaurant of the same name is on a loud, busy street corner. If you're set on barbecued meats, try *Roda Viva* (Av. Ajuricaba 1005A, Cachoeirinha; phone: 232-2687).

BEST EN ROUTE

BELÉM

Thanks to the government's program to promote tourism in Brazil, tourist facilities are improving. In major cities, such as Belém, Santarém, and Manaus, visitors will find a few high-caliber and moderate hotels and many *pensions.* Prices are generally higher here due to the high cost of transporting food, materials, and personnel to this remote part of the country. In hotels categorized as expensive, expect to pay $50 to $60 a night for a double for a private bath, air conditioning, television, radio, restaurant, pool, hairdressers, nightclubs; moderate from $20 to $45 per night for a private shower, air conditioning, television; and inexpensive, below $15 per night for hotels ranging in quality from the bare minimum to adequate, sharing a shower, no restaurants, bars, and television. Telephone numbers (changeable) have been included where they exist.

Hilton Internacional Belém – The most luxurious hotel in Belém, this new property pampers guests with a swimming pool with hydromassage, sauna, exercise room, hair salon, barbershop, and coffee shop. Av. Presidente Vargas 882 (phone: 223-6500). Expensive.

Novotel Belém – A new 121-room hotel near the river, it is fully air conditioned, with wheelchair access, pool and sauna, boating facilities, restaurant, and meeting space for 300. Av. Bernardo Sayao 4804 (phone: 0912-226-8011). Expensive to moderate.

Equatorial Palace – A modern, first-class hotel, renovated in 1980: 230 rooms with refrigerators and air conditioning, pool, tennis courts, nightclub, restaurant, and snack bar. Av. Braz de Aguiar 612 (phone: 0912-224-8855). Moderate.

Excelsior Grao Pará – It offers 140 air-conditioned rooms overlooking Praça da República, excellent dining in well-decorated rooms, a bar, hairdressers, private telephone, and television in rooms. Av. Presidente Vargas 718 (phone: 0912-222-3255). Moderate.

Vanja – A downtown hotel with 105 air-conditioned rooms. It has dining facilities, a bar, beauty salon, barber, and television in rooms. Rua Benjamin Constant 1164. Moderate.

ILHA DO MOSQUEIRO

Chapeu Virado – Small hotel directly on the beach of Mosqueiro with nicely decorated rooms, each with private bath. Praia do Virado (phone: 771-1202). Moderate.

Murubira – Across the street from the beach, this place also has a pool and a fairly good restaurant. Av. Beira-Mar (phone: 771-1256). Moderate.

Farol – This small hotel on the beach has 12 double rooms without private baths. Praia do Faros (phone: 771-1219). Inexpensive.

SANTARÉM

Tropical Santarém – The best in the city and hard to beat for luxury in the Amazon region. The 120 air-conditioned rooms all have balconies. The facilities include a circular tiled pool, a nightclub, casino, game rooms, movie theater, indoor-outdoor restaurant, and a houseboat cruiser for day or overnight trips. Mendonça Furtado 4120 (phone: 091-522-1583); contact Varig Airlines for reservations. Expensive.

Nova Olinda – With six rooms and two showers. Av. Adriano Pimentel 150 (phone: 091-522-1531). Inexpensive.

MANAUS

Tropical Hotel Manaus – The largest and one of the most exclusive resorts in South America, with 358 air-conditioned rooms with colonial furnishings of natural wood. The grounds, on the Rio Negro, are beautifully landscaped, with 40,000 orchid plants, tropical patios, a natural zoo, a casino, shops, a floating river bar, and cruisers for jungle river trips. On the beach of Ponta Negra, 12 miles (19 km) from downtown (contact Varig Airlines, 092-234-0251; or the hotel, 092-238-5757). Expensive.

Novotel Manaus – Adequate, 110-room establishment, 10 minutes from the city center; air conditioning and refrigerator in rooms, pool, and restaurant with dining terrace. Av. Mandii 4, Grande Rotula (phone: 092-237-1211). Expensive.

Amazonas – Hotel with a pool; near shops and docks downtown. The property, while nothing special, has 153 air-conditioned rooms, a bar, and a restaurant. Praça Adalberto Valle (phone: 092-234-7679). Expensive.

The Northeast

The Northeast of Brazil — or O Nordeste, as it's called in Portuguese — is composed of nine states: Ceará, Rio Grande do Norte, Piauí, Paraíba, Pernambuco, Bahía, Alagoas, Sergipe, and Maranhão. Together they form the bulge of Brazil's coastline that includes its most easterly point, which is the continental spot closest to Africa in the Western Hemisphere. This geographical fact has profoundly influenced the culture of certain sections of the Northeast.

An area of over one million square miles harboring one-third of Brazil's population, the Northeast has been and still is the scene of great joy and heartbreak for Brazil. Sixty out of every 1,000 babies in the Northeast die in their first year; life expectancy is 38 years; the illiteracy rate ranges from 33.8% in urban areas to 66.2% in rural areas. These are overall statistics, though. The Northeast is actually made up of two distinct regions, the Northeast coast and the *sertão,* which have developed separately and unequally due to one factor: rainfall. The 150-mile-wide Northeast coast is bordered by the Atlantic on the east and by Brazil's Great Escarpment on the west, extending from Ilhéus in the southern part of Bahía to Fortaleza in Ceará. The early Portuguese sailors quickly realized that its rich soil and humid tropical climate tempered by ocean breezes would be ideal for the cultivation of sugarcane, as indeed it was. The crop flourished, and by the mid-1600s, Portugal's colony was a power on the world's sugar market. The areas of Olinda in Pernambuco and Salvador in Bahía became especially prosperous as a result, and great individual fortunes were made by the end of the century.

This wealth attracted the Dutch, who took advantage of Portugal's temporary domination by Spain in the 1630s to invade and hold the area. By 1654, the Portuguese, who had once again gained control of their portion of the Iberian Peninsula, succeeded in driving the Dutch from the region. Unfortunately for the Northeast, the invaders who had been expelled carried the knowledge they had acquired during their occupation to the Antilles. There, along with Jewish technicians who had been driven from Brazil during the Inquisition, they started their own sugarcane plantations. By the 1750s, the sugar grown on these farms, together with the English and French West Indian production, cut into Brazil's sugar markets. While the crop is still important today, it has been in a slow decline for the last 200 years.

The societies that grew up along the Northeast coast can be compared to those that formed around the southern cotton plantations in the U.S. Large tracts of land were often presented to favorites of the Portuguese crown as rewards for helping rid the area of bandits. Within the family-owned sugarcane plantations (*fazendas*) there developed a semifeudal world, complete with aristocracy, slaves from Africa, and free laborers and artisans who were dependent on the *fazendeiro* for protection. These semi-independent economic units scattered along the coast usually consisted of the *fazendeiro's* mansion, shacks for the slaves, small houses and shops for the artisans and laborers, and the ever-present church. Additionally, each *fazenda* usually had its own sugar refinery, cattle, and crops. In these closed communities, incest and miscegenation were a matter of course. Paralleling the Virginia plantations in the US, the *fazendas* produced many of the statesmen of the day.

By the end of the nineteenth century, the family-owned *fazenda* began to lose its place as the foremost economic institution of the Northeast. With the development of large steam-powered refinery equipment, the smaller farmers, whose profits had been slipping anyway, found themselves being usurped by the large concerns that eventually became the huge corporations that today control sugar production.

Remnants of the wealth that sugar brought to the region can still be found in the *fazendas* with their abandoned sugar mills that dot the countryside and in the magnificent baroque-tiled buildings that adorn Salvador and Recife. Probably the most enduring and colorful vestiges of the sugar era are the surviving elements of African culture that arrived with the slaves, brought by the thousands to work in the sugarcane fields. Slavery in Brazil, while perhaps not as brutal as that in North America, was certainly more widespread. Africa's presence can be felt not only in the areas surrounding Salvador and Recife, where huge slave markets existed, but in the African-rooted samba that is popular throughout Brazil. In Rio de Janeiro, *macumba,* a fusion of West African voodoo elements with Christianity, is widely practiced. Two cousins of *macumba* that have many adherents are *candomblé* in Bahía and *xango* in Pernambuco.

Also from Africa is *capoeira,* which in Angola was originally a type of one-on-one combat and today is a dance performed in the midst of a clapping circle of onlookers in streets all over the Northeast. Planters forbade the original kicking duel, which could permanently injure one of the contestants. The participants, however, learned how to mask their battles. When the *fazendeiro* came too close during a *capoeira* duel, the combatants would pull their kicks up short of landing and brush their legs just over the opponent's head, feigning harmless exercise. This disguised form of combat has evolved into the high leg-sweeping, hip-spinning, tumbling ballet that is performed to the twangy beat of the *berimbau,* a one-stringed African instrument.

African cuisine has become a tasty, permanent fixture in the Northeast. The following dishes are most characteristic of the state of Bahia, which has the most slave descendants in Brazil: *vatapá,* a creamy shrimp dish made with *dendê,* an oil from a certain type of palm tree; *acarajé,* a deep-fried shrimp and bean batter mixture served with extremely hot sauce; *carurú,* okra with fish or shrimp and minced herbs and spices; *abará,* banana leaves surrounding a stuffing of bean paste, peppers, and palm oil; *xinxim,* a chicken ragout; and *cocada,* a sweet made from coconuts and sugar.

Oral traditions are also rich with African folklore — stories of goblins, spells and fantastic journeys. The hand-carved, sacred wood sculptures make you wish you had some extra room in your suitcase.

The area in southern Bahía surrounding Ilhéus is considered a subregion of the Northeast coast. It had its own single-crop boom — cacao. For many years the dense forests and hostile Indians kept settlers away, but by the late 1800s, migrants from drought-stricken regions of the Northeast had cleared land for small farms. Cacao transplanted from the Amazon did not do particularly well, but by 1907, with the introduction of sturdy Ceylonese cacao and the wide markets provided by the burgeoning chocolate industry in the US and Europe, a major boom was under way.

A violent era followed, with clan wars, assassinations, and false documents used to usurp precious cacao lands. Brazil's gifted Jorge Amado, born in Ilhéus in 1912, has written several novels of the cacao days, including *Cacao* and *São Jorge dos Ilhéus.* In the latter, he describes the city in its heyday:

Ilhéus and the cacao zone swam in gold, bathed in champagne, slept with French ladies from Rio de Janeiro. At the Trianon, the city's most chic cabaret, Colonel Maneca Dantas lit cigarettes with 500,000-reis bills, repeating the gesture of all the country's rich fazendeiros during the previous rises in coffee, rubber, cotton, and sugar prices.

The most precious and certainly the most famous of Amado's treatments of the epoch is in *Gabriela, Clove and Cinnamon,* which portrays the end of the violent days and the beginning of "civilization" in Ilhéus through a rich cast of characters headed by the splendid Gabriela, a mulatto migrant from the drought region.

Large *fazendas* developed here, as they did in the north, but with a difference. The resident slaves were replaced by mobile migrant workers from other sections of the Northeast, who left when the harvest was in. A mercantile elite developed among the *fazendeiros,* known as "colonels," who passed on their great estates to their heirs.

But soil erosion and foreign competition put an end to Ilhéus's glory. Prices fell and land changed hands as exporters bought farms from ruined *fazendeiros.* Today, Ilhéus has only its old palatial mansions to attest to the era.

Along the shores from Ilhéus to Natal and then on to Fortaleza and São Luís are some of the most varied, beautiful, and isolated beaches in South America (and perhaps the world). You can pick from white sand, red sand, yellow sand, flat shores that let you walk out a mile, steep coconut-studded dunes, built-up beaches with modern facilities, desolate expanses where the only footprints you see are your own, pounding surf or little laughing waves. If you care to get away from the more "civilized" beaches that surround the larger cities, you can head for an outlying fishing village and enjoy a more down-home surfside scene. If you are adventurous, you can put on a broad-brimmed hat, pack some supplies, and start hiking in one direction or another from a fishing village down miles of uninhabited beach. Eventually, one day or the next, you will hit another village. Along the way is ample opportunity for uninhibited abandonment. Watch out for the sun, though. In many areas of the Northeast, the ultraviolet rays are so intense from 11 AM to 3 PM that all but the minimum exposure can be dangerous.

THE SERTÃO

Things have not been nearly as cheery in this drought-plagued region of Brazil's Northeast, sometimes referred to as the "other" Northeast. It is an arid land of low mesas and sloping terrain spotted with scrub forest called *caatinga,* thorny bushes, and cactus beginning 150 miles from the coast. The *sertão,* which means "hinterland," is often referred to as *opolígono das sêcas* ("the polygon of drought") in government studies due to the rough geometric shape of the region.

Rainfall here is completely unpredictable, but when it does arrive, violent torrents run quickly through the eroded soil, providing minimal relief. Droughts run in cycles and can last from 1 to 5 years. During these periods, when the last drops of water have disappeared and the scrawny cattle that form the fragile economic backbone of the region have died off, there are mass migrations to the Amazon Valley, the mountains, or the coast to find relief and work. Over the years, these unfortunate migrants have been brutally exploited upon their arrival in more prosperous areas.

A typical migration will mean the movement of from 15,000 to 20,000 people, but the numbers can swell. During the devastating drought from 1877 to 1879, over 100,000 *sertanejos* were forced to leave their homes and as many as 500,000 died. In *Barren Lives,* Graciliano Ramos writes with stunning vividness of one destitute farmer and his family during the drought of 1938 — a story of their journey to nowhere. This book has been made into a classic Brazilian film.

Today, the Northeast migrant is often recruited as a laborer for the great building boom in the south, especially in Rio and São Paulo. For 2 to 3 years he will leave his family and head for the big city, where he lives and eats in a shed right on the job site and is paid from 35¢ to 50¢ per hour, depending on how skilled he is. He hopes that at the end of his job he will have something to bring back to his family in the north.

Strangely enough, with all the adversity of this region, the *sertanejo* still seems to love his home. When the drought ends, he can once again be found returning to the *sertão,* which has the highest rural population density in Brazil.

The *vaqueiro,* a hearty, horse-riding, dust-covered cowboy shrouded in worn leather, is the economic mainstay of the *sertão.* He usually tends the cattle herds for an absentee landlord. His life is often seminomadic, and, as is true of many of the people of the region, he is usually a squatter on the land that he does occupy. The *vaqueiro* probably does some farming to feed his family, and when he is not doing that or tending the herds, he will be collecting *canaúba* and *licuri,* which are a source of wax, and *oiticica,* used in the production of paint and varnish, from local trees.

The history of the *sertão* is similar in some respects to the holdups (or "bangie-bangie," as Brazilians like to call it) of the American Wild West. Bandits roamed the region as hired guns for the *fazendeiros* or robbed the gold and diamonds transported through the *sertão* from the mines in Minas Gerais.

These bandits, who sensed the inequality between the landowners and the landless, were an early breed of South American revolutionary. Like Robin Hood, they were transformed into legendary figures. The most famous of these was Virgulino Ferreira da Silva, better known as Lampião (the lightning), who, from 1920 until he was killed in 1938, tore through the countryside stealing from merchants and giving amply to charities while urging the people to wake up to what was happening around them.

In this land of suffering and uncertainty, the people have often embraced a messianic leader to help them through troubled times. The village of Canudos, under the direction of its "savior" Antonio Conselheiro, battled the federal government for years in a struggle for secession that ended finally in its crushing defeat in 1896. This struggle has been described effectively by Euclides de Cunha in *Rebellion in the Backlands.*

Another popular figure at the turn of the century was Padre Cicero in Juazeiro do Norte. Even though he had been excommunicated by the Church, he had 50,000 followers when he tried unsuccessfully to take over the state of Pernambuco.

More recently, in the early 1960s, peasant leagues were formed under the leadership of Francisco Julião. These groups took possession of some Northeast lands by legal expropriation and helped the peasants pay their debts. Sensing a threat in the growing political awareness that the poor gained from their exposure to the leagues, the government has moved to placate the people by creating an economic development program called SUDENE. Various projects of SUDENE, such as the construction of dams and hydroelectric plants, have been started to provide relief and alleviate some of the devastating effects of drought.

Other books that give some historical perspective on the region are: *The Devil in the Backlands,* by João Guimarães Rosa; *Death in the Northeast,* by Josue de Castro; *Sharecroppers of the Sertão,* by Allen W. Johnson.

Because the *sertão* is so severe an area and probably of more interest to the sociologist or anthropologist than the casual traveler, our tour will primarily follow the more pleasant route, along the sands of the Northeast coast. The roads in this region (BR-101, 116, 222, 343), generally two-lane blacktop, are by far the best found in the more remote areas of South America. Travel is almost exclusively via buses, which are at least as comfortable in Brazil as any you will find in the US. And though not all are air conditioned, you can usually travel at night, when the air is cool. There is the occasional inconvenience caused by a washed-out bridge, especially in the midst of the rainy season. This may require putting your bus on a barge to ford the river or taking a potholed detour on a dirt road. The journey begins in Ilhéus.

ILHÉUS: With a population of 130,000, this city lies 118 miles (190 km) south of Salvador. As noted above, its history is rich, but its present state is not particularly glorious. The beautiful beaches and visits to the abandoned cacao *fazendas* in the countryside make it a nice place for a short visit.

  En Route from Ilhéus – Heading northwest, you soon pass Itabuna (pop. 150,000), the trading center for the cacao region. From there, take the newer BR-101 rather than the Rio-Bahía highway, passing through some magnificent elevated countryside of Brazil's Great Escarpment, with villages that still retain a colonial flair, such as São Felix, Cruz das Almas, and Cachoeira. Feira de Santana is 20 miles (31 km) beyond Cachoeira and 70 miles (112 km) northwest of Salvador. Try to arrive here for the Monday market, which is quite colorful and offers some excellent leather handicrafts and other native products. (For more information, see *Salvador* in THE CITIES.) Continue north across Bahía's border into the tiny state of Sergipe and stop off in Aracaju, 203 miles (327 km) north of Salvador.

ARACAJU: The capital of Sergipe, Aracaju has a population of 293,000. While this symmetrical city has no great tourist attractions, it is a good base from which to explore some wonderful nearby beaches. Offshore oil rigs can be seen from the town's waterfront and are just a part of the industry that has been attracted to the region through financial incentives.

  En Route from Aracaju – Continuing on BR-101 on the way to Maceió, you cross the Rio São Francisco between Propria and Pôrto Real do Colegio. From Maceió, via Palmeira dos Indios — or in a bit more complicated fashion from Penedo, a nice little town 37 miles (60 km) east of Propria off BR-101 — the Falls of Paulo Alfonso on the river can be reached by bus and boat.

THE FALLS OF PAULO ALFONSO: Upstream on the Rio São Francisco, this set of four falls cascades 260 feet and is separated by spires of boulders, a very spectacular sight. Centuries of gushing water have polished the granite walls of the cavern through which the falls flow, creating caves and a deep gorge that has inspired many local Indian legends. The surrounding area, a mat of tropical vegetation, is now a national park. The falls are most grand in the wet months of January and February. The Alagoas bank to the north offers the best view.

Returning to the land route and crossing into the tiny state of Alagoas, you arrive at its capital, Maceió, 121 miles (195 km) north of Aracaju.

MACEIÓ: This sugar port has a population of 400,000. Here (and throughout the Northeast) you will see baroque colonial buildings with familiar red-tiled roofs. Though high-rises do dot the skyline, Maceió has managed to preserve some of its earlier flavor. There is a lighthouse in the center of town, near the Government Palace and the Church of Bom Jesus do Mártires, all worth a visit. The recently refurbished waterfront, where large cargo ships are berthed, is very pleasant, as are the seafood restaurants, the town lake, and Pajucara Beach. All the beaches in this area are delightful, with coral reefs ½ mile offshore to keep the water calm. From December 20 to January 6, regional folk plays and dances are performed in the public squares.

In Maceió also are fishermen, called *jangadeiros,* who can be seen on their strange *jangada* boats all along the coast to Belém. They just manage to squeeze out a living on these raft-type sailboats made of six logs 24 feet long, fitted together with wooden pegs and tapered at one end to form a bow.

Sometimes out for days at a time, the *jangadeiros* and their rafts bob like floats on the water, usually anchored to a good fishing spot with a stone. When they finally return home, they use two dry logs on the beach as rollers on which to haul their *jangadas* past the high tide's reach.

Continue north through several tiny fishing towns, enter the state of Pernambuco, and 121 miles (195 km) from Maceió you'll reach the state capital of Recife.

RECIFE: With a population of 1,200,000, this city is the main port and commercial capital of the Northeast and the largest city on the route. Though the Brazilian tour brochures proclaim Recife to be the Venice of Brazil, a bit of an overstatement, waterways do run through the city. Split by the Capirabe and Tejipiú rivers, Recife, meaning "reef" and named for the great natural coral mass that lies off its shore, is made up of three sections: Freguesia do Recife, which is a peninsula; Santo Antônio, an island between Freguesia do Recife and the mainland; and Boa Vista, on the mainland. Bridges of stone and iron connect the three sections. In 1975, the Capirabe and Tejipiú catastrophically flooded Recife, but a series of dams have since been constructed that should prevent such a recurrence.

The city was founded by fishermen and sailors in the first half of the 16th century and grew quite rapidly as sugarcane cultivation became profitable. As the closest point in Brazil after João Pessoa to West Africa, Recife became a huge center for the slave trade, and much of its present population are descendants of those slaves. Sugar and cotton are still the main crops of the region.

Recife is still expanding rapidly, and it is getting more and more crowded as skyscrapers nudge out the beautiful colonial mansions, monuments to the sugar era. Wide boulevards, such as Ruas Nova and Imperatriz, have been built to try to cope with the intense traffic jams, but more construction will be necessary to alleviate the problem. As the poor people of the countryside continue to stream in looking for employment, a more *tranquilo* Recife does not seem to be in the cards.

Several very special folkloric traditions of the Northeast are centered in this city: *Frevo* is wildly accelerated music with syncopated rhythms, and its name comes from the Portuguese *ferver,* "to boil," which is just what it does. *Maracatu* is a traditional dance drama, similar to the Portuguese *fandango,* practiced usually during Carnival by the impoverished people of the surrounding area who come to the city to celebrate and forget about their troubles for a while. *Caboclinha* groups perform their folkloric dance in bright feathers, red tunics adorned with medals, and animal-tooth necklaces. Theirs is a leaping, spinning performance played to the beat of banging bows and arrows.

Recife boasts more than 60 splendid churches that deserve a look. A few of the best are Nossa Senhora da Conceição dos Militares, built around 1710 in a baroque-rococo style, on Rua Nova in Santo Antônio; Nossa Senhora do Livramento on Rua do Livramento, built in 1692 and refurbished in 1735, has a classic style with interiors worked in granite and wood; and Capela Dourada on Rua Imperador, completed in 1734, is another of baroque design with some splendid gold-leaf paintings and carved cedar.

Some other attractions in Recife include Fort Brum, erected by the Portuguese and finished by the Dutch when they took over the city; Fort São Tiago das Cinco Pontas, built by the Dutch and completed by the Portuguese in 1677 in the shape of a pentagon; Patio de São Pedro, in the center of the city across from the Church of São Pedro dos Clerigos, a gathering place of the intellectual and artistic crowd of Recife, with good restaurants nearby, weekend folk music concerts, and poetry readings; Sitio da Trinidade, in the districts of Casa Amarela and Parnamirim, the nicest park in town and the former site of the Dutch invasion. The Sugar Museum (Av. 17 de Agosto) has examples of colonial sugar mills, slave torture devices, and many other historical, social, and scientific exhibits related to sugar production. Boa Viagem is the fashionable southern suburb that sports a 5-mile ocean promenade, scenic views, coconut palms, and villas of the wealthy. Some good eating establishments are here, too.

Beaches are one of the area's greatest attractions and the major reason for a visit to Recife. Those within the city limits include Pina, to the south and Boa Viagem, mentioned above. Farther south, in an area filled with coconut palms and clean sand, are: Piedade, Venda Grande, Candeias, and Barra de Jangada. Still farther, near the town of Cabo, 20 miles (34 km) from Recife, are: Itapuama, with interesting rock formations, lots of coconuts, and full facilities for the traveler; and Gaibu, the most famous in the area and perhaps the most beautiful. There are natural spring pools here, and it is possible to rent *jangadas.* Nazaré is even more remote, with ruins of an old lighthouse and a church built in 1612. Suape is also an isolated blue cove surrounded by green hills and miles of empty beach.

Another excursion from Recife is to Olinda, the original capital of Pernambuco. Founded in 1537, it lies just 4 miles (6 km) north of Recife. It is a delightful town built on hills and has been preserved in its early elegance. Many local artists have chosen to live on its windy cobblestone streets lined with tile-faced buildings. The spirit of the old days returns each November during Olinda's colonial festival.

This place abounds in old churches, convents, and monasteries. Some of the recommended spots for exploration include the monasteries of São Bento and São Francisco, full of wood carvings and paintings; the Pernambuco Contemporary Art Museum, with a good collection of painted ceramic figurines; the Church of Nossa Senhora do Rosario dos Pretos, built in 1715; and Bica de São Pedro, the colonial public fountain.

Clean local beaches are: Barro Novo, Carmo, Casa Caida, Farol, Rio Doce, São Francisco, and Milagres.

ITAMARACÁ: This is a small, pretty island 38 miles (50 km) from Recife just off the mainland and reached easily via causeway. Fort Orange, built by the Dutch in 1631, is one of the attractions, but its fame lies in its beaches. Vila de Pilar is the main town on the island, shared on weekends by poor fishermen and wealthy vacationers from Recife. It has a tourist hotel and plenty of good seafood. The cleanest and most remote beaches are reached by walking beyond Jauaripe, a tiny village just a mile or so from Vila de Pilar.

FAZENDA NOVA: This is a tiny town 2 hours west of Recife. The sole reason to visit this place in the middle of the arid region is to see its open-air theater-town of Nova Jerusalem, which has been constructed as a replica of Ancient Jerusalem. During Easter Week each year, thousands flock to the village to witness the spectacular Passion of Christ play. Hotels, complete with air conditioning and swimming pools, have now been built to handle all the tourists.

CARUARU: If you are visiting Fazenda Nova, you will want to stop here, too; it is just a few miles away. The Saturday market offers some good buys in the leather and pottery of the region. Visit the Mestre Vitalino Museum in homage to the sculptor responsible for creating the traditional distinctive clay figures of peasants sold at the market. From December 23 to January 1, the city hosts a festival featuring Pernambuco folklore, and from March 13 to 19, an International Handicraft Week is held.

En Route from Recife – The road north toward João Pessoa passes through some lovely coconut palm–filled country. Just 20 miles (32 km) from Recife, Igaraçu is reached. Filled with colonial buildings, including the first church built in Brazil, much of the town has been declared a national monument. It is a pleasant place to stop for a few hours.

Continuing north, you will arrive at Paulista, yet another old city with some nice inviting beaches. The last stop before João Pessoa is at Goiana, 44 miles (70 km) from Recife. It has churches dating back to 1595, and the clean, easygoing beaches of Catuama, Carne de Vaca, and Pontas de Pedras are not far away. After 70 miles (113 km) and about 2 hours of travel, you arrive at João Pessoa on the Paraíba River.

JOÃO PESSOA: With a population of 330,000, this is the capital of Paraíba state. Again, there is the juxtaposition of high-rises and the baroque, wealthy homes of a city on the move. Plenty of palms still line the streets, but the state government is providing many incentives to attract business to this region, which has as its major industries fishing, cattle breeding, and the cultivation of cotton, sisal, pineapples, corn, beans, and sugar. Huge stacks of modern sugar mills can be seen on the outskirts of town.

Continuing up the coast, you will be constantly tempted to try a new succulent variety of tropical fruit. Sometimes the same fruit will bear a different name in a town just 100 miles away. Besides the old standbys like bananas, watermelons, and pineapples, in João Pessoa you might experiment with tastes you've never tried before, like *graviola, bacuri, açai, manga, cupuaço, goiaba,* or *maracujá.* The fruit is put into a blender with some milk and made into a smooth drink called a *suco.*

October is the beginning of the summer season, which is greeted by the election of the Queen of the Beaches, jalopy races, a *jangada* regatta, and plenty of *batidas,* a favorite Brazilian drink combining the local firewater, *cachaça,* with any of the above-mentioned fruits.

Tambaú is a beach resort just half an hour from town. The beach is extensive, the fishing and bathing excellent, the palm trees sway constantly, and all complemented by excellent facilities. Caso Branco is another beautiful nearby spot.

Campina Grande is 2 hours west of João Pessoa and another fast-growing sugar manufacturing center. Its Saturday market is quite lively and a good place to pick up artifacts from the Northeast.

Juazeiro do Norte lies another 250 miles (400 km) west of Campina, deep in the heart of the *sertão,* but its elevation makes it an oasis of green. Here, Padre Cicero's stand against the government is commemorated by an open-air mass and pilgrimage to his statue each Novemeber 2. It is from Juazeiro — if you care to skip the rest of the Northeast — that you can take a relaxing 9- to 10-day paddlewheel boat ride 500 miles down the Rio São Francisco to Pirapora in Minas Gerais. This river valley is actually a subregion of the *sertão,* and forms a navigable waterway that has served to unite the north and south of the region. Along its banks and within its narrow flood plain, river agriculture avoids the droughts that afflict the rest of the *sertão.* Bring malaria pills and a hammock for a glide through some inspirational countryside that is still much as it was in the days of Lampião.

As the road moves away from the shoreline a bit, you pass Guarabira and 113 miles (180 km) farther north arrive at Natal, the capital of the state of Rio Grande do Norte.

NATAL: Sitting on the Rio Potengi just inland from the coast is this city of 416,000 people. The surrounding area is the largest sea salt–producing region in Brazil, and huge, flat tracts of the white salt dominate the countryside in Macau to the north. Important regional products are manioc, sugarcane, black beans, and fruit. The recent discovery of oil off the coast indicates a potential economic boom.

Natal is a pleasant city that still has a lot of green foliage. Its beaches are its real claim to fame, with Praia do Genipabu the finest. Huge sand dunes are shaded by coconut palms that offer an ideal place to camp.

En Route from Natal – As the elevation drops and the temperature rises, you move closer to the equator along this route to Fortaleza. Try to travel during the night. About 90 miles (150 km) outside Fortaleza, after you have passed Mossoro, a salt-processing center for the area, and have crossed the border into Ceará, you arrive at the turnoff for the tiny fishing village of Canoa Quebrada.

CANOA QUEBRADA: While there are no formal facilities for the traveler here, this is the perfect spot for someone who cares to rough it a bit and get to know the local people. The beaches are magnificent and unspoiled and the fishermen hospitable, offering you space in their simple homes and food for a ridiculously low price.

Continuing beyond Canoa Quebrada for a few hours brings you to Fortaleza, the capital of Ceará.

FORTALEZA: This port of almost 1 million people grew as a center for the export of sugar, caraúba wax, cotton, castor oil, and salt. Today, lobsters and cashew nuts, both marketed worldwide, are the most important sources of income. Fishing is also excellent here, and the state government is constructing new port facilities to protect the fishing fleets and lessen layover times for large cargo ships. While the city does have some old colonial buildings and plenty of red tiles on its roofs, it does not possess the historic and artistic flavor of the other colonial cities in the Northeast.

Many *jangadeiros* of Fortaleza became famous in Brazil for refusing to carry slaves from shore to ship after 1850, when the importation of slaves was banned and the local *fazendeiros* sought to make a profit by bringing their slaves to Rio de Janeiro for sale. Today, the *jangadeiros* can be seen from Iracema beach bringing in their catch at sunset.

The Northeastern Handicraft Fair is held in Fortaleza at a different time each year. Local art is displayed, and folk groups perform. At Christmas, a nativity play with singing and dancing is enacted.

There are several sights in Fortaleza worth seeing, such as the *Mercado Central,* where you can bargain for stunning handmade lace, embroidery, and hammocks (the best in Brazil), and the *Tourist Center,* in Fortaleza's old prison, with an interesting popular art museum, shops that sell folkloric items, and good restaurants.

The beaches in and around Fortaleza are excellent. Within 7 miles (12 km) of town are Iracema, Meirelles, Mucuripe, do Futuro, and Caça e Pesca. More outlying beach-combing awaits in Aquiraz, 20 miles (31 km) away, on the beaches of Prainha and Iguape; Beberibe, 49 miles (78 km) away, with the beaches of Morro Brabco combining sand dunes and freshwater waterfalls; and in Cascavel, 37 miles (62 km) away, with Capanga beach.

Another quite worthwile trip is the 19-mile (30-km) drive to the mountain of Serra de Maranguape, which has tropical vegetation and an excellent view of the city.

En Route from Fortaleza – You travel deep into the *sertão* on your way to São Luís, the final stop on this route. After passing the city of Sobral, the climate becomes pleasantly cool as you ascend Serra da Ibiapaba. As if by magic, the arid scrub landscape becomes a lush green tropical scene, complete with banana and mango trees. The pleasure is short-lived, through, as the descent from the hills plunges you into the even hotter and dustier environment of the state of Piauí. On BR-222, between Piracuruca and Piripiri, are the Sete Cidades.

SETE CIDADES (THE SEVEN CITIES): This national park is a strange moonlike area of dried eroded earth formations that are symmetrically arranged over 11.4 square miles and look like the ruins of seven cities intersected by streets and avenues. Even stranger are the carvings on some of the formations — hands, animals, and other figures. Scientists have been unable to identify their origin, but some feel that they may have been left by ancient Phoenicians.

A waterfall with some refreshing bathing pools is right on the site, and you can camp for a nominal fee.

En Route from Sete Cidades – There is no good road that leads directly to São Luís, so you will have to continue south to Terezina, a brutally hot, dry city of 378,000 that offers nothing particularly appealing to the traveler, then north toward the cool breezes of the coast once again. Roughly 350 miles (560 km) from Fortaleza, you arrive at São Luís, the capital of Maranhão.

SÃO LUÍS: Technically, this city of 450,000, sitting on an island between the bays of São Marcos and São José, is considered part of northern Brazil, but because it is such a nice spot, it makes a good finish for the Northeast tour route.

A pleasant, low-key place with a minimum number of high-rise buildings, São Luís has managed to preserve a bit of its past. The older part of town, built on steep flagstone streets, still has many beautiful baroque mansions, complete with blue tile façades, interior gardens, wrought iron, and hand-carved woodwork. The narrow, winding avenues have plenty of palm shade cover.

Claimed in 1612 by Frenchman Daniel de la Touche for the French regent Maria de' Medici, who desired a tropical paradise of her own, the city was named in honor of King Louis XIII. The port is now too shallow to accommodate modern ships, unlike in the beginning of the 19th century, when hundreds of boats entered and left the harbor annually. These ships hauled the tons of cotton that were the source of the tremendous one-crop boom that shook the area just as sugar and cacao stimulated other sections of the Northeast. Supported by slave labor, the São Luís region flourished, producing enough writers and poets to be called the Athens of Brazil. As with all the single-crop booms that Brazil has experienced, this one crashed ultimately as a result of the large-scale cotton production on US plantations. Today, the most important products of the area besides cotton are babacu nuts, rice, and manioc.

There are some 380 miles of tranquil water beaches to the east and west of São Luís. Some extend out for miles when the tide is low, and, closer to town, others are the scene of perpetual parties. Dune buggies cruise up and down the shoreline past the many *barzinhos* (little bars), most of which serve delicious seafood.

The region never seems to get too hot; even after the winter rains have ceased in April and the sun begins to shine for 8 months, a gentle breeze keeps the air circulating almost constantly. The city is now the scene of a reverse migration, moving from south to north, as many *paulistas* (people from São Paulo), disheartened with the fast-paced life, look for a more relaxed existence in the north.

From June 23 to July 10 is a special time. The festival of Bumba-Meu-Boi is celebrated with a pastoral play. Its principal theme, the death and resurrection of the bull, has a mixture of Portuguese, African, and native elements. The players are divided into three classes: human, animal, and fantasy. They dance, sing, and talk to the accompaniment of percussion instruments.

A 1½-hour boat ride across the Bay of São Marcos brings you to Alcântara, a tiny, quiet fishing community. With its rich treasury of colonial buildings, it has been designated a historical monument. There are many nice beaches here, too. For those who want to visit and return, the boat leaves at 7 AM and returns around 1 PM.

BEST EN ROUTE

The Northeast is still developing facilities for tourism, and present hotels range from a few top-quality places in the major cities to the most primitive accommodations in general. Restaurants, when they exist in hotels, have Continental cuisine with specialties of regional dishes, primarily seafood. Hotels categorized as expensive will cost from $45 per day for a double room; moderate, from $20 to $45 per day; and inexpensive, under $15 per day.

ILHÉUS

Ilhéus Praia – A comfortable hotel with air conditioning, TV, and refrigerators in the rooms. Praça D. Eduardo (phone: 073-231-2533). Moderate.

Britania – All 39 rooms are clean and have air conditioning; some have a private shower. No credit cards. Rua 28 de Junho 16 (phone: 073-231-1722). Inexpensive.

ARACAJU

Beira-Mar – Right on the beach, this hotel is pleasant, and it has a nightclub. Accepts all credit cards. Av. Rotary, Atalaia Velha (phone: 079-223-1819). Moderate.

Palace – Comfortable and the newest in town. Has good restaurant, bar, 74 air-conditioned rooms. Accepts all credit cards. Praça General Valadao (phone: 079-222-3111). Moderate.

Oasis – Hotel is in central part of town. Private bath, air conditioning. No credit cards. Rua São Cristavão 466 (phone: 079-224-2125). Inexpensive.

PENEDO

São Francisco – Hotel in this small stop has 52 rooms, all with private bath and air conditioning. The hotel has a bar and restaurant. Accepts Elo credit card. Av. Floriano Peixoto. Moderate.

MACEIÓ

Jatiúca – For luxury, try this hotel on the beach. It offers volleyball and tennis courts. Accepts all credit cards. Lagoa da Anta 220 (phone: 082-231-2555). Expensive.

Beiriz – Hotel with air conditioning, bar, and 71 rooms with showers. Accepts Nacional credit card. Rua João Pessoa 290. Moderate.

FALLS OF PAULO ALFONSO

Grande Hotel Paulo Alfonso – First-rate hotel at the falls in a national park. Has good restaurant, bar, pool, air conditioning. All 46 rooms have private bath. Accepts Diners, Nacional, Credicard. Parque da CHESF. Expensive.

Guararepes – Hotel is in commercial district. 102 rooms with private bath, air conditioning, restaurant, bar. Accepts all credit cards. Rua da Palma 57. Moderate.

Miramar – Well situated on a beach. The 120 rooms have a private bath, music, air conditioning. The hotel has a pool, international restaurant, nightclub, bar, hairdressers. All credit cards. Rua dos Navegantes 364. Expensive.

Grande – Fully air-conditioned hotel with bar and restaurant. All 107 rooms have private bath. All credit cards. Av. Marins de Barros 593. Moderate.

RECIFE

Internacional Othon Palace – A member of the countrywide Othon chain, and a good one, on Boa Viagem beach with 258 rooms. American Express and Master-Card accepted. Av. Boa Viagem 3722 (phone: 081-326-7225). Expensive.

Miramar – With 120 rooms, this beachfront hotel is also first class, with facilities that include a sauna. Av. 363 Rua dos Navegentes (phone: 081-326-7422). Expensive.

Quatro Rodas–Recife (Olinda) – One of the nicest resorts on the Atlantic coast, this property of the Quatro Rodas chain is just outside Recife, in Olinda. The hotel is most attractive, as are the beachfront grounds, which include a large pool with snackbar and refreshments. Rooms face the sea, and the service is attentive, with a mostly English-speaking staff. Hotel boutiques offer unusually good selections. Av. José Augusto Moreira 2200 (phone: 081-431-2955). Expensive.

JOÃO PESSOA

Tambaú – The best in town, right on the beach. All 110 rooms have a private bath, with air conditioning, TV, radio. Hotel has great restaurant, pool, bar. All credit cards. Av. Alm. Tamandare 229 (phone: 083-226-3660). Expensive.

CAMPINA GRANDE

Rique Palace – 41 rooms have private shower, TV. Hotel has bar and restaurant. No credit cards. Venancio Neiva 287. Moderate.

Ouro Branco – The 60 rooms have private baths, TV, radio. Bar and restaurant. No credit cards. Rua Cor. João Lourenco Portoa 20. Moderate.

NATAL

Ducal – Tall, round modern hotel in the center of downtown. A quick cab ride gets you to the beach. Av. Rio Branco 634 (phone: 084-222-4612). Expensive.

Reis Magos – Great location overlooking the ocean. Has good restaurant, pool, bar, nightclub. All 61 rooms have private baths, TV, air conditioning. All credit cards. Av. Cafe Filho 882 (phone: 084-222-2055). Expensive.

FORTALEZA

Imperial Othon Palace – Very modern. The 117 rooms have private baths, music, TV, air conditioning. The hotel has a bar, pool, restaurant, and nightclub. Accepts Credicard, Elo. Av. Pres. Kennedy 2500 (phone: 085-224-7777). Expensive.

Colonial Praia – Comfortable 40 rooms with private baths, bar, restaurant, sauna, pool. Rua Bar. de Aracati 145 (phone: 085-244-3333). Expensive.

Esplanada Praia – This is a new, modern 244-room property with balconies overlooking the sea. The hotel also has two pools. Av. Pres. Kennedy 2000 (phone: 085-224-8555). Expensive.

Beira-Mar – A pleasant hotel on the main drag. The pool and outdoor restaurant are good for people watching. Av. Pres. Kennedy 3130. Moderate.

São Pedro – One of the best in town. Has great restaurant, bar, pool, hairdresser, and 102 rooms with private showers. All credit cards. Rua Castro e Silva 81 (phone: 085-211-9911). Moderate.

Iracema Plaza – On the beach. Good restaurant, bar, hairdresser. All 76 rooms have private showers. Av. Pres. Kennedy 746. Moderate.

TERESINA

Luxor Hotel do Piauí – First-class hotel. All 87 rooms have private baths, air conditioning, TV, music. Facilities include good restaurant, bar, pool. All credit cards. Praça Mar. Deodoro 310. Expensive.

Terezina Palace – 95 comfortable rooms have private showers, air conditioning, TV. Has a bar-restaurant. Rua Paissandu 1219. Inexpensive.

SÃO LUÍS

São Luís Quatro Rodas – Very exclusive. The 112 rooms have private baths, TV, music, refrigerator, and air conditioning. Has top restaurant, bar, nightclub, pool, hair salon. All credit cards. Praia do Calhau (phone: 098-227-0244). Expensive.

Vila Rica – Near the old colonial section of the city, this comfortable hotel offers easy access to cobblestone streets along which you'll find museums and "hidden-away" restaurants. The hotel itself has a coffee shop, sauna, and hairdresser. Praça Dom Pedro II 299 (phone: 098-222-4455). Expensive to moderate.

Central – Simple hotel. The 108 rooms are available with a variety of bathroom facilities. Has a restaurant, bar. Av. Dom Pedro II 258 (phone: 098-222-5644). Inexpensive.

Lord – The 59 rooms have varying service. No restaurant. Rua Joaquim Tavora 258 (phone: 098-222-5544). Inexpensive.

Rio de Janeiro to Belo Horizonte

The 290-mile (464-km) route from Rio de Janeiro to Belo Horizonte is one of the most scenic and historic in South America. Starting at Avenida Brasil in Rio, BR-040 winds its way through tropical and subtropical flora and spectacular mountains to the nineteenth-century "imperial" city of Petrópolis (pop. 240,000), 40 miles (64 km) from Rio and 2,748 feet above sea level.

In Petrópolis you can already see the odd mixture of tropical, subtropical, and even temperate-zone flora that excited the scientific interest of Brazil's great post-independence ruler Dom Pedro II. From Petrópolis to Belo Horizonte is another 250 miles (400 km) of increasingly temperate but continuously mountainous terrain. Crossing the border between the states of Rio de Janeiro and Minas Gerais just after Três Rios, 50 miles (80 km) from Petrópolis, you enter the industrial region around Juiz de Fora. Approaching the state capital of Belo Horizonte, the land begins to take on the iron-red color that is typical of Minas Gerais (which means literally General Mines), one of the great mineral centers of the world.

A recent estimate placed the state's iron ore reserves at an astounding 38½ billion tons, but Minas Gerais also produces nickel, tin, chrome, silver, gold, and diamonds. The state's fabulous mineral production and processing industry is also of interest to tourists, since metalwork handicrafts as well as precious and semiprecious stones are traditionally good buys.

In the hilly, red-tinted Serra da Mantiqueira region between Juiz de Fora and Belo Horizonte, a distance of 150 miles (240 km), lies one of Brazil's most important historical treasures, the Old Minas region, which includes the colonial cities of Ouro Preto, São João Del Rei, Tiradentes, Congonhas, and Mariana, preserved for the benefit of historians and tourists.

It was in 1695 that gold was first discovered in Minas Gerais, which led, in the eighteenth century, to the first significant development of the state. Many of the cities and towns of Old Minas trace their beginnings to the time of the gold rush and to the long period of prosperity that followed. It was also here in 1789 that a group of merchants, clergymen, and planters plotted the famous Inconfidência Mineira (independence movement), one of the first colonial revolts against the Portuguese crown. The political leader, Joaquim da Silva Xavier, better known as Tiradentes (literally "tooth-puller," for he was a dentist), was arrested and executed in Rio de Janeiro. Tiradentes is one of the great heroes of Brazilian history, and his name is used liberally for towns, plazas, and roads throughout the state.

In more contemporary times the state of Minas Gerais (Brazilians usually say simply "Minas") has served as one of the political and economic capitals of Brazil, supplying the nation with presidents, artists, and some of the nation's most distinguished bankers. The people of Minas, with their distinctive accent, are regarded by other Brazilians as being somewhat stubborn and tenacious, although extremely courteous and intelligent.

The state is also one of the most important artistic centers of the nation. In Ouro Preto, Congonhas, and the other towns of Old Minas, some of the best-preserved and most important works of Brazil's baroque and rococo periods in art, sculpture, and architecture can be seen. Particularly noteworthy are the world-famous sculptures of Antônio Francisco Lisboa, known as Aleijadinho ("the Little Cripple"), whose eighteenth-century religious works are among the highlights of any visit to Brazil. Belo Horizonte, on the other hand, is more modern. During a characteristically energetic urban renewal campaign in the early 1940s, Belo Horizonte's mayor, Juscelino Kubitschek (who served as Brazil's president from 1956 to 1961), commissioned world-famous architect Oscar Niemeyer to design a number of structures in the city's Pampulha District that still today seem futuristic.

The highway from Rio to Petrópolis is extremely steep, but the road is new, and conditions are generally good. The entire route from Rio to Juiz de Fora has been widened to four lanes and provides good driving conditions. After Juiz de Fora, the highway has two lanes and passes through mountains for its entire length, although it is not as steep as the initial Rio-Petrópolis segment.

The best local tourist guide to the region is the trilingual — English, Portuguese, Spanish — *Guia Quatro Rodas,* which includes detailed information on routes, attractions, and accommodations for the entire country. It can be purchased at newsstands for about $5.

PETRÓPOLIS: This historic 19th-century city (named after Brazil's two emperors, both named Pedro) lies 40 miles (64 km) west of Rio de Janeiro on the well-paved but sinuous highway BR-040. At an altitude of 2,748 feet, the city is noted for its moderate climate and rich flora.

Petrópolis was founded in 1843 by Dom Pedro II, the second emperor of Brazil, and its earliest settlers were Germans. A number of street and district names — Westfalia, Bingen, and Darmstadt — still reflect this heritage. During the latter part of his 49-year reign, Emperor Pedro II used the city as his summer residence. It was here in 1889 that the liberal monarch was first informed that Brazil's First Republic had been proclaimed in Rio de Janeiro. He left the city for the last time in November of that year and died in exile in France two years later. Since 1940, his summer palace has been an official historical site, and in 1947 it was the meeting place for the signing of the Hemispheric Mutual Assistance Treaty — the historic "Rio Pact," which has aligned US and Latin American military and political interests ever since.

The junction of the Petrópolis-Teresópolis bypass road and BR-040, 7 miles (11 km) outside the city, affords a spectacular view of the tropical valleys below and the heights of the Serra Fluminense ahead. After reaching the plateau a few miles beyond, the road approaches the first important suburb of Petrópolis, Quitandinha, the site of the memorable, Normandy-style *Quitandinha Club*. Once one of the most elegant hotels in the world, the picture-postcard structure is now a private club.

Busy Avenida Quincede Novembro is the heart of Petrópolis. On the west side is the emperor's lushly overgrown Botanic Gardens, and just beyond, on Avenida 7 de Setembro, is the Imperial Palace. Open from noon to 5 PM every day except Monday, the interior of the palace has been faithfully preserved as its last occupant left it. The major attraction is the room that houses Pedro's crown — a remarkable work of craftsmanship that sparkles with 77 pearls and 629 diamonds. Across the street is the private residence of the Braganza family, the legitimate heirs to the Brazilian throne.

Up the street from the palace is the Catedral de São Pedro de Alcântara on Avenida Tiradentes, a Gothic cathedral that is Pedro I's burial site. Farther up the road, beyond the turnoff to Itaipava, is the Crystal Palace, erected by the royal family for musical and horticultural exhibitions. The entire glass and metal structure was imported from France in pieces and assembled in Brazil.

Also worth seeing are the Santos Dumont House, a museum on Avenida Robertó Silveira, and the castle-like Weapons Museum, on BR-040 12 miles (19 km) from the city on the Rio side. Largely forgotten outside Brazil, Santos Dumont was the father of Brazilian aviation, one of the most important inventors and daredevils of the early days of flying. His home, built in 1918, features a collection of aviation relics and memorabilia. The Weapons Museum is noted for its collection of early military hardware as well as for its commanding valley view.

En Route from Petrópolis – Six miles (10 km) beyond Petrópolis on BR-040 is *Tarrafa's Churrascaría*, which features reasonably priced barbecue dishes according to the traditional Brazilian *rodizio* plan ("running skewer" — all you can eat of a variety of meats) and, at night, entertainment by nationally known musicians. On the highway 2 miles before *Tarrafa's*, look for the turnoff to *Florilândia* on Rua Barão do Rio Branco, a marvelous, almost hidden rose garden with an alpine-style restaurant and a well-stocked but high-priced gift shop.

Another 13 miles (21 km) down BR-040 is Itaipava, a small town noted for its good buys in ceramics and home decorations. Itaipava marks the junction of BR-040 and BR-486, the northern cutoff that extends 25 miles (40 km) through magnificent scenery to the city of Teresópolis, in the heart of Serra dos Orgãos National Park.

TERESÓPOLIS: With a population of about 98,000, Teresópolis stands at an elevation of little more than 3,000 feet, but it is surrounded by an impressive set of sheer peaks that are collectively known as the Dedos de Deus ("fingers of God"), the highest of which is the 7,422-foot Pedra do Sino. Also notable here is the Von Martius Natural History Museum, inside the park 8 miles (13 km) from the city. Good restaurants include the *São Moritz* (also a hotel), in the park itself, and the *Lararium* (Praça Kennedy 10), in Teresópolis's "upper city." Other restaurants are on Avenida Lúcio Meira downtown. Rugged RJ-130 begins east of the city and runs 66 miles (106 km) to Nova Friburgo.

NOVA FRIBURGO: At 2,778 feet above sea level, Nova Friburgo is the third city of the Serra Fluminense. In both its architectural and its natural setting, Nova Friburgo retains the alpine aspect that first drew Swiss settlers to its picturesque valley in the early 19th century. The city is noted for its mountain scenery and its resorts, which offer sports, mountain climbing, and hiking programs. The highest mountain is the 7,575-foot Pica da Caledônia. A 2,132-foot cable car takes passengers from Praça dos Suspiros downtown to Morro da Cruz, which commands views of the city and countryside. Restaurants are around Praça Getulio Vargas.

En Route from Nova Friburgo – The Petrópolis–Belo Horizonte road continues for another 62 miles (100 km) to the Rio-Minas border, passing a small railroad museum near Paraíba do Sul on the Rio side of the border. After another

27 miles (43 km) of well-paved, four-lane highway you arrive in the industrial city of Juiz de Fora (pop. 300,000) in Minas.

JUIZ DE FORA: Set in a deep valley at an elevation of 2,227 feet, Juiz de Fora can be a good stop for lunch. Try the *Brasão* at Avenida Rio Branco 2262 in the heart of downtown. Mariano Procópio Museum, a former mansion containing a number of Brazilian and European paintings, is set on a swan-graced lake. Its original owner was the engineer who built the first Rio-Petrópolis highway in the 19th century. Three miles (4 km) outside town is a statue of Christ atop the Morro do Imperador similar to the statue in Rio de Janeiro.

En Route from Juiz de Fora – BR-040 is two lanes all the way to Belo Horizonte, a distance of 150 increasingly rugged miles (241 km). Driving at night can be particularly hazardous since reckless truck drivers dominate the road. Beyond Santos Dumont (25 mi/40 km from Juiz), the road begins to climb again until you reach the horticultural center of Barbacena, 50 miles (80 km) from Juiz.

BARBACENA: Nine miles (14 km) before the city lies an area of small rose and chrysanthemum farms that form the basis of a unique export industry. The farms, some of which can be visited on request, produce 150,000 dozen roses a month from October to March. Most of the crop is shipped to Rio in refrigerated trucks; some are sold there, and some are placed in refrigerated containers and flown on to Europe. Every October this city of 86,000 celebrates its major industry with a three-day Rose Festival in Senador Bias Fortes Exposition Park. Worth visiting for a good lunch is the *Grogotó Restaurant* 2 miles (3 km) from town on the main road. The busy spot is completely staffed by service trainees and hence is reasonably priced. In the middle of town, on Praça Dom Bosco, is the Basílica de São José Operario, and in the city's shops you'll find good buys in leather, ceramics, and wood handicrafts.

En Route from Barbacena – A "must" side trip for anyone on this route is a journey into the historic region of Old Minas, accessible via BR-265 to the west of Barbacena. You first come to São João Del Rei, the beginning of the historical and artistic heart of Minas. The rich history of Old Minas is open today to the tourist. The hilly, red-tinted setting is bracing and spectacular. Unlike most of Brazil, the Old Minas region is often quite cool during the winter, with temperatures averaging in the 60s F and sometimes dipping into the 50s or 40s F. During the summer, average temperatures are in the 70s F.

Like most Brazilians, the *mineiros* love to eat, and unique local dishes are served everywhere. The dairy products here are the best in Brazil, originating in the rich pasturelands in the western part of the state. *Feijão tropeiro* (black beans in bean sauce), *frango ao molho pardo* (brown sauce and chicken), and *lombo do porco e torresmo* (luscious pork loin and sauce) are among the most popular.

SÃO JOÃO DEL REI: Famous for its baroque churches, this city of 60,000 is 36 miles (59 km) west of Barbacena, at an altitude of 2,942 feet. Its most notable church is the Igreja de São Francisco de Assis on Praça Frei Orlando, built in 1774. It contains several works by Aleijadinho, and visitors should know that the priests have been known to bar tourists who wear short-sleeved blouses or shorts. Nossa Senhora do Pilar on Rua Getulio Vargas, noted for its gold-encrusted altars, was opened in 1721. Nossa Senhora do Carmo on Praça Carlos Gomes, completed in 1732, includes a small museum. The city is one of the oldest in Minas and has 11 churches in all, but, unlike nearby Tiradentes or Ouro Preto, it has also been penetrated by modern buildings. Good buys here include wood, silver, and tin handicrafts. Eight miles (13 km) away is the Fazenda Pombal, where the patriot Tiradentes was born. An interesting sidelight is the *María Fumaça,* a coal-burning train that runs weekends and holidays to Tiradentes at 10 AM and 2:15 PM from the RFFSA station, Hermilio Alves 366.

TIRADENTES: Nine miles (14 km) from São João Del Rei and 33 miles (53 km) from

Barbacena, this city boasts an almost completely preserved 18th-century façade. Places worth seeing include the baroque Igreja de Nossa Senhora das Mercês on Praça das Mercês and the Tiradentes House on Praça Berço da Liberadade. Some of the churches contain furnishings that were uniquely crafted, without either nails or glue. The city is also noted for its many fountains and is surrounded by picturesque hills.

CONGONHAS: Seventy-two miles (116 km) from São João Del Rei on BR-383 or 60 miles (96 km) from Barbacena on BR-040 is Congonhas, one of the most important cities of Old Minas. With a population of 30,000 and elevation of 3,243 feet, it is the home of the Church of the Good Child Jesus (Sanctuário do Bom Jesus) on Praça da Basílica. Outside the church are famous statues of the *Twelve Prophets,* and inside, 66 sculptures of the Passion of Christ. All the soapstone statues are the work of Aleijadinho, who completed them in his early sixties. The incredible figures seem to come alive as the viewer approaches them, and the graceful esplanade that is the showcase for the *Twelve Prophets* is a work of art in itself. The city is also noted for its festivals, including the annual Aleijandinho Jubilee in the first half of September, but the *Prophets* are the town's main attraction. Other notable churches include Nossa Senhora da Conceição on Praça 7 de Setembro and Rosario on Rua do Rosario.

OURO PRETO: The capital of Old Minas until 1897, Ouro Preto ("black gold") is a perfectly preserved 18th-century colonial city, 60 miles (98 km) from Belo Horizonte or 85 miles (136 km) from Congonhas on the circuitous BR-040 cutoff route. Ouro Preto is the home of some of the most important artistic and historical treasures of Brazil. Begin the journey through Ouro Preto at the Igreja de São Francisco de Assis, the most important church in the city, in the heart of town on Largo de São Francisco. The church contains works by Aleijadinho and his noted associate Ataíde, including the latter's *Glorification of the Blessed Virgin.* Also interesting is the Minerology Museum, formerly the governor's palace, at Praça Tiradentes 20. The palace was finished in 1742 and is now part of the state Minerology School. The baroque church of Nossa Senhora do Carmo, on Rua Costa Sena, includes some of Aleijadinho's last works. The tile paintings there were done by Ataíde. Nossa Senhora de Conceição on Rua Bernardo Vasconcelos is the site of Aleijadinho's tomb and includes a museum annex devoted exclusively to the great artist. Nossa Senhora do Pilar, on Praça Monsenhor Castilho Barbosa not far from the central Praça Tiradentes, houses the city's silver museum whose interiors are rich in gold and silver work. The most imposing museum in town is the Museu da Inconfidência on Praça Tiradentes. Half the sights are open mornings, half afternoons; check at the tourist office.

Ouro Preto is a town to be walked through and savored. In addition to the main attractions, there are countless 18th-century houses and public buildings along the cobbled streets and hills. In 1933 Ouro Preto was declared a historical city, and justly so. It has 13 churches, 11 chapels, 18 fountains, and numerous byways such as Rua São João and Rua Conde de Bobadela, where you'll find the famous *Calabouço Restaurant,* which got its name from the fact that it used to be the city jail (Bobadela 132). The *Casa de Ouvidor,* at Rua Claudio M. da Costa 22, is also a good spot for a meal. Festivals here include several events during July as well as Tiradentes Day (April 21, the date of his execution in 1792) and Holy Week. Another interesting date is April 21, when Ouro Preto becomes the state capital again — for one day. Good buys include soapstone statues at prices much lower than in the big cities.

MARIANA: Only 11 miles (19 km) from Ouro Preto along a steep road, Mariana (pop. 29,000; elevation 2,286 feet) is said to be the oldest town in Minas (founded in 1696). The Igreja de São Francisco de Assis on Praça João Pinheiro includes paintings by Ataíde. The Catedral on Praça Dr. Cláudio Manoel has works by both Aleijadinho and Ataíde and maintains an ancient organ that is operated by a hand bellows. Praça João Pinheiro is also the site of Nossa Senhora do Carmo and of the old Governor's

Palace. The bargains here are in rugs. One of Brazil's few remaining active gold mines is just outside of town.

SABARÁ: Another city on the Old Minas circuit is Sabará, 15 miles (25 km) outside Belo Horizonte off BR-262. From the hilltop just before you reach the town, you'll set a magnificent view of Belo Horizonte and the surrounding countryside. The Igreja Nossa Senhora do Carmo on Rua do Carmo includes works by Aleijadinho, most notably his famous *Four Evangelists.* On a hill overlooking the town is the noted Intendência de Ouro Gold Museum on Rua da Intendência. Rua Pedro II has some of the best colonial homes. Rua Caquende is the site of the legendary Caquende Fountain, but don't sample it: The legend says that those who drink from its waters will never leave Sabará. Below the Gold Museum on Largo de Nossa Senhora de O is the church of the same name, displaying an uncanny Oriental influence. Holy Week in Sabará is especially festive.

BELO HORIZONTE: The state capital of Minas since 1897, Belo is one of the great cities of Brazil and the first to be completely planned and built from scratch in the country's interior. The city also went through a significant facelift in the 1940s during the administration of Mayor Juscelino Kubitschek. The two most important changes were the creation of an industrial park in the Contagem District and the opening of a modernistic park area around Pampulha. Downtown Belo Horizonte is a busy financial and administrative center, with the Municipal Park (bordered by Avenida Afonso Pena, the city's main street, and Alameida Ezequiel Dias) as its heart. Overlooking the park is the *Othon Palace* hotel. The park is noted for its 2,000 varieties of trees, its beautiful gardens and ponds, and a Sunday morning arts and crafts fair that offers bargains in all types of handicrafts. Tree-lined avenues radiate from the park.

A few blocks away is the Praça de Liberdade, the Governor's Palace, and the city's library. The approach to the plaza is impressively lined with royal palms. Important churches in downtown Belo include Nossa Senhora de Lourdes on Rua Espírito Santo, featuring attractive stained-glass windows; and the nearby Nossa Senhora de Boa Viagem, which has a plant fair and sale every Saturday. In sharp contrast to this part of downtown Belo is its modernistic Pampulha District, 7 miles (12 km) outside town around a beautiful lake. The setting there is dominated by the new Governor Magalhães Pinto Stadium — known locally as Minerão. The stadium is understood to be the second largest in the world (surpassed by the Maracanã in Rio de Janeiro), seating 110,000 noisy soccer fans. On another part of the lake is the famed Igreja de São Francisco de Assis. Its rounded surfaces portend the stylistic breakthroughs made later by its architect, Oscar Niemeyer, when he designed Brasília. Inside are works by Brazil's great 20th-century artist Candido Portinari. Other notable structures include the Casa do Baile and the Modern Art Museum, both designed by Niemeyer as well. Slightly removed from this area is the city zoo and, on the opposite side of the lake, the Pampulha Airport. The entire district was laid out and landscaped by another noted Brazilian artist, Burle Marx, who also participated in the design of Brasília some 15 years later. The Art Museum, incidentally, was a gambling casino until gambling was outlawed in Brazil in 1947.

BEST EN ROUTE

This region of scenic towns and panoramic views is fast becoming a heavily traveled route for both Brazilian and foreign tourists, so there are modern, sophisticated hotels. You should try to make advance reservations during the summer, December-March, especially in the smaller towns, that do not have many places to stay. Hotels listed as expensive will cost $50 per night and up; moderate, $25-$45 per night; and inexpensive, usually under $25.

PETRÓPOLIS

Casa do Sol – Just outside the city, this hotel has a nice view, a swimming pool, and sauna. Estrada Rio, Quitandinha 115 (phone: 43-5062). Expensive.

Margaridas – Good food and accommodations with pool. Rua Monsenhor Bacelar 274 (42-4686). Moderate.

NOVA FRIBURGO

Bucsky – Good food, pool, sports, horseback riding. Nova Friburgo–Niteroi Hwy. (RJ-116), 3 miles (5 km) from city. Call 252-5053 in Rio de Janeiro. Expensive.

Sans Souci – Good restaurant, sports, pool, horseback riding and movies. Jardim Sans Souci, 1 mile from city (phone: 22-77-52; in Rio de Janeiro, 239-2089). Expensive.

Mury Garden – Good restaurant, pool, boutique, horseback riding. Credit cards accepted. Nova Friburgo–Niterói Hwy., 5 miles (8 km) from city (phone: 5222; in Rio de Janeiro, 224-7435). Moderate.

Camping CCB – Comfortable camping facilities with exceptional natural beauty. Nova Friburgo, Niteroí Hwy. (RJ-08), km 69. Inexpensive.

JUIZ DE FORA

Imperial – A simple hotel, with restaurant. Rua Batista de Oliveria 605 (phone: 212-7400). Moderate.

BARBACENA

Grogotó Senac – Highly recommended, the *Grogotó* is both a hotel and a restaurant, and is staffed by hotel and restaurant students from government training programs. Service is excellent and it's hard to get a table. BR-040, km 699, 2 miles from the city (phone: 331-4111). Moderate.

SAO JOÃO DEL REI

Novotel Pôrto Real – This pleasant hotel has a restaurant featuring international cuisine. Brazilian credit cards accepted. Av. Eduardo Magalhães 254 (phone: 371-1201). Moderate.

TERESÓPOLIS

São Moritz – Good food, pool, sports facilities, and boutique. At km 41 of the Teresópolis–Nova Friburgo Hwy. (RJ-130), 16 miles (26 km) from the city. Reservations can be made in Rio de Janeiro by calling 265-7991. Expensive.

Caxanga – A pleasant hotel with restaurant, pool, and sports facilities. Rua Caxanga 68 (phone: 742-1062; in Rio de Janeiro, 240-9122). Moderate.

TIRADENTES

Alpina – A chalet-style hotel, with pool, tennis courts, sauna, and a restaurant serving German food. At km 3, Bila Imbui (phone: 742-5252).

Solar da Ponte – Recommended, but has no restaurant. The address is simply Praça das Mercês; to phone, just dial 10. Moderate.

OURO PRETO

Luxor Pousada Ouro Preto – Historic hotel converted from a colonial mansion, with simple, rustically furnished, air-conditioned rooms with refrigerator and phone; popular restaurant and bar. Praça Antonio Dias 10 (phone: 031-551-2244). Expensive.

Grande Hotel Ouro Preto – Lodgings but not the restaurant recommended. Built in modern style by famed South American architect Oscar Niemeyer. Major credit cards accepted. Rua Senador Rocha Lagoa 164 (phone: 551-1488). Moderate.

Pouso Chico Rei – A colonial home converted into a 4-room hotel, but without a restaurant. Highly recommended. Accepts Brazilian credit cards. Rua Brigadeiro Mosqueira 90 (phone: 551-1274). Moderate.

BELO HORIZONTE

Brasilton Contagem – Newest hotel in the area (an affiliate of Hilton International), with 145 rooms in a resort setting 9 miles out of town; pool, health club, entertainment. Rod. Fernao Dias, CP 2220 (phone: 031-351-0900). Expensive.

Del Rey – Considered one of the best hotels in town, it includes shops, convention room, and restaurant. Accepts Brazilian credit cards. Praça Afonso Arinos 60, downtown (phone: 222-2211). Expensive.

Horsa Excelsior – A 250-room property in the center of town, but quiet; panoramic rooftop restaurant and bar. Rua Caetes 753 (phone: 031-201-2600). Expensive.

Othon Palace – The newest unit in the Othon chain, opened late in 1978. Features complete hotel services and a view of the city's park. Major credit cards accepted. Av. Afonso Pena 1050 (phone: 031-226-7844). Expensive.

Normandy – Noted for its fine restaurant. Accepts Brazilian credit cards. Rua Tamoios 212, downtown (phone: 201-6166). Moderate.

Belo Horizonte to Brasília

From Belo Horizonte to Brasília there is a long stretch of relatively new road built to link the new inland capital with the rest of the country. While the 472-mile (740-km) trip can be made in 12 to 14 hours with few stops, you have to make some lengthy detours to see the main sights.

Route BR-040 takes you diagonally across the state of Minas Gerais (shortened to "Minas" by residents), one of the most historically important areas in Brazil and the center of vast mineral deposits. From Belo Horizonte the terrain is mountainous, with peaks of 9,000 feet that contain the state's valuable deposits of iron ore, gold, limestone, manganese, and bauxite. This is Brazil's hottest and driest region, where temperatures of 100°F (38°C) are common during the dry season (May to November) and unpredictable torrential downpours cause extensive flash-flooding.

In 1698, gold was discovered in Minas by explorers from São Paulo, starting a great influx of Brazilian and Portuguese settlers in search of quick wealth. In the early 1700s, large quantities of diamonds were found in what is now the city of Diamantina, north of Belo Horizonte. In the next hundred years, the mines in this state yielded over 3 million karats of diamonds and 100 tons of gold. The mineral reserves were so important to the Brazilian economy that in 1763 the capital was moved from Salvador to Rio de Janeiro, the main port and access route to Minas. Today, iron ore is the source of wealth for the state, accounting for 10% of Brazil's total exports. Although the amount has greatly diminished, gold and diamonds are still mined there as well as semiprecious stones, such as topaz, aquamarine, and tourmaline.

En Route from Belo Horizonte – Instead of taking the main highway, BR-040, north from Belo Horizonte, you might consider making a visit to Gruta de

Lapinha and Gruta de Maquiné, two of the 400 caves in the whole of Minas. Take the road from Belo Horizonte to Vespianino and Lagoa Santa. The first group of caves is at Gruta de Lapinha, only 25 miles (40 km) from the city. The caves themselves, with colorful stalactites and stalagmites, are open from 9 AM to 5 PM. At the nearby town of Lagoa Santa there is a lake with a sandy beach and good camping facilities. *Praia Bar* (Av. Getulida Vargas 8) is a good place to eat. From Lagoa Santa you can continue directly to Diamantina, almost a must for the traveler going to Brasília.

DIAMANTINA: This town, as its name suggests, was the very center of Brazil's diamond mining industry and is well worth a visit. You may find that while Diamantina is probably the best-preserved colonial town in Brazil, it does not have the splendor of Ouro Preto (see *Rio de Janeiro to Belo Horizonte*). This town of 36,000 is the birthplace of Juscelino Kubitschek, builder of Brasília. The town's economy still centers around the mining and processing of semiprecious stones, and these are good buys if you know quality. There is a Museum of Popular Art (Praça Juscelino Kubitschek 10), part of the city public library. There are several good hotels and restaurants, including *Xica da Silva,* specializing in regional cooking, on the ground floor of the *Dalia Hotel* (Praça Juscelino Kubitschek 13).

En Route from Diamantina – You must return to the main Belo Horizonte–Brasília highway to reach the federal capital. The road passes just below the hydroelectric dam that contains the waters of the Rio São Francisco to form Tres Marias Lake. The small town of Pirapora, 200 miles (320 km) from Belo, is the next stopping place, a point where the river becomes navigable. Here the wood-burning, paddlewheel riverboats end their inland journey of 6 or 7 days from Juazeiro in Bahía.

BRASÍLIA: Since the beginning of the 19th century, successive Brazilian governments have planned to move the federal capital to the central plateau. But it was only with the government of Juscelino Kubitschek in the late 1950s that the dream became a reality. The former capital, Rio de Janeiro, had become so overcrowded that enlarging the various ministries was physically impossible. An equally important reason for moving the capital inland was to develop the interior of this immense country, where to this day 80% of its 131 million people live within 50 miles of the seacoast. It was felt that the new location would start people looking inland for their inspiration instead of toward Europe or North America.

In Brazil, where until recently governments changed every four years, a president has had to move quickly to ensure that a project be near enough completion so that it cannot be abandoned by his successor. Kubitschek, born in the state of Minas (which would most benefit from the building of Brasília), started the project with the construction of BR-040 to the site of Brasília. To ensure the inauguration of the city during his presidency, Kubitschek got the buildings up as rapidly as possible; today some of the original buildings of the city are already showing serious signs of age and the forced timetable of building. Many have had to be partially rebuilt due to flaws such as cracking cement. Sidewalks have been replaced and roads rebuilt.

Brasília is designed for tours by car; it is almost impossible to see it on foot. It has been built on the principle that there is plenty of space that should all be used, resulting in long distances between buildings. The contest to design the city was won by Lucio Costa, who laid it out in the shape of an airplane, spacing residential districts out along the "wings" and the major government buildings on the "fuselage." The well-known Brazilian architect Oscar Niemeyer designed the major public buildings, including the National Theater and the houses of government. The major commercial districts — including banks, hotels, office buildings, cinemas, and shops — are at the intersection of the "wings" and the "fuselage," near the busy Brasília bus station.

Flying into Brasília, you have a very good panoramic view of the city, spreading out in a sort of giant bowl with the artificial Lake Paranoa as a backdrop. If you are arriving by car, you come upon a city that looks like an enormous oasis — a mirage that you cannot believe is true, especially after the very long and rather tedious drive from Belo Horizonte. As you approach, the first signs of habitation are the new lots marked for development on the fringes of the city; building within the confines of Brasília itself is strictly limited. The original area of the city — the Pilot Plan, as it is called — is completely developed now, and there are almost as many residents on the outskirts of Brasília as there are in the city proper.

Coming from Minas, you enter the city itself at the southern tip. To get to the center where the hotels are, there are several routes to choose from. The fastest way is to travel along the Eixo Monumental, but you can follow the Avenida das Nações (Avenue of the Nations) if you wish to pass closer to the lake and see the elegant embassies that line its shore. The street numbering and names are quite confusing to the newcomer, but once the code has been deciphered, getting around the city is very easy indeed. Brasília is divided into a series of blocks running from the center to each "wing" tip: They go from 1 to 16. This number forms the last two digits of a three-digit locating number. The first digit indicates where buildings lie on several parallel roads. There are also letter symbols for each of the various central districts. SHS, for example, is Setor Hotelera Sul, the hotel area in the southern "wing." SCS is Setor Commercial Sul, the southern commercial sector. All the hotels are in the same area and all business is done within one very small area, which does simplify locating the buildings. After selecting a hotel, make a quick tour of the city to get your bearings.

The easiest course is to drive around the Eixo Monumental (Monumental Axis), a one-way route where virtually all the buildings of importance and interest in central Brasília lie. Leaving your hotel, drive north along the axis, following the signs to Palacio Burity. The whole city is linked by fast expressways, and there are very few intersections with traffic signals to slow you down.

The first major building is the 600-foot-tall Torre de Televisão (television tower), in the very center of the axis near the bus station. This is one of the tallest communications towers in the world; you can take an express elevator to a viewing platform 225 feet above the ground. Another elevator takes visitors to a restaurant and bar with a panoramic view of the city. At the highest level you can see as far as the horizon. This is one of the best places for you to get an idea of Brasília's layout. The best time to visit the tower is near sunset, when the whole city and the surrounding areas are illuminated with a beautiful golden light. It is the perfect time to take color photographs of the downtown area, stretched away from the tower to the Praça dos Tres Poderes (Square of the Three Powers), where the congressional buildings, the president's palace, and other major administrative buildings are located. Because Brasília is not yet overcrowded by tourists, the TV tower is seldom busy. On the distant horizon you may see columns of smoke rising where areas of scrubland are being cleared for new building projects. At the foot of the TV tower on Saturdays, Sundays, and public holidays, a handicraft fair is held, with articles from all of Brazil for sale. Particularly good buys are handmade leather shoes and sandals, glasswear, metal and semiprecious stones, jewelry, leather, furniture, and baskets. You will also find the famous dried flowers of Brasília, although a better selection is available daily on the square in front of the cathedral.

The next building of interest on the axis is the convention and leisure center, completed in 1979, with an auditorium for 2,000 delegates and other conference facilities. But part of this building is now also open to the general public, thereby providing the large public gathering place that has been absent so long in Brasília. There is a large recreation area with a tree-lined "lovers meeting area," complete with an open-air bar and dance floor. The city's planetarium is part of this complex, which has a number of pools and waterfalls — particularly welcome in a city that is bone dry most of the year.

Opposite the convention center is Brasília's sports area, with a soccer stadium with seating for 100,000 spectators and a gymnasium. Nearby is a motor racetrack. On the axis at Praça do Cruzeiro is the recently constructed Juscelino Kubitschek monument in honor of the capital's founder.

Continuing on the axis to its end, the last building is the railway station, one of the select buildings designed by architect Oscar Niemeyer. At this point, turn around and head back on the southern side of the axis road. Leaving the TV tower on the left, the road passes beside the Estação Rodoviária (bus station). This dilapidated building is worth a visit because it is the point of arrival and departure for the majority of Brasília's residents, who have come far to live here. Here you see the city as it really is. Long-distance buses arrive and depart for the distant Northeast, Amazonas, and the more civilized southeast. Some of the vehicles, many of which are old and battered, will be traveling on rough direct roads for the next 48 hours or more, running through deep mud in the rainy season. If you do not want to drive around the city by car anymore, you can take the city bus to points of interest. With few exceptions, all the bus lines in Brasília start and finish here, and there are some circular trips that take you around the city. Buses marked "Três Poderes Universidade de Brasília" (Brazilian University), "Avenida das Nações" (Avenue of the Nations), and "Aeroporto" (Airport) are among the most interesting. Also in the bus station is one of the stores run by FUNAI, the Indian foundation. Here you can purchase pottery, baskets, bows and arrows, musical instruments (notably flutes), and ornaments. These latter are generally made from fish scales and bones as well as from a wide range of berries and nuts from the forest, feathers, and butterfly wings, all at very reasonable prices. The Tourist Office is also in the bus station, adjacent to the Indian shop. The staff will make hotel reservations for the visitor in need of a room as well as provide maps and guides to the city.

Continuing past the bus station toward the Três Poderes, the first major building is the Cathedral of Brasília. This building is in the form of a crown of thorns, and the nave is below ground. The roof is surrounded by water, making this one of the many places in Brasília where the visitor may find relief from the dry, hot city. Before reaching the main circular nave you still follow a darkened passage called the Passage of Reflection. The St. Peter statue, suspended from the roof, is one of the main features in this light and airy structure. The marble altar and marble blocks spaced around the nave for temporary seating are prominent features in the rather stark but restful interior. The glass panels of the roof reflect the water in the surrounding pool, and the buildings of the city beyond shimmer in the pool's reflection.

Proceeding farther down the axis, the foreign ministry, Itamarati Palace, the last of these buildings on the way to the Three Powers Square, should not be missed. This is one of Brasília's most notable buildings, rising out of beautiful water gardens that hold Brasília's best-known and most-photographed piece of sculpture, the Meteor. In the Itamarati Palace is one of the best collections of Brazilian art, including magnificent paintings by Portinari, Brazil's major painter. Register at the reception desk a day before visiting. In the center of the Monumental Axis just below Itamarati Palace are the Congress buildings, comprised of the House of Deputies, the Senate, and the various offices housed in a huge, marble-coated tower, also rising out of the lake. These buildings can be visited by arrangement, between 10 AM and 4 PM. Black and white swans glide peacefully on the lake.

Behind the Congress is the actual square of the Three Powers. On one side is the Planalto Palace, the office of the president; the other holds the Supreme Court. There are several important pieces of sculpture on the square, including the *Two Warriors* and a statue of justice. There is also a curious-shaped dovecote, the home of hundreds of pigeons. The birds can sometimes be persuaded to fly in the right direction for taking interesting photographs of the buildings in the foreground. The Planalto Palace (Uplands Palace) is one of the most graceful buildings in Brasília, its roof supported by one of the several varieties of marble pillars that are the hallmark of the Brasília architecture. Changing-of-the-guard ceremonies take place in front of the palace on Mondays and Thursdays at 8:30 AM and 5:30 PM.

Just below Three Powers Square is the capital's giant flagstaff, a controversial structure of steel that rises 300 feet from the ground and holds a massive 3,000-square-foot flag. On the first Sunday of each month, the flag is lowered and replaced by a new one, donated by the governors of each of Brazil's 22 states in turn. From this end of the Monumental Axis, the visitor can either turn around and travel back up the axis, visiting the buildings on the other side, or make a short drive to the president's residence, the Alvorada (Dawn) Palace, one of the most beautiful buildings in Brasília. Designed by Niemeyer and set on the banks of Paranoa Lake, it cannot be visited, but you can get a good view from the main gates. En route to the palace, you pass one of the best restaurants in the city, *Churascaría do Lago* (*Lake Barbecue*). At this restaurant the usual procedure is to have a *rodizio* meal, where you pay a set price and are served assorted barbecued cuts of beef, chicken, and sausage as well as plates of assorted salads, rice, vegetables, and garnishings. The price for this typical meal ranges between $4 and $6, a very good value. *Rodizio,* however, should be avoided if you just want a light meal. There are other clubs on the lakeside, usually restricted to members, but several are housed in spectacular buildings, notably those of the various armed forces. On the way back to the Monumental Axis, you should next stop at the Palácio da Justiça (Ministry of Justice), another of Niemeyer's structures. This building is remarkable because of the huge water shoots emerging from its walls at different levels and cascading to a delightful water garden below. This building, its water gardens, and vegetation are open to the public Tuesdays thruogh Fridays, 9 to 11 AM and 2 to 5 PM.

At the intersection of the avenue with the main east-west throughway is the Teatro Nacional (National Theater). This building was left unfinished for many years, but its three auditoriums, restaurant, and exhibition area opened to the public in March 1979. It has one of the finest stages in the country in its main auditorium, and the building itself, shaped like an elongated Aztec pyramid, is one of the most interesting in the city. The new rooftop restaurant is one of Brasília's most attractive and inviting eating places, comparable to the TV tower restaurant.

The Galeria dos Estados (Gallery of States) is a section of town that can only be seen on foot. It links the central commercial district of business buildings with the banking district and has shops for each of Brazil's 22 states. This 200-yard-long mall has displays of handicrafts at reasonable prices. The most beautiful wares are from Pernambuco, Ceará, Maranhão, Pará, and Bahía. The Ceará shop has good buys on hammocks and handmade lace. The Amazon state of Pará has some of Brazil's most interesting pottery, which has its roots in Indian designs. Other states whose stores are especially good are those of Rio Grande do Norte, Maranhão (for baskets), Mato Grosso, and Goiás, Brasília's home state.

Several impressive buildings are nearby, including the huge bulk of the Banco Central (Central Bank), completed in 1979. This building has a money museum on the first floor, is shaped in the design of a doubloon, and is the largest structure in Brasília.

There are three drives around the city that are worth taking. One is along Avenida das Nações where the majority of the foreign embassies have been built on land donated to each country by the Brazilian government. Competition to build an outstanding structure has produced some delightful variations in architecture. It all depends on one's taste, but the Spanish and some of the Middle Eastern and Asian embassies all have been called the best.

If time permits, a fun trip in Brasília is the drive around Lake Paranoa, a 50-mile (80-km) excursion. On the far side of the lake are some of the most impressive individual homes, where the very wealthy and foreign ambassadors live. There is also a dam that holds back the waters of the artificial lake. The Dom Bosco Chapel, near the dam, is a nice place from which to view the city outline rising up from the lake.

The University of Brasília has many notable buildings of futuristic, even extravagant, architecture. These include the main library and lecture hall, which are nicknamed "the worm" because they are almost a quarter-mile long and curve unevenly. If you are interested in architecture, the refectory and the exact science faculty are worth a visit.

A visit to Brasília would not be complete without a short visit to the superquadro residential area. Brasília was designed so that a group of blocks of flats, none of which can be more than six floors high, would have all facilities available to residents, thereby avoiding travel to other areas for necessities. Each block has a school, shops and restaurants, and other utility buildings within easy reach of all the complexes. Each block, sometimes with dozen or so in a group, forms a superquadro. There are also gardens and play areas between each block. The access of vehicles is controlled so that the whole area is safe for children's play, something that is especially welcome to Brazilians from crowded cities. If you do not want to stay in a hotel in Brasília, there is a large campsite behind the sports area and the motor racetrack. Rogerio Puthon Park is a favorite spot for picnickers, and there are other sporting facilities, including a swimming pool with a wave-making machine for those nostalgic for the beaches of Copacabana, Ipanema, and Flamengo.

From Brasília, you can drive to Salvador in the Northeast or to the less-developed state of Mato Grosso in the west.

BEST EN ROUTE

There are few hotels of any note before Brasília, but the federal city itself has modern facilities in all price ranges, built within the last 20 years in either the Southern or Northern Hotel District. While not as luxurious as the tourist hotels of resort areas (few contain pools and other recreational facilities), they are on the whole modern and efficient. Hotels listed as expensive will cost $50 per night and up for a double room; moderate, $30–$45 per night; and inexpensive, below $30.

DIAMANTINA

Tijuco – The best in town, with a bar, restaurant, private showers. Major credit cards. Rua Macau de Meio 211 (phone: 031-222-2268). Moderate.

Dália – Small hotel with restaurant, television, and private showers. Praça Juscelino Kubitschek 13. Inexpensive.

Grande – Another small hotel with a restaurant. Rua da Quitanda 70. Inexpensive.

PIRAPORA

Canoeiros – Moderately comfortable hotel near the river. Av. Salmeron 3. Inexpensive.

BRASÍLIA

Nacional – Brasília's best hotel, with prices to match, it has a nightclub, good restaurants, swimming pool, air conditioning, sauna, hairdressers. Beneath it is one of the city's best shopping arcades. Major credit cards accepted. Southern Hotel Sector (phone: 061-226-8180). Very expensive.

Carlton – Facilities include fine, top-class health club, bar and restaurant. Southern Hotel Sector (phone: 061-224-8819). Expensive.

Eron Brasília – One of Brasília's most spectacular hotels, with an elevator made of glass for a good view of the city outside. All 203 rooms have air conditioning and refrigerators. Other features are a hairdressing salon and nightclub. Major credit cards accepted. Northern Hotel Sector (phone: 061-226-2125). Expensive.

Torre Palace – One of Brasília's better hotels, with swimming pool and refrigerators in each of the 160 rooms. Southern Hotel Sector. Expensive.

Americas – Modern hotel with 154 rooms, all with air conditioning and refrigerator. Major credit cards accepted. Southern Hotel Sector. Moderate.

Aracoara – A comfortable hotel with 165 rooms, all air conditioned and with refrigerators. Southern Hotel Sector. Moderate.

Aristus – A small hotel with 50 rooms. Near the Conjunto Nacional shopping center, Northern Hotel Sector. No credit cards. Inexpensive.

El Pilar – A very basic but comfortable hotel, with 70 rooms. Northern Hotel Sector. No credit cards. Inexpensive.

Planalto – A simple hotel with few facilities. Major credit cards accepted. Southern Hotel Sector. Inexpensive.

Brasília to Cuiabá: The Mato Grosso

Traveling from Brasília to Cuiabá through the Central West region of the Federal District — the states of Goiás, Mato Grosso, and Mato Grosso do Sul — is like weaving through a time warp. The area holds much of human history, combining the futuristic capital and Stone Age Indians, satellite stations and wild frontier towns like those of pre-1900 Texas, *artesanatos,* or handicraft fairs and remnants of the colonial Portuguese past, luxurious hot spring spas, primeval swamps, and forests untouched by man.

The 700-mile (1,147-km) route west across this region of striking contrasts begins 3,500 feet above sea level on the red earth of the central plateau that covers much of the territory. In Goiás, the terrain slopes gently in alternating levels of hilly plateau, scrub-grass flatlands, and tropical riverbeds carved by the many tributaries that flow north to the Amazon or south to the Paraná–La Plata system. At the eastern border of Mato Grosso the route crosses the Rio Araguaia before climbing to the plateau, where the elevation offsets the heat of the latitude. Near Rondonópolis the road begins a final descent to Cuiabá and the low-lying plain and swamps of the Pantanal that cover most of southwestern Mato Grosso and northwestern Mato Grosso do Sul.

The 936,000 square miles of the Central West region was first visited in the sixteenth and seventeenth centuries by *bandeirantes* (pioneers) from São Paulo, who traveled in tightly organized, armed expeditions in search of Indian slaves and precious stones. These adventurers rarely formed permanent settlements, but their discovery of gold in the early eighteenth century brought an influx of people who established colonial towns like Cuiabá and Goiás near the mines. By the nineteenth century, a primitive grazing economy had been developed on the savannah plains of southern Goiás and Mato Grosso do Sul, but the dense tropical forests in the northern part of both states remained inhabited exclusively by primitive Indians.

It was only at the beginning of this century that the Central West region began to be integrated with the rest of the country. Under the leadership of Candido Rondon, telegraph wires were laid across the territory, and 150,000 Indians were subdued, opening up the area to settlers with their families. Rondon, who was part Indian and twice nominated for the Nobel Peace Prize, established the Indian Protection Service at the government's request and organized 100 service posts in the interior. The peaceable Rondon told his agents, "Die if you must, but never kill." Despite his motto and principles, the destruction of Indians and their way of life has continued throughout this century, reducing tribes like the Paco d'Arco from 3,000 to one old woman with bitter memories.

While this area has been Brazil's fastest-growing region in the past 25 years, with new roads, railroads, airports, and modern cities like Brasília rising rapidly on the plains, the gains have often been made at the cost of human life and dignity.

It is best to begin the journey in the cool, dry months of July through September if you intend to take side trips on the dirt roads that lead off the paved highways. This is particularly true when exploring the Pantanal, where rivers overflow and cause flooding from October to early April. Brazilians also suggest, half kiddingly, that the safest way to begin your journey is with a brief detour to a suburb north of Brasília called Vali do Amanhaçer (Valley of Dawn). Here you may seek the blessings of a religious cult started by a woman truck driver, a *macumbista,* or practicioner of the popular religion that combines voodoo with Catholicism. That visit, plus a *figa,* the common clenched-fist amulet designed to ward off the evil eye, should guarantee a good trip into the wild west.

En Route from Brasília – Begin your drive in the southern part of the city on Route 40-50-60 that starts near the zoological garden. A short distance ahead on the right is Saida Norte (north exit), a single-lane exit road that joins the Brasília-Belém highway and is paved all the way to the mouth of the Amazon 1,450 miles away. A little farther on the left is the single-lane paved road that becomes 40 and 50 going south to Belo Horizonte, but you should continue on the double-lane highway 60 toward Anápolis.

Route 60 is heavily trafficked but in good condition, passing through an urban area that is 9 miles (14 km) from the capital. On your left is a city officially called Nucleo Bandeirante, but generally known as Cidade Livre (Free City).

CIDADE LIVRE: Prior to the building of Brasília, the unskilled, uneducated northeasterners flocked here to escape the drought and poverty of their own region. Desperate for food and money, they lived in wooden shacks and worked 15 hours a day to build Brasília in 3 years.

Cidade Livre, which quickly grew to 100,000 people, was a dusty, rough city, reminiscent of Hollywood's version of a Wild West town. Its clapboard storefronts had false second stories; hundreds of bars served hordes of men who arrived in Jeeps instead of on horseback. On payday, lines formed at the bordellos at the far end of town, where men often fought over the few prostitutes in residence.

Government officials planned to dismantle Cidade Livre after the completion of the Brasília, but it stands today as an unofficial monument to the men who built the new city. In fact, it remains because the capital's planners did not realistically allocate housing for anyone earning less than $10,000 a year.

En Route from Cidade Livre – Continuing on Route 60, you pass additional satellite communities such as Taguatinga, Ceilandia, and Brasiandia, which hold the overflow of poor migrants from the Northeast. Take the turnoff to Gama (which ends in Belo Horizonte), bypassing the dirt road exits for Cidade Eclectica and Santo Antonio do Descoberto. The shift to these dirt roads reflects with sociological precision the emergence of slums around the metropolis. The most primitive and recent are farthest out, with housing of cardboard and tin that will someday become adobe when the occupants have some economic success. The next wave of migrants will begin the process again as squatters in a new ring of slums even more remote from the employment that initially drew them to the city.

After the turnoff to Gama and Belo Horizonte, Route 60 becomes a single-lane road all the way to Cuiabá. The road is kept in good condition, with well-marked signs and asphalt exits. After leaving the Federal District at Luzania and entering the state of Goiás, the road starts to wind as you lose altitude. The landscape is the same arid red earth found in Brasília, with low scrub brush and twisted trees that barely cover the soil. A number of small streams intersect the route, and the vegetation along their banks is more tropical. Here you may see monkeys, parrots, and snakes if you decide to wander along one of the streams.

Along this route before Anápolis, there is little to see except the small towns of Alexania and Abadinania, where the only attractions are filling stations and stores with the most basic supplies. Here there are also meat stores that attract people from Brasília, who buy at less expensive prices to try to offset their very high cost of living. Just outside Anápolis, take the main highway to the right — the main road to Belém.

ANÁPOLIS: Some 92 miles (150 km) from Brasília, Anápolis is a growing city of 180,000. It is a prime example of the economic boom that came to the region with the building of Brasília. The city has become a manufacturing center, supplying Brasília with processed food, furniture, fabrics, ceramics, and beer, as well as a center of agricultural produce. The area around Anápolis is a region of large farms that produce Brazilian staples such as rice, beans, eggs, and dairy products.

Besides the military, manufacturing, and agricultural installations here, there is little to see, but interesting excursions can be taken to Jarágua and Pirenópolis, two colonial towns near the old gold mines north of Anápolis.

JARÁGUA: About 55 miles (90 km) from Anápolis, this city has provincial architecture and two churches of note, Igreja da Concicao and Igreja do Rosario. Prior to Carnival, the Feast of St. Sebastian is celebrated in January and features street dancing and arts and crafts. Hotels and dining spots are pretty bad (for emergency use only).

PIRENÓPOLIS: About 40 miles (63 km) from Anápolis, this town of 30,000 has more extensive examples of colonial architecture, including the Igreja do Carmo in the downtown area and the Museum of Religious Art and the Igreja do Matriz, built in 1728, in the central district. The city is also the site of the Calvalhada, a medieval pageant that originated in Portugal and is still celebrated with jousting tournaments, clowns, and jesters. The festival, which takes place 40 days after Easter, lasts for 1 week.

En Route from Anápolis – Take Route 60 for the 30-mile (47-km) journey to Goiânia through low, rolling hills. The main approach to the city is startling — you top a hill of scrub brush and find a city of skyscrapers rising before you.

GOIÂNIA: This growing city of 717,000, capital of the state of Goiás, was one of the first planned cities in Brazil and was created in 1937 as a result of President Getulio Vargas's "to the West" campaign. The charismatic president, affectionately called "Father of the Poor," broadcast radio messages urging western expansion to change the economic lot of the millions of peasants flooding to southeastern cities.

City planners designed Goiânia with symmetrical streets marked with white divisions for bus lanes. Although the city was planned for easy movement of automobiles, the population grew way beyond the original dimensions. Goiânia has a large number of parks, botanical gardens, and areas for outdoor relaxation. Educativo do Goiânia (Av. das Rosas) has a good zoo, playground, and park. Mutirama, also a park, has a large amusement area for children. You can water ski in Jão Reservoir. Locally made arts and crafts are displayed each Sunday morning in the Praça Civica at the Feira do Hippi (Hippie Fair).

Several restaurants have good reputations for indigenous food. For regional dishes, there's *Forno de Barro* (Rua 83, No. 570). Try *Recanto do Gaucho* at Mutirama Park for *churrascaría* and *Chopin* on the agricultural fairgrounds. Goiânia is a cosmopolitan city and has a good Chinese restaurant, *Shang Hai* (Rua 20, No. 717).

Centrally located Goiânia is a good starting point for trips into less-populated areas — the more remote regions of the Araguaia and Tocantins rivers for wildlife; Goiás, the old state capital and former gold-mining center; and Caldas Novas, an area known for luxurious hot springs resorts. If you wish to travel in a group, several tourist agencies in Goiânia can arrange tours, including Incatur (Av. Goiás 151) or Turisplan (Rua 8, No. 388). Both sponsor fishing and hunting packages.

If you wish to visit Caldas Novas, an area of therapeutic hot springs, take BR-153 south from Goiânia through broad farmland. The two-lane highway is paved and kept in good condition. Turn left at Morrinhos to complete the 110-mile (176-km) journey to Caldas Novas. Near the city are two other well-known mineral bath resorts, Fontes de Pirapetinga, a few miles away, and Rio Quente, which has the most luxurious accommodations. The temperature of these springs ranges from 98° to 115°F (36° to 46°C) as the bubbling water emerges from caverns in the base of the adjacent mountains and meanders through natural pools and lakes.

Goiás, the former state capital, is well worth visiting for its colonial architecture. Take the road from Goiânia; the paved road ends midway on the 90-mile (145-km) trip. Goiás (pop. 43,000) has narrow, winding streets with low, two-story houses. The most spectacular of its churches is Igreja de Nossa Senhora da Boa Morte, now a museum of sacred art featuring the works of José da Veiga, as well as many works in gold. Igreja de São Francisco (Praça Zaqueu Alves de Castro) is the oldest in town, erected in 1761. The Museum of the Bandeiras, dedicated to the early explorers, is on Praça Brasil Caiado, to the right of the central water fountain. Around the city you can still see remains of the mortarless stone walls built by the slaves of landowners.

There are several adequate restaurants here, including *Vila Boa* (Morro Chapeu do Padre), with a spectacular view, and *Serra Dourado* (Moretti Foggia 7) for *churrascos.*

If you're set on exploring the Aruana and wildlife preserves by car, be prepared for primitive travel. Many roads are unmarked and unnumbered. The dirt road from Goiás north is in poor condition, and the village of Aruana (pop. 7,000) has few tourist facilities. Get a good supply of gas in Goiás for the 90-mile (144-km) trip and plenty of insect repellent, since Aruana is on the Rio Araguaia. It is the central point for river fishing and hunting expeditions and has a few basic tourist lodges, eating spots, and camping facilities. Located 15° south of the equator, the town's favorite activity is swimming off the white sandy beaches that line the river, but beware: Some of the warmer, stagnant pools near shore have piranha. The area also has sting rays that measure up to 2 feet in diameter, with long, poisonous tails. If you must swim, keep kicking.

You are almost guaranteed a good catch of fish on the Araguaia, especially at dawn or sunset, when the calm river is tinged reddish yellow. You will find a variety of unusual fish, including striped *tucanares,* with their large painted mustaches; dogfish with enormous teeth used by the Indians for decorative purposes; *soia,* a fish with only one eye; *poraque,* an electric fish; and *tabarana,* considered by many to be the area's most powerful fighting fish. Fishermen boast of catches of all sizes, from the tiny *pacu* to the *pirarucu* that are sometimes 6 feet long and weigh 200 pounds.

You can rent small motorboats with a guide for about $10 a day. Larger excursion boats that make 1- and 2-week trips on the river can be reserved through tourist agencies in Goiânia or Brasília. Boatels — hotels constructed on large, flat-bottomed boats — are more comfortable. You can also combine a weekly river excursion with an escorted trip to the Rio Tocantins valley, which has good hunting.

On a river excursion through a rain forest, you will see wildlife such as turtles, parrots, gulls, and alligators along the banks as the widening river approaches the

Amazon. You will also pass the world's largest river island, Bananal, which measures 8,000 square miles. Inhabited by Carajás and Javaes Indians, the island is a good stopping point and has small villages with tourist lodgings. The Carajá make interesting orange and black clay dolls and feather headdresses. You'll find them very hospitable to visitors. Remember, however, to get permission to visit them from FUNAI (the national Indian Foundation) in Brasília, which maintains strict control over outsiders mingling with Indians to protect them against disease. The common cold, a routine illness of non-Indians, killed 177 Meinaco Indians one year, and when measles carried by a traveler broke out among Gaviao Indians on the Rio Tocantins, 60 died overnight. Be very sure you are in good health before visiting any tribe even if you do have permission.

En Route from Goiânia – Rejoin Route 60 and travel west through the farming areas characteristic of this region. The two-lane highway is still heavily traveled and well maintained, with gas stations approximately every 25 miles. You may want to visit Pirenópolis, a small community a few miles off the main road, that celebrates a tournament between Moors and Christians 40 days after Easter. There is little to do in these small towns, so the inhabitants make annual celebrations big events. The St. John's Day celebration on June 23 is dedicated to the saint believed to have enjoyed good music and drink. Bonfires and firecrackers at night are thought to awaken him so he will join in the fun of mock marriages performed by drunken priests and irate fathers holding shotguns.

Continuing on Route 60, you pass through the small farming communities of Guapó and Posselandia and the town of Indiara, which is intersected on the right by a dirt road that leads to Parauna, 38 miles (60 km) away. Parauna is one of the best places to view the eroded rock sculptures typical of the red rock highlands north of this route.

You cross the Capivari and Turvo rivers on Route 60, but unlike in less-developed regions, there are bridges instead of ferries. You might want to stop for a swim or to fish in one of the rivers, although there are few tourist facilities here or at the Rio Verdao beyond Acreun. After crossing the Verdao, you will pass the town of Santo Antonio da Barra and two paved highways before Rio Verde.

RIO VERDE: After leaving Goiânia, you'll find this city of 74,000 is one of the best and most interesting places to stop for food. It has a large community of Mennonites, who fled Prussia, the Ukraine, and other European countries and who have maintained their strict religion. The Japanese, a major immigrant group to Brazil since World War II, own many of the outlying farms, where they grow vegetables and fruit. This area, known as *campo cerrado,* has become an important area for agriculture despite the fact that the red soil and arid climate have to be enhanced by fertilizers and irrigation.

Here, as in most of Brazil, agriculture is characterized by huge landholdings. Some 37% of the farmland is owned by 1% of the population. These enormous properties are typical of the Central West region. The only group that protests land distribution is the Catholic Church.

En Route from Rio Verde – Continuing on Route 60, the next stretch is a long haul as you pass through the flat plains typical of the cattle country in the western and southern parts of the region. The 300-mile (480-km) route has few diversions before Rondonópolis, but road conditions are good and there is little traffic. At Jataí, the road changes to Route 364, and there is a good alternative overnight and restaurant stop. The most adequate restaurant is *Rosana* (at the exit road for BR-364). On the longest stretch of the road, between Portelandia and Alto Araguaia, you cross the border into the state of Mato Grosso.

RONDONÓPOLIS: This town of 82,000 was named after the first Indian protector, Candido Rondon, who attempted to save vanishing Indians from the advances of white settlers. The town makes a good stop on this long stretch of road. There are a number of Indian crafts for sale, and you can try to get permission to visit nearby tribes at the local FUNAI office. The town's Indian historian, Carmelita Cury (Rua 15 de Novembro 61), can tell you how to get to the Bororo Indian tribe, who live on a reservation 3 miles (5 km) away.

Several restaurants serve *churrascos,* including *Los Pampas* (Rua 13 de Maio 286), *Gaucha* (Av. Amazonas 1128), and *David* (Rua Fernando Correia da Costa 615).

About 500 miles north of Rondonópolis is one of the largest Indian reservations in the world, the Xingu National Park. In an area the size of France, the remains of a once-enormous tribe continue their civilization. There are an estimated 30,000 Indians here and perhaps 8,000 more who have not yet made contact with the white man. It is very doubtful that FUNAI will permit you to visit this reservation.

En Route from Rondonópolis – The last stretch of Route 364 crosses a flat plateau with cotton, rice, bean, corn, and soybean farms and an increasing number of cattle ranches. You will pass through the small farming communities of Santa Elvira, Juscimeira, Dom Auino, S. Pedro da Cipa, and Jaciara. A possible stopping point on this 132-mile (211-km) trip is Aqua Quentes, which has health resorts and hot mineral baths. Then the road twists as you enter the flood plain. Cuiabá lies in a basin, abutted on the south by low mountains.

CUIABÁ: The capital of the state of Mato Grosso, a sparsely populated area of 353,000 square miles, Cuiabá grew as a center of gold mining in the 18th century but today gets its wealth from the Amazon rain forest as the center of rubber and palm nut harvest. Mato Grosso has been integrated into the Amazon region to benefit from the area's federally funded projects. Before 1978, Mato Grosso also included Mato Grosso do Sul, which is now a separate state with a population of 1,370,000.

Cuiabá is a modern city of 213,000 on the Rio Cuiabá. Except for the cost of meat, prices are much higher than those in São Paulo. Cuiabá is the geographic center of South America, but to add a little cultural confusion, the city also has a large community of Middle Eastern people and a large mosque near Praça Moreira Cabral. There are three museums worth visiting, including the FUNAI Indian Museum (Rua Barao del Melgaco 1174), Pedras Ramis Bucair Museum (Rua Pedro Celstino 213), and the Museum of Popular Culture and Art (Bloco del Tecnologia). Indian handicrafts can be purchased in shops and at an outdoor market on Saturdays. The environment in the surrounding region is the real point of interest here. Travel agencies, like Cuiabá-Tur (Rua Joaquim Murtinho 551; phone: 322-8732) can arrange excursions to outlying areas.

There are several very good restaurants in town, such as *Maria Taquara* at the *Hotel Excelsion,* which has international cuisine, and the *Aurea Palace* (Rua General Mello 63; phone: 322-3637).

Two hours south of the city are the tablelands of Guimares — mountains suitable for climbing with a spectacular waterfall, the Veu da Novia (Bride's Veil), which is 180 feet high.

The Pantanal, a swampland with a wide variety of birds and animals, is half the size of Minnesota and can be crossed on the Transpantaneira Highway. The trees along this wet savannah make natural aviaries for many bird species, including the spoonbill, the red wood ibis, and the gray heron. The region also has alligators, deer, capybara, and jaguars. It is one of the country's best hunting areas but only for group outings.

Rio Teles Pires is one of the best rivers in Brazil for fishing, although the area does not have the extensive facilities for groups and individuals that other rivers have.

The Port Velho Road is treacherous driving but has several interesting towns — Vihelna, Pimenta, Bueno, Cacoal — that will give you a good taste of contemporary frontier life. Southwest of Vihelna on the Rio Galarea are archaeological ruins currently under excavation. The caves, which are not open to tourists at this time, have walls carved with symbols that indicate the people were sun- and women-worshipers.

The Interior, north of Vihelna, is the area Theodore Roosevelt explored by canoe in search of the lost Inca treasure, described in his book *In the Brazilian Wilderness*. Nearby is the site where British Colonel Percy Fawcett mysteriously disappeared, leaving behind accounts of a white god of the Xingu tribe. The area is only a little tamer now. It is spotted with FUNAI posts, such as Serra Morena; research centers like Humboldt Scientific City; and homesteading towns like Aripuana. This area and the region farther north are crossed by the Trans-Amazonia Highway and are slowly being developed. It can be explored by air taxis out of Cuiabá via government planes that usually fly in supplies. Get a yellow fever vaccination, antimalaria medicine, and plenty of insect repellent. If you are adventurous and do not mind some discomfort, this is where the trip to the Wild West really begins.

BEST EN ROUTE

Since this is not one of the more heavily traveled parts of Brazil, there are few hotels, and most are in the larger cities. Exceptions are the resorts around health spas. Hotels listed as expensive will run about $40 per day and up; moderate, about $20 to $30 per night; and inexpensive, under $15 per night.

ANÁPOLIS

Itamarty – A pleasant hotel with 34 rooms; private baths, telephone, television, breakfast included in the price. Rua Manoel da Abadia 209. Inexpensive.

Principe – Another simple hotel, with 25 rooms, all with private bath, hot water. Rua Cons. Portela 165. Inexpensive.

GOIÂNIA

Castor Park – The best in town, with a health and fitness center including European-style vapors. Av. Republica do Libano 1520 (phone: 223-7707). Expensive.

Bandeirantes – Comfortable hotel in the center of town, with air conditioning, a bar, boat rental, and a decent restaurant with international cuisine. Av. Anhanguera 3278 (phone: 224-0066). Expensive to moderate.

Umuarama – A comfortable hotel with convention facilities, parking, air conditioning, and a bar. The restaurant serves average food. Rua 4 No. 492 (phone: 224-1555). Expensive to moderate.

CALDAS NOVAS

Posada do Rio Quente – One of the best in the hot springs area, in a scenic park with a swimming pool, boat, football field, playground, bar, and simple restaurant. Estr. P/Morrinhos, km 28 (phone: 062-421-2244). Expensive.

Tourismo – In a scenic park setting, with pool, air conditioning, bar, and a simple restaurant. Estr. P/Morrinhos. Expensive.

GOIÁS

Vila Boa – A small hotel with panoramic views, a restaurant, bar, pool, air conditioning, and playground. Morro Chapeu do Padre. Expensive.

PIRENÓPOLIS

Rex – A basic hotel. Praça Emanoel Jaime Jopes 3. Inexpensive.

Municipal Campsite – Has capacity for 50 tents. Rio das Almas. Inexpensive.

ARUANA

Recanto Sonhado – A simple hotel, nicely located on the river. Av. Altamiro Caio Pacheco. Inexpensive.

RIO VERDE

Campos – Another basic hotel with 12 rooms with private showers. Praça 5 de Agosto 31. Moderate.

JATAÍ

Itamaraty – Here you can choose from 10 rooms with private showers. Rua José Carvalho Bastos 100. Moderate.

RONDONÓPOLIS

Thaani – A reasonably comfortable hotel with bar, air conditioning, and sauna. Av. Amazonas 472. Moderate.

Rondonópolis Palace – Plain but adequate, with air conditioning and a bar. Rua Fernando Correia da Costa 601. Moderate.

CUIABÁ

Aurea Palace – In the downtown area, this comfortable hotel has a coffee shop, color TV, and refrigerators in the rooms. Av. General Mello 63. Expensive.

Santa Rosa Palace – The best in town, all rooms have private showers and air conditioning. It also has a bar, pool, and dining room. Av. da Getulio Vargas 370 (phone: 322-9044). Expensive.

Centro America – All 10 rooms have private showers. Praça da República 297. Moderate.

São Paulo to the Uruguay Border

There are many places of interest in the three southern states of Brazil, and the road from São Paulo to Porto Alegre passes within a stone's throw of almost all of them. There is little of special interest in the first half of the trip from São Paulo to Curitiba, but the rewards farther south make the journey a memorable one, for the route passes through mountains that skirt the sea and a series of beaches. The city of Curitiba is pleasant, and from there to Porto Alegre you drive through lovely towns populated by German- and Italian-speaking people to the scenic beaches of Santa Catarina and its capital city of Florianópolis. The road takes you through summer resorts along the coast before becoming a modern highway for the final 60 miles (96 km) to Porto Alegre, a city with many tourist attractions.

With all the interesting side trips possible on this route, you may want to devote a week to seeing the area. It will take the better part of one day to cover the 250 miles (400 km) from São Paulo to Curitiba. You will probably want to spend two nights in Curitiba, with a day's side trip to Paranaguá. A third night could be spent in one of the towns that has retained its German influence, such as Joinville or Blumenau. Plan to stop in Florianópolis for at least a big lunch of seafood at one of the restaurants by the lake. If you want to avoid metropolitan areas such as Porto Alegre, you can try one of the resort hotels in Gramado, stop in the wine region at Caxias do Sul, or stay in a seaside resort in Camboriu or Torres. From Porto Alegre you will find modern, paved roads to Montevideo, Uruguay, a distance of 530 miles (850 km), and to Buenos Aires, 641 miles (1,025 km) away.

The best tourist guides and maps in Brazil are the trilingual Quatro Rodas Guides, published annually by Editora Abril. The editions for the coming year appear on the newsstands by December and sell out in a few months. Most of the guides are published in Portuguese, with a condensed portion in English at the end of each book. Bring a dictionary. The most useful guide for southern Brazil is the Quatro Rodas *Guia do Sul* (*Guide to the South*), which covers the states of Paraná, Santa Catarina, and Rio Grande do Sul as well as parts of Paraguay, Uruguay, and Argentina. The *Guia do Sul* contains more descriptive information about the south than the *Guia Quatro Rodas do Brasil,* which covers the whole country.

The best time to visit southern Brazil is in summer, from November to April, when the climate is warm and dry, much like southern Europe. Many tourist facilities close in the winter, when you may even find occasional snow in the far south.

En Route from São Paulo – From the center of São Paulo, take Ipiranga Avenue south to Consolação Avenue, which turns into Rebouças Avenue, crossing the Rio Pinheiros. Beyond the Jockey Club, turn left onto Professor Francisco Morato Avenue and begin route BR-116 to Curitiba. For the first 19 miles (31 km) the highway is divided. The town of Embú, 16 miles (26 km) from São Paulo, is a historical town with a noteworthy church, Nossa Senhora do Rosario, dating to 1680. Once the divided highway ends, driving is tedious because of heavy traffic and slow-moving trucks. Fortunately, on most hills there is a third lane, and trucks obligingly move over, but there are many steep inclines and much traffic. São Paulo lies at an elevation of more than 2,500 feet, and by the time the road reaches the Rio Juquia and the town of Registro, 15 miles (24 km) away, you are at sea level.

REGISTRO: This town of 12,000 is the largest between São Paulo and Curitiba. It lies on the south bank of the Rio Juquia, about 40 miles from the Atlantic, and is a river town with a port for shipping much of the produce from the region. The largest industry is tea processing, and the area is a major agricultural region; its principal crops are rice, bananas, and tea. Several truck stops along BR-116, such as *Petropen* and *Guácha Altaneira,* serve big steak dinners at low prices.

CURITIBA: They say that the *paulistas,* the residents of São Paulo, work all the time so that the *cariocas,* the residents of Rio, can play all the time. Of the *curitibanos,* one could say that they live all the time, for Curitiba is one of the most livable cities in Brazil. In fact, with adequate space for its people and no pollution, Curitiba is often cited by Brazilians as a model of how to do things right. The city center with its pedestrian mall has often been copied by other cities, but with less success. Here, cars are prohibited, and special bus lanes move commuters back and forth efficiently. Even the climate is more moderate, cooler in the summer than Porto Alegre. It is only about an hour's drive to the beaches along the coast, and Iguaçu Falls is less than 6 hours west over a well-paved road (which does not explain why many *curitibanos* have never made the visit). The city has no spectacular tourist sights, but by visiting it you are able to see a modern, well-organized Brazilian city that is moving with its people in a progressive direction. One of the several museums worth visiting is the Paranaense, in the old city hall built in 1916. Here you will find paintings, sculptures, weapons, and coins. It is on the Generoso Marquês Plaza downtown.

There are several day trips from Curitiba; the best is the rail ride down to the major coffee-exporting port of Paranaguá. Trains leave Curitiba from the station on Av. Afonso Camargo at 7 AM and 8:10 AM, but be sure to check the time of departure the day before (phone: 234-8441). There are many short tunnels and fine views of the seacoast during the 3-hour trip through the mountains. Have lunch at *Danúbio Azul* (Rua 15 de Novembro 91) in Paranaguá, which features inexpensive seafood and has a panoramic view. After lunch, take a taxi to the port or walk to the Archaeology and Popular Arts Museum, which dates from 1740 and is housed in a Jesuit monastery (15 de Novembro 567; closed Mondays). The train station in Paranaguá is on Avenida Arturo de Abreu, with departures every day at 4:30 PM.

Take another worthwhile excursion to the state park of Vila Velha, 50 miles (80 km) from Curitiba. Wind has eroded the red sandstone rocks into grotesque and fantastic shapes, and a trail threads around their bases for several miles of wonderful hiking. There are also daily tour buses and public buses to the park.

En Route from Curitiba – You can rejoin Route BR-116 to get to Porto Alegre, but the more scenic route, the coastal BR-376, is much more interesting for sightseeing. This route leaves BR-116 just south of Curitiba. Signs are few and far between as you leave Curitiba; if you think you're lost, stop and ask for the road to Joinville or Florianópolis. Because the paved two-lane road is heavily trafficked, plan for a slow but scenic drive.

Watch for the striking Paraná tree, called *aracauria* locally. This unique member of the pine family has a long, straight, limbless trunk with beautiful uplifting branches at the top. In April the trees bear fruit; their large cones are composed of many long, narrow nuts that taste like roasted chestnuts when cooked. Roadside vendors sell them by the quart for a pittance. About 50 miles (80 km) from Curitiba the road crosses the border into Santa Catarina State, an agricultural region with many German communities. At this point the road number changes to BR-101.

JOINVILLE: This city, settled in the 19th century by German immigrants, is 77 miles (129 km) from Curitiba. Joinville is one of the best known of the German communities and worth an overnight stop. Though it has become a bustling industrial center, many original buildings with their European architecture have been maintained. Joinville has more bicycles per inhabitant than any other city in Brazil.

There are several museums of note, including Museu de Arte de Joinville (Rua 15 de Novembro 147), with a permanent exhibit of art, sculpture, and prints, and Museu do Sambaqui (Rua Dona Francisca 600), with local archaeological finds. If you like flowers, be sure to visit the private orchid collection at the Orquidario Voinvilense (Rua Placido Gomes 590; open daily).

Two very good restaurants feature German food: *Tante Frida* (Rua Visconde de Taunay 1174) is open daily and takes all credit cards. *Bierkeller* (Rua 15 de Novembro 497) is closed Tuesdays and takes Credicard, Elo, and Nacional.

En Route from Joinville – The road is almost flat after Joinville and soon reaches the sea and Santa Catarina's beautiful beaches. Rice and bananas are the principal crops of this area. At the summer resort towns of Picarras and Penha there are many sandy beaches. If you prefer quiet and miles of secluded beach, stay along here; if you prefer wall-to-wall people on the beach, lots of young folks, night life, and classier hotels, push on to Camboriu.

THE ITAJAI VALLEY: Before reaching Camboriu, the road passes the city of Itajai at the mouth of the Rio Itajai, 123 miles (206 km) from Curitiba. Itajai, an important fishing and boatbuilding center, was settled by German immigrants whose architecture, customs, and language have survived. The most important town in the valley and the best known of all the German towns in Brazil is Blumenau, 26 miles (44 km) from Itajai. Locally made linens and crystal are good buys, and there are several decent hotels and restaurants, most of which have been built recently to accommodate the increasing numbers of tourists to the town. For restaurants, investigate the good German cuisine of *Cavalhinho Branco* (Av. Rio Branco 165); the touristy *Moinho do Vale* (Rua Paraguai 66), with its imitation Dutch windmill; or the fantastic views of the river valley from the hilltop *Frohsinn* (on Morro do Aipin), ½ mile from town.

BALNEARIO DE CAMBORIU: Camboriu, 10 miles (16 km) beyond Itajai, offers Brazil's most "in" beach south of Ipanema. The 4-mile stretch of sand is lined with restaurants, hotels, bars, houses, and condominiums, most of which went up in the past 10 years. Reservations are a must in summer, but in winter the place is deserted. If Camboriu Beach itself is too crowded, there are others in both directions (though the surf gets a bit rough to the north).

En Route from Camboriu – Beyond this point, the road follows the sea and is very scenic, with beautiful beaches and resorts at every turn. At 141 miles (235 km), there is a beach worth visiting at Itapema. The road continues past several other small towns before reaching Florianópolis, the state capital.

FLORIANÓPOLIS: Part of this city is situated on an island and part on the mainland. To reach the city center, turn left off the main road and take one of the two bridges to the island, where the downtown section is quieter than that on the mainland. On the island are many fine beaches, a Jesuit monastery, several forts, and a beautiful blue lake, the Lagoa da Conceição. Excellent shrimp is available at the seafood restaurants along the lake, such as *Oliveira* or *Saveiros.* If steak is your meat, try *Ataliba,* on the beach (Rua Jaú Guedes da Fonseca), instead.

En Route from Florianópolis – The road continues along the coast, but the sea itself is not visible until you reach Imbituba, 224 miles (373 km) from Curitiba. Imbituba is in a coal-mining region and has several nice beaches. The next important town is Tubarão (Portuguese for "shark"), another coal-mining town with many hot springs nearby. To reach the popular hot springs at the town of Gravatel, turn right on the paved road at Tubarão for a 12-mile (19-km) side trip. The road beyond Tubarão passes many small villages before reaching Ararangua at 301 miles (502 km), a town with long, sandy beaches and good fishing. At 334 miles (557 km), the road crosses the border into the state of Rio Grande do Sul, a cattle ranching area with cowboys similar to the gauchos of the Argentine pampas. Rice, corn, wheat, and grapes are also grown here. Just beyond the border there is a mobile information booth on the right side of the road during the summer. Stop there for maps and free brochures.

TORRES: This resort town, also just beyond the state border, is named after the basalt towers that jut out into the sea and afford fine views of the area. Both the long beach and the towers can be reached on foot from the town's hotels. From May to October, it is just too cool to lie on the beach, and Torres and other resort towns to the south shut down for the winter.

En Route from Torres – Beyond Torres, the road runs between the sea on the left and several lakes on the right, passing the turnoffs to other beach resort towns. However, these are overcrowded because of their proximity to Porto Alegre. If you are going to stay at the beach, stay in Torres or in Santa Catarina. At the town of Osorio, BR-101 becomes a modern, divided toll highway for the rest of the drive to Porto Alegre, turning westward away from the coast and changing its number to BR-290. Osorio is 411 miles (657 km) from Curitiba and just 64 miles (103 km) from Porto Alegre. The highway turns into Avenida Bento Gonçalves as it approaches downtown Porto Alegre.

PORTO ALEGRE: This is the largest city in South Brazil and the state capital of Rio Grande do Sul. It is a booming, modern industrial center on the banks of the Rio Guaiba with access to the sea via the Lagoa dos Patos.

For a good view of this hilly city, take a boat trip to the islands in the Rio Guaiba. Porto Alegre has several museums, including the Varig Airlines Museum (Rua 18 de

Novembro 800), which has a collection of airplane parts and miniature airplanes. For the shopper, Porto Alegre is a good place to pick up leather goods, agates, and mounted butterflies.

The city has many fine restaurants that feature giant portions of steak and local wines. Some of the best local beef is served at *Quero Quero* (Otavio Rocha Plaza 47) and *Capitao Rodrigo* (*Plazo São Rafael* hotel) and the German influence is still strong at *Ratskeller,* on the outskirts of town in Floresta (Rua Cristovao Colombo 1564).

While you are in Rio Grande do Sul, don't fail to take an excursion to the mountain region just north of Porto Alegre. The trip can be made in a day, but an overnight stay is recommended. Take BR-116 north from Porto Alegre through the heavily industrialized northern suburbs. The last of these, Novo Hamburgo, 28 miles (46 km) north of Porto Alegre, offers good buys in shoes at its factory outlets. Farther north, the road rises rapidly into the hills, reaching an altitude of 2,000 feet in the town of Nova Petrópolis 64 miles (103 km) from Porto Alegre. Turn off here to the twin mountain resort towns of Gramado and Canela, literally "the grassy place" and "cinnamon town." In summer, the roadside is covered with beautiful hydrangeas.

GRAMADO and CANELA: Gramado is 22 miles (36 km) from Nova Petrópolis on a paved road that continues 5 miles (8 km) to Canela. These towns have attractive gardens and Bavarian architecture, and the road is dotted with shops offering original handicrafts. There is a striking waterfall in the Caracol State Park on the outskirts of Canela that should not be missed. The water cascades over the lip of a giant cave and crashes on the rocks more than 300 feet below. Spend the night in Gramado.

CAXIAS DO SUL: To reach the wine country, retrace your route to Nova Petrópolis and continue north on BR-116 for 20 miles (33 km) to Caxias do Sul. The city has several wineries open to the public, such as the Alianca (Rua Feigo Filho 164), open every weekday morning and afternoon. All the wineries have a tour and free samples (they are all closed on weekends). You can also visit the Experimental Grape and Wine Center, where new varieties of grapes are grown and tested. In February, there is an annual wine festival in Caxias do Sul. For some good food, try *Don Jon* (Rua Sinimbu 2302).

To get to the vineyards, take the newly paved road west past the village of Farroupilha and turn north, when the road forks, to the town of Bento Gonçalves. Surrounded by vineyards, this town has several wineries of its own and an annual wine festival to rival the one in Caxias do Sul. The next stop is the ski slope at Garibaldi, 6 miles (10 km) south of Bento Gonçalves. To return to Pôrto Alegre, either retrace your steps to Caxias do Sul or continue south on the paved road from Garibaldi for 46 miles (73 km) until the road rejoins BR-116 just below Novo Hamburgo. If you want to stay overnight in the grape-growing region, do so in Caxias do Sul.

The complete trip from São Paulo to Porto Alegre, including the round-trip excursion to the mountains from Porto Alegre, is 928 miles (1,486 km).

BEST EN ROUTE

Since this is one of the more heavily traveled areas of Brazil and more developed due to European immigrants, hotels tend to be more modern and numerous, including facilities such as swimming pools, television, and good restaurants. Hotels categorized as expensive will cost about $50 per night and up; moderate, about $25 to $45 per night; and inexpensive, below $20 per night.

EMBÚ

Rancho Silvestre – To avoid downtown São Paulo or get a head start on your way south, this is the place to stop. On the outskirts of Embú about 45 minutes from downtown São Paulo in a parklike setting, the *Rancho* has only 42 rooms, so reservations are a must. Facilities include a tennis court, swimming pool, playground, and sauna. Visa accepted. Estrada Votorantim 700 (phone: 494-2911; in São Paulo, 210-1440). Expensive.

CURITIBA

Iguaçu Cauipéstre – The newest and best in town. Sauna, massage, mini golf, and lake fishing. BR-km 92 (Alto), 5 miles from the city (phone: 262-5313). Expensive.
Caravelle Palace – Centrally located hotel with 99 rooms. Reservations recommended. Major credit cards accepted. Rua Cruz Machado 282 (phone: 223-4323; in Rio de Janeiro, 257-1950). Expensive.

JOINVILLE

Colón Palace – A comfortable, clean hotel with 84 rooms, a small pool, and a good restaurant. Rua São Joaquim 80 (phone: 22-6188). Inexpensive.

PIÇARRAS

Imperador – A pleasant resort hotel on the beach. Its 109 rooms are full most of the summer, and reservations are recommended. No credit cards. Av. José Temistocles de Macedo 380 (phone: 4-5176). Moderate.

BLUMENAU

Plaza Hering – Owned and operated by the Hering family, which also owns the large Hering Glass Company. It is a large, modern facility with 134 rooms, a swimming pool, and a swanky restaurant. Reservations recommended in summer. Major credit cards accepted. Rua 7 de Setembro 818 (phone: 22-1277). Expensive.
Grande Hotel Blumenau – On the left just as the road enters town, with 76 rooms and a swimming pool. Reservations recommended in summer. Major credit cards accepted. On the crossroads of Rio Branco and Av. 15 de Novembro (phone: 22-0366). Moderate.

BALNEARIO DE CAMBORIU

Maranbaia – Right on Camboriu Beach, where the action is. *Maranbaia*'s 117 rooms are full all summer. It has a swimming pool if you tire of the beach and a good restaurant. Major credit cards accepted. Av. Atlantico 300 (phone: 66-0099; in São Paulo, 258-6587). Moderate.
Fischer – A pleasant hotel, right on the beach, with a restaurant. Reservations necessary in summer. No credit cards. Av. Atlantico 4770 (phone: 66-0177). Moderate.

ITAPEMA

Plaza Itapema – A first-class beach resort hotel, fancier than anything along the more frequented Camboriu Beach. It has 118 rooms, a pool, nightclub, and tennis. Reservations are a must in summer. Ilhota Beach, about 1 mile from town (phone: 44-2222). Expensive.

FLORIANÓPOLIS

Florianópolis Palace – A simple, downtown hotel; has a good restaurant. Reservations recommended. Major credit cards accepted. Rua Artista Bittencourt 2 (phone: 22-9633). Moderate.

GRAVATEL

Gravatel Termas – At the hot springs near the village of Gravatel. Many Brazilians come here from as far away as Porto Alegre and Curitiba to bathe in the hot spring, which many believe have therapeutic value. It's a country resort hotel, with a satisfactory restaurant, and room rates that normally include all meals; 114 rooms, tennis court, swimming pool, and sauna. Major credit cards accepted. About 2 miles from town (phone: 4-2145; in Porto Alegre, 33-2776). Moderate.

ARARANGUA

Morro dos Conventos – On the beach, with its own restaurant. No credit cards. Reservations recommended in summer. About 8 miles (13 km) from Ararangua (phone: 22-0608). Moderate.

TORRES

Dunas – The best hotel in Torres, but back from the beach. Good restaurant. Reservations are a must in summer. Major credit cards accepted. Rua 15 de Novembro 247 (phone: 664-1211). Moderate.

Do Farol – Beautiful views of the beach and the sea from the *Lighthouse* hotel. Good restaurant. Reservations are a must in summer. Major credit cards accepted. Rua José A. Picoral 240 (phone: 664-1240). Moderate.

PORTO ALEGRE

Plaza São Rafael – This is the most luxurious hotel in Porto Alegre, a large downtown property with 214 rooms and two fine restaurants. Reservations are a must. Major credit cards accepted. Av. Alberto Bins 514 (phone: 21-6100). Expensive.

Plaza – Another good, large downtown hotel with a good restaurant, it has 182 rooms. Reservations recommended. Major credit cards accepted. Rua Senhor dos Passos 154 (phone: 26-1700). Moderate.

Porto Alegre City – Still another good downtown hotel, with 146 rooms. Good restaurant. Major credit cards accepted. Rua José Montauri 20 (phone: 24-2988). Moderate.

GRAMADO

Serrano – A resort hotel in a garden setting in the mountain town of Gramado. This hotel's 40 rooms are full all summer. Swimming pool. Reservations are a must. Major credit cards accepted. Rua Presidente Costa e Silva 1112 (phone: 286-1332). Moderate.

Serra Azul – Definitely second place behind the *Serrano,* but a good choice nonetheless. Good restaurant, closer to town than the *Serrano.* Swimming pool. Reservations necessary in summer. Major credit cards accepted. Rua Garibaldi 152 (phone: 286-1082). Moderate.

CAXIAS DO SUL

Samuara – This beautiful hotel is in the forest on the road to Farroupilha. Swimming pool. Reservations a must during summer and fall. Good restaurant; most guests eat at the hotel. Major credit cards accepted. Six miles (10 km) from downtown (phone: 221-7733). Moderate.

Alfred Palace – A pleasant hotel with sauna, bar, hairdresser, and wine cellar. Rua Sinimbu 2302 (phone: 221-8655). Moderate.

Iguaçu Falls

Three waterfalls in the world surpass the rest: Niagara, Victoria, and Iguaçu. While the argument as to which of the three is the most spectacular may never end, one thing is for certain: Iguaçu is unsurpassed. The tropical rain forest provides the ideal setting for the torrents of water that fall and crash with a thunderous noise onto the rocks below, sending spray shooting back up to make beautiful rainbows. The Rio Iguaçu, a tributary of the Paraná, widens to a distance of 2 miles just above the precipice over which the river drops almost 200 feet, to create Iguaçu Falls. Since the lip of the precipice is uneven, the water doesn't fall in one great curtain, but rather in dozens of cataracts, interspersed with jungle greenery. The most spectacular cataract is *Garganta do Diabo,* or Devil's Throat.

The panoramic view of these falls from the Brazilian side is awesome, but perhaps even more thrilling is the walk along the Argentine side. In 1965 the Argentine government built a system of catwalks alongside and over the falls. Each step on the catwalk affords an excellent view of the cataracts; every time you round a bend, you're surprised by a vista even more beautiful than the last.

While any time is a good time to go to Iguaçu, the optimum months are August to November when you can climb around the falls more easily than during the highwater months of May and June. However, during this period the air is filled with butterflies, including many in lovely iridescent blues. The Rio Iguaçu forms the border between Brazil and Argentina and the areas on both sides of the river are national parks.

Iguaçu is served by two airports. The larger of the two is the international airport on the Brazilian side, midway between the falls and the city (in the border town of Foz do Iguaçu). Varig has daily flights from Rio de Janiero and São Paulo, Brazil, and from Asunción, Paraguay, to Iguaçu. The airport on the Argentine side, serving both the falls and border town of Puerto Iguazú, has daily flights to and from Buenos Aires on Aerolineas Argentinas. Cruzeiro do Sol flies from Buenos Aires to Iguaçu Falls, Brazil. You can also take the bus from Asunción to the falls, crossing the international bridge at Puerto Stroessner into Brazil at Foz do Iguaçu. A full 48 hours is recommended if you wish to see the falls from both sides. If you only see them from one side you have only seen half the show, since the two views are completely different.

IGUAÇU — THE BRAZILIAN SIDE: The best panoramic view of the falls is immediately in front of the *Hotel das Cataratas* in the national park. The well-manicured path and steps down to the falls start directly in front of the hotel. The steps lead to the very edge of the river, and at one point a catwalk goes right out over the river. Wear a raincoat or rent one from a vendor on the path. The path leads to the head of the falls, where an elevator takes you to the top for a small fee. From here it is a short walk upstream to the small boats that will take you out in the river for an even closer look. To return to the hotel, either retrace your steps or walk along the paved road; it's about 1 mile each way. Take your movie camera.

En Route from the Brazilian Side – This trip to the Argentine side takes a full day, a couple of hours each way over and back and at least 2 hours on the catwalks, which go past many waterfalls before stopping just short of the Devil's Throat, the most violent waterfall of them all. Add 1 hour for lunch, 1 hour for shopping, plus time to rest, and you have had a full day. To cross the Rio Iguaçu you must take the ferry about 10 miles downstream from the falls. Ask at your hotel if they provide transport to the ferry. If not, take a taxi to the ferry at a place called Pôrto Meira. You will have to go through customs here as you are leaving Brazil. If they stamp your passport when you leave, which is unlikely, make sure it is stamped again when you return. The ferries run at frequent intervals between approximately 8 AM and noon, and 2:30 and 6 PM. Just remember that there are no ferries during the long siesta or in the evening.

Once on the Argentine side you need to go through customs. After that, take a taxi to the falls some 12 miles away. Only a short distance from the river is the town of Puerto Iguazú. Soon after leaving the town, the road enters the national park. The parking lot is next to an aging hotel, and the falls are a short walk across a field.

Once you have crossed the field, it is more than a mile on the catwalks leading past various falls out to the Devil's Throat. Take along suntan lotion, a hat, a camera, and perhaps a canteen or flask of water to keep you refreshed. The catwalks are all on the level above the falls leading to the Devil's Throat. There are other catwalks that descend immediately from the field to the bottom of the falls.

By the time you get back to the hotel you will be ready for lunch and a good rest (a light lunch of a sandwich or two is suggested). Sit on the veranda, eat sandwiches, write postcards (no stamps available), and watch the other tourists. In due course, hail a taxi and head back to the ferry. Stop at the village of Puerto Iguazú to shop, especially if you do not make it to Montevideo or Buenos Aires. Puerto Iguazú's shops carry beautiful wool sweaters, sheepskin coats, and leather goods. There is no need to have Argentine pesos; you can pay with Brazilian cruzeiros, dollars, traveler's checks, and perhaps even with an American Express credit card. From here it is only a 5- or 10-minute walk down the hill to the ferry. Once again, it's time to go through Argentine customs, ride the ferry, and go through Brazilian customs. If transportation back to the hotel was not prearranged, taxis are available.

IGUAÇU — OTHER ATTRACTIONS: If you enjoy gambling, there is a full-fledged casino nearby in Paraguay, in the border town of Ciudad Presidente Stroessner. Transportation is available at all hotels on the Brazilian side for an evening across the Rio Paraná at the gambling tables. Many Brazilian and Argentine tourists visit Stroessner by day to buy Scotch whisky, French perfumes, and Japanese calculators at low prices. (Prices are not low by American standards, and therefore this border town holds no particular attraction for the American tourist.)

The Brazilian border town Foz do Iguaçu (referred to simply as Foz by the local folks) is not much better. It is growing by leaps and bounds and now boasts several high-rise apartment buildings. The construction boom is due only in part to the tourist industry. Not far upstream from the confluence of the Iguaçu and Paraná rivers at Foz do Iguaçu, the Itaipú Dam is now completed, with a generating capacity of 12.6 million kilowatts, making it the largest hydroelectric power generating facility in the world. Organized tours are available, and tour buses will probably be permitted to drive across the top of the dam. Check at your hotel for more information or in downtown Foz at the offices of Itaipú Binacional, a commission composed of an equal number of Paraguayans and Brazilians responsible for the Itaipú project. The better vantage points for viewing are on the Brazilian side, where a giant canal was carved out of the rock and the entire Rio Paraná was diverted into it on October 20, 1978. The new dam flooded, doing away with the Sete Quedas, or Seven Falls, once rated by *The Guinness Book of World Records* as the greatest waterfall in the world. A tour boat leaves from Porto Meira below the Iguaçu Falls and runs down the Rio Iguaçu, to the confluence of the Paraná, and then runs up the Paraná to the Itaipú construction site. Inquire at your hotel or at Porto Meira when crossing over to see Iguaçu Falls from the opposite side.

BEST EN ROUTE

You're going to pay for the comfort you seek at Iguaçu Falls, and it doesn't matter what side you're on: Argentine, Brazilian, Paraguayan. The most expensive rate is around $50; moderate is about $30 to $40; and anything under $30, inexpensive. All the hotels are in excellent condition and have spacious rooms with private baths, swimming pools, and that extra-plus amenity of a wonderful view of the falls. Make reservations before you visit, since the falls are one of South America's most breathtaking attractions.

BRAZILIAN SIDE

Das Cataratas – Because of its location alone, this is the outstanding choice of hotels on this side. Reservations hard to obtain. This 110-room hotel has front rooms with a view, private baths, and a restaurant that has a smorgasbørd every evening. Right on the *cataratas* (phone: 74-2666; in São Paulo: 289-7422; or write *Hotel das Cararatas,* Foz de Iguaçu, Paraná, Brazil). Expensive.

Bourbon – This new luxury motel has 180 rooms, a swimming pool, and a tennis court. The property is about 4 miles (7 km) from Foz de Iguaçu on the road to the falls (phone: 74-1313; in São Paulo, 223-2244). Moderate.

San Martín – 141-room motel has a swimming pool. About 10 miles (16 km) from the falls and from Foz de Iguaçu, near where the road to the airport branches off (phone: 74-2577). Inexpensive.

Salvatti – For those who prefer to stay in the city of Foz, rather than on the road between the city and falls, this hotel is centrally located, with adequate facilities. Rua Rio Branco 577 (phone: 74-2727). Expensive.

ARGENTINE SIDE

Esturion – This first-class resort hotel near the riverbank has 122 air-conditioned rooms with private bath; facilities include a restaurant, nightclub, swimming, and tennis courts. Av. Tres Fronteras 650 (phone: 2020 or 2161). Expensive.

Internacional Iguazú – A hotel with grand views of the falls and jungle (ask for a falls view); its 180 rooms have air conditioning and private baths, and facilities include a bar, casino, restaurant, and pool. Make reservations in Buenos Aires. Reconquista 585 (phone: 2790 or 2748). Expensive.

PARAGUAY SIDE

Acarai – This hotel is well known for its gambling casino. It also has a swimming pool and features live entertainment in its dining room. Turn left as you go up the main street of the town from the Rio Paraná, then follow the signs for about 1 mile on an unpaved road to the hotel, which has a fine view of the river. Puerto Presidente Stroessner (phone: Presidente Stroessner 2302). Moderate.

Chile

Chile, a 2,600-mile-long country on the southwestern edge of South America, extends from Perú and Bolivia in the north to Tierra del Fuego in the south. Its eastern boundary with Argentina is formed by the Andes; its western border by the Pacific Ocean. Within its borders, Chile contains some extremely varied terrain: from the Atacama Desert in the north to the rich vineyards and farmlands of the Central Valley, where Santiago, the capital, is located. About four million of the country's ten million inhabitants reside in the capital; nearly three-quarters of the population lives in the central valley. (For a complete report on the capital, see *Santiago*, THE CITIES.) To the south of Santiago are the lake district and the fjords and glaciers of Patagonia and the Tierra del Fuego archipelago. Easter Island, the site of mysterious giant stone figures called *moai*, is a Chilean possession, as are the Juan Fernández Islands, the supposed setting of *Robinson Crusoe*.

The climate, too, varies considerably from region to region. The central area is temperate, with seasons reversed from those in the Northern Hemisphere. Summer temperatures average in the 80s F (27°C) between November and March; winter temperatures between May and October can get as cold as the 20s F (−7°C). Spring and fall are in the 60s and 70s F (16° to 21°C). Visitors are attracted to Chile's beaches, especially those at the resort city of Viña del Mar, and to Portillo, the most famous ski resort in South America. The Atacama Desert is hot and dry throughout the year. Southern Chile is rainy even during the summer. During the winter, heavy snows are frequent.

Tawantinsuyo, the Inca Empire, extended as far south as Chile's Río Maule, but the Incas were unable to conquer the Araucanian Indians, who inhabited most of present-day Chile. In 1531, a colleague of the Spanish conquistador Francisco Pizarro headed south from Perú into what is now Chilean territory, but it wasn't until Pedro de Valdivia arrived in 1541 that the first Spanish settlement was built in Santiago. His path of conquest came to an abrupt and brutal end in 1544 with his capture by Araucanians. The conflict between settlers and Indians continued until the seventeenth century. Chile became part of the viceroyalty of Perú and remained under Peruvian jurisdiction until the late eighteenth century when immigrants from Spain, Great Britain, and Germany arrived to settle the country. Bernardo O'Higgins, a Chilean patriot, initiated a revolt against Spain in 1810, and the Argentine General José de San Martín helped Chile gain independence. In 1879, Chile seized control of nitrate fields in the Atacama Desert that belonged to Bolivia. Waging a successful military campaign, the Chilean armed forces gained control of Bolivia's Pacific seaport Antofagasta and the coastal town of Arica, which had been part of Perú. The enduring enmity among these three countries continues to this day, a legacy of the War of the Pacific that ended in 1883.

Until 1973, Chile prided itself on a 150-year tradition of democracy in which presidents and legislators were freely elected. Unlike other Latin American countries, Chile was not prone to military takeovers of the government, except during rare, brief periods of crisis. But after a period of strikes, riots, and economic troubles, the elected government of Marxist President Salvador Allende was overthrown in a military coup on September 11, 1973. Since then, a junta headed by General Augusto Pinochet has imposed tight state control and rule by military decree. The political climate in Chile today is considerably more relaxed than it was several years ago, and a number of political exiles who were forced to leave the country after the coup have started to return. But Chile still has not returned to its historic democratic government.

The Pan-American Highway is the country's main road. It is used primarily by commercial vehicles such as trucks and buses. There are very few service stations along the route and even fewer on the side roads, which are not paved. At Puerto Montt, you can get a boat or plane farther south to Tierra del Fuego or, from November to March, to Antarctica via Punta Arenas. Easter Island and the Juan Fernández Islands are only accessible by air or sea. Because of the long distances involved in traveling north-south, it is advisable to fly from one major city to another, then take a bus, train, or *colectivo* to nearby towns or resorts. If you are driving, be sure you carry spare parts and that your insurance papers and *carnet* are in order (see *Touring by Car,* GETTING READY TO GO).

The nine routes in this chapter crisscross the country. The North takes you south from the Peruvian frontier at Arica through the Atacama Desert, to the port city of Antofagasta (pop. 200,000), and through the resort town of La Serena. The Central Valley runs from Valparaíso (pop. 250,000), Santiago's port, to the seaside resort of Viña del Mar. Portillo leads from Santiago to South America's best ski resort, with a description of facilities and slopes. Ovalle to Talca explores the country's fertile farming and ranching region; Concepción to Laja Falls runs through the country's third largest city. The Lake District route passes through mountain lake resort towns, including Temuco, Valdivia, Osorno, and Puerto Montt. Chilean Patagonia and the Tierra del Fuego archipelago describes a journey through the glaciers and fjords leading to the Chilean Antarctic. Easter Island, its statues and settlements, and the Juan Fernández archipelago are described in detail.

The North

The northern third of Chile, that 1,640-mile stretch from Arica to La Serena, encompasses the Atacama, the driest desert in the world. It looks like no-man's-land but don't let it fool you. The desert's story is a dramatic and often bloody one, filled with tales of fortunes made and lost, of vicious battles fought for the enormous mineral wealth stored beneath the rock and sand. The Incas were the first to know of the desert's secrets; they mined copper from the open pit of Chuquicamata long before conquistador Diego de Almagro claimed it for the Spanish throne in 1536. (According to legend, de Almagro had his horses shod with copper shoes here when he led his troops back to Cuzco.) Eventually, the Spanish exploited the area's mineral wealth. While they found nothing like the rich gold and silver deposits of Bolivia, there was still ample silver treasure in the Inca Huantahaya mines.

The Spanish were exultant over this mineral discovery, but nothing could beat the mining boom that followed the 1809 discovery that the sodium nitrate found on the altiplano (desert plateau) near Iquique could be converted into gunpowder. At the time, Iquique belonged to Perú, as did all of Chile north of Antofagasta (the territory south of the city belonged to Bolivia). Demand for the gunpowder dropped after the colonial independence wars in the 1820s, however, and a mining lull continued until the next decade, when nitrate became important for its value as a fertilizer.

A century of profit taking began following this discovery, but territorial rivalry over the desert's mineral wealth brought about the War of the Pacific in 1879. During the 6-year conflict, Chilean troops pushed as far north as Lima in an attempt to gain independence from Perú. The soldiers successfully occupied the city and claimed for themselves the rich nitrate fields in the desert, which Chile holds to this day.

You can travel the arid, 66°F (18°C) Atacama by picking up the Pan-American Highway (Rte. 5) at the Peruvian border and continuing south. You'll enter Chile about 12 miles (19 km) north of the seaport of Arica, but be careful: The border dispute between Chile and Perú heats up from time to time, and border guards may be tense at checkpoints. Also, the area is mined, so don't stray off the road.

If you're entering from Perú, you'll receive a 90-day tourist card (renewable for another 90 days). The route south leads through Arica to the seaport of Iquique, to the copper mine of Chuquicamata and its mining town, Calama, then on to Copiapó. These towns are in the Norte Grande (Great Desert) part of the Atacama, where there is no rainfall. The next 200 miles (321 km) south through La Serena to Ovalle is Norte Chico (Little Desert), where you can swim and fish off La Serena's beaches or visit Vicuña, the home of the late Nobel Prize–winning poet Gabriela Mistral. In the Atacama's Norte Chico, rainfall makes the desert sprout with vineyards, olive groves, and mango and papaya trees.

Like other South American highways, Chile's road network is often unmarked and unpaved. The Pan-American Highway, however, is, for the most part, in excellent condition: two lanes, often with concrete siding. Because there are few gas stations in the Norte Grande, make sure your car is checked out before you leave Arica, and be sure to carry extra gas. You should also expect primitive conditions in many of the Atacama hotels. However, first-class hotels do exist in the Atacama, although few and far between, mainly in Arica and La Serena, but also in Calama, Antofagasta, Iniuique, and Copiapó.

What you lack in physical comfort will be made up for in sights. In this flat and tan-gray desert land, you'll find wildlife ranging from the near-extinct giant condor of the Andes to mountain lions, vultures, llamas, alpacas, vicuñas, skunks, falcons, pheasants, and hummingbirds. When you reach the Pacific coastline, look for dolphins, whales, sea lions, penguins, and otters, among other sea mammals and birds. A trip through the Atacama may appear boring; it steadily becomes a diversified and fascinating excursion.

ARICA: A constantly sunny climate where the temperature hardly ever dips below 66°F (18°C) has earned this town the nickname City of Eternal Spring. Arica means "desired land" in Quechua. The northernmost city of Atacama, it is really an oasis filled with flowering gardens on the edge of the Pacific. The white beaches are good for swimming, for, unlike most Chilean shores, Arica's waters are warm. Neighboring and land-locked Bolivians are particularly fond of Arica because it serves as their main port and seaside resort.

If you're not intending to snooze on the beach all day, go see some of the historical monuments in the area. The most famous spot is El Morro, a high bluff overlooking the sea, where the Chileans won one of the most decisive battles of the War of the Pacific (1879–1883). Legend has it that the Chilean soldiers downed a concoction of *aguardiente* (sugar whiskey) and gunpowder. Cushioned for war with the devil, they scaled the steep precipice of El Morro successfully to attack and defeat the Peruvians. This legend, however, is more macho myth than reality. History books show that the Chileans actually took a less harmful route up a gradual incline at the side of the hill, away from the sea. You can climb El Morro, too, but take the back route. The hill offers a good view of the town and coast. There's also a small museum on the hilltop, with arms, uniforms, flags, and other war memorabilia on display.

On the plaza near El Morro is the Church of San Marcos, built in 1868 to replace the original 1640 church, which was razed and pulled into the sea by a tidal wave. The second church was actually shipped prefab from England, and the iron steeple was designed by Alexandre Gustave Eiffel years before he built his famous Paris tower.

For shoppers, Arica has some local craft centers where goods are reasonably priced. About 10 years ago, the Chilean government initiated the Galerías Artesanales CEMA Chile. CEMA is the Centro de Madres, or Mothers' Center, designed to aid women in impoverished areas earn money for their households, and it has developed into the best chain distributor of typical artisan goods. In the Arica CEMA (Baquedano 331), you can purchase ceramics whose shapes and designs are modeled after artifacts of the pre-Inca cultures.

One good restaurant in Arica is *Da Aurelio* (21 de Mayo 459), a cozy eaterie specializing in Italian food. While you're in town, enjoy some of the local fruits and dishes. Mangoes, guayabas, and midget bananas are grown throughout the area. Local seafood dishes are tasty: Try *perol de mariscos* (seafood pot) with locos, mussels, clams, sea urchins, and rock lobsters (*langostinos*). You can also have swordfish in black butter (*albacora a la mantequilla negra*).

To wash it down, try *pusitunga,* the local aperitif made from an inland *aguardiente; pisco* sours are made with lemon, beaten egg white, and *pisco,* a grape brandy. Wine fermented in the Codpa Valley 30 miles from Arica is known as *pintantini.*

There are two railway stations in Arica: One services trains to Tacna, Perú (M. Lira 1071); the second is the terminus for trains to La Paz, Bolivia (21 de Mayo 51). While the company coaches, with their gas lights and wood paneling, may look like the original cars from 1913, travel on these two routes is comfortable and the views are spectacular. The day trip to Tacna is a 10-hour ride; it also takes 10 hours from Arica to La Paz. (This La Paz run originates in Calama, the best point to begin the sky-high rail ride; advance Pullman reservations are recommended for the overnight trip.)

The Arica tourist office is at Calle Prat 375 (phone: 32-10-1). You can take two side trips from Arica. The first is a 7-mile (11-km) trek east of the city along a paved road to the Azapa Valley. The San Miguel de Azapa Archaeological Museum here contains a collection of items from pre-Inca cultures dating back to 5000 BC.

The second side trip is about 50 miles (80 km) east of Arica on Route 11, a gravel road. The altiplano scenery includes snowcapped volcanoes and a variety of wildlife, including Darwin's fox, *pudu* (small deer), and pumas.

En Route from Arica – The 180-mile (290-km) ride south on the Pan-American to Iquique takes you through the arid Atacama, so be sure your tank is full and your car is in good shape. The highway is paved, but it's a boring ride, more so with no gas stations around. Be sure to pack a sweater: Nights can reach a chilly 57°F (14°C).

To reach Iquique, take Route 16 at the Pan-American junction and continue west.

IQUIQUE: Arriving here is like landing a small plane. The steep, winding descent from the coastal plain to the city is abrupt, and the bright reaches of the ocean come as a big surprise. Iquique, with 85,000 people, is the capital of the first region (Perú to Copiapó) and the site of numerous annual underwater fishing competitions. The city has a duty-free import zone, but there's a catch: Leaving the area, you run right into a customs check. If you're carrying more than US $240 in purchased goods (check with the *carabineros* — customs officers — as the limit changes periodically), you have to pay some stiff taxes, and bribery in Chile will get you nowhere.

One cautionary note about Iquique: The breezes off the ocean lower the heat to an average temperature of about 67°F (19°C); but the sun is still fierce. Bring a hat for protection.

Of all of Iquique's beaches, the best is Cavancha, north of the sailor's monument, a memorial to the naval battle of May 21, 1879, during the War of the Pacific. The Chilean naval hero Arturo Prat captained the *Esmeralda,* which was rammed by a Peruvian ship until it sank offshore here. Prat died when he jumped aboard the Peruvian ship as it hit the *Esmeralda.* Plaza Prat, named for the hero, houses Casino Español; the building's architecture is as Moorish as the Alhambra.

There are two museums in Iquique: the Museo Regional (Bauquedano 930) and the Archaeological Museum (Serrano 579). Both contain pre-Columbian relics and artifacts, plus mementos of naval battles.

Iquique's wide streets and brick houses seem odd to visitors. Homes were all wood frame during the nitrate boom years, and it wasn't until the 1920s that bricks were used. Set on narrow streets, the wooden houses were fire traps, and serious fires in 1875 and 1880 wiped out large portions of the city. In rebuilding the city, architects borrowed English Georgian, rococo, and Greek revival styles. A French visitor in 1866 wrote home to say that the balconies and small colonnades made the houses look like opera stages.

En Route to Chuquicamata – Continuing east on Route 16 to the Pan-American, you come to the small town of Pozo Almonte, sitting by itself on the vast expanse of the nitrate fields, or Pampa de Tamarugal. There is a small museum here, with exhibits pertaining to the nitrate boom and mementos from the War of the Pacific. In nearby Santa Laura you can visit an old nitrate office that was left exactly the way the English left it, complete with cricket field.

La Tirana, near the Route 16–Pan-American junction, is the scene of the annual July 16 feast honoring the Virgin of Carmen. Thousands of pilgrims come here for the colorful festivities; townsfolk dance wearing costumes and masks, and people walk barefoot or on their knees into town to repay their *mandas* (promises) to the Virgin for granted favors.

South of La Tirana, the Pan-American passes through Salar de Pintados, a dry salt lake. About 150 miles (241 km) outside Iquique, a paved turnoff (Rte. 24) heads both east and west. Continuing 43 miles (69 km) west on the highway takes you to Tocopilla, renowned for its deep-sea fishing. The eastbound lane of the road takes you to Chuquicamata.

CHUQUICAMATA: The green slopes of cast-off ores that make up the embankment around the world's largest pit copper mine — a 9,840-foot hole — is startling against the tan and gray Atacama Desert. An Inca mine before the Spaniards claimed it, the pit was further developed by the US Guggenheims. The mine now produces about 49,000 tons of copper annually. Tours can be arranged through the public relations office near the mine.

It is a 9-mile (14-km) drive south to Calama, the mine's support town. As you approach, posters promoting Chile's copper business dot the roadside. Once you see them, you know you're near Calama.

CALAMA: About half of the town's 70,000 residents work in or around the mine, and the city resembles the hybrid of a Pennsylvania mining town and a frontier town out of the Old (US) West. Tiny stone houses are close together; there are wooden sidewalks, saloons with swinging doors, general stores, and even a brothel or two.

Calama is set on an oasis along the bank of the Río Loa, the only river running through the Norte Grande. In town, a small archaeological museum on Ramirez Street, above the library, contains a chronologically arranged collection of pre-Inca artifacts (pottery, utensils, and so on). Also of interest is the Indian village of Chiu-Chiu, 20 miles (32 km) southeast of Calama. Follow the dirt road east through Lasana, another Indian village with low, adobe houses that was once a *pucara* (Indian fortress settlement), then swing south.

Ayquina, 35 miles (55 km) east of Chiu-Chiu (by dirt road), is famous for its September 8 religious feast day honoring the Virgin of Guadalupe. A statue of the Virgin is carred on bearers' shoulders up a hill to the town's shrine, and the people are blessed. Afterward there is a lot of dancing, merrymaking, and fireworks. Pilgrims attend masses and leave tokens of thanks at the shrine.

From Ayquina, Route 23 runs south to San Pedro de Atacama, 60 miles (96 km) away.

SAN PEDRO DE ATACAMA: This Spanish-Indian town, built on an oasis of the Río San Pedro, is famous for an archaeological museum founded in 1963 by a Belgian priest known throughout Chile as Padre La Paige. He worked for years collecting artifacts from the area, which is estimated to have been inhabited some 10,000 years ago. On display are several mummies that have been well preserved by the desert dryness and Indian ponchos over 1,000 years old.

En Route from San Pedro de Atacama – To continue to Antofagasta, retrace your route to Calama. From there, take the paved Route 55 southwest 66 miles (106 km) to the Pan-American. Then it's another 66 miles (106 km) to Antofagasta.

ANTOFAGASTA: This city of 125,000, which may strike you as unexpectedly modern, exports nitrates and the copper from Chuquicamata. There are beaches, deep-sea fishing, and three museums: the regional museum (Av. Argentina 1595), the archaeological museum (Prat 482), and the Professor Humberto Fuenzalida Museum (António Toro 956). At the last one there are plant and animal fossils more than 140 million years old and mineral samples from the desert.

Antofagasta is filled with strange attractions. Plaza Colón contains a replica of Big Ben, presented by the British in 1910. If you take a walk along Avenida Brasil, look closely at its gardens: The soil comes from different parts of the world, carried as ballast on boats that returned home loaded with nitrates. At the port, the old customs house (Balmaceda and Bolívar streets — the tourist office is here) resembles a strange combination of Spanish colonial and Swiss chalet architecture. It was built during the last century with prefabricated materials so it could be taken apart and moved. Drydocked on the Avenida Costanera, *El Galeón* is an old ship converted into a disco bar.

Antofagasta's major holiday is the June 29 feast day of San Pedro, the fishermen's patron saint. A statue of the saint is carried across the water in a motorboat procession, and a blessing is given for the fishermen's catch and well-being. A festival is held afterward. From Antofagasta, there is steamer service to Valparaíso, Iquique, and Arica; LAN-Chile operates weekly service here from Santiago en route to the US (Miami).

But you'll probably want to stay in Antofagasta for a few days before starting on your second long journey down the Atacama: the 340-mile (548-km) trip through the Norte Grande to Copiapó and La Serena in Norte Chico.

En Route from Antofagasta – You've reached the fringe of the Atacama when you've arrived in Copiapó, an oasis on the river of the same name. While no rain falls in the Norte Grande, the Norte Chico gets occasional sprinkles. Temperatures are mild, and there are valleys running east-west along the length of the desert that are good planting grounds for olive trees and grapevines. As you travel south on the Pan-American, you'll pass through Taltal, once an important nitrate port, now mainly known for the large swordfish and sea bass caught off its shores.

COPIAPÓ: The Pan-American Highway turns inland at Copiapó; you get a better feel for what an oasis is really like here. In Copiapó, you're surrounded by sand dunes as far as the eye can see. A city of some 60,000, it was founded by Pedro de Valdivia in 1540. It wasn't until the 1700s, however, that silver and gold were actually discovered, and in 1832, Juan Godoy found the rich Chanarcillo silver mines south of the city. Plaza Godoy bears a statue of the prospector, and Copiapó's other plaza, Plaza Prat, is considered one of the prettiest in all of Chile, complete with its own pool of Carrara marble imported from Italy.

The Regional Museum of Atacama (Calle Atacama 630) is in a colonial-style house built at the end of the 1800s; it displays minerals and metal tools used by the Indians and old mining equipment. The School of Mines, 1 mile north of the city, has a geological museum with more than 12,000 specimens of Chilean minerals.

En Route from Copiapó – Continue on the Pan-American for 200 miles (323 km) to reach La Serena. About 80 miles (129 km) south of Copiapó, you pass through Vallenar on the Río Huasco, a town noted for its various gardens. The soils along the Huasco are rich; there are vineyards, fruit orchards, and cattle grazing areas. From the grapes, the people of Huasco make *pajarete,* a strong, sweet wine, and *pisco.*

The Huasco Museum (Colchagua and Prat streets) houses archaeological artifacts from the preceramic Huentelauquen Indian culture and from the agricultural El Molle and Diaguita cultures, all pre-Columbian tribes that once thrived in the Norte Chico. Fossils and a regional history section are also featured here. From Huasco, you'll have to retrace your path to the Pan-American to continue on to La Serena.

LA SERENA: On entering the city, you can't miss the Alameda Francisco de Aguirre Boulevard; there are more than 37 marble sculptures lining the street like an open-air art museum. The road is indicative of the rest of the city. Founded in 1544, La Serena has preserved or remodeled old buildings in the Spanish colonial style, and there are many churches and museums. A 16th-century cathedral can be found keeping watch over the central Plaza de Armas; the 17th-century San Francisco church sits serenely on Balmaceda Street. The Archaeological Museum (Cordovez and Cienfuegos streets) contains an extensive collection of pottery and tools from the pre-Inca Atacama and Diaguita Indian cultures, and a history section preserves manuscripts of Chile's Nobel Prize–winning poet, Gabriela Mistral. The Ignacio Domeyko Geological Museum (Benavente 970) houses more than 2,000 mineral specimens. For more information, the tourist office is at Calle Infante 560.

Atop the garden-covered Santa Lucia Hill sits a *moai,* a giant, 25-foot stone man brought back from Isla de Pascua (Easter Island).

If you follow the Pan-American Highway south for 5 miles (8 km) you'll come to Coquimbo, La Serena's twin city. It's a port with little for the tourist except a recently refurbished gambling casino, Casino de Peñuelas, with roulette tables, slot machines, and dining facilities, and La Herradura (Horseshoe) Beach.

Because of the clarity of the atmosphere, three international observatories are near La Serena, and in 1986 it was a popular site for viewing Halley's Comet. Cerro Las Campanas, 86 miles (138 km) north on the Pan-American, is open to the public Mondays through Fridays; the Cerro La Silla observatory is 75 miles (120 km) north; Cerro Tololo observatory is 53 miles (85 km) east down a paved road (also open on weekdays). Visits to the observatories can be arranged.

En Route from La Serena – Winding up your tour of the Atacama, you'll want to take Route 43 east of La Serena and travel the 50 paved miles (80 km) to Ovalle. Along the way, you'll pass the town of Andacollo, which is the site of three yearly festivities. December 25, the festival honoring the Virgin of Andacollo, is the most noted feast day in the Norte Chico. The statue of the Virgin carried through the streets is said to have been found by miners who were trapped underground for 5 days and managed to survive. It reportedly belonged to a Spanish soldier who got lost in the foothills of the Andes. July 16 is the festival of the Virgin of Carmen. During October there's the Fiesta Chica, the equivalent of the German Oktoberfest.

From Andacollo, it's on to Ovalle, and the start of your journey through the Central Valley.

BEST EN ROUTE

Any hotels you find on your journey through the Atacama will be small, frequently without private bathing and sanitary facilities, except in larger towns. If you land a hotel with all the facilities in your room, however, expect to pay an expensive rate of $40 to $50 or a moderate rate, about $20 to $30 a night. Those without are very inexpensive, between $10 and $15. In most cases, rooms are doubles, with breakfast included in the price. Some hotels have no address or phone, so check with the local tourist offices. Reservations aren't usually needed unless it's holiday time.

ARICA

Hostería Arica – This 90-room hotel offers private baths and a dining room. Expensive.

Azapa Inn – 71 rooms, some deluxe, all with private bath. Swimming pool. Calle Guillermo Sánchez, Valle de Azapa (phone: 42612). Expensive.

El Paso – Small hotel with 40 double rooms. Expensive.

IQUIQUE

Hostería de Cavancha – Just about the best on the North Zone beach, the hotel has 43 rooms. Los Rieles 250. Expensive.

Arturo Prat – Hotel offers small, comfortable rooms. Av. Anibal Prat. Expensive.

Ben Ezer – You can get an American-style breakfast in this hotel, a rarity among rarities in Chilean hospitality. Beachfront. Moderate.

ANTOFAGASTA

Turismo Antofagasta – 108-room hotel offers a swimming pool, breakfast in bed, and a view of the city and port. Beachfront. Expensive.

Valparaíso and Viña del Mar

On your Chilean tour, you should leave Santiago and head 70 miles (112 km) northwest to the major seaport of Valparaíso and its sister city, Viña del Mar. Actually, these two cities are more opposite than they are alike. Valparaíso is a brawling seaport, filled with closely built, weatherbeaten houses crawling over numerous hills. Nicknamed "Pancho" by its residents, the city preserves its past in English street names and European architecture. Viña del Mar, 5 miles (8 km) north across the bay, is more a tourists' town, with clean, well-tended gardens, a casino, and long stretches of beach along a 10-mile coastal highway.

Viña del Mar is the spawn of Valparaíso, which precedes the town by more than 350 years. Founded in 1536 by Diego de Almagro, Valparaíso and the surrounding area was already inhabited by the Changos, an Indian tribe that lived off the sea and traveled the shore in canoes made of sea lion skins. The port lived a rather dull, uneventful life until English pirateers started to plunder the South American coastline in attacks against the Spanish throne. Sir Francis Drake robbed, among other things, the chalice out of Valparaíso's church in 1578, and Richard Hawkins pillaged his way down the coast 15 years later. Finally the Spanish had to build the town's first real fortress, San José, overlooking the sea.

A lot of Chilean firsts happened in Valparaíso. The first Chilean newspaper, *Aurore de Chile,* was published here on the country's first printing press in 1811, at the start of the Independence War; Valparaíso celebrated its first battle in 1813. After the war, Chile's first naval squadron sailed from here in 1818 under the command of Captain Manuel Blanco Encalada. The first steamship to sail the Pacific arrived in Valparaíso in 1822, and Charles Darwin passed through during his 6-year voyage on the HMS *Beagle* in 1834.

But it wasn't until 1874 that little Viña del Mar was even a gleam in Valparaíso's eye. That year, the town government gave José Francisco Vergara the go-ahead to build from village plans he had submitted. (Before then, Viña del Mar was no more than the hacienda of a wealthy port resident.) The resort was founded in 1878; since then, it has become popular with affluent tourists from all over Latin America.

The climate in Valparaíso and Viña del Mar is milder than that of Santiago; the temperature rarely falls below 30°F (-1°C) in winter and averages about 59°F (15°C) throughout the year. The summer heat (if any) is tempered by constant ocean breezes, and the Humboldt Current–chilled waters make sunbathing more popular than swimming along the beaches.

To reach these two cities from Santiago, the best route is to take a 90-minute scenic trip along Route 68 northwest, going through the Lo Prado tunnel instead of over the hill. Along the way, you'll pass the town of Curacavi, known for its meringue sweets, and the small farming town of Casablanca, with its Lo Vasquez church. Every December 8 you share the road with pilgrims approaching church, many on their knees, for the annual observance of the Feast of the Immaculate Conception. There is one expensive toll along this route (about $4), so make sure you have your money ready.

VALPARAÍSO: The first thing that strikes you when entering the city is that Avenida Argentina, the city's major road, is lined with monuments dedicated to, among others, Christopher Columbus, Lord Cochrane, Admiral Blanco Encalada, and the French and British colonists who settled here in the 19th century. Once you reach the downtown area, park your car and walk the city's narrow, one-way streets.

The city center is Plaza Sotomayer, with the main entrance to the port on one side and the gracious, wedding-cake Government House (Intendencia) on the other. In the middle is a monument to the Heroes of Iquique (1879), where Captain Arturo Prat and the others who died in the Battle of Iquique are buried. Every May 21 the Chilean navy stages commemorative events at the monument.

If you cross the plaza to the front of the Intendencia and turn right, you're headed south on Serrano Street, the oldest in the city. Two blocks down is the Plaza Echaurren, where the La Matriz Church stands at the site where the first chapel in Valparaíso was built in 1559. The current church was built in 1842, but the statue of Christ is from the 1600s.

Four blocks farther is the Plaza Aduana, with the old customs building. From here you can take a funicular railroad up to the top of Cerro Artilleria, where there's a terrace (Paseo 21 de Mayo) overlooking the city and bay. While you're in the port area, you can climb some of the other hills. To the right of the Intendencia as you face it is Cerro Cordillera, which houses the Lord Cochrane Sea Museum.

A longer walk around Valparaíso will take you along the coast road west. From the Plaza Aduana, take Avenida Antonio Varas, which becomes Avenida Altamirano when it reaches the shore. There are a number of restaurants in this area. *El Membrillo* (Av. Altamirano 1569) is a fisherman's cooperative and has fresh seafood at low prices. As you walk back to the main dining room, a bare porch over the water, you'll see the beach where the fishermen draw up their long, brightly painted boats, guarded by a statue of St. Peter (San Pedro), which is taken out to sea every June 29 (the saint's feast day) to bless the water, the catch, and the fishermen. While you're here, try the *sopa de mariscos,* a seafood and shellfish soup. Here, as elsewhere in Valparaíso and Viña del Mar, you can get *congrio* (conger eel), *corvina* (sea bass), *almejas* (clams), and *cholgas* (mussels).

By the way, you'll want to be here on New Year's Eve, when the city greets the new year with the wailing of ships' horns accompanying fireworks set off over the port. A good place to be is the Mirador de O'Higgins, a lookout point behind the city, where the roads from Viña del Mar and Valparaíso meet before heading on to Santiago.

Transportation is such in Valparaíso that you could go anywhere you want in the world, with steamers available to Los Angeles and New York; London; Guayaquil, Ecuador; or to Punta Arenas and Arica here in Chile. Rail express service is available on a regular basis to Santiago, Concepción, and Puerto Montt; buses also run between here and Viña del Mar, Santiago, and Concepción.

Leaving Valparaíso, take the paved road north to Viña del Mar, the little resort of 280,000 that is one of the most popular adult playgrounds in Chile.

VIÑA DEL MAR: This resort is interesting from the moment you enter it: You'll pass a sundial of flowers planted on a small, raised plot of land; it keeps perfect time and is the resort's hallmark. North of the clock overlooking the water is the summer presidential home, Cerro Castillo, a Spanish colonial mansion on the former site of the Collao fort. After Cerro Castillo, you will come to the Naval Museum (Av. Marina), which is installed in an English Tudor castle-like building, Castillo Wulff, on a small peninsula overlooking the sea. The museum contains paintings and drawings, uniforms, medals, books, maps, and documents all pertaining to Chile's naval history. Avenida Marina ends at a bridge crossing the Marga-Marga inlet; to the left is Avenida San Martín, which runs north to the beaches.

On the left of Avenida San Martín as you cross the bridge is a casino, open every night during the summer season (mid-September to mid-March), and weekend nights the rest of the year. The casino is a gambler's haven for blackjack, baccarat, and roulette tables; there's also a gaming room for *tragamonedas* (one-armed bandits), a bar, dining facilities, and a floor show. You do have to pay admission at the door (a small gamble for a good time), and you have to pay for a membership card that gives you access to the game room. The minimum roulette bet is $1; $10 for blackjack and baccarat.

If you turn right from Avenida Marina and nix the casino, you'll find yourself on Schroeders Street. At the end of the second block, turn right onto Valparaíso Street, which will take you into the town's main shopping center and Plaza Vergara, where you can trot around in a colorful, horse-drawn carriage (victoria) decked with roses.

At one side of the plaza is the municipal theater, built during the town's early years. There are concerts here on Thursdays, from 6 PM on, and on Sundays, from 11 AM on. Just south of the Plaza Vergara, one block past the railroad tracks, is a large garden park, the Quinta Vergara. Here the fine arts museum is in the mansion where the founding Vergara family lived. The building was badly destroyed in the 1971 earthquake but has been repaired and looks much as it did when the family lived there. There is a large collection of European and Chilean paintings and antique furniture.

Take Avenida Libertad from the Plaza Vergara across the bridge and take a left at Calle 3 Norte; three blocks down on Quillota is the archaeological museum, in the Rioja mansion in Rioja Park. There's a collection of pre-Columbian ceramic art from Perú, silver Araucanian jewelry, and items from Easter Island and from the Indian part of Chile's central zone. There's also a natural history collection, with stuffed species of Chilean wildlife.

Three blocks from Rioja Park is the Sporting Club, with its racetrack and playing fields for rugby, tennis, hockey, polo, and soccer. Nearby is the Sausalito Lake, a popular spot for picnics, and the Sausalito Stadium, with a capacity of 30,000. Around the lake are old willow trees, and you can take a boat ride on the lake. Beyond the lake is the municipal park, the golf club, and the Granadilla Country Club.

There are many restaurants and cafés in Viña del Mar, but a traditional gathering spot is the *Samoiedo* shop (Av. Valparaíso 637). You'll know it when you see it — it's the one with the stuffed animals in the window and crowds of young people outside. *Viñamarinos* and tourists take tea and cocktails here about 5 PM every day; one Chilean cocktail to try is a sherry punch, *vaina,* made with egg, milk, and sherry.

Hotel reservations are always recommended during the summer season, but especially in February, when Viña del Mar hosts its annual popular music festival in the Quinta Vergara Greek Theater. Attracting singers from all over the world, the event gets sold out and it's even difficult to find a camping spot in the area. The town goes crazy, with mobs of young people jamming the streets and having a good time.

If you're heading out to the beach — and usually you'll have to wait until early afternoon if you want sun — take Avenida Libertador north to the end and turn left at the Regiment Coracero onto Calle 15 north. In one block you're on Avenida Jorge Montt, the road along the coast.

The coastal ride is exhilarating: You drive along a winding road over the crest of Viña del Mar's rocky shoreline, the surf pounding to your left and a cliff with woods or houses with colorful gardens on the right. The first beach is Las Salinas; farther down the road is Reñaca, one of the most popular beaches, with a fairly wide strip of sand and a series of little shops selling ice cream and beer. As you hit the Reñaca area, a honky-tonk conglomeration of pizza parlors, hamburger dens, and dancing spots remind you of the crowded US Atlantic coast.

On the hill above Reñaca beach is the area's most famous discotheque, *Topsy-Topsy*. Perched at the top of a very high cliff, one of the discotheque's many rooms has a superb view of the bay, with the lights of Valparaíso in the distance. Each room is decorated differently; in one, you skip over little ponds to dance and retire for your drinks to little caves. There's a two-story slide to take you from one floor to another.

En Route from Viña del Mar – The fastest way back to Santiago is east on Route 68. However, you might want to take the scenic Agua Santa road that winds around the hills of Viña del Mar back to that route rather than return to Valparaíso to pick up the same road. If you leave Viña del Mar in the evening at sunset, you'll see a phenomenon for which Valparaíso is noted. The setting sun reflected on the windows of Valparaíso's homes seems to set the city's hills afire.

If you want to explore a bit more of the coastline east of Santiago, take the road that turns south off Route 68 just a few miles beyond Casablanca. This will take you to Algarrobo, a less noted, less crowded, and now fashionable beach resort, and on to the quiet and progressively less fashionable beaches of El Quisco, El Tabo, Las Cruces, and Cartagena.

From here, it's about 25 miles (40 km) from the turnoff to Algarrobo and another 25 miles (40 km) to the port of San Antonio, Chile's fourth largest seaport (pop. 50,000). Isla Negra, where Pablo Neruda had his home, is a little south of El Quisco. Despite its name, Isla Negra is not an island, and you can visit Neruda's home and the women there who make the small, embroidered-cloth and hand-sewn scenes of rural Chilean life, the *bordadores de Isla Negra*. Just south of San Antonio is the small summer town of Rocas de Santo Domingo, a garden spot perched on a cliff overlooking the sea. This is a summer village of private homes of well-off Chileans.

From San Antonio you can return to Santiago in about 2½ hours, taking Route 78 through the Central Valley farming district. Include a visit to one of the local vineyards, such as Viña Concha y Toro.

BEST EN ROUTE

In the resort area you'll need advance reservations, more so in the summer months (mid-September to mid-March) and especially in February, when Viña del Mar hosts its annual popular singing festival. Hotels in Valparaíso are a lot less expensive than those in Viña del Mar — you can find a comfortable, clean room for about $15 a night — but the better properties are in the resort town and it is expensive. Viña del Mar hotels are from over $50 (expensive) to $35 (moderate) per person, but you get private baths, telephones, and often coastal views and excellent service.

VALPARAÍSO

Condell – 50-room hotel features comfortable facilities and amenities. Piramede and Condell (no phone). Moderate.

Prat – 100 rooms facing bay and sea. Condell 1443 (phone: 25-30-81). Moderate.

VIÑA DEL MAR

Miramar – 100-room hotel features single and double rooms, private baths, phones, dining rooms, bars, terraces, and walk-ups to rocky cliffs overlooking the ocean. Caleta Abarca (phone: 66-4077). Very expensive.

O'Higgins – 300-room hotel offers private baths, phones, a dining room, bar, valet service, and other amenities. Plaza Vergara (phone: 88-20-16). Expensive.

Alcazar – 75-room hotel near railroad station offers a friendly atmosphere. Alvarez 646 (phone: 68-51-12). Moderate.

San Martín – 120-room hotel offers private baths and phones. A dining room and bar service are there when you need them. Av. San Martín and Calle 8 Norte (phone: 97-25-48). Moderate.

ROCAS DE SANTO DOMINGO

Las Rocas – Basic, clean, friendly, on a cliff overlooking the sea, it is the traditional hotel in town. La Ronda 180 (phone: 31-34-8). Moderate.

Portillo

Ski enthusiasts throughout the world smile knowingly or wistfully at the mention of Portillo, Chile's renowned ski resort nestled in the highest peaks of the Chilean-Argentine Andes. Just 80 miles (129 km) northwest of Santiago, looming 9,230 feet above sea level, beginners and pros alike have challenged the jagged, hair-raising slopes. The extra thrill for North Americans is skiing at its best — in July and August. There's something in Portillo for everyone: You can live a life of leisure and hang out by the fire in the *Portillo* hotel and skate on Laguna del Inca; or you can brave the toughest slope in the world — 2,405-foot Roca Jack, its slope inclined half its length. If the thought of descending on a near-45° angle doesn't scare you, then perhaps the local lore about the slope will: "Jack" was a old-time local skier who used to ascend the slope every morning, then stand there and admire the Andean view until he had enough guts to parallel down.

Since Portillo has the best ski slopes around, the best skiers converge here annually to keep themselves in shape. It is the summer home for national ski teams from the US, Canada, and Europe; its ski school is operated by former international ski champions. There are trails for skiers of all classes, but the most famous runs are one going 9 miles cross-country to the Christ of the Andes monument on the Argentine border and another 4-mile track down Mt. Ojos de Agua. The *Gran Hotel Portillo* has been owned by Robert Purcell since 1961. Purcell is a Rockefeller-affiliated investment banker who fell in love with the area while here on business. Today, his nephews operate the resort. Purcell himself has been known to sneak a few snowplows down the slopes on several occasions.

The skiing season here lasts from May through October, with the Ski Carnival held in August. Several airlines, including LAN-Chile, offer 14- to 28-day ski packages to Portillo alone or to Portillo and Bariloche, Portillo's resort rival east across the Andes in Argentina. All flights bring you into Santiago; from there, you're bused up into the mountains or you can rent your own car.

Before packing yourself off to the plane, however, there are two important things to keep in mind. First of all, part of the resort, except for a small restaurant, is shut down from November through January; after that, several rooms containing bunk beds are opened from January through May for any visitors trekking through. The beds are in an octagonal building near the main hotel, where the downstairs cafeteria is opened for dining. A few years ago, the hotel ownership initiated summer activities, which included horseback riding and hiking, but these were abandoned due to a lack of interest. The only entertainment you'll get during the summer is swimming in the resort's pool or gazing at the clear, Andean scenery — and it is superb.

The second important reminder is this: If you do visit Portillo during the winter, be prepared to overstay. Snowstorms are known to hold up activities, and if you're snowed in beyond your reservation, you're going to have to pay for the extra time spent there. One particular blizzard in 1978 lasted 20 days, and traffic to and from the hotel was cut, period. Desperate skiers who were either broke or suffering from cabin fever were finally flown out by helicopter.

There are two routes to Portillo. You can take the Pan-American Highway northwest out of Santiago to La Calera, exploring some of the Central Valley towns before heading on to San Felipé and Los Andes; or you can take paved Route 57 north from Santiago to Los Andes, making a 10-mile (16-km) detour west to visit San Felipé before heading on to Los Andes and Portillo on Route 60 once again.

The first route takes you 43 miles (69 km) out of Santiago to your first stop, the small village (10,000 people) of Llay-Llay. The town received its name from the way the Indians said the wind sounded as it blew through the valley.

A few miles south of La Calera on Route 62 are three swimming holes. Farther south are the garden hills of Quillota and Limache; during the September 18 and 19 *fiestas patrias,* the rodeo shows are fun. East of Limache on a gravel road is Olmue, where there's a *huaso* festival during the second half of January and rodeos in November and February. From here, return to Llay-Llay and continue east on Route 60 to San Felipé, where you will find a small archaeological and historical museum containing mementos of José de San Martín and Bernardo O'Higgins. Continuing west on Route 60 you'll reach Panquehue and the vineyards that produce some of Chile's best wine.

A paved route north from San Felipé runs to the small colonial town of Putaendo, where the 4,000-strong army of liberators San Martín and O'Higgins rested in February 1817 after crossing the Andes from Argentina. From here, the troops marched to the south side of Chacabuco Hill to stage a comeback by defeating the Spanish. East of San Felipé on a paved road are two small copper-, gold-, and silver-mining towns, Santa María and Catemu; north of Santa María are the Jahuel hot springs. If you take the Route 60 stretch east of San Felipé for about 15 miles (24 km) you'll reach Curimon, where a Franciscan colonial church (Calle Real) houses a colonial religious museum. From here, it's on to Los Andes.

LOS ANDES: Founded in 1791, this town of 28,000 is an important transportation center for rail and road traffic to Argentina. The road from here that crosses the border is the only link between La Serena and Talca, and much of the Chile-Argentina tourist trade passes this way.

There's little for a tourist to do here other than wander through the town's plazas and rest before taking the steep ascent from Los Andes, 2,400 feet above sea level, to Portillo. One place you can check out (if you're stuck in a snowstorm and need some overnight fun) is the *El Silo* disco (Av. Tocornal), housed in a converted silo.

  En Route from Los Andes – It's about 40 miles (64 km) — all uphill — from here to Portillo. The sky gets increasingly bluer, reaching an astonishing intensity for eyes used to gazing up through city pollution. The paved road parallels the Río Aconcagua to Río Colorado. You then follow the Aconcagua past the Salto del Soldado waterfall and on to Río Blanco, where the Blanco and Juncal rivers join to form the Aconcagua. The road then runs along the Juncal to Portillo; it is increasingly steep, with many hairpin turns. During the winter, the snowdrifts reach above the roof of a small car, and sometimes the road is blocked. But it's paved all the way and in good condition.

PORTILLO: Despite the altitude, the bright yellow *Gran Hotel Portillo,* a curved slice of sunshine at the end of the road, is set in a valley with mountain peaks that tower to great heights on three sides. To the right as you come up the hill are the beginner and intermediate slopes; to the left, the craggy face of Roca Jack.

By the time you get this far, you'll be able to get a glimpse of Mt. Aconcagua, which at 22,834 feet is the highest mountain in South America, just over the border in Argentina.

Portillo gets its name from the original name of the Portillo Cordillera in Argentina, higher than the separate Peuquenes Ridge on the Chilean side. A short distance beyond Portillo, along paved Route 60, the border is marked by a large statue of Christ the Redeemer, erected in 1904. The statue, cast from the bronze of cannon used in the independence wars against Spain, bears the legend: "These mountains will crumble before Argentines and Chileans break the peace sworn at the feet of Christ the Redeemer." Well, the mountains haven't crumbled yet, the northern Atacama Desert dispute between Chile and Perú is quiet for the moment, and the southern Beagle Channel argument between Chile and Argentina has been resolved by a treaty negotiated by the pope — so the ridges aren't rumbling much now.

Behind the hotel is Laguna del Inca, 3 miles long and about 1 mile wide. If you're here in the spring and hear some strange groans coming from the lake, don't worry: It's only the ice. That is, white men say it's the ice, but Indian legend says otherwise. Actually, that's Indian Illi Yunqui you hear, crying for his lover Kora-llé, who lies at the bottom of the lake. She died when she fell from one of the precipices surrounding the water, and poor Illi decided the only fitting burial place for her was in the lake. As Kora-llé's body sank to the bottom, the water turned emerald green, taking the color of her eyes. The lake, with three snow-covered mountains rising from its shores, is one of the most dramatic scenes in Chile.

Skiing is of prime interest. The ski school is currently managed by Hartmut Helmstreit, and offers group and private lessons for beginning, advanced, and expert skiers. Ski equipment can be rented. You can also spend your days lounging and tanning on the deck; swimming in the heated pool, outdoors, or shooting pool indoors. Or you can dine, take in a movie, disco, or simply keep watch at the bar (open from 11 AM to 10 PM). There's just one rule at the hotel: Wear a jacket to dinner. You can't escape this even if you're on a national ski team.

When you really can't stay in Portillo much longer, and if you don't have a car, there is scheduled bus service, a 2-hour trip one way, operated by Gray Line (Agustinas 1173; phone: 696-0518 or 72-3923). Buses leave from either the *Sheraton Carrera* or *Crowne Plaza* hotels; fare is approximately $20.

BEST EN ROUTE

The best service in any Chilean hotel is rendered at the only hotel in Portillo. Guests have to pay the price, whether it be the basic $28 and $100 reservation fee for a bunk with common bath or the $654 ski-week rate, double occupancy. Reservations are mandatory. Keep in mind that the *Gran Hotel Portillo* shuts down from November through January, with only some accommodations open from January until May, the start of the ski season.

LOS ANDES

Continental – Second-class hotel, offering a common bath and comfortable bed. Esmeralda 211 (phone: 21510). Inexpensive.

PORTILLO

Gran Hotel Portillo – A 220-unit hotel with everything: ski lessons, rentals, and slopes; swimming, ice skating, pool tables, Ping-Pong, disco, bar, and other amenities included. The address in Santiago is Roger de Flor 2911, Las Condes (phone: 231-3411).

Basic bunks are also available in the train station, where you share baths. Inexpensive.

Ovalle to Talca

The 400-mile (645-km) stretch of land from Ovalle south to Talca leads to the heart of Chile's Central Valley, comfortably sandwiched between the Chilean Andean Cordillera (ridge) and the Pacific coast. More than 70% of Chile's population of 12 million lives here, 4 million alone in the Greater Santiago area (for detailed information, see *Santiago* in THE CITIES). Considered a fringe town of the Atacama, Ovalle is the meeting point of desert and fertile valley; a number of oases here have been transformed into national parks, including Parque Fray Jorge and Parque Talinay. When you head south on the Pan-American Highway and reach La Ligua, 150 miles (240 km) away, you run into the start of a mild, rainy zone that stretches past Talca to the southernmost end of the desert and Concepción (see *Concepción to Laja Falls*). Vegetation becomes greener south of Santiago, thanks to the many rivers that irrigate the area. You'll cross water a dozen times between here and Talca. This part of the valley is the country's fruit-growing, grain-raising, and cattle district — a multitude of *fundos* (farms). The valley is breathtaking: rows of alamos bending in the southwesterly winds; groves and groves of eucalpytus trees; and an occasional weeping willow drooping by the water.

Agriculturally, Chile is a fairly well-developed country, and during recent years exports of agricultural produce have increased substantially, due to improvements in agricultural techniques. As recently as 1969, however, there existed large haciendas where the majority of wealthy, absentee owners exploited peasant labor; Araucanians who were previously indentured into serfdom on the farms gave in to the *inquilino* (tenant farmer system) rather than work in the owner's employ.

An agricultural reform program instituted under the presidency of Eduardo Frei (1964–70) continued through the ill-fated leadership of Salvador Allende (1970–73) and, despite the military junta led by General Augusto Pinochet Ugarte that deposed Allende, continued to the end of 1978. An active government policy to stimulate agricultural exports may eventually modernize farming in the Central Valley, but it may also mean that small farmers and cooperatives will fold as modern agro-industry spreads.

Chile's colonial heritage is strongly felt in the Central Valley: Landowners descended from the early Basques and Castilians were pushed strongly for independence from Spain and the viceroy of Lima, who ruled colonial Chile. Many of the independence war's important battles were fought here, and on February 12, 1818, Bernardo O'Higgins signed Chile's declaration of independence at Talca.

Continuing your tour from the Atacama on the Pan-American, you'll pass through some of the oldest towns in Chile. Talca dates back to 1592; San Fernando, 1742; Rancagua and Curicó, 1743. Most of these towns are craft towns, and you can pick up a variety of ponchos, baskets, and ceramics. At times, the highway will flirt with the Pacific coast, taking you to some small resorts, including Papudo and Zapallar, known for their fishing and sailing. While you're in Rancagua, see if you can arrange a tour of the El Teniente copper mine; the public is invited on occasion.

OVALLE: This small town of 37,000 people signals the start of the Central Valley. The arid desert of the Atacama blends into green, fertile valleys and pastures; the area around Ovalle is ripe with orchards of various fruit, from apples to oranges and mangoes; there are even vineyards.

Ovalle's biggest attraction is its privately owned Archaeological Society (Vicuña MacKenna 521), which displays pre-Inca items from an Indian cemetery discovered at a stadium construction site in 1962. Pieces include artifacts and relics from various preceramic cultures, including the Valle del Encanto, Huentelauquen, Ell Molle, and Diaguita.

The town is a good base for visiting the nearby national parks, which are reached by paved roads. Parque Fray Jorge is 18 miles (29 km) west of Ovalle; it is a natural forest in the middle of the Atacama fringe. Parque Talinay, another oasis-type park, is 35 miles (56 km) southeast.

If you prefer, you can take a short, 20-mile (32-km) ride down the Pan-American south of Ovalle until you come to a small, paved road that will take you in less than a mile to Termas de Socos, noted for thermal, therapeutic springs.

   En Route from Ovalle – A paved road leads to the coast, where you can pick up the Pan-American south to La Ligua. On the way you'll pass thin, rocky beaches and Huentelauquen, site of the excavated Indian cemetery and famous for its cheese. About 100 miles (162 km) south of Ovalle is Los Vilos, a fishing village with 5,000 inhabitants and wide, sandy beaches (camping is permitted). A short road north from the village leads to Conchali Bay, where the beach is protected from coastal winds by a cover. Some 15 miles (22 km) south of Los Vilos, Pichidangui Beach offers deep-sea fishing and diving. From here, it's another 30 miles (48 km) to La Ligua.

   If you prefer, you can take an alternate paved road to La Ligua and skip the beach. This road parallels the Pan-American, traveling over some rough, hilly territory that eventually leads to Combarbalá. Forty-five miles (72 km) south of Combarbalá on the same road is Illapel, a small town of 12,000 on the Río Choapa. A nearby petrified forest contains *petroglifos* (rock etchings). From Illapel, another road southwest leads into Los Vilos and the Pan-American, which you'll ride until you come to La Ligua.

LA LIGUA: This small, heartland town is famous for its brown and gray vicuña and alpaca garments: ponchos, sweaters, jackets, coats, and even bolt wool. And you can forget about your diet: the *alfajores,* cookies made with layers of *manjar blanca* (blancmange) from cooked milk, are irresistible. Both clothing and food are sinfully inexpensive.

After you've finished indulging yourself, a 12-mile (19-km) drive northeast along a dirt road will take you to Cabildo, where you'll digest while wandering among the old-style Araucanian houses of straw and adobe. Fifteen miles (24 km) southwest of La Ligua on the same road are the beach resorts of Papudo and Zapallar. Six miles (9 km) apart, both are noted for water skiing and sailing. While Papudo caters to the middle-class resorter, Zapallar is visited by a more wealthy clientele, who own large homes that date back 100 years. At Zapallar, you can grab the boat ride to nearby Isla de los Lobos and watch the sea lions.

You'll have to return to La Ligua before continuing south on the Pan-American another 147 miles (237 km) through Santiago to Rancagua.

En Route from La Ligua – Via the Pan-American you'll reach the Río Colina and Huechun Reservoir, about 25 miles (40 km) north of Santiago. There's good trout fishing here, so if you've packed your rod, you'll find some action. From here you can take a road northeast toward Santiago's own little ski resort, an area containing three slopes: Parva, Farellones, and El Colorado. The slopes are connected by lifts, and there is skiing for the beginner, novice, and pro alike. Next you go southwest on Route 78 to Maipú, where the decisive battle of the independence war was fought against the Spaniards in 1817. Legend says that liberator Bernardo O'Higgins, who later became Chile's first head of state, prayed to the Virgin of Carmen before the battle and promised that, if the Chileans won, he would erect a shrine in her name on that site. Today, the ground floor of the shrine houses a museum of colonial weapons, furniture, clothing, and historical documents. Religious embroidery from the 12th to the 19th century and a collection of horse-drawn carriages are also featured.

Continuing southwest along Route 78 are two small villages famous for their crafts. Talagante, 26 miles (41 km) southwest of Santiago, makes ceramic figurines representing the traditional Chilean *huaso* (cowboy) festival, which takes place throughout central Chile on Cuasimodo, the Sunday after Easter. The brightly painted figures portray the ceremony, which includes a priest carrying the Host throughout town to the bedridden faithful accompanied by *huasos* on horseback or, where villages are more modern, on bicycles and motorcycles.

Another road you can take southeast from Santiago goes through the Cajón del Maipo (Maipo Canyon). This road stretches about 60 miles (96 km), then ends at the Morales hot springs, Baños Morales, at the fringe of the Cordillera, the Andes mountain range. The springs are 6,800 feet above sea level, with temperatures ranging as high as 77°F (25°C). The springs are recommended for rheumatism, bronchial problems, and nerves.

RANCAGUA: Essentially, this is the support town for the El Teniente copper mine, Chile's third largest mine, 42 miles (67 km) northeast of the city. About one-half of the city's 140,000 people depend directly on the mine for their livelihood. Founded in 1743, Rancagua was the site of the famous 1814 battle between Bernardo O'Higgins's revolutionary troops and Spanish royalists in which the Chilean forces were defeated. The plaza, known as the Plaza de Héroes, is significantly different from other plazas in Chile in that two main streets form a cross through the middle, where a statue of O'Higgins stands. The colonial museum on the corner of Estado and Ibieta streets, installed in an 18th-century house, the Casa del Pilar de Piedra (House of the Stone Pillar), contains many O'Higgins items.

You can eat well-prepared Chilean food in the *Mi Ruca* restaurant (Av. Cachapoal). If you prefer to eat on the road outside of town, ask for the *Munich* restaurant at the tourist office (Ferman Riesco 277).

Rancagua and the area south are known as *huaso* land, strong in cowboy tradition, and many places have a *media luna* (corral), with weekend rodeos. Rancagua's *media luna* is the most important in Chile, and every March the national rodeo championship is held here.

There are a few noteworthy towns east of Rancagua, where you can go for a day trip. Machali does a good tourist trade during the *fiestas patrias,* the September 18 and 19 commemoration of Chilean independence. The town becomes an incarnation of the *huaso* tradition, with dancing and *chicha* drinking in the small town *ramadas,* open-air huts covered with tree branches. *Chicha* is brewed from the first grapes of the season and goes down as easily as punch — a wallop, that is.

About 13 miles (20 km) west of Rancagua is the town of Doñihue, where elaborately embroidered and woven *huaso chamantos* (ponchos) are made. Eight miles (11 km) farther east is the turnoff for the Cauquenes hot springs, where the hot waters vary from 104° to 122°F (40° to 50°C) and are good for kidney, skin, and nerve disorders.

En Route from Rancagua – The area around the 60-mile (96-km) stretch of the Pan-American Highway between Rancagua south to Curicó is strewn with little towns devoted to some type of craft, whether it be wicker, straw works, weaving, pottery, or making the massive, wooden Chilean stirrups. You'll pass the broom-making town of Rengo first, 18 miles (29 km) from Rancagua. Farther on, you'll be greeted by a short stretch of wicker furniture lining the road, obviously begging to be bought. This is Chimbarongo, where prices are about a third of what they are in Santiago. If you're in the market for artisan goods, however, an alternative is to wait until you hit the markets at Curicó.

CURICÓ: The market in this town of 41,000 takes up an entire block between Rodríguez and Pena streets. Here you'll find basketry from Panimavida, pottery from Cauquenes, blankets and capes from Talca, ponchos and shawls from Quinamavida, and stirrups from La Lajuela. Smoked delicatessen meats can also be purchased, and you can even hail a taxi — a horse-drawn carriage, that is.

From Curicó it's a 40-mile (64-km) drive to Talca.

TALCA: Many mementos from the War of Independence are preserved here. In the crypt near the main altar of the small town's brick and concrete cathedral is the birth certificate of Bernardo O'Higgins. The historical museum on the main street (Calle Uno Norte 875) was the headquarters of Chile's first government junta in 1813: This is where O'Higgins signed the act of independence. The museum houses other colonial items and a collection of Chilean paintings.

You can buy some local goods at the marketplace, but the area menu outshines the baskets. The dish to sample is *chancho en piedra,* a pork dish with a sauce of tomato, onion, garlic, and *aji.* The recipe's name is derived from how it's made, on a grinding stone. If you don't care to try it in the market, then ask for it in any of the restaurants that line the Río Claró, near Urzua Park. The tourist office is in the Edificio Intendencia and is happy to assist you.

About 95 miles (153 km) southeast of Talca down a paved road is Maule Lake, a popular spot for trout fishing and camping. On the coast east of Talca is the beach resort of Constitución, at the mouth of the Río Maule, surrounded by small hills covered with pine trees. On the north bank of the river are the Quivolgo and Junquillar beaches, with some striking rock formations: seagulls, a church, and a lover's arch. The restaurants here are known for their seafood, especially sea bass, sea urchins (*erizos*), and *locos.*

As you leave Talca and Constitución and continue south, you're going to hit Chile's rainy regions. Be forewarned and carry rain gear, even in the summer.

BEST EN ROUTE

You're going to run into more so-so hotels than good ones in this part of the Central Valley. Fortunately, prices are moderate — about $25 to $35 — for a double room and meal. The smaller, more primitive hotels cost anywhere from $10 to $20 a night; they aren't listed here because of their poor quality. If you're staying in this area, your best bet would be to make reservations in Santiago.

OVALLE

Turismo Ovalle – A first-class hotel that offers both single and double rooms. Victoria 295 (phone: 159). Moderate.

TERMAS DE SOCOS

Termas de Socos – A health resort that offers one first-class hotel for rest and recuperation. Pan-American Hwy. Km. 368 (464). Moderate.

TALCA

Plaza – This 45-room property is the best in town. Antonio Varas 708 (phone: 33591). Moderate.

Concepción to Laja Falls

There's a bit of blood and gore in everyone's past, and Chile is no exception. The Pan-American Highway, heading south from Concepción to Laja Falls where the Central Valley meshes into the start of the forest and Lake District, is laced with horror stories of the Spanish attempt to dominate the Indians. One such tale belongs to conquistador Pedro de Valdivia, who in 1551 crossed the Río Bío-Bío and set up cities at Imperial, Angol, Villarrica, and Valdivia, and forts at Tucapel, Buren, and Arauco.

Now de Valdivia, who founded Concepción the previous year, was after the heads (if not the hearts) of the Araucanian Indians, otherwise known as Mapuches. The Mapuches put up stiff resistance, and when they destroyed the forts at Tucapel and Arauco under the leadership of Cacique (Chief) Caupolicán, de Valdivia rushed to Tucapel with reinforcements. Cacique Lautaro, whom de Valdivia had imprisoned at Concepción, escaped and went on to lead his tribe in bloody battle in December 1555. Not one Spaniard escaped alive, and de Valdivia was captured as he fled from the battleground. As he pleaded mercy from Caupolicán and Lautaro, another chief came up from behind and bashed his head in with a club. Lautaro's troops then overran Concepción and moved on to take Santiago; Lautaro, however, was betrayed by one of his men on the banks of the Río Mataquito, outside Curicó. His head was carried off by the Spanish on a pike to Santiago. Caupolicán himself was impaled on a stake after he was taken prisoner in 1558.

The area's violent history continued into recent years in the fights between a revolutionary peasant movement and the landowners (1971–73), followed by incidents between the military and the leftists following the 1973 coup deposing President Allende.

Despite the past violence, the countryside has a peaceful atmosphere, with golden wheat fields and groves of eucalyptus, pine, and the native alerce and araucaria trees. Native hardwoods unknown to the rest of the world — coigüe, raulí, lingue, canelo — appear. The only thing missing is the wildlife, largely exterminated as farmers cleared the land for planting and pasturing domestic animals. A number of rivers irrigate the land, and fish, including several varieties of trout, pejerrey, and perch, are abundant.

This route will take you from Talca south to Concepción, a city largely populated by the descendants of the German immigrants who came here in the 1800s. From Concepción, you will go through the coal mines of Coronel and Lota to Cañete and a small lake district, then on to Laja Falls, a popular honeymoon area. Any travel assistance needed can be acquired at the tourist office in Concepción (Anibal Pinto 460; phone: 29-20-1). The first city you'll come to on the Pan-American is Linares.

LINARES: This small town of 38,000 is worth a stop if you're interested in colonial history. One of the first battles of the Independence War was fought in the Plaza de Armas; the art and artisan museum (Av. Valentin Letelier 580) contains works of Chilean artists dating back to the 1820s. The town's cathedral is the replica of one in Milan, Italy, and the mantel altar was partly donated by Pope Pius XII.

   En Route from Linares – The Pan-American from Linares to Chillán is another 60 miles (90 km); along the way, you'll come to Parral, the birthplace of Chile's second Nobel Prize–winning poet, Pablo Neruda (1905–73); the house where Neruda was born is near the railroad station. From here, you can take Route 128 west to Cauquenes, some 33 miles (56 km) away, where artisans from Pilen, a town 25 miles (40 km) west of here, sell their light red clay pottery at the Saturday market. If you follow a dirt road 24 miles (42 km) northwest, you'll come to Pelluhue, a small beach with black sand. You can eat seafood — raw or cooked — brought in by the fishermen right at the wharves. A gravel road east along the Pacific coast leads to Constitución (see *Ovalle to Talca*). If you retrace your steps, the Pan-American will lead into Chillán.

CHILLÁN: This rather modern city of 130,000 is noted for its famous natives: Bernardo O'Higgins; Captain Arturo Prat; contemporary pianist Claudio Arrau; painter Pacheco Altamirano; and writer Marta Brunet.

The marketplace (5 de Abril 779) is a good place to sample the local dishes. You can try pork with *pebre* (a spicy onion-tomato sauce), sea bass filled with sausage, and two ground corn dishes: *humitas* (corn wrapped in leaves) and *pastel de choclo* (corn pie). Some of the local drinks include *malicia* (coffee laced with the local *aguardiente*) and *chicha* made from *michai,* a local bush. Crafts sold in the *Feria Libre* adjoining the market include black and white pottery from Quinchamali, horsehair and vegetable fiber figures from Rari, and baskets from Mehuin.

Leaving Chillán en route to Concepción, follow the Pan-American south for about 16 miles (25 km) before turning west onto Route 148. From the turnoff, it's about 50 miles (80 km) to Concepción.

CONCEPCIÓN: The third largest urban center in Chile, this city of 250,000 (mostly German descendants) is 354 miles (580 km) southwest of Santiago and is known for its sometimes violent rainstorms. Not unduly cold, summer temperatures range from 57° to 75°F (14° to 23°C); during the extended rainy season (April to September), the temperatures drop to between 46° to 66°F (8° to 19°C).

One of Concepción's prime tourist attractions is the Universidad de Concepción. The landscaped school grounds are a park in themselves, with a pond sheltering black-necked swans from the Chilean south. The Pinacoteca Museum in the university contains a large collection of paintings by well-known Chilean artists.

The Plaza Independencia, the largest of seven plazas here, houses the city's cathedral, built in 1940 with a gold and ceramic mosaic in the central nave. Six blocks from the plaza you can climb the 300-foot Cerro Caracol for a good view of the city.

Concepción is a city with good seafood; try the shrimp *al pil pil* (in garlic juice) at *El Galeon. Da Salvatore* (O'Higgins 448) specializes in Italian food.

Train service is available from Concepción to Santiago, Temuco, and Valdivia daily;

to Puerto Montt, it runs on a thrice-weekly basis, so check schedules. A mural depicting the city's history is painted on the wall at the railroad station. LAN-Chile offers daily service to Santiago (connections in Valdivia and Puerto Montt) year-round; if you prefer, you can hop a bus for the 9-hour trip to Santiago. The National Tourist Office is at Anibal Pinto 460, near Plaza Independencia.

You might want to venture out of Concepción to the Hualpen Farm, a few miles from the city overlooking the mouth of the Río Bío-Bío. This museum is the house of famed adventurer Pedro del Río Zanartu and contains items he collected during his four round-the-world voyages. He donated everything to the city on his death in 1918.

South from here along a progressively impoverished road is Lebu, founded as a village-fortress by the Spanish and twice destroyed by the Araucanians. Lebu has a nice beach you can get to by motorboat; near the beach is a large rock formation known as the Cave (it's shaped like one).

You'll have to head back by Route 148 to Chillán from Concepción before continuing the 170 miles (274 km) to Temuco, with a stop some 45 miles (72 km) south of Chillán at the Laja Falls.

LAJA FALLS: These falls are considered one of Chile's most beautiful natural attractions; you can spot them from the highway before you reach them. Salto del Laja falls about 120 feet before crashing into a rocky gorge, a rainbow forming above them in the constant fine spume.

En Route from Laja Falls – Continue east another 19 miles (30 km) to Los Angeles, where you can stop at the clubhouse of the local fishing club. From here, you can take a side road 111 miles (179 km) northeast to the Antuco Volcano and its three ski runs.

Then you can get on the Pan-American, which leads east onto a gravel road to the hot springs of Tolhuaca and Río Blanco. Returning to the Pan-American takes you into Temuco and Chile's favorite lake resort area.

BEST EN ROUTE

From Concepción into the Lake District, you're going to have to make hotel reservations beforehand, since the area is popular with Chileans and foreigners alike. Most of the hotels listed below lack telephones, so you'll have to make arrangements with the local tourist offices or with recommended organizations. Don't expect a small-town hotel to be the Ritz, but you can have very comfortable accommodations (with or without private baths) in most places for an expensive $40 or a moderate $20 to $30. As you get into the Lake District prices are going to rise, and you'll probably find yourself paying about $10 more for a room here than you would up north.

LINARES

Linares – This 28-room hotel offers private baths and sitting as well as dining rooms. Central. Moderate.

CHILLÁN

Termas de Chillán – In a Shangri-la setting at the base of the Chillán volcano, 5,400 feet above sea level, this beautiful 100-room resort, long famed for its thermal springs, has achieved prominence as one of the leading ski centers in South America and one of the most popular resorts in Chile. Guests enjoy an unusually wide range of amenities, including lounges with fireplaces, a comfortable dining room, a disco, and a video cinema. Best of all, after a demanding day tired skiers can ease their tired muscles in the heated outdoor pool or in the individual or family indoor thermal baths. Advance reservations are essential and best booked through Santiago tour operators. 50 km east of Chillán. Expensive.

Isabel Riguelme – A 68-room hotel that offers single and double rooms with private baths; additional amenities include smoking and dining rooms. Moderate.

CONCEPCIÓN

Araucano – A 300-unit hotel that provides private baths, telephones, swimming pool, restaurant, and disco. Caupolican 51. Expensive.

LAJA FALLS–LAJA

Mariscal Alcazar – A 25-room hotel with private baths and a dining room, in the center of town. Expensive.

Motel del Laja Falls – Hotel offers swimming pool, bar, and dining room with an added, wonderful amenity — it's right next to the falls. Expensive.

LOS ANGELES

Two ski lodges on the Antuco Volcano offer accommodations, and you can make reservations either here in town or in Concepción at the *Club de Ski de Los Angeles* or at the Universidad de Concepción.

The Lake District

The Pan-American route between Laja Falls and Temuco signals the start of Chile's Lake District, called the South American Switzerland, with snow-capped mountains, clear lakes, and wooded hillsides. The only difference between the European and Chilean settings, however, is that the inhabitants here are not the rich, St.-Moritz type you find on the Alps. On the contrary, the 1.3 million people living here are poor, and the "Swiss" scenery is marred by ox teams pulling heavy loads along rain-gutted roads, often stalling your journey. Be grateful for the animals, however, since these ox teams are known to have rescued sinking cars from the treacherous mud.

Let's face it: It rains in Temuco. Unlike dry Santiago, the rainfall averages about 100 inches a year here, so be prepared and bring a raincoat. Most of the roads you'll be taking will be gravel or dirt, and the constant rain makes for muddy driving. Although there are many campsites in the south, you're better off camping only during the drier, summer months of December and January. Even then, however, be prepared for a shower or two, and if the rain doesn't get to you, the horseflies will, so bring plenty of repellent.

You'll find that you can spend the day here just admiring the view. The lakes (and there are 10 major ones) are magnificent, ranging from crystal to green to blue, reflecting the mountains (some of which are dormant volcanoes) of the eastern Andean Cordillera (range). When glaciers receded from the earth, the large depressions became lakes and rivers set deep into forests of cypress, alerce, coigüe, raulí, and canelo. You'll see an occasional fox slither up to a lakeshore and *peucos* (one-banded buzzards) and *choroyes* (slender-billed parakeets) winging overhead.

The people here are just as colorful. There is a high concentration of Araucanian Indians (150,000) living around Temuco (noted for their silver jewelry and handwoven rugs) and the German descendants of immigrants are centered around the Puerto Montt and Valdivia areas. (The Germans first came to Chile in 1850 at the urging of the Chilean government, which set up an immigration office in Kassel, Germany, in 1848 to lure settlers to the region.) As in Concepción (see *Concepción to Laja Falls*), you'll probably be stunned to hear these fair-haired folk speaking Spanish like native Castilians.

You can take this journey through the Lake District and turn it into four separate routes that will take about 3 days each. The first takes you from Temuco south to Valdivia along the Pan-American. From Valdivia, you follow a gravel road to Lake Villarrica, Calafquén, Panguipulli, and Riñihue. The second route returns you to the Pan-American north to Valdivia. From there you take the highway southeast to Paillaco, then go northeast along a gravel road to Lakes Ranco Llifén and Maihue. Once again, you return to the Pan-American east (toward Argentina) for the third route, through Osorno east on Route 215 to Coihue, south to Lake Puyehue, and east to Puyehue National Park and the Argentine Andes; then turn southeast along a gravel road to Antillanca (a ski resort), south to Entre Lagos and Lake Rupanco and Llanquihue, where you continue south to Puerto Octay to Frutillar and Puerto Varas, picking up Route 225 to Ensenada. Retrace your route to Puerto Varas for the fourth and final route south down the Pan-American to Puerto Montt and the island of Chiloé.

TEMUCO: You're going to meet up with many Araucanian men here, wearing their diamond-patterned Mapuche rugs draped off their shoulders. Sometimes they'll offer the rug off their backs for sale. Buy it, since you'll get a better offer from the individual seller than you will at any of the blanket stores here.

Temuco is a large city of 200,000. It's of little importance to travelers, save that it houses the largest Indian population in Chile. The Museo Araucano Regional de La Frontera (Av. Alemania 084) contains a collection of Araucanian pottery and tools and a photographic history of the area. Shopping is another Temuco attraction: Try the *Galerías Artesanales de Chile* (Balmaceda and Caupolicán streets), the municipal market (Aldunate and Rodríguez streets), and the *Feria Libre* (Av. Aldunate and Rodríguez). If you're fond of German food, try *Club Alemán* (Calle Prat 743).

Less than 1 mile north of the Plaza de Armas, Cerro Ñielol is a hill covered with copihue, Chile's national red, bell-shaped flower. From here, you can see the entire city and the Río Imperial, which flows through the city. On one side of the hill sits Agua Santa (Holy Water), a small lake: Legend decrees that if you drink the water three times from a cupped hand, all your worldly aspirations will come true.

The rustic Casino Ñielol near the lake has a wooden, Araucanian woman stationed near the door to greet you. Two miles (3 km) outside town, it offers a dining room along with a golf course, tennis courts, and swimming pool. Visitors are always welcome.

From Temuco, travel 50 miles (80 km) east along a gravel road (that branches off to the Pan-American, north of the city) to the 10,153-foot Llaima Volcano.

En Route from Temuco – Leaving the city, continue south along the Pan-American for 18 miles (28 km) until you reach Freire, where you take a southeast turn and head along a paved road for 35 miles (56 km) to Villarrica, at the southwestern tip of Villarrica Lake. You'll know you're there when you see the towering, 9,230-foot active volcano on the southeastern edge of the lake.

VILLARRICA: This town of 25,000 is one of Chile's favorite resorts; you can swim in the chilly Andean waters or rent a boat for skimming over it. If you follow the southern shore around the lake for 16 miles (25 km) you'll reach Pucón.

From Pucón, you can take a gravel road 10 miles (16 km) south to a ski site on the slopes of the Villarrica Volcano. There are five runs, the longest nearly 6,200 feet long, served by chair and tow lifts. Then take Route 11, a gravel road, 50 miles (80 km) east to Junín de los Andes in Argentina. Have your passport ready.

En Route from Villarrica – A rough, gravel road will take you south, then east, from Villarrica into Lican-Ray on the shores of Lake Calafquén, a small, summer resort of about 800 people, mostly Chileans who own or rent small cottages lakeside; Main Street is nothing but a dirt road with a few grocery stores and a bus station. From here, you can rent a boat and take a swim across the lake. Looking to your north, you'll see the Villarrica Volcano; to the east, Argentina's Lanín Volcano towers above you.

Camping is available along the eastern road, which takes you to the lake's eastern tip at Conaripe. From there, you can turn onto a dirt road and head south to a string of lakes: Panguipulli, Riñihue, and Pirehueico. Here you can opt for a 30-mile (48-km) trip along another gravel road or an 18-mile (29-km) jaunt down a paved road to the Pan-American, continuing south another 27 miles (43 km) to Valdivia, the start of your second Lake District route.

VALDIVIA: The broad, rolling Río Valdivia calmly flows by this city of 109,000. Founded by Pedro de Valdivia in 1552, Valdivia became more European than South American in the late 1800s when the Germans built Chile's first factory, the Anwandter Brewery. Most of the houses in Valdivia are made of lumber, in contrast to the concrete and stucco in the northern areas. There's a lumber factory on Teja Island, in the middle of the Río Valdivia, and a historical and archaeological museum is filled with exhibits depicting the city's Spanish and German origins and silver Mapuche jewelry.

A small café in the center of town recommended for its *kuchen,* the German open pie with fruit filling that Chile has adopted as its own, is *Café Haussmann* (O'Higgins 394).

The docks are a short walk from town, and the morning activities there are lively. Large rowboats pull up with catches of fresh fish and loads of fresh vegetables and fruit, all of which are sold in stalls on the concrete promenade along the riverbank. From the docks slightly upriver (from the fruit and fish stands), passenger boats steam downriver to the villages of Niebla, Corral, Mancera, Amargos, and Cancahual. You can take either a fancy cruiser or one of the standard small ferries.

Daily rail service is available from Valdivia to Santiago (express) and Puerto Montt; LAN-Chile also offers regularly scheduled service to Santiago from Pichouy Airport.

En Route from Valdivia – The second Lake District route will take you around the lake area from here to Osorno. Take the Pan-American Highway 27 miles (43 km) southeast to Paillaco, where you continue on a gravel road 50 miles (80 km) across the northeastern sector of Lake Ranco to Llifén. While you're here, try the Río Calcurrupe for fishing.

Continuing on, take the gravel road to the town of Quillaico at the lake's southeastern point, then drive 30 miles (48 km) to Río Bueno, where there is a small historical and archaeological branch of the Valdivia museum. Return to the Pan-American and continue another 25 miles (40 km) to Osorno to begin your third Lake District excursion.

OSORNO: Founded in 1552 by de Valdivia, this city of 120,000 is another major German immigrant town. German is the second language here, and more often than not, you'll find it on a street sign beside the Spanish name. There are a few sites of interest here. At the Plaza de Armas, a canelo tree was planted by poet Gabriela Mistral in honor of the Mapuche Indians. The municipal museum (Calle Manuel Antonio Matta 809) contains Indian and German exhibits, and on the banks of the Río Rahue is the Spanish Maria Lewis Fort (1793).

The tourist office here is in the provincial government building, near the main plaza.

En Route from Osorno – Take paved Route 215 east 26 miles (41 km) to Coihue and the Pilmaiquen waterfall, where you can fish in the Río Pilmaiquen.

From here, a 25-mile (40-km) gravel road takes you east along the southern shore of Lake Puyehue, in a national park. A short distance from the town of Puyehue (southern shore) are the Puyehue hot springs. From here, the gravel road runs another 26 miles (41 km) to the Argentine border. North of here stands the 7,300-foot Puyehue Volcano.

Along the lake's southern road is Entre Lagos; from here, take the gravel road south to Rupanco, where the Río Rahue flows into Lake Rupanco. From here, you can get a good eyeful of the Osorno Volcano, the district's largest volcano, wedged between Lake Llanquihue, and the green, green waters of Lake Todos los Santos. To reach Llanquihue, take the gravel road south to Puerto Octay. A 112-mile (180-km) road encircles the lake; as you travel around, you'll see both the Osorno Volcano and another 6,549-foot volcano, Calbuco.

PUERTO VARAS: Eleven miles (17 km) north of Puerto Montt, this is the City of Roses, and in season (summer) you'll be struck by the profusion of flowering arbors. From here, you can take boat rides across Lake Llanquihue to the small towns of Frutillar and Puerto Octay, or simply stay in port and try your luck at the gambling casino, which is open from September through March (there's dining and dancing, in addition to betting and beating the odds). You can also stroll to the top of Monte Calvario for a splendid view of the volcanoes and lake.

You can pick up paved Route 225 to tiny Ensenada, at the southeastern tip of the lake; from here, a 10-mile (16-km) gravel road takes you to some waterfalls and Petrohue, a small Indian settlement at the western edge of the green waters of Lake Todos los Santos. From Petrohue, it's about a half-hour's walk uphill to the crater of the Osorno Volcano.

There's camping in Petrohue and a few basic hotels, but not much more, not even a grocery store. You can take motor- and sailboat rides along the lake to the town of Vuriloche or to a beach at Cayutue, where you can rent horses and trot out into the open woods. There's also a ferry to Peulla on the eastern edge of the lake, from which Route 225, another gravel road, continues east to the Argentine border and the Perez Rosales pass.

From Puerto Varas you can take either a gravel road or the Pan-American Highway south to Puerto Montt, the beginning of your fourth and last route in the Lake District.

PUERTO MONTT: This city of 120,000 is reminiscent of a Bavarian village; the small houses are unpainted, like German houses, and the ocean meets the island's shore with a roaring, almost Teutonic crash, unlike other, quieter surfs along the Chilean coast.

Small but vital, Puerto Montt is the beginning of the Chilean Patagonian region and the starting point for tour groups crossing the lakes to Argentina. The town maintains communication with the rest of Chile through good transportation. Rail and bus service to Puerto Varas, Osorno, and Santiago is scheduled regularly; LAN-Chile and LADECO offer flights to Santiago, Valdivia, Concepción, Punta Arenas, and others. From here, you can also book a cabin on one of the steamers heading south into Patagonia and Punta Arenas.

In 1978, a tourist cruiser began to make weekly trips from Puerto Montt to the fjords to the south for a look at the glacier scenery. The luxury cruiser *Skorpios* leaves Puerto Montt at 10 AM Saturday morning for a 6-day trip to the Laguna de San Rafael. It stops in Puerto Chacabuco for lunch in Puerto Aysén one day and then continues to Coyhaique, where tourist buses take you on a trip around the countryside for the afternoon. The boat runs from mid-September to the end of April and has space for 70 guests. The company makes arrangements for your car in Puerto Montt. From December through February, the prime sailing months, prices are approximately $850 per person for a double inside cabin and $1,000 for an outside cabin. You can stay over on the boat the Friday night before your trip for an extra charge. Reservations should be made months ahead. In Santiago, the cruise is offered by *Turismo Cocha,* Agustinas 1173 (phone: 698-3341). In the US, the cruise is offered by *LADATCO,* 2220 Coral Way, Miami, FL 33145 (phone: in Florida, 800-432-9049; elsewhere, 800-327-6162). Also operating this program is *Tara Tours,* 6596 NW 36th St., Miami Springs, FL 33166 (phone: in Florida, 800-228-5168; elsewhere, 800-327-0080).

You can take a short trip from the docks at Puerto Montt to Tenglo Island, right off the coast, for a picnic, and view the area from the top of the island's hill. If you're in luck, they'll be serving *curantos,* a mixed bag of seafood and shellfish steamed over rocks and leaves nestled in a sand pit.

En Route from Puerto Montt – If you're up to an interesting 4-hour trip, you're ready for Chiloé Island. You can get there by boat through the Chacao Channel to the port of Ancud; or you can drive south to Bahía Pargua along the Pan-American and cross the channel to the island's extension, some 35 miles (56 km) from Ancud.

CHILOÉ ISLAND: Foggy and chilly — a constant 50°F (10°C), the island is rich with hardwood and evergreen forests and fjords. Founded in 1567, Ancud and Castro were stopping places for ships continuing through the Strait of Magellan. The island was the last Spanish royalist stronghold in Chile. Today the island's 120,000 people (a few live on the surrounding, smaller islands that make up the province of Chiloé) fish or raise domestic livestock and welcome the occasional traveler.

Ancud, with 25,000 people, is the first village you'll hit. This is the site of Fort Antonio, the Spanish stronghold. There's a small museum in the area, too, displaying colonial items, but you have to ask for its location and hours. From Ancud, there's a paved road that leads 46 miles (74 km) southwest to Castro (pop. 25,000), where there's a municipal museum (Blanco St.) containing archaeological and natural history collections.

You'll have to return to Puerto Montt to proceed by car to the Chilean Patagonia and the Tierra del Fuego archipelago.

BEST EN ROUTE

You know you're in the Lake District the moment you start paying over $50 per person a night for a hotel room (at the *Antumalal* hotel in Villarrica). If you want a private bath and a hotel dining room (and the occasional casino), you have to pay for it. This is the area where expensive means anything between $60 and $100; moderate, anything between $30 and $50. A room for $15 should be considered downright inexpensive, although you'll probably wind up with a very nice, very small room in a secluded lake village. Since the district is a big Chilean tourist center in summer, it's best to make reservations well in advance. Check with the local national tourist office or ski clubs if telephones and addresses aren't listed. There are also a number of camping sites available throughout the area. (Note that prices are higher in season).

TEMUCO

La Frontera – This 60-room hotel offers private baths. M. Bulnes 733 (phone: 31-26-6). Moderate.

PUCÓN

Antumalal – This 18-room, secluded hotel on Lake Villarrica has welcomed Queen Elizabeth II and numerous other international dignitaries. PO Box 6-D, Pucón (phone: 2). Expensive.

Pucón Gran – A 130-room hotel that offers private baths, dining, swimming, game room, tennis, and horseback riding. Lakeside. Expensive.

Camping is available in nearby Lorena, Millaray, and Narquemalil.

LAKE CALAFQUÉN

Calafquén – A 53-room hotel that features private baths, dining, swimming, fishing, and hunting. Lakeside. Expensive.

Camping is available on the eastern road to Conaripe.

VALDIVIA

Schuster – Old, Victorian hotel offers comfortable amenities. Maipú 60 (phone: 32-72). Moderate.

Pedro de Valdivia – An 85-room hotel that offers private baths, dining room, and a bar. Carampagne 190 (phone: 29-31). Moderate.

Melillanca – Simple hostelry featuring 43 rooms, all with private bath and color TV. Av. Alemania 675 (phone: 3416). Moderate.

Villa del Río – The best in Valdivia, with 60 rooms and cabañas. Av. España 1025 (phone: 6292). Moderate.

OSORNO

Gran – A 100-room hotel with private baths and a dining room. O'Higgins and Ramirez (phone: 21-71). Expensive.

ANTILLANCA

A ski lodge is on the slope; make reservations in the *Club Andino* offices in Osorno. Moderate.

PUERTO VARAS

Cabañas del Lago – Considered the best in Puerto Varas, it offers 10 cabañas and 20 first-class double rooms, all with private bath and fantastic views over Lake Llanquihue and magnificent Osorno volcano. Klenner and Bellavista (phone: 291). Moderate.

Gran – 106-room giant of a hotel offers dining, bar, casino, and view of the Osorno Volcano. Klenner 141. Expensive.

PETROHUE

Two ski lodges sit atop the Osorno Volcano. Reservations: *Club Los Punas* or the *Tuski Club,* both in Osorno. Moderate.

Camping is available in the area.

RALÚN

Ralún – On the Reloncavi Estuary, it's a wonderful modern timber lodge, beautifully decorated and grandly comfortable. There is a choice of rooms in the main building or separate cabins, all overlooking gardens, water, and mountains. The food is excellent, and excursions along the estuary to nearby villages, as well as fishing trips, are organized by the hotel. For reservations, write to the Hotel Ralún, Casilla 9391, Santiago (phone: 72-4495 or 8-1881). Expensive.

Chilean Patagonia and the Tierra del Fuego Archipelago

Few but the hardiest travelers venture into the South American Patagonia and Tierra del Fuego archipelago, the southernmost section of the continent shared by Chile and Argentina. It is a gray land filled with forest and moor where the sun does not shine until 9 AM in the winter; most days are drizzly and hazy, and cold, biting winds more often than not whip through the summer terrain at 70 to 85 miles an hour.

Every explorer to brave this area has had rough going. The first was the Portuguese Fernão de Magalhães — Ferdinand Magellan — who, in the employ of the Spanish crown, discovered the area in 1520 as he was traveling east to west along a narrow, 330-mile waterway that separated the mainland from a large, rocky island from which bonfires filtered through the haze. The waterway became known as the Strait of Magellan; the island, Tierra de los Fuegos (or Tierra del Fuego). The mainland was christened Patagonia after the big-footed Indians on the coast (*patagones* means "big feet"). Eventually Spain took possession of the strait for both Spain and Chile.

For political purposes, the Spanish kept the strait a well-guarded secret until Francis Drake led an expedition through in 16 days, giving English names to the islands. English ships continued to use the passage until 1594, when the Spanish took control of the seas by force and the British pirate raids along the South American coast ceased.

Despite the dangers and hardships of the strait, its passage was an impressive experience, especially for Charles Darwin, who wrote extensively on the area after the HMS *Beagle*'s voyage, during which the captain, Robert Fitz Roy, discovered the Beagle Channel. The passage, to the south of the strait, has been long disputed by both Chile and Argentina. Stopping short of war over possession of three tiny islands in the channel, both parties accepted the papal mediation of Pope John Paul II and signed a treaty.

Leaving Puerto Montt, you take a rough road southeast to Punta Arenas, the southernmost city in Chile, across from Porvenir on Tierra del Fuego. A ferry takes you to the island town; from here, you can retrace your steps to Patagonia, where Pan-American alternate Route 9 leads northwest toward Puerto Natales.

If you don't care to drive (side trips in Patagonia may require a horse or a good pair of feet if you venture into the heart of the area), then it's recommended that you fly via LAN Chile or LADECO from either Santiago or Puerto Montt into Punta Arenas. Or book passage aboard the freighter *M/V Evangelistas* for a beautiful 3-night sail between Puerto Montt and Punta Arenas.

PUNTA ARENAS: A stark little port that is the capital of the Magallanes region, this town of 80,000 people is the entry point into Lower Patagonia. Five Indian tribes inhabited this area at one time, primarily on Tierra del Fuego: the tall Tehuelches, the first to be seen by Darwin, who wore virtually nothing except guanaco capes over their shoulders, their faces painted with red and white bands and charcoal streaks; the Onas, the last of the tribes, who disappeared only a few years ago; the Huash; the Yaganes; and the Alcalufes.

There are several museums in Punta Arenas: the Museum of Patagonia (Plaza Muñoz Gamero 745) and the Mayorino Borgatello Museum (Av. Bulnes 374), both of which contain remnants of the Indian cultures that once thrived here; the Mayorino Borgatello Museum, kept by Salesian friars, also has a magnificent collection of flora and fauna of the region, and the new Magellan Regional Museum, with seven display rooms devoted to the history of the region. Also not to be missed is the city cemetery, with its monumental mausoleums.

In town, walk up Cerro La Cruz and look at the hillside planted with an assortment of native flowers and plants. Punta Arenas's municipal park is named after Maria Behety, of one of the founding families; it has a small zoo housing small guanacos, penguins, and *nandu,* a variety of ostrich native to the area. About 3 miles (4 km) from the center of town, along the northward strip of Avenida Bulnes, is an open-air museum with vehicles, machinery, and tools once used by pioneers in the mid-19th century. Traveling south from Punta Arenas for 45 miles (72 km), you reach Fort Bulnes, which has been restored and contains a museum with documents and artifacts from the colonization period.

Back in town, try some of the local seafood specialties in the town's restaurants, especially the *Austral* (Fagnano 595) and *Sotitos* (O'Higgins 1116). The big treat here is king crab, generally eaten as an appetizer with mayonnaise or salsa verde; *ostiones* (large oysters) are served with parmesan cheese *(a la parmesana)* or in a garlic-flavored juice, *al pil-pil.* You can also try *congrio* (sea bass) in cognac butter or black butter or a *chupe de mariscos* (seafood casserole). Squid from Tierra del Fuego are eaten in their ink, with rice and *erizos* (sea urchins) in a soup with onions, celery, lemon, and white wine. You should also try the strongly flavored roast mutton.

When your stomach's filled, shop at the CEMA store (Av. Colón) for local wood and shell carvings or at the artisan stores *Tehueltur* (Plaza Munoz Gamero 1035) and *Koyaten* (21 de Mayor 11570). About 1½ miles (2½ km) north of town is the *Instituto de la Patagonia,* with artisan exhibits and textiles, pottery, and regional handicrafts on display and for sale.

There's no shortage of winter or summer sports in Punta Arenas. About 5 miles (8 km) south of town you can enjoy the ski slope on Mirador Hill; it's the world's southernmost run, and the season lasts from May through October. Remember: Daylight hours are short, from 9AM to 4PM, during much of the skiing season, so ski early. In midwinter (the second week in July), a winter festival is celebrated throughout Patagonia.

Though there's little time for winter skiing, the 19-hour summer days (4 AM until 11 PM) are great for water sports: Deep-sea fishing, sailing, and other aquatic delights are offered at the Nautical Club, about 20 miles (32 km) south of Punta Arenas.

If you want, you can take tours to the Antarctic and around the Tierra del Fuego archipelago from here before proceeding onto the island to Porvenir. The schedule depends on the weather; during the summer, there are frequent boat tours to Puerto Williams, Whiteside Channel, the d'Agostini Fjord, and the Beagle Channel. Check with Skartour at Plaza Munoz Gamero 1013 (phone: 21-24-7) and Turismo Comapa, Av. Independencia 830 (phone: 22-59-9). You can also inquire about renting small planes for flights over the archipelago.

Cargo boats go from here to Puerto Montt and may take some passengers; if you're interested in returning to the north in this manner, check with EMPREMAR, at Lautaro Navarro 1336. LAN-Chile offices are here, too; the National Tourist Office is on Calle Waldo Seguel 689.

From Punta Arenas, you can take the four-times-daily ferry across the strait (it leaves at low tide) to Porvenir.

PORVENIR: This port town (pop. 4,600) is the jumping-off point for exploring both the Chilean and Argentine sides of Tierra del Fuego. From Porvenir, you drive across the flat, Chilean side of the island to Penguins National Park, about 22 miles (35 km) northwest of Punta Arenas. The park has 37 square miles and is made up of coigüe and canelo forests; both trees are native hardwoods and take centuries to grow. Near the park are the smaller islands of Magdalena and Santa Maria, where penguins line the coasts standing guard while sea lions and dolphins frolic in the waters.

Another side trip from Porvenir is to the oil camps at Cerro Sombrero and Manantiales, where the Chileans first discovered oil in 1945. En route, you'll pass the Lago de los Cisnes (Lake of the Swans), where the black-necked birds seem to mirror the drab landscape; the depressing picture is enlivened, however, by pink flamingos.

From the lake, backtrack to Porvenir and the ferry, and return to Punta Arenas for the northern trip along Pan-American alternate Route 9 to Puerto Natales, 145 miles (220 km) away on the mainland.

PUERTO NATALES: This small town of 18,000 sheepherders and coal miners (who work in the Río Turbio mines across the border in Argentina) is famous for its Cueva del Milodon (the Mylodon Cave), 15 miles (22 km) east. Discovered in 1896, the cave contained the well-preserved remains of a prehistoric animal, the mylodon, otherwise known as the giant sloth. You can visit the cave, but you can't see the beast's bones, since they were shipped back to the British Museum in London.

Back in town, go see the Monseñor José Fagnano High School (De Agustine 665); maintained by Salesian priests, it contains a small museum where local wildlife (rhea, cormorants, flamingos, black-necked swans) is displayed.

You can take an 85-mile (136-km) drive north of Puerto Natales to Paine National Park, where the Torres de Paine (Towers of Paine) rise 7,000 feet over hilly Patagonia. The sharp, twisted rock formations jut up, usually into a layer of clouds. At the foot of the towers rest the ever-present sheep, an integral part of the Patagonian landscape and the major industry in the area.

East of Puerto Natales on Route 250, you can head for Río Turbio in Argentina. On Last Hope Sound, this mining town is where most of the Puerto Natales working population earns its keep. Or you can return to Puerto Natales and Punta Arenas and catch a LAN Chile jet back to Santiago.

PUERTO WILLIAMS: Claimed by Chileans to be the southernmost city on the continent, which it is (Argentinians claim Ushuaia is), Puerto Williams is actually on Isla Navarino in the Beagle Channel. You can fly from Puerto Arenas on Tuesdays, Thursdays, and Saturdays, and stay in comfort at the *Hostería Wala.*

BEST EN ROUTE

First-class hotels throughout Patagonia and Tierra del Fuego will cost between $50 and $60 a night, depending on whether you take a single or double room (singles cost more). First-class hotels may be scarce, but their service is first quality. There are some second-class, inexpensive ($10 to $15) hotels here; if you don't have a private bath, at least you'll have a clean room and friendly service. Wherever you stay, however, it's a good idea to reserve well in advance. If you're looking for a handout, there is at least one Salvation Army in Punta Arenas; for about $5 a night, you'll either wind up on a mattress or find yourself sleeping on the floor. If you're roughing it, you can camp anywhere in the area; that's the norm in the Patagonian heartland.

PUNTA ARENAS

Cabo de Hornos – Luxury in the wilds: private baths, phones, a restaurant, and bar. Plaza Muñoz Gamero 1025 (phone: 22-13-4). Very expensive.

Los Navegantes – This modern hotel has a bar, restaurant, central heating, and 50 rooms with private bath. José Menendez 647 (phone: 22134). Expensive.

PUERTO NATALES

Capitán Eberhard – The best hotel in town offers you a spectacular view of the fjord and glaciers. Pedro Montt 25 (phone: 208). Expensive.

Hostería Patagonia Inn – Small, comfortable hotel holds up to 38 guests; you share bathrooms. (Managed by *Cabo de Hornos,* above). Expensive.

PAINE NATIONAL PARK

Hostería Pehoé – First-class hotel offers single and double rooms. The only hotel in the national park. Expensive.

PORVENIR

Hostería Los Flamingos – Hotel offers single and double rooms in a pleasant atmosphere. Teniente Merino (phone: 80-04-9). Expensive.

Easter Island

Easter Island isn't quite as isolated as it was 20 years ago, when virtually its only contact with the outside world was a Chilean warship that visited once a year with provisions. Still, despite the advent of organized tourism, the island remains far from civilization: 2,300 miles west of the Chilean coastline and 1,200 miles from the nearest speck of land, Pitcairn Island.

Adding to its isolation is its landscape: The island was formed when three volcanoes emerged from the sea to form a triangular wedge, with the cone of Rano Kao Volcano at the southwestern point of the triangle, Pu Katiki at the eastern point on the Poike Peninsula, and Rano Aroi forming the third point toward the north. The island is hardly anything more than a barren sweep of land covered with volcanic black rock and ash and with two small sand beaches — one at Anakena Bay on the island's northern coast and the second, under the cliff at Ovake, where the surf is treacherous.

Easter Island received its name from the Dutch explorer Jacob Roggeween, who anchored his three ships at the island on Easter Day, 1722. His crew went ashore — the first Europeans to step onto the island. They were met by what appeared to be a tall, racially mixed group of natives, some with dark skins and others quite fair. They were all naked, with tattoos of birds and other figures across their bodies. Some wore reed hats on their heads; others wore feathers. They lived in reed huts; kept fowl as domestic animals; raised bananas, sugarcane, and sweet potatoes; and traveled about in canoes. A simple enough culture, but their origins remain an intriguing mystery to this day. Some anthropologists believe they came from Polynesia or Malaysia; others contend they were a pre-Inca Indian culture from Perú that moved to the island to escape either natural disaster or internal war, although this theory has been disproven. Artifacts discovered in Perú indicate a similar culture did exist there in the last 1,500 years.

If the natives are intriguing, their *moai* — the stone men that line the island's coast — are more of a mystery. Apparently some 600 *moai* were erected along the coast, standing sentry on *ahus* (pedestals), with some reaching as high as 160 feet. The monoliths were carved from stone at the Rano Raraku Volcano; about 53 are still affixed to the rock there. The details of the face and body were finished before the statues were chipped away at the back and set loose from the stone. *Moai* still dot the roadway, waiting for some long-gone transport to the shore below the quarry, where there seemed to be a storage lot from which they were taken to their final destination, atop the *ahus*.

Although legend decrees that the *moai* walked to their destination, archaeological diggings reveal that they were transported on wooden boards pulled like a sled by ropes made of tree fibers. At dry spots, cooked potato was rubbed along the bottom of boards to make them more slippery. Other *moai* might have been transported by being rolled on two round logs, with one log placed ahead of the other until the destination was reached. There, the *moai* were hoisted into place by ropes.

You can reach Easter Island by either plane or boat. LAN-Chile flies to the island every Wednesday and Sunday, with returns on Mondays and Saturdays. You should have confirmed reservations for leaving the island if your time is limited; there have been reports of overbooked flights, and some travelers have remained on the island longer than they wished. All flights depart from Santiago, and you can make reservations at LAN offices there or in the US.

Tour operators also include Easter Island in their South America programs. Among them are *Lindblad Travel*, Westport, CT; *Society Expeditions*, Seattle, WA; *Travcoa*, Chicago, IL; *Unique Adventures*, San Francisco, CA (see tour listings on pages 34 and 36, or call the LAN-Chile tour desk in Miami at 800-327-7192).

The island is about 70 miles square, and the most comfortable way to get around is on horseback. About 2,000 people live on the island. Some are from the mainland; the others appear to be of Polynesian origin. The main settlement is at Hanga-Roa, and here and there you'll see small children, three at a time, astride horses trotting across the rocky terrain. The weather brings everybody out: Winter temperatures never fall below 60°F to 65°F (15° to 18°C), and summer temperatures are a comfortable 72° to 83°F (22° to 28°C). Rainfalls may be heavy at times, but they're always brief.

In addition to visiting the Rano Raraku Volcano and the *moai*, you can go to Orongo, next to the Rano Kau Volcano at the southeastern tip of the island. This was the site of the ceremonial village, and stone carvings still remain that depict the island's "birdmen." From the Orongo cliff, the island's young men would dive into the sea to swim on reed floats out to three tiny islands offshore in search of the first egg of the year laid by the sooty tern. The lucky guy who found it became a god — the "birdman" — for almost a year. His head was shaved and painted red, and he was taken to a hut at the foot of Rano Raraku, where he was given anything and everything he wanted. The only catch was that he wasn't allowed to mingle with the villagers during that time.

You'll also want to see some of the caves where the villagers lived during what is believed to have been long periods of civil war on the island. The Atan Cave (near Hanga-Roa), the Lazaro Cave (near Hanga O Teo at the north point of the island), and the Santiago del Este Cave (at Vaihu) all housed villagers fleeing from ravages and death, which included cannibalism. A cave of more temperate times is the Cave of the White Virgins, in the northeast sector of the island. Young girls were hidden here from the sun for years to keep their skin white. These "bleached" girls then exhibited their white bodies during ceremonial occasions.

Reservations are advised if you plan to remain on the island. Since tourism is an established trade, everything, from local items to imported food, beer, and wine, has a high price tag.

BEST EN ROUTE

The only hotels on Easter Island are in Hanga Roa. One, the *Hanga Roa* (noted below), towers above the others in Western amenities, and in price. The cost of everything here is at least three times mainland prices. Lodgings can run from $60 to $120 a night, with meals. Reservations should be made in advance. If you prefer, you can stay at an islander's house or rent a tent from a hotel and camp out.

Hanga Roa – Considered by many to be the best hotel on the island, this property sleeps 120 guests, and meals are included. Av. Ponto (phone: 99). Very expensive.

Hotu Matua – A smaller hotel that offers clean accommodations. Av. Ponto (phone: 42). Expensive.

Residencial Rosita – Another small hotel in the village that offers clean and comfortable lodgings. Te Pito Te Henua (phone: 50). Expensive.

The Juan Fernández Archipelago

Just 403 miles west of Valparaíso in the green Pacific, the three volcanic islands of the Juan Fernández archipelago — Robinson Crusoe, Alejandro Selkirk, and Santa Clara — offer a quiet haven to anyone seeking isolation, lush green surroundings, and warm, 71°F (21°C) swimming waters. Discovered in 1574 by the Spanish navigator Juan Fernández, the islands' outward calm belies their historic notoriety: Spanish, English, and Dutch pirate ships harbored here in the sixteenth, seventeenth, and eighteenth centuries.

The islands' most famous resident was an English seaman who asked to be stranded here because he couldn't stand the mistreatment he was receiving from his ship's captain. Alexander (or Alejandro) Selkirk was marooned by the Cinque Ports in 1704; four years later, he was rescued by another English ship and returned to England, where tales of his island exploits inspired Daniel DeFoe to write *Robinson Crusoe*, published in 1719. DeFoe changed the location of the island, but it's generally accepted that Selkirk was the Crusoe prototype, and the cave where he allegedly lived on Robinson Crusoe Island is shown to visitors today.

More than one man suffered hardship here. The survivors of two English shipwrecks lived on Robinson Crusoe for 5 months in 1721; the island also served as a prison camp for both Chilean patriots in the Independence War and for Spanish prisoners once the war was won. Both parties lived wretchedly in caves that can still be seen along the Bay of Cumberland. Colonial settlements were also started at this time.

There is one amusing chapter in the islands' history. In 1877, German Baron Alfredo de Rodt arrived and fell in love with the archipelago. He decided to stay, and died here at the age of 65. Not only does his ship remain, but numerous de Rodts — the blue-eyed descendants of the baron's two wives — thread the tiny, 800-person census of Robinson Crusoe Island.

Robinson Crusoe is the only island visited by travelers. The main industry on the island is lobster fishing, and the catch is considered the tastiest in the world. Until 1966, the only way you could reach the archipelago was by boat or seaplane, but the construction of an airstrip now allows surface landings. The islands are linked to the mainland by a few boat trips monthly from Valparaíso during the summer season and the periodic plane service of Linea Aerea Taxpa, Ltda. Although the fleet of bimotor light planes — Piper Navajos, Cessna 310s, and Aerocommanders — flies here daily from December through February (vacation time), service out of season is irregular. The planes make the trip from Cerrillos Airport in Santiago to Robinson Crusoe Island in about 3 hours. Charters are also available, but there is a 6-passenger limit. Passage is booked at Taxpa's downtown Santiago office, 10th floor, Nueva York 53 (phone: 696-1833 or 57-26-32). You'll have to give fixed dates for going and returning when you book.

ROBINSON CRUSOE ISLAND: Formerly known as Mas a Tierra (Closer to Land), this island is small — about 36 square miles — and west of Alejandro Selkirk Island, or Mas Afuera (Farther Out Island), by about 109 miles, a desolate place visited only during the lobster season (December to April) by fishermen. This island doesn't expect tourism competition from Santa Clara Island, either — a tiny southwesterly speck with no vegetation and no water.

The starting point for adventure here is Juan Bautista village in the Bay of Cumberland, a small area that takes in the entire island population. Robinson Crusoe is triangular, with one angle pointing north; the bay is on the northeastern slope of the triangle. Selkirk, who spent his island vacation in the bay, was merely "let off" at the stop, so to speak, armed with his Bible, gun, knife, ax, gunpowder, tobacco, and clothes; you'll have to take a 90-minute motorboat ride from the landing strip on the southeastern tip of the island. (Be prepared to pay about $20 for the jaunt.) You'll be impressed during the trip by the striking, nearly vertical cliffs of up to 1,000 feet that ring the island. Only at the Bay of Cumberland and three other spots does the ground slope gently to the sea, providing access to the island. In the center of the cliffs' towers is the 3,000-foot Yunque (Anvil) Hill, the island's highest peak, which is always covered by clouds.

Since there are tourists (few) in the summer, the island does provide accommodations in the Cumberland Bay area. If you're dealing with islanders, take into consideration that they are not cash-oriented. Until a few years ago, the main currency was lobster. There is still no bank on the island, so money doesn't have much value. Even today, islanders may choose to rent you a horse or take you fishing or deep-sea diving on their motorboats in exchange for some item you have that strikes their fancy. And whether you can rent a horse to ride or take that boat trip will depend on the islander's whim: Sometimes you can and sometimes you can't. And if you do rent something, say, for 8 AM, don't get upset if it doesn't show up on time. Islanders have no conception of such demands; they are known for showing up with their goods as late as the following day.

If you do go fishing, you're in for a treat. Archipelago waters are noted for their abundance of fish — pompano, tuna, moray eel, rock salmon, dogfish, flying fish, and octopi. You're also going to see a lot of sea lions, *lobos marinos de dos pelos;* these little fellows at one time numbered about 3 million, but North American sealing expeditions in the 19th century rapidly diminished that number. A 1970 census showed only 700 in existence; it's estimated, however, that the number will increase slowly during the coming years.

Unfortunately, the island's fragrant sandalwood tree was never given the opportunity to propagate; the trees were all chopped down by traders. Today, the Chilean government protects the *palmera chonta* (hardwood tree) to keep it from the same fate, but items made of the dark wood (thinly stripped with tan) can occasionally be bought in Chile. One natural feature still thriving in the constant 67°F (19°C) weather, fortunately, is the giant fern. More than 40 varieties of fern grow on the island, and some even grow to tree size. In fact, because of the vegetation, Darwin, who made the archipelago one of his many stops during the *Beagle*'s voyage, later commented that he was more impressed with these islands than with the Galápagos archipelago.

You can get a good look at the vegetation by taking a 90-minute climb from the Bay of Cumberland to the top of Selkirk's old lookout, the Mirador de Selkirk. A slightly shorter walk to the west from the bay will bring you to Bahía del Ingles and the Robinson Crusoe Cave. On the Bay of Cumberland, at one end of Juan Bautista village, are buried some sailors from the *Dresden,* a German ship that retired to the island for repairs during World War I. With the approach of some British ships in 1915, however, the *Dresden* was burned, and the crew stayed here for the rest of their lives. Parts of the ship were resurrected in 1964, and on clear days the ship's towers can be spotted in the bay where it sank. A few pieces of Krupp artillery from World War II and some old cannons are also buried in the bay.

The ruins of two other forts are a good hike from Cumberland Bay. Centinelas Fort ruins are near Bahía del Ingles; the ruins of San Carlos are at the extreme eastern tip of the island at Puerto Frances.

Once you've seen the fort and lookout, you've seen most of the island's attractions. Your best bet would be to rest and enjoy the island's beauty and quiet.

BEST EN ROUTE

You're going to pay a lot for a room in a first-class hotel on Robinson Crusoe Island, and there are no other choices. Brace yourself for $200 per night for a double with meals. If you stay at one of the two smaller hotels, expect to pay about 25% less; if you arrange to stay with an islander, expect to pay anything — from money to your camera to your false teeth and water wings, if the islander is fascinated with them. Whatever, make reservations before you arrive; they're mandatory. You can arrange them at the Taxpa offices in Santiago.

ROBINSON CRUSOE ISLAND

Hostería Robinson Crusoe – Just outside town, this 25-room hotel serves 47 guests, provides private baths, hot water, and electricity, and offers a choice of rooms: single, double, small, medium, or a suite. Expensive.

Aldea Daniel DeFoe – A smaller, modest hotel that provides basic lodgings. Expensive.

Don Rino – Small hostería that provides the same services as *Aldea Daniel DeFoe.* Expensive.

Colombia

Colombia covers 440,000 square miles of tropical and mountainous terrain. Bordered on the north and west by the Caribbean, Panamá, and the Pacific, on the south by Ecuador and Perú, on the east by Brazil, and on the northeast by Venezuela, it is well known around the world as the country that produces fabulous emeralds, delicious coffee, and pure cocaine. The country's great variety of attractions, from the towering peaks of the Sierra Nevada chain to the tiny ports bordering two seas, as well as the treasures of a rich pre-Columbian and colonial past, are less publicized and deserve attention.

Out of a national population of 28 million, about 6,500,000 people live in the capital, Bogotá. In the center of the country in an Andean valley, Bogotá stands at an elevation of 8,640 feet above sea level. Here is the Gold Museum (Museo del Oro), which contains one of the most impressive and complete collections of gold objects in the world. Despite this wealth, shantytowns called *barrios* surround the city. Overflowing with poor migrants from rural areas, they typify the abysmal contrast between wealth and poverty that is common in Latin American society. In recent years, the Colombian government has instituted a number of programs to improve living conditions in the *barrios*. Electricity, sewage systems, and home improvement projects have helped somewhat, as have community action programs that enable *barrio* residents to participate in municipal activities. (For a complete report on Bogotá, see THE CITIES.)

Colombia has three Andean ridges: the Cordillera Occidental (Western Range), the Cordillera Central (Central Range), and the Cordillera Oriental (Eastern Range), plus an independent group of mountains along the Caribbean shore called the Sierra Nevada de Santa Marta. The second largest city in the country, Medellín (pop. 1,700,000), the self-proclaimed orchid capital of the world, stands in a Central Cordillera mountain valley. The country's third largest city, Cali (pop. 1,400,000), is in a western Andean valley. Nearly half of all Colombians reside in these particular Andean valleys.

Bordering both Pacific and Caribbean coasts, Colombia has a couple of resort areas, Santa Marta (pop. 600,000) and Cartagena (pop. 850,000), as well as a thriving Caribbean port, Barranquilla (pop. 800,000). See DIVERSIONS for more about them.

A large section of Colombia is covered by jungle, as at Leticia (pop. 15,000), southern Colombia's Amazon port.

Historically, Colombia is the land that gave the world the legend of El Dorado (literally, "the gilded one"). The myth that attracted the gold-hungry Spaniards in the sixteenth century came from an actual ritual in which Muisca Indians dipped the chief of their tribe in gold dust. In 1500, Alonso de Ojeda was the first Spaniard to sail into Cartagena, but the Indians drove him away. In 1538, Gonzalo Jiménez de Quesada founded Santa Fe de

Bogotá. Later, when Colombia became the Kingdom of New Granada and Panamá (under Spanish rule), the country went through a relatively peaceful colonial era during which prosperity was insured by regular shipments of gold to Spain. Except for the problems of piracy, Colombia remained undisturbed until early in the nineteenth century, when the first battles for independence began. Simón Bolívar, the Liberator, waged a lengthy campaign on Colombian soil in 1812, but it was not until December 17, 1819, that he was able officially to declare the country's independence from Spain. He established the Republic of Gran Colombia, which included Venezuela, Colombia, Panamá, and Ecuador, but he was unable to maintain a cohesive whole. In 1885, the Colombian constitution went into effect. Despite some periodic internal strife, there has been no substantial modification in the constitution since its inception. A novel constitutional arrangement has institutionalized a periodic sharing of the government between the two historic political parties, the Conservatives and the Liberals. Today Colombia is considered a democracy in which the electoral process assures an open, though not often orderly, transfer of office.

Although it's possible to drive through Colombia yourself, the country has an extensive system of buses, *colectivos* (chauffeured cars that carry four or five passengers), railroads, and internal domestic airlines that connect even the most remote towns and villages. The use of public transportation is recommended because road services are few and far between, and Colombia is not the safest place in which to have a breakdown. (The country's illicit drug traffic has contributed to its reputation as a particularly dangerous place, where muggings and thefts are common; anyone planning to visit should be especially careful of valuables — whether on the open road or on a city street.) Those who do drive should be sure to have their *carnets* and insurance policies in order and easily accessible should there be an accident. Also, bring spare parts and be prepared to make repairs without outside help.

This chapter contains five routes. The first runs along the lovely Caribbean coast from Cartagena to Baranquilla. The next, Riohacha to Villa de Leyva, explores a not-often-traveled route through tough smugglers' territory — Santa Marta to the Venezuelan coast. Bogotá to Medellín travels through Colombia's agricultural region, where there are huge orchards and fields of coffee beans. Neiva to Cali includes several Colombian archaeological zones. The Amazon section gives some suggestions for exploring that region.

Cartagena and the Caribbean West Coast

There's a lot of fun, mystery, and history waiting on Colombia's Caribbean coast. The white sand beaches from Cartagena north to Santa Marta, with their sunny climate and picturesque colonial buildings, invite visitors to leave the mountains of Bogotá behind and spend several days — or weeks — prowling the coastline, lying on the sands, or partying with the *costeños* (coastal inhabitants of both the Pacific and Caribbean).

Don't come to the Caribbean to sit indoors, mope, and read a book. Come here to be happy, eat good meals, and spend the days relaxing in the sun or exploring the jagged *páramos* (plateaus) of the Sierra Nevada and the nights dancing in a disco or gambling at a casino. If you're here for the pre-Lenten Carnival, then so much the better, and even more so in Barranquilla. This is the time to do what you want, when you want.

There are a number of ways to start this Caribbean journey. There is airline service from New York and Miami to Barranquilla or Cartagena. If you intend to drive through Colombia, however, it's best to start out straight from Cartagena. From there, continue north to Barranquilla and on to Santa Marta, the oldest European-founded settlement in South America. Along this route live many different types of people: white and mestizo, black (slave descendants), mulatto (black and white), and Zamba (black and Indian). *Costeño* music — like the people — is a happy blend of black and Spanish, sounding more like *salsa* and African tribal than Andalusian or Castilian Spanish.

To drive the entire Colombian route, be sure to have a Mobil road map or the Codazzi Institute's set of route maps covering main highways and highlighting places of interest. There are a lot of highways in Colombia, but only about half of the 30,000-mile network is paved; the rest is narrow, often poor, and unmarked. Any travel assistance needed, as well as maps, can be obtained from the National Tourist Office in Bogotá (Calle 28, No. 13A-15, piso 15; phone: 283-9466) or from the US office (140 E 57th St., New York, NY 10022, phone: 212-688-0151).

Just one word about this route: Petty crime is an ugly fact marring the Caribbean's beauty. Pickpockets and muggers thrive in most of the large cities, so be prepared, and try not to wander about alone. Have a good time, but guard your personal belongings. If you do get robbed, report it to the authorities, but don't be surprised if they don't do anything about it immediately. Theft is an everyday occurrence hereabouts, particularly in Cartagena, and the police have developed a rather lackadaisical attitude toward it.

CARTAGENA: Founded by Pedro de Heredia in 1533, the "Heroic City" was built as a Spanish base for the conquest of the continent — an impregnable port with a heavily armed garrison to protect the gold routes and slave trade established by the Spaniards. Within 30 years, a branch of the Río Magdalena joining the Bay of Cartagena to the main channel 90 miles inland was made into a canal; the Canal del Dique made Cartagena the main port for merchandise shipped from Spain for the conquest of the South American north and for treasures shipped back to the mother country. The city was also granted a royal monopoly as a slave port and market.

While the canal theoretically could have prevented direct attacks by outside forces, Cartagena did have its share of buccaneers: It was sacked by pirate Robert Baal in 1544, then by Martin Côtes a few years later; other English, French, and European pirates also put in their bit of aggravation. The most famous (or infamous) of these renegades was the English privateer Sir Francis Drake, who pillaged the port in 1586, then "mercifully" decided not to burn the city to the ground once he was presented with 10 million pesos, which he ferried home to Queen Elizabeth. He also took with him an enormous emerald, which he gave to the Virgin Queen as a New Year's Day gift.

By the 17th century, the Spaniards finally built thick walls around the city. An adjacent circle of walls was constructed around the neighborhood of Getsemaní in

1656, and the small, eight-cannon Castillo de San Lázaro became the formidable Castillo de San Felipé de Barájas, bristling with 70 pieces of artillery. It was the strongest fort in all the Spanish colonies.

Today, Cartagena has expanded in every direction and has recently been declared a World Cultural Heritage Site by UNESCO. Broad avenues, elegant residential areas, and tall, tourist complexes border the Caribbean. It's a dynamic city of 850,000, but the walled citadel has changed very little. It's a great place for a walking tour, beginning with the inner walled city at the Clock Tower Entrance (Torre del Reloj). The portal is near Plaza de los Coches, once a slave market, which now houses the city hall and some arcades. Plaza de la Aduana, the city's old parade ground, contains a stone statue of Christopher Columbus. Behind it are the narrow streets of El Centro, an elegant little neighborhood with two-story, balconied colonial buildings. Plaza San Pedro Claver, behind El Centro, houses a church and monastery built by the Jesuits in 1603 and later dedicated to San Pedro Claver, a Spanish-born priest who ministered to the blacks brought from Africa as slaves. Claver, whose body rests in a glass coffin on the church's high altar, was the first person to be canonized in the New World.

There are a number of colonial churches and buildings in the San Pedro area. At the Palace of the Inquisition (Plaza Bolívar), the Holy Office held court starting in 1610. The present building dates from 1706. It's a wonderful example of colonial baroque, with balconies, cloisters, patios, stone entrances, and wooden doors. Rather than housing monsignors carefully scrutinizing the sins of *cartageneros,* however, the office today offers travelers a museum and library. The palace is open daily (closed from noon until 2 PM for siesta), and admission is free.

The city's cathedral, also in Plaza Bolívar, was started in 1575, but was partly destroyed by Francis Drake in 1586. The church has a fortlike exterior, and its museum houses models made by the English admiral John Vernon, who laid siege to the city in 1741. The church of Santo Toribio de Mongrovejo (Calle del Sargento Mayor) sports a real Vernon memento — a cannonball that fell into the church while mass was being said. To this day, it's lodged in one of the central columns. Santo Domingo (Calle de la Universidad) is reputedly the oldest church in the city; it was taken over by the Cartagena University in 1827. Santa Clara (Parque de San Diego) was a monastery transformed into a hospital, but the church still retains its carved altar.

The Plaza de las Bovedas provides a good idea of the strength of the city walls — they're 40 feet high and 50 to 60 feet thick; 24 bombproof vaults are faced with an elegant neoclassical portico that now contains shops for tourists. The *ruanas,* or woolen ponchos, at *Artesanías Bochica* No. 3 are a good bet.

The plaza marks the end of the "inner walled" tour and the start of a walk through Getsemaní (named after the olive grove where Jesus Christ prayed after the Last Supper), the outer walled city. Today, the only part walled in here is the eastern section, where the working class lived in single-story *casas bajas,* typical of colonial architecture. Here, visit the Chapel of Espíritu Santo (Calle Espíritu Santo) and the colonial church of Santisima Trinidad on its own colonial plaza.

Outside the walls, across Puente Heredia on La Popa Hill, look into the Castillo de San Felipé de Barájas which has a *son et lumière* (sound and light show — the equivalent of an audiovisual presentation) Saturdays at 8 PM, featuring the history of Cartagena and San Felipé. The fort's remarkable network of tunnels and passageways, its water system, its storage and munitions rooms — the sheer mass and ingenuity of the battlements and fortifications — make for a fascinating visit. Outside the fortress stands an enormous pair of shoes honoring poet Luis Carlos Lopez, who once said in a poem that the city inspired as much affection and comfort as an old pair of shoes.

Bus tours to the fort are available in Spanish and English for about $6, or take a taxi to get there on your own. Also visit Manga Island to view the turn-of-the-century and older architecture, where some of the mansions are still occupied by Cartagena's first families. The old fort there, San Sebastian de Pastelillo, is now the *Club de Pesca* (*Fishing Club*), which serves a good seafood dinner (try the *paella* — a hodgepodge of rice, clams, mussels, and lobster). Then take a 2-hour trip to Boca Chica (the eastern waterway that provides the only outside access to Cartagena) for swimming and sunning: The beaches are cleaner and fresher here than on Boca Grande. There are also two colonial forts, San Fernando and the Batería San José.

While out on Boca Grande, check the *Willis F. Bronkie* gem store (which sells those famous Colombian emeralds for a pretty fair price) and the leather goods at *Land Leather* and *Boots and Bags*. If you like seafood, the *Don Boris, Nautilus,* and *La Fonda Antioqueña* restaurants are guaranteed to satisfy your palate with their lobster, mussel, and clam dishes. Afterward, try your luck at the *Caribe Casino* roulette wheels and baccarat tables.

There is a short side trip of interest, to the fishing village of Boquilla, about 20 minutes northeast of Cartagena past the Crespo airport. You can also reserve launch space for a day trip to the Rosario Islands for sunbathing, swimming, and sailing. Bird lovers should take a boat trip through the Canal del Dique for some of the best birdwatching in the world.

Cartageneros love to party, and some big ones are held during the year. In addition to the standard Roman Catholic and political holidays, Cartagena has its own fiestas, with plenty of eating, drinking, dancing, and general hell-raising. Cartagena goes crazy during Carnival season, before Lent. September 9 is the feast of San Pedro de Claver and features religious processions. From November 11 to 14 is the city's Independence Day feast when a national beauty queen is selected. Around Christmas time, there's one helluva custom that takes place between friends: Two groups agree to meet at an appointed place, then everybody dresses in identical costumes. When both sides meet, everyone has to guess who the leader of the other group is. The first one to do so yells *"Mis aguinaldos!"* ("My presents!"), and the loser either has to pay up or throw a party.

Hotels in Cartagena are of mixed quality. Some are small, in need of renovation, lacking hot water and shower stalls, and more often than not, lacking in security. Also, rates rise 25% during the holiday seasons; reservations for these times should be made well in advance. Other than that, hotel service is good, and prices are quite good for what is returned.

Before taking a 90-mile (145-km) drive along the coastal Route 2 to the larger port of Barranquilla, you might fly from Cartagena to the island of San Andrés, 298 miles north of the Colombian coast.

SAN ANDRÉS: White beaches, palm trees, and blue skies aren't all that lure travelers to this happy Caribe resort island: Welsh privateer Henry Morgan harbored here during his 17th-century raids on Spanish strongholds. Legend has it that he left over $1 billion worth of gold bullion buried in a cave, either here or on one of the island's many tiny adjacent cays. You're welcome to hunt for the booty, but most people prefer to skip the cave and relax instead in the 75°F (24°C) weather, tempered by trade winds.

Discovered in 1527 by Spanish explorers on the eve of the Feast of St. Andrew, the tiny island — 8 miles long and 2 miles wide — became part of Colombia in 1827. Its population of 30,000, a mix of black slave descendants, English, and Spanish, is boosted by a large number of foreign and Colombian tourists. The island was cut off from any constant form of communication with the mainland until the 1950s, when regular domestic flight service was established.

Sightseeing and water sports are the island's biggest draws. It's possible to hire a taxi or your own minijeep, motorbike, or even bicycle for as low as $15 a day for a jaunt around the island's paved coastal road. Along the way, stop and visit Morgan's Cave and the Blowhole, formed by compressed air spouting through an opening in the sea floor near a number of underground tunnels.

As for sports, you can rent scuba gear from the *Sea Horse Inn* and go diving for

Morgan's fabled treasure or deep-sea fish for marlin, sailfish, bonita, or red snapper. The *Bahía Marina Resort* (PO Box 597) provides charters for fishing, water skiing, scuba diving, and snorkeling that cost anywhere from $12 an hour to $110 a day.

If you prefer, simply wander around the downtown area of the island. The free port area has over 600 stores containing foreign imports and domestic crafts, from china and porcelain to watches, jewels (plenty of Colombian emeralds), liquor, and even canned goods. Some of the stores worth browsing through include the *Carolina Duty-Free Shop* (Av. Costa Rica Colón) for porcelain, watches, and jewelry; *Casa Amberes* (Av. Colón 2-131) and *Artesanías de Colombia* (Av. Colón 2-144) carry handicrafts from all over Colombia.

A $4 fare will purchase a ride on the public launch to Johnny Key for a picnic. Plan to go on Sunday, however, when there's a fish fry, and you wine and dine to the strumming guitars of wandering musicians. There's plenty of singing and dancing, and the day turns into a mini-fiesta for no reason except the fun of it all. For nightlife, the main island has a quiet assortment of entertainment that ranges from dining to catching a show at the cinema.

Don't miss trying some of the local dishes. *Miss Bess* offers home-cooked specialties, including crab soup and *cebiche* (marinated fish that makes palates smart). *Patacones* (fried plantains), *rondón,* a vegetable stew, and coconut bread are also on the menu. *La Fonda Antioqueña* features interior Colombian dishes such as *mondongo* (tripe), *sobrebarriga con papas* (Creole potatoes and steak), and *arepa* (corn cakes). Also try *La Tortuga* for seafood with an Italian twist. Incidentally, in the Spanish-English patois spoken in San Andrés, seafood is known as *sifú.*

San Andrés hotels are clean, and comfortable. Although some provide private baths, hot water is scarce, and the drinking water is putrid. (In fact, water is a big island problem.) All of the hotels are geared toward the tourist and include a number of game rooms, water sport equipment, discos, and bars.

From San Andrés, it's possible to fly to Providencia, a mountainous rural island with good swimming and few accommodations. Or fly to Cartagena, where you can pick up the highway route or continue by jet up to Barranquilla, Colombia's number one port, at the mouth of the Río Magdalena.

BARRANQUILLA: Unless you're a quiet introvert who can't stand crowds, you're going to love the madness, mayhem, and assorted carryings-on that accompany this city's best-known and best-loved fiesta, Carnival. Colombia's major port, 8 miles from the Caribbean on the west bank of the Magdalena, goes wild during the 4-day festival, calling itself Ciudad Loca (Crazy City) with puffed-up pride. After all, not only do the city's 800,000 inhabitants disguise themselves and roam the noisy, music-filled streets, but a lot of other people from neighboring Caribbean towns stagger in for the fun, as do the hard-core celebrants from Bogotá. Everyone, it seems, stages balls; every neighborhood schedules at least one parade filled with flower-decked floats. Water bombs blast passersby, and wandering, inebriated groups go from door to door in search of more rum and *aguardiente.* If you're invited to join a *parranda* (revel), go along and don't ask questions; after all, Carnival is the equivalent of an adult's mischief night, so ease your conscience and have some fun — everyone else does.

The rest of the year, skip Barranquilla. Founded in 1629, it is an industrial city that produces textiles, glassware, perfume, beer, and ships. There really is little to do here but visit the colonial cathedral (Plaza Bolívar), wander through Parque 11 de Noviembre, and look around the interesting port zone.

The tourist office, should you need it, is on Carrera 52 No. 72-46 (phone: 57378).

   En Route from Barranquilla – Leaving the city, head up coastal highway Route 2 north to Santa Marta, crossing the long bridge over the Río Magdalena that connects the city to the Salamanca Island National Park. Along the way, you'll see marsh and sea birds, turtles, alligators, and howler monkeys. Forty miles

(64 km) north of Barranquilla is Ciénaga, a small agricultural town of 68,000 people that produces bananas, cotton, and cocoa. Eighteen miles (30 km) beyond Ciénaga is Santa Marta and the jagged Andean spur of the Sierra Nevada that juts out of the Caribbean coastline.

SANTA MARTA: The sight of a snowcapped, 16,420-foot Cordillera rising out of the ocean will probably astound you the way it did conquistador Rodrigo de Bastidas, who founded this first settlement in Colombia in 1525. Eleven years later, fellow Spaniard Gonzalo Jiménez de Quesada set off from here into the interior in his search for the mythical El Dorado. Later, the blue-watered harbor became the final resting ground of Simón Bolívar, who died in 1830 at the age of 47 at nearby Quinta San Pedro Alejandrino.

Today, the town (pop. 600,000) has some fine colonial buildings to show the traveler, but they're not as well preserved as those in Cartagena. Hacienda de San Pedro Alejandrino, where Bolívar died broke and very disillusioned with the collapse of his dream of a Gran Federación, sits on a road 2½ miles (4 km) northeast of the city, and today houses a museum dedicated to Bolívar. His body was kept in the town's cathedral for 30 years before it was removed to Caracas, but his heart remained in Santa Marta, at the request of the townspeople, in a leaden casket that mysteriously disappeared when the cathedral went up in flames in 1872.

Actually, people go to Santa Marta not for what's in the city but for what's outside it. The semicircular El Rodadero, a few miles south, is Colombia's most fashionable beach. On a more rugged jaunt into the Sierra Nevada, jaguars, pumas, and bright-colored parrots that live in the dense forests can be seen. The Sierra sits at the foot of the bleak, black *páramos* that precede the snowcapped peaks. You can also take a 21-mile (35-km) ride northeast of Santa Marta on Route 2 into Tayrona National Park, an area on the beach that has been left in its virgin state. A more adventurous and rugged excursion climbs high into the Sierra, once the home of the wild and primitive Tayrona Indians, whose society flourished on gold. They were reduced to slavery during the first period of colonization, although their resistance was fierce and prolonged. There are five crystal-clear lakes in the park, and overnight camping is available, although the trip is less than 1 day out of Santa Marta.

From El Rodadero you can charter a boat for $15 an hour, or $30 daily, and go out for sailfish, wahoo, kingfish, amberjack, or red snapper. The boats are rented from Captain Ospina in his beachstand. If you'd prefer to skip the fishing, the jolly skipper will be happy to take you on a tour into the Sierra for an afternoon romp. A number of other tours are offered by Sportour, which will take visitors to the quaint Sierra village of Minga. Another point of interest in the area is the fishing village of Taganga, where a Quijote-inspired Frenchwoman has opened a restaurant and hotel called *La Ballena Azul (The Blue Whale)*.

The *El Cocodrilo* in downtown Santa Marta sells soapstone statuettes of Tayronian gods, chiefs, men, and animals, along with other Colombian crafts.

The tourist office is in Rodadero at Apartado Aereo 5064 (phone: 5045).

En Route from Santa Marta – You can continue your Colombian excursion in one of two directions. The first way is to backtrack to Ciénaga and Barranquilla, where you can either hop a plane to Bogotá or take Route 11 east to Route 61, continue southeast on Route 51 via Pamplona, then pick up Route 71, alias the Simón Bolívar Highway, alias the Pan-American Highway (all to be discussed in *Riohacha to Villa de Leyva*). But if you take this route, you're missing a trip around the northern Caribbean coast and the semi-arid Guajira Peninsula, a weird, definitely romantic spot with its own Indians, beaches, and history. If you're in the mood for a little adventure — and possibly a lot of problems — delay your flight to Bogotá for a few days, and head north along the coast, where the first stop will be Riohacha, capital of the Department of La Guajira.

BEST EN ROUTE

The chances of netting a West Caribbean hotel room without hot water, air conditioning, and/or a bath compared to those of getting one with all these features is about 50-50. Hotel prices in this part of Colombia are $40 to $60 (expensive); $30 to $40 (moderate); and $15 to $20 (inexpensive) per person. In Cartagena, the expensive range is $50 to $85; and keep in mind that rates go up at least 25% during Carnival, for everybody, not just tourists. Most of the hotels have telephone numbers; however, it's better to write or make arrangements through a travel agent or the local tourist office, since phone connections from the US to Colombia are frequently bad. Once you're at the hotel, don't forget to keep an eye on personal belongings, since resident security in Colombian hotels is minimal.

CARTAGENA

Cartagena Hilton International – This is the city's best, with 298 balconied rooms, 2 pools, 3 tennis courts, and a good, if small, beach. El Laguito, Bocagrande (phone: 959-50660). Very expensive.

Capilla del Mar – 263-room hotel has television, French restaurant, coffee shop, disco, and meeting facilities. Carrera 1, No. 18-59 (phone: 51033). Expensive.

Las Velas – Probably the only hotel in Colombia to offer kosher cooking, it has 100 rooms, with air conditioning, private baths, suites with kitchenettes, pool, rooftop bar, directly on beach. Calle 1, No. 1-160 (phone: 50000). Moderate to expensive.

El Caribe – This traditional Cartagena hotel, recently totally renovated, is by, not on, the sea, and convenient to town. Carrera 1, No. 2-87 (phone: 55555). Moderate.

Barlovento – Close to the beach, it offers 48 rooms with air conditioning, a bar, pool, and restaurant. Carrera 3, No. 6-23 (phone: 53966). Moderate.

Plaza Bolívar – A restored colonial-style hotel with 54 rooms; some have air conditioning, others fans. In town on the old square called Plaza Bolívar. Calle 33, No. 3-98 (phone: 40431/2). Inexpensive.

SAN ANDRÉS

El Acuarium – A delightful spot, with 12 bungalows constructed on pilings over the water. Also good food. (Reservations in Bogotá only; phone: 282-0691). Expensive.

Isleño – A 42-room hotel with fans and stall showers, but no hot water. Av. Colombia, No. 5-117 (phone: 6590). Expensive.

Abacoa – This 62-room hotel has new and old wings: The new wing has air conditioning; the old one doesn't. All rooms, however, are doubles with combination baths, and there's a restaurant with nightly entertainment and a casino. Av. Colombia (phone: 6313). Expensive to moderate.

El Dorado – The 30 bungalows here have fans and no hot water; property also has a casino and restaurant. Av. Colombia, No. 1A-25 (phone: 6201). Moderate.

Los Delfines – Recently opened, with 23 suites with kitchenettes, air conditioning, TV, and balcony. Swimming pool, good dining room, and probably the friendliest service on the island. Av. Colombia (phone: 4083; or to make reservations in Cali, 804317). Moderate.

Malibu – This 22-unit hotel provides air conditioning, hot water, and a restaurant. 4-65 Av. Nicaragua (phone: 6542). Moderate to inexpensive.

PROVIDENCIA

Aury – Clean and comfortable, and the island's largest. Providencia is a scuba diver's and snorkeler's paradise — the fish and plant life off its shores are fascinating. Call the Colombia Tourist Office in New York City for help in making reservations (phone: 212-688-0151). Moderate.

BARRANQUILLA

El Prado – Large, suburban hotel has 171 rooms (single and double), nightclub, swimming pool, and tennis courts. Carrera 54, No. 70-10 (phone: 456533). Expensive.

Cadebia – Barranquilla's only five-star hotel, with 110 very large rooms, color TV, conference rooms, supper club, pool, shops, and casino. Calle 75 No. 41D-79 (phone: 344817). Expensive to moderate.

Royal Lebolo – In the El Prado area, it has 74 rooms, a bar, pool, restaurant, and disco. Carrera 54, No. 68-124 (phone: 357800). Expensive to moderate.

Caribana – 170-room centrally located hotel offers reasonable singles and doubles, including private baths and occasionally hot water. Carrera 41, No. 40-02 (phone: 414782). Moderate.

TAYRONA NATIONAL PARK

Campgrounds are available with hot water, electricity, and a restaurant.

SANTA MARTA

Irotama – The 60 cottage-type units have single and double rooms, air conditioning, living and dining rooms. There's also a restaurant. Best choice in the area. Km 14, Rte. 2 (phone: 27643). Expensive to moderate.

La Sierra – 74-room hotel with seafood restaurant is on El Rodadero beach (phone: 27197). Moderate.

Tamacá Inn – 72-room hotel has single and double rooms, swimming pool, casino, dining rooms, and coffee shop. At Rodadero Bay. Carrera 2, No. 11A-98 (phone: 27015). Moderate.

Sompallón – 14-room hotel is simple, without air conditioning, but has a good restaurant. 10B-57 Carrera 1, El Rodadero beach (phone: 33000). Moderate.

Residencia Île de France – 17-room hotel with air conditioning is two blocks from the beach. 22-106 Carrera 2, El Rodadero (phone: 2877). Inexpensive.

Riohacha to Villa de Leyva

Rimmed by the Caribbean and blessed with groves of graceful coconut palms, the highway east of Santa Marta to the Venezuela border belies its gentle appearance: Only rugged, risk-loving (and, frankly, irresponsible) travelers should venture on this course. The isolated area, ripe for smuggling cocaine, marijuana, and other contraband that includes emeralds, cattle, and electrical appliances, has recently been transformed into a battlefield for warring smugglers and local authorities. Police constantly patrol the border and the entire desert, and even the Caribbean Sea is watched by the Colombian and US navies on the lookout for any ships ferrying their illegal cargo up to Panamá and the eastern US coast. For this reason, the police are edgy, nervous, and highly suspicious.

You can avoid this route and travel from Santa Marta back to Barranquilla, taking the Barranquilla-Bogotá highway southeast to Bogotá, and reversing the route described below. The more diehard traveler, however, will continue along Route 2 through Riohacha, capital of the Department of La Guajira, east across the desert to Maicao and Cúcuta.

Entering the area that is near the Venezuelan border, the route ascends steadily up into the mountainous range of the Eastern Cordillera, the Andean ridge that continues through Colombia south to the Ecuador border. Encompassed in the Cordillera's *páramos* are the coffee-, oil-, and emerald-rich departments of Norte de Santander and Santander, named after Colombia's revolutionary hero, General Francisco de Paula Santander. The route winds down these departments by a number of good highways that intertwine with the Pan-American (Route 71) — through the Santander capital of Bucaramanga, where you can sample the local delicacies of fried and jellied ants, on through Boyacá, a rich historical department. In the Battle of Boyacá Bridge in 1819, the forces of Simón Bolívar were victorious over the royalist troops, thus defeating Spain's last attempt to hold Colombia. Set high in the Cordillera at 9,000 feet, Tunja was once the home of one of the Chibcha chieftains who was annually initiated in ceremonies that produced the legend of El Dorado. The route from Tunja goes south to the small market villages of Chiquinquirá and Raquira, through the Candelaria Desert, and into Villa de Leyva, an exquisitely preserved, colonial town. The whole lovely province of Boyacá can be visited easily by car or local bus from Bogotá.

RIOHACHA: Once the pearling center of Colombia, this port of 45,000 did not escape the licks of Francis Drake when he ravaged Santa Marta, 104 miles (160 km) to the east, in 1586. Today, the pearlers have all but disappeared, and Riohacha's role is that of a seaport and fishing town on the fringe of the semiarid peninsula. The temperature rarely dips below 90° to 95°F (32° to 35°C), and the dry, listless land is laced with occasional palm and almond trees.

The Guajira is the home of the very independent, nomadic Guajira Indians; they can be seen in town or in the peninsula desert. The Indians basically keep to themselves by farming or cattle and goat raising. They used to be housekeepers and servants for the colonists in the peninsula and later intermarried with the Spaniards. They live in white, thatched-roof houses; the women are distinguished by their long, loose flowing dress, the *manta guajira.* They also weave a number of bright belts, sashes, and bags that can be purchased in the Indian market at Riohacha.

Other than wander through the town or play on the white sand beach, there isn't much to do in Riohacha.

En Route from Riohacha – Route 2 leads east some 40 miles (65 km) to the small town of Maicao, near the Venezuelan border. At least three and a half times the size of Riohacha, Maicao's numbers are inflated by approximately 10,000 ladies and gentlemen whose sole occupation is smuggling. Contraband goods are ferried in and out of Colombia. This is a rugged, really seamy town that should be glanced at, gulped at, and gotten out of — or better yet avoided. But before leaving, check the legal Guajira market and some of the local dishes, like *friche* (goat) and fish stew. If you're interested in crossing the border into Venezuela, do so legally by obtaining a visa (either in Cartagena or Barranquilla) and an exit stamp from Colombia and an entry stamp into Venezuela.

From Maicao, follow Route 167 southwest for 90 miles (145 km) to Valledupar;

the highway turns into Route 51 and proceeds another 155 miles (208 km) until you reach the junction of a paved road that heads east some 110 miles (177 km) to the frontier town of Cúcuta.

CÚCUTA: This city of 375,000 and capital of the Department of Norte de Santander is another smugglers' hangout. Founded in 1724, Simón Bolívar passed through during his 1813 campaign, and a statue marks the spot where he addressed his soldiers. Most of the colonial buildings were destroyed by an earthquake in 1875, so many of the buildings are modern.

Unlike the region of La Guajira, some parts of Norte de Santander, such as Pamplona, have a cold, brisk climate; temperatures remain at about 48°F (9°C), so bring an extra sweater or two.

From Cúcuta, either travel northeast into Venezuela (get the necessary exit stamp at the immigration office, Av. S. Calle 15) or drive south along the Pan-American Highway — known here as Route 71 — some 42 miles (67 km) to Pamplona.

PAMPLONA: Unlike Cúcuta, this town of 30,000 is chilly, and most of its colonial buildings were also wiped out in the 1875 earthquake, although the former monasteries of San Agustín, San Francisco, and Santo Domingo are still intact. The recently restored cathedral is a colonial jewel.

From Pamplona, there are two routes to follow down to Tunja. One continues on the Pan-American, passing through the small towns of Concepción, Malaga, and Capitanejo; Route 61 west, however, is better, continuing south through Chitagá to Bucaramanga, the next stop.

BUCARAMANGA: The capital of Santander, this city of 500,000 was founded in 1622 by a member of the party of the German explorer Nicolás Federmann, although this fact doesn't actually explain the local perchant for eating those all-time favorites, fried and jellied ants. An archaeological museum, where Bolívar lived for 2 months during his 1813 campaign, now houses pre-Columbian pottery and other artifacts.

Bucaramanga has an airport, and there are flights back to Bogotá; buses for the 9-hour trip are also available.

En Route from Bucaramanga – Continuing south on Route 61, you'll pass Aratoca, a colonial town that looks the way it did during the settlement period. Fourteen miles (23 km) south is San Gil. The weather gets warmer as you head into the Central Valley in the Department of Boyacá: San Gil and Socorro and Barbosa are in fruit- and coffee-producing areas.

From here, continue south on Route 61 until it merges with the Pan-American Highway (Route 71) and leads to Tunja.

TUNJA: Only 90 miles (148 km) north of Bogotá, this was once the home of one of the two legendary Chibcha kings, the Zaque, renowned for the legend of El Dorado. Settled by the Spanish in 1539, this city of 100,000 is a chilly one when the harsh Cordillera winds blow through its avenues filled with white colonial haciendas, stone churches, and tree-filled plazas.

Today, Tunja retains the colonial elegance it had when it was founded by Captain Suarez Rendón, and many of the original 16th-century mansions and cathedrals are intact or are undergoing restoration. Many of the house façades still contain the carved coats of arms of their conquistador owners and are open to the public for small admission fees (about 25¢). Rendón mansion, across from Plaza de Bolívar (open daily from 8:30 AM to 6 PM, with 2 hours off for siesta, beginning at noon), contains vivid gold and red frescoed ceilings in the second-floor salons which overlook an enclosed courtyard filled with red geraniums. The mansion of Don Juan de Vargas (Calle 20), the oldest son of the first governor general, Don Diego de Vargas, also has elegant frescoes of red, gold, and blue (open from 8:30 AM to 6 PM; closed between 12:30 and 2:30 PM). The mansion of Don Juan de Castillanos, a major poet of the 16th century, is also worth seeing (Calle 1).

Tunja's churches are as lavish as its mansions. The cathedral (Plaza de Bolívar), was built between 1576 and 1607 and contains a very splendid gold, rococo repository. Built in 1574, Santa Clara Convent (Calle 19) was a former mansion whose paneled roof is typical of Sevillan churches from that period. Next to the convent choir is the cell of Sister Francisca Josefa, a famous writer and mystic known as the Colombian St. Theresa.

The capital of the Department of Boyacá, Tunja was one of the first Colombian cities to declare war against Spain during the battle for independence. Plaza de Bolívar contains a statue of Simón Bolívar, who stayed in the nearby Holguin Maldonado House (now the private Club Boyacá) when he came here prior to the Battle of Boyacá: visits are allowed only with permission of the club's manager. The office of the National Tourist Board, on the central square, can assist in obtaining this permission.

You'll want to drive north through the city to the Teacher's College and Donato's Well. According to Chibcha legend, the well was formed after Chief Unzahue fell in love with his sister and they ran away together. When they returned some months later, the daughter got into a dispute with her mother, who gave her a good wallop, knocking over *chicha* she was mixing with a wooden spoon. The spilled corn beer formed the pond, which the Chibcha believed was bottomless. Don't try drinking its water, though, since you're likely to walk away with a case of Chibcha Mama's Revenge. A few kilometers west of the city is Los Cojines (the Pillows), a 60-foot semicircle hewn out of rocks, used by the Chibcha chieftains in their homage to the sun god. The stone throne was used by the priest officiating at the rite.

Both bus and car service are available from Tunja south to Bogotá for about $5 (bus) or $8 (car). Or delay continuing to the capital and take a short side trip 50 miles (80 km) along a paved road to Lake Sochagota, where you can swim, fish, sail, and water ski. Also, there is a good Indian Market and Archaeological Museum at Sogamoso. If you make this side trip, be sure to include a visit to two quiet colonial villages, Tópaga and Monguí, and to Lake Tota, high in the mountains, for a lunch of freshly caught trout. There are good accommodations in both Tota and Duitama, down the road. It's necessary to return to Tunja, however, before proceeding to Villa de Leyva.

En Route from Tunja – Continuing south along the Pan-American, you come next to Puenta Boyacá, where, on August 6, 1819, Bolívar defeated the royalists during the Battle of Boyacá. From here, continue on an unpaved road west to Villa de Leyva, or backtrack through Tunja for the 45-minute drive to Villa de Leyva on a paved road. A more attractive alternative, however, is to take the unpaved road west past Lake Fuquene to the craft market town of Chiquinquirá, where green-glazed earthenware as well as *tagua* (ivory-type) figurines are sold. The town also holds two important religious celebrations: October 7 is the Feast Day of the Virgin of Chiquinquirá, patroness of Colombia; December 8 is the Feast of the Immaculate Conception. On both occasions, pilgrims flock to the cathedral on their knees to pay their respects and hear mass.

From Chiquinquirá, continue west along this unpaved road to Raquira, another market town, where you can purchase ceramic statuettes of the Magi and small animals. The area around Villa de Leyva, the Candelaria Desert, is named after the Candelaria convent founded in 1604 by Friar Mateo Delgado, which is a short distance past Raquira. The church, now a historic monument, contains many paintings from the 17th century and is open to the public daily, from 8 AM to noon and from 2 to 6 PM. The Candelaria may be the most fertile desert in the world. A rich, olive-growing basin where the temperature never exceeds 65°F (18°C), it is surrounded by barren, fossil-filled mountains.

VILLA DE LEYVA: Founded in 1572, this town was the home of several Colombian patriots, including Antonio Nariño, who helped start the independence movement when he translated Thomas Jefferson's *Rights of Man* into Spanish in 1794. His home

— open to the public daily, except Mondays, from 8 AM until noon and from 2 to 6 PM — contains colonial memorabilia. It's also possible to visit the Iglesia Mayor, the 16th-century manor house where Colombia's first Congress met in 1812. The houses are set between a number of picturesque, cobblestone plazas, and many fossils are imbedded in the buildings. One "fossil" that gives the town an ironic air is the carved Spanish coat of arms that is over the main entrance to the Royal Distillery. The still is gone and so are the royalists; today the building houses a small museum (open 8 AM to noon, then 2 to 6 PM, except Sundays). Another convent, Santo Ecce Homo, was founded in 1620 by the Dominicans. It is worth a visit for its adobe and stone Andean type of architecture.

   En Route from Villa de Leyva – It's necessary to backtrack to the Pan-American Highway to reach the outskirts of Bogotá, where you'll pick up Route 1 northwest to Manizales, a drive that leads through Colombia's more fertile region, the Magdalena Valley.

BEST EN ROUTE

Hotels on this route are small and simple (some lack private baths and hot water), but clean, comfortable, and very moderately priced, with per person rates of no more than $30 (moderate), and many under $20 (inexpensive), except in the province of Boyacá, where rates can go as high as $60 for expensive accommodations. While not necessary, it's still a good idea to phone ahead for reservations. There are lovely country inns in old colonial homes in the Boyacá region. Some of the hotels have offices in Bogotá, so you can call there rather than risk poor connections in the smaller towns. Try not to linger in Riohacha or Cúcuta because of the contraband and drug problem, and remember, to avoid irritating the police, do not accept any items — even wooden nickels — from a Guajiró Indian unless you're buying at an Indian market or a legitimate store.

RIOHACHA

Gimaura – This 36-room hotel offers breakfast and clean, beachfront accommodations. Av. La Playa (phone: 26). Inexpensive.

CÚCUTA

Tonchalá – This 100-room hotel has air conditioning, a pool, Turkish baths, and sauna. Calle 10 and Av. 0 (phone: 22205). Moderate.

Bolívar – This 94-room motel has a swimming pool, comfortable accommodations. Av. Demetrio Mendoza (phone: 43991). Moderate.

Villa Antigua del Rosario – A clean hotel with 42 small rooms. Autopista San Antonio (phone: 42128). Inexpensive.

PAMPLONA

Cariongo – This new 32-room hotel is quiet and provides good service. Carrera 5, No. 9-10 (phone: 2645). Moderate.

BUCARAMANGA

Bucarica – Has 80 rooms, a pool, and a restaurant. Calle 35-Carrera 19 (phone: 23111). Moderate.

Chicamocha – Offers 200 air-conditioned rooms, pool, TV. *Bar Cepitá* is decorated like a local farm house and is the place to try the area's delicacy, fried or jellied ants. Calle 34, No. 3124 (phone: 343000). Moderate.

San Juan de Gíron – Clean, 80-room hotel, with a swimming pool and restaurant. Km 6, Autopista a Gíron (phone: 366430; for reservations in Bogotá, 257-3311). Moderate.

Andino – New 74-room hotel provides good service. 18-44 Calle 34 (phone: 22142). Inexpensive.

SAN GIL

Belle Isla – Small hotel has pleasant double rooms and a swimming pool. Contact Bogotá office (phone: for reservations in Bogotá, 257-3311). Inexpensive.

TUNJA

Hunza – Comfortable hotel has 55 rooms, with a swimming pool and Turkish bath. 10-66 Calle 21-A (phone: 4111; or in Bogotá, 283-2200). Expensive.

Centenario – This 29-room hotel has a restaurant. 16-81 Calle 10 (phone: 2271). Inexpensive.

BOYACÁ

Reservations for most hotels in the area can be made by contacting Boyacá Servicios Hoteleros, Carrera 15, No. 77-90, Local 204, in Bogotá (phone: 218-0321).

PAIPA/LAKE SOCHAGOTA

Estelar Paipa and Centro de Convenciones – 200 rooms, pool, thermal baths, convention center with 1,000-person capacity, and a striking view of the lake (phone: for reservations in Bogotá, 232-8250). Expensive.

Sochagota – A 57-room hotel with a swimming pool and a recently opened convention center. Lakeside (phone: 211, for reservations in Bogotá, 212-2200). Moderate.

Panorama – A total of 32 rooms, with pool, thermal baths, sauna, and spa. The decor is definitely of the plastic persuasion, but it is a good buy (phone: for reservations in Bogotá, 235-8976). Inexpensive.

TOTA

Rocaslindas – 14 rooms on the edge of the lake; fresh trout a specialty. The weather up this high is nippy, and in the evenings you'll be grateful for the roaring fire in the lounge and the handwoven blankets on the beds (phone: for reservations in Sogamosa, 2245). Moderate.

DUITAMA

San Luis de Ucuengá – An old converted farmhouse with 12 rooms, surrounded by breathtakingly beautiful rose gardens. Family owned and run, with good food and peaceful atmosphere (phone: for reservations in Bogotá, 218-0376). Moderate.

VILLA DE LEYVA

Hostería el Molino la Mesopotamia – Restored old mill has 26 rooms with bath and telephones, a restaurant, swimming pool, and great atmosphere. Calle del Silencio (phone: 35). Expensive.

Mesón de la Plaza Mayor – As the name indicates, this 20-room hotel, in an ancient building, is right on the main square. Huge rooms, boiling hot water, and delicious food make guests feel right at home (phone: for reservations in Bogotá, 218-1671). Inexpensive.

Bogotá to Medellín

The next route through Colombia begins in the Tunja-Bogotá area of the Eastern Cordillera and travels through some of the country's most fertile valleys. One of these, the Magdalena, is wedged between the Eastern and

Central Cordilleras and borders Río Magdalena, which flows 1,000 miles to the Caribbean Sea. Honda, once a principal port on the west bank of the river, is today the heart of the fruit-producing valley; its warm (84°F/29°C) temperature and mild rainfall are ideal for growing coconuts, papayas, and other tropical tidbits.

The trip from the valley over the jagged, snowcapped *páramos* of the Central Cordillera is breathtaking as well as chilly — about 30° lower than in Honda. Above, the black and white Andean peaks fill the blue, cloud-laced sky; below stretches the valley and the river — a mere silver sliver wandering through the green orchards. Manizales straddles the Cordillera like a man with a leg caught in the mud: Its buildings stand on stilts, and their backs slope down, down, down into the mountainside. This is coffee-growing country. Small farms dot the area, their coffee beans ripening for harvest under the shade of trees planted for the sole purpose of protecting them from the strong equatorial sun.

Isolated deep in the heart of Colombia, this area had little involvement in the country's fight for independence, but its prominent department, Antioquia, was founded through curious circumstances. In the mid-seventeenth century, a group of Jews from Bogotá came here to escape the onslaught of the Spanish Inquisition, which was intent on purifying members of the Roman Catholic church and persecuting anyone who was not. As time passed, the immigrants became excellent farmers, heavily propagating among themselves to strengthen their work force, refusing to own slaves, and building up a reputation as hard workers with successful businesses. A wave of migration into the southern section of central Colombia during the nineteenth century resulted in the formation of additional departments, including Caldas, Tolima, and Valle. Medellín, the Antioquian capital, is today also renowned as the orchid capital of the world.

En Route from Bogotá – Start this phase of the journey by taking Route 1 west from Bogotá through Facatativá, a small town of 22,000 about 25 miles (40 km) from the capital. Here, visit the Piedras de Tunja, an amphitheater formed by stones; then continue west across the ridge until you overlook the wide chasm of the Magdalena Valley. From this point, the snows of the Nevado del Tolima and Nevado del Ruiz in the Central Cordillera are visible. The eruption in November 1985 of the latter resulted in an avalanche of melted snow and volcanic mud that destroyed the town of Armero and caused great loss of life and property damage. Descending into the valley, you come into the coffee belt, pass the small towns of Sasaima and Villeta, then cross the broad valley of Guaduas into the Magdalena Valley itself and Honda.

HONDA: Known as the city of bridges because 14 of them span the Río Magdalena, this was an important port until the start of the 20th century. Now it's primarily a fishing town, and a number of Bogotá residents and other Colombians flock here every February with their bait, rods, and tackle. They gather in numbers along the west bank of the river, playing and chatting in the warm, 84°F (29°C) weather like children playing hooky.

Honda also has some colonial buildings in its downtown area, including the El Rosario Church, Casa Consistorial, and Calle de las Trampas (Street of the Traps), built for defensive purposes.

En Route from Honda – The scenery in the Magdalena Valley is remarkable: Flat cotton fields broken by strangely eroded table mountains skirted with jungle growth. Heading west toward Manizales, you'll come to Mariquita, the valley's fruit-producing area, known for its mangoes, papayas, pineapples, and coconuts.

Leaving Mariquita, you enter the rest of the fruit-bearing region, stretched out along a number of gently rolling hills not unlike those of Kentucky. You reach the small town of Fresno, the first of a series of towns set into the mountains of the Central Cordillera.

The view from the Cordillera is great: Black, snowcapped *páramos* loom high above the green valley of sparkling river waters and ripe fruit orchards. The highest point of the highway is at 10,000-foot Páramo de Letras. A left turn north leads below the snowline of El Ruiz Mountain. From here, the route dips down the other side of the Cordillera into the Department of Caldas and its capital of Manizales.

MANIZALES: Sitting on the side of the Cordillera at 7,000 feet above sea level, this city's population of 400,000 dwells in two-story buildings that stand on stilts, then slope backward into the mountains to become three and four stories tall. It is surprising to learn that all of these buildings are made out of concrete and stone, thanks to a local ordinance imposed after two separate fires virtually wiped out the entire city's wooden structures in the 19th century.

Founded in 1848 by peasants from Medellín, which is 164 miles north, the largest industry here is coffee. Introduced in 1865, the beans thrive in the moist, 60°F (16°C) temperature and mild rainfall of the Cordillera and are grown mostly on the 8-acre farms owned by *campesiños* (peasants), who are exemplified in Colombian folklore by Juan Valdez. The National Federation of Coffee Growers runs an experimental farm in Chinchiná, 15 miles (24 km) outside Manizales; it is open to the public Mondays through Fridays. This small town also suffered considerable damage from the November 1985 eruption.

En Route from Manizales – From Manizales it's possible to go in one of two directions: Traveling south, you go through the Cauca Valley into the archaeological parks of San Agustín and Tierradentro (discussed in *Neiva to Cali*). Otherwise you can continue along Route 1 west toward Medellín, picking up the Pan-American Highway at Risaralda. There is heavy traffic on this route, which only recently was paved all of the way into the city. The road winds up the Alta de Minas Pass at 8,000 feet, then winds down over the Central Cordillera until it descends 5,000 feet into Medellín.

MEDELLÍN: This city of 1.7 million people, aptly nicknamed "the City of Flowers, Friendship, and Eternal Spring," is the orchid kingdom of the world; its mild (70°F/21°C) temperature and its rainfall are perfect for floral cultivation and for the growth of coffee beans on the slopes of the mountains. Medellín also ranks second to Bogotá in industrial importance, being a major manufacturer of textiles, pharmaceuticals, woodwork, metallurgical products, and rubber goods.

Founded in 1675, most of the settlers here were Jewish refugees seeking isolation and a chance to develop their own way of life without too much pressure from Spanish feudal overlords. Contrary to the pattern set by the conquerors who exploited slave and serf labor, the settlers did their own work. The few Indians in the area were primitive nomads who made poor agricultural laborers, and the settlers refused, on ethical grounds, to use black slave labor. The land was therefore divided into small, family-size farms; the *antioqueños,* as they are called, maintained an extremely high birthrate in order to increase the work force, and there was very little intermarriage with the Indians or blacks.

Medellín has a number of museums. Museo de Antioquia (Calle 52 at Carrera 53) contains paintings by local artists and Indian pottery; it is open, with an admission fee, Tuesdays through Saturdays from 9 AM to 6 PM (closed from 1 to 3 PM for siesta). Fernando Botero, Colombia's number one painter/sculptor, recently donated 15 of his finest paintings and 24 sculptures to this museum, making it a *must* stop for anyone visiting Medllín. Museo de Antropología, on the campus of Antioquia University, contains pre-Columbian pottery; it is open Mondays through Fridays from 10 AM to 6 PM (closed from noon to 2 PM); admission is free. Museo de Ciencias Naturales (Calle 55 No. 30-1) exhibits over 300 stuffed animals, birds, and insects from the area. The museum is closed to the public, but private tours can be arranged (phone 390417 for an appointment). Museo El Castillo (Loma los Balsos in El Poblado) contains a collection of European and American art, crystal, porcelain, and priceless rugs. It is in the former mansion of Don Diego Echevarria Missas, an entrepreneur, and is open from 1 to 5 PM daily.

One place not to be passed up is the Jardín Botánica Joaquin Antonio Uribe (Carrera 52 No. 73-298), where there is a collection of orchids under the Orquideorama, a pavilion designed for growing and maintaining orchids. The gardens also house a replica of a colonial Antioquian village, an azalea patio, fern gardens, and aviaries. Open daily from 9 AM to 5:30 PM; admission is 15¢ for adults, 10¢ for children. On a visit to the Santa Fe Zoo (Carrera 52 No. 20-63), you'll come face to face with South American apes, rare black jaguars, and the fierce, almost extinct Andean condor. Open daily from 9 AM to 5 PM; admission is 20¢. Cattle auctions are held here Tuesdays and Thursdays; admission is free.

There are many colonial churches in Medellín. Basilica Metropolitana (Carrera 49, No. 56-44) is a huge, 15,000-foot Romanesque structure, with a 3,425-flute organ and marble altars; Basilica de la Candelaria, built in 1766, is more moderate in style, displaying a gentler Creole touch in the altar's silverwork. Iglesia de la Veracruz (Calle 51 at Carrera 52) is a 17th-century church with a stone façade surrounded by pillars and arches.

There is still one public place here that is off limits to women through a centuries-old custom: The European-Mediterranean sanctuary of the café is for men only, and while women travelers stomp their feet and pout outside, their male companions are welcome to wander inside, grab a cold beer or quaff some *tinto* (demitasse coffee served black), while having their shoes shined, and can even buy a ticket to the lottery. More obliging — and less sexist — are the numerous discos in the city, including *Carousel* (Centro Commercial San Diego), *El Infierno* (Calle 50 No. 69-20), *Timaná* (Calle 50 No. 71-190), and *2002* (Calle 50 No. 651-30), all of which are open until dawn. But for some real high life, don't miss *Kevin's* (phone: 249-3420), a vibrant mixture of restaurant, art gallery, disco, bar, and more. On a high hill near the *Inter-Continental Medellín,* its surrounding glass walls provide a panoramic view of the sparkling city lights.

Downtown Medellín is a shopping complex in itself, and travelers can pick up a number of craft items, from the Antioquian *carriel,* a leather pouch used by both men and women, to the *ruana* (poncho) and other leather and woolen items. Flea markets are also reaching popular proportions here, especially the *Mercado Popular Los Toldos de San Alejo,* held in Bolívar Park on the first Saturday of every month; you can buy rare coins, antiques, Indian artifacts, and even exotic pets like ocelots and *pericos ligeros,* koala-like bears found in the high sierra. Even those not shopping will want to visit the Villa Nueva shopping center, which recently won an international architectural prize for its conversion from a staid old brick seminary to a modern shopping complex. One of the attractions is an excellent restaurant in what was once the chapel. Called *The Chapel,* it has waiters dressed as monks and Gregorian chants for background music. Beverages other than holy water are, however, available. Avenida Oriental and Carrera 50.

Golf and tennis are available at Medellín's private clubs, so if you're a member of a club at home, bring along a letter from your home pro or club president requesting hospitality and reciprocity. One unusual game open to the public is the cockfight; it's legal throughout South America, although it's been banned in the US. There are three cockfighting arenas in town: *Guadelajara* (Calle 52 No. 89-49), *Cantaclara* (Carrera a Bello), and *Villa Julia* (Carrera 52 No. 11SA-45). Fights are scheduled regularly; check the newspapers.

The people of Antioquia are no somber lot. They love to party, and at least 6 major festivals are held in Medellín throughout the year. The Feria de la Candelaria, held in February, commemorates the feast of the city's patronness with bullfights, and 8 days of parades and musical celebrations. It's an occasion to don Spanish Coroban hats and shawls. The Festival del Tango in June commemorates the death of Argentine singer Carlos Gardel, who was killed in an airplane crash at the Medellín airport in 1935. The city goes tango crazy, and everybody, from professionals to the bar drunks, tangos all day and all night. Antioquia's independence is celebrated in the Desfile de los Silletros in August; parades are filled with floats of orchids, carnations, and other flowers; there are bands, singers, horsemen, and the typical gathering of beauties for the trip. The Festival del Recuerdo is a "nostalgic" festival, commemorating the city's past, held at different times throughout the year. The Christmas holidays are celebrated from December 20 through January 7; everyone, it seems, comes to the mountains on vacation, and dinners are flavored with aniseed *aguardiente*, and parades take place around the city. Feria Colombiana de la Confección, held in September, is a salute to the textile and garment industries.

As in Cartagena, Barranquilla, Bogotá, and the other big cities, the professional pickpockets have a field day in Medellín, so watch your belongings. Don't wander into slums if you can avoid it; and try not to hail just any old cab in the city — use the green and off-white cars assigned to hotels or you may be taken for a real ride. If you're doing your own sightseeing, rent a car from *Hertz*, Carrera 43A, No. 23-50 (phone: 232-4864), where you can get a Renault or other make for about $40 a day, or $200 a week, plus mileage. Other rental car agencies are *Alqui-Car*, Calle 53, No. 43-32 (phone: 393281), and *Renta Car*, Calle 58, No. 49-50 (phone: 254-5766).

The tourist office is at Calle 55 No. 49-84 (phone: 454525) if you need assistance. Unlike some Colombian cities, there are a number of good restaurants in Medellín. On the menu at *La Posada de la Montana* (Carrera 35 No. 16-22) are local dishes including *arepas*, *frijoles* (red beans cooked with pork), *mazamorra* (corn soup that's very thick), *patacones* (fried plantains), and *chorizos* (sausages). *La Res* (Calle 50 No. 69-A51) specializes in barbecued kidneys and Argentine grilled steaks. Strangely enough, this city far from the coast boasts an excellent seafood restaurant, *Frutos del Mar* (Carrera 43B, No. 11-51).

Some side trips from Medellín include a ride to El Ranchito, 7 miles (11 km) south of Medellín on the Pan-American in the small town of Itaquí, which has over 50,000 orchids. About one mile before El Ranchito is Envigado, where craftsmen still make the traditional *carriel*. Bello, 4 miles (7 km) north of Medellín up the Pan-American, houses the hut where Marco Fidel Suarez, president of Colombia from 1918 to 1922, was born. The hut is encased in glass to preserve it. If there's time, make a side trip (about 3 hours each way) down the mountainside to Santa Fe de Antioquia, on the banks of the Cauca river. Founded in 1541, this perfectly preserved colonial town takes you back to a time of cobbled streets and thick-walled houses surrounding flower-filled patios. This jaunt may be done as an all-day excursion, or there are pleasant accommodations at *Hostería Mariscal Robledo* and *Hotel Lago Tours.*

En Route from Medellín – For the next leg of the Cauca Valley adventure and the mysteries of San Agustín and Tierradentro, there are several choices. Either drive back to Manizales and Bogotá, or fly (Avianca has daily flights from the new José María Cordóva Airport, which is over an hour away from downtown Medellín). Another possibility is to drive directly from Medellín to semitropical Cali; the road is good and well paved.

BEST EN ROUTE

As in the previous route, hotels in this part of Colombia are economical in small towns and reasonable in cities, ranging up to $80 (expensive), $30 to $50 (moderate), and under $25 (inexpensive). Most of the hotels in larger cities have private baths and hot showers in double and single rooms; some have fairly good restaurants. Here, as everywhere else in Colombia, it's a good idea to make reservations beforehand and to check security at the hotel to make sure your belongings will be safe.

HONDA

Campestre Cabañas El Molino – A 23-room hotel with cabins, five swimming pools, and a game room. Carretera a Mariquito (phone: 3165; for reservations in Bogotá, 235-2105). Inexpensive.

Ondama – This 58-room hotel has a swimming pool and comfortable rooms. Calle 16 at Carrera 13A (phone: 3127). Inexpensive.

MANIZALES

Hostería Villa Kempis – A 30-room retreat house on the city's outskirts is very quiet and provides a view of the city from its hillside site. Salida a Pereira (phone: 42961). Moderate.

Las Colinas – This 65-room hotel is clean and comfortable. Carrera 22 at Calle 20 and 21 (phone: 42009). Moderate.

Tama Internacional – A 61-room hotel next to the city's cathedral. Calle 23, No. 22-43 (phone: 22273). Inexpensive.

MEDELLÍN

Amaru – New, with 93 air-conditioned rooms, a good restaurant, cozy bar, and shopping arcade. Carrera 50A, No. 53-45 (phone: 231-2232). Expensive.

Inter-Continental – The best hotel in town, although outside the center, with single and double rooms, a bar, health club, tennis courts, dining room, and Turkish bath. Variante Las Palmas (phone: 266-0680). Expensive.

Nutibara – This 328-room hotel offers single and double deluxe rooms with tile baths and antique furniture; there's also a sidewalk café, nightclub, casino, and restaurant serving T-bone steaks for under $3.50. 50-46 Calle 52A (phone: 319111). Expensive to moderate.

Gran – Thys hotel has 112 rooms, bar, restaurant, and homey service. Set right downtown, it's popular with the executive crowd. Calle 54, No. 45-92 (phone: 251-9951). Moderate.

Europa Normandie – A small hotel with 154 rooms, singles and doubles, private baths, hot water, large closets, and a dining room. 49-100 Calle 53 (phone: 241-9920). Inexpensive.

Veracruz – This 120-room hotel features private baths and hot water, open bar, restaurant, and swimming pool. 54-18 Carrera 50 (phone: 242-0805). Inexpensive.

SANTA FE DE ANTIOQUIA

Lago Tours – Twenty minutes away from Santa Fe de Antioquia, this pleasant country hotel has 10 bungalows, each with a tree growing through its roof, and 15 regular rooms. Good dining room, pool with giant slide, cockfighting pit, lake with all water sports, and billiard room (phone: 62004; for reservations in Medellín, 232-3069). Moderate.

Hostería Mariscal Robledo – Named for the founder of the town, with 32 big, high-ceilinged rooms; Olympic-sized pool; and surprisingly good dining room.

A block away from the central square. Calle 10 and Carrera 12 (phone: 1609). Inexpensive.

Neiva to Cali

The next route south from Bogotá leads through the lower part of the Magdalena Valley into the humid Department of Huila and the archaeological zone of San Agustín National Park. The site of many mysterious stone monoliths of men, monsters, and beasts was left by an isolated culture that cropped up between 600 BC and AD 1200, then suddenly disappeared. Very little is known about who or what these people were, but the 30 or so sites unearthed by archaeologists have determined that the Indians were farmers who harvested corn, yucca, and peanuts. The men wore loincloths; the women, short skirts, and they adorned themselves with necklaces, bracelets, and pectorals. They were devoted to death rites, burying their dead in elaborate tombs and artificial mounds, according to their status within the society. They had a polytheistic religion, and strolling along the park's forest paths, you will come upon a host of gods, including monkeys (fertility), eagles (fire and light), and cats (the underworld). A similar mystery is Tierradentro, some 100 miles (162 km) northeast of San Agustín, where several underground chambers housing human bones have been discovered; these possibly relate to the one situated at San Agustín. Their similarities can be seen in the carvings embedded in the *hypogeiums* (chambers).

It takes a few days to explore and enjoy these sites. The "fastest" way to reach them is to take a plane from Bogotá to Neiva, then drive for about 5 hours down a paved highway to San Agustín.

From there, continue a round-robin circuit that heads west over the Central Cordillera into the fertile Pubenza and Cauca valleys, a springlike area where the 70°F (21°C) climate is good for farming. The northern section of the valley is green and wet enough to grow sugarcane; along the 84-mile (136-km) stretch of the Pan-American north from Popayán to Cali there are bamboo and palm trees. Ducks, doves, and partridges fly in the blue skies, into which juts the 18,860-foot Nevado de Huila, a snowcapped, wintry contrast to the tropical scenery.

Some of the oldest Colombian cities are in this area, founded in the midsixteenth century by conquistadores in their search for El Dorado: Popayán was the birthplace of a number of Colombian patriots; Cali, the most important city, is a large producer of sugar, rice, coffee, and cattle, and has just celebrated its 450th birthday. This is the "hottest" nightlife spot and ranks in the number one position as Colombia's Sport City, with a huge, multistadia sports complex constructed for the Pan-American Games of 1971. Leaving Cali, either return to Bogotá by plane (25 minutes) or continue east by car to the capital, completing the surface route.

Along this route, like all others in Colombia, there are good and bad roads, hotels with and without baths and hot water, and poor to fine restaurants. Actually, be prepared for excellent to horrible in all three categories. If any assistance is needed along the way, contact the tourist offices in any of the major cities and at points of interest such as San Agustín National Park. Also remember that the chance of exchanging a car route for an air itinerary is in your favor, since Colombia's 24 private carriers provide better passage than its roads in most cases.

NEIVA: This city of 90,000 was founded in 1539 by Sebastián de Belalcázar, while en route to Bogotá from Popayán. The climate is relatively warm (80°F/26°C), and the city is a major producer of coffee. Many holidays are celebrated here, including Bambuco (June 19–28), the national dance festival, which lures Colombians from every part of the country. Sandwiched into the event schedule is the June 20 Feast of San Pedro y San Pablo and the June 24 Feast of San Juan. On both days there are masses and religious processions followed by the usual merrymaking, fireworks, and bullfights.

Neiva's airport, La Manguita, has flights to and from Bogotá. You can also catch a bus to the capital; the trip, however, takes about 6 hours.

En Route from Neiva – Proceeding to San Agustín National Park on Route 61 south, the highway leads toward the headwaters of the Río Magdalena. Along the way are a number of small, green valleys and towns that include Garzon and Pitalito, about 88 miles (142 km) south of Neiva. From here, drive into the town of San Agustín: The national park is 3 miles (5 km) away. It's a minimum 5-hour drive from Neiva.

SAN AGUSTÍN NATIONAL PARK: Hire a horse or Jeep, or take the tour on foot to spend at least a full 1 or 2 days wandering along the park's well-tended forest paths crossed by small silvery streams. At each turn is another delightful surprise. The monoliths and carvings stand randomly throughout the area, as though the original dwellers here left them for our amusement. Be sure to take a walk through the Bosque de las Estatuas (Forest of Statues). Here stands the carved statue of a lizard, eyes glaring, ready to flick its tongue; here is a carved man who looks more like a primitive baseball player than an Indian, clutching a long, batlike stick in his hands. Salamanders squiggle underfoot, and they, along with lizards and various wizened humans, scurry across the face of the *lavapatas,* the foot-washing fountain, a water-washed basin that was once a shrine dedicated to the water gods. Not far from the fountain on the path is a stone toad, who seems to be pointing a finger at the fountain. Some 15 miles away is the Salto de Bordones waterfall.

A short drive 19 miles (30 km) north of the park leads to the town of San José de Isnos, where Alto de los Idolos site is covered with statues, coffins, and tombs decorated in red, black, and yellow. These were discovered just recently. North of the area and near the same town is Alto de las Piedras, which contains monuments to the local fertility goddess. Northeast of here you can cross El Estrecho, a small wedge through which the Río Magdalena flows furiously.

San Agustín's inhabitants were believed to be preoccupied with death: Villagers were buried according to social rank; the greater their affluence, the more elaborate the tomb. Similar to the ancient Egyptian practice of entombing a dead pharaoh's wealth with him, the dead here were also buried with their jewels, chains, necklaces, and ceramics. There is a good map of the ruins and guidebook available at the park entrance or at the tourist office in San Agustín (11-41/45 Calle 3A).

En Route from San Agustín – From here, it is best to backtrack to Garzon before continuing to Tierradentro. Along the way are the small towns of Inzá and La Plata, where you'll find the Cascada Azufrada, a sulfurous waterfall. From La Plata, drive 40 minutes to San Andrés de Pisimbala, the central town of Tierradentro.

TIERRADENTRO: Literally "beneath the ground," this archaeological zone contains up to 200 burial chambers that house bones of still other, unidentified ancient inhabitants of the area. Like the monoliths of San Agustín, the *hypogeiums,* or underground tombs, are carved with designs similar to those of the other statues, hinting that some type of Agustinian influence was felt here. Again, you can hire a horse or walk up steep inclines to the areas of interest.

The museum in San Andrés de Pisimbala, the center of the burial area, displays various ceramics discovered in the tombs. About 15 minutes from the museum is Segovia, the most prominent site in the area, with about 15 tombs. Various *hypogeiums* are found in El Duende and Alto de San Andrés, both of which are within a 30-minute walk from the museum. You can also take a 90-minute hike up El Aguacate, a mountain from which the entire area, and the most elaborate tombs, can be seen.

San Andrés de Pisimbala is interesting in itself as the home of the Paez Indians, the tribe that now inhabits the area but has no relation to the pre-Columbian culture that left the tombs. The Indians, once fierce opponents of the white man, are today farmers and weavers, and a number of their crafts are for sale during the Wednesday market here.

En Route from Tierradentro – The 140-mile (257-km) drive on Route 68 west to Popayán is over rough, unpaved road and takes at least 4 hours. Along the way, stop in the Puracé National Park, where you can horseback ride beneath or walk around the Coconuco volanoes, a string of snowcapped craters with Puracé at one end and Pan de Azúcar (Sugar Loaf Mountain) at the other. There are a number of waterfalls and thermal springs here as well as wildlife, including the Andean condor, eagles, hummingbirds, black bear, rabbit deer, and tapir. From here, it's just a few short miles to Popayán.

POPAYÁN: Founded in 1536 by de Belalcázar in the rich and temperate Pubenza Valley, this city of 106,000 people somehow managed to guard its colonial beauty throughout the years. In 1983, on Good Friday, the town's sleepy atmosphere was disrupted by a massive earthquake that severely damaged all its two-story, Spanish colonial buildings, churches, and museums. However, thanks to numerous international donations, the town has risen from the ruins, even more sparklingly white than before.

It won't be the first time the town has had to recover from a crisis. After surviving the vicious attacks of the Pijao Indians in the early years, Popayán went on to become a major social and cultural center. By 1540, it was a provincial capital, subject to the Audencia de Quito, and was an obligatory stopover between Cartagena and Quito. In addition, the city attracted the wealthier Spanish families from the tropical sugar estates to the north, who came to live in the better climate and establish an aristocratic and cultural center by founding schools and a university. The city was an important gold-producing area until the mid-1750s. It managed to change hands at least 22 times during Colombia's fight for independence and was the birthplace of seven presidents and some outstanding citizens, including Francisco José de Caldas, who discovered how to determine altitude by the variation in the boiling point of water.

Be sure to visit the churches, cloisters, and museums in Popayán. The Church of San Francisco (Calle 4 and Carrera 9) has a bell that can be heard from one end of the valley to the other; its pulpit is carved with the delightfully graceful figure of the *canefora americana,* a Creole girl carrying a basket of tropical fruit on her head. Other masterpieces of baroque wood sculpture are the *retablo* (altarpiece) of the Señor de la Coronación and Bernardo de Lagarda's Virgin of the Immaculate Conception, who seems to dance as she triumphs over the devil. In contrast to the baroque splendor of these works are the simple and highly spiritualized stone carvings on the outside of the church, done by the contemporary soldier-sculptor Roque Navarrete. The sacristy also has some treasures, including the stone-studded, gold monstrance by José de la Iglesia.

The Church of San Agustín (Calle 7 and Carrera 6) also contains a stone monstrance;

Santo Domingo (Calle 4 and Carrera 5) has a carved colonial doorway; the cloistered Monastery of San Francisco, now the *Monasterio* hotel (Calle 4 and Carrera 10), and that of the Dominicans, next to the entry of Santo Domingo, have fine colonial architecture. The Dominican monastery now houses the university, founded in 1640.

Popayán has several interesting museums, including the Casa Mosquera Colonial Museum (Carrera 5 with Calle 3), which contains an ethnological section. The Museo Guillermo Valencia (Carrera 6 No. 2-69), and the Natural History Museum, opposite Cauca University, are also worth a visit.

Popayán is famous for its Holy Week celebrations, which vie with those of Spain in splendor and solemnity. The first procession occurs on Palm Sunday, when two images are brought down from the Chapel of Belén to the cathedral; every evening there are processions, with bearers carrying 11 or more images at a time.

In recent years, a Festival of Sacred Music with top rank musicians has been organized during Holy Week. The celebrations attract country folk in their typical dress from a wide area; they also attract Colombians from all over the country and many foreign visitors.

The tourist office is at 5-72 Calle 3A (phone: 2251), if you need any assistance.

One incredibly good restaurant in the city is *May Chow* (6-74 Carrera 6A, phone: 2604), which serves Chinese dishes — a welcomed contrast to the staid Colombian diet of rice, potatoes, and, too often, tough beef. An ice cream shop on the main square offers tasty flavors, too, including *arequipa* (milk pudding). Also try *La Herrería* restaurant, a converted blacksmith shop under the Humilladero Bridge. For a starter, ask for *empanadas de Pipian,* small meat pies with a peanut sauce.

Take a side trip to Silvia, 40 miles (64 km) northeast of Popayán on the dirt turnoff from the Pan-American at the town of Piendamo. Silvia is the small settlement of the skilled Guambino Indians. You can buy their carpets, woolen products, *chaquiras* (beads), and pendant crosses of beaten silver at the Tuesday morning market.

En Route from Popayán – The road leads in one of two directions: south to Pasto and the Ecuador border, or north to Cali, both of which are off the Pan-American Highway. Heading south to Pasto, the trip is 155 miles (248 km) and takes about 5 hours. The capital of the Department of Nariño, Pasto lost many of its colonial structures to modernization. Today a city of 113,000, it was very active during the independence battle. During the early days of the fighting, Antonio Nariño, a Colombian patriot, attempted to take the royalist stronghold here. He was deserted by half his army, led to Pasto, clapped in irons, and shipped off to Spain to rot in prison for 6 years. When independence had been won in the rest of Colombia, Pasto put up a long and bitter resistance; later, when Ecuador split from Gran Colombia, the people here wanted to go with it but never did.

Those continuing on to Ecuador must stop in Ipiales and the customs post (6-19 Carrera 6) to have their *carnets* stamped. The Colombian exit stamp is obtained from the DAS at the frontier post of Rumichaca, about 2½ miles (4 km) south.

Nearby is the Santuario de Nuestra Señora de Las Lajas, an incredible, castle-like church built directly over a deep chasm. It resembles a medieval structure poised over a moat rather than a church. It's awesome and eerie, more so if you stand on its bridge and look down. It has been described by a famous poet as "a triumph of faith over gravity."

Going north from Popayán, it's a short, 90-mile (145-km) trip through Santander de Quilichao, a town inhabited only by blacks, descendants of runaway slaves.

CALI: The third largest city in Colombia, with a population of well over a million people, Cali is a thriving center of commerce and industry and is filled with lively and friendly people who make the good life mandatory. Founded by de Belalcázar in 1536, the city is modern with a matching mentality, and since the arrival of the railway early in this century, it has ridden a remarkable economic boom. It's the sugar capital of the country and has developed a dynamic commercial sector of paper production and publishing.

There are a number of special places in Cali, ranging from the historic to the scenic to the lively. Plaza Caicedo, with tall palm trees, contains a statue of Joaquin Caicedo y Cuero, one of the leaders of the Independence movement. The cathedral, next to the plaza, is the oldest church in the city, revamped through the ages from the baroque style to the neoclassic.

Cali sits on the banks of the Río Aquacatal, and you can visit El Orquideal, a garden filled with thousands of orchids. For shopping, try the market around the plaza, which overflows with woolen goods from *ruanas* to skirts, *carriels* and other leather goods, and even emeralds.

If it's nightlife you're after, there are a number of discos and clubs between Calle 9 and Carrera 3 — the neon area has quickly earned a reputation as the city's "sinpot" or "fire zone." On Sundays in the daytime, the town goes crazy at Juanchito, a small port on the Río Cauca just a few minutes from downtown. There's plenty of eating, dancing, and drinking. Try the *sancocho de gallina,* a rich soup made from fowl, plantains, and other mysterious things.

Cali is known as the sports center of Colombia, and everything, it seems, is available here. The Pan-American Sports Complex, built in 1971 for the internationally acclaimed games, contains the 60,000-seat Pascual Guerrero Stadium, a 7,000-seat gymnasium, a 4,000-seat baseball diamond, swimming pools, a field hockey stadium, and a track for bicycle racing. A number of tennis clubs and golf clubs are spread throughout the city as well.

Cali is blessed with a number of good restaurants. *Cali Viejo,* near the *Inter-Continental,* offers *tamales* and *empanadas* for sampling; they're not as spicy as the Mexican versions, but just tasty enough. Also try some *pan de bono* (cassava bread) while being serenaded by a band of roving musicians. *Embajada Embajada* (3-25 Carrera 4A Oeste; phone: 893534) and *Las Torres,* in the Chipre section of the city, feature regional dishes that include red beans served with pork, a favorite dish from the Department of Antioquia. *El Campanario,* also near the *Inter-Continental,* has seafood and rice specialties along with a wine cellar. *Carnes do Brasil* serves beef in seven different varieties in a type of all-you-can-eat buffet. With scantily clad waitresses and samba music, it truly resembles Rio de Janeiro (Av. 8 Norte and Calle 18 Norte).

If you haven't a car already (or want to drop off the one you've been using), then rent from *Hertz* (Av. Colombia 2-72; phone: 822-428) or *Rayda Rent-a-Car* (*Inter-Continental Hotel;* phone: 881-971). Renaults and other makes are available from $40 per day, and from $200 per week, plus mileage. Additionally, there are lots of flights between Cali and Bogotá and other Colombian cities. International carriers serving Cali include Avianca and Eastern.

One good side trip to take before heading to Ibagué and back to Bogotá is to the Pacific port of Buenaventura, about 54 miles (87 km) west of Cali. The warm (84°F/ 29°C) port is the major Pacific center for exporting coffee and sugar. The port is reachable either by car or by taking a bus (for about $5) over the Western Cordillera mountains or through the jungle. Then continue by launch: The port is on an island 10 miles out in Buenaventura Bay. From here, backtrack to Cali or fly to Bogotá.

   En Route from Cali – Take the Pan-American and continue through the Cauca Valley over the Central Cordillera to the Magdalena Valley and Ibagué, the capital of the cattle-raising Department of Tolima, at the foot of the Nevado del Tolima. A city of 226,000, Ibagué hosts the National Folklore Festival held annually during the last week of June.

   From Ibagué, it's a short 141 miles (224 km) to Bogotá and the completion of the circuit.

BEST EN ROUTE

With the exception of Cali, most of the hotels in this route are inexpensively priced (about $20). Cali's hostelries, however, are more like $40 and up to $80 for a double at the *Inter-Continental*. Most hotels are clean and comfortable and offer hot water, baths, and air conditioning. It's wise to make reservations before arrival, more so during the festivals from January through June. Also, don't forget to guard your belongings, since pickpockets are rampant throughout Colombia.

NEIVA

Hostería Matamundo – This 27-room converted hacienda has air conditioning and a restaurant. Carretera al Sur (phone: 22037). Moderate.

Plaza – Offers 142 air-conditioned rooms and a swimming pool. 4-62 Calle 6 (phone: 23980). Moderate.

Residencias Pacande – This 30-room hotel has a swimming pool. Calle 10, No. 4-39 (phone: 29140). Inexpensive.

SAN AGUSTÍN

Yalconia – A state-owned hotel with a swimming pool; camping is permitted on the grounds, between San Agustín and the park. Make reservations with the *Monasterio* hotel in Popayán (phone: 22191). Moderate.

Cabañas Alto de las Guaduas – Cabins hold up to four people each. Make reservations in Neiva at 5-07 Carrera 9 (phone: 23430). Inexpensive.

Osoguaico – Strictly for campers, but it has a good dining room. Via Parque Arqueológico (phone: 15).

SAN ANDRÉS DE PISIMBALA

Refugio de Pisimbala – A 7-room hotel that is comfortable and provides hot water. In the archaeological park (no phone). Inexpensive.

POPAYÁN

Camino Real – Owned by a North American, this restored colonial mansion has 12 balconied rooms and a restaurant serving US-style cuisine. Charming and comfortable. Calle 5, No. 5-59 (phone: 21546). Moderate.

Monasterio – A converted monastery with 50 rooms, doubles and singles, with high ceilings and tiled baths. Calle 4 between Carreras 9 and 10 (phone: 22191). Moderate.

La Plazuela – Another restored colonial house, this one with 8 rooms. It is so small, its restaurant so excellent, and the service so friendly that stopping here feels more like visiting friends than staying in a commercial establishment. Calle 5, No. 8-13 (phone: 21084). Moderate.

Los Balcones – A new, smaller hotel with 15 rooms, all very comfortable. 6-80 Calle 3 (phone: 21814). Inexpensive.

Residencias Americanas – This 25-room hotel has private baths. 2N-12 Calle 6 (phone: 21645). Inexpensive.

SILVIA

Turismo – A small, centrally located, 27-room hotel that is clean and comfortable. Make reservations in Cali (phone: 771677). Inexpensive.

PASTO

Agualongo – A hotel with 70 rooms, doubles and singles. Carrera 25 with Calle 18 (phone: 35578). Moderate.

Morascuro – Offers 60 rooms, doubles and singles. 17-30 Carrera 23 (phone: 35019). Moderate.

IPIALES

Pasaviveros – This 20-room hotel is clean and has hot water. 16-90 Carrera 6 (phone: 2622). Inexpensive.

Hostería Mayasquer – This 31-room hotel is on the road (Pan-American) to the frontier (phone: 2643). Inexpensive.

CALI

Inter-Continental – Large, deluxe hotel with 258 double and single rooms, air conditioning, a swimming pool, tennis courts, Turkish baths, and sauna. 2-72 Av. Colombia (phone: 813811). Expensive.

Dann – There are 62 air-conditioned rooms, with spectacular views of the city. Restaurant, bar, pool, and downtown location make it a favorite with business-people. Av. Colombia No. 1-40 (phone: 814400). Expensive to moderate.

Americana Cali – This small hotel has 53 double and single rooms with tiled baths, cafeteria, and bar. 8-73 Carrera 4a (phone: 893171). Moderate.

Aristi – This hotel has 172 double and single rooms, with air conditioning, tile baths, shower stalls, rooftop pool, and a restaurant. 10-04 Carrera 9 (phone: 822521). Moderate.

BUENAVENTURA

Estación – The traditional choice at this Pacific port, it has recently been restored to its turn-of-the-century splendor. 4 stories with 45 air-conditioned, balconied rooms overlooking a pool and palm trees. Calle 2, No. 1A-08 (phone: 23935). Moderate.

IBAGUÉ

Ambalá – This 135-room hotel has air conditioning, a nightclub, sauna, and Turkish bath. 2-60 Calle 11 (phone: 32822). Moderate.

Lusitania – A 54-room hotel with air conditioning. 15-55 Carrera 2 (phone: 39166). Inexpensive.

The Amazon

The Amazon Basin lies deep in the southeastern section of the country. The teeming, dense jungle, filled with giant liana vines, comes alive with the screech of monkeys and green parrots, the snorting of wild boars, the splashing of angry alligators, and the quiet slithering of boa constrictors and the deadly fer-de-lance. Adventurers love superlatives, and the Amazon is full of them. The 3,700-mile network literally flows from one ocean to the other, and each country it encompasses has dozens of wild tales of lost tribes, Amazonian women warriors, primitive headhunters, and pots of gold some-where over the jungle rainbow.

Some of the stories are taller than others. Take, for instance, the story of

Francisco de Orellana, the first white man ever to trek down the river's course. Maybe he did meet a tribe of macho lovelies, but he didn't name the Colombian port of Leticia after a woman he captured. In fact, the port was named after the lost sweetheart of an engineer in the party of the Peruvian Captain Benigo Bustamante, who founded the port in 1867. Once part of Perú, Leticia was ceded to Colombia by treaty in 1922; it was retained by Colombia even after a bloody border skirmish in the 1930s was settled by the League of Nations. Today, the town is a lively frontier outpost with over 15,000 inhabitants. It's a good place to purchase a number of Colombian and imported items, not to mention a few handicrafts made by the local Ticuna, Yagua, and Chama Indians, including bark masks, necklaces, blow guns, arrows, and snake and jaguar hides.

It's not possible to get to the Amazon and Leticia by car from Bogotá, more than 620 miles (1,000 km) to the northwest. The best option is to take a plane from the capital to Leticia, then take a cab into town for about $3.50. Or interrupt your flight at Villavicencio, the capital of the Department of Meta. Here, a long stretch of *llanos orientales* — the grassy, cattle-raising plain roamed by *vaqueros,* the Colombian version of the US cowboy — is on the side of the Eastern Cordillera that separates the rest of the country from the Amazon. With the exception of short, local roads, major highways simply don't exist in the Amazon.

Once in Leticia, hire a boat and driver for local river excursions or take part in one of the many safaris offered by Turamazonas (through the jungle, to Monkey Island, up nearby tributaries), or book a fascinating 3-day stay with the Yagua tribe. Don't just roam through Leticia, however, for there are a lot of things to do. Go catch butterflies in the surrounding jungle; take a 3-hour cruise upriver to the Taraporto lakes, where you can fish for your own dinner of yellow catfish, *pirarucu,* trout, and amberjack; simply gape at the giant lily pads that grow in the nearby Yaguacaca lakes: They grow to as much as 5 feet in diameter. *Turamazonas*'s tour can very well wind up in the Brazilian villages of Marco and Benjamin Constant for a tour of a rubber plantation. You'll also be taken in to Arara Village, where the Ticuna Indians live; if you're lucky, you'll get a glimpse of one of the ceremonies that include the *pelazon,* an initiation rite where young women have their hair plucked out by family and friends. Or hike or drive the short distance into Brazil or cruise 30 minutes downriver to the Brazilian Ticuna village at Mariacú. More primitive, however, are the Yaguas of the Río Atacuari, which forms the natural border between Colombia and Peru; these people still hunt with blow guns. Hunting, by the way, shouldn't be missed here, so try your luck at bagging alligator (*Turamazonas* arranges night hunts), deer, boar, jaguar, or ocelot.

If you do not want to return or proceed to Bogotá from Leticia, take a short ride to the Tabatinga Airport on the Brazil side of the jungle and fly to Manaus, but secure your entry visa in advance. Otherwise, either fly from Tabatinga to Iquitos in Perú or take a 3-night Amazon cruise. For information, contact Tara Tours, 6595 NW 36th St., Miami Springs, FL 33126 (phone: in Florida, 305-871-1246; elsewhere, 800-327-0080).

BEST EN ROUTE

Make reservations before traveling to the Amazon; there are very few hotels, and they get filled with adventure-seekers very quickly. These hotels range from $15 to $20 per person a night — inexpensive even for the Amazon. They are small and lack hot water, but are air conditioned.

LETICIA

Parador Ticuna – This 31-room hotel has refrigerators, a bar, swimming pool, and a formal dining room that creates American comfort in the jungle, though the hotel is getting run down. Av. Libertador 6-03 (phone: 7243).

Anaconda – This 33-room hotel offers large rooms and all the cold water you can take. Carrera 11 at Calle 7 (phone: 7005; for reservations in Bogotá, 218-4830).

MONKEY ISLAND

Monkey Island Lodge – This 31-room lodge runs on full-pension plan, with free service to and from Leticia, and all the chattering monkeys, parrots, and wild orchids on the island are at your disposal. Make reservations at *Parador Ticuna* (above).

Ecuador

Sitting directly on the equator, Ecuador (Spanish for "equator") is bordered by the Pacific Ocean in the west, Colombia on the north, and Perú to the south. It is a geographical meeting place of high sierra, Amazon Basin jungle, and coastal plain. Traveling north to south, the traveler is treated to the sight of the snowcapped volcanoes of the Andes, which stretch 410 miles in two parallel ridges called the Western and Eastern Cordilleras. The tallest mountain, Chimborazo, towers at an altitude of 20,577 feet. Wedged between the Cordilleras is the sierra, or mountain highlands. This is the most fertile area of Ecuador. Here, grains are harvested for domestic and foreign use along with the production of livestock, poultry, maize, sugar, and other products. Small Indian villages dot the highway, and some, such as Otavalo, are inhabited by people who were there long before the Incas or the Spanish and whose men and women wear distinctive clothing and are well known for their excellent handicrafts. These include ponchos, shawls, sweaters, embroidered blouses, and wood carvings sold at traditional weekly markets in the villages on different days.

About 45% of Ecuador's more than 9 million people live in the sierra; of the entire population, 40% are Caucasian; 45% are mestizo (part Indian, part Caucasian); 10% are pure Indian; and the remaining 5% are the descendants of black colonial slaves ferried in from Africa. While the sierra is considered to be the agricultural center of Ecuador, only 5% of it has been cultivated, and food supply and distribution to the country's people remains a major problem. For the most part, the rural population lives in small, thatch-roofed huts, and produce moves on the backs of the inhabitants from family farms to central villages. In hopes of raising the low standard of living, government job programs have been instituted recently in low-income areas. East of the Cordilleras lies the Oriente, a lowland covered with jungle vegetation and laced with Amazon tributaries of the Napo, Pastaza, and Curanay rivers. This area produces a wealth of tropical fruits that include avocados and papaya and is inhabited by exotic animals, such as pumas, jaguars, and deer that roam through forests of cedar, mahogany, and rubber trees. To add to the primeval atmosphere, the Aucas (or, more formally, the Huaouranis), another pre-Incan tribe — who in the past were rather savage — live deep within this jungle. The Oriente is also the home of the Jivaro, or Shuar, Indians, whose previous head-shrinking methods still baffle today's scientists.

Unlike the Oriente, the tropical coastal lowlands (El Litoral) benefit from the Pacific's proximity and are cooler and milder. Guayaquil, Ecuador's largest city (pop. 2 million), is also the country's major exporting seaport; the nearby beaches of Salinas and Playas provide *guayaquileños* with year-round seaside recreation. Ecuador's climate is relative to its altitude, and two seasons prevail — dry and rainy. The rainy season in the highlands lasts from

December through March, and temperatures vary, from the sierra's 40° to 60°F to the Litoral's 90° to 95°F. If this sounds paradisal, there is a catch: Ecuador, like all Andean countries, suffers from occasional earthquakes; the last one destroyed the country's crucial Transandean oil pipeline in 1987.

For the total feel of Ecuador, there is nothing like the drive south from Colombia, on the Pan-American Highway, crossing the border into Ecuador at Tulcán, continuing through the Indian villages of Ibarra and Otavalo to Quito (for detailed information see *Quito,* THE CITIES). Beyond, there is a beautiful drive down the Valley of the Volcanoes to Ambato. Then you can take the highway west at Cajabamba, beyond Riobamba, to the coastal region and Guayaquil. If you're arriving in Ecuador by plane or steamer at Guayaquil, you may want to explore the coast first, then take the highway east to the Pan-American. Excursions into the Amazon Basin can also be made from Quito, east, then south through the jungles until the Oriente highway links up with the Pan-American outside Cuenca.

Traveling the Pan-American south of Quito, you drive along Ecuador's fascinating El Camino Real, the Royal Road that connected Quito with the Inca capital of Cuzco in Perú. The narrow path was a footroad used by teams of relay runners carrying messages between both kingdoms; following Spanish colonization, the road was paved with cobblestones and was later converted to the narrow, usually two-lane Pan-American.

Be prepared for some rough riding in Ecuador if you're traveling by car. Generally, 87% of Ecuador's 12,400-mile road network is passable year-round; the remaining 13% can wash out during the rainy season. This doesn't mean the road system is mostly a modern one. The Pan-American is a two-lane road, often good and just as often poorly paved (and sometimes unpaved). Ecuadorian highways are poorly marked and gravelly; through many villages, the highway is the main street. More often than not, they appear where no roads are indicated on the map. Still, you need a map, available in bookstores (there's a good one in the *Colón* hotel) and at the tourist office headquarters (DITURIS) in Quito (at the Mariscal Sucre Airport; phone: 246-232) or at the office in Guayaquil (Malecón 2321Y, Av. Olmedo; phone: 518-926).

The North: Tulcán to Machala

From the Colombian border at Tulcán to the Peruvian border at Huaquillas, through the tiny Indian villages and marketplaces, this exciting and beautiful route leads through the remnants of the ancient civilizations of the Andes. Along the way, the most famous of the Indian markets is Otavalo, where traditional Indian goods are sold by the weavers of the region.

TULCÁN: Leaving Colombia, you travel over the natural stone bridge of Rumichaca. Papers are checked at the immigration office at the bridge. The border is supposed to be open 24 hours a day, but to be on the safe side, it is advisable to cross during the day. Busloads of tourists and trucks with cargo can lengthen the time it takes to have your passport stamped. There is no exit tax when leaving Ecuador overland.

You will pas through Tulcán, a small village with 35,000 inhabitants, and of little historical or cultural interest, although the cemetery's hedges are trimmed in the odd topiary shapes of animals, birds, and geometric designs.

En Route from Tulcán – Continuing south to Ibarra on the Pan-American, you pass Lago Yaguarcocha, the Lake of Blood. Legend has it that the lake waters turned red with the blood of the native Caras Indians after they were tossed into the waters by their foes, the Incas.

IBARRA: Every Saturday morning the village comes alive around 5 AM, when Indian merchants flock here to sell their produce and handicrafts. The village streets become cluttered with ground displays of ponchos, shawls, embroidered blouses, rope sandals, and wood carvings from neighboring San Antonio de Ibarra. Prices are reasonable, and this local market draws fewer tourists than the one in Otavalo. Here and there, you see the native Indian men (and a few women) sipping *chicha,* the local beer fermented from dried corn. Needless to say, there are a few happy, singing voices — and headaches — by the end of the morning.

When traveling through Ecuador, try some of the local potions — they're quite good. One excellent beer is Cerveza Pilsenar; *hervidas* are cocktails made with rum and fruit. As you near the larger cities, what looks like the soy sauce on your restaurant table is probably liquid instant coffee. Just pour it into your cup of boiled water and stir.

You can catch a bus in Ibarra and head to Otavalo and Quito.

OTAVALO: The Saturday morning markets have become very popular with visitors, and rightly so, for Otavalo has become rather the supermarket of regional markets. Goods come from all over the country, just as the *otavaleños,* world-famous weavers, travel all over the world with their produce. You can often spot them in South American airports, where they wear the traditional provincial dress. For the man, it's white calf-length pants, white shirt, and blue woolen poncho, and hair drawn into one single braid falling down his back. The woman's costume is no less colorful. She wears two dark woolen skirts, a brightly embroidered blouse, strands of colored glass and coral beads entwined around her neck, and brightly colored woven belts wrapped around her waist.

One big square in the market has nothing but textiles, some now made on big Spanish looms with synthetic fibers and dyes. However, some have only weavings of pure sheep's wool, hand carded, vegetable dyed, and woven in the traditional patterns on ancient backstrap looms.

Other squares have the food and animal markets and instant alfresco "kitchens" are in business all day. On one corner the dealers haggle over sacks of squeaking *cuyes* (guinea pigs), and in another, over trays of the ubiquitous coral or glass beads worn by the women. (Ecuador markets start at sunrise, and the action is over by 1 PM.)

Otavaleño sport is rough; illegal in the US, cockfights are habitual here and throughout Ecuador; bullfights are normally held in June, along with regattas on nearby Laguna de San Pablo.

En Route from Otavalo – Continuing south, the Pan-American takes you through the winding, up-and-down countryside of the sierra on your way to Quito and the equatorial line.

Guayllabamba grove is noted for its harvest of avocados. In Cayambe, a dairy products center, there are shops selling good cookies and cheese.

Nineteen miles (30 km) north of Quito, Caldéron is noted for its painted bread-dough sculptures, modeled after the decorated breads made in Ecuador commemorating November 2, Día de los Muertos (Day of the Dead). The bread sculptures reproduce religious images: the Magi, the Holy Family, shepherds, and angels — as well as more secular objects.

EQUATORIAL LINE: You can't feel it or see it (save for one, lone monument), but the equatorial line is about 15 miles (24 km) north of Quito at the village of San Antonio. The monument is set at the line determined by the French explorer Charles de la Condamine in 1735. Condamine, however, was not totally accurate, for the imaginary line dividing the Northern from the Southern Hemisphere actually runs several hundred feet away. Nevertheless, the monument has never been moved, probably out of respect for Condamine's well-educated guess.

A sun museum in the nearby village of San Antonio contains two entrances, one on each side of the line. One door is marked NORTHERN HEMISPHERE; the other, SOUTHERN HEMISPHERE. You might try entering one door and exiting through the other, just for fun. The museum also contains information concerning the Inca sun cult that existed before the Spaniards came. From San Antonio it is just a few scenic miles to Rumicucho, a pre-Inca fortress now excavated.

A new, paved road leads from the monument south to Quito; if you prefer, you can continue on the Pan-American Highway into the city.

QUITO: (For a detailed report on the city, its hotels and restaurants, see *Quito,* THE CITIES.) After you've enjoyed the city, you can then resume your trip. You can either continue south to Cuenca, then southwest to Malachi; or drive south to Cajabamba and pick up the paved road that runs to Guayaquil; or continue on the Pan-American highway south to Perú.

En Route from Quito – Machachi, 25 miles (40 km) south of Quito, is noted for its therapeutic mineral springs. The water here has gone somewhat the way of commercialism, for it is bottled and sold under the name Agua Güitig. You can try the village's fresh cheeses or catch a cockfight on Sunday afternoon.

South of Machachi, a minor road turns east off the highway toward Parque Nacional Cotopaxi. Here, you can see the famous Cotopaxi, the world's highest active volcano, its snowcapped peak towering 19,347 feet above sea level. Returning to the Pan-American Highway, you'll pass San Agustín Hill, believed to be a pre-Columbian pyramid. In Latacunga, the soil is laden with gray lava rock; it's used to build houses and public buildings. This town of 45,000 inhabitants has its own markets on Saturdays (the big one) and Tuesdays.

Northwest of Latacunga sits Saquisili, a Thursday market place — a riot of fresh fruit and vegetable colors. Its eight plazas become jammed with people examining various merchandise (ponchos, shawls, rope shoes, and so on); the regional Indians can be identified by their red ponchos and white felt hats.

You can visit a host of smaller towns before returning to the Pan-American. Most of these places, however, lie deep in the mountains of the Western Cordillera on almost nonexistent roads. It's best to take a bus into this area or, better yet, a guided tour, and let the natives do the driving — to the Sunday market at Pujili, or to Zumbahua, where there is a good Saturday market with a lot of llama selling; and you can hike the volcanic crater filled lake at Quilota.

AMBATO: A major earthquake in 1949 destroyed this city of 110,000; the survivors picked themselves up, dusted themselves off, and reconstructed the area. The fourth largest city in Ecuador and a 2½-hour drive from Quito, Ambato was once known as the "Garden City," probably because the colonists lined the streets with parks and flowers. Ambato still has a Festival of Flowers and Fruits every February. The rich suburb of Miraflores is on the Río Ambato; from here, you can see the peaks of both Chimborazo and Tungurahua volcanoes.

Market day (the biggest in Ecuador) is Monday; most of the buying and selling is carried on in the center plaza. Try to arrive the night before to watch the produce markets being set up. Crafts are grouped separately, with weavings the most abundant item.

Don't forget to try some local dishes while you're in the sierra. *Llapingachos* is a treat of mashed potatoes and cheese, and *secos* are tasty chicken, lamb, or goat stews served with rice and potatoes. Another interesting specialty is *fritada y mote,* fried chunks of pork with hominy served in newspaper.

For those interested, mountain climbing expeditions can start from Ambato (or Riobamba) for Chimborazo or other mountains. Take adequate mountain-climbing equipment and make sure you know what you're doing. Chimborazo is not for the sometime-climber; arranging for an expedition and guide in advance is recommended. A side trip 8 miles (14 km) east of Ambato will bring you to Salasaca, the village of the Salasaca Indians, whom the Incas brought from Bolivia as laborers in the 15th century. The natives here dress in white shirts, black ponchos, and flat white, wide-brimmed hats.

RIOBAMBA: In order not to miss the Saturday market here, drive the 4-hour trip (slower if you visit along the way) from Quito on Friday and spend the night. By 9 AM there's selling and bartering in all of the town's 11 plazas, each one reserved for different merchandise: ponchos, shawls, leather goods, animals, food, and so on. If you're hungry, grab a snack at one of the open-air restaurants: the local favorites are roast pig and grilled guinea pig. If you stay in Riobamba on Saturday night, drive out on Sunday to the Indian market at Lake Colta for the most vivid local color.

A major religious center, Riobamba (population 85,000) is particularly interesting during Holy Week. However, anytime is right for visiting the beautiful Museum of Sacred Art, housed in a cloister of the Sisters of the Conception. A guide who may speak some English will show you about; there is a small entrance fee of 40 sucres. From Riobamba, there is a wonderful rail running south to Guayaquil and north to Quito. The southern section is being repaired after recent floods in the Delta, but the northern trip to Quito follows the country's most scenic route. There is a single-car train called the *autoferro* on this run daily except Sundays, and a special *Expreso* with a refitted parlor car operated by Metropolitan Touring in Quito. There is also regular bus service to Quito and to the coast, as well as special tourist itineraries.

CAJABAMBA: Actually, this is the site of the original Riobamba. Founded in 1534, the town was leveled by an earthquake in 1797; the new Riobamba was moved 12½ miles (20 km) northeast.

En Route from Cajabamba – The Pan-American running south to Cuenca passes through scores of little scenic villages. Guamote is on little Lake Colta; Alausi is a popular mountain resort. Trains from Guayaquil to Quito stop here for passengers who wish to disembark and continue the trip by car or bus.

Azogues, the start of the southern sierra, is a somewhat drab town; the Indians wear black, and the area has poor, infertile land. There is only one notable item here: This is one of the Ecuadorian centers of the Panamá hat manufacture.

CUENCA: Eighty-eight miles (141 km) south of Azogues sits the country's third largest city (195,000) people); it is a charming colonial town, surrounded by four rivers — the Tarqui, Yanuncay, Tomebamba, and Machangara.

Founded in 1557, the city is filled with squares, monuments named for poets, streets named after literary figures, little museums, and historical churches. El Carmen, a Carmelite convent (Calle Sucre 533), dates to 1682 and contains much of its original furniture. Nuns will sometimes take you through the building, showing you the dining room and "doctor's room," where nuns used to receive medical treatment. A small Nativity scene enclosed in a wooden box, with wooden figures adorned in silver and gold brocade, highlights the tour. Check with the tourist office for permission to visit the convent. Two cathedrals, one lofty and new and the other old, face each other on Calderon Square in the center of the city; the older cathedral, built in 1557, is particularly interesting during the various saints' days celebrations.

One of Cuenca's most colorful citizens, Padre Crespi, founder of the former Salesian Museum, had some interesting theories about early Ecuadorians. He believed that the Phoenicians and other Mediterraneans entered Cuenca from the mouth of the Amazon around 1000 BC. He said that expeditions he led in the Oriente produced pharaonic Egyptian chairs and artifacts from the Babylonians, Greeks, Etruscans, and even Mesopotamians! His collection has been moved to the Archaeological Museum of the Banco Central, next to the Puma Pungo ruins, which are thought to be the remains of a Huayna-Capac palace. Restoration of this site is still in progress, but the Museum is open Mondays through Saturdays.

In contrast to Crespi's collection, the Municipal Museum is tame. It contains Inca ceramics, stone and metal weapons, and oil portraits of late, great local officials.

The San José de la Merced Church and Convent (Calle Rafael Arizaga 1306) is a smaller replica of the church and convent of La Merced in Quito. The main altar contains small sculptures and silver heads, arms, and legs — small tokens of thanks to the saint for granting favors.

Cuenca is a major handicraft center and the original home of the Panamá hat. The museum of CIDAP (Centro Interamericano de Artesanías Populares) gives an excellent overview of regional crafts. Such clothing as handwoven shawls with macrame fringe and embroidered blouses are sold in shops, and pottery and ironwork are also produced in open workshops where the visitor is welcome. Market days in Cuenca are Thursdays and Sundays, and there are many different markets (named for the streets on which they're located) scattered about the city. The 3rd of November market has fruits; the 12th of April, baskets and sweaters.

INGAPIRCA: A 2-hour trip from Cuenca and 10 kms off the Pan-American takes you to Ecuador's only major Inca monument. Ingapirca is a stone fortress-like inn erected for the Inca king when he journeyed between Cuzco and Quito. The Incas set the stones together in a circular shape without any binding material between them; the stones themselves are engraved. One of the great mysteries raised by Ingapirca is how the Incas managed to move the stones to the site from a far-away quarry, since they had not yet discovered the wheel. This is an excellent archaeological site, well worth a visit, with artifacts from the excavations housed in the convent on the little plaza until a local museum is built.

Among the artifacts remaining at Ingapirca are two Intinahui (Eyes of the Road) — stone faces that seem to guard the fortress. The Ingachungana (Inca Game) is a stone chair that contains canals carved into the armrests; circular objects were apparently rolled down them to entertain royal guests.

From the road to Ingapirca, make a short detour to Biblián, whose pilgrimage cathedral is cut high into the rocks above the town. It is worth the climb up the stairs to the church. Here, September 8 is fiesta day, honoring Our Lady of the Dew.

An hour from Cuenca is the craft village of Gualaceo and, just beyond, Chordeleg, both of which have good Sunday markets. Although the latter is known for its ceramics, the selection is somehow better in Cuenca, except for the atelier on the road to the right as you enter town.

BEST EN ROUTE

In most smaller villages of Ecuador, hotels are small, and many lack private bathrooms. For the most part, hotels are inexpensive — about $15 per person a night. The better hotels are in the larger cities and are a moderate $20 to $40. Unless you're in Quito, or maybe Guayaquil, you won't pay much more than this.

OTAVALO AREA

La Mirage – Exclusive new hostelry, with 10 rooms, all with private baths. In Cotacachi. Expensive.

Hostería Chorlavi – A hacienda-style hotel where advance bookings are necessary for Fridays in its 37 rooms; good food and lovely grounds. Near Otavalo. Moderate.

Mesón de las Flores – Attractive 15-room country inn with private bathrooms. In Cotacachi. Moderate.

Parador Cusin – Charming farmhouse, with main rooms and upstairs bedrooms furnished with antiques and overlooking flowering patio. Six miles (10 km) from Otavalo (phone: in Quito, 525-380). Moderate.

Ajaví – Comfortable 60-room hotel with modern amenities, including telephone and bar-restaurant. Just outside the town of Ibarra. Moderate.

Cabañas del Lago – Here, 15 comfortable bungalows, all with private baths, are set on the shore of Lake San Pablo. Water sports available. In San Pablo del Lago. Moderate.

Otavalo – Friendly, modest hotel, but lacks bathing facilities, and beds are scare on Fridays without reservations. The Saturday morning market brings people in the night before. Calle Roca (phone: 415). Inexpensive.

Pension Vaca No. 2 – Friendly hotel is similar to the *Otavalo*. Inexpensive.

LASSO

Hostería La Ciénega – Between Quito and Ambato, this former colonial estate has 8 double rooms and 3 suites, all with private bath. A popular place with the local people on weekends. Book through *Adventure Associates,* 13150 Coit Rd., Dallas, TX (phone: in Texas, 214-907-0414; elsewhere, 800-527-2500).

AMBATO

Ambato – Opened in 1985, this modern 60-room hotel offers a host of amenities, including telephone, color TV, restaurant, coffee shop, casino, and conference rooms. The best in town by far. Expensive.

Miraflores – A 50-room hotel with private baths, a restaurant, and bar. Av. Miraflores 71. Moderate.

RIOBAMBA

El Troje – Part of a tourist complex, this country inn features 29 rooms, all with private bath, as well as a swimming pool, tennis courts, good restaurant, and bar-lounge. Definitely the best in the area. Approximately 5 km from Riobamba on the road to Chambo. Expensive to moderate.

Chimborazo – A new hotel with 33 comfortable rooms, all with private bath. Bar-restaurant on the premises. The best alternative to *El Troje.* Downtown, one block from Galpón. Moderate.

El Galpón – A new hotel with about 20 rooms, some with three or four beds, and all with bathrooms. There's also a first-class dining room, where dinner should start by 8 PM, and a bar. The best in town and, though not very efficient, friendly and comfortable. Moderate.

CUENCA

La Laguna – A lovely hotel whose attractive guest and public rooms overlook a lake, it is Swiss managed and very well run. Just outside the city center; 60 rooms, 3 restaurants, pool. Expensive.

El Dorado – First-class hotel in the city center; has 49 rooms with carpeting, telephone, TV, and private baths. Moderate.

Crespo Internacional – This 44-room hotel has telephones, private baths, and a dining room. Moderate.

Presidente – New 60-room property with modern amenities such as phone, TV, restaurant, and bar. Moderate.

Hostería Uzhupud – An hour from Cuenca in Paute, this is a charming, hacienda-style country inn. Lovely rooms, as well as a pool, sauna, steambaths, bar lounge, and a good restaurant. Expensive to moderate.

The Oriente

Some North American oilmen and South American Indians in Ecuador have one thing in common: They occupy the Oriente, that wild, tropical stretch of jungle east of the sierra that makes up at least 50% of Ecuador. Primarily undeveloped, the region saw few white men — other than Spanish explorers and heathen-converting Roman Catholic missionaries — until the twentieth century. Then the discovery of oil deposits near Lago Agrio sent US corporations scurrying to the *selva* (jungle) for their stake in "black gold."

The white man first came here in search of golden treasure in the sixteenth century; Francisco Pizarro's brother Gonzalo dispatched Francisco de Orellana into the *selva* to search for the precious metal in 1541. Orellana trekked off with his men and disappeared, drifting down the Río Napo toward the mainstream of the Amazon River — the first white explorer to dare the jungle and survive. He didn't find his gold, but he had an amazing adventure, braving jaguars, pumas, snakes, and a host of primitive tribes, including the headhunting Jivaros. In fact, Orellana loved the trip so much that he went back a second time around 1546, never to be seen again.

Had Orellana been a modern explorer, he really might have struck it rich, for large petroleum deposits were discovered in 1967. Five years later, an oil pipeline was laid between the Oriente and the Pacific port of Esmeraldas, 311 miles away. Texaco and Gulf Oil set up a consortium with the Ecuadorian government to maintain the fields. Today the US investment in Ecuador is more than $850 million, and the Oriente provided a major economic boom for Ecuador, though it may not last as the surplus of oil continues.

Shell-Mera and other petroleum towns look rather like a cross between a North American frontier town and the Panamá hat and ceiling fan images often depicted in "banana republic" films: There are boardwalks for sidewalks, saloons with swinging doors, and even an occasional brothel or two. Such stereotypes, however, are somewhat modified by the appearance of discos in town and military security checkpoints at the Shell-Mera airport.

The road network in the Oriente is, to say the least, not first class. Long stretches of road are paved but very narrow, and some eventually wander into dirt tracks that turn to mud during the rainy season. While the temperature in the *selva* isn't impossibly hot — 85° to 90°F (29° to 32°C) — the humidity is very high, and the dust of the roads clings to you and your sweat-dampened clothes. Anyone venturing into the Oriente would be wise to bring a backpack, sleeping bag, mosquito repellent, and netting. Also, the deeper you wander into the jungle, the worse the roads get, until they're nothing but footpaths smothered in jungle flora. It's best to plan your trek around canoe or motorboat transport once you get near the rivers and let one of the missionaries or natives guide you around. Weekly 4- or 5-day Oriente jungle tours aboard the *Flotel Orellana* down the Río Napo are also offered by Metropolitan Touring out of Quito (Amazonas 239; phone: 560-550; in the US: Adventure Associates, Dallas; phone: 800-527-2500).

Small-plane service is available to the Oriente from Quito and Guayaquil: ECUAVIA and TAME offer private and chartered flights to Shell-Mera. There is bus service, as well, to some interesting gateway towns such as Baños and Puyo.

PUERTO FRANCISCO DE ORELLANA: At the mouth of the Coca and Napo rivers, the port was named after the conquistador. (Ecuadorians still use its former name, Coca.) Here you can rent a canoe and drift down the river to Limóncocha and the Peruvian border post of Nueva Rocafuerte (passports stamped here). If you prefer, you can reach the port of Coca via a 10-hour bus ride from Quito.

Retracing your steps to Lago Agrio then west to the Quito–Lago Agrio Highway will bring you to a fork halfway along the route. Continuing west, you will reach Quito. Continuing south, you will arrive in Tena.

TENA: The capital of Napo province is quiet; the town is inhabited by the Yumbos Indians, who have been here longer than the white man. They speak Spanish, but generally the common language is the Inca-culture dialect Quechua. More often than not they reside in houses of bamboo and grass, making their living harvesting *naranjillas* (tomato-like oranges) and selling them to truckers. Some goldpan in small streams. Between 30,000 to 50,000 Yumbos are thought to live in the Oriente today.

PUYO: Today a major Oriente center, this was once a frontier town, and the swinging saloon doors still remain. The shops sell a variety of souvenirs, ranging from stuffed animals to feathers, baskets, and interesting pottery. The drive to Puyo from Tena or Baños is on a rough but scenically splendid road. The best road travel in this region is by bus or chauffeur-driven car.

SHELL-MERA: Thirty-one miles (50 km) west of Baños, this oil camp houses an airport and an Ecuadorian military checkpoint. (At one time, special passes were needed to enter the Oriente.) There's a bar and disco in town.

A ride south along the Río Pastaza brings you out of the Oriente to Baños.

BAÑOS: More on the fringe of the Eastern Cordillera than in the Amazonian plains, Baños is a health resort, noted for its thermal baths and hot springs. The church here has interesting murals depicting Nuestra Señora de Santa Agua performing miracles; you can sightsee or, if you're in hearty shape, take a walk up the Tungurahua volcano and camp there for the night.

From Baños, you can continue either west to Ambato and pick up the Pan-American Highway or eastward to the Oriente, where your next stop is Macas.

MACAS: The Sangay volcano and the Salesian Sevilla and Don Bosco missions upriver on the Río Upano are the major attractions in this village. One note about the Amazonian tributaries: Unlike some rivers around Ecuador, you can swim in these (many others are very polluted).

SUCUA: This upriver village is the home of the "tamed" Jivaro, or Shuar, Indians. They're a very passive, Christianized lot these days, but still display their shrunken heads. This much is known about the head-shrinking process: The skull is removed, and the skin is dried out by a hot stove. This way, the skin shrinks yet retains its features. The mouth is sewn shut. Any head-hunting performed today is done for the tourist trade. The victims are animals, their hides turned into souvenirs that the gullible are led to believe is really a human head.

Both Quechua- and Spanish-speaking, there are only about 13,000 Jivaros left in the Oriente. They are, for the most part, farmers, growing crops of cotton, tobacco, and fruit, and raising guinea pigs. Though Christianized, they still honor pagan ways, and their sociological system is rather chauvinistic: Women are either sold to their husbands or the prospective grooms are employed by future fathers-in-law for a certain period of time before the ceremony.

These Jivaros share the jungle with their cousins, the Aucas, once a fierce, uncivilized tribe that murdered several missionaries in the 1960s. Both of these tribes, however, reside deep in the jungle, and they should be visited only on an escorted tour.

When you're ready to leave Sucua, a turn west will lead you back to the Pan-American Highway and Cuenca. You can now continue south to Perú.

BEST EN ROUTE

There are very few places offering accommodations in the Oriente. Your best bet is to plan to camp or to stay at one of the several missions that dot the jungle. If you camp, be sure to bring plenty of mosquito repellent and/or netting with you, as well as anti-malaria quinine pills. If you take Metropolitan Touring's boat tour on the Río Napo, then you will remain on board the Flotel Orellana overnight.

Any hotels will be very primitive and inexpensive — about $8 to $10. Check their availability with the Quito tourist office (Reina Victoria y Roca) or with a local travel agency.

LIMÓNCOCHA

A rustic, dormitory lodge is now operating here, mostly for Flotel passengers. Check with Metropolitan Touring office at Amazonas 239.

TENA

Amazónico – A jungle hotel, where you'll get a bed and be able to sleep safe and sound from things that go bump in the *selva* night. Inexpensive.

Danubio – Another jungle hotel, as above. Inexpensive.

BAÑOS

Villa Gertrudis – Comfortable, spacious rooms, all with private bath. Normally booked with meals, which are surprisingly good. Moderate to inexpensive.

Cabañas Bascún – A new resort featuring 50 A-frame bungalows, all with private bath, surrounding a swimming pool. Restaurant on premises. Moderate to inexpensive.

Sangay – This hotel in a health resort offers tennis courts and showers. Inexpensive. A rustic, dormitory lodge is now operating here, mostly for *Flotel* passengers. Check with Metropolitan Touring office at Amazonas 239.

MISAHUALLI

Anaconda Lodge – From Misahualli, it's an hour's ride downriver via motorized canoe. Comfortable accommodations in attached bungalows with bath and shower; central lodge for meals. Excursions arranged through Metropolitan Touring, Amazonas 239, Quito (phone: 56-05-50).

El Litoral

The easiest way to proceed southwest from the sierra to the coastal region (El Litoral) of Ecuador is to follow the Quito-Guayaquil Highway from Cajabamba and the Pan-American Highway. The 290-mile (464-km) journey will take you from the cattle ranges of the Western Cordillera through the marshy rice plantations that cover the lowlands. The 350-mile coast that stretches from Esmeraldas to Guayaquil is the heartland of Ecuador's major exports.

Barely 100 miles wide, El Litoral encompasses the provinces of Esmeraldas, Manabí, Los Ríos, Guayas, and El Oro, a mix of jungle, rolling hills, lowlands, beach, and desert. Hot and humid, El Litoral is tempered by the cool Humboldt Current. The average yearly temperature is 79°F (26°C) and is, in fact, about 10° warmer but more comfortable than the Oriente, where the high humidity often makes it feel as though you're immersed in an eternal steambath. El Litoral is warmer than the Andes, since the temperature increases about 1° for every 320-foot descent. The coastal plains are also the home of a number of colorful animals, ranging from the coatimundi, kinkajou, fox, and otter to the weasel and skunk.

There are several seaports along the Pacific coast. The farthest north, Esmeraldas exports wood and bananas and houses the terminal of the 311-mile Transandean petroleum pipeline from the Oriente. At one time, the Santa Elena Peninsula south of Guayaquil contained a large number of oil deposits, but that quantity has declined, leaving the deposits in the Oriente to be explored and exploited. Manta and Puerto Bolívar, south of Esmeraldas, export frozen fish, coffee, and castor beans.

But it is Guayaquil, Ecuador's largest city (pop. approximately 2 million) and seaport, that handles up to 65% of all exports and 90% of the imports. Passing through Guayaquil's Puerto Nuevo are bananas, sugar, beans, cocoa, fish, wood, Panamá hats — a list of everything from soup to nuts. Guayaquil is seated on the west bank of the Río Guayas; ships ply in and out from the Gulf of Guayaquil, which eventually leads to the Pacific Ocean.

While not rich in gold, El Litoral exports a host of other minerals. Azuay province has large copper and limestone deposits. Gold has been mined in Portoviejo in El Oro province since the sixteenth century; silver and salt deposits can be found in Guayas province.

Shrimp, which have become one of Ecuador's major exports, and fish, especially tuna, are taken from "national" waters that the government says extend 200 miles into the Pacific. Several US fishing boats have been picked up by Ecuadorian patrols within the last several years in this never-ending dispute over high seas sovereignty.

More than 52% of Ecuador's 8 million people live in El Litoral; of these, nearly 2,000 are Indians from the Cayapa and Colorado tribes along with a few migrant Yumbos from the Oriente and Coayqueros from Colombia. Most of them live in the jungle or along riverbanks; many are farmers and fishermen, although the Cayapas are known for their basket weaving. They rarely mingle with whites, are baptized Roman Catholics, and live in houses of thatched roofs and open walls. The rest of the coastal population is made up of *montuvios* — coastal mestizos — who are mostly farmers and fishermen. The white population is generally concentrated around Guayaquil, Manta, and the resorts of Salinas and Playas.

Like the rest of Ecuador, the roads in El Litoral are partly paved, partly incomplete, unmarked, often impassable in the rainy season, with one or two lanes, and are, in general, poor. The most interesting drive is from Quito to Guayaquil, which will take you past the river towns of Babahoyo and Daule, down into the port. From Guayaquil, you can journey to the resort towns of Playas, Salinas, and Punta Carnero, continue up the coastal highway to Manta, then inland to Quevedo, Santo Domingo de los Colorados, and north to Esmeraldas.

There are a number of flights to Guayaquil daily from Quito and Cuenca. The best way to make this scenic excursion is on the Quito-Guayaquil railroad, a roller-coaster ride that passes beneath the Cotopaxi and Chimborazo volcanoes through the Urbina Pass and tacks back and forth on a switchback line down the Nariz del Diablo (Devil's Nose), a 45° incline leading down to the coastal plains of Bucay and Duran. The train passengers take a ferry from here to Guayaquil. The trip is a real treat; it's the engineering feat of two North Americans engineers, Arthur and John Harmon. Unfortunately, both men died before the road was completed in 1908, but you remember them every time that train creeps down a steep *cerro* or makes a vertical climb. (Note that at this writing, the rail line was being repaired from Riobamba to Guayaquil, so that passenger traffic is running only on the line from Riobamba to Quito. Check rail conditions before you make the trip.)

Depending on which train you take, the trip takes from 11 to 12 hours. Be sure to bring extra food with you, although a wide variety of local produce is sold on platforms at train stops. Full food service is available twice weekly in the *Expreso Metropolitan* deluxe car that runs on the scenic route between Riobamba to Quito twice weekly. The *autoferro,* a kind of one-car rail bus, travels both ways between Quito and Riobamba daily except Sundays. It allows you to sit on the roof with the baggage in case you want to take pictures or get away from the crowd. The cars, which carry a maximum of 40 passengers, can be specially chartered from the bus company's offices in Quito (Bolívar 443; phone: 216-180).

GUAYAQUIL: Ecuador is the largest banana exporter in the world, and it is through Guayacuil that the nation's most important commodity is shipped; so Guayaquil is used to heavy cargo traffic as a way of life. Still, the city's new port, Puerto Nuevo, is reputed to be the cleanest harbor in the world, despite the tons and tons of animals, minerals, crops, equipment, and people that plow through it daily. The first steamboat ever to run in Latin America was made here; also, the first submarine, the *Hippopotamus,* was tested in the Gulf of Guayaquil.

Guayaquil played an important role in Ecuadorian independence in the 19th century. A military junta was formed against Spanish rule in 1820 after the signing of a declaration of independence; liberators José de San Martín and Símon Bolívar were invited to join the revolt. An army dispatched by San Martín helped overthrow the Spanish government in Quito in 1822. Soon afterward, San Martín and Bolívar held a secret meeting in Guayaquil. San Martín, it appears, wanted Guayaquil to become part of Perú, but Bolívar thought differently: He wanted it as part of his own Gran Colombia Federación. A committee was called in to vote on the decision, and Guayaquil became part of Bolívar's federation. San Martín exiled himself to Europe and never returned.

A waterfront monument (Av. 9 de Octubre and Malecón) commemorates the secret meeting between the two heroes. The rotunda of the monument is erected in such a way that two people can stand at opposites sides, whisper, and hear one another.

If you like museums, then visit the two here. The Municipal Museum (Calle Diez de Agosto y Pichincha) houses pre-Columbian artifacts discovered along the coast, including clay seals, molds for gold masks, and shrunken heads of *tzantzas.* The Museum of the Ecuadorian House of Culture (Av. 9 de Octubre) contains a gold exhibit, with objects such as snake-shaped bracelets, nose rings, chest shields, and masks. Both museums are open daily, except Mondays, but are closed from noon to 2:30 PM for siesta. Most of the gold artifacts in these museums were taken from recent excavations in the Santa Elena Peninsula area; dating suggests that the pre-Columbian culture may be more than 5,000 years old. Also worth a visit is the Anthropological Museum of the Banco Central (Av. 9 de Octubre 1503), which houses some very interesting artifacts from ancient cultures.

You can also wander through Guayaquil's churches. The cathedral (Calle 10 de Agosta between Boyacá y Chimborazo) is a modern, Gothic church with white towers. In the old district of Las Peñas is the church of Santo Domingo, the first church erected in Guayaquil, in 1543.

The *barrio*, called Las Peñas, is famous for its winding stone streets and cramped houses. It is on the *malecón*, a waterfront drive where small riverboats dock for excursions down the Guayas. The Government Palace is on this drive, too, which changes into Avenida 9 de Octubre at the last pier on the northern side of town. The city cemetery, with its opulent marble tombs and statuary, is also worth a visit.

Guayaquil isn't renowned as a shopping spot; if you do look for souvenirs and bargains, keep away from the Inca relics now being paraded in various shops — they're as authentic as fool's gold.

As in other parts of Ecuador, Guayaquil celebrates the national holy days and festivals. There's a lot of merrymaking, and people have a good time, drinking beer and *aguardiente* (moonshine sugarcane whiskey); but stay away on July 24, the city's Foundation Day. Hotel prices skyrocket, and you're better off out of the crowds.

Since Guayaquil is Ecuador's largest port, a number of steamers arrive in the harbor daily from all over the world. Símon Bolívar Airport, near the center of the city, handles daily jet arrivals from around the world. Ecuador has many carriers of its own: Ecuatoriana, which provides international service between North and South America; TAME (Transportes Aéreos Militares de Ecuador), the largest domestic carrier, which flies to some 20 cities; and, in addition, SAN (Servicios Aéreos Nacionales) and SAETA, which offer daily jet service to Quito and Cuenca from Guayaquil.

You may have traveled past Babahoyo and Daule on your way into Guayaquil by bus or car, but you can rent a boat and journey up the Guayas for a look at these riverfront villages.

Babahoyo, 119 miles (193 km) north of Guayaquil, is uninteresting in itself, but its tropical setting sells it. It's all there — the river, flocks of parrots and toucans brightening the jungle trees, plantations of rice, cocoa, sugar, and bananas (all you need is a gin and tonic, a Panamá hat, and a Humphrey Bogart film). A few miles down the river, Daule, filled with banana plantations, is a pictorial repeat of Babahoyo.

Returning to Guayaquil, you're ready to pack your bags and head on to the resorts.

PLAYAS: Less than 60 miles (96 km) south of Guayaquil down the Peninsula Highway, this resort was once a lively fishing village. Today, fishermen still return in the afternoon with their catch stacked high on their canoes, but for the most part, the inhabitants here are sun-seeking *guayaquileños*.

SALINAS: About 40 miles (64 km) west of Playas, this modern resort, well regarded by locals, sits on a crescent-shaped beach and offers an abundance of black marlin fishing. In recent years, Salinas has hosted a number of fishing competitions and regattas.

PUNTA CARNERO: About 6 miles (10 km) south of Salinas on the Santa Elena Peninsula, this resort has a 9-mile beach and plenty of surf and black marlin, dolphin, and bonito deep-sea fishing.

En Route from Punta Carnero – The coastal route forks at Santa Elena village; from here, you can head back to Guayaquil or continue north as far as Manta. This coastal road, however, is not very good during the rainy season — in fact, it disappears entirely. If you take it, do so in the dry season, and at low tide only.

MANTA: This port in Manabí province has grown steadily to handle almost 10% of the country's fruit and fish exports. There really isn't much to see here, but Manta does have a beach where you can go swimming and watch the shrimp fleets off on the horizon. Vast shrimp beds were discovered about 10 miles off the coast 10 years ago.

Bahía de Caráquez, a small port north of Manta, is the home of its tennis club and world tennis star Pancho Segura. There are also some nice beaches and reasonable accommodations in neighboring San Vicente.

En Route from Manta – From Manta, you can continue inland south through Portoviejo, then north to Santo Domingo de los Colorados, where the highway (if you can call it that) eventually leads you northeast to Esmeraldas.

Jipijapa, the first town on this route, is a small fruit-processing center famous for Panamá hats. Hats have been made here since the 1500s, using the same procedure. Leaves from the *paja toquilla,* a palm tree, are dried, then woven. Montecristi, 20 miles (32 km) north of Jipijapa, also produces the hats.

PORTOVIEJO: The road leading north from Montecristi eventually reaches this farm-produce processing center of 120,000 people. There isn't much to see; so, unless making a pit stip here, most travelers would continue on.

QUEVEDO: This town of 70,000 is a junction for routes leading to Quito, Guayaquil, and Esmeraldas. It is known for its small population of Chinese who have settled here over the years and established themselves as shopkeepers and wholesale produce sellers.

Ecuador has a number of interesting overseas minority groups: A large, established Lebanese community resides in Guayaquil (where they are known as *turcos,* or Turks); and several thousand Germans and Spanish immigrated here during World War II and the Spanish Civil War. Here and there you'll also find native Ecuadorians with English, Irish, and French surnames.

SANTO DOMINGO DE LOS COLORADOS: The most colorful attraction here is the Colorado Indians. They paint their bodies with red dye from the *achiote* plant, thought to ward off unfriendly spirits. The men, who wear brief skirts and cloths slung over their shoulder, keep their hair short, parted in the middle, and smeared with the same red paint, giving a clay effect. The women wear their hair and skirts long. In the old days, many of the women romped around bare-breasted; because of a few missionaries, however, more and more are concealing themselves.

Most of the Colorados farm for their living; others supplement their incomes posing for *turista* photographs for a few sucres. They're a very docile group and even appear to enjoy mingling with foreigners. In fact, they have mingled too much and tribal customs are now mostly for show. You can buy bananas and other produce at the Sunday morning markets.

If you're returning to Quito by road — a 79-mile (129-km) trip — watch out: The road washes out during the rainy season. Landslides in the early 1970s made it impassable for days. The road is better on its route northwest to Esmeraldas.

ESMERALDAS: A long, 279 miles (450 km) from Guayaquil, the "emerald" province is continuously green — lush, tropical vegetation grows down to the shore of the Pacific. It's not as hot and humid here as it is in Guayaquil; temperatures stay at a constant 80°F (26°C).

The second largest seaport in Ecuador (pop. 80,000), its prime exports are wood, bananas, cocoa, and tobacco, and the Transandean pipeline ends at Balao Port.

Lately, Esmeraldas has become a popular tourist spot for Ecuadorians. Its main boulevard is closed to traffic between 7:30 and 9:30 PM, so you can stroll through the street without worrying about being hit by a car, bus, or a rickety truck laden with bananas. Most of the Esmeraldans you'll meet here are blacks, the descendants of shipwrecked and freed slaves brought in by Spain during the 16th century to work the plantations. Spanish-speaking, they have been assimilated into the main Ecuadorian "white" culture, although their native music and the rhythmic beat of the marimba gives Ecuadorian music its own distinctive style.

There are a number of small white beaches nearby where you can step into the Pacific for a swim or simply bask in the sun. Atacames and Sua are about 15 miles (24 km) south of the city and make an excellent day trip when the sun is shining (almost always).

For pre-Columbian treasures, visit La Tolita (Little Indian Mound) in the far north pocket of the province. A number of artifacts, including fishing, agricultural, sculpting, and metalworking tools were discovered during an excavation: They are estimated to have been in use between 500 BC and AD 500.

Another side trip from Esmeraldas is north to the banana-exporting town of Limones, where you can see the Cayapa Indians in their bright print shirts and bathing suit–type dress. Like the Colorados, Cayapa women wear long skirts and nothing else.

Transportation along the coast between Guayaquil and Esmeraldas is available via surface transport, car, or scheduled bus service. Air service between Esmeraldas and Guayaquil or Quito is also available.

BEST EN ROUTE

El Litoral has the widest variety of hotels found in Ecuador; it's possible to book a first-class, sanitized room (with private bathroom) in Guayaquil for an expensive $50 or more a night; a first-class, modern room with bath in a gulf hotel for a more moderate $25 a night; or a small, second-class, not-so-private affair in a small town for about $10. Some of these hotels have telephones; others do not. If you can, make reservations at the city hotels in advance, and *don't* — repeat, *don't* — be in Guayaquil for Foundation Day on July 24, unless you don't mind sleeping on the sidewalk. Hotels, by the way, add the standard nationwide 20% tax. Guayaquil's hotels are more expensive than Quito's.

GUAYAQUIL

Oro Verde – Guayaquil's first really deluxe hotel is now open, with 200 rooms, outdoor pool, sauna, gymnasium, several restaurants, and a fun and friendly casino. 9 de Octubre y García Moreno (phone: 37-21-00). Expensive.

Casino Boulevard – Besides a popular casino, there are 60 suites, all with private bath, kitchenette, and wet bar, as well as a restaurant. 9 de Octubre and Chimborazo (phone: 30-67-00). Expensive.

Continental – This 91-room downtown hotel offers private baths, air conditioning, a cocktail lounge, a good restaurant, conference rooms, service shops, and car rentals. Chile y 10 de Agosto , Apdo. 4510 (phone: 32-92-70). Expensive.

Grand Hotel Guayaquil – This 160-room hotel is fully climate-controlled and offers private baths, telephones, a dining room, casino, dancing, and nightclub entertainment, plus a swimming pool (with poolside bar), valet, laundry service, and garage. Boyacá 10 de Agosto y C. Ballen, Apdo. 9282 (phone: 32-96-90). Expensive.

Unihotel – Part of a downtown shopping complex, this new deluxe hotel has 77 rooms and 42 suites with kitchens. Facilities include 3 restaurants, 24-hour room service, solarium with whirlpool, sauna, gym, and casino. Calle Ballen y Chile (phone: 32-71-00). Expensive.

Ramada – A comfortable hotel overlooking the Río Guayas, with 110 rooms, restaurant, and shopping. Malecón and Orellana (phone: 31-22-00). Moderate.

Humboldt Internacional – This 77-room hotel offers air conditioning and central heating, private baths, and telephones; nightclub entertainment, casino, and bar. *Malecón* 2309 (phone: 52-12-00). Moderate.

Palace – An 80-room hotel that features private baths, air conditioning, a casino, nightclub, and 24-hour cafeteria. Calle Chile 216, Apdo. 608 (phone: 32-10-80). Moderate.

Plaza – Comfortable and conveniently located downtown, it has 47 rooms, all with private bath. Chile 414 y Calle Ballén. Moderate to inexpensive.

Rizzo – A small, first-class hotel that contains private baths in rooms. Calle Ballén 319 y Chile (phone: 51-12-10). Inexpensive.

SALINAS

Miramar – Resort hotel offers private bathrooms and telephones. Best in town. Moderate.

Salinas – Hotel right off the beachfront boulevard offers private baths and telephones, like the *Miramar*. Moderate.

PUNTA CARNERO

Punta Carnero Inn – This 45-room hotel features private baths, air conditioning, and balconies overlooking the sea. Guests can play tennis or charter a deep-sea cruise, and there's nightclub entertainment with casino gambling during local vacation periods, December through April (phone: 78-53-77). Expensive.

SANTO DOMINGO DE LOS COLORADOS

Tinalandia – This hotel outside town features a golf course, swimming pool, bird watching, and a restaurant. Expensive.

Zaracay – This 44-room hotel features a restaurant and swimming pool surrounded by gardens (Apdo. 50). Expensive.

The Galápagos Islands

They have been called everything from bewitched to paradisial. They have harbored Spanish explorers, buccaneers, and avaricious whalers. They are ugly clusters of volcanic rock, glazed with algaeic slime from the ocean, smothered by coarse, yellow grass inland. They are inhabited by species of wildlife so unique that almost half of them cannot be found anywhere else, providing the basis for man's theory of evolution. They are the fascinating Galápagos Islands, 13 major islands and dozens of smaller islets some 600 miles west of Ecuador, comprising a 3,029-square-mile natural wonderland, and they may be the only remaining habitat of substantial size where man has conserved huge quantities of wildlife before completely abusing the natural balance of nature.

Discovered by the explorer Thomás de Berlanga in 1535, the islands were named Galápagos, the Spanish word for the giant, lethargic tortoises that sunned themselves on the rocks. They were later nicknamed the Bewitched Isles, or Las Islas Encantadas. The meeting of the cold, antarctic Humboldt Current with the warm, northerly El Niño Current churned the waters to create the hypnotic illusion that the gray, jagged boulders were swaying. During the sixteenth, seventeenth, and eighteenth centuries, buccaneers landed on the islands' shores en route to search for treasure on mainland South America. More savage visitors harbored there in the nineteenth century: Whalers, and later oilers, moored in the island coves for the sole purpose of slaughtering tortoises (and thanks to these human predators, the *galápagos* are nearly extinct today).

A more pacific visitor did explore the islands in 1835 — 26-year-old Charles Darwin, who was serving as a naturalist aboard the HMS *Beagle* during its 6-year voyage around the world. Darwin was fascinated with the local wildlife, and the variety of subspecies of animals and birds helped him formulate his theory about natural selection and the process of evolution; that is, animals, plants, and birds adapt to an environment for survival. About 50% of the animals — mostly iguanas, tortoises, and sea mammals — were original residents of the islands, and other bird and marine species were eventually carried here by wind or water currents.

The islands are estimated to be more than 3 million years old; tortoises and iguanas here may be the descendants of prehistoric animals. The land and marine iguanas look like miniature dinosaurs, and their scaly hides give them a beastly appearance (the land iguana turns itself from gold to brownish red). These lizards and other island inhabitants are virtually tame, however, with a tendency to be drawn to, rather than away from, two-legged visitors.

The list of wildlife tenants is endless: In addition to tortoises and iguanas, there are flightless cormorants, penguins, albatrosses, red- and blue-footed boobies, finches (13 varieties), frigate birds, swallow-tailed gulls, and more. Some "imported" trees and fruits crop up along some of the inhabited islands: bamboo, bromeliads, breadfruit, papaya, avocado, and orange. Here and there a tropical rain forest adds lushness to the bare lava landscape.

Claimed by Ecuador in 1832, the Galápagos (also known as Archipelago Colón) were designated one of Ecuador's 20 governmental provinces during the 1970s. In 1959, the Charles Darwin Foundation, with the aid of the Ecuadorian government and UNESCO, established a biological research station on Santa Cruz Island. The entire Galápagos territory was designated a national park shortly afterward.

Of all the islands, only five are inhabited, mostly by Ecuadorians and English and German immigrants. Half of that population resides on the capital island of San Cristóbal; the rest live on Santa Cruz (the central island), Baltra (the air base), Isabela, and Floreana. Most of the islands have both Spanish and English names: Chatham (San Cristóbal), Indefatigable (Santa Cruz), Seymour (Baltra), Albemarle (Isabela), and Charles (Floreana). Isabela, 75 miles long, is the largest island; it and the uninhabited islands of Fernandina, Santiago, Marchena, and Pinta have their own active volcanoes.

A visitor can come to the islands by plane from Quito and Guayaquil to Baltra (via TAME) or to San Cristóbal (via SAN). Other than a few scheduled departures offered by tour operators, there is little in the way of regular boat service for those traveling from the mainland. There are erratic departures of local cargo ships (the *Iguana* and the *Piguino*), but they do not always accept passengers. Metropolitan Touring in Quito operates several of the most popular of the Galápagos charter yachts and cruises and its fleet includes the *Santa Cruz,* which carries 90 passengers in 45 staterooms, the 16-passenger *Isakela,* and the *Amigo I,* which carries 14. The company's US representative is Adventure Associates, 13150 Coit Rd., Suite 110, Dallas, TX 75240 (phone: 800-527-2500). In addition, the 90-passenger ship, the *Buccaneer,* operates weekly island cruises and is represented in the US by Galapagos, Inc., 7800 Red Road, South Miami, FL 33143 (phone: 800-327-9854).

Visitors can also fly to Santa Cruz or San Cristóbal, stay in one of a few small hotels on either island, and take day trips to neighboring islands. A traveler should check upon arrival with the local captains at the harbor, who are in turn required to be accompanied by a local naturalist-guide from the Darwin Station. There is a national park fee of $40 to visit the islands.

Some of the islanders will be happy to take you on a tour of the islands, providing you're a serious naturalist. There are limited but good accommodations in Santa Cruz. Camping is available, but check with the National Park office first for authorized sites.

Below are descriptions of some of the prominent islands.

SANTA CRUZ (INDEFATIGABLE): If you fly to Baltra, take a 1½-hour bus ride into Academy Bay to visit the Charles Darwin Biological Research Station. Open to visitors Mondays through Saturdays (9 AM to 4 PM), the station, among other things, houses a tortoise egg hatchery, tortoise pens, and even incubators. Few of the *galápagos* are alive today, thanks to the marauding whalers, but the station hopes to regenerate the species through controlled reproduction and replacement in natural breeding grounds.

Soon after the islands were established as a national park, the foundation formulated a master plan for the area in an attempt to set up a comfortable balance between the ecosystem and invading travelers. As a result, the islands were separated into zones. For instance, Academy Bay and the Darwin Research Station, along with the residential village (pop. 2,000) and hotels, are open to visitors, but the rest of Santa Cruz is restricted. The master plan has a schedule for developing tourism. Within the last few years, the number of tourists visiting the islands has increased to as many as 20,000 annually. Under the plan, not more than 20% of these may remain overnight; they either sleep on the ships or return to the mainland. Present tourists are also prohibited from touching or feeding the animals (a huge temptation when the animals waddle, stroll, or slink right up to you) or from taking chunks of lava home with them.

At the station, you'll be able to get a good look at the tortoises. They set themselves on the rocks, their old-man necks protruding from their shells, squinting at the sun — and you — through half-shut eyes. They look like they're bearing the weight of the world on their backs — but so would you if you had to tote a 500-pound shell around for 400 years or so. On Santa Cruz you can also take a guided tour of the Tortoise Reserve in the Highlands.

You can camp on the island, but check with the rangers to make sure you're not in a restricted area.

From Santa Cruz, you can book day trips (or longer) on small yachts. The islands are widely scattered, so be prepared for some rides that last up to 6 or 7 hours; if you get seasick, bring along the Dramamine.

SAN CRISTÓBAL (CHATHAM): The administrative capital of the Galápagos, the island houses about 2,500 people in the village of Puerto Baquerizo.

PINTA: With an active volcano, this tiny island cannot be visited.

ISABELA (ALBEMARLE): The archipelago's longest island; an active volcano erupted here in April 1963. Until 1958 there was a convict colony on Isabela, and today about 1,000 people (all free and respectable) reside on the southern tip of the island. The unpopulated portion of the island has been set aside as National Park land.

This is a good place to observe the land iguana, along with a few fur seals, penguins, and some of the 13 finch varieties that Darwin managed to classify.

BARTOLOME: It has a good swimming beach and is famous for its volcanic landscape and Pinnacle Rock, which you can climb for a superb view of the islands.

JAMES: Fur seals and thousands of marine iguanas are at home here on the black lava rocks. The lava formations at Buccaneer Cove are also intriguing, as are the lovely coral-colored flamingos standing in quiet groups at the island's inland lakes.

FLOREANA: In the 18th century, whalers opened a post office here in a barrel, and letters have been dropped off and carried onward ever since. Point Cormorant is a bird-watcher's dream.

HOOD: Almost every species of bird, including blue-footed and masked boobies and albatross, are found on this island, and its wild cliffscapes are alive with iguana and sea lions.

PLAZA: This tiny island is packed with splendid vegetation and all kinds of rare Galápagos wildlife — sea lions, iguanas, and many tropical birds.

BEST EN ROUTE

Unless you're moving with a boat tour, the only place to stay comfortably is in the tourist area on Santa Cruz Island at Academy Bay. Private houses offer some type of accommodation, but it's best to check first with the Darwin station. (Visitors arriving without advance arrangements will have to inquire at Balta Airport about how to cross to Santa Cruz Island; it's not always easy.) Expect prices to be anywhere from an expensive $50 with meals to an inexpensive $10. The *Delfin* hotel and the *Galápagos* hotel have a new program that combines a 3-day cruise aboard the *Santa Cruz* and 2 nights on land. This gives visitors a chance to visit the Darwin Research Station (a tour is included in the price) and to take an optional tour to the Tortoise National Reserve in the highlands.

These days, it's recommended that plans for a Galápagos tour be made 6 months in advance, since the islands are becoming popular and boat tours fill up rapidly. Tour operators hold blocked space for their programs, but they must release cabins 45 days prior to departure. So check them for cancellations.

SANTA CRUZ (INDEFATIGABLE)

Delfin – Choose from 16 attached bungalows and rooms with private baths. Amenities include central dining, bar, and lounge area, three meals daily (picnics packed for boat excursions); cove beach swimming. There are plans in the works to expand this property. Expensive.

Galápagos – This hotel has the best island accommodations — 14 cottage rooms with hot showers and laundry service. The central building, with a fine view of Academy Bay, is where meals are served, and it also has a bar and library. Expensive.

Solymar – This hotel has cabin accommodations for 20 people that are divided into doubles, triples, and quadruples. Nice simple oceanfront restaurant. Moderate.

Ninfa – Accommodates 60 guests in cabins that are divided into doubles and triples, all with private bath. There are optional day trips available on the yacht *Ninfa I*. Moderate to inexpensive.

Cabiñas de Gusch Angermayer – 20 beds offered by a German immigrant. It's best to ask about reservations at the Darwin station. Inexpensive.

French Guiana

French Guiana, that tiny, 35,135-square-mile relative of Suriname (its western neighbor) and Guyana, is meant to satisfy the traveler seeking an exotic, offbeat spot in the Western Hemisphere. After all, it has all the components to thrill the most jaded explorer: a jungle that is penetrable only by motorized, native canoe; exotic birds that include parrots and macaws; stunning orchids that block your way along the river path; Amazonian varieties of jaguar, ocelot, tapir, anteater, caiman (the South American alligator), the frightening howler monkey; snakes (including the anaconda); and the passive, lovely, blue morpho butterfly. Humid and constantly rainy (the best months to visit are from late June to November), the country sits slightly north of the equator, bordered to the south and east by Brazil (400 years ago, it was part of Brazil) and by the Atlantic on the north. Cayenne, the country's capital, sits about 6 miles (10 km) inland, on the banks of the Cayenne River. If the name Cayenne sounds familiar to you, you're probably a cook: Cayenne is the red, hot pepper exported from French Guiana from as far back as the seventeenth century. More modern exports include bauxite (huge quantities were discovered in the east), rice, and rum.

No stranger to European eyes (the Guianas were first sighted by Amerigo Vespucci in 1496), French Guiana was settled by the French in 1604. After that, its history is a stormy one, the land of jungle, marsh, and sand constantly passing back and forth among the French, Dutch, and English. Captured by the Dutch in 1676, the country was finally returned to the French, then taken by the English; a final resolution (thanks to the Treaty of Vienna of 1815, following the Napoleonic wars) returned the land to the French. Today, French Guiana is an Overseas Department of France, with its own prefect (or governor) sitting in Cayenne.

Despite the lure of its jungle, French Guiana — with a minuscule population of about 75,000 (90% scattered around Cayenne), a mixture of Creoles, Asians, whites, Amerindians, and Bushnegros — presently lacks extensive tourist accommodations. Travelers now have the amenities of modern air-conditioned hotels in Cayenne, Kourou, and St.-Laurent. Aiding in the development of the coast is the French space center at Kourou, which launches and monitors satellites. In addition, many new all-year roads have been built to exploit the boundless tracts of lumber and other resources to be extracted from the bush.

Any adventure in French Guiana starts in Cayenne. Before heading off into the jungle, take a look around the capital as well as Kourou and St.-Laurent. Whatever you do, *don't* — repeat, *don't* — forget a trip to Devil's Island, the infamous French penal colony, also known as the Dry Guillotine, about 12 miles (19 km) off shore from Kourou.

If you do intend to travel into the jungle, it's wise to plan far in advance for local guides and boatmen. On a typical trip upriver, expect to visit lumber camps that bustle during the harvest of jungle hardwood logs that are floated down river in rafts. Also you will see picturesque Indian and Bushnegro villages, where one can purchase very interesting handicrafts. Farther upriver comes the reward of wildlife, roaring cataracts, and rapids during the rainy season from late December to early August.

Camping is the rule upriver. Don't expect easy living here: Sleeping is in hammocks strung from the uprights of *carbets* (a jungle version of a lean-to), and sleeping on the ground is not recommended. There are few pesky insects, however, and mosquitoes are not a big problem as long as the swampy areas are avoided. Actually, the scourges of malaria and yellow fever are now mostly a thing of the past, but it's best to get inoculations and pills anyway. Today, the biggest health problem for the traveler is overexposure to the sun. When sitting in a dugout engrossed in photographing, birding, and observing, it is easy to forget the strength of the equatorial sun. Essentials for any river trip include a good insect repellent, sunscreen lotion, long-sleeve shirts and long trousers, sunglasses, sun hats, a poncho or rain suit, plenty of plastic bags to protect cameras, and so on. An inflatable cushion (most dugouts have no seats) and camping equipment, including hammocks, are available locally: Consult with tour operators on other items, since proper equipment is most important. Dugouts or *pirogues* can only carry so much, and at many points portages must be made to bypass rapids and cataracts. The best time to observe birds and animals is early in the morning or late in the afternoon, when the jungle life seems to gravitate to the riverbanks to drink and feed.

Additional tour information is available from the French Government Tourist Office, 610 Fifth Ave., New York, NY (phone: 212-757-1125), or from the prefect's offices in Cayenne, 3 Pl. Schoelcher (phone: 31-09-00). The office is near the zoo and is open weekdays, 9 AM to noon and 4 to 6 PM.

If you prefer not to rough it on your own, be aware that tour operators occasionally book tours through the area and cruise ship itineraries sometimes include Devil's Island. If you prefer to wait until you're in Cayenne, contact Takari Tours (phone: 31-19-60) at the *Hotel du Montabo,* or write BP 513, Cayenne 97300. Local travel agents ready and willing to help you in Cayenne include: Somarig, 2 Pl. de Grenoble (phone: 31-29-57); Sainte Claire et Cie, 8 Rue de Remire (phone: 31-00-23); Relais de Brousse, 11 Rue Malouet (phone: 31-36-41); and Air France, 5 Pl. de Grenoble (phone: 31-27-40).

You can ferry-drive your way into French Guiana from neighboring countries, or take a Suriname Airways or Cruzeiro do Sul flight in from Paramaribo, Suriname. Both carriers have regular service to Cayenne and weekly flights from Belém, Brazil; Air France offers flights from Lima, Perú. If you're flying from the US, you have to make connections with an Air France flight in Martinique, Puerto Rico, Haiti, or Guadeloupe.

If you do fly, start by driving or taking a taxi or bus in from Rochambeau International Airport, about 11 miles (18 km) outside of the capital.

CAYENNE: The first sight to greet you in this city of 38,000 people is the imposing statue of Felix Adolphe Eboué (1884–1944), the African Free French sympathizer who served as governor-general of Martinique and Equatorial Africa. He stands in the Place des Palmistes, the city's main palm-filled square. Surrounding the square are sidewalk cafés, and beyond the square is the city's main street, with little shops and a museum (closed Mondays). Adjoining Place des Palmistes is Place de Grenoble, equally picturesque with its old whitewashed governor's mansion, post office, and the Air France office. Down the main street one can visit the city cemetery, the hospital, and a small botanical garden–zoo.

A few blocks west of the main street is the older part of town, called La Crique after a tidal creek that flows through the area and provides safe haven for multicolored Brazilian fishing boats, called Les Tapouilles. Here indeed is the color of Cayenne, with its animated market, selling pottery, spices (including pepper), parrots and other tropical birds, as well as pelts of ocelot, carman, and jaguar. Chinese and Lebanese shops supply the surrounding populace, as well as the lumber camp workers and miners of the hinterland. Hence weekends are particularly animated in Cayenne compared to working days, which are dull except after dusk when the sidewalk cafés come to life in the evening cool.

> **En Route from Cayenne** – Leaving town, you cross a new, long bridge spanning the Cayenne River, then travel northwest along the paved coastal highway 40 miles to Kourou. As you speed along the lush jungle plain, which alternates with a few patches of cultivated clearing, you suddenly approach a horizon filled with antennas and tracking mechanisms, used by the nearby space center for tracking the communications and weather satellites orbited here.

KOUROU: Once a small fishing village, the town you now see was built near its "older brother" on reclaimed, swampy land, spreading out at the very mouth of the river on a peninsular point. This Kourou is a modern whitewashed concrete town, with several shops (where you can buy jewelry, butterflies, and cigarettes), boutiques, bank, and post office. There are the ever-present cafés, all catering to a community of about 2,000, the majority being either employees at the space center or French Legionnaires who come to town to relax.

Sit back and enjoy the river view here: Marsh and sea birds zoom into its banks for landings among the thick mangroves along the shoreline. You can rent a dugout canoe at the *Des Roches* hotel for cruising.

You should definitely arrange at the hotel for the 1-hour launch ride out to Devil's Island (one of Les Îles de Salut); reservations are recommended, since space on the boat is limited, and space center employees and Legionnaires like to laze away their weekends on the islands. The boat departs at 8 AM and returns at 4 PM, depending on the tide.

DEVIL'S ISLAND: Les Îles de Salut (the Isles of Salvation) are really a trio of islands: Royale (the largest), St. Joseph, and Devil's. Its name originated in the 17th century, when settlers fled the mainland to take refuge from the disease-ridden jungle.

On Royale, you can visit the commandant's house and houses of the prison staff, the hospital, chapel, children's cemetery, lighthouse, and space center tracking station, and perhaps swim in a sheltered, ocean-fed pool, constructed by the prisoners for the staff. Overnight accommodations are provided in the converted guards' quarters. The entire island is circled by a passable footpath that can be walked in an hour (at a slow pace).

From Royale, a short motor launch takes you to St. Joseph, where there are the remains of the huge, solitary confinement compound, with cells and a common area with its roof almost rusted away. Huge tree roots and vines make it difficult to enter. Facing the ocean is the prison staff cemetery and rocky beach, a cool place to picnic.

Tide and currents permitting, you may be lucky enough to visit Devil's Island itself, which now contains the ruins of 13 cottages once used for political prisoners, including Alfred Dreyfus, the Jewish French army officer who was convicted of treason and imprisoned here in 1895 until further investigation proved his innocence. Almost completely cut off from Royale and St. Joseph, the prisoners here raised their own vegetables and poultry. Today, the incarcerated have been replaced by rather aggressive bees.

En Route from Devil's Island – Returning to Kourou, you can visit the space center, which stretches 6 miles (10 km) west along the coast. Owned by the French and maintained by an international force of civilian scientists from NATO, the center launches weather and communication satellites. Employees there boast that their location is far better than that of Cape Kennedy in Florida, since it is closer to the equator, and the greater thrust of the earth's rotation here makes launches easier and more successful. Visitors are allowed on the site for tours on Wednesday mornings at 8 AM except during launches (phone: 33-44-82). Tours are in French, but there is a 30-minute film in English. From the center, the coastal highway proceeds northwest along the plain, passing small farms and fishing villages. At Sinna Mayr, on the river of the same name, there is a Javanese settlement. One favorite restaurant here is Indonesian with an Art Nouveau decor, owned and operated by a retired Javanese soldier named Papa Chef. After leaving you will pass two more small villages, Inracoubo and Organaba, and come to the city of St.-Laurent on the Maroni River, which divides French Guiana from Suriname.

ST.-LAURENT-DU-MARONI: This frontier town is the starting point for a trip down the Maroni River, the supply route of many Indian and Bushnegro villages dotting the shore. The quay is bustling with activity: boats loading provisions as well as ferry traffic from the town of Albina, across the river in Suriname. Parquet flooring is the main industry here.

St.-Laurent was a larger community during the prison era: It was the receiving station for sentenced prisoners. The remnants of the prison still stand. Prisoners were received, classified, and served sentences here; incorrigibles were shipped to the Salvation Islands. Today some of the buildings are used as dwellings by local Creoles. Except for the busy waterfront, St.-Laurent still maintains a sleepy look, enlivened in the evening when the bistros come to life. Here one makes a final check of supplies and equipment for the trip up the Maroni River.

En Route from St.-Laurent – The river is about 3 miles wide at St.-Laurent, and as you proceed upriver, the width, with a few exceptions, stays fairly constant. Close to the banks you get a good view of life along the river, with chattering naked children playing and bathing; women washing clothes and carrying water, firewood, and other unbelievable loads on their heads. The tailored, clean villages always have ornately carved decorations on the individual doors and walls and a ceremonial hut and granary that is always more ornate than the common dwellings.

For the next 130 miles (209 km) upriver you pass Bushnegro and Boni (an African tribe) villages; you may be lucky enough to buy a painted paddle called a *pagaie,* a two-bladed affair with one end handsomely carved in a beautiful symmetrical design and the blade on the opposite end painted in a multicolored design. These paddles are an intricate part of village life, and usually the carving and painting carry deep meaning. For example, a *pagaie* with a house painted on it means a proposal of marriage when presented by a young man to the maiden of his choice.

After 3 or 4 days of river travel you arrive at Maripasoula, where accommodations are provided at a simple riverside inn. Maripasoula is the gateway to the Wayana Indian country, which stretches south upriver for hundreds of miles into Brazil. The Wayana culture is based on hunting (rarely with the use of firearms), sacred tribal rituals in colorful head regalia, and a natural red, rougelike paste called *roucou.* The Wayana are a hospitable people, so much so that even though one's visit may break their daily routine, you would never be aware of the imposition. Since Maripasoula has an airstrip, you can either return to Cayenne in a small, single-engine plane, or retrace your route downriver.

BEST EN ROUTE

Tourist facilities in French Guiana are few and far between. Hotels outside of Cayenne and Kourou offer simple accommodations (small rooms and often no private baths). However, what you get is comfortable and, if you're not fussy, likable. The most expensive places will run at least $50 a night; more moderate prices are between $15 and $25; and anything under $15 is considered inexpensive. It's a good idea to make reservations; if you're booking with a tour, it will be done for you.

CAYENNE

Novotel Cayenne – Two miles outside town, on the sea, Cayenne's newest hotel has 100 air-conditioned rooms, with 4 equipped for handicapped guests. Amenities include a pool, 2 tennis courts, a restaurant that is nothing to write home about, bar, and conference facilities. Route de Montabo (phone: 30-38-86). Expensive.

KOUROU

Des Roches – A large hotel with 100 rooms and 10 seafront bungalows, an elegant and very good restaurant, swimming pool, and tennis courts. Bord de Mer, BP 18, 97310 (phone: 32-00-66). Expensive.

DEVIL'S ISLAND

L'Auberge de l'Île Royale – Once the administration building for the French penal colony, it now offers guestrooms, all with balconies and private bath, in dormitory accommodations (phone: 33-45-30). Inexpensive.

ST.-LAURENT-DU-MARONI

Atyp – This small hotel provides clean, simple accommodations. 97320 St.-Laurent-du-Maroni (phone: 34-10-84). Inexpensive.
Peslier – Similar to the *Atyp*. 97320 St.-Laurent-du-Maroni (phone: 34-10-59). Inexpensive.

Guyana

Guyana is a country for serious adventurers only and is not to be visited casually, for there is very little in the way of a visitor infrastructure. The wild beauty of its jungle interior is visited at a price of rigorous — and sometimes dangerous — effort. Though only 83,000 square miles in area (about the size of Idaho or Kansas), travel is difficult. The rain forests and savannahs make air or river travel the only viable means of transport. Few of Guyana's 825,000 residents venture into the jungle interior; those who do contend with tropical heat and humidity (temperatures range from 63° to 105°F, and rainfall averages as much as 105 inches annually), tropical insects, and (hardly surprising in such jungle) the risk of malaria.

Bordered by Venezuela to the west, Suriname to the east, Brazil to the south, and the Atlantic Ocean on the north, Guyana ("Guy" as in "eye") was called British Guiana before it gained independence in 1966. Since then, it has developed a socialist government that appears to discourage tourism. The truth is that large-scale tourism is hardly a question in Guyana. There is a lamentable shortage of accommodations outside Georgetown, the capital, and the rush of bad press at the time of the Jonestown massacre in November 1978 brought with it some disturbing rumors about the stability of parts of the interior, rumors the government has gone to some trouble to lay to rest. For whatever reason, strangers — and that includes any travelers — are met in most interior towns and river ports by the police, who take a careful look at entry papers. The police are friendly and helpful, but vigilant. In Georgetown, foreigners have complained of attacks by "choke and grab" thugs on the city's streets. The attacks certainly occurred, but there seems to be no pervasive pattern in such incidents. Just be particularly careful after dark, even in a taxi.

Guyana is an Indian word meaning "land of many waters," and those many waters are the major thoroughfares of the country. All tours to the interior begin in Georgetown, the nation's port of entry by air or sea. With only two roads of any consequence (one along the coast, the other joining Georgetown to the bauxite mines in Linden, 65 miles away), visits to the interior must be made by air. Once there, travel is by boat, horse, or Jeep.

Despite its small size, Guyana offers a variety of landscape and vegetation. It is fanned by trade winds that keep the temperatures almost bearable along the 270-mile coast. In many places, the land is below sea level. The ingenuity of the first Dutch settlers (the first Europeans to colonize the country in 1621) is still evident in the form of flood gates, or *kokers,* set around Georgetown.

Because so many rivers empty into the Atlantic along Guyana's coast, the coastal waters are for the most part murky and muddy, a long shot from the fine Caribbean beaches that bring so many swimmers, divers, and sun worshipers to the Venezuelan and Colombian shores west of Guyana. But if sun worshippers are disappointed, river lovers thrive here.

Guyana's interior is forest, mountain, and savannah. Most mountainous is the southwestern corner of Guyana's border with Venezuela, where the mountains are characteristically primordial, steep and sharp along the inclines, and flat on top. Mt. Roraima, the 9,094-foot mountain near the juncture of the Guyanese, Venezuelan, and Brazilian borders, so caught Sir Arthur Conan Doyle's imagination that after seeing it he wrote *The Lost World,* envisioning the mountaintop inhabited by prehistoric animals.

The savannahs, in the northeast and southwest parts of the country, sustain cattle herds tended by cowboys who are really Indians. In fact, agriculture is one of the country's first, and still major, industries. Following the Dutch colonization and the founding of the Dutch West India Company, slaves were imported to work the plantations, which still produce sugar, cotton, and coffee. Today, more than 150,000 people are involved in the sugar industry; rice, rum, and timber are also profitable trade.

Mining is another major industry. The production of bauxite started in Linden in 1916 is still going strong but not at great profit because of low prices on the world market. In more isolated areas, gold and diamonds are mined by single adventurers who string out along the country's rivers with nothing more than gold pans and the clothes on their back.

Romantic? Exciting? Wild? Yes. But one must remember that a trip to Guyana is no fool's holiday. Certain precautions should be taken while traveling here. Visitors are warned to dress in field gear in the interior. Rainwear and insect repellent are requisite, and tennis shoes, not boots, should be worn for river transportation (boots are hazardous if a canoe tips over). Malaria tablets are essential, and a yellow fever inoculation is required when entering from Venezuela or Suriname.

To ease the trials of a visit, visitors are urged to arrange travel, sightseeing, and accommodations through Guyanese travel agents. The best of these services are offered by Guyana Overland Tours, 6 Av. of the Republic, PO Box 10173, Georgetown (phone: 69876), or Sprostons, 26 Main St. (phone: 6-3974). The Guyana Tourist Board, in the Bank of Guyana Building on the Avenue of the Republic (phone: 6-3096), will also answer queries.

GEORGETOWN: At the mouth of the Demerara River in the center of the coastline, Georgetown is the capital and commerical heart of Guyana; in November 1978 it was the unfortunate site of the mass suicide of more than 900 people, many from California, who were members of a religious sect called the People's Temple. The city covers an area of 1,612 acres and has a population of 190,000, nearly one-quarter of the national total.

The entry point for all travelers, Georgetown is a quaint combination of Victorian elegance — the legacy of its British heritage — and tin-roofed mining town. Both aspects are worth a visit, and you can plan to spend a couple of days roaming the town. A walking tour should begin at the seawall near the *Guyana Pegasus* hotel on High Street (a stop at the top floor of the *Pegasus* will give you an overall view of the city). The seawall was originally built in 1882 to protect the city, which is 5 feet below the high-tide mark.

Leaving the hotel, observe the large, circular thatched building to your right. Patterned after the dwellings of the Indians in the interior, it was built a few years ago at the request of the government to be used as an auditorium; it is a good example of

Guyanese architecture. In contrast, colonial homes on High Street are trimmed in Victorian gingerbread.

When you reach the railroad track, note the station, built in 1848 — the first such erected on the South American continent. At the tracks, High Street changes to Main Street and passes more Victorian homes; you can peer through the guarded hedge at Guyana House, home of the presidents, but you can't enter the grounds. By the time you reach the *Park* hotel, on the right at the corner of Main and Middle streets, you'll probably be ready to take a break at the hotel, an ideal resting spot. The *Park* is a glorious old hotel with a huge, wooden porch. Sit under the rotating ceiling fans in a wicker chair, order a drink made with the local rum (rated "E" for "Excellent"), or indulge in tea and cakes. It is the tropical life as played out in a dozen different novels. There are often some miners or other breed of fortune hunter nearby, and they'll eagerly share some of their adventures with you, usually for the price of a cool drink and willing ear.

If you can pull away, resume your trip along Main Street to the *Tower* hotel on the left (74 Main). Straight ahead is the Bank of Guyana, the place to cash checks and change currency. A bit farther, Main Street once again becomes High Street.

Off Church Street is the Georgetown Museum. Open daily except Sundays, the museum contains exhibits on the country's prehistory, history, and flora and fauna.

St. George's Anglican Cathedral, across Main Street, is considered by the Guyanese to be the tallest wooden building in the world. That is probably an exaggerated claim, but the church, which opened in 1892, towers a magnificent 142 feet above the street. Inside, a huge stained-glass window casts a many-colored glow on the simple wooden pews. Over half the Guyanese population is Christian, with Anglicans predominating. One third of the citizens are Hindus; slightly under 10% are Moslem. English, however, is the official language.

Beyond the cathedral, High Street becomes the Avenue of the Republic. On your right is the tiny, charming police station that resembles a Victorian dollhouse and several other gingerbread buildings, including the city hall (1887) and Tudor-style law courts.

The Botanic Garden and Zoo, on Vlissegen Road, completes the walking tour. The 180-acre garden is covered with bougainvillea, flamboyant trees, orchids, and other tropical plants. Afloat in the ponds are huge, umbrella-sized lily pads. The zoo, open daily from 6 AM to 6 PM, has another pond loaded with sea cows, which swim over to take grass from your hand. Band concerts are held on Sunday afternoons around the little gazebo. Adjacent is the new and excellent Cultural Centre, which suffers only from underuse.

Shopping is a "don't miss" in Georgetown. Upon reaching Brickdam Street, take a right and pass the Parliament Building. Straight ahead is *Stabroek Market,* a glorious display of agricultural products and some handicrafts, but not the safest place for foreigners.

Two other fascinating shops carry only local handicrafts at absurdly low prices. Next door to the market (1 Water St.) is the *Amerindian Handicrafts Centre,* run by the Interior Development Department. On the second floor of an austere, gray building, it looks more like a museum than a shop. Spears, blowpipes, beadwork, carvings, and feather headdresses made by the Indians are available. The *Guyana Crafts Co-op,* at the corner of Brickdam and the Avenue of the Republic, has lovely baskets and hammocks.

En Route from Georgetown to Linden – Bauxite mining, a major Guyanese industry, was started in Linden in 1916. Visitors can visit the nationalized plants there via a 65-mile highway or by buses that leave frequently from Georgetown's *Stabroek Market.* A tour at the mines is a 2-hour affair.

En Route from Georgetown to the Interior – You can't be warned enough to make early reservations for any flights into the interior. The schedule has been chaotic in recent years. Guyana Airways' planes, serving some 20 domestic airfields, hold 19 passengers each, and rising fuel costs have made some routes almost prohibitive. For example, the cost of a 1-day tour from Georgetown to the country's major tourist attraction, Kaieteur Falls, doubled, then tripled, in recent years. At one time, the government curtailed travel there completely. Anyone going into the interior must make sure arrangements have been made for the return trip and should inquire in advance whether the airline accepts credit cards (some don't). Double-check the schedules, and verify return flights with the local agents in any towns visited outside Georgetown.

And make sure to get clearance through a travel agent to visit the interior, because many areas are off limits. The government does not want Jonestown to become a tourist attraction for obvious reasons, and some Indian reservations are also restricted. When you arrive in the outposts, show your credentials to the police, who will probably meet you at the plane, anyway. Most of them will steer you to nearby attractions; they are also there for your protection in areas that sometimes resemble the wild, wild American West.

KAIETEUR FALLS: On the Potaro River, a tributary of the Essequibo, about 150 miles from Georgetown, the Kaieteur Falls, 740 feet high and nearly five times as high as Niagara, are Guyana's most famous attraction. Guyana Airways offers a round-trip visit to the falls every Sunday from Georgetown. (The flight leaves from Temehri Airport, the international airport 25 miles from Georgetown, instead of from smaller Ogle Airport, only 6 miles from the city.) The trip lasts 4½ hours (9 AM to 1:30 PM), giving the traveler an hour at the falls.

The airline recently planned to extend the tour to a full day to visit Orinduik Falls on the Ireng River, which separates Guyana and Brazil. Travelers should check current schedules.

The trip to Kaieteur should certainly not be missed. The small plane will bump to a landing on a rocky strip. The traveler is then left to walk across a desolate area and through a dense jungle — the plane's stewardess leads the way along a trail surrounded by towering trees draped in moss. After a 10-minute walk, which includes clambering over rocks, the jungle opens, and you see the falls roaring below.

Sometimes diamond and gold miners congregate in tents at the top of the falls on the smooth, rocky bluff, and they usually can be persuaded to part with their finds for cash. But the falls is the main attraction. It varies considerably in size from the rainy to the dry season (the rainy seasons run from April to August and November to January), but is spectacular when flowing deep and fast. The water is stained brown by decaying vegetation, and branches of trees are swept along the cliff to oblivion at the falls' bottom. Dense spray rises from the white foam as the waves crash onto the boulders at the base of the gorge, and rapids twist away from the falls. Tiny birds flit around the edge of the falls to reach the huge cave that has been carved out underneath by years of erosion.

A day trip to the falls costs about $75; a 3-day, air-overland trip, about $200.

The truly adventurous don't have to make the return trip immediately. They can wait and spend several days camping with the miners at the top of the falls. The climb from the river to the top of the falls takes about 2 hours. There are no provisions in the area (except a plenitude of water), but the stay will allow time to follow the path to the base of the falls and along the roaring river downstream. If you come prepared, it can be an exceptional, otherworldly stay. But be sure your return flight is assured on another plane.

IMBAIMADAI: A trip to Imbaimadai is also time well spent. The Old West must have been much like this diamond- and gold-mining town on the Mazaruni River in western Guyana. The town consists of shanties, three bars (where gin in condensed milk is a popular breakfast drink), the diamond buyers' office — and a pool table.

Along the Mazaruni are dredges for gold mining. Divers spend entire days at the bottom of the river, handling the hoses that suck mud to the surface. The mud is strained, then panned by hand to separate the grains of gold, which are melted down in coffee cans.

The diamond hunters operate mainly along the riverbanks, digging holes and sifting the sand for the tiny glittering gems. Most of the diamonds are small, but they are of excellent quality. Usually a man will spend several weeks in the bush collecting, sell his finds, spend the money in a few days, then go into the wilds again. It is a cruel life — as cruel, it would seem, as the wild Guyanese environment surrounding the miners. Not even the three men who discovered Guyana's largest diamond have enough money to buy shoes today. (The eight-karat gem was discovered 20 years ago, only to mysteriously disappear. One of those three discoverers frequently passes through Imbaimadai, still searching for new riches.)

Peters' Guest House is run by a pork knocker (the traditional bush term for a miner) who first visited Imbaimadai in 1938 in search of diamonds, gave up the hunt in 1961, and opened a store. He expanded the store into a guesthouse 7 years later.

The Indians or some of the miners in the town — which has a population of only 200 — are happy to guide travelers to Imbaimadai's tourist attractions: Maipuri Falls (*maipuri* is the Arawak Indian word for the tapir), 80 feet high and 90 feet wide; and the Temehri cliff drawings, on the way to the falls; and nearby Kawaio Indian villages. The falls and the cliff drawings must be reached by the river, and at least two Indian paddlers — both familiar with the river — are necessary. Don't try to go by yourself.

The Temehri cliff paintings date from the 14th century, and the Indians claim the glistening, quartzite cliff was painted not by men, but by the god Ama Livaca, who visited Guyana during a great flood. The paintings extend over a width of 50 feet to a height of 25 feet, and they depict animals, groups of dancing figures, and hundreds of handprints. The half-hour hike from the river to the cliff is as impressive as the paintings themselves. The trail leads through the heart of the rain forest and across a chasm, stopping on the way only for a cool drink from a cold spring in a cave.

To get to the Indian villages, it is a good idea to have a motor rather than paddle boat. Gasoline is expensive because it must be flown in from Georgetown, but the trip is fascinating. The chief of the village will take you on the tour himself, showing you the peanut farm and the women making cassava bread (cassava is the plant whose root provides the stock for making tapioca).

Again, make sure you have advance reservations to and from Imbaimadai by Guyana Airways. The flight over the jungles, past the flat-topped mountains encircled by mist, is awesome.

A 3-day trip to Imbaimadai costs about $225, including flight, accommodations, and the trip to Maipuri Falls and the cliffs.

THE RUPUNUNI SAVANNAH: In the southeast corner of Guyana, bordering Brazil, the Rupununi is part of the vast Río Branco savannah. One hour's plane ride from Georgetown to the town of Lethem brings you to the savannah and Mrs. Margaret Orella's *Manari Ranch* hotel. One popular trip from the ranch goes by Jeep to a tropical forest of the Kanuku Mountains to visit one of the oldest Indian settlements in the country. The Wai-Wai Indians, a branch of the Amerindian tribe, are known for their colorful use of bird feathers in their dress. Nearby, the Macushi Indians will take you on a 20-minute walk from the village to Moco Moco Falls, which has clear swimming pools surrounded by boulders.

In Lake Pan, you can go swimming or fish for *lukunani,* tasty fish that are easily caught with fly gear from the shore. If you're too lazy for the sport, however, then you can watch the natives fish for giant *arapaima* the old-fashioned way, with bows and arrows.

One word about the Rupununi waters: Beware when you bathe; some very unfriendly creatures lurk here. The *perai* is a 6- to 9-inch creature lured by the smell of fresh blood. Stingrays and electric eels — the 500-volt variety — also inhabit the otherwise tranquil waters.

Another short excursion from the *Manari Ranch* takes you to Schomburgk's Peak. The 3,000-foot climb to the top takes about 4 hours, winding past huge trees, balata and wild cocoa, covered with orchids.

Near Lethem is the Takatu River, the border with Brazil. Many floating shops can be found anchored along the Brazilian side.

A 3-or-more-day visit to Lethem from Georgetown should cost about $250.

BEST EN ROUTE

A visit to Guyana is fun, if rugged, when planned properly. Accommodations are adequate in Georgetown, where the best hotel, the *Guyana Pegasus,* runs $100 a night, while lodging in the interior borders on the primitive and can be disproportionately expensive. *Peters' Guest House* in Imbaimadai, for instance, costs about $40 a night for a room with oil lamps and an outhouse. Expect to pay $20 to $30 for more moderately priced hotels; under $20 for inexpensive ones.

GEORGETOWN

Guyana Pegasus – A 109-room property, owned and operated by Trust House Forte, with air conditioning, a swimming pool, restaurant, pub, and cocktail lounge. Seawall and High St. (phone: 5-2856; for information and reservations in the US: 800-223-5672). Expensive.

Tower – This first-class hotel has 90 rooms, swimming pool, and restaurant. 74 Main St. (phone: 7-2011). Moderate.

Park – A colonial-style hotel with a new annex (recommended), it has 46 rooms, restaurant, bar, and garden (phone: 6-3001). Inexpensive.

IMBAIMADAI

Peters' Guest House – Provides rugged accommodations that aren't recommended for the pampered life. No reservations needed. Expensive.

LETHEM

Manari Ranch – This guesthouse is 6½ miles (12 km) outside Lethem, with good accommodations, fishing, swimming, and horseback riding. Reservations are recommended through local authorities. Moderate.

Panamá

Traversing the 340-mile section of the Pan-American Highway linking the Costa Rican frontier at Paso Canoa with the Panamá Canal provides a very different perspective of this 28,753-square-mile republic (about the size of South Carolina) of 1.8 million people. This is the Panamá of lush mountain ranges, dormant volcanoes, trout-filled streams, and wide beaches, where the Guaymi Indians still farm and practice native arts of embroidery and hand-crafted jewelry and live in houses of thatched roof and bamboo construction, as their ancestors have for ten centuries.

It's not until the highway winds its way east to Arraiján, and then drops a few miles down forest-cool slopes to the Bridge of the Americas across the Canal, that travelers get a taste of the more traditional Panamá — Columbus, Spanish gold-seekers, Henry Morgan's pirates, Colombian profiteers, and French and US canal builders.

Spain's interest in Panamá as anything more than an interoceanic short cut was perfunctory. What little gold the isthmus yielded was mined mostly in what today is the Colombian border area. The interior — in Panamanian usage, that part of the republic between the Canal and the Costa Rican border entry at Paso Canoa, on the Pacific side of the Continental Divide — meant nothing to Madrid's gold-mad bureaucrats. Anyone who settled there was on his own.

Independence in 1821 brought a marginal change of status from a Spanish colony to a distant province of politically unstable Colombia. Bogotá's bureaucrats cared no more than their Madrid predecessors for anything Panamanian, except rapid transit. *Interioranos* were still on their own until 1903, when US President Teddy Roosevelt proved an adept puppeteer in the separation of Panamá from Colombia.

So the Panamá the road traveler sees between Paso Canoa and the Canal, with Panamá City close beside it, is not . . .

the Panamá of Balboa's discovery of the Pacific Ocean in 1513 — that's 93 miles (150 km) beyond the Canal;

the Panamá of treasure raids by those "redistribute the wealth" economists, Sir Francis Drake and Lieutenant Governor Sir Henry Morgan;

the Panamá of the Canal — the crushing French failure of Suez-builder Ferdinand de Lesseps, followed by the triumph of Teddy Roosevelt's US engineers and, most of all, the US doctors who controlled malaria and yellow fever;

the Panamá of two world wars and the passenger liner era, when ingenuous itinerants' tall tales promoted the city as rife with honky-tonks on a par with those of Port Said, Marseilles, and Macao.

No. The Panamá glimpsed from the Pan-American Highway formed its character as a farming frontier, with no proud fortresses, no costly social pretensions. Self-reliance was the only way to get from one rugged day to the next.

Which has much to do with why the proud Texan-type folks of Chiriquí, the rich farm province adjoining the Costa Rican border, have been heard to scoff at three generations of to-ing and fro-ing between the US and Panamá over Canal issues. "Turn control of the republic over to us *chiricaños,*" they say, "and it would be so abundantly ranched that the Canal would not matter much one way or the other."

This sturdy spirit has culinary consequences. For most of the way along the highway, it is hitching-rail cuisine. Diners don't show up on cow ponies (pickups, four-wheel-drive farm vehicles, and trailer rigs, yes), but Pan-American Highway roadside restaurants — many of which double as open-air dance halls on weekends — are for hard, hard men. Hotel-hopping is, therefore, prudent — at least until the highway crosses the Río Hato airstrip and sets off along the beach resorts, about 70 miles (112 km) from Panamá City.

The best tourist guide is the twice-yearly *Focus on Panamá,* which is available at the Paso Canoa frontier post and in the better hotels. At Paso Canoa, the Tourist Information Office also hands out a road map. It's not as informative as the Shell road map of Panamá, but since the latter is only available from the company's Panamá City office, you may have to make do with what you can get.

One phone book serves the whole country. The number of any hotel in any town is there on its pages and can be dialed directly for reservations.

Street addresses are less helpful. Newly installed mayors in Panamá come with a built-in compulsion to manifest their authority. Since the municipal coffers usually tend to be empty, the least expensive way to exercise this urge is to change the names of the streets. In Panamá City, for example, it is not uncommon to see a street sign bearing three names or numbers.

Another thing to keep in mind: The Pan-American Highway is not just part of Panamá's highway system. It *is* the system. No sector of the interior, whether of tourist, industrial, farming, or commercial significance, can be reached by land from either the Costa Rican frontier or the capital without traveling part of the way on the Pan-American. However, the highway has any number of convenient turnoffs that lead to most of the nation's major attractions.

By and large, the signs on the highway are clear and accurate. But there is no guarantee that a given signpost might not suffer a little adversity the night before you come rolling by, so signposts should be augmented by a good map.

Panamá is, with a single exception (La Herradura), bereft of trailer parks — an aspect of tourism that has yet to take root here. While an annual convoy of campers and motor homes from the US is given special treatment — much as Portobelo used to arouse from its slumbers to greet the Spanish galleons bearing treasure centuries ago — today's camper would do better to navigate from hotel to hotel, where power and water are assured.

As a frontier town, Paso Canoa is as ramshackle a place as Dodge City ever was. The border runs down its one and only street, and Panamanians and Costa Ricans buy whatever is least expensive in the cinderblock stores lining each side of the border. It is, however, one of Latin America's less nitpicking frontiers for international travelers. A busload can be cleared through both Costa Rican and Panamanian customs and immigration posts in about an hour. For those moving by car, motorbike, or thumb, the frontier delay is a matter of luck — depending on how many trucks, buses, and other vehicles are in line. It can be as brief as 5 minutes on a light traffic day.

There's a Paso Canoa tale that, in a statesmanlike effort to speed up the customs process, the two countries agreed to synchronize the lunch hour of border officials. Noon to 1 PM was decided upon, rather than the previous noon to 1 PM for the Costa Ricans and 1 to 2 PM for the Panamanians. So everyone lunched from noon to 1 PM, an exercise in bureaucracy that extended the midday border closing time from 1 to 2 hours. Someone had forgotten that, year-round, Panamá is on Eastern Standard Time, Costa Rica on Central Standard. Well, it's a funny story, but these days the frontier is a 24-hour operation, traffic having increased twentyfold over the past 10 years.

Panamá has undergone some heat over the treaty, which (in the year 2000) changes the US authority over the Canal to control by the republic. While Panamanians are delighted with the new pact, some resident Americans have left the Canal Zone, disenchanted. Others have taken early retirement and moved into one of the condominiums proliferating in the republic. But most of the Americans employed and living in the Canal Zone have stayed on, rather than uprooting families and jobs.

The Pan-American Highway

PUERTO ARMUELLES: Turn right off the Pan-American Highway about 2 miles after entering Panamá and head for Puerto Armuelles, one of the republic's chief ports, on the coast of the Gulf of Chiriquí in the Pacific Ocean. Created (and at one time owned) by United Brands (formerly United Fruit), the town is one of the few in the area with a population of more than 10,000 and is now controlled by national authorities.

If you've never seen one of Central America's big-time banana farms, Puerto Armuelles rates a look. Most of the plantations are today owned by those who work them. But the Chiriquí Land Company, the local arm of United Brands, remains the only customer of consequence and keeps a close eye on quality control. Chiquita Banana's Big Brother is almost always watching.

A question not to ask in Puerto Armuelles: "Where is the best hotel and restaurant?" They don't exist. Instead, take the question back to David, 55 miles (88 km) northeast, the capital of Chiriquí province.

VOLCÁN and CERRO PUNTA: The turnoff into the hills of Concepción, 17 miles (28 km) from the Costa Rican frontier, leads 22 miles (35 km) up into the hills to El Hato del Volcán, the rarely mentioned full name of the little town everyone calls Volcán. Bring a sweater; the altitude here is 5,000 feet. Farther up the road, about 11 miles (18 km), is Cerro Punta, 1,000 feet higher than Volcán.

If you've spent recent days in the green, crisp uplands of Costa Rica, Volcán and Cerro Punta may be a repetition. But for someone who has just barreled across Central America's scorched coastal plains, these two towns are a lofty haven where not only is the air like wine, but the strawberries are like strawberries. It doesn't take long to understand why the Indians called the region *Chiriquí,* the Valley of the Moon.

The volcanic soil of the slopes of the extinct El Volcán Barú volcano, at 11,411 feet Panamá's highest mountain, and the farming skills of Yugoslav and Swiss communities that settled the high valleys generations ago, have made the region Panamá's fruit and vegetable garden. Nowhere else in the country is there land so meticulously tilled. Nor, except in air-conditioned city offices, do Panamanian girls wear woolen ponchos. It is roughly equivalent, in improbability, to an Aleut maiden in a bikini.

What to do in the area today? The steadiest tourist trade from the US is bird-watching groups. Though it is only the fourth largest country in the mid-Americas area (after El Salvador, Belize, and Costa Rica), Panamá has close to 800 species of native birds. Another 200 or so spend the northern winter here or stop over on their southward migration. Chiriquí is the southernmost habitat of the quetzal, a gorgeous Central American bird with brilliant bronze, green, and red plumage.

Hunters and fishermen also head for the Chiriquí hills. Favorite targets are the torcaza (a white-tailed pigeon) and migratory waterfowl. The torcaza is known locally as *rabiblanco.* To explain to immigration officials that you are visiting the country to shoot *rabiblancos* will not quite do. The term is also slang for members of Panamá's wealthy, traditional ruling class.

The fishing runs from brown trout — not found in the warmer, slothful streams where the Continental Divide dips toward the Canal — to black bass, found in the tarns around Volcán. In both Volcán and Cerro Punta, horses can be hired for trail riding.

Climbers can try El Volcán Barú. Guides are available. Groups should make it a 2-day venture, camping out overnight on the mountain. The climb is more like an uphill march than an alpine feat, but it's man against mountain all the way. Keep in mind there are no cabins or comforts of any sort along the trails. Bring what you need.

Volcán can also be reached by a road that runs up the line of the Costa Rican frontier from Paso Canoa to Río Sereno, and from there along the hillsides to Volcán. Sections of this route are slide-prone. The road from Concepción is more reliable.

DAVID: Sixteen miles (26 km) along the Pan-American Highway from Concepción, David (pop. 50,000) is Panamá's principal city before the Canal area, as well as Chiriquí's capital. Many highway-riding tourists make it their first Panamá stopover.

David refuses to let tourists get on its nerves. It proudly remains a nine-bank, unreconstructed farm town. To capture its flavor, don't look for theaters or art galleries. Check the number of pickup trucks in the parking lots of the *Nacional,* David's *Waldorf-Astoria.*

The big civic event of the year is the mid-March Feria de San José de David. It goes on for a week or more, and Costa Ricans and other Central Americans participate. Dancing in the streets till dawn? Feckless jubilation? Hardly. Cattle, farm equipment, and produce. Regional handicrafts, such as saddles, is what the David fair is all about.

Chiriquí looks to the future. Its Cerro Colorado copper deposits are said to be among the largest in the world. Under construction near Cerro Colorado is Panamá's costliest hydroelectric dam, the $236 million, 255-megawatt La Fortuna project.

David's San José church stands as a symbol of the town's self-reliance. Built centuries ago, the structure's belfry was set apart from the church as a defense against hostile Indians.

The best David has to offer in the currency of the past are a small archaeological museum in the José Felix Olivares School (most exhibits of Chiriquí's pre-Columbian art are in museums in Panamá City) and a modest historical display in the house where Francisco Morazán lived for a while between his 1838 ouster as the last president of the United Provinces of Central America and his subsequent engagement with a firing squad in Costa Rica. Central Americans, the majority of David's foreign tourists, do not come to Panamá to inspect mementos of presidents who got shot. They can do that at home. Tourist attractions are the stores with household appliances and electronic equipment, either unobtainable or heavily taxed at home.

For non-drivers, transport from David to Panamá City is abundant. Three flights daily, on Copa and Aeroperlas, offer a total of about 200 seats. Trunkline buses, some air conditioned with reclining seats, make the run down the Pan-American Highway in about 5 hours. No-frills buses that pick up and deposit passengers along the way, and stop for meals, take a little longer.

BOQUETE: At an altitude of 3,800 feet, Boquete is a half-hour drive up into the foothills from David. It's the tranquil preference of many visitors having business in David, of escapees from the Canal hotlands, of Pan-American Highway travelers, of bird-watchers, fern collectors, orchid fanciers, and of hunters of the feathered species.

Locals call Boquete and the misty mountain walls of its half-hidden valley the Land of the Rainbows. At times, seven rainbows can be seen at once. And in a way, it does come with a pot of gold for some. Some of the Forty-niners who reached Panamá bound for the California gold fields decided that life in these hills would be somewhat steadier than in the gun-toting West. As a result, the Boquete section of the phone book carries a larger proportion of non-Spanish names than is true in most small Panamanian communities.

This place is known as the flower capital of Panamá. The Flower Fair in mid-April, the brightest event of its kind in the republic, draws exhibitors from Central American neighbors and even from Japan.

As in Volcán and Cerro Punta, guided ascents of El Barú can be arranged.

BOCAS DEL TORO and CHANGUINOLA: They say that Bocas del Toro and Changuinola are "somewhere over the rainbow," probably because the only way to get here is by plane. Bocas Town, as natives refer to it, is in northwest Panamá, some 300 miles from Panamá City on the Atlantic side of the isthmus, directly across from Boquete. Access from David is by DC-3.

Columbus stopped by Bocas del Toro on his fourth and final voyage in 1502, and not much has happened since. The archipelago of Bocas del Toro and the Chiriquí Lagoon, its islands' guard, provide as fine an anchorage as can be found on the coast. Fittingly, it's named Bahía Almirante (Bay of the Admiral). Unhappily, once a ship is moored here, there is nothing much for it to load except bananas from the Chiriquí Land Company's Changuinola farms (Chiquita's headquarters) and cocoa.

For the tourist there's reef fishing, skin diving, turtle steaks, a largely English-speaking population, and no danger of getting caught in traffic.

Copa and Aeroperlas fly from Bocas del Toro to Panamá City. For those tired of the highway and happy to devote a day or so to watching an 18-inch tide rise and fall, take this detour en route to Panamá City.

En Route from David-Boquete – During the drive from the David-Boquete intersection down the Pan-American Highway, use one of the several gas stations thereabouts to ready car and riders for the 188-mile (300-km) run down a fine stretch of highway to Santiago de Veraguas, the next town in which gas stations and restaurants will be found.

This leg of the journey follows a gentle roller coaster over what was empty land until a new section of the highway opened a few years ago. The first 44 miles of road hugs the base of the mountains, passing La Chorcha waterfall, a lovely sight when it is rushing, full of rainy-season water. On the right, Panamá's richest cattlelands stretch to the sea. The San Felix turnoff leads to the beaches of Las Lajas, where seaside tourism facilities are planned for the future. This shoreline is so attractive that, during major Panamanian fiestas, as many as 10,000 holidaymakers camp here despite the lack of organized accommodations. The next highway turnoff of significance is at Guabalá, about 7 miles (12 km) farther on. This turnoff was the old central highway to Santiago, through Sona, and it's in rough condition compared to the highway that replaced it. It has its attractions for the pastoral-minded, despite what the road does to car and passengers. The area serves fine farmland that one day will be brought into production by farmers cashing in on the Pan-American Highway access.

Tolé, gathering place of the Guaymi Indians, is just a few hundred yards off the Pan-American Highway, 3 miles (5 km) past the Guabalá turnoff. The Guaymi definition of a *casería,* or village, comprises a couple of huts on one ridge, a couple more on another (with a 2,000-foot gorge between them), and a farther hut up a slope and virtually hidden by clouds. Some of these villages are as much as 14 trail hours by pack pony from the nearest road.

Saturdays and Sundays are market days in Tolé. The Indians gather to sell produce, buy goods, and gossip. Guaymi women wear floor-length, shapeless, varicolored, Mother Hubbard dresses. Among the best buys from the Guaymi is the *chaquira,* a shoulder-wide collar in beaded geometrical patterns, and the *cháorra,* also known as *mochila,* basically a string bag. Drivers buying souvenirs don't even have to go into Tolé. Close to the turnoff, the Indians have set up souvenir booths near the highway.

From the Tolé turnoff to Santiago, 59 miles (95 km) of empty land lies ahead. One consolation: The Panamá National Guard's Highway Patrol is helpful and well intentioned if you get stranded for any reason.

SANTIAGO: This city is the capital of Veraguas, Panamá's only sea-to-shining-sea province, in the center of the republic. Across the range lies Belén (sometimes called Bethlehem), where, at the mouth of the river of the same name, Columbus established Panamá's first European community. Since 1914, Santiago has been the educational center of the republic. The Normal School was moved here in that year, and since then it has been the sole supplier of the republic's public school teachers. The decentralized National University has a campus here. General Omar Torrijos Herrera, president of Panamá for 10 years (a record in this category) until his resignation in 1978, was born and raised near Santiago. Both his parents were teachers.

About 7 miles (12 km) down the highway toward the Canal is the turnoff for Atalaya. The village church there is probably the nearest thing to a Panamanian shrine. Panamanians from all social strata come here to solicit or give thanks for divine favors.

AZUERO PENINSULA: Down the highway 23 miles (37 km), mostly running between sugar fields, is Divisa, the turnoff for the Azuero Peninsula. The region is sketchily developed. Los Santos, a little beyond Chitré and 27 miles (44 km) from Divisa, is old Spanish Panamá, tile-roofed and charming. It is the site of Panamá's 1821 proclamation of independence from Spain, and its little museum recalls those times.

Business-oriented Chitré, a six-bank farming center, makes no effort to lure the tourist. It serves more as a hot water base from which to prowl the peninsula. The hometown airline, Chitreana, flies twice daily to Panamá City's downtown Paitilla Airport, a 40-minute flight.

The most enduring of Panamá's music and dance stem from Azuero's mestizo heritage. Increasingly, Panamá's Carnival, virtually a week-long fiesta that folds at sunup on Ash Wednesday, is shifting into the interior in general and to Azuero in particular. Hotel space at this time is scarce. Easter is the other time of year when the chance of finding an empty hotel room in the interior is slender. The where-to-stay problem is not insoluble. Guararé in mid-September and Ocú in mid-January celebrate their respective saint's day with small-town happiness. Hotel rooms will be available in Santiago or Chitré or Penonomé or Aguadulce or Los Santos or Las Tablas, none of which is more than a few hours' drive from these festivities.

After folkloric celebrations, Azuero's major attraction is broad miles of people-free beaches. Local folk, busy with cows and crops, take the beaches for granted.

AGUADULCE: Fourteen miles (22 km) down the Pan-American Highway from Divisa is Aguadulce. Both the decor and the menu of the *Interamericano* hotel are attractive to veteran travelers, who make this their prime dining spot on the run between the Canal and David. Aguadulce's additional claims to fame include: a salt industry based on running the Pacific tide of up to 20 feet into salt pans and letting the sun evaporate it; a small river port; the heart of the republic's sugar industry; and a battlefield from the Colombian civil war, the War of 1,000 Days.

En Route from Aguadulce – Through the sugar fields 6 miles (10 km) down the highway is Natá, and what some say is the oldest church in continuous use on the American continent. While the claim is questionable, there's no question that the church reflects its age and warrants a visit. In contrast to the venerable edifice is the nearby Nestlé plant, the biggest processor of Panamanian agricultural products.

PENONOMÉ: This area, 11 miles (18 km) farther east along the highway, was the heart of Panamá's Indian culture long before (and during) the time Columbus was setting up a handful of grass huts in Belén as a symbol and example of Western civilization. For archaeologists, it has been the most fruitful site on the isthmus, and a considerable proportion of the exhibits in the Museum of the Panamanian, probably Panamá City's best museum, are from Penonomé. *Huacas,* the gold ornaments that traders promoted into symbols of Panamá in days gone by, were obtained for the most part by grave-robbing in the area of the Penonomé Indian civilization.

LA PINTADA: A short drive into the hills from Penonomé leads to La Pintada, home of the Panamá hat. These straw hats, worn by Panamanians and other isthmus residents, have a black pattern woven into the white straw with multicolored cords and thongs. In La Pintada a visitor can be measured and order a hat bearing the buyer's name and/or any pattern. Delivery takes a while, though.

FARALLÓN: Where the highway runs plumb across the Río Hato airstrip, about 12 miles (19 km) down the highway from Penonomé, it is close to history of modern vintage. By the seaward end of the strip, right on the beach of the Gulf of Panamá, is the home that ex-President Torrijos used as his Camp David during the Canal treaty negotiations. Named Farallón, for the islet off the end of the airstrip, it was here that US senators, congressmen, negotiators, and assorted VIPs came for treaty talks. Farallón is not a national monument battlefield; it's a National Guard post. Close by, however, is the *Farallón* hotel, the westernmost property in the chain of beach resorts that stretches 50 miles along the Pacific coast to Punta Chamé.

As beaches, those between Farallón and Punta Chamé are neither so broad nor so beckoning as those of the Azuero Peninsula or Las Lajas.

En Route from Farallón – From west to east, after Farallón, the beaches with cabins and other holiday facilities are: Santa Clara, 71 miles (115 km) from Panamá City, with *Muu Muu* and *Vista Bella* cabin complexes; Río Mar, 58 miles (93 km) from Panamá City, with swimming in both river and ocean, and the *Río Mar* cabins and restaurant; El Palmar, 57 miles (92 km) from Panamá City, with cabins; San Carlos, practically contiguous with El Palmar, retains a rural charm with shaded tables and a restaurant among beach facilities set up by the national tourist office; Coronado, 50 miles (80 km) from Panamá City, is Panamá's most ambitious beach development. Many of the houses would be elegant in any exclusive suburb. The golf course is one of the three best on the isthmus, and facilities include an airstrip and supermarket, and its restaurant is the best for maybe 50 miles in any direction. Rentals, including apartments in a multi-story building, can be negotiated at the development manager's office. Gorgona, 43 miles (70 km) from Panamá City, features the *Jayes* hotel and the *Ocean Blue Cabins.* Punta

Chamé is reached from a highway turnoff at Bejuco, 40 miles (64 km) from Panamá City. To get to the development at its western tip requires about 12 miles (19 km) of backtracking down the Chamé Peninsula. There's ocean swimming on the southern side of this 10-mile tongue of sandy land, and calmwater swimming on the north side on the bay. By air, this is the closest resort beach to the capital. By road, Gorgona is the closest beach.

EL VALLE: Once tired of the beaches, you might swing off the highway 3 miles (5 km) before the Río Mar turnoff, cross the mountains, and drive up to El Valle, at an altitude of 2,000 feet. The Sunday morning market here is the interior market best known to "Canalsiders," and a good proportion of the shoppers are US citizen-residents of the isthmus. Bright bead necklaces, straw items, soapstone animal carvings, and all manner of produce are sold. Golden frogs are said to leap about beneath the area's odd, squarish trees, though they are rarely seen outside of the bush.

En Route from El Valle – Getting back on the Pan-American Highway at the Bejuca turnoff (the entrance to the Punta Chamé resort), it's about a 40-mile (64-km) drive to Chorrera, a sprawling dormitory for Panamá City, where the road turns into the patched and potholed remains of a time-worn thoroughfare. About a 10-minute drive farther is La Herradura, Panamá's only trailer park, with plug-in facilities, a pool, restaurant, and riding horses for hire. Mobile home and camper travelers stop off here in the countryside to rest up and organize before heading on to Panamá City, where standard mobile home facilities are nonexistent.

PANAMÁ CITY: For a detailed report on the city, its hotels, and restaurants, see *Panamá City*, THE CITIES. As the Pan-American Highway winds its way to Arraiján, and then on down the cool, green slopes of Ancrón Hill, you'll come upon "the Crossroads of the World," Panamá's number one city with a population of a half-million, standing near the Pacific entrance to the Canal. This place hasn't had an easy time of it since its 1519 founding by the Spanish on the Atlantic side of the Canal.

Sacked by Henry Morgan and his merciless cutthroats in 1671, the Spanish picked up the pieces and took the city 7 miles inland on the Pacific side, set it up on a peninsula, and surrounded it with huge walls to keep out the likes of Morgan and his rowdies. As a center of commerce, Panamá prospered until the late 18th century, when Spain decided to reroute its vessels around the Horn. Things looked bleak until the gold rush of 1849. Prosperity returned as settlers went through Panamá on their way to the West Coast. But the rush was short-lived, and the town's economic fortunes declined until the Canal began to be built in earnest in 1903.

The result of the trauma undergone by the city is that today it wears three faces: Old Panamá, comprising the few remnants left by Morgan (the King's Bridge, the ruins of the Convent and Church of San José, and the Cabildo); colonial Panamá, with its 108-year-old cathedral, iron-laced balconies, cobblestone streets (remnants of the walls still stand); and modern Panamá, with wide boulevards, elegant shops, restaurants, hotels, casinos, and modern office buildings. A marble statute of Balboa looks out at the ocean he discovered.

En Route from Panamá City – Beyond Panamá City, the highway is in good shape for about 62 miles (100 km), passing the new Tucumen International Airport and going on to where it bridges the lake backed up behind the Bayano hydroelectric dam and comes to an end. Roadbuilding continues, with plans to extend the highway through Darién, the republic's easternmost province, to connect it with Colombia. As it is, the swamps and wilderness of Darién today are harder to traverse than when Balboa crossed to stand silent upon a peak. Balboa had more Indians — therefore more trails and guides.

SAN BLAS ISLANDS: Off Panamá's coast in the Caribbean are the San Blas Islands and their Cuna Indians, among Panamá's most exotic attractions. The island chain is a sort of 130-mile, bamboo-hutted, coral-based Venice. Panamanians say there are as many islands as there are days in the year. About 30 are permanently inhabited, and on them it's 100% occupancy — no room to build another hut.

Until recently, there was a viable and wonderful vacation spot at Pidertupo Village, but a local Indian skirmish burned out the hotel and all facilities. Visitors can fly over for a single-day excursion or make arrangements to stay at one of the hotels mentioned below. Canoes can also be hired for day trips to small atolls. There have been no recent recurrences of incidents like the one at Pidertupo. The islands are indeed lovely and interesting, with rustic, but comfortable, accommodations, and the Cunas welcoming. Check with Margo Tours (phone: 64-9739); Gordon Dalton Travel Agency (phone: 28-2555); Agencias Giscome (phone: 62-0111); Turista Internacional (phone: 64-8682); or Caribe Travel (phone: 69-3011). All are in Panamá City.

Uncommon among Indian races, the Cunas can take civilization or leave it alone. A Cuna who has lived and worked on a Canal Zone army post with color TV in his barracks (and many have) returns to his island lifestyle without any apparent sense of loss. One aspect of this lifestyle, as closely adhered to in the islands as in the Canalside cities, is a firm commitment to cash. While the men work on plantations on the mainland or fish, the women make *molas* — hand-stitched in reverse appliqué, and multicolored — which they price in line with big-city inflation. Photos of *mola*-clad Cuna women will cost about 25¢ per person photographed — so count your change before they line up 6 children to pose for your picture.

COLÓN: The second city of Panamá (pop. 73,000) is at the northern terminus of the Canal. This place could have itself declared a monument to Joseph Conrad and Somerset Maugham — it could easily serve as a movie set for any of their novels of men and mores coming ungummed in the tropics. There's nothing much for a tourist to do around Colón except to savor its raunchy disarray and watch his wallet. A tour of the city takes about 15 minutes.

Getting to Colón is the fun. The Panamá Railroad, for which the town was created as a California gold rush terminal, follows a scenic route beside the Canal, and the trip is recommended. The air-conditioned ride across the isthmus on the hemisphere's oldest transcontinental railroad costs $2. The city has two good restaurants: the *VIP* on Front Street, right by the railroad crossing; and the *Canal Zone Yacht Club,* beside the failed French canal in adjacent Cristóbal.

PORTOBELO: Some 30 miles (47 km) northeast of Colón, Portobelo was one of the great treasure ports of the Spanish Main. Then for two centuries or more it became a sort of Brigadoon, awakening only once a year for its October 21 festival. The town (whose fair, when the treasure fleet was in, handled the silver and gold of Perú and the products of the wealthiest cities of Europe) in these two sleeping centuries did not even have a road to Cólon. The road exists now. You can ride to see the forts that blasted away at the all-star buccaneers of their era. You can also see the harbor mouth islet near which Drake was buried at sea, after dying aboard his ship in the harbor. There are good beaches and fine wreck scuba diving here, but no hotels.

BEST EN ROUTE

There are a number of especially fine or interesting accommodations at your disposal in Panamá, for the most part in the moderate, $20 to $40 price range for a double with bath. The going rate for a double with bath which we classify as expensive is $50 to $100; $7 to $17 is inexpensive. Some of these prices are based on the American plan, which includes three meals a day. Most of the larger hotels accept major credit cards. Except where noted, rooms are modest and low key.

VOLCÁN

Dos Ríos – A mountain rill ripples clear and cool below the bedrooms, past the bar and dining room. Beside it the soil is rich and the grass is soft and the flowers are bright. The 16-room hotel is at the western end of the village, where the road heads for Río Sereno. Both American and European plans are available (phone: 5-0271). Expensive.

Bambito – A modern hotel, complete with resort facilities that include tennis courts and a pool, as well as such activities as horseback riding, fishing, and hunting. Reservations through Utell in the US (phone: in New York, 212-757-2981; elsewhere, 800-223-9868) or Moonlight, Inc., Calle Girardo Ortega #6, Panamá 4 (phone: 23-50-84). Expensive.

California – A motel with no frills, no discomforts. Patronized by independents who rise and rest at eccentric hours, such as hunters and bird-watchers. The restaurant and bar are sympathetic to them. 26 rooms (phone: 5-0272). Inexpensive.

DAVID

Nacional – It has 76 rooms and the best restaurant in town; it's air conditioned and equipped with a tennis court, pool, bowling alley and casino. Apdo. 37 (phone: 5-2221). Moderate.

BOQUETE

Panamonte – Almost two generations of Canalside Americans have sublimated their longing for the soft, quiet hills of home at this gracious, 21-room haven. An old residence among flowers and close to the coffee plantations, its contrast with company housing and sun-scorched locks is therapy. In the bar-lounge is the rediscovery of a household fixture that youngsters from the hot country may never have seen — a fireplace. Both European and American plan available, depending on time of year (phone: 5-5327). Moderate.

Los Fundadores – Not a hotel beside a dancing stream so much as a hotel bestraddling a dancing stream. The brook is as all-pervading at 25-room *Fundadores* as a better-known waterway is farther down the isthmus (phone: 5-5327). Inexpensive.

LOS SANTOS

La Villa – The most picturesque town on the Azuero Peninsula deserves the most pleasant hotel on the peninsula. With 49 rooms, it is air conditioned and has a bar and restaurant (phone: 6-4845). Inexpensive.

RÍO MAR

Río Mar Cabins – The 13 cabins are as unadorned as a surfboard. The restaurant, on a bluff with a clear view out to sea, is held by many to offer the best eating along the 50-mile suntan lotion coast. San Carlos (phone: 64-2985). Moderate.

CORONADO

Villas-Golf Club – Set on the republic's most ambitious beach development, the eight 2- and 3-bedroom villas are élegant. Bar, restaurant, pool, and tennis. The golf course is one of the three best on the isthmus. Apdo. 4381, Pan. 5 (phone: 23-1342). Expensive.

GORGONA

Jayes – The closest approximation to a hotel rather than beach cottages between Farallón and Punta Chamé, though a casual, seaside style prevails. Hammocks swing lazily around the pool, and a band entertains. Air conditioning (phone: 23-7775). Moderate.

PUNTA CHAMÉ

Punta Chamé – A 20-room cabin-style motel, with restaurant and bar on the beach where you can fish, boat, surf, hike, and skin dive. The chef will cook your deep-sea catch to your taste while you take in the terrific view of the mountains across the water. Apdo. 10520, Pan. 4 (phone: 23-1747). Moderate.

EL VALLE

Club Campestre – A lodge-like property set back against the valley wall in ample grounds, with a view over the valley and most that goes on therein. Not much does. Visitors here are content to exchange a civil nod with such golden frogs that may chance by their rockers and to contemplate the growth rate of any square trees to be seen from the porch or bar. Huge fireplaces and a color TV in an adjacent sitting room. 22 rooms (phone: 25-4707). Moderate.

SAN BLAS ISLANDS

Posada Anai – On Wichub Walla Island, all the rooms in the two-story building around the pool are comfortable and have electricity; only some have bath. Boat transfer from the Porvenir Airport. Moderate.

San Blas – On Nalunega Island. Very rustic accommodations in thatched huts with candlelight, bathing in open-air showers, and toilet facilities in a separate hut; hammocks hang outside the cottages. The hotel is run by Luis Burgos, who will organize canoes to take guests fishing, snorkeling, and island-hopping. Meals in the dining cottage or daytime picnics packed. Boat transfer from Porvenir. Moderate.

COLÓN

Sotelo – While there's nothing fancy here, the 45-room hotel is comfortable, sits in the heart of town, and the price is right. Casino, restaurant, bar, coffee shop. Av. Amador Guerrero y Herrera (phone: 47-6700). Inexpensive.

Paraguay

Paraguay, like her northwestern neighbor, Bolivia, is a landlocked nation. Relatively unknown, Paraguay shares her other borders with Argentina to the south and Brazil to the east. Its 157,047 square miles contain primarily barren plains, subtropical farmland, and thick jungle. Temperatures are in the 90s and 100s F (32° to 39°C) from November through March, and in the 70s and 80s F (21° to 28°C) the rest of the year. About 650,000 inhabitants out of a national total population of 3,600,000 live in the capital, Asunción, a port on the Río Paraguay (for a complete report, see *Asunción,* THE CITIES).

When discovered by the Spanish conquistador Diego de Solis in 1524, Paraguay was inhabited by the Guaraní Indians, a mellow group who welcomed the Europeans. During the next two centuries, the Jesuits exerted a strong presence in the southern part of the country, where they built a number of missions with the cooperation of the Indian workers and craftsmen. Paraguay gained independence from Spain in 1811, a liberation that came more peacefully than the devasting War of Triple Alliance against Brazil, Uruguay, and Argentina 50 years later. During the 1930s, Paraguayan forces fought the Bolivians in the Chaco Wars and gained new western territory. Since independence, Paraguay's history has featured a cast of flamboyant, insular dictators. The latest and longest lasting in the line of *caudillos* (leaders) is President General Alfredo Stroessner, who has been in the Presidential Palace since 1954.

Although it is possible to drive through Paraguay, with the exception of the Golden Triangle, roads are not well surfaced or in reasonable condition, and it is recommended that you fly or take bus or river transport to the interior. If you do drive yourself, bring spare parts and be prepared to make your own repairs. Road services are few and far between. And be sure to have proper insurance, and check that your *carnet* and insurance papers are in order and easily accessible (see *Touring by Car,* GETTING READY TO GO).

There are four routes in this chapter: The Golden Triangle takes you on a circuit in the region of Asunción and includes the towns of Tobatí, where a famous carver fashions wooden statues of saints, and Itauguá, where *ñandutí* lace is made. To tour the Chaco region west of the Paraguay River, you fly from Asunción to Filadelfia, visit the Mennonite farms, and return to the capital. The Jesuit Trail runs from Asunción through Encarnación, and among the fascinating missions, the Jesus Mission is the largest. The Paraguay side of Iguazú Falls, the giant cataracts on the Paraguay–Brazil–Argentina border, is briefly covered; for a more detailed description of the entire area, see *Brazil.*

The Golden Triangle

To travel through eastern Paraguay is to turn the clock back a century or more. The landscape is dotted with neat little villages, many as old as 300 years, each with its own central plaza and large Catholic church. Crude oxcarts and horse-drawn carriages are a common sight, and women wash the family clothes in streams at the side of the road, with jagged rocks as their only clotheslines. One-horsepower sugarcane refineries stand beside simple, thatch-roofed homes.

But even in rural Paraguay times are changing. Tractors are an increasingly common sight, and the introduction of modern farming techniques is increasing the production of cotton, tobacco, soybeans, and sugarcane on the fertile soil of the Paraguay and Paraná river valleys. Just east of Asunción is beautiful Lake Ypacaraí: The area here abounds with pretty waterfalls and is a center of the fine Paraguayan handicrafts, including *ñandutí*, the delicate spiderweb lace.

A newcomer, Paraguay really didn't make the international tourist scene until about 10 years ago, with the completion of a network of roads that formed a triangular route joining various lakes and other attractions. Hence the area became known as Circuito de Oro, the Golden Circuit or Golden Triangle, as it is more commonly known in English. It's very possible to cover this route in 1 day and, fortunately for the tourist, the entire route is a paved, two-lane highway: You can either rent a car in Asunción or take one of the many mini-bus tours operated by the larger tourist agencies, including the Mennonite-owned Menno Travel S.R.L., 551 Azara St. (phone: 41-210).

If you do prefer to go it alone, then obtain a map from the Instituto Geografico y Militar, available at all stationery stores (*librerias*) in Asunción. You might also want to do a little reading; try *The Land of Lace and Legend,* available in most bookstores in the capital.

En Route from Asunción – Follow the main highway that starts at Asunción and runs due east to Brazil. About 5 miles (8 km) from the city, Paraguay's second major highway branches off to the southeast, and it is here that the Golden Triangle begins. The first leg takes you through rolling hill country; small farms dot the landscape, and you pass several houses with sugarcane refineries in their yards. A single horse provides the power to drive the machine that crushes the cane. About 20 miles (32 km) from Asunción the highway passes through the town of Ita, a center of pottery production. Because most shops sport their wares right on the curb, you won't miss them as you drive through town. There is a large variety of decorative pieces as well as functional items that you can buy here. The hand-painted hens are popular, but you can also pick up other animal figures, flower pots, water jugs, bowls, and so on. The pottery is unfired, so be careful, since unfired means fragile.

About 7 miles (11 km) beyond Ita is the ancient colonial town of Yaguarón.

YAGUARÓN: Founded in 1530 (two years after Asunción), this town is known mainly for its church, which is on the right just beyond the center of town. Completed in 1720, it took 50 years to build and remains a prime example of Spanish colonial architecture: The large edifice is flanked by covered verandas, and a bell tower sits in front of it. The intricate carvings on the altar and elsewhere are interesting. There is a small museum near the church in the restored home of Dr. José Gaspar Rodríguez de Francia, who ruled Paraguay from its independence in 1811 until his death in 1840. Since the museum's hours are irregular (it's officially open on Tuesday, Thursday, Saturday, and Sunday afternoons, as well as Sunday mornings), inquire at the church for opening times.

En Route from Yaguarón – Continue 9 more miles (15 km) through the rolling hills to the town of Paraguarí and turn left, onto the second leg of the triangle — the narrow, winding road that eventually ends at the Asunción-Brazil Highway. From Paraguarí, the road climbs steadily higher into the hills, offering fine views of the countryside. The local folk call these rather modest hills La Cordillera (the Ridge).

Continue on the highway for another 14 miles (23 km) to a sign for Chololo Falls and a restaurant, *Chololo,* on your left. The restaurant is a fine place to stop. Not only does it have a good view of Chololo Falls, but the dining room itself was constructed over a small stream that tumbles across the rocks and through lush, tropical shrubbery among which the tables are set. If you want to swim in the lake, there are bathhouses, complete with showers, for changing your clothes.

About 1½ miles (2 km) farther is the turnoff to the right for the Pirareta Falls. The entrance is marked by an archway and sign for the Pirareta Farm (Colonial Pirareta). From here, it's a long 6 miles (10 km) over a rough road to Pirareta, which is somewhat larger than Chololo. The pools here are large enough for real swimming, but you'll have more fun at Chololo.

From Pirareta, the narrow, winding road continues north past the town of Piribebuy, which has another church; from here, it's about 9 miles (14 km) to the junction with the Asunción-Brazil Highway. Turn left at the dead end, and you are now on the third leg of the Golden Triangle. After 6 miles (10 km) on this busy two-lane road you enter Caacupé.

CAACUPÉ: The holiest of Paraguay's shrines is the Catholic church at Caacupé, with its Blue Virgin. Every December 8 (feast of the Immaculate Conception), thousands of the faithful descend on Caacupé from all directions, starting out on foot after work on the evening of the seventh and arriving in Caacupé at sunrise, in time for the first mass on the morning of the eighth. The less faithful, less healthy, or less adventuresome make the trip by bus or car, and the president of Paraguay visits the shrine by helicopter.

The church with the Blue Virgin is one block above the main plaza, on your left as you drive through town. The Virgin stands above and behind the altar in her blue robes. Street vendors peddle religious souvenirs at the side of the church. If you want a hardy meal, go to the *Uruguayo* hotel in the center of town.

If you have time, you can take the side trip from Caacupé to the village of Tobatí, 10 miles (16 km) over a dirt road. Turn right (north) at the main plaza in Caacupé at the sign for Tobatí: This road takes you even farther into the hinterland. The chief attraction in Tobatí is the saint maker (*santero*), who carves small wooden statues of saints. His teams of oxen (as many as six) and oxcarts laden with logs are beautiful, but too large to fit in your suitcase. There are also animal and bird statues and a variety of pots and vases, but the saint maker is best known for his holy images, which are unique and small enough to take with you. In other villagers' homes you can purchase crude wooden masks. You can also visit the old church on the plaza or the Shrine of the Virgin off the road at the base of a cliff that is on your left on the road from Caacupé to Tobatí.

En Route from Caacupé – As you leave Caacupé, you slowly climb a long hill with large eucalyptus trees on either side. This is the National School of

Agronomy, a center for agricultural research and training. Note the nicely contoured fields on both sides of the road — a rare sight in Paraguay. As you cross the crest of the hill and start down, you will catch your first glimpse of Lake Ypacaraí. At the bottom of the hill turn off the highway onto the paved road for about 1 mile to reach the town of San Bernardino on the lake's shore. The lake was once the weekend home of prominent families from Asunción; now it is polluted, and swimming can be recommended only in the pools of the luxurious *Casino San Bernardino* hotel or one of the several country clubs.

If you retrace your steps to the main highway and turn right, you can continue on the Asunción, passing the lakeside town of Ypacaraí. Continue until the town of Itauguá, just 18 miles (30 km) east of Ascunción.

ITAUGUÁ: This is the place to purchase the beautiful, finely woven *ñandutí,* as it is known in the Guaraní Indian vernacular. Legend has it that the original *ñandutí* lace was spun by a spider to rescue a servant girl who had accidentally ruined her mistress's mantilla. In fact, the art of making *ñandutí* was introduced from Spain and Portugal by the nuns, who then taught it to the Indian women. The delicate lacework is embroidered in small circular and floral patterns on large looms and comes in white or colors such as violet, yellow, and red. It is not to be confused with *Aó Po'i* embroidery, designs embroidered on clothing and pieces of cloth.

You'll see the large (10 feet long) *ñandutí* lace tablecloths draped over wooden racks at the roadside. They're quite inviting, but before you purchase one, be advised that they are difficult to iron. They say in Asunción that the Paraguayan Embassy in London used to return the lace tablecloths to Paraguay by ship to be washed, pressed, and stretched on the racks in Itauguá after each dinner party. Fortunately, there is a great variety of smaller items from which to choose; prices do vary, so shop around. The less pretentious looking shops often have the same quality goods at lower prices. However, there is no uniformity of quality, so check the workmanship of each place mat, napkin, or whatever before you buy. There is some room for bargaining.

En Route from Itauguá – It is only about 25 minutes back to downtown Asunción. The highway becomes increasingly crowded, and there is little of special interest along the way.

BEST EN ROUTE

On all routes in Paraguay, hotels are few and far between, and those that do exist tend to be small, comfortable, and often cost under $20 a night. Most travelers prefer to spend their nights back in Asunción, but for those who plan to overnight on the road, it's wise to make careful advance reservations in any one of the hotels listed below. If there are no phone numbers, then make arrangements through your travel agent or the tourist office in Asunción.

CAACUPÉ

Uruguayo – This small, clean hotel has a restaurant famous for its hearty meals. In the center of town (phone: 222 Caacupé).

LAKE YPACARAÍ

Del Lago – An old hotel with a rustic atmosphere that will remind you of a bygone era, in much the same way as does the *Gran Hotel del Paraguay* in Asunción (no wonder, since both are under the same management). Lakeside (phone: 201, San Bernardino).

Casino San Bernardino – Surrounded by gardens, this deluxe lakeside property has a swimming pool, restaurant, casino, and discotheque. Lakeside (phone: 391-4, San Bernardino).

The Chaco

The area to the west of the Río Paraguay is a harsh, desolate plain called the Chaco, encompassing all of the western section of the country and extending into Bolivia and Argentina. It's a hot area — about 100°F (37°C) — dry and windy. The first 150 miles (241 km) are grasslands, and beyond that are scrubby forests. The Chaco is best known for the bloody Chaco War that Paraguay and Bolivia fought to a standoff in the early 1930s.

Sparsely populated, the principal settlement in the Chaco is the area around the towns of Filadelfia and Loma Plata, about 300 miles (483 km) northwest of Ascunción via the Trans-Chaco Highway. Most of the people are Mennonites, who came from Canada, Russia, Germany, and other countries searching for freedom to practice their religion, which includes, among other things, exclusion from military service. Today, there are about 10,000 Mennonites in the Chaco; their principal language is German rather than Spanish. Despite the harsh living conditions, they manage to battle the constant dust storms and have developed a thriving economy based mostly upon soybeans, peanuts, dairy products, and cattle.

The Chaco is an interesting place to visit — for about 2 days. There is only one way to get to Filadelfia and that is by road, and there is only one place to go to make proper arrangements — the Menno Travel agency in Asunción (551 Azara St.). The mailing address is Casilla 713, Asunción (phone: 41-210). The agency will arrange for your round-trip NASA bus tickets, as well as your stay in Filadelfia at the *Floridá,* the only hotel in the area.

It is possible, however, to drive the Trans-Chaco Highway to Filadelfia yourself. Sections of the so-called highway are now paved, but part of it is not. Four-wheel-drive vehicles are recommended to negotiate the other parts; when it rains, the army closes the road and you're stuck — either in a mudhole or at a police barricade. In good weather, however, the trip can be made in 6 to 7 hours.

FILADELFIA: About 25 miles (40 km) north of the Trans-Chaco Highway, here you will want to visit the small, flourishing agribusinesses, including the cheese-making and peanut oil factories. If you can, hire someone to drive you out to see the farms in the surrounding area. The most important crops, besides soybeans and peanuts, are castor beans and cotton. Beef and dairy cattle are also raised, and the meat and dairy products are shipped out to Asunción.

While driving around, you can also visit the other Mennonite settlement, Loma Plata, south toward the highway. Back in Filadelfia you can sit in on a Mennonite service if you wish. You'll enjoy the singing even if you don't understand what is being said.

BEST EN ROUTE

There's only one place to stay in the Chaco — the *Floridá* hotel in Filadelfia, with its new wing, which has rooms with bath and air-conditioning (in the old wing, baths are shared). Breakfast included. It's best to make reservations before you get there.

The Jesuit Mission Trail

In 1600 the Spanish (actually, the Jesuit order of priests) began to filter into Paraguay. They found the area already occupied by the Guaraní Indians, a nomadic and pacific people who did not resist the Spanish invaders. Instead, the Guaranís formed an alliance with the Spanish, intermarried, and even went so far as to defend the Spanish forts against marauding Indians from nearby Brazil. Because the Guaranís didn't war with the Spanish, like other South American tribes, they were not destroyed. Indeed, they prospered. Today, there are some 27,000 Guaranís left as well as 23,000 other Indians, who, combined, represent 2% of the entire Paraguayan population. Guaraní is still a prominent language here, as Quechua is in the Andes.

The Jesuits set up numerous *reducciones,* or missions; they taught the Guaranís how to farm and speak Spanish and converted them to Catholicism. In return, the Indians built great stone churches in the forests. The construction of these churches, however, was halted in the mid-eighteenth century, when the Jesuits began to criticize the divine right of the Spanish throne. Angered at their "rebellion," King Charles III of Spain ordered them out of Paraguay in 1767. After the Jesuits left, the *reducciones* were taken over by the Dominicans and four other orders.

Today, these fine churches and missions — in southern Paraguay, southwestern Brazil, and northeastern Argentina — lie in ruins, but bit by bit are being restored. (The most extensive restoration, and the mission most visited today, is San Ignácio Mini, in the town of San Ignácio, across the Río Paraná in the Mesopotamia section of Argentina.) Two of the missions in Paraguay, Trinidad and Jesús, are accessible from Asunción via Encarnación; the trip takes 2 nights (or 3 days), and tours are available from the major tourist agencies in Asunción. If you need any help, contact the National Tourism Office in Asunción (ground floor, corner of Calle Oliva and Calle Alberti).

The following route takes you from Asunción to the Paraguayan ruins and back over the Asunción-Encarnación Highway. For the first 38 miles (63 km) of this trip between Asunción and Paraguarí, you take the first leg of the Golden Triangle. Instead of turning left at Paraguarí, however, continue straight ahead through the town of Carapegua until you reach Villa Florida, on the banks of the Río Tebicuary, almost 100 miles (162 km) southeast of Asunción.

VILLA FLORIDA: If fishing is your thing, then 1 or 2 days here should be a joy. Paraguay's rivers are teeming with fish, but the rivers are for the most part inaccessible and facilities completely undeveloped, with the exception of Villa Florida. The prize catch is the *dorado,* which often weighs 15 to 20 pounds, puts up quite a fight, and makes excellent eating. Other fish commonly caught in the Tebicuary are the catfish (*surubí*), often larger than the prized *dorado,* and the infamous piranha fish, which is often used in soups. There are several places to stay, and you can get a good meal at the restaurant adjoining the Shell station on the lefthand side of the street as you drive through Villa Florida.

En Route from Villa Florida – Just 11 miles (20 km) beyond is the small village of San Miguel, one place in Paraguay where handwoven woolen articles are still found. In the shops you'll find roughly finished blankets and sweaters that are very inexpensive.

From San Miguel, you enter the Jesuit mission area. The towns bear the names given to them by the Jesuits: San Juan Bautista, San Ignácio (not to be confused with the better-known San Ignácio, Argentina), and Santa Rosa. The next 75 miles (121 km) are an important cattle-raising area. Toward the end of this stretch the highway passes through rolling hills, where you will catch your first glimpses of the Río Paraná and Encarnación.

ENCARNACIÓN: Although this is Paraguay's third largest city, its population is only about 60,000; the city's size, however, is steadily increasing due to the construction of the Yacyreta hydroelectric complex, a short way downstream. The lower part of Encarnación will be flooded once the Yacyreta Dam is completed. While not as high as the Itaipú Dam now under construction farther up the Paraná, Yacyreta will be about 60 miles wide, to prevent the mighty Paraná from going around the dam on either side. While there is nothing of particular interest to the tourist here, those wishing to spend the night will find modern and comfortable accommodations in the *Novotel.* Alternatively, those willing to push on another 12 miles (19 km) toward the Paraguayan Jesuit ruins can stay at the *Tirol,* a resort hotel built of stone.

Or you can cross the Paraná on the ferry and stay in the city of Posadas, Argentina.

En Route from Encarnación – To reach the Paraguayan Jesuit ruins and the *Tirol Hotel,* take the new Encarnación–Presidente Stroessner Highway. Ciudad Presidente Stroessner is Paraguay's second largest city, on the border of Brazil near Iguazú Falls. The recently completed 150-mile (241-km) route was opened in 1985 and affords some very interesting sightseeing.

At the 12-mile (20-km) mark, take the right-hand turnoff for the *Tirol* and continue for 6 miles (10 km), where you will come to the village of Trinidad and the first major Jesuit mission in the area. The mission is the best preserved in Paraguay: Most of the original walls are still standing, and some of the statuary has been restored. Completed in 1745, the church contains many fine examples of the excellent stone carvings usually found in Jesuit churches throughout Paraguay.

From Trinidad, go 7 miles (11 km) down a dirt road off the left-hand turnoff of the highway to the tiny village and ruins of Jesús.

JESÚS: The largest of all the Jesuit missions, this church was not yet completed when the Jesuit order was expelled from Paraguay in 1767. The tropical vegetation and tree roots still cover much of the unrestored ruins.

Jesús is the far point of your trip, some 250 miles (420 km) from Asunción. After a night or two at the *Tirol,* retrace your steps for an easy day's drive back to Asunción.

BEST EN ROUTE

While a few hotels along the Jesuit trail cost more than $30, most are less. Hotels are small, but have comfortable rooms with private bath.

VILLA FLORIDA

Las Mercedes – This small hotel is a rugged little fisherman's lodge. About 2 miles (4 km) from the highway — watch for the sign and the dirt road to the left before crossing the Río Tebicuary (no phone).

Del Seguro Social – The newest hotel around offers private baths, a restaurant, and a swimming pool. It's on your left as you approach Villa Florida from Asunción, just before you cross the Tebicuary (no phone).

Parado – This small motel offers clean rooms and private baths. On your left just after you cross the river (no phone).

ENCARNACIÓN

Tirol – This resort-type hotel has stone buildings and a motel-like structure with spring-fed swimming pools. Six cabins hold up to eight people each, and a large dining room, sitting room, game room, bar, and veranda overlook the valley. Rooms aren't air conditioned, but they have fans. Km 19, Hoenau (no phone).

Novotel – A first-class hotel with 102 rooms. Along Rte. 1 (phone: 071-4221/25, 4131/35). Moderate.

Iguazú Falls

One of the major land crossings for those entering Paraguay is via the Puente de la Amistad Bridge from Brazil and another is from Argentina. At the meeting of these two countries is Ciudad Stroessner, a fast-growing city with nearly 100,000 residents. While visitors staying at the Falls on the Brazilian side (which affords better views and offers more comfortable accommodations) often come here to gamble at the *Casino Acaray,* the newest attraction is Itaipú, the new hydroelectric dam, about 12 miles north of the city. Local travel agents can arrange interesting visits to the site, including hydrofoil rides on the reservoir lake.

BEST EN ROUTE

Casino Acaray – Understandably popular with gamblers and comfortable enough, it is about the best in town. Av. 11 de Septiembre and Río Paraná (phone: 2555).

Perú

Few countries in the Americas can match Perú in diversity of historic and natural attractions. Covering 496,223 square miles, the country is bordered by the Pacific Ocean to the west, Chile to the south, Bolivia and Brazil to the east, and Colombia and Ecuador to the north. Geographically, Perú is divided into three distinct regions: a narrow coastal strip of desert that extends the entire length of the country; the Andean sierra, where nearly half the Peruvian population of 15 million people live; and the jungle, which accounts for nearly two-thirds of the land.

Three climatic zones correspond to the topographical regions. Along the coast, temperatures climb into the 80s F (around 28°C) between October and May, then drop to around 50°F (10°C) between June and September. In the Andes, winter, which runs from June through September, is the dry season, with temperatures frequently falling into the 20s F (−9°C) at night and daytime highs in the 60s F (17°C). During the rainy season, from November through April, temperatures are somewhat warmer. The jungle, which starts along the eastern slopes of the Andes, has temperatures ranging from the 80s to the 100s F (27° to 40°C) throughout the year. It rains constantly, but most heavily between November and April.

Although it's in the arid coastal region, Lima, the capital for about 6 million people, is enshrouded in fog (called the *garúa*) roughly from June to October. (For a complete report, see *Lima,* THE CITIES.) Perú's other major cities are: Trujillo, the most important northern city; Arequipa, in the southern highlands; Iquitos, the leading Amazon port; and Cuzco, the former Inca stronghold.

While the Inca civilization with its headquarters in Perú is far and away the best known in South America, it was the last of an illustrious line of pre-Columbian cultures. The Chavín, Chan-Chan, and Nazca Indians predated the Inca by many centuries. However, when Spanish conquistadores Francisco Pizarro and Diego de Almagro arrived in Perú in 1532, the Inca empire extended from Ecuador in the north to Chile in the south. The conquistadores killed the head Inca, Atahualpa, and went on to found Lima in 1535.

Perú was one of the most important centers of the Spanish colonial realm in the New World until the early nineteenth century, when the struggle for independence began. Helped to a large extent by the Argentine General José de San Martín and the Venezuelan Simón Bolívar, Perú gained liberation from Spain in 1826 after years of fighting. In 1879, Perú allied with Bolivia against Chile to fight the War of the Pacific, which ended in 1883 with Perú's loss of the coastal town of Arica (now in northern Chile) and a strip of the Pacific coast. The hostility between Perú and her southern neighbor has never completely abated, and both countries have installed armaments along their mutual frontier in anticipation of renewed fighting.

In the twentieth century, no election system has been particularly successful in Perú, and military intervention has frequently occurred in national political affairs. The most recent military junta seized power in 1968, toppling the regime of President Fernando Belaunde.

In 1975, a shift in military factions resulted in the overthrow of General Juan Velasco by General Francisco Morales Bermúdez. The Morales government failed to assert effective financial and economic control, and Perú was officially on the verge of default in May 1978, when the International Monetary Fund instituted austerity programs designed to stabilize the country in the face of the emergency. Since then, Perú experienced some nominal political stability with the reelection of Fernando Belaunde to the presidency in 1980 and the 1985 election of the young and charismatic Alan García. During the last couple of years, however, conditions in Perú have deteriorated seriously, and there is growing frustration with the government's failure to deal with mounting terrorism and violence — especially that committed by the Maoist "Shining Path" guerrillas. As of press time, warnings issued by the US Department of State in response to recent urban terrorist activity as well as incidents in southern Perú, including parts of the Inca Trail, were still in effect, and tourists were advised to travel with caution.

Driving in Perú can be scenically fascinating and physically frustrating for car and driver: The roads are badly maintained, seasonally impassable, and lacking in auto service stops. When driving long distances, plan ahead for gas and service emergencies; carry spare parts, insurance, and your *carnet* (see *Touring by Car,* GETTING READY TO GO). Perú has an extensive network of buses, *colectivos* (chauffeured cars that carry four or five passengers), railroads, and internal domestic airlines that connect even remote towns and villages. The use of public transportation as an alternative to driving is strongly recommended. And if travel plans include stopovers at any of the small, state-owned hotels, advance reservations through EnturPerú or a Lima travel agency are also strongly recommended.

The seven routes in this chapter are: the Outskirts of Lima, which describes several trips into the surrounding countryside, to the beach resorts of Ancón and Santa Rosa, and to the mountain resort towns of Chaclacayo and Chosica; Lima to Chan-Chan takes you north from Lima along the Pan-American Highway to the city of Trujillo and the ruins at Chan-Chan; Lima to Arequipa describes a trip south of the capital to the curious area where the huge line drawings appear in the Nazca Desert, and from there to Arequipa, the lovely colonial city in the southern part of the country — and an explanation of how to arrange for a flight over the Nazca line drawings; Cuzco and the Inca Ruins, which takes you from the colonial city and its surrounding Inca fortress to the lost city of Machu Picchu and the peaceful Urubamba Valley; Cuzco to Puno, which takes you southeast through the altiplano (mountain plain) to the shores of Lake Titicaca; and the Amazon and Madre de Dios, which describes trips through the jungle regions where oil and gold are mined, monkeys chatter in the trees, and life is generally uncluttered.

The Outskirts of Lima

When Francisco Pizarro, the Spanish conqueror of Indian Perú, established the City of the Kings — now called Lima — beside the Río Rimac in 1535, he bypassed the existing large native population center of nearby Pachacámac. Apparently Pizarro wanted a capital that would be completely Spanish in its physical design and social character from the beginnings: hence imperious, arrogant, viceregal, Spanish Lima.

Lima has already been discussed in a chapter all its own (see *Lima,* THE CITIES). A circuit around the outskirts of the capital is your next destination, and the trip takes you in just about every interesting direction. To reach Pachacámac, you travel south on the Pan-American Highway into the Rimac and Lurín valleys, which once housed the Cuisamancu kingdom, a pre-Columbian civilization known to us only through remaining artifacts. Continue down the Pacific coast to the cotton-growing Cañete Valley and Herbay Bajo Hacienda (the Palace of the Inca King) and other Inca ruins, all about 68 miles (113 km) from Lima. If you continue north along the highway, you reach the Peruvian beaches of Santa Rosa and Ancón. An alternate northern route leads you to Canta, a small mountain town. Cantamarca, a bit outside of the town, is a mysterious archaeological site that was at one time a deserted fortress, town, or temple. The 2,000-foot climb to the ruins is strictly for the hearty. Keeping in step with the archaeological mood, Ancón itself houses the remains of a Paleolithic tribe that existed 9,000 to 10,000 years ago, and bones of the one-time tribesmen were discovered in a burial tomb. Nearby, San Pedro is reputedly the oldest inhabited site in the entire country.

The three major highways in Perú that lead south, north, and into the center form a great T-shaped figure. The central part or the Central Highway (otherwise known as Route 2) connects Lima with the lands in the eastern Andean slopes. Leaving Lima and heading east, you begin to climb steadily, flanked by the peaks of the Andes. This part of the route will take you to Chosica, a mountain resort very popular with the *limeños* 80 years ago, and, much farther, to Huancayo, a central business village where farmers and manufacturers in the area come every Sunday to sell their wares. The highways in all directions are asphalted, but, alas, are only two lanes wide.

For short trips, you can stay in Lima (see *Lima,* THE CITIES). This doesn't mean other accommodations are terrible, however — many hotels are owned by the state and have excellent service and clean rooms; they are inexpensive and also more comfortable than the primitive accommodations you'll get on other routes in Perú.

Your first route from Lima goes south, to the mysterious Pachacámac. The easiest way to reach the highway is via either Avenida Javier Prado or the Avenida Primavera to the Pan-American. Alternatively, VISTA offers daily guided bus tours to the ruins. For reservations, phone 27-66-24 or contact a local travel agent. Pachacámac is 19 miles (31 km) outside the capital. Since the highway parallels the Pacific Ocean, you can get some good views of the fishermen going out to net the elusive anchovies that end up in fishmeal plants in Callao. The weather along the way will be wonderful — it's similar to that of Southern California, about 73°F (23°C) from December to March and about 55°F (13°C) the rest of the year.

PACHACÁMAC: What remains of the temple was probably built by the faithful under the orders of the head of the Cuisamancu kingdom around the middle of the 1300s, although archaeological data show this was an important pilgrimage center several hundred years before the beginnings of Christianity. Hernando Pizarro, Francisco's brother and the first Spaniard to view the massive shrine, called it a mosque (having known the Moorish mosques in southern Spain); and indeed it was in the sense that it was "Mecca" for the peoples of the various kingdoms before and after their conquest by the Inca. They came from as far north as Ecuador and from as far south as Chile. Truces were arranged among the warring kingdoms so that the pilgrims could fulfill their religious duties to the great god and his oracle.

The ruins, which are open daily except Mondays from 9 AM to 5 PM, encompass the Temple of Pachacámac, the Inca Temple of the Sun, the House of the Virgins of the Sun (also an Inca addition), the remains of the surrounding city, and other secondary temples. Hidden under the drifting sands are the remains of a large, ceremonial-like square. The first temple is a pyramid constructed of small adobe bricks. Climbing it, you reach the holy chamber where sacrifices of llamas in honor of the god were made; you can gaze upon the pedestal where the wooden image of the god, blood-spattered by the sacrificers, rested, and the remains of the four columns from which hung a curtain woven of gold thread.

The quadrangular Temple of the Sun is particularly attractive because of its massive stone foundations, upon which were erected the five great adobe brick platforms at varying levels. At the top you get a striking view of the Pacific and of the lush surrounding valley.

Hernando Pizarro, and later his brother, came seeking the temples' legendary treasures. Both went away disappointed, for if there were great golden stores, they had been well hidden by the temple priests. Atahualpa, the conquered Inca, had sent Hernando to Pachacámac to collect the gold necessary for the Inca's presumed ransom.

When the Pizarros first approached Pachacámac, the city had a population of 30,000. The year the fifth viceroy arrived in Lima, 1569, the city's population had been reduced to 100. Thus the "barbarian" Inca empire was tamed by the "civilized" Europeans.

En Route from Pachacámac – Continuing south on the Pan-American, you come upon some of the more pleasant and less crowded beaches near Lima: Punta Hermosa, Punta Negra, and San Bartolo, all about 28½ miles (46 km) from Lima; another 20 miles (33 km) bring you to the beaches of Santa María del Mar and Pucusana. If the weather is good, bring along a picnic lunch and enjoy a swim and some restful hours. Along the highway are many small, very modest restaurants that serve local seafood dishes; they're not very clean, however, and for hygienic reasons aren't recommended.

If you really want to take a good day's outing, continue south another 68 miles (113 km) to the Cañete Valley, on a seacoast bluff on what was known as the Herbay Bajo Hacienda, or the Palace of the Inca King, as it was called in the 1800s. From what little remains of the adobe walls and foundations, you cannot visualize what kind of structure once stood here, but there is an early testament from the chronicler Pedro Cieza de León (and in 1863, with the eyewitness report of E. G. Squier, an American archaeologist) that this was the site of the "most beautiful and ornate citadel to be found in the whole kingdom of Perú, set upon great square blocks of stone, and with very fine gates, entranceways, and large patios." From the top of this royal edifice, a stone stairway descends to the sea. By the time Squier saw it, the adobe walls, the 15-foot-high doorways, and some of the roof beams remained; the stone upper structure had long since disappeared.

Fifteen miles (24 km) inland, following the road along the Río Cañete, you reach Incahuasi, once called New Cuzco by its Inca founder. This is a great complex of buildings, including the Houses of the Chosen Women, ceremonial sites and residences, a large storage area, and a square where apparently sacrifices took place. Incahuasi (House of the Inca) is the largest area of Inca constructions on the entire coast; the site covers some 5 square miles.

The best restaurants in Cañete are in the Plaza de Armas. They're modest, offering good food at low prices, and clean. It can be safely said that if this type of restaurant (*del pueblo:* of the people) has decent hygienic services, it usually offers good food. Just stay away from uncooked food such as lettuce, tomatoes, and unpeelable fruit. The food is normally prepared in pots of cooking oil, which makes it a bit greasy for North American stomachs, but it is savory. Try *Oasis* (Plaza de Armas) or *Le Paris;* no reservations are necessary at either.

From here, you have to return to Lima to continue north. For a day trip from Lima in this direction you have the choice of two routes: Either turn off onto the asphalt road that leads to Santa Rosa de Quives and Canta, or continue straight ahead to the Santa Rosa beach and Ancón. If you have to make a choice, choose the trip to Canta, since the Río Chillón valley is wonderfully green after the monotony of the coastal desert. The road is good, though winding (one should drive with care and sound the horn before arriving at the curves). Forty-six miles (75 km) later, you'll arrive at Santa Rosa de Quives, a bucolic spot with a small, graciously built church in honor of St. Rose of Lima, who spent part of her short life here more than 300 years ago.

Though you may not have noticed, you have been climbing steadily since the turnoff from the north Pan-American Highway; when you reach Canta, some 24 miles (38 km) ahead, you will be 12,600 feet above sea level. Because the climb has been gradual and slow, you should not experience even slight *soroche* (altitude sickness).

Canta will give you your first taste of small-town Andean life. On weekdays it is rather deserted, for the majority of people are busy with their farming duties outside town. There is nothing exceptionally inviting about Canta, but a bit farther is Cantamarca, the principal reason for coming here.

CANTAMARCA: This is one of those mysterious archaeological sites that abound in Perú, a deserted town or fortress or temple, abandoned but intact except for the ravages of the passing centuries. When you arrive, you will have to climb about 1,000 feet to reach the fortress-town (this climb is recommended only for the stout of heart with strong lungs). If you don't want to climb, be sure to bring binoculars so you can get some impression of the town at the top. Once you reach the peak, you discover a series of cylindrical stone structures, the doors of which are set so low that you have to crouch to get inside. The interior roof beams are stone and spokelike and go from the outside wall to a central pillar that incorporates a small fireplace with its flue. The roofs are sod placed on top of the beams: The grass growing on top of the sod must have served as camouflage. Before leaving this area, which archaeologists believe to be at least 1,000 years old, take a good look into the surrounding valleys to understand why the unknown builders chose this site for their town. It could have been conquered only by a prolonged siege that would starve out its inhabitants. The scenery is indeed overwhelming — a good introduction to the majestic beauty of the Andes. The climb up takes about 2 hours; the walk-at-a-run down will take less than ½ hour.

En Route from Cantamarca – If you want to find the place where Lima's beautiful people water-frolic with great style and much display, it's at Santa Rosa Beach; beyond km 35 turn left for Ancón.

ANCÓN: As you approach the resort, you will be surprised to see skyscrapers of residential apartments and many seaside villas sprouting up out of the dry desert sands, with the crude houses of the fishermen off to one side. The bay that has tamed the battering Pacific waves is flanked by a grand esplanade, along which the aristocracy of Lima — formerly known as the oligarchy because of their possession of both political and economic power — promenade in the cool sea breezes of the summer evenings.

Archaeologically, Ancón is an important area because remains of Paleolithic man have been discovered in the area. An extensive burial ground has been found and thousands of artifacts and mummies recovered, though many will never find a legitimate home in the museums of Lima.

En Route from Ancón – When you return to the Pan-American, be sure to stop briefly to visit the ruins of a small town on the site of the mountain called San Pedro. This town is considered by some archaeologists to be the earliest inhabited area on the South American continent. Many remains of the various Peruvian cultures that predate the Christian era have been discovered.

From here, you once again return to Lima to start the next excursion: the Central Highway. Your first stop will be Puruchuco.

PURUCHUCO: With San Pedro behind you, head straight out the Central Highway (which badly needs some repaving) to Km 8 to visit the reconstructed country mansion and farm center of an Indian chief. According to the many relics that have been found, the original house dates from the 900s. Built of adobe, the customary construction material used on the coast, the house is a geometrical triumph of straight lines and right angles and trapezoidal niches in the walls. The numerous corridors and alleys, with horseshoe-shaped doors and windows, add to the enchantment of the restored farm center. The adjacent museum displays artifacts, costumes, and musical instruments excavated in the area; they represent all the generations who have lived here — pre-Inca, Inca, conqueror, and colonial. Open daily, except Mondays, from 9 to 11 AM and from 2 to 5 PM.

En Route from Puruchuco – Continuing east on the Central Highway for 2 miles (3½ km), you come to a road on the left. This will take you to the ruins of a mystery site like the one at Cantamarca. When discovered by the Inca, the huge complex of walls, squares, underground storage areas, and houses was empty. Who lived here and in what era is not known, not because these questions cannot be answered archaeologically, but because Perú lacks the archaeological and financial resources to investigate them thoroughly.

Back on the Central Highway and continuing toward the Andes to the east, you go less than 1½ miles (2½ km) to find another group of ruins on the right-hand turnoff. This group is called Pariachicuiyo, built in a style similar to that of Puruchuco. The complex consists of two large residences and a group of isolated houses. The large residence has been restored, so you can appreciate the large rectangular patio, with its two successive platforms united by a short ramp. From the platforms you enter a group of rooms by a series of passageways.

Chaclacayo, a small town of about 30,000 people, is a favorite winter weekend spot of *limeños,* but there is more to see in Chosica, Chaclacayo's neighbor.

CHOSICA: City of the Sun and the Gateway to the Andes, this city of Victorian houses was Lima's winter resort 80 years ago. Access to Chosica was easy then because it was only an hour away by train. However, as more indigenous people settled in and around Chosica, its desirability as an exclusive winter resort lessened drastically, and the old families built new houses in Chaclacayo.

Chosica, though somewhat faded, remains charming. Its very large plaza is especially handsome because of the many palm trees that give it both shade and impressiveness. Because it is 656 feet higher than Chaclacayo, its air is clearer and winter skies sunnier. It is worthwhile visiting the public market to get an idea of how the mountain markets function in relation to the daily lives of the people.

If you're tired of the sun at Chosica, then you can push on up the Central Highway for 24 miles (40 km) east to Matucana solely for the sheer joy and excitement of knowing a little bit more of the fantastic variety of cultivated plants, wild flowers and trees, and chameleon-colored rocks of the Andes. The small city of Matucana is an enchanting introduction to the simplicity of life and the physical vastness of the Andes Mountains and valleys. The climate is dry and brisk. When the sun shines in the Andes, it is normally hot from 10 AM to 2 PM. But as soon as you pass from sun to shadow, after 2 or 3 in the afternoon you will feel the chill after the heat.

En Route from Matucana – From Matucana the Central Highway, or Route 2, winds southeast to become Route 7 to Huancayo (pop. 110,000) — the major marketing center for the central Peruvian highlands. Some 192 miles southeast of Lima, this city, at 10,750 feet above sea level, has many chilly afternoons, cold nights, and tempestuous rains. If you'd rather skip the car ride (and it's a hairy one), then backtrack to Lima and take the train. It leaves Lima every morning except Sundays at 7:40 AM and arrives at 10:50 AM. The train itself has a narrow gauge, and this is the highest of its kind in the whole world: When the train reaches Ticlio, it has climbed almost 16,000 feet. Small oxygen tanks are on board, and the stewards are trained to operate them for any passenger who can't handle the thin air.

A good time to get to Huancayo is in time for the Sunday market (that means going on Saturday); Indians from neighboring villages flock here to sell their llama and alpaca wool, ponchos, rugs, blankets, pottery, and other items. As there are many thefts, it's best to go empty-handed, wearing a money belt. Thieves often work in teams, so be wary of distractions. In addition, you can take a run to the Santa Rosa Monastery in Ocopa, 17 miles (28 km) outside Huancayo. The monastery alone is worth the trip, with beautiful carved cloisters and an impressive library.

In the morning, take the train back to Lima; it's an interesting ride because of the many switchbacks the train makes, an impressive engineering feat accomplished under the direction of an eccentric North American named Henry Meiggs. By taxi is also a good way to travel — this is a beautiful road trip.

BEST EN ROUTE

All the hotels you'll come across on this route are small, with the basic accommodations (room, bed, maybe a private bath, and meals) for about $15 a night. It's a good idea to make reservations before you go. Most of the hotels listed below have telephones; in some cases, however, you'll have to write to them.

SANTA ROSA DE QUIVES

Turistas – Comfortable rooms and dining room are provided by this government-owned hotel. Centrally located (phone: 72-19-28, 40-46-30, 72-82-27).

CHACLACAYO

Los Condores Tambo Inn – Garcilaso de la Vega 900-902, Los Condores (phone: 91-07-86; in Lima, 61-08-15).

CHOSICA

Fidel – This 12-room hotel provides private baths, a dining room, and a swimming pool in its garden. Av. Las Flores 200 (phone: 91-01-06).

HUANCAYO

Turistas – This small, state-owned hotel provides clean rooms and meals. Ancash 729 (phone: 23-10-72; in Lima, 72-19-28).

Presidente – No restaurant, but clean, reliable, and the best in town. Calle Real 1138 (phone: 23-12-76).

Kiya – Rooms with baths, restaurant for lunch and dinner; clean and neat, but noisy. Calle Giraldez 107 (phone: 23-1431).

Lima to Chan-Chan

A voyage to Perú brings the traveler into contact with the mysteries of human origins on the South American continent: There are almost as many theories about those beginnings as there are books about early Peruvian civilizations. Although we know a great deal about the Inca Empire, there is precious little exact knowledge of the pre-Inca Andean cultures and of the coastal kingdoms other than what their buildings (mostly ruins) and their tombs (now largely plundered) have revealed to archaeologists. The use of Carbon 14 in arriving at dates has been significant, but because apparently none of the Peruvian civilizations left written documents, scholars have had to construct their cultural dimensions from findings of ceramics, textiles, jewelry, food remains, metallurgy, building styles, and materials.

The Peruvian coast, from Nazca in the south (see *Lima to Arequipa*) through the valleys clustered around modern Lima (see *The Outskirts of Lima*) to Piura close to the northern frontier of Perú, is of singular interest to the traveler who is fascinated not only by the discovery of his own roots in history but also by the encounter with the roots of mankind in the Americas. Touring the coast from Lima to Trujillo offers the opportunity to learn of and appreciate the majesty and the mystery of the ancient Peruvian coastal kingdoms. In addition, this is the region of Creole Perú, an area with a distinctly black flavor because of the great number of slaves brought here to work the sugar and cotton plantations centuries ago. Within the first few years following Pizarro's arrival in 1532, the majority of the coastal Indians perished — victims of European diseases, firearms, and swords.

The trip north from Lima to Trujillo covers a distance of 341 miles along the asphalt Pan-American Highway. The best way to travel is by car so you can stop and savor the pre-Columbian and post-Conquest towns and cities at your own pace. You can rent a car in Lima (see Sources and Resources, *Lima,* THE CITIES). There is good bus service, but you will only get glimpses of the fragments of early Peruvian culture. Turismo Empreso Pullman Tepsa (Paseo de la República 119; phone: 32-12-33 or 32-65-05) offers modern, comfortable service. Reservations are necessary to guarantee your seat. If you prefer to travel with a guide, contact a local tour operator who can also provide transportation. Reputable operators are listed in the *Perú Guide,* which is available for free at all major hotels and tourist information centers. APOTUR, the organization of local tour operators, can also provide information on reliable operators (Av. Tacna 665, office 506, Lima; phone: 27-50-37). Vista

(Belén 1040, Lima; phone: 27-66-24) provides the only available group bus tours to the north. If you have little time, you can take the 60-minute flight to Trujillo instead. Once you arrive, you can at least tour Chan-Chan, the adobe city, and its nearby temples. Faucett Airlines (Plaza San Martín; phone: 27-5000) and AeroPerú (Plaza San Martín; phone: 31-7626) offer daily flights. Book ahead, and get to the airport early — especially on Friday evenings and Monday mornings.

Accommodations en route are comfortable and modern: Some even have private baths. If you need any assistance, contact the tourist office in the *Tambo de Oro* restaurant at Calle Belén 1066 (phone: 32-3559).

You proceed north along the Pan-American; before reaching the turnoff for Ancón (see *The Outskirts of Lima*) you arrive at a bypass called Variante Pasamayo, 10½ miles (17 km) long; at its end are the Banos de Boza, recommended for their curative sulfurous waters. Crossing the Río Chancay, you find yourself in one of the usually narrow but lush coastal valleys where the coastal cultures began and flourished. Because the major portion of the Peruvian coast is desert, these small valley oases were essential to the survival of the settlers. Therefore, the inhabitants devoted great time and effort to developing irrigation canals to bring precious water from the mountains in order to increase the amount of cultivatable land. Some say that before the Spanish arrived there was more coastal land under cultivation than there is today because the Spaniards let the irrigation systems deteriorate. The beginnings of the Chancay culture, which is closely related to that of the Lurin and Rimac valleys, date back to 300 BC. You can see some handsome relics representative of Chancay ceramics in the Museo Amano in Lima (160 Calle Retiro, Miraflores; phone: 41-29-09).

This city of 20,000 farmers and fishermen is about 51 miles (82 km) north of Lima: A number of factories are devoted to processing fishmeal, one of Perú's biggest exports. Near the main square, you encounter the well-known *Castillo de Chancay,* a colonial building that is now a restaurant serving shellfish (mainly shrimp). This is a good place for an early lunch. Two other restaurants, both at kilometer 82, also feature local seafood: *Astoria* and *Marco.*

Continuing north, you go through the village of Las Salinas de Huacho, filled with salt deposits.

HUACHO: Ninety-one miles (148 km) north of Lima, this fishing center of 37,000 inhabitants is a picturesque old sea town and offers a good spot to stop and rest. The restaurant in Hotel Centenario (Av. 28 de Julio 836; phone: 30-12 or 27-28) and Restaurant La Libertad (Av. 28 de Julio 600; phone: 29-46) serve particularly good river shrimp. Try the chupes de camarones (heavy, freshwater shrimp soup).

En Route from Huacho – Three miles (5 km) north you'll pass the small village of Huaura, known to Peruvians as the capital of la guinda, a delicious if oversweet liquor made from the guinda fruit, which grows abundantly in this area. Here you can see the balcony of the house where General José de San Martín first proclaimed Perú's independence from Spain on July 28, 1821. The house is open daily.

As you travel north, you will be struck by the aridity of the surrounding desert area between the valleys. Often the wind will have formed sand drifts across the highway or heaped the sand into dunes. The soil of this desert is very rich; it just lacks water. By the time you reach Supe, 115 miles (179 km) north of Lima, you will have concluded that through fishing and farming, the Peruvian coastal people have sustained themselves for some thousands of years; only the clothing, buildings, and language have changed. Supe is well known for its tamales, which you can safely buy in any of the restaurants if you want a snack.

Beyond Supe lie the towns of Barranca and Pativilca, the latter with a well-preserved colonial center.

At kilometer 199 is a road that goes to the Andean zone called Callejón de Huaylas. The valley is in the Central Highlands and is nicknamed the Peruvian Alps. A few miles north of Pativilca is the great adobe fortress-temple of Paramonga and the southern frontiers of the one-time kingdom of Chimú.

PARAMONGA: Built of adobe and forming a series of ascending terraces, the Paramonga fortress-temple is one of the best-preserved ancient buildings on the coast. A silent witness to the majesty and power of the kingdom of Chimú, it has beautifully decorated exterior walls, ceremonial terraces, subterranean passages, immense foundations, and a number of small rooms at the top where the walls bear some faint hints of their once brightly painted birds and animals. From the fortress-temple, its priests and soldiers had a commanding view of both the land and sea approaches. The Inca found it exceedingly difficult to break the resistance of the defenders of Paramonga in their first try at conquering the Chimú territories; but around 1470, the fortress was breached by the Inca armies coming from the north, and the kingdom of Chimú was reduced to a province of the Inca Empire. On the hills around Paramonga are other buildings, probably houses and storage areas and granaries.

En Route from Paramonga – Leaving the small valley, follow the Pan-American Highway across one of the most desolate sections of the northern desert coast, 49 miles (80 km) of dunes and arid wasteland.

Halfway between Lima and Trujillo is Huarmey, a small town of 12,000 people that enjoys a pleasant climate and almost endless sunshine in 80°F (26°C) weather. From here, the 54-mile (87-km) trip to Casma is of little interest.

CASMA: A small city of 22,000 inhabitants; this crossroads handles commerce to and from the north and the south with Huaraz, 91 miles (140 km) — a 4-hour trip — to the east in the Callejón de Huaylas. Because of its hot, dry climate and fertile farmland, Casma is a center of the production of cotton and vegetables. Four miles (7 km) east, on the highway to Huaraz, are the formidable ruins of Sechín. This was probably a temple site influenced in design and decoration by the famous temple at Chavín de Huantar, which was an important pilgrimage site around 1,200 years ago.

Sechín in its present state probably dates to approximately the same period; however, there are indications that people were building in the area in about 500 BC. What you find now is a temple consisting of two great terraces, the smaller one imposed upon the lower and larger terrace. The upper terrace is striking for the catlike figures painted there, but the lower terrace is truly impressive for the stone carvings representing priests and warriors. Sechín is still being excavated, and its recently opened museum is well worth a visit.

In the Casma Valley, visit other ceremonial centers equally important in that early period: Moqeke and Pallka as well as the Canquillo Fortress and Monte Grande, a sanctuary that occupies about 7½ acres. (Before beginning your tour of the Casma Valley, inquire in Casma itself about these last-named ruins since they are not usually visited by people other than archaeologists and therefore are not entered on maps.) All the temples are built in the pyramid style, with slight variations.

En Route from Casma – Thirteen miles (21 km) north of Casma on the Pan-American is a cutoff toward the ocean that leads to Tortugas (Turtles), a pleasant town with sandy beaches: Take a swim in the Pacific right here, if you like. When you return to the highway, you travel north to another sideroad that turns left and brings you to the town of Nepeña and the ruins of Pañamarca, which date to the period between AD 600 and 900. The temple remains are your first introduction to the Moche culture and its art and architecture, probably the most significant of coastal origin. Note the murals that present rites probably performed in the temple. There are agricultural terraces irrigated by a system considered a prime example of the hydraulic engineering skills of the coastal peoples.

Return north to the highway and you get to Chimbote, the capital of the fishing and steel industry in Perú.

CHIMBOTE: This sleepy fishing village boomed 30 years ago with the development of meal from the anchovies that flourished ago off the northern coast. The city now has over 200,000 inhabitants, many of whom are unemployed today because the anchovy catch has declined due to changes in the ocean currents and overfishing.

There is really not much reason for spending any time in Chimbote unless you are hungry or need a place to stay — the strong fishy odors that permeate the city some days will drive you away. If you are hungry, try the *Riviera Roof Garden* (that's really its name) on Calle Elías Aguirre 385 (phone: 32-2571), which serves excellent fish and shellfish. You can also enjoy a pleasant snack or meal at the *Turistas* hotel, Galvez 109 (phone: 32-37-21).

En Route from Chimbote – Before reaching Trujillo, you pass through the Viru Valley, where some of the earliest remains of prehistoric Perú have been found. (Supposedly, the name Perú is derived from the name of this valley; somehow it was given to the whole territory of the Inca in a case of mistaken identity on the part of the Spaniards.) Ruins dating back to AD 200 have been discovered in the valley, and there are 14 pyramidal sanctuaries in the area.

From here, it's a short, 30-mile (48-km) trip up the Pan-American to Trujillo, founded in 1535 by the Spaniards near the monumental city of Chan-Chan.

TRUJILLO: Francisco Pizarro named this after his home town in Spain. With an excellent climate, Trujillo averages 70°F (27° C) December through April, and 58°F (14°C) the rest of the year, disturbed only by the high humidity that can make your tour through its colonial buildings a damp but enjoyable romp.

Because the surrounding Moche Valley is agriculturally rich, great plantations devoted to the cultivation of sugar, cotton, rice, and cereals semicircled the city to the north, west, and south. They brought great wealth to the area, and plantation owners maintained elegant Spanish-style homes with large patios, luxurious reception rooms, and magnificent façades of sculpted wooden balconies and lovely lacelike wrought-iron window grilles. In the old city, which was surrounded by high walls topped with 28 watch towers, there are still traces of the aristocratic luxury that was once synonymous with this viceroyal city, probably the most Spanish of all the Peruvian cities during the colonial period.

The agrarian reform inaugurated in 1969, which expropriated farmland to government control, first affected the immense plantations in the Trujillo area (Casa Grande, the property of a German immigrant family, was as large as the state of Rhode Island). The proud manorial families have either left the country or retired to their mansions in the wealthy sections of Lima. But it seems at present that this has helped greatly in the industrialization and modernization of the city and the surrounding area.

Trujillo has some handsome colonial churches and monasteries, but most of what is worth seeing can be done in a day.

The Plaza de Armas, which must surely be the largest in Perú, is dominated by an ugly fountain and group of sculptures. On one corner is the cathedral, which is not particularly interesting in itself; it does have some fine paintings of the School of Quito, Ecuador. However, the Monastery and Church of Carmen, on the corner of Jirón Bolívar and Jirón Colón, offer the best example of high colonial religious art in Trujillo. The wooden altars are covered with gold leaf, and the pulpit and the pictures as well as the pieces sculpted in Huamanga stone are of good quality.

While visiting the churches, you will also chance upon the better-preserved colonial mansions: Casa de la Familia Ganoza (on the sixth block of Jirón Independence across the street from the Church of San Francisco); Casa del Mayornzgo (on the third block of Jirón Pizarro); Palacio Iturregui (Jirón Pizarro 680; note the beautiful window grilles); and the Casa Urquiaga (Jirón Pizarro 428 on the Plaza de Armas). There is no regular pattern of visiting hours, so take a chance and walk in to see what each has to offer. The University Archaeological Museum (Jirón Bolívar 446) offers an excellent collection of pre-Columbian art (check with your hotel for its visiting hours), and the Museo José Cassinelli (Jirón Nicolás de Piérola 601) exhibits about 1,200 ceramics from the various ancient Peruvian civilizations. The museums are open Mondays through Saturdays from 8:30 AM to noon and from 2 to 6 PM.

Surely you will get hungry as you stroll around Trujillo, but apart from the restaurants attached to the better hotels, there are no first-class eating places. However, the restaurant *Gamarra* (Jirón Gamarra 777), the bar-restaurant *Demarco* (Jirón Pizarro 725, phone: 29-91), and the bar-restaurant *Romano* (Jirón Pizarro; phone: 24-45) can be recommended for the quality of their food, their cleanliness, and their moderate prices.

The tourist office is at Independencia 509.

There may be no nightlife in Trujillo, for people entertain at home, but there are good beaches. Just 2½ miles (4 km) from the city is Buenos Aires beach, probably the best in the area; closest to town is Huanchiquito beach, with a good restaurant, *Las Sirenas.* Along the beach are several good restaurants that specialize in seafood, as do the restaurants along Las Delicias beach at Moche, about 4 miles (7 km) south of Trujillo. About 7½ miles (11 km) north of the city is the port of Huanchaco, which also has a decent beach. One of its attractive features is the *caballito del mar* (little seahorse), a reed-constructed boat made by the residents and used for fishing; the boat's history goes back over 1,000 years, for replicas are depicted in pottery of the pre-Columbian Moche tribe. A good restaurant here is *El Poseidón.*

If you're looking for fiestas, plan to be in Trujillo during the third week in January, when the Festival of La Marinera is celebrated. *La Marinera* is a dance of African and Hispanic origins and is one of the most elegant dances found on the coast. It reminds one of the Spanish flamenco, but it is performed in a more leisurely manner. All schoolchildren on the coast learn the *marinera* at an early age, and its graceful (if strenuous) steps are Perú's major contribution to the ballet-like dance form. To discover what colonial social life was really like, visit Trujillo's Spring Festival, held from September 22 through 30. It offers all kinds of music and dance presentations, bullfights, cockfights, horse shows, competitions, and lots of food and drink.

Your last stop in this area should be at Chan-Chan, one-time capital of the ancient kingdom of Chimú, about 2½ miles (4 km) from Trujillo.

CHAN-CHAN: In its heyday, around AD 1300, this site was larger in size and population than any European city. Try to turn back the clock 750 years and imagine yourself, for the first time, descending the Andean mountain slopes to the Pacific Ocean. There, spread out over many square miles, sits the sophisticated city of your royal masters. Surrounded on all sides, as far as the eye can see, by emerald green fields crisscrossed by aqueducts and irrigation channels, the city is a great bouquet of red, yellow, orange, and green embellished by the continual glinting of gold and silver that adorn the palaces and temples.

Completely encircled by walls almost 50 feet high, immensely thick and covered with glowingly painted bas-reliefs, the splendor of the city will make you gasp, for nowhere in the Andean province is such a marvel to be seen. You enter by one of the massive gates and find yourself caught up in the swirl of the city's busy life. To the right and left are small artisan factories where skilled hands are creating beautiful costume jewelry; hand-painting delicate pottery; renewing the weapons of the royal army; or weaving, with intricate patterns, soft mantles and shirts. Patient women are chewing the corn that ferments with their saliva. This chewed corn is deposited in great earthen vessels and becomes the *chicha* (beer) so cherished by ruler and commoner alike.

As you enter each of the ten districts of the clay and adobe city, the pattern of life is repeated. The plan of each district is basically the same: The great central plaza is the center of political and religious life; the temples of the Moon Goddess and lesser gods and the palaces of the princes; the courts of justice, where an "eye for an eye and a tooth for a tooth" punishments are dealt out; the marketplace with immense water reservoirs; the cemeteries, principally reserved for the notables. The considerable pedestrian traffic is constantly halted to allow the richly adorned litters of the nobles and the judges to pass by. On the steps of the palaces and the temples your attention is overwhelmed by the stylish dress and ornaments (gold and silver nose and ear rings, colorful turbans topped by proud sprays of exquisitely colored plumes) of those who dominate this kingdom — truly an empire, for its political and economic power spread far beyond its territorial limits, Paramonga in the south and Tumbes in the north.

What were the origins of this splendid city and kingdom? According to archaeological studies, its great predecessor was the Moche civilization (sometimes called the Mochica culture), which flourished in the first eight centuries of this era. Fortresses and temples in the Moche style (pyramidal) abound throughout the Trujillo area. The most important remnants of this civilization are its marvelous ceramics and wall bas-reliefs, which provide us with a complete panorama of the daily life of the Moche people: ceremonial rites (both religious and political), work and recreational habits, war and hunting procedures, sexual practices, and burial customs. If you did not get to the Larco Herrera Archaeological Museum in Lima (Av. Bolívar 1515; phone: 61-1312), be sure to do so upon your return, for it has a fine collection of Moche pottery.

Chan-Chan today has suffered destruction at the hands of the gold- and relic-seekers and from the rare torrential rain that occurs on the Peruvian coast. With roofs long rotted away by the humid and salty air, the buildings no longer were protected. However, you can still perceive the magnificence that was Chan-Chan in the several restored portions and in the monstrously thick walls, now somewhat reduced in height. And near Chan-Chan are the great Moche temples of the Sun and the Moon, the first constructed of about 500 million adobe bricks. Do not wander off alone into the ruins at Chan-Chan; stick with the guided groups. The same applies to the pyramids of the sun and the moon. There have been a number of robberies recently.

In the same area are the Temple of the Dragon (its walls adorned with bas-reliefs of the dragon symbol, so common to the ancient Chinese and Mesopotamian civilizations) and the Emerald Temple. Other Moche and Chimú urban centers and irrigation projects are near Trujillo; their remains offer further confirmation of the political, economic, and artistic heights reached by these two ancient Peruvian cultures.

BEST EN ROUTE

Accommodations on this route are priced in the same range as those on the Lima-Arequipa route: $20 to $30, expensive; $11 to $19, moderate; and under $10, inexpensive. Expect clean rooms, some private baths, and restaurants on the premises. Again, make reservations before traveling.

CASMA

Hostal El Farol – Centrally located and very basic, but clean (no phone). Inexpensive.

HUACHO

Centenario – This small hotel has a restaurant where seafood is the specialty. Av. 28 de Julio 840 (phone: 32-3731). Moderate.

HUARMEY

Turistas – A state-owned hotel with clean rooms and good service. Centrally located (phone: 72-1928, 40-4630, or 72-8227). Moderate.

CHIMBOTE

Turistas – Modern, pleasant, and recently restored, with private baths, restaurant, and bar. Calle Galvez 109 (phone: 32-3721, or call EnturPerú in Lima, 72-19-28). Moderate.

TRUJILLO

El Golf – New, elegant hotel has pleasant rooms, restaurant, and bar. It's some distance from the center of town, but free transportation downtown is provided hourly. Urbanización El Golf, Manzana 1-1 (phone: 24-2592). Expensive.

Turistas – The oldest hotel in town has a good bar and restaurant service, with a bit of the "old days" flavor to it. Independencia 485 and Plaza de Armas (phone: 23-2741, or in Lima, 72-19-28). Moderate.

Opt Gar – Small, central hotel offers clean rooms, a restaurant, bar, and good service. Jirón Grau 525 (phone: 24-2192). Moderate.

Chan-Chan – A new hotel with spacious rooms, restaurant, and bar. Av. Sinchi Roca and Huayna Capac 201-304 (phone: 24-2964). Inexpensive.

Hostería El Sol – A warm, comfortable small hotel where many visiting archaeologists stay. Los Brillantes 224, Urbanización Santa Inez (phone: 23-19-33). Inexpensive.

Lima to Arequipa

This route takes you from Lima south on the Pan-American to the valleys of the Pacific coast. The area is an archaeological treasure trove, filled with the remains of pre-Columbian cultures that developed here at least 9,000 to 10,000 years ago. No one knows the origins of the Nazca and Paracas groups. Presumably Asian, they settled here after migrations across the Bering Strait — probably a land bridge at the time — and down the American continents, settling in nomadic fashion on the coast here. As they progressed from a survival existence based upon fishing, hunting, and food gathering, they began to lay the agricultural foundations of what would become the great Peruvian coastal and highland civilizations.

Perhaps the more mysterious culture of the two was the Nazca, whose people settled in five valleys along the coast: Nazca, Santa Cruz, Palpa, Ingenio, and Poroma. Very little is known except that they emerged between 1,000 BC and AD 500, a group of master craftsmen who made pottery in the shape of animals, men, and vegetables. The designs etched into the Nazca Pampa Colorado plains — figures of men, circles, and birds that can only be seen in their entirety from the air — are faithful to the designs found on Nazca ceramics and textiles. Although the who, when, and how of the making of the Nazca lines is becoming clearer, scientists and anthropologists still have many questions to answer.

The Paracas Peninsula, a dry, windswept piece of land about 125 miles south of Lima, was the center of Paracas culture. Like the Nazca, the Paracas became master artisans. Little is known about this group except that once in about 300 BC people (Paracas or otherwise is not known) began to use the peninsula as a burial ground. They interred their mummified dead in huge baskets in chambers receding into the Cerro Colorado, a huge, reddish mountain. The tombs within the cerro were also discovered to be like those of the Egyptians, with anterooms, patios, and main chambers.

In addition to the Nazca and Paracas ruins, you can also visit a more "modern" ruin, that of the Inca village of Chala (known as *la quebrada de la vaca*), some 252 miles (403 km) north of Arequipa, the Ciudad Blanca (White City), renowned for its buildings made of *sillar*, or white volcanic rock, from nearby El Misti, a still active volcano. *Chasquis* (Inca messengers) used to run from coastal Chala with fresh fish and seaweed, in a relay that took them all the way to Cuzco and the Royal Court, in two days. (The Inca road system, which crisscrossed at Arequipa, was taken over by the Spaniards in 1538.)

Today, Arequipa is a modern yet peaceful city, still renowned in Perú for its eternal springlike weather that manages to stay between 77°F (25°C) and 55°F (13°C) year round.

You can travel this route either by car, which you can rent in Lima, by *colectivo*, or by bus. (Any way, it's a long and difficult drive from Paracas to Arequipa.) Before leaving, however, prepare yourself for a trip where accommodations are going to be quite simple. Gas stations are usually found only within the small cities and towns along the Pan-American Highway and do not operate after 7 or 8 PM. If you are driving, confine your touring to the daylight hours in order to have enough gas and to get yourself situated for the night. Since this is an essentially rural route, people go to bed early and get up early, and night life is virtually nil. Road conditions are satisfactory, but drive with care; Peruvian drivers aren't the best in the world, and the road becomes quite narrow along the coast and can be slippery when sand scurries across it when it's misty in winter.

If you bus it, plan your trip with stops at the most important towns and archaeological sites — Ica, Nazca, Paracas, Chala, Camaná, and Arequipa. If you don't speak Spanish, arrange the route with a travel agency in Lima (see the *Outskirts of Lima*).

Traveling in the daytime, summer clothing is comfortable at any time of the year; however, from April through November you had better carry along a couple of sweaters, one light and one heavy, and either a jacket or a raincoat.

To start your route, take the Pan-American south to Cañete, 89 miles (144 km) from Lima. Another 33 miles (55 km) south is Chincha Alta, a town of about 80,000 inhabitants and once the center of the small Chincha Empire, a pre-Columbian culture composed of the neighboring Chincha, Pisco, Ica, and Nazca valleys. In its heyday, the empire was renowned for its fierce soldiering. Tambo de Mora, the one-time capital of the empire, 7 miles (11 km) to the west, is now a small port and has several ruins, including a temple. The port's original adobe structures have survived the centuries well because of the dry desert air. Nearby is the site of La Centinela, a well-preserved Inca Temple of the Sun.

Nineteen miles (31 km) south of Chincha Alta you'll arrive at Pisco; before you enter the city, however, take the left-hand side road marked Humay-Castrovirreyna. About 29 miles (48 km) inland, you will come upon Tambo Colorado, a well-preserved Inca city lacking only its thatched roofs. The many bright yellow and red walls once again testify to the excellent preservative quality of the desert air.

Returning to Pisco, continue south for about 11 miles (18 km) until you reach Paracas, where sifting sand moves lightly across the one-time city and necropolis of the pre-Columbian Paracas culture.

PARACAS: Were a traveler to walk about this peninsula, innocent of any knowledge of its history, he might be shocked to find an occasional human bone in his path. He would soon find out that this desolate area was once a great burial ground, dating back some 2,500 years.

This extensive city of the dead was unearthed in 1925 by Julio C. Tello and Toribio Mejia Xesspe, leading archaeologists in Lima. They unearthed priceless ceramics and textiles made of vicuña and alpaca wool and fine-spun, coastal cotton — a long fiber and one of the best for weaving in the whole world. Mummies, buried in a sitting position, were placed in reed baskets and covered with cotton blankets. At the Julio C. Tello Museum, you can see burial displays of mummies, along with other items found at the dig, including brightly woven mantles, some embroidered with purple and red wool, with checkerboard or condor patterns. Two hours away by boat is Ballestas Island, a nature preserve for sea lions, guano birds, pelicans, and penguins.

En Route from Paracas – You have to backtrack to Pisco before continuing 48 miles (78 km) inland to Ica, one of those wondrous, fertile valleys that enliven the long Peruvian desert coast. Famous for 400 years for its grapes and its wines (Tacama and Ocucaje wines, both very good, are exported to North America and within South America), the Ica valley was prized both by the Incas and the conquistadores. The climate here is dry, but not excessively hot — about 85°F (29°C). At its height, the pre-Columbian culture (between AD 400 and 1000) that existed here was definitely related to the Nazca culture, and there are still remains of the ancient city of Pampa de Tate. Backtrack about 2½ miles (4 km) toward the ocean and you'll arrive at Huacachina, which has medicinal waters once frequented by the Inca and still popular with Ica residents. The odor is sulfurous, but the site is handsome: The spa is a small lake surrounded by sand dunes and palm trees.

South of Ica are desolate desert regions that lead to the valleys of Nazca, Santa Cruz, Palpa, Ingenio, and Poroma. This is a most important archaeological zone, influenced both by Paracas and by the Wari. The various developments in the Nazca culture reveal a homebound people, democratically inclined (at least in death, for there are no marked distinctions among the graves), without any strong authoritarian influences in their public life (there are no pharaonic public works such as you find under the government of the Inca), with sufficient leisure time to produce remarkable ceramics and textiles. The potteries are delicately colored in varying pastel shades and reveal an unexpected elegance. The Nazca textiles are among the finest in workmanship and design.

Some 53 miles (85 km) after Ica, you approach the Quebrada de Santa Cruz (Canyon of the Holy Cross). Within it is a ruin that fills the entire canyon. To get a good idea of its immensity and various structures, climb above it and look down. When the highway intersects with the Río Ingenio, turn to the left to investigate the Tambo (way station) El Ingenio, a typical Inca construction, but of adobe.

After passing the small town of Palpa, about 3 miles (5 km) later, you will come upon the Pampa Colorada.

PAMPA COLORADA: This is the site of the famous Nazca lines, which were carved into the plain as much as 5,000 years ago. There has been much speculation as to exactly who drew these lines on the dry desert floor. Perhaps the most fantastical theory is that of Erich von Daniken, who speculated in his book *Chariots of the Gods* (Putnam; 1970) that the lines were drawn with the aid of extraterrestrial beings: One of the drawings even depicts a man that resembles an astronaut with a life-support system strapped to his back. A more recent theory, developed in 1975 by members of the Explorers Society of Coral Gables, Florida, says that the Indians — or whoever they were — first strung out the lines on small plots of land, then were guided in drawing the finished products by observers — fellow Indians — who flew above them in hot-air balloons filled with smoke, acting as supervisors. The society even went so far as to reconstruct a Nazca balloon with the help of drawings found in Nazca burial chambers and *totora* reeds (cattails) from the shores of Lake Titicaca (see *Cuzco to Puno*).

You can fly up and see the Nazca lines for yourself in AeroCondor's tours above the plains in a single-engined plane. Takeoff is from Lima, Ica, or Nazca; reservations can be made at the AeroCondor offices in Lima (*Sheraton* hotel, Galerías Comerciales; phone: 32-90-50) or at *Aeróica,* Nicolas de Pierola 677, Office 702, Lima (phone: 27-37-77, 28-22-43). It's a breathtaking tour. From above, the lines appear to be purposeful: a series of rectangles, squares, circles, and apparent drawings of fish, whales, insects, and birds. The interpretation of the lines probably depends upon your own imagination and knowledge. Because coastal peoples worshiped the "cool" moon (night brought daily relief from the desert heat), it is possible that the lines do have astronomical significance.

The small city of Nazca itself is modern and has 40,000 inhabitants. Before you leave, take a visit southeast to Cahuachi, where there is an unusual forest of planted, cut trunks of trees placed in orderly lines; its purpose is puzzling. The trunks and stakes have been here for more than 500 years — or maybe twice that long.

En Route from Nazca – Some people prefer to continue south to Chala, having timed their visit to the Nazca lines and ruins so they can arrive in Chala by 6 PM. That means an early sightseeing start, because Chala, on the ocean, is another 109 miles (172 km) south. The village is small (about 1,500 people), but the fresh ocean air is enlivening and the delicious shellfish and "fin" fish plates, inviting. There are very basic accommodations at *Hostal Melchorita* in Punta Lomas, halfway between Nazca and Chala.

From Chala, the city of Arequipa is 252 miles (420 km) farther south. The area around Chala and the next important town, Atico, was important to the Imperial City of Cuzco because here was harvested and dried the seaweed that the mountain people prized for its iodine content. From this area the *chasquis,* the postal runners of the empire, ran fresh fish in relays to the court of the Inca.

Between Atico and Ocoña, the land gets drier; all vegetation disappears; the desolation seems more absolute; and the only sound comes from the ocean and its shrieking birds — a picturesque and thrilling scene: But keep going, for now you are beginning to descend into the green Majes Valley and soon will be entering the fishing town of Camaná, rebuilt inland after the original coastal town was destroyed in a 1599 earthquake. Camaná, attractive on a brisk summer's day, is prized in the Arequipa area because of its large freshwater shrimps.

The Pan-American Highway then shoots east and up toward Santa Isabel de Sihuas and crosses the Valley of Vitor; where it arches back down toward the ocean there is a cutoff that leads into Arequipa through the Uchumayo Valley. As you ease down the last hills, you will see one of Perú's most beautiful cities, Arequipa, richly colonial in its white volcanic stone mansions and churches, magnificently surrounded by several towering volcanoes, supremely serene, and politically and spiritually independent.

AREQUIPA: Diego de Almagro, Francisco Pizarro's first partner and later, bitter enemy (because of a dispute over dividing the riches of the Inca Empire), was probably the first Spaniard to enter Arequipa. It was a small but very important junction in the Inca road system: The Chilean road came from the south, and toward the north, it went through the now-pacified coastal kingdoms; eastward it ascended the high Andean passes to arrive at Cuzco.

The Spaniards established a small community in what is known today as the barrio of San Lázaro, the name of the first church erected. In 1540, the principal square was laid out, and the Spanish town of Arequipa was formally established. In 1541 King Carlos gave "Beautiful Town of Arequipa" the rank of a city. "This city," writes Cieza de Leon, "is situated in the best and coolest spot suitable . . . and the location and climate of this city are so good that it is reputed the healthiest and pleasantest in which to live." And 438 years later his words still ring true.

Arequipa, 7,590 feet above sea level, is one of the world's few cities where "eternal springtime" reigns. Temperatures vary between 54° and 70°F (12° and 22°C) throughout the year, and the city rarely has a day where at least a few hours of brilliant sunshine do not illuminate turquoise skies and warm the *sillar* colonial houses and churches in the heart of the old city. *Sillar* is the white volcanic stone resulting from the lava overflow of the several volcanoes that surround the city and that were immensely active centuries ago. Even today El Misti, Arequipa's Vesuvius (and the resemblance to Vesuvius is striking), smokes from time to time.

Because of the *sillar* material, the city is called La Ciudad Blanca (the White City). But there are some who point out that the real origin of that title lies with the town edict passed a few years after the city's founding, limiting residency within the city to the Spanish whites and their Indian servants. All other Indians who had business in the city (artisans, mechanics, builders, and manual laborers) had to leave at the close of each day to their encampments beyond the city walls. Be that as it may, Arequipa merits its title today more than ever for the concerted effort to restore to their pristine loveliness the *sillar* mansions and churches that abound in the center. Arequipa merits a visit of at least 3 or 4 days.

Like the tourist arriving in Cuzco by airplane, the visitor flying to Arequipa may experience a bit of *soroche.* Because almost all the magnificent architecture is centrally located, a tourist can do practically all sightseeing on foot. Except for the market of San Camilo and the immediately surrounding streets, Arequipa is still a safe city for tourists; obviously, one should still take precautions. If you want to rent a car, get in touch with *Avis/Arequipa Rent-a-Car* (Calle Piérola; phone: 21-43-30). If you have come by car and want a checkup, try Servicentro 2001 (Av. Jesús 318; phone: 21-6575), or consult your hotel. The tourist office, open Mondays through Fridays, is at La Merced 117, second floor.

The Plaza de Armas is among the most beautiful central-city squares in all Perú. Besides its trees and pretty fountain, the plaza is enhanced by the liveliness of the constant flow of people just taking a short rest on its many benches. From the plaza you get a good view of the mountains that form Arequipa's background: the famous El Misti and the Chachani and Pichupichu. The cathedral dominates the plaza; rebuilt in the last century, after one of Arequipa's numerous earthquakes, its unusual façade is oddly impressive. The interior is 19th-century pseudo-baroque.

The heart of the plaza, although not immediately on it, is the Jesuit church, La Compañía. The church, begun in 1650 and finished 48 years later, has a front and side entrance, both remarkable for the *sillar* carvings above the doors. The interior of the church shines with quiet dignity because of the unadorned *sillares;* it's further distinguished by the principal and side altars of carved wood covered with gold leaf.

At the upper end of the left-hand aisle are two sacristies. Passing through the first, which is adorned with not unusual paintings, you will enter the second, which must be one of the most beautiful rooms in the entire country. If you can speak some Spanish (or use sign language), ask the caretaker to turn off the lights so that the second sacristy is dim when you go in. Then ask him to turn on the lights and you will literally gasp at the brillance, freshness, and vividness of the colors. The sacristy, also known as St. Ignatius's Chapel, is a polychromatic "high." It must not be omitted from your visit to Arequipa. The church is open from 9 to 11:30 AM and from 3:30 to 5:30 PM; there is an admission fee of about $1.

On the Morán Street side of La Compañía are the church's cloisters. Recently restored, these cloisters breathe the starkness of the spiritual exercises of Loyola, the founder of the Jesuits, and contrast sharply with the exotic beauty of the Chapel of St. Ignatius in the church. However, the columns and their crowns offer excellent examples of the high artistic level that stone carving had reached in 17th-century Spanish Perú.

Among other churches and cloisters worth the visitor's detailed study are Santo Domingo (the corner of Calle Santo Domingo and Calle Piérola) and San Francisco (in the small plaza and at the end of the street). Both churches are *sillar,* but what is most attractive is the combined use of red brick and white *sillar* within. The main altars are of sculpted wood covered with thin sheets of beaten silver. San Francisco has spacious cloisters; those of Santo Domingo are more intimate and garden-like. The art museum in San Francisco offers some fine examples of both the 17th-century *limeño* and *cusqueño* schools of painting. Also you will see two illuminated psalters with pages of lamb's skin. The Chapel of the Sorrowful Virgin in the Church of San Francisco is another of those small chapel jewels one discovers in the dimly lit corners of so many of Perú's churches, especially in the Andes. An interesting ecclesiastical "novelty" is the group of saints and angels surrounding the image of the Virgin. The whole scene is mounted in a gilt Cinderella-like coach, which was drawn through the streets of colonial Arequipa on the Franciscan-inspired Feast of the Immaculate Conception of the Virgin on December 8.

The most interesting colonial architectural complex is the Convent of Santa Catalina, on the street of the same name (301). It was founded in the 1570s as a cloister principally for the daughters of well-to-do families. Except for the daily tolling of its bells, Santa Catalina meant little to the vast majority of the population until 1971, when the government opened a large portion of the ancient cloisters for visitors. The few nuns who were left retired to the new convent built for them in one corner of the extensive grounds, leaving the rest for visitors to discover that 400 years of history had bypassed this corner of Arequipa.

Santa Catalina Convent is really a small, late-16th-century Peruvian city of mestizo architecture. It has houses, streets, cooking areas, cloisters, a church, and the traditional isolated cells. The wealthy young women who entered Santa Catalina in its first 250 years of existence brought their serving maids and cooks with them, as well as large dowries. You can judge the social and financial status of some of the sisters by the size and richness of their quarters, the spiritual values of others by the ascetic cast of their cells. The church is open from 9 AM to 5 PM, and there's a small admission fee. The staff of girl guides is well informed. The other churches are open from 7 AM to noon and from 4 to 7 PM, but check with your hotel first to verify the time — like the names of Peruvian streets, Peruvian schedules have a habit of changing.

Your choice of restaurants in Arequipa is far more diverse than anywhere else on this route. *La Chopería* (San José 103, Cerro Colorado; phone: 21-76-7) serves German and Peruvian dishes. A great place for lunch outdoors is *Restaurant Campestre El Labrador* (at Km 3.5 of Camino Chilina; phone: 22-84-74) where you get a beautiful view of the surrounding mountains. *Restaurante Picanteria Sol de Mayo* (Jerusalén 207, Yanahuara; phone: 22-55-46) is also worth a visit, as is *Chez Nino* (Calle San Francisco

125; phone: 23-44-52), one of the city's great restaurants, serving a wide variety of regional specialties.

Among many of the *picanterías,* country-type restaurants, which only serve long, leisurely afternoon lunches, you can try *Sol de Mayo* (Jerusalén 207), in the suburb of Yanahuara, *El Roho* in the suburb of Tiabaya, and *La Capitanita* in the suburb of Antiquilla. (Any taxi driver will know where the last two are.) At times, these places could offer more in the way of cleanliness in both kitchens and bathrooms, but as long as you stick to cooked foods and beer or soft drinks (or mineral water), you should come out safely. The *picantería* serves typical *arequipeñan* food treats, with or without hot sauce, that include *chicharrones* (fired bits of pork or chicken), *ocopa* (boiled potatoes with a piquant peanut sauce), *rocotto relleno* (hot red peppers, boiled and stuffed with ground beef, onions, raisins, and boiled egg), and *cuychactado* (fried pressed guinea pig; you might want to remove the head and paws before eating).

Perhaps because of the usually cold nights (except in the summer) or because of the tradition of parties and dances at home or at the *Club de Arequipa,* nightlife in Arequipa barely swings. However, some of the discotheques more favored by the younger residents are the following: *Olimpo Club Discoteca* (Calle Rivero 113-A); *La Miel* (San Francisco 203); *Papillón* (Av. Para 112; phone: 23-64-8).

If you like sweets, buy some chocolates at *La Ibérica,* on the corner of Morál and Jerusalén. Among the better artisan shops are: *Arte Perú,* at Los Claustros of La Compañía (the Jesuit Cloisters); *Artesanías del Perú,* the government-managed organization that sells directly for the artisans (Santo Domingo 120, beside the entrance to the Jesuit Cloisters); *Casa Sechi* (Calle Mercaderes 111); *Inti* (Calle Zela 202, across from the small square beside the Church of San Francisco); and a fascinating antique shop without a name, across from the entrance to Santa Catalina (Santa Catalina 206). You will find two other artisan shops in the passageway behind the cathedral, *Quero Arte Popular* at 199 and *Artesanías* at 119. *The Galerías Colonial,* in the second block of Calle San Juan de Dios, has a number of small shops specializing in particular handicraft products, like leather goods, for which Arequipa is famed. *Alpaca 111* (San Juan de Dios 111; phone: 21-23-47) sells fine fabrics, yarn, sweaters, scarves, and furs.

The best way to see the old suburbs of Arequipa is to take a taxi. Arrange this through your hotel — for route, hours, and price. One route takes you through Yanahuara on to Cayma and then to Yura, where there is a pleasant *Hotel de Turistas* and thermal baths (not always too clean). Yanahuara and Cayma have impressive colonial churches, built with the ubiquitous *sillar* and with graciously sculpted portals. The plaza in Yanahuara is singularly beautiful and offers a good view of the city. In Yura you can have a good lunch at the hotel and enjoy the gardens if not the sulfur baths. By another route you can go out to Tingo and Tiabaya, famous for their *picanterías,* which specialize in delicacies such as *chicharrones, cuychactado,* boiled corn and lima beans served with cheese, and beer and *chicha.* Also see Sabandía, which is close to the city and has a lovely restored flour mill.

En Route from Arequipa – If you have time, go up to the province of Cailloma. It's a 4-hour drive up into the high Andes behind Arequipa and El Misti. The highway, although unpaved, is one of the better ones in southern Perú because of the work on the Majes irrigation project. The highway circles up and around El Misti, giving you a striking look at that old firehorse that spewed out so many tons of lava over the past centuries. You drive a little above 13,120 feet across a cold and desolate *puna* (mountain plateau) where often in the distance you will see a herd of scurrying vicuña, and down into the enchanting Colca Valley, which has been settled for centuries.

The Collahua tribe was, in spite of the province's proximity to Cuzco, one of the last of the Andean peoples to be conquered by the Inca. On both sides of the valleys you will find tremendous pre-Inca farming terraces; in the small villages are traces of an indigenous civilization centuries old, though modified by Spanish feudalism. This is an extraordinary trip.

BEST EN ROUTE

Accommodations along this route are the standard Peruvian fare — prices range from $40 or more (very expensive); $20 to $35 (expensive); between $11 and $19 (moderate); and under $10 (inexpensive). Most hotels, especially the *Turistas* owned by the state, are clean, with good-sized rooms, modern facilities (private baths), and restaurants. As elsewhere, it's a good idea to reserve your rooms before you arrive, either phoning directly or through your travel agent.

PARACAS

Paracas – This first-class hotel has bungalow accommodations, private baths, swimming pool, and meeting facilities. Bahía de Paracas (phone: 22-20; in Lima, 46-48-65). Very expensive.

ICA

Las Dunas – A very good hotel-cum-resort in an interesting area with a good year-round climate. Accommodations are large modern rooms with bath, and facilities include tennis, golf, pool, and a landing pad for air service to nearby Nazca. Excursions to the Paracas Peninsula easily arranged. At km 300 of Panamericana South, Ica (phone: 23-10-31). Reservations through the office at Las Magnolias 889, San Isidro, Lima (phone: 42-41-80 or 42-30-90), or in the US, through American Express (phone: 800-327-7737, or 800-327-3573). Very expensive.

Centro Vacacional – Small hotel offering clean, comfortable rooms. Av. La Angostura s/n (phone: 20-01). Moderate.

Turista – This state-owned hotel has clean rooms, a swimming pool, and a restaurant. Av. Los Maestros sn (phone: 23-33-20; or call EnturPerú in Lima, 72-19-28). Moderate.

NAZCA

Turistas – Small, cozy hotel with a restaurant where you can order a nice, thick, shrimp soup. Av. Bolognesi s/n (phone: 60; or call EnturPerú in Lima, 72-19-28). Moderate.

AREQUIPA

Crismar – Centrally located hotel with clean rooms and good service. Calle Morál 105 (phone: 21-52-90). Expensive.

Turistas Arequipa – A lovely, large hotel just outside the city but within comfortable walking distance. Plaza Bolívar (phone: 21-55-30). Reservations can be made through EnturPerú in Lima. Expensive.

El Portal – Modern hotel on the Plaza de Armas, with a good bar and restaurant; some rooms have balconies with a view. Portal de Flores 116 (phone: 21-55-30). Expensive.

Turistas de Colca – Recently opened, this hotel is the only (and very pleasant) place to stay in the Colca Valley if you want to enjoy the natural wonders of the valley and canyon. Reservations must be made through EnturPerú (phone: 72-19-28). Expensive.

Posada del Puente – A cozy downtown hostelry. Av. Bolognesi 101 (phone: 21-74-44). Moderate.

Viza – A small hotel near the bus station. Calle Perú 202 (phone: 23-23-01). Moderate.

Cuzco and the Inca Ruins

The year was 1479, and Indians from as far as the arid Pacific coast, from the magnificent waters of Lake Titicaca, from the distant kingdom of Quito, and from the steamy jungles of the lower eastern slopes were arriving at the brink of the Cuzco hills and throwing themselves on their knees as they contemplated the gold and silver spectacle below them. Gazing down at the narrow valley, they cried out their pounding faith and burning reverence: "Cuzco, oh Great City, we Salute You!" For that was the year the empire of the Incas was reaching its apex under the masterly rule of Capac Inca Túpac Yupanqui, which translates to "The One and Only Child of the Divine God of the Sun." In 1445 his father, Pachacutec, had begun the great expansion of the Inca's small principality of Cuzco, spreading eastward to encompass all of Bolivia and the northern provinces of Argentina. It was an almost incredible military feat, one considered to be on a par with the great conquests of Alexander the Great, the Romans, and Napoleon.

Unfortunately, Inca domination over indigenous Indian groups throughout that area was relatively brief and not strong enough to counter the 1532 "invasion" of Francisco Pizarro. With his small band, Pizarro destroyed the mightiest empire ever built in the Western Hemisphere.

The following year, the Spaniards entered Cuzco itself; within 30 years, the city no longer existed — apart from some walls of the various palaces and temples and the great fortress of Sacsayhuamán — once the jewel of the City of the Sun. From 1534, Inca Cuzco was replaced by Spanish mansions and squares and churches. However, the Spaniards never quite replaced the Inca spirit of the city, even to this day, which you can note by listening to the people on the street: The Quechua language, the lingua franca of the Inca empire, is as prevalent as Spanish among the people today.

To put the record straight, the Spanish under Pizarro probably could not have captured this mighty empire as easily as they did had it not been for the fratricidal war between the two sons of Huayna Capac — Huascar, the legitimate heir, and Atahualpa, the pretender at least to Quito and the northern territories of Tahuantinsuyo, or the Kingdom of the Four Quarters, as the Inca called their empire. The Spanish arrived at the moment when Atahualpa not only had destroyed the armies of Huascar but also had fatally abolished the governing principle of the Inca empire — namely, that the Inca emperor was the child of the sun and, therefore, divinely appointed to his authoritarian role as the one and only ruler of these great provinces that formed the empire. Once Huascar, the "son of the sun," was captured and imprisoned by Atahualpa, the underlying basis of all Inca rule was destroyed. The Sun God either no longer had the power to protect his divine child or he had withdrawn his supernatural support. The empire began to collapse from within, a process that began even before the Spanish arrived.

The conquerors' primary motive was the search for the great stores of gold hidden throughout the empire. They had no interest in Inca culture and almost casually destroyed the great palaces and temples. The destructive process was accelerated when the conquerors fell to disputing among themselves over the distribution of lands and treasures, quarrels that eventually erupted into full-scale war between the followers of Pizarro and those of Diego de Almagro in 1538.

The chaos that prevailed in and around Cuzco and throughout the empire in these turbulent years included the demolition of the great infrastructure of communications (namely, the roads) and of the planned economy whereby the agricultural system and the interchange of all kinds of merchandise adequately served the needs of all the citizens of the empire. Many of the marvelous terraces were torn down by the Spaniards, so that great areas of arable lands were lost. Irrigation systems were either rendered useless or completely neglected, and the storehouses of food and clothing were burned. The result: death through both war and starvation.

This very capsuled view of the events that occurred in this historic area 500 years ago may not prepare you for the Cuzco of the late twentieth century. A city of 200,000 people, Cuzco is a blend of Indian, Spanish, and mestizo, a charming city 11,000 feet above sea level. What is encountered today are subtle reminders of its 1,000-year-old history at the turn of almost every corner. Sit on a bench in the Plaza de Armas, close your eyes, and you can be carried back to when this square was called Huacaypata and was bounded on all sides by the sumptuous palaces of the dead and mummified Inca and the imperial residences of the living Inca. If you listen carefully, you will hear the muffled drums and the mournful wails of the great days of penance, when all foreigners were forced outside the city while the Inca and his people begged for forgiveness and release from their evils from the Creator God Viracocha and from Inti, the Sun God. Or your eyes will be caught by the rich and dazzling colors worn by members of the court and by the glitter of shields, spears, and images, as the Feast of Inti Raymi (June 24), the day of the return of the Sun to his people in Cuzco, is celebrated with joyful songs, animated dancing, and drinking. Off in a far corner you see the somber, finely cut walls of the House of the Chosen Women, where some 3,000 women and girls serve their divine spouse, the Sun, or wait to be called by their earthly spouse, the Sapa Inca.

The reveries of yesterday are dissolved by the shouts of the plaza's ice cream peddlers or shoeshine boys, and you open your eyes to the magnificent sight of the cathedral. The House of the Chosen Women has become the Monastery of Santa Catalina, while the palaces have been replaced by Spanish mansions whose first floors are occupied by small stores and restaurants. The hoofbeats of the conquerors' horses no longer ring against the square's cobblestones; the clashing swords and thundering blunderbuses have been silent for four centuries.

Despite its beauty and brilliant history, Cuzco today suggests a poverty that rages through Perú. Its population grows daily with the arrival of more and more disillusioned Indian peasants who can no longer survive on the land. The city also has a sizable floating population of foreigners and young Peruvians from the coast who come for a few months or even years to soak up the "spiritual" atmosphere of Cuzco, Machu Picchu, and Urubamba. Cocaine plays a large part in attracting some of these semipermanent residents. Coca tea, legal in Perú, is offered to visitors as an effective aid in acclimating to the altitude, and most Indians in the Andes chew coca leaves. However, cocaine use is illegal and the penalties extremely stiff, especially for foreigners who are often accused (rightly or not) of smuggling (see *Drinking and Drug Laws,* GETTING READY TO GO).

Cuzco can be reached by road from Lima via the Central Highway to Huancayo, although this is not recommended because it goes through Ayacucho, where terrorist activity is on the rise. You can also drive via Nazca–Puquio–Abancay, if you are prepared for the extremely rough road. The journey is difficult and will take from 3 to 5 days, depending on the weather. The best way to reach Cuzco is by plane (AeroPerú and Faucett have daily flights from Lima), which only takes about 50 minutes.

Traditionally, tourists have dedicated 2 days and 2 nights to Cuzco, arriving early in the morning from Lima (see *Lima,* THE CITIES). They plan on a few hours of rest to accustom themselves to the altitude, then spend an afternoon briefly touring the interior city and later explore the Inca ruins in the city's outskirts. One day is devoted fully to visiting Machu Picchu — by a 3-hour train ride, either alone or with a tour group. Travelers should remember, however, that Machu Picchu is a heavily visited site. Below the ruins there is a small *Turistas* hotel, which offers its guests a chance to have Machu Picchu to themselves from 3 PM, when the train to Cuzco departs, until 1 PM, when the next train arrives, and is well worth the extra time. Reservations are a must and can be made in Lima through EnturPerú (phone: 72-19-28) or any local travel agency.

Like other cities in Perú, hotels in Cuzco offer a mixed choice of accommodations — some excellent, most comfortable, and some bathless. Outside Lima, there is little to be found in the way of sophisticated hotels, restaurants, or nightclubs. The attraction of the area is in its pre-Columbian and colonial artifacts and architecture; a tourist's comfort is considered secondary. To get a feel for the area before you visit, you might look at any of a number of books, including *The Ancient Civilizations of Perú,* by J. Alden Mason (Plata Publishing Ltd., Switzerland); *Perú under the Incas,* by C. A. Blurland (Putnam's); *Lords of Cuzco,* by Burr Cartwright Brundage (University of Oklahoma Press); *The Conquest of the Incas,* by John Hemming (Macmillan); *The Royal Road of the Inca,* by Victor W. Von Hagen (Gordon and Cremonesi, London); and *The Incas of Pedro de Cieza de León,* translated by Harriet de Onis (University of Oklahoma Press). Also highly recommended is *Exploring Cuzco,* by Peter Frost. An excellent book on walking tours through Cuzco was published by William G. Evans (Editorial Universitario Lima); copies are still available in some of the mustier Cuzco bookshops. The *Lima Times* office also has a very good collection of hard-to-find Cuzco guidebooks at Carabaya 928, 3rd floor, Lima (phone: 28-40-69).

Because the center of Cuzco, where all the main tourist attractions are, is not very big, it is easy to get around on foot — that is, if climbing up and down hills does not bother you at such a high altitude. We strongly suggest that you spend a few hours walking around the town, soaking in Cuzco's very special atmosphere. Travel with a friend to the central market area, near the station for the trains to Machu Picchu. There are plenty of pickpockets about, awaiting the unwary solitary tourist. This is also true of the train station itself here, and the other one for Puno departures. In Cuzco, as in similar cities with many tourists, plenty of self-taught guides will show you around and help you to spend more money on handcrafts than the goods merit. If you don't know enough Spanish for making your purchases, you are better off sticking to the well-known artisan shops in the center of the city.

On-the-spot tourist information can be had from the Ministry of Tourism, Galerías Turísticas, Av. El Sol 103, Mondays through Fridays from 8 AM to 5:30 PM; Saturdays, 8:30 AM to 12:30 PM. In addition, many travel agencies in Cuzco can provide information and make arrangements, although these should preferably have been made from Lima before your arrival in Cuzco.

CUZCO: Start your tour of the city with the cathedral and its accompanying churches of El Triunfo and the Holy Family. On the site of Viracocha's Palace, the church is considered by many to be the finest in the Western Hemisphere, principally because it reflects the mixing of the Spanish Renaissance style and Indian stonemason skills. The cathedral took almost 100 years to build, and many of its stones were quarried at Sacsahuamán, the immense Inca fortress overlooking the Sacred City. Many sculptures and paintings are within the building; of particular interest is the flame-blackened image of Christ Crucified, revered by the *cusqueños* under the title of the *Lord of the Earthquakes*. The famous Maria Angola bell in the north tower, cast in 1659 from a mixture of gold, silver, and bronze, weighs over a ton and is the largest bell in South America: It has a melodic and deep tone that can be heard up to 25 miles away. The church is open to the public from 6 AM to noon and from 3 to 6:30 PM daily.

To the right of the cathedral is El Triunfo, the first church built by the Spanish in Cuzco; the present building dates from 1733. Originally the church commemorated the victory of the Spanish soldiers over the troops of Manco II, who in 1536 was determined to expel the Spaniards from his capital once and for all. Manco II had besieged them hiding within a storage tower that stood where the church is, and he was ready to burn the heavy thatched roof and smoke them out. The desperate conquistadores, however, called upon the help of the Virgin Mary, and especially their patron of Spain, St. James the Apostle, both of whom appeared to save them, preventing the roof from blazing up and frightening the Indian soldiers.

The Church of the Holy Family is on the other side of the cathedral but is without much historical importance, dating back only to 1733. Looking up the hill beside the Holy Family Church, you will see an imposing Spanish mansion, the so-called Palace of the Admiral, which proudly overlooks the Spanish colonial city of Cuzco. Built in the early 1600s, the house was badly damaged in the 1950 earthquake and is now being restored by the government. Following this street past the Palace of the Admiral, which houses the Museum of Art (or Regional Historical Museum), you reach the Plaza de las Nazarenas. On the left, across the square, is the House of the Serpents, so called because of the seven snakes carved on the wall; they supposedly protected the house and its occupants from evil. The house is open from 9 AM to noon and from 3 to 6 PM daily.

Turn right on the Calle Palacios leading off the plaza and walk downhill to the Museum of Religious Art, originally the site of the Palace of Inca Roca, the sixth Inca. The museum is a lovely example of the finest in Peruvian architecture and merits close observation: the carved doors and balconies, the Moorish patio and fountain, the tiles throughout the building. In addition, there is a fine collection of paintings belonging to the so-called Cuzco school that flourished from the 16th through the 18th centuries. The paintings offer a fine example of the crossbreeding (*mestizaje*) in art; that is, Catholic religious scenes peopled by saints with Indian faces.

Outside the principal door of the museum, to the right and a few paces up, you will discover embedded in the foundation wall the magnificent Twelve-Angled Stone, a fabulous example of the best in Inca stonecutting. The imperial stonemasons had mastered the art of fitting irregular stones so perfectly that no mortar was needed. Open from 9 AM to noon, and 3 to 5 PM, except Sundays.

The Church of San Blas, which is above the art museum on the same street, is especially noted for its wood pulpit, carved from a single block of wood in the 18th century. The church is open from 9 AM to noon and 3 to 5 PM daily except Sundays. In this section of the city you will discover the splendid little studios used today by Cuzco artists.

Returning to the Plaza de Armas you will find the Jesuit church, La Compañía, considered by many to be the most beautiful church in Cuzco. If not the most beautiful, it is certainly the most representative of Cuzco baroque architecture. The church took almost 100 years to complete because of its intricate interior; gold leaf covers the finely carved wood of the altars and the balconies. On the other side of this narrow street (once called the Street of the Sun, because it led from Cuzco's main plaza to its most sacred structure, Coricancha, the Temple of the Sun) is the wall of what was the House of the Chosen Women. The church is open daily from 9 AM to noon and 3 to 5 PM daily except Sundays.

Cross the street at the foot of Loreto and follow the Pampa del Castillo to Coricancha, now the site of Santo Domingo Church, actually built on the foundations of the Temple of the Sun. Coricancha means "Enclosure of Gold" and included not only the Sun's home but also that of the Moon Mother, Rainbow, God of Thunder, Lightning, Rain, and the Morning Star. There were smaller houses or chapels for the lesser gods, including those of the captured peoples of the empire.

The Enclosure of Gold must have been the most impressive group of buildings in the holy city of Cuzco. Walls were sheeted with gold; a garden of flowers and animals was cast in silver and gold, as was the area where both llamas and young children were kept to be sacrificed to the gods. You can get some idea of the structural plan of Coricancha by the restorations taking place within the cloisters of Santo Domingo. It's open from 9 AM to noon and from 2 to 5 PM daily except Sundays.

Back on the Plaza de Armas, turn right onto the Calle Santa Catalina Angosta to visit the House of the New Chosen Women, the cloistered Catholic Dominican nuns who came from Arequipa in 1605 to establish a convent in the House of the Chosen Women of the Sun. Recently much of the convent has been restored and is now open to the public Mondays through Saturdays from 9 AM to noon and from 3 to 5 PM.

The Church and Cloisters of Our Lady of Mercy — La Merced — merit a place on your tour, especially the cloisters, which are among the most beautiful of viceregal Perú. The most famed possession of the cloister is the religious vessel known as La Custodia, made of 48 pounds of pure gold and containing 1,518 diamonds and some 600 emeralds, pearls, topazes and rubies. The church is open from 5 to 10 AM and 6 to 8 PM daily; the cloisters and Religious Art Museum, from 9 AM to noon and 3 to 5 PM daily except Sundays.

When budgeting your sightseeing time, be sure to leave some for the Museum of Archaeology of the National University of Cuzco (Calle Tigre 165), which was founded in 1848 and has some excellent collections from various Peruvian cultures. Don't forget to ask to see the gold and silver figures that represent some of the Inca gods. The museum is open weekdays from 8 AM to noon and from 3 to 5:30 PM.

The stores in Cuzco have touristy merchandise and specialize in alpaca and sheep's wool products. The *Galerías Turisticas* (Av. El Sol 103) has a good display of the most typical handicraft products of the Cuzco area. Fine pottery is available in the *Fábrica de Artesanías de Ruiz Caro* (Calle El Triunfo 387; phone: 22-43-61), and beautiful alpaca skin rugs, bedspreads, and the like can be obtained in the *Fábrica de Artesanías de Federico Alarco* (Calle Pavitos 567; phone: 22-54-11) and at *Artesanías Pérez* (Av. Ejercito 1640; phone: 23-24-96). If you want something special, do go to the *Plazoleta,* San Blas 634 (behind the church of the same name), to make a choice from the delicate but at times crude pottery figures made by the family of the late Hilario Mendivil. Other fine artisans also work in the area; just walk around and look.

For entertainment, two small theaters specialize in the folkloric dances of the area, *Centro Qosco* (Av. Sol 604; phone: 22-79-01) and *Peña Folklórica* (Montero 114). Presentations at both theaters begin at 8 PM. If you'd rather do the dancing yourself, there is the disco *El Muki* (Santa Catalina Angosta 114), half a block from the Plaza de Armas and decorated to simulate a salt mine. Its two dance floors are filled with younger *cusqueños* and tourists until 4 AM. The only nightclub in town is *El Truco* on the Plaza Regocijo; it has both a small restaurant and live entertainment (phone: 23-24-41).

One of the newest and most interesting night spots is the *Qhatuchay* in the Plaza de Armas (Portal Confitería 233, 2nd floor). The attractiveness of the place is not so much in the surroundings but in its clientele and its show, which sticks to Andean and coastal and Latin American music. There's no rock 'n' roll. Beer and *pisco* are the only beverages served, accompanied by tasty, often hot hors d'oeuvres and bread and cheese. The *Qhatuchay* is a special meeting place for tourists who did not come thousands of miles to spend an evening in a discotheque listening to music indigenous to England and the US, but who are interested in hearing the *huaynos* of the sierra and the *marineras* of the coast. Open from 8 PM until 4 AM; you have to go early to get a table.

While Cuzco has relatively decent hotels, restaurants are only fair and often poor. Around the Plaza de Armas, try *Paititi* or *Victor. El Truco* (the nightclub with a restaurant) is decent, but the rest are dismal. There are good, but far from hygienic, restaurants that cater to the local people. Recommended are *Pizzería La Mama, Mesón Espaderos, Mesón Alhambra,* and for delicious local fare try *Quinta Eulalia.* See the *Perú Guide* for details. One particularly good one is at the *El Dorado,* which offers marvelous native food that is tempered to the non-Cuzco palate. Recommended are the *chupes* (heavy soups) and local Andean lake trout. For some reason, most of the eateries forget travelers like to taste the native dishes, so their food comes out as Cuzco-Norteamericano.

To get around, local bus service is good in Cuzco but only if you can ask directions and understand the Spanish answers. Car rentals are available through the major hotels and through *Avis Rent-a-Car* (Av. El Sol 900; phone: 22-79-01) or *National Rent-a-Car* (Santa Catalina Angosta 139; phone: 22-45-91). All the better hotels have their own bus service meeting each flight at the airport. Organized group or private tours are available through local tour operators. Check the *Perú Guide* for a list of the best operators in Cuzco. To get around, taxis are available and usually inexpensive (about $5 an hour in town); but with the help of someone from the hotel or tourist agency, fix the price for the trip before starting out.

En Route from Cuzco – After a good look at Cuzco, get out into the hills and visit the Inca ruins. A pleasant, second-day circuit will take you through the Sacred Valley of the Inca, the Urubamba. For this tour, you had better hire a car and give yourself lots of time, starting at 8 AM. Your first stop will be at the overpowering Pucara of Sacsayhuamán, or the Fortress of the Speckled Hawk, on the northern outskirts of Cuzco, within walking distance of the city.

SACSAYHUAMÁN: One of the most stupendous structures of pre-Columbian America, it is a fortress begun by the first great conqueror of the known worlds, Pachacutec, sometime after 1445. Seventy-five years later it was still under construction, during the reign of the last of the pre-Conquest Inca, the unfortunate Huascar. When the Inca were not off warring somewhere in their vast empire, there were probably 20,000 construction workers constantly adding to the vast edifice — quarrying the great blocks of stone, dragging them on log rollers to the site, and fitting them in place. Sacsayhuamán is an incredible heap of engineered masonry, and before its destruction by the Spaniards — who used it as a quarry for the stone needed to build Cuzco — it was the most wondrous building in the whole of the Kingdom of the Four Quarters (of the World). The modern reproduction of the ancient Inca feast of Inti Raymi on June 24 is staged with this brooding fortress as a background.

Of all the holidays observed throughout Perú and especially the Cuzco area, Inti Raymi is perhaps the most important. Coinciding with the Feast Day of San Juan Bautista (St. John the Baptist), this was once the time for the Inca observance of Inti Raymi, the feast commemorating the winter solstice. The week leading up to the feast is a time for partying, parading, drinking, and dancing. On the 24th, there's a costumed replay of the ancient procession and a symbolic sacrifice to the sun. (Hotel space in Cuzco is at a premium at this time.)

The shrines around Cuzco are linked to the Inca calendar, according to a study conducted about 5 years ago. There are 328 shrines in all, set in a circular pattern around Cuzco. They are believed to be spread out along 41 lines, each shrine representing one day of the Inca year; the lines, representing one week, and three sets of lines representing 1 month (the Inca year was 12 months divided into 3 weeks, or 36 weeks a year).

Inti Raymi is not the only Inca holiday celebrated in Perú; Kapaq Situa, the Inca month of purification, occurs in August, and various acts of penance are performed by the Indians. The Festival of the Queen, Koya Raymi, coincides with the September 8 Feast of the Nativity of the Blessed Virgin; festivities center around Cuzco's Twelve-Angled Stone.

En Route from Sacsayhuamán – About 4 miles (7 km) east is Quenko, another Inca shrine that dates back to the days of Huayna Capac; its prosaic use, however, goes back further. Take a look at the great stone block almost 18 feet high.

Puca-Pucará, about 3½ miles (6 km) north of Cuzco on the road to Pisac, is what's left of a small fortress that probably guarded the road down to Pisac and the Sacred Valley of the Inca. You get another view of the hillside terraces, stairways, tunnels, and towers so common to Inca architecture.

Tambo Machay, a bit farther north, was a bathing place for the Inca and royal women of the court. A handsome place, it offers in miniature some of the rich engineering details of the architecture of the Inca.

Leaving behind these lovely Inca ruins, you head down the road — and it really is down, for you will be descending almost 1,500 feet — to the village of Pisac in the Urubamba Valley. It is advisable that in the rainy season you find a driver who has a happy relationship with hairpin curves on the descent. Pisac itself has glorious terraces climbing up the mountainside, which is topped by the largest Inca fortification in the valley.

Pisac offers not only ruins and a Sunday Market (a bit touristy), but often a chance to hear a church mass in Quechua. About 50 miles from Cuzco at Chinchero is an interesting Indian market, which is also held on Sundays and features some very fine weaving. Because weekly markets break up around noon, the distance between the two makes it difficult to do both the Chinchero and Pisac markets on the same day. The area fishing is good, and you might like to match wits with the fighting trout of the Vilcanota River.

Continuing from Pisac you pass through the village of Urubamba. Particularly pleasant for lunch is the *Hotel Alhambra 111* in Yucay.

But your destination is the great fortress of Ollantaytambo (about 45 mi/72 km from Cuzco), one of the very few Inca towns still distinctively Inca and inhabited. The fortress, intricate and elegantly constructed, is one of those dozen places in Perú that lends itself to dreaming of the great empire that was Tahuantinsuyo. The ruins here include temples, baths, and military defenses.

Now go back to Cuzco to depart for the most famous of them all — Machu Picchu. Or you can also reach Machu Picchu from Ollanta; the autowagon and local train both stop here, but if you chose to the autowagon, be sure to arrange for your Ollanta pick-up in Cuzco.

MACHU PICCHU: Nothing written in the Spanish chronicles, which depended upon the oral histories of the Indians, prepares you for this dramatically isolated city of the Inca, unseen by Occidental eyes for centuries. Apparently the Indians who lived in the vicinity knew of the citadel, so loftily placed above the Río Vilcanota and shrouded by clouds that envelope the more than 200 buildings of the city during the rainy season. As the crow (or the condor) flies, Machu Picchu is only about 15 minutes from the cold heights of Ollantaytambo, but it has the climate of the semitropical, richly foliaged, eastern slopes of the Andes.

The theories about the city are varied, but each one, though somewhat romantic in detail, is basically sound in itself. It *could* have been one fortress in a chain of fortresses erected by the Inca to protect the jungle flanks of the empire from the savages who made sporadic raids into the national territory; it *could* have been a great religious sanctuary administered by a group of Chosen Women of the Sun, for the skeletons of mainly women have been found in its burial places; it *could* have been a training school for the noble youth of the empire; it *probably* was the last way station for the final Inca ruler and his nobles as they escaped from the Spaniards into what appeared to be the security of Vilcabamba in the jungle.

All we *know* is that Machu Picchu is an imposing architectural complex set in an awesome natural setting; it deservedly has helped Cuzco earn fame as a major archaeological capital of the world. Its granite forts, temples, altars, squares, fountains, and aqueducts were the site of a 1977 signing of a charter by world architects and planners to improve universal living conditions, so inspirational were the ruins, so fascinating its own, anonymous blueprints to them.

Machu Picchu lies 70 miles (112 km) northwest of Cuzco; the only way to get there is by the oft-times crowded narrow-gauge railroad that leaves Cuzco's San Pedro Station each day at 7 AM, arriving at approximately 10:30 AM. Because the return train leaves at 3 PM, bring your lunch with you from Cuzco or grab a bite at the *Hotel de Turistas,* recently expanded to better accommodate lunch guests and overnight visitors, and a wonderful place to be after the tourist train leaves. The trip to Machu Picchu is striking and full of scenic contrasts; try to sit by a left-hand window. Be prepared for rain from December through March; but even in the rain, the citadel is awe-inspiring.

Do everything you can to get a room at the one and only hotel on the mountain-top. The small *Hotel de Turistas* has recently grown from 17 to 31 rooms — scarcely enough supply to meet the demand. The hotel is fair, the food is just as fair, and neither factor is important as long as you can have the ruins basically to yourself when the tourist train leaves before sunset. Sunrise is even more spectacular. That peak you see in photographs of Machu Picchu is called Huayna Picchu. It's a steep climb, but the view from the top is hard to beat. Another more level walk follows the original Inca trail behind the ruins — about 2 hours to what may have been the entrance gate to the site.

If you spend one night or more, you can take the local train back to Cuzco at 1 PM instead of the tourist train at 3 PM. Although more picturesque, the trip is longer. You share the car with resident Peruvians and even their live produce. Book first class for a cushioned seat and take a lunch packed by the hotel.

From the rail station, you can look up to the mountain and see a now idle construction site. Conservationists lost their long-time lobby against building a new hotel on Machu Picchu, but the mountain won. The rock foundations turned out to be too soft to hold the planned 200-room inn.

There is one other way to reach Machu Picchu; the way its discoverer, US Senator Hiram Bingham, did in 1911, and that is on foot. Treks are organized from Cuzco; you take the train to km 88 and walk the next 65 miles. Depending on your stamina, you can take the high or low road, and organized expeditions are complete with the mandatory guide and a dozen or more bearers. There are no supply points along the way, so do not attempt the Inca trail alone (see *The Wild Continent,* DIVERSIONS).

BEST EN ROUTE

Hotels in and around Cuzco are very tourist-oriented. Several are very good, but some are poorly maintained and space can be hard to find. They generally provide hot water but no private baths; there's an occasional restaurant. What hurts, however, it that you pay for what you don't get: Prices for a double room range from an expensive $45 to $65; for moderate, figure $25 to $45; and anything under $25 is inexpensive. Make reservations beforehand, more so if you plan to be in the area in June during the feast of Inti Raymi.

CUZCO

Libertador – In Los Cuatro Bustos, a colonial mansion, this 131-room hotel is elegant. The *pisco* sours in the restaurant are better than the food or service. San Agustín 400 (phone: 23-26-01 or 23-19-61; in Lima, 42-01-66 or 42-19-95). Expensive.

Picoaga – You'll find pleasant accommodations and receive good service here. The bar and restaurant offer a great view of the surrounding mountains but not very good food. Santa Teresa 344 (phone: 22-76-91; in Lima, 28-63-14). Expensive.

Savoy – This property has 130 rooms, double and single, with private bath and shower. It's rather far from the center of town and requires a taxi ride to and from the main plaza. Av. El Sol 954 (phone: 22-43-22; in Lima, 47-81-88). Expensive.

El Dorado Inn – In the heart of town, it offers heated guestrooms with private bath, colonial-style public rooms, and a dining room and bar. Av. El Sol 395 (phone: 23-25-73 or 23-31-12). Expensive.

Alhambra – Here are 26 rooms with bath, as well as a restaurant that presents a nightly folklore show during dinner. Av. El Sol 594 (phone: 22-48-99). Expensive to moderate.

Hostal Inti – This hotel has recently been redecorated, and its 26 rooms have private baths. Its restaurant and its location are both good. Calle Matara 260 (phone: 22-84-01). Moderate.

San Agustín – Centrally located, it has 53 rooms, each with bath and telephone. Calle Maruri 300 (phone: 23-10-01; in Lima, 23-60-06). Moderate.

Espinar – Only a block from the Plaza de Armas, it has 36 rooms with private bath, and its restaurant has a fine view of the plaza. Portal Espinar 142 (phone: 23-30-91). Inexpensive.

Hostal Garcilaso – This small, 27-room colonial mansion has hot water and an elegantly arched patio. Calle Garcilaso 233 (phone: 23-35-01). Inexpensive.

PISAC

Chongo Chico – A small hotel with clean rooms, good food, and breathtaking view of the ruins. Centrally located (no phone). Moderate.

URUBAMBA

Hostal Naranjachayoh – This lovely hacienda has clean rooms and good food. On the road between Pisac and Urubamba (no phone). Moderate.
Alhambra 111 – A lovely little hotel in Yucay (no phone). Moderate.

MACHU PICCHU

Hotel de Turistas – The one and only place to stay at Machu Picchu has recently been remodeled and rooms have been added. It is now perfectly comfortable, and its restaurant can accommodate up to 300 people for self-service lunch. At the ruins. Reservations must be made through EnturPerú in Lima (phone: 72-19-28). Expensive.

Cuzco to Puno

The Inca Atahualpa could certainly be said to have been worth his weight in gold, for he cost his kingdom over $9.65 million in ransom and loot the conquistadores greedily possessed following his capture. But the greatest riches that the Spaniards took from the New World to Europe were its agricultural products. Many of the foods that make up the basic US diet originated in the Andean highlands, the richly fertile irrigated valleys in the coastal desert, and the low-lying slopes leading into the Amazon jungle. The Irish and the Idaho potatoes are of Peruvian ancestry, as are beans, sweet potatoes, yucca, hot and sweet peppers, tomatoes, cocoa, papaya, pineapple, and various nuts. Peruvian cotton is one of the most exquisite fibers in the world and alpaca and vicuña wool come from Perú. Great deposits of guano (the bird droppings fertilizer found on the offshore Peruvian islands), enormous quantities of copper and other minerals, and rich fishing grounds made the Land of the Four Quarters one of the world's naturally wealthy countries.

Sadly, Perú's later conquerors — the English, French, German, Italian, and North American as well as native Peruvians, Bolivians, Chileans, and Ecuadorians — have made enormous fortunes through their sacking of the Inca Empire, an exploitation that has continued through this century.

Yet even with its great natural resources, Perú is a desperately impoverished country. Someone wrote that Perú is a "beggar sitting on a mountain of gold"; he might have added that Perú is a beggar because it has never recovered from the conquistador mentality, which considers the national territory fair game for personal and corporate exploitation. However autocratic and despotic the Inca were — and they were both — they never neglected the cardinal rule necessary to maintain autocracy: Give the people enough food, decent work that reinforces their sense of human dignity, and ceremonial leisure.

When the Inca began their historic conquests in the 1430s, their kingdom consisted of little more than Cuzco and the immediate countryside. When, 50 years later, Túpac Inca Yupanqui completed the essential formation of the empire through conquest, the Land of the Four Quarters contained about 350,000 square miles of area and almost 3,000 miles of coastline. He and his father, Pachacutec, must be ranked beside Julius Caesar, Philip of Macedon, and Alexander. But not only did they conquer great landmasses, they also unified the many groups of people into a unique political organization.

The empire was divided into four political areas: Chinchasuyo (the Andean area from Cuzco to Quito), Anti Suyo (the Andean area to the east of Cuzco, descending into the beginning of the Amazon region), Contisuyo (coastal Perú from north of Arequipa to Tumbes), and Collasuyo (southern Perú, both mountains and coast; Bolivia; a small part of Paraguay; the Andean zone in Argentina-Tucumán; and Chile, to 35°S latitude). Collasuyo was the largest of the Four Quarters and probably the most important, both because of its agricultural and mineral wealth and because of the difficult political opposition that the Inca encountered there during their conquest.

The road from Cuzco to Puno follows more or less the major Inca highway that united Collasuyo to its Inca lords. Capac Ñan, the beautiful road, as the Inca called their 15,000 miles of major and connecting roads that physically knit the vast expanses together, probably surpassed the magnificent Roman road system, according to the information we have from both chroniclers of the Spanish conquest and archaeologists.

The departments of Cuzco and Puno, with a combined population of approximately 1.6 million, were referred to publicly as *la mancha india* (the Indian strain) until recently because the majority of their inhabitants are of primarily Indian ancestry. They spoke either Aymará or Quechua. Unfortunately, coastal and Lima residents have a tendency to look down upon the poor, illiterate Indians of the Andes.

The Quechua- and the Aymará-speaking Indians of the Andes live mainly on the fringe of modern political, social, and economic Perú. Having seen so many saviors come and go since the Conquest, they have little trust in the various rescue plans presented, whether they be by Peruvian civil or military rulers or by European and North American secular or religious missionaries.

A legend to remember as you are crossing the altiplano to Puno and come upon the solitary Indian pasturing his flock of sheep and alpaca or plowing his barren and rocky field is the following, recalled at countless feasts that began with the offering of a glass of *chicha* to Pachamama (Mother Earth). According to ancient Indian beliefs, the end of a historical age (the apocalypse) and the beginning of a new one (the renovation) occurs every 500 years. The apex of the Inca Empire happened in the reign of Túpac Inca Yupanqui, in the last years of the fifteenth century, which was also the beginning of the end of the Inca rule. At the end of the twentieth century another cataclysm should occur, and the world inaugurated by the Spanish invaders will be destroyed; a new creation, presided over by a spiritual descendant of Túpac Inca Yupanqui, will surge into being and the Indians, the true Peruvians, will be given back their land and their glory.

There are three ways of getting from Cuzco to Puno: train, car, or bus; the last two travel southeast along the Cuzco-Puno road. If you take the train, be prepared for a real humdinger of a trip — it leaves daily (except Sundays) at about 7 AM and arrives in Puno around 6 PM. The 11-hour trip is actually a roller-coaster ride, climbing up and down Andes and antiplano with some 30 stops — a real *loco* local. The ride one way costs about $10 first class; make reservations beforehand at the Huanchac Railroad (Av. Sol) in Cuzco. The first part of the trip is lovely, for the train passes through the Huatanay and Vilcanota valleys, both of which have many trees and rich farmlands. Once you reach the Continental Divide at La Raya, at 14,000 feet above sea level, and ease down onto the altiplano, with an average altitude of 12,500 feet, the terrain becomes a moonscape of cold and forbidding plains outside the train window. There is an otherworldly aspect to this part of the ride. Be sure to buy a reservation ticket for the midday meal served in the dining car to first-class passengers or take your own lunch. Note that the trains to Puno from Cuzco leave from a different rail station than do the trains to Machu Picchu. Keep careful track of your luggage when boarding the train, and if you are taking the train in from Puno to Cuzco, be particularly watchful. The train arrives after sundown, and there are many "porter" types who board to help you off the train. Carry everything you can yourself, particularly camera bags.

Going by car is not recommended in the rainy season months of November through April, since only a small portion of the highway is asphalt. Don't forget warm clothing; the morning hours on the altiplano are usually temperate, but after about 2 PM the air gets chillier, and by nighttime it's downright cold: Puno's average temperature is 47°F (8°C). If you want to travel by road but not rent a car, you can get a taxi, but this would be very expensive. However, you can go by bus, but the trip will be much like the one on the train, except less time-consuming. Check with a tourist agency in Cuzco. Two poor bus lines operating daily from Cuzco to Puno are Transportes Morales MORALITOS, SA (Calle Belén 451; phone: 22-86-51), which goes only as far as Juliaca (taxis complete the trip), and Transportes San Cristóbal, (Av. Muascar 120; phone: 31-84). If you want to continue on to La Paz, Bolivia, or down to Arequipa, these bus companies provide transport to either place. (There are no bathrooms along this route.) Transturin (Portal de Panes 109 in Cuzco; phone: 22-23-32) provides a tourist trip from Cuzco to La Paz, with a lunch stop at Copacabana on the Perú-Bolivia border and a motor launch ride across Lake Titicaca to Huatajata, where another bus takes passengers on to La Paz; the cost is approximately $50.

En Route from Cuzco – Your first stop is San Sebastian, a small town just 3 miles (5 km) southeast of Cuzco on the Cuzco-Puno Highway: Its Avenida de la Cultura boasts a beautiful colonial church constructed by the indigenous architect Manuel de Sahuaraura and contains many valuable paintings of the Cusqueño School, whose painters included Indians and mestizos of the 17th and 18th centuries. Continuing, you pass through San Jeronimo, which has a handsome church, and the town of Oropesa. From here, you on to Piquillacta, about 20 miles (33 km) from Cuzco.

PIQUILLACTA: This is literally called "flea town" in the Quechua tongue; it's a very large town, probably pre-Inca because of the use of uncut and undressed stone in the construction of terraces, retaining walls, and many houses. What is unique about the construction is the lack of doors and windows; perhaps the Inca used the buildings for storage. If so, one Peruvian engineer calculates that the 620 buildings would have held approximately 32,000 tons of food supplies.

En Route from Piquillacta – Four miles (7 km) south on the Cuzco-Puno Highway you enter the rich agricultural valley of the Rió Vilcanota and the town of Andahuailillas, a small town with an interesting church, supposedly built on the remains of an Inca temple. The ceiling is richly decorated, and there are many murals and paintings. The 17th-century organ is adorned with paintings of angels playing musical instruments. Back on the road, you pass through Urcos, once an important crossroads in the empire, and the towns of Quiquihana (house of crystal), Cusipata (beautiful region), and Combapata, formerly important way stations when the sovereign Inca went forth upon his beautiful road to visit his subjects in the Colla Quarter.

Tinta, a few miles south of Combabata, was the scene of a 16th-century revolt against tax burdens of the colonial administration in Lima led by Cacique (Chief) Condorcanqui, a direct descendant of the last ruling Inca. Taking the title of his distinguished ancestor, Condorcanqui called himself Túpac Amaru II. Under this name he, with thousands of Indian followers, revolted against the rapacious local administrators who, through taxes and the reduction of the Indians to practical slavery on the large haciendas and in the mines, had become odious masters, particularly in the Andean highlands. The rebellion began in 1780 and was immediately successful. The young Túpac Amaru II and his followers reached the heights overlooking Cuzco and then faltered. By failing to follow through and to conquer the imperial city, they lost the overwhelming military advantages they had had at the outset and were soon captured by the arrival of the better-armed professional royal troups.

You leave Tinta behind, practically unchanged since the time of Túpac Amaru II, and continue on to Racchi, where you'll see the imposing ruins of the Temple of Viracocho just before reaching town. Then you'll proceed through San Pedro, a small Indian village where, in the 1960s, a bored Peace Corps Norteamericano named Meester Williams decided to paint some crazy designs on water pumps and doors. The faded remains of American flags and psychedelic drawings can still be seen. From here, it's another 12 miles (19 km) to Sicuani.

SICUANI: A very bleak, tough Indian town where a lot of drinking and brawling occurs on Saturday nights, this can be an unfriendly place toward gringos unless you've acquired that burnished, been-around look that serious travelers get after a while. A truck stop on the Cuzco-Puno route and an embarkation point for trucks carrying gold panners into Madre de Dios, Sicuani was the subject of an extensive anthropological study about the effect the British Industrial Revolution had on traditional social structures and wool marketing procedures. The results of the study have been published in a book called *Alpacas, Sheep, and Men,* by Benjamin Orlove (Academic Press; 1977).

Don't even try to look for a hotel here — any in existence are small and simply awful. About the only other interesting attractions are the daily market, a Rotary Club near the railroad tracks, and a Chinese restaurant, *La Chifa,* which serves large portions of decent food. Just outside of town stands a burnished copper–colored mountain that stands out from all the rest. If you get stuck in Sicuani for a few hours, you will notice the red mountain changing colors. Watching this phenomenon is far and away the most pleasant way to pass the time here.

En Route from Sicuani – Beyond Sicuani, as you start the climb to the altiplano, you'll notice that the vegetation gets thinner, the air is cooler, and in the distance you get clearer glimpses of the shining snow peaks of the Vilcanota knot of mountains. Around kilometer 180 on the highway, you are at the highest point, La Raya, a mere 13,700 feet above sea level.

About 130 miles (209 km) southeast of Cuzco, you pass through Santa Rosa; some 25 miles (40 km) farther is the village of Ayaviri, a not very exciting provincial capital that was an important way station along the royal road some 500 years ago, with a great palace for the Inca, a Temple of the Sun, and sundry storehouses. These have all disappeared, but you can visit the Bosque de Pedro (stone woods) in Tinajani (the devil's bath), a strange, stone city with imposing walls, great columns, and scattered heaps of red sandstone.

A side road near Ayaviri takes you to the village of Nuñoa, the central site of an altitude study performed in 1968 by scientists from Pennsylvania State University in collaboration with the Instituto de Biología Andina. The study examined the effect of high-altitude living upon indigenous groups (humans can live in the altiplano as high as the snow line, at 17,590 feet). The study determined that a high percentage of those tested suffered from malnutrition, hypocia, and a slow growth rate (better attributed to malnutrition than high altitude). The local Nuñoa residents (mostly Quechua Indians) took part in the study, for which they were paid, until a medical team arrived and took some blood samples. The Indians refused to participate further on the grounds that taking someone's blood placed the receiver in power over the donor.

At kilometer 285 on the Cuzco-Puno Highway is Pucará, an archaeological site interesting for the stone and adobe remains of what was a great fortress and temple precincts, probably dating from the 2nd century AD. What is physically impressive about this village is the immense red sandstone rock, 1,000 feet high, which rises behind the town. The name of this village is now synonymous with its famous ceramic bulls, which actually are made in a nearby village called Santiago de Papujá. From here, it's another 40½ miles (67 km) to Juliaca.

JULIACA: The commercial and transportation center of the southern Peruvian Andes, this town has long been an important crossroads. At one time it even had its own imperial Inca residence. It seems to be a place that has kept up with the times, however, shedding first its pre-Inca heritage, then its Inca vestiges, and finally its colonial character, so that the Juliaca of today is a bare, rather ugly Andean market town. Market days are Sunday and Monday here: Among its best woolen buys are llama ponchos. There's also a large llama market.

Other than the market, there's not much reason for stopping here unless you're on business. But you should know that Juliaca has air service connecting it with Lima and Arequipa; train service with Cuzco, Puno, and Arequipa; and an excellent medical center, La Clinica Adventista de Juliaca at Calle Loreto.

From here, it is 28½ miles (46 km) to Puno.

PUNO: At 12,500 feet above sea level, Puno is the highest town on the route. Rest easy, eat lightly, avoid exertion for a while, and drink coca tea. Eventually, climb slowly up Muajsipate, the hill three blocks from the main square for a fine view of the city and Lake Titicaca.

Founded by the Spaniards in 1668, Puno itself is not noteworthy architecturally, and what there is to be seen can be done in less than one day. On the Plaza de Armas is the cathedral, which dates from 1757, which is late colonial baroque and has a lovely main altar with a silver-plated frontal, and is open daily from 9 AM to noon and from 3 to 5 PM. While you are on the Plaza de Armas you can look inside the museums there, all in the same building. The Museo Municipal has some pre-Inca and Inca pottery. All the museums are open daily, except Sundays. After 6 PM, you can visit a museum that belonged to Señor Carlos Dreyer (Calle Conde de Lemos 233); his excellent collections were left to the city upon his death.

If finding independent restaurants in Cuzco is a problem, it is an even greater one in Puno. The safest choices for decent food prepared under hygienic conditions are the restaurants of the hotels (see *Best en Route*). However, if, in spite of the cold, you want to eat outside your hotel, the best food at low prices is at the *Café Internacional,* on the square. Other choices are *Restaurant Sillustani* at Calle Maguegua 190 and *Samary Restaurant* on Jirón Deustua.

As for shopping, you might well be captivated by the marvelous representations of the masks used in some of the folk dances, reproduced on a smaller scale. If you did not get to Pucará, you will find the famous "bulls" and other ceramic items from that area. There is a good selection of these and other handicrafts at the *Sociedad de Artesanos* at Calle Arequipa in front of the Municipal Theater. Other places to pick up similar items are the *Artesanías Puno-Corpuno* at Calle Lima 544; *Artesanías La Sirena* at Jirón Deustua 576; *Artesanías Folklóricas de Perú Andino* at Jirón Lambayeque 44; and *Artesanías Puno* on Teodoro Valcarcel.

Puno's fame rests on its cultural traditions. It has been rightly named by one of Perú's best modern writers, José María Arguedas, the symbolic capital of Latin American dance. The many Puno folk dances (in this context Puno refers to the whole department) find their inspiration in the daily life of fishing, farming, hunting, and sheep herding. The dances also give the Aymarás (the largest ethnic group in the Titicaca region) an opportunity to make a spectacular comment on their history since the Conquest and at the same time to affirm their own group identity.

The principal fiesta is that of the Virgin of Candelaria, which begins on February 2 and lasts an entire week. The Diablada (the devil's dance) is performed with giant masks and elaborate costumes and is the catalyst of a whole series of dances; the *pandilla,* the Puno version of the lively coastal *marinera;* the *kallahuaya,* the medicine men's dance; and many others. Carnival season offers the next big folkloric explosion of dancing, performed with such exuberance in the streets and plazas that some think the color and high spirits equal those in Rio de Janeiro. Each month, except February and April, in some part of the department there is least one fiesta featuring one or more of the special costumed dances, which number at least 200.

Three particularly interesting trips are available outside the city: the floating islands of the Uros on Lake Titicaca, the burial towers at Sillustani, and the churches of Juli and Pomata. You can combine the first two in one day, with a morning trip to the islands, and an afternoon trip to the towers. Actually, Puno is the most important Peruvian town on Lake Titicaca, renowned as the highest navigable lake in the world at 12,506 feet above sea level. This lake was especially precious to the Inca, whose first ancestors, Manco Capac and his wife, Mama Occlo, supposedly were created by Father Sun on the Isla del Sol where Inca ruins are still to be found. But the most famous ruins are those of Tiahuanaco, apparently a religious center that had great influence on other cultures throughout Perú some 1,000 years before. These islands today are in Bolivian territory, but you can see them after passing the border guards on the other side of the lake.

At the mouth of the Río Huili (which leads into Lake Titicaca), the floating islands house a tribe of some 600 Uros Indians, a very old lake civilization famous for its use of the indigenous totora reeds in building huts, boats, and rafts. The islands themselves are large enough to accommodate one family, and each island contains a small, cone-shaped reed hut and a small plot for potatoes and other tubers, which, along with fish, make up the daily diet. The Uros rarely leave their islands, visiting the mainland only on religious occasions. They have little contact with others except for the Adventist missionaries, who provide them with a clinic and school (on rafts floated by oil drums) and with the tourists who venture out to see them to purchase some small replicas of their sailing boats or weavings.

Seventeen miles (28 km) north of Puno on Lake Umago, the burial tombs of Sillustani, called *chullpas,* were built probably before the Inca conquests of the Colla tribes. Either round or square, they are of adobe or stone and sometimes a combination of both. One of these mausoleum towers is 40 feet high. When the towers were filled with the cadavers and all the paraphernalia they needed for the next world (including wives and servants as well as food, drink, and clothing), they were closed.

En Route from Puno – Since there are no car rental services available in Puno, we recommend that you arrange a tour to Juli and Pomata through a local tourist agency. This is a "must" trip. The road, dusty and curvy, follows the shoreline of Lake Titicaca, and the background of the magnificent snowcapped Andes off in the direction of Bolivia offers some wonderful scenery. In Ancora are both a fine colonial church and more burial tombs. Farther on, in the town of Ilave, is the handsome façade of the local church. But the high point is Juli, 51 miles (83 km) south of Puno, where there are five magnificent churches: San Juan, originally built by the Dominicans at the end of the 16th century and later remodeled by the Jesuits, and the four Jesuit churches. These churches, as well as the one at Pomata, 25 miles (40 km) beyond Juli, are superb examples of the blending of Spanish and Indian genius for art and architecture. The sculptured arches and portals with their wealth of detail of animals, birds, and fruit are exotically exuberant. Twenty-five miles (40 km) beyond Pomata one reaches Desaguadero and the Bolivian border. From here, it is possible to cross into the lakeside resort of Copacabana to take a launch ride out to the Isla del Sol and to drive to the Tiahuanaco ruins in Bolivia.

BEST EN ROUTE

There really are no restaurants or hotels worth recommending in the towns between Cuzco and Juliaca. Those that do exist are not particularly clean and would be close to slum dwellings in most of North America. It's probably best, if traveling by car, to plan your trip so that you leave Cuzco early in the morning and arrive in the evening at Juliaca. Buy fresh fruit, bread, cheese, and cold meat in Cuzco and lunch along the way. While hotels in Juliaca are passable, it's better to wait until you're in Puno. Again, don't expect regal accommodations. Most of the hotels have hot water, but no central heating, and you'll pay about $25 (moderate) to under $15 (inexpensive) for a room for 1 night. Advance reservations are not absolutely essential unless you're arriving during festival times.

JULIACA

Turistas – A clean and comfortable small hotel, with a restaurant and good bar service. Av. Manuel Prado 355 (phone: 435; or call EnturPerú in Lima, 72-19-28). Moderate to inexpensive.

Arce – A passable hotel offering rooms with private baths, a restaurant, and parking spaces. Arapa and Plaza 1 de Mayo (phone: 139). Inexpensive.

PUNO

Isla Esteves – This comfortable, new, first-class hotel on the island of Esteves is connected by a causeway and is convenient to weekly markets and Indian festivals. Expensive.

Don Miguel – It has a restaurant and 20 comfortable rooms with private bath. Av. La Torre 545 (phone: 724 in Isla Esteves; or call EnturPerú in Lima, 72-19-28). Moderate.

Sillustani – This is the newest hotel in town, with a restaurant that has fair food and service. Jirón Lambayeque and Tarapaca (phone: 792). Moderate.

Ferrocarril – A small, characterless hotel that offers private baths and good service. Folklore shows are performed Mondays, Wednesdays, and Fridays. Av. La Torre 185 (phone: 409). Inexpensive.

The Amazon

Perú's Amazon territory is a vast watershed of rivers and canopied rain forest in which more than a thousand species of unique plant and animal life flourish. Exceeding the size of Spain, France, and West Germany combined and covering almost 60% of Perú's landscape, La Selva (as it is known locally) is the home of some half-million people, largely adventurers, explorers, romantics, missionaries, and members of 35 known indigenous Indian tribes who have only superficial contact with the modern world.

This eastern Peruvian jungle consists of the basins of four great rivers. Far to the north, the Río Putumayo rises in the Colombian Andes and stretches itself as the border between Perú and Colombia. In the south, the Madre de Dios begins in the Andes near Cuzco and has as its major port Puerto Maldonado, near the Bolivian border (see *Madre de Dios*). Between these two rivers is the Infierno Verde (Green Hell) watered by the Marañón and Ucayáli.

Peruvians have long dreamed of colonizing the Amazon territory, but the jungle, with its allies of rivers and mountains, has proven to be a worthy adversary. In the northeast, the important port of Iquitos, Perú's navigation outlet to the Atlantic, has no connecting road system — the idea of building a road from the Pacific west coast has been abandoned as an impossible dream. During certain months of the year, the Río Marañón rises 30 to 60 feet, flooding everything in its path; so even if the Andes could be conquered, the river cannot.

For travelers, Perú's Amazon region spells adventure but not danger to all but the foolhardy. Jaguar and other large animals have retreated deep into the rain forest; boa constrictors, fer-de-lance, and bushmaster snakes successfully avoid man; dangerous Indian tribes are few and are almost never encountered even by those that seek them out. In the river, electric eels, rays, piranha, carnero, and crocodiles are hazardous — but there are some safe swimming areas.

What travelers will encounter is a pioneer spirit among residents and the knowledge that here nature, not man, is in charge. A curtain of green vegetation is everywhere, as are the hum, squeak, screech, and buzz of bird and insect life. Indians with brightly painted faces and bodies, only two generations removed from headhunters, smile and offer to trade goods. And then there is the ever-present heat and humidity, 82°F (28°C) average.

There are several ways to reach the Amazon and Iquitos from Lima. You can fly directly to the town on one of the four daily flights offered by AeroPerú and Faucett, or you can take one of those carriers to Pucallpa, 489 miles from Lima, finishing your trip by riverboat down the Ucayáli; you can travel by air to either Huánuco or Tingo María (about halfway to Pucallpa) mixing air and surface travel, or you can go all the way from Lima to Pucallpa by ground along the Carretera Central (Central Highway, also known as Route 2), traveling east from Lima. The highway starts immediately with an upgrade through naked hills and mountains, following an old Inca road and the less ancient tracks of the Central Railway, the highest climbing standard-gauge railroad in the world. It reaches 15,981 feet before descending, and then rises again to 14,371 feet at Cerro de Pasco, where the railroad tracks end and the road continues.

The road crosses successive ranges of the Cordillera de los Andes for some 233 miles before reaching the harsh, but lush, Caja de Montaña on the eastern slopes of the Cordillera. Then it descends to the green-blanketed Pampa de Sacramento and the jungle floor to Pucallpa. Until 1937, the road went only as far as Huánuco, 265 miles from Lima — at the time, no one expected it to go any farther. That year, however, engineers did an ingenious thing: They used an account of a 1757 expedition by Fray Alonso Abad and discovered a pass through the Cordillera Azul that wasn't visible from the air. The pass, the Boqueron Abad, with perpendicular walls 6,000 feet high, was used to extend the road to Pucallpa by 1941. It was, and still is, the only overland route to the Amazon territory, recommended for four-wheel-drive vehicles only, and only during the dry season.

There are several ways to travel by road to Pucallpa. You can hitchhike, but this is almost impossible, since trucks only pick up paying passengers, and there are few family cars along the route. Hitchhiking is called *tirar dedo* (literally, "to throw a finger") here, and isn't illegal, simply inconvenient. You can travel by *camion* (truck); the price is about as rock bottom as the comfort and is a long, dragged-out affair since the truck driver starts and stops anywhere he likes, depending on how far he's going and how long he decides to take getting there. The trucks are usually 4-ton types with wooden slat sides: They hold a lot of cargo, human and otherwise, and because they're open, they can be absolutely miserable in wet and cold weather. You "rent" one of these by simply standing along the road and flagging one down.

Or you can go by autobus. Since this is not a popular tourist route, the vehicle may resemble a rejected school bus and is just as noisy. It is likely to be outfitted with a luggage rack on the roof, overhead racks inside, and a shrine to the Blessed Virgin on the dashboard (the way the road is, and the way the driver controls the bus, you'll need it). There may or may not be springs in the seats, mufflers, or headlights, and the quarters are tight. This method of traveling is a real endurance test; the buses seldom stop for meals, so when one pulls into a town, vendors flock to the windows with food for hardy stomachs. Needless to say, do not count on onboard toilet facilities.

Actually, the best way to get to the Amazon is either by *colectivo* (sedan-type taxis that take a group of not more than five people) or by car rental. Each, however, has its disadvantages. The *colectivos* make frequent, 45-minute stops at little cafés for lunch and dinner: They also have specific runs, which means you have to hunt for another car when one segment ends. Prices, however, are inexpensive and negotiable. The car rental, on the other hand, might mean making the return trip by car or finding someone to drive it back for you if you decide to return to Lima by air. Make sure insurance comes with the rental, and find out beforehand who pays for what if damages occur (it might also be a good idea to get flares.) A valid license and credit card are enough to rent a car, and rates should be about the same as in the US because of rapid inflation and gasoline rationing in Perú.

This is not a route for the comfort-seeking traveler, but the scenery is perhaps the most extraordinary in Latin America. You cross mountains, plateaus, and ravines. Vegetation is bright or nonexistent; the terrain is harsh and chipped or soft and flowing. There are mountain villages lying in pastoral surroundings and homes hanging dangerously from cliffs.

Larger cities have adequate (no luxury or first-class) hotels, and restaurants are modest, to say the least. Gasoline is available, but there are few repair shops and even fewer parts, except in the cities. A knowledgeable mechanic makes the best driver.

Since this is an important commercial route, there are more trucks than cars on the road, and except for the run between Lima and La Oroya, potholes are everywhere (around mining areas such as Cerro de Pasco, potholes are ditches), and at least one flat tire is the norm. Peruvians mark the road with patches of grass or rocks to indicate a disabled car: Be different and drive the car off the road and put out a flare. Because the road is often very narrow, because many cars and trucks go without lights (or only one at best), and because of the ditches or animal and people movement on the road — do not drive at night.

A direct trip by car can take as little as 20 to 24 hours nonstop, but double that time is the average. The trip should be made in three sections of three days. The first stage, Lima to Huánuco, should take 10 hours. Next, it's Huánuco to Tingo María in four or more hours. And finally, it's Tingo María to Pucallpa in 10 hours, more or less.

To avoid the heavy rains that cause havoc in the mountains and jungle, the best time to travel is from April to November. In fact, from July to November would be even better. By this time, the rock slides should be removed and the washouts repaired.

For special information, road maps, and itineraries, contact Touring y Automóvil Club del Perú, César Vallejo 699, Lince, Lima (phone: 40-32-70).

Advice, good sense, and arrangements are also provided by Lima Tours (Belén 1040, Lima); and Receptour (Rufino Torrico 889, Lima); and Viajes Vía (in the Galerías Comerciales of the *Lima Sheraton* hotel).

Now that you've been prepared for the horrors and excitement of traveling to and through the Amazon, there are two books you should read to get the feel of it. One, *The Rivers Amazon,* by Alex Shoumatoff (Sierra Club Books; 1978), is a fascinating account of a young naturalist's voyage down the Amazon and its tributaries and his encounters with various Indian tribes. A bit more bizarre is *Keep the River on Your Right,* by Tobias Schneebaum (Grove Press; 1969), an account of self-discovery in the jungle. It has been an underground cult favorite for many years.

From the suburbs of Lima, it's only 5 miles (7 km) down the Central Highway to Puruchuco.

PURUCHUCO: A pre-Inca administration center, the restoration of this ruin started in 1953. Set into the hillside, it's easily recognizable: The exterior walls, standing about 23 feet high, have no windows. The entrance is a ramp that leads to a ground-level patio surrounded by high passageways. A museum at the site displays ceramics and textiles discovered here, and folkloric dances are presented in the summer months.

   En Route from Puruchuco – Continuing north on the Central Highway, you'll pass the industrial town of Vitarte (pop. 54,000). Seven miles (11 km) on your left (to the west) is the turnoff to Cajamarquilla, the ruins of the largest pre-Columbian settlement in the Lima Valley. Much of the ancient settlement is covered with soil and rock from constant mud slides, but excavations are under way, and citadels, streets, and large squares are visible.

   Back on the Central Highway, about 10 miles (16 km) out of Lima to the east is a series of ruins similar to Puruchuco on the San Juan Hacienda. The ruins consist of two residences and a group of isolated houses. The larger residence has been restored.

Two miles (3 km) farther on are the ruins of Huaycan-Tambo.

HUAYCAN-TAMBO: This urban community sits at the foot of the Huaican Mountains, whose highest peak is 7,590 feet. At the bottom of the slopes is an Inca citadel, consisting of a large number of corridors, enclosures, and *colcas* (granaries) that have been restored. Stretching up the foot of the hills for several hundred feet are the remains of a *tambo,* the stopping place for *chasquis* (Inca runners), with terraces on the hillside; this was the last stop for a messenger in this journey from the sierra, a one-day walk from the Rimac Valley and the village of Lima, where the Plaza de Armas now stands.

En Route from Huaycan-Tambo – The fashionable resorts of Chaclacayo and Chosica are 19 miles (30 km) and 25 miles (40 km) respectively north of Lima at altitudes just under 3,000 feet. Both are havens in which wealthy Lima residents can escape the city's humidity.

From Chosica, the Rimac Valley becomes narrow and steep, the terrain rocky and barren. The Central Highway continues its upgrade, passing the Andean villages of Matucana, Tambo de Viso, and San Mateo, all known for their curative mineral waters. By now you are at an altitude of 10,382 feet.

Seven miles (11 km) north of San Mateo is a turnoff to Casapalca in the Río Blanco valley. This is the Andean *puna* (plain), where all traces of vegetation disappear, the altitude having risen to 13,728 feet. You won't reach the highest point of your journey, however, until you reach Ticlio, *la cima* (the peak) of Anticona Gorge — at 15,981 feet, on the highest paved road in the world; glaciers of neighboring peaks provide the backdrop for this spectacular view.

Try to contain your *soroche* here — it's not long before the highway descends into the Mantaro Valley. Six miles (10 km) down the road is the turnoff for Morococha, a mining center at the foot of the snowcapped mountain of Yanasinga; not far from here is La Oroya.

LA OROYA: The mining center of central Perú, the town itself is rather drab, but you can take a number of side trips from La Oroya before heading back to the highway. Jauja, some 46 miles (74 km) south of the city on a branch road, was the second city in Perú founded by Pizarro and was the capital for one year (1534), until Lima won the prominent title. Legends of rivers of gold and mountains of silver brought hundreds of European adventurers here in the 16th century. In the nearby Paca Lagoon, it is said, natives deposited a fabulous treasure in gold when they heard of the death of the Inca Atahualpa — it was to have been part of the king's ransom. Outside the city, if you follow the road south, you enter the fertile Mantaro Valley, a beautiful, green sight after the brownness of the highlands.

In the 1460s, the native Huancas tribe was conquered by the army of Inca general Capac Yupanqui, and the area developed under Inca rule. Today, it is an agricultural center with a population of some 200,000. The valley ends at Huancayo, an important commercial and handicraft center (see *The Outskirts of Lima*).

East of La Oroya, a branch road (one of Peru's worst roads) leads to Tarma, 20 miles (32 km) from the turnoff, a beautiful spa founded in 1545 in the center of an equally beautiful irrigated valley some 10,000 feet above sea level. Tarma is known for its folkloric traditions — a curious blend of Catholicism and Indian myth. During holy weeks, the city's streets are covered with decorative flower carpets that all but stop motor traffic. A few miles outside the city, near the village of Palcamayo, is the grotto of Huapango, with startling limestone natural sculpture. Surrounding the area is an archaeological zone with the important pre-Inca and Inca ruins of Shoguemarca, Yanamarca, Huayipirca, Huancoy, Cachi-Cachi, Tarmatambo, and the fortress of Vilcabamba in various degrees of ruin and restoration.

Following the same road east for 75 miles (120 km) you reach San Ramón, the first base for air service to Iquitos and the *selva*. La Merced, 7 miles (11 km) from San Ramón, is in the Valley of Chanchamayo and supports coffee, pineapple, and orange plantations; continuing another 15 miles (24 km) you reach San Luis de Shuaro, a fruit-producing area and departure point for roundabout river navigation to Iquitos. From here, you can continue 36 miles (58 km) to Oxapampa, with grand haciendas of large coffee plantations in the area of the Río Bocaz, where a nearby road (there's a sign) leads to the Pueblo de Villa Rica, a turn-of-the-century German settlement that is more European than Peruvian. The road continues to the small agricultural villages of Huancabamba and Pozuzo.

En Route from La Oroya – You have to backtrack to La Oroya before you can continue your journey on the Central Highway. Traveling north, there is a sharp upgrade to the immense Pampa de Junín at an altitude of about 13,000 feet. Here, in an area called Bosque de Piedras (Stone Forest), where wind and rain have carved hundreds of extraordinary figures in "rock trees," the forces of Simón Bolívar, Sucre, and Miller beat the royalists in the first battle to end Spanish domination of the continent.

Some 35 miles from La Oroya is the city of Junín, at 13,530 feet. The city was known as Pueblo de los Reyes until changed by Simón Bolívar to Heroica Villa de Junín in honor of the Battle of Junín on August 6, 1824. The surrounding landscape is mountainous and monotonous, but it is broken every now and then by herds of cattle and sheep and by flocks of wild ducks traveling to nearby Lake Junín, the source of the Río Mantaro. The lake is important for its fish and bird life, and boats and tackle can be hired in the city for a day's outing. There is a small hotel with a most pleasant restaurant. From the city of Junín, the road continues to ascend, stretching over valleys and plateaus for 46 miles (74 km) to Cerro de Pasco.

Nine miles (14 km) from Cerro de Pasco, a road from Lima joins the Central Highway. The road leaves Lima, heading north through the city of Canta and crossing the Cordillera Occidental Andina at La Viuda before entering the highway. It is the shortest route to Cerro de Pasco from Lima but not recommended because of the high altitude and sparsely populated area. Four miles (6 km) from the turnoff, a sharp left leads to Cerro de Pasco.

CERRO DE PASCO: To Peruvians, this is a city of the future — which means prosperity is just around the corner. It is an area of fabulous mineral wealth, the base of the largest copper mining concern in the country. Mine shafts burrow into the bare brown earth, miners' houses and huts climb the hillside, and a great smelter spews flames. Some years ago, the Congress passed a law allowing the townspeople (and corporation) to move the city to another location. The new city of San Juan is a mile away, and they are mining under the old city.

Cerro de Pasco, the capital of the province of Pasco, was founded by order of the Viceroy Amat y Juniet in 1771. In the days of national independence, it was a patriotic center and was destroyed by the Spanish. Rebuilt in 1840, it was named La Opulenta Ciudad de Cerro de Pasco because of its large population (now about 40,000) and mineral wealth. It has a 300-year-old cathedral that displays the first clock ever made in Perú. For the most part, the city lacks the amenities required by most tourists. Because of its altitude (about 14,000 feet), it is generally cold (it sometimes snows), and *soroche* poses a problem for visitors. The city is surrounded by ranches and farms.

En Route from Cerro de Pasco – A small road bypasses the Central Highway, following the course of the Río Pallanchacra, going through little villages including Tingo, Pachac-Rahuay, and Hualancayo for 30 miles (48 km) until rejoining the Central Highway.

Back on the Central Highway, the road descends, taking you through small, stark villages like Salcachupán and following the course of the Río Huallaga by obscure towns such as San Rafael and Ambo before reaching Huánuco, gateway to the *montaña,* some 148 miles (238 km) from La Oroya and 72 miles (116 km) from Cerro de Pasco.

HUÁNUCO: The capital of the department of the same name, this city of some 45,000 people lies in a mountain valley 6,300 feet above sea level. It sports a temperate climate and is a popular tourist center for people of the *montaña.* As in all the cities of the *montaña,* what is oldest and best preserved are the churches, and two good examples of colonial architecture are San Cristóbal and San Francisco (they are, however, no match for the great cathedrals of the major cities).

The city is known for its folkloric festivals and especially its popular ballet — *Negritos de Huánuco* — seen on January 8 and 16 and on other festive days. The Dance of the Negroes reenacts slaves calling for their liberation. Each dancer wears a mask to represent certain characters — the overseer, traveler, and nobleman. The music seems Afro-Hispanic.

The city is irrigated by the Huallaga and Huigueras rivers and is surrounded by large hills and green, spreading fields of sugarcane and grain. For the angler, the rivers are filled with fish; arrangements can be made at the hotels for tackle and bait.

The Huánuco area abounds in ruins. Just before entering the city, a turnoff to the left leads to Cotosh, an important, pre-Inca temple that is still undergoing restoration. Following a small road (ask directions) from the city center to adjacent flatlands will bring you to a series of ruins known as Huánuco Pampa, that cover an area some ¾ mile wide. Here you'll find an Inca fortress, a royal palace, and baths, all badly decayed.

En Route from Huánuco – Two roads, one following the left bank of the river (passing the airport) and the other following the right bank, join the Central Highway again. The road continues its ascent through a terrain of cacti and small shrubs into the foothills of the Carpish Mountains, some 32 miles (51 km) from Huánuco. Here there is dense forest and a long tunnel (badly lit), which opens up into wooded hills and lush vegetation at an altitude of some 9,000 feet.

A side road leads to the top of Puente Pardo, some 12 miles (19 km) from the Central Highway. The dirt road is narrow and vegetation clogged; the climb, steep. The prize at the end is Cueva de las Lechuzas, or the Owls' Cave, inhabited by large birds known as *guancharos,* which are distant relatives to owls and almost extinct.

Back on the Central Highway, you reach the small village of Bella. Here on the banks of the Río Huallaga is the Playa de Bella, a beautiful white sand beach surrounded by wild flowers. It's worth a swim (although a bit cold), but you must hire someone at the village to take you there because there is no road. From Bella, the Central Highway descends sharply to Tingo María.

TINGO MARÍA: Born in various stages of this century, the city lies in the rainy Coja de Montaña. Its population of some 25,000 man the coffee and tea plantations and the farms producing sugarcane and bananas. The Río Huallaga widens at this point, providing an area for recreation. The city is nominally under the control of the Bureau of Montaña Lands and Colonization, which has had some success in encouraging people to settle in the area. Japanese immigrants have already demonstrated that tea plantations can be run successfully.

It is the surrounding scenery, not the city itself, that attracts, for this area is a paradise of lush, subtropical green vegetation. Called the *ceja,* or eye, of the *montaña,* magnificent glaciers extend into the clouds. The Peruvian *montaña* covers some 30,000 square miles of virtually unsettled area, but its rich, well-watered soil and temperate climate — about 70°F (21°C) — offer incredible potential for both agriculture and tourism (if recreational facilities can be developed).

It is from Tingo María that the Marginal Highway to Puerto Maldonado, near Cuzco, will be built — if it ever becomes more than a proposal.

En Route from Tingo María – The Central Highway heads toward the northeast with varying degrees of construction under way along the route to Pucallpa (a likely state of affairs for several years). Little villages on the road such as Naranjillo, Pumahuasi, and Las Delicias on the banks of the Río Huallaga are passed before the road begins an ascent into the Cordillera Azul, passing by great areas of coffee and tea cultivation. At La Divisoria, 39 miles (63 km) away at 5,000 feet, there is a marvelous panoramic view: On a clear day to the east, the green-blue plain of the Pampa de Sacramento is visible, and it is here that the Amazon plain begins.

The road descends slowly as it comes to and passes through the incredible natural pass, Boquerón Abad, which has to be one of the natural wonders of the world. The green-covered rock cliffs jut straight up, almost blocking out sunlight. Once through the pass, you are out of the Andes.

The road passes through magnificent vegetation and over the Río Aguaytia by way of the longest bridge in South America (2,290 feet). There is another bridge over the Río San Alejandro before the road ends at Pucallpa on the Río Ucayáli.

PUCALLPA: This cluster of mud and thatched buildings, on the west bank of the wide, muddy-green Río Ucayáli, thrives — in heat, humidity and frontier spirit — as the second most important riverport in the jungles of Perú (Iquitos is first).

The oil camps, scattered throughout the basin into northeastern Perú, are groups of huts spread out in a village-type grid. Some are no more than tents; all, however, have their general stores (or huts) and even shacks for their "girls" (local women contracted to act as prostitutes for the men). If you're a woman, and manage to come upon one of these *barrios,* ignore the macho stares, whistles, and occasional propositions that will be thrown at you.

Most of Perú's oil fields, located near the Ecuadorian border, were, by the way, captured in a bloody border skirmish in 1922. Every once in a while controversy flares up anew between these two old adversaries, and feelings of hostility will hang in the air until negotiations settle disputes between the two countries or until tempers simply cool down.

But why worry about international affairs now — you're in Pucallpa, on the fringe of the Amazon, where everything has that smell of slow rot of earth and vine. The city's population of 60,000 is a rather off-and-on group of rejects, pioneers, semicivilized Indians, and less civilized mestizos. Along the river is a collection of canoes, *peque-peques* (motorized launches), barges, houseboats, small steamers, and workers loading and unloading a collection of jungle goods, including round gray-black balls of wild rubber from Ibena up north.

On musty store shelves everything is for sale: Japanese radios, English chocolate, stuffed crocodiles, pinned butterflies and beetles, feathered arrows, blowguns, and insect repellent (the latter may be the most important buy of all, because the Ucayáli is not nicknamed the Mosquito River without reason).

In the city, sightseeing is limited to the exotic riverfront cargo and the Hospital Amazónico Albert Schweitzer, a 28-plus-bed hospital and research center devoted to helping jungle people, mostly members of the Shipibo and Cashiba Indian tribes. A staff member will be happy to show visitors around.

About 2½ miles (4 km) back on the route to Huánuco, a dirt road leads you 6 miles (9 km) to the lake, the basic center of activity around Pucallpa. Once an arm of the Río Ucayáli (it's still possible to get out to the river during high tide), the lake offers boating, fishing, and a look at the natives.

The main village of the Shipibos, San Francisco, is about 6 miles (9 km) from Pucallpa by boat. En route, the mestizos have shacks along the reedy margin of the lake, and the warm waters break with leaping dolphins. Soon, the wood and palm-leaf houses of the Shipibos are visible. They are open-sided, have bamboo floors, and are high off the ground to prevent rats and snakes from entering. The Shipibos wear clothing with geometric designs that are also patterned on their famous *telas,* enormous glazed pots. Dugout canoes line the banks; on land one must travel over log bridges that often seem more rotten than sturdy. In the village, yuca beer is made, and a cooking pot may contain a brightly colored toucan, with beak and head attached. Often the Shipibos will trade their 8-foot blowguns for something you have that they like.

Ten minutes or so by canoe takes one to the off-and-on settlement of a band of Cashibas, a tribe that generally is found farther west. It is best to ask if they are around before venturing out into the jungle.

Lake Yarinacocha is also the base of the Summer Institute of Linguistics, a Wycliffe mission of translators who adapt the Bible into aboriginal tongues. From here the missionary-linguists fan out to work with some 35 jungle tribes of the *selva.* In the main office of the screened bungalow settlement, an orientation greets the visitors with the institute's philosophy: "To help prepare Indians for the severe adjustment they face as roads and planes threaten their isolation." The institute can be reached by writing Instituto Linguistico de Verano, Casilla 2492, Lima 100, Perú. Also devoted to "saving" the Indians is Texas millionaire Robert G. Le Tourneau. In 1952 Le Tourneau, a fundamentalist lay preacher and promoter of "industrial-missionary enterprises," obtained a concession on almost one million acres of jungle for development some 21 miles from Pucallpa, off the main road. In this majestic valley Le Tourneau has created Tournavista, his colonization center established by Socio de Dios — God's associate.

By Yarinacocha, live comfortably in the jungle at *La Brisa Lodge* and take river expeditions and bird-watching trips in dugout canoes. The lodge was lovingly built, and is run, by California attorney Connor Nixon; accommodations are in two-story screened bungalows or in the main lodge. Casilla 202 (phone: 6551). For information in the US, call *LADATCO Tours* in Miami (phone: in Florida, 800-432-9049; elsewhere, 800-327-6162).

Do anything you want in Pucallpa, but don't stop your Amazon trip here: On the contrary, the best part, that trek into the roadless jungle, is just beginning.

En Route from Pucallpa – Flying to Iquitos from Lima may be the fastest and easiest way to get to your next destination, but you're losing out on the fun. The 533-mile journey downriver via the Ucayáli to the Amazon's principal port is wearisome but exotic. At best, the trip takes 4 to 5 days in highwater April to November, when the river is filled with vessels of all types taking advantage of the freight-carrying waters from the summer rains.

In the other months, when the water is low, the trip often takes 8 days, because sandbars make travel at night impossible. From the voyage's beginning to its end, the riverbanks are covered with jungle growth. There are always the vibration of the ship's motor and the cries of the jungle animals. River plantations with grazing cattle, the inevitable dugout canoe with Indians, fishermen hauling nets, the small, stilted houses of jungle villages are passed. Occasionally crocodiles are visible, as are tapirs and flocks of birds. There are also the plague of mosquitoes and flies and intense heat that is only pacified by river breezes.

No matter how one gets downriver, there will be problems. The biggest is booking. There is virtually no way to book before reaching Pucallpa, and then one must negotiate with the captain of the vessel (generally the monies become his sole property).

Almost any type of vessel takes passengers if there is room. There are Peruvian army steamships, oceangoing vessels, and *lanchas* (two-story houseboat-barge combinations). Passage on these will mean a bunk (if there is one) or a place to hang a hammock (your own). Food will be from the jungle and water from the river, so antidysentery medicine and canned food are mandatory. One can always travel by *colectivo* (large motorized passenger canoes or barges that function as water taxis). Several *colectivos* will have to be taken to make the entire trip, and nights will be spent in a hammock on the porch of an Indian's hut (visitors are a welcome sight on the river). Food must be brought or bought, and a sleeping bag, hammock, and tarpaulin are recommended.

Besides Iquitos, connections may be made for the downriver ports of Contamana, Reguena, and Omaguas on the Ucayáli and Yurimaguas on the Huallaga. Upstream are the ports of Puerto Bermudez and Atalaya.

IQUITOS: Some 2,000 miles from the mouth of the Amazon River and the Atlantic Ocean and almost 1,000 miles from Lima, Iquitos would seem the most isolated of places. Yet even before "Slim" Faucett opened up the air lanes between Lima and Iquitos in 1922 (today there are more than four flights daily), the city had a memorable history.

Started as the Jesuit Mission of Santa María de Iquitos in the 1750s, the town suffered the raids of the headhunting Jivaro Indians. In 1876, Iquitos had only 1,500 permanent residents, hardly a reason for the city to be called the Pearl of the Amazon. But just 4 years and 24,000 residents later, this steaming capital of the District of Loreto was indeed the Pearl.

From 1880 to 1917, Iquitos lavished in the rubber boom, as steamers as large as 1,000 tons called regularly from New York and Liverpool. There were resident consuls from ten foreign countries. The city imported everything from common foodstuffs to champagne and caviar, and the *Gran Hotel Malecón Palace,* a luxury hotel, was imported from Paris in pieces and reassembled on the banks of the Amazon. Its ballroom boasted performances of Sarah Bernhardt and the French Grand Opera. Not to be outdone by the latter performance, a rubber baron bought a building designed by Eiffel (of the tower fame) and had the cast-iron structure transported to Iquitos. By 1918, it was all over. Rubber from Malaya, grown from seeds stolen from Brazil, was less expensive and easier to obtain.

Today, Iquitos's 100,000-plus inhabitants hope for a new boom from oil recently discovered by PetroPerú. In the meantime, lumber, orchids, raw rubber, wicker furniture, medicinal plants, barbasco (the source of Rotenone for insecticides), and tropical fish are the main exports.

The port on the left (north) bank of the river is merely a shadow of its past. The Malecón, the river promenade, with its balustrade and wrought-iron lanterns, guards a certain antiquity, but vegetation and the river have already undermined its foundation. The grandiose houses along the Malecón, with cupolas, façades of Portuguese azuelo tile, and ornate wrought-iron balconies from England are now military headquarters. Statues to forgotten men stand in neglected squares. And the building designed by Eiffel is now the home of the Iquitos Social Club (Plaza de Armas). Squeaky stairs and sagging floors must be ignored.

The center of Iquitos, one block from the riverfront, is the Plaza de Armas — the business and social center. It was from the plaza that the city grew to its present dimensions. Santa Ana Church, the Municipal Hall, banks, retail stores, and restaurants face the plaza, and the main business district is centered on three streets extending south. If a sense of sophistication is evident, this is dispelled by a list of what's available at the market: sapodillas, mangoes, papayas, melons, and hearts-of-palm are recognizable. But there are also spiny fruits, nuts, roots, and cacti competing for space on the stalls with armadillos, snails, grubs, slugs, monkeys, piranhas, turtles, and rats, not to mention love charms, coagulant bark, coca leaves, curare poison, and even popular aphrodisiacs.

Besides decaying old buildings and the large market, Iquitos itself offers limited sights. For a look at stuffed denizens of the jungle plus popular crafts and archaeological items, there is the rather overcrowded Amazon Museum (Jirón Lima 349). And to see what's in the waters surrounding Iquitos, a visit to the Aquarium (Jirón Ramirez Huitado 16) is worthwhile.

Perhaps the most picturesque and at the same time the most desperate site in Iquitos is the waterfront slum of Belén. This floating village of some 15,000 people is made up of balsa rafts held in place with long poles. The average rise and fall of the Amazon here is about 40 feet, with the low in August and September, when Belén sits on a bed of mud. At all times the village is a mass of humanity, but at high tide its floating market, with canoes canopied with palm thatch, serves as a store for bananas, coconut, fish, and vegetables grown upriver. The whole scene reminds one of an exotic bazaar.

It is outside the city that the attraction of Iquitos is strongest. The jungles of the coffee-colored Amazon River offer visits to Yagua and Jivaro camps. The Yagua, the most numerous tribe in the area, are famous blowgun hunters, and the highlight of their native dress is the men's colorful rush skirts, which, it is now believed, caused early explorers to mistake them for women — thus the famed Amazons of the jungle and the name of the great river.

The Jivaro, in the Río Napo area, were the once-feared headhunters of the jungle. Now peaceful and quite civilized, they live in small village units much as they always did, without headhunting.

On the river there are commercial fishermen with huge nets suspended between boats, native dugouts and water taxis, occasional barges, and military boats. Along the shore the green wall of trees is broken now and then by clearings where cattle graze, a stilted river house stands, or where there's a government school whose pupils arrive by native canoe. Every now and then the water breaks from the leap of a freshwater porpoise, which, a native will tell you, is the most dangerous of animals. Pink dolphins emerge from the water at night, dress up in male drag, and go about town with perfect ease and seduce girls. They take them on a picnic at the water's edge or to a restaurant overlooking the river. There they lull them with sweet talk and take them home to a watery grave. This is the way of the jungle.

BEST EN ROUTE

Hotels in the Amazon region of Perú are a mixed lot, ranging from rustic to adequate to very comfortable. In some places, accommodations come with private bath and hot water, but in the interior, lodging can be very basic. The price of a double room listed here as expensive is about $40; moderate, $20 to $30; and less than $15, inexpensive. Jungle lodges are generally booked for two-night stays; prices include all meals and, when necessary, transport to the lodge (in Iquitos particularly, book ahead, preferably through a US travel agent or through a travel agent in Lima).

HUÁNUCO

Hotel de Turistas – This 34-room hotel provides private baths and a dining room. Damaso Beraun 775 (phone: 2410; or call EnturPerú in Lima, 72-19-28). Inexpensive.

TINGO MARÍA

Turistas – Offers hot water and private baths with its clean, comfortable rooms. Km 1 of Carretera Tingo María (phone: 2047; or call EnturPerú in Lima, 72-19-28).

PUCALLPA

Turistas de Pucallpa, Jr. – San Martín 522 (phone: 6381). Reservations can be made through the Lima EnturPerú office. Moderate.

LAKE YARINACOCHA

La Brisa – This lodge on an island in the middle of the lake offers bungalows in thatch-roofed huts, a restaurant, swimming, and river tours. In Lima, call 27-66-24, or write to Connor Nixon, Casilla 202, Pucallpa, Perú (phone: 6551). Moderate.

La Cabana Lodge – A lakeside bungalow-resort that offers water sports, food service, jungle trails. Travelers usually reserve in 3-day packages. Moderate.

IQUITOS

Explorama Inn – The newest and best in the Iquitos area, this is the only lodge on the main Amazon River. Each of its 25 separate bungalows has a private bath and shower, and more are now being constructed. The flora and fauna here are unsurpassed in the greater Iquitos area (phone: 23-57-31). Expensive.

Amazonas – This 120-room hotel provides swimming pool, tennis courts, and rooms with private baths. About 4 miles (7 km) outside Iquitos. Expensive.

Turistas – This government-owned hotel retains the musty, frontier ambience that has made it a long-time favorite with visitors. All of its 80 rooms have private baths, and there is a bar and dining room. Malecón Tarapaca (phone: 23-10-11 or 23-13-22). Moderate.

Hostal Acosta – A small hotel, it also has a restaurant. Calles Huallaga and Araujo (phone: 23-17-61). Moderate.

Hostal Ambassador – Another small hotel, it has 25 rooms, a convenient location, and fairly good service. Calle Pevas 260 (phone: 23-31-10). Moderate.

DOWNSTREAM

Explorama Lodge – Divided into ten pavilions, each with 10 rooms and 5 baths; there is a hammock pavilion as well. The dining room has 24-hour service, and a folklore show is presented every evening in the bar. Associated with the big lodge is the smaller *Explornapo Lodge*, a 5-hour trip from *Explorama* and a favorite with birdwatchers and fauna followers. It has accommodations in tented pavilions. Even more remote is the *Adventurama Lodge*, 7 hours from *Explorama* and ideal for the adventurer in search of the pure Amazon experience. Book through Explorama Lodge, Camana 851, Lima (phone: 24-47-64).

Amazon Lodge – Provides accommodations for 90 people in thatch-roofed huts, and it has a bar and restaurant, as well as walking trails. River trips, visits to an Indian village, and outings to fish or spot crocodiles can be arranged. Ninety minutes downstream from Iquitos (phone: in Lima, 41-91-94).

Amazon Safari Camp – Thatch-roofed accommodations with semiprivate bath, central dining, and jungle walks. On Río Momon tributary, 45 minutes from Iquitos's dock. Reservations through SA Travel Reps, Los Angeles, California (phone: 800-423-2791; or in Lima, 40-72-02).

Jungle Amazon – Some 30 miles from Iquitos — a 1½-hour trip downriver and some 3 hours back — it has 29 bungalows with private bath, as well as a restaurant and bar. Make reservations through Jungle Amazon, Av. Garcilazo de la Vega 732, oficina 401, Lima (phone: 32-50-96).

Amazon Village – A new village, with 34 bungalows, a thatch-roofed common house, and open-air bar — all on the Momon River. For information, contact the US sales office of *Hotels Promoting Peru* (phone: in Florida, 305-261-3024; elsewhere in the US, 800-327-3573; or in Lima, 40-72-02).

The Madre de Dios

Cuzco is the jumping-off place (by air or truck) for Perú's southeastern jungle of the Río Madre de Dios, a 700-mile-long tributary of the Amazon that runs northeast through Perú. The department of Madre de Dios, established in 1912, is a wide, 29,640-square-mile area no different than the Amazon — hot and humid, with a drenching rainy season. It has, in recent years, attracted oil and gold prospectors who daily combat jungle conditions in their search for fortune and fame. The rest of the area's 40,000 inhabitants are farmers, who grow *cascarilla, castañas,* Brazil nuts, vanilla, cacao, coffee, cotton, and sugarcane. In addition, there are *siringeros,* the rubber farmers of the Río Tahuamanu near the town of Iberia on the Bolivian border, who still tap and produce *goma,* or organic rubber, using old-fashioned methods. Oddly enough, many of these rubber farmers are Japanese, descendants of the immigrants during the organic rubber boom of the nineteenth century.

The best way to see the Madre de Dios area is to take a boat trip from Puerto Maldonado, the capital of the department, 350 miles downriver, across the Bolivian border to Riberalta, an isolated Bolivian rubber-tapping center some 40 miles from the frontier. It's a glorious adventure, especially if you've ever dreamed of floating down a mammoth, muddy jungle river where shy, soft-spoken Indians shoot crocodiles with bows and arrows. The old-fashioned way to travel is by dugout canoe, taking about 7 days to complete the journey. By motorized launch, you can reach Riberalta in about 4 days. Although no regular transport service exists along the river, it isn't difficult to charter a boat, complete with necessary jungle river travel amenities that include a guide, cook, hammock, and (most importantly) a mosquito net. If you're looking for a detailed published route, forget it!

Even if you do not intend to embark upon a major Amazonian adventure, Puerto Maldonado is the logical point of departure for a jungle sortie. Unfortunately, it is not a pleasant town in which to relax. The people are friendly, but a quick walk around the square, grid layout of the dusty streets and the unexciting clapboard architecture should help inspire you to explore further.

There are a number of ways to reach Puerto Maldonado. You can fly (depending on weather) from Cuzco (AeroPerú and Faucett) or you can fly as far as Quincemil; then, take the Quincemil-Maldonado route — a real honey, 65 miles (104 km) of the 155-mile (250-km) trek is incomplete between kilometers 27 and 92. The excursion normally takes 24 hours, but when it rains, about 14 days. At one point, the highway is so narrow that the road becomes one way; as a result, the highway alternates between east and west on certain days. Trucks taking the route normally gather in Urcos, a town only a few miles west of Quincemil, then set out in caravan. You reach Urcos by taking the Central Highway south from Cuzco. You can ride in a truck from Cuzco or Sicuani.

However you go, consume a fair number of vitamin B_1 pills (*tiamina*) as a deterrent against mosquitoes (it works) and quinine pills to ward off malaria. A medicine kit with antiseptic, a snakebite kit, and some antifungus cream might also be a good idea. There is little formal health care: Madre de Dios has a population of 40,000 and only three doctors. Otherwise, the International Red Cross conducts boat cruises of the Madre de Dios system.

QUINCEMIL: This mining town of about 15,000 people is a rugged little place, founded during the 1930s at the height of a gold rush. Its name is based on legend: Some poor soul one night lost 15,000 soles (or *quince mil* soles) during a card game. After that rush, things quieted down here somewhat until the early 1970s, when a new boom along the river and its Inambiri and Tambopata tributaries brought discoveries of up to $13 billion in gold. The miners pan during the dry season, April to October, when the rivers are lowest. Actually, the gold doesn't come from the jungle area itself but from the mountains — it's washed downstream in the waters.

En Route from Quincemil – There isn't much to see here, and for the rest of the route you'll have to content yourself with a bumpy truck ride over potholes until hitting Puerto Maldonado.

PUERTO MALDONADO: The sleepy, ramshackle, riverside port is the shipping point for jungle products from the deepest reaches of the rain forests. But other than dock confusion and the often exotic cargo of jungle vegetation, there is little worth seeing in the port.

In the surrounding area, about 3 hours by river, is the Tambopata Natural Wildlife Preserve, established in 1977. Here is the place for jungle safaris and visits to the villages of the Huaraya Indians. Their main village lies on the Palma Real, a red-soil plateau overlooking the Madre de Dios. It is a clearing of huts with nearby fields under cultivation in the slash-and-burn method. The Indians are peaceful, but have had only limited contact with civilization.

Farther into the rain forest is the Manu National Park, a 30-minute plane ride from Cuzco or several days by boat from Puerto Maldonado. The park comprises some 4,800 square miles and extends from altitudes of 1,000 to 12,000 feet. The base of the Direction Forestal of Perú, which runs the park with financial aid from the World Wildlife Fund, is where the Panahua and Manu rivers join.

Much of the park is unexplored cloud forest where bear, puma, and other large animals roam. Also in the area are hostile Amahuacas Indians, said to occupy the area of the Río de las Piedras near the Isthmus of Fitzgerald. In the lowland jungle are such rare animals as giant otter and black caimans. Around Lake Cochacascho, the forestry department has built an observation post that has become the best spot in the *selva* for viewing rare hoatzin, a reddish yellow marsh bird, and oropendola.

Another of the forestry department's bases is at Takakume, en route to Sotilya Lake (a giant otter haven), a good day's canoe ride from Panahua. Near the base is the only known collective settlement of the Machiguenga Indians, who generally live in separate family units. These primitive hunters have only had contact with the outside world for the last 20 years; they were the subject of a survey 2 years ago in which was studied the amount of free time primitive cultures have compared to people in Western civilization. The findings concluded that these Indians spend more than 40% more time simply doing nothing.

Unescorted treks into the park are discouraged; arrangements for safaris can be made in Cuzco, Puerto Maldonado, Lima, or, better, further in advance. Miraculously, Puerto Maldonado and the immediate vicinity are not excessively plagued by mosquitoes and bugs. Cool nighttime breezes periodically sweep down from the not-too-distant snowcapped Andes and keep the insect population down. However, equip yourself with mosquito nets and long-sleeved shirts when you go on any expedition.

The temperature hovers in the 85°F to 90°F (29°C to 33°C) range year-round, but the months of June, July, and August constitute South American winter. Occasionally the "southern winds" will blow for 3 or 4 days and the temperature will dip to about 50°F (15°C). Although the locals complain about these cold spells (called *friaje*), they are most definitely welcome. Most important, avoid visiting the area during the summer rainy season, which lasts from November through March.

En Route from Puerto Maldonado – Sightsee here and take the side trips, but the natural termination of this trip is downriver at Riberalta, Bolivia. You'll see lots of fascinating wildlife once you're on the river: Black bears roam the jungle recesses and you can encounter freshly killed, ferocious-looking jungle cats. On some occasions baby vicuña, a rare species, stride down to drink at the river at sunset. You'll also see furry, two-toed sloths hanging upside down by their over-sized claws. Armadillos, tapirs, crocodiles, and turtles also live in the area, and if you stop at a village (be prepared to stay since you'll be warmly invited), you might be treated to a bit of one of these as a snack.

The river is literally swarming with fish. Piranha are not particularly numerous since they favor clearer waters, where the oxygen content is higher, but other equally noxious aquatic specimens — such as the freshwater sting ray — are prevalent. Three species of crocodiles exist, although their numbers are dwindling. July is the time for the migration of large schools of fish that the locals call salmon. These tasty 20-pound monsters can be hooked as they swim up the clearwater tributary side streams to spawn. July and early August is also when the turtles lay their eggs on the sandbars at night.

Probably the noisiest and most colorful of the nonhuman inhabitants are the birds. This is an area where birdlife proliferates, yet little ornithological work has been done. Butterflies glide past in rainbow-colored clouds, enveloping the equally breathtaking orchids that dangle from the fallen tree trunks along the banks. The air sparkles, and the scent of flowers is magical.

Before leaving Puerto Maldonado, be sure you have received your official stamps and *laissez passer* exit papers that will be required at the frontier post at the Perú-Bolivia border. The terrain for 50 miles (80 km) on either side of Puerto Heath is the wildest area of the entire route. The merchant boats do not pass through this section of Madre de Dios, and consequently, occasional isolated settlements of pure-blood, non-Spanish-speaking Amerindians have remained almost untouched in this part of the jungle. One such civilization is at Pan Marial, a population of less than 1,000 who retain their traditional language, religion, and customs and are extremely hospitable. Essentially oblivious to the cash economy and the outside world, they eke out a subsistence livelihood from their untamable environment in much the same way that their ancestors did.

RIBERALTA: This fairly pleasant town, whose economy is based on rubber and nuts, is perched at the confluence of the Beni and Madre de Dios rivers. A passable dirt road crosses the border from Brazil at Guayaramerin. No road, however, links the town with the rest of Bolivia. Consequently, although the dirt streets are wide and symmetrical, there are very few automobiles. Motorcycles, on the other hand, are quite common. For less than 50¢ you can go almost anywhere on one of the many "moto-taxis" that cruises throughout the municipality.

Unless you enter Riberalta by bus or Jeep from Brazil, the only access is via airplane. Several passenger and cargo flights arrive every week from La Paz, Cochabamba, and Trinidad. The restaurants on the plaza all serve palatable food. There is even an ice cream and coffee shop serving delicious cappuccino.

The town is better maintained than Puerto Maldonaldo. Pickup trucks spray the dirt streets and keep the dust to a minimum. The main center of activity is the tastefully laid-out central plaza. During the cool evening hours, the entire population strolls up and down the plaza. The hottest night spot is *El Disco,* just off the plaza. It is a neon-decorated, thatched-hut nightclub with genuine American soul music.

Forty-five minutes away by moto-taxi is the spectacular lake of Tumi Chucua, a perfect place to swim during the heat of the day. An American missionary group (the Wycliffe Bible translators) has established a small open colony at this heavenly spot. In blatant contradiction to the jungle setting, there are washing machines, hot dogs, diving boards, and Styrofoam sailboats.

Riberalta and its immediate environs have a rather congenial frontier atmosphere. Very few tourists venture this far into the jungle, so the townspeople are extremely friendly and eager to meet visitors. Don't be surprised at dinner invitations or entering into conversations with strangers at neighboring tables.

The best time of year to visit is during the first 10 days of August, when the Bolivian Independence Day is celebrated. For 4 days, August 4–7, all business activities shut down. All the *riberalteños,* in a truly hedonistic South American frontier style, take to the streets, eating, drinking, dancing, and laughing all through the night.

BEST EN ROUTE

Transient accommodations are virtually nil along this route. With the exception of one hotel in Puerto Maldonado and some jungle lodges, there are no decent properties; even these, although inexpensive (about $14 a night and under), provide no hot water. You must also write to them for the required reservations or try to get them through your travel agent.

PUERTO MALDONADO

Turistas Amazonas – This lodge on the Río Tambopata provides basic room and food service. Contact: EnturPerú in Lima (phone: 72-19-28).

DOWNSTREAM

Cuzco Amazónico Lodge – This jungle lodge 50 miles (80 km) downstream of Puerto Maldonado provides thatch-roofed accommodations, and package rates include meals. Trails lead into the surrounding jungle; hiking and canoe rides are offered. Stays are available in 1- and 4-day packages (phone: in Lima, 46-27-75).

TAMBOPATA NATURAL WILDLIFE PRESERVE

Explorer's Inn – Bungalow huts in the middle of the jungle park offer mosquito protection (netting), and the food is good; meals are included in 3-day package rates. Planned activities include jungle walks, visits to Indian camps, animal- and bird-watching, alligator-spotting at night, and trips to Cocococha to see toucans, parrots, monkeys, and boas. Contact Explorer's Inn, Av. Garcilazo de la Vega 1334, Box 10088, Lima 1 (phone: 31-30-47).

RIBERALTA

Riberalta – A small hotel that offers clean rooms. In the center of town.
Santa Rita – This small hotel in the center of town provides clean rooms and air conditioning.

Suriname

A tiny, 63,037-square-mile piece of land on the northern coast of South America, Suriname — alias Dutch Guiana — is one of those countries you don't just drive into. It cannot be reached by car from the surrounding countries: Neither Guyana (to the west) nor French Guiana (to the east) is connected with the Pan-American Highway. And there is little reason to go to the expense of shipping a car in and out. Although there are good coastal highways (for the most part paved), they are cut by large rivers flowing from the mountains in the south to the Atlantic Ocean; the roads often can be crossed only by ferry.

Suriname itself is not an old country, gaining total independence from the Netherlands as recently as 1975. But its roots stretch back as far as the late sixteenth century, when Dutch expeditions repossessed Spanish territory that included not only Suriname, but Guyana (formerly British Guiana). The Dutch did their best during the next 400 years to preserve their stronghold, but to no avail. Constant British attacks against the coast and an unsuccessful slave revolt in the mid-1700s contributed to the erosion. Suriname was finally lost to the British in the seventeenth century, and the Dutch only gained it back — named Surreyham by the British — when they traded it for their island of Manhattan in 1665. In 1863, an already torn Suriname endured a successful slave revolt that resulted in the Dutch granting the colony its own parliament. This ultimately led to the country's total independence in 1975, and ended a long period of civil stress and racial strife.

The Suriname of today is a cultural melting pot of Bushnegroes (the term is absolutely valid, since it stems from the 1863 fight for independence by ex-slaves-turned-guerrillas who hid out in the jungle bush), Chinese, Indonesians (descendants of laborers brought to work on the tobacco, rice, and coffee plantations), Amerindians (or Suriens, descendants of the indigenous tribes), and Europeans (Dutch, Portuguese, and Jews). The official language is still Dutch, although Spanish is spoken as well as Sranan-tongo, or Negro English. Most of the country's 350,000 inhabitants are centered around Paramaribo, the coastal capital.

The country itself is a tropical, pretty place: a blend of forest-covered land, savannahs, sparkling rivers and streams, sandy beaches, lagoons, mangrove forests, and murky swamps. The leading industries are bauxite mining and aluminum processing along with forestry and the production of cocoa, coffee, sugarcane, rice, bananas, and maize. Tourism is almost nil — there were only 10,000 visitors last year — but the country maintains a few tourist offices overseas in an endeavor to attract more people.

Recent political events may continue to leave tourism at an absolute standstill. American visitors will not find it easy or inexpensive to arrange interesting tours to the interior. Until violence hit the capital in December 1982, Suriname had been a peaceable kingdom, living in serenity with a racial mix that has proved explosive in other parts of the world. But at this writing, it is only possible to say that, politics aside, Suriname is a fascinating country, and then outline the directions visitors can take.

The easiest way to get there is on Suriname Airways, the national carrier, with service between Miami and Paramaribo. Air France, KLM, BWIA, and ALM all have connecting flights from the US via Caribbean points. Bus and train service from Paramaribo is available into the country's interior, and there is daily service by launch across the Corantijn River separating Suriname from Guyana.

The main road from Paramaribo south crosses, after some 75 miles (120 km), the Afobaka Dam, which backs up the waters of the Suriname River to form an artificial lake to generate electrical power on behalf of the bauxite mining industry. Whoever wants to go farther south into the jungle, where there are still quite a number of Amerindian and Bushnegro villages (Bushnegroes and their tribes — including chiefs — are recognized by the central government), must travel either by outboard canoe or plane. Airstrips built for survey and development work are numerous in the interior, and many are open to tourists.

The best place to start a tour through Suriname is from Paramaribo. Any questions you have can be answered by Suriname Airways, 6501 NW 36th St., Miami, FL 33166 (phone: 305-871-2637), before you leave the US, or at the board's office in Paramaribo (Kerkplein 10; phone: 73733). Unless you're the rugged type, stay in a hotel, not in a guesthouse, which often lacks private baths and comfort.

Paramaribo is about 30 miles (48 km) from Zanderij, the international airport. The drive will take 45 minutes. The airport lies in a savannah where the trees do not grow very tall and the land is interspersed by white sand and swamp water. Alongside the road some Bushnegroes have set up small workshops where they produce wood carvings. Made on a flat cedar board, each intricately carved piece is different, depending on what the artist wants to express. Love and eroticism play a large role in this, as in daily life. The men produce these carvings for their women, using them to express their feelings. Crude utensils such as forks, combs, ladles, and paddles are also made (the last do not necessarily express feelings).

Near the Creole settlement of Onverwacht, one passes the ruins of the main station of what was the railway to the abandoned gold mines farther south. Nearby lies Bernharddorp, an Amerindian village, where on festive occasions the women may still don traditional brightly colored dresses. Nearer the city, stretched across both sides of the road, Hindustanis (as the East Indian immigrants are called) have small vegetable farm plots. There are also several Hindu temples. A few miles before reaching Paramaribo lies the nine-hole golf course of the Golf Club Paramaribo. Tourists may be introduced by members and pay only a small fee for using the well-kept course.

As the city comes into view above the water tower, the main reservoir of the waterworks sticks out above the surrounding buildings. The industrial area, it includes the plant of the British-American Tobacco Company and, by the river, the mills of the Bruynzeel Lumber Company. After crossing the Saramacca Canal, you are in Paramaribo.

PARAMARIBO: This interesting city has many wooden buildings in the typical colonial style, particularly in the center of the old town. In Sranang-tongo, the native lingua franca, Paramaribo is called Foto, "fort," since the city was built around Fort Zeelandia, lying in a bend of the wide Suriname River some 12 miles from the ocean. Fort Zeelandia was initially a small garrison of French colonists; later it became the English Fort Willoughby and then was captured by Abraham Crynssen from Zeeland in 1667. Strengthened afterward, the stone walls of the pentagonal fort are many feet thick and have bastions at the corners. When there was no further use for the fort as such, Zeelandia was used as a prison, then restored as a museum and, sadly, now reoccupied by the military. The area around the fort is lovely, with tall mahogany, mango, and tamarind trees, and the old residences of the officers — still in use — have been well maintained. To the left of the fort, the former army barracks, built in 1970, now house the Ministry of Economic Affairs. Behind the fort are the modern buildings and grounds of the *Society Club Het Park,* with a good restaurant open to visitors. This club, where the country's elite meet, looks out not only on the river but, on the land side, on Independence Square, one of the most beautiful squares on this side of the ocean. In the old times it used to be called Esplanado or Place d'Armée, for the army used to parade there, but the name was changed several times — for instance, into Government Square and Oranjeplein (after the Dutch House of Orange) — until the country became independent. The large grass field — a gathering place on festive occasions — is dominated by the People's Palace, the home of the president of the republic, built in 1730 but repeatedly remodeled and expanded since then.

The west side of the square is taken up by three old, typical colonial buildings: the Court of Justice, the Ministry of Finance, and the Ministry of the Interior. The first was built with red brick stone, which was brought to the country as ballast in sailing ships. The imposing Ministry of Finance in the center, with tall columns and a 104-foot tower, was originally the Town Hall. The Ministry of the Interior, built with wood, is at least as old as the Court of Justice (1774).

Visitors do not have far to go to find quiet in the middle of the busy city. Right behind the People's Palace are the Palm Gardens, with hundreds of tall royal palms. Coming back past the palace and turning into the Gravenstraat, other colonial buildings, each 2 to 3 centuries old, catch the eye: the Parliament Building, on the corner with the Grote Combeweg, and the Ministry of General and Foreign Affairs, where the prime minister has his office. Farther down the street is the Roman Catholic cathedral of St. Peter and St. Paul, with its tall spires. It is said to be the largest completely wooden cathedral in South America. Recently restored, it forms quite a contrast to the modernistic building of De Surinaamsche Bank next door. Go inside and admire its unpainted cedar interior with high curved ceilings in neo-Romanesque style, its pillars and high, glass-paneled windows each in a different pattern and the carved gate to the baptismal font.

Around the corner on Kerkplein (where the tourist office is located) is the Reformed Church, an octagonal building that dates from 1835. Inside, the pews rest on historical gravestones covering the floor. With an old mahogany pulpit, brass chandeliers, and a big organ, it is only natural that Suriname's independence was proclaimed here in the presence of Queen Juliana of the Netherlands and that the University of Suriname also uses it on special occasions. Other interesting religious buildings include Hindu temples at Koningstraat, a mosque at Keizerstraat, and a synagogue, built over a century ago, at Herenstraat.

The Kerkplein is surrounded by some modern buildings, including the ABN Bank, the Central Post Office, a department store, and the main office of the electrical company.

Orlando's Coffee Shop, with its coffee terrace, is a gathering place for lunching hotel guests. To have a hearty lunch or dinner, one only has to cross the street to *Iwan's Restaurant,* which specializes in Chinese dishes.

On the other hand, if you're hankering for native dishes, ask for *Roline's* restaurant. Take a taxi for the 5-minute drive to the northern border of the city. The dining room is small, but the food is great. Some of the dishes you'll want to try are *pol,* which contains fried chicken and a potato-like vegetable, and *nasi goreng,* with either meat or chicken with vegetables, all ingredients fried.

In the center of the city are several cafeterias, including *Spanhoek* soda fountain, *Joly Fountain,* and, in the Domineestraat (the main shopping street), the *Hola* cafeteria, where you can sit and look down on the city's busiest intersection, the girls driving by on their fast scooters and the vendors selling their shaved ice cream. The *Hola* is next to a supermarket of the same name.

For those wishing to try the Indonesian *rijsttafel,* a multicourse dish including the *nasi goreng,* try the *Deli* on Saramaccastraat or *Sarinah's* on Verlengde Gemenelaudsweg. Order a taxi to go there, however, for *Sarinah's* is quite a distance beyond Via Bella, with its modern villas.

Surrounding Paramaribo are the modern residential areas, including Zorg en Hoop and Elisabethshof. Driving beside the Suriname River toward the ocean one also sees beautiful villas on the Anton Dragtenweg all the way to Leonsberg, where the *River Club* hotel with its cozy restaurant and lively *Blue Bell* discotheque are located. On the edge of the river rests another bar-restaurant-discotheque, the *Leonsberg* bar. But go upstairs unless you want to mix with the local boys having a good time or waiting for the ferry to cross to Fort Nieuw Amsterdam and its open-air museum. (But upstairs the prices are higher!)

What you should not miss in Paramaribo is the central market, where you will see all the different people of the country, all the produce with its exotic smells and the stalls with fish brought in every morning from the river or barbecued if you want. Also, at the central market you can hear all the languages being spoken in the country.

From the central market all your shopping is available within a few blocks. It is better to walk here, as it is difficult to find a parking place. There is much variety — from large department stores to small souvenir and jewelry shops. There are also imports from the Orient such as batik, jade, and ivory as well as dress material from all over the world.

En Route from Paramaribo – Traffic in Suriname drives on the left. When driving to Albina, a border town on the broad Marowijne (Maroni) River, look out, since the neighbors in French Guiana drive on the right and may forget when they cross the border.

Traveling from Paramaribo, you have to cross the Suriname River first by car ferry to Meerzorg. From there, the East-West Highway leads straight to Albina, some 90 miles (145 km) away. The road leads past Hindustani settlements, with their temples and mosques, as well as the large, Indonesian village of Tamanredjo.

The widest river to cross in between is the Commewijne, but since a bridge has been built, people are no longer held up by the ferry, which was used for over 15 years. Apart from small farms and a few Bushnegro huts, there is not much to see between the Commewijne and the bauxite-mining town of Moengo. The Suriname Aluminum Company, a subsidiary of Alcoa, runs this American-style community. Stopping on the hill beyond the bridge over the Cottica River, one can see a small golf course, a ranch with the best cattle anywhere in Suriname, and a milk plant as well; to the left, down the Cottica River, are the smokestacks of the bauxite-crushing plant. If time permits, drive around Moengo; be sure not to miss the White House, the company club, situated on a hill and surrounded by a valley.

Near Moengo also lies the Indonesian village of Wonoredjo, where on occasion one may witness Javanese dances to the tinkling of *gamelan* music. Going on to Albina, one passes the bauxite mines and several Bushnegro villages. At one of them called Negerkreek, Bushnegro fire dances are staged (if arrangements have been made in advance). It is usually too costly for individuals to do so, therefore tour operators do it for groups only.

Nearing Albina, one crosses a hill: The town can be seen with the river behind it and St.-Laurent-du-Maroni on the other side.

ALBINA: Although a favorite vacation spot for Surinamers, this village so far has only small guesthouses that are not recommended. There are also some small restaurants. *Soebkhi* specializes in Indonesian simple dishes at reasonable prices. The best food can be found at the *Government Guesthouse* on the waterfront.

At night, the *Anjoemara Club,* on a river beach, offers disco music. Tastefully decorated with driftwood and other crude material, it is practically the sole place of entertainment apart from a movie house.

On Albina's waterfront — which gets a constant breeze — you can hire a canoe to travel either down river to some Amerindian village or to the beaches where the turtles lay their eggs, or upriver to other Amerindian and Bushnegro villages. A real adventure is the canoe trip to Stoelmansisland and beyond, up the Tapanahony River to the Gran Holo Falls, which takes several days. It may be easier to fly from Paramaribo on Suriname Airways for a 3-day tour.

En Route from Albina – If you backtrack to Paramaribo and take the highway west, you come to Nieuw Nickerie, a town on the western border nestled between the Nickerie and Corantijn rivers, the latter forming a natural border with Guyana. The road is dotted with many small farms; although a bridge now crosses the Saramacca River, you have to cross by ferry at the mile-wide Coppename Estuary. On the other side of the river lies the Coronie district, called the land of milk and honey because of its coconut groves. The district is inhabited mainly by Creoles and Indonesians; signs along the road bearing Scottish names such as Inverness and Totness remind you of the first settlers.

Soon you reach the Nickerie district. Wageningen is the biggest fully mechanized rice farm in the world, and the polders, where rice is grown, seem endless. When you come to the Nickerie River, you again have to cross by ferry, only to reach more rice fields before getting to the town of Nieuw Nickerie itself, which looks much like a western boom town.

You can take a trip to Brownsberg, a 14,820-acre nature park about 3 hours south of Paramaribo, which you can get to by driving yourself, taking a combination bus and van tour, or by a scenic, 6-hour steam train ride. The park is a tropical rain forest filled with giant toads, communal spiders, monkeys, jaguars, jacamars, macaws, and the colorful, wide-billed toucan. An admission fee is charged.

The park is operated by Stinasu, the foundation for nature preservation in Suriname. Maps are available at the park office, and a guidebook to the birds in Brownsberg may be purchased at the Stinasu office in Paramaribo. For added adventure, you can rent a canoe and go fishing for walappa, patakka, and koemapari in the Brokopondo Reservoir.

Actually, the best fishing is done from February to April, then from August through November — the dry seasons. You need a special permit if you're going to sport fish; it can be obtained in the tourist office in Paramaribo. If you want to go hunting (game includes tapir, deer, and wild boar), licenses are necessary, as are gun licenses (you are allowed to hunt in Suriname with shotguns only). The hunting season runs officially from May through December, although jaguar and caymana, considered dangerous animals, may be hunted year-round. For further information on animal hunting and for tips on bird hunting, contact the tourist office in Paramaribo, Grote Combeweg 99 (phone: 71163, 78421).

Another reserve northeast of Paramaribo, the Wia-Wia Reserve, offers you a look at five species of turtles (the reserve is their nesting ground), and some wonderful bird life, including wild ibis, flamingos, spoonbills, kites, terns, and storks. To get to the reserve from Paramaribo, take a riverboat in the morning to Alliance up the Commewijne River, transferring to a Stinasu launch for the 2-hour trip. The trip costs around $15 one way.

BEST EN ROUTE

There are two types of accommodations in Suriname: the tourist-style hotel (which you should frequent if you like comfortable quarters) and the guesthouse (which you should avoid if you don't like rugged, spare rooms, and in many cases, the lack of private baths and/or air conditioning). Rates are comparable to US prices and can range anywhere from $70 (expensive); between $30 and $50 (moderate); and under $25 (inexpensive). Your best bet is to stick to the hotels in Paramaribo, Suriname's capital, although there are some acceptable guesthouses in the villages you will visit. As usual, you're better off reserving accommodations well ahead of time.

PARAMARIBO

Krasnapolsky Paramaribo – The 85 air-conditioned rooms here contain private baths; European and American plans are both offered. Centrally located (phone: 75050; in New York, 212-247-7950). Expensive.

Suriname Torarica – This 135-room hotel has gambling casino, swimming pool, meeting facilities, and a restaurant. About 5 minutes from downtown (phone: 71500; in New York, 212-247-7950). Expensive.

River Club – This 70-room hotel has air conditioning, showers, and 16 bungalows with kitchenettes. Bar, restaurant, lounge, swimming pool, and golf, tennis, and other sports facilities are also on the premises. On the river estuary about 7 minutes outside the city. Reservations: Box 914 (phone: 51959). Moderate.

Palace – A pleasant, 32-room hotel that features some air conditioning and private baths (depending on your room), a casino, and a nightclub. Independence Sq. (phone: 72815). Moderate.

Guesthouse "Fanna" – This 10-room hotel has private baths. Prinsessestr 31 (phone: 76789). Inexpensive.

Lashley – A 13-room hotel with small, comfortable rooms. Corner of Watermolenstr (phone: 77013). Inexpensive.

NIEUW NICKERIE

There are a few comfortable guesthouses worth checking out, including *Amer Ali's, Dorien,* and *Sjiem Fet* (all inexpensive); others in the area are not recommended.

BROWNSBERG PARK

Central Lodge – Cottages and bungalows sleep eight to ten people and provide kitchen facilities, showers, toilets, and beds. In the park. Moderate to inexpensive.

Uruguay

The smallest country in South America, Uruguay covers only 72,172 square miles of hilly meadows, broken by streams and rivers and a strand of beaches along the coast. A triangular country, it is bordered by Argentina on the west and south, Brazil on the north, and the Atlantic Ocean on the east and south. The capital, Montevideo, has a population of 1.5 million out of a national total of 3.1 million.

Most of the country is grazing land for sheep and cattle. Salto (pop. 60,000) is the center of the cattle-raising area. Uruguay's colorful cowboys, the gauchos, congregate here. Punta del Este is the major seaside resort. Uruguay has a temperate climate, with summer temperatures climbing as high as 90°F (32°C) between November and March, dropping to the low 40s F (around 5°C) between June and August.

The Spanish explorer Juan de Solís landed in Uruguay in 1516, but he and his band were promptly attacked and killed by Charruas Indians. The first real exploration took place in 1520, when Ferdinand Magellan sailed up the Río de la Plata and discovered the site on which Montevideo now stands. Although accurate records of the exact date have been lost, the capital was founded sometime in the early eighteenth century. Until the early nineteenth century, Uruguay was little more than a buffer zone between rival Spanish and Portuguese interests.

José Gervasio Artigas led a grass-roots movement for independence from Spain between 1811 and 1821, but Uruguay was annexed to Brazil until 1928, when independence was finally declared formally.

Uruguayans have experimented with various democratic institutions of government and, for a time, were popularly known as the Swiss of South America — because the country was run by a Swiss-inspired national council from the 1920s until 1966. During the 1970s, Uruguay suffered from horrific outbreaks of urban violence, and the adoption of dictatorial methods by President Juan María Bordaberry proved inadequate to quell the disorder. He was ousted in 1976 by a military coup that restored a certain amount of stability but has now itself become a government of oppression. However, the first popular election in years was held recently, and Uruguay now has a civilian president.

As you drive through the countryside, you'll discover a wide variety of wildlife. Green parakeets nest high in eucalyptus trees; partridges can be seen walking across the road; red oven birds' two-room nests perch on telephone posts; *nandues* (a species of small ostrich) gallop in the fields; and wood pigeons are practically everywhere. You can also see, among others, the small *apereá* (a ratlike rodent) scurrying into the bushes as the cars approach, hares in the fields, skunks, and the tasty *mulita* (a breed of small armadillo).

For the most part, Uruguay maintains the pace of the small, agrarian society that it is. English is rarely spoken in any of the smaller villages. Although you can change dollars at some banks in the interior, it is usually best to do so in Montevideo; credit cards are of little value anywhere except in Punta del Este, where the most useful ones are American Express, Diners Club, and Visa. Wayside restrooms are very spartan, and you should carry toilet paper with you.

The best way to get around Uruguay is to rent a car. *Autorent* in Montevideo (Yaguarón 1683; phone: 90-8778/82) is reliable; however, you must be 23 years old and pay a $100 deposit. Expect, however, to pay more than you would in the US for the rental and for gas. When traveling in the interior, don't count on frequent wayside cafés or service stations; most of these are in towns. If you do plan to drive, bring spare parts and be prepared to make repairs yourself. But in case of need, don't hesitate to flag down a car; the friendly and courteous Uruguayan can be approached with perfect confidence. Whatever little traffic there is on the roads, do drive carefully and remember that you are in another country where driving habits differ.

The long-distance bus service is an efficient alternative to driving. Buses are comfortable and reliable, though you may have to buy your ticket in advance. The biggest bus company is ONDA; in Montevideo it is on Plaza Libertad. Railroads are slow and should be avoided. If you do drive, be sure you have proper insurance and that your *carnet* and insurance papers are easily accessible and in order (see *Touring by Car,* GETTING READY TO GO).

Any assistance can be acquired at the tourist office in Montevideo (Av. Agraciada 1409; phone: 91-43-40), the tourist information center (Plaza n Cagancha; phone: 90-52-16), or at the office in the Carrasco Airport (phone: 50-22-61).

The two routes detailed below run from Montevideo to Salto and from Montevideo to La Coronilla. The Montevideo-Salto route heads west from the capital through the potato farms of Rincón del Pino, through Nueva Helvecia (also known as Colonia Suiza, a Swiss pioneer town founded in the 1860s where *Nirvana,* Uruguay's finest country inn, is located), to Colonia (founded in 1680), to the sixteenth-century cattle-ranching town of Carmelo, to Mercedes and Paysandú (both agribusiness centers), and to the gaucho town of Salto, with thermal springs and two Laguna Negra fishing areas.

The route from Montevideo to La Coronilla takes you east from Montevideo along the Riviera of the South American coast, past the summer residences of Piriápolis, to Punta del Este, with its casino and nightclubs, to La Paloma, a smaller resort, and to La Coronilla and nearby Santa Teresa National Park.

Montevideo to Salto

Most tourists come to Uruguay from neighboring Argentina and Brazil in search of the good vacation life: sun, beaches, food, wine, and song. If this is what you want, you should take off to the eastern Atlantic coastline, for there you will find the beaches (see *Montevideo to La Coronilla*). If, however, you are more interested in learning about Uruguay's grasslands and gauchos (cowboys) you should explore the river coastline west from Montevideo.

This route leads through the vast, fertile grasslands that produce the country's main exports, beef and wool. The most dramatic figure you'll see on this gentle landscape is the gaucho himself; and you'll see gauchos everywhere, confidently astride their horses, trekking cattle by the roadside. Under wide-brimmed hats, with a poncho, wide *bombachas* (pantaloon-type pants gathered at the ankles), leather boots, *facón* (knife) carried in their belt, and spurs jangling, they make impressively romantic figures. Uruguay's plains are famous for their ranches (called *estancias*), although it is most difficult to visit one without a private invitation. However, there are some 60 cattle auctions held every month throughout the country, and even if you don't plan to take a cow home, you should attend one to get a flavor of Uruguay's cattle world. Large cattle auctions are always well advertised in the newspapers (try *El País*), and as cattle markets dot the countryside, it is easy to plan a visit to one en route.

The trip from Montevideo to Salto described here can be done easily in 5 days. The places of most interest to the tourist are Colonia, Paysandú, and Salto, and none of these very different towns should be missed. Although you can do this trip at any time of the year, the countryside is possibly most attractive in the middle of spring (November). Hotel reservations are a good idea.

Route 1 due west begins just beyond the toll bridge over the Río Santa Lucía. It takes you through Libertad, Rincón del Pino (where most of Uruguay's potatoes are grown), and on to Colonia Valdense, where there is a good wayside restaurant, *Brisas del Plata.* Turn right along Route 53 to Nueva Helvecia (New Switzerland).

NUEVA HELVECIA: Known as Colonia Suiza and founded in the 1860s by Swiss pioneers, the town bears the profound imprint of its founders and is well known for the cheese, cold meats, and wine it produces. Make a quick visit to the home of Eva Leitch de Muller (Camino de la Totorra) to see her antiques. This is a private home, but Mrs. de Muller is usually delighted to show visitors her collection of music boxes, coins, and lace.

Follow Route 51 back to Route 1 for the 35-mile (56-km) trip to Colonia del Sacramento.

COLONIA DEL SACRAMENTO: Known simply as Colonia, the town was founded in 1680 (before Montevideo) by Portuguese seeking to gain control of the Río de la Plata estuary. It was conquered by the Spaniards and became the most important city of southwestern Uruguay and a crossing point to Buenos Aires, which it remains today, with many daily crossings to the Argentine capital by ferry or airplane. Colonia has a few small industries and is a strategic port, but its main interest for a visitor is the colonial architecture, carefully restored and protected, that is part of the original 17th-century city known as Ciudad Vieja. Well worth a visit, here are the lighthouse, Calle de los Suspiros (Street of Whispers), the city walls, and the section's three museums. The Museo Municipal (Del Comercio 77) specializes in documents of the colonial period, while the Museo del Período Español (San José, corner of España) and the Museo del Período Portugués (25 de Mayo 124) each has collections of relics from the Spanish and Portuguese periods of colonization. Colonia also possesses Uruguay's only bullring (Real de San Carlos), now a piece of historic architecture since it has not been used in over 50 years (bullfighting was abolished shortly after the ring was built). Near the bullring is an enormous building that houses the only South American court of *cesta-punta,* a deadly Basque ball game; international matches are held here in the summer. Colonia is also a good place for river fishing because of the Río Uruguay. There are beaches, but remember that although the Río de la Plata is 25 miles (40 km) wide at Colonia, it is still a river and has very muddy waters at times.

If you want to eat beef (you should in Uruguay), try *Pulpería de los Faroles* (Del Comercio 102) in the old part of town. It has juicy steaks. *El Colonial* (Flores 440) is also a good steak house. Nightlife is restricted to gambling at the *Miramar Hotel.*

En Route from Colonia del Sacramento – Take Route 21 north, but if it rains heavily, you'll have to wait for the flooded Manga stream to recede or take the much longer route through the town of Tarariras. About 12 miles (20 km) out of Colonia there is a turnoff left for the national park of Anchorena, a great place for a picnic lunch. If you are quiet, you may see wild pig or deer roam nearby. On the grounds you will find the president's vacation residence and a watch tower that offers a wonderful view of the park and the Río Uruguay. From here it is just over 31 miles (50 km) along Route 21 north to Carmelo.

CARMELO: Now a small, sleepy agricultural town, it has had surprising importance in the past. Just south, at Arroyo de las Vacas, cattle were introduced into Uruguay in the 16th century. The parents of José de San Martín, the Argentine national hero, lived here (you can visit the ruins of their farmhouse in Calera de las Huérfanas); and both Charles Darwin and Giuseppi Garibaldi (Italy's liberator) visited here in the 19th century. Today the town offers little for a visitor, but it does have a lively yachting harbor in the summer.

As for restaurants, there is little choice apart from the *Casino* hotel and *La Fragata* (19 de Abril, corner Solís).

From Carmelo, follow Route 21 for some 62 miles (100 km) to Mercedes.

MERCEDES: An important center of business for the surrounding agricultural community, Mercedes has a few agribusinesses, including a sugar mill and milk pasteurizing plant. A drive along the riverfront is worthwhile, and the colonial cathedral on the main square is also interesting. The Castillo Mauá, built in 1857, gives you an idea of how fortress-like the farmhouses were when Uruguay was settled.

For a meal, try *El Estribo de Castro y Carreaga* (corner of Artigas) or the *Club Remeros* on the riverfront — both specialize in steaks.

En Route from Mercedes – From here, follow Route 2 north 20 miles (32 km) to Fray Bentos, a small town that grew as a result of its meat packing plant. From here, you can cross to Argentina by means of a new bridge 3 miles (5 km) north; the distance by road from the bridge to Buenos Aires is just over 186 miles (300 km).

The road north to Paysandú from Fray Bentos, Route 24, is not in the best condition and does not have many gas stations, so fill up in Fray Bentos before leaving.

PAYSANDÚ: This town was founded as a European village in 1769, although certain Indians, now extinct, are known to have lived in the area previously. In the 19th-century wars of independence, it was a center of much fighting; in the early decades of this century, it became the main industrial town of the interior. Today, it maintains this position, though threatened by the recent growth of Salto. The industries that form the backbone of Paysandú are mostly related to agriculture (leather, wool, sugar, beer, and milk).

The attractive cathedral on the main square is reputed to have one of the best organs in the country. The old cemetery (Monumento a la Perpetuidad) has a great number of statues and massive mausoleums.

Fishing on the Río Uruguay, mostly for dorado, boga, dientudo, and surubi, is said to be very good. From here, you can cross by the bridge for a day in Argentina.

For restaurants, *Artemio's* (18 de Julio 985) is regarded as the best (try the pepper steak), followed by *El Águila* (18 de Julio, corner Montecaseros) and *Kiwi* (18 de Julio, corner Dr. L. A. de Herrera). You should not leave Paysandú without trying its famous *postre chajá* (buy it across the road from the Centro Bar), a delicious cream cake.

   En Route from Paysandú – Follow Route 3 north; at kilometer 404 there is a turnoff to the small waterfall of the Río Queguay, a lovely place to have a picnic and fish. About 25 miles (40 km) farther along Route 3 are the camping grounds of Guaviyú. The main attractions here are the thermal springs, but there are even better facilities farther north in Arapey. On kilometer 463 of Route 3 is a turnoff to the "Meseta de Artigas." This is the place where Artigas (the national hero) made his headquarters in 1815; it is an attractive spot from which to watch the Río Uruguay. Some 28 miles (35 km) farther is Salto.

SALTO: Until recently, this was almost exclusively a cattleman's town, serving the surrounding department as an administrative and commercial center. Lately Salto has had noticeable growth, mostly due to the hydroelectric dam (one of the largest in the world) being built on the Río Uruguay. The power generated is being shared by Uruguay and Argentina and will help supply Montevideo and Buenos Aires. It is a most impressive structure and well worth a visit, with excellent guided tours around the works twice a day (no need to book in advance). Once the dam is completed, a large tourist complex is to be built on the reservoir.

The people of Salto pride themselves on the cultural facilities in their town. There are a number of museums worth visiting: Museo de Bellas Artes y Artes Decorativas (Uruguay 1067), which exhibits mostly paintings, sculptures, and wooden cabinets (by Pacot); Museo Histórico Municipal (Av. Paraguay y Ruta General Artigas), which has items pertaining to the history of the city itself; and the new Museo del Hombre (Brazil and Zorrilla), which deals with anthropological topics. The theater, Teatro Larrañaga, built in 1882, was famous for its early acoustical design and lack of columns. There are also the ruins of two meat-salting plants that date back to the 1870s (Costanera Sur), where meat was salted and sent to feed slaves in Cuba and northern Brazil. Watch for attractive pieces of raw amethyst or polished agate in the shops.

The thermal grounds near Salto are worth a visit. The nearest is at Dayman, 12 miles (19 km) north of Salto, with rather limited facilities. The best is called Termas del Arapey, 60 miles (96 km) northeast of Salto (it is signposted from Route 3). The facilities there are very good. Not only can you have therapeutic baths, but you can play tennis, basketball, or football. You can either camp or rent bungalows. Long-distance buses go straight to Dayman from Montevideo, but reservations at the spa are always a must.

A pleasant drink at night can be had by the river at *Parador Ayuí* (Costanera Norte). For restaurants, try the *Gran Hotel Salto, Chef Restaurant* (Uruguay 639), *Los Pinguinos* (Uruguay 708), or *Club Remeros* (Uruguay 457). For a good piece of barbecued meat, try *Parrillada El Cerro* (Zorrilla 619).

   En Route from Salto – There are three ways to return to Montevideo, all different from the way you came. The fastest way is to take Route 3 south until it meets Route 1 and then head east to Montevideo. The distance is 310 miles (500 km) and normally takes 6 hours (there is a very bad stretch of road just before the town of Trinidad). A modification of this choice is to take Route 3 to a point 16 miles (26 km) south of Paysandú, then follow Route 24 to Route 2. Follow Route 2 to Route 1, then east to Montevideo. A good place to stop for lunch is Cardona, at the *Hotel Elizondo;* ask if they have partridge (*perdiz*). The difference between the two alternatives is that this is 16 miles (26 km) longer than the first route.

Your third alternative is much longer — about 416 miles (670 km) — and involves coming down the center of the country. Take Route 3 south (with a full tank) to take Route 26 on to Tacuarembó. This route is well surfaced, but has almost no traffic — and no gas stations. The terrain is different, consisting mostly of small basalt hills. From here you could go north toward Brazil and the border town of Rivera. If not, take Route 5 south to Montevideo, nearly 248 miles (400 km) away.

BEST EN ROUTE

Hotels on this route are about the same price as those in Montevideo. Those classified as expensive will cost about $50 per night; moderate, from $20 to $30; and inexpensive, under $15. It's a good idea to make reservations before arriving.

COLONIA SUIZA

Nirvana – One of the best hotels in the country is set in 60 acres of lovely grounds. Tennis, horseback riding, and swimming are offered in the summer, and the restaurant features Swiss food. Follow the signposts off Route 1 at Km 118 (phone: Colonia Suiza 175, 81, or 52). Expensive.

COLONIA

Posada del Gobernador – Formerly an elegant private colonial home, this hotel has very cozy and comfortable rooms, all with private baths. 18 de Julio 205/209 (phone: 3018-2718). Expensive.

Mirador – This modern hotel features a swimming pool, tennis courts, and a casino at night. The food is very good, especially the cold buffet. Av. Roosevelt (phone: Colonia 2004 and 2552). Expensive.

Leoncia – A small, comfortable hotel that offers clean rooms and private baths. Rivera, corner Flores (no phone). Inexpensive.

Onda – Reasonably comfortable. Flores 2081 (no phone). Inexpensive.

CARMELO

Casino Carmelo – A large hotel set in a pleasant park by the Río Uruguay. Offers good cooking and casino (phone: Carmelo 314). Moderate.

Bertoletti – This smaller hotel offers spacious rooms. Uruguay, corner Lavalleja (phone number not available). Moderate.

MERCEDES

Brisas del Hum – A very plain hotel, on the main square, that features comfortable rooms (phone: Mercedes 2740 or 2741). Moderate.

FRAY BENTOS

Gran Hotel Fray Bentos – A pleasant hotel that looks onto the Río Uruguay. Calle Paraguay (phone: Fray Bentos 358). Moderate.

PAYSANDÚ

Gran Hotel Paysandú – A centrally located, functional hotel with good dining facilities and a popular coffee room. 13 de Julio and 19 de Abril (phone: Paysandú 3400 or 2614). Moderate.

Nuevo Paysandú – Reserve ahead, if possible. No credit cards. L. A. de Herrera, corner Leandro Gómez (phone: Paysandú 3062 and 3063). Inexpensive.

SALTO

Gran Hotel Salto – This hotel on the square has air conditioning and a good restaurant. 25 de Agosto, corner Uruguay (phone: Salto 3250 and 3251). Moderate.

Los Cedros – A modern hotel with meeting rooms. Uruguay 657 (phone: Salto 3984 and 3985). Moderate.

TACUAREMBÓ

Tacuarembó – A pleasant hotel with a swimming pool. Centrally located. 18 de Julio 133 (phone: 2104/2105). Expensive.

Montevideo to La Coronilla

From Montevideo to the Brazilian border is a coastline of nearly 218 miles filled with many wonderful beaches that attract *montevideanos* who want a relaxing weekend by the sea and foreign visitors who want the traditional summer seaside vacation. The farthest resort, La Coronilla, is only 6 hours from Montevideo by car, and the highways are well surfaced and marked. Book hotels well in advance.

The first 68 miles (110 km) of the road to Piriápolis is a continuous series of small villages with summer houses, owned by Uruguayan families who idle away the summer months by the sea. The largest resort along the way is Atlántida. Twenty-four miles (38 km) east of Piriápolis is Punta del Este, the internationally famous resort with casinos, nightclubs, and a pleasant beach. La Paloma, 142 miles (230 km) from Montevideo, is set around a beautiful cove and tends to attract those fleeing the larger resorts. La Coronilla, about 186 miles (310 km) from Montevideo, is quiet even at the height of the summer season and sufficiently near the Santa Teresa National Park to attract those interested in camping in such beautiful surroundings. You can rent a car in Montevideo (see Sources and Resources, *Montevideo,* THE CITIES) or take a bus.

The route really begins at Atlántida, 31 miles (50 km) from Montevideo.

ATLÁNTIDA: Surrounded by pine and eucalyptus forests, this small resort, so near Montevideo, attracts people year round. The genial atmosphere of the town is as calm as the waters along its beaches, with such pleasant diversions as golf and tennis and tea at the town's best restaurant, *Country Club* (on Route 11, just north of the Interbalnearia). A small casino in the center of town opens at night.

En Route from Atlántida – Some 23½ miles (38 km) past Atlántida (just past the second toll on the Interbalnearia), take the turnoff left and drive through the seaside village of Solís. If you stop to eat, you must go to the well-decorated *Chajá* (the only hotel and restaurant actually in town). Then, as the road turns left along the beach, you'll see the waves breaking just over ½ mile from the road.

As you drive through the hamlet of Las Flores, look for the houses built of pebbles. Six miles (10 km) farther lies Piriápolis.

PIRIÁPOLIS: This is a well-planned town laid out in wooded hills. It's a popular resort for people with very young children because the waters of the bay are protected, quiet, and safe. Fishing is good off Punta Fría. San Antonio Hill has a chair lift up to the top, where there's a restaurant and tearoom, discotheque, swimming pool, and the view of the whole bay, town, and surrounding countryside; you can drive up if you prefer. Sugar Loaf Hill on the outskirts of town (take Route 37 north) has only a very steep footpath in the bush leading up to the cross that crowns the hill. The view is spectacular and worth the 2-hour climb, but beware of snakes.

As for the food, the *Argentino Hotel Casino* is excellent. For simpler food try *El Grillo* (Rambla) or one of the small cafés on the coast road famous for shellfish. Uruguay's most popular sandwich, *chivito* (beef tenderloin garnished with ham, cheese, lettuce, tomato, and peppers) is available at every restaurant and snack bar.

En Route from Piriápolis – You can take either Route 37 or Route 93 to get onto the Interbalnearia. On the left, at about kilometer 120, you pass a large lake, Laguna del Sauce, near an air force base (which also serves as the commercial airport for Punta del Este). The lake is a good place for boating and fishing. Farther on you will come to the steep climb up Punta Ballena; at the top take a camera stop, for the view of Portezuelo Bay is beautiful. On Punta Ballena itself (take the first right after the climb off the Interbalnearia) you will find an excellent site for snorkeling, and you can visit Casapueblo, a beautifully designed Moorish house. Clinging to the cliff, is the spectacular home of Carlos Paez Vilaró, a well-known Uruguayan artist. It is open to the public in summer, and you can buy paintings and ceramics. From Punta Ballena you can view Punta del Este across the bay, only 10½ miles (17 km) farther along the Interbalnearia.

PUNTA DEL ESTE: This is one of the world's best seaside resorts, yet it is one of the least known, possibly because Uruguay itself is so far off the jet set's flight pattern. On a peninsula that juts out into the sea (here the Río de la Plata officially ends and the Atlantic Ocean begins), Punta del Este is surrounded by lovely pine forests. When it began as a resort area almost 100 years ago, houses were built only on the peninsula itself. Now the town has spread out, but there are still relatively few high-rises. In the last 10 years, some very beautiful mansions have been built. The town has a permanent population of about 10,000, but in summer as many as 400,000 people visit the resort; most of the summer visitors rent houses or apartments, and many stay for the whole summer.

On the western side of the peninsula (Playa Mansa), the waters are safe and calm enough to allow water skiing (try renting at L'Marangatú Beach), but on the eastern side (Playa Brava), the Atlantic Ocean throws waves of 10 feet down the beach; great for surfing, but intimidating for many swimmers. The two beaches are about a 20-minute walk from each other.

Punta del Este has an excellent golf course (just off Av. del Golf), which often hosts international tournaments. Tennis is available at many locations (Cantegril Country Club has excellent courts); and horses can be rented at Parque Jaguel near Jaguel Airport. Fishing all along the coast is excellent due to the confluence of the Río de la Plata and the Atlantic Ocean. You can roll-cast from the coast or rent a boat from the Yacht Club for deep-sea castings. There is fishing in inland lakes such as Laguna del Sauce, Laguna Garzón, or Lago José Ignacio (famous for pink flamingos in summer).

For the person who only has a day to spend in Punta del Este, there are three "must do" activities: Go to the beach — Playa Brava — for a midmorning swim-and-sun; after a good meal take a taxi or drive yourself through the neighborhoods around the *San Rafael* hotel and the Golf Club to see some of the gorgeous houses; and in the evening, take a walk down Gorlero to get a feeling for the place and look at the shops. No matter how long you stay, be prepared to dine late — from 10 PM on.

There are four sidetrips from Punta del Este for a visitor with more time. Gorriti Island is about 2 miles (3 km) off Punta del Este in the bay. This quiet island has not only two protected beaches, but also the ruins of an 18th-century colonial fortress. A second trip is to another island, Isla de Lobos, 6½ miles (10 km) off Punta del Este, a government-run natural reserve for some 500,000 sea lions. It is literally covered with animals. You can go to both islands by boats from the Yacht Club, but buy your tickets the day before. You should also visit La Barra de Maldonado and its inverted W-shaped bridge some 6 miles (10 km) east of Punta del Este on the mainland. It is a growing suburb of the resort that is a resort in itself. Manantiales, a few miles farther east, is also becoming fashionable and has some beautiful Spanish-Moorish houses. A fourth trip to Maldonado, 3 miles (5 km) due north of Punta del Este, will show you how the other half lives; here, most of the population are year-round residents. The town is full of shops (less expensive than Punta del Este) and has a beautiful cathedral on the main plaza that is well worth visiting at night to see the dancing waters of the musical fountain. There are also colonial ruins, such as the Watch Tower (El Vigía) and the windmill, as well as the Museum Mazzoni (Ituzaingó 789).

Eating in Punta del Este should be considered seriously, for there is a great choice of excellent restaurants (in which everyone dresses informally). For seafood, the best restaurants are: *Mariskonea* (Calle 26 No. 850) and *Posta del Cangrejo* (Barra de Maldonado). *London Grill* (Gorlero, corner No. 27) is good for both fish and meat. *Catari* (at the *Palace*) has good Italian food; *Bungalow Suizo* (Av. Roosevelt and the rail tracks) is well known for Swiss food; and the *Chino* restaurant (Av. Roosevelt and Parada 7) is an excellent Chinese restaurant. *Il Papagallo* (in the *Playa* hotel) boasts a famous cook, Mrs. Gori Salaverri; *La Tabla del Rey Arturo, La Bourgogne,* and *El Floreal* (across the street from each other on Pedragosa Sierra) are famous for haute cuisine. A good inexpensive restaurant is *Club Ciclista* (Calle 20, corner No. 27); try the *mejilliones a la provenzal* (fresh mussels in parsley sauce), washed down with white wine.

At night Punta del Este has a refreshing breeze (you will need a sweater). Its nightlife is mostly geared for couples, with good discotheques such as *Ezequiel* at the *Cantegril Country Club, Rainbow* (Parada 40), *Le Club* (San Rafael Beach), *L'ete* (Punta Ballena), and *Swan.* Another form of entertainment is found in clubs like *Caras y Caretas* at the port, the *Mozart Piano Bar* at La Barra, and *Au Piano Bar,* downtown on Maldonado, where you can have a few drinks and see a floor show. There is gambling every night, at the *Casino Hotel San Rafael* (a coat is required for men) or at the *Casino Nogaró* (Gorlero and Calle 31). There are roulette tables, blackjack, and baccarat.

En Route from Punta del Este – Drive to Maldonado and then north toward San Carlos. Drive through San Carlos and take Route 9 to Rocha. If you are tempted to visit Lago José Ignacio, be warned that the turnoff from Route 9, about 15½ miles (25 km) from San Carlos, is a very bumpy road. On the outskirts of Rocha you will come across the groves of palm trees that are dotted about the eastern part of the country — an unexpected sight. From Rocha, turn south along Route 15 for another 15½ miles (25 km) until you come to La Paloma.

LA PALOMA: This small summer sports resort is set in a beautifully wooded area surrounding a small bay protected by an island, a convenient natural design that allows water skiing in the bay and surfing on the beaches outside the bay. There is an excellent port and even better fishing — deep sea or shore casting. Species in local waters include anchoa (anchovy), bonito, pargo, sargo, brótola, pescadilla, pejerrey, manta, luna, corvina blanca, cazón, palometa, pez martillo (hammer fish), tiburón (shark), and raya (ray fish). There are facilities for tennis and golf and a very popular camping site, Parque Andresito, that is within walking distance of both the center of town and the beach. You can rent bungalows here very inexpensively.

Try the fish in the restaurant of the *Cabo Santa María* hotel (Av. Nicolás Solari). Nightlife is somewhat restricted to the *Casino* (Av. Nicolás Solari and Titania) and various modest discotheques.

En Route from La Paloma – You have two possibilities from here. The first is to go back to Rocha and then turn east along Route 9 to Castillos, a 53-mile

(85-km) trip that can be done in a little over an hour. The second is to take Route 10 east from La Paloma. Although it is about the same distance, the road is unpaved and the journey takes longer. There are, however, two very worthwhile side trips from this road: Some 3 miles (5 km) out of La Paloma you will drive through La Pedrera, a tiny resort suddenly becoming very popular with Argentines. It resembles Biarritz (c. 1905!). Some 28 miles (45 km) beyond you will come to a sign reading Cabo Polonio. Don't attempt driving there unless you have a four-wheel-drive vehicle. Sooner or later, a horse-drawn taxi service will appear out of the sand dunes. Take it. After 6 miles (10 km) of going through the dunes you come upon the Atlantic Ocean and approach the cape and a lighthouse, where you will see thousands of sea lions; their playful roars rise above the dry crying of the seagulls and the thunder of the ocean waves. Unfortunately, there is nowhere to stay in the adjacent fishermen's village.

Once back on Route 10, on your way to Castillos, you come to Aguas Dulces, an unusual summer village; the houses are thatched, wooden, and cramped (a few feet from the ocean) on the beach itself. You can have a snack of fried fish at one of the small cafés on the main street. Don't bother to stop in Castillos, but follow Route 9 for 28 miles (45 km) and turn left at the sign for Punta del Diablo. Follow the unpaved road to this small fishing village, whose economy is based on sharks caught from little boats out at sea. The fish are gutted and sun-dried into what is wrongly called *bacalao* (cod). This is consumed in vast quantities during Holy Week, when Uruguayans reluctantly leave their meat dishes aside and eat fish. Unsurprisingly, you can find interesting handicrafts made of shark's teeth and vertebrae here. There is a restaurant, *Restaurante del Mar,* looking onto the sea. Once back on Route 9, the turnoff for Santa Teresa National Park is only 6 miles (10 km) away.

PARQUE SANTA TERESA: This is a lovely national park with many kinds of vegetation and over 300 different species of trees. It is the ideal place for those who enjoy camping, although you can also rent cottages in summer. Among the two million trees in the park are scattered hothouses, a bird sanctuary, and some delightful freshwater swimming pools. Nearby is Laguna Negra, an excellent lake for fishing. The main attraction, though, is the colonial fortress built by the Portuguese in 1761. It changed hands many times among Spaniards, Uruguayans, Argentines, and Brazilians. Restored in 1921, it is now a museum of the colonial period.

If you do not want to camp, you can stay at one of the hotels in La Coronilla, only 9 miles (15 km) away.

LA CORONILLA: A collection of summer houses with some good hotels right on the beach, this is a good base for visiting Parque Santa Teresa and Chuy as well as for enjoying the beach itself. The beaches here are vast and wild, and the fishing probably the best in Uruguay. There is little nightlife, (except for the *Casino* at the *Costas del Mar* hotel) and few restaurants (try the one at the *Gure Exté* hotel), but these are not the main reason for a visit.

There is a side trip worth your time to the border town of Chuy, which is half Brazilian and half Uruguayan. Then take Route 19 north for 6 miles (10 km) and visit the Park and Fortress of San Miguel, built in the same period as the Fortress of Santa Teresa but by the Spaniards. It is smaller and very well kept, and free (as are most museums in Uruguay). Ask to see a small carriage museum in the grounds. You can have a good meal or even stay at the attractive hotel called *Parador San Miguel.*

En Route from La Coronilla – You have three alternatives. First, you can return to Montevideo along Route 9, which will take about 6 hours. The second, a longer (by 62 mi/100 km) but more picturesque way to Montevideo (going first through marshland and then hilly terrain), is to take Camino de los Indios (Routes 16, 14, 15, and 13) through to Aigua and then Route 8 to Montevideo, which will take close to 9 hours due to the gravel roads on the first third of the journey. (A good spot for lunch is an isolated restaurant just outside Aigua called *Pororó.*) Your third alternative is to drive through Chuy to Brazil, but you must first clear the car's papers at customs. (A rented car will eventually have to be returned to Uruguay.)

BEST EN ROUTE

Hotels in Uruguay's coastal resorts are a little more expensive than those found in Montevideo. Double accommodations can run as high as $80 to $110 (expensive); between $50 and $75 (moderate); and under $50 (inexpensive). Most are clean, comfortable, have private baths, restaurant, and a variety of sports. Before coming here, it's a good idea to make reservations, especially in the summer. (In season, the rates at Punta del Este and neighboring hotels can go even higher.) Room rates include breakfast, but a 20% value-added tax is additional.

BELLA VISTA

Hostería Bella Vista – A good hotel on the beach, run by an English-speaking management, it offers bungalows and a good cuisine, but a restricted menu for the day. Tennis courts and horseback riding are other amenities. 3 miles (5 km) from Solís toward Piriápolis (phone: Solís 52). Moderate.

PIRIÁPOLIS

Argentino Hotel Casino – This large hotel on the seafront has a saltwater swimming pool, cuisine á la carte, and casino action at night. Rambla (phone: Piriápolis 6). Moderate.

PUNTA BALLENA

Solana del Mar – Quiet, attractive, and modern, in a lovely setting with pine forest behind and ocean and beach below. Expensive.

PUNTA DEL ESTE

Casino San Rafael – A large, beautiful, first-class hotel, on the seafront, with facilities for meetings (usually held in winter). Rooms are comfortable, but not luxurious; a swimming pool and casino are extras. Rambla Lorenzo Batlle (phone: Maldonado 82161 to 66). Expensive.

L'Auberge – This very small, exclusive hotel has excellent service. Barrio Parque del Golf (phone: Maldonado 82601). Expensive.

La Posta del Cangrejo – A small hotel, very near the beach on the outskirts of Punta del Este, that provides clean, airy rooms. It is famous for seafood. Barra de Maldonado (phone: La Barra 2021). Expensive.

Palace – In the heart of Punta del Este, this is a well-run hotel with comfortable rooms. Gorlero, corner of Calle 14 (phone: Maldonado 82519). Expensive.

San Marcos – This beautiful first-class hotel has comfortable rooms, all with a private bath and telephone, a swimming pool, tennis courts, barbecue, restaurant, and meeting facilities. Av. Mar del Plata, corner Buenas Artigas (phone: 8-2251). Expensive.

Playa – This spacious hotel is in front of the beach, but within walking distance of the center of Punta del Este. It has a restaurant, *Il Papagallo.* Continuación Gorlero (phone: Maldonado 82231). Moderate.

La Capilla – Small, but very comfortable, and only two blocks from the beach. Besides very good service, there is a swimming pool and an excellent restaurant. Viña del Mar, corner Buenas Artigas (phone: 84059, 81843). Moderate.

Nuevo España – A small but comfortable hotel in downtown Punta del Este. All rooms have private baths. Calle 9, No. 160 (phone: 40228). Moderate.

Embajador – One block from the beach, this hotel provides standard accommodations, including private bath and phone. Risso, corner La Via (phone: 81008). Inexpensive.

Grumete – Standard accommodations two blocks from the beach. Calle 20, No. 797 (phone: 41009). Inexpensive.

LA PALOMA

Casino Cabo Santa María – The best hotel in town, it has large rooms, private baths, and a good restaurant, where you should try the fish. The casino is open at night. Av. Nicolás Solari (phone: La Paloma 92 or 4). Moderate.

Portabello – All the guests at this new, oceanfront hotel enjoy a splendid view of the sea and the pool. Las Tres Marías (phone: 6159). Moderate.

PUNTA DEL DIABLO

Hostería del Pescador – You will need a car, as there is almost no public transport. Small, family-type hotel is ideal if you want quiet. Good food (phone: Santa Teresa 17). Moderate.

LA CORONILLA

Costas del Mar – This small hotel faces the sea and is open all year. There is a good restaurant, and the casino is open at night. Beachfront (phone: Coronilla 11). Moderate.

PARQUE SAN MIGUEL

Gure Exté – A small, well-run hotel, only a half-block from the beach. Guests can dine at the fine restaurant here. Moderate.

Venezuela

For a range of geographical spectacles in a relatively small, accessible area, no South American nation can match Venezuela. Covering 352,150 square miles, this tropical nation, with a fairly steady average yearly temperature in the 80s F (27°C), is bordered by the Caribbean Sea to the north, Colombia to the southwest, Brazil to the southeast, and Guyana to the east. In Caracas, the capital, which stands at an elevation of 3,400 feet about 12 miles from the Caribbean, reside about 4 million of the country's 14 million inhabitants (for a complete report, see *Caracas,* THE CITIES).

In the southeast are the Guayana Highlands, a vast and beautiful wilderness of giant sandstone plateaus that soar above the green jungle and cover almost half the country. To the botanist, the highlands are a paradise; to diamond miners, an El Dorado. The source of many rivers, the Guayana Shield is the oldest land formation on the face of the earth. Here, free-falling over ½ mile, are the Angel Falls, the highest waterfall in the world.

To the north stand the Andes. In its northward stretch to the sea from Tierra del Fuego, this longest of mountain ranges bunches in southern Colombia into a complex volcanic knot that eventually unravels into several spurs in Venezuela. One, the Sierra de Perijá, tracks north to the Goajira Peninsula on Venezuela's northwestern frontier; the other, the Cordillera de Mérida, makes a broad northeasterly arc, falling into the Caribbean just northeast of Caracas. Within the V formed by the two spurs is Lake Maracaibo, lying in a vast depression that is the major source of Venezuela's oil and thus the location of the generally excellent highways traversing Venezuela. A lesser spur, the Cordillera de la Costa, runs just to the south of Caracas, entering the sea off eastern Venezuela on a line with the Windward Islands.

Between the Andean highlands to the west and north and Guayana to the south is an immense area of low alluvial plain called the *llanos,* the basin of the Orinoco and Apure rivers. A harsh land, it is flooded 6 months of the year, drought-stricken the other 6 months, and always hot.

The land was discovered, so to speak, by Columbus, on his third voyage in 1498. He sailed along the coast of the Delta Amacuro (where the Orinoco empties into the Atlantic) and rounded the Paria Peninsula in the east. The following year, Alonzo de Ojeda and Amerigo Vespucci mapped the coast of the Guianas and Venezuela to Lake Maracaibo. Here, at what is now Sinamaica, they found the indigenes living on the water in palm-thatched huts supported by stilts, a phenomenon found also in the Delta Amacuro. All commerce was conducted by water and dugout canoe, as it still is today. Overcome by some nameless impulse, they named the land Venezuela, which means "little Venice." From 1500 on, adventurers from Spain began roaming the difficult terrain in a relentless search for gold.

As early as 1510, a settlement of pearlfishers was established on the island of Cubagua off the northeastern coast, and a small settlement on the mainland followed 3 years later at Cumaná. The Germans assumed control of the land for a time and produced a couple of notable explorers, but they also fought a great deal and founded no towns. A Spanish colonizer from Curaçao founded Coro on the western coast in 1523, but he was forced to flee. There were two main thrusts of colonization, one from the region of Coro and the other from Pamplona (founded 1849), in what is now Colombia. This latter founded the elevated eyries of Mérida and Trujillo in 1558 and San Cristóbal 3 years later. Colonizers from the coast founded Barquisimeto in 1552, pushed east to Valencia (1555), also in an Andean valley, and, under the command of Diego de Losada, entered the valley of Caracas in 1561. The *cacique* (chieftain) of the Caracas Indians, Guaicaipuro, defended his emerald paradise fiercely but eventually was killed near what is now La Carlota Airport and his head paraded about on a spear. Nonetheless, such was the ferocity of his resistance that Guaicaipuro is considered one of Venezuela's greatest heroes. The city of Santiago de León de Caracas was founded, and within a few decades every sizable valley along the spine of the Andes had bred a settlement.

The Andes gave birth to the *caudillos* who, until well into modern times, ruled their lofty valleys as fiefdoms, paying tribute to no one, least of all to one another. As late as the 1890s, the *caudillo* of Petare, now a suburb of Caracas, could be at war with the president of the republic in Caracas. A hardy, serious people, known disrespectfully as *gochos,* the Andinos work hard to eke a precarious living from the stony soil in great contrast to the determinedly unburdened *costeños,* the people of the coast. The Andinos, with few exceptions, have always ruled.

At the end of a century of dictatorship, Venezuela has been Latin America's showcase democracy for the past 20 years. *Caudillismo* persists, however, resulting in an extremely centralized government somewhat attenuated by oligopoly. A founding member of OPEC, the country is rich, but with the problems that attend accelerated development — most notably deeply rooted bureaucratic corruption (which won't affect the casual traveler) and an overly hectic capital.

Successive administrations have had a fairly ambivalent attitude toward foreign tourism; partly as a result, the traveler in remote regions will find a shortage of good accommodations. The people, on the other hand, are unambivalent in their friendliness and helpfulness to foreigners (whom they call, disrespectfully, *musiús,* the legacy of an earlier French influence). They take almost nothing seriously, least of all the sensibilities of others or of themselves. In their speech they occasionally say please, rarely say thank you, and almost never use the formal address. They love to talk, especially of politics and baseball.

Although Venezuela has an extensive road network, driving in the interior is a rugged experience. Gasoline, although inexpensive, is not sold in every town. Road services of any kind are scarce (or nonexistent) in the interior. If you do drive, carry the spare parts needed and be prepared to make repairs yourself. Be sure to have proper insurance and that your insurance papers and *carnet* are in order and easily accessible. When driving in the interior, you must stop at *alcabalas* (military checkpoints). Venezuela has good airlines and bus companies connecting the capital with many parts of the country.

The ten routes in this chapter are designed to enable you to plan different itineraries through the Venezuelan countryside. The first one, Caracas to San Francisco de Yare, goes from Caracas to the sulfur springs at San Juan de los Morros, home of the *llanero,* the Venezuelan cowboy, to Lake Valencia, the mountains around Cata, to the town of Valencia, to the Bavarian village of Colonia Tovar, to the secluded beach area of Barlovento, Higuerote, the village of San Francisco de Yare in the Tuy River valley, and Los Roques Islands. The second route, the Andes, goes from Valencia through the cowtowns of San Carlos, Acarigua, and Guanare, to the garden village of Boconó, to La Puerta, a hill resort, through the Aguilar pass of the Andes to the Apartaderos Andean valley, to the mountain village of Santo Domingo, the fishing area of Laguna Negra, the historic mountain city of Mérida, with its cable car (teleférico) to the Pico Espejo, 15,500 feet above sea level, to Los Nevados, the restored colonial village of Jají, the city of San Cristóbal, and the Segovia Highlands where people worship the Indian goddess María Lionza. The third route, the Western Coast, goes from Valencia to Tucacas along the Morrocoy reef, the sand dunes of Coro, and the Paraguaná desert. The fourth route describes a trip around the Maracaibo region off the Guajira Peninsula where oil was discovered in 1917, changing the entire Venezuelan economy. The fifth route, the Eastern Venezuelan Coast, goes from Caracas east to Barcelona and Puerto La Cruz, a vast beach resort (see *Luxury Resorts and Special Havens,* DIVERSIONS), Cumaná, the first Hispanic settlement in Venezuela, the Cariaco Gulf, the Paria Peninsula, and the Guácharo Cave. The sixth route, the Lower Orinoco, goes through Ciudad Bolívar, a river port, along the Río Paragua, through Ciudad Guayana, the Guarao Indian town of Tucupita and through the Orinoco delta to Barrancas. The seventh route, the Gran Sabana, goes through the pink massifs and tropical highlands of one of the most isolated sections of Venezuela, travels through the savannah town of Upata, the pretty jungle town of El Callao, the former penal colony where Papillon lived, El Dorado, up the escarpment to the Gran Sabana, the town of Santa Elena, to the Brazilian frontier. The eighth route describes a trip to Canaima, site of Angel Falls. The ninth route covers Margarita Island, Venezuela's most famous Caribbean resort. The tenth route explores the Venezuelan Amazon.

Caracas to San Francisco de Yare

This route is a series of day trips around the Caracas outskirts, starting in the west with the dry, grassy *llanos* (plains) and continuing east along the Caribbean coast. Wedged between the base of the snowcapped Andes and marshy lowlands of the 1,700-mile Orinoco River, the *llanos* harbor a special breed of Venezuelan — the *llanero* (cowboy). He is an independent, proud character who rides his horse barefoot, herding his *zebu* (hump-backed cattle) through duststorm and flood and braving the dangers of the ever-present rattlesnake. The *llanero* is quite a contrast to the lazy, somewhat suspicious, action-seeking resident of Barlovento, the quiet backwater that claims most of the country's central coast — an area filled with steep, mountainous roads and silver streams.

En route to the ocean is Lake Valencia, the second largest lake in Venezuela. Here, Juan Vicente Gomez, one of the last, great, infamous *caudillos,* made the lakeside city of Maracay his capital after deciding Caracas was just ungovernable. This sentiment was shared by the *libertador,* Simón Bolívar, who was born just 57 miles west of Caracas, in the village of San Mateo, in 1883.

There is no train service in Venezuela, so it's better to rent a car in Caracas (see Sources and Resources, *Caracas,* THE CITIES) and drive from there. There are hotels in most of the major towns on this route, and their rooms — spacious, catering to double occupancies, and supplied with private showers — are adequate.

For tourist information in Caracas, go to the Venezuelan Tourism Corporation on Plaza Venezuela, Capriles Center, 7th Floor (phone: 781-83-11); Venezuelan Airlines Assn. (ALAV), Urdaneta Ave., Edificio Phelps (phone: 81-64-29); and the National Association of Hotels (ANAHOVEN), Capriles Center (ground floor), Plaza Venezuela (phone: 51-14-94). The best maps are found in gas stations.

En Route from Caracas – Take the Caracas-Valencia *autopista* (freeway) or the Panamericana, which leaves the *autopista* at the suburb of Coche, between Los Proceres and the Rinconada Racecourse.

At La Victoria, 50 miles (80 km) west of Caracas, there is a turnoff to Colonia Tovar; or else continue on another 7 miles (11 km) west to San Mateo, where the hacienda of Simón Bolívar is open to visitors. This is where El Libertador was raised, where he returned with his bride from Europe in 1802, and from whence he fled to Paris after her death. From La Encrucijada, 1 mile away, Route 5 leads south to San Juan de los Morros, 30 miles (48 km) away.

SAN JUAN DE LOS MORROS: This town, named for the shape of the nearby mountains (which resemble Moorish castles with their tall, spiral peaks), is noted chiefly for its 1,500-gallon-per-hour, 95°F (35°C) sulfur springs; it is also the gateway to the *llanos* (flats). The *llanero,* or cowboy, will tell you that he is the true Venezuelan and his hardy and happy people herd some 5 million head of cattle (*zebus*) under immensely trying conditions. For 6 months of the year, the 125,000-square-mile plains are largely under water, and the herds must be moved to higher ground. The *llanero* rides barefoot (because wet feet don't rot, but wet feet inside soggy boots are subject to fungus infections) with the big toe hooked through a small ring stirrup. The other 6 months the plains are dry, and the herds are driven into the Central Highlands and fattened for sale. The music of the *llanos* is the best in Venezuela: passionate ballads relating the tales of hell-bent men and evil women, odes to the ubiquitous rattlesnake (murder, literally, to a barefoot people) and to the *llanero*'s principal enemy, the jaguar. These songs are belted out by a soloist (preferably female), accompanied by marracas, *cuatro* (ukulele), and a harp, Venezuela's national instrument. There is a dance called the *joropo,* involving the vigorous stomping of feet. Another tradition is the *toros coleados,* a kind of rodeo whose object is (believe it or not) to throw a bull by its tail.

En Route from San Juan de los Morros – Continue north on Route 5 to the junction of Route 9, and north toward the town of Cata, 36 miles (57 km) from Maracay. On the eastern shore of Lake Valencia is Maracay, a commercial center of no particular interest to the traveler.

The lake itself is the second largest in Venezuela, covering some 140 square miles with 22 islands. Unfortunately, however, it is drying up.

Twelve miles (18 km) from San Juan de los Morros is San Sebastian and the so-called Murciélagos (Bat) Cave. It is 650 feet long and 350 feet wide. Despite its name, the dry, vast cave is inhabited only by spiders.

From here, the road runs 36 miles (50 km) north by way of a spectacular mountain drive, built with pick and shovel by prisoners, ordered by Gomez as an escape route to the sea. These mountains are in the Henry Pittier National Park, the highest about 4,200 feet. The region is beautiful, thickly forested with giant figs, liana, and tree ferns. There are at least fourteen identifiable vegetation zones, surmounted by one of the world's rare cloud forests. Along the road is Rancho Grande, an unfinished mansion ordered by Gomez for purposes that were never clear. Part of it is now a natural history museum (not generally open to the public), part a laboratory, and the rest the range of forest wildlife.

This road ends at the resort village of Cata.

CATA: Very popular and one of the most beautiful beaches in Venezuela, Cata sits on a wide, blue bay with fine white sands and coconut palms — now rather spoiled by two very ugly condominiums rising above the beach. It is a good day excursion, with an overnight at the *Inter-Continental Valencia.*

En Route from Cata – A few miles east of Cata is Choroní. There is no coast road. Approach to Choroní is from Maracay, 36 miles away along the Valencia highway. Coming directly to Chroní from Caracas, take the route via the Henri Pittier Park, luxuriant with tropical plants. Choroní is a lovely colonial town with accommodations available in reconstructed old houses. The best beaches in this area are reached by outboard launches, available in town.

Thirty-nine miles (62 km) west of Maracay on Route 9 is the city of Valencia.

VALENCIA: Today an industrial city of nearly 500,000 people, Valencia is on the banks of the Río Cabriales, near Valencia Lake. It is a historical treasure trove, with a 400-year-old cathedral, a 1772 state capitol originally built as a convent, an 1894 theater resembling a scaled-down Paris Opera House, and the second largest bullring in Latin America (after Mexico City's Plaza de Toros). About 15 miles (24 km) south of the city is the battleground of Carabobo, where two battles were fought during the Independence Wars: one in 1814, the other in 1821, and both led and won by Bolívar. Shortly after the first war, Thomas Boves ("The Butcher") charged from the *llanos* (plains), slaughtering thousands and driving Bolívar clear out of the country. The second victory, won with the aid of the lancers of Boves's heir José Antonio Paez, definitively established Venezuela's independence. There is a large and impressive monument on the field that depicts scenes from the battle in high relief. Shortly before the field is a safari park, with many black bears, animals from Africa (giraffes and the like), and Bengal tigers.

There are a few side trips from Valencia. The first follows a small road 18 miles (29 km) north to Vigirima, where there are petroglyphs; it's one of the many pre-Columbian sites to be found in the Valencia Valley. South of the lake, near Belén and Gualamaya, are a number of dark, damp, uninhabitable caves.

En Route from Valencia – If you retrace your steps east to Caracas on Route 9 and take the Junquito road right before Vista Alegra and then continue for 35 miles (56 km), you'll reach Colonia Tovar, a village as Bavarian as Bavaria. As an immigration experiment, farmers from Germany were brought here to start a colony in 1843. The present inhabitants are their descendants who grow coffee, fruit, and vegetables and speak the same Black Forest German. Set at 5,900 feet above sea level in nicely wooded ranges, the village is unquestionably beautiful. All the buildings here are made of timber and stone, conforming strictly to the old-country style.

Colonia Tovar has become a weekend tourist trap of late, but it is still the best place to buy German bread and sausages.

From here, return to Caracas and head east to Barlovento, a secluded beach area set on the seacoast that stretches from Los Caracas on the Litoral (see *Caracas, THE CITIES*) to the town of Higuerote.

BARLOVENTO: For those in search of isolated beaches, this is a good one. The holiday camp of Los Caracas has its own, guarded entrances (all you have to do, however, is tell the guard you're passing through, and he'll let you by). Here there is an old mule track, winding up, down, and around steep headlands, fording several streams; the road is very rough, so take care. In the occasional ravines are small villages with names like Quebrada Seca (Dry Gulch), Osma, and Oritapo — each looking like the other: one bar, one cop, and one stereo at full volume. All the inhabitants except the cops are the black descendants of slaves. The older generation is made up of fishermen; the younger hangs around, smartly dressed, and does little of anything.

HIGUEROTE: This is a pleasant, bustling resort on a magnificent bay of long, white beaches. Its appearance is tranquil despite the rush to development. Everything seems to be more expensive in this part of the coast, so watch how you spend your money, especially around the tourist season and the festival of San Juan.

According to tradition, the festival's origin dates back to the days of slavery, when liberty was granted for one day each year on the feast of San Juan. The festival is one of the most popular in Venezuela, with its focal point here in Higuerote and in nearby Curiepe. Otherwise known as the Tambores de San Juan (tambores is a set of African drums — usually two big and three small drums), this feast is a wild one, beginning at noon on June 23 with the eruption of ringing bells and the pounding of the large drums. Rum is consumed like oxygen; the dancing in the streets and the constant pounding beat never stop until dawn on June 26, when this world falls suddenly, desperately silent.

En Route from Higuerote – From here, retrace your steps back to Caracas and proceed east on Route 9 through the Tuy Valley, following the Río Guaire valley to Santa Teresa, 34 miles (54 km) away — a pleasant drive. Continue another 9 miles (16 km) up the Tuy to San Francisco de Yare.

SAN FRANCISCO DE YARE: The best time to come to the town is in June, around the Feast of Corpus Christi, for the 2-day festival of the devils. The devils, in this case, are men wearing large red masks of durable papier-mâché and shaped like nightmarish animals. Each has two or more horns, and the more elaborate ones are fitted with the teeth of asses. The devils dance in front of the church, repent, defy the church again, and again repent. In the end, they say the hell with it, and everyone gets drunk.

Sadly, the origin of this festival is obscure, although it is assumed to have been invented by a medieval-minded missionary who imagined — and rightly so — that such a thing might prove diverting to the heathen.

BEST EN ROUTE

Hotels along this route are inexpensive even when they are expensive. Occasionally, one runs a very high $50 or $60, but they mostly cost from $30 to $40 a night (expensive); $20 to $30 (moderate); and under $20 (inexpensive). They're small, clean, and comfortable, and many have private baths. It's a good idea to make reservations in advance, especially during the festival season.

SAN JUAN DE LOS MORROS

Ana – A small, 14-room hotel with double rooms and private baths. Av. Los Puentes (phone: 038-35-037). Moderate.

Santa Monica – A 45-room motel with swimming pool and private baths in double rooms. At the entrance of town (phone: 038-35-691). Moderate.

VALENCIA

Inter-Continental – A 172-room hotel, extraordinary for this route, with private baths, a restaurant, bar, and a swimming pool. Av. Juan Alar, Urb. La Vina (phone: 041-10-33). Expensive.

Aparthotel Ucaima – There are 75 air-conditioned suites with kitchenettes, TV, pool. Av. Boyacá 141-80 (phone: 041-22-20-11). Moderate.

Continental – A 22-room hotel with private baths, restaurant, and double rooms. Av. Boyacá (phone: 041-83-014). Inexpensive.

COLONIA TOVAR

Freiburg – An 11-room hotel offering private baths, a restaurant, and double rooms. Centrally located (phone: 033-51-313). Credit cards not accepted. Expensive.

Selva Negra – A 36-room hotel with all the conveniences of the *Freiburg*. Centrally located (phone: 033-51-415). Expensive.

HIGUEROTE

Sol Mar – A 14-room hotel providing clean, double rooms for the night. Beachfront (phone: 034-21-030). Moderate.

Barlovento – A 28-room hotel and swimming pool. Beachfront (phone: 034-21-161). Moderate.

The Andes

The elevated lands of Mérida are the frosty crown of the Venezuelan Andes. The *páramos,* or lands beyond the treeline, known to geographers as the alpine moors, is a starkly beautiful region of endless mountain after mountain, falling here and there into narrow valleys beneath the snowcapped peaks. The principal vegetation is a fur-covered plant with yellow flower called the *frailejón* (great friar). The cold, gray *páramos,* carpeted with these *frailejónes* in flower, is a breathtaking sight. These combine with mountain streams and mirror lakes filled with trout to attract fisherman and hikers alike.

The seasons are reversed in the Andes. Summer (November to May) is wet, rainy, often snowy; while winter (May to November) is cold, dry, crisp, and clear.

The best way to reach the Andes is by car, shunning the bus that takes travelers up and down what seems like a shaky roller-coaster ride over the dozens of sharp zigzags, or switchbacks, along the Andean highway. The crafty traveler gets up at dawn to start his route and catch the morning light, saving his dining for the middle of the day, when the glare of an ultraviolet haze sets in and remains until late afternoon.

En Route from Caracas – Start this trip by heading south along Route 5 on the Pan-American Highway out of Caracas; continuing south through Valencia in the Central Highlands through the *llanos,* skirting the foothills. Overnight buses from Caracas make San Cristóbal in 13 hours.

Heading south from Valencia, you pass through the small towns of San Carlos, Acarigua, and Guanare (cowtowns all) whose streams offer fishing (as well as piranha). Guanare is the worship center of the country's patron saint (since 1942), the Virgin of Coromoto.

GUANARE: The Virgin first appeared in the area in 1561, when the Indian *cacique* (chief) Coromoto spied a splendid lady with a radiant infant walking toward him on the surface of a stream. He was less impressed, perhaps, than he should have been, but after soliciting advice he commanded the baptism of everyone in his tribe, except himself. Obviously displeased, the Virgin appeared to him again, whereupon he lunged for her and she disappeared — leaving in his hands her image on parchment. Today, that same parchment is still venerated, and the faithful make pilgrimages here in January and September.

En Route from Guanare – Four miles (7 km) out of Guanare, you leave the Pan-American and the heat and scrub of the *llanos* to climb to the cool, rich green of the Andes. This is a land of flowering trees and coffee plantations clinging to the side of precipitous ridges; tiny villages perch on little plateaus that jut out over terrible gorges. A bizarre artwork — the painted skeletons of cattle — occasionally decorate fronts of houses. More bizarre, perhaps, are the boys on the side of the road who will sell baby *cachecamos* (armadillos), considered tasty morsels.

At the village of Biscucuy the road once agains swings south, continuing to Boconó.

BOCONÓ: This garden town is reputed to have the prettiest girls in the country. The valley, set at the waters of the Río Boconó, is very narrow, and the town seems to tumble down the side of a long steep ridge. Trees sprout Spanish moss in the plaza, and mosses and airplants cling about the church.

The market is worth a visit here for its good, traditional earthenware: pots, cups, bowls. There is also a hand-loom industry recently started by a German couple, who sell a variety of wool *ruanas,* blankets, and cushion covers.

En Route from Boconó – About 45 miles (72 km) north by northwest (the road winds itself in these directions, so don't worry about turns) is the turnoff for Trujillo; although the capital of this state, it is small and economically unimportant but old — dating back to 1558. About 20 miles (32 km) from the turnoff, continuing west through Trujillo, is Valera, the wheat and coffee center of the Andes. It is an extremely unattractive town, but set in an attractive valley that's ringed by heavily forested mountains above and the Río Monay below.

Valera, sadly, is a maze of one-way streets that make it a cartographer's nightmare. Once in, it's difficult to find the way out.

Another 14 miles (22 km) southwest is La Puerta.

LA PUERTA: Aptly named "the Door," this village is filled with the high, steep ridges of the *páramos,* which suddenly recede to reveal a broad, green glade. La Puerta is a hill resort for the people of Maracaibo; at one end of town is a resort of prefabricated, concrete, Bavarian houses, a popular modern style in Venezuela but rather ugly compared to the traditional.

Stores are filled with stocks of Andean *ruanas* and blankets. Visit the discotheque if you're not squeamish; it's filled with papier-mâché spiders.

En Route from La Puerta – An early morning drive that winds through 14 miles (22 km) of zigzags from here to Timotes is a spectacular trip. Etched starkly in the morning light, the alluvial terraces are visible — small, and improbable — suspended from the sides of mountains on the edge of deep and narrow gorges; they are cultivated right to the edge by farmers using wooden plows and oxen.

Timotes is a good place to have breakfast. Try the regional specialty of wheat *arepa,* a kind of unleavened bread that's very tasty — in contrast to the maize *arepa* found in the rest of Venezuela, which is definitely an acquired taste. *Arepas* can be eaten plain, with butter, or filled with cheese, meat, chicken, or *caraotas* (black beans).

From Timotes, it is about 28 miles (45 km) south to the Águilar Pass, where in 1819 Simón Bolívar crossed — in the hazardous snows of winter — to do battle against Royalist forces in Colombia on the plains of Boyacá. The zigzags in the road are occasionally severe, but on the whole it is a slow ascent, passing from verdant ranges to the harsh moonscape of the Páramo de Mucuchíes, where only *frailejónes* can grow. On occasion, there appears a deep valley supporting wheat and some vegetables, and in the middle of nowhere you may find a small Indian girl selling carrots by the road. Usually very shy, such young salesgirls are often accompanied by their grandmothers, who look like their mothers — the *andinos* age well in the crisp, clear air.

There comes a point in the wasteland where you reach a rise overlooking a long rugged valley and catch the first sight of snow on the cap of Pico Mucuñuque — miles away behind Laguna Negra. The peak to the left is Gavilán, at 14,000 feet, and off to the right is the Pico del Águilar at 13,500 feet. The Águilar Pass farther on is cold, very windy, and impassible in snow. Águilar means "eagle," and here is an eagle monument to Bolívar. Here also is a pleasant way station where hot chocolate for the cold and glucose for altitude sickness are dispensed. About 4 miles (7 km) farther is the valley of Apartaderos.

APARTADEROS: In the arid brown landscape of the *páramos,* the sides of this valley are extremely steep and eroded, and a crystal stream runs by several small villages. Their houses are old and whitewashed, with worn red-tiled roofs that with time have sagged to gentle undulations. Massive stone fences crisscross the valley. The people are poor but not badly off; they grow wheat on the sides of the ridges, and in January they thresh the grain on round, stone threshing floors as they have done for centuries. By night, the *páramo* resembles a forbidding moonscape and is very silent and eerie when the fog rolls in.

Overlooking the valley from a 12,000-foot pass on the left is the *Hotel Sierra Nevada;* across the road is an Andean handicrafts display and cafeteria where *ruanas* and *gorros,* a kind of Andean *balaclava* much more elegant than the Turkish variety, are sold. Near the *Macubají* hotel in the valley is an antique shop.

From here, the road leads southwest to the pretty village of Santo Domingo at 7,000 feet in wooded surroundings. From Apartaderos, take the road past the *Sierra Nevada* hotel heading south 15 miles (22 km) and down. En route is *Los Frailes* (the friars) hotel, formerly a monastery founded in 1620. The valley is somewhat wooded with the *páramo* only a step away; furry llamas roam with dignity — and at will. Horses are for hire at the hotel, which has elegant old buildings and walls surrounding a compound built about a brook. The rooms are exquisite and heated, with thick plastered walls and heavy exposed beams.

Return to Caracas from Santo Domingo via Barinas on the *llanos* about 40 miles (64 km) from Santo Domingo, 64 miles (103 km) west of Guanare.

LAGUNA NEGRA: Down the ridge from the *Sierra Nevada* is the trail to the Black Lagoon, a mirror lake at the foot of a tall and snowcapped peak (a lure to photographers and trout fishermen). Aim to be at the lake before 10:30 AM when the sun strikes it. The early morning sun is strong and hot while frost crackles underfoot.

A 20-minute walk (or shorter drive) leads first to the Laguna Macubají, not much bigger than an extravagant duck pond. Take it easy, though, because at this elevation you can tire easily or succumb to *soroche* (altitude sickness). Within 10 minutes there is a fork in the trail: Bear right and upward. Ten minutes later you overlook a rugged valley and a beautiful lake. Filled and emptied by stepped waterfalls, the lake is fed by the snows of Pico Mucuñuque, standing behind it at 15,000 feet. Above it is another lagoon, the Laguna de los Patos, which is worth a visit if you feel up to the climb.

En Route from Laguna Negra – About 38 miles (61 km) south the road comes down to the town of Mérida. On the way, the vegetation changes, but the villages remain much the same: old whitewashed cottages with weathered, red-tiled roofs. The largest village (several blocks in size and very old) is Mucuchíes, a name lent to a breed of Andean dog. Mucuchíes, at an elevation of 10,000 feet, has one hotel.

At the approach to Mérida, the valley broadens to include stately trees and manicured pines lining the stony beds of streams. Except for the peaks that soar steeply and ruggedly on either side, you could believe this was England. To the south is the Sierra Nevada de Mérida, the only range in the Venezuelan Andes that is snowcapped all year-round. Crowning the sierra is Pico Bolívar, at 16,427 feet the highest mountain in Venezuela.

MÉRIDA: Founded in 1558, this is one of the oldest cities in Venezuela. Unhappily, little of the colonial town remains. It has one of the oldest universities in the Americas — the University of the Andes, founded in 1785 — and many gardens, museums, and parks. The Parque Los Chorros de Milla is quite beautiful. According to legend, its springs and cascades are the tears of Princess Tibisay, shed for her love, the *cacique* Murachí, who was struck down by conquistadores. The cathedral on the Plaza Bolívar has statues of dour, bloody saints, crucified Christs (with blood pouring out of heads and wounds), and suffering martyrs of the church, all grotesquely real. This must also be one of the few places in the world where you will find a portrait of God. Architecturally, the cathedral is uninteresting ("rebuilt colonial," twice destroyed by earthquakes). Fiesta Week here falls around December 8.

Actually, the beauty of Mérida is in the Sierra Nevada, whose inhabitants — presumably related to the Chibcha Indians of Bogotá — are set in their Andean traditions. They are a tough people: short, serious, supremely self-sufficient. They emerge from the mists to greet you, then melt away to their own business.

Travelers going into the sierras should bring a map; one is available at the Mérida climber's supply store. The map outlines walking trails — often blazing with wildflowers — across the *páramos,* the ascent to the Pico Bolívar, and takes in the length of the valley and sierras from Santo Domingo to Mérida.

Those preferring not to walk can see the sierras via a fantastic cable car ride.

SIERRA NEVADA DE MÉRIDA: Mérida boasts the highest *teleférico* (cable car) in the world, running from an elevation of 5,000 feet to Pico Espejo (Mirror Peak), 15,500 feet high. It operates daily, except Mondays and Tuesdays, but is occasionally out of commission. If it's not running one day, return the following morning; mechanical difficulties are often minor. Get in line early, by 7 AM at the latest. The 4-stage ascent takes 1 hour, if you go straight to the top. The first car leaves at 8 AM, the last at 2 PM.

The view from Pico Espejo is magnificent. With the massive splintered rock pile of the Andes all around and the alluvial plain of Mérida far below, you feel you are standing on top of the world. Far to the south is a haze, which is the heat rising up from the *llanos,* yet it is cold and windy. Across the gap and 1,000 feet above is Pico Bolívar.

There are four well-known ascent routes from Pico Espejo, none of them exceptionally difficult for experienced climbers, but beware — ice-climbing equipment is necessary. The north face is the hardest, ice all the way with an unbroken fall of several thousand feet. The south face, Ruta Weiss, is the easiest. On top of the peak is a bronze bust of Bolívar. The next two peaks along are Jahn and Abanico. The south face of Abanico (16,000 feet) is almost vertical and a favorite with rock climbers. The Club Andino de Mérida takes parties of a maximum of three people to the top (ask at the alpinists' store). You should camp at the *teleférico* station on Pico Espejo and set out at dawn. Permits from the local forestry commission and the Defensa Civil are necessary.

The Glacier de los Timoncitos is between Jahn and Abanico. It has a spectacular ice cave that shouldn't be missed (a 2-hour walk). Looking east, the twin conical peaks of Humboldt and Bonpland are visible, both in the 16,000-foot range. The walk from Espejo to the summits of Humboldt and Bonpland is a straightforward one. You should allow more than a day (there are refuges on the trail) and should not have a medical history of heart problems.

From here, there is a trail heading south to the hidden village of Los Nevados. A half-day walk will get you there, but there is an easier way of doing it.

LOS NEVADOS: At 12,500 feet, this is the country's highest village, sitting on a steep and sunny cultivated slope 1,000 feet above the Río de Nuestra Senora. The village is very old, very neat, and totally isolated. Its contact with the outside world depends on mules and the *teleférico*. It takes time to arrange the trip. Discuss the matter with Señor Castillo, who will take you from the second *teleférico* station, provided his mules aren't needed for hauling provisions. The smaller party has a better chance.

Departure is from the third *teleférico* station, at a gentle climb. Traversing a spur, you pass the Lagunas Los Anteojos, mirror lakes that reflect the snows of Pico Bolívar. Here the mules begin a steep climb through the wastes of the Páramo de la Media Luna, a beautiful and harsh landscape with rushing falls and *frailejónes* (flowers) growing under the stark gray faces of cliffs. It's constantly cold — about 47°F (14°C) — and winds are often savage. Here and there you see *andinos* in traditional garb: *ruanas* and broad-brimmed hats, trousers rolled up to the knees, and *alpargatas* (a type of leather sandal). You reach the path at 14,500 feet and begin a gentle descent into the sunlight of Los Nevados.

There are no stores and no hotels; bring your own food and bedding. You share Señor Castillo's stables with the mules and wash in their drinking water. It's necessary to return to Mérida before traveling west to Jají, a small town some 35 miles (54 km) away.

JAJÍ: A 1-day excursion from Mérida, Jají is built on a point overlooking a valley and appears snow white in a blazing sun, with old buildings, a grassless plaza (named Bolívar, not surprisingly), and a church. The entire town surrounds the plaza. Small boys in the plaza hire out mule rides; little girls peddle traditional Andean sweets made from fruit and milk; and stores stock diverse souvenirs. Two restaurants serve Andean trout.

En Route from Jají – Return to Mérida and continue west through the tranquil valley of the Río Chama. From here, head toward the state of Táchira, an isolated, backwoods region where no one lives except a town full of smugglers: As with all border areas in Venezuela (and this one's near Colombia), there is a quality of anarchy here.

Believe it or not, Táchira has been more influential on Caracas than Caracas on Táchira. It is home of the great *caudillos* and a provincial mountain culture with the remnants of a peculiar sort of feudalism that remembers and reveres the 19th-century, tyrannical *caudillos*. Their portraits hang in the *bodegas* (grocery stores), and it becomes very clear that the democratic hurly-burly of Caracas is, indeed, far away.

Actually, even Mérida is far away — the road more or less disappears at Bailadores, just short of the Táchira line, about 60 miles (96 km) west of Mérida.

BAILADORES: This small, neat village lies at the end of a fertile valley; its plaza, smothered with flowering trees and bougainvillea, is among the prettiest in the country.

Just out of the town in a forest is a small park, built up, but in a minimal way, with paths, bridges, and shelters, and there is a fan-shaped waterfall. The *Toquisai* hotel is one of the nicest in the country and the principal reason for stopping here. The restaurant is very good, and at night the locals drink at the bar. In this convivial atmosphere you find yourself sharing a table with *contrabandistas* and the relatives of infamous guerrillas, all stout fellows and apparently upright. This is not yet Táchira, but in the *bodega* on the plaza is a portrait of former dictator Pérez Jiménez.

En Route from Bailadores – The roads into Táchira are not good. Fourteen miles (22 km) from Bailadores is the Mérida-Táchira border, and here the paved road ends. Go left, continuing to the end at La Grita, on a twisting road that is paved in some stretches, gravel in others.

La Grita (the Cry) is over 400 years old, a major trading center for the area and not very attractive. Thirteen miles (20 km) farther is El Cobre, a very tiny village in an arid landscape on the side of a ridge, sweltering under a hot midday sun with no trees in sight. The houses are very old, and through a quality of the local stone the entire village is pink. The inhabitants on the whole are old, serious, and photogenic; youth has fled this little pueblo; ultimately, perhaps, it will die.

Another 35 miles (56 km) south is San Cristóbal, an equal distance from the Colombian border.

SAN CRISTÓBAL: Founded in 1561, some colonial streets remain in this town, but on the whole it is a modern, thriving city, attractive only in parts. Built on a terraced plateau in the broad, rolling valley of the Río Torbes, it has many parks and plazas. The cathedral (in the center of town) appears colonial, but the façade was rebuilt.

In late January, there is a week-long festival that is vastly overrated but features good bullfights. At that time of the year it is very difficult to find a room, so make reservations before coming.

En Route from San Cristóbal – The country to the south is wild with vegetation, tangled, and lush: This is the home of many of the *caudillos* who rose to such power that they were able to leave their separate states and capture the executive power of the presidency for a long time. From San Cristóbal, take the Pan-American Highway to San Antonio del Táchira, along the Colombian border, and then move on to Cúcuta; no visa is needed. Cúcuta is very unattractive, but a good spot to buy Colombian wares, notably leather goods. Watch out — Cúcuta is notorious for pickpockets. Visitors intending to spend any time in Colombia must have their passports stamped in San Antonio. Eight miles (12 km) north of San Antonio is Ureña, with thermal springs, and the *Aguas Calientes* hotel.

The Pan-American from San Cristóbal offers two routes; one to Maracaibo in the north; the second, heading south, leads to Llanos, returning to Caracas.

SEGOVIA HIGHLANDS: If you are feeling really jaded, bored with Haitian voodoo rites and *macumba* on the Copacabana, and seek something more macabre, visit the Sorte Mountains, in the northeastern Andean foothills in the state of Yaracuy (its capital is San Felipe). This is the home of the semipagan cult of María Lionza, whose statue stands in the middle of an eight-lane *autopista* in Caracas. Atop a 20-foot column, she sits naked astride a rampant tapir — a warrior queen brandishing aloft the bones of a female pelvis. Called Queen, Mother, and Goddess, María Lionza was an Indian princess whom her people thought a witch and cast out. It came to pass that she was loved by a serpent. There was a great flood, and she was saved from drowning, nursed, and raised by a tapir. As a result she is renowned as mistress of the elements. Should you make a pact with her, she grants you favors, including riches — if they are shared with the poor. She demands fierce fidelity.

Her altars include a distinguished pantheon: Jesus, Mary, and the Roman Catholic saints (especially Peter); the great Indian *caciques;* Simón Bolívar; the Negro Primero, Pedro Camejo (a slave who rose to be a general under Bolívar); the Negro Miguel, who led a slave revolt in 1552 (and who is sometimes identified as María Lionza's husband); and José Gregorio Hernández, a doctor who lived at the turn of the century and whose Roman Catholic sainthood is currently pending. Several divinities are imported directly from the Santería Cubana cult, which is said to have had its origins in Nigeria. Commanding all this is María Lionza, who is occasionally represented on the altar by a photograph, said to have been posed for by a medium of 1930s vintage who was a concubine of the dictator Gómez.

The supplicant seeks intercession through mediums through whom the appropriate spirit acts. The supplicant goes barefoot, perhaps on his knees. Men are bare to the waist. Rum is used liberally as a purifier, and cigars are a major tool. Faith healing is common.

The cult is not considered dangerous, and it has a wider following than a stranger might suspect. The newspaper space reserved for paid ads proclaiming gratitude to the Holy Ghost for favors granted generally include several addressed to María Lionza. Scattered around Caracas are little "pharmacies" dealing solely in magic potions — love, fortune, health, and what have you — in countless combinations. People come in with prescriptions written on paper torn out of an exercise book.

A visitor interested in learning more might starting by asking around, checking newspapers, and inquiring at the Universidad Central about the local leader of this cult. She calls herself Beatriz Veit-Tane and heads up the Asociación Civil y Filosofico de María Lionza (it is not listed in the telephone book). Beatriz Veit-Tane claims to have been the statuesque model for the famous monument.

San Felipe is about 78 miles (125 km) from Valencia on the Pan-American Highway. Take Route 5 heading south, turning right on Route 11 some 10 miles (16 km) later. Alternatively, take Route 3 to the coast as far as Morón, then Route 1 west.

BEST EN ROUTE

There are a lot of hotels in the Andes; most are small, but comfortable, providing modern facilities and clean accommodations. They're not expensive; figure about $35 (expensive); $10 to $20 (moderate); and under $10 (inexpensive). Make reservations in advance.

GUANARE

Coromoto – A 76-room hotel and a swimming pool. Av. Miranda (phone: 057-53-442). Moderate.

BOCONÓ

Country Steinberg – Very pleasant, 18-room hotel, with private showers. El Otro Iado (phone: 072-52-195). Moderate.

Colonial – Offers 20 small, clean rooms. Av. Miranda (phone: 072-52-281). Inexpensive.

TRUJILLO

Trujillo – A 32-room hotel with private baths, restaurant, and a pool. Av. Carmona (phone: 072-21-201). Expensive.

LA PUERTA

Guadalupe – A comfortable 30-room hotel, with private baths and food (no phone). Moderate.

Los Andes – A 27-room hotel, similar to the *Guadalupe.* Keep away from the hotel restaurant: The food is poor (no phone). Moderate.

TIMOTES

Las Truchas – A 10-room hotel providing excellent service, food, and facilities. On the La Puerta edge of town (phone: 074-89-158). Moderate.

APARTADEROS

Macubají – A quaint and clean 16-room hotel, overlooking the valley on the southern edge of town (no phone). Moderate.

Sierra Nevada – A pleasant 15-room hotel offering food. Near the *Macubají* (no phone). Moderate.

SANTO DOMINGO

Los Frailes – Considered one of the best in Venezuela, this 41-room hotel has private baths, central heating, and a restaurant. On the highway between Santo Domingo and Apartaderos. Book in Caracas with Hoturvensa hotel organization (phone: 562-30-22). Expensive.

Moruco – A 60-room hotel that is as popular, but not as pretty, as *Los Frailes.* In the center of town. Book in Mérida (phone: 074-24-380). Expensive.

MÉRIDA

Prado Río – With 60 rooms, a pool, lovely gardens, and a mountain setting, this is one of the nicest hotels in town. Hollada de Mella (phone: 2-4380/1). Expensive.

Holiday Inn Mérida – A recent addition to the hotel scene, with 111 rooms and modern facilities. In the downtown area near the university. Calle 37 at Av. Gonzalo Picom (phone: 743-3828). Expensive.

Valle Grande – Eight miles outside Mérida, in a deep pine forest, this combination of lodge-plus-bungalows provides cozy accommodations, and the dining room serves fine food. Carretera El Valle, Mérida (phone: 2-4265). Moderate.

La Sierra – An old, 37-room hotel, providing excellent service. Calle 23 and Av. 2 (phone: 074-23-625). Moderate to inexpensive.

JAJÍ

La Posada de Jají – A small, 5-room hotel. Very pleasant and personal. Book in Mérida (phone: 074-35-182). Moderate.

BAILADORES

Toquisai – A 20-room hotel with excellent service, good rooms, and private baths. On the edge of town (phone: 074-71-818). Moderate.

SAN CRISTÓBAL

El Tama – This is a 98-room hotel with an Olympic-size swimming pool. Av. 19 de Abril, overlooking the town (phone: 076-51-371). Moderate.

Las Lomas – A 50-room motel with a swimming pool. Av. Libertador (phone: 076-31-225). Moderate.

Hamburgo – There are 21 good-sized rooms and fairly good service. Av. Libertador (phone: 076-34-060). Inexpensive.

URENA

Aguas Calientas – A 28-room hotel with private baths, pool, and restaurant (phone: 076-86-391). Expensive.

The Western Coast

This route travels along the western Venezuelan coastline, starting some 27 miles (43 km) north of Valencia at Puerto Cabello, continuing on to the

Paraguaná Peninsula, an arid area, barely above sea level. Inland it is described as the dank, cave-filled badlands, inhabited only by rattlesnakes, oil birds, and burros, but once the home of leftist guerrillas. A dry, often desolate route, this would be a boring trip if not for the small, picturesque resort towns fringing the Caribbean coast.

From Valencia, the Pan-American Highway leads some 27 miles (42 km) north to El Palita, then 7 miles east to Puerto Cabello.

PUERTO CABELLO: Set amid miles of palm-shaded beaches, this port of 70,000 people figured importantly in the 19th-century Venezuelan Wars of Independence. The El Águila monument in the town's colonial section marks the site where North American mercenaries, paid by Venezuelan hero Francisco de Miranda to help overthrow the Royalists, were executed in 1806. The Castillo Libertador was a Royalist prison; and in this century was infamous as a prison of cruel dictators.

En Route from Puerto Cabello – Continuing 31 miles (44 km) north, you soon reach the resort town of Tucacas, a small, rundown place of about 50,000 inhabitants noted as a jumping-off point for a trip into the palm-shaded, lush cays scattered here and there around the coral-reefed lagoon. Arrange launch transportation at the docks. Out beyond Boca Grande are the coral islands. The largest is Cayo Sombero, where the clear waters team with multicolored fish, lobster, squid, barracuda, and stonefish. The islands are also recommended for snorkelers and scuba divers. At present, camping is allowed in the cays.

Another 125 miles (201 km) west on the Pan-American is the port of Coro and the Paraguaná Peninsula.

CORO: Like Puerto Cabello, this town saw action during the independence battles. Founded in 1523, a large section of its colonial buildings have been preserved, along with cobblestone streets and grand old houses of sunburned brick and red-tiled roofs. The cathedral, constructed in 1583, has a tower that once doubled as a fort during the privateer attacks of Francis Drake, Henry Morgan, and Walter Raleigh.

North of the city, at the base of the low-lying desert of the Paraguaná Peninsula, are the famous *medanos* of Coro, a 30-square-mile region of giant sand dunes. Constantly shifted by unceasing winds, the dunes have already consumed three roads and are working on a fourth. The Paraguaná Peninsula itself is a vast, low desert connected to the mainland by only a narrow strip of sand. Its greater part is barely above sea level. The peninsula's highest point, rising abruptly to 2,500 feet from an immense flat plain, is the Santa Ana Mountain. At the foot of the mountain, 37 miles (59 km) from Coro, is the village of Santa Ana, founded about 1546.

En Route from Coro – Ferries on irregular schedules leave from Punto Fijo and Coro for the islands of Curaçao and Aruba in the Netherlands Antilles.

To the south of Coro are the badlands. These are dry and brittle ranges bristling with cactus and inhabited largely by goats, burros, rattlers, and, until recently, guerrillas; a traditional refuge of subversives, dictators always appointed their abler generals to govern this state. About 35 miles (56 km) inland are the hill resorts of Coro in the Sierra de San Luis. These ranges are riddled with caves, of which at least 96 are known, not all of them explored, and some inhabited with guácharos (oil birds). Detailed maps are classified. The best-known cave is the Bellard Cave near Santa Cruz de Bucaral, 90 miles (144 km) from Coro: This majestic cavern can be entered by rubber raft.

The southern road continues to Barquisimeto, 180 miles (290 km) from Coro in the Andes. En route is the turnoff to Siquisique, notable only in lending its name to the local tequila — a brew more commonly known as *miche,* which means "micturate of skunk," more or less.

The highway west of Coro leads to Maracaibo, 158 miles (250 km) away.

BEST EN ROUTE

Hotels in the western coastal area generally lack hot water, but have cold showers, double rooms, and, in some cases, restaurants. They are reasonably priced — ranging from $15 to $25 (moderate); and under $10 (inexpensive). Make reservations before arriving.

PUERTO CABELLO

Suite Caribe – The newest hotel in Puerto Cabello, but not on the beach. Air conditioning. Av. Salom 21 (phone: 042-5479). Expensive.

Balneario Canaima – A 42-room hotel with cold showers, on the beachfront near Puerto Cabello. Urbanizaciíon Palma Sol (phone: 042-71-395). Moderate.

Miramar – A 14-room hotel on its own beach. El Palito (phone: 042-38-53). Inexpensive.

TUCACAS

Manuare – A 25-room hotel with restaurant, double rooms, and cold showers. Av. Silva (phone: 042-84-286). Moderate.

Camping is available out in the cays.

CORO

Miranda – An 86-room hotel with a restaurant and pool. Av. Josefa Camejo, opposite the airport (phone: 068-59-114). Expensive.

Caracas – An old, elegant 14-room hotel with a beautiful courtyard. Calle Toledo, on the edge of the colonial section (phone: 068-59-545). Moderate.

The Guajira Peninsula

Fed by Andean streams in the south and open to the Gulf of Venezuela in the north, 5,000-square-mile Lake Maracaibo is the largest in South America. Its shores are heavily forested in the south (with the highest rainfall in the entire country) and desert-covered to the north — a desert that is hot, windless, and humid, but laden with riches. Oil was discovered here in 1917, and for a long time Venezuela — with an estimated crude oil reserve of 750 million barrels — was the world's leading exporter of petroleum.

A few words best describe this area: desert, oil-rich, and dangerous. The peninsula, shared by Venezuela and neighboring Colombia to the west, has for years been a smugglers' haven; drugs, like cocaine and marijuana, have just about replaced the emeralds, cattle, and electrical appliances in such high demand during the 1960s. So much illegal traffic has crossed the borders recently that war has erupted between the authorities and the *contrabandistas,* transforming what was an interesting desert circuit into a dangerous travel risk.

This route, which starts with lakeside Maracaibo, is approachable from the Andes or from Coro on the western Caribbean coast. Some 438 miles northwest of Caracas, it has its own Indians, the Guajiras, who are related to the Colombian Guajiras, and whose women wear the long, colorful *mantas,* or flowing robes. Both Colombian and Venezuelan groups are nomadic and extremely independent. The Spanish heard along this route is almost incomprehensible — a quaint, archaic form of Castilian. Predominant in the culture is the *gaita,* often heard throughout the country during Christmas, a song filled with humorous verses that are generally topical and often political. More than one political *gaita* has been banned from the radio. *Gaitas* are rendered by a soloist and chorus, and are accompanied by *cuatros* (a type of ukulele), marracas, drums, and *ferrocos* (a drum with a pole extending vertically from the hide, played by moving the hand up and down the pole).

The first stop is Maracaibo.

MARACAIBO: On the western shore of the lake, this city is only 25 feet above sea level and extremely hot — tempered only by a breeze that moves in at about 5 PM. Founded in 1570, Maracaibo ranks highly in the bygone romantic histories of Caribbean ports, but only around the docks is any trace of the colonial past still to be found.

One enters the city across the mouth of the lake via the 5-mile Rafael Urdaneta Bridge, with the longest prestressed concrete span in the world.

Predominant among the Indians in the city are the Guajira, who live in the native quarter of Ziruma. A very proud race, the Guajira adapted well to Western ways, and their weavers make a tidy living selling brightly colored hammocks, dresses, wall hangings, and rugs — some of which have been exhibited in the US.

En Route from Maracaibo – A road heading north from Maracaibo leads toward the Guajira desert beaches on into Colombia.

Off to the right is the 17th-century fortress of San Carlos, which saw action and lengthy siege against pirates and republicans and which, under the dictatorships, became a notorious prison. Twenty-five miles (40 km) from Maracaibo is the mouth of the lagoon at Sinamaica, the "little Venice" described by Alonso de Ojeda when naming the country. The Indians here live in houses woven from reeds and supported on stilts.

Fifty-three miles (85 km) from Maracaibo, 12 miles (19 km) short of the Colombian frontier, is Paraguaipoa, a Guajira town with markets selling the same goods found in Maracaibo but at a better price.

The larger part of the wild and arid Guajira Peninsula is in Colombia. The road goes through Maicao, 7 miles (11 km) beyond the frontier, and on about 45 miles (72 km) to Riohacha on the northern coast. No visa is necessary until you reach Riohacha.

It was with the nomadic Guajiras that the infamous Papillon, a prisoner on Devil's Island, hid out during his first (unsuccessful) escape from the compound in French Guiana.

The peninsula, remember, is crawling with bandits and drug smugglers; the traveler is advised never to stop on this road for any reason, definitely not to stop in Maicao, and even consider avoiding the whole region.

BEST EN ROUTE

Hotels on this route are few — mostly in Maracaibo — and are more expensive compared to those on other routes, ranging from $50 (expensive) to $25 (moderate) to under $10 (inexpensive) for a double room.

CABIMAS

Cabimas Hilton – On Lake Maracaibo, this new *Hilton* has 125 rooms and a full range of amenities and facilities. Av. Andres Bello (phone: 064-45-692). Expensive.

MARACAIBO

Inter-Continental del Lago – A 364-room hotel on Lake Maracaibo, with 2 pools, a gym, sauna, several restaurants, and 8 meeting rooms. Av. El Milagro (phone: 061-91-20-22). Expensive.

Holiday Inn Maracaibo – The newest deluxe property in the city, this 279-room hotel offers recreation facilities and business meeting rooms. Av. El Milagro (phone: 061-913-645). Expensive.

Kristof – This 187-room hotel has the same features as the *Del Lago*. Av. Santa Rita (phone: 061-72-911). Moderate.

Astor – A 25-room hotel with cold showers and double rooms. Calle 78, opposite Plaza Republica (phone: 061-74-770). Inexpensive.

Venecia – A 40-room hotel providing the same amenities as the *Astor*. Av. 31 (phone: 061-71-605). Inexpensive.

The Eastern Venezuelan Coast

The eastern coast of Venezuela far outranks its western counterpart in terms of scenery. There are the sparkling, deep lagoons and coconut palm trees of Costa Azul; the vast, salt flats of the Araya Peninsula; and the deep, dank, Guácharo Cave, home of the blind guácharo, or oil bird. The stretch along the Caribbean is a noted tourist area, although not developed enough to handle the weekend vacation crowd that streams in from Caracas to laze on the beaches, swim, and deep-sea fish for the coast's renowned marlin. So popular is the area, in fact, that a mass tourist development along the coastal region between Barcelona and Puerto la Cruz is being built.

Start this route by heading east out of Caracas along the recently completed *autopista* that runs through the Central Highlands (Caracas to Guarenas) and to Route 9, an alternate of the Pan-American Highway, continuing along the flat, steamy, lagoon-filled coast until reaching Barcelona, 198 miles (319 km) away. It's another 6 miles (10 km) to the resort town of Puerto la Cruz.

PUERTO LA CRUZ: This pleasant, bustling resort less than 50 years old is renowned for its perfect 82°F (28°C) weather, and it is swamped with hotels.

A huge coastal development is visible as you approach Puerto la Cruz from Barcelona: This is the El Morro tourist complex.

By backtracking all the way to Barcelona, you can take a highway south to the lower Orinoco River. From Puerto la Cruz, a ferry leaves for Margarita Island.

En Route from Puerto la Cruz – This 51-mile (82-km) drive east to Cumaná winds around the steep headlands of the spectacular "La Ruta del Sol." Standing along the coast are great jagged rocks eroded from the coastline. There are several good beaches, notably the Playa Colorada, 22 miles (32 km) outside Puerto la Cruz — a long blue lagoon with red sands lying in the shade of coconut palms. There is a small entrance fee; camping is permitted and there is a restaurant. Also worth a visit is Mochina National Park, with beautiful secluded beaches that are accessible only by boat. Shortly before Cumaná the road cuts through the mountains along "the highway of the *munecas*" (dolls).

CUMANÁ: The first Hispanic settlement on Venezuelan soil was perhaps the first in South America, dating as far back as 1520 or 1521, when the military landed. However, ecclesiastical history records a settlement here in 1513 by two Dominican friars who were massacred, but a group of Franciscans returned in 1515 and somehow managed to survive. Cumaná, at the mouth of the Cariaco Gulf, has had a devastating history of war, revolution, and earthquake. The newer section of town by the airport is barren and unpleasant, with the exception of the San Luis Beach. The older section clusters about the foot of a high steep hill dominated by the town's fortress, Castillo de San Antonio. The houses here are wattle and daub, many deteriorating. Through the center of town runs the Río Manzanares, with the Parque Ayacucho and markets to either side. Except for the river and coconut plantation in the center of town, the terrain is stone desert with cacti.

The Castillo de San Antonio is floodlit by night. Standing on the parapets by the rusting guns, you gaze over the bright clear blue of the Caribbean Sea from where pirates and republicans stormed ashore long ago. Across the gulf is the arid Araya Peninsula, long the source of Venezuela's salt. The salt harvester's lot, evidently, was an unhappy one (laboring naked in the glaring salt flats — naked because clothing is destroyed by salt).

Conferry also offers ferries from here to Margarita Island.

En Route from Cumaná – A road leads south from here to the Guácharo Cave. Before heading there, however, take the coastal highway some 42 miles (69 km) east, skirting the shore of the Cariaco Gulf, where dry, thorny ridges seem to plunge into the water; across the gulf is the ridge of the Araya Peninsula.

In the shallows is a variety of marine life, notably a grazing mollusk as big as a hand, very attractive and soft to the touch. The largest town is San Antonio del Golfo, with neither luxury hotels nor tourists. At the eastern end of the gulf is Cariaco, with an unpaved road that goes to Araya 60 miles (97 km) away. A winding road through the highlands returns to the coast at the lovely port town of Carúpano, 74 miles (120 km) from Cumaná.

CARÚPANO: This town flourishes with beautiful woods and prosperity and dates to the 1500s with narrow streets, old and elegant buildings, and tree-shaded plazas. It was here in 1816 Simón Bolívar freed the slaves on the condition they join him in fighting.

Carúpano is far from Caracas, and its people are more gentle and civilized, tolerant and friendly; it's also the only place in Venezuela where there is still a traditional pre-Lenten Carnival, with days of dancing and long fiestas and even *negritas* — women in black who are completely masked, free to do as they please and with whom, for just one night of the year. Their enthusiasm is probably enhanced by the best rum in the country, distilled here in Carúpano.

Carúpano's beach is wide and desolate. Other beaches lie to the west but are not very good for bathing since they are filled with shells. To the east is the Paria Peninsula; to the south, in the highland, is the Guácharo Cave.

THE PARIA PENINSULA: The stretch between Carúpano and the marshes of the Paria Gulf (about 34 mi/54 km) is a startlingly luxuriant lowland forest, quite unusual for the Venezuelan coast. Feathered stands of tall bamboo crowd against the road, and great trees fringed with Spanish moss arch over the isolated, drab houses. Six miles (10 km) from Carúpano, rounding a headland, you see El Morro de Puerto Santo, a tiny village on a narrow strip of sand between a rocky island offshore and the coast. A turnoff 7 miles (11 km) farther leads to Río Caribe, a small, old fishing port, with houses neatly painted in pastel colors. From here, descend into the forest and on to the gulf, where the terrain becomes drier.

Sixty-three miles (100 km) from Carúpano on the gulf is Irapa, in a field of coconut palms. It was here that Papillon landed after his escape from Devil's Island in 1945. Another 31 miles (50 km) brings you to Guiria, a rundown town where the streets are in a perpetual state of disrepair, often appearing as a great expanse of mud.

A major fishing port, there is no fresh fish; ironically, frozen marlin is the local staple. It is a dismal area. There is a boat across the Dragon's Mount to Trinidad, if there are a sufficient number of passengers. It generally leaves on Mondays.

En Route from Irapa – Head back to Carúpano and then go south, then northwest to get to the Guácharo Cave, 166 miles (267 km) away, just outside the town of Caripe. The cave, first described by missionaries in 1657, is over 8,500 feet long from mouth to source. In 1799, Alexander von Humboldt penetrated it to a depth of 1,550 feet and it was tracked to its source by cave explorers in 1957.

This cave is one of the several known haunts of the guácharo (*Steatornis caripensis*) or the oil bird, a blind, nocturnal, and noisy specimen that flies from the mouth of the cave at dusk to feed in Guyana 200 miles away, returning to the cave at dawn. The birds have improvised their own radar system by clacking their beaks.

The first part of the cave is a tubular gallery 2,500 feet long and 150 feet in diameter called the Hall of the Guácharos. Stalactites and stalagmites abound. There are guácharos and rats and spiders, plus a vegetation sown by the birds. Contrasting with the boisterous uproar here is the Hall of Silence, 800 feet long, with a diameter of 6 to 20 feet. Farther on is a complex arrangement of galleries called the Salón Precioso; most notable is the Hall of the Caribe Vidal, renowned for stalactites as transparent as ice. The celebrated Well of the Wind, 3,300 feet from the entrance, is a 22-foot passage, 10 feet high and 5 feet wide. Stalagmites make the passage difficult to negotiate. About 230 feet farther is the most spectacular part of the cave, the Great Hall of the Landslide, a gallery 650 feet long, 150 feet wide and 80 feet high. Here is a silent enclosed moonscape of mountains and crags with enormous stalactites in red and white marblized colors. In the center is the smaller Hall of Towers, celebrated for its 10 cream stalagmites. Another 4,000 feet or so beyond is the source of the cave, well worth the trip but dangerous after a heavy rainfall.

BEST EN ROUTE

Accommodations along the eastern coastal route are comfortable and usually reasonable, ranging from $60 to $90 (expensive); to between $30 and $50 (moderate); and under $30 (inexpensive). Most are beachfront hotels with cold showers; make reservations before arriving.

PUERTO LA CRUZ

Melia – A deluxe, 221-room hotel on the beach with a bar and restaurant. Tennis and golf facilities are available. Paseo Colón (phone: 081-69-13-11). Expensive.

Doral Beach Villas – A huge development with 386 rooms and suites on the Caribbean coast at Ponzuelo Bay. Facilities include an 18-hole golf course, tennis, all water sports, miniclub for children, restaurants, bars, and disco (phone: 081-66-63-33). Expensive.

Riviera – A 40-room hotel on a private beach. Paseo Colón (phone: 081-22-268). Moderate.

San Remo – A 26-room hotel with pleasant service and double rooms. Calle Simón Rodriquez (phone: 081-22-289). Inexpensive.

CUMANÁ

Cumanagoto – A 136-room hotel with a swimming pool and private beach. Av. Universidad (phone: 081-24-591). Expensive.

Villamar – A smaller hotel with 30 rooms and a swimming pool. Beachfront on Av. Universidad (phone: 081-22-147). Inexpensive.

CARÚPANO

Lilma – A 46-room hotel offering food service, cold showers. Av. Independencia (phone: 81-22-538). Inexpensive.

CARIPE

El Guácharo – A 34-room hotel with a swimming pool. Centrally located (phone: 092-51-288). Moderate.

The Lower Orinoco

The Orinoco River is the second largest river in South America and the third largest in the Americas. Rarely narrowing to less than a mile, it widens in places to as much as 10. Its waters rise at a height of about 3,000 feet in the Sierra Parima on the far southeastern border of the Amazonas territory and fall down the western edge of the Guayana watershed (putting out a branch to the Amazon) to meet the Apure River. There it becomes a big brown stream that meanders across the scrubby flats of the *llanos,* then spills into the Atlantic 1,300 miles from its source. In its several-thousand-square-mile delta, canoes are the usual means of transport, and Indian villages are built on stilts along its banks. The paddle steamers that plied the river for decades exist no more, and only in the lower and upper reaches do boats take passengers any great distance.

It is an immense tropical river, for the most part free of deadly animals, but dangerous and impressive in flood. Here is the home of the Orinoco crocodile, and the freshwater dolphin, as bottle-nosed as any found in the sea.

This route traverses the central *llanos,* south from San Juan de los Morros in the Central Highlands to Ciudad Guayana, on the river. A number of tours into this area can be arranged by Happy Tours. They can be contacted in Puerto Ordaz (Calle Urbaba, Edificio Tony, 1st Floor, No. 8; phone: 23-257), or at the Happy Tours office in Caracas (phone: 781-50-10).

En Route from San Juan de los Morros – Starting out, a 31-mile (50-km) drive south from San Juan de los Morros brings you to the crossroads of Los Caminos. Here, swing east toward El Tigre, 259 miles (417 km) across the *llanos.* The road is a speedway, flat and fairly straight, and you make good time (but beware of *alcabalas,* the Venezuelan military checkpoints). El Tigre, the center of an old and sizable oil field, is reminiscent of a US midwestern town — until the clerks come rushing out at midday to hang their hammocks at siesta time.

Here the road joins the Pan-American to Ciudad Bolívar, a fast 81 miles (130 km) away. However, there is an alternative route to El Tigre on the Pan-American south from Barcelona on the eastern coast. But the coastal road is heavily trafficked, especially on weekends and holidays; nevertheless, the 104-mile (167-km) stretch from Barcelona to El Tigre is fast and straight.

CIUDAD BOLÍVAR: On the banks of the Orinoco River, this is an old, very romantic town, steeped in history. The capital of Bolívar is a major port and trading center for rubber from the forests and gold and diamonds gouged from the rivers and flats of Guayana. It retains much of its colonial character and has a Bolívarian museum, as well as a fine collection of kinetic art at the Museo de Arte Moderno Jesús Soto. It was here, in 1817, that Bolívar established his capital after a series of defeats suffered under the Royalists. He was soon joined, however, by legionnaires from Britain and the greatly feared and bloodthirsty *llaneros* of José Antonio Paez (the Centaur), who formerly fought for the Spanish Crown. From here Gran Colombia was declared independent, and from here Bolívar marched a ragged, starving army of 2,500 men across the sweltering *llanos* and over the Andes to engage a 5,000-strong Spanish army on the heights of Boyacá, near Bogotá. The Battle of Boyacá was the turning point in the Independence Wars that in the end took the lives of one-quarter of the entire Venezuelan population.

During Bolívar's time, Ciudad Bolívar was called Angostura (Narrows), because the Orinoco slims down to less than a mile wide here; today it is spanned by the white and elegant Angostura suspension bridge. The city is very hot, but at 4 in the afternoon a delightful breeze blows in from the river. Beyond the waterfront there is little of interest, but the waterfront teams with activity — markets, gold and diamond buyers, Indians peddling bows and arrows, baskets, and sebucanes (basket-woven presses used to extract the poison juices from cassava root).

Looking out over the river it's common to see lazy dolphins cavorting in pairs. A short and intense fishing season begins at the rainy season (about June), when the very tasty sapoara migrate to spawn. The river is so thick with them, they say, that the rattle of scales against scales can be heard as they fight their way upstream. Here the river rises as much as 45 feet during the flood season.

This city is the best place in Venezuela to buy gold. A common though not so attractive souvenir is a brooch hand-beaten from green, pink, and yellow gold into the shape of the national orchid. It's rare, however, to find a bargain in diamonds.

Ciudad Bolívar can be a jumping-off point for some excursions. One is a trip to the Gran Sabana and Canaima and Angel Falls. A shorter trip, however, is the 130-mile (209-km) drive south on a very scenic road to the Río Paragua. En route is Cerro Bolívar, the great iron mountain that is the crux of Venezuela's second industry, iron. The Río Paragua is a major source of diamonds, and a very primitive, strictly dry-weather track on the far side leads to the diamond camps. Five miles (8 km) short of the Paragua there is a dirt road leading east to San Pedro de las Bocas, 34 miles (50 km) away, at the confluence of the Paragua and the Caroní rivers. The best gemstones come from San Pedro.

Happy Tours in Puerto Ordaz runs a 4-day car and canoe tour to a campsite on the Paragua fields (minimum eight people). You can tour the mines and Indian villages, and fish.

En Route from Ciudad Bolívar – The industrial complex of Ciudad Guayana lies downstream from Ciudad Bolívar, about 67 miles (108 km) by road. After 43 miles (69 km) there is a crossroads. The right-hand fork is an alternative route to the Paragua; continuing straight ahead leads to the Río Caroní (crossed by punt), and on to the town of Upata, 49 miles (79 km) away, en route to the Gran Sabana, but the left goes to Ciudad Guayana.

CIUDAD GUAYANA: This is an iron boom town of about 275,000 people, a planned complex encompassing Puerto Ordaz and the San Félix complex farther downstream. Puerto Ordaz is new, and what little sightseeing can be done is found in the old port town of San Félix. It is old and rotting, which is expected of river towns, and far from salubrious. Nonetheless, it has a very pretty plaza with flowering poinciana where schoolgirls congregate at midday.

The river here is 2 to 5 miles wide and populated with tiny islands. The waterfront is exceedingly run down and very wet, with a number of rats lying dead in the street. (The photographic possibilities shouldn't be underestimated — more so if you like cinema vérité.)

A couple of hours downstream from Ciudad Guayana are the Castillos de Guayana, two deteriorating Spanish forts. One was built in the 17th century on a rock in the river; the other, on a hill above the town in 1734. History has it that in 1618 Sir Walter Raleigh, ailing and his fortunes waning, sent a party through here in search of gold. There was a clash with the Spaniards, and Raleigh's elder son was killed. Raleigh himself was beheaded later the same year by James I. The forts, the presumed site of the clash, lie about 22 miles (35 km) from San Félix via dirt road. A boat can occasionally be secured by bargaining with a likely boatman, but it is a very casual, spontaneous affair.

En Route from Ciudad Guyana – A car ferry crosses the Orinoco — here about 2 miles wide — at San Félix. From here, proceed north to the Mata Negra crossroads 42 miles (67 km) away. (This road goes on through a vast oil field to the eastern coast.) This is all low-lying *llanos,* very wet and humid cattleland. Another 40 miles (64 km) southwest, then 34 miles (54 km) northeast brings you to Tucupita in the Delta Amacuro.

TUCUPITA: There is something that seems purposeless and disorganized about this town of 25,000. The inhabitants seem to consist wholly of government officials or Guaro (or Waras) Indians, forced out of their former homes by the 1.2 million-kilowatt Guri Dam, over 200 miles (320 km) away on the Caroní. The dam went into operation in 1968, sufficiently slowing the Orinoco's momentum so that salt from the Atlantic backed into the delta, ruining the fishing and farmland of the Guaro Indians. Some have been relocated on government land (expropriated, with difficulty, from the cattlemen) closer to Tucupita. For whatever reason, the Indians don't adjust to life here. Some live unhappily in a large compound on the town's waterfront, a sad people, their children malnourished; some work for dismal wages harvesting the palm hearts that enliven our salads. Fine craftsmen, they make baskets of such durability, utility, and beauty that they have been exhibited in New York.

All transport here is by river: speedboat, barge, dugout canoe. Go to the compound and ask for Vicente or Jesús: Neither may actually be there, but knowing a name will alleviate suspicion and find you a boat.

The delta, which has its own population of 50,000, is a maze of narrow and mile-wide channels, great and little islands, tangled vegetation and marshes. Traffic is considerable. Indians can be seen transporting their small cattle herds tied down in dugout canoes. One moment the river is like glass, the next it is very choppy. One moment you are solidly drenched by a sudden rainstorm, then the steam rises off you under a blazing sun. Dolphins frolic through the water, as occasionally do babas (small alligators), and many birds are visible. At the Indian villages there are tame peccaries (wild pigs), toucans, parrots, and agoutes (little rodents); women weave baskets from the fiber of the *moriche* palm; and men carve animals from balsa wood. A missionary on a houseboat may invite you to tea. There is a 2-day journey to Pedernales, a National Guard outpost and sometime prison on the far northern coast of the delta, less than 30 miles (48 km) across the Serpent's Mouth from the coast of Trinidad.

Tucupita is the best place to buy hammocks woven from *moriche* fiber; they are very comfortable and somewhat elastic.

About 40 miles (64 km) upriver lies Barrancas.

BARRANCAS: The Orinoco widens to a mouth before spilling into the delta at this village. Though the view is obscured by islands, the river here is at least 10 miles (16 km) across at its lowest point. Barrancas is a small town, fairly clean, and very quiet. A day-long journey to the island of Curiapo is rather sobering but worth the effort. Lying in the mouth called the Boca Grande, Curiapo is the largest Indian village in the delta.

From the Orinoco, head back to Caracas, and prepare for the next route along the eastern coast of Venezuela.

BEST EN ROUTE

Expensive hotels here run as high as $60 a night, double occupancy. More moderate hotels cost from $20 to $40; inexpensive accommodations cost under $20. It's best to make reservations before arriving.

CIUDAD BOLÍVAR

Gran Hotel Bolívar – A 63-room hotel with all conveniences except a swimming pool. Paseo Orinoco, the waterfront (phone: 085-20-100). Moderate.

Valentina – In the best residential section of the city, this spot originally occupied two small houses and has been expanded, redecorated, and air conditioned. Av. Maracay 55 (phone: 085-22-145 or 23-490). Moderate.

Italia – An old, comfortable, 30-room hotel. Waterfront (phone number not available). Inexpensive.

CIUDAD GUAYANA

Inter-Continental – There are 195 rooms and a pool on a beautiful lagoon at Puenta Vista, between Puerto Ordaz and San Félix (phone: 086-22-217). Expensive.

Rasil – A 159-room hotel with a pool and a good restaurant. Centro Civico (phone: 086-22-688). Moderate.

Dos Ríos – An 82-room hotel and pool. Calle México (phone: 086-20-679). Inexpensive.

Plaza – About 10 rooms and a good restaurant. Plaza in San Félix (phone number not available). Inexpensive.

TUCUPITA

Gran Hotel Amacuro – A fairly good 42-room hotel. Calle Bolívar (phone: 087-21-057). Inexpensive.

The Gran Sabana

The highlands of Guayana, the original "Lost World" immortalized in Sir Arthur Conan Doyle's novel of the same name, became cherished by and enchanting to Victorian England. Although the highlands extend along the southern frontiers of the three Guianas — French, Suriname, and Guyana — along the northern border of Brazil and into Venezuela to the Orinoco River, their greater and more interesting part is in Venezuela, where they are known as simply Guayana. The ancient tabletop mountains, or *tepuyes,* are still awesome to man, erupting from the vast Precambrian plain, scattering an area of more than 500,000 miles square and towering over the surrounding savannahs. Their sides are so vertical that many have yet to be climbed and several are considered impossible. Their summits are tabletop but seldom flat, often laced with streams and treacherous crevices; some are scrubby at the top; others, swampy or forested. Around the base are steep escarpments called *talus,* the accumulation of rubble and great sandstone blocks that have split from the cliffs in ages past.

The *tepuyes* are a bonanza to ornithologists and botanists. More than 7,000 varieties of orchids are known, and the entire region is a major source of diamonds. There are great differences between the highlands in the west and those in the east. *Tepuyes* scattered in the west rest on a peneplain 325 feet above sea level, while those in the east are level and clustered, rising from a much higher base.

So broad and extensive are the highlands that this route will focus on only one of the principal areas, a low *tepuy* of enormous area in the east, the 10,000-square-mile Gran Sabana. Its northern escarpment lies about 230 miles south of San Félix on the lower Orinoco, stretching some 120 miles south to the Brazilian border, 800 miles south of Caracas.

Although buses are available from Ciudad Bolívar to Santa Elena, the town near the Brazilian border, schedules are irregular, and the length of the trip (12 to 14 hours) depends on the weather. It's better to rent a four-wheel-drive vehicle or Volkswagen in Caracas (see Sources and Resources, *Caracas,* THE CITIES) and drive yourself, or take one of the Aeropostal flights to Santa Elena (check for schedules) from Ciudad Bolívar. A more economical approach to this route is to hitchhike. In reality, this is a no-problem alternative, even for young, unescorted women in this region ruled by gold and diamond gamblers and fugitives, where unethical behavior can get you shot; if you do hitchhike, however, take the bus as far as El Dorado and be prepared to wait it out at the *alcabala* on the Río Cuyuni to have your papers checked before proceeding.

En Route from San Félix – Leaving San Félix, a 35-mile (56-km) drive through lone, rolling savannah brings you to the township of Upata, a good place to halt when coming from Caracas at the end of a 10- or 12-hour trip. There are no really good hotels, but one restaurant at the *Hotel Comercio* (Calle Ayacucho) is very good. Nowhere in Guayana is there hot water, and water of any temperature is severely rationed in Upata.

A 65-mile (102-km) drive from Upata takes you to Guasipati, a little town of no great note. By now, you have left the savannah and are driving through a thick lowland forest. Ten or 12 miles (16 or 18 km) farther is El Callao.

EL CALLAO: Though only a couple of hundred yards off the road on the other side of the Río Yuruari, the forest here is so high and thick you can't see the town and could drive right by. But that would be a mistake: El Callao is a pretty, romantic little place, one of the loveliest in the country and certainly the loveliest in any jungle. The town is not much bigger than the plaza. It is very clean, the houses are brightly painted, and the obligatory rusted iron roofs are picturesque. In the cool of the evening the townsfolk gather in the plaza for the traditional Latin stroll, when young men contrive to catch the eye of a strolling maiden. Here also a Trinidadian population, going back several generations, brings an exotic, calypso flavor to the pre-Lent February carnival. Because of the recent reopening of gold mines, you will find no shortage of handguns visibly stuffed in waistbands. There is one restaurant, which serves chicken-on-a-spit and beer.

En Route from El Callao – A fast drive on a straight road across the broad alluvial plain of the Yuruari leads to the town of El Dorado, 67 miles (108 km) south of El Callao. The town swelters on the forested banks of the Río Cuyuni. It continues to exist by sheer persistence and by virtue of its gas station. Life was easier before the gold ran out and before they let the prisoners go. Here, on an island surrounded by rivers and swamp, is the prison where Papillon — Henri Charrière — served the last of his many prison terms, imprisoned by the Venezuelan authorities after his escape from Devil's Island.

An Englishman, Sidney Coles, owns the *El Dorado* hotel and tourist camp. He will arrange 1-day and half-day river expeditions. Until recently he would arrange long river journeys, but he is noticeably less enthusiastic about it now; however, a party of 9 or 10 people who are already equipped could persuade him.

Erich Irady, an operator in Puerto Ordaz, also arranges river tours for 10 to 15 people. Passengers travel up the Cuyuni to the highlands, down to the Guayanese frontier, up the Yuruari to the Paraván Falls. Along the way *tepuyes,* gold mines, orchids, howler monkeys, parrots, toucans, and rivers the color of cognac can be seen.

En Route from El Dorado – This town marks the end of the paved portion of the highway; from here, head back out of town to the north and take a sharp switchback to the south. In the beginning the road is severely rutted, but it improves, changing into a sandy, red soil.

The forest recedes to a scrub and, after a while, the great wall of the Gran Sabana rises before you. Fifty-five miles (88 km) from El Dorado is an isolated outpost called Km 88, at the foot of the Escalera (staircase), the pass leading up to the Gran Sabana.

KM 88: This directly abuts the *talus* of the Gran Sabana. The rim of the plateau proper is about 25 miles (40 km) away by road up the Escalera, but only a mile or so away laterally and a bit over a mile vertically.

The size of Km 88 belies its importance. Not long ago, there was nothing here except a rough dirt track at the end of which lived a *brujo* (witch doctor) named Albilio. Twenty-seven cars and two buses, they say, were coming here daily to see the *brujo* when Señor Varga, a miner, opened his *bodega* (general store) 20 years ago. Now there is a garage next door to the *bodega,* a gas station, and several houses. Gold miners who inhabit the forest emerge from time to time to restock. There is a certain amount of military and tourist traffic, and trucks haul timber in from Brazil. A restaurant on the porch of the *bodega* serves excellent meals.

En Route from Km 88 – This is the last chance to fill up with gas before heading on to Santa Elena, 140 miles (225 km) south (fill up with gas at every opportunity along this route). Plan on a 6-hour drive; the first 40 miles of this stretch, by the way, must be driven in first gear.

Now you start your journey up the Gran Sabana's Escalera. For many decades, Km 88 was considered the end of the road; diamond prospectors would stock up on provisions and then set out for the plateau, searching for the pass that was known to exist (by the Indians) but not always found. Many never returned, falling prey to jaguars, snakes, disease, the elements, or simply to gravity. From time to time, at the bidding of various dictators, convicts were ordered to build a road, but they were always defeated by the hard sandstone that couldn't be blasted. In the end, the task was undertaken by a corps of army engineers under the command of Colonel Antonio Llabanera, who retired in 1973 and now lives in Santa Elena himself. The road, an essential link in the now-almost-completed Pan-American Highway, was opened in 1973.

If you don't have a Volkswagen or a Jeep, and if it has just rained, it may well be difficult to reach the top. Go ahead anyway; you can rely on the national guard or another traveler to pull you through. The plateau escarpment is thickly forested, teeming with orchids, flowers, and the long, hanging nests of turpials, the national bird. On the left near the top is a stream and a set of falls called the Salto Danto (*danto* means "tapir"). A very pretty spot with moss and mists, it is a sampling of what a rain forest offers. From the top, the stream seems deceptively gentle, but it narrows and rifles through a gap like a breaking dam.

A pathway leads to the bottom. From above the falls you look north across 100 miles of forest and savannah splashed with the pink and yellow of *apamate* and *araguaney,* and you see that you're hanging from the almost vertical side of a great sandstone mountain rising from the wilderness: Welcome to the Gran Sabana.

THE GRAN SABANA: When you emerge from a close, heavily timbered fissure onto the open, rolling savannah of the Gran Sabana, the effect is startling. This is one of the most silent places on earth. Nothing lives here, save the occasional grasshopper by day, lightning bugs at night, and small, bony fish in the streams. The vegetation, except for trees along watercourses and *moriche* palms on the far escarpments, is largely confined to bromeliads. A great bushfire that swept through here in the 1920s is partly responsible for its sparseness.

You should come prepared to spend the night under the stars. Find firewood and stack it under the car in the hope that it will dry sufficiently by dawn (in the crisp morning air you will appreciate a fire). When the morning mist lifts, if it lifts far enough, you see great *tepuyes* rising several thousand feet from the rim of the plateau. Off to the west lies a vast highland crowned by the massifs of Sororopentepuy and Ptaritepuy, the latter the highest at 8,500 feet, its summit considered inaccessible. Other *tepuyes* lie to the southwest. To the east, on the border with Guyana only a couple of miles away, is the Cerro Venamo, quite low at 6,200 feet.

Your view across the savannah is impeded by low ridges; from the higher ones you can see a surface broken by the gorges of streams. These are tributaries of Venezuela's second river, the diamond-rich Caroní, which rises here on the Gran Sabana.

A couple of hundred yards from the top of the Escalera you find a campsite with round thatched huts, now considerably deteriorated. But there is no fresh water, and you'd be better off pitching a tent by the side of any stream. A few miles farther is a large *alcabala,* and just beyond that a track leading to the west that takes you, after a half-day's drive, to the Cabanayén mission on the Río Camá, which has facilities for travelers at a price. En route you pass the impressive 300-foot falls on the Río Aponguao (or Apanguao). From Cabanayén you can see the great bulk of Auyantepuy rising from the forest.

En Route from the Gran Sabana – Farther south (on the road to Santa Elena) is the Río Yurnaní, also with falls and fine for swimming. This is called Quebrada Pacheco, 23 miles (38 km) south of the Camá. As you cross a vast open plain between here and the slopes, you may see, off to the left, the massive formation that includes Roraima. The mountain to the left and closer is Irutepuy. The long, monstrous formation on the right is Roraima; contiguous with it on the left is Cuquenán (for the energetic these are worth a side trip). South is a deep, fast stream that is crossed by punt powered by passengers (pulling on a rope) and an outboard-rigged *curiara* (dugout canoe). The system looks a trifle unsafe, but a cable to windward so far has arrested the tendency of the vessel to escape downstream. The system closes down after a heavy rain and you can find yourself stranded on the wrong side of the river. Above the crossing are thundering horseshoe falls that can be reached by a path on the northern bank.

A little farther, lying out on a flat, is the Indian settlement of Yurnaní. The Indians will sell you baskets, bows, and arrows. A few hundred yards south is a track leading off to the left. This is the starting point for a trip to Roraima. About 6 miles (10 km) from the village is San Ignacio.

You descend the southern slopes through a region of *moriche* palm to reenter the forest near the Brazilian frontier. In the midst of the forest is the fascinating mining and frontier town of Santa Elena de Uairén.

SANTA ELENA DE UAIRÉN: About 37 miles (59 km) south of San Ignacio. Lucas Fernández Peña set out on foot in 1923 from Ciudad Bolívar to look for diamonds. He crossed the savannah and unexplored forest of the lowlands, ascended the Escalera, and in the forest near Brazil he found his fortune. He built a house, a large thatched structure of wattle and daub, and founded a town. He lives here still, in the same house, with his daughter Elena, the eldest of his 27 children.

It is a small town (population of a few hundred), but here you find every race of man — refugees (from Eastern Europe, war, justice, the din of Caracas, ulcers), miners, prospectors, diamond buyers.

Next door to the *Mac-King* hostelry is a very pleasant little restaurant called *La Gran Sabana,* and of the several watering holes, *Fanny's* bar is the best.

Prospectors come and go here. For 20 years now they've been tramping through the forest, searching, with the aid of diverse occult devices, for the "pipe," a volcanic formation that is the presumed source of the diamonds that sprinkle the greater length of the Río Caroní. Living on the plaza with his crippled houseboy is Colonel Llabanera, who fell in love with this beautiful wilderness while building the road up the Escalera.

It rains at least 9 months of the year, and all is mud. Small diesel plants generate electricity, and there are no phones. Rather quiet through the week, Santa Elena comes alive on a Saturday night, when miners emerge from the jungle, drink copiously, almost never fight, and strive to overcome their shyness to dance with the four or five available women.

About 2 miles outside town toward Brazil stands a big, red house called El Manguito, the principal whorehouse. At the edge of town, on the same road, is a pool and a small waterfall.

En Route from Santa Elena – It's not difficult to hitch a ride to Icabarú. You take the exit toward Brazil, then a marked fork to the right that directs you on a westerly course along the southern frontier. It's a 60-mile (96-km) drive. For a time you pass through a tall, impenetrable jungle, which is very dark when the sky is overcast. The foot-long structures hanging from the trees are the nests of turpials, and the darting patches of iridescent blue you see a mile away are the fabulous morpho butterflies. About halfway along this road you reach a high point, a desolate region of *tepuyes* and sparse savannah, the birthplace of the Río Surucán. This is a region famous for diamonds and the source of the largest ever found in Venezuela. The 154.15-karat stone (about 1 inch in diameter), called the Barrabas, or Libertador, was discovered by Jaime Hudson (also called Barrabas) in 1942. Four stones were cut, and the largest, a 40-karat emerald cut, was subsequently sold in New York for $185,000. Six miles (10 km) farther is Pauji, inhabited by a number of Europeans and Americans. You descend toward the source of the Icabarú, an area very rich in diamonds.

Icabarú is a smaller, muddier version of Santa Elena, with few amenities. The mining here is typical of the Río Caroní. Large rafts carrying suction pumps are anchored on the water, with divers directing operations. The divers work in darkness at depths of 50 to 100 feet — and it's dangerous work. Another town near Santa Elena is the Tauripan Indian settlement of Peraitepuy.

PERAITEPUY: A day's walk from the Santa Elena Road (the name Peraitepuy is derived from the *paray,* an uncomfortable footwear used during the dry season by the villagers). The road to the Río Chirimá is negotiable by Volkswagen or short-wheelbase Jeep. Life here is semiprimitive; the houses are thatched-roof wattle and daub; water is fetched by hand from streams 1½ miles away and several thousand feet down; and the little desks in the schoolhouse and the occasional sheet of galvanized iron have been carried on foot from Santa Elena, some 70 to 80 miles (112 to 129 km) away.

Peraitepuy's *cacique,* or chief, Eugenio Ortíz, gravely greets you upon your arrival and may offer you a shot of *cachire* — a semi-fermented drink concocted from yams — in a calabash, and he will certainly place a hut at your disposal. If you need anything else, however, you will have to pay or trade for it. Cast-off clothes and shoes make the best trades. Through the *cacique* you may negotiate the help of a guide, probably a member of the Ayusco tribe, who generally do not speak Spanish, but instead Tauripen, the local dialect.

From here you can proceed up the Roraima Formation, the region's largest summit area of about 18 square miles. The north face of Roraima Mountain itself (an extremely difficult climb) was first scaled in 1973; however, there is a manageable ascent route from Paraitepuy.

Some distance out of the village you reach a high point of 4,500 feet and begin your descent, fording several streams. Four hours later you come upon an old Mines Ministry camp that can be reached in a day from the Chirimá. Two hours farther you reach the Río Cuquenán in the shadow of the massifs. Just short of the crossing is a trail to the left that leads to Cuquenán. En route is a cave, ideal for camping.

If the river is high, you lose half a day by crossing at a ford downstream. A steep 2,500-foot climb from the river brings you to a meadow (suitable for camping) at the foot of the cliffs, just to the right of the falls. The ascent begins in a wood at the northern edge. A rather unpleasant scramble through the wet, dank forest, over and under boulders, across tree trunks and treacherous vegetation, takes you higher, to the beginning of an ascending ledge. Five hundred feet up, the ledge maneuvers around three spurs and descends to a point where a stream from the mountain falls onto the path. Traversing this obstacle, you ascend sharply toward the summit on a path that can prove very slippery. You pass between the cliff face and great flakes that form a false front. At 8,625 feet you reach the summit.

The sight is staggering. You are in a vast amphitheater of rippled stone, occupied by great black boulders and pinnacles eroded into fantastic shapes. From any vantage point they stretch as far as you can see. Exploring this trackless labyrinth is dangerous at any time, but especially when the mist settles in. Here and there are small streams, waterholes and marshes, no trees, and few animals. Close to the top of the ledge the Río Camaiwá leaps from the mountain.

The current *comandante* of the region asks travelers to report their departure and return to the *alcabala* at San Ignacio.

BEST EN ROUTE

For the most part, hotel accommodations along this route are very rustic. Cold showers are provided; in some cases, there are a few private baths. The most expensive hotel costs about $20 a night; all, therefore, can be considered inexpensive. The only camp in this region, *Cantarrana,* is between Santa Elena and Icabarú. Run by a German painter and her Venezuelan husband, it is really a small farm, with thatched-roof houses, a waterfall, fresh food, homemade bread, and organized trips to Indian villages.

EL CALLAO

Italia – This centrally located 10-room hotel provides cold showers (no phone). Inexpensive.

EL DORADO

El Dorado – A small, 6-room hotel in a beautiful location at the confluence of two rivers. It has its own beach (no phone). Inexpensive.

SANTA ELENA

Fronteras – A 40-room hotel with private baths and a restaurant. Centrally located (no phone). Inexpensive.

Mac-King – An 8-room, rustic hotel, providing one bed per room plus rings for slinging hammocks (bring your own) and food (until it runs out). Center of town (no phone). Inexpensive.

KM. 88

La Clarita – An 8-room hotel with three beds to each room and two bathrooms. Hurricane lanterns are provided. Centrally located (no phone). Inexpensive.

Angel Falls

In 1935, an adventuresome American bush pilot named Jimmy Angel flew up the canyon of the Río Cherún Merú and saw below him the great waterfall that now bears his name — Angel Falls. At the time, however, Angel was more interested in the mountain from which it sprang, the massive *tepuy* (table mountain) of Auyantepuy, about 160 miles (258 km) due south of Ciudad Guayana. For Jimmy Angel was looking for a mountain of gold. Two years later, with a small party that included his wife, he attempted a landing on the summit; his plane, until recently, was a tourist attraction, standing on its nose on top of the mountain.

Eleven days after the crash, when the party emerged from the forest at whatever point that then passed for civilization, the major treasures they had discovered were the 15 or 20 highest waterfalls in the world. The tallest, Angel asserted, was a mile high. In 1949, a private expedition set out to verify the matter, concluding that Angel Falls were indeed the highest in the world, with an unbroken fall of 2,648 feet and a total height of 3,212 feet. Since that measurement was only three-fifths of a mile, Jimmy Angel was disappointed, despite the fact that the falls were 15 times taller than Niagara Falls.

Equally celebrated in this interior part of Venezuela are the names Rudy Truffino and Charlie Baughan. Baughan (who founded the diamond-mining town of Icabarú on the Gran Sabana — see *The Gran Sabana*) was also a pilot and discovered the beautiful wine-red lagoon about 2 days downstream from Angel Falls on the Río Carrao. He named it Canaima, and he and Truffino founded a tourist camp on its shores. They befriended the Indians (the Camaratas, a people renowned for their gentleness) and introduced fruit cultivation. Today, the name Canaima refers to the entire region, a 6-million-acre national park. The traveler with a taste for the jungle and the wild natural beauty of southern Venezuela should stay there.

For the most part, the only practical access to Canaima is by air. Avensa flies a DC-9 in daily for a price that includes airfare, accommodations, and meals. Weather permitting, passengers on these flights have a chance to see the spectacular park and waterworks as pilots make several passes by the falls and over the mountain's summit. In Caracas, you can book the excursion package with Avensa (phone: 81-52-51-59; in Puerto Ordaz, 25-780, 25-957). In the US, book through Avensa Airlines (phone: in Miami, 305-381-8001; elsewhere, 800-872-3533) or Viasa Airlines (phone: in New York, 212-421-7722; elsewhere, 800-221-2150). The private pilots of *Aerotaxis Tanca* offer 3-passenger Cessna plane flights for a day over Angel Falls and Canaima. From Puerto Ordaz, 5-passenger, 1-hour Cessna flights are offered over and around the falls.

This route starts by flying into the Avensa-run Canaima campsite from Caracas, a 1½-hour flight, stopping in Ciudad Bolívar.

CANAIMA: Baughan and Angel are now dead (both having died with their flying goggles on), and "Jungle Rudy" Truffino has his own camp at Ucaima, above Hacha

Falls, an hour's walk upstream from here. The Avensa camp is on a beach at the lagoon. Fed by seven rose waterfalls and set against a backdrop of two *tepuyes,* the lagoon is breathtaking and wonderful for swimming. There is water skiing, and a boat can be taken into a cave behind one of the falls. Jungle Rudy's camp at Canaima is a smaller, friendlier operation, more expensive and more intimate than other lodgings. Skiing and sunfish sailing are available.

En Route from Canaima – There are several half- and one-day river excursions both upstream and down from both camps (about $35 per person a day). You shoot rapids, swim in the river, see a variety of wildlife (notably the macaws), and sail along the battlements of Auyantepuy. The highlight is a 5-day round-trip river journey to the foot of Angel Falls.

Auyantepuy (the setting for some parts of the movie *Green Mansions*) is one of the largest of the *tepuyes,* almost 9,000 feet high. The falls spring from the northern wall. A fairly easy route up the southern escarpments has been known since 1938, but the overhanging northern wall wasn't climbed until 1971 (by alpinist David Nott); standing at the foot of the falls you can't help but be a bit overwhelmed. The twin plums of water shoot out into space from a summit gorge — about 200 feet deep — to strike the earth with a thundering roar. There are good pools for swimming. Rudy Truffino arranges the journey at Canaima (very professional); at Canaima see Canaima Tours or an Indian outfit called Camarata Tours.

The journey is possible only during the wet season (which is not particularly wet — from June to December), and you must book ahead. During the dry season (when much of the river becomes unnavigable), Truffino has a 17-day excursion (or less, depending on how far you want to go) overland and by river to the source of the Cherún Merú on top of Auyantepuy. The summit is sometimes boggy, but for the most part it is a spectacular green moonscape, severely fractured, with smaller *tepuyes* and great ravines. On any excursion you might met Alejandro Laime, who has been living in the area now for more than 30 years and who guided the 1949 expedition to the foot of the falls. He lives in a cabin looking out on the mountain's soaring wall, decorated with a dozen glittering cascades — undoubtedly the most spectacular front yard in the world.

From here, you return by plane to Caracas.

BEST EN ROUTE

There are only two places to stay at Angel Falls: Avensa's 150-bed camp at Canaima, where 1- or 2-night package tours are available, including airfare, accommodations (cold showers), and good meals (if you provide your own transportation, you can stay at the camp at a per diem rate); and Rudy Truffino's 8-room camp at Ucaima on the Carrao River, where meals are also included. Reservations are necessary at both sites. Contact either the Avensa offices in Caracas (phone: 815-2515-59) or Rudy, also in Caracas (PO Box 61879, Caracas 106; phone: 561-9153).

Margarita Island

A large, 325-square-mile island, 17 miles north of the Araya Peninsula off the eastern Venezuelan coast, Margarita Island is the country's favorite tourist spot. Venezuelans flock here in droves on weekends, attracted by its fine beaches, mangrove lagoons, and free-port status. The weather is excellent, with almost no rain (water is piped in from the mainland), and the mean temperature never exceeds 82°F (28°C). Traditionally, residents were both fisherman and pearl divers, but the oyster beds, once famous throughout the country, have diminished. Only the fishermen remain.

It's very easy to reach Margarita, although the hydrofoil from the Caracas port of La Guaira seems to have been abandoned for the time being (after an unfortunate encounter with a whale). There are several daily flights from Caracas via *Avensa* or *Aeropostal,* or a straight-through ticket can be purchased at the Nuevo Circo bus station in the capital. From there you'll be driven to Puerto La Cruz, then ferried out to Margarita. *Conferry* (Edificio Banhorient, Av. Casanova, Sabana Grande, Caracas) arranges ticket reservations for those taking their own cars (phone: 782-85-44); offices are also in Puerto La Cruz (phone: 22-145), Cumaná (phone: 22-986), and in Porlamar on Margarita (phone: 22-611). Round-trip reservations are essential at Carnival time, during Holy Week, July 1–September 15, and December 15–January 6.

This route starts by ferrying from Caracas into the former fishing port of Punta de Piedras, then taking the *autopista* east to Porlamar, some 20 miles (32 km) away.

PORLAMAR: Founded in 1536 by a Franciscan priest, this was once a quiet fishing port and is now a thriving commercial and tourist center. There is a bustling and pleasant shopping mall (closed to traffic), but the city is very congested with vacationers and shoppers here for duty-free imported bargains.

Hotels line the stretch of beach bordering El Morro Bay, and you can buy anything you want here — from Parisian perfume and Colombian emeralds to Andean *ruanas.*

En Route from Porlamar – The fast, straight *autopista* west of the city returns you toward Punta de Piedras; 4 miles (6 km) short of Punta de Piedras is a road leading off toward the Macanao Peninsula. You skirt the Tetas de María Guevara, two conical hills shaped rather like breasts (*tetas*) that once served to identify the island to mariners. About 8 miles (12 km) along is a bridge crossing the sea mouth of La Restinga Lagoon, and on the other side is the port of Boca del Rio on the peninsula.

La Restinga is a narrow, 12-mile (19-km) lagoon enclosed to the north by a long narrow isthmus constructed, apparently, mostly of seashells. It is thick with whimsical channels and mangroves and is swarming with seabirds. La Restinga, along with the lagoon of Morrocoy on the western coast, is also a noted sanctuary for the scarlet ibis.

The large Macanao Peninsula is wilder, drier, and more mountainous than the rest of Margarita, very photogenic, and little inhabited; there are many secluded beaches, particularly at the western end near Boca de Pozo.

From here, return to Porlamar for a trip around the northern end of Margarita, where your first stop is La Asunción, 5 miles (9 km) outside Porlamar.

LA ASUNCIÓN: Coastal residents, who were constantly menaced by pirates, founded this inland capital in 1565. It is a quaint and quite beautiful town with a number of fine old colonial buildings in the Santa Lucía Valley. The old San Francisco Convent, Parish Church, Puente de Piedra (Stone Bridge), sun dial, and what is now the Nueva Cádiz Museum (formerly the seat of government and later a jail) all date back to the 16th and 17th centuries. The restored fortress of Santa Rosa, built between 1677 and 1683, saw action during the Independence Wars.

Between Porlamar and La Asunción is El Valle (the Valley) with an oft-visited shrine, the sanctuary of the Virgin of the Valley. Legend has it that she appeared in a cave in what is now called the Valley of the Holy Ghost and is considered the patroness of eastern Venezuela. Her festival is held from September 7 to 15.

Between Porlamar and La Asunción on the coastal road is the deepwater port of Pampatar. Here two forts overlook the sea, the smaller called Caranta and the larger, the fortress of San Carlos Borromeo (17th century). There are several stillwater beaches here; Pampatar is the home of *Christ of the Safe Voyage,* venerated by fishermen. To the north of Pampatar, reached by road from La Asunción, is an ocean beach at Guacuco.

En Route from La Asunción – A road leads north from La Asunción to Manzanilla, 12 miles (19 km) away on the island's northern extremity. About 8 miles (12 km) along is the fishing port of Puerto Fermín, also called El Tirano (the Tyrant) after Lope de Aguirre, a bloodthirsty rebel-adventurer who took the island by storm in 1561. At both Manzanilla and El Agua, a couple of miles south, are long ocean beaches with a powerful surf and fairly narrow shelf. Manzanilla is generally the more pleasant of the two; El Agua can be very windy. The sun is very strong, and here, as at all beaches on Margarita, there is little shade. The Los Frailes Islands lie off the coast to the northeast.

A 9-mile (13-km) drive northwest of La Asunción leads to the village of Pedro González, on a quiet little bay with a stillwater beach and an ocean beach not far away in the village of Las Arenas. A few miles southwest, beyond the town of Santa Ana (known as Villa del Norte in accounts of the Independence Wars) is the beautiful bay and town of Juangriego, celebrated for its vivid sunsets. The town is fairly large by island standards, and the beach is long, white, popular, and attractive. Overlooking the town is the Galeria Fort.

About 8 miles (12 km) down the coast is La Guardia Isthmus, on the eastern end of the seashell spit that doubles as the sole connection between the main island and the Macanao Peninsula and as the wall separating La Restinga from the sea. Seven miles (11 km) inland, east of La Guardia, is the village of San Juan Bautista, an area of large date plantations.

This road then returns to the east-west *autopista* and Punta de Piedras, where you can take a ferry home. Two islands worth visiting are Coche and Cubagua, between Margarita and the mainland. Coche has major salt mines and pearl fisheries; its town, San Pedro, is on a beautiful bay with quite nice beaches.

Ferries to Coche leave Punta de Piedras in the morning, returning in the late afternoon. Somewhere off the shores of the island lies the Spanish warship *San Pedro Alcantara,* sunk in 1815 during the Independence Wars.

Cubagua, Coche's twin, is deserted now since the pearls ran out in the 17th century. Here can be seen the ruins of Nueva Cádiz, incorporated as a city in 1528 (although sizable settlement goes back to 1510) and destroyed by a succession of earthquakes and tidal waves in 1541 and 1543. Nueva Cádiz was the subject of a study conducted by oceanographer Jacques Cousteau in 1979. There is no regular ferry service to Cubagua, but there are boats for hire in Porlamar.

BEST EN ROUTE

Expect accommodations to be as costly on Margarita Island as on the mainland, skyrocketing as high as $80 a night, double occupancy, to a more moderate $35 to $45; inexpensive here can be considered anything under $25. Since the island is one of Venezuela's more popular tourist and shopping haunts, it's wise to make reservations before arriving. There are reasonably priced vacation packages available from Avensa and Viasa Airlines, if booked in the US.

PORLAMAR

Concorde – A 446-room luxury hotel with a swimming pool, tennis, a marina, and its own beach. El Morro Bay (phone: 095-61-3333). Expensive.

Bella Vista – This hotel (the new wing is best) has 240 rooms with cold showers, its own swimming pool, and a private beach. A 10-minute walk from town (phone: 095-22-292). Moderate.

Granada – A 30-room hotel providing cold showers. The only thing missing here is the swimming pool. Calle Igualdad (phone: 095-23-332). Inexpensive.

Plaza – Quaint 24-room hotel. Av. 4 de Mayo (phone: 095-23-332). Inexpensive.

JUANGRIEGO

La Posada del Sol – On the beach, offering 12 cabins, complete with electricity and cold showers. Galería Bay (phone: 95-54-354). Moderate.

Residencias Clarry's – There are 6 air-conditioned rooms for rent in owner-manager Antonio Begnini's family house, said to offer the best and least expensive accommodations in town. There are also housekeeping units with kitchens behind the house (phone: 54-037). Inexpensive.

The Upper Orinoco
(The Venezuelan Amazon)

The wild, not entirely explored Amazonas Territory is Venezuela's last frontier and your next route, also known as the other half of the unique Roraima Formation, a little-inhabited region of vast, trackless jungle and marvelous wildlife, rivers, falls, *tepuyes* (tabletop mountains), and nomadic Indians. Leading the geographic highlights is the Orinoco River itself. As early as 1531 the Orinoco was navigated to half its 1,700-mile length to the mouth of the Meta River, widely considered at the time to be the site of El Dorado by Diego de Ordaz; by the middle of the eighteenth century its larger tributaries had been explored, including the sprawling Ventuari basin in the northern half of Amazonas and the Casiquiare, the channel joining the Orinoco to the Amazon River system.

But for centuries, as with the White Nile in Africa, the source of the Orinoco remained a great mystery. It wasn't until 1950 that a joint Venezuelan-French expedition tracked the last unexplored 120 miles of its course to the Sierra Parima on the eastern frontier with Brazil. There, at a height of 3,400 feet trickling down the side of a mountain they called Delgado Chalbaud, was a small rivulet, the source of the Orinoco River.

With the notable exceptions of the Atures and Maipures rapids, the greater part of the upper Orinoco is navigable by small craft. The Casiquiare connection is also navigable, and in 1956 a couple of Americans successfully (give or take some problems with authorities who locked them in jail for a short time) canoed from the Orinoco to the Río de la Plata in Argentina. The Ventuari is largely navigable, with a couple of fairly spectacular falls in its upper reaches.

Among the more spectacular mountains is Sarisariñama, one of a cluster of *tepuyes* near the southern frontier in Bolívar state at the source of the Río Caura. About 130 square miles in area and about 7,200 feet high, the mountain is thickly forested on the summit and figures greatly in widespread Indian legend, which claims a manlike beast — a giant — lived in the forest. At night he would come down from the mountain and eat people, making a *sari sari* sound as he munched.

It was first climbed by the explorer and naturalist Felix Cardona in 1942. In 1964, a bush pilot named Harry Gibson discovered the phenomenon for which Sarisariñama has since become famous: two gigantic holes punched violently into the emerald green surface of the plateau. They are 1,000 feet deep and 800 feet wide with vertical walls. The first descent into the larger hole was made in 1975 by the explorers Charles Brewer Carias and David Nott.

Toward the northern border of the Amazonas Territory is the *tepuy* (or *jidi*, as this type of mountain is called by the Indians of this region) called the Autana. This 4,000-foot column resembles nothing so much as the trunk of a petrified tree. About 300 feet from the summit is a complex system of caves passing clear through the mountain, and it is said that at a certain time of year the setting sun shines directly through the hole. The caves were first explored in 1971 by Brewer Carias, who descended from the top, aided by a helicopter (the Autana has not been climbed). The Autana caves and the holes on Sarisariñama point to the existence of a vast underground river system in epochs past.

On the southern frontier of Amazonas (shared with Brazil) is the Sierra de la Neblina, the highest non-Andean mountains in Venezuela and the highest mountains in Brazil: The highest point, a few hundred yards inside Brazil, is Pico Phelps, with a height of just under 10,000 feet. Though La Neblina belongs to the Roraima Formation, it is not in the classic *tepuy* mold, but presents a fantastic vista of mountains rising up from mountains, of vertical walls and impenetrable forests, and of a great canyon, which one visitor described in 1956 as rivaling the Grand Canyon of North America. The summit of La Neblina is about 230 square miles.

Among the several Indian nations here are the very proud Maquiritare, who dwell north of the Ventuari but travel freely throughout Amazonas. The fierce Yanomamo, living on the southern frontier with Brazil, are an isolated people with a primitive culture that includes the use of *yope,* a drug that is snorted through the nose, like cocaine.

All transport in the Amazonas Territory is by river, air, or on foot, and the only good overland way to get to Puerto Ayacucho, the territorial capital, is by air. A short flight you can take is from San Fernando de Apure, on the Río Apure, a major tributary of the Orinoco itself, which can be reached by road from San Juan de los Morros in the central highlands, a 164-mile (232-km) drive. As an alternative to flying, a cargo vessel can be hitched from San Fernando down the Apure and up the Orinoco, a trip that takes 3 days. Near the mouth of the Apure is Caicara, on the Orinoco, also connected to the north by road. You can take a vessel from Caicara to Puerto Ayacucho.

PUERTO AYACUCHO: On the edge of the forest, this is your typical jungle town: small, new, fairly rough, and very hot — about 100°F (37°C). It has a population of 8,000 (compared to the entire Amazonas population of 30,000). The Atures rapids are just south of town, and there is quite a good road to the impressive rapids at Maipures, about 40 miles (64 km) away.

En Route from Puerto Ayachucho – Amazonas on the whole offers little to the casual tourist but much to the rugged adventurer. Several small pueblos have a fairly regular air service — San Fernando de Atabapo, an old rubber trading town where the Atabapo meets the Orinoco (pop.: about 1,600); San Simon de Cocuy, in the deep south on the borders of Venezuela, Colombia, and Brazil; La Esmeralda on the upper Orinoco near the 8,000-foot Mt. Duida; and Cacuri on the upper Ventuari. Downstream from Cacuri are the Oso Falls and Tencua Falls, the latter about 300 feet high and very impressive.

About 80 miles (129 km) upstream from La Esmeralda and deep in the virgin forest is the mission of Platanal, which has costly ($40 a night) accommodations for travelers. There are also accommodations in the camp at Yutajé.

YUTAJÉ: Due east of Platanal, in the rugged highlands of the northern Amazonas at the source of the Río Mapaniare, this is a very beautiful area, long considered bewitched with spirits by the Indians. The camp is set in the V between the Mapaniare and its short tributary, the Río Yutajé; both rivers tumble over falls at their source. The word *yutajé* in the Piaroa dialect means "twin falls," and the spectacular falls on the Yutajé, only 10 minutes by boat from the camp, are reckoned to be the second highest (Angel Falls ranks first) in Venezuela (exact height as yet unknown).

The camp has accommodations for about 35 people in thatch-roofed cabins, with a restaurant and bar. You can choose between sleeping quarters: a rectangular, enclosed version and a round, Indian-style hut open to breezes. The principal attraction at Yutajé is the fishing, including night fishing with spotlight and spear. Canoes, pedal-boats, swampboats (for the flooded areas beside the rivers), wagons, and horses are available, and there is swimming in a broad deep pool below the falls of the Mapaniare (which produce a foam considered by the Indians to be good for the skin) and in shallower pools below the falls on the Yutajé.

Excursions include a 3-day (return) hike to the top of the giant falls and a 3-day stay at an Indian village as guests of the Maquiritare. Among the wildlife thriving in the area are the beautiful macaws and parrots, peccaries, tapir, monkeys, and giant anteaters.

BEST EN ROUTE

Except for the inexpensive, but impressive, colonial *Amazonas* in Puerto Ayacucho, which has a bar, restaurant, swimming pool, and air-conditioned rooms, accommodations along the upper Orinoco River are difficult to arrange. There are several river camps, but they are privately owned and don't seek publicity: The best you can do is ask around. Some camps that once existed are either temporarily or permanently closed. About the only place you'll find accommodations is at the mission at Platanal ($30 a night); Rudy Truffino arranges reservations: Call him in Caracas: (561-9153). The camp in Yutajé, with room for 30 guests, offers a restaurant and bar for about $100 a night including meals. For a minimum stay of 3 days, groups of ten can stay for $80 to $90 a night. For reservations, call Johann Mikuski in Caracas (phone: 72-37-35, 72-37-27).

Index